Organizational Behavior

Steven L. McShane
The University of Western Australia

Mary Ann Von Glinow
Florida International University

 **Irwin
McGraw-Hill**

Boston   Burr Ridge, IL   Dubuque, IA   Madison, WI   New York   San Francisco   St. Louis
Bangkok   Bogotá   Caracas   Lisbon   London   Madrid   Mexico City   Milan
New Delhi   Seoul   Singapore   Sydney   Taipei   Toronto

McGraw-Hill Higher Education

A Division of The **McGraw-Hill** Companies

ORGANIZATIONAL BEHAVIOR

Copyright © 2000 by The McGraw-Hill Companies, Inc. All rights reserved. Printed in the United States of America. Except as permitted under the United States Copyright Act of 1976, no part of this publication may be reproduced or distributed in any form or by any means, or stored in a database or retrieval system, without the prior written permission of the publisher.

This book is printed on acid-free paper.

2 3 4 5 6 7 8 9 0 WCK/WCK 9 0 9 8 7 6 5 4 3 2 1 0

ISBN 0-256-22896-5

Vice president/Editor-in-chief: *Michael W. Junior*
Executive editor: *John E. Biernat*
Developmental editor: *Christine Scheid/Burrston House, Ltd.*
Marketing manager: *Ellen Cleary*
Project manager: *Jim Labeots*
Production supervisor: *Kari Geltemeyer*
Designer: *Laurie J. Entringer*
Cover image: *© 1997 Robert Shaw/The Stock Market, PhotoDisc*
Senior photo research coordinator: *Keri Johnson*
Senior supplement coordinator: *Marc Mattson*
Media technology developer: *Barb Block*
Compositor: *GAC Indianapolis*
Typeface: *10/12 New Aster*
Printer: *World Color*

Library of Congress Cataloging-in-Publication Data

McShane, Steven Lattimore.
   Organizational behavior / Steven L. McShane, Mary Ann Von Glinow.
     p.   cm.
   Includes index.
   ISBN 0-256-22896-5 (alk. paper)
    1. Organizational behavior.   I. Von Glinow, Mary Ann Young, 1949–
  II. Title.
  HD58.7.M42   2000
   658—dc21   99-37328

http://www.mhhe.com

Dedicated with love and devotion to Donna,
and to our wonderful daughters,
Bryton and Madison
—S.L.M.

And to my family and my virtual family,
you know who you are!
—MAVG

ABOUT THE AUTHORS

Steven L. McShane

Steven L. McShane is Professor of Management in the Graduate School of Management at the University of Western Australia (UWA). He has also served on the business faculties at Simon Fraser University and Queen's University in Canada. Steven receives high teaching ratings from MBA and doctoral students both in Perth, Australia, and in Singapore, where he also teaches for UWA. He is also a popular course instructor and facilitator in executive development programs.

Steven earned his Ph.D. from Michigan State University, a Master of Industrial Relations from the University of Toronto, and an undergraduate degree from Queen's University at Kingston, Canada. He has served as President of the Administrative Sciences Association of Canada and Director of Graduate Programs in the business faculty at Simon Fraser University. Steven has pub-

lished several dozen articles and conference papers on diverse issues, such as the socialization of new employees, gender bias in job evaluation, wrongful dismissal, and media bias in business magazines. His work has appeared in equally diverse journals, including *Industrial and Labor Relations Review, Journal of Rehabilitation*, and *Journal of Occupational and Organizational Psychology*. Steven has written other textbooks in the management field, which include McGraw-Hill Ryerson's top selling Organizational Behavior book in Canada for 1998.

Along with teaching and writing, Steven enjoys spending time with his wife and two daughters. In particular, he spends his leisure time swimming, body surfing, canoeing, skiing, and traveling.

Mary Ann Von Glinow

Mary Ann Von Glinow is a Professor of Management and International Business and the Director of the Center for International Business Education and Research (CIBER) at Florida International University. Previously on the Business School Faculty at the University of Southern California, she has an MBA and Ph.D. in Management Science from The Ohio State University. Dr. Von Glinow was the 1994–95 President of the Academy of Management, the world's largest association of academicians in management and is a member of eleven editorial review boards.

In addition to *Organization Behavior,* she has authored over 100 journal articles and seven other books: *Organizational Learning Capability,* Oxford University Press, 1999; *International Technology Transfer and Management,* Tsinghua University Press, 1993; *United States—China Technology Transfer,*

Prentice Hall, 1990; *A Resource Guide for Internationalizing the Business School Curriculum,* AACSB/CIBER Publication, 1993; *Technology Transfer in International Business,* Oxford University Press, 1991; *Managing Complexity in High Technlogy Organizations,* Oxford University Press, 1990 and *The New Professionals: Managing Today's High Technology Employees,* Ballinger, 1988. She is presently writing up a decade's worth of work based on the international consortium she heads of researchers delving into "Best International HRM Practices."

Mary Ann consults for a number of domestic and multinational enterprises, and holds a Mayoral appointment to the Shanghai Institute of Human Resources in China. Since 1989, she has been a consultant in General Electric's "Work-Out" and "Change Acceleration" programs, and has led change initiative activities throughout the world. She serves on the Board of the Fielding Institute, Friends of Bay Oaks, Animal Alliance in Los Angeles, and is a Senior Advisor to Miami's One Community One Goal, having worked extensively in their jobs-creation process. She is actively involved in animal welfare organizations from Miami to Los Angeles, and won the 1996 Humanitarian Award of the Year from Adopt-A-Pet.

BRIEF CONTENTS

CONTENTS

Chapter Three
Foundations of
Employee Motivation   64

Chapter Four
Applied Motivation Practices

Chapter Five
Stress Management

Part Three

Individual and Interpersonal Behavior

Chapter Six

Perception and Personality in Organizations

Chapter Seven
Workplace Emotions, Values, and Ethics

Chapter Eight
Communicating in Organizational Settings

Part Four
Team Processes

Chapter Nine
Team Dynamics 266

Chapter Twelve
Organizational Power and Politics   368

Chapter Thirteen
Organizational Conflict and Negotiation

Chapter Fourteen
Organizational Leadership   432

Part Five
Organizational Processes

Chapter Fifteen
Organizational Change and Development   466

Chapter Eighteen
Organizational Structure and Design

PREFACE

here's a revolution going on in the workplace. Knowledge is replacing infrastructure. Self-leadership is replacing direct supervision. Networks are replacing hierarchies. Virtual teams are replacing committees. Companies are looking for employees with emotional intelligence, not just technical smarts. Globalization has become the mantra of corporate survival. Co-workers aren't down the hall; they're at the other end of an Internet connection. Chances are they live somewhere else on the planet.

Organizational Behavior is written with this revolution in mind. This book describes organizational behavior (OB) theories and concepts in the context of current and emerging workplace realities. For example, we learn that telecommuters experience a new type of organizational politics, that clashing corporate cultures can sink a global merger, and that the Internet is driving fundamental changes in the way organizations are structured. We also discuss emerging concepts that are reshaping the field of organizational behavior, such as knowledge management, emotional intelligence, and appreciative inquiry. Throughout this book, we emphasize that these organizational behavior ideas are for everyone around the globe, not just managers in one country.

Emerging Issues and Concepts

If there was ever an ideal time to write a new organizational behavior textbook, this is it. Certainly, it's exciting to write a new book for a new millennium. But the real opportunity is to write a new organizational behavior book that captures and reflects the revolutionary changes in the workplace. *Organizational Behavior* highlights emerging issues and concepts in this rapidly changing work environment. For example, you will discover how self-leadership is replacing the traditional carrot-and-stick approach to employee motivation (Chapter 4), how the traditional topic of work attitudes has an increasing emphasis on workplace emotions (Chapter 7), how the "law of telecosm" and other information technology concepts are revolutionizing communication (Chapter 8), how the job-for-life model of career development is being replaced by employability (Chapter 17), and how network alliances are redrawing organizational structures (Chapter 18).

Knowledge management is another emerging concept that flows throughout *Organizational Behavior.* This increasingly popular way of viewing organizations is discussed in detail at the beginning of this book (Chapter 1). It is also considered when we look at several topics, such as attracting and retaining employees (Chapter 2), communicating across work units (Chapter 8), involving employees in corporate decisions and improving quality (Chapter 10), and designing organizations (Chapter 18).

Globalization, information technology, and ethics *Organizational Behavior* carefully integrates three other emerging workplace realities: globalization, information technology, and ethics. This book adopts a global perspective because we believe that the most interesting examples are found anywhere in the world, not just in New York or San Francisco. For instance, you will discover how Hongkong Telecom employees are developing their emotional intelligence, how Finland's Nokia has evolved from a manufacturer of toilet paper to a designer of high-tech cellular telephones, how Canada's Nortel Networks is improving employee communication by tearing down the walls and turning its headquarters into a cityscape, and how Japan's Pan

Pacific Hotel supports emotional labor by hiring for attitude. *Organizational Behavior* also emphasizes globalization through frequent discussion of diversity and cross-cultural issues.

Computer-based information technology is another important theme woven throughout this book. The Internet, computer systems, and other emerging forms of information technology now play an integral role in organizational life, so it has a similar level of integration in *Organizational Behavior*. For instance, you will learn how information technology leads to technostress, improves and hinders communication, alters team dynamics, and leverages the potential for new forms of organizational structure. This book also recognizes the importance of ethical issues in various topics of organizational behavior, such as monitoring employee performance, stereotyping employees, using peer pressure, engaging in organizational politics, applying organization development practices, and influencing organizational culture.

Linking Theory with Reality

Every chapter of *Organizational Behavior* is filled with real-life examples to make OB concepts more meaningful and reflect the relevance and excitement of this field. For example, you will read about how St. Luke's, the British advertising firm, fashions its organization after a medieval guild, how employees at Billabong USA minimize stress by taking "surf breaks," how perceptual errors almost prevented the original *Star Wars* from becoming a blockbuster movie, how Amazon.com's frugal corporate culture is evident from tables made of old doors, and how computer programmers fulfill their needs by creating hidden "easter eggs" in software programs.

These anecdotes appear in many forms. Every chapter of *Organizational Behavior* is filled with photo captions and in-text stories about work life in this new millennium. Each chapter also includes "Connections," a feature that "connects" OB concepts with events in real organizations. Another feature, called *Fast Company Online*, highlights exciting and entertaining anecdotes from the award-winning business magazine. The *Business Week* Case Study in each chapter is another feature that encourages students to understand how OB concepts relate to workplace reality. The organizations described throughout this book have a balanced regional representation throughout the United States and around the world. Moreover, they represent a wide range of industries—from software to city government—and from small businesses to the Fortune 500.

Contemporary Theory Foundation

Organizational Behavior has a solid foundation of contemporary and classic scholarship. As you can see in the references, each chapter is based on dozens of articles, books, and other sources. The most recent literature receives thorough coverage, resulting in what we believe is the most up-to-date organizational behavior textbook available. Moreover, some of these references reveal that we have reached out to information systems, marketing, and other disciplines for new ideas. At the same time, this textbook is written for students, not the scholars whose work is cited. Consequently, we avoid detailed summaries of specific research studies and seldom mention in the text the names of researchers or their affiliations. Our purpose is to present OB scholarship in ways that students will remember long after the final examination.

Organizational Behavior Knowledge for Everyone

A distinctive feature of *Organizational Behavior* is that it is written for everyone in organizations, not just "managers." The philosophy of this book is that everyone who works in and around organizations needs to understand and make use of organizational behavior knowledge. The new reality is that people throughout the organization—systems analysts, production employees, accounting professionals—are assuming more responsibilities as companies remove layers of bureaucracy and give teams more autonomy over their work. This book helps everyone to make sense of organizational behavior, and gives them the tools to work more effectively within organizations, no matter where they are located globally.

Supporting the Learning Process

Organizational Behavior supports student learning through several innovative pedagogical elements. We believe that these learning elements will make this book even more enjoyable to read, and make the OB material more memorable.

Fast Company Online   Every chapter includes a *Fast Company Online* feature that summarizes articles from *Fast Company*, the popular business magazine dedicated to describing the workplace revolution. For example, students learn how employees at Pixar Animation Studios (creators of *A Bug's Life*) handle the stress of tight deadlines (Chapter 5) and how a Xerox communications manager relied on savvy political tactics to develop a company web-based information resource (Chapter 12). *Fast Company Online* includes questions for class discussion and self-learning. The feature is also linked to the full-text article available through *Organizational Behavior's* student online learning center web site.

Business Week case studies   Found at the end of each chapter, *Business Week* case studies introduce the online full-text article and provide critical thinking questions for class discussion or assignments. These cases encourage students to understand and diagnose real world issues using organizational behavior knowledge. For example, one case study describes how investment firm Charles Schwab is redefining customer service in the industry by relying on teams rather than individual brokers to serve clients (Chapter 9). Another case study reveals the forces that drive and constrain organizational change at France Telecom (Chapter 15).

Experiential activities   Experiential exercises and self-assessments represent an important part of the active learning process. *Organizational Behavior* facilitates that process by offering one or two team exercises in every chapter as well as a self-assessment exercise in most chapters. Many of these learning activities are not available in other organizational behavior textbooks, such as a not-so-trivial game of cross-culture communication and etiquette (Chapter 8) and an assessment of your self-leadership skills (Chapter 4).

Chapter cases and additional cases   Every chapter includes one short case that challenges students to diagnose issues and apply ideas from that chapter. Four additional cases appear at the end of the book for more comprehensive analysis. Many cases are new to this book. Others, such as Perfect Pizzeria, are classics that have withstood the test of time.

Video cases   Every chapter includes a video segment from the NBC News Archives and the Irwin/McGraw-Hill management library. These video clips, which range from two to seven minutes, focus on critical issues in *Organizational Behavior*, such as the potential for clashing cultures in the newly merged DaimlerChrysler (Chapter 16) and giving employees at the Los Angeles Dodgers the power to make better decisions (Chapter 12).

Connections and photo captions   *Organizational Behavior* is grounded in the philosophy that students learn by connecting theory with real-world situations. One way that we provide this connection is through a feature called "Connections," which illustrates the relevance of organizational behavior theories and concepts. For example, you will learn how AARP, Sprint, Volvo and other firms go to extraordinary lengths to have fun at work (Chapter 7) and how a Campbell's Soup executive in Canada generates constructive conflict. *Organizational Behavior* is also filled with fully-captioned photos that bring organizational behavior concepts to life. Specific questions accompany most photo captions to encourage critical thinking and stimulate classroom discussion.

Student online learning center (www.mhhe.com/mcshane1e)   *Organizational Behavior* offers a comprehensive web site to complement the textbook and further support every student's learning experience. The student OLC includes direct links to the full-text *Fast Company* articles featured in each chapter, direct links to the full-text *Business Week* case studies in each chapter, study questions similar to those found in the test bank, links to relevant organizational behavior web sites, and other valuable resources for students.

Indexes, margin notes, and glossary   *Organizational Behavior* tries to avoid unnecessary jargon, but the field of organizational behavior (like every other discipline) has its own language. To help you learn this language, key terms are highlighted in bold and brief definitions appear in the margin. These definitions are also presented in an alphabetical glossary at the end of the text. We have also developed a comprehensive index of content, names, and organizations described in this book.

Instructor Support Materials

Organizational Behavior includes a variety of supplemental materials to help instructors prepare and present the material in this textbook more effectively. Some restrictions may apply, so please consult your McGraw-Hill representative regarding these resources.

Instructor online learning center   Along with the Student OLC, *Organizational Behavior* incorporates on its web site many materials for the instructor. These include downloadable supplements, sample syllabi, links to OB news, online updates to chapter material from the authors, and even a Teaching Tips Bulletin Board for you to share with other colleagues interesting classroom approaches and ideas.

PowerPoint® presentations   *Organizational Behavior* includes a complete PowerPoint presentation package with one file of PowerPoint "slides" for each chapter. Each PowerPoint file has more than a dozen overheads relating to the chapter, complete with builds and transitions. Most files include one or more photographs from the textbook.

Instructor's resource manual   The *Instructor's Resource Manual* is written entirely by the textbook authors to ensure that it represents the textbook's content and supports instructor needs. Each chapter presents the learning objectives, glossary of highlighted words, a chapter summary, complete lecture outline (in larger typeface!), solutions to the end-of-chapter discussion questions, notes for the cases and experiential exercises, summary sheets for the

PowerPoint file, and other support materials. The *Instructor's Resource Manual* also includes a very large set of transparency masters and notes for the end-of-text cases.

Test bank   The *Test Bank* manual includes more than 1,400 multiple choice, true/false, and essay questions. All questions were written by the textbook authors and the majority have been tested in large class examinations. Each question has a page reference, as well as a difficulty level, many of which are based on actual student results.

Computerized test bank   The entire *Test Bank* manual is available in a computerized version for Windows. Instructors receive special software that lets them design their own examinations from the test bank questions. It also lets instructors edit test items and add their own questions to the test bank.

Acknowledgments

Organizational Behavior involves dozens of people, not just the two co-authors whose names appear on the front cover. In fact, this project illustrates the power of organizations to accomplish incredible tasks.

John Biernat, our senior sponsoring editor, had the uncommon combination of faith, determination, and support to ensure that we created an innovative organizational behavior textbook for the new millennium. He also established the association between Mary Ann and Steve that resulted in this productive and effective partnership. At the risk of sounding vain, we doubt that anyone could have picked a better combination of co-authors.

Christine Scheid (developmental editor), Charles Olson (copy editor), Jim Labeots (project manager), Laurie Entringer (designer), and the folks at Burrston House provided excellent service and support throughout this project. Christine has the most incredible diplomatic skills for keeping textbook authors on schedule. Charles's keen copy editing skills made *Organizational Behavior* almost completely error-free. Jim had nerves of steel as he expertly balanced the production schedule with our need for one more change to the manuscript. Laurie Entringer, in spite of the many directions and changes that were thrown at her, designed a truly stunning interior and cover. Glenn Turner and his staff at Burrston House orchestrated a large and diverse group of manuscript reviewers and provided valuable ideas to align this book with student needs and expectations. Thanks to you all. This has been an exceptional team effort!

Several colleagues provided valuable suggestions as reviewers of *Organizational Behavior*. We were energized by their positive feedback, and very grateful for their numerous suggestions for improvement. Their feedback reshaped many parts of this book and resulted in substantial improvements throughout. Our sincerest thanks go to all of them:

Joe Anderson
Northern Arizona University

Karen Eboch
Bowling Green State University

Lady Hanson
Calif State Polytechnic University–Pomona

Loren Kuzhara
University of Wisconsin–Madison

Anne O'Leary
University of Arkansas

Richard Peterson
University of Washington

Marcia Pulich
University of Wisconsin–Whitewater

Raymond Read
Baylor University

Katherine Ready
University of Wisconsin–Eau Claire

Joel Rudin
University of Central Oklahoma

Holly Schroth
University of California–Berkeley

Richard Sebastian
St. Cloud State University

Miles Smayling
Mankato State University

Mary Van Snell
Oakland University

Ron Stephens
Central Missouri State University

Steve would also like to extend special thanks to his students for sharing their learning experience and assisting with the development of *Organizational Behavior*. These include undergraduate students at Simon Fraser University in Canada, master of business administration students at the University of Western Australia, and officers attending the command and staff college in the Singapore Armed Forces. They have been warmly receptive to emerging OB concepts, cases and exercises, examination questions, and other pedagogical features of this book. An author could not ask for richer or more diverse audiences in which to put this book to the test. Special thanks also go to Professor David Plowman and other colleagues at the University of Western Australia's Graduate School of Management for their support, as well as to colleagues at Simon Fraser University in Vancouver, Canada. Finally, Steve is forever indebted to his wife Donna McClement and to their wonderful daughters, Bryton and Madison. Their love and support give special meaning to his life.

Life has a strange way of intruding while you are making other plans. So it is with heartfelt gratitude that Mary Ann acknowledges a few of the people who have been incredibly supportive during this learning journey: Janet, Peter, Anisya, Bill, Linda, Joanne, Pam, Candy, Deb, Leslie, Mary, and Michael. And of course Mary Ann's family—John, Rhoda, Lauren, Lindsay, and Christy—are owed apologies for her not having been around enough. Thank you all!

Organizational Behavior

Introduction to the Field of Organizational Behavior

Learning Objectives

After reading this chapter, you should be able to:

- Define organizational behavior.
- Identify three reasons for studying organizational behavior.
- List six emerging trends in organizational behavior.
- Diagram an organization from an open systems view.
- Define knowledge management and intellectual capital.
- Identify four common ways that organizations acquire knowledge.

John Chambers, CEO of Cisco Systems, strapped on an apron as he prepared for a quarterly ritual: distributing ice cream to corporate headquarters staff. "Hi, my name is John Chambers: corporate overhead here at Cisco," Chambers announces with wry humor as he passed out ice-cream bars.

Cisco Systems builds most of the Internet's plumbing—the hidden network of routers and other technologies that connect the World Wide Web. The San Jose, California firm is one of the fastest-growing companies in history. Many believe that it is also the organization of the future. "The structure of Cisco is directed chaos," says a Cisco executive. "It's kind of like the Internet—people are gluing stuff on all over the place."

Cisco's glue is an egalitarian, fun-oriented, and customer crazy corporate culture. There are no special offices or first class airline tickets for executives. Cisco's headquarters looks more like a college campus than the home of the world's leading Internet technology corporation. The incongruence is even more apparent when the CEO gives out ice cream bars and the company hires Ringling Brothers to entertain employees with an exclusive circus event. Although Cisco employees have lots of fun, they are dead serious about customer satisfaction. CEO John Chambers devotes at least 55 percent of his time to customers, and employees are partly rewarded by customer satisfaction survey results.

Cisco also uses its own information technology to glue together a global network organization. Seventy percent of Cisco's products are purchased over the Internet, then are processed by suppliers, contractors, and other partners without any direct involvement from Cisco's employees. Job applicants usually apply online. Current employees become virtual buddies with these applicants during the selection process.

Most Cisco employees also spend some time telecommuting, so they depend on the company's Intranet to keep them connected. Promising applicants who don't want to move to California might be hired anyway. Cisco will quickly hook them into the network from where they prefer to live. "We are the best example of how the Internet is going to change everything," says Chambers.[1]

isco Systems has leveraged the power of the Internet, but its real power comes from the effective application of organizational behavior theories and concepts. More than ever, organizations are relying on these ideas and practices to remain competitive. For example, Cisco Systems empowers employees with autonomy and responsibilities to get the work done. It has a flexible organizational structure. The company is driven by a strong corporate culture. Reward systems, socialization practices, and John Chambers' effective leadership keep Cisco Systems employees aligned with these values.

This book is about people working in organizations. Its main objective is to help you understand behavior in organizations and to work more effectively in organizational settings. Organizational behavior knowledge is not only for managers and leaders. It is relevant and useful to anyone who works in and around organizations. In this chapter, we introduce you to the field of organizational behavior, outline the main reasons why you should know more about it, describe the fundamental perspectives behind the study of organizations, and introduce the concept that organizations are knowledge and learning systems.

The Field of Organizational Behavior

organizational behavior
the study of what people think, feel, and do in and around organizations

Organizational behavior (OB) is the study of what people think, feel, and do in and around organizations. OB researchers systematically study individual, team, and structural characteristics that influence behavior within organizations. Through their research, OB scholars try to understand and predict how these behaviors help companies succeed.

By saying that organizational behavior is a field of study, we mean that scholars have been accumulating a distinct knowledge about behavior within organizations—a knowledge base that is the foundation of this book. Most OB texts discuss similar topics, which shows that OB has evolved into a reasonably well-defined field of inquiry. This is really quite remarkable considering that OB is still in its infancy.

By most estimates, OB emerged as a distinct field around the 1940s.[2] However, its origins can be traced much further back in time. Plato, the Greek philosopher, wrote about equity in work relationships. Another Greek philosopher, Aristotle, spoke about the elements of persuasive communication. The writings of the 16th-century Italian philosopher Niccolò Machiavelli laid the foundation for contemporary work on organizational power and politics. In 1776, Adam Smith advocated a new form of organizational structure based on the division of labor. One hundred years later, German sociologist Max Weber wrote about rational organizations and initiated discussion of charismatic leadership. Soon after, Frederick Winslow Taylor introduced the systematic use of goal setting and rewards to motivate employees. In the 1920s, productivity studies at Western Electric's Hawthorne plant reported that an informal organization—employees casually interacting with each other—operates alongside the formal organization. So you can see that OB ideas have been around for a long time; they just weren't organized into a unified discipline until after World War II.

What Are Organizations?

Organizations are as old as the human race. Archaeologists have discovered massive temples dating back to 3500 B.C. that were constructed through the organized actions of many people. The fact that these impressive monuments were built suggests not only that complex organizations existed, but that the people in them cooperated reasonably well.[3]

We have equally impressive examples of contemporary organizations, such as Hong Kong's new island airport at Chek Lap Kok, the Hibernia oil platform off the East Coast of North America, and that complex network of computer connections we call the Internet. "[A] company is one of humanity's most amazing inventions," says Steven Jobs, CEO of Apple Computer and Pixar Animation Studios. "It's totally abstract. Sure, you have to build something with bricks and mortar to put the people in, but basically a company is this abstract construct we've invented, and it's incredibly powerful."[4]

organizations groups of people who work interdependently toward some purpose

So what are these powerful constructs that we call **organizations?** They are groups of people who work interdependently toward some purpose.[5] Organizations are not buildings or other physical structures. Rather, organizations are people who work together to achieve a set of goals. Employees have structured patterns of interaction, meaning that they expect each other to complete certain tasks in a coordinated way—in an *organized* way.

Organizations have a purpose, whether it's building an island airport or selling books. Some organizational behavior scholars are skeptical about the relevance of goals in a definition of organizations.[6] They argue that an organization's mission statement may be different from its true goals. Also, they question the assumption that all organizational members believe in the same goals. These points may be true, but imagine an organization without goals: it would consist of a mass of people wandering around aimlessly without any sense of direction. Our view is that organizations do have a collective sense of purpose, even though it may not be fully understood or agreed upon.

Hailed as the world's largest construction project, Hong Kong's new airport at Chek Lap Kok is a symbol of how complex organizations can become. Thousands of people used half the world's dredging equipment to build an airport site from the 300-foot-high island of Chek Lap Kok and a smaller, neighboring island. Others constructed the world's largest airport terminal building, miles of expressways, tunnels and light-rail lines, and the world's longest road-and-rail suspension bridge between the island airport and Hong Kong. Of course, complex organizations are not infallible, and Chek Lap Kok is no exception. A software glitch disrupted the flight-information display system on the opening day, leaving thousands of passengers wondering which gate their flight departed from. Up to 10,000 pieces of luggage were separated from their owners in the mix-up. In the cargo dispatch area, another computer problem left thousands of air freight containers, many with perishable contents, unclaimed on the tarmac. Fortunately, many of Chek Lap Kok's teething pains were corrected by the second week, which further illustrates the amazing capacity of people to coordinate and solve problems in organizational settings.[7]
[Courtesy of CORBIS/Michael S. Yamashita and South China Morning Post]

Why Study Organizational Behavior?

You are probably reading this book as part of a course in organizational behavior. Aside from diploma or degree requirements, why should you or anyone else study OB? After all, who ever heard of a career path leading to a "Vice-President of OB" or a "Chief OB Officer"?

The main reason for studying organizational behavior is that most of us work in organizations, so we need to understand, predict, and influence the behaviors of others in organizational settings (see Exhibit 1.1). Marketing students learn marketing concepts and computer science students learn about circuitry and software code. But everyone needs organizational behavior knowledge to address the people issues that we face when trying to apply marketing, computer science, and other ideas.

Satisfying the need to understand and predict   Every one of us has an inherent need to know about the world in which we live. This is particularly true in organizations, because they have a profound effect on our lives. We want to understand why organizational events occur and to more accurately predict what to expect in the future.[8] In other words, we need to map out organizational events so that we can participate more fully and comfortably in that area.

The field of organizational behavior uses scientific research to help us understand and predict organizational life. This is not to say that OB knowledge offers a perfectly clear crystal ball. The decisions and actions that people make in organizations are determined by a complex combination of factors. Moreover, the field of organizational behavior is not a pure science. Nevertheless, OB helps us to make sense of the workplace and, to some extent, predict what people will do under various conditions in organizations.

OB also helps us to test personal theories of the world that we develop through previous observation and learning. Some of these personal theories may be quite accurate and predict behavior in many situations. Even so, the theories and concepts presented in this book will further clarify or crystallize these personal views of the world. Of course, some of our personal theories are inaccurate or overly simplistic for the real world. The field of organizational

Exhibit 1.1
Reasons for studying
organizational behavior

behavior uses scientific methods and applied logic to test the accuracy of personal theories in organizational settings. This book gives you the opportunity to deconstruct—to question and rebuild—your personal theories, thereby establishing more accurate and complete models on which to base your future actions in organizational settings.

Influencing organizational events Although it is nice to understand and predict organizational events, most of us want to influence the environment in which we live. Whether you are a marketing specialist or a computer programmer, you need to know how to communicate effectively with others, manage conflict, make better decisions, build commitment to your ideas, help work teams operate more effectively, and so on. OB theories and concepts will help you to influence organizational events.

Although organizational behavior generally takes a prescriptive view, it does so in the context of theory and research. OB scholars use scientific research to build strong theory that provides the foundation for effective practice. In other words, the best organizational practices are those built on sound organizational behavior theory and research.[9]

This book takes the position that organizational behavior knowledge is for everyone—not just managers. Indeed, as organizations reduce layers of management and delegate more responsibilities to the rest of us, the concepts described in this book will become increasingly important for anyone who works in and around organizations. We all need to master the knowledge and skills required to influence organizational events. That's why you won't find very much emphasis here on "managing people." Yes, organizations will continue to have managers, but their roles have changed and, more important, the rest of us are now expected to manage ourselves. As one forward-thinking organizational behavior scholar wrote many years ago: Everyone is a manager.[10]

Emerging Trends in Organizational Behavior

There has never been a better time to learn about organizational behavior. The pace of change is accelerating, and most of the transformation is occurring in the workplace.[11] Let's take a brief tour through a few of the emerging organizational behavior issues discussed in this textbook: globalization, the changing workforce, emerging employment relationships, information technology, work teams, and business ethics.

Globalization

Cisco Systems, described in the opening story, doesn't just compete with other U.S. firms. The network giant's emerging competitors—Alcatel, Nortel, Ericsson, and Siemens—are based in France, Canada, Sweden, and Germany, respectively.[12] Cisco and other organizations operate in a global economy. Some participate in tightly integrated partnerships; others have become their own global enterprises through mergers and acquisitions.

ABB Asea Brown Boveri, Ltd., is a classic example of the global enterprise. The $35 billion manufacturer of electrical equipment and electronic control systems is based in Switzerland, yet claims to have no national identity. Its 200,000 employees work in 1,000 facilities and 140 countries. ABB's board of directors looks like a United Nations, with representatives from Japan, United States, Germany, and other countries. ABB became a global powerhouse by merging dozens of companies and by organizing employees into 5,000 small profit centers so that they stay close to the local market.[13]

ABB and Cisco are large multinational corporations, but information technologies now allow smaller firms to compete in the global economy.[14] Yahoo!, the Internet search and portal site, was just a hobby that Stanford University students David Filo and Jerry Yang started in 1994. Today, Yahoo! has sites around the globe and is the world's best-known Internet address. Amazon.com has also leveraged the power of the Internet to compete globally. Amazon.com didn't exist before 1994 and still operates out of a small four-story brick building in downtown Seattle. Yet it quickly became the world's most popular on-line bookstore with a higher market capitalization than the major bookseller Barnes and Noble.[15]

Globalization also takes the form of tightly woven worldwide organizational networks. A dress shirt made at J.C. Penney, for example, consists of yarn made in Korea, which is woven and dyed in Taiwan, and then shipped to Thailand for final assembly. The entire process is coordinated from Hong Kong by TAL Apparel Ltd. TAL is directly connected to every J.C. Penney store. If a store in, say, Ft. Lauderdale gets low on a particular size of dress shirt, TAL quickly prepares another delivery from its Hong Kong warehouse.[16]

Implications for organizational behavior

What does globalization mean for organizational behavior? Plenty! For the past 40 years, OB scholars have warned that organizational practices in the United States may not be applicable elsewhere because of different cultural, religious, and ethnic belief systems.[17] With increasing globalization, corporate leaders must heed these warnings and adjust their OB practices accordingly. For instance, we cannot assume that people throughout the world hold the same implicit employment relationship expectations. Nor can we assume that everyone in a globally diverse workforce will embrace work teams, employee involvement, reward systems, or other practices that are widely adopted in North America.[18]

This doesn't mean that we have to reinvent organizational behavior. Rather, globalization emphasizes the need to recognize the contingencies of effective OB practice in a diverse workforce. (The contingency anchor of OB is discussed later in this chapter.) At the same time, we must not assume that OB practices that work in one culture won't work elsewhere. Phillip Ashkettle, CEO of North Carolina-based Reichhold, recently discovered this when he was warned that employees in France don't feel comfortable in question-and-answer town hall sessions with executives. Sure enough, there was dead silence during Ashkettle's first meeting with employees at Reichhold's French operations. Rather than give up, Ashkettle invited the French employees to watch videotapes of question-and-answer sessions in North America. When Ashkettle returned one year later, the French employees asked more questions than he normally received in North America.[19]

Globalization has important implications for how we learn about organizational behavior. We can no longer rely on U.S. businesses as exclusive role models of effective organizations. The best performing companies may be in Hong Kong, Finland, or Germany, not just in Illinois or California. That's why you will encounter numerous examples of international businesses in this book. We want you to learn from the best, no matter where their headquarters are located.

The Changing Workforce

You don't have to visit a global organization to find a diverse workforce. Most companies operating exclusively within the United States have a multicultural workforce because of the country's increasing demographic diversity. Minorities represent over one-quarter of the American workforce, and this is projected to increase substantially over the next few decades. The Hispanic population is now one of the fastest-growing groups in the United States and, within the next decade, will replace African Americans as the second largest

Walk into the offices of Roesling Nakamura Architects, Inc. (RNP) in San Diego and you may think you've entered the United Nations building. The architectural firm's 20 employees have extremely diverse backgrounds—the United States, Japan, Mexico, the Philippines, Macao, China, Italy, and Canada. This cultural mix makes good business sense because RNP works with diverse clients around the world. "We do a lot of projects where we have to be sensitive to the kind of people who live in those communities," explains Kotaro Nakamura (front), RNP's president. For example, it helps to know that an architect is really a developer in Mexico. "By having people from Mexico in the office, we'll know what's expected when a client comes to us," says Nakamura.[20] In what other ways does a diverse workforce improve organizations? What problems might Roesling Nakamura Architects face with this amount of diversity?
[Courtesy of Roesling Nakamura Architects]

ethnic grouping.[21] Within the next 50 years, according to some estimates, one in four Americans will be Hispanic, 14 percent will be African American, and 8 percent will be Asian American.

The labor force participation of women has also surged since the 1950s. Women now represent nearly 50 percent of the paid workforce and have strongly influenced organizational practices. Moreover, gender-based shifts are now occurring within occupations. For example, women represented only 17 percent of accountants in the United States in the 1960s. Today, over half of the accountants are women. Only 9 percent of medical school students in 1970 were women. They now account for 43 percent of medical school enrollments. This is a significant increase, considering that medical economics journals in the 1960s published articles about whether medical training was wasted on women![22]

Another form of diversity comes from younger people entering the workforce.[23] While the baby-boomers are starting to think about retirement, Generation-X employees—those born between 1965 and 1977[24]—are seeking out meaningful career opportunities. Gen-Xers also bring new ways of thinking about the world of work and preferred employment relationships. For example, one organizational behavior scholar frequently heard Gen-Xers say "We are not living to work but working to live, choosing a life that we want to have as opposed to just bringing home a paycheck."[25]

Implications for organizational behavior An increasingly diverse workforce presents both opportunities and challenges in organizations. Diversity can become a competitive advantage by improving decision making and team performance on complex tasks.[26] For many businesses, a diverse workforce is also necessary to provide better customer service in the global marketplace. "Diversity in our company is itself a business imperative—vital to our ongoing renewal and our competitiveness into the 21st century," states Jack Krol, president and CEO of chemical giant DuPont.[27]

As we will learn in several chapters of this book, workforce diversity also brings new challenges with respect to communication, team dynamics, and dysfunctional conflict. Moreover, employers need to support employees as "whole people" by realizing that work and nonwork are interdependent spheres. People do not park their personal lives at the door, and Generation-X employees are particularly unwilling to do so.[28] Employers also need to adjust to emerging workforce expectations by replacing command-and-control leadership with empowerment—giving employees more freedom to get the job done.

Gen-X employees are discovering that some organizations aren't yet making these changes. Consider Ivan Pulleyn, a 20-something job applicant who interviewed for a software developer's job at Electronic Data Systems Corp. (EDS). When Pulleyn caught a glimpse of the rows of cubicles and people tapping robotically on PCs, he knew the EDS job wasn't for him. "I walked into EDS and it felt like the Death Star," Pulleyn recalls. Although EDS offered him the job, Pulleyn accepted a lower-paying position with a company that was more in tune with his needs.[29]

Lastly, workforce diversity creates increasing concerns about workplace discrimination and harassment. According to one recent survey, 81 percent of African-American professionals believe that discrimination in the workplace is still common.[30] Recent reports of discrimination at Circuit City Stores, Denny's, Shoney's, and Texaco support these perceptions. We look at the organizational behavior issues of discrimination and harassment in several chapters, including stress (Chapter 5), perceptions (Chapter 6), and organizational power (Chapter 12).

Emerging Employment Relationships

America's workforce isn't the only thing that's changing. After more than 100 years of relative stability, employment relationships are being redefined. In the wake of downsizing, restructuring, and contracting out noncore activities, many organizations are reluctant to hire people for the long term. Replacing the job-for-life contract is a "new deal" called **employability.** Employees perform a variety of work activities rather than hold specific jobs, and they are expected to continuously learn skills that will keep them employed. Several chapters in this textbook will discuss the effects of this emerging employment relationship on organizational loyalty, career dynamics, and workplace stress.[31]

Contingent work is another emerging employment relationship. Contingent work includes any job in which the individual does not have an explicit or implicit contract for long-term employment, or one in which the minimum hours of work can vary in a nonsystematic way.[32] By some estimates, more than 15 percent of the U.S. workforce is employed in some sort of contingent work arrangement. Many of these people would rather be in stable, well-paying jobs, but an increasing percentage of them are finding new freedom in being their own boss. This new breed of "free agents" rely on their knowledge rather than physical labor to thrive in this fast-paced world.[33] As our *Fast Company Online* feature describes, free agents enjoy liberation from the stifling regiments of traditional employment. An entire section of Chapter 17 is devoted to the contingent workforce and its ramifications for organizational behavior.

employability the 'new deal' employment relationship in which the job is a temporary event and employees are expected to continuously learn skills that will keep them employed in a variety of work activities

contingent work any job in which the individual does not have an explicit or implicit contract for long-term employment, or one in which the minimum hours of work can vary in a nonsystematic way

Telecommuting   Vicki Hall used to commute more than two hours each day to and from VISA's San Francisco headquarters. She has now cut down that travel time to about 10 seconds. With the aid of a company-paid PC, fax, ISDN phone line, storage shelves, and spare bedroom at her home, Hall has turned her daily commute into a telecommute. "Telecommuting gave me back my life," she says.[34]

FAST COMPANY
Online

□ Living in a Free Agent Nation

Theresa Fitzgerald missed the fun as she rose from low-level designer to creative director at United Media. She earned more money and received more responsibility at the New York company that syndicates columns and comic strips. But she also moved further away from what she loved most: doing art.

David Garfinkel left the corporate hierarchy to become part of the free agent nation.

So, at the top of her career, Fitzgerald left United Media and joined the 25 million or more Americans who belong to the free agent nation. She became her own boss, designing children's clothing, toys, and promotions for Playskool, Scholastic Publishing, and Major League Baseball. "I'm a doer," says Fitzgerald. "I would have very busy days at United Media, but I wouldn't have *done* anything."

Instead of accepting the old terms, free agents are demanding new ones. Through their independence, free agents are discovering that people can achieve a beautiful synchronicity between who you are and what you do in the workplace.

"A large organization is about submerging your own identity for the good of the company," says David Garfinkel, who previously worked as a bureau chief for business publisher McGraw-Hill. "The appearance and title of the job were exciting," Garfinkel recalls, "but the job wasn't using the best part of me. I felt like I was out of touch with who I really was." He's now a free-agent marketing strategist, copywriter, and author of an audio seminar on copywriting.

Sue Burish agrees. After working at Southern Pacific Railroad, Crocker Bank, and electronics manufacturer Raychem Corporation, Burish became a free agent to achieve integration between who she is and what she does. "In free agency," says Burish, who now designs training programs, "people assume their own shape rather than fit the shape of some corporate box."

ONLINE CHECK-UP

1. This *Fast Company Online* feature describes one of the three rules for free agents: Work is personal. What are the two other rules identified in the full text of this *Fast Company* article?
2. These free agents claim that traditional employment prevents them from being themselves. Explain how free agents are able to achieve this alignment or integration better than in traditional employment. What, if anything, can employers do to help employees create a better alignment or integration of self and work in traditional employment?

Get the full text of this *Fast Company* article at www.mhhe.com/mcshane1e

Source: Adapted from D. H. Pink, "Free Agent Nation," *Fast Company,* Issue 12 (December–January 1998). □

telecommuting (also called *teleworking*) performing work at home or another location away from the office, usually with a computer or other telecommunications connection to the office

Vicki Hall is among the tens of millions of people who have altered their employment relationship through **telecommuting** (also called *teleworking*)—working from home, usually with a computer connection to the office. As we move from an industrial to a knowledge-based economy, the number of people who take the information highway to work each day will continue to increase. Moreover, technology has untethered some employees so completely from the employer's physical workspace that clients and co-workers no longer know whether they are calling an employee at an office or on a deserted island.[35]

Telecommuting is potentially a win-win situation for both employees and employers. Just look at Cisco Systems. Telecommuters at the world's leading provider of business-to-business computer networks say they love the freedom of working by their own schedule, skipping rush hour, and being in comfortable surroundings. Telecommuting has improved the productivity of Cisco's employees, reduced overhead costs, and retained key employees who might otherwise have left. It has created more flexible expectations about the employment relationship. "It's surprising the number of engineers who will respond to a question at 11:00 on a Saturday night," says a Cisco executive. "We can solve a problem that would not have been solved until Monday morning."[36]

Telecommuting raises organizational behavior issues that we discuss in this book. For instance, executives must learn to evaluate employees for their results, not for their "face time"—the amount of time the employee is physically in the workplace.[37] Meanwhile, employees must learn to get things done through **virtual teams**—cross-functional groups that operate across space, time, and organizational boundaries with members who communicate mainly through electronic technologies.[38] They must also learn to motivate themselves through self-leadership, which is described in Chapter 4.

virtual teams cross-functional teams that operate across space, time, and organizational boundaries with members who communicate mainly through electronic technologies

Information Technology and OB

Information technology is shaking up organizations and forcing organizational behavior scholars to reexamine their concepts in light of these revolutionary changes. We have already noted how this technology has given rise to virtual teams and telecommuting, and has made it possible for small businesses to compete in the global marketplace. More generally, information technology challenges traditional business logic regarding how employees interact, how organizations are configured, and how they relate to customers.

One of the critical effects of information technology on organizational behavior concerns the way people perform their tasks and work with each other. Consider Verifone, the Hewlett-Packard subsidiary that makes secure payment systems. Verifone's employees are connected around the globe so that work processes follow the sun. For example, Verifone's software development group in India develops new code, then

"Can't talk now. I'm in a seminar about improving communication with technology."

© 1996 Ted Goff

electronically sends it at the end of their day to Dallas for testing. This work is then forwarded to employees in Hawaii who integrate the code with existing software. By combining information technology with global coordination, Verifone is faster than its competitors at bringing products and services to market.[39]

Information technology has also reshaped organizations and their interactions with other entities. We are now witnessing the emergence of the **network organization**—an alliance of several organizations for the purpose of creating a product or serving a client. Cisco Systems illustrates this trend. As we learned in the opening story, Cisco is really a constellation of suppliers, contract manufacturers, assemblers, and other partners connected through an intricate web of information technology. Cisco's network springs into action as soon as a customer places an order (usually through the Internet). Suppliers send the required materials to assemblers who ship the product directly to the client, usually the same day. Seventy percent of Cisco's product is outsourced this way. In many cases, Cisco employees never touch the product.[40] Some writers predict that skyscrapers will become obsolete as information technology forms more durable and flexible network organizations around the globe.[41]

Teams, Teams, and More Teams

Visit Kemet Electronics Corp.'s ceramic capacitors plant in Monterrey, Mexico, and you will soon discover that people don't work alone. "We have 2,000 employees and 2,000 teams," explains plant manager Ed Raygada. "But they aren't one-person teams. Most of our employees participate in multiple teams. You can be a leader of one team and a member of another team. Our goal is to have every employee serving on five teams."[42]

At Kemet and many other companies, teams are replacing individuals as the basic building blocks of organizations.[43] Some teams design products or services; others are responsible for complete work processes. For example, Kaiser Aluminum's Tennalum plant in Jackson, Tennessee, is operated by self-directed work teams with their own team leaders. AES Corp., the Virginia-based electrical power company, also relies on teams to run the business. "Everything in the company is divided up into teams, small groups of people that are multidisciplinary in nature," explains Dennis W. Bakke, CEO and cofounder of AES

network organization an alliance of several organizations for the purpose of creating a product or serving a client

Kaiser Aluminum's Tennalum plant in Jackson, Tennessee, is operated completely by self-directed work teams. The aluminum screw machine stock manufacturer organizes teams around work processes (such as making a product) and encourages employees to learn several skills. The Tennalum plant has no supervisors. Teams make most decisions, help select new employees, and perform preventive maintenance. This team-based structure works so well that Tennalum is considered one of the top-performing manufacturing operations in the United States and recently won the Tennessee Quality Achievement Award.[44] In your opinion, why would teams make the Tennalum facility so effective?

[Courtesy of Tennalum]

Corp. "They have total authority to make all decisions: I mean total, complete authority on every aspect of business."[45]

Organizational behavior scholars have long argued that teams can be more effective than individuals working alone in many situations. Diverse work groups can potentially resolve complex problems more creatively than if those team members had worked individually. Moreover, by giving teams direct responsibility for coordination and control of work activities, companies can increase responsiveness and remove unnecessary layers of management. However, teams are not appropriate in every situation. The costs and problems associated with team work can sometimes offset its benefits. We will learn much more about team dynamics and team decision making in Chapters 9, 10, and 11.

Business Ethics

Check out your favorite newspaper or Internet news site and you will almost certainly read about an organization accused of unethical business conduct. Microsoft Corp. has come under scrutiny for allegedly undermining competition and forcing computer makers to bundle its products. Eastman Chemical and Archer Daniels Midland Co. recently admitted that they engaged in price fixing—colluding with other companies in order to keep prices above competitive levels. A court concluded that several male firefighters at the Kansas City Fire Department had sexually harassed female firefighters and support staff. Royal Dutch/Shell actively fights against corruption in the oil industry, yet the energy giant fired several employees after investigating 23 cases of bribery in one year.[46]

ethics the study of moral principles or values that determine whether actions are right or wrong and outcomes are good or bad

social responsibility a person's or organization's moral obligation toward others who are affected by his or her actions

Ethics refers to the study of moral principles or values that determine whether actions are right or wrong and outcomes are good or bad. We rely on our ethical values to determine "the right thing to do." **Social responsibility** is related to business ethics, but has a broader meaning. It refers to a person's or organization's moral obligation toward others who are affected by his or her actions. Geon is considered a socially responsible company because of its self-imposed strict standards against pollution. "For our company, environmental performance is our license to practice our art in society," explains William Patient, CEO of the polymer manufacturer. "We do not presume we have a right to do business unless society gives us that right."[47]

One of the dilemmas organizational leaders face is that the distinction between ethical and unethical behavior is not black and white. It depends on several factors, such as the person's intent for engaging in the behavior, specific conditions in that culture, the influence of external factors on the behavior, and so forth. Consider the recent practice by Doak Dermatologics, a New Jersey-based pharmaceutical company that offered doctors a free Beanie Baby for every prescription written for some of its products. Some people might view this as an innovative marketing strategy. Others suggest that this is unethical because it is a conflict of interest. "This thing with the Beanie Babies is a true kickback," said Dr. Robert M. Tenery, a Dallas ophthalmologist and chairman of the Council on Ethics and Judicial Affairs.[48]

Throughout this book, you will discover numerous topics that relate to business ethics, such as monitoring employee performance, rewarding people equitably, stereotyping employees, using peer pressure, engaging in organizational politics, and applying organization development practices. We will also cover the topic of ethical values and behavior more fully in Chapter 7.

The Five Anchors of Organizational Behavior

Globalization, the changing workforce, new employment relationships, computer technologies, work teams, and business ethics are just a few of the issues

Exhibit 1.2

Five conceptual anchors of organizational behavior

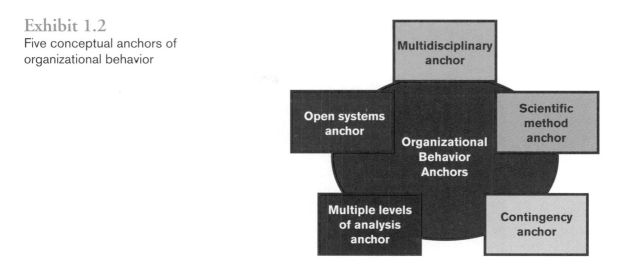

that we will discuss in this textbook. To understand these and other topics, organizational behavior scholars rely on a set of basic beliefs or knowledge structures (see Exhibit 1.2). These conceptual anchors represent the way that OB researchers think about organizations and how they should be studied. Let's look at each of these five beliefs that anchor the study of organizational behavior.

The Multidisciplinary Anchor

As part of the social sciences, organizational behavior is anchored around the idea that it should draw on knowledge from other disciplines rather than just its own isolated research base.[49] In other words, OB should be multidisciplinary. The upper part of Exhibit 1.3 identifies the traditional disciplines that have had the greatest impact on organizational behavior knowledge. Of these, the fields of psychology and sociology have contributed the most to current OB knowledge. The field of psychology has aided our understanding of individual and interpersonal behavior. Sociologists have contributed to our knowledge of team dynamics, organizational socialization, organizational power, and other aspects of the social system.

Anthropology has mainly helped us to understand organizational culture, whereas political science contributed ideas regarding power and politics in organizations.[50] Engineering played an early role in OB with productivity issues. Economists influenced early OB writing on organizational power, negotiations, and decision making. However, as recent economics concepts are applied to OB writing, some scholars warn that economics offers only one of many ways to view organizations.[51]

The bottom part of Exhibit 1.3 identifies some of the emerging fields from which organizational behavior might acquire knowledge. The communications field is currently helping us to understand the dynamics of electronic mail, communicating corporate culture, and socialization processes. Information systems writers are exploring the effects of information technology on team dynamics, decision making, and knowledge management. Women's studies scholars are studying power relations between men and women in organizations, as well as perceptual biases.

The true test of OB's multidisciplinary anchor is how effectively OB scholars continue to transfer knowledge from traditional and emerging disciplines. History suggests that fields of inquiry tend to become more inwardly focused as they mature.[52] Hopefully, OB will avoid this tendency by continuing to recognize ideas from other disciplines.

Exhibit 1.3
Multidisciplinary anchor of
organizational behavior

Disciplines	Relevant OB topics
Traditional	
Psychology	Motivation, perception, attitudes, personality, job stress, job enrichment, performance appraisals, leadership
Sociology	Team dynamics, roles, socialization, communication patterns, organizational power, organizational structure
Anthropology	Corporate culture, organizational rituals, cross-cultural dynamics, organizational adaptation
Political science	Intergroup conflict, coalition formation, organizational power and politics, decision making, organizational environments
Economics	Decision making, negotiation, organizational power
Industrial engineering	Job design, productivity, work measurement
Emerging	
Communications	Electronic mail, communicating corporate culture, employee socialization
Information systems	Team dynamics, decision making, knowledge management
Women's studies	Organizational power, perceptual biases

The Scientific Method Anchor

A second anchor of organizational behavior relates to the way we study organizations. For the most part, OB researchers test their hypotheses about organizations by collecting information according to the **scientific method.** The scientific method is not a single procedure for collecting data; rather, it is a set of principles and procedures that help researchers to systematically understand previously unexplained events and conditions. Appendix A at the end of this book summarizes the main elements of the scientific method, as well as various ways to conduct research.

scientific method a set of principles and procedures that help researchers to systematically understand previously unexplained events and conditions

The Contingency Anchor

"It depends" is a phrase that OB scholars often use to answer a question about the best solution to an organizational problem. The statement may frustrate some people, yet it reflects an important way of understanding and predicting organizational events, called the **contingency approach.** This anchor states that a particular action may have different consequences in different situations. In other words, no single solution is best in all circumstances.

Many early OB theorists have proposed universal rules to predict and explain organizational life, but there are usually too many exceptions to make these "one best way" theories useful. For example, in Chapter 14 we will learn that leaders should use one style (e.g., participation) in some situations and another style (e.g., direction) in other situations. Thus when faced with a particular problem or opportunity, we need to understand and diagnose the situation, and select the strategy most appropriate *under those conditions.*[53]

contingency approach the idea that a particular action may have different consequences in different situations; that no single solution is best in all circumstances

Although contingency-oriented theories are necessary in most areas of organizational behavior, we should also be wary about carrying this anchor to an extreme. Some contingency models add more confusion than value over universal ones. Consequently, we need to balance the sensitivity of contingency factors with the simplicity of universal theories.

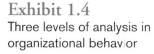

Exhibit 1.4
Three levels of analysis in organizational behavior

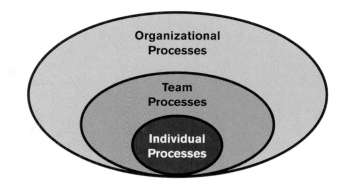

The Multiple Levels of Analysis Anchor

Organizational events are usually studied from three common levels of analysis: individual, team, and organizational (see Exhibit 1.4). The individual level includes the characteristics and behaviors of employees as well as the thought processes attributed to them, such as motivation, perceptions, personalities, attitudes, and values. The team level of analysis looks at the way people interact. This includes team dynamics, decisions, power, organizational politics, conflict, and leadership. At the organizational level, we focus on how people structure their working relationships and on how organizations interact with their environments.

Although an OB topic is often pegged into one level of analysis, it usually relates to all three levels.[54] For instance, communication includes individual behaviors and interpersonal (team) dynamics. It also relates to the organization's structure. Therefore, you should try to think about each OB topic at the individual, team, and organizational levels, not just at one of these levels.

The Open Systems Anchor

Phil Carroll likes to think of himself as an ecologist for the organization. The chief executive officer of Royal Dutch/Shell believes that all executives should take this view because they are responsible for organizations and their interactions with the environment. "Perhaps my real job [as CEO] is to be the ecologist for the organization," Carroll explains. "We must learn how to see the company as a living system and to see it as a system within the context of the larger systems of which it is a part."[55]

open systems organizations and other "systems" with interdependent parts that work together to continually monitor and transact with the external environment

Phil Carroll is describing the fifth anchor of organizational behavior—the view that organizations are **open systems.** This means that organizations consist of interdependent parts that work together to continually monitor and transact with the external environment.[56]

Exhibit 1.5 represents a simplified image of organizations as open systems. An organizational system acquires resources from its external environment, including raw materials, employees, information, financial support, and equipment. Technology (such as equipment, work methods, and information) transforms these inputs into various outputs that are exported back to the external environment. The organization receives feedback from the external environment regarding the use of these outputs and the availability of future inputs. It also receives more resources in return for its outputs. This process is cyclical and, ideally, self-sustaining, so that the organization may continue to survive and prosper.

To understand the open systems anchor better, think about its opposite: closed systems. A closed system exists independently of anything beyond its boundaries. In other words, it is closed off from the outside environment and

Exhibit 1.5
Open systems view
of organizations

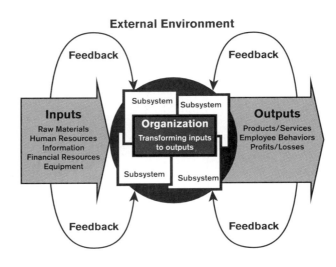

has all the resources needed to survive indefinitely. Organizations are never completely closed systems, but those operating in very stable environments tend to become relatively closed by ignoring their surroundings for long periods of time. For example, monopolies are relatively closed systems because they don't need to respond to customers or other stakeholders very much.

Systems as interdependent parts　A few years ago, Lane Nemeth decided that her company, Discovery Toys Inc., should branch out from toys into children's clothing. Nemeth paid close attention to clothing design and market research, resulting in a successful product in terms of quality and customer satisfaction. Unfortunately, Nemeth did not foresee huge problems in warehousing and inventory control, which caused considerable frustration among the company's independent sales reps. "We made a complete mess out of our computer," says Nemeth, "and we should have known it would happen." She discontinued the line after a year, taking a significant loss.

This incident at Discovery Toys highlights another important feature of open systems thinking: Organizations have many interdependent parts (called subsystems) that must coordinate with each other in the process of transforming inputs to outputs. Subsystems include various processes (such as communication and reward systems), task activities (such as production and marketing), and social dynamics (such as informal groups and power dynamics). Organizational decision makers need to monitor these subsystems to ensure that they are aligned with each other and with the external environment.[57] Moreover, all employees need to anticipate how changes in one subsystem affect other subsystems.

As organizations get larger, they develop more subsystems, and relationships among them become more complex. That's why even the best-laid plans are paved with unintended consequences. Subsystem interdependence is so complex that an event in one department may ripple through the organization and affect other subsystems. Making employees aware of this can minimize those unintended consequences. British Airways used some innovative approaches to teach employees this open systems view, as Connections 1.1 describes.

Open systems thinking is an important anchor in how we view organizations. However, it has traditionally focused on physical resources that enter the organization and are processed into physical goods (outputs). This was representative of the industrial economy, but not of the emerging knowledge-based economy. Organizational behavior scholars increasingly recognize that knowledge is the driving variable in an organization's survival and success.

knowledge management
any structured activity that improves an organization's capacity to acquire, share, and utilize knowledge that enhances its survival and success

Consequently, they have created an entire subfield of research dedicated to the dynamics of **knowledge management.**

Knowledge management develops an organization's capacity to acquire, share, and utilize knowledge in ways that improve its survival and success.[58] It provides a foundation for a stronger learning capability—generating a large number of learning opportunities, generalizing the learning beyond the individual to others across the organization, and building a motivation and opportunity to learn from others.[59] Let's look closely at the dynamics of knowledge management.

Knowledge Management

There is a story about a factory engineer who became a consultant after being laid off by his employer. A year later, the plant manager where the consultant had worked called him in to fix a broken piece of equipment. As his former boss anxiously looked on, the consultant scratched his head, closely studied the machine from different angles, and thought for a moment. He then reached for a small hammer and tapped twice at a particular spot. The lights came back on and the machine sprang to life. When the consultant presented an invoice for $1,000, the irate plant manager demanded that the bill be itemized. The consultant took the invoice and wrote: "Tapping machine with hammer, $1. Knowing where to tap, $999."[60]

Connections 1.1 ◻ **British Airways Flies High with Systems Thinking**

British Airways is a vanguard organization in the application of open systems thinking. One of the airline's innovative ways to teach employees about open systems is by encouraging departments to host "A Day in a Life" seminars. People from other parts of the company attend these sessions which describe the department's activities. For example, the reservations group might give pilots a tour of the reservations system. Flight attendants might help accountants learn more about working on an aircraft.

Another open systems learning tool at British Airways is Domino, an interactive computer simulation. This simulation challenges employee teams to get "Granny" on a flight from London, England so that she can visit her new grandchild somewhere in North America. The trick is to make Granny a happy British Airways passenger without disrupting other areas of the company.

When Domino participants select a course of action, the computer shows the impact of this decision on other departments in the organization. For example, if participants decide to lure Granny to a particular flight with bonus air miles, the computer explains that the marketing department must now decide how to communicate the bonus plan to Granny and other potential customers.

Few companies have gone as far as British Airways in helping employees develop an open systems perspective. The results are apparent. As one employee commented, British Airways has been transformed from a "bloody awful" government-controlled company to "the world's favorite airline."

Sources: E. P Lima, "Pioneering in People," *Air Transport World,* April 1995, pp. 51–54; "British Airways Encourages Employees to Be Conceited," *Travel Weekly,* October 8, 1992, pp. 41–42; K. Macher, "Creating Commitment," *Training and Development Journal* 45 (April 1991), pp. 45–52; J. Aspery, "British Companies Meet the Challenge of Change," *IABC Communication World* 7 (December 1990), pp. 39–41. ◼

As this story illustrates, brains have replaced brawn as the primary source of corporate wealth creation. According to some estimates, nearly 80 percent of American jobs involve knowledge work rather than manual labor. In other words, workers are worth more than their tools. Organizations gain competitive advantage in the external environment through knowledge management; that is, by effectively acquiring, sharing, and utilizing knowledge.

Intellectual Capital

intellectual capital the knowledge that resides in an organization, including its human, structural, and customer capital

The knowledge that resides in an organization is called its **intellectual capital.** Intellectual capital is the sum of an organization's human capital, structural capital, and customer capital.[61]

- *Human capital*—This is the knowledge that employees possess and generate, including their skills, experience, and creativity.
- *Structural capital*—This is the knowledge captured and retained in an organization's systems and structures.
- *Customer capital*—This is the value derived from satisfied customers, reliable suppliers, and other external sources that provide added value for the organization.

An organization's knowledge—its intellectual capital—is its main source of competitive advantage. Software companies, for example, have few assets other than the knowledge held by their employees. Some firms, including Scandia AFS, a Swedish financial services company, realize that intellectual capital does not show up in financial statements, so they try to measure it in some way. This isn't easy, however. It took Scandia several years to develop "Navigator," its model to measure intellectual capital. It may take even longer for senior executives in some organizations to understand and implement this amorphous perspective of corporate wealth.[62]

Whether or not accountants will be able to quantify the value of a company's knowledge, organizational behavior scholars are beginning to understand the process of acquiring, sharing, and utilizing intellectual capital.

Knowledge Management Processes

organizational learning an organization's capacity to acquire, disseminate, and apply knowledge for its survival and success

As previously noted, knowledge management develops an organization's capacity to acquire, share, and utilize knowledge so that it can survive and succeed. This is often called **organizational learning** because companies learn about their internal and external environments in order to survive and succeed through adaptation.[63] The "capacity" to acquire, share, and utilize knowledge means that companies have established systems, structures, and organizational values that support the knowledge management process. Let's look more closely at some of the strategies companies use to acquire, share, and utilize knowledge (see Exhibit 1.6).

Knowledge Acquisition

Knowledge acquisition includes the organization's ability to extract information and ideas from its environment as well as through insight. Four of the most common ways organizations acquire knowledge are through individual learning, environmental scanning, grafting, and experimentation.

Individual learning
Production employees at Motorola, Inc., plant in Illinois recently spent the day driving around the back of a Chicago police car. They hadn't broken any laws. Rather, they wanted to know how police officers use the emergency communications equipment Motorola manufactures.[64] Knowledge flows through individuals, so Motorola and other organizations are

Exhibit 1.6
Elements of knowledge management

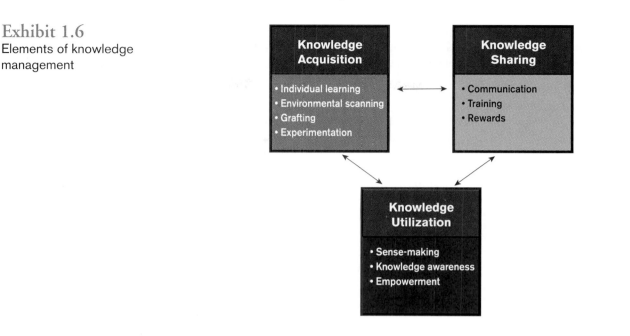

using innovative ways to help employees acquire knowledge through individual learning. Chapter 2 looks at how individual employees learn through reinforcement, feedback, observation, and experience. The quality management practices of benchmarking and continuous improvement, described in Chapter 10, also involve individual learning. The main point here is that organizations acquire knowledge more effectively by assisting the process of individual learning.

Environmental scanning

environmental scanning receiving information from the external and internal environments so that more effective strategic decisions can be made

Environmental scanning involves receiving information from the external and internal environments so that more effective strategic decisions can be made. Environmental scanning helps build new perceptual models of the world, which we describe in Chapter 6. There are many forms of environmental scanning. Pricewaterhouse Coopers, the accounting and management consulting firm, regularly scans media clippings for any mention of its clients. Consultants who serve that client receive the news item so that they are kept informed. USAA, Xerox, and other companies regularly survey customers to find out what market changes are likely to occur. For internal scanning, many firms survey employees, as we discuss in Chapter 8.

Grafting

grafting the process of acquiring knowledge by hiring individuals or buying entire companies

Microsoft Corp. has an incredible amount of intellectual capital that it has translated into successful products and services. However, did you know that some of Microsoft's best-known products were acquired rather than developed in-house? For example, PowerPoint™ presentation software was developed by Forethought, Inc. before the company was bought by Microsoft in the 1980s. More recently, Microsoft acquired Vermeer Technologies Corp. so that it could quickly add the Web editor Frontpage to its product list.[65]

The process of acquiring knowledge by hiring individuals or buying entire companies is called **grafting.**[66] Microsoft is not unique in acquiring information through grafting. Every company hires new employees, who bring fresh ideas as well as technical knowledge with them. Mergers and acquisitions are classic examples of grafting, particularly in software and other knowledge-based industries where intellectual capital is the only resource worth acquiring. "Most people forget that in a high-tech acquisition, you really are acquiring only people," says John Chambers, CEO of Cisco Systems.[67] Of course, grafting an acquired company onto an existing one creates problems with merging different organizational cultures, as we shall learn in Chapter 16.

Experimentation   The previous three activities primarily collect information from elsewhere. However, knowledge acquisition also comes from within the person through insight. This insight is the result of experimentation and creative processes.[68] Corporate leaders need to establish a learning capability. This means that they must create infrastructures that help employees gain insight from their own experiences as well as the experiences of others, then generalize these ideas beyond their own confined boundaries. For example, organizations must welcome critical inquiry and allow employees to make reasonable mistakes. These and other issues are discussed in the context of creativity in Chapter 11.

Knowledge Sharing

Many organizations are reasonably good at acquiring knowledge but waste this resource by not effectively disseminating it. More than one CEO has recently lamented: "I wish we knew what we know."[69] Recent studies report that knowledge sharing is usually the weakest link in knowledge management. For example, only 13 percent of executives in major corporations think that they are adept at transferring knowledge held by one part of the organization to other parts.[70] Valuable ideas sit idly—rather like unused inventory—as hidden pockets throughout the organization. One organizational unit might apply useful ideas to improve customer service, whereas a nearby unit is unaware of these better practices.

How do companies share knowledge? Many corporate executives believe that training is the main element of knowledge management. However, this overstates the role of training. Formal training is useful, but most knowledge sharing occurs through communication processes that quickly and fluidly share meaningful information across organization boundaries.[71] Ford Motor Company uses a Web-based database to tear down its "silos of knowledge." When a work unit posts details about a new way to apply paint, other Ford paint shops around the world automatically receive this information. Recipients indicate whether they plan to use the information and expected cost savings.[72]

Teams also play an important role in knowledge sharing.[73] Organizations disseminate knowledge by seeding teams with new members who bring valuable experience from successful teams in the past. Another strategy is to form **communities of practice.** These informal groups consist of people who live, breathe, and love a particular field of knowledge. Chevron has effectively leveraged knowledge sharing in this way. Dozens of communities of practice groups have sprung up around customer satisfaction measurement, training, safety, quality, and a variety of technical issues.[74]

Of course, many employees are reluctant to share knowledge, fearing that they will lose power (see Chapter 12). Reward systems potentially reduce this problem. Arthur Andersen rewards employees with amounts up to several thousand dollars a year for regularly contributing to the consulting firm's knowledge database. Buckman Labs, a pioneer in knowledge management, took the top contributors of its knowledge management system to a resort. Participation in the specialty chemical company's online forums spiked immediately following the event, and it has never dropped off.[75]

communities of practice
informal groups of people who are connected by their mutual interest in a particular field of knowledge

Knowledge Utilization

Acquiring and sharing knowledge are wasted exercises unless knowledge is effectively put to use. This involves making sense of the information received and applying it to employee behaviors either directly or through organizational systems and structures. It seems obvious that useful information should be applied, but several conditions need to exist.

First, employees need to realize that they possess information to potentially improve customer service or product quality. This requires clear role perceptions, which we discuss in Chapter 2. Second, employees must be able to make sense of the information they receive. They must adopt common perspectives of the world so that everyone makes sense of the information in similar ways (see Chapter 6). "We're not constrained by information; we are constrained by sense making," says Bipin Junnarkar, director of knowledge management at Monsanto. "We are not constrained by ideas but by what to do with them."[76] Third, employees need to have the freedom to apply their knowledge. Thus, knowledge utilization requires employee empowerment, which we discuss in Chapter 4.

Organizational Memory

When NASA officials went to the United States Congress to fund its next-generation launch vehicle, someone asked why the space agency didn't simply rebuild its successful Saturn 5 rocket. NASA had invested $50 billion in that rocket, which had carried the Apollo space capsule and astronauts to the moon. NASA officials investigated this option, but they soon discovered that the agency didn't have a complete set of plans, tools, or dies for the rocket. Moreover, most engineers in the Saturn project had since retired or died.[77]

organizational memory the storage and preservation of the organization's intellectual capital

NASA learned an expensive lesson—that intellectual capital can be lost as quickly as it is acquired. Corporate leaders need to recognize that they are the keepers of an **organizational memory.** This unusual metaphor refers to the storage and preservation of intellectual capital. It includes information that employees possess as well as knowledge embedded in the organization's systems and structures. It includes documents, objects, and anything else that provides meaningful information about how the organization should operate. In other words, organizational memory is the stock of knowledge an organization possesses at any given time.

How do organizations retain intellectual capital? One way is by keeping good employees. Microsoft is so serious about retaining knowledgeable employees that the company recently formed a department in human resources to focus solely on it, even though the software giant's annual attrition rate is only seven percent. "Our assets go home at night," explains a Microsoft executive. "If enough of them don't come back in the morning, the corporation is in danger."[78]

It is important to keep knowledgeable employees, but it is arguably even more important to transfer their knowledge into structural capital.[79] This includes bringing out hidden knowledge, organizing it, and putting it in a form that can be available to others. Knowledge mapping is a potentially effective way to do this. *Knowledge mapping* identifies what knowledge is important for the delivery of a product or service, and directs us to where this knowledge may be found.[80] For example, a knowledge map might identify everything the organization knows about a particular raw material, including the key people and places where this information is stored. As Connections 1.2 describes, Hewlett-Packard has been a pioneer in retaining organizational memory through knowledge mapping. Notice how this practice captures knowledge from human capital and transfers it to structural capital where it is more easily stored and retrieved for future use.

Before leaving the topic of organizational memory and knowledge management, we should tell you that successful companies also unlearn. Sometimes it is appropriate for organizations to selectively forget certain knowledge.[81] This means that they should cast off the routines and patterns of behavior that are no longer appropriate. Employees need to rethink their perceptions, such as how they should interact with customers and which is the "best way" to perform a task. As we shall discover in Chapter 15, unlearning is essential for organizational change.

The Journey Begins

This chapter gives you some background about the field of organizational behavior. But it's only the beginning of our journey. Throughout this book, we

Connections 1.2 ▫ Knowledge Mapping at Hewlett-Packard

Knowledge mapping helps Hewlett-Packard employees share knowledge more effectively.
[Courtesy of Hewlett-Packard Company]

Hewlett-Packard (HP) wants employees to share their knowledge as much as possible. But to share knowledge effectively, the high technology company had to create road maps where co-workers can quickly identify what knowledge is needed and where it is located. These road maps are developed through a process called knowledge mapping.

"Knowledge Mapping is a process that identifies knowledge, skills, collateral, and tools needed to sell or deliver a solution," says Marilyn Martiny, Knowledge Services Manager at Hewlett-Packard's consulting division. "The map is used as a guide to what knowledge is important and where it can be found."

A typical knowledge mapping process brings together experts within the organization, who identify what knowledge is needed, what gaps exist in current knowledge capabilities, and what skills are required for a particular project or work activity. It creates a collective view of the knowledge and skills required to successfully perform each step in the work process. This framework is a valuable resource for knowledge sharing and utilization because it enables others to quickly identify and retrieve knowledge.

Sources: N. Venkatraman and J. C. Henderson, "Real Strategies for Virtual Organizing," *Sloan Management Review* 40 (Fall 1998), pp. 33–48; M. Martiny, "Knowledge Management at HP Consulting," *Organizational Dynamics* 27 (Autumn 1998), pp. 71–77; R. M. Fulmer, P. Gibbs, and J. B. Keys, "The Second Generation Learning Organizations: New Tools for Sustaining Competitive Advantage," *Organizational Dynamics* 27 (Autumn 1998), pp. 6–20. ■

will challenge you to learn new ways of thinking about how people work in and around organizations. We will also rely on a broad range of firms. You will recognize some companies—like Microsoft, Continental Airlines, and Nike. But we also introduce you to many firms that you probably haven't heard about. Some, such as SEI Investments and Cisco Systems, are emerging forces in today's fast-paced world of work. (Cisco employees like to joke that they work at the most important company that nobody has heard of!) Still others, such as Gregory Communications and Buddy's Natural Chickens, Inc., are small organizations. Chances are that you will work in a small business, so it makes sense that we should learn about organizational behavior in these operations.

Chapter Summary

Organizational behavior is a relatively young field of inquiry that studies what people think, feel, and do in and around organizations. Organizations are groups of people who work interdependently toward some purpose.

OB concepts help us to predict and understand organizational events, adopt more accurate theories of reality, and influence organizational events more effectively. They let us make sense of the work world, test and challenge our personal theories of human behavior, and understand ways to guide organizational activities.

There are several emerging issues and changes in organizational behavior. Globalization requires corporate decision makers to be more sensitive to cultural differences. The workforce is becoming increasingly diverse. Companies and employees must adjust to emerging employment relationships. Computer technology has created virtual teams and network organizations. Employees are expected to work in teams rather than alone. Ethics and social responsibility in business continues to be important.

Organizational behavior scholars rely on a set of basic beliefs to study organizations. These anchors include beliefs that OB knowledge should be multidisciplinary and based on scientific method, that organizational events usually have contingencies, that organizational behavior can be viewed from three levels of analysis—individual, team, and organization—and that organizations are open systems.

Knowledge management develops an organization's capacity to acquire, share, and utilize knowledge in ways that improve its survival and success. Intellectual capital is knowledge that resides in an organization, including its human capital, structural capital, and customer capital. It is a firm's main source of competitive advantage.

Knowledge acquisition occurs through individual learning, environmental scanning, grafting, and experimentation. Knowledge sharing occurs mainly through communication and training. Knowledge utilization is more effective when employees are aware they have certain knowledge, are able to make sense of that knowledge, and have sufficient freedom to apply that knowledge. Organizational memory refers to the storage and preservation of intellectual capital.

Key Terms

Communities of practice, p. 22
Contingency approach, p. 16
Contingent work, p. 10
Employability, p. 10
Environmental scanning, p. 21
Ethics, p. 14
Grafting, p. 21
Intellectual capital, p. 20
Knowledge management, p. 19
Network organization, p. 12

Open systems, p. 17
Organizational behavior, p. 4
Organizational learning, p. 20
Organizational memory, p. 23
Organizations, p. 5
Scientific method, p. 16
Social responsibility, p. 14
Telecommuting, p. 12
Virtual teams, p. 12

Discussion Questions

1. A friend suggests that organizational behavior courses are only useful to people who will enter management careers. Discuss the accuracy of your friend's statement.

2. Look through the list of chapters in this textbook and discuss how computer technology could influence each organizational behavior topic.

3. "Organizational theories should follow the contingency approach." Comment on the accuracy of this statement.

4. Employees in the water distribution unit of a major city were put into teams and encouraged to find ways to improve efficiency. The teams boldly crossed departmental boundaries and areas of management discretion in search of problems. Employees working in other parts of the city began to complain about these intrusions. Moreover, when some team ideas were implemented, the city managers discovered that a dollar saved in the water distribution unit may have cost the organization two dollars in higher costs elsewhere. Use the open systems concept to explain what happened here.

5. After hearing a seminar on knowledge management, an oil company executive argues that this perspective ignores the fact that oil companies could not rely on knowledge alone to stay in business. They also need physical capital (such as pumps and drill bits) and land (where the oil is located). In fact, these two may be more important than what employees carry around in their heads. Discuss the merits of the oil executive's comments.

6. Fully describe intellectual capital, and explain how an organization can retain this capital.

7. BusNews Inc. is the leading stock market and business news service. Over the past two years, BusNews has experienced increased competition from other news providers. These competitors have brought in Internet and other emerging computer technologies to link customers with information more quickly. There is little knowledge within BusNews about how to use these computer technologies. Based on the knowledge acquisition processes for knowledge management, explain how BusNews might gain the intellectual capital necessary to become more competitive in this respect.

8. Of what importance is communication in knowledge management?

CASE STUDY

An untimely incident at Ancol Corp.

Paul Sims was delighted when Ancol Corp. offered him the job of manager at its Lexington, Kentucky, plant. Sims was happy enough managing a small metal stamping plant with another company, but the headhunter's invitation to apply to the plant manager job at one of the leading metal fabrication companies was irresistible. Although the Lexington plant was the smallest of Ancol's 15 operations, the plant manager position was a valuable first step in a promising career.

One of Sim's first observations at Ancol's Lexington plant was that relations between employees and management were strained. Taking a page from a recent executive seminar that he attended on building trust in the workplace, Sims ordered the removal of all time clocks from the plant. Instead, the plant would assume that employees had put in their full shift. This symbolic gesture, he believed, would establish a new level of credibility and strengthen relations between management and employees at the site.

Initially, the 250 production employees at the Lexington plant appreciated their new freedom. They felt respected and saw this gesture as a sign of positive change from the new plant manager. Two months later, however, problems started to appear. A few people began showing up late, leaving early, or taking extended lunch breaks. Although this represented only about five percent of the employees, others found the situation unfair. Moreover, the increased absenteeism levels were beginning to have a noticeable effect on plant productivity. The problem had to be managed.

Sims asked supervisors to observe and record when the employees came or went and to discuss attendance problems with those abusing their privileges. But the supervisors had no previous experience with keeping attendance and many lacked the necessary interpersonal skills to discuss the matter with subordinates. Employees resented the reprimands, so relations with supervisors deteriorated. The additional responsibility of keeping track of attendance also made it difficult for supervisors to complete their other responsibilities. After just a few months, Ancol found it necessary to add another supervisor position and reduce the number of employees assigned to each supervisor.

But the problems did not end there. Without time clocks, the payroll department could not deduct pay for the amount of time that employees were late. Instead, a letter of reprimand was placed in the employee's personnel file. However, this required yet more time and additional skills from the supervisors. Employees did not want these letters to become a permanent record, so they filed grievances with their labor union. The number of grievances doubled over six months, which required even more time for both union officials and supervisors to handle these disputes.

Nine months after removing the time clocks, Paul Sims met with union officials, who agreed that it would be better to put the time clocks back in. Employee-management relations had deteriorated below the level it was when Sims had started. Supervisors were overworked. Productivity had dropped due to poorer attendance records and increased administrative workloads.

A couple of months after the time clocks were put back in place, Sims attended an operations meeting at Ancol's headquarters in Cincinnati. During lunch, Sims described the time clock incident to Liam Jackson, Ancol's plant manager in Portland, Oregon. Jackson looked surprised, then chuckled. He explained that the previous manager at his plant had done something like that with similar consequences six or seven years ago. The manager had left some time ago, but Jackson heard about the earlier time clock incident from a supervisor who attended his recent retirement party.

"I guess it's not quite like lightning striking the same place twice," said Sims to Jackson. "But it sure feels like it."

Discussion Questions

1. Use the systems theory model to explain what happened when Ancol removed the time clocks.

2. This case illustrates poor knowledge management. Use the knowledge management concepts in this chapter to explain what went wrong and how this type of problem might be minimized in the future.

© Copyright 2000 Steven L. McShane. This case is based on actual events, but names and some facts have been changed to provide a fuller case discussion. ■

Knowledge management: taming the info monster

BusinessWeek

As the World Wide Web accelerates the Information Economy, know-how is replacing labor and capital as the profit engine. Corporate survival requires faster and better knowledge acquisition, dissemination, and utilization. The quest for knowledge management means tearing down walls between departments and individuals, inside and outside the company. It also requires innovative strategies for knowledge sharing.

This *Business Week* case study describes how organizations remain competitive through knowledge management. It looks at technologies that support knowledge sharing, as well as barriers that companies face as they

move to knowledge management. Read through this *Business Week* case study at www.mhhe.com/mcshane1e and prepare for the discussion questions below.

Discussion Questions

1. According to the authors of this article, what is probably the most important skill required in the Information Economy?

2. Identify several knowledge management strategies described in this article, and indicate where they logically fit in the model presented in the textbook.

3. What is one of the main problems organizations face when encouraging knowledge sharing? How are companies overcoming these problems?

Source: G. McWilliams and M. Stepanek, "Knowledge Management: Taming the Info Monster," *Business Week,* June 22, 1998, pp. 170–71. ■

VIDEO CASE

Southwest Airlines

 Southwest Airlines is the most profitable and productive airline in the United States. It boasts an annual growth rate of 15 percent while at the same time offering seats at one-third less than its competition. It has the lowest operating costs, lowest employee turnover rates, and the fewest customer complaints of any airline in the industry. It is also the only airline ever to win the coveted Triple Crown Award from the Department of Transportation, for Best On-Time Performance, Best Baggage Handling, and Fewest Customer Complaints. Clearly this airline is doing something right. Herb Kelleher, CEO of Southwest, is convinced that "something right" lies in the power of his people.

Discussion Questions

1. Identify the organizational behavior topics that Southwest Airlines seems to leverage to its advantage.

2. Use systems theory to explain how Southwest is effectively aligned with its environment. ■

TEAM EXERCISE

Developing knowledge from mistakes

Purpose

The problem that people make from their mistakes isn't so much the mistake itself. Rather, it's that they do not take the time to learn from those mistakes. This exercise is designed to help you understand how to gain knowledge from past mistakes in a specific situation.

Instructions

This activity requires teams of five or six people, a situation identified by the instructor, and personal mistakes in that situation.

1. The instructor will identify a situation that students would have experienced and, therefore, probably have made mistakes. This could be the first day at work, the first day of a class you attended, or a social event, such as a first date.

2. After the topic has been identified, each team member writes down an incident in which something went wrong in that situation. For example, if the topic is the first day of classes, someone might note how they were late for class because they forgot to set their alarm clock.

3. Each student describes the mistake to other team members. As an incident is described, students should develop a causal map of the incident. They should ask why the problem happened, what were the consequences of this incident, did it happen again, and so on. The knowledge might not be as obvious as you think. For example, in the incident of being late, the learning might not be that we should ensure the alarm clock is set. It may be a matter of changing routines (going to bed earlier), rethinking our motivation to enroll in a program, and so on.

4. As other incidents are analyzed, the team should begin to document specific knowledge about the incident. Think of this knowledge as a road map for others to follow when they begin their first day of class, first day at work, first date, and so on.

Source: This exercise was developed by Steven L. McShane, based on ideas in P. LaBarre, "Screw Up, and Get Smart," *Fast Company,* Issue 19 (November 1998), p. 58. ■

SELF-ASSESSMENT EXERCISE

It all makes sense?

Purpose

This exercise is designed to help you understand how organizational behavior knowledge can help you to understand life in organizations.

Instructions

Read each of the statements below and circle whether each statement is true or false, in your opinion. The class will consider the answers to each question and discuss the implications for studying organizational behavior. After reviewing these statements, the instructor will provide information about the most appropriate answer. (Note: This activity may be done as a self-assessment or as a team activity.)

1. True False A happy worker is a productive worker.

2. True False Decision makers tend to continue supporting a course of action even though information suggests that the decision is ineffective.

3. True False Organizations are more effective when they prevent conflict among employees.

4. True False It is better to negotiate alone than as a team.

5. True False Companies are most effective when they have a strong corporate culture.

6. True False Employees perform better when they don't experience stress.

7. True False The best way to change an organization is to get employees to identify and focus on its current problems.

8. True False Female leaders involve employees in decisions to a greater degree than do male leaders.

9. True False Male business students today have mostly overcome the negative stereotypes of female managers that existed twenty years ago.

10. True False Top-level executives tend to exhibit a Type A behavior pattern (i.e., hard-driving, impatient, competitive, short-tempered, strong sense of time urgency, rapid talkers).

11. True False Employees usually feel overreward inequity when they are paid more than co-workers performing the same work. ■

Individual Behavior and Learning in Organizations

Learning Objectives

After reading this chapter, you should be able to:

- Describe the four factors that influence individual behavior and performance.
- Identify five types of work-related behavior.
- Define learning.
- Describe the A-B-C model of organizational behavior modification.
- Explain how feedback influences individual behavior and performance.
- Identify five elements of effective feedback.
- Describe the three features of social learning theory.
- Discuss the value of learning through experience.

H ow does an organization with 18,000 employees, 3 million customers, and 350,000 customer calls *every day* provide exceptional customer service? For USAA, the San Antonio–based insurance and financial services company, the magic recipe is hiring and keeping the best people, supporting knowledge acquisition and sharing, and providing lots of customer service training.

Rated as one of America's best companies for employees, USAA is very good at hiring and keeping exceptional people. Applicants are attracted by child care facilities and other generous benefits, competitive salaries, and a friendly workplace. "It's important for us to attract and retain the best employees the community can provide," explains a USAA executive.

USAA's second ingredient is a work environment that encourages knowledge acquisition and sharing. A powerful computer system links USAA staff throughout the country so that everyone has instant access to product and customer information. Equally important, call center employees use this system 2,000 times each week to share information about nonroutine customer issues. "Action agents" analyze the information to discover emerging market trends, competitive information, and new product ideas.

Extensive customer service training is the third ingredient in USAA's recipe for success. Employees complete 800,000 person-hours of training, including 10 weeks for every new employee and plenty more for USAA employees throughout their career. To maintain this learning culture, USAA continually recognizes and rewards those who develop their skills and knowledge.

"We take a holistic view toward our employees and their careers here at USAA," says Tony Rivera, USAA's vice president of workforce development. "We know that if they're well-trained and well taken care of, they will serve our customers to the best of their abilities. That benefits everyone."[1]

USAA provides exceptional customer service by attracting people like George Jones, shown here with his daughter at USAA's child development center.
[Courtesy of Kevin Elliott,
The Virginian-Pilot]

SAA applies several organizational behavior concepts to ensure that employees provide exceptional customer service. The company recognizes that customer service depends on the four elements of individual behavior that we will learn about in this chapter: motivation, ability, role perceptions, and situational contingencies. USAA also depends on individual behavior to apply the knowledge management concepts introduced in Chapter 1. For example, the company provides extensive training, including role modeling, to share subtle knowledge about serving clients. Employees also receive plenty of performance feedback, and their learned behaviors are reinforced through recognition and rewards.

This chapter introduces the dynamics of individual behavior and learning in organizations. We begin by introducing a model of individual behavior and performance as well as the main types of work-related behavior. Most elements of the individual behavior model are influenced by individual learning, so the latter part of this chapter discusses the concept of learning and describes four perspectives of learning in organizational settings: reinforcement, feedback, observation, and experience.

Model of Individual Behavior and Performance

USAA depends on its employees to perform their jobs in a way that satisfies customers and fulfills other organizational objectives. How can organizations ensure that all employees provide exceptional customer service and fulfill their other work obligations? To answer this question, let's begin with the model of individual behavior and performance, shown in Exhibit 2.1. As illustrated, four factors directly influence an employee's voluntary behavior and performance—motivation, ability, role perceptions, and situational contingencies.

The model also shows that these four factors have a combined effect on behavior and performance. If any factor weakens, employee performance will decrease. For example, highly qualified salespeople who understand their job duties and have sufficient resources will not perform their jobs as well if they aren't motivated to market the company's products or services. Let's briefly examine these four influences on individual behavior and performance.

Exhibit 2.1
Model of individual behavior and performance

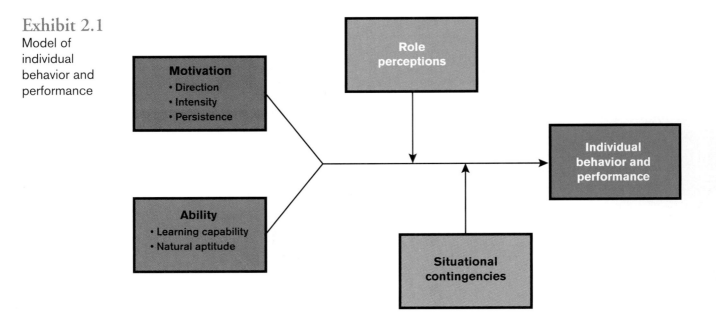

Employee Motivation

Opel, General Motors' German subsidiary, recently announced that employee motivation is essential for its long-term success: "Employee motivation represents one of our largest competitive reserves and is therefore a key element for increasing the international competitiveness of German automobile manufacturers."[2] **Motivation** represents the forces within a person that affect his or her direction, intensity, and persistence of voluntary behavior.[3] *Direction* refers to the fact that motivation is goal-oriented, not random. People are motivated to arrive at work on time, finish a project a few hours early, or aim for many other targets. *Intensity* is the amount of effort allocated to the goal. For example, two employees might be motivated to finish their project a few hours early (direction), but only one of them puts forth enough effort (intensity) to achieve this goal. Finally, motivation involves varying levels of *persistence,* that is, continuing the effort for a certain amount of time. Employees sustain their effort until they reach their goal or give up beforehand. Chapter 3 looks more closely at the conceptual foundations of employee motivation, while Chapter 4 presents some applied motivation practices.

motivation the forces within a person that affect his or her direction, intensity, and persistence of voluntary behavior

Ability

A second influence on individual behavior and performance is the person's ability. **Ability** includes both the natural aptitudes and learned capabilities required to successfully complete a task. *Aptitudes* are the natural talents that help employees learn specific tasks more quickly and perform them better. For example, people with finger dexterity tend to quickly learn how to manipulate small objects using their fingers. You cannot learn finger dexterity; rather, some people have a more natural ability than others to adeptly manipulate small objects with their fingers. There are many different physical and mental aptitudes, and our ability to acquire skills is affected by these aptitudes. *Learned capabilities* refer to the skills and knowledge that you have actually acquired. This includes the physical and mental skills you possess as well as the knowledge you acquire and store for later use.

ability the natural aptitudes and learned capabilities required to successfully complete a task

Competency approach to employee performance

For many years, companies hired and promoted people with learned and natural abilities for a specific job. Now, they want employees who are flexible enough to work in many jobs, and their talents must fit the needs required by customers, coworkers, and stakeholders. Consequently, organizations are quickly moving toward a competency-based approach to employee performance. **Competencies** are the characteristics of people that lead to superior performance.[4] Along with natural and learned abilities, competencies include the person's values and personality traits. Ultimately, competencies must be evident through employee behaviors.

The main feature of the competency-based approach is to identify the generic competencies that distinguish outstanding performers across the organization or broad job groups rather than specific jobs. Holiday Inn developed a list of competencies for executives, managers, technical, and administrative employees. The process began when top management at the hotel chain identified the characteristics and behaviors wanted in its future leaders. Then, about 30 outstanding performers throughout the company were interviewed to determine what distinguished them from their peers.[5]

competencies the abilities, values, personality traits, and other characteristics of people that lead to superior performance

Person-job matching

Whether an organization relies on broad competencies or job-specific measures, there are basically three ways to match

EMC relied on a list of generic competencies when it recently hired over 4,000 employees. This "Employee Success Profile" includes technical competence, goal-orientation, sense of urgency, accountability, customer responsiveness, cross-functional behavior, and integrity. "We've held fast to those attributes as the core nuggets" of hiring, says John Ganley, EMC's director of corporate staffing.[6] Although successful at EMC, what problems might occur when using generic competencies to hire people?
[Courtesy of EMC Corporation]

individuals with job requirements.[7] One strategy is to select applicants whose existing competencies best fit the required task. A second approach is to re-design the job so employees are only given tasks within their capabilities. For instance, new employees might initially be assigned to clients with less complex problems or requests. This is usually a temporary strategy, although jobs may be permanently changed to provide reasonable accommodation for employees with disabilities.

The third strategy, training and development, is one of the most effective ways to improve employee performance. Recent studies confirm what USAA and other companies have practiced for several years: that employees provide significantly better customer service after they receive appropriate technical and customer values training.[8] Training and development also increases employee flexibility by ensuring that they acquire the abilities to perform several different tasks and can therefore be moved to different jobs as work demands require. Long term development involves providing learning opportunities throughout the employee's career, as we will discuss in Chapter 17.

Role Perceptions

role perceptions a person's beliefs about what behaviors are appropriate or necessary in a particular situation, including the specific tasks that make up the job, their relative importance, and the preferred behaviors to accomplish those tasks

Role perceptions are a person's beliefs about what behaviors are appropriate or necessary in a particular situation. Employees have accurate role perceptions when they understand the specific tasks assigned to them, the relative importance of those tasks, and the preferred behaviors to accomplish those tasks. Sales staff at a clothing store understand that they serve customers and stock shelves, but they might have poor role perceptions regarding the relative importance of these tasks.

Inaccurate role perceptions cause employees to exert effort toward the wrong goals, and ambiguous role perceptions lead to lower effort.[9] These misperceptions occur when employees receive no information or conflicting information about task responsibilities and the relative importance of those responsibilities. More accurate role perceptions develop when the required tasks are described clearly, employees are trained in the most appropriate way to accomplish those tasks, and they receive frequent and meaningful performance feedback.

Situational Contingencies

situational contingencies

environmental conditions beyond the employee's immediate control that constrain or facilitate employee behavior and performance

Job performance depends not just on motivation, ability, and role perceptions. It is also affected by **situational contingencies.** Situational contingencies are conditions beyond the employee's immediate control, at least in the short term, that constrain or facilitate his or her behavior and performance.[10] Some factors—such as time, people, budget, and physical work facilities—are controlled by others in the organization. It is important to identify these conditions so that the work environment is optimized for employee performance. Lockheed Martin's jet fighter production facility in Fort Worth does this by asking employees to identify obstacles created by management that prevent them from performing effectively.[11]

Other situational contingencies—such as consumer preferences and economic conditions—originate from the external environment and, consequently, are beyond the employee's and organization's control. For instance, a sales representative may have more difficulty selling the product or service when the economy enters a recession or the demographics of the sales area indicate fewer people would purchase the item. Rather than create a defeatist attitude, some companies encourage employees to focus on things they can control, rather than these external situational contingencies. "What [insurance agents] can control," says a New York Life executive, "is booking new appointments, doing a certain number of fact-finders per month, . . . or even blocking time [to make] prospecting calls. Those things are all controllable. If they do those things, then hopefully the business will come in."[12]

The four factors that we just described—motivation, ability, role perceptions, and situational contingencies—affect all conscious behavior in the workplace. In the next section, we introduce the five categories of work-related behavior.

Types of Work-Related Behavior

People engage in many different types of behavior in organizational settings. Exhibit 2.2 highlights five types of behavior discussed most often in the organizational behavior literature: joining the organization, remaining with the organization, maintaining work attendance, performing required tasks, and exhibiting organizational citizenship.

Exhibit 2.2

Types of work-related behavior

Joining the Organization

Companies need qualified people to complete required tasks and acquire valued knowledge. In fact, an organization's success at attracting and retaining talented employees is one of the top five (from a list of 39) nonfinancial factors used by Wall Street's decision makers to pick stocks.[13] Organizations cannot perform well if they are unable to hire qualified people. Texas Instruments faces this problem. Executives at the high-technology company are scrambling to hire people, but low unemployment and the resulting shortage of talent is hampering Texas Instruments' ability to design new products as quickly as it had hoped.[14] Moreover, to benefit from a diverse workforce, companies need to recognize that people with different backgrounds look for jobs in different ways. They need to recruit at different colleges, rely on ethnic networks rather than the traditional "old boy" network, and advertise in different sources.

Of the four previously described factors that influence behavior, motivation seems to be most important in terms of joining the organization. And in today's tight labor market, many organizations are going to extraordinary lengths to attract skilled and knowledgeable people. Some have jazzed up their Web sites to show potential applicants that the company is in tune with the needs and expectations of today's workforce. Others provide signing bonuses to applicants who accept job offers. For example, people who join Burger King as area managers in Tampa, Florida, receive signing bonuses of up to $10,000. Corey Thomas, a senior at Vanderbilt University, was offered a $5,000 bonus if he accepted a job offer within 10 days with accounting and consulting firm Deloitte & Touche. Jeff Finney was enticed by the BMW roadster that his new employer, Revenue Systems Inc., leased for him over the next two years.[15]

Sally Katovsich (left) and Sue Schroeder are almost drowning in the attention they receive from companies trying to recruit them. Nestlé delivered chocolates; General Mills shipped off cereals; S. C. Johnson & Son sent them a stash of cleaning supplies. Campus recruiters also wined and dined the students in the hope they will join their organization. "At one point I was going out to dinner two, three times a week or more," says Katovsich, a University of Michigan MBA student.[16] In your opinion, do these incentives motivate people to join their organization? What are the limitations of this recruiting strategy?
[Courtesy of D. Strick. Used with permission.]

Each of these strategies might motivate applicants to join the organization. However, as we will learn in Chapter 17, recruiting strategies that lead to unrealistic expectations about the job may result in job dissatisfaction and reduced organizational loyalty. Moreover, these problems lead to other problems with the second set of organizational behaviors: remaining with the organization.

Remaining with the Organization

When Jim Huling became chief information officer of a worldwide software provider in the mid-1990s, he was shocked to find that the company's information technology employees had an annual turnover rate of 63 percent. "When I started, the ones who were still there were only there because they hadn't found another job yet," Huling says. "We were on the brink of disaster. If three or four more people had left, the organization would have collapsed."

Fortunately, Huling was able to instill a sense of respect and loyalty. Only one employee in his 200-person group resigned over the next three years.[17]

Jim Huling and other corporate leaders know that organizations need to do more than hire employees; they also need to keep them. As we learned in Chapter 1, the knowledge employees carry in their heads represents a large portion of an organization's intellectual capital. Long-service employees have valuable knowledge about work processes, corporate values, and customer needs. Thus, knowledge management involves ensuring that valuable employees stay with the organization. "At 5 P.M., 95 percent of our assets walk out the door," says an executive at SAS Institute, a leading statistics software firm. "We have to have an environment that makes them want to walk back in the door the next morning."[18]

Unfortunately, with historically low unemployment levels in the United States, firms are finding it increasingly difficult to keep good employees. According to a recent survey, 53 percent of workers expect to leave their jobs voluntarily within the next five years. Approximately the same percentage of employers admit that they have difficulty retaining staff.[19]

job dissatisfaction a person's evaluation of his or her job and work context

Why do people quit their jobs? **Job dissatisfaction,** which we discuss more fully in Chapter 7, is a major factor. Employees become dissatisfied with their employment relationship, which motivates them to search for and join another organization with better conditions.[20] The labor market is another factor. Even if employees are dissatisfied with their jobs, they remain until another job offer comes along. Some scholars have identified a "hobo phenomenon" as another influence on employee turnover. The hobo phenomenon refers to the idea that some people have short job patterns because they reject the idea that long-term employment with one organization is a sign of career success.[21]

Maintaining Work Attendance

Even if employees don't quit, companies still need them to show up for work at scheduled times. Absenteeism rates have fallen to about 3 percent, but some firms are still struggling with chronic attendance problems. As we see in Connections 2.1, Chrysler is fighting to reduce absenteeism, whereas Honda of America and Toyota have fewer problems with absenteeism in their plants.

What causes people to be absent from work? Situational contingencies certainly influence work attendance. For instance, we often hear employees say they missed work due to poor weather conditions and lack of transportation.[22] Family responsibilities, which now account for one-quarter of all absences, is another reason why people (particularly female employees) miss work.[23]

[© W. Graham Harrop. Used with permission]

Connections 2.1 ◻ Fighting Absenteeism at Chrysler, Honda, and Toyota

Chrysler Corp. is fighting an uphill battle against employee absenteeism. The company recently announced that absenteeism has risen to 6.05 percent, up from 5.2 percent the previous year. In some Chrysler work units, monthly absentee rates have reached 15 percent. Industry experts say that GM and Ford have similar or higher absenteeism levels, but neither company releases this information.

"It's a chronic, contagious, and costly way of doing business that we have yet to get our hands around," said John S. Franciosi, general manager in charge of Chrysler's manufacturing program.

Chrysler has tried various ways to curb this problem. At one time, employees earned up to $600 in attendance bonuses. Then, attendance counselors were hired to pay special attention to those with a chronic attendance problem. Chrysler recently introduced a "no-fault" attendance procedure which allows up to nine absences per year before triggering a mandatory 10-day layoff. The automaker is also developing a selection test that identifies job applicants with a strong attendance motivation.

Perhaps Chrysler should look at the attendance policies at Honda of America and Toyota. With absenteeism rates below 2 percent, both companies are more cost competitive and face fewer quality problems from temporary workers.

Clear attendance standards keep absenteeism low at Toyota's Georgetown, Kentucky, plant.
[Courtesy of Toyota]

Honda of America employees receive up to $2,000 for good attendance, but the company mainly credits its mandatory attendance targets for the low absenteeism. "Our policy is the simplest in the industry with a minimal acceptable attendance level of 98 percent—or 4.5 absences a year," explains Tim Garrett, Honda's assistant vice-president of administration in Marystown, Ohio. "If workers can't adapt to our standards, we eventually have to part company. We make that clear from the very beginning."

Pete Gritton echoes this view. "We have to set a high standard," says the vice-president at Toyota's Georgetown, Kentucky, plant. "If you consistently have to rely on a labor pool, you send a message to workers that they don't necessarily have to come to work."

Sources: Adapted from D. Phillips, "Worker Attendance: Carmakers Get Tough on Absentees," *Detroit News,* July 27, 1997, p. C1; K. Showalter, "Group Bonuses Foster Team Efforts in Manufacturing," *Business First of Columbus,* May 5, 1997. ◻

Ability is also a source of absenteeism, such as when we are incapacitated by illness or injury. Employee motivation to attend is a third factor. Attendance motivation mainly explains why absenteeism is higher in companies with generous sick leave benefits and among those who are dissatisfied with their jobs or experience a lot of work-related stress. For these people, taking time off is a way to temporarily withdraw from stressful or dissatisfying conditions.[24]

Performing Required Tasks

People are hired to perform tasks above a minimum standard. **Task performance** refers to goal-directed activities that are under the individual's control.[25] These include physical behaviors as well as the mental processes leading to behaviors. For example, foreign exchange traders at Citibank make decisions and take actions to exchange funds. These traders have certain *performance standards;* that is, their behaviors and outcomes of those behaviors must exceed a minimum acceptable level.

In most jobs, employees are evaluated on several performance dimensions.[26] Foreign exchange traders, for example, must be able to identify profitable trades, work cooperatively with clients and co-workers in a stressful environment, assist in training new staff, and work on special telecommunications equipment without error. Each of these performance dimensions requires specific skills and knowledge. Some are more important than others, but only by considering all performance dimensions can we fully evaluate an employee's contribution to the organization.

Exhibiting Organizational Citizenship

For the past 50 years, management writers have known that an organization's success depends on more than just satisfactory job performance. It also relies on **organizational citizenship.**[27] Organizational citizenship behaviors extend beyond required job duties. They include avoiding unnecessary conflicts, helping others without selfish intent, gracefully tolerating occasional impositions, being involved in organizational activities, and performing tasks that extend beyond normal role requirements.[28] For example, good organizational citizens work cooperatively with co-workers and share resources. They forgive others for mistakes and help co-workers with their problems.

How do employees become good organizational citizens? Various forms of recognition may encourage these behaviors, but research has identified two conditions that are essential for organizational citizenship. One is the perceived fairness of the company's treatment of employees. Organizations encourage organizational citizenship by correcting perceptions of injustice in the workplace. Employees feel a higher sense of obligation to "walk the extra mile" when organizations distribute rewards fairly and have a process in place to correct problems when employees feel unfairly treated. One way to improve organizational citizenship through perceived fairness is to involve employees in decisions that affect them.[29]

The second condition is the degree to which employees hold strong ethical values, particularly a sense of social responsibility or conscientiousness.[30] **Social responsibility** refers to a person's or organization's moral obligation toward others who are affected by his or her actions. People with a strong social responsibility norm are more motivated to assist others, whether or not this assistance will ever be repaid, and avoid behaviors that interfere with others' goals. It is a value learned through lifelong socialization, so organizations might try to hire people with this value.

The model of individual behavior and performance, as well as the five types of behaviors described above, will be mentioned throughout this textbook. However, probably the most important influence on this model is individual

task performance goal-directed activities that are under the individual's control

organizational citizenship employee behaviors that extend beyond the usual job duties: avoiding unnecessary conflicts, helping others, tolerating impositions, being involved in organizational activities, and performing tasks beyond normal role requirements

social responsibility a person's or organization's moral obligation toward others who are affected by his or her actions

learning because it affects employee ability, role perceptions, and motivation. The rest of this chapter examines the topic of learning in organizational settings.

Learning in Organizations

Most employees appreciate a good paycheck, but an increasing number of them seem to place at least as much value on the opportunity to learn new things at work. "The people and the learning are what's primary," says Tracy Amabile, a thirty-something employee. "I've been provided a lot of opportunities, lots of challenging work in different industries." John Waterman has similar thoughts. "I'm here because I keep learning," he says. "Whenever I start to get a little bored, a new project comes along with opportunities for learning."[31]

learning a relatively permanent change in behavior (or behavior tendency) that occurs as a result of a person's interaction with the environment

Learning is a relatively permanent change in behavior (or behavior tendency) that occurs as a result of a person's interaction with the environment.[32] Behavior change is our only evidence of learning. For example, if a team leader had a tendency to be blunt or rude toward co-workers but doesn't act this way anymore, then we say that he or she has *learned* to interact with others more effectively. Learning occurs when behavior change is due to interaction with the environment. This means that we learn through our senses, such as through study, observation, and experience. Notice, too, that learning requires a relatively permanent change in behavior. This distinguishes learning from situational contingencies that cause short-term behavior changes.

Learning influences ability, role perceptions, and motivation in the model of individual behavior and performance. With respect to ability, employees develop competencies through formal and informal learning processes. They clarify role perceptions through learning. Lastly, learning is a basic assumption behind many theories of motivation. For example, employees learn to expect certain rewards (or less favorable outcomes) following their behavior and performance. They develop or lose confidence by learning whether their effort results in desired performance. Feelings of accomplishment and other forms of need fulfillment would be difficult or impossible if employees did not receive information about their work and reactions from co-workers.

knowledge management any structured activity that improves an organization's capacity to acquire, share, and utilize knowledge that enhances its survival and success

Along with its role in individual behavior, learning is essential for **knowledge management.** As we explained in Chapter 1, knowledge management develops an organization's capacity to acquire, share, and utilize knowledge in ways that improve its survival and success.[33] USAA, described in the opening story, provides superior customer service by providing a foundation for a strong learning capability. Specifically, it motivates employees to acquire and share knowledge from their interactions with customers, and provides opportunities for them to learn from others.[34]

Learning Explicit and Tacit Knowledge

When employees learn, they acquire both explicit and tacit knowledge. Explicit knowledge is organized and can be communicated from one person to another. The information you receive in a lecture is mainly explicit knowledge because the instructor packages and consciously transfers it to you. Explicit knowledge can be written down and given to others. However, explicit knowledge is really only the tip of the knowledge iceberg.

tacit knowledge knowledge embedded in our actions and ways of thinking, and transmitted only through observation and experience

Most of what we know is **tacit knowledge.**[35] Tacit knowledge is the idea that we know more than we can tell. You have probably said to someone: "I can't tell you how to do this, but I can show you." Tacit knowledge is embedded in our actions and ways of thinking, but it is not clearly understood and therefore cannot be explicitly communicated. The knowledge and skills you want to give to others are not sufficiently articulated, so they cannot be communicated through verbal messages. And because tacit knowledge isn't documented, it is quickly lost when employees leave the organization.

Tacit knowledge is acquired through observation and direct experience.[36] For example, airline pilots do not learn how to operate a commercial jet through lectures. They master the necessary skills by watching the subtle details as others perform the tasks, and by directly experiencing this complex interaction of behavior with the machine's response. Similarly, organizations acquire tacit knowledge when employees experiment with new technologies or work on unique problems for clients. Most knowledge in organizations is tacit, but this does not mean that it should remain so. On the contrary, one of the critical challenges in knowledge management is to make tacit knowledge explicit so that it may be stored and shared more easily.

Learning—both tacit and explicit—occurs in many ways. The rest of this chapter introduces four perspectives of learning: reinforcement, feedback, social learning (observation), and direct experience. These activities are not completely different; for example, feedback can be viewed as a form of reinforcement. Rather, they provide different views of the learning process and, by understanding each of these perspectives, we can more fully appreciate the dynamics of learning.

Behavior Modification: Learning through Reinforcement

behavior modification a theory that explains learning in terms of the antecedents and consequences of behavior

The definition of learning recognizes that people learn through their interaction with the environment. This idea is central to one of the oldest perspectives of learning, called **behavior modification** (also known as *operant conditioning, operant learning,* and *reinforcement theory*). Behavior modification argues that we learn from previous interactions with the environment to alter our behaviors in such a way that we maximize positive consequences and minimize adverse consequences. In other words, past experience teaches us how to "operate" on the environment so that we receive desired consequences from that environment.[37]

All learning perspectives that we describe in this chapter recognize the role of environment, but behavior modification takes this to the extreme. Specifically, behavior modification argues that all learning is dependent on the environment. It does not question the notion that thinking is part of the learning process, but views human thoughts as unimportant intermediate stages between behavior and the environment.[38]

Behavior modification emphasizes voluntary behaviors. Researchers call them *operant behaviors* because they "operate" on the environment—they make the environment respond in ways that we want.[39] For example, you put a certain amount of money in a soft drink machine and press a certain button so that the machine will provide a particular can of pop. You learned from past experience how to cause the environment (the soft drink machine) to deliver that brand of soft drink. Operant behaviors are different from *respondent behaviors,* such as automatically withdrawing your hand from a hot stove element or having your eyes automatically contract when you turn on a bright light. These are uncontrollable responses to the environment. The environment causes respondent behaviors, whereas people voluntarily engage in operant behaviors to cause environmental responses. Our attention in this book is on operant behaviors because they represent most learned behaviors in organizational settings.

law of effect a principle stating that the likelihood that an operant behavior will be repeated depends on its consequences

Behavior modification is based on the **law of effect.** According to the law of effect, the likelihood that an operant behavior will be repeated depends on its consequences. If a behavior is followed by a pleasant experience, then the person will probably repeat the behavior. If the behavior is followed by an unpleasant experience or by no response at all, then the person is less likely to repeat it. The law of effect explains how people learn to associate behaviors with specific environmental responses. Let's now look at a behavior modification model that highlights these environmental contingencies. After that, we will examine the types of contingencies and schedules of reinforcement, and finish up by describing the practical implications and limitations of this perspective of learning.

A-B-C's of Behavior Modification

Behavior modification helps us to understand how environmental contingencies influence learning and behavior. There are two contingencies of behavior: the antecedents that precede behavior and the consequences that follow behavior. Together, these elements form the A-B-C model shown in Exhibit 2.3. The central objective of behavior modification is to change behavior (B) by managing its antecedents (A) and consequences (C).[40]

Antecedents are events preceding the behavior, informing employees that certain behaviors will have particular consequences. An antecedent may be a sound from your computer signaling that an e-mail has arrived, or a request from your supervisor to complete a specific task by tomorrow. These antecedents signal employees to establish certain behaviors in order for certain consequences to occur. Notice that antecedents do not cause behavior. Only respondent behaviors are caused by the environment, whereas our discussion is around operant behaviors. The computer sound doesn't cause us to open our e-mail. Rather, the sound is a cue telling us that certain consequences are likely to occur if we engage in certain behaviors.

Although antecedents are important, behavior modification mainly focuses on the consequences of behavior. Consequences are events following a particular behavior that influence its future occurrence. This concept is based on the law of effect that we mentioned previously. If a behavior is followed by a pleasant experience, then the person is more likely to repeat the behavior. If the behavior is followed by an unpleasant experience or by no response at all, then the person is less likely to repeat it. Over the next few pages, we will look at

Exhibit 2.3
A-B-C's of behavior modification

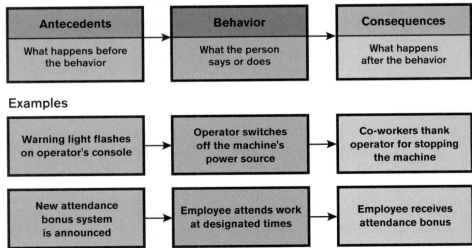

Sources: Adapted from T. K. Connellan, *How to Improve Human Performance* (New York: Harper & Row, 1978), p. 50; F. Luthans and R. Kreitner, *Organizational Behavior Modification and Beyond* (Glenview, IL: Scott, Foresman, 1985), pp. 85–88.

the four types of consequences and the five schedules to administer these consequences.

Contingencies of Reinforcement

Behavior modification identifies four types of consequences, collectively known as the *contingencies of reinforcement,* that strengthen, maintain, or weaken behavior. As we see in Exhibit 2.4, these contingencies are positive reinforcement, negative reinforcement, punishment, and extinction.[41]

positive reinforcement occurs when the introduction of a consequence increases or maintains the frequency or future probability of a behavior

negative reinforcement occurs when the removal or avoidance of a consequence increases or maintains the frequency or future probability of a behavior

punishment occurs when a consequence decreases the frequency or future probability of a behavior

extinction occurs when a target behavior decreases because no consequence follows it

- **Positive reinforcement** occurs when the *introduction* of a consequence *increases* or *maintains* the frequency or future probability of a behavior. Receiving a bonus after successfully completing an important project usually creates positive reinforcement because it typically increases the probability that you will use those behaviors in the future.

- **Negative reinforcement** occurs when the *removal* or *avoidance* of a consequence *increases* or *maintains* the frequency or future probability of a behavior. Supervisors apply negative reinforcement when they stop criticizing employees whose substandard performance has improved. By withholding the criticism, employees are more likely to repeat behaviors that improve their performance.[42] Negative reinforcement is sometimes called escape or avoidance learning because employees engage in the desired behaviors to escape or avoid unpleasant consequences (such as being criticized by your supervisor or being fired from your job).

- **Punishment** occurs when a consequence *decreases* the frequency or future probability of a behavior. As Exhibit 2.4 illustrates, punishment may occur by introducing an unpleasant consequence or removing a pleasant consequence. An example of the former would be threatening an employee with a demotion or discharge after treating a client badly. The latter form of punishment would occur when a salesperson must give a cherished parking spot to another employee who has a higher sales performance for the month.

- **Extinction** occurs when a target behavior decreases because no consequence follows it. For example, if an employee makes practical jokes that are potentially dangerous or costly, this behavior might be extinguished by

Exhibit 2.4
Contingencies of reinforcement

	Consequence is introduced	No consequence	Consequence is removed
Behavior increases or is maintained	**Positive Reinforcement** Example: You receive a bonus after successfully completing an important project.		**Negative Reinforcement** Example: Supervisor stops criticizing you when your job performance improves.
Behavior decreases	**Punishment** Example: You are threatened with a demotion or discharge after treating a client badly.	**Extinction** Example: Co-workers no longer praise you when you engage in dangerous pranks.	**Punishment** Example: You give your cherished parking spot to another employee who received top sales this month.

Exhibit 2.5
Comparing punishment with
negative reinforcement

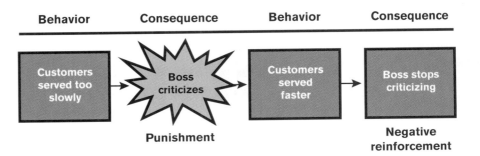

discouraging others from praising the employee when he or she engages in these pranks. Behavior that is no longer reinforced tends to disappear or be extinguished. In this respect, extinction is a do-nothing strategy.[43]

Negative reinforcement and punishment are easy to mix up. As we see in Exhibit 2.5, punishment reduces the frequency or likelihood of a behavior. For instance, after your boss criticizes your performance, you are less likely to do things (such as chatting with co-workers) that cause slow service. Negative reinforcement, on the other hand, increases the frequency or likelihood of a behavior. Thus, you are more likely to repeat the behaviors that provide speedier customer service.

Comparing reinforcement contingencies

All four reinforcement contingencies are found in organizations, but which is best? Conventional wisdom says that we should follow desired behaviors with positive reinforcement and follow undesirable behaviors with extinction (do nothing or withholding the positive reinforcer). This is because there are fewer adverse consequences when applying these contingencies compared with punishment and negative reinforcement.

However, punishment and negative reinforcement are sometimes necessary. For extreme behaviors, such as deliberately hurting a co-worker or stealing inventory, some form of punishment (e.g., dismissal, suspension, demotion) seems more likely. Moreover, some writers suggest that punishment is a necessary part of organizational life because it maintains a sense of fairness.[44] Research indicates that employees who are disciplined believe this action maintains justice in the workplace. Co-workers are often eager to hear about an employee's punishment through the grapevine because it fulfills their need for social justice.

Unfortunately, organizations tend to be inconsistent in their administration of punishment, so justice through discipline is an elusive goal.[45] Moreover, punishment is usually an emotionally charged event that creates negative feelings and undermines the employee's ability to learn from the punishment.[46] In extreme cases, employees develop hostilities toward the organization that may result in aggression and other forms of dysfunctional behavior. This happened at a Frito-Lay plant where punishment was so widely accepted by management that 58 of the 210 employees were fired for various reasons in one year. The remaining employees retaliated by putting obscene messages in the potato chip packages.[47]

Schedules of Reinforcement

Along with the types of consequences, behavior modification identifies the schedule that should be followed to maximize the reinforcement effect. In fact, there is some evidence that scheduling the reinforcer affects learning more than the size of the reinforcer.[48]

continuous reinforcement a schedule that reinforces behavior every time it occurs

Behavior modification theorists have identified five schedules of reinforcement. One of these is **continuous reinforcement**—reinforcing every occurrence of the desired behavior. This produces the most rapid learning of the targeted behavior. When the reinforcer is removed, extinction also occurs very quickly. Continuous reinforcement is most effective for employees learning new behaviors. When practicing new skills, trainees might receive immediate computer reinforcement whenever they perform the correct action.

The other four schedules of reinforcement are intermittent because reinforcement does not occur every time or with every behavior. Instead, intermittent schedules apply the reinforcer after a fixed or variable time (interval) or number of target behaviors (ratio). As illustrated in Exhibit 2.6, a fixed schedule means that the reinforcer occurs after the same number of behaviors or time units, whereas variable means that the reinforcer varies randomly around an average number of behaviors or time units.

fixed interval schedule a schedule that reinforces behavior after it has occurred a fixed period of time

variable interval schedule a schedule that reinforces behavior after it has occurred for a variable period of time around some average

The **fixed interval schedule** occurs when behavior is reinforced after a fixed time. Most people get paid on a fixed interval schedule because their paychecks are received every week or two weeks. As long as the job is performed satisfactorily, a paycheck is received on the appointed day. The **variable interval schedule** involves administering the reinforcer after a varying length of time. Promotions typically follow this schedule because they occur at uneven time intervals. The first promotion might be received after two years of good performance, the next after four years, and the third after 18 months, and so on. Promotions are interval-based because they are typically received after a period of time rather than after a desired number of behaviors.

fixed ratio schedule a schedule that reinforces behavior after it has occurred a fixed number of times

variable ratio schedule a schedule that reinforces behavior after it has occurred a varying number of times around some average

The **fixed ratio schedule** reinforces behavior after it has occurred a fixed number of times. Some piece-rate systems follow this schedule where employees get paid after they produce a fixed number of units. The **variable ratio schedule** reinforces behavior after it occurs a varying number of times. Salespeople experience variable ratio reinforcement because they make a successful sale (the reinforcer) after a varying number of client calls. They might make four unsuccessful calls before receiving an order on the fifth one. This is followed by 15 unsuccessful sales calls before another sale is made. One successful sale might be made after 10 calls, on average, but this does not mean that every 10th call will be successful.

Exhibit 2.6
Schedules of reinforcement

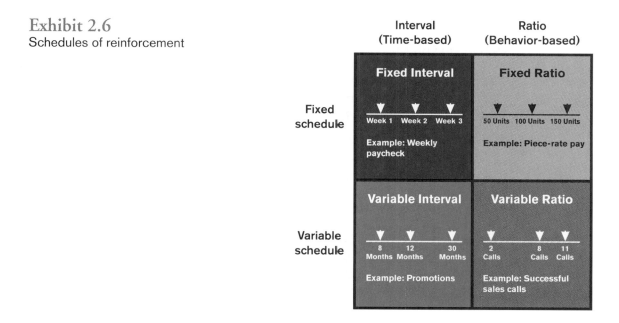

Behavior that has been reinforced with a variable ratio schedule is cost effective because employees are rewarded infrequently. It is also highly resistant to extinction. Suppose your boss walks into your office at varying times of the day. Chances are that you would work consistently better throughout the day than if your boss visits at exactly 11 A.M. every day. If your boss doesn't walk into your office at all on a particular day, you would still expect a visit right up to the end of the day if previous visits were random.

Shaping Complex Behavior

Behavior modification learning is more easily applied to simple, routine behaviors. Complex tasks, on the other hand, are difficult to master quickly, so learners receive little reinforcement. Yet, without some early reinforcement, employees become frustrated as they continually fail to produce the ideal behavior.

Scholars generally argue that social learning theory, described later in this chapter, provides a better template for learning complex activities.[49] However, behavior modification does advocate a process, called **shaping,** that minimizes some problems with the lack of reinforcement on complex behaviors. Shaping involves initially reinforcing crude approximations of the ideal behavior, then increasing the standard until only the ideal behavior is reinforced.[50] For instance, a trainee might be praised initially for backing a dump truck anywhere near the desired dump location. As the trainee improves, the supervisor would provide praise only as the truck is placed close to the dump location and eventually only when the vehicle is driven to the ideal location.

shaping initially reinforcing crude approximations of the ideal behavior, then increasing reinforcement standards until only the ideal behavior is rewarded

Behavior Modification in Practice

Organizational behavior modification has been widely used in industry as a formal process of learning and behavior change. For example, Dana's auto parts plant in Hopkinsville, Kentucky, reinforces safe work behaviors through a game called safety bingo. Employees can draw a number for their bingo card for every day that the plant has no accident. The first employee to fill a bingo card wins a television set.[51]

Organizational behavior research has generally found that behavior modification significantly improves learning and task performance in work settings.[52] One recent study demonstrated how a roofing crew reduced labor costs by 64 percent when employees received positive reinforcement daily for goal accomplishment. The same crew significantly improved compliance with safe behaviors when a behavior modification reinforcement system was introduced. Another study reported how behavior modification practices improved performance of the banquet staff at a hotel in Texas. Specifically, the group's quality and timeliness of setup jumped from 68.8 to more than 99.0 percent.[53]

Limitations of behavior modification   In spite of these favorable results, behavior modification isn't always cost effective, and it certainly has a number of limitations.[54] Here are the main problems with behavior modification:

• *Can't reinforce nonobservable behavior*—Behavior modification may work with easily observed behaviors, such as work attendance, but it's more difficult to reinforce conceptual activities, such as making good decisions.

• *Reinforcer tends to wear off*—Behavior modification programs often suffer from "reward inflation," in which the reinforcer either is quickly forgotten or is eventually considered an entitlement. In other words, a bonus that was once an unexpected surprise becomes an expected part of the employment relationship. Withholding the reinforcer may represent extinction, but it feels like punishment![55]

- *Variable ratio schedule is a form of gambling*—The variable ratio schedule may be best for maintaining behavior, but it also resembles a lottery. Some people worry about the ethical nature of this schedule because employees are essentially betting that they will receive a reinforcer after the next behavior. A forest products firm that tried a variable ratio schedule discovered that some of its employees held strong antigambling beliefs and were repulsed by these behavior modification practices.[56]

- *Ethical concerns about perceived manipulation*—Some critics say that behavior modification tries to manipulate employee behavior and treat people as animals with low intelligence.[57] This perception occurs largely because behavior modification focuses on behaviors and therefore pays less attention to human thoughts. However, behavior modification experts point out that any attempt to change employee behavior is a form of manipulation. No matter how valid this counterargument, behavior modification has an image problem that will remain for some time to come.

Learning through Feedback

feedback any information that people receive about the consequences of their behavior

When the Conference Board asked human resource executives to identify the primary causes of poor performance, the top-ranked problem was poor or insufficient feedback to employees.[58] **Feedback** is any information that people receive about the consequences of their behavior. Feedback may be an antecedent or a consequence, if we look at it from a behavior modification perspective. However, our discussion of learning through feedback will take a broader view by considering how it affects employee thoughts as well as behaviors.

As with other forms of learning, feedback has a powerful effect on behavior and job performance by improving role perceptions, ability, and motivation.[59] With respect to role perceptions, feedback lets people know what behaviors are appropriate or necessary in a particular situation.[60] For example, your boss might remind you to spend more time on a certain activity and less on another. Feedback improves employee ability by frequently providing information to correct performance problems.[61] Employees develop better skills and acquire job-related information by watching instrument dials or nonverbal cues from customers. This is known as *corrective feedback*, because it makes people aware of their performance errors and helps them correct those errors quickly.

Feedback is a source of motivation. As we shall learn in Chapter 3, positive feedback fulfills personal needs and makes people more confident that they are able to accomplish certain tasks. Connectix, Inc. (maker of RamDoubler) uses feedback in this way: The software company distributes letters from happy customers to its employees. This customer feedback has a powerful effect on employee motivation. Whenever a difficult problem arises, the letters boost a product team's confidence and drive to get the job done.[62]

Feedback Sources

360-degree feedback performance feedback is received from a full circle of people around the employee

Feedback can originate from social or nonsocial sources. Social sources include supervisors, clients, co-workers, and anyone else who provides information about the employee's behavior or results. Pepsi-Cola, Whirlpool, Federal Express, Claremont Technology Group, and Nortel are some of the firms that use multisource feedback, in which employees receive performance feedback from several people.[63] This is often called **360-degree feedback,** because feedback is received from a full circle of people around the employee (see Exhibit 2.7). At Pepsi-Cola Company, managers receive feedback from five

Exhibit 2.7
360-degree feedback

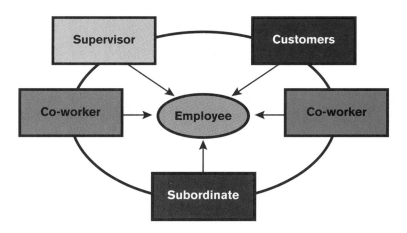

salespeople, three managers at their level, and their immediate supervisor. Managers at Claremont Technology Group in Beaverton, Oregon, ask employees to complete an Intranet-based feedback form which is sent anonymously directly to them. In other organizations, feedback is submitted to a more senior person who combines the results into a single performance appraisal report.[64]

Research suggests that multisource feedback improves employee performance.[65] The main reason is that this type of feedback provides more complete and accurate information than from supervisors alone. Supervisors may have the best view of the employee's task orientation, but not customer service skills. This feedback may be best observed by co-workers or customers themselves. Subordinates may have the best information about the employee's leadership and interpersonal skills. As our *Fast Company Online* feature describes, some people go out of their way to get meaningful feedback from various sources.

Along with social sources, employees usually receive nonsocial sources of feedback. With a click of the computer mouse, a marketing manager at Xerox can look at the previous day's sales and compare them with the results from any other day over the previous year. At Carpenter Technology, Inc., a computer monitoring system lets any employee receive feedback on the productivity of any machine and the status of any work order going through the specialty metals plant.[66] The job itself can also be a source of feedback. Many employees see the results of their work effort by looking directly at the results of their work.

The preferred feedback source depends on the purpose of the information. To learn about their progress toward goal accomplishment, employees usually prefer nonsocial feedback sources, such as computer printouts or feedback directly from the job.[67] This is because information from nonsocial sources is considered more accurate than from social sources. Corrective feedback from nonsocial sources is also less damaging to self-esteem. This is probably just as well because social sources aren't very accurate when communicating negative feedback. To minimize conflict and avoid the awkwardness of confronting poor performers, social sources tend to delay negative information, leave some of it out, and distort the bad news in a positive way.[68]

When employees want to improve their self-image, they seek out positive feedback from social sources. It feels better to have co-workers say that you are performing the job well than to discover this from a computer printout.[69] Positive feedback from co-workers and other social sources mainly motivates because it fulfills our need for social recognition (see Chapter 3).

Giving Feedback Effectively

Whether feedback is received from a supervisor or computer printout, it should be specific, sufficiently frequent, timely, credible, and relevant.

• *Specific feedback*—Feedback should include specific information such as "you exceeded your sales quota by 5 percent last month" rather than subjective and general phrases such as "your sales are going well." This helps employees redirect their effort and behavior more precisely and gives them a greater sense of accomplishment when the feedback is positive. Also, notice that

FAST COMPANY
Online

◘ Fannie Mae Executive Uses "Spotters" to Get Great Feedback

LeRoy Pingho, a vice president at mortgage giant Fannie Mae, never complains about not getting enough feedback. For several years, he's organized annual 360-degree reviews. This is not an official company program; it's his personal program. He selects a cross-section of colleagues—a boss, a subordinate, a customer—and asks them each to assess his performance. "Some things are 'flat spots' for me," says Pingho. "I can struggle with them alone or get help."

Last year Pingho took his review process a step further. He wrote an assessment based on the feedback he received, and then distributed copies to 50 people: bosses, peers, direct reports, his wife. He sent everyone the same message: "You work with me, so you should know my strengths and weaknesses. Also, I'm going to ask four of you to help me work on the things I'm not good at."

Pingho dubbed those four people his "spotters." He chose two at his level, one above him, and one below him. He met with each of the spotters to review the "flat spots" he'd identified. Then he told them that he wanted to focus on getting better at two of those weaknesses. (He didn't think he could tackle five at once.) One was active listening: "When I'm in meetings, I am already through the presentation before the presenter has gotten to the first page." The second was empowerment: "I want to use the input I get from people instead of disregarding it."

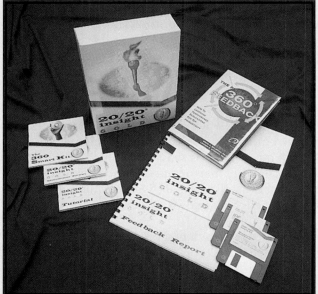

There are many commercial 360-degree systems, but LeRoy Pingho relies on his spotters for feedback.
[John Thoeming]

He asked his spotters to alert him when they saw behavior that related to those improvement goals: "I said, 'You don't have to do this in a formal way. But if you see something, tell me.' It's like being on the high bar. Just knowing that there's somebody to make sure you don't fall helps you become more self-confident."

ONLINE CHECK-UP

1. LeRoy Pingho has developed an elaborate 360-degree feedback system. What might prevent Pingho from receiving meaningful feedback in this situation?
2. The full text of this *Fast Company* article identifies five features of effective feedback in performance management. Identify these five points and note which one is supported by 360-degree feedback.

Source: G. Imperato, "How to Give Good Feedback," *Fast Company,* Issue 17 (September 1998). ◘

Get the full text of this *Fast Company* article at www.mhhe.com/mcshane1e

specific feedback is focused on the task, not the person. This reduces the person's defensiveness when receiving negative feedback.

- *Frequent feedback*—Feedback should be continuously available to employees from nonsocial sources so they can adjust the feedback frequency to suit their needs. If feedback must be provided by someone else, the optimal frequency depends on the task cycle (how long until the task is completed) and task uniqueness. Cashiers and assembly line workers have very short cycles (they finish working with a customer or product unit in a few minutes), so they should receive feedback more often than people with long cycles such as executives and salespeople. Employees working on unique tasks should also receive more frequent feedback because they require more behavior guidance and reinforcement.

- *Timely feedback*—Feedback should be available as soon as possible so that employees see a clear association between their behavior and its consequences.[70] Computers and other electronic monitoring systems can sometimes provide timely feedback, but usually only for routine behavior.

- *Credible feedback*—Employees are more likely to accept feedback (particularly corrective feedback) from trustworthy and credible sources.[71] Multisource feedback has higher credibility because it comes from several people. Employees are also more likely to accept corrective feedback from nonsocial sources (e.g., computer printouts, electronic gauges) because it is not as judgmental.

- *Relevant feedback*—Feedback must relate to the individual's behavior rather than to conditions beyond the individual's control. This ensures that the feedback is not distorted by situational contingencies.[72] Feedback is also relevant when it is linked to goals. Goals establish the benchmarks (i.e., what ought to be) against which feedback is judged.

Seeking Feedback

So far, we have presented the traditional view that supervisors and others give feedback to employees. However, employees do not just passively receive feedback; they actively seek it.[73] The most obvious way to do this is through *inquiry*—asking other people about our performance and behavior. This feedback-seeking tactic tends to be used when individuals have high self-esteem, expect to receive positive feedback, and work in an organization that values openness.

Direct inquiry is a powerful form of feedback in a private setting and occurs when the person providing the feedback communicates the information clearly, yet diplomatically. However, many people have difficulty with direct inquiry when someone has performed a task poorly. As we noted earlier, supervisors and co-workers tend to provide inaccurate feedback when the information is negative. Moreover, it is more difficult to save face when receiving negative feedback in response to a direct request. A third problem is that inquiry is only possible when someone else is available and has time to answer questions.

Thus, employees often use other feedback-seeking tactics. The most common of these is *monitoring*. This involves scanning the work environment and the behavior of others for information cues. Executives monitor corporate data to determine whether their strategies have worked. Salespeople monitor the nonverbal cues of customers during a transaction. Monitoring usually occurs at any time and can be more efficient than relying on others to transmit the information. For instance, production employees can continuously monitor the quality of their work quickly and independently. And although monitoring nonverbal cues of clients and co-workers creates the risk of misinterpreting meaning (see Chapter 8), it has the advantage of avoiding problems with saving face.

Ethics of Employee Monitoring

If you work in a medium- or large-size organization today, chances are that someone is monitoring your behavior or performance. According to one study, nearly two-thirds of large and midsize companies monitor employee telephone conversations, transactions, keystrokes, Web hits, completion time, or other forms of behavior on the job.[74] Transit companies time bus drivers along their routes. General Electric admits that it uses small fisheye closed-circuit television lenses in walls and ceilings to watch employees. Iams in Vandalia, Ohio, listens to some phone calls of sales personnel for customer-service development and coaching. DuPont monitors loading docks with hidden, long-range cameras. In Little Rock, Arkansas, Alltel Corp. requires employees to use specific log-off codes whenever they go to the bathroom or otherwise leave their desks.[75]

Critics argue that monitoring is an invasion of employee privacy, but employers have wide latitude to monitor behavior in the workplace. One court recently decided that video surveillance cameras at the Puerto Rico Telephone Company did not violate employee privacy rights because the cameras were aimed at a public workspace. Another court concluded that Pillsbury could look at employee e-mails even after the firm apparently assured employees that e-mail communications were confidential and privileged. "When you walk into your workplace, you check your privacy rights at the door," says Beth Givens at Privacy Rights Clearinghouse, a consumer-information and advocacy program in San Diego.[76]

Companies argue that workplace monitoring gives employees more accurate feedback to improve product or service quality. It also protects company assets and provides a safer workplace. AT&T claims that its high-quality customer service is partly due to employee monitoring. "Our quality is quite high, and that's why," says AT&T spokesman Jim McGee. "We keep quite an eye on them."[77] A few studies have confirmed that employees see monitoring as a necessary evil. They are worried about invasion of privacy, but are willing to be monitored when the information only provides developmental feedback.[78]

Social Learning Theory: Learning by Observing

social learning theory a theory stating that learning mainly occurs by observing others and then modeling the behaviors that lead to favorable outcomes and avoiding behaviors that lead to punishing consequences

Feedback and organizational behavior modification mainly consider learning through direct experience with the environment. However, we also learn by observing the behaviors and consequences of other people. **Social learning theory** states that much learning occurs by observing others and then modeling the behaviors that lead to favorable outcomes and avoiding behaviors that lead to punishing consequences.[79] There are three related features of social learning theory: behavioral modeling, learning behavior consequences, and self-reinforcement.

Behavioral Modeling

People learn by observing the behaviors of a role model on the critical task, remembering the important elements of the observed behaviors, and then practicing those behaviors.[80] Behavioral modeling works best when the model is respected and the model's actions are followed by favorable consequences. For instance, recently hired college graduates should learn by watching a previously hired college graduate who successfully performs the task.

Behavioral modeling is a valuable form of learning because tacit knowledge and skills are mainly acquired from others in this way. Earlier in this chapter, we explained that tacit knowledge is the subtle information about required behaviors, the correct sequence of those actions, and the environmental consequences (such as a machine response or customer reply) that should occur after each action. The adage that a picture is worth a thousand words applies here. It is difficult to document or verbally explain how a master baker kneads dough better than someone less qualified. Instead, we must observe these subtle actions to develop a more precise mental model of the required behaviors and the expected responses. Behavioral modeling also guides role perceptions. Leaders model the behavior that they expect from others, for example.

Behavior modeling and self-efficacy

self-efficacy a person's belief that he or she has the ability, motivation, and situational contingencies to complete a task successfully

Behavioral modeling is also valuable because it enhances the observer's **self-efficacy.** Self-efficacy refers to a person's belief that he or she has the ability, motivation, and situational contingencies to complete a task successfully.[81] People with high self-efficacy have a "can do" attitude towards a specific task and, more generally, with other challenges in life.

Behavioral modeling increases self-efficacy because people gain more self-confidence after seeing someone else do it than if they are simply told what to do. This is particularly true when observers identify with the model, such as someone who is similar in age, experience, gender, and related features. You might experience this when working in a student support group. You form a "can-do" attitude when another student similar to you describes how he or she was able to perform well in a course that you are now taking. You learn not only what has to be done, but that others like you have been successful at this challenge.

Self-efficacy is also affected by initial experiences when practicing the previously modeled behavior. Observers gain confidence when the environmental cues follow a predictable pattern and there are no unexpected surprises when practicing the behavior.[82] For example, computer trainees develop a stronger self-efficacy when they click the mouse and get the same computer response as the model did when performing the same behavior. The expected response gives trainees a greater sense of control over the computer because they can predict what will happen following a particular behavior.

Learning Behavior Consequences

A second element of social learning theory says that we learn the consequences of behavior in ways other than through direct experience. In particular, we learn by logically thinking through the consequences of our actions and by observing the consequences that other people experience following their behavior. On the first point, we often anticipate desirable or adverse consequences through logic. We expect either positive reinforcement or negative reinforcement after completing an assigned task and either punishment or extinction after performing the job poorly because it is a logical conclusion based on ethical values.

We also learn to anticipate consequences by observing the experiences of other people. Civilizations have relied on this principle for centuries, by punishing civil disobedience in public to deter other potential criminals.[83] Learning behavior consequences occurs in more subtle ways in contemporary organizations. Consider the employee who observes a co-worker receiving a stern warning for working in an unsafe manner. This event would reduce the observer's likelihood of engaging in unsafe behaviors because he or she has learned to anticipate a similar reprimand following those behaviors.[84]

Self-Reinforcement

The final element of social learning theory is *self-reinforcement*. Self-reinforcement occurs whenever an employee has control over a reinforcer but doesn't "take" the reinforcer until completing a self-set goal.[85] For example, you might be thinking about taking a work break after you finish reading the rest of this chapter—and not before! You could take a break right now, but you don't use this privilege until you have achieved your goal of reading the chapter. The work break is a form of positive reinforcement that is self-induced. You use the work break to reinforce completion of a task. Numerous consequences may be applied in self-reinforcement, ranging from raiding the refrigerator to congratulating yourself for completing the task.[86] Self-reinforcement has become increasingly important because employees are given more control over their working lives and are less dependent on supervisors to dole out positive reinforcement and punishment.

Learning through Experience

Corporate leaders traditionally view learning as a process of information delivery from a knowledgeable source, such as an instructor or book, to someone who lacks this knowledge. It implies that knowledge is mostly explicit, organized, and stored with a long shelf life in some form of corporate memory bank. This is certainly an efficient and controlled approach to learning. However, it overlooks the fact that most organizations operate in rapidly changing environments, and, consequently, they need to adapt quickly by developing a learning capability. They must encourage employees to question the status quo and to continuously discover new knowledge through direct experience and experimentation.[87]

With this reality in mind, many organizations are discarding the notion that learning is measured by the number of hours employees spend in the classroom. Instead, most learning occurs when employees directly interact with their environment, whether it is experimenting with a new software program or learning better forestry practices on-site from a trained co-worker. "The more you separate learning from the job, the less effective and competitive you're going to be," says Apple Computer's training director.[88]

The classroom is surrounded by trees at International Forest Products (Interfor). The forest products company introduced a peer trainer program in which specially trained employees provide hands-on, just-in-time learning to co-workers right in the forest. Rather than going to off-site lectures, Interfor employees can now learn a new skill on the job when they need it from a peer trainer. Interfor has less downtime and its employees receive a more thorough understanding of the training topic through direct experience.[89] What concepts about learning presented earlier in this chapter help to explain why Interfor's employees tend to learn more effectively in the woods rather than in the classroom?
[Courtesy of International Forest Products Ltd.]

implicit learning acquiring information about the environment through experience without any conscious attempt to do so

Learning through experience is important because tacit knowledge and skills are acquired through experience as well as observation. Thus, much of our learning takes place while practicing new behaviors and watching the environmental responses to our actions. This also relates to the concept of **implicit learning.** Implicit learning occurs when we acquire information about relationships in the environment without any conscious attempt to do so.[90] In other words, we aren't even aware of much of the information we acquire. Most implicit learning occurs when we interact with the environment, such as when we work with customers or operate a machine. Less implicit learning occurs off the job because knowledge about the environment is indirect.

Practicing Learning through Experience

Learning through experience must occur within a learning culture. The organization or immediate work unit must value the process of individual and team learning. It does this by establishing an environment that rewards experimentation and recognizes mistakes as a natural part of the learning process. Without these conditions, mistakes are hidden and problems are more likely to escalate or reemerge later.[91] Coca-Cola recently *celebrated* the 10th anniversary of the launch of New Coke to demonstrate the value of making mistakes. "We celebrated the failure because it led to fundamental learning and showed that it's okay to fail," explains Neville Isdell, president of Coca-Cola's Greater Europe Group. Mistakes are thoroughly studied so that Coke employees learn from them, but the errors are viewed as part of the experiential learning process.[92]

action learning a form of on-site, experiential-based learning in which participants investigate an organizational problem or opportunity and propose recommendations

Action learning is another form of on-site, experiential-based learning. Action learning typically involves the formation of cross-functional teams that investigate an organizational problem or opportunity, write up their recommendation, and meet with senior executives to discuss their results.[93] A recent study of leadership development concluded that strategically oriented action learning was one of the key features of the best performing companies.[94]

Motorola has embraced action learning to such an extent that many of its training initiatives look more like new business development proposals than classic educational programs. Motorola views learning as an active ingredient in organizational change. Through action learning projects, employees participate in new ventures and develop innovative solutions to unique problems. For example, one of Motorola's action learning teams spent several months learning how to create and manage a software business. Team members interviewed customers, industry representatives, and experts both within and outside an existing network for the company.[95] As we read in Connections 2.2, other organizations have replaced or supplemented classroom training with action learning. In each case, the learning process resulted in organizational change, not just the transfer of individual knowledge.

Why have so many companies embraced action learning? The answer is mainly that this form of experiential learning captures both tacit and explicit learning concepts that we described earlier. It forces employees to enter new situations, to learn from their mistakes in controlled settings, and to rethink current work practices. At the same time, the results of action learning potentially add value to the organization in terms of a better work process or service. As Motorola has discovered, action learning contributes to the organizational change and renewal process, not just to individual learning.

Action learning and other forms of experiential learning will become more important as organizational leaders recognize the value of knowledge acquisition and sharing for corporate competitiveness. However, knowledge does not provide value unless it is translated into action, so we must consider all four drivers of individual behavior: motivation, ability, role perceptions, and situational contingencies. The next two chapters look at the conceptual foundations and applied strategies of employee motivation.

Connections 2.2 ◻ **Action Learning at Britvic and Carpenter Technology**

Robert Cardy, CEO of Carpenter Technology, wanted his $1 billion firm to become a global competitor that seeks out, rather than responds to, market opportunities. Traditional classroom education wouldn't solve the problem because few managers at the Reading, Pennsylvania, steel manufacturing firm have international experience.

Instead, Carpenter Technology's senior executives were assigned to one of three action learning teams and asked to assess the potential of three major strategic initiatives: entry into India, a new distri-

Britvic Soft Drinks initiated a series of action learning projects that helped nonmanagement employees develop leadership skills and save money for the organization.
[Courtesy of Britvic Soft Drinks]

bution channel, and leveraging Carpenter's existing international network to enter new markets. Two of these projects have resulted in major new initiatives for the organization.

"Through action learning, our people are now focusing on strategic issues that are important to us and coming up with plans to solve them," says Cardy.

Michael L. Shor, Carpenter's vice president of manufacturing operations, agrees. "In my MBA program, we learned something, took a test, and it was over," says Shor, who was assigned to the India team. "Here we were given a real opportunity to change the company, and I developed a much broader perspective of the business than I ever had before."

Britvic Soft Drinks, the second largest soft drink manufacturer in the United Kingdom, successfully used action learning to develop leadership competencies among nonmanagement employees. Thirty people, ranging from sales team leaders to line operatives, were initially selected for the leadership development program, called "Developing to Lead" (DTL). The teams identified changes that eventually saved Britvic more than $4 million. Over half of the employees in Britvic's action learning pilot program were subsequently promoted.

Roger Birkett was one of them. Birkett was a Britvic truck driver who had never written a formal report or investigated management practices before completing the action learning project. His experience in the program resulted in promotions to team leader and then to distribution supply manager. "If I hadn't completed DTL," says Birkett, "I would have been going nowhere, just from drop to drop in a green Britvic lorry."

Sources: Adapted from A. L. Stern "Where the Action Is," *Across the Board* 34 (September 1997), pp. 43–47; M. Meehan and J. Jarivs, "A Refreshing Angle on Staff Education," *People Management*, July 1996, pp. 38–39. ◻

Chapter Summary

Individual behavior is influenced by motivation, ability, role perceptions, and situational contingencies. Motivation consists of internal forces that affect the direction, intensity, and persistence of a person's voluntary choice of behavior. Ability includes both the natural aptitudes and learned capabilities to perform a task. Role perceptions are a person's beliefs about what behaviors are appropriate or necessary in a particular situation. Situational contingencies are environmental conditions that constrain or facilitate employee behavior and performance.

These four factors influence various types of behavior, including joining the organization, remaining with the organization, maintaining work attendance, performing required job duties, and exhibiting organizational citizenship.

Learning is a relatively permanent change in behavior (or behavior tendency) that occurs as a result of a person's interaction with the environment. Learning influences ability, role perceptions, and motivation in the model of individual behavior. The four main perspectives of learning in organizations are reinforcement, feedback, social learning, and direct experience.

Behavior modification focuses on behavior rather than thoughts and is based on the law of effect. According to this view, behavior change occurs by altering its antecedents and consequences. Antecedents are environmental stimuli that provoke (not necessarily cause) behavior. Consequences are events following behavior that influence its future occurrence. Consequences include positive reinforcement, negative reinforcement, punishment, and extinction. The schedules of reinforcement also influence behavior.

Feedback is any information that people receive about the consequences of their behavior. It affects role perceptions, learning (through corrective feedback), and employee motivation. Employees prefer nonsocial sources of feedback to learn about their goal progress. They prefer positive feedback from social sources to improve their self-image.

Effective feedback is specific, frequent, timely, credible, and relevant. Employees seek out feedback, rather than just passively receive it. Although employee monitoring is sometimes necessary for feedback, it raises ethical concerns.

Social learning theory states that much learning occurs by observing others and then modeling those behaviors that seem to lead to favorable outcomes and avoiding behaviors that lead to punishing consequences. It also recognizes that we often engage in self-reinforcement. Behavioral modeling is effective because it transfers tacit knowledge and enhances the observer's self-efficacy.

Many companies now use action learning and other experience-based methods of employee learning. Learning through experience is an effective way of acquiring tacit knowledge and skills and is consistent with the implicit learning process.

Key Terms

Ability, p. 33
Action learning, p. 54
Behavior modification, p. 41
Competencies, p. 33
Continuous reinforcement, p. 45
Extinction, p. 43
Feedback, p. 47
Fixed interval schedule, p. 45
Fixed ratio schedule, p. 45
Implicit learning, p. 54
Job satisfaction, p. 37
Knowledge management, p. 40
Law of effect, p. 41
Learning, p. 40
Motivation, p. 33

Negative reinforcement, p. 43
Organizational citizenship, p. 39
Positive reinforcement, p. 43
Punishment, p. 43
Role perceptions, p. 34
Self-efficacy, p. 52
Shaping, p. 46
Situational contingencies, p. 35
Social learning theory, p. 51
Social responsibility, p. 39
Tacit knowledge, p. 40
Task performance, p. 39
Variable interval schedule, p. 45
Variable ratio schedule, p. 45
360-degree feedback, p. 47

Discussion Questions

1. An insurance company has high levels of absenteeism among the office staff. The head of office administration argues that employees are misusing the company's sick leave benefits. However, some of the mostly female staff members have explained that family responsibilities interfere with work. Using the model of individual behavior and performance, as well as your knowledge of absenteeism behavior, discuss some of the possible reasons for absenteeism here and how it might be reduced.

2. Organizational citizenship behaviors occur in a variety of settings. Identify specific organizational citizenship behaviors that you have encountered when working with other students on team projects and assignments.

3. You notice that sales representatives in the Midwest made 20 percent fewer sales to new clients over the past quarter than salespeople located elsewhere. Use the model of individual behavior to identify possible reasons why their overall performance was lower than that of salespeople in other regions.

4. Imagine that you are learning to use a new version of your word processing software. Use the A-B-C model of behavior modification to describe the process of learning this software.

5. When do employees prefer feedback from nonsocial rather than social sources? Explain why nonsocial sources are preferred under those conditions.

6. Senior officials in a manufacturing firm are increasingly concerned about the liability they face if any of their supervisory staff engage in sexual harassment. The company's attorney says that this risk may be minimized by monitoring supervisory staff with hidden cameras. Discuss the dilemmas that this company faces in monitoring employees in this situation. What is the best solution here?

7. The person responsible for training and development in your organization wants to build a new training center where all employees can receive instruction in new skills and knowledge. Why might this idea be an ineffective approach to learning?

8. A consulting firm has recommended that Big Rock Mining Company should rely on action learning to prepare its technical staff for leadership positions in the organization. The executives complain that action learning takes too long, whereas they could have consultants provide several classroom sessions in less time and with less expense. Discuss the merits of their arguments against action learning.

CASE STUDY

Pushing paper can be fun

A large metropolitan city government was putting on a number of seminars for managers of various departments throughout the city. At one of these sessions the topic to be discussed was motivation—how we can get public servants motivated to do a good job. The plight of a police captain became the central focus of the discussion:

> I've got a real problem with my officers. They come on the force as young, inexperienced rookies, and we send them out on the street, either in cars or on a beat. They seem to like the contact they have with the public, the action involved in crime prevention, and the apprehension of criminals. They also like helping people out at fires, accidents, and other emergencies.
>
> The problem occurs when they get back to the station. They hate to do the paperwork, and because they dislike it, the job is frequently put off or done inadequately. This lack of attention hurts us later on when we get to court. We need clear, factual reports. They must be highly detailed and unambiguous. As soon as one part of a report is shown to be inadequate or incorrect, the rest of the report is suspect. Poor reporting probably causes us to lose more cases than any other factor.
>
> I just don't know how to motivate them to do a better job. We're in a budget crunch and I have absolutely no financial rewards at my disposal. In fact, we'll probably have to lay some people off in the near future. It's hard for me to make the job interesting and challenging because it isn't—it's boring, routine paperwork, and there isn't much you can do about it.
>
> Finally, I can't say to them that their promotions will hinge on the excellence of their paperwork. First of all, they know it's not true. If their performance is adequate, most are more likely to get promoted just by staying on the force a certain number of years than for some specific outstanding

act. Second, they were trained to do the job they do out in the streets, not to fill out forms. All through their career it is the arrests and interventions that get noticed.

Some people have suggested a number of things, like using conviction records as a performance criterion. However, we know that's not fair—too many other things are involved. Bad paperwork increases the chance that you lose in court, but good paperwork doesn't necessarily mean you'll win. We tried setting up team competitions based upon the excellence of the reports, but the officers caught on to that pretty quickly. No one was getting any type of reward for winning the competition, and they figured why should they bust a gut when there was no payoff.

I just don't know what to do.

Discussion Questions

1. What performance problems is the captain trying to correct?

2. Use the model of individual behavior and performance to diagnose the possible causes of the unacceptable behavior.

3. Has the captain considered all possible solutions to the problem? If not, what else might be done?

Source: T. R. Mitchell and J. R. Larson, Jr., *People in Organizations*, 3rd ed. (New York: McGraw-Hill, 1987), p. 184. Used with permission. ■

CASE STUDY

How'm I doing? No, really!

BusinessWeek

Lou Hoffman felt something was missing in his work life—a boss to tell him how he was doing. Just because Hoffman was top dog of a Silicon Valley public relations firm didn't mean he was above the need for an annual review. So, in a wild leap of faith, the small business owner asked his 54 employees to give him some meaningful performance feedback. Although the initial results were generally positive, Hoffman's workers trashed their genial boss for his internal communications skills, rating him a dismal three out of 10. Still, Hoffman believes the process is important.

This *Business Week* case study describes how Lou Hoffman and other senior executives are receiving feedback from employees to improve their leadership performance. The author examines the methods used to collect feedback, as well as some of the risks and problems that emerge during this process. Read through this *Business Week* article at www.mhhe.com/mcshane1e and prepare for the discussion questions below.

Discussion Questions

1. Describe a typical process of collecting feedback information from employees.

2. What might prevent employees from giving their boss accurate and meaningful feedback? How can these problems be minimized?

3. Are there times or situations in which these upward feedback sessions would be inappropriate?

Source: S. M. Beck, "How'm I Doing? No, Really," *Business Week*, Online. September 1, 1997. ■

Workplace perks: More companies provide fitness

 At Cigna Insurance Company, Philadelphia, Earl Knight puts in 10-hour workdays. The last thing that either he or his working wife wants to do at the end of the day is cook. However, at Cigna, ordering take out is not exactly what you think. For $10 a dinner, the company chef cooks for the family.

In New York if you work long, stressful days at Salomon Brothers on Wall Street and catch the flu, you can see your own primary care physician right in the building. If you need medicine, fax your prescription to the neighborhood pharmacy and a few hours later your antibiotic walks in the door.

With working hours up and job security down many companies offer a range of attractive and unusual benefits from onsite dry cleaning to lactation rooms for nursing mothers. For example, in Charlotte, North Carolina, Patty Carter takes her laundry to her $7 an hour assembly line job at the Connor Packaging Company. That's because her company does the laundry for her. This company also likes to give money away—15 dollars a week per child, for example, for day care. There's also an emergency loan fund for people who say their light or heating is about to be turned off, with a little free counseling thrown in to prevent it from happening again. All of these benefits combined cost the company $30 a week per employee.

Is this good business? Wilton Connor, owner of Connor Packaging Co., thinks so. He said, "Absolutely it's good business. It's good hard-nosed business. Treat people as if they are human beings with needs and concerns and you will get back loyalty and good work." Hattie Carter, a Connor employee, agreed with his comments. She said, "We try to make him as happy in every way we can because he's been very good to us."

In Chicago at Andersen Consulting you needn't take time for life's small tasks. A company concierge will do them for you. Employees pay $5 per day for concierge services. Andersen pays $2 per day per employee. The company says it's a cost-effective way of keeping busy employees happy and more focused on work.

At the Centers for Disease Control and Prevention (CDC) in Atlanta employees participate in a sponsored fitness program. Dr. Gregory Heath, an epidemiologist at the CDC, said, "Increased levels of regular physical activity is related to the prevention of premature heart disease." A new study by the CDC says that 30 minutes of moderate exercise five times a week will dramatically lower the risk of heart disease, still the nation's number one killer, claiming half a million deaths per year. Dr. Heath noted, "Coronary heart disease alone costs upwards in excess of $47 billion a year." The study estimates that $5.7 billion of that is spent on patients that could have avoided the disease if they had exercised.

The study demonstrates that healthcare costs have been dramatically reduced for companies that provide fitness programs for their employees. One of those is Coca Cola. Arlene Kirchoffer, Coke's health promotion manager, said, "We did find that employees that participate in our fitness center have less health care costs. Something like $500 dollars a year less." That adds up to a saving of $1.2 million a year at Coke's headquarters in Atlanta alone.

Many employees now consider fitness programs an important fringe benefit. And the companies that provide them are finding that they not only save money but win the appreciation and loyalty of employees as well.

Questions for Discussion

1. According to research, 53 percent of employees expect to leave their jobs voluntarily in the next 5 years. Do you think the Connor Packaging Company can keep its people longer than that? Explain.

2. Do you think that employees who have the benefits of those at Cigna or the Centers for Disease Control will exhibit higher levels of organizational citizenship than persons in firms that don't offer such benefits? Explain.

3. Explain how employee behavior might be positively affected by the benefits in this video using social learning theory. ■

Task performance exercise

Purpose

This exercise is designed to help you understand how specific behaviors are associated with job performance and how people may have different standards or expectations about which behaviors constitute good performance.

Instructions

The instructor will identify a job that all students know about, such as a bank teller or course instructor. Students will focus on one performance dimension, such as service skills among cafeteria cashiers, technical skills of computer lab technicians, or lecture skills of professors. Whichever performance dimension or job is chosen for your team, the following steps apply:

- *Step 1:* The instructor identifies a specific job and students are placed into teams (preferably four or five people).

- *Step 2:* Working alone, each student writes down five specific examples of effective or ineffective behavior for the selected job and performance dimension. Each incident should clearly state the critical behavior that made it effective or ineffective (e.g., "Instructor sat at desk during entire lecture." "Bank teller chewed gum while talking to client"). The statements should describe behaviors, not attitudes or evaluations.

- *Step 3:* Members of each team jointly number each statement and delete duplicates. Each behavior statement is read aloud to the team and, without any discussion, each team member privately rates the statement using the seven-point behaviorally anchored rating scale accompanying this exercise. When all statements have been rated, the ratings for each statement are compared. Discard statements about which team members significantly

Exhibit Performance standards scale for performance dimension

disagree (such as when ratings are two or three points apart).

- *Step 4:* Average the ratings of the remaining statements and write them at the appropriate location on the accompanying seven-point behaviorally anchored rating scale. An arrow or line should point to the exact place on the scale where the statement's average score is located. (You may want to put the seven-point rating scale and your results on an overhead transparency or flip chart if your results will be shown to the class.)

- *Step 5:* Each team presents its results to the class and describes areas of disagreement. Other class members will discuss their agreement or disagreement with each team's results, including the quality of the statements (e.g., behavior-oriented) and their location on the performance scale. ◻

SELF-ASSESSMENT EXERCISE

Assessing your self-efficacy

Purpose

This exercise is designed to help you understand the concept of self-efficacy and to estimate your general self-efficacy.

Overview

Self-efficacy refers to a person's belief that he or she has the ability, motivation, and situational contingencies to complete a task successfully. Self-efficacy is usually conceptualized as a situation-specific belief. You may believe that you can perform a certain task in one situation, but are less confident with that task in another situation. However, there is also evidence that people develop a more general self-efficacy that influences their beliefs in specific situations. This exercise helps you to estimate your general self-efficacy.

Instructions

Read each of the statements below and circle the response that best fits your personal belief. Then use the scoring key to calculate your results. This self-assessment is completed alone so that students rate themselves honestly without concerns of social comparison. However, class discussion will focus on the meaning of self-efficacy, how this scale might be applied in organizations, and the limitations of measuring self-efficacy in work settings.

General self-efficacy scale

To what extent does each statement describe you? Indicate your level of agreement by circling the appropriate response on the right.

1. When I make plans, I am certain I can make them work.	Strongly Agree	Agree	Neutral	Disagree	Strongly Disagree
2. One of my problems is that I cannot get down to work when I should.	Strongly Agree	Agree	Neutral	Disagree	Strongly Disagree
3. If I can't do a job the first time, I keep trying until I can.	Strongly Agree	Agree	Neutral	Disagree	Strongly Disagree
4. When I set important goals for myself, I rarely achieve them.	Strongly Agree	Agree	Neutral	Disagree	Strongly Disagree
5. I give up on things before completing them.	Strongly Agree	Agree	Neutral	Disagree	Strongly Disagree
6. I avoid facing difficulties.	Strongly Agree	Agree	Neutral	Disagree	Strongly Disagree
7. If something looks too complicated, I will not even bother to try it.	Strongly Agree	Agree	Neutral	Disagree	Strongly Disagree
8. When I have something unpleasant to do, I stick to it until I finish it.	Strongly Agree	Agree	Neutral	Disagree	Strongly Disagree
9. When I decide to do something, I go right to work on it.	Strongly Agree	Agree	Neutral	Disagree	Strongly Disagree
10. When trying to learn something new, I soon give up if I am not initially successful.	Strongly Agree	Agree	Neutral	Disagree	Strongly Disagree

11. When unexpected problems occur, I don't handle them well. -------	Strongly Agree	Agree	Neutral	Disagree	Strongly Disagree
12. I avoid trying to learn new things when they look too difficult for me. -------	Strongly Agree	Agree	Neutral	Disagree	Strongly Disagree
13. Failure just makes me try harder. -------	Strongly Agree	Agree	Neutral	Disagree	Strongly Disagree
14. I feel insecure about my ability to do things. -------	Strongly Agree	Agree	Neutral	Disagree	Strongly Disagree
15. I am a self-reliant person. -------	Strongly Agree	Agree	Neutral	Disagree	Strongly Disagree
16. I give up easily. -------	Strongly Agree	Agree	Neutral	Disagree	Strongly Disagree
17. I do not seem capable of dealing with most problems that come up in life. -------	Strongly Agree	Agree	Neutral	Disagree	Strongly Disagree

Source: M. Sherer, J. E. Maddox, B. Mercandante, S. Prentice-Dunn, B. Jacobs, and R. W. Rogers, "The Self-Efficacy Scale: Construction and Validation," *Psychological Reports*, 51 (1982), pp. 663–671.

Scoring key for general self-efficacy scale

To calculate your score on the general self-efficacy scale, assign the appropriate number to each question from the scoring key below. Then add up the numbers.

For statement items 1, 3, 8, 9, 13, 15:	For statement items 2, 4, 5, 6, 7, 10, 11, 12, 14, 16, 17:
Strongly Agree = 5	Strongly Agree = 1
Agree = 4	Agree = 2
Neutral = 3	Neutral = 3
Disagree = 2	Disagree = 4
Strongly Disagree = 1	Strongly Disagree = 5 ◼

Foundations of Employee Motivation

Learning Objectives

After reading this chapter, you should be able to:

- Explain why motivating employees is becoming more challenging.

- Define motivation and distinguish between content and process theories.

- Compare and contrast the four content theories of motivation.

- Discuss the practical implications of content motivation theories.

- Explain how each component of expectancy theory influences work effort.

- Discuss the management implications of expectancy theory.

- Explain how employees react to inequity.

- Describe the five characteristics of effective goal setting.

Greg Matusky has learned that younger employees at Gregory Communications thrive on entrepreneurship, not contrived pressure from the boss. "I think they're looking for ways to develop themselves," says the founder of the seven-person public relations firm in Ardmore, Pennsylvania. "As an employer, you've got to feed that need."

Bridgit Smith, a twenty-something marketing graduate who works at Gregory Communications, believes that Matusky is doing the right things. "I like having responsibility and being in charge of my own destiny," says Smith. "I don't know if I'd like lots of bureaucracy and politics. By working for a small company, you have more opportunity to prove yourself."

Generation-X employees—the 52 million Americans born between 1965 and 1977—may prefer small, entrepreneurial workplaces, but that hasn't stopped retail giant J. C. Penney. "It occurred to us that Gen-Xers will work 90 hours a week if they have their own business," explains Debbie Heard, J. C. Penney's college relations manager. To make this happen, managers across the retailer's 1,200 stores nationwide watched a live broadcast on how to motivate Gen-Xers through a more entrepreneurial environment.

"After the broadcast, I came back to my office and my e-mail was flooded," says Heard. "'Thank you, thank you, thank you, they finally understand me,' the younger managers told me. And our older managers thanked me, too, because they finally understood where their employees are coming from."[1]

motivation the forces within a person that affect his or her direction, intensity, and persistence of voluntary behavior

Motivation is one of the key ingredients in employee performance and productivity. Even when people have clear work objectives, the right skills, and a supportive work environment, they won't get the job done without sufficient motivation to achieve those work objectives. **Motivation** refers to the forces within a person that affect his or her direction, intensity, and persistence of voluntary behavior.[2] Motivated employees are willing to exert a particular level of effort (intensity), for a certain amount of time (persistence), toward a particular goal (direction).

Motivating employees has never been more challenging. One reason is that the workforce is changing. As we learned in the opening story, Generation-X employees bring different needs and expectations to the workplace than their baby-boomer counterparts.[3] Meanwhile, baby boomers' needs are shifting as they enter new stages of their life. There is some evidence that companies have not yet adjusted to these changes. A recent survey indicates that only 37 percent of employees feel that their bosses know what motivates them. "The greatest obstacle preventing Xers from giving our best in the workplace is that we are severely misunderstood," complains Bruce Tulgan, the management consultant who has helped J. C. Penney, Wendy's Restaurants, and other companies find better ways to motivate people in this generation.[4]

Motivating employees is also more challenging at a time when firms have dramatically changed the jobs that people perform, reduced layers of hierarchy, and jettisoned large numbers of employees throughout the process. These actions have significantly damaged the levels of trust and commitment necessary for employees to put out effort beyond the minimum requirements. Some organizations have completely given up on motivation from the heart and rely instead on pay-for-performance and layoff threats. These strategies may have some effect (both positive and negative), but they do not capitalize on the employee's motivational potential.

Lastly, as companies flatten their hierarchies to reduce costs, they can no longer rely on supervisors to practice the old "command-and-control" methods

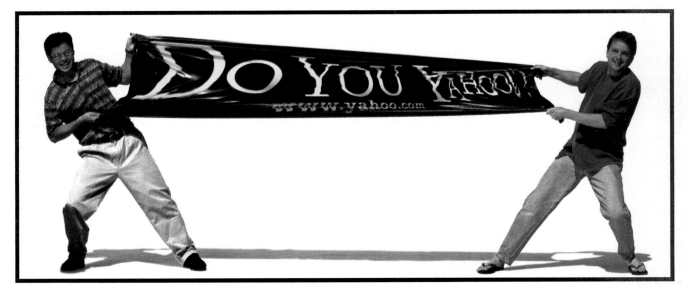

Yahoo! Web-search founders Jerry Yang and David Filo are role models for Generation-Xers. Experts say that Gen-Xers are more motivated by entrepreneurial opportunities and have a greater affinity for risk than baby boomers. Does this mean that Gen-Xers are less motivated by money than older employees? Or, in your opinion, are Gen-Xers and baby boomers motivated by different types of financial rewards?

[Photo by Phil Saltonstall as it appeared in Upside Magazine]

content theories of motivation theories that explain the dynamics of employee needs, such as why people have different needs at different times

process theories of motivation theories that describe the processes through which need deficiencies are translated into behavior

of motivating employees. This is probably just as well, because direct supervision is incompatible with the values of today's educated workforce. Still, many businesses have not discovered other ways to motivate employees.

In this chapter, we look at the foundations of employee motivation. Motivation theories fall into two main categories: content theories and process theories. **Content theories of motivation** explain the dynamics of employee needs, such as why people have different needs at different times. By understanding an employee's needs, we can discover what motivates that person. **Process theories of motivation** do not directly explain how needs emerge. Instead, they describe the processes through which needs are translated into behavior. Specifically, process theories explain why someone with a particular need engages in a particular direction, intensity, and persistence of effort to reduce the need tension.

Content Theories of Motivation

needs deficiencies that energize or trigger behaviors to satisfy those needs

Most contemporary theories recognize that motivation begins with individual needs. **Needs** are deficiencies that energize or trigger behaviors to satisfy those needs. At some point in your life, you might have a strong need for food and shelter. At other times, your social needs may be unfulfilled. Unfulfilled needs create a tension that makes us want to find ways to reduce or satisfy those needs. The stronger your needs, the more motivated you are to satisfy them. Conversely, a satisfied need does not motivate. Let's now look at the four content theories of motivation that dominate organizational thinking today.

Maslow's Needs Hierarchy Theory

needs hierarchy theory Maslow's content motivation theory of five instinctive needs arranged in a hierarchy, whereby people are motivated to fulfill a higher need as a lower one becomes gratified

One of the earliest and best-known content theories to explain why people have different needs at different times is Abraham Maslow's **needs hierarchy theory.** Maslow identified five basic categories of human needs and placed them in a hierarchy.[5] At the bottom were *physiological needs,* which include the need to satisfy biological requirements for food, air, water, and shelter. Next came *safety needs*—the need for a secure and stable environment and the absence of pain, threat, or illness. *Belongingness* includes the need for love, affection, and interaction with other people. *Esteem* includes self-esteem through personal achievement as well as social esteem through recognition and respect from others. At the top of the hierarchy is *self-actualization,* which represents the need for self-fulfillment—a sense that the person's potential has been realized.

satisfaction-progression process a process whereby people become increasingly motivated to fulfill a higher need as a lower need is gratified

An employee's behavior is motivated simultaneously by several need levels, but Maslow argued that behavior is primarily motivated by the lowest unsatisfied need at the time. As the person satisfies a lower level need, the next higher need in the hierarchy becomes the primary motivator. This is known as the **satisfaction-progression process.** Even if a person is unable to satisfy a higher need, he or she will be motivated by it until it is eventually satisfied. Physiological needs are initially the most important and people are motivated to satisfy them first. As they become gratified, safety needs emerge as the strongest motivator. As safety needs are satisfied, belongingness needs become most important, and so forth. The exception to the satisfaction-progression process is self-actualization; as people experience self-actualization, they desire more rather than less of this need.

Maslow's needs hierarchy is one of the best-known organizational behavior theories, but the model is much too rigid to explain the dynamic and unstable characteristics of employee needs.[6] Researchers have found that individual needs do not cluster neatly around the five categories described in the model.

ERG theory Alderfer's content motivation theory of three instinctive needs arranged in a hierarchy, in which people progress to the next higher need when a lower one is fulfilled, and regress to a lower need if unable to fulfill a higher need

existence needs a person's physiological and physically related safety needs, such as the need for food, shelter, and safe working conditions

relatedness needs a person's need to interact with other people, receive public recognition, and feel secure around people (i.e., interpersonal safety)

growth needs a person's self-esteem through personal achievement as well as self-actualization

frustration-regression process process whereby people who are unable to satisfy a higher need become frustrated and regress back to the next lower need level

Moreover, gratification of one need level does not necessarily lead to increased motivation to satisfy the next higher need level. Although Maslow's model may not predict employee needs as well as scholars initially expected, it provides an important introduction to employee needs and lays the foundation for Alderfer's ERG theory which has better research support.

Alderfer's ERG Theory

ERG theory was developed by Clayton Alderfer to overcome the problems with Maslow's needs hierarchy theory.[7] ERG theory groups human needs into three broad categories: existence, relatedness, and growth. (Notice that the theory's name is based on the first letter of each need.) As we see in Exhibit 3.1, existence needs correspond to Maslow's physiological and safety needs. Relatedness needs refer mainly to Maslow's belongingness needs. Growth needs correspond to Maslow's esteem and self-actualization needs.

Existence needs include a person's physiological and physically related safety needs, such as the need for food, shelter, and safe working conditions. **Relatedness needs** include a person's need to interact with other people, receive public recognition, and feel secure around people (i.e., interpersonal safety). **Growth needs** consist of a person's self-esteem through personal achievement as well as the concept of self-actualization presented in Maslow's model.

ERG theory states that an employee's behavior is motivated simultaneously by more than one need level. Thus, you might try to satisfy your growth needs (such as by serving a client exceptionally well) even though your relatedness needs aren't completely satisfied. However, ERG theory applies the satisfaction-progression process described in Maslow's needs hierarchy model, so one need level will dominate a person's motivation more than others. As existence needs are satisfied, for example, relatedness needs become more important.

Unlike Maslow's model, however, ERG theory includes a **frustration-regression process** whereby those who are unable to satisfy a higher need become frustrated and regress back to the next lower need level. For example, if existence and relatedness needs have been satisfied but growth need

Exhibit 3.1   Content theories of motivation compared

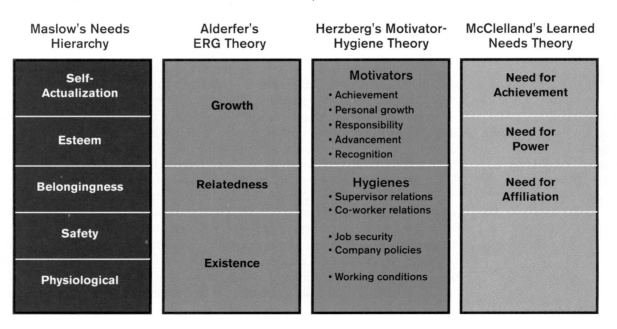

Maslow's Needs Hierarchy	Alderfer's ERG Theory	Herzberg's Motivator-Hygiene Theory	McClelland's Learned Needs Theory
Self-Actualization	Growth	**Motivators** • Achievement • Personal growth • Responsibility • Advancement • Recognition	Need for Achievement
Esteem			Need for Power
Belongingness	Relatedness	**Hygienes** • Supervisor relations • Co-worker relations	Need for Affiliation
Safety	Existence	• Job security • Company policies	
Physiological		• Working conditions	

fulfillment has been blocked, the individual will become frustrated and relatedness needs will again emerge as the dominant source of motivation.

Although not fully tested, ERG theory seems to explain the dynamics of human needs in organizations reasonably well.[8] It provides a less rigid explanation of employee needs. Human needs cluster more neatly around the three categories proposed by Alderfer than the five categories in Maslow's hierarchy. The combined processes of satisfaction-progression and frustration-regression also provide a more accurate explanation of why employee needs change over time. Overall, it seems to come closest to explaining why employees have particular needs at various times.

Herzberg's Motivator-Hygiene Theory

motivator-hygiene theory
Frederick Herzberg's theory that employees are primarily motivated by growth and esteem needs, not by lower level needs

job satisfaction a person's evaluation of his or her job and work context

Frederick Herzberg's **motivator-hygiene theory** differs from Maslow's and Alderfer's needs hierarchy models because it does not suggest that people change their needs over time. Instead, Herzberg proposes that employees are primarily motivated by growth and esteem needs, such as recognition, responsibility, advancement, achievement, and personal growth. These factors are called *motivators* because employees experience **job satisfaction** when they are received and are therefore motivated to obtain them. In contrast, factors extrinsic to the work, called *hygienes,* affect the extent that employees feel job dissatisfaction. Hygienes include job security, working conditions, company policies, co-worker relations, and supervisor relations. Improving hygienes will reduce job dissatisfaction, but they will have almost no effect on job satisfaction or employee motivation.[9]

A unique characteristic of motivator-hygiene theory is that it does not view job satisfaction and dissatisfaction as opposites. Improving motivators increases job satisfaction, but it does not decrease job dissatisfaction. Improving hygienes reduces job dissatisfaction but it does not increase job satisfaction. Moreover, job satisfaction is produced by growth fulfillment and other work content outcomes, whereas job dissatisfaction is produced by the work context. Thus, Herzberg differs from Maslow's and Alderfer's hierarchy models by suggesting that growth needs represent the only source of motivation.

Limitations of motivator-hygiene theory   Motivator-hygiene theory provides a unique perspective of employee motivation, but many scholars have concluded that Herzberg's findings are mainly due to problems with the methodology he used. Other studies relying on more appropriate methods don't support Herzberg's hypothesis that work content and recognition are the only sources of employee motivation.[10]

Moreover, financial rewards and other hygiene factors are widely used to motivate people to join the organization, attend work on time, perform their jobs better, and learn new skills. For example, many high-technology firms have found that younger recruits are motivated as much by a "cool" work environment as by the work they will perform. The work must be interesting, but so should the workplace. Thus, many companies provide game rooms, free pizza, and plenty of opportunity to customize their work space.[11]

Herzberg recognized that money has a complex effect on individual needs, but he generally viewed it as a hygiene factor. As we will learn in Chapter 4, financial rewards are potentially powerful motivators.[12] Robert B. Reich, former U.S. Secretary of Labor, highlights this fact in our *Fast Company Online* article. The people cited in his article clearly indicate that money motivated them to join and stay with an organization. And although money isn't always enough to motivate people to work in boring jobs, neither is an interesting job enough to motivate people to accept low-paid work.

So, why do we include Herzberg's theory here? Motivator-hygiene theory is worth mentioning because it casts a spotlight on job content as a dominant source of employee motivation. Before Herzberg's work was published, many researchers were preoccupied with the physical and social context of work. Few writers had addressed the idea that employees may be motivated by the work itself. Motivator-hygiene theory changed this view and has led to

FAST COMPANY
Online

◘ Who Says That Money Doesn't Motivate?

For most people who are trying to decide which company to join, the name of the game today is stock options. Chalk it up as another legacy of Microsoft and that company's now-legendary cadre of millionaires.

Across the landscape of the new economy, young, well-educated, talented businesspeople are joining up to get a piece of the action. They're willing to forgo larger salaries at bigger and better-established firms in favor of stock options in upstarts that may be worth a great deal down the road. The result: Even small, little-known enterprises can compete for top talent. In fact, startups promising high risk and huge gain are winning.

"Obviously, it's not just compensation that motivates people to come to work here," says David Stewart, 30, head of human resources at Tripod, a Web company (http://www.tripod.com) based in Williamstown, Massachusetts. "But stock options are a big motivator." Founded in 1992, Tripod employs 60 people, produces one of the 10 most heavily trafficked sites on the Web, and boasts more than 2 million members. To keep ahead of the competition, Tripod depends on talent.

Money played a role in bringing Kara Berklich to Tripod as the company's director of communications. Berklich knew Bo Peabody, Tripod's CEO and founder, from her college days and would have joined up right after graduation— but at that point, Tripod not only couldn't offer options; it couldn't even offer a livable salary. When Tripod was able to put together a package that included options, the company suddenly became much more attractive. "You think that eventually those options will become publicly traded stocks, whether through an IPO or through a buyout by a public company," says Berklich.

Stock options motivated Kara Berklich to join Tripod, long before the Web company could afford to offer livable salaries.
[Photo by Larry Ford]

ONLINE CHECK-UP

1. Former U.S. Secretary of Labor Robert B. Reich raises one of the long-standing questions in organizational behavior: whether money is a motivator. Are his arguments and examples in this article convincing that money motivates? Why or why not?

2. In the full text of this *Fast Company* article, Robert B. Reich identifies several other conditions that motivate talented people to join and stay with organizations. Read through the online copy of this article to identify these other motivating conditions.

3. Go to the web sites of Tripod and other organizations described in the full text of this article. What information do you find that describes how these organizations motivate employees?

You can download the full text of this article at www.mhhe.com/mcshane1e

Source: Adapted from R. B. Reich, "The Company of the Future," *Fast Company,* Issue 19 (November 1998). ◘

considerable study into the motivational potential of jobs.[13] We will look more closely at motivational aspects of job design in Chapter 4.

McClelland's Theory of Learned Needs

The content motivation models described so far look at the individual's primary or instinctive needs and their relative importance in life. However, people also have secondary needs or drives that are learned and reinforced through childhood learning, parental styles, and social norms. Several learned needs can motivate us at the same time. David McClelland devoted his career to studying three secondary needs that he considered particularly important sources of motivation: need for achievement, need for affiliation, and need for power.

need for achievement (nAch) a learned need in which people want to accomplish reasonably challenging goals through their own efforts, like to be successful in competitive situations, and desire unambiguous feedback regarding their success

Need for achievement (nAch)   The most widely studied learned need is **need for achievement (nAch).** People with a high nAch want to accomplish reasonably challenging goals through their own efforts. They prefer working alone rather than in teams because of their strong need to assume personal responsibility for tasks. High nAch people also like to be successful in competitive situations and have a strong need for unambiguous feedback regarding their success. High nAch people are therefore most satisfied when their jobs offer challenge, feedback, and recognition.[14]

Research indicates that high nAch people are mainly motivated by the expectation of satisfying their need for achievement. Money is a relatively weak motivator for them, except to the extent that it provides feedback and provides recognition for their success. In contrast, employees with a low need for achievement perform their work better when money is used as a financial incentive.

A substantial body of research has found that successful entrepreneurs tend to have a high nAch. This is possibly because high nAch people establish challenging goals for themselves and thrive on competition.[15] High nAch people also perform better in other occupations with competitive environments. For instance, research at PepsiCo suggests that they perform well in subsidiaries of large organizations that face competition and have few layers of management. However, corporate and team leaders should have a somewhat lower nAch because they must delegate work and build support through involvement (characteristics not usually found in high achievers).[16]

One of the most fascinating streams of research on need for achievement has been its effect on the economic growth and decline of civilizations. One study measured nAch from stories in children's primary school readers and found that nAch scores were associated with economic growth in those countries over the next 20 years. Another study that estimated nAch from popular literature in Europe between 1400 and 1830 found that a rise in nAch preceded economic growth by as much as 50 years. A third study reported that nAch (as measured by fourth-grade readers) predicted the number of patents recorded in the United States between 1800 and 1950.[17] Overall, there is convincing evidence that need for achievement is a powerful factor in the success of organizations and societies.

need for affiliation (nAff) a learned need in which people seek approval from others, conform to their wishes and expectations, and avoid conflict and confrontation

Need for affiliation (nAff)   **Need for affiliation (nAff)** refers to a desire to seek approval from others, conform to their wishes and expectations, and avoid conflict and confrontation. People with a strong nAff want to form positive relationships with others. They try to project a favorable image of themselves and take other steps to be liked by others. Moreover, high nAff employees actively support others and try to smooth out conflicts that occur in

Desi Kepe (left) and Robert Kepe became entrepreneurs at an early age. When Togo's restaurant chain let the two brothers own one of Togo's Los Angeles area restaurants a few years ago, the teenagers became the youngest Togo's owners in the company's two-decade history. Today, their sandwich shop employs nearly two dozen people. Like most successful entrepreneurs, Desi and Robert Kepe have a strong need for achievement. Organizational behavior scholars say the need for achievement is learned (rather than instinctive) through parents and early childhood experiences. This is certainly true of the Kepe brothers. Their parents, immigrants from Slovenia, raised their sons in an entrepreneur-friendly household. Their father owns a construction business and both parents own real estate. The common question around the dinner table was, "So how's the business going?"[18] If need for achievement is learned, how might this need be developed later in life?
[Michael O. Baker/Los Angeles Daily News]

meetings and other social settings. As Exhibit 3.1 illustrated earlier, need for affiliation is similar to Maslow's belongingness need and Alderfer's relatedness need. The main difference, however, is that need for affiliation is learned rather than instinctive.

High nAff employees tend to be more effective than those with a low nAff in coordinating roles, such as helping diverse departments work on joint projects. They are also more effective in sales positions where the main task is to cultivate long-term relations with prospective customers. More generally, employees with high nAff prefer working with others rather than alone, tend to have better attendance records, and tend to be better at mediating conflicts.

Although people with a high nAff are more effective in many jobs requiring social interaction, they tend to be less effective at allocating scarce resources and making other decisions that potentially generate conflict. For example, research has found that executives with a high nAff tend to be indecisive and are perceived as less fair in the distribution of resources. Thus, people in these decision-making positions must have a relatively low need for affiliation so that their choices and actions are not biased by a personal need for approval.[19]

need for power (nPow) a learned need in which people want to control their environment, including people and material resources, to benefit either themselves (personalized power) or others (socialized power)

Need for power (nPow)   **Need for power (nPow)** refers to a desire to control one's environment, including people and material resources. People with a high nPow want to exercise control over others and are concerned about maintaining their leadership position. They frequently rely on persuasive communication (see Chapter 8), make more suggestions in meetings, and tend to publicly evaluate situations more frequently.

McClelland and his colleagues claim that the need for power takes two forms: personalized and socialized.[20] People with a high need for *personalized power* enjoy their power for its own sake and use it to advance their career and other personal interests. They desire loyalty from others and gain satisfaction from conquering or dominating them. This contrasts with people who have a high need for *socialized power*. The latter seek power to help others, such as improving society or increasing organizational effectiveness. People with a high need for socialized power want power, but they also have a strong sense of altruism and social responsibility. They are concerned about the consequences of their own actions on others.

Corporate and political leaders have a high nPow because this motivates them to influence others—an important part of the leadership process (see Chapter 14).[21] However, McClelland argues that effective leaders should have a high need for socialized rather than personalized power. In other words, leaders must exercise their power within the framework of moral standards. The ethical guidance of their need for power develops follower trust and respect for the leader, as well as commitment to the leader's vision.[22]

Learning needs   McClelland argued that achievement, affiliation, and power needs are learned rather than instinctive. Accordingly, he developed training programs that strengthen these needs. In his achievement-motivation program, trainees review imaginative stories written by high-achievement-need people and then practice writing their own achievement-oriented stories. They practice achievement-oriented behaviors in business games and examine whether being a high achiever is consistent with their self-image and career plans. Trainees also complete a detailed achievement plan for the next two years and form a reference group with other trainees to maintain their new-found achievement-motive style.[23]

These programs seem to work. For example, need achievement course participants in India subsequently started more new businesses, had greater community involvement, invested more in expanding their businesses, and employed twice as many people as nonparticipants. Research on similar achievement-motive courses for North American small business owners reported dramatic increases in the profitability of the participants' businesses.

Practical Implications of Content Motivation Theories

Content theories of motivation suggest that different people have different needs at different times. Some employees are ready to fulfill growth needs, whereas others are still struggling to satisfy their minimum existence needs. Needs change as people enter new stages of their life.

Moreover, as the opening story to this chapter indicated, different generations bring a unique set of needs that have been influenced by experiences while they were growing up. According to a recent report from consulting firm McKinsey and Co., many companies don't realize that the strategies that motivated baby boomers are outdated and inappropriate for Gen-X employees. "[Corporate leaders] think they're entitled to have a workforce that works like their parents did," warns McKinsey partner David Friedman.[24] Thus, companies must realign their motivational practices to fit these changing needs.

Most organizations distribute the same reward, such as a salary increase or paid time off, to all employees with good performance. But rewards that motivate some people have less effect on those with different needs. Thus, content motivation theories advise organizations to offer employees their choice of rewards. Those who perform well might trade part of the bonus for extra time off. The result of a flexible reward system is that employees can create a reward package with the greatest value to them. This principle is also found in flexible benefits systems, in which employees alter their pensions, vacation time, and other benefits to match their particular needs.

Content theories of motivation also warn us against relying too heavily on financial rewards as a source of employee motivation.[25] As we noted earlier, some content theories may have been too critical of money as a motivator. However, these theories correctly point out that there are other forms of motivation. For instance, most software programmers make good money, but their real reward seems to be the respect and fun of hiding Easter eggs in their software. As Connections 3.1 describes, these nuggets of graphical graffiti satisfy a programmer's need for recognition by peers or users. The point here is that organizations must recognize nonfinancial as well as financial sources of motivation.

Process Theories of Motivation

At the beginning of this chapter, we distinguished the content theories presented above from process theories of motivation. Content theories explain why people have different needs at different times, whereas process theories describe the processes through which need deficiencies are translated into behavior. Three of the most popular process theories of motivation are expectancy theory, equity theory, and goal setting.

Expectancy Theory of Motivation

expectancy theory a process motivation theory stating that work effort is directed toward behaviors that people believe will lead to desired outcomes

Expectancy theory is a process motivation theory based on the idea that work effort is directed toward behaviors that people believe will lead to desired outcomes.[26] Through experience, we develop expectations about whether we can achieve various levels of job performance. We also develop expectations about whether job performance and work behaviors lead to particular outcomes. Finally, we naturally direct our effort toward outcomes that help us fulfill our needs.

Expectancy theory emerged from the writings of Kurt Lewin and other social psychologists in the 1930s.[27] Victor Vroom is generally credited with introducing expectancy theory to organizational settings in 1964, although his version of the model is unnecessarily complex and often described incorrectly. The version of expectancy theory presented in this book, developed by Edward E. Lawler, is equally effective at explaining employee motivation, yet avoids the unnecessary complexity of Vroom's original model.[28]

Expectancy Theory Model

Lawler's expectancy theory model is presented in Exhibit 3.2. The key variable of interest in expectancy theory is *effort*—the individual's actual exertion of energy. An individual's effort level depends on three factors: effort-to-performance (E→P) expectancy, performance-to-outcome (P→O) expectancy, and outcome valences (V). Employee motivation is influenced by all three components of the expectancy theory model. If any component weakens, motivation weakens.

effort-to-performance (E→P) expectancy an individual's perceived probability that a particular level of effort will result in a particular level of performance

E→P expectancy The **effort-to-performance (E→P) expectancy** is the individual's perception that his or her effort will result in a particular level of performance. Expectancy is defined as a *probability,* and therefore ranges from 0.0 to 1.0. In some situations, employees may believe that they can

Connections 3.1 ◻ **Fulfilling Needs through Cyber Easter Eggs**

Computer programmers like a good paycheck, but they love the recognition found in Easter eggs. Easter eggs are nuggets of graphical graffiti left behind by programmers in most software programs. Click in the right place or type in a special command and a secret message or image will appear.

Microsoft programmers are infamous for sticking Easter eggs in their software, including Windows95, Word, Excel, and Internet Explorer. Easter eggs are "just kind of quirky," explains a Microsoft spokesperson. "It's just something [programmers] leave users to discover."

Many Easter eggs are the inspiration of individual programmers who sneak them by the quality inspectors. The more elaborate the Easter egg, the harder it must have been for the programmers to slip it unnoticed into the product, and the more respected they will be by their peers.

Other Easter eggs are created by the entire development team to fulfill their need for public recognition. Microsoft's Internet Explorer 4.0, for example, contains a secret multimedia show several minutes long about the people who built it. Excel 97, Microsoft's popular spread-

7.5.3 Core Project Team: Bala Akella, Wendy Chiou, Doug Clarke, Mike Crawford, Michael ...

Hidden in a recent Macintosh operating system is an elaborate Easter egg showing Apple's headquarters.

sheet package, has a hidden flight simulator. Fly across its landscape to the right mountain and you can see a list of the programmers' names.

A recent version of the Macintosh OS had perhaps the most elaborate Easter egg. By dragging a special phrase onto the desktop, the operating system revealed a virtual reality image of Apple's headquarters, complete with a flag that waved in the direction of the user's mouse.

One of the earliest known eggs was found in an Atari game developed in 1977. The programmer left a permanent signature by spelling out his name on the walls of one room.

Sources: Adapted from L. Gornstein, "Software Harbors Treasures," *Arizona Republic,* March 9, 1998, p. E1; T. Standage, "Easter Eggs beyond a Joke," *Daily Telegraph* (London), February 19, 1998, p. 4. Some information was also collected from web site http://www.eeggs.com ◼

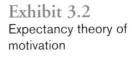

Exhibit 3.2
Expectancy theory of
motivation

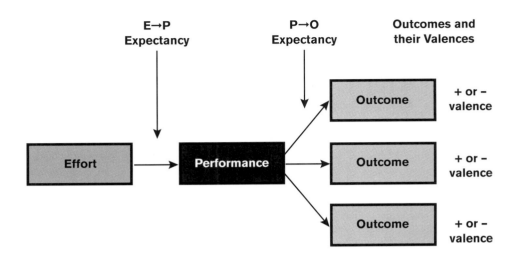

unquestionably accomplish the task (a probability of 1.0). In other situations, they expect that even their highest level of effort will not result in the desired performance level (a probability of 0.0). In most cases, the E→P expectancy falls somewhere between these two extremes.

performance-to-outcome (P→O) expectancy an individual's perceived probability that a specific behavior or performance level will lead to specific outcomes

P→O expectancy   The **performance-to-outcome (P→O) expectancy** is the perceived probability that a specific behavior or performance level will lead to specific outcomes. This probability is developed from previous learning. In extreme cases, employees may believe that accomplishing a particular task (performance) will *definitely* result in a particular outcome (a probability of 1.0), or they may believe that this outcome will *definitely not* result from successful performance (a probability of 0.0). More often, the P→O expectancy falls somewhere between these two extremes.

One important issue in P→O expectancies is which outcomes do we think about? We certainly don't evaluate the P→O expectancy for every possible outcome. There are too many of them. Instead, we only think about outcomes of interest to us at the time. One day, your motivation to complete a task may be fueled mainly by the likelihood of getting off work early to meet friends. Other times, your motivation to complete the same task may be based more on the P→O expectancy of a promotion or pay increase. The main point is that your motivation depends on the probability that a behavior or job performance level will result in outcomes that you think about.

valence the anticipated satisfaction or dissatisfaction that an individual feels toward an outcome

Outcome valences   The third element in expectancy theory is the **valence** of each outcome that you consider. Valence refers to the anticipated satisfaction or dissatisfaction that an individual feels toward an outcome. It ranges from negative to positive. (The actual range doesn't matter; it may be from -1 to $+1$, or from -100 to $+100$.) An outcome valence is determined by the strength of the person's basic needs that are associated with the outcome. Outcomes have a positive valence when they directly or indirectly satisfy the person's needs, and have a negative valence when they inhibit the person's need fulfillment. If you have a strong social need, for example, then outcomes that likely fulfill that need will have a strong positive valence to you. Outcomes that move you further away from fulfilling your social need will have a strong negative valence.

Notice that some outcomes directly fulfill personal needs, whereas other outcomes indirectly fulfill those needs. You might be motivated to achieve the highest sales in your company this month because "it feels great." This is the direct outcome of growth need fulfillment. At the same time, you might want to be the top sales person because you will be mentioned in the company magazine, thereby indirectly fulfilling your social needs.

Expectancy Theory in Practice

One of the appealing characteristics of expectancy theory is that it provides clear guidelines for increasing employee motivation by altering the person's E→P expectancies, P→O expectancies, and/or outcome valences.[29] Several practical implications of expectancy theory are listed in Exhibit 3.3 and described below.

Increasing E→P expectancies
E→P expectancies are based on self-esteem and previous experience in that situation.[30] Consequently, employees should be given the necessary competencies, clear role perceptions, and favorable situational contingencies to reach the desired levels of performance so that they form higher E→P expectancies. This involves properly matching employees to jobs based on their abilities, clearly communicating the tasks required for the job, and providing sufficient resources for them to accomplish those tasks.

Even when employees have the capacity and resources to perform the work, they may have low E→P expectancies because of low self-confidence. Counseling and coaching may be advisable so that employees develop confidence that they already possess the skills and knowledge to perform the job. Similarly, E→P expectancies are learned, so positive feedback typically strengthens employee self-efficacy.[31] Shaping and behavioral modeling also tend to increase E→P expectancies in many situations.

Exhibit 3.3   Practical applications of expectancy theory

Expectancy theory component	Objective	Applications
E→P expectancies	To increase the belief that employees are capable of performing the job successfully	• Select people with the required skills and knowledge. • Provide required training and clarify job requirements. • Provide sufficient time and resources. • Assign simpler or fewer tasks until employees can master them (shaping). • Provide examples of similar employees who have successfully performed the task. • Provide counseling and coaching to employees who lack self-confidence.
P→O expectancies	To increase the belief that good performance will result in certain (valued) outcomes	• Measure job performance accurately. • Clearly explain the outcomes that will result from successful performance. • Describe how the employee's rewards were based on past performance. • Provide examples of other employees whose good performance has resulted in higher rewards.
Valences of outcomes	To increase the expected value of outcomes resulting from desired performance	• Distribute rewards that employees value. • Individualize rewards. • Minimize the presence of countervalent outcomes.

Increasing P→O expectancies

The most obvious ways to improve P→O expectancies are to measure employee performance accurately and distribute more valued rewards to those with higher job performance. This is not as easy as it may sound. As we shall see in Chapter 4, reward systems sometimes have little effect on employee motivation or, worse, may inadvertently motivate undesirable behaviors.

P→O expectancies are perceptions, so employees should *believe* that higher performance will result in higher rewards. Having a performance-based reward system is important, but this fact must be communicated. When rewards are distributed, employees should understand how their rewards have been based on past performance. More generally, companies need to regularly communicate the existence of a performance-based reward system through examples, anecdotes, and public ceremonies.

Increasing outcome valences

Performance outcomes influence work effort only when they are valued by employees.[32] This brings us back to a conclusion of the content theories of motivation; namely, that companies must pay attention to the needs and reward preferences of individual employees. They should develop more individualized reward systems so that employees who perform well are offered a choice of rewards.

Bob finally gets the recognition he deserves.

[FARCUS is reprinted with permission from Farcus Cartoons Inc. All rights reserved.]

© 1992 Farcus Cartoons/dist. by Universal Press Syndicate   WAISGLASS/COULTHART

Expectancy theory also emphasizes the need to discover and neutralize countervalent outcomes. These are performance outcomes that have negative valences, thereby reducing the effectiveness of existing reward systems. For example, peer pressure may cause some employees to perform their jobs at the minimum standard even though formal rewards and the job itself would otherwise motivate them to perform at higher levels.

Does Expectancy Theory Fit Reality?

Expectancy theory has been a difficult model to test because it must recognize almost every possible performance level and outcome that employees could imagine. Most of the early studies also suffered from measurement and research design problems.[33] Some critics have suggested that expectancy theory is an imperfect theory because it doesn't predict spontaneous behaviors (such as making a rude remark to a co-worker).[34] One could argue that expectancy theory accounts for spontaneous behaviors because they are learned from past experience, but expectancy theory needs further clarification on this point.

In spite of its limitations, expectancy theory offers one of the best models available for predicting work effort and motivation. For example, recent studies have shown that expectancy theory predicts a person's motivation to use a decision-support system, leave the organization, and work with less effort in a group setting.[35] All three components of the model have received some research support. There is particularly good evidence that P→O expectancies influence employee motivation.

Equity Theory

A technical manager in a large telephone company was confronted one day by several of his employees about the starting pay of a new co-worker. The employees learned that the manager offered the new recruit $500 a year above the normal starting rate—the rate they received a few years earlier. The manager explained that the slightly higher starting pay was necessary to compete with another job offer the new employee was considering. Still, the current employees, who now earned much more than the starting rate, felt that the manager's decision was inequitable.

As this true story illustrates, the emotional tension created by feelings of inequity motivates employees to act on those emotions. **Equity theory** explains how people develop perceptions of fairness in the distribution and exchange of resources. As a process theory of motivation, it explains what employees are motivated to do when they feel inequitably treated. In this incident, perceived inequities motivated several employees to complain to the telecommunications manager and try to change the source of the perceived inequity. Let's look more closely at the four main elements of equity theory: outcome/input ratio, comparison other, equity evaluation, and consequences of inequity.[36]

equity theory a process motivation theory that explains how people develop perceptions of fairness in the distribution and exchange of resources

Outcome/Input Ratio

Inputs include skills, effort, experience, amount of time worked, performance results, and other employee contributions to the organization. Employees see their inputs as investments into the exchange relationship. Outcomes are the things employees receive from the organization in exchange for the inputs, such as pay, promotions, recognition, or an office with a window.

Both inputs and outcomes are weighted by their importance to the individual. These weights vary from one person to the next. To some people, seniority is a valuable input that deserves more organizational outcomes in return. Others consider job effort and performance the most important contributions in the exchange relationship, and give seniority relatively little weight. Similarly, equity theory recognizes that people value outcomes differently because they have different needs. For example, it accepts that some employees want time off with pay whereas others consider this a relatively insignificant reward for job performance.

Comparison Other

Equity theory states that we compare our situation with a comparison other.[37] However, the theory does not tell us who the comparison other is in a particular situation. It may be another person, group of people, or even yourself in the past. It may be someone in the same job, another job, or another organization. Most of the time, we tend to compare ourselves with others who are nearby, in similar positions, and with similar backgrounds.[38] Employees in lower-level positions tend to compare themselves with others within the same firm, possibly because they develop firm-specific skills. Moreover, it is easier to get information about co-workers than from people working elsewhere.

People in more senior positions compare themselves more with their counterparts in other organizations. For example, the chief executive of a company has no direct comparison within the firm, so he or she tends to look to CEOs in other organizations. Some research suggests that employees frequently collect information on several referents to form a "generalized" comparison other.[39] For the most part, however, the comparison other varies from one person to the next and is not easily identifiable.

Equity Evaluation

We form an equity evaluation after identifying our outcome/input ratio and comparing this with the comparison other's ratio. A familiar example will help to explain the evaluations that may occur. Let's assume that you are assigned to a project with another student in your class. Let's keep the example simple by also assuming that both of you receive the same project grade, whether or not one of you contributes more than the other. This means that your outcomes are the same as the other student's outcomes.

In the *equity condition*, both of you contribute the same effort and value to the project, in your opinion. As illustrated in Exhibit 3.4(a), this means that you and the comparison other (the other student) have the same outcome/ input ratios. Now, let's consider the situation that produces *underreward inequity*. As shown in Exhibit 3.4(b), you believe that you contributed more time, effort, knowledge, resources, and other inputs than the comparison other. Since the outcomes are identical in our example, the result is that the comparison other's ratio is higher than your ratio. Finally, imagine a situation in which you have contributed less to a project than the other student

Exhibit 3.4
Equity theory model

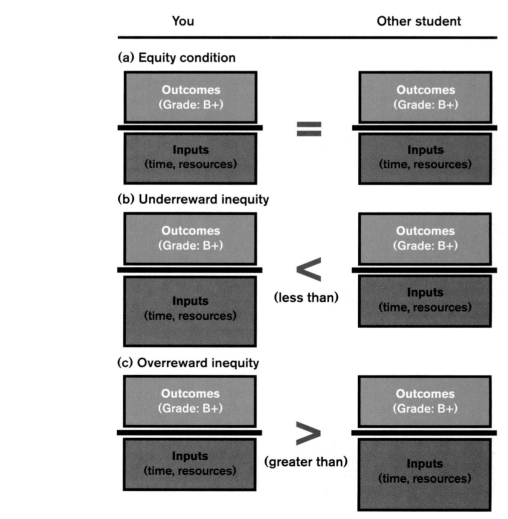

contributed, illustrated in Exhibit 3.4(c). This represents an *overreward inequity* condition for you (and an underreward inequity if the other student noticed that you were slacking off). Both of you receive the same grade, but the other student contributed more time, effort, and other inputs to the work.

The student project example had the same outcome for both you and the comparison other. However, the equity theory model recognizes that we make more complex equity evaluations where you and the comparison other have different outcomes and inputs. By comparing outcome/input *ratios*, the model states that equity occurs when the amounts of inputs and outcomes are proportional. They don't necessarily have to be the same amount. For instance, we feel equitably treated when we work harder than the comparison other and receive proportionally higher rewards as a result.

Consequences of Inequity

Employees are motivated to reduce or eliminate their feelings of inequity by correcting the inequitable situation. There are six possible ways to reduce feelings of inequity.[40] Notice, however, that the strategy used depends on the person's past experience as well as whether they are under- or overrewarded.

1. *Changing inputs*—Underrewarded workers tend to reduce their effort and performance if these outcomes don't affect their paycheck. Overpaid workers sometimes (but not very often) increase their inputs by working harder and producing more.
2. *Changing outcomes*—People with underreward inequity might ask for more desired outcomes, such as a pay increase. If this does not work, some are motivated to join a labor union and demand these changes at the bargaining table.[41] Others misuse sick leave for more paid time off. At the extreme, some people steal company property or use facilities for personal use as ways to increase their outcomes.[42]
3. *Changing perceptions*—Employees may distort inputs and outcomes to restore equity feelings.[43] Overrewarded employees typically follow this strategy because it's easier to increase their perceived inputs (seniority, knowledge, etc.) than to ask for less pay!
4. *Leaving the field*—Some people try to reduce inequity feelings by getting away from the inequitable situation. Thus, equity theory explains some instances of employee turnover and job transfer. This also explains why an underrewarded employee might take more time off work even though he or she is not paid for this absenteeism.
5. *Acting on the comparison other*—Equity is sometimes restored by changing the comparison other's inputs or outcomes. If you feel overrewarded, you might encourage the referent to work at a more leisurely pace. If you feel underrewarded, you might subtly suggest that the overpaid co-worker should be doing a larger share of the workload.
6. *Changing the comparison other*—If we can't seem to alter the outcome/input ratio through other means, we might eventually replace the comparison other with someone having a more compatible outcome/input ratio. As was mentioned earlier, we sometimes rely on a generalized comparison other, so feelings of inequity may be reduced fairly easily by adjusting the features of this composite referent.

Equity Theory in Practice

Equity theory has received considerable support in research and practice. The model helps us to understand why baseball players change teams, why employees steal from their employer, why people become hostile at work, and why employees enact numerous other behaviors.[44] One of the clearest lessons from equity theory is that we need to continually treat people fairly in the distribution of organizational rewards. If feelings of inequity are sufficiently strong, employees may put less effort into the job, leave the organization, steal resources or time (e.g., absenteeism), or join a labor union to correct these inequities.

Unfortunately, maintaining feelings of equity is not an easy task. Employees have different opinions regarding which inputs should be rewarded (e.g., seniority versus performance) and which outcomes are more valuable than others.[45] Moreover, as the workplace becomes more diverse, organizations are developing customized employment relationships. For example, many firms give employees with family obligations more flexible work hours. However, some employees without families feel that this privilege is unfair to them. We can try to improve equity perceptions by telling employees how rewards are distributed, but we also need to understand the inputs and outcomes that are most important to people.

The ethics of inequity   Inequity in the workplace extends beyond employee motivation to the organization's ethical conduct. In fact, a fundamental ethical principle, called the *distributive justice* rule, applies the concept of equity and equality.[46] Specifically, this principle suggests that inequality is acceptable if (1) everyone has equal access to the more favored positions in society and (2) the inequalities are ultimately in the best interest of the least well off in society. The first part means that everyone should have equal access to higher paying jobs and other valued positions in life. The second part says that some people can receive greater rewards than others if this benefits those less well off. For instance, employees in risky jobs should be paid more if this benefits others in society.

The distributive justice principle explains why discrimination in the workplace is unethical. Discrimination creates inequalities and denies equal access to more favored positions in the organization even when people are qualified for those jobs. The distributive justice principle also provides a foundation for the ethics of executive compensation. As Connections 3.2 describes, employees, shareholders, CEOs, and others feel that some executives receive so much compensation that these payments are unethical.

Goal Setting

When Soren Gyll became chairman of Volvo, the Swedish automaker, he gave each of his senior executives a watch with three numbers stamped on the straps: 25, 50, and 100. The numbers represented the goals that Gyll expected them to achieve: 25 percent return on assets, 50 percent reduction in project time, and 100 percent attainment of corporate vision. "If you set objectives and go for things," says Gyll, "you can accomplish goals the books say are impossible."[47]

Goal setting is one of the most effective and widely practiced theories of motivation in organizations.[48] **Goals** are the immediate or ultimate objectives that employees are trying to accomplish from their work effort. **Goal setting** is the process of motivating employees and clarifying their role perceptions by establishing performance objectives. Notice that goal setting potentially improves employee performance in two ways: (1) by stretching the intensity and persistence of effort and (2) by giving employees clearer role perceptions so that their effort is channeled toward behaviors that will improve work performance.

Goal setting is widely used to motivate employees. At the Telecommunications Products Division of Corning Inc., corporate performance goals are

goals the immediate or ultimate objectives that employees are trying to accomplish from their work effort

goal setting the process of motivating employees and clarifying their role perceptions by establishing performance objectives

selected by a cross-functional Goal Sharing Team that consists of 8 to 10 people from all levels of the company. The city manager in La Palma, California, arranged a goal-setting workshop so that city council members and staff could more effectively identify goals and develop a plan to implement them. And at the U.S. Army Chemical Biological Defense Command, teams develop a list of specific goals at the beginning of each year, along with the steps needed to achieve those goals. Team members are empowered to accomplish their goals without supervisory intrusion.[49]

management-by-objectives (MBO) a participative goal setting process in which organizational objectives are cascaded down to work units and individual employees

Some companies apply goal setting through a formal process known as **management-by-objectives (MBO).** There are a few variations of MBO

Connections 3.2 ◻ **Fair Pay in the Executive Suite**

The perceived equity of executive compensation is making headlines as some CEOs pull down record-breaking earnings from salary and stock options. Disney CEO Michael Eisner recently exercised a $565 million options package. Henry Silverman, chief executive of HFS Inc. (which owns Home Shopping Network), holds options worth more than $700 million.

Disney CEO Michael Eisner recently took home $565 million from his stock option pay package. Many people think that he and other executives are overpaid.
[AP Wide World]

Many people are starting to complain that executives are overpaid. The United Farm Workers recently campaigned against the $4.4 million annual paycheck that went to Monsanto CEO Robert B. Shapiro. The union argued that Shapiro is overpaid when compared to the $10,000 a year earned by pickers at Monsanto-owned strawberry farms.

A few senior executives also question the equity of executive pay. "Frankly, I've been amazed, appalled and awed by the levels of compensation of a number of CEOs that have walked away with incredibly munificent packages clearly not based on performance," exclaims John N. Lauer, head of Oglebay Norton Co. Lauer works without a salary at the Cleveland-based industrial sands and shipping firm. Instead, he receives dividends from $1 million worth of shares bought with his own money as well as bonuses from specific performance-based targets.

What is a fair level of pay for corporate executives? The Greek philosopher Plato felt that no one in a community should earn more than five times the lowest-paid worker. In the 1970s, management guru Peter Drucker suggested that 20 times the lowest-paid worker's earnings was more reasonable. Corporate leaders cherish Drucker's wisdom on many issues, but not on fair pay. According to consulting firm Towers Perrin, CEOs in large American corporations today receive an average annual paycheck of $4.3 million, 130 times more than the average (not the lowest) manufacturing employee.

Sources: T. W. Gerdel, "Paying for the Privilege," *Cleveland Plain Dealer*, February 15, 1998, p. H1; W. Hamilton, "Eisner's Payout Just the First of Hefty Rewards," *Los Angeles Times*, December 5, 1997, p. D1; D. C. Johnston, "Execs' Pay Far Outstrips Rise in Profit," *Commercial Appeal* (Memphis), September 2, 1997, p. B6; A. Bernstein, "An Embarrassment of Riches?" *Business Week*, April 21, 1997, p. 64; R. C. Longworth, "Mega-Pay Foreign to Most Execs," *Chicago Tribune*, September 2, 1996, p. C1; G. S. Crystal, *In Search of Excess: The Overcompensation of American Executives* (New York: W. W. Norton, 1991). ◼

programs, but they generally identify organizational objectives, then cascade them down to work units and individual employees.[50] Employees are actively involved with their supervisors in goal formation as well as clarifying the means to reach the agreed-upon goals. MBO also includes periodic review and feedback. Although the process frequently creates too much paperwork, MBO can be an effective application of goal setting in some parts of the organization.

Characteristics of Effective Goals

Goal setting is more complex than simply telling someone to "do your best." Instead, organizational behavior scholars have identified five conditions, diagrammed in Exhibit 3.5, that are necessary to maximize task effort and performance.[51]

Specific goals   Employees put more effort into a task when they work toward specific goals rather than "do your best" targets. Specific goals have measurable levels of change over a specific time, such as "reduce scrap rate by 7 percent over the next six months." Specific goals communicate more precise performance expectations, so employees can direct their effort more efficiently and reliably.

Results-oriented goals   Results-oriented goals improve work performance more than process-oriented goals. A results-oriented goal is one that directly refers to the person's job performance, such as the number of customers served per hour. Process-oriented goals refer to the work processes used to get the job done. An example of a process-oriented goal would be finding one way to reduce the time for customers to describe their problems. Research indicates that these process-oriented goals encourage employees to think about different ways to get the job done, but they seem to block them from choosing

Exhibit 3.5   Characteristics of effective goal setting

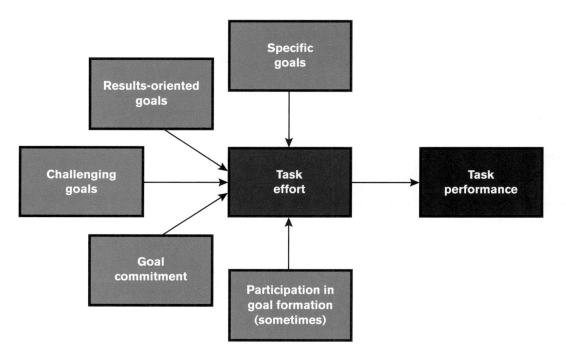

one method and getting on with the job. Therefore, results-oriented goals tend to be more effective.

Challenging goals   Employees tend to have more intense and persistent work effort when they have challenging rather than easy goals. Challenging goals also fulfill a person's need for achievement or growth needs when the goal is achieved.[52] Some organizations, such as General Electric and Daimler-Chrysler, like to use "stretch" goals—goals that are challenging enough to stretch the employee's abilities and motivation toward peak performance. Stretch goals are effective if employees receive the necessary resources to accomplish them and do not become overstressed in the process.[53]

Goal commitment   Of course, there are limits to challenging goals. At some point, a goal becomes so difficult that employees are no longer committed to achieving it. At that point, work effort falls dramatically, as we see in Exhibit 3.6. This is the same as the E→P expectancy that we learned about in the section on expectancy theory.[54] The less the E→P expectancy that the goal can be accomplished, the less committed (motivated) the employee is to the goal.

The optimal level of goal difficulty is the area in which it is challenging but employees are still committed to achieving the goal.[55] John Westrum, founder and CEO of Westrum Development Co., tries to maintain this balance between challenge and commitment by establishing intermediate goals. When the initial goals are accomplished for two years in a row, then employees at the Blue Bell, Pennsylvania, home-building firm agree to "raise the bar" by moving to more challenging goals. "If you set unrealistic goals in the beginning, people will be discouraged," advises Westrum.[56]

self-efficacy a person's belief that he or she has the ability, motivation, and situational contingencies to complete a task successfully

Another influence on goal commitment is the employee's **self-efficacy.** Recall from Chapter 2 that high self-efficacy employees have a "can-do" attitude. They are confident that they can perform the tasks facing them. There is some evidence that high self-efficacy employees are more likely to accept their goals because they believe they can choose successful strategies to reach those goals.[57] Those with low self-efficacy, on the other hand, tend to be in a panic when given a unique goal where the means to achieve that goal isn't obvious.

Exhibit 3.6
Effect of goal difficulty on performance

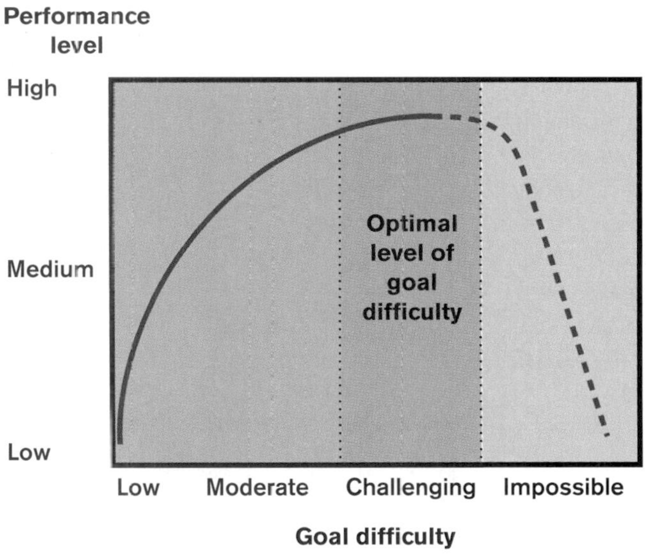

Participation in goal formation   Another way to build or maintain commitment to goals is to ensure that employees are involved in the goal setting process.[58] Participation in goal formation tends to increase goal commitment because employees take ownership of the goal, compared to goals that are merely assigned by supervisors. In fact, today's workforce increasingly expects to be involved in goal setting and other decisions that affect them.

Participation may also improve goal quality, because employees have valuable information and knowledge that may not be known to those who initially formed the goal. For example, some organizations have employees throughout a work area review the unit's future goals. This process ensures that employees buy into those goals and have the competencies and resources necessary to accomplish them.

Goal feedback   Feedback is another necessary condition for effective goal setting. As we discussed in Chapter 2, feedback is a powerful source of learning. In terms of goal setting, feedback lets us know whether we have achieved the goal or are properly directing our effort toward it. Feedback is also an essential ingredient in motivation because our growth needs can't be satisfied unless we receive information on goal accomplishment.

Goal Setting Applications and Limitations

Goal setting is one of the "tried and true" theories in organizational behavior. It is widely supported by research and is generally successful in practice. However, we must keep the contingency approach to organizational behavior in mind. Goal setting does not work for everyone in every situation.

The Defense Systems and Electronics Group (DSEG) at Raytheon is strongly committed to goal setting, and it relies on a form of "catchball" to ensure that employees buy into that commitment. Goals are initially formed by the teams responsible for them (e.g., product reliability). Once formed, every person along the work process "receives" the goal and decides whether or not it is acceptable. If someone feels that he or she cannot achieve the goal, the barriers to goal accomplishment are documented and sent along with the goal to the next person in the work process. The team that developed the goal receives the final documentation and determines whether a goal will be adjusted.[59] Are there some goal setting situations where this catchball process is more important and valuable?

[Courtesy of Raytheon Systems]

One problem with goal setting is that when goals are tied to monetary incentives, some employees are motivated to select easy rather than difficult goals.[60] In some cases, employees have negotiated goals with their supervisor even though they have already been completed! Employees with high self-efficacy and need for achievement tend to set challenging goals whether or not they are financially rewarded for their results. However, employers should typically separate goal setting from the pay-setting process.[61]

implicit learning acquiring information about the environment through experience without any conscious attempt to do so

A second concern is that goal setting can interfere with job performance on new or complex tasks.[62] The best explanation we have for this is that working on a new or complex task requires a large amount of **implicit learning** (as we discussed in Chapter 2). We use our unconscious learning strategies to sort out the best work processes for these tasks. Unfortunately, goal setting interferes with implicit learning by shifting our attention to more explicit (and cumbersome) learning processes. On the other hand, goal setting is effective for simple or routine tasks because the best work processes are already known or are quickly learned without much thought.[63]

Comparing Motivation Theories

Exhibit 3.7 summarizes the central ideas behind the four content and three process theories of motivation presented in this chapter. As you can see, each of the process theories provides a unique perspective of employee motivation. Each looks at different variables in the workplace and the minds of employees. As for the content theories, Alderfer's ERG theory builds on Maslow's needs hierarchy theory. McClelland's learned needs theory is somewhat more distinctive because it suggests that some needs are acquired (learned) rather than instinctive.

Are Motivation Theories Culture Bound?

Are the motivation theories presented throughout this chapter relevant across cultures? A few scholars don't think so. They argue that most theories of

Exhibit 3.7   Comparing employee motivation theories

Motivation theory	Type	Central idea
Maslow's Needs Hierarchy	Content	People try to satisfy higher need when lower need is fulfilled (satisfaction-progression).
Alderfer's ERG Theory	Content	Satisfaction-progression (above) and people focus on lower need if unable to satisfy higher need (frustration-regression).
Herzberg's Motivator-Hygiene Theory	Content	Motivators (job content, recognition) motivate and satisfy, whereas hygiene factors (work relations, work environment) create dissatisfaction but do not motivate.
McClelland's Learned Needs	Content	Some needs are learned rather than instinctive, and more than one need can motivate at the same time.
Expectancy Theory	Process	Motivation is determined by perceived expectancies, outcome values, and a rational decision making process.
Equity Theory	Process	Perceived equity is formed from outcome/input ratios with a comparison other, and people are motivated to reduce perceived inequities.
Goal Setting	Process	Clear, relevant goals increase motivation and performance by stretching the intensity and persistence of effort and by clarifying role perceptions.

motivation were developed by American scholars and tested on Americans, so they reflect the values of Americans and don't readily apply to cultures with different values.[64]

Some of this criticism has focused on older content theories (e.g., Maslow's Need Hierarchy) that were rejected by organizational behavior theorists long ago. It doesn't make sense to complain about the relevance of motivation theories abroad if they don't work in the United States, either. Another criticism has been that people in other cultures have different needs. However, research has revealed that needs for achievement and interesting work are the two most important motivating factors in several cultures (e.g., China, Germany, United States). Employees in different cultures may have different absolute levels of need for achievement, for example, but their relative strength is similar. Moreover, the conceptual structure of need for achievement is consistent across several different cultures, suggesting that its meaning is relevant in other societies.[65]

Expectancy theory has also been criticized as culture bound.[66] Some critics argue that expectancy theory only works in the United States and other cultures where people have strong feelings of personal control. Others claim that expectancy theory applies to individual motivation and consequently doesn't work in cultures where people place a higher value on group membership. In reality, expectancy theory requires neither of these conditions. First, expectancy theory does not assume that people feel complete control over their lives. On the contrary, the E $\rightarrow$ P expectancy directly varies with the employee's perceived control over the work situation. Second, expectancy theory applies to team and organizational outcomes, not just individual performance. Research indicates that expectancy theory predicts employee motivation in different cultures.[67]

Equity theory also allows for individual differences and consequently seems to apply equally well to other cultures. We know that people in some cultures are more sensitive than people in others to perceived inequities. For example, some cultures value equality more than equity. However, feelings of inequity exist even in more egalitarian cultures. Equity theory also allows for the fact that the most important inputs and outcomes can vary from one culture to the next.[68]

The debate over the cross-cultural relevance of motivation theories will continue for some time. Certainly, we must not automatically assume that a theory successfully tested in the United States will apply equally well in other societies. We need to continuously evaluate motivation theories and other organizational behavior concepts in other cultures. Future research will hopefully throw more light on the topic by evaluating the cross-cultural relevance of expectancy, goal setting, and other contemporary motivation theories. In the meantime, it is not clear (at least, not as clear as the critics believe) that contemporary motivation theories are culture bound.

Chapter Summary

Work motivation refers to the forces within a person that affect his or her direction, intensity, and persistence of voluntary behavior in the workplace. Companies need to rethink their motivational practices because of an increasingly diverse workforce, turbulent changes in employment relationships, and flatter organizational structures that require less reliance on direct supervision to control employee behavior.

Content motivation theories explain why people have different needs at different times. Process theories of motivation describe the processes through which needs are translated into behavior.

According to Maslow's needs hierarchy, the lowest needs are initially most important, but higher needs become more important as the lower ones are satisfied. Alderfer's ERG theory is a content motivation theory that groups human needs into a hierarchy of three broad categories: existence, relatedness, and growth. Herzberg's motivator-hygiene theory suggests that people are only motivated by characteristics of the work itself. McClelland studied need for achievement, need for power, and need for affiliation. These needs are learned rather than instinctive, and more than one need may motivate a person at the same time.

Expectancy theory states that work effort is determined by the perception that effort will result in a particular level of performance (E→P expectancy), the perception that a specific behavior or performance level will lead to specific outcomes (P→O expectancy), and the valences that the person feels for those outcomes.

The E→P expectancy increases by improving the employee's ability and confidence to perform the job. The P→O expectancy increases by measuring performance accurately, distributing higher rewards to better performers, and showing employees that rewards are performance based. Outcome valences increase by finding out what employees want and using these resources as rewards.

Equity theory explains how people develop perceptions of fairness in the distribution and exchange of resources. The model includes four elements: outcome/input ratio, comparison other, equity evaluation, and consequences of inequity. The theory also explains what people are motivated to do when they feel inequitably treated.

Goal setting is the process of motivating employees and clarifying their role perceptions by establishing benchmarks against which growth needs are fulfilled. Goals are more effective when they are specific, results oriented, challenging, accepted by the employee, and accompanied by meaningful feedback. Participative goal setting is important in some situations. Goal setting is usually less effective when tied to financial rewards and when applied to new or complex tasks.

We must not automatically assume that an employee motivation theory successfully tested in the United States will apply equally well in other cultures. However, there is increasing support for the cross-cultural relevance of the motivation theories described here.

Key Terms

Content theories of motivation, p. 67
Effort to performance (E→P) expectancy, p. 75
Equity theory, p. 79
ERG theory, p. 68
Existence needs, p. 68
Expectancy theory, p. 74
Frustration-regression process, p. 68
Goal setting, p. 82
Goals, p. 82
Growth needs, p. 68
Implicit learning, p. 87
Job satisfaction, p. 69
Management by objectives (MBO), p. 83

Motivation, p. 66
Motivator-hygiene theory, p. 69
Need for achievement (nAch), p. 71
Need for affiliation (nAff), p. 71
Need for power (nPow), p. 73
Needs, p. 67
Needs hierarchy theory, p. 67
Performance-to-outcome (P→O) expectancy, p. 76
Process theories of motivation, p. 67
Relatedness needs, p. 68
Satisfaction-progression process, p. 67
Self-efficacy, p. 85
Valence, p. 76

Discussion Questions

1. This chapter begins by saying that motivating employees has never been more challenging. Do you agree with this statement? Are there any other reasons why employees might be more (or less) difficult to motivate today than, say, 20 years ago?

2. Think about your personal level of need for achievement, power, and affiliation. What factors in your past have caused you to experience high, moderate, or low levels of each? Which of these would you like to increase or decrease in the future?

3. As a team leader, you notice that one employee isn't putting much effort into the team project because she doesn't believe she has the ability to contribute anything valuable. Using your knowledge of expectancy theory's E → P expectancy, identify four ways that you might increase this person's motivation to contribute to the team.

4. Use all three components of expectancy theory to explain why some employees are motivated to show up for work during a snowstorm whereas others don't make any effort to leave their home.

5. Several service representatives are upset that the newly hired representative with no previous experience will be paid $1,000 a year above the usual starting salary on the pay range. The department manager explained that the new hire would not accept the entry-level rate, so the company raised the offer by $1,000. All five reps currently earn salaries near the top of the scale ($10,000 higher), although they all started at the minimum starting salary a few years earlier. Use equity theory to explain why the service representatives feel inequity in this situation.

6. This chapter provided one example of potential inequity in the classroom (i.e., two students receive the same grade on a team project). Identify other classroom situations in which you had feelings of inequity. How might course instructors minimize these inequitable situations?

7. Last year, Xtra Cellular Inc. introduced a goal-setting program to improve motivation and performance among its salespeople. In January each year, salespeople are assigned a set of specific goals to improve work processes (e.g., submitting sales notes on time; say the customer's last name in conversations). After the first year, however, senior management decided to cancel the goal-setting program because sales did not improve even though competitors did well. Use your knowledge of the characteristics of effective goals to explain why goal setting may not have been effective at Xtra Cellular.

8. In at least one African country, many employees believe that pay levels should be partly determined by the number of children that employees have. The argument is that employees with more children need more money to support their families. Discuss this idea in the context of the equity theory model.

CASE STUDY

Steelfab Corp.

Jackie Ney was an enthusiastic employee when she began working in the accounting department at Steelfab Corp. In particular, she prided herself on discovering better ways of handling invoice and requisition flows. The company had plenty of bottlenecks in the flow of paperwork throughout the organization and Jackie had made several recommendations to her boss, Mr. Johnston, that would improve the process. Mr. Johnston acknowledged these suggestions and even implemented a few, but he didn't seem to have enough time to either thank her or explain why some suggestions could not be implemented. In fact, Mr. Johnston didn't say much to any of the other employees in the department about anything they did.

At the end of the first year, Jackie received a 6 percent merit increase based on Mr. Johnston's evaluation of her performance. This increase was equal to the average merit increase among the 11 people in the accounting department and was above the inflation rate. Still, Jackie was frustrated because she didn't know how to improve her chances of a higher merit increase the next year. She was also upset that another new employee, Jim Sandu, received the highest pay increase (10 percent) even though he was not regarded by others in the finance department as a particularly outstanding performer. According to others who worked with him on some assignments, Jim lacked the skills to perform the job well enough to receive such a high reward. However, Jim Sandu had become a favored employee of Mr. Johnston and they had even gone on a fishing trip together.

Jackie's enthusiasm toward Steelfab fell dramatically during her second year of employment. She still enjoyed the work and made friends with some of her co-workers, but the spirit that had once carried her through the morning rush hour traffic had somehow dwindled. Eventually, Jackie stopped mentioning her productivity improvement ideas. On two occasions during her second year of employment, she took a few days of sick leave to visit friends and family in Vermont. She had used only two sick days during her first year and these were for a legitimate illness. On one occasion, even her doctor had urged Jackie to stay at home. But by the end of the second year, using sick days seemed to "justify" Jackie's continued employment at Steelfab. Now, as her second annual merit increase approached, Jackie started to scout around seriously for another job.

Discussion Questions

1. What symptom(s) exist in this case to suggest that something has gone wrong?

2. What are the root causes that have led to these symptoms?

3. What actions should the organization take to correct these problems?

As workers turn into risk-takers . . . one plant really turns on the steam

BusinessWeek

Andrzej Blikle had a problem. He wanted to introduce Western quality-control concepts to his baked-goods plant in a Warsaw suburb. But the best of the "motivational" slogans sounded too much like discredited socialist mantras to Polish employees. Instead, Blikle found that he could motivate his employees by gathering them together for weekly troubleshooting meetings. David Bailey, who heads International Paper Company's operations in Poland, is also looking for new ways to motivate employees. His main strategy is pushing the Poles to take risks.

This *Business Week* case study describes how organizations are finding new ways to motivate employees in Poland. These strategies range from involving employees so that they fulfill their growth needs to setting goals to improve quality. Read through this *Business Week* case study at www.mhhe.com/mcshane1e and prepare for the discussion questions below.

Discussion Questions

1. What motivation theory best describes the strategy used at the Warsaw Marriott Hotel? What other practice might it consider within the framework of this motivation theory?

2. This article describes an incident in which a Polish manager, Alfred Trepow, visited a plant in the United States and realized that it was possible to double production back in Poland. Analyze this incident in terms of expectancy and goal-setting theories.

3. What cultural values are identified in this article that organizations need to recognize when attempting new strategies to motivate Polish employees?

Source: P. Simpson, "As Workers Turn into Risk-Takers . . . One Plant Really Turns on the Steam," *Business Week*, December 15, 1997. ■

Dishonesty in America: Lie, cheat, and steal

 Cheating in the workplace has become a serious problem for American managers. When employees abuse their workplace, everyone suffers. Theft in retail leads to higher prices for the consumer. Cutting corners on qual-

ity leads to shabby or, worse, unsafe products, And the list goes on.

How can companies reduce employee cheating? According to an NBC News poll, 54 percent of American workers say a better work environment would fix things up, 27 percent say increased penalties for wrongdoers would help, and 13 percent say increased surveillance and security would be an effective deterrent. One of the worst kinds of dishonesty at work is stealing from an employer.

For example, consider the case of Denver dentist, Dr. James MacIntyre. He was the perfect victim. He takes great care of his patients. His office manager, Cindy Roe, did that and much more. Convicted of embezzling more than $64,000 over a three-year period, Roe forged the doctor's signature 44 times on checks all payable to herself. The check stubs all showed the money going to suppliers, but Roe hid the cancelled checks from the accountants.

The office manager pleaded guilty to theft and in exchange for no jail time she promised to make restitution. Dr. MacIntyre pleads guilty to having trusted Roe. He said, "She was a good people person. It was a total betrayal. She betrayed me, she betrayed all the other employees here."

An insolated case? Not by a long shot. Joseph Wells, a certified fraud examiner, said, "If you're in business, you're going to have people steal from you. It's that simple." The Association of Certified Fraud Examiners found, after a 2½-year study, that employee fraud and abuse costs U.S. businesses $400 billion a year—that's nine dollars a day for every worker on the job.

Theft in the workplace is not limited to office supplies, but also cash stuffed into a blouse, a load of mattresses, and worse. Security cameras even caught a security guard breaking into a safe. Wells said, "In the United States about a third of employees steal on the job regularly. About 6 percent of all revenues are lost to employee thefts."

Who steals? Of the reported cases, employees twice as often as managers, but owners like to put their hand in the cookie jar too. Why? One prisoner convicted of workplace theft said: "I had figured that I wasn't getting what I was worth." Another prisoner said, "It was just so simple that it was child's play."

And the problem is getting worse. In Denver alone, in 2 years, 190 cases were tried involving $4.5 million. Fifty more cases are under investigation now. Wells said, "It's the tip of the iceberg. The most vulnerable is the small business." For Dr. MacIntyre his losses were covered by employee theft insurance. It's not new, but it's getting popular. One company says claims are coming in fast. The experts say "bosses watch the books and watch your employees like a hawk."

Questions for Discussion

1. Which of Maslow's needs do you think employees who steal in the workplace are most likely trying to satisfy?

2. Do you think employee crime can be understood from the position of equity theory? Explain.

3. Can employee crime be understood from the perspective of McClelland's theory of learned needs? Explain. ◼

TEAM EXERCISE

Bonus decision making exercise

Purpose

This exercise is designed to help you understand the elements of equity theory and how people differ in their equity perceptions.

Instructions

Four managers in a large national insurance company are described below. The national sales director of the company has given your consulting team (first individually, then together) the task of allocating $100,000 in bonus money to these four managers. It is entirely up to your team to decide how to divide the money among these people. The only requirements are that all of the money must be distributed and that no two branch man-

agers can receive the same amount. The names and information are presented in no particular order. You should assume that economic conditions, client demographics, and other external factors are very similar for these managers.

Step 1: Students will form teams of four or five people. Working alone, read information about the four managers. Then fill in the amount you would allocate to each manager in the "Individual Decision" column.

Step 2: Still working alone, fill in the "Equity Inputs Form." First, in the "Input Factor" column, list in order of importance the factors you considered when allocating these bonus amounts (e.g., seniority, performance, age). The most important factor should be listed first and the least important last. Next, in the "Input Weight" column estimate the percentage weight that you assigned to this factor. The total of this column must add up to 100 percent.

Step 3: After individually allocating the bonus money and determining the input factors and weights, team members will compare their results and note any differences. Then, for each job, team members will reach a consensus on the bonus amount that each manager should receive. Write these amounts in the "Team Decision" column.

Step 4: The instructor will call the class together to compare team results and note differences in inputs and input weights used by individual students. Discussion of these results in terms of equity theory will follow.

Manager Profiles

Bob B. Bob has been in the insurance business for over 27 years and has spent the past 21 years with this company. A few years ago, Bob's branch typically made the largest contribution to company profits. More recently, however, it has brought in few new accounts and is now well below average in terms of its contribution to the company. Turnover in the branch has been high and Bob doesn't have the same enthusiasm for the job as he once did. Bob is 56 years old and is married with five children, three of whom are still living at home. Bob has a high school diploma as well as a certificate from a special course in insurance management.

Edward E. In the two years that Edward has been a branch manager, his unit has brought in several major accounts and now stands as one of the top units in the country. Edward is well respected by his employees. At 29, he is the youngest manager in the region and one of the youngest in the country. The sales director initially doubted the wisdom of giving Edward the position of branch manager because of his relatively young age and lack of experience in the insurance industry. Edward received an undergraduate business degree from a regional college and worked for five years as a sales representative before joining this company. Edward is single and has no children.

Lee L. Lee has been with this organization for seven years. The first two years were spent as a sales representative in the office that she now manages. According to the regional director, Lee rates about average as a branch manager. She earned an undergraduate degree in geography from a major university and worked as a sales representative for four years with another insurance company before joining this organization. Lee is 40 years old, divorced, and has no children. She is a very

ambitious person but sometimes has problems working with her staff and other branch managers.

Sandy S. Sandy is 47 years old and has been a branch manager with this company for 17 years. Seven years ago, her branch made the lowest contribution to the company's profits, but this has steadily improved and is now slightly above average. Sandy seems to have a mediocre attitude toward her job but is well liked by her staff and other branch managers. Her experience in the insurance industry has been entirely with this organization. She previously worked in nonsales positions, and it is not clear how she became a branch manager without previous sales experience. Sandy is married and has three school-aged children. Several years ago, Sandy earned a diploma in business from a nearby community college by taking evening courses.

Bonus allocation form

Name	Individual decision	Team decision
Bob B.	$_____	$_____
Edward E.	$_____	$_____
Lee L.	$_____	$_____
Sandy S.	$_____	$_____
Totals:	$100,000	$100,000

Equity inputs form

Input factor*	Input weight**
_____	_____%
_____	_____%
_____	_____%
_____	_____%
_____	_____%
Total	**100%**

*List factors in order of importance, with most important factor listed first.
**The weight of each factor is a percentage ranging from 1 to 100. All factor weights together must add up to 100 percent.

© 2000, 1983 Steven L. McShane ◻

SELF-ASSESSMENT EXERCISE

Measuring your growth need strength

Purpose

This self-assessment is designed to help you to estimate your level of growth need strength.

Instructions

People differ in the kinds of jobs they would most like to hold. The questions in this exercise give you a chance to say just what it is about a job that is most important to you. For each question, two different kinds of jobs are briefly described. Please indicate which of the two jobs you personally would prefer if you had to make a choice between them. In answering each question, assume that everything else about the jobs is the same. Pay attention only to the characteristics actually listed. After circling each answer, use the scoring key to calculate your results for this scale. This exercise is completed alone so students assess themselves honestly without concerns of social comparison. However, class discussion will focus on the growth need strength concept and its implications.

Growth need strength scale

JOB A	Circle the number indicating the degree to which you prefer Job A or Job B	JOB B
1 A job where the pay is very good.	1-----------2-----------3-----------4-----------5 Strongly Slightly Neutral Slightly Strongly Prefer A Prefer A Prefer B Prefer B	A job where there is considerable opportunity to be creative and innovative.
2 A job where you are often required to make important decisions.	1-----------2-----------3-----------4-----------5 Strongly Slightly Neutral Slightly Strongly Prefer A Prefer A Prefer B Prefer B	A job with many pleasant people to work with.
3 A job in which greater responsibility is given to those who do the best work.	1-----------2-----------3-----------4-----------5 Strongly Slightly Neutral Slightly Strongly Prefer A Prefer A Prefer B Prefer B	A job in which greater responsibility is given to loyal employees who have the most seniority.
4 A job in a firm which is in financial trouble and might have to close down within the year.	1-----------2-----------3-----------4-----------5 Strongly Slightly Neutral Slightly Strongly Prefer A Prefer A Prefer B Prefer B	A job in which you are not allowed to have any say whatever in how your work is scheduled, or in the procedures to be used in carrying it out.
5 A very routine job.	1-----------2-----------3-----------4-----------5 Strongly Slightly Neutral Slightly Strongly Prefer A Prefer A Prefer B Prefer B	A job where your co-workers are not very friendly.
6 A job with a supervisor who is often very critical of you and your work in front of other people.	1-----------2-----------3-----------4-----------5 Strongly Slightly Neutral Slightly Strongly Prefer A Prefer A Prefer B Prefer B	A job which prevents you from using a number of skills that you worked hard to develop.

7	A job with a supervisor who respects you and treats you fairly.	1----------------2----------------3----------------4----------------5					A job which provides constant opportunities for you to learn new and interesting things.
		Strongly Prefer A	Slightly Prefer A	Neutral	Slightly Prefer B	Strongly Prefer B	
8	A job where there is a real chance you could be laid off.	1----------------2----------------3----------------4----------------5					A job with very little chance to do challenging work.
		Strongly Prefer A	Slightly Prefer A	Neutral	Slightly Prefer B	Strongly Prefer B	
9	A job in which there is a real chance for you to develop new skills and advance in the organization.	1----------------2----------------3----------------4----------------5					A job which provides lots of vacation time and an excellent benefits package.
		Strongly Prefer A	Slightly Prefer A	Neutral	Slightly Prefer B	Strongly Prefer B	
10	A job with little freedom and independence to do your work in the way you think best.	1----------------2----------------3----------------4----------------5					A job where working conditions are poor.
		Strongly Prefer A	Slightly Prefer A	Neutral	Slightly Prefer B	Strongly Prefer B	
11	A job with very satisfying teamwork.	1----------------2----------------3----------------4----------------5					A job which allows you to use your skills and abilities to the fullest extent.
		Strongly Prefer A	Slightly Prefer A	Neutral	Slightly Prefer B	Strongly Prefer B	
12	A job which offers little or no challenge.	1----------------2----------------3----------------4----------------5					A job which requires you to be completely isolated from co-workers.
		Strongly Prefer A	Slightly Prefer A	Neutral	Slightly Prefer B	Strongly Prefer B	

Source: Developed by J. R. Hackman and G. R. Oldham as part of the Job Diagnostic Survey instrument. The authors have released any copyright ownership of this scale (see J. R. Hackman and G. Oldham, *Work Redesign* [Reading, MA: Addison-Wesley, 1980], p. 275).

Scoring the growth need strength scale

Step 1: The Growth Need Strength Scale yields a number from 1 ("Strongly Prefer A") to 5 ("Strongly Prefer B"). Write your circled numbers for the items indicated below and add them up:

_____ + _____ + _____ + _____ + _____ + _____ = _____
  (#1)   (#5)   (#7)   (#10)   (#11)   (#12)   Subtotal A

Step 2: The remaining items in the Growth Need Strength Scale need to be reverse-scored. To calculate a reverse score, subtract the direct score from 6. For example, if you circled 4 in one of these items, the reverse score would be 2 (i.e., $6 - 4 = 2$). If you circled 1, the reverse score would be 5 (i.e., $6 - 1 = 5$). Calculate the *reverse score* for each of the items indicated below and write them in the space provided. Then calculate Subtotal B by adding up these reverse scores.

_____ + _____ + _____ + _____ + _____ + _____ = _____
  (#2)   (#3)   (#4)   (#6)   (#8)   (#9)   Subtotal B

Step 3: Calculate the total score by summing Subtotal A and Subtotal B.

_____ + _____ = _____
(Subtotal A) (Subtotal B)   TOTAL ◼

Applied Motivation Practices

Learning Objectives

After reading this chapter, you should be able to:

- Discuss the advantages and disadvantages of the four types of rewards.
- Give an example of an individual, team, and organizational level performance-based reward.
- Describe Kohn's five main concerns with rewards in organizations.
- Discuss the advantages and disadvantages of job specialization.
- Diagram the job characteristics model of job design.
- Identify three strategies to enrich jobs.
- Describe the five elements of self-leadership.
- Explain how mental imagery improves employee motivation.

I t's an understatement to say that BMC Software rewards its employees well. The Houston-based maker of database support software pays its software developers up to 5 percent of their product's revenues over the first five years. They earn 2 percent of revenues by updating the product. This can add up to a lot of money.

"We're not talkin' $40,000 year-end bonuses," explains Max Watson, BMC's chairman. "We're talkin' money that'll make their grandkids happy." In fact, 30 employees recently earned over $500,000 a year in cash and stock awards from BMC's generous royalty-based reward system. The average person—excluding executives—earns over $85,000 per year.

Employees at Kingston Technology also know about megabonuses. Soon after company owners David Sun and John Tu sold 80 percent of the company to Softbank Corp., they decided that staff should share some of the windfall based on their length of service. Employees with good job performance and the longest service got checks worth two-and-a-half times their annual salaries. The average bonus at the Fountain Valley, California, computer memory manufacturer was over $75,000.

Kingston's employees were delighted but not exactly surprised. "Several times a year David and John just make these spontaneous gestures," says product manager Nahid Casazza. "There's an envelope on your desk. And you open it and say, 'Thank God I work for this company.' And then you put the envelope away and start working twice as hard."[1]

BMC Software Chairman Max Watson (*front*) with some of the company's happy and increasingly wealthy employees. Some programmers earn $500,000 in cash and stock awards in a year.
[*James McGoon © 1999*]

hether it's writing software code at BMC or designing memory chips at Kingston Technology, employees are being rewarded more for their performance these days than for just showing up to work. As we will learn in the first part of this chapter, there are many types of rewards that serve different purposes. Moreover, reward systems are quickly changing away from a model of entitlement and status to competence and performance. We will also discover that as companies increase their use of performance-based rewards, they face new challenges that may interfere with the objectives of employee motivation and commitment.

Of course, reward systems are not the only way to motivate employees. This chapter also examines the dynamics of job design, specific job design strategies to motivate employees, and the effectiveness of recent job design interventions. Then we turn to the emerging concept of self-leadership. This final section explains how employees motivate themselves through personal goal setting, constructive thought patterns, designing natural rewards, self-monitoring, and self-reinforcement.

Reward Systems

Financial rewards are a fundamental part of the employment relationship. Organizations distribute money and other benefits in exchange for the employee's availability, competencies, and behaviors. Rewards help to align individual goals with corporate goals and to provide a return to the individual's contribution. This concept of economic exchange can be found across cultures. The word for "pay" in Malay and Slovak means to replace a loss; in Hebrew and Swedish it means making equal.[2] No matter which culture, a paycheck means giving back or rebalancing the employee's contribution to the employer.

Exhibit 4.1 identifies the four main types of organizational rewards: membership and seniority, job status, competency, and performance. Although Western culture dominates current thinking on this topic, various rewards exist across cultures. For example, there is increasing evidence that individuals in most cultures value some amount of performance-based pay, rather than a fixed salary alone. One survey reports that 65 percent of large employers throughout Asia already use some form of performance-based reward system. Incentives are most popular in Thai companies and least likely to be found in Indonesian firms.[3]

Exhibit 4.1
Types of organizational rewards

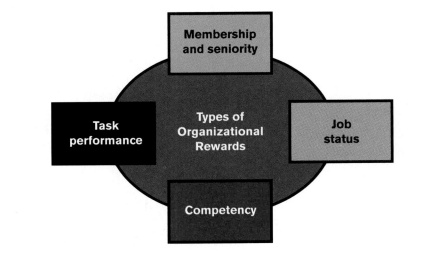

Membership and Seniority-Based Rewards

The largest portion of most paychecks is based on membership and seniority. Employees receive fixed hourly wages or salaries, and many benefits are the same for everyone in the firm. Other rewards increase with the person's seniority in the firm. Most organizations offer longer vacations to those with higher seniority. Base pay sometimes increases with the number of years in a job. Japanese firms usually move employees into a higher pay rate for each year on the job or their age.[4]

Company pension plans emphasize seniority because those who leave within the first five years typically forfeit some or all of the company's contribution to the pension plan. Some firms offer special perquisites to employees above a certain seniority level. As we learned in the opening story, employees at Kingston Technologies received a special bonus based in part on their years of service. NewAge Industries, a plastics and material testing manufacturer in Willow Grove, Pennsylvania, offers employees a complimentary meal *every* month at a local upscale restaurant, but only to those with five or more years of seniority.[5]

Advantages and disadvantages Membership-based rewards may attract job applicants, particularly when the size of the reward increases with seniority. Seniority-based rewards reduce turnover because the cost of quitting increases with the employee's length of service. One problem with membership-based rewards is that they do not directly motivate job performance. Another problem is that membership-based rewards discourage poor performers from leaving voluntarily because they seldom have better job offers. Instead, the good performers are lured to better-paying jobs. Lastly, we will learn in Chapter 7 that golden handcuffs—financial incentives that discourage people from leaving the organization—tend to undermine their loyalty and job performance to that organization.

Job Status-Based Rewards

Almost every organization rewards employees for the status of their jobs in the organization. Firms with many employees typically use **job evaluation** systems to evaluate the worth of each job in terms of its required skill, effort, responsibility, and working conditions.[6] Jobs that require more skill and effort, have more responsibility, and have difficult working conditions would have more value and consequently would be placed in higher pay grades. Organizations that don't rely on job evaluation still tend to reward job status based on pay survey information about the external labor market.

A senior engineer typically earns more than, say, a purchasing clerk because the work performed by the engineer is worth more to the organization. It has more value (calculated by a job evaluation system or pay survey) and therefore employees in that job receive more status-based rewards in the organization. People in some higher status jobs are also rewarded with larger offices, company-paid vehicles, and exclusive dining rooms.

Advantages and disadvantages Companies reward job status to maintain feelings of equity (see Chapter 3). Job evaluation systems try to maintain *internal equity;* that is, to ensure that employees feel their pay is fair when compared to how much other jobs in the organization are paid. This process also minimizes pay discrimination.[7] Pay surveys generally try to maintain *external equity;* that is, to ensure that employees feel their pay is fair when compared to how much people in other organizations are paid. Job status-based

---

job evaluation

systematically evaluating the worth of jobs within the organization by measuring their required skill, effort, responsibility, and working conditions. Job evaluation results create a hierarchy of job worth

rewards also motivate employees to compete for positions further up the organizational hierarchy.

Despite these advantages, job status-based rewards have received much criticism. They motivate employees to increase their job's worth by exaggerating job duties and hoarding resources. These political behaviors may increase the job's pay rate through a job evaluation system, but they don't help the organization.[8] Job status-based rewards also cause employees to focus on narrowly defined tasks rather than broader organizational citizenship and customer service behaviors. Job status-based benefits, such as executive dining rooms and golf memberships, create a psychological distance between employees and management, thereby inhibiting communication between these groups. Some companies try to minimize these problems by closing executive dining rooms and removing other status-based benefits. There is also a strong trend away from rewarding employees for their job status and toward competency-based rewards.

Competency-Based Rewards

competencies the abilities, values, personality traits, and other characteristics of people that lead to superior performance

The emerging reward system strategy is to pay employees more for their competencies than for the tasks they perform at a particular time. Recall from Chapter 2 that **competencies** are the underlying characteristics of people that lead to superior performance.[9] Competency-based pay rewards employees for their skills, knowledge, and traits that lead to desired behaviors. Employees are expected to have several competencies, and these competencies are evaluated by observing specific behavior patterns.

How does competency-based pay differ from job status-based pay? Companies with traditional status-based rewards have many pay grades, each with a narrow range between the lowest and highest pay. Employees might see their pay increase somewhat by moving within a pay grade, but they are mainly rewarded through promotions to a higher job and a higher pay grade. In contrast, companies with competency-based systems use fewer pay grades with very wide ranges between the lowest and highest pay rates within each grade. These wide pay ranges allow more room to reward employees for their competencies rather than the specific jobs they hold.[10] For example, some competency-based systems allow highly competent employees to earn more than their supervisors or team leaders. Similarly, this motivates employees to acquire skills and knowledge by moving laterally through several jobs, rather than waiting for promotions up a career ladder.

skill-based pay (SBP) pay structures in which employees earn higher pay rates with the number of skill modules they have mastered

Skill-based pay (SBP) plans represent a variation of competency-based pay. In SBP plans, employees earn higher pay rates with the number of skill modules they have mastered.[11] Through special training and job rotation, employees learn how to operate another machine or complete another set of tasks. The employee's pay rate depends on the number of skill modules that he or she has mastered, not on the specific job performed on a particular day.

To illustrate how a skill-based pay plan works, lets look at how production employees are paid at Marley Cooling Tower Co. The Olathe, Kansas, cooling tower manufacturer has more than 30 skill modules in its production operations. Each skill module is worth between 30 and 75 cents per hour, depending on its level of difficulty. Unskilled workers at the plant start at $6.30 an hour, and this rises to $15.50 an hour for those who have mastered all 30 skill modules. Some skill modules are learned quickly, whereas others require special training at a community college. Everyone must pass written and hands-on tests before earning the higher pay. Marley employees perform only one skill module at a time, but they are paid for the number of skill modules they are capable of performing.[12]

Advantages and disadvantages   Competency-based rewards have been praised for developing a better-skilled and more flexible workforce. Customer needs are met more quickly because employees can move into different jobs as demands require. Product or service quality tends to improve because employees who have work experience in several jobs are more likely to know where problems originate. Moreover, employees find it easier to discover ways to improve the work process as they learn more skills and tasks in that process.[13] Competency-based rewards are also consistent with the emerging view that people are hired into organizations, not specific jobs. Rather than paying people for their ability to perform a specific job, competency-based rewards ensure that the best-paid employees are those who can adjust to new situations because they possess the capabilities across jobs and circumstances.

However, competency-based rewards have their limitations. Competencies are supposed to be measured by assessing the employee's specific behaviors, but some critics worry that this can deteriorate into subjective personality assessments.[14] It is difficult enough to measure personality traits through scientific measures (see Chapter 6); casual assessments by co-workers and team leaders of someone's personality would be less accurate. Skill-based pay systems measure specific skills, so they are usually more objective and accurate. However, SBP plans are expensive because they motivate employees to spend time learning new tasks. Also, it's not uncommon to have most employees eventually reach the highest pay rate because few firms have established ways to reduce pay rates when employees get rusty on specific skills.

Performance-Based Rewards

In the early 1990s, 90 percent of a typical manager's pay at Sears Roebuck and Co. was straight salary. Now, it's 80 percent and dropping as the retail giant moves to performance-based pay. For some top executives, performance bonuses can exceed their base salary. "I wanted to move away from an entitlement mentality—put pay at risk and increase it over time to motivate and drive people," says Sears CEO Arthur Martinez.[15]

Sears is following the trend toward performance-based rewards rather than purely membership and seniority-based rewards. Although this shift is most apparent in North America, companies in Europe and Asia are also paying employees more for their performance than ever before. For instance, in a recent survey of 210 large firms in Tokyo, Japan, 24 percent currently awarded pay increases on the basis of performance rather than seniority.[16]

Performance-based rewards are not new, but they now come in more flavors than ever before. Exhibit 4.2 lists the most common types of individual, team, and organizationwide performance-based rewards.

Exhibit 4.2
Types of performance-based rewards

Individual rewards Individual rewards have existed since the time of Babylon in the 20th century B.C.[17] The oldest of these is the *piece rate,* which calculates pay by the number of units the employee produces. For example, glass installers at Safelite Glass Corp. of Columbus, Ohio, receive $20 per unit installed. *Commissions* pay people based on sales volume rather than units produced. Many real estate agents and automobile salespeople are paid straight commission. *Royalties* pay individuals a percentage of revenue from the resource or work ascribed to them. For instance, some mining companies pay royalties to their exploration geologists from the mineral deposits they discover. BMC Software, described in the opening story to this chapter, pays its software developers a percentage of their product's revenues over the first five years.

Merit pay—increasing the individual's pay based on performance appraisal results—was common during times of high inflation. However, merit pay has been replaced in many firms by reearnable *bonuses* for accomplishing specific tasks or achieving certain goals. Although these bonuses are often determined from team or organizational performance, they may also result from satisfactory completion of individual goals.

Companies also reward top performers with gifts. IBM, Hewlett-Packard, Nortel, and others send their top salespeople on exotic trips. The Hong Kong office of DHL International gave sales staff miniature air cargo containers to put on their desks. Each month, those who exceeded their sales target at the courier company received small blocks that would be put into the containers. Travel prizes were awarded to those who filled their containers. This visual incentive was so successful that most sales staff exceeded their targets by 40 percent. Now the sales staff at DHL's offices in Taiwan and China want a similar incentive plan.[18]

Jim Williams, an auto glass installer in Cambridge, Massachusetts, earns $20 for each windshield he installs. After Williams's employer, Safelite Glass, switched from hourly wages to piece rates, productivity jumped by 20 percent and installers took home an average of 10 percent more pay. "It adds an extra $300 a week to what I used to make," says Williams, one of Safelite's better performers. The company also reports lower absenteeism and turnover among those with the best performance. Why do piece rate rewards seem to work well for Safelite's installers? What problems might this piece rate system create? Where would it be difficult to apply this type of reward?[19]

[© Matheny/Christian Science Monitor]

Team rewards Organizations increasingly rely on teams to get the work done (see Chapter 9). Consequently, they are rewarding team performance to support these team-based structures.[20] Some teams are rewarded with special bonuses or gifts if they collectively achieve specific goals. At the San Antonio Marriott River Center, for example, general manager Arthur Coulombe offered sales staff a four-day trip to Padre Island, Texas, if they achieved $1 million in group room revenue over a six-month period. Coulombe sent buckets of sand or fishing lures to employees' homes every couple of weeks to remind them of the reward. The sales team brought in $1.5 million in revenue, well beyond anyone's expectations.[21]

gainsharing plan a reward system that rewards team members for reducing costs and increasing labor efficiency in their work process

A **gainsharing plan** is a type of team reward that motivates team members to reduce costs and increase labor efficiency in their work process. Gainsharing plans use a predetermined formula to calculate cost savings and pay out a bonus to all team members. Typically, the company shares the cost savings with employees for one or two years. For example, 911 dispatchers in Howard County, Maryland, were recently awarded bonuses up to $400 for significantly reducing the time to answer a call and send out an emergency crew. The increased productivity avoided hiring two more dispatchers, and employees shared the savings with taxpayers.[22] Similarly, Connections 4.1 describes how gainsharing successfully improved morale and productivity among employees in Baltimore County, Maryland.

Gainsharing plans create a reasonably strong performance-to-outcome expectancy (see expectancy theory in Chapter 3) because much of the cost reduction and labor efficiency is within the team's control. In other words, team members quickly learn that their work efficiencies increase the size of the gainsharing bonus. However, costs do occasionally increase beyond the team's control, such as when demand for the product or service drops quickly, thereby increasing costs per unit.

Organizational rewards J. Robert Beyster believes that the best way to motivate employees is to instill an "ownership culture." The founder and chief executive officer of San Diego-based Science Applications International Corp. (SAIC) has done that by forming an **employee stock ownership plan (ESOP)** in which employees own over 90 percent of the company's stock. Beyster believes that this ownership has helped the company's phenomenal success. From just 6 employees in 1969, SAIC now employs 25,000 people and has annual revenues of $3.4 billion. "We turn employees into stakeholders," Beyster says. "I really believe it makes a difference, and I think it's fair."[23]

employee stock ownership plan (ESOP) a reward system that encourages employees to buy shares of the company

There are currently 10,000 ESOPs representing 10 million employees throughout the United States. Most of these are in privately held companies, such as SAIC, but you will also find ESOPs at Microsoft, Home Depot, Cisco Systems, and other publicly traded firms.[24] Most ESOPs give employees a small stake in the firm, with most stocks held by the founder or outside shareholders. However, employees own a majority of all the stock at SAIC, United Airlines, Avis, and about 3,000 other ESOP firms. The U.S. federal government relied on an ESOP to privatize the OPM Office of Investigations, which conducts background checks of employees for federal agencies. This service, now called U.S. Investigations Services, Inc., is owned by its 700 former civil servants.[25]

ESOPs encourage employees to buy stocks of the company and reward them through dividends and market appreciation of those stocks. With a financial stake in the firm's success, employees tend to work smarter to reduce costs and increase customer service. They align their behaviors more closely to organizational objectives and build commitment to the firm. According to one study, productivity rises by 4 percent annually at ESOP firms, compared with only 1.5 percent at non-ESOP firms. However, it is difficult to motivate employees with ESOPs when stocks are depressed due to economic downturn,

◻ Baltimore County Employees Bounce Back through Gainsharing

"Dutch" Ruppersberger (center) with some Baltimore County maintenance employees who reduced costs through gainsharing.
[Courtesy of Baltimore County, Maryland]

As a member of the Baltimore County Council, "Dutch" Ruppersberger noticed that declining employee morale was affecting service quality. He was convinced that both would improve if department heads challenged employees with achievable cost-saving goals, and then paid them appropriately for meeting or exceeding those goals.

Ruppersberger decided to take up this challenge by campaigning for the Baltimore County Executive job on a platform of improving employee productivity and morale. His secret weapon: gainsharing. Labor union officials and employees were initially skeptical that a gainsharing plan would make a difference, but voters liked the idea enough to put Ruppersberger into office.

Soon after, Ruppersberger identified the 13-person Dietary Division and the 87-employee Maintenance Division to test the gainsharing plan. After receiving training in teamwork and conflict resolution, both groups drafted strategies to reduce costs. These were reviewed by an oversight committee and an outside panel of representatives from the community.

With minor modifications, both plans were implemented, with a resulting saving of more than $400,000. Labor union officials began to praise the plan, particularly as they saw how gainsharing increased employee incomes and avoided privatizing some work performed by union members. "All in all, it worked out much better than we expected," said James Clark, president of the Baltimore County Federation of Public Employees. "It certainly increased morale and brought some things to light that management should have been aware of all along."

It has also given employees the opportunity to earn extra money. Cooks and cafeteria workers in Baltimore County's Dietary department each received a $7,540 gainsharing bonus. They reduced costs when serving inmates through better portion control, improved recipes, and better food preservation methods. Grass cutters at the parks department pocketed up to $815 by using more efficient mowing equipment and other techniques to save $193,447 over two years.

The gainsharing plan has now been expanded to Public Works employees where savings of $700,000 are anticipated next year.

Sources: Adapted from S. Wilson, "Counties Try Productivity Bonuses," *Washington Post*, March 26, 1998, p. M1; J. Fox and B. Lawson, "Gainsharing Program Lifts Baltimore Employees' Morale," *American City & County* 112 (September 1997), p. 93. Information updated by Melissa Boone, Baltimore County Gainsharing Program Manager. ◼

"bear" market sentiments, and other factors beyond the control of individual employees. For instance, the ESOP at Weirton Steel in West Virginia has not been successful because the company faces tough competition in a difficult product market.[26]

profit sharing a reward system in which a designated group of employees receives a share of corporate profits

Profit sharing, another type of organizational level reward, awards a share of corporate profits to designated employees. These plans are most often found in firms that use teams and face plenty of competition.[27] British Airways is one of those organizations. The London-based airline recently paid every eligible employee a profit-sharing bonus equivalent to three weeks pay. Profit sharing tries to motivate employees to reduce waste and improve performance. Unfortunately, like ESOPs, profit sharing generally has a weak performance-to-outcome expectancy because economic conditions, competition, and other factors beyond the immediate control of employees significantly influence the organization's profitability. The clearest benefit of profit sharing is to automatically adjust employee wages with the firm's prosperity, thereby reducing the need for layoffs or negotiated pay reductions during recessions.[28]

The Trouble with Rewards

Performance-based reward systems have become tremendously popular, but a few scholars claim that these incentives might do more harm than good for organizations. One strong critic of workplace rewards is Alfie Kohn, an educational researcher and writer.[29] Although Kohn identifies many concerns, he mainly links reward systems to the behavior modification problems that we discussed in Chapter 2. He even suggests that praise is unhealthy when applied as a reinforcer. Kohn's five main arguments against the use of performance-based rewards are as follows:

- *Rewards punish*—Kohn suggests that there are punitive features built into every reward. First, when rewarding people, we are also demonstrating our control over them. This can eventually assume a punitive quality by making the reward recipient feel subservient. Second, after being rewarded, employees come to expect that reward in the future. If their expectation is not met, they feel punished.

- *Rewards rupture relationships*—Kohn complains that individual rewards create jealousies and competition. In other words, rewards usually lead to feelings of inequity (see Chapter 3) because people invariably compare their rewards to others. Team rewards aren't any better because they encourage peer pressure. Rewards also create a psychological distance between the person giving and receiving the reward. Taken together, rewards disrupt the collaboration needed for organizational learning.

- *Rewards ignore reasons*—Employers need to spend time discovering the cause of behavior problems. Instead, according to Kohn, they use incentives as quick fixes. We can see this in situations where companies use incentives for the most trivial reasons. For example, an Arizona company hands out cash to employees who arrive early at company meetings and fines those who arrive late.[30] The company would be better off identifying the causes of lateness and changing the conditions, rather than using money to force a solution to the problem.

- *Rewards discourage risk taking*—Kohn cites evidence that rewards motivate people to do exactly what is necessary to get the reward and nothing more. Incentives dampen creativity because employees no longer explore new opportunities outside the realm of rewarded behavior or results. In other words, rewards motivate employees to get rewards, not to discover better ways to help the organization.

- *Rewards undermine intrinsic motivation*—Kohn's greatest concern with reward systems is that they kill a person's motivation found in the work itself. This intrinsic motivation relates to fulfilling growth needs, which are the most powerful and sustaining sources of motivation (see Chapter 3). Kohn reports studies indicating that employees are less intrinsically motivated to perform a task after they have received an extrinsic reward for performing it. Critics point out that these studies were not conducted in real work situations. However, until more precise research indicates otherwise, we should be concerned about the risk of losing intrinsic motivation when extrinsic rewards are introduced.

Should we abandon rewards, based on Alfie Kohn's arguments? Probably not. Organizational behavior scholars have known for years that performance-based rewards are imperfect.[31] Even with these concerns, the OB literature generally concludes that properly implemented financial rewards do motivate employees.[32] And what about Alfie Kohn's criticisms? Our opinion is that they must be viewed as caveats of performance-based rewards, but not an outright dismissal of them.

agency theory an economic theory that assumes company owners (principals) and employees (agents) have different goals and interests, so rewards and other control systems are required to align the agent's goals with those of the principals

One additional argument for performance-based rewards comes from the economic concept called **agency theory**.[33] According to agency theory, company owners (principals) and the executives and employees representing the owners (agents) have different goals and interests. For example, companies typically want to provide a good return on investment to stockholders, serve customers effectively, and meet government obligations. Agency theory argues that agents will not support the owner's goals unless they happen to coincide with their personal goals or there is a compelling incentive to fulfill those goals. Reward systems are designed to successfully align employee goals and actions with the owner's interests.

Minimizing Reward Problems

As we said, reward systems do motivate—but only if we can avoid the problems that often plague performance-based reward systems in organizational settings. Here are some of the more important strategies.

Measure performance accurately   Rewards won't work unless companies learn how to measure employee performance and tie that information to the reward. This strengthens the performance-to-outcome expectancy (see Chapter 3) because accurate performance measurement increases the probability that employees who perform well are correctly identified and thereby receive larger rewards. Unfortunately, recent surveys indicate that only about one-third of U.S. employees believe there is a clear link between job performance and pay increases.[34] This occurs partly because it is difficult to measure the many elements of job performance and organizational citizenship. Moreover, evidence suggests that performance pay decisions are biased by organizational politics. Employees with organizational connections (e.g., friendships with senior management) tend to receive higher increases.[35]

Ensure that rewards are relevant   Companies need to align rewards with performance within the employee's control. For example, Sears rewards senior executives for corporate performance because they have some control over the company's overall success. Bonuses for department sales managers, on the other hand, are based on profits and customer satisfaction in their departments but not on Sears' overall corporate performance.[36] Reward systems also need to correct for situational contingencies. Salespeople in one region may have higher sales because the economy is stronger there than elsewhere, so sales bonuses need to be adjusted for these economic factors.

Use team rewards for interdependent jobs

Organizations should use team (or organizational) rewards rather than individual rewards when employees work in highly interdependent jobs.[37] One reason is that we can't identify or measure individual contributions very well in these situations. For example, you can't see how well one employee in a chemical processing plant contributes to the quality of the liquid produced. It is a team effort. A second reason is that team rewards tend to make employees more cooperative and less competitive. People see that their bonuses or other incentives depend on how well they work with co-workers, and they act accordingly.

The third reason for having team rewards in team settings is that they support employee preferences for team-based work arrangements. This was found in a recent study of Xerox customer service representatives. The Xerox employees assigned to teams with purely team bonuses eventually accepted and preferred a team structure, whereas those put in teams without team rewards did not adapt as well to the team structure.[38]

Ensure rewards are valued

Employers often introduce a reward without considering whether employees really value it. This point relates to the valence concept in expectancy theory (see Chapter 3). If a reward isn't valued, then it won't motivate. Moreover, we need to determine whether there are counter-valent factors related to the reward that undermine its motivational value. A British firm failed to do this when it asked staff to choose an employee-of-the-month. Everyone thought that the incentive was so tacky that they chose the worst employees for the award. "The company was surprised at the choices," explains a consultant familiar with the case, "but it didn't dawn on them what was going on."[39] Employees may have appreciated praise, but the "uncool" nature of this reward easily offset its benefits.

Watch out for unintended consequences

Performance-based reward systems sometimes have an unexpected—and undesirable—effect on employee behavior.[40] Employee behavior is a complex combination of needs, competencies, role perceptions, and situational factors, so it is often difficult to foresee the unexpected results when reward systems are introduced. Consider the pizza company that decided to reward its drivers for on-time delivery. The plan got more hot pizzas to customers on time, but it also increased the accident rates of its drivers because the incentive motivated them to drive recklessly.[41] Connections 4.2 describes a few other examples where reward systems had unintended consequences.

Job Design

job design the process of assigning tasks to a job, including the interdependency of those tasks with other jobs

Reward systems are not the only way to motivate people. As we mentioned in Chapter 3, OB scholars usually emphasize the job itself as the preferred source of motivation. It is also an important factor in work efficiency, work-related stress, and various other employee outcomes. The process of assigning tasks to a job, including the interdependency of those tasks with other jobs, is called **job design.** A *job* is a set of tasks performed by one person.[42] Some jobs have very few tasks, each requiring limited skill or effort. Other jobs include a very complex set of tasks and can be accomplished by only a few highly trained tradespeople or professionals.

We are currently seeing something of a revolution in the way jobs are designed. Information technology has reshaped the type of work that organizations now require (e.g., more information processing, less physical labor) as well as the degree of control that people have over the work they perform. Some critics argue that computers increasingly control the pace of work and

Connections 4.2 ▫ **When Rewards Go Wrong**

[John Thoeming]

There is an old saying that "what gets rewarded, gets done." But what companies reward isn't always what they had in mind. Here are a few dramatic examples:

• Toyota rewards its dealerships based on customer satisfaction surveys, not just car sales. What Toyota discovered, however, is that this motivates dealers to increase satisfaction scores, not customer satisfaction. One Toyota dealership received high ratings because it offered free detailing to every customer who returned a "Very Satisfied" survey. The dealership even had a special copy of the survey showing clients which boxes to check off. At another dealership, a recently hired salesperson was found pleading with customers to give him a good rating so that he didn't lose his job. This increased customer ratings, but not customer satisfaction.

• Donnelly Mirrors, the automobile parts manufacturer, introduced a gainsharing plan that motivated employees to reduce labor but not material costs. Employees knew that their work took longer as the diamond grinding wheels started to wear down, so they reduced labor costs by replacing the expensive wheels more often. This action reduced labor costs, thereby giving them the gainsharing bonus, but labor savings were easily offset by much higher costs for diamond grinding wheels.

• When AES Corp. purchased the majority share of Tisza Power in Hungary, it wanted to cut the 5,050-person workforce by half. To do this, all employees who voluntarily quit were offered a cash reward of Ft 100,000 (US$500) along with up to 26 months' severance. Someone miscalculated the value of this incentive. Over two-thirds of the employees signed up for the buyout package, leaving Tisza's operations short by 1,000 staff. At one point, AES management convened a meeting to persuade some employees to stay. "These people have never seen Ft 100,000 cash in their life," said Jozsef Montagh, head of the electricity union at Tisza's plant in Berente, Hungary. "They went crazy about it, without thinking about what they are going to do after the money dries up."

• An insurance company wanted salespeople to contact potential clients, so it devised an incentive that rewarded them based on the number of telephone calls made each month to prospective clients. The salespeople made significantly more calls under this plan, but they didn't sell any more insurance policies. Instead, the company had fewer sales and a much larger telephone bill.

Sources: Adapted from M. S. Gaspar and J. O'Leary, "Power Co. Golden Parachute Works Too Well," *Budapest Business Journal*, January 27, 1997, p. 3; F. F. Reichheld, *The Loyalty Effect* (Boston: Harvard Business School Press, 1996), p. 236; D. R. Spitzer, "Power Rewards: Rewards That Really Motivate," *Management Review*, May 1996, pp. 45–50; E. E. Lawler III, *Strategic Pay* (San Francisco: Jossey-Bass, 1990), p. 120. ▪

reduce the employee's freedom on the job. However, others claim that corporate leaders can influence the way jobs are designed around information technology and that work can be redesigned with employee needs in mind.[43]

Jobs are also being transformed as companies move toward a more flexible workforce. The trend toward **employability,** which we introduced in Chapter 1, means that many organizations now expect employees to perform a variety of work activities rather than hold specific jobs, and employees are expected to continuously learn skills that will keep them employed. In terms of job design, this means that employees are no longer hired into specific, narrowly defined jobs. Instead, they hold generic titles (associate, team member) and are expected to perform several clusters of tasks.[44]

Whether the change occurs through information technology or workforce flexibility, job design often produces an interesting conflict between the employee's motivation and ability to complete the work. To understand this issue more fully, we begin by describing early job design efforts aimed at increasing work efficiency through job specialization.

employability the "new deal" employment relationship in which the job is a temporary event and employees are expected to continuously learn skills that will keep them employed in a variety of work activities

Job Design and Work Efficiency

Mary Strang sees plenty of windshields, about 72 of them every hour. Mary and her assembly-line partner mount one windshield onto a Dodge Neon every 45 seconds. That's more than 500 windshields on each work shift, five days each week, and two Saturdays every month.[45]

These sewing machine operators at a United International Garment plant in Saipan (a U.S. territory in the Pacific Ocean) have a high degree of job specialization. An employee might complete each work unit (a piece of clothing) in a few minutes. This specialization improves work efficiency, but it can also lead to boredom and repetitive strain injuries. How does job specialization improve work efficiency for sewing machine operators?
[AP/Wide World]

job specialization the result of division of labor in which each job now includes a narrow subset of the tasks required to complete the product or service

Mary works in a job with a high degree of **job specialization.** Job specialization occurs when the work required to build a Neon car—or any other product or service—is subdivided into separate jobs assigned to different people. Each resulting job includes a very narrow subset of tasks, usually completed in a short "cycle time." A cycle time is the time required to complete the task before starting over with a new work unit. For Mary, the cycle time is less than a minute.

The economic benefits of job specialization were popularized over 200 years ago in Adam Smith's famous example of pin manufacturing.[46] According to Smith, there are several distinct operations in pin manufacturing, such as drawing out the wire, straightening it, cutting it, sharpening one end, grinding the other end, putting on the head, and whitening the head. In one factory where these tasks were divided among 10 people, Smith reported that the work team could produce almost 4,800 pins a day. But if the same 10 people made their own pins separately and independently, they would produce only 100 to 200 pins a day!

Why does job specialization potentially increase work efficiency? One reason is that employees have fewer tasks to juggle and therefore spend less time changing activities. A second explanation is that employees require fewer physical and mental skills to accomplish the assigned work, so less time and resources are needed for training. A third reason is that employees practice their tasks more frequently with shorter work cycles, so jobs are mastered quickly. Lastly, work efficiency increases because employees with specific aptitudes or skills can be matched more precisely to the jobs for which they are best suited.[47]

Adam Smith was mainly writing about *horizontal job specialization,* in which the basic physical behaviors required to provide a product or service are divided into different jobs (see Exhibit 4.3). With horizontal job specialization, employees perform fewer tasks. *Vertical job specialization,* on the other hand, refers to separating physical tasks from the administration of these tasks (i.e., planning, organizing, scheduling). In other words, vertical job specialization divorces the "thinking" job functions from the "doing" job functions.

Scientific Management

scientific management the process of systematically determining how work should be partitioned into its smallest possible elements and how the process of completing each task should be standardized to achieve maximum efficiency

One of the strongest advocates of job specialization was Frederick Winslow Taylor, an industrial engineer who introduced the principles of **scientific management** in the early 1900s.[48] Taylor described scientific management as a revolutionary way for management and workers to view their respective roles. In practice, it involves systematically determining how work should be partitioned into its smallest possible elements and how the process of completing

Exhibit 4.3
Horizontal and vertical job specialization

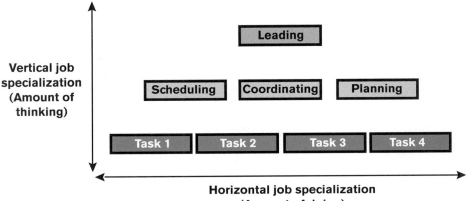

each task should be standardized to achieve maximum efficiency. Taylor advocated vertical job specialization so that detailed procedures and work practices are developed by engineers, enforced by supervisors, and executed by employees. He also applied horizontal job specialization, such as narrowing the supervisor's role to such a degree that one person manages operational efficiency, another manages inspection, and another is the disciplinarian.

Scientific management ideas can be found throughout industry today. For instance, Taylor popularized goal setting, employee training, incentive systems, and other practices described in this book. Frank and Lillian Gilbreth were enthusiastic followers of the scientific management philosophy and are largely credited with developing procedures known as **methods-time measurement** (also called *time-and-motion study*).[49] Methods-time measurement involves systematically observing, measuring, and timing physical movements to identify more efficient work behaviors. Industrial engineers use these practices to identify the best way to lay bricks, prepare hamburgers in fast-food restaurants, or engage in any other observable behavior. For example, National Sea Products Ltd., a Canadian fish-processing company, relies on methods-time measurement to improve efficiency in its fish-processing plants.[50] Some forms of methods-time measurement are also used for continuous improvement in quality management (see Chapter 10).

methods-time measurement the process of systematically observing, measuring, and timing physical movements to identify more efficient work behaviors

There is ample evidence that scientific management has improved efficiency in many work settings. One of Taylor's earliest interventions was at a ball-bearing factory where 120 women each worked 55 hours a week. Through job specialization and work efficiency analysis, Taylor increased production by two-thirds, using a workforce of only 35 women working fewer than 45 hours a week. Taylor also doubled the employees' previous wages. No doubt, some of the increased productivity can be credited to improved training, goal setting, and work incentives, but job specialization has also contributed to the success of scientific management.

Problems with Job Specialization

Job specialization tries to increase work efficiency, but it doesn't necessarily improve job performance. The problem is that job specialization ignores the effects of job content on employees.[51] One effect is that highly specialized jobs are usually tedious, trivial, and socially isolating. "Specialization is the root of a lot of boredom," explains Dennis Bakke, cofounder of AES Corp., the Virginia-based electrical power company that takes pains to avoid specialized jobs.[52]

Job specialization was supposed to let companies buy cheap, unskilled labor. Instead, many companies must offer higher wages—some call it *discontentment pay*—to compensate for the boredom of narrowly defined work.[53] Labor unions have also been effective at organizing and negotiating higher wages for employees in specialized, short-cycle jobs. Job specialization also costs more in terms of higher turnover, absenteeism, sabotage, and mental health problems.

Work quality has become another major concern. Employees in specialized jobs usually see only a small part of the process, so they can't identify with the customer's needs. As one observer of General Motors' traditional assembly line reported: "Often [workers] did not know how their jobs related to the total picture. Not knowing, there was no incentive to strive for quality—what did quality even mean as it related to a bracket whose function you did not understand."[54]

Perhaps the most important reason why job specialization has not been as successful as expected is that it ignores the motivational potential of jobs. As jobs become specialized, the work tends to become easier to perform but is less motivating. As jobs become more complex, work motivation increases but the ability to master the job decreases. Maximum job performance occurs somewhere between these two extremes, where most people can eventually perform the job tasks efficiently, yet the work is interesting.

Job Design and Work Motivation

motivator-hygiene theory
Frederick Herzberg's theory that employees are primarily motivated by growth and esteem needs, not by lower level needs

job characteristics model a job design model that relates five core job dimensions to three psychological states and several personal and organizational consequences

Industrial engineers may have overlooked the motivational effects of job characteristics, but it is now the central focus of many job design changes.[55] Frederick Herzberg is credited with casting more of the spotlight on job content as a dominant source of employee motivation. As we learned in Chapter 3, Herzberg's **motivator-hygiene theory** proposed that employees are primarily motivated by job content factors (e.g., responsibility, achievement, and personal growth) but not by job context factors (e.g., job security, supervisory relations, company policies).[56] This might seem rather obvious to us today, but it was radical thinking when Herzberg proposed the idea in the 1950s.

As we noted in Chapter 3, there are problems with Herzberg's motivator-hygiene theory. However, Herzberg's writing is significant because it led to considerable study into the motivational potential of jobs.[57] Out of that research has emerged J. Richard Hackman and Greg Oldham's **job characteristics model.** This model, shown in Exhibit 4.4, details the motivational properties of jobs as well as specific personal and organizational consequences of these properties.[58] The job characteristics model identifies five core job dimensions that produce three psychological states. Employees who experience these

Exhibit 4.4
The job characteristics model

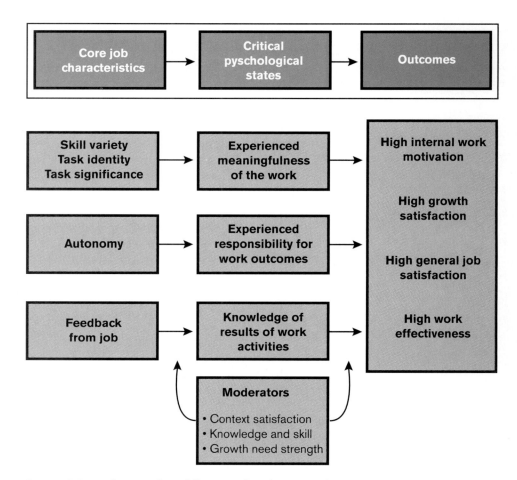

Source: J. R. Hackman and G. Oldham, *Work Redesign* (Reading, MA: Addison-Wesley, 1980), p. 90. Used with permission.

psychological states tend to have higher levels of internal work motivation (motivation from the work itself), job satisfaction (particularly satisfaction with the work itself), and work effectiveness.

Core Job Characteristics

Hackman and Oldham have identified five core job characteristics (see Exhibit 4.4). Desirable work outcomes increase when jobs are redesigned such that they include more of these characteristics.

skill variety the degree to which a job requires employees to use different skills and talents to complete a variety of work activities

task identity the degree to which a job requires completion of a whole or identifiable piece of work

task significance the degree to which the job has a substantial impact on the organization and/or larger society

autonomy the degree to which a job gives employees the freedom, independence, and discretion to schedule their work and determine the procedures to be used to complete the work

job feedback the degree to which employees can tell how well they are doing based on direct sensory information from the job itself

- **Skill variety** refers to the use of different skills and talents to complete a variety of work activities. For example, sales clerks who normally only serve customers might be assigned the additional duties of stocking inventory and changing storefront displays.
- **Task identity** is the degree to which a job requires completion of a whole or identifiable piece of work, such as doing something from beginning to end, or where it is easy to see how one's work fits into the whole product or service. An employee who assembles an entire computer modem rather than simply soldering the circuitry would develop a stronger sense of ownership or identity with the final product.
- **Task significance** is the degree to which the job has a substantial impact on the organization and/or larger society. For instance, air traffic controllers would have a high degree of task significance because the quality of their work affects the safety of others.
- **Autonomy** is the degree to which the job provides employees with freedom, independence, and discretion in scheduling the work and determining the procedures to be used to complete the work. In autonomous jobs, employees make their own decisions rather than rely on detailed instructions from supervisors or procedure manuals.
- **Job feedback** is the degree to which employees can tell how well they are doing based on direct sensory information from the job itself. Airline pilots can tell how well they land their aircraft and physicians can see whether their operations have improved the patient's health.

Critical Psychological States

The five core job characteristics affect employee motivation and satisfaction through three critical psychological states.[59] One of these is *experienced meaningfulness*—the belief that one's work is worthwhile or important. Skill variety, task identity, and task significance directly contribute to the job's meaningfulness. If the job has high levels of all three characteristics, employees are likely to feel that their job is highly meaningful. Meaningfulness drops as the job loses one or more of these characteristics.

Work motivation and performance increase when employees feel personally accountable for the outcomes of their efforts. Autonomy directly contributes to this feeling of *experienced responsibility*. Employees must be assigned control of their work environment to feel responsible for their successes and failures. The third critical psychological state is *knowledge of results*. Employees want information about the consequences of their work effort. Knowledge of results can originate from co-workers, supervisors, or clients. However, job design focuses on knowledge of results from the work itself.

Individual Differences

Job redesign doesn't increase work motivation for everyone in every situation. Employees must have the required skills and knowledge to master the more challenging work. Otherwise, job redesign tends to increase stress and reduce job performance. A second condition is that employees must be reasonably satisfied with their work environment (e.g., working conditions, job security, salaries) before job redesign affects work motivation.

A third condition is that employees must have strong growth needs. As we learned in Chapter 3, people with strong growth needs have satisfied their relatedness or existence needs, and are looking for challenges from the work itself. In contrast, improving the core job characteristics will have little motivational effect on people who are primarily focused on existence or relatedness needs.[60]

Increasing Work Motivation through Job Design

Three main strategies potentially increase the motivational potential of jobs: job rotation, job enlargement, and job enrichment. As we will learn in this section, there are also several ways to implement job enrichment.

Job Rotation

job rotation the practice of moving employees from one job to another, typically for short periods of time

Job rotation is the practice of moving employees from one job to another. Consider a typical "one hour" photofinishing retail outlet where one employee interacts with customers, another operates the photofinishing machine, and a third puts the finished product into envelopes and files them for pickup. Job rotation would occur where employees move around those three jobs every few hours or days. This form of job redesign is widely practiced in North America.[61] At US West, for example, teams are responsible for handling batches of mail from beginning to end, and individual team members are rotated through the various tasks in that process. Toyota Motors Manufacturing (TMM) in Georgetown, Kentucky, also rotates employees through various jobs every few hours or days.[62]

Toyota and US West recognize that job rotation reduces boredom, but they also want to reduce the incidence of repetitive strain injuries. By engaging in different tasks, employees use different muscles, thereby minimizing these injuries. A third reason for introducing job rotation is to develop a flexible workforce. Job rotation helps employees learn new tasks and thereby increase their ability to move to jobs where they are needed. At Memorial Medical Center in Las Cruces, New Mexico, cooks are expected to do catering and pot washers to do some cooking. This job rotation ensures that co-workers can cover for each other's absences. "Some employees don't like switching around like this and some have left the department because of it," explains Memorial Medical Center's manager in charge of food services. "But we have to do [job rotation] to build in flexibility."[63]

Job Enlargement

job enlargement increasing the number of tasks employees perform within their job

Instead of rotating employees through different jobs, **job enlargement** combines tasks into one job. We might combine two or more complete jobs into one, or just add one or two more tasks to an existing job. Either way, the job's skill variety has increased because there are more tasks to perform.

An example from NationsBank will help illustrate how job enlargement operates. Until recently, the tasks required to prepare a letter of credit at the Charlotte, N.C.–based financial institution were divided into four distinct jobs. One person prepared the letter of credit for issuance; a second person amended it; a third person negotiated payment; and a fourth person processed the debit or credit to the customer's account. This process was slow, resulted in occasional mix-ups, and frustrated customers who didn't know whom to call regarding the status of their letter of credit. Today, each NationsBank clerk handles all activities in a letter-of-credit transaction.[64]

Exhibit 4.5

Comparing job rotation and job enlargement

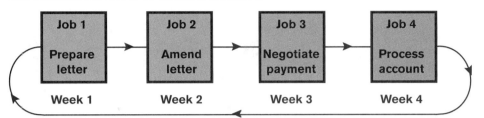

Job Rotation for Letter-of-Credit Transaction

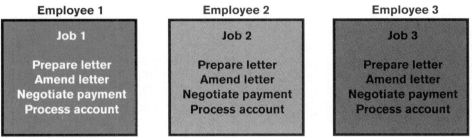

Job Enlargement for Letter-of-Credit Transaction

Exhibit 4.5 illustrates job enlargement at NationsBank and how this job design differs from job rotation. Under job rotation, the tasks for the letter-of-credit work process are divided into four jobs, and employees would move around these different jobs from time to time. Job enlargement, on the other hand, combines the tasks from all four jobs into one job so that one employee is responsible for the entire work process. The exhibit shows that the company has created three of these jobs to keep pace with the number of letters of credit required.

Job enlargement significantly improves customer service in NationsBank's letter-of-credit work process. This occurs partly because assigning all tasks to one employee minimizes coordination problems. However, research indicates that simply giving employees more tasks won't affect motivation, performance, or job satisfaction. Instead, these benefits result only when skill variety is combined with more autonomy and job knowledge (which NationsBank did as well as enlarge the jobs).[65] In other words, employees are motivated when they have a variety of tasks *and* have the freedom and knowledge to structure their work to achieve the highest satisfaction and performance. These job characteristics are at the heart of job enrichment.

Job Enrichment

job enrichment assigning responsibility for scheduling, coordinating, and planning work to employees who actually make the product or provide the service

Job enrichment occurs when employees are given more responsibility for scheduling, coordinating, and planning their own work. Although some writers suggest that job enrichment is any strategy that increases one or more of the core job characteristics, Herzberg said that jobs were enriched only through autonomy and the resulting feelings of responsibility. At least, skill variety was not recognized as a way to enrich jobs.[66] Notice that our definition of job enrichment relates directly to *vertical job loading* because it reverses vertical job specialization that we described earlier. There are numerous ways to enrich jobs, but we will discuss three of the most popular methods: empowerment, forming natural work units, and establishing client relationships.

empowerment the feeling of control and self-efficacy that emerges when people are given power in a previously powerless situation

Empowering employees   Corporate leaders like to use the term **empowerment** to describe how employees are given more autonomy over the work process. This includes letting jobholders decide work methods, check quality, establish work schedules, decide how to solve problems, and receive information about and control over financial budgets.

Empowerment refers to a feeling of control and self-efficacy that emerges when people are given power in a previously powerless situation.[67] Empowered employees are given autonomy—the freedom, independence, and discretion over their work activities. They are assigned work that has high levels of task significance—importance to themselves and others. Empowered employees also have control over performance feedback that guides their work. Notice from the definition that empowered employees also have feelings of self-efficacy; that is, they believe that they are capable of successfully completing the task (see Chapter 2).[68]

Empowerment has become such a popular practice that it is in danger of being labeled a fad. Moreover, some companies claim they practice empowerment, but haven't introduced the changes necessary to make this a reality. This may explain why some studies have not found any improvements after corporate leaders have allegedly "empowered" employees.[69]

Fortunately, many companies have truly implemented empowerment. One of the best examples is AES Corp. As the *Fast Company Online* feature for this chapter describes, the electric power company based in Arlington, Virginia, empowers employees far beyond most other organizations. This philosophy isn't limited to its operations in the United States. AES also empowers its employees in South America, eastern Europe, and other parts of the world.

FAST COMPANY Online ▪ AES Corp.'s Power Comes from Empowerment

AES Corp. empowers Oscar Prieto (center), his co-workers at this construction project in Brazil, and other AES employees around the globe. *[Christopher Hartlove. Used with permission.]*

Oscar Prieto was visiting AES Corp.'s headquarters in Arlington, Virginia, when a senior executive asked for a volunteer to sit in a meeting. Prieto, a recently-hired AES engineer from Argentina, raised his hand. He was soon negotiating with a large European power company over a joint venture in Brazil. Now, two years later, Prieto heads an AES division in Rio de Janeiro that supplies electricity to 8 million homes and businesses. "That's what happens when you raise your hand around here," says Prieto with a smile.

At most companies, Oscar Prieto's personal odyssey would be a fairy tale—far too much new responsibility, far too early in his tenure. At AES, the fast-growing electric power company, it is standard operating procedure. Many companies talk about empowering employees and pushing responsibility out from headquarters, but few push as hard or as far as AES. For instance, when AES raised $350 million to finance a joint venture in Northern Ireland, two control-room operators led the team that raised the

Forming natural work units   Another way to enrich jobs is to organize tasks into a natural grouping, such as completing a whole product. Assembling an entire toaster rather than just some parts of it is an example of forming a natural work unit. Another example is to rearrange tasks around specific clients. For example, most human resource departments assign their staff to specialized jobs, such as recruiting or compensation. These jobs would be redesigned around natural work units by having each employee take responsibility for all human resource activities for a specific group of employees. One human resource person would be responsible for recruiting, compensation, and other human resource activities involving technical staff, another person would be responsible for production staff, and so on.

By forming natural work units, jobholders have stronger feelings of responsibility for an identifiable body of work. They feel a sense of ownership and therefore tend to increase job quality. Forming natural work units increases task identity and task significance because employees perform a complete product or service and can more readily see how their work affects others.

Establishing client relationships   As mentioned, some natural work units assign employees to a specific client group. However, establishing client relationships takes this one step further by putting employees in *direct contact* with their clients rather than using the supervisor as a go-between. These

funds. Indeed, most of the $3.5 billion that financed 10 new AES power plants was brought in by decentralized teams, not finance specialists.

"The modern manager is supposed to ask his people for advice and then make a decision," says Dennis Bakke, who cofounded AES with Roger Sant in the early 1980s. "But at AES, each decision is made by a person and a team. Their job is to get advice from me and from anybody else they think it's necessary to get advice from. And then they make the decision."

Oscar Prieto and other managers are quickly learning to continue that power-sharing tradition. When AES took over Argentina's Cabra Corral power plant, Prieto removed the time clocks and bosses, and empowered employees to operate the business. "I trust people—without fear or hesitation," he says. "The best way to let them perform is with absolute freedom: I release you of all constraints, including the constraints imposed by your boss."

ONLINE CHECK-UP

1. AES Corp. is a very successful company, partly because it engages in radical power sharing with its employees. But certain conditions must exist to make empowerment effective. From your reading of this excerpt, what conditions are necessary to ensure that empowerment creates a motivated and productive workforce?

2. The full text of this *Fast Company* article describes how AES encourages skill variety. Read the entire article and discuss how this generalist approach to work gives AES a competitive advantage over organizations that value specialization.

You can download the full text of this article at www.mhhe.com/mcshane1e.

Source: Adapted from A. Markels, "Power to the People," *Fast Company,* Issue 13 (February–March 1998). ■

clients submit work and provide feedback directly to the employee rather than through a supervisor.[70] Brooklyn Union, the New York gas company, has enriched the jobs of field distribution crews by establishing client relationships. At one time, these crews would only install pipes from the main lines to the house. A customer service representative would then come into the house to finish the work. Now, the distribution employees do the entire job and work directly with customers. After the distribution employees have installed the pipes, they clean off their shoes and enter the house to unlock the gas, relight the pilot light, and check the results. The customer deals with one person or crew and the field staff feel a stronger sense of obligation to their client.[71]

Job Design Prospects and Problems

Job rotation, enlargement, and enrichment are now fairly common activities and have a much higher survival rate than most work interventions.[72] In most situations, they keep organizations competitive and fulfill employee needs. Employees with high growth needs have higher job satisfaction and work motivation, along with lower absenteeism and turnover. Productivity is also higher when task identity and job feedback are improved.[73] Error rates, number of defects, and other quality indicators tend to improve because job enrichment increases the jobholder's felt responsibility and sense of ownership over the product or service. Quality improvements in production and service are particularly evident when the job enrichment intervention involves completing a natural work unit or establishing client relationships.[74]

Obstacles in Job Design

In spite of these potential benefits, job design is not easy to implement. One concern is how to measure the core job characteristics accurately. Objectively measuring job content is expensive and difficult, so the most popular tool for measuring job content asks employees to describe their *perceived* job characteristics. Scholars are concerned that these perceptions are biased by job satisfaction (which may be caused by factors other than job content) and by what co-workers say to us about our work.[75] Until we find an accurate and cost-effective way to measure job content, job design experts will have trouble pinpointing which jobs require changing and how well job design strategies are working.

Our current knowledge about job design is also limited by its focus on individual jobs. In particular, the literature tends to overlook job design characteristics that apply to team settings.[76] Moreover, many work settings require team-based job redesign because the technology is fixed or the work is too complex for one person to complete alone. For example, one employee would not make an entire automobile or operate an entire petrochemical process. We will consider some of these issues in our discussion of employee involvement (Chapter 10) after introducing team dynamics in Chapter 9.

Job design interventions also face resistance to change. Some supervisors don't like job redesign interventions because they change their roles and may threaten job security.[77] Labor union leaders have been bitter foes of job specialization and scientific management, yet they complain that job enrichment programs are management ploys to get more work out of employees for less money. Unskilled employees may lack the confidence or growth need strength to learn more challenging tasks. Skilled employees are known to resist job redesign because they believe the intervention will undermine their power base and force them to perform lower-status work.[78]

Kellogg's, the U.S.-owned cereal company, recently experienced this problem at its production plant in Australia. The company wanted to enlarge and enrich jobs for a more flexible workforce, but maintenance employees refused to let production employees do simple maintenance tasks. "We had negotiated to lift the skill levels of operators through a comprehensive multiskilling program only to have the maintenance unions continually renege on that," says Clyde Morgan, Kellogg's Australian human resource manager. To remove this barrier, the company contracted out the entire maintenance work.[79]

Lastly, an ongoing dilemma with job design is finding the ideal balance between job enrichment and specialization. There are several competing factors to consider. Specialized jobs may improve work efficiency, but job performance may decline as employee motivation falls. Job enrichment may increase motivation, but performance may fall if employees lack the skills necessary to complete more challenging tasks. Job enrichment may increase recruiting and training costs, whereas job specialization may increase compensation costs if companies provide discontentment pay to entice people into boring jobs.[80] Job enrichment improves product quality, but error rates may increase when tasks become so challenging that employees lack the necessary skills or experience stress.[81] Of course, job specialization also increases stress if employees do not make effective use of their talents in narrowly defined jobs, as we will learn in Chapter 5.

Motivating Yourself through Self-Leadership

While most companies are busy finding new "carrots" to motivate employees, Steelcase, Inc., is teaching its employees to motivate themselves. The Grand Rapids, Michigan, office furniture company uses a process in which employees confirm their responsibilities, set their own goals corresponding to those responsibilities, and track their own goal accomplishment. "If you can give [employees] the tools to improve self-management, it's a plus," explains Daniel Wiljanen, Steelcase's vice president of human resources.[82]

Most literature on workplace motivation assumes that companies must do things to motivate employees. Yet the truth is that employees motivate themselves most of the time. Realizing this, Steelcase and other companies are adopting an employee-centered performance management model by teaching employees how to guide their own behavior more effectively. This is increasingly important as companies try to become less reliant on direct supervision over employees. Moreover, direct supervision is incompatible with the emerging ideals of egalitarianism (minimal status differences) and empowerment. The emerging view is that employees can take care of themselves.

self-leadership the process of influencing oneself to establish the self-direction and self-motivation needed to perform a task, including personal goal setting, constructive thought patterns, designing natural rewards, self-monitoring, and self-reinforcement

Self-leadership is an emerging organizational behavior concept that captures this overlooked perspective of employee motivation and performance. Self-leadership refers to the process of influencing oneself to establish the self-direction and self-motivation needed to perform a task.[83] This concept includes a toolkit of behavioral activities borrowed from social learning theory (Chapter 2) and goal setting (Chapter 3). It also includes constructive thought processes that have been extensively studied in sports psychology. Overall, self-leadership takes the view that individuals mostly regulate their own actions through these behavioral and cognitive (thought) activities.

Although we are in the early stages of understanding the dynamics of self-leadership, Exhibit 4.6 identifies the five main elements of this process. These elements, which generally follow each other in a sequence, include personal goal setting, constructive thought patterns, designing natural rewards, self-monitoring, and self-reinforcement.[84]

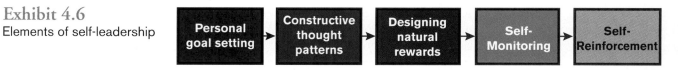

Personal Goal Setting

The first step in self-leadership is to set goals for your own work effort. This applies the ideas we learned in Chapter 3 on goal setting, such as identifying goals that are specific, results oriented, and challenging. The only difference between personal goal setting and our previous discussion is that goals are set alone, rather than assigned by or jointly decided with a supervisor.[85] According to the self-leadership literature, effective organizations establish norms whereby employees have a natural tendency to set their own goals to motivate themselves.[86]

Constructive Thought Patterns

Before beginning a task and while performing it, employees should engage in positive (constructive) thoughts about that work and its accomplishment. In particular, employees are more motivated and better prepared to accomplish a task after they have engaged in self-talk and mental imagery.

self-talk talking to yourself about your own thoughts or actions, for the purpose of increasing self-efficacy and navigating through the decisions required to get the job done effectively

Self-talk
Do you ever talk to yourself? Most of us do, although perhaps not out loud. **Self-talk** refers to any situation in which we talk to ourselves about our own thoughts or actions.[87] These self-statements affect our self-efficacy which in turn can influence our behavior and performance in a particular situation.[88] In other words, self-talk creates a "can-do" belief and thereby increases motivation by raising our $E \rightarrow P$ expectancy. We often hear that professional athletes "psyche" themselves up before an important event. They tell themselves that they can achieve their goal and that they have practiced enough to reach that goal. They are motivating themselves through self-talk.

Self-talk also affects how well we figure out the best way to accomplish new or complex tasks. People who tell themselves "I can do this job well; I've got the necessary skills!" are more effective at navigating through the decisions required to get the job done effectively. In contrast, people who make negative self-statements tend to have more difficulty deciding how to complete new or complex tasks.[89] Thus, increased self-efficacy seems to improve not only a person's motivation to accomplish a task, but also how to determine the best way to accomplish that task.

mental imagery mentally practicing a task and visualizing its successful completion

Mental imagery
You've probably heard the phrase, "I'll cross that bridge when I come to it." Self-leadership takes the opposite view. It suggests that we need to mentally practice a task and imagine successfully performing it beforehand. This process is known as **mental imagery**.[90]

As you can see from this definition, mental imagery has two parts. One part involves mentally practicing the task, anticipating obstacles to goal accomplishment, and working out solutions to those obstacles before they occur. By mentally walking through the activities required to accomplish the task, we begin to see problems that may occur. We can then imagine what responses would be best for each contingency.[91]

While one part of mental imagery helps us to anticipate things that could go wrong, the other part involves visualizing successful completion of the task. We imagine the experience of completing the task and the positive results that

As one of the world's leading neurosurgeons, Dr. Ben Carson uses mental imagery to visualize each medical operation he performs—up to 500 of them each year. "I think through every procedure: how I expect it to go, how long each phase will last, when I can move on to the next one," explains the chief of pediatric neurosurgery at Baltimore's Johns Hopkins Hospital. Carson also imagines the worst thing that could happen, what he should do to make sure the worst doesn't happen, and what he would do if it does. "I always anticipate the worst-case scenario," says Carson.[92] How might Dr. Carson apply other elements of the self-leadership model in his work?
[Keith Weller]

follow. Everyone daydreams and fantasizes about being in a successful situation. You might imagine yourself being promoted to your boss's job, receiving a prestigious award, or taking time off work. This visualization increases goal commitment and motivates us to complete the task effectively.

Designing Natural Rewards

Self-leadership recognizes that employees can find ways to make the job itself more motivating.[93] One way is to think about how the work affects co-workers, customers, and others. Production employees who mount wheels on new cars might keep in mind that mounting wheels properly ensures customer safety. By consciously thinking about the effects of one's work, employees can increase the perceived task significance of their work.

There are other ways to build natural rewards into the job. One strategy is to alter the way a task is accomplished. People often have enough discretion in their jobs to make slight changes to suit their needs and preferences. For instance, you might prefer to drop by a co-worker's office to discuss an issue rather than to send him or her an e-mail. The visit fulfills your social needs and is a natural reward of performing the task. Another example would be trying out a new software program to design an idea, rather than sketching the image with pencil. By using the new software, you are adding challenge to a task that might otherwise be mundane.

Self-Monitoring

Self-monitoring is the process of keeping track of one's progress toward a goal. In the section on job design, we learned that feedback from the job itself communicates whether we are accomplishing the task successfully. Self-monitoring includes the notion of consciously checking that naturally occurring feedback at regular intervals.

Self-monitoring also includes designing artificial feedback where natural feedback does not occur. Salespeople might arrange to receive monthly reports on sales levels in their territory. Production staff might have gauges or computer feedback systems installed so they can see how many errors are made on the production line.

Self-Reinforcement

Self-leadership includes the social learning concept of self-reinforcement. Recall from Chapter 2 that self-reinforcement occurs whenever an employee has control over a reinforcer but doesn't "take" the reinforcer until completing a self-set goal.[94] A common example is taking a break after reaching a predetermined stage of your work. The work break is a self-induced form of positive reinforcement.

Self-reinforcement also occurs when you decide to do a more enjoyable task after completing a task that you dislike. For example, after slogging through a difficult report, you might decide to spend time doing a more pleasant task, such as scanning web sites for information about competitors.

Self-Leadership in Practice

Does self-leadership improve motivation and performance? It's too early to say that every component of the model is useful, but the overall results are impressive. For instance, one recent study reported that new employees who practiced self-set goals and self-reinforcement had higher internal motivation.[95]

Studies of self-talk and mental imagery, mostly from sports psychology, indicate that constructive thought processes improve individual performance. For example, research found that young skaters who received self-talk training improved their performance one year later.[96] Self-talk and mental imagery are also effective in organizations. Employees at America West Airlines who received constructive thought training experienced better mental performance, enthusiasm, and job satisfaction than co-workers who did not receive this training. This self-leadership training was particularly useful because America West was under bankruptcy protection at the time of the study.

Employees with a high degree of conscientiousness have a more natural tendency to apply self-leadership strategies compared with people with lower conscientiousness scores. Conscientiousness is a personality trait (see Chapter 6) and one of the key elements of organizational citizenship behavior (Chapter 2). People with a high degree of conscientiousness are meticulous, careful, organized, responsible, and self-disciplined. However, one of the advantages of self-leadership is that it can be learned. Training programs have effectively improved self-leadership skills in those with lower conscientiousness scores.[97] Overall, self-leadership promises to be a valuable concept and practice for improving employee motivation and performance.

Self-leadership, job design, and rewards are important ways to motivate people in organizational settings. However, they are not the only ways. Recall from Chapter 3 that motivation is derived from a person's unique combination of natural and learned needs. Each of these needs can be fulfilled in many ways and from various sources. Many of the topics covered later in this book—such as team cohesiveness, work-related values, and corporate culture—also affect employee motivation.

Chapter Summary

Organizations reward employees for their membership and seniority, job status, competencies, and performance. Competency- and performance-based rewards are increasingly popular. Job status-based rewards are becoming less important because they are inconsistent with the need for a flexible workforce.

There are many types of individual, team, and organizational rewards. However, these performance-based rewards have also been criticized for doing more damage than good to employee motivation. Performance-based rewards tend to work better when companies measure performance accurately, recognize and adjust for situational contingencies in job performance, use team rewards for interdependent jobs, ensure rewards are valued, and minimize unintended consequences.

Job design involves assigning tasks to a job and distributing work throughout the organization. Job specialization subdivides work into separate jobs for different people. This increases work efficiency because employees master the tasks quickly, spend less time changing tasks, require less training, and can be matched more closely with the jobs best suited to their skills. However, job specialization may reduce work motivation, create mental health problems, lower product or service quality, and increase costs through discontentment pay, absenteeism, and turnover.

Contemporary job design strategies reverse job specialization through job rotation, job enlargement, and job enrichment. Hackman and Oldham's job characteristics model is the most popular foundation for recent job redesign interventions because it specifies core job dimensions, psychological states, and individual differences. Companies often enrich jobs through empowerment, forming natural work units, and establishing client relationships.

Self-leadership is the process of influencing oneself to establish the self-direction and self-motivation needed to perform a task. This includes personal goal setting, constructive thought patterns, designing natural rewards, self-monitoring, and self-reinforcement.

Constructive thought patterns include self-talk and mental imagery. Self-talk refers to any situation in which people talk to themselves about their own thoughts or actions. Mental imagery involves mentally practicing a task and imagining successfully performing it beforehand.

Key Terms

Agency theory, p. 106
Autonomy, p. 113
Competencies, p. 100
Employability, p. 109
Employee stock ownership plan (ESOP), p. 103
Empowerment, p. 115
Gainsharing plan, p. 103
Job characteristics model, p. 112
Job design, p. 107
Job enlargement, p. 114
Job enrichment, p. 115
Job evaluation, p. 99
Job feedback, p. 113

Job rotation, p. 114
Job specialization, p. 110
Mental imagery, p. 120
Methods-time measurement, p. 111
Motivator-hygiene theory, p. 112
Profit sharing, p. 105
Scientific management, p. 110
Self-leadership, p. 119
Self-talk, p. 120
Skill-based pay (SBP), p. 100
Skill variety, p. 113
Task identity, p. 113
Task significance, p. 113

Discussion Questions

1. As a consultant, you have been asked to recommend either a gainsharing or profit-sharing plan for employees who work in the four regional distribution and warehousing facilities of a large retail organization. Which reward system would you recommend? Explain your answer.

2. Educational researcher Alfie Kohn claims that rewards punish. Describe two ways that this may be true.

3. Wichita Technologies, Inc. has redesigned its production facilities around a team-based system. However, the company president believes that employees will not be motivated unless they receive incentives based on their individual performance. Give three explanations why Wichita Technologies should introduce team-based rather than individual rewards in this setting.

4. Under what conditions would job specialization be most appropriate?

5. Most of us have watched pizzas being made while waiting to pick up a pizza from a pizza shop. What level of job specialization do you usually notice in

these operations? Why does this high or low level of specialization exist? If some pizza shops have different levels of specialization than others, identify the contingencies that might explain these differences.

6. You have been asked by the senior administration at your college or university to identify ways that instructors can "empower" students in the classroom. What specific recommendations would you provide? Your answer should identify specific things that instructors should do to generate empowerment.

7. Tomorrow, you present your first report to senior management to extend funding for your unit's special initiative. All of the materials are ready for the presentation. Following the five steps in self-leadership, describe how you can prepare for that meeting.

8. Several elements of self-leadership are derived from concepts presented earlier in this book. Identify those concepts and explain how they are applied in self-leadership.

CASE STUDY

Vêtements Ltée

Vêtements Ltée is a chain of men's retail clothing stores located throughout the province of Quebec, Canada. Two years ago, the company introduced new incentive systems for both store managers and sales employees. Store managers receive a salary with annual merit increases based on sales above targeted goals, store appearance, store inventory management, customer complaints, and several other performance measures. Some of this information (e.g., store appearance) is gathered during visits by senior management, while other information is based on company records (e.g., sales volume).

Sales employees are paid a fixed salary plus a commission based on the percentage of sales credited to that employee over the pay period. The commission represents about 30 percent of a typical paycheck and is intended to encourage employees to actively serve customers and to increase sales volume. Because returned merchandise is discounted from commissions, sales staff are discouraged from selling products that customers do not really want.

Soon after the new incentive systems were introduced, senior management began to receive complaints from store managers regarding the performance of their sales staff. They observed that sales employees tended to stand near the store entrance waiting for customers and would occasionally argue over "ownership" of the customer. Managers were concerned that this aggressive behavior intimidated some customers. It also tended to leave some parts of the store unattended by staff.

Many managers were also concerned about inventory duties. Previously, sales staff would share responsibility for restocking inventory and completing inventory reorder forms. Under the new compensation system, however, few employees were willing to do these essential tasks. On several occasions, stores experienced stock shortages because merchandise was not stocked or re-order forms were not completed in a timely manner. Potential sales suffered from empty shelves when plenty of merchandise was available in the back storeroom or at the warehouse. The company's new automatic inventory system could reduce some of these problems, but employees must still stock shelves and assist in other aspects of inventory management.

Store managers tried to correct the inventory problem by assigning employees to inventory duty, but this has created resentment among the employees selected. Other managers threatened sales staff with dismissals if they did not do their share of inventory management. This strategy has been somewhat effective when the manager is in the store, but staff members sneak back onto the floor when the manager is away. It has also hurt staff morale, particularly relations with the store manager.

To reduce the tendency of sales staff to hoard customers at the store entrance, some managers assigned employees to specific areas of the store. This also created some resentment among employees stationed in areas with less traffic or lower-priced merchandise. Some staff openly complained of lower paychecks because they were assigned to a slow area of the store or were given more than their share of inventory duties.

Discussion Questions

1. What symptom(s) exist in this case to suggest that something has gone wrong?

2. What are the root causes that have led to these symptoms?

3. What actions should the organization take to correct these problems?

© Copyright. Steven L. McShane. ■

Talent trawl: what's the best bait?

BusinessWeek

Jonathan King was an employer's dream catch. The 26-year-old had already run his own successful Internet design business and was happily employed as a well-paid securities lawyer at one of Chicago's more prestigious firms. Yet when American Information Systems Inc. (AIS) approached him with something better, King took the bait. What would entice King to work for a 60-person Internet consulting company? The opportunity to work on exciting projects in a hot industry was the main factor. But not far behind for King was a stock option deal that could make him rich if the company ever goes public.

This *Business Week* case study describes how money and benefits are motivating talented people to join organizations with the best offers. It details the limitations of pension plans as well as ways that employees receive stock options. Read through this *Business Week* case study at www.mhhe.com/mcshane1e and prepare for the discussion questions below.

Discussion Questions

1. Why would stock options attract talented people to join an organization like American Information Systems Inc.? Use your knowledge of expectancy theory from Chapter 3 to help answer this question.

2. Suppose that you were offered attractive stock options for a job that you didn't particularly like? To what extent would the financial motivation to join the firm offset the lack of motivation from the work itself? Are these two factors completely separate from each other in this case?

3. The full text of this *Business Week* case study explains that the U.S. government rules imply that everyone in a job group should receive the same employee benefits. What type of reward in Exhibit 4.1 does this create and what are its implications for attracting talent to the organization?

Source: L. Stern, "Talent Trawl: What's the Best Bait?" *Business Week*, December 7, 1998, p. 22.

Increasing number of companies are offering workers flextime

 In an attempt to ease the work versus family time crunch, more and more companies are offering their employees flexibility in their schedules. One of the most popular choices is, believe it or not, the dawn patrol, working the early morning hours. *Working Mother* magazine tells you how to make this work for you and your boss. *Working Mother* editor-in-chief Judsen Culbreth noted that many companies are allowing their employees to work the early bird shift. She said, "It's such a popular benefit that 70–80 percent of Fortune 500 companies now offer flextime. Flextime reduces absenteeism, people can be more productive. Sometimes, firms can extend their service hours, they can open an office earlier, for example, or deal with clients on another coast. So it does have a lot of advantages for companies."

Besides advantages to the firm, there are advantages for employees. Culbreth said, "You can eliminate rush hour traffic because you are on the road before the other cars are. It also cuts down child care costs and, if you're an early bird, that's your most productive time. So that's a big benefit." Cutting down on rush hour driving is a great benefit to some. Culbreth noted, "People are commuting longer and longer. The average commuter spends 204 hours a year on the road."

Many workers would like to have flextime but don't know how to approach their managers about the topic. Culbreth offered this advice to employees who would like to introduce the idea into their workplaces: "Well you should look at it as how is it going to benefit the company. Don't say 'well this would be great for me,' say 'this would be great for the company' and show them what the real savings are in terms of turnover and absenteeism. Make it a win-win situation for the boss."

One of the benefits to an employer from introducing flextime arrangements is increased loyalty from employees. One employer who uses this approach is American Management Systems (AMS), an international information technology consulting firm in Fairfax, Virginia. One employee who benefits from AMS's flextime system is Debra Bailey, who works the dawn patrol. Her boss is AMS CEO Paul Brans.

Bailey said, "Basically what I do is I manage our company stock, which means I need to be available at all times to answer questions from employees. I get up usually at 5:30 and I'm in the office at 7:00 and my work day ends at 2:45. Usually I'm running out the door at that time to pick up my first grader, Brittany, from school." After she picks up her child, Bailey makes additional work-related calls from home. She noted, "Usually I get home at 3:30 and I'll start dinner or get my daughter going on her homework, but at the same time I'm always able to check my voice mail and also the company has provided me with a modem so I can check my e-mail through home."

AMS has a number of employees like Bailey who use the flextime system. Brans said, "We have a number of AMSers, and it's not just the early morning shift. There are some that come in later in the day. The key I think

for us has been offering a flexible work environment and it has many, many advantages for us. One of the key points, as you know, is that today AMS is in the technology and consulting business. It's a challenging business. We have frequent travel and tight deadlines. And one thing the flexible work place offers us is the ability to hire and retain top quality people." Bailey added, "Everyone's needs are different. At AMS it's not at all uncommon to see people deviate from the standard 8–5 or 9–6 work day or actually work from home a lot of days."

Culbreth stated that she expects the flextime trend to continue for the foreseeable future, "I think flextime works very well, often for small companies, but it's more likely in the service industries. In manufacturing you don't see as much flexibility when everyone has to be there at the same time producing the product, but with any service industry whatever the size it's really catching on. It is the most popular employee benefit right now."

Discussion Questions

1. The video states that flextime is used primarily in the service industry. Do you think flextime could be used in manufacturing?

2. Explain how flextime leads to employee motivation using the three critical psychological states of personal motivation.

3. How does flextime relate to the trend toward empowering workers? What benefits does the firm receive from empowering employees in this manner? ■

TEAM EXERCISE

Is student work enriched?

Purpose

This exercise is designed to help students learn how to measure the motivational potential of jobs and to evaluate the extent that jobs should be further enriched.

Instructions

In several ways, being a student is like having a job. You have tasks to perform and someone (such as your instructor) oversees your work. Although few people want to be students most of their lives (the pay rate is too low!), it may be interesting to determine how enriched your job is as a student.

Step 1: Students are placed into teams (preferably four or five people).

Step 2: Working alone, students complete the Job Diagnostic Survey. Then, using the guidelines below, they individually calculate the score for the five core job characteristics as well as the overall motivating potential score for the job.

Step 3: Members of each team compare their individual results. The group should identify differences of opinion for each core job characteristic. They should also note which core job characteristics have the lowest scores and recommend how these scores could be increased.

Step 4: The entire class meets to discuss the results of the exercise. The instructor may ask some teams to present their comparisons and recommendations for a particular core job characteristic.

Job diagnostic survey

Circle the number on the right that best describes student work.	Very little ▼		Moderately ▼			Very much ▼
1. To what extent does student work permit you to decide on your own how to go about doing the work? 1	2	3	4	5	6	7
2. To what extent does student work involve doing a whole or identifiable piece of work, rather than a small portion of the overall work process? 1	2	3	4	5	6	7
3. To what extent does student work require you to do many different things, using a variety of your skills/talents? 1	2	3	4	5	6	7
4. To what extent are the results of your work as a student likely to significantly affect the lives and well-being of other people (e.g., within your school, your family, society)? 1	2	3	4	5	6	7
5. To what extent does working on student activities provide information about your performance? 1	2	3	4	5	6	7

Circle the number on the right that best describes student work.	Very inaccurate ▼		Uncertain ▼			Very accurate ▼
6. Being a student requires me to use a number of complex and high-level skills. 1	2	3	4	5	6	7
7. Student work is arranged so that I do *not* have the chance to do an entire piece of work from beginning to end. 7	6	5	4	3	2	1
8. Doing the work required of students provides many chances for me to figure out how well I am doing. 1	2	3	4	5	6	7
9. The work students must do is quite simple and repetitive. 7	6	5	4	3	2	1
10. How well the work of a student gets done can affect many other people. 1	2	3	4	5	6	7
11. Student work denies me any chance to use my personal initiative or judgment in carrying out the work........................ 7	6	5	4	3	2	1
12. Student work provides me the chance to completely finish the pieces of work I begin. 1	2	3	4	5	6	7
13. Doing student work by itself provides very few clues about whether or not I am performing well. 7	6	5	4	3	2	1
14. As a student, I have considerable opportunity for independence and freedom in how I do the work. 1	2	3	4	5	6	7
15. The work I perform as a student is *not* very significant or important in the broader scheme of things. 7	6	5	4	3	2	1

Source: Adapted from the Job Diagnostic Survey, developed by J. R. Hackman and G. R. Oldham. The authors have released any copyright ownership of this scale (see J. R. Hackman and G. Oldham, *Work Redesign* [Reading, MA: Addison-Wesley, 1980], p. 275).

Scoring key for the motivating potential score

Scoring Core Job Characteristics

Use the following scoring key to estimate the motivating potential score for the job of being a student. Use your answers from the Job Diagnostic Survey that you completed above.

Skill Variety (SV) $\dfrac{\text{Question } 3 + 6 + 9}{3} = \underline{\hphantom{xxxx}}$

Task Identity (TI) $\dfrac{\text{Question } 2 + 7 + 12}{3} = \underline{\hphantom{xxxx}}$

Task Significance (TS) $\dfrac{\text{Question } 4 + 10 + 15}{3} = \underline{\hphantom{xxxx}}$

Autonomy $\dfrac{\text{Question } 1 + 11 + 14}{3} = \underline{\hphantom{xxxx}}$

Job Feedback $\dfrac{\text{Question } 5 + 8 + 13}{3} = \underline{\hphantom{xxxx}}$

Calculating Motivating Potential Score (MPS)

Use the following formula and the results above to calculate the motivating potential score. Notice that skill variety, task identity, and task significance are averaged before being multiplied by the score for autonomy and job feedback.

$$\left(\frac{\text{SV} + \text{TI} + \text{TS}}{3}\right) \times \text{Autonomy} \times \text{Job feedback}$$

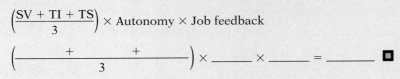

$$\left(\frac{\underline{\hphantom{xx}} + \underline{\hphantom{xx}} + \underline{\hphantom{xx}}}{3}\right) \times \underline{\hphantom{xxxx}} \times \underline{\hphantom{xxxx}} = \underline{\hphantom{xxxx}} \ \blacksquare$$

SELF-ASSESSMENT EXERCISE

Assessing your self-leadership

Purpose

This exercise is designed to help you understand self-leadership concepts and to assess your self-leadership tendencies.

Instructions

Read each of the statements below and circle the response that you believe best reflects your position regarding each statement. Then use the scoring key to calculate your results. This exercise is completed alone so that students assess themselves honestly without concerns of social comparison. However, class discussion will focus on the meaning of each self-leadership concept, how this scale might be applied in organizations, and the limitations of measuring self-leadership in work settings.

Self-leadership questionnaire

Circle the number that best reflects your position regarding each of these statements.	Describes me very well ▼	Describes me well ▼	Describes me somewhat ▼	Does not describe me very well ▼	Does not describe me at all ▼
1. I try to keep track of how I am doing while I work.	1	2	3	4	5
2. I often use reminders to help me remember things I need to do.	1	2	3	4	5
3. I like to work toward specific goals I set for myself.	1	2	3	4	5
4. After I perform well on an activity, I feel good about myself.	1	2	3	4	5
5. I seek out activities in my work that I enjoy doing.	1	2	3	4	5
6. I often practice important tasks before I do them.	1	2	3	4	5
7. I usually am aware of how I am performing an activity.	1	2	3	4	5
8. I try to arrange my work area in a way that helps me focus positively on my work.	1	2	3	4	5
9. I establish personal goals for myself.	1	2	3	4	5
10. When I have successfully completed a task, I often reward myself with something I like.	1	2	3	4	5
11. When I have a choice, I try to do my work in ways that I enjoy rather than just trying to get it over with.	1	2	3	4	5
12. I like to go over an important activity before I actually perform it.	1	2	3	4	5
13. I keep track of my progress on projects I am working on.	1	2	3	4	5
14. I try to surround myself with objects and people that bring out my best behaviors.	1	2	3	4	5
15. I like to set task goals for my performance.	1	2	3	4	5
16. When I do an assignment especially well, I like to treat myself to something or an activity I enjoy.	1	2	3	4	5
17. I try to build activities into my work that I like doing.	1	2	3	4	5
18. I often rehearse my plan for dealing with a challenge before I actually face the challenge.	1	2	3	4	5

Source: C. C. Manz, *Mastering Self-Leadership: Empower Yourself for Personal Excellence* (Englewood Cliffs, NJ: Prentice Hall, 1992). Used with permission of the author. The scale presented here excludes the self-punishment dimension found in the SLQ1 instrument because it is not calculated in the SLQ1 total score. The designing natural rewards dimension presented here is measured by items in the third dimension of the SLQ2 instrument.

Scoring key for self-leadership questionnaire

To calculate your score on the Self-Leadership Questionnaire, assign the appropriate number to each question
from the scoring key below. Then add up the numbers
for that dimension. The self-leadership total score is calculated by adding up all scores on all dimensions.

Self-leadership dimension	Calculation	Your score
Personal goal setting	Item 3 + Item 9 + Item 15 =	_____
Mental practice*	Item 6 + Item 12 + Item 18 =	_____
Designing natural rewards	Item 5 + Item 11 + Item 17 =	_____
Self-monitoring**	Item 1 + Item 7 + Item 13 =	_____
Self-reinforcement	Item 4 + Item 10 + Item 16 =	_____
Cueing strategies***	Item 2 + Item 8 + Item 14 =	_____
Self-Leadership Total	Add up all dimension scores =	_____

*Mental practice is similar to constructive thought patterns, but does not represent self-talk and
mental imagery as clearly.

**Self-monitoring is called "Self-Observation" in the SLQ1.

***Cueing strategies represent activities that help us behave in certain ways. Although not
explicitly described in Chapter 4, it is similar to "antecedents" in the A-B-C model of
organizational behavior modification described in Chapter 2. The only difference is that
these antecedents are self-developed or self-controlled rather than introduced and controlled
by others. ◻

Stress Management

Learning Objectives

After reading this chapter, you should be able to:

- Define stress and describe the stress experience.
- Outline the stress process from stressors to consequences.
- Identify the different types of stressors in the workplace.
- Explain why a stressor might produce different stress levels in two people.
- Discuss the physiological, psychological, and behavioral effects of stress.
- Identify five ways to manage workplace stress.

Michael Dobler is under continuous pressure to plow through the electronic and other information he receives. This work-related stress contributes to his migraine headaches.

[Ricky Chung. Used with permission of the **South China Morning Post.***]*

Every day, Michael Dobler is bombarded with information. The Hong Kong-based technical manager for a Swiss-based multinational firm looks through dozens of faxes, e-mail messages, computer print-outs, and other sources of information. The large volume of information takes up to four hours to get through and gives Dobler migraine headaches. "It really is painful and I have to stop working and go home and take medicine," Dobler explains. "My work is definitely a factor that causes it."

Dobler is not alone. A recent study sponsored by Pitney Bowes, Inc., reports that 71 percent of Fortune 1000 employees feel overwhelmed by the incessant demands of electronic communication. Little wonder that "technostress"—stress caused by information technology—has become one of the leading health hazards in the workplace.

Bill Baker blames his high blood pressure on technostress. "How could you not be stressed when you're expected to wear a beeper on your hip 24 hours a day?" complains Baker. "I'm chained to my beeper—I can't get free of it." As management information director at TIMCO, a Greensboro, North Carolina, aircraft maintenance company, Baker says he has trouble keeping up with all the new information coming his way. "The information is endless. I feel very inadequate—I don't keep up with it very well."[1]

ork-related stress, whether due to information technology or other causes, is now considered an epidemic in the workplace. According to the American Institute of Stress, 78 percent of Americans describe their job as stressful. Over half of American adults say they experience high levels of stress at least once each week.[2] The Families and Work Institute reported that 42 percent of the 3,400 workers surveyed felt burned out or "used up" at the end of the workday. Perhaps the greatest worry comes from a detailed international medical study which concluded that people born after 1955 are up to three times as likely to experience stress-related disorders as were their grandparents.[3]

Work-related stress costs American businesses somewhere between $200 and $300 billion each year in lower productivity and higher absenteeism, turnover, alcoholism, and medical costs. It can also cost employers in arbitration awards, court decisions, and workers' compensation claims. Workers' compensation claims have become so widespread that most States have changed their laws to limit these claims.[4]

Chronic work-related stress is not just an American affliction. In the United Kingdom, 83 percent of human resource managers indicate that stress is a problem in their organizations. UNUM, a long-term disability insurer in the United Kingdom, reported that 20 percent of its claimants suffer from stress-related problems. At the Escorts Heart Institute in Delhi, India, routine cardiac screenings indicate that most executives are in fairly advanced stages of stress. "Corporate India is finally waking up to the fact that a lot of human potential is being drained away because of stress and burnout," says Shekhar Bajaj, CEO of Bajaj Electricals, a consumer electronics manufacturer.[5]

In this chapter, we look at the dynamics of work-related stress and how to manage it. The chapter begins by describing the stress experience. Next, the causes and consequences of stress are examined, along with the factors that cause some people to experience stress when others do not. The final section of this chapter looks at ways to manage work-related stress from either an organizational or individual perspective.

What Is Stress?

stress an adaptive response to a situation that is perceived as challenging or threatening to the person's well-being

Stress is an adaptive response to a situation that is perceived as challenging or threatening to the person's well-being.[6] As we shall see, stress is the person's reaction to a situation, not the situation itself. Moreover, we experience stress when we believe that something will interfere with our need fulfillment. Stress has both psychological and physiological dimensions. Psychologically, people perceive a situation and interpret it as challenging or threatening. This cognitive appraisal leads to a set of physiological responses, such as higher blood pressure, sweaty hands, and faster heartbeat.

We often hear about stress as a negative consequence of modern living. People are stressed from overwork, job insecurity, information overload, and the increasing pace of life. These events produce *distress*—the degree of physiological, psychological, and behavioral deviation from healthy functioning.[7] There is also a positive side of stress, called *eustress*, that refers to the healthy, positive, constructive outcome of stressful events and the stress response. Eustress is the stress experience in moderation, enough to activate and motivate people so that they can achieve goals, change their environments, and succeed in life's challenges. In other words, we need some stress to survive. However, most research focuses on distress, because it is a significant concern in organizational settings.[8] Employees frequently experience enough stress to hurt their job performance and increase their risk of mental and physical health problems. Consequently, our discussion will focus more on distress than on eustress.

WHISGLASS/COULTHART © 1993 Farcus Cartoons/dist. by Universal Press Syndicate

". . . now let's see how you react to scenes of your employees leaving early."

general adaptation syndrome a model of the stress experience, consisting of three stages: alarm reaction, resistance, and exhaustion

General Adaptation Syndrome

The stress experience was first documented 50 years ago by Dr. Hans Selye, a pioneer in stress research.[9] Selye determined that people have a fairly consistent physiological response to stressful situations. This response, called the **general adaptation syndrome,** provides an automatic defense system to help us cope with environmental demands. Exhibit 5.1 illustrates the three stages of the general adaptation syndrome: alarm, resistance, and exhaustion. The line in this exhibit shows the individual's energy and ability to cope with the stressful situation.

Alarm reaction   In the alarm reaction stage, the perception of a threatening or challenging situation causes the brain to send a biochemical message to various parts of the body, resulting in increased respiration rate, blood pressure, heartbeat, muscle tension, and other physiological responses. The individual's energy level and coping effectiveness immediately decreases in response to the initial shock. Extreme shock, however, may result in incapacity or death because the body is unable to generate enough energy quickly enough. In most situations, the alarm reaction alerts the person to the environmental condition and prepares the body for the resistance stage.

Resistance   The person's ability to cope with the environmental demand rises above the normal state during the resistance stage because the body has activated various biochemical, psychological, and behavioral mechanisms. For example, we have a higher than normal level of adrenaline during this stage, which gives us more energy to overcome or remove the source of stress. However, our resistance is directed to only one or two environmental demands, so that we become more vulnerable to other sources of stress. This explains why

Exhibit 5.1
Selye's general adaptation syndrome

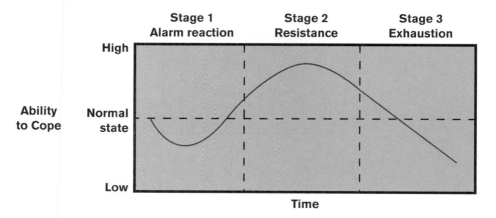

Source: Adapted from J. L. Gibson, J. M. Ivancevich, and J. H. Donnelly, *Organizations: Behavior, Structure, Processes,* 7th ed. (Burr Ridge, IL: Richard D. Irwin, 1994), p. 265.

people are more likely to catch a cold or other illness when they have been working under pressure.

Exhaustion   People have a limited resistance capacity and, if the source of stress persists, they will eventually move into the exhaustion stage as this capacity diminishes. In most work situations, the general adaptation syndrome process ends long before total exhaustion. Employees resolve tense situations before the destructive consequences of stress become manifest, or they withdraw from the stressful situation, rebuild their survival capabilities, and return later to the stressful environment with renewed energy. However, people who frequently experience the general adaptation syndrome have increased risk of long-term physiological and psychological damage.[10]

The general adaptation syndrome describes the stress experience, but this is only part of the picture. To effectively manage work-related stress, we must understand its causes and consequences as well as individual differences in the stress experience.

Stressors: The Causes of Stress

stressors any environmental conditions that place a physical or emotional demand on the person

Stressors, the causes of stress, include any environmental conditions that place a physical or emotional demand on the person.[11] There are numerous stressors in organizational settings and other life activities. Exhibit 5.2 lists the four main types of work-related stressors: physical environment, role-related, interpersonal, and organizational stressors.

Physical Environment Stressors

Some stressors are found in the physical work environment, such as excessive noise, poor lighting, and safety hazards. For example, a recent study of textile

Exhibit 5.2
Causes and consequences of stress

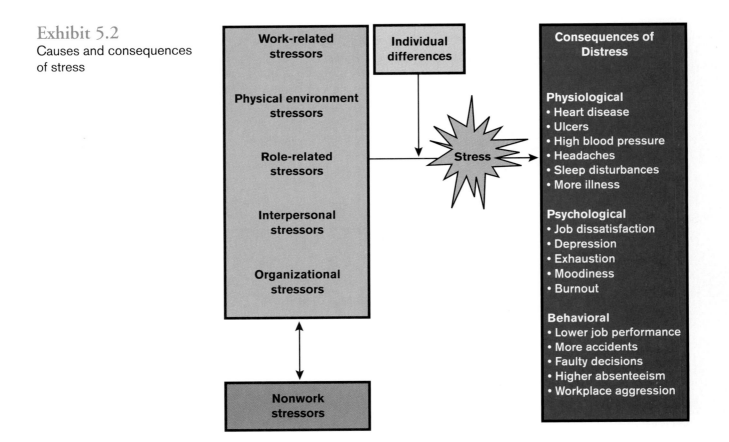

workers in a noisy plant found that their levels of stress measurably decreased when supplied with ear protectors.[12] Logging truck drivers wear mouthguards because they would otherwise grind their teeth down from stress while driving the fully loaded rigs along treacherous mountain roads. Physical stressors are also becoming apparent in office settings, including poorly designed office space, lack of privacy, ineffective lighting, and poor air quality.

Role-Related Stressors

Role-related stressors include conditions where employees have difficulty understanding, reconciling, or performing the various roles in their lives. The four main role-related stressors are role conflict, role ambiguity, workload, and task characteristics.

role conflict a situation whereby people experience competing demands, such as having job duties that are incompatible with their personal values, or receiving contradictory messages from different people

    Role conflict occurs when people face competing demands.[13] There are several types of role conflict in organizational settings. *Interrole conflict* occurs when an employee has two roles that are in conflict with each other. For example, most of us experience some interrole conflict because our work time or behavior conflicts with nonwork role expectations. *Intrarole conflict* occurs when the individual receives contradictory messages from different people. For example, this stressor would occur when your boss wants you as team leader to take greater control over the team's decisions, whereas employees on your team urge you to give them more freedom. *Person-role conflict* occurs when organizational values and work obligations are incompatible with personal values. Many employees experience person-role conflict when they must demonstrate emotions (e.g., compassion) toward a client even though they do not actually feel these emotions toward the person. Others face this stressor when their personal values are incompatible with the values that are widely held and supported by the organization.[14]

role ambiguity uncertainty about job duties, performance expectations, level of authority, and other job conditions

    Role ambiguity exists when employees are uncertain about their job duties, performance expectations, level of authority, and other job conditions. This tends to occur when people enter new situations, such as joining the organization or taking a foreign assignment, because they are uncertain about task and social expectations.[15] They cannot rely on past routines (e.g., how to greet people) so they concentrate on their actions and carefully monitor responses from others.

    Workloads represent another role-related stressor. Nearly half of American workers claim to have excessive workloads. This likely occurs because many companies have reduced their workforce and restructured work, leaving the remaining employees with more tasks and fewer resources or time to complete them.[16] Although less common, work underload can also cause stress. Work underload occurs when employees receive too little work or are given tasks that do not make sufficient use of their skills or knowledge. For example, people in very boring or repetitive jobs sometimes experience work underload.

    Task characteristics represent another type of role-related stressor. Tasks are most stressful when they involve decision making, monitoring equipment, or exchanging information with others. Lack of control over work activities, technostress, and work environment also fall into this category.[17] Bill Baker, described in the opening story, experiences stress from this lack of control because he can't get free from his beeper. As we learn in Connections 5.1, heavy traffic congestion is a major stressor for salespeople, real estate agents, bus drivers, and anyone else who must face this as part of their job (including commuting). And as traffic intensity increases in the future, so will stress levels.

Interpersonal Stressors

Our interaction with others produces interpersonal stressors, including poor supervision, office politics, and conflict with co-workers and clients.

Interpersonal stressors will likely become increasingly common as the workforce becomes more diverse and as organizations rely more on teams than individuals working alone to perform the work (see Chapter 1). *Diversity stress* occurs when employees lack the personal resources to both understand and respond effectively in this increasingly multicultural workforce.[18] For those who are unprepared, diversity creates feelings of ambiguity and conflict about how co-workers from different backgrounds will respond to their decisions and actions (see Chapter 13). The trend toward teamwork also seems to generate more interpersonal stressors because employees must interact more with

Connections 5.1 ▫ **Traffic Jams Stress the Urban Workforce**

Tim Blackwood considers himself a commuter casualty. The Detroit-area salesman gets headaches and sleeplessness from the traffic congestion he faces every day.

[Reprinted with permission from The Detroit News]

Tim Blackwood considers himself a commuter casualty. The Detroit area salesman is sick of traffic gridlock—and he is sick *because* of the gridlock. Blackwood suffers brain-splitting headaches, neck spasms, and back pain. He is restless and irritable at home and has trouble sleeping. "I'll get home and feel like I've been in a fistfight," says Blackwood regarding his bouts with traffic congestion.

Traffic tie-ups are getting urban dwellers stressed even before they get to work. Traffic congestion now ranks second to crime in many polls of what bothers Americans. And it's going to get worse. Highway traffic has been growing five times faster than new highway construction in recent years. Traffic congestion is projected to increase by 30 percent or more over the next 20 years. The five worst places for traffic-related stress are Los Angeles, Washington, D.C., San Francisco-Oakland, Miami, and Chicago. Detroit ranks seventh on the list.

Research indicates that those who commute at least 20 miles and 45 minutes have higher blood pressure and worse job performance up to two hours after the commute. Telecommuting—working at home—is a solution for some, but not for most workers. Salespeople, real estate agents, and bus drivers must face traffic problems throughout their workday. One study of British bus drivers found that stress increases as traffic congestion increases. A Danish study reported that traffic intensity was the strongest predictor of death or heart problems among bus drivers.

Sources: Adapted from R. French, "Worsening Gridlock Is Enough to Make Metro Commuters Sick," *Detroit News*, March 31, 1998, p. A1; Texas Transportation Institute, "10-Year Study Shows Most Cities Losing the Battle with Traffic Gridlock," news release, October 21, 1997 (at web site: http://tti.tamu.edu/mobility/); F. Greve, "Americans Get Together—in Traffic Jams," *Herald-Sun* (Durham, NC), August 13, 1997, p. A1; G. W. Evans and S. Carrere, "Traffic Congestion, Perceived Control, and Psychophysiological Stress among Urban Bus Drivers," *Journal of Applied Psychology* 76 (1991), pp. 658–63; B. Netterstrom and K. Juel, "Impact of Work-Related and Psychosocial Factors on the Development of Ischemic Heart Disease among Urban Bus Drivers in Denmark," *Scandinavian Journal of Work and Environmental Health* 14 (1988), pp. 231–38. ▫

co-workers. For instance, employees at Westrail, the government-owned rail transportation company in Western Australia, experienced higher stress when they were formed into work teams.[19]

Sexual harassment   Laura Flannery was getting stressed out at her sales job. She loved the work she performed at the small Long Island manufacturing plant. The cause of stress was an older male co-worker who would frequently drop by her office to boast about his sexual prowess and to proposition her. Flannery tape recorded some of his lewd remarks so that the company owner would stop the problem, but no action was taken. "I was miserable whenever I saw him," says Flannery, "but I needed the job."[20]

Laura Flannery has experienced the stress of **sexual harassment.** Sexual harassment refers to unwelcome conduct of a sexual nature that detrimentally affects the work environment or leads to adverse job-related consequences for its victims. One form of sexual harassment, called *quid pro quo*, includes situations in which a person's employment or job performance is conditional on unwanted sexual relations (e.g., a male supervisor threatens to fire a female

sexual harassment
unwelcome conduct of a sexual nature that detrimentally affects the work environment or leads to adverse job-related consequences for its victims

Kathleen Kline (above) and Anne Wedow knew that fighting fires was stressful. But the firefighters didn't anticipate the further stress of sexual harassment at the Kansas City Fire Department. Wedow testified that male firefighters would try to fondle her, even when she was an acting battalion chief. Kline received sexually graphic pictures anonymously through interoffice mail and had her locker defaced with obscene messages. Recruitment posters with her picture on it were altered when someone placed a picture of a nude woman's body beneath Kline's face. A U.S. district court eventually awarded damages to both women, but these stressors had already taken a heavy toll. "Fifteen years of incidents like this can wear a person out," says Kline. "It can work on your self-confidence, your patience, your mental state."[21]
[Rich Sugg. Used with permission from The Kansas City Star.*]*

employee if she does not accept his sexual advances). Laura Flannery experienced the second and more common form of sexual harassment, called *hostile work environment*. This includes sexual conduct that unreasonably interferes with an individual's work performance or creates an intimidating, hostile, or offensive working environment.[22]

Sexual harassment is more widespread than we once thought. According to various estimates, about one-quarter of U.S. and Canadian women have been sexually harassed at work. The Equal Employment Opportunity Commission receives 16,000 sexual harassment complaints annually. Unlike Laura Flannery's boss, most corporate leaders are taking steps to minimize harassment. However, they have been slow to recognize that harassment is more than a legal issue; it is a costly interpersonal stressor.[23] Victims of sexual harassment experience trauma (especially from rape or related exploitation) or must endure tense co-worker relations in a hostile work environment. Moreover, they are expected to endure tense relations while corporate officials investigate these incidents.

Workplace violence and aggression   Another serious interpersonal stressor is the rising wave of physical violence and aggression in the workplace.[24] The U.S. Bureau of Justice Statistics reports that more than 1,000 employees are murdered at work each year in the United States. It is the most common cause of work-related death for women and the second most common for men. However, homicides represent a very small percentage of dangerous behaviors in the workplace. Overall, more than 2 million people experience some form of violence at work each year.[25] These include assaults, rape, and threats using a weapon (e.g., robberies).

Employees who experience violence usually have symptoms of severe distress after the traumatic event.[26] It is not uncommon for these primary victims to take long-term disability. Some never return to work. But workplace violence is also a stressor for those who observe the violence. After a serious workplace incident, counselors work with many employees, not just the direct victims.

Employees who have not directly experienced or observed violence may also show signs of stress if they work in high-risk jobs.[27] For example, one study reported that the greatest cause of work-related stress among British bus drivers was their perceived risk of physical assault. Similarly, the threat of a bank robbery is a major stressor for employees at Comerica Inc., which has an average of two robberies each week at its 140 Detroit area branches. "We're certainly in a business and location where robberies can occur," acknowledges an executive at the financial services holding company. "The possibility of knowing a robbery can occur is a stressor."[28]

If we are fortunate enough to escape physical violence or aggression, most of us will still experience some form of verbal aggression from our boss, co-workers, or clients. For example, call center employees feel stressed from dealing with uncooperative customers; "260 calls a day from rude and angry people . . . it's hard to deal with at times," concludes one employee from a call center in Canada. Other threats come in the form of bullying from bosses and co-workers. The problem is serious enough for some Scandinavian countries to pass laws protecting workers against workplace bullying.[29]

Organizational Stressors

Organizational stressors come in many forms. As we shall learn in Chapter 15, most forms of organizational change are stressful. Downsizing (reducing the number of employees) is a stressor not only for those who lose their jobs, but for the survivors. Specifically, survivors experience higher workloads, increased job insecurity, and the loss of friends at work. Restructuring, privatization, mergers, and other forms of reorganization are stressful because employees face increased job insecurity, uncertain work demands, and new forms of interpersonal conflict.[30]

Nonwork Stressors

Work is usually the most stressful part of our lives, but we also experience numerous stressors outside organizational settings. Relationship problems, financial difficulties, and the loss of a loved one usually top the list of nonwork stressors. New responsibilities, such as marriage, birth of a child, and a mortgage, are also stressful to most of us. Why are these nonwork stressors discussed in a book about behavior in organizations? Because we do not park these stressors at the door when we enter the workplace. They carry over and ultimately affect our behavior at work.

But the connection between work and nonwork stressors is more complex than this. The stress model shown in Exhibit 5.2 has a two-way arrow between work and nonwork stressors. This indicates that work and nonwork activities spill over into the other domain and often conflict with each other. For instance, almost half of the North American workforce experiences some type of work-family stressor. Increasingly, employees without families also express their need to balance work with personal life. There are three main work-nonwork stressors: time-based, strain-based, and role behavior–based conflict.[31]

Time-based conflict
Dennis DeMari knows all about work-nonwork conflicts. The technical services manager at Factory Mutual Engineering & Research Corp. in Norwood, Massachusetts, is often called away from his home life to solve an emergency technical problem. He even had to leave his family during vacation at Walt Disney World to repair a client's computer network.[32] DeMari has to contend with *time-based conflict*—the challenge of balancing the time demanded by work with family and other nonwork activities.

Time-based conflict largely explains why stress increases with the number of hours of paid employment and the amount of business travel or commuting time. Inflexible work schedules and rotating shift schedules can also take a heavy toll because they prevent employees from effectively juggling work and nonwork.[33] Time-based conflict is more acute for women than for men. One estimate is that working mothers devote 79 hours each week to paid employment, child care, household chores, and personal chores, whereas working fathers spend 69 hours on these activities. The difference occurs because women have 31 hours of child care and household work each week whereas men have only 15 hours.[34] Until men increase their contribution to homemaking and business learns to accommodate the new social order, many of these "supermoms" will continue to experience superstress.

Strain-based conflict
Strain-based conflict occurs when stress from one domain spills over to the other. Death of a spouse, financial problems, and other nonwork stressors produce tension and fatigue that affect the employee's ability to fulfill work obligations. This problem works the other way as well. Stress at work spills over to an employee's personal life and often becomes the foundation of stressful relations with family and friends. Research indicates that fathers who experience stress at work engage in dysfunctional parenting behaviors. Similarly, men who are stressed at work cause their female partners to experience more stress, even when stress from the female partner's job is

taken into account. Another study suggests that female managers experience more work-family stress caused by strain-based conflict than by other work-family stressors.[35]

Role behavior conflict   A third work-nonwork stressor, called *role behavior conflict,* occurs when people are expected to enact different work and nonwork roles. People who act logically and impersonally at work have difficulty switching to a more compassionate role in their personal lives. For example, one study found that police officers were unable to shake off their professional role when they left the job. This was confirmed by their spouses, who reported that the officers would handle their children in the same manner as they would people in their job.[36]

Stress and Occupations

Several studies have attempted to identify which jobs have more stressors than others.[37] These lists are not in complete agreement, but Exhibit 5.3 identifies a representative sample of jobs and their relative level of stressors. You should view this information with some caution, however. One problem with rating the stress of occupations is that task characteristics and job environments differ considerably for the same job in different organizations and societies. A police officer's job may be less stressful in a small town, for instance, than in a large city where crime rates are higher and the organizational hierarchy is more formal.

Another important point to remember when looking at Exhibit 5.3 is that a major stressor to one person is insignificant to another. In this respect, we must be careful not to conclude that people in high-stress occupations actually experience higher stress than people in other occupations. They are exposed to more serious stressors, but careful selection and training can result in stress levels no different from those experienced by people in other jobs. The next section discusses individual differences in stress.

Individual Differences in Stress

In Exhibit 5.2 we saw that individual characteristics moderate the extent to which different people experience stress or exhibit a specific stress outcome in a given situation. Two people may be exposed to the same stressor, such as the

Exhibit 5.3
Stressors in occupations

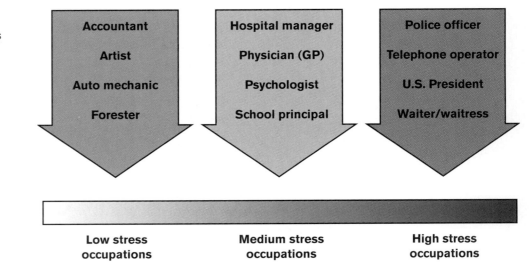

Accountant	Hospital manager	Police officer
Artist	Physician (GP)	Telephone operator
Auto mechanic	Psychologist	U.S. President
Forester	School principal	Waiter/waitress

| Low stress occupations | Medium stress occupations | High stress occupations |

threat of job loss, yet they experience different stress levels or different stress symptoms.[38]

People exposed to the same stressors might have different stress symptoms for three reasons. First, each of us perceives the same situation differently. People with high self-efficacy (see Chapter 2), for instance, are less likely to experience stress consequences in that situation because the stressor is less threatening.[39] Similarly, some people have personalities that make them more optimistic, whereas others are more pessimistic. Those with pessimistic dispositions tend to develop more stress symptoms, probably because they interpret the situation in a negative light.[40]

A second reason why some people have more stress symptoms than others in the same situation is that they have lower thresholds of resistance to a stressor. Younger employees generally experience fewer and less severe stress symptoms than older employees because they have a larger store of energy to cope with high stress levels. As we shall learn later, people who exercise regularly and have healthy lifestyles (e.g., diet, sleep) are also less likely to experience negative stress outcomes.

A third reason why people may experience the same level of stress and yet exhibit different stress outcomes is that they use different coping strategies.[41] Some employees tend to ignore the stressor, hoping that it will go away. This is usually an ineffective approach, which would explain why they experience higher stress levels. There is some evidence (although still inconclusive) that women cope with stress better than their male counterparts. Specifically, women are more likely to seek emotional support from others in stressful situations, whereas men try to change the stressor or use less effective coping mechanisms.[42] However, we must remember that this is not true for all women or men.

Type A/Type B Behavior Patterns

One of the most frequently cited individual differences is the Type A/Type B behavior pattern. In the 1950s, two cardiologists noticed that patients with premature coronary heart disease exhibited common behaviors that were collectively labeled a **Type A behavior pattern.** Type A people are hard-driving, competitive individuals with a strong sense of time urgency. They tend to be impatient, lose their temper, talk rapidly, and interrupt others during conversations (see Exhibit 5.4).[43]

In contrast, those with a **Type B behavior pattern** are less competitive and less concerned about time limitations. Type B people may be just as ambitious to achieve challenging tasks, but they generally approach life more casually and systematically than Type A people. They tend to work steadily, take a relaxed approach to life, and be even-tempered. The important distinction, however, is that Type B people are less likely than Type A people to experience distress and its physiological symptoms (such as heart disease) when exposed to a stressor. For example, a study reported that Type A nurses experienced significantly greater job stress and work overload than Type B nurses.[44]

Regarding job performance, Type A people tend to work faster than Type B people, choose more challenging tasks, have higher self-motivation, and are more effective in jobs involving time pressure. On the other hand, Type A people are less effective than Type B people in jobs requiring patience, cooperation, and thoughtful judgment.[45] Type A people tend to be irritable and aggressive, so they generally have poorer interpersonal skills. Studies report that middle managers tend to exhibit Type A behaviors, whereas top-level executives tend to have Type B behaviors.[46] One possible explanation is that Type B people receive more promotions because of their superior human relations skills.

Type A behavior pattern a behavior pattern associated with people having premature coronary heart disease; Type As tend to be impatient, lose their temper, talk rapidly, and interrupt others

Type B behavior pattern a behavior pattern of people with low risk of coronary heart disease; Type Bs tend to work steadily, take a relaxed approach to life, and be even-tempered

Exhibit 5.4
Characteristics of Type A
and Type B behavior
patterns

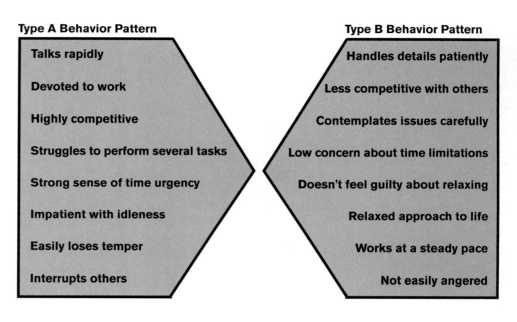

Exhibit 5.4
Characteristics of Type A and Type B behavior patterns

Type A Behavior Pattern	Type B Behavior Pattern
Talks rapidly	Handles details patiently
Devoted to work	Less competitive with others
Highly competitive	Contemplates issues carefully
Struggles to perform several tasks	Low concern about time limitations
Strong sense of time urgency	Doesn't feel guilty about relaxing
Impatient with idleness	Relaxed approach to life
Easily loses temper	Works at a steady pace
Interrupts others	Not easily angered

Consequences of Distress

For more than 25 years, Rick Venturi had been able to handle the stress of coaching professional football. But while recently serving as defensive coordinator for the Cleveland Browns, Venturi pushed himself too far. "I got to where I was working 20 hours a day, and sleeping 3, 4 hours a night," Venturi recalls. "I was staying awake on coffee and cigarettes. And finally I got to a point where there wasn't anything left. I was running on empty." Venturi became inflexible with his players and had lost his edge as a teacher. So, under advice from friends and team doctors, he temporarily relinquished his duties and took a mini-vacation. Venturi didn't require hospitalization, just time out. "I never collapsed or anything like that. I was just frizzed out. I was fried out."[47]

As we learned from the general adaptation syndrome at the beginning of this chapter, chronic stress diminishes the individual's resistance, resulting in adverse consequences for both the employee and the organization. Rick Venturi suffered from exhaustion and lower job performance, but fortunately he withdrew from the stressors before matters got worse. Some of the more common outcomes or symptoms of work-related stress were listed earlier in Exhibit 5.2 and are discussed here.

Physiological Consequences

Stress takes its toll on the human body.[48] As we noted earlier, people are more susceptible to disease when under pressure from stress. For example, studies have found that medical students who are anxious about their exams are more susceptible to colds and other illnesses.[49] Michael Dobler (described in the opening story to this chapter) experienced tension headaches due to stress. Others get muscle pain and related back problems. Both physiological ailments are attributed to muscle contractions that occur when people are exposed to stressors.

Cardiovascular diseases represent one of the most disturbing effects of stress in modern society. Bill Baker (also described in the opening story) is among the one-third of Americans who have hypertension (high blood pressure), much of which is the result of anxiety and worry. Coronary heart disease (including strokes and heart attacks) was virtually unknown a century ago but is now the leading cause of death among American adults. Medical researchers believe that the long-term effect of stress on heart disease goes

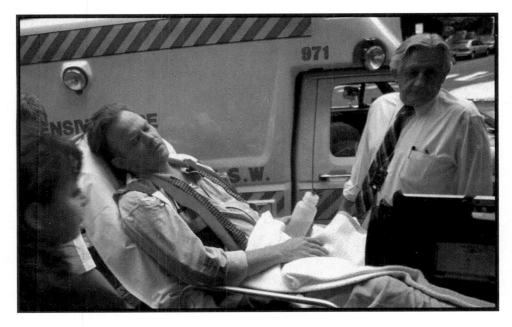

something like this: Whenever people are stressed, their blood pressure goes up and down. That frequent pressure causes injury to the blood vessel walls, which eventually makes them constrict and function abnormally. Over time, this leads to heart disease. Unfortunately, we often don't realize when we are biologically stressed. Researchers have found that people think they are normal when, in fact, their palms are sweating and blood pressure has risen.[50]

Psychological Consequences

Probably the most common psychological symptom of work-related stress is lower **job satisfaction,** which represents a person's evaluation of his or her job and work context.[51] Employees with a high level of stress also tend to be moody and depressed.[52] Emotional fatigue is another psychological consequence of stress and is related to job burnout.

job satisfaction a person's evaluation of his or her job and work context

Job burnout   Amy (not her real name) needs to take "mental health days" from her teaching job at Westside Middle School in Los Angeles. She also sees a therapist and is planning a career change. When Amy started in this profession, she didn't experience the student problems that she now faces. Fearing verbal abuse and physical attack, Amy says that she is no longer confident about how to deal with her students. "I'm burned out," she admits.[53]

The expression "job burnout" didn't exist 40 years ago. Now, it is commonly heard in everyday conversations, possibly because many people experience some level of job burnout. For example, a recent study reported that public-sector employees in several countries typically suffer from advanced stages of burnout.[54]

job burnout the process of emotional exhaustion, depersonalization, and reduced personal accomplishment resulting from prolonged exposure to stress

Job burnout refers to the process of emotional exhaustion, depersonalization, and reduced personal accomplishment resulting from prolonged exposure to stress.[55] It is a complex process that includes the dynamics of stress, coping strategies, and stress consequences. Burnout is caused by excessive demands made on people who serve or frequently interact with others. In other words, burnout is mainly due to interpersonal and role-related stressors.[56] For this reason, it is most common in helping occupations (e.g., nurses, teachers, police officers).

Exhibit 5.5
The job burnout process

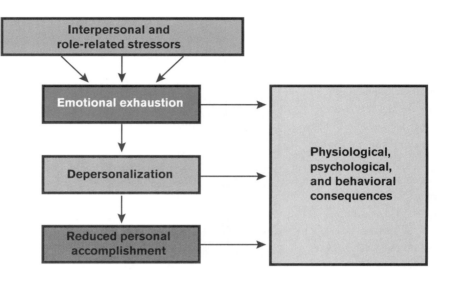

Exhibit 5.5 diagrams the relationship among the three components of job burnout. *Emotional exhaustion* represents the first stage and plays a central role in the burnout process.[57] It is characterized by a lack of energy and a feeling that one's emotional resources are depleted. Emotional exhaustion is sometimes called compassion fatigue because the employee no longer feels able to give as much support and caring to clients.

Depersonalization follows emotional exhaustion and is identified by the treatment of others as objects rather than people. Burned-out employees become emotionally detached from clients and cynical about the organization. This detachment reaches the point of callousness, far beyond the level of detachment normally required in helping occupations. For example, a burned-out nurse might coldly label a kidney transplant patient as "the kidney in room 307." Depersonalization is also apparent when employees strictly follow rules and regulations rather than try to understand the client's needs and search for a mutually acceptable solution.

Reduced personal accomplishment, the final component of job burnout, refers to the decline in one's feelings of competence and success, and is observed by feelings of diminished competency. In other words, the person's self-efficacy declines (see Chapter 2). In these situations, employees develop a sense of learned helplessness as they no longer believe that their efforts make a difference. Amy, the Los Angeles teacher described above, experiences this because she is no longer confident about how to deal with her students.

Behavioral Consequences

When stress becomes distress, job performance falls and workplace accidents are more common. High stress levels impair our ability to remember information, make effective decisions, and take appropriate action.[58] You have probably experienced this in an exam or emergency work situation. You forget important information, make mistakes, and otherwise "draw a blank" under intense pressure.

Overstressed employees also tend to have higher levels of absenteeism. One reason, as we saw with Michael Dobler at the beginning of this chapter, is that stress makes people sick. The other reason is that absenteeism is a coping mechanism. At a basic level, we react to stress through fight or flight. Absenteeism is a form of flight—temporarily withdrawing from the stressful situation so that we have an opportunity to reenergize. Companies may try to minimize absenteeism, but it sometimes helps employees avoid the exhaustion stage of the stress experience (see Exhibit 5.1).[59]

Workplace aggression   Workplace aggression is more than the serious interpersonal stressor that we described earlier. It is also an increasingly worrisome consequence of stress.[60] Aggression represents the "fight" (instead of flight) reaction to stress. In its mildest form, employees engage in verbal conflict. They "fly off the handle" and are less likely to empathize with co-workers. Occasionally, the combination of an individual's background and workplace stressors escalates this conflict into more dangerous levels of workplace hostility.

Co-worker aggression represents a relatively small proportion of workplace violence, but these violent acts are not inconsequential. Consider the following incidents that occurred recently within one month of each other: An Equal Opportunity officer at the Colorado Department of Transportation was gunned down in her office by an employee who was there for a disciplinary meeting. Distraught about being fired, an employee at Chemical Lime Co.'s plant near Las Vegas went on a rampage, using a bulldozer to crush his supervisor, destroy buildings, and smash vehicles before police shot and killed him. At Electric Boat, a Connecticut shipbuilder, an employee and a union steward argued over shift schedule assignments. The employee was punched and knocked to the ground, and died from head injuries a few days later.[61]

Like most forms of organizational behavior, co-worker aggression is caused by both the person and the situation.[62] While certain individuals are more likely to be aggressive, we must also remember that workplace stressors trigger many of these aggressive acts. Moreover, stress can lead to aggression in employees who have no previous behavior problems. In other words, employee aggression is a consequence of extreme stress, not just the temperament of certain individuals.[63] In particular, employees are more likely to engage in aggressive behavior if they believe they have been treated unfairly, experience other forms of frustration beyond their personal control, and work in physical environments that are stressful (e.g., hot, noisy).

Managing Work-Related Stress

Alvin Schulzberg didn't realize that his job was making him stressed out until a particularly troublesome project spiraled out of control. As pressure mounted, the New York book manufacturing consultant felt his stomach churn and his insides knot. Then, one morning, Schulzberg had a heart attack. After moving to North Carolina, Schulzberg participated in a Duke University study where he learned to take life more casually and not assume everyone else's problems. "I learned to relax, totally relax," says Schulzberg. Recently, when another project with the same client was getting out of control, Schulzberg took the problem in stride. "I've told myself, if necessary, I'll just dump it, and throw it back on the people causing the problem."[64]

Everyone needs to manage stress. Unfortunately, many of us deny the stress until it is too late. This avoidance strategy creates a vicious cycle because the failure to cope with stress becomes another stressor on top of the one that created the stress in the first place. The solution is to discover the toolkit of effective stress management strategies presented in this section, and to determine which ones are best for the situation.[65] As described in the *Fast Company Online* feature for this chapter, employees at Pixar Animation Studios have their own stress management strategies that suit their personalities and lifestyles.

Several different stress management strategies are described over the next few pages (see Exhibit 5.6). Each of these can be introduced as corporate initiatives, but they also represent ways that each of us can personally learn to cope with stress at work. As we look at each approach, keep in mind that effective stress management often includes more than one of these strategies.

Remove the Stressor

Exhibit 5.6 identifies several stress management strategies, but some writers argue that the *only* way companies can effectively manage stress is by removing the stressors that cause unnecessary tension and job burnout. Other stress management strategies may keep employees "stress-fit," but they don't solve the fundamental causes of stress.[66]

There are many ways to remove stressors in the workplace. One of the best solutions is to empower employees so that they have more control over their work and work environment (see Chapter 4).[67] Task-related stressors can be minimized through more effective selection and placement of employees so that their competencies are compatible with job requirements. Noise and

F\ST C\MPANY
Online

▫ Recharging Batteries at Pixar Animation Studios

Andrew Stanton, co-director of *A Bug's Life*, has learned how to shake off stress with a good laugh.
[Courtesy of Pixar Animation Studio]

The word "PANIC" is taped to Katherine Sarafian's office door. The creative-resources manager at Pixar Animation Studios is racing to prepare a pressure-packed presentation while still working part-time in her previous position as manager of Pixar's art

Exhibit 5.6
Stress management
strategies

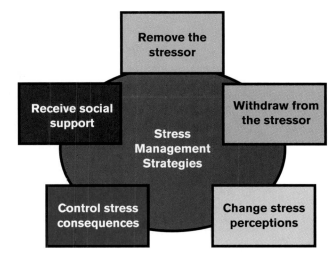

department. "I'm the one who can't get down the hall fast enough, so I sprint," says Sarafian. "Burnout? I'm high risk."

But Sarafian is convinced that easing up won't help. "I don't have time for a lot of slowdown-type things," she says. Today, Sarafian attends the weekly improvisational-acting class at Pixar University. She also plays in a highly competitive basketball league and takes an amateur drawing class. "When I first signed up for improv, a friend told me that I was insane—that I should try yoga instead. But yoga doesn't calm me down; it calms down the person next to me. When I play hoops or go to improv class, I usually get results."

Andrew Stanton also knows about impossible deadlines. The co-director of *A Bug's Life* has just four months to get this film ready for public release. Stanton's every working minute is booked. His wife and two kids are near-strangers to him. But is Stanton running on empty? Hardly. In fact, he looks almost carefree.

Stanton's prescription for preventing burnout is simple: Laugh hard, twice daily. "Something is horribly wrong," he says, "if I don't crack up at least a couple of times a day." Most of the time, "fun" at Pixar isn't forced. It's allowed to flow freely, such as impromptu Nerf battles, scooter races in the corridors, and toy action-figure jousts. With tight deadlines, Stanton doesn't have much time to goof off right now. But that doesn't stop him from creating some levity. "Say we've got five minutes left in a production meeting and 10 more people to talk to," he explains. "Right around then, the 12-year-old in me takes over. Afterward, nobody seems to mind working hard all over again. Myself included."

ONLINE CHECK-UP

1. Among the five stress management strategies described in this chapter, where would you classify the activities used by Katherine Sarafian and Andrew Stanton?

2. The full text of this *Fast Company* article describes how three other employees at Pixar Animation Studios manage stress. Which types of stress management strategies are they using?

3. Go to your favorite web search engine and look for sites that specialize in stress management. Which types of stress management seem to be most common among the sites that appear in the results list?

Get the full text of this
Fast Company article at
www.mhhe.com/mcshane1e   Source: Adapted from T. Balf, "Out of Juice? Recharge!" *Fast Company* 16 (August 1998). ■

safety risks are stressful, so improving these conditions would also go a long way to minimize stress in the workplace. Companies can diffuse aggression by establishing procedures that minimize dysfunctional conflict and ensure that workplace decisions are perceived as fair.

Of course, employees can also take an active role in removing stressors. If we experience stress due to ambiguous role expectations, for example, we might seek out more information from others to clarify these expectations. If a particular piece of work is too challenging, we might break it into smaller sets of tasks so that the overall project is less threatening or wearing. We can also minimize workplace violence by learning to identify early warning signs of aggression in customers and co-workers and by developing interpersonal skills that dissipate aggression.

Family-friendly and work/life initiatives

Chris Kunkel, an electric utility technician in Beaumont, Texas, racked up 400 hours of overtime last year. While the extra money was nice, Kunkel believes companies are squeezing too much time out of their employees. "We just can't keep up," complains Kunkel. "You've got to have a life."[68]

Fortunately, many companies have introduced work/life initiatives to help employees do just that: help employees to balance their work and nonwork roles. Most of these programs began as "family-friendly" benefits that provided a more flexible workplace for employees (particularly women) with children. However, organizations now realize that time-based conflicts between work and nonwork extend beyond employees with families.

Baxter Healthcare recently discovered this when a survey revealed that 42 percent of its employees were thinking of quitting because work conflicted with their personal lives. This was startling news because the health products manufacturer has one of the better family-friendly workplaces in America. The problem was that the greatest complaints came from singles and dual earners without kids, not from working mothers. So, Baxter changed its work-family program into a "work/life" program and has begun to evaluate managers on how well they help *all* employees maintain this balance. The goal is to ensure that all employees, not just those with children, lead more balanced lives.[69]

Family-friendly and work/life initiatives remove or reduce the stressors that cause time-based conflict. Two recent studies reported that employees who participate in work/life programs were significantly more satisfied with their jobs and experienced lower levels of stress in balancing work, family, and personal lives.[70] Five of the most common family-friendly and work/life initiatives are flextime, job sharing, telecommuting, personal leave, and child care facilities.

- *Flexible work time*—Many firms let employees decide when to begin and end their workday so that they can more easily balance personal and work activities. For example, employees at Eli Lilly and Company, the pharmaceutical company, can start work as early as 6 A.M. and finish at 3 P.M., or they can start as late as 9 A.M. and work until 6 P.M.[71]

- *Job sharing*—Job sharing splits a career position between two people so they experience less time-based stress between work and family. The two typically work different parts of the week with some overlapping work time in the weekly schedule to coordinate activities. This works well for some people, but the major challenge is finding a partner with a compatible work style and pace.[72]

- *Telecommuting*—As we learned in Chapter 1, tens of millions of people have altered their employment relations through **telecommuting**— working from home, usually with a computer connection to the office.

telecommuting (also called *teleworking*) performing work at home or another location away from the office, usually with a computer or other telecommunications connection to the office

Pamela Johnson and Christine Bridgham share the job of bankruptcy officer at the NationsBank dealer finance headquarters in Greensboro, North Carolina. They each work two-and-a-half days a week, meeting at lunch on Wednesdays to keep one another updated. Job sharing splits a career position between two people so they experience less time-based stress between work and family. "When we come to work, we're focused and energized," says Pamela Johnson. "We don't burn out because we have enough time to be with our children."[73] What are the limitations of job sharing? Are there any jobs that might make job sharing difficult?

[© 1997 Jim Stratford]

Although most telecommuting arrangements require employees to spend some days at the office, they significantly reduce the time and stress of commuting to work, thereby allowing more time for personal activities. Telecommuting often makes it easier to switch between work and non-work activities during the day, such as temporarily leaving the home-office to pick up the kids from school. Overall, there is growing evidence that employees are more productive with this arrangement and experience a healthier balance between work and nonwork roles.[74]

- *Personal leave programs*—Governments in the United States, Canada, Australia, and several other countries require employers to provide paid or unpaid maternity leave. For example, the U.S. Family and Medical Leave Act gives expectant mothers (and anyone considered to have an "illness") 12 weeks of unpaid, job-protected leave.[75] Work/life employers typically offer extended or partially paid maternity, paternity, and personal leaves to care for a new family or take advantage of a personal experience. Increasingly, employees are using personal leave to care for elderly parents and other relatives who need assistance.

- *Child care facilities*—On-site child care centers have existed since World War II, when women worked in war factories. Today, child care facilities can be found at Hewlett-Packard, IBM, Nynex, Pricewaterhouse Coopers, and many other companies.[76] On-site (or nearby) child care facilities save parents time and worry and might allow them to spend a little time with children during the day.

Withdrawing from the Stressor

Removing the stressor may be the ideal solution, but it is often not feasible. One alternative strategy is to permanently or temporarily remove employees from the stressor. A permanent solution is to transfer employees to jobs for which they are better suited. A more drastic action is to have the employee leave the organization if a suitable position is not available.

Temporary withdrawal strategies The 72 employees at Billabong USA work long hours with challenging deadlines. Fortunately, the Costa Mesa,

Cigna Corp. encourages employees to take 15-minute "Fast Breaks" during the day to combat work-related stress. Employees at the Philadelphia-based insurance company choose from seven programs, such as "Move to Music," "Tackle Tension," and "Sanity Stretch" (shown in photo). These activities provide a temporary withdrawal from work-related stressors.[77] To what other stress management strategy does this activity apply? [Don Tracy. Courtesy of Cigna Corp.]

California, maker of surfwear also encourages staff to take "surf breaks" in the middle of the day to temporarily get away from the stress. "People rarely call in sick here," says Paul Gomez, Billabong's director of marketing and promotions. "People are not afraid of putting in long hours, but if the work gets done with time to spare, then you have extra time at lunch to go surfing."[78]

Whether a coffee break or a surf break, withdrawing temporarily from stressors is the most frequent way that employees manage stress. Vacations represent another form of temporary withdrawal from workplace stressors. Netscape, Silicon Graphics, and a few other firms offer paid sabbaticals to help long-term employees restore their capacity to cope with stressful work experiences. Although some firms (including Apple Computer and Compaq) have withdrawn these two- or three-month paid absences, others swear by them. "If you've been in any organization six to seven years, you face burnout," says Ric Edelman, chairman of Edelman Financial Services in Fairfax, Virginia. "You need to relax, smell the roses." Month-long sabbaticals are mandatory in Edelman's company.[79]

Employees typically experience stress when living and working in another culture. Lacking common assumptions and expectations, expatriates must pay constant attention to how others react to their behaviors. For example, expatriates say that Vietnam is the most stressful Asian nation in which to live and work because it is difficult for expatriates and Vietnamese to communicate and understand each other's goals. To manage this stress, some expatriates retreat into a stabilization zone—any place similar to the home country where they can rely on past routines to guide behavior.[80] These may include attending an "American night" at a club in the foreign country or having dinner with friends from the home country.

Changing Stress Perceptions

Employees often experience different levels of stress in the same situation because they perceive it differently. Consequently, stress can be minimized by changing perceptions of the situation. This does not mean that we should ignore risks or other stressors. Rather, we can strengthen our self-efficacy and self-esteem so that job challenges are not perceived as threatening.

Several elements of self-leadership described in Chapter 4 can alter employee perceptions of job-related stressors. For example, mental imagery can reduce the uncertainty of future work activities. A study of newly hired accountants reported that personal goal setting and self-reinforcement can also reduce the stress that people experience when they enter new work settings.[81] Positive self-talk can potentially change stress perceptions by increasing our self-efficacy and developing a more optimistic outlook, at least in that situation. As we noted earlier, a person's optimism can minimize the effects of stressors.

Controlling the Consequences of Stress

Another way that we can cope with workplace stress is to control its consequences. One of the most obvious ways to do this is by keeping fit. The majority of U.S. companies encourage employees to practice this stress management activity by providing either on-site fitness centers or financial support for off-site fitness programs. For instance, the City of Victoria, Texas, has started an annual fitness testing program for its 590 employees and reimburses them up to 50 percent for health club membership costs.[82] Physical exercise helps employees lower their respiration, muscle tension, heartbeat, and stomach acidity, thereby reducing the physiological consequences of stress.

Lifestyle programs extend the objectives of fitness programs by helping employees learn how to live a healthier lifestyle. This includes learning how a balanced diet and good sleep habits combat the adverse effects of stress. There is increasing evidence that fitness and lifestyle programs help employees control the dysfunctional consequences of stress.[83]

Another way to control the physiological consequences of stress is through relaxation and meditation. Generally, these activities try to decrease the person's own heart rate, blood pressure, muscle tension, and breathing rate. For example, Acacia Life Insurance Co. offers a meditation room where employees at the Bethesda, Maryland, firm can remove themselves from any distractions.[84] As we see in Connections 5.2, companies around the world are adopting these practices to minimize workplace stress. Research suggests that relaxation and meditation programs are effective, particularly in reducing blood pressure levels and muscle tension.[85]

employee assistance programs (EAPs)

counseling services that help employees cope with personal or organizational stressors and adopt more effective coping mechanisms

Sometimes, employees cannot control the effects of stress on their own. They often need help overcoming dysfunctional stress coping tactics, such as alcoholism and drug abuse. Many companies have responded to this need by offering **employee assistance programs (EAPs).** EAPs are counseling services that help employees overcome personal or organizational stressors and adopt more effective coping mechanisms. Most EAPs began several decades ago as programs to overcome alcoholism. Today, most are "broad-brush" programs that counsel employees on work or personal problems. Family problems often represent the largest percentage of EAP referrals, although this varies with industry and location.[86]

Receiving Social Support

Social support from co-workers, supervisors, family, friends, and others is one of the more effective stress management practices.[87] Social support refers to the person's interpersonal transactions with others and involves providing either emotional or informational support to buffer the stress experience.

Social support reduces stress in at least three ways.[88] First, employees improve their perception that they are valued and worthy. This in turn increases their self-esteem and perceived ability to cope with the stressor; for example, "I can handle this crisis because my colleagues have confidence in me." Second, social support provides information to help employees interpret, comprehend, and possibly remove the stressor. For instance, social support might reduce a new employee's stress because co-workers describe ways to handle difficult customers. Finally, emotional support from others can directly help to buffer the stress experience. This last point reflects the idea that "misery loves company." People seek out and benefit from the emotional support of others when they face threatening situations.[89]

Social support is an important way to cope with stress that everyone can practice by maintaining friendships. This includes helping others when they need a little support from the stressors of life. Organizations can facilitate social support by providing opportunities for social interaction among employees as well as their families. People in leadership roles also need to practice a supportive leadership style when employees work under stressful conditions and need this social support.

Connections 5.2   ◻ **Meditation and Relaxation Become Global Stress-Busting Mantras**

Around the world, people are turning to meditation and relaxation techniques to offset the stressors of work. Steve Jones, who works for the City of London, England, uses meditation to avoid getting stressed out at work. "I work in a very high-pressure environment," Jones explains. "If I know I'm going to have a really heavy day, then I meditate before I go into work. It keeps me calm and clear-headed."

Many Japanese companies have corporate meditation programs. McDonald's Restaurants and Levi Strauss in the United States also have meditation rooms where employees chant mantras to release pent-up tension. Phatra Thanakit, one of Thailand's top finance and securities companies, sent stressed-out staffers to a one-week retreat in a Buddhist monastery. The monastic setting cuts employees off from contact with the outside world while they take courses in meditation, contemplation, breathing, and basic Buddhism.

Seventy members of the India Club, an exclusive club of senior executives in India, recently participated in a one-day workshop on rhythmic breathing, conducted by the Vedanta Academy. K. K. Khandelwal, chairman and managing director of Hermann Electronics Ltd, was a skeptic before attending the session. Now, he is a regular at the Vedanta Academy. "After a couple of sessions (of Vedanta discourses) I felt galvanized. There are no signs of stress or fatigue now, and my efficiency at work has increased."

Sources: Adapted from H. Jones, "Walk This Way to a Better Business," *The Independent* (London), March 18, 1998, p. C2; N. Chowdhury and S. Menon, "Beating Burnout," *India Today*, June 9, 1997, p. 86; P. Janssen "Refresher Course at Temple," *Asian Business*, August 1995, p. 25. ◼

Chapter Summary

Stress is an adaptive response to a situation that is perceived as challenging or threatening to the person's well-being. Distress represents high stress levels that have negative consequences, whereas eustress represents the moderately low stress levels needed to activate people. The stress experience, called the *general adaptation syndrome*, involves moving through three stages: alarm, resistance, and exhaustion.

The stress model shows that stress is caused by stressors. However, the effect of these stressors depends on individual characteristics. Stress affects a person's physiological and psychological well-being, and is associated with several work-related behaviors.

Stressors are the causes of stress and include any environmental conditions that place a physical or emotional demand on a person. Stressors are found in the physical work environment, an employee's various life roles, interpersonal relations, and organizational activities and conditions. Conflicts between work and family obligations represent a frequent source of employee stress.

Two people exposed to the same stressor may experience different stress levels because they perceive the situation differently, have different threshold stress levels, or use different coping strategies. Employees with Type A behavior patterns tend to experience more stress than those exhibiting Type B behaviors.

High levels of prolonged stress can cause physiological symptoms, such as high blood pressure, ulcers, sexual dysfunction, headaches, and coronary heart disease. Behavioral symptoms of stress include lower job performance, poorer decisions, more workplace accidents, higher absenteeism, and more workplace aggression. Psychologically, stress reduces job satisfaction and increases moodiness, depression, and job burnout. Job burnout refers to the process of emotional exhaustion, depersonalization, and reduced personal accomplishment resulting from prolonged exposure to stress. It is mainly due to interpersonal and role-related stressors and is most common in caregiving occupations.

Many interventions are available to manage work-related stress. Some directly remove unnecessary stressors or remove employees from the stressful environment. Others help employees alter their interpretation of the environment so that it is not viewed as a serious stressor. Fitness and lifestyle programs encourage employees to build better physical defenses against stress experiences. Social support provides emotional, informational, and material resource support to buffer the stress experience.

Key Terms

Employee assistance programs (EAPs), p. 153
General adaptation syndrome, p. 135
Job burnout, p. 145
Job satisfaction, p. 145
Role ambiguity, p. 137
Role conflict, p. 137

Sexual harassment, p. 139
Stress, p. 134
Stressors, p. 136
Telecommuting, p. 150
Type A behavior pattern, p. 143
Type B behavior pattern, p. 143

Discussion Questions

1. Several web sites describe problems that people experience at work. Scan through at least one of these web sites and determine what type of work-related stressor is most commonly described.

2. Sally works as an attorney for a leading Washington, D.C., law firm. She was married a few years ago and is currently pregnant with her first child. Sally expects to return to work full time a few months after the baby is born. Describe two types of work-nonwork conflict that Sally will likely experience during the first year after her return to work.

3. Police officer and waiter are often cited as high-stress jobs, whereas accountant and forester are low-stress jobs. Why should we be careful about describing these jobs as high or low stress?

4. Two recent graduates join the same major newspaper as journalists. Both work long hours and have tight deadlines to complete their stories. They are under constant pressure to scout out new leads and be the first to report new controversies. One journalist is increasingly fatigued and despondent, and has taken several days of sick leave. The other is getting the

work done and seems to enjoy the challenges. Use your knowledge of stress to explain why these two journalists are reacting differently to their jobs.

5. Do people with Type A personalities make better managers? Why or why not?

6. A friend says that he is burned out by his job. What questions might you ask this friend to determine whether he is really experiencing job burnout?

7. How might fitness programs help employees working in stressful situations?

8. A senior official of a labor union stated, "All stress management does is help people cope with poor management. [Employers] should really be into stress reduction." Discuss the accuracy of this statement.

CASE STUDY

Jim Black: Sales representative

Jim Black impatiently drummed the steering wheel and puffed a cigarette as his car moved slowly northbound along the Washington Parkway. Traffic congestion was normal in the late afternoon, but it seemed much heavier today. In any event, it was another irritation that was going to make him late for his next appointment.

As a sales representative at Noram Corp., Jim could not afford to keep clients waiting. Sales of compressed oxygen and other gases were flat because of increased competition. Other compressed gas suppliers were eager to grab new accounts and it was becoming more common for clients to switch from one supplier to another. Jim pressed his half-finished cigarette against the ash tray and accelerated the car into another lane.

Buyers of compressed gases knew that the market was in their favor and many were demanding price discounts and shorter delivery times. Earlier in the week, for example, one of Jim's more demanding customers telephoned for another shipment of liquid oxygen to be delivered the next morning. To meet the deadline, Jim had to complete an expedited delivery form and then personally convince the shipping group to make the delivery in the morning rather than later in the day. Jim disliked making expedited delivery requests, even though this was becoming increasingly common among the reps, because it often delayed shipment of Noram's product to other clients. Discounts were even more troublesome because they reduced his commission and, except for very large orders, were frowned upon by Noram management.

Meanwhile, at Noram headquarters where Jim worked, senior managers were putting more pressure on sales reps to produce. They complained that the reps weren't aggressive enough and area supervisors were told to monitor each sales rep's monthly numbers more closely. Jim fumbled for another cigarette as the traffic stopped momentarily.

Two months ago, the area sales supervisor had "a little chat" (as he called it) with Jim about the stagnant sales in his district and loss of a client to the competition. It wasn't exactly a threat of being fired—other reps also received these chats—but Jim felt nervous about his work and began having sleepless nights. He began making more calls to potential clients, but was only able to find this time by completing administrative paperwork in the evenings. The evening work wasn't helping relations with his family.

To make matters worse, Noram's parent company in Germany announced that it planned to sell the U.S. operations. Jim had heard rumors that a competitor was going to purchase the firm, mainly to expand its operations through Noram's western U.S. sales force and production facilities. The competitor was well established in the eastern United States where Jim worked, and probably wouldn't need a larger sales force there. Jim's job would be in jeopardy if the acquisition took place. Jim felt another headache coming on as he stared at the endless line of red taillights glimmering along the highway ahead.

Even if Jim kept his job, any promotion into management would be a long way off if the competitor acquired Noram. Jim had no particular desire to become a manager, but his wife liked the idea because it would involve less travel and provide a salary that was less dependent on monthly sales. Business travel was a nuisance, particularly for out-of-town appointments, but Jim felt less comfortable with the idea of sitting behind a desk all day.

The loud honk of another car startled Jim as he swerved into the exit lane that he was supposed to take (but almost missed). A few minutes later, he arrived at the client's parking lot. Jim rummaged through his briefcase for some aspirin to relieve the headache. He heaved a deep sigh as he glanced at his watch. Jim was 15 minutes late for the appointment.

Discussion Questions

1. What stress symptoms is Jim experiencing?

2. What stressors can you identify in this case?

3. What should Jim do to minimize his stress?

© Copyright 2000. Steven L. McShane. ■

CASE STUDY

Work and family

BusinessWeek

Many Americans, caught between the crush of demanding employers and their dual-income, sandwich-generation families, feel abused and angry. An employee at KPMG Peat Marwick observed, "My company has programs that should make balancing family life and work better. But the reality is, we are a service organization, and when a client says jump, our firm does not care about flexible schedules." Comments like this suggest that work-family programs aren't working very well. They are often applied halfheartedly with cursory executive support and at odds with corporate culture.

This *Business Week* case study describes the issues and concerns that companies and employees face when trying to accommodate the stress of balancing work with nonwork. Some organizations seem to be getting it right, but most aren't. Read through this *Business Week* case study at www.mhhe.com/mcshane1e and prepare for the discussion questions below.

Discussion Questions

1. What are the main barriers identified in this *Business Week* case study to making work-family or work/life programs effective?

2. If you could choose one factor that, more than anything else, distinguished the successful from the unsuccessful work-family programs described in this case study, what is that factor?

3. Go to the web sites of Cigna, MBNA, and other companies mentioned in this article. Are its work-family policies mentioned anywhere? Does the description at the web site reflect the company's commitment to helping employees balance work and nonwork?

Source: K. H. Hammonds, "Work and Family," *Business Week*, September 15, 1997, pp. 96–100. ■

VIDEO CASE

Take this job ... How stress can be fought on the job

 On the job we all feel it: too much to do, too much monotony, too much uncertainty, too little control. Today, there is so much stress in the workplace that some managers have actually taken up arms. At the S.C. Johnson Wax Company in Racine, Wisconsin, customer service employees fight stress by grabbing their master blasters and letting loose. There are hazards, but stalking and dousing the boss can pay off.

Emergency room surgeon Roxanne Roberts, doesn't have the luxury of playing games. Despite the latest bells and whistles, she is constantly hobbled by stress. Roberts says, "You just run on adrenaline until there is some break in the action. Sometimes you just go home with your tail between your legs." Or worse.

In Madison City, Iowa, insurance claims adjuster, Frank Dunlavy was hospitalized for depression after a new supervisor kept loading him down with crushing amounts of work. Dunlavy said, "I never thought of stress before in the work that I did. But it can jump up and bite you in a hurry." Dunlavy argued workplace stress caused his breakdown; he sued and won over $300,000. Others take a different approach.

To prevent employees from "going postal" some companies now target workplace stress, which one survey found affects 46 percent of workers. To stem absenteeism and increase production the Cigna Corp. even provides an on-the-spot exercise physiologist. The program costs employees just $25 a month and pays big dividends.

The question is not whether stress busters like this work; the question is why doesn't corporate America use them more often. Dr. Joyce Keen, Iowa Methodist Medical Center, said, "There are notable exceptions but, in general, corporate America is still quite toxic to human well being."

In the 90's, however, a number of businesses have discovered that pampering rank and file employees pays dividends. In Philadelphia, Earl Knight puts in 10 hours a day at the Cigna Insurance Company. The last thing that either he or his working wife wants to do is cook. For $10 a dinner, Mr. Knight can order a dinner from the company chef.

In New York if you work long and stressful hours at Solomon Brothers on Wall Street and catch the flu, you can see your own primary care physician right in the building, fax your prescription to the neighborhood pharmacy, and a few hours later your antibiotic leaves the pharmacy and walks in the door. With working hours up and job security down, about 1000 companies offer a range of attractive and unusual benefits from on-site dry cleaning to lactation rooms for nursing mothers.

In Charlotte, North Carolina, at 5:30 A.M., Patty Carter takes her laundry to her $7 assembly line job at the Wilton Connor Packaging Co. That's because the factory does her laundry for her at $1 a load, 25 cents for ironing. The company gives employees $15 a week per child for day care. There's also an emergency loan fund for people who, for example, might be faced with their lighting or heating about to be turned off. The company also throws in free counseling to prevent it from happening again. All of these benefits combined cost the company $30 a week per employee. Is this good business? Wilton Connor, owner of Connor Packaging Co., thinks so. "Absolutely it's good business. It's good hard-nosed business. Treat people as if they are human beings with needs and concerns and you will get back loyalty and good work." Listen to Hattie Carter, a loyal Connor Packaging Co. employee, "We try to make him happy in every way we can because he has been very good to us."

The federal government is telling companies that paying for their employees' fitness now can save billions later. Dr. Gregory Heath, epidemiologist at the U.S. Centers for Disease Control, said, "Increased levels of activity, or regular physical activity, is related to the prevention of premature heart disease." A new study by the centers says thirty minutes of moderate exercise five times a week will dramatically lower the risk of heart disease, still the nation's number one killer claiming half a million deaths a year.

Dr. Heath says, "Coronary heart disease alone can cost in excess of $47 billion dollars a year." The study estimates that $5.7 billion of that is spent on patients who could have avoided the disease if they had exercised. It points out that health care costs have been dramatically reduced for companies that provide fitness programs for their employees. One of those is Coca Cola. Adrienne Kirchnoffer, health promotion manager at the soft drink giant said, "We did find that employees that participate in our fitness center have less health care costs. Something like $500, $530 a year less." That adds up to a saving of $1.2 million a year at Coke's headquarters in Atlanta alone.

Giving employees the opportunity to work out and improve their health at the workplace provides another benefit, as Coke's Kirchnoffer pointed out, "If they are healthier we know that they are going to work better, their productivity is going to be up, they are going to be absent a lot less."

Many employees now consider fitness programs an important fringe benefit. And the companies that provide them are finding that they not only save money, but win the appreciation and loyalty of employees as well.

Questions for Discussion

1. Why don't more companies offer the kind of workplace benefits highlighted in the examples in this case? What might convince companies to develop benefit programs like the ones in this case?

2. What benefits do you think you would want in the workplace that don't currently exist? Why? Can these benefits be justified?

3. What are the advantages of these types of benefits for a company? What are the disadvantages? ◼

Stressed out or "no problem"?

Purpose

This exercise is designed to help students understand how people will have different stress reactions to the same stressors.

Instructions

Students individually indicate their responses to each of the incidents on the scoring sheet for "Stressed Out or 'No Problem'?" Then, the instructor places students into groups (typically four or five people) to compare their results. For each incident, group members should discuss why each person feels more or less stress. They should pay particular attention to the reasons why some students would feel little stress. Specifically, they should examine the extent that each person:

a. Perceives the situation differently.
b. Has more or less tolerance to stressors due to health or need to cope with other problems.
c. Would use different coping strategies to deal with any stress related to the incident.

After group members have diagnosed these results, the instructor brings the class together to compare results and discuss why people react differently to stressors.

Stressed out or "no problem"?

Circle the number on the right that best describes the extent that you would feel stressed in this situation.	Very little ▼		Moderately ▼			Very much ▼
1. Your final exam for Economics 200 is in 48 hours and a bad case of the flu and other class assignments have prevented you from studying for it. You know that the instructor will not accept your illness and other assignments as an excuse to have the examination at another time.	1	2	3	4	5	6	7
2. You started work last month as a sales clerk in a small clothing store (men's or women's) and have been asked to mind the store while the other two clerks take their lunch break elsewhere in the shopping mall. During this usually slow time, four customers walk in, each one of them wanting your immediate attention.	1	2	3	4	5	6	7
3. You and two friends are driving in an older van with snow tires to a ski resort in the Canadian Rockies. You took over driving duty at 8 P.M., two hours ago. Your friends are asleep in the backseat while you approach a steep mountain pass. It has been snowing so heavily that you must drive at a crawl to see where you are going and to avoid sliding off the road. You passed the last community 30 miles back and the resort is 40 miles ahead (nearly two hours at your current speed).	1	2	3	4	5	6	7
4. You work as an accountant in a large insurance company and for the past month have received unwanted attention several times each week from your supervisor, a married person of the opposite sex. The supervisor regularly touches your shoulder and comments on your looks. You are sure that they are advances rather than just friendly gestures.	1	2	3	4	5	6	7

SELF-ASSESSMENT EXERCISE

Behavior activity profile: The Type A scale

Purpose

This exercise is designed to help students estimate the extent that they follow a Type A behavior pattern. It also shows the specific elements of Type A patterns in various life events.

Instructions

This is a self-diagnosis exercise that you complete alone. For each of the 21 sets of descriptions, circle the number which best describes the way you feel, behave, or think.

The interpretation of results is provided, along with norms for both women and men. After you have scored your results, the instructor may want to determine, by a show of hands, how many are Type A's, Type B's, and Type X's (in between). The discussion can then turn to whether students would like to have more or less Type A behavior than what they are currently like. While few people would want to be extreme Type A's, there are benefits to some Type A characteristics in some jobs and other life activities.

Experiential exercise

1.	I'm always on time for appointments.	7 6 5 4 3 2 1	I'm never quite on time.
2.	When someone is talking to me, chances are I'll anticipate what they are going to say, by nodding, interrupting, or finishing sentences for them.	7 6 5 4 3 2 1	I listen quietly without showing any impatience.
3.	I frequently try to do several things at once.	7 6 5 4 3 2 1	I tend to take things one at a time.
4.	When it comes to waiting in line (at banks, theaters, etc.), I really get impatient and frustrated.	7 6 5 4 3 2 1	Waiting in line doesn't bother me.
5.	I always feel rushed.	7 6 5 4 3 2 1	I never feel rushed.
6.	When it comes to my temper, I find it hard to control at times.	7 6 5 4 3 2 1	I don't seem to have a temper.
7.	I tend to do most things, like eating, walking, and talking, rapidly.	7 6 5 4 3 2 1	I tend to do most things slowly.

Total score 1–7 _____ = S

8.	Quite honestly, the things I enjoy most are job-related activities.	7 6 5 4 3 2 1	Leisure-time activities are what I most enjoy.

9. At the end of a typical workday, I usually feel like I needed to get more done than I did.   7 6 5 4 3 2 1   I accomplished everything at work I needed to.

10. Someone who knows me very well would say that I would rather work than play.   7 6 5 4 3 2 1   I'd rather play than work.

11. When it comes to getting ahead at work, nothing is more important.   7 6 5 4 3 2 1   Many things are more important than work.

12. My primary source of satisfaction comes from my job.   7 6 5 4 3 2 1   I regularly find satisfaction in nonjob pursuits, such as hobbies, friends, and family.

13. Most of my friends and social acquaintances are people I know from work.   7 6 5 4 3 2 1   Most of my friends are not connected with my work.

14. I'd rather stay at work than take a vacation.   7 6 5 4 3 2 1   Nothing at work is important enough to interfere with my vacation.

Total score 8–14 _____ = J

15. People who know me would describe me as hard-driving and competitive.   7 6 5 4 3 2 1   Most people would describe me as relaxed and easygoing.

16. In general, my behavior is governed by a desire for recognition and achievement.   7 6 5 4 3 2 1   I do what I want to do—not by trying to satisfy others.

17. In trying to complete a project or solve a problem, I tend to wear myself out before I'll give up on it.   7 6 5 4 3 2 1   I tend to take a break or quit if I'm feeling fatigued.

18. When I play a game (tennis, cards, etc.) my enjoyment comes from winning.   7 6 5 4 3 2 1   My enjoyment comes from the social interaction.

19. I like to associate with people who are dedicated to getting ahead.   7 6 5 4 3 2 1   I like people who are easygoing and take life as it comes.

20. I'm not happy unless I'm always doing something.   7 6 5 4 3 2 1   Frequently, "doing nothing" can be quite enjoyable.

21. What I enjoy doing most are competitive activities.   7 6 5 4 3 2 1   Noncompetitive pursuits are what I most enjoy.

Total score 15–21 _____ = H

Impatience (S)	Job involvement (J)	Hard driving and competitive (H)	Total score (A) = S + J + H
_____ +	_____ +	_____ =	_____

The Behavior Activity Profile attempts to assess the three Type A coronary-prone behavior patterns, as well as provide a total score. The three a priori types of Type A coronary-prone behavior patterns are shown:

Items	Behavior pattern		Characteristics
1–7	Impatience	(S)	Anxious to interrupt Fails to listen attentively Frustrated by waiting (e.g., in line, for others to complete a job)
8–14	Job involvement	(J)	Focal point of attention is the job Lives for the job Relishes being on the job Immersed by job activities
15–21	Hard driving/competitive	(H)	Hardworking, highly competitive Competitive in most aspects of life, sports, work, and so on Racing against the clock
1–21	Total score	(A)	Total of S + J + H represents your global Type A behavior

Score ranges for total score are:

Score	Behavior type
122 and above	Hard-core Type A
99–121	Moderate Type A
90–98	Low Type A
80–89	Type X
70–79	Low Type B
50–69	Moderate Type B
40 and below	Hard-core Type B

Percentile score Percentage of individuals scoring lower	Raw score	
	Males	Females
99%	140	132
95	135	126
90	130	120
85	124	112
80	118	106
75	113	101
70	108	95
65	102	90
60	97	85
55	92	80
50	87	74
45	81	69
40	75	63
35	70	58
30	63	53
25	58	48
20	51	42
15	45	36
10	38	31
5	29	26
1	21	21

Percentile scores

Now you can compare your score to a sample of over 1,200 respondents

CHAPTER SIX

Perception and Personality in Organizations

Learning Objectives

After reading this chapter, you should be able to:

- Outline the perceptual process.
- Explain how we perceive ourselves and others through social identity.
- Discuss the accuracy of stereotypes.
- Describe the attribution process and two attribution errors.
- Diagram the self-fulfilling prophecy process.
- Discuss the objectives and limitations of diversity management programs.
- Explain why personality is relevant to organizational behavior.
- Identify the "Big Five" personality dimensions.
- Discuss the psychological dimensions identified by Jung and measured in the Myers-Briggs Type Indicator.

When Texas Instruments closed its Austin plant, Robert Mitchell didn't think he would have a problem finding another job. Mitchell saw lots of jobs listed in his specialization, and high-technology firms were scrambling to hire talented workers. But Mitchell didn't figure that his age would get in the way. "I sent out 75 résumés and I got one interview," says the 51-year-old.

Corporate leaders say that there is no age bias, just a few older employees whose skills don't fit current needs. But Greg Kokoska will tell you otherwise. Kokoska and dozens of other sales representatives were laid off a few years ago by Monsanto only to be replaced by younger staff. Almost all of the terminated employees were over 40 years old and most had good work records. Kokoska and others sued Monsanto for age discrimination and won large out-of-court settlements.

Age bias also seems to be a problem facing script writers in the television industry, according to Larry DiTillio, chairman of the Writers Guild age awareness committee. "There is a perception held by some network executives that you have to be young to write young," he says. "And when you have Gary David Goldberg [creator and executive producer of ABC's "Spin City"] being quoted in *TV Guide* as saying, 'Don't send me any writers over 29,' it hurts."[1]

Robert Mitchell sent out 75 résumés and got one interview after his former employer left the area. "I hate to say it, but I think it was the amount of experience," says the 51-year-old. "They said, 'Oh, this is probably an old, fat, bald guy.'"

[*S. Park,* Austin American-Statesman]

perception the process of receiving information about and making sense of our environment. This includes deciding which information to notice as well as how to categorize and interpret it

he Greek philosopher Plato wrote long ago that we see reality only as shadows reflecting against the rough wall of a cave.[2] In other words, reality is filtered through an imperfect perceptual process. **Perception** is the process of receiving information about and making sense of the world around us. It involves deciding which information to notice, how to categorize this information, and how to interpret it within the framework of our existing knowledge.

As we saw in the opening vignette, the perceptual process often leads to inaccurate assumptions and inappropriate behaviors toward people who are different from us. Young recruiters may rely on inaccurate stereotypes, for example, and thereby assume that older workers aren't as productive as younger applicants. With an increasingly diverse workforce, we need to pay closer attention to the perceptual process to minimize these misperceptions. "No matter who you are, you will have to work with someone different from yourself," says Ted Childs, the executive who engineered IBM's worldwide diversity strategy.[3]

This chapter begins by describing the perceptual process; that is, the dynamics of selecting, organizing, and interpreting external stimuli. Social identity theory is introduced, including how this process influences our self-perceptions and the perceptions of others. Social identity theory lays the foundation for our coverage of stereotyping, prejudice, and discrimination. The perceptual processes of attribution and self-fulfilling prophecy are described next, followed by an overview of strategies to minimize perceptual problems. Our perception of others, as well as most other organizational behavior processes, is influenced by our personality. The final section of this chapter introduces this important concept and its relevance to organizational behavior.

The Perceptual Process

As Exhibit 6.1 illustrates, the perceptual process begins when environmental stimuli are received through our senses. Most stimuli are screened out; the rest are organized and interpreted based on various information-processing activities. The resulting perceptions influence our emotions and behavior toward those objects, people, and events.[4]

Exhibit 6.1
Model of the perceptual process

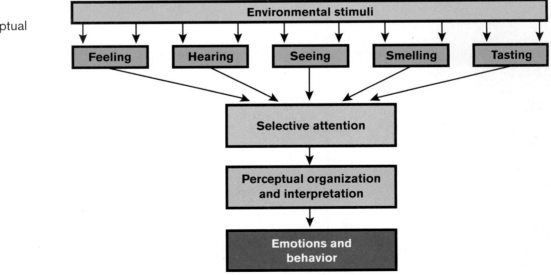

Selective Attention

Our five senses are constantly bombarded with stimuli. Some things get noticed, but most are screened out. A nurse working in postoperative care might ignore the smell of recently disinfected instruments or the sound of co-workers talking nearby. Yet, a small flashing red light on the nurse station console is immediately noticed because it signals that a patient's vital signs are failing. This process of filtering information received by our senses is called **selective attention.**

selective attention the process of filtering (selecting and screening out) information received by our senses

One influence on selective attention is the size, intensity, motion, repetition, and novelty of the target (including people). The red light on the nurse station

Protecting the President of the United States and other dignitaries is a difficult perceptual job. Secret Service agents must somehow ensure that their selective attention process takes in as much information as possible to identify potential security risks. How do they do this? They practice "splatter vision"—scanning everything and focusing on nothing. As one agent explains, "Never look through the crowd to find a potential assailant. The sheer number of people will leave you snow blind." When agents focus on one suspicious character, they develop expectations that focus their attention. This in turn causes them to unconsciously screen out most of the other stimuli from the crowd. But with splatter vision, agents don't concentrate on a particular person, so their perceptual process doesn't filter out potentially valuable information.[5] How would splatter vision be useful in organizational settings?

[REUTERS/Win McNamee/Archive Photos]

console receives attention because it is bright (intensity), flashing (motion), and a rare event (novelty). As for people, we would notice two employees having a heated debate if co-workers normally don't raise their voices (novelty and intensity).

Notice from the example of two people arguing that selective attention is also influenced by the context in which the target is perceived. We probably wouldn't notice two people arguing in a noisy bar, but they stand out in a quiet office. Similarly, you might be aware that a client has an Australian accent if the meeting takes place in New York, but not if the conversation took place in Melbourne, Australia, particularly if you had been living there for some time. On the contrary, it would be your American accent that others would notice!

Characteristics of the perceiver   Selective attention is partly influenced by the perceiver's emotions. We tend to remember information that is consistent with our attitudes and ignore information that is inconsistent. For example, interviewers who develop positive feelings toward a job applicant early in the interview tend to subsequently screen out negative information about that candidate.[6] In extreme cases, our emotions screen out large blocks of information that threaten our beliefs and values. This phenomenon, called **perceptual defense,** protects our self-esteem and may be a coping mechanism to minimize stress in the short run.[7]

Our expectations, which are shaped by preconceived ideas, also condition us to be "ready" for certain events and to ignore others.[8] If we believe that professors are forgetful, for instance, then we notice information that confirms this belief and tend to screen out contradictory evidence.

Perceptual Organization and Interpretation

After selecting stimuli, we usually simplify and "make sense" of it. This involves organizing the information into general categories and interpreting it. Organizing information mainly occurs through the process of **perceptual grouping.** We rely on perceptual grouping principles to organize people and objects into recognizable and manageable patterns or categories. One grouping principle is closure, such as filling in missing information about what happened at a meeting that you missed (e.g., who was there, where it was held). Another perceptual grouping principle is identifying trends. Marketing analysts try to identify consumer trends from seemingly random information. A third grouping principle is based on a target person's similarity or proximity to others. We might assume that a particular employee is inefficient because he or she works in a department where employees tend to be inefficient.

Perceptual grouping helps us to make sense of the workplace, but it can also inhibit creativity and open-mindedness. It puts blinders on our ability to organize and interpret people and events differently. Perceptual grouping is influenced by our broader assumptions and beliefs, known as mental models.

Mental models   Communications guru Marshall McLuhan once wrote that people wear their own set of idiosyncratic goggles. In his colorful way, McLuhan was saying that each of us holds a unique view of what the world looks like and how it operates. These idiosyncratic goggles are known as **mental models.**[9]

Mental models represent the information acquired from past experience that we organize in a meaningful way.[10] They are the broad world views or "theories-in-use" that people rely on to guide their perceptions and behaviors. For example, most of us have a mental model about attending a college lecture or seminar. We have a set of assumptions and expectations about how people arrive, arrange themselves in the room, ask and answer questions, and so

perceptual defense a psychological process that involves subconsciously screening out large blocks of information that threaten the person's beliefs and values

perceptual grouping the perceptual organization process of placing people and objects into recognizable and manageable patterns or categories

mental models the broad world views or "theories-in-use" that people rely on to guide their perceptions and behaviors

forth. We can create a mental image of what a class would look like in progress.

Mental models are beneficial because they guide our perceptions and enable us to make decisions more quickly. They create the screens through which we select information, the boxes we use to contain that knowledge, and the assumptions we use to interpret events. Effective decision makers rely on their mental models to quickly identify discrepancies and to find solutions to those discrepancies. In our classroom example, we would immediately notice if there is something out of the ordinary (such as a student sitting on a desk rather than on a chair). In organizational settings, these discrepancies cue us to take appropriate action.

However, mental models that give us a rich or efficient understanding of one environment may blind us to alternative and potentially better perspectives of the world when that environment changes.[11] For instance, when soundtracks first appeared for movies in 1927, Harry Warner of Warner Brothers Studios boldly asked: "Who the hell wants to hear actors talk?" In the 1970s, General Motors continued to build big gas-guzzling cars even though oil prices had significantly altered what consumers were looking for in a vehicle. And as recently as 1996, Microsoft's Bill Gates mocked the commercial viability of the Internet.[12]

How do we develop new mental models? It's a tough challenge. After all, we have developed models of the way things work based on years of experience and reinforcement. Certainly, we need to be aware of the limitations of mental models and to constantly question our existing assumptions. The creative decision process that we will describe in Chapter 11 helps in this regard. Working with people from diverse backgrounds is another way to break out of existing mental models. Some companies try to form new mental models by hiring outsiders—people who have not worked in the industry and are therefore free of the dominant perceptions that blind industry veterans. As our *Fast Company Online* feature for this chapter describes, Sony's North American video game group successfully launched PlayStation by breaking away from long-established views of the market. Sony hired people with little or no experience in the video game industry so that the group could see opportunities differently.

Social Identity Theory

social identity theory a theory that explains self-perception and social perception in terms of our unique characteristics (personal identity) as well as membership in various social groups (social identity)

The perceptual process is more than just placing other people into groups. It is an interactive dynamic between our self-perceptions and perceptions of others. **Social identity theory** explains this process of self-perception and social perception.[13] According to social identity theory, people develop their self-perceptions through personal identity and social identity. *Personal identity* includes the individual's unique characteristics and experiences, such as physical appearance, personality traits, and special talents. An unusual achievement that distinguishes you from other people becomes a personal characteristic with which you partially identify yourself.

Social identity, on the other hand, refers to our self-perception as members in various social groups. For example, one person might have a self-identity as an American, a graduate of the University of Vermont, and an employee at Acme Widget Company. This social categorization process helps us to locate ourselves within the social world (see Exhibit 6.2).

Some scholars argue that self-concepts are derived almost completely from social perceptions.[14] However, the research evidence seems to suggest that people adopt degrees of personal and social identity, depending on the situation. If your organizational behavior class has several students with your gender, race, and specialization (e.g., marketing, finance), then you would tend to identify yourself in terms of personal identity characteristics in that context (e.g., "I'm probably the only one in this class who has trekked through

FAST COMPANY
Online

◻ Sony Changes the Game

Until recently, the global video game market was dominated by two seemingly invincible giants: Nintendo and Sega. Then came PlayStation—the most successful new product from Sony since the Walkman. In its first three years, Sony's video game business unit shipped over 16 million PlayStation units and over 100 million pieces of game software.

How did Sony become a force in the video game industry? By bringing in people who didn't have existing mental models of the industry. This strategy worked for Sony's enormously successful music division. When that venture was created in the 1980s, it was staffed almost entirely with people from outside the music industry.

Sony succeeded in the video game market with PlayStation by hiring people who didn't have a set mental model of that industry.
[John Thoeming]

"We didn't want people from the record business," explains Kazuo Hirai, Sony's top executive in North America for video games. "They would just bring their old ways with them. We wanted people who would have to figure things out all over again, who would question everything, people who 'didn't know any better.'"

Sony took the same approach with PlayStation. Half the unit's top personnel, including Hirai, came from Sony Music rather than the video game business. "The last thing I want to hear is, 'We tried that last year and it didn't work,'" Hirai says. "Our business changes constantly. What didn't work a year ago might work today."

Sony hired lots of young people for the same reason. "Young people don't have preconceived notions about how things should be done," says Phil Harrison, Sony video group's vice president for third-party relations and research and development. "They just come up with solutions—without even realizing that they've arrived at success in a 'strange' way."

ONLINE CHECK-UP

1. Sony's strategy of bringing in people from outside the industry seems to avoid the limitations of mental models. However, what problems might arise from this strategy, in both the short and long term?

2. The full text of this Fast Company Online feature describes how the Sony Video game group in Foster City, California, is highly autonomous. How would this autonomy affect employee perceptions of their work, senior executives, and the video game market?

Get the full text of this
Fast Company article at
www.mhhe.com/mcshane1e

Source: Adapted from P. Roberts, "Sony Changes the Game," *Fast Company,* Issue 10 (1997). ◼

Exhibit 6.2
Self-perception and social perception through social identity

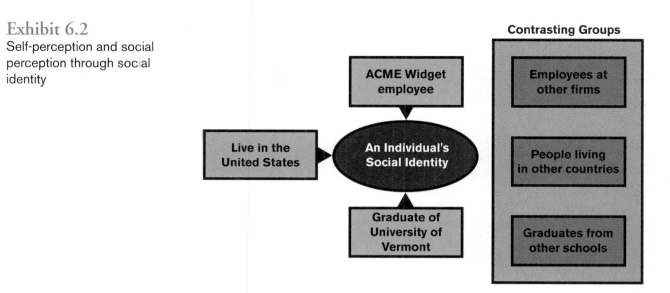

Malaysia's Cameron Highlands!"). On the other hand, if you are one of the few computer science students in a class with business students, then your group membership—your social identity—would dominate your self-perception. In this situation, you would define yourself more by your field of specialization ("I'm from computer science") than by any personal identity characteristics. As your distinguishing social identity becomes known to others, they too would likely identify you by that feature.

We tend to perceive ourselves as members of several groups, not just one or two. In this respect, social identity is a complex combination of many memberships determined by personal priorities. Also, we are motivated to create and present a positive self-image. According to social identity theory, this occurs by identifying ourselves with groups that have a positive public reputation. This explains why medical doctors usually define themselves in terms of their profession, whereas people in low-status jobs are less likely to do so. It also explains why some people like to mention their employer while others never mention where they work.[15] At one time, Continental Airlines had such a terrible reputation that some employees removed the company labels from their uniforms. Now that the airline is successful again, employees proudly wear Continental's logo on their uniforms and buy lots of labeled items for home use from the company store.[16]

Perceiving Others through Social Identity

Social identity theory doesn't just explain how we develop self-perceptions. It also explains the dynamics of social perception—how we perceive others. In particular, it describes how and why we categorize others into homogeneous and often less favorable groups. Social identity is a *comparative* process, meaning that we define ourselves in terms of our differences with people who belong to other groups. To simplify this comparison process, we tend to *homogenize* people within social categories. We think that people within our group share certain traits, and people in comparison groups share a different set of traits. This may be partly true, but we further exaggerate these differences. For example, students from one college often describe students from a rival school (particularly before a football, basketball, or other sports competition) as though they come from a different planet!

Comparison and homogenization explain why we perceptually group other people and overgeneralize their traits. But we also tend to develop less positive (or sometimes downright negative) images of people outside our social identity group. This occurs because our self-identity involves contrasting the groups we belong to with other groups. To maintain a positive self-image, we usually construct favorable images of our own social identity group and, as a result, less favorable images of people belonging to other social categories. This is particularly true when the groups are in competition and conflict with each other. The negative image of opponents preserves our self-image while the threat exists.[17]

To summarize, the social identity process explains how we perceive ourselves and others. We partly identify ourselves in terms of our membership in social groups. This comparison process includes creating a homogeneous image of our own social groups and different homogeneous images of people in other groups. We also tend to assign more favorable features to our own groups and less favorable features to other groups. This perceptual process makes our social world easier to understand. However, it also becomes the basis for stereotyping people in organizational settings.

Stereotyping in Organizational Settings

stereotyping the process of using a few observable characteristics to assign people to a preconceived social category, and then assigning less observable traits to those persons based on their membership in the group

Stereotyping is an extension of social identity. It is the process of assigning traits to people based on their membership in a social category.[18] In other words, stereotypes define people by the demographic and organizational groups to which they belong. Exhibit 6.3 illustrates the three steps in the stereotyping process. First, we develop social categories and assign traits that are difficult to observe. For instance, students might form a stereotype that professors are both intelligent and absent-minded. These unobservable traits are, to some extent, formed from personal experiences, but they are anchored more in public images, such as movie characters and public figures.

Next, people are assigned to one or more social categories based on easily observable information about them, such as their gender, appearance, or physical location. Observable features allow us to assign people to a social group quickly and without much investigation. Lastly, the cluster of traits linked to the social category is assigned to people identified as members of that group. For example, we unconsciously assume that the professors we meet are intelligent and absent-minded, at least until we know them better.

How Accurate Are Stereotypes?

Early writers warned that stereotypes were almost completely false or, at best, exaggerated the traits of people in those groups. Scholars now take a more

Exhibit 6.3
The stereotyping process

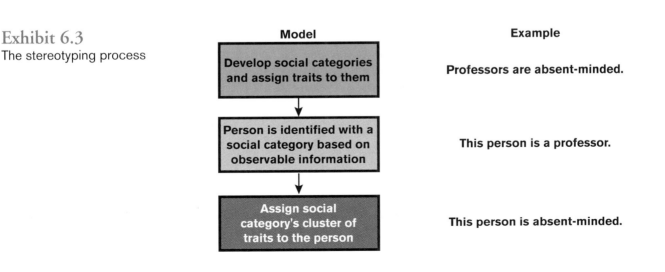

moderate view. They say that stereotypes generally have some inaccuracies, some overestimation or underestimation of real differences, and some degree of accuracy.[19] Still, we should remember that stereotypes are never as accurate as our personal knowledge of a person.

One problem with stereotyping is that stereotyped traits do not accurately describe every person in that social category. For instance, research has found that people with physical disabilities are stereotyped as being quiet, gentle-hearted, shy, insecure, dependent, and submissive.[20] While this may be true of some people, it is certainly not characteristic of everyone who has a physical disability. Another concern with stereotypes is that we often ignore or misinterpret information that is inconsistent with the stereotype.[21] Stereotypes are notoriously easy to confirm because they include abstract personality traits that are supported by ambiguous behaviors.

Female police officers face plenty of stereotypes. "There is the perception the job is too physical, and there is an old and wrong perception that women who would do this job somehow are not feminine," says Sgt. Kathy Copeland in Glendale, Arizona. In reality, most police work involves problem solving, conflict management, and collecting information (as Phoenix officer Pam Haas is doing here). Moreover, increasing the percentage of policewomen tends to reduce police violence and improve police force effectiveness.[22] How can police departments change these stereotypes and misperceptions?
*[Mark Henle/*Arizona Republic*]*

People also develop inaccurate stereotypes under *certain conditions*. One condition is the degree to which we interact with people in that group. If we don't communicate with and directly observe people, then we tend to rely on distorted public images of them. Second, stereotypes are less accurate when we experience conflict with members of that group. Conflict creates an "us-versus-them" emotional state that unconsciously distorts the information we assign to the group.

The third problem is that we develop inaccurate stereotypes of groups that enhance our own social identity. Recall from social identity theory that our self-perception is developed by identifying with certain social groups and contrasting them with other groups. This creates less favorable images of other groups, which involves unconsciously assigning inaccurate traits to people in those different groups.[23]

At this point, you might think we should avoid stereotyping altogether. Unfortunately, it's not that simple. Stereotyping is a natural process we use to economize mental effort.[24] By remembering information about categories of people rather than every individual we meet, stereotyping saves a lot of investigative work. Moreover, this perceptual process fills in missing information when we lack the opportunity or motivation to directly know others. The good news is that the more we interact with someone, the less we rely on stereotypes to understand the individual. Stereotyping occurs when we lack personal information about the individual or the information is ambiguous. As we get to know someone better, we remove our stereotypical perceptions of that individual.[25]

Ethical Problems with Stereotyping

Stereotypes may be part of the perceptual process, but inaccurate stereotypes raise serious ethical concerns. Perhaps the greatest concern is that

prejudice unfounded negative emotions toward people belonging to a particular stereotyped group

stereotyping lays the foundation for **prejudice**—unfounded negative emotions toward people belonging to a particular stereotyped group.[26] For instance, more than a dozen African-American employees at a Wonder Bread bakery in San Francisco recently claimed that they constantly received disparaging remarks and racial slurs, such as being called "too lazy" and "welfare people."[27] Similar complaints have been raised at Circuit City, Denny's, Shoney's, and Texaco over the past few years. Not surprisingly, 81 percent of African-American professionals believe that discrimination in the workplace is still common.[28]

Although these examples of overt prejudice still exist, it is probably fair to say that most people try to avoid discriminatory behaviors. They support the notion of equality and try to act consistently with this equality value. People tend to monitor their own emotions and suppress prejudices arising from ingrained stereotypes, although some are better than others at containing their prejudices.[29]

Unfortunately, even when prejudices are minimized, subtle discrimination occurs because people rely on stereotypes to establish notions of the "ideal" person in specific roles.[30] In the opening story to this chapter, we read that some older people have difficulty getting a job. It's not that recruiters are overtly prejudiced against older people. Rather, their implicit image of an ideal job candidate is a young person. Similarly, many women executives in large U.S. companies feel that their careers have been hampered by negative preconceptions and stereotypes of their professional capabilities.[31] In support of this view, several recent studies indicate that male business students continue to hold a masculine stereotype of successful middle managers. As long as they keep these images of the ideal manager, women will be evaluated less favorably in these positions.[32]

sexual harassment unwelcome conduct of a sexual nature that detrimentally affects the work environment or leads to adverse job-related consequences for its victims

Before leaving this topic, we should note that stereotyping is also partly responsible for **sexual harassment.** As we learned in Chapter 5, sexual harassment refers to unwelcome conduct of a sexual nature that detrimentally affects the work environment or leads to adverse job-related consequences for its victims. Sexual harassment is mainly caused by the harasser's abuse of power, as we will discuss in Chapter 12. However, recent studies also emphasize that sexual harassment is more prevalent where the harasser (typically a man) holds sexist motives based on paternalism and gender stereotyping.[33] In other words, harassment is more likely to occur among people who stereotype the victim as subservient and powerless. For example, a study of female firefighters reported that sexual harassment is much more prevalent in fire departments where men hold strong sex stereotypes of women.[34]

Attribution Theory

attribution process a perceptual process whereby we interpret the causes of behavior in terms of the person (internal attributions) or the situation (external attributions)

Our discussion so far has mainly looked at the dynamics of grouping, including social identity and stereotyping. A different perceptual activity, called the **attribution process,** helps us to interpret the world around us. The attribution process involves deciding whether an observed behavior or event is largely caused by internal or external factors.[35] Internal factors originate from within a person, such as the individual's ability or motivation. We make an *internal attribution* by believing that an employee performs the job poorly because he or she lacks the necessary competencies or motivation. External factors originate from the environment, such as availability of resources, supportiveness of co-workers, or just luck. An *external attribution* would occur if we believe that the employee performs the job poorly because he or she doesn't receive sufficient resources to do the task.

How do people determine whether to make an internal or external attribution about a co-worker's excellent job performance or a supplier's late shipment? Basically, they rely on the three attribution rules shown in Exhibit 6.4. Internal attributions are made when the observed individual behaved this way in the past (high consistency), usually behaves like this toward other people or in different situations (low distinctiveness), and other people do not behave this way in similar situations (low consensus). On the other hand, an external attribution is made when there is low consistency, high distinctiveness, and high consensus.

The following example will help to clarify the three attribution rules. Suppose that an employee is making poor quality products one day on a particular machine. We would probably conclude that there is something wrong with the machine (an external attribution) if the employee has made good quality products on this machine in the past (low consistency), the employee makes good quality products on other machines (high distinctiveness), and other employees have recently had quality problems on this machine (high consensus). We would make an internal attribution, on the other hand, if the employee usually makes poor quality products on this machine (high consistency), other employees produce good quality products on this machine (low consensus), and the employee also makes poor quality products on other machines (low distinctiveness).[36]

Consequences of Attribution

Attributing behavior to internal versus external factors affects our subsequent reactions to that event.[37] One study of union grievances reported that arbitrators rely on the attribution process to decide whether employees are responsible for wrongdoing. In particular, arbitration decisions favor the employee

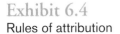

Exhibit 6.4
Rules of attribution

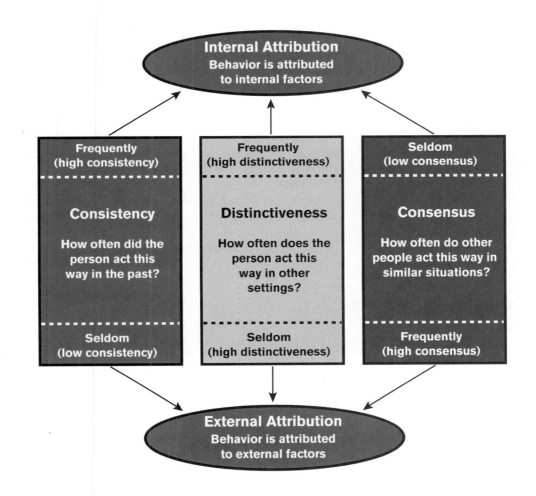

when other employees have committed the same error and the employee has not previously been guilty of the wrongdoing.[38]

Attribution decisions also affect the implications of performance feedback and reward allocation. Employees receive larger bonuses or pay increases when decision makers attribute good performance to the employee's ability or motivation.[39] Employees also develop a stronger self-efficacy and tend to have higher job satisfaction when they believe positive feedback relates to events within their control rather than to external causes.[40]

Attribution Errors

fundamental attribution error the tendency to incorrectly attribute the behavior of other people to internal more than to external factors

The attribution process is far from perfect. The most fundamental error we make in attribution is called (not surprisingly) **fundamental attribution error.** This refers to the tendency to attribute the behavior of other people to internal factors more than external factors. If an employee is late for work, observers are more likely to conclude that the person is lazy than to think that external factors may have caused this behavior. Fundamental attribution error mainly occurs because we typically have limited information about the situational contingencies affecting other people. Meanwhile, the person performing the behavior is naturally more sensitive to situational contingencies affecting that behavior. This can lead to disagreement over the degree to which employees should be held responsible for their poor performance or absenteeism.[41] The observer blames the employee's lack of motivation or ability, whereas the employee does not feel responsible because the behavior seems to be due to factors beyond his or her control.

self-serving bias a perceptual error whereby people tend to attribute their own success to internal factors and their failures to external factors

Another attribution error, known as **self-serving bias,** is the tendency to attribute our favorable outcomes to internal factors and our failures to external factors. Simply put, we take credit for our successes and blame others or the situation for our mistakes. The existence of self-serving bias in corporate life has been well documented. In a unique study of corporate annual reports, researchers discovered that organizational successes were typically explained by internal attributions such as management strategy, workforce qualities, and research/development efforts. But when explaining corporate problems, the annual reports relied more on external attributions such as bad weather, strong competition, and inflationary pressures.[42]

Aside from these errors, attributions vary from one person to another based on personal values and experiences. For instance, female managers are less likely than male managers to make internal attributions about their job performance.[43] Japanese and Chinese employees are less likely to engage in self-serving bias than American employees. In cultures where group membership is important, individuals try to maintain harmony among group members, so they make more external attributions about another employee's poor performance.[44] Overall, we need to be careful about personal and systematic biases in the attribution process within organizations.

Self-Fulfilling Prophecy

When Henry Quadracci started Quad/Graphics in the 1970s, he could only afford inexperienced employees, many of whom had low self-esteem. "When they come into the employment office, they're not looking at the stars," Quadracci observed. "They're looking at their shoes." But Quadracci saw the potential of these new hires, and continually treated them as winners. The strategy worked. Quad/Graphics employees developed confidence and exceptional performance, and this has made the printing firm one of the largest and most successful in America.[45]

self-fulfilling prophecy a phenomenon in which an observer's expectations of someone causes that person to act in a way that is consistent with the observer's expectation

Henry Quadracci has been practicing a powerful perceptual process called **self-fulfilling prophecy.** Self-fulfilling prophecy occurs when our expectations about another person cause that person to act in a way that is consistent with those expectations.[46] In other words, our perceptions can influence reality. If a supervisor believes a new employee won't be able to perform the job, this expectation influences the supervisor's behavior toward the employee and, without realizing it, may cause the recruit to perform the job poorly. Consequently, the supervisor's perception, even if originally incorrect, is confirmed. Exhibit 6.5 illustrates the four steps in the self-fulfilling prophecy process, using the example of a supervisor and subordinate.[47]

• *Expectations formed*—The supervisor forms expectations about the employee's future behavior and performance. These expectations are sometimes inaccurate, because first impressions are usually formed from limited information.

• *Behavior toward the employee*—The supervisor's expectations influence his or her treatment of employees.[48] Specifically, high-expectancy employees (those expected to do well) receive more emotional support through nonverbal cues (e.g., more smiling and eye contact), more frequent and valuable feedback and reinforcement, more challenging goals, better training, and more opportunities to demonstrate their performance.

• *Effects on the employee*—The supervisor's behaviors have two effects on the employee. First, through better training and more practice opportunities, high-expectancy employees learn more skills and knowledge than low-expectancy employees. Second, the employee develops a stronger **self-efficacy.**[49] Recall from Chapter 2 that high self-efficacy employees believe that they have the ability, motivation, and situational contingencies to complete a task successfully.[50] This results in higher motivation because employees develop stronger effort-to-performance expectancies and set more challenging goals for themselves.

• *Employee behavior and performance*—With higher motivation and better skills, high-expectancy employees are more likely to demonstrate desired behaviors and better performance. This is observed by the supervisor and reinforces the original perception.

self-efficacy a person's belief that he or she has the ability, motivation, and situational contingencies to complete a task successfully

The self-fulfilling prophecy effect extends beyond supervisor-subordinate relationships. Some of the earliest work reported that teacher expectancies influenced the subsequent behavior and performance of elementary school children. Courtroom research has found that judges influence jury decisions

Exhibit 6.5
The self-fulfilling prophecy cycle

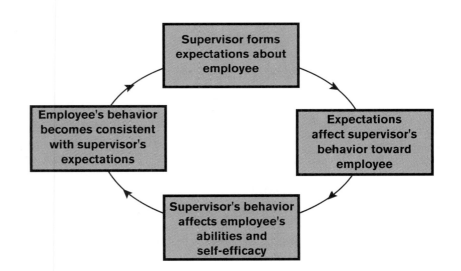

by nonverbally communicating their expectations. And while self-fulfilling prophecy is an interpersonal effect, it also operates at a macro level in the stability of financial institutions. The stability of a bank, for instance, depends on the public's expectation that it will be stable. As soon as people begin to doubt this belief, the financial institution has a "run on the bank" that threatens its survival.[51]

Self-Fulfilling Prophecies in Organizations

In organizational settings, employees are more likely to be victims of negative self-fulfilling prophecy than benefactors of positive self-fulfilling prophecy.[52] This is unfortunate because, as Henry Quadracci knows, self-fulfilling prophecy is a potentially valuable strategy to maximize employee performance and satisfaction. Researchers have reported, for example, that hard-core unemployed trainees were more likely to find work and poor-performing sailors in the United States Navy were more likely to improve their performance when instructors or supervisors formed positive expectations about them.[53]

One of the best examples of self-fulfilling prophecy took place in an Israeli Defense Force combat command course. Course instructors were told that one-third of the incoming trainees had high command potential, one-third had normal potential, and the rest had unknown potential. The trainees had been randomly placed into these categories by the researchers, but the instructors were led to believe that this was accurate information. As predicted, high-expectancy soldiers performed significantly better by the end of the course than did others. They also had more favorable attitudes toward the course and the instructor's leadership effectiveness.[54]

How can organizations harness the power of positive self-fulfilling prophecy? Like Henry Quadracci, corporate leaders must exhibit more contagious enthusiasm and, although providing accurate feedback, continue to express hope and optimism in each employee's potential.[55] In some situations, researchers have found that these positive expectations spread from one or two employees to the entire group. To block negative self-fulfilling prophecy, companies need to fight negative stereotypes and avoid first impressions. They should also develop more objective performance measures and provide fair access to challenging assignments and training opportunities.

Other Perceptual Errors

Perception is an imperfect process. This is already apparent from our discussion of stereotyping, attribution, and self-fulfilling prophecy. Some of the other troublesome errors that distort our ability to perceive people and events include primacy, recency, halo, and projection.

Primacy Effect

primacy effect a perceptual error in which we quickly form an opinion of people based on the first information we receive about them

Primacy effect relates to the saying that "first impressions are lasting impressions." It is our tendency to quickly form an opinion of people based on the first information we receive about them. This rapid perceptual organization fulfills our need to make sense of others and provides a convenient anchor to integrate subsequent information. For example, if we first meet someone who avoids eye contact and speaks softly, we quickly conclude that the person is bashful. It is easier to remember the person as bashful than to recall the specific behaviors exhibited during the first encounter.

Under the right circumstances, primacy effect can be beneficial. Many organizations take extra care to ensure that customers have a positive first experience. They also make sure that employees have a good first impression when they join the firm. Later, customers and employees are more likely to tolerate and forget minor organizational conflicts if they have already established a positive first impression. Unfortunately, once an inaccurate first impression is established, it is difficult to change because people pay less attention to subsequent information after the impression has been formed and they tend to completely ignore information that contradicts the first impression.[56] Thus, the person we think is bashful will have difficulty shaking this first impression.

Recency Effect

recency effect a perceptual error in which the most recent information dominates our perception about the person

The **recency effect** occurs when the most recent information dominates our perception of others.[57] This effect is stronger than the primacy effect when there is a long delay between the time when the first impression is formed and the person is evaluated. In other words, the most recent information has the greater influence on our perception of someone when the first impression has worn off with the passage of time.

The recency effect is found in performance appraisals, for which supervisors must recall every employee's performance over the previous year. Recent performance information dominates the evaluation because it is the most easily recalled. Some employees are well aware of the recency effect and use it to their advantage by getting their best work on the manager's desk just before the performance appraisal is conducted.

The folks at Starbucks Coffee know that you never get a second chance to make a good first impression. That's why they put a lot of effort into welcoming new employees. The Seattle-based coffee company hires about 500 people each month across its 1,600 stores. Yet new recruits repeatedly hear how much they're valued during the 24 hours of training in their first 80 hours of employment. The company hopes that this initial first impression will help newcomers form a clear idea that Starbucks cares about them and their contribution to the company. "I think you have to engage the employee early on by sharing how much you care about what you do," explains Howard Schultz, Starbucks' CEO and chairman. "For people joining the company, we try to define what Starbucks stands for, what we're trying to achieve, and why that's relevant to them."[58] In what other ways can the primacy effect be beneficial in organizational settings?

[Corbis/Wolfgang Kaehler]

Halo Error

halo error a perceptual error whereby our general impression of a person, usually based on one prominent characteristic, biases our perception of other characteristics of that person

Halo error occurs when our general impression of a person, usually based on one prominent characteristic, colors our perception of other characteristics of that person.[59] If we meet a client who speaks in a friendly manner, we tend to infer a host of other favorable qualities about that person. If a colleague doesn't complete tasks on time, we tend to view his or her other traits unfavorably. In each case, one trait important to the perceiver forms a general impression, and this impression becomes the basis for judgments about other traits. Halo error is most likely to occur when concrete information about the perceived target is missing or we are not sufficiently motivated to search for it.[60] Instead, we use our general impression of the person to fill in the missing information.

Halo error has received considerable attention in research on performance appraisal ratings.[61] Consider the situation in which two employees have the same level of work quality, quantity of work, and customer relations performance, but one tends to be late for work. Tardiness might not be an important factor in work performance, but the supervisor has a negative impression of employees who are late for work. Halo error would cause the supervisor to rate the tardy employee lower on *all* performance dimensions because the tardiness created a negative general impression of that employee. The punctual employee would tend to receive higher ratings on *all* performance dimensions even though his or her performance level is really the same as that of the tardy employee. Consequently, halo error distorts our judgments and can result in poor decision making.

Projection Bias

projection bias a perceptual error in which we tend to believe that other people hold the same beliefs and attitudes that we do

Projection bias occurs when we believe other people have the same beliefs and behaviors that we do.[62] If you are eager for a promotion, you might think that others in your position are similarly motivated. If you are thinking of quitting your job, you start to believe that other people are also thinking of quitting.

Projection bias is usually a defense mechanism to protect our self-esteem. If we break a work rule, projection justifies this infraction by claiming that "everyone does it." We feel more comfortable with the thought that our negative traits exist in others, so we are quick to believe that others also have these traits. Similarly, projection maintains the credibility of our goals and objectives. When we want an organizational policy changed, we tend to believe that others also have this goal.

Improving Perceptions

We can't bypass the perceptual process, but we should make every attempt to minimize perceptual biases and distortions. As we learned earlier, perceptual biases potentially cause employment discrimination as well as the stress and career limitations that go with this problem. Perceptual biases also threaten the organization's survival. When employees screen out or perceptually distort information about the organization's environment, they cannot make the best decisions to keep the organizational system aligned with that environment. This section introduces five strategies to improve our perceptions: introducing diversity management programs, learning to empathize with others, postponing our impression of others, comparing our perceptions with others, and becoming more aware of our values, beliefs, and prejudices.

Diversity Management Programs

In Chapter 1 we learned that the labor force has become more diverse. Moreover, companies acquire a more diverse workforce as they extend operations globally. The challenge for corporate leaders is to leverage the benefits of this diversity while minimizing the perceptual and behavior problems that tend to accompany heterogeneity. "We see language differences, religious differences, the graying of the workforce," says Elaine Grossinger Eddis, the first woman president of the American Hotel and Motel Association. "It's a business imperative to get people to work together."[63]

To get employees to work together more effectively, over 75 percent of Fortune 500 companies, as well as many smaller organizations, have introduced diversity management programs. Typically, these training programs serve two purposes. First, they communicate the value of diversity. For example, participants learn how a multicultural workforce potentially improves corporate decision making and customer service. Second, diversity management programs help participants become aware of their perceptual biases and gives them more accurate information about people with different backgrounds.

Diversity management sessions are not intended to correct deep-rooted prejudice or intolerance. In fact, they could make matters worse because highly prejudiced employees are likely to view these sessions as a form of coercion if they are required to attend them.[64] Rather, they help employees learn, and eventually overcome, the more subtle forms of bias that emerge from distorted stereotypes. As Connections 6.1 describes, employees at Barnett Bank (now with NationsBank) have benefited from diversity management programs in their relations with co-workers and clients.

Diversity management programs typically include interpersonal exercises because participants need to experience their subtle biases in order to correct them. In one such exercise, small teams of employees with diverse backgrounds (including one "blind" person who is blindfolded) are assigned a challenging task, such as building a miniature water system. While the teams are focused on building a system that doesn't leak, the judges evaluate them on how well they work productively together. If the blind person or any other team member is left out, the team loses. Some participants don't realize their exclusionary behavior until the debriefing session afterwards.[65]

In most organizations, diversity management programs mainly increase employee awareness of differences. More awareness can be helpful, but some experts are calling on companies to introduce the "next level," that is, moving beyond awareness to a deeper level of understanding and sensitivity. There isn't a single solution on how to do this, but one strategy is through greater interaction. At Hoechst Celanese, each of the company's top two dozen officers joined two organizations in which they are an ethnic minority. "The only way to break out of the comfort zones is to be exposed to other people," explains Ernest Drew, CEO of the large chemical company. Adds vice president Charles

Connections 6.1 ◻ Diversity Management at Barnett Bank

Anthony Robinson shares some of his thoughts during a diversity management workshop for Barnett Bank employees in Fort Lauderdale, Florida.
[With permission of Knight-Ridder Tribune]

At a recent diversity awareness session, Maureen O'Neil learned that Haitians avoid eye contact as a sign of respect, not evasiveness. "You do think of someone not looking at you in the eye as looking a bit sneaky or having something to hide," acknowledges the employee of Barnett Bank (now with NationsBank). She adds that the training session made her more aware of these differences. "You learn not to prejudge people."

Barnett Bank's workforce and clientele have become more diverse, so the Fort Lauderdale-based financial institution is preparing employees for this emerging reality through diversity awareness training. Barnett employee Mauro Sabarillo believes diversity awareness training will improve cross-cultural relations among employees at the bank. "I'm glad Barnett Bank has developed this training," says the Philippine-born Sabarillo, "because even where I work, you can sometimes feel some tension in the air."

Anthony Robinson agrees. The African-American teller at Barnett Bank says he has faced lifelong discrimination in the workplace. "The banking industry doesn't tend to value diversity, so I was pleasantly surprised that Barnett is taking the initiative," says Robinson.

Along with the diversity training sessions, Barnett Bank measures progress toward diversity awareness through a "Diversity Report Card" with information from employee surveys. It also has a Diversity Council made up of senior and midlevel officers, including the corporate ombudsman, that sets the direction of new diversity initiatives.

In spite of the optimism from Barnett's employees, diversity consultants recognize that these programs do not dissolve prejudices or stereotypes overnight. Rather, they make people aware of their differences and begin the journey toward tolerance and ultimately acceptance of these differences.

"You can't change a person's feelings overnight," explains Isabel Fernandez, a Barnett Bank diversity trainer. "What [diversity training] does is start a lot of dialogue that may not normally occur."

Source: Adapted from F. Santiago, "Diversity Awareness Makes Inroads into Corporate Culture," *Houston Chronicle*, February 16, 1997, p. 3; S. Caudron and C. Hayes, "Are Diversity Programs Benefiting African Americans?" *Black Enterprise*, February 1997, pp. 121–32. ◼

Langston, "Joining these organizations has been more helpful to me than two weeks of diversity training."[66]

Another form of interaction is to improve communication through formal dialogue sessions. Dialogue is based on the idea that people develop a common mental model as they continually engage in conversations to understand each other.[67] American President Lines (APL) got serious about dialoguing after its diversity awareness program had limited success. Several employees were trained as facilitators in dialogue. Then they recruited other employees to be involved in the year-long series of dialogue sessions. "It's amazing how when the session is over, we find ways to access each other and we see each other differently," says Ralph Dechabert, APL's director of diversity and employee development.[68]

Digital Equipment Corporation has been a leader in diversity management with its "Valuing Differences Program." One of its pioneering practices has been to encourage dialogue among employees from different cultural backgrounds. These groups meet regularly to discuss and learn to appreciate their differences.[69] How would dialoguing relate to the perceptual errors that were introduced in this chapter? [Courtesy of Digital Equipment Corp.]

empathy a person's ability to understand and be sensitive to the feelings, thoughts, and situation of others

Empathize with Others

Moving to the "next level" in diversity management programs involves learning how to empathize with people from different backgrounds. **Empathy** refers to a person's ability to understand and be sensitive to the feelings, thoughts, and situation of others. This is particularly useful for reducing attribution errors because empathy makes us more sensitive to external causes of another person's performance and behavior.[70]

Empathy comes naturally to some people. However, the rest of us can develop empathy skills by receiving feedback on how well we seem to empathize.[71] Another approach is to work closely with others and spend time participating in their environment. For instance, directors and employees at Memorial Health System in South Bend, Indiana, participate in three or four "plunges" each year so that they keep in touch with the local community. Plunges are outreach projects, such as assisting seniors or helping to rebuild a neighborhood, that put Memorial's staff closer to people in the community. "Our goal is to provide an education, an experience, so we are not working off statistics, but instead can put a name and face to an issue," says Phil Newbold, Memorial's president and CEO.[72]

Along with community plunges, some corporate leaders are spending time in the jobs performed by their employees. As Connections 6.2 describes, these activities increase the leader's empathy with employees and clients by "walking in their shoes."

Postpone Impression Formation

It is very tempting to put people into boxes as soon as possible. After all, the sooner we have labeled them, the sooner we can simplify the world and reduce the tension of uncertainty. Unfortunately, this practice of forming impressions with limited information forces us to rely on inaccurate and overgeneralized stereotypes. A much better perceptual strategy is to postpone impression formation until more information is collected about the individual or situation. By delaying closure, we rely less on stereotyped inferences to understand others.

When working with people from different cultural backgrounds, for instance, we should constantly challenge our stereotypic expectations and actively seek out contrary information. By blocking the effects of stereotypes, first impressions, and other perceptual blinders, we are better able to engage in a developmental learning process that forms a better understanding of others.[73]

Connections 6.2 ◾ Increasing Empathy by Being There

Miami-Dade Schools superintendent Roger Cuevas (center) and other corporate leaders are bringing their perceptions back into focus by working alongside other employees and customers.
[C. W. Griffin. With permission of the Miami Herald.]

As superintendent of Miami-Dade Schools, Roger Cuevas has his hands full with administration and politics. He also has his hands full of dough—teaching adult vocational students the fine art of baking.

Along with his regular duties, Cuevas has been guest teaching in dozens of schools. Today, he donned a baker's hat and taught culinary arts students how to bake Cuban bread. Next month, he visits five elementary schools to teach reading. It's part of Cuevas's campaign to make classrooms, rather than school bureaucracy, the center of attention. It's also an effective way for him to understand the real issues in the organization he leads.

Many executives and professionals are developing a better empathy for employees and customers by spending time in front-line jobs. Senior management at Continental Airlines become flight attendants and reservation agents every three or four months. Corporate leaders at AES Corp. work in the electrical plants for a week each year. "We felt we had to do this to give us a feel for what that operating experience was like," explains AES cofounder Roger Sant.

One of the most enthusiastic supporters of working in front-line jobs is William Malec, chief financial officer of the Tennessee Valley Authority. Malec devotes one day each month scrubbing toilets, sorting mail, or performing other nonmanagement jobs while hearing the concerns of employees who work in that department.

A vivid illustration of his perceptual awakening came one day when Malec delivered mail to a manager who was always sugary sweet when Malec served in his chief financial officer job. But the manager didn't recognize Malec in his temporary role as mailroom employee, and rudely snubbed him. The incident helped Malec see that reality looks different from the top of the corporate ladder. The abrupt manager also learned in his next performance review how to improve his behavior toward employees.

Sources: Adapted from J. M. Farrell, "Schools Chief Teaches How to Make Career Rise," *Miami Herald*, January 23, 1998, pp. B1–B2; L. Rittenhouse, "Roger W. Sant: Visionary Internationalist," *Electricity Journal*, January–February 1998, pp. 40–47; J. M. Feldman, "Structure," *Air Transport World*, November 1994, pp. 30–38; T. Gutner, "Meeting the Boss," *Forbes*, March 1, 1993, p. 126. ◾

Compare Perceptions with Others

Another useful way to reduce perceptual bias is to compare our perceptions with the perceptions other people have about the same target. By sharing perceptions, we learn different points of view and potentially gain a better understanding of the situation. If our colleagues have different backgrounds but similar perceptions of the situation, then there is reason to be more confident in our interpretation. Of course, there is no way to know for sure that our perceptions are correct, but they are less likely to be wrong if people with different backgrounds have the same general interpretation of the situation.

Know Yourself: Applying the Johari Window

A powerful way to minimize perceptual biases is to know yourself—to become more aware of your values, beliefs, and prejudices.[74] For example, suppose that you dislike a particular client who treated you badly a few years ago. If the client meets with you to reestablish the relationship, you might be more open-minded about this business opportunity if you are conscious of these emotions. Moreover, if your colleagues are also aware of your unique values and past experiences, they are more likely to understand your actions and help you to improve in the future. If you act harshly toward the troublesome client, for example, your colleagues are likely to understand the reason for your behavior and draw this to your attention.

Johari Window a model of personal and interpersonal understanding that encourages disclosure and feedback to increase the open area and reduce the blind, hidden, and unknown areas of oneself

The **Johari Window** is a popular model for understanding how co-workers can increase their mutual understanding.[75] Developed by Joseph Luft and Harry Ingram (hence the name *Johari*), this model divides information about yourself into four "Windows"—open, blind, hidden, and unknown—based on whether your own values, beliefs, and experiences are known to you and to others.

As we see in Exhibit 6.6, the *open area* includes information about you that is known both to you and others. For example, both you and your co-workers may be aware that you don't like to be near people who smoke cigarettes. The *blind area* refers to information that is known to others but not to yourself. For example, your colleagues might notice that you are embarrassed and awkward

Exhibit 6.6
Johari Window

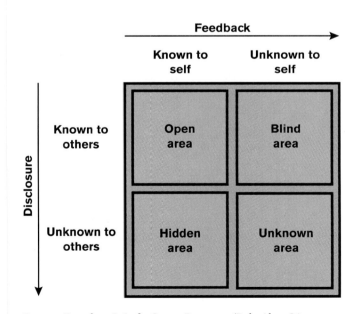

Source: Based on J. Luft, *Group Processes* (Palo Alto, CA: Mayfield, 1984).

when meeting someone confined to a wheelchair, but you are unaware of this fact. Information known to you but unknown to others is found in the *hidden area*. We all have personal secrets about our likes, dislikes, and personal experiences. Finally, the *unknown area* includes your values, beliefs, and experiences that aren't known to you or others.

The main objective of the Johari Window is to increase the size of the open area so that both you and colleagues are aware of your perceptual limitations. This is partly accomplished by reducing the hidden area through *disclosure*—informing others of your beliefs, feelings, and experiences that may influence the work relationship. Disclosure must be reciprocal among team members; that is, they should provide information about themselves as you reveal information about yourself. Fortunately, self-disclosure by one person tends to cause others to make a self-disclosure.[76] The open area also increases through *feedback* from others about your behaviors. This information helps you to reduce your blind area, because co-workers often see things in you that you do not see. Finally, the combination of disclosure and feedback occasionally produces revelations about information in the unknown area.

Johari Window in practice   The Johari Window can be found in the diversity awareness programs that we described earlier. By learning about cultural differences and communicating more with co-workers from different backgrounds, we gain a better understanding of their behavior patterns. The 360-degree feedback process, described in Chapter 2, also applies to the Johari Window process because it represents a structured way to provide feedback from others.

A third strategy is to engage in open dialogue with co-workers. As we communicate with others, we naturally tend to disclose more information about ourselves and eventually feel comfortable providing candid feedback to them. Swedbank followed this approach soon after it was created out of mergers with 11 Swedish savings banks. Consultants helped the 17 members of the executive team to achieve a level of openness through ongoing discussion. Although initially reluctant to give each other feedback, the executives eventually engaged in open debates about the strengths and weaknesses of executives in the group.[77]

The Johari Window may work well in some situations, but the model ignores cultural differences in openness, egalitarianism, and face-saving. It is more difficult to implement in Asia, for example, where feedback and self-disclosure are less acceptable than in the United States. Similarly, some colleagues from Mexico may have difficulty with the Johari Window because of their stronger cultural norm of saving face. Lastly, in any country, we must remember that everyone needs to have a hidden self. Unfortunately, some individual development practices cross this ethical boundary by trying to invade that private space (see Chapter 15).

No matter which steps are taken to improve the perceptual process, we need to recognize that our perceptions of the world are partly structured by our personality. In fact, an individual's personality traits play a pervasive role in almost every aspect of organizational behavior, from learning processes to one's willingness to adopt a company's cultural values. Let's now turn to the topic of personality in organizations.

Personality in Organizations

Steve Jobs is a personality to reckon with in the high-technology industry. Some have described the founder of Apple Computer, Pixar Animation Studios, and Next Computers as an intimidating, mercurial dictator—an individualistic egomaniac who pushes everyone too hard. His intensity, arrogance,

Steve Jobs's personality is a driving force behind the success of Pixar Animation Studios and the turnaround of Apple Computer. Some say he is a mercurial dictator, while others claim his wilder personality traits have mellowed over the years. Why do we describe Jobs and other people in terms of their personality? Are we usually accurate in our perceptions of personality?

[Reuters/Mousse Archive Photos]

and obscenity-laced tirades are infamous. Others say that Jobs is charismatic and charming. His wilder personality traits have mellowed over the years, particularly after being fired from Apple in the mid-1980s and experiencing difficulties with Next Computers. "He is more tolerant, less impatient—the kinds of things you would expect that come with age," says a long-time acquaintance.[78]

It is difficult to describe Steve Jobs—or anyone else—without referring to the concept of **personality.** Personality refers to the relatively stable pattern of behaviors and consistent internal states that explain a person's behavioral tendencies.[79] Personality has both internal and external elements. The external traits are the observable behaviors that we rely on to identify someone's personality. For example, we can observe Steve Jobs's sociability by how often he interacts with other people and how comfortable he acts in those social settings. The internal states represent the thoughts, values, and genetic characteristics that we infer from the observable behaviors.

An individual's personality is relatively stable. If it changes at all, it is only after a very long time or as the result of traumatic events. Personality explains behavioral tendencies, because a person's behavior is influenced by the situation as well as personality traits. Personality traits are less evident in situations where social norms, reward systems, and other conditions constrain our behavior.[80] For example, talkative people spend much of their time in conversations when free to do so, but not when they are explicitly told to keep quiet.

An individual's personality is both inherited and shaped from the environment.[81] Our personality is partly inherited genetically from our parents. However, these genetic personality characteristics are altered somewhat by life experiences. Steve Jobs's personality is partly handed down genetically from

personality personality refers to the relatively stable pattern of behaviors and consistent internal states that explain a person's behavioral tendencies

his parents, but it has also been shaped by a variety of life experiences, such as the traumatic events of being fired from the company he cofounded (Apple Computer) and the difficulties of his subsequent venture, Next Computers.

Personality and Organizational Behavior

Most people use personality traits to describe colleagues and anticipate their future behavior. But does personality really help us to understand behavior in organizational settings? At one time, the answer seemed obvious. Scholars commonly explained employee behavior in terms of personality traits, and companies regularly administered personality tests to job applicants.

Then, in the 1960s, researchers reported that there is a very weak relationship between personality and job performance.[82] They cited problems with measuring personality traits and explained that the connection between personality and performance exists only under very narrowly defined conditions. Companies stopped using personality tests due to concerns that these tests might unfairly discriminate against people of color and other identifiable groups.

Over the past decade, personality has regained some of its credibility in organizational settings.[83] Recent studies have reported that certain personality traits predict certain work-related behaviors, stress reactions, and emotions fairly well under certain conditions. Scholars have reintroduced the idea that effective leaders have identifiable traits and that personality explains some of a person's positive attitudes and life happiness. Perhaps most important is that personality traits seem to help people find the jobs that best suit their needs. Many organizations use personality tests to help them become more aware of themselves (rather like the Johari Window described earlier) and find better career directions.[84]

Does this mean that companies should rely on personality tests to hire people? Probably not. At best, specific personality measures might supplement current selection methods. One reason for this caveat is that a person's skills, work experience, and previous job performance are usually better than abstract personality traits at predicting on-the-job behavior and performance.[85] In other words, how you acted in your previous job is a better indicator of your future behavior than the score on a personality test.

There are also ongoing concerns about the accuracy of personality tests. Some tests are fairly easy to fake and some traits are so broadly defined that it's difficult to measure them accurately. For these reasons, many test developers warn that their measures should be used for counseling and development, not selecting job applicants and other forms of evaluation.[86] With these caveats in mind, let's look at the main personality traits and dimensions currently studied in organizational settings.

"Big Five" Personality Dimensions

Since the days of Plato, scholars have been trying to develop lists of personality traits. However, about 100 years ago a few personality experts tried to catalog and condense the many personality traits that had been described over the years. They found thousands of words in *Roget's Thesaurus* and *Webster's Dictionary* that represented personality traits. They aggregated these words into 171 clusters, then further reduced them to five abstract personality dimensions. Using more sophisticated techniques, a recent investigation identified the same five dimensions—known as the **"Big Five" personality dimensions**.[87] As Exhibit 6.7 shows, these five dimensions include:

• *Conscientiousness*—**Conscientiousness** refers to people who are careful, dependable, and self-disciplined. Some scholars argue that this dimension also includes the will to achieve, rather like the need for achievement described in

"Big Five" personality dimensions the five abstract personality dimensions under which most personality traits are represented. They are conscientiousness, emotional stability, openness to experience, agreeableness, and extroversion

conscientiousness a "Big Five" personality dimension that characterizes people who are careful, dependable, and self-disciplined

Exhibit 6.7
The "Big Five"
personality traits

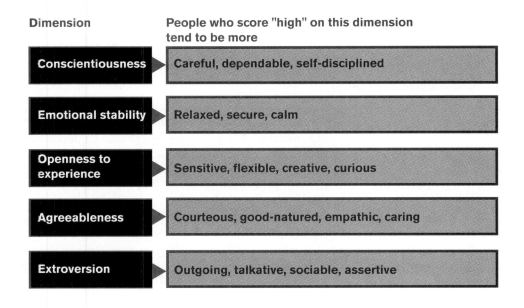

Dimension	People who score "high" on this dimension tend to be more
Conscientiousness	Careful, dependable, self-disciplined
Emotional stability	Relaxed, secure, calm
Openness to experience	Sensitive, flexible, creative, curious
Agreeableness	Courteous, good-natured, empathic, caring
Extroversion	Outgoing, talkative, sociable, assertive

Chapter 3. People with low conscientiousness tend to be careless, less thorough, more disorganized, and irresponsible.

• *Emotional stability*—People with high emotional stability are poised, secure, and calm. Those with emotional instability tend to be depressed, anxious, indecisive, and subject to mood swings.

• *Openness to experience*—This dimension is the most complex and has the least agreement among scholars. It generally refers to the extent that people are sensitive, flexible, creative, and curious. Those who score low on this dimension tend to be more resistant to change, less open to new ideas, and more fixed in their ways.

• *Agreeableness*—This includes the traits of being courteous, good-natured, empathic, and caring. Some scholars prefer the label of "friendly compliance" for this dimension, with its opposite being "hostile noncompliance." People with low agreeableness tend to be uncooperative, short-tempered, and irritable.

• *Extroversion*—**Extroversion** characterizes people who are outgoing, talkative, sociable, and assertive. The opposite is **introversion**, which refers to those who are quiet, shy, and cautious. This does not mean that introverts lack social skills. Rather, they are more inclined to direct their interests to ideas than to social events. Introverts feel quite comfortable being alone, whereas extroverts do not.

Several studies have found that these personality dimensions affect work-related behavior and job performance.[88] Champions of organizational change (people who effectively gain support for new organizational systems and practices) seem to have high levels of the five personality dimensions described above.[89] People with high emotional stability tend to work better than others in high stressor situations. Those with high agreeableness tend to handle customer relations and conflict-based situations more effectively.

Conscientiousness has taken center stage as the most valuable personality trait for predicting job performance in almost every job group. Conscientious employees set higher personal goals for themselves and have higher performance expectations than employees with low levels of conscientiousness. Moreover, as we learned in Chapter 2, employees with high conscientiousness tend to engage in more organizational citizenship behaviors. Conscientious employees are necessary for emerging organizational structures that rely on empowerment rather than the traditional "command and control" system. This

extroversion a "Big Five" personality dimension that characterizes people who are outgoing, talkative, sociable, and assertive

introversion a "Big Five" personality dimension that characterizes people who are quiet, shy, and cautious

personality trait also plays an important role in customer service, along with agreeableness and emotional stability.[90]

Jung's Psychological Types and the Myers-Briggs Type Indicator

Myers-Briggs Type Indicator (MBTI) a personality test based on Jung's theory that identifies people into sixteen types based on how they focus their attention, collect information, process and evaluate information, and orient themselves to the outer world

During the 1920s, Swiss psychiatrist Carl Jung proposed a personality theory that identifies the way people prefer to perceive their environment as well as obtain and process information. Twenty years later, the mother and daughter team of Katherine Briggs and Isabel Briggs-Myers developed the **Myers-Briggs Type Indicator (MBTI),** a personality test that measures each of the traits in Jung's model.[91]

The MBTI measures how people prefer to focus their attention (extroversion versus introversion), collect information (sensing versus intuition), process and evaluate information (thinking versus feeling), and orient themselves to the outer world (judging versus perceiving). Extroversion and introversion were discussed in the previous section, so let's examine the other dimensions:

• *Sensing/Intuition*—Some people like collecting information through their five senses. Sensing types use an organized structure to acquire factual and preferably quantitative details. In contrast, intuitive people collect information nonsystematically. They rely more on subjective evidence as well as their intuition and sheer inspiration. Sensers are capable of synthesizing large amounts of seemingly random information to form quick conclusions.

• *Thinking/Feeling*—Thinking types rely on rational cause-effect logic and the scientific method (see Appendix A) to make decisions. They weigh the evidence objectively and unemotionally. Feeling types, on the other hand, consider how their choices affect others. They weigh the options against their personal values more than rational logic.

• *Judging/Perceiving*—Some people prefer order and structure in their relationship with the outer world. These judging types enjoy the control of decision making and want to resolve problems quickly. In contrast, perceiving types are more flexible. They like to adapt spontaneously to events as they unfold and want to keep their options open.

The MBTI questionnaire combines the four pairs of traits into 16 distinct types. For example, corporate executives tend to be ESTJs, meaning that they are extroverted, sensing, thinking, and judging types. Each of the 16 types has its strengths and weaknesses. ENTJs are considered natural leaders, ISFJs have a high sense of duty, and so on. Also, these types indicate a person's preferences, not the way they necessarily behave all of the time.

Effectiveness of the MBTI

Is the MBTI useful in organizations? Many business leaders think so. The MBTI is one of the most widely used personality tests. It is used by most counseling centers for career assessment. Many organizations also use this instrument to select people for particular positions. It is so popular in some companies that employees are encouraged to reveal their four-letter type so that co-workers can better understand their personality.

Yet, in spite of its popularity, evidence regarding the effectiveness of the MBTI and Jung's psychological types is mixed.[92] The MBTI does a reasonably good job of measuring Jung's psychological types. There is also some indication that a person's type predicts his or her preferences for particular occupations. For example, people who score high on intuition tend to prefer careers in advertising, the arts, and teaching. Some popular press sources claim that the MBTI predicts business success; one indirect analysis of a dozen successful people who founded successful firms (e.g., Sony, Price Club, Microsoft, Honda) determined that all were intuitive thinkers.[93] However, other evidence

At a recent semiannual retreat in Maine, employees at Thompson Doyle Hennessey & Everest did more than run rapids. Everyone at the Boston real estate company completed the Myers-Briggs Type Indicator and learned how their personalities can help them to more effectively relate to each other. For example, the assessments revealed that salespeople don't mind working in a crazed atmosphere, whereas support staff prefer a calmer environment. Both groups now understand each other better.[95] How is the MBTI being used here? Is this an effective use of this instrument?
[Courtesy of Thompson, Doyle, Hennessey & Everest]

is less supportive regarding the MBTI's ability to predict job performance.[94] Overall, the MBTI seems to be useful for career development and self-awareness, but probably should not be used in selecting job applicants.

Other Personality Traits

The Big Five personality dimensions and the MBTI don't capture every personality trait. A few others are frequently cited in the organizational behavior literature, such as the Type A and Type B behavior patterns, described in Chapter 5, and the learned needs introduced in Chapter 3. Two other personality traits that you should know are locus of control and self-monitoring.

locus of control a personality trait referring to the extent that people believe what happens to them is within their control

Locus of control
Locus of control refers to a generalized belief about the amount of control people have over their own lives. Individuals who feel that they are very much in charge of their own destiny have an *internal locus of control;* those who think that events in their life are due mainly to fate or luck have an *external locus of control.* Of course, externals believe that they control many specific events in their lives—such as opening a door or serving a familiar customer—but they have a general belief that outside forces guide their fate. This is particularly apparent in new situations in which the person's control over events is uncertain.

People perform better in most employment situations when they have a moderately strong internal locus of control. They tend to be more successful in their careers and earn more money than their external counterparts. Internals are also more satisfied with their jobs, cope better in stressful situations, and are more motivated by performance-based reward systems.[96]

Internals are particularly well suited to leadership positions and other jobs requiring initiative, independent action, complex thinking, and high motivation. Two studies reported that firms led by internals pursued more innovative strategies than firms led by executives with a more external locus of control. The internals invested more in research and development, introduced new products more quickly than the competition, and made more drastic product line changes. They also pursued more aggressive strategies and planned further into the future.[97]

self-monitoring a personality trait referring to the extent that people are sensitive to situational cues and can readily adapt their own behavior appropriately

Self-monitoring **Self-monitoring** refers to an individual's level of sensitivity and ability to adapt to situational cues. High self-monitors can adjust their behavior quite easily and therefore show little stability in other underlying personality traits. In contrast, low self-monitors are more likely to reveal their moods and personal characteristics, so it is relatively easy to predict their behavior from one situation to the next.[98]

The self-monitoring personality trait has been identified as a significant factor in many organizational activities. Employees who are high self-monitors tend to be better conversationalists, better organizational leaders, and better in boundary-spanning positions (i.e., positions in which incumbents work with people in different departments or organizations). They are also more likely than low self-monitors to be promoted within the organization and to receive better jobs elsewhere.[99]

Self-monitoring, locus of control, conscientiousness, and the many other personality traits help to explain the dynamics of organizational behavior. At the same time, we must be careful about using personality traits to oversimplify a more complex world. Too often, we see problems as "personality clashes" rather than diagnosing the situation to discover the underlying causes. These labels can become perceptual blinders that label people even after their personal dispositions have changed. As Nobel prize-winning scholar Herbert Simon warned many years ago, personality is often overused as "a magical slogan to charm away the problems that our intellectual tools don't handle."[100] Personality is only one of the many concepts that we need to understand in organizational behavior.

Chapter Summary

Perception involves selecting, organizing, and interpreting information to make sense of the world. Selective attention is influenced by characteristics of the target, the target's setting, and the perceiver. Perceptual grouping principles organize incoming information. This is also influenced by our emotions and existing mental models.

According to social identity theory, people perceive themselves by their unique characteristics and membership in various groups. They also develop homogeneous, and usually positive, images of people in their own groups, and usually less positive homogeneous images of people in other groups. This leads to overgeneralizations and stereotypes.

Stereotyping is the process of assigning traits to people based on their membership in a social category. Stereotyping economizes mental effort and fills in missing information, but it often results in incorrect perceptions about others. These misperceptions may lead to prejudice, employment discrimination, and harassment.

The attribution process involves deciding whether the behavior or event is largely due to the situation (external attributions) or personal characteristics (internal attributions). Two attribution errors are fundamental attribution error and self-serving bias.

Self-fulfilling prophecy occurs when our expectations about another person cause that person to act in a way that is consistent with those expectations.

We can improve our perceptions in organizational settings through diversity awareness programs, empathizing with others, postponing our impression of others, comparing our perceptions with others, and becoming more aware of our values, beliefs, and prejudices. Diversity management programs communicate the value of diversity and increase awareness of perceptual biases, but they do not correct deep-rooted prejudices.

Personality refers to the relatively stable pattern of behaviors and consistent internal states that explain a person's behavioral tendencies. It is shaped by both heredity and environmental factors. Personality traits are important for some job design activities, championing organizational change, and matching people to jobs. However, some concerns remain about relying too heavily on personality traits to understand and predict behavior in organizations.

Most personality traits are represented within the "Big Five" personality dimensions: conscientiousness, emotional stability, openness to experience, agreeableness, and extroversion. Based on Jung's theory of psychological types, the Myers-Brigg Type Indicator measures how people prefer to focus their attention, collect information, process and evaluate information, and orient themselves to the outer world. Locus of control and self-monitoring are two other traits that influence organizational behavior.

Key Terms

Discussion Questions

1. You are part of a task force to increase worker responsiveness to emergencies on the production floor. Identify four factors that should be considered when installing a device that will get every employee's attention when there is an emergency.

2. Erie Publishing Inc. has just acquired a major competitor in the industry. Although senior executives expected a smooth transition, they soon discovered that employees at each company viewed each other with suspicion and had generally negative perceptions of each other's skills and motives. Use social identity theory to explain why this problem exists.

3. During a diversity management session, a manager suggests that stereotypes are a necessary part of working with others. "I have to make assumptions about what's in the other person's head, and stereotypes help me do that," he explains. "It's better to rely on stereotypes than to enter a working relationship with someone from another culture without any idea of what they believe in!" Discuss the merits and problems of the manager's statement.

4. At the end of an NHL hockey game, the coach of the losing team is asked what happened. "I dunno," he begins. "We've done well in this rink over the past few years. Our busy schedule over the past two weeks has pushed the guys too hard, I guess. They're worn out. You probably noticed that we also got some bad breaks on penalties tonight. We should have done well here, but things just went against us." Use attribution theory to explain the coach's perceptions of the team's loss.

5. Self-fulfilling prophecies are common in organizations, but much of the research originated in schools. Discuss how this perceptual process occurs in a college course. How might instructors use self-fulfilling prophecy beneficially?

6. You are the leader of a newly formed project team that will work closely together over the next three months. The seven team members are drawn from as many worldwide offices. They do not know each other and come from different professional specializations. Describe the activities of a one-day retreat that would minimize perceptual errors and potential communication problems among the team members.

7. Nile Technologies Inc. wants to hire employees for its new production plant. Employees will have a high degree of autonomy because the plant uses self-directed work teams. The work also requires employees who are careful because the materials are sensitive to mishandling. Identify one personality trait from the Big Five that may be appropriate for selecting people for

these jobs. Describe the trait and fully explain your answer.

8. Look over the four pairs of psychological types in the Myers-Briggs Type Indicator and identify the personality type (i.e., use four letters) that would be best for a student in this course. Would this type be appropriate for students in other fields of study (e.g., biology, fine arts) or in graduate programs?

CASE STUDY

Nupath Foods Inc.

James Ornath, vice-president of marketing at Nupath Foods, Inc., read the latest sales figures with a great deal of satisfaction. He was pleased to see that the marketing campaign to improve sagging sales of Prowess cat food was working. Sales volume of the product had increased 20 percent in the past quarter compared with the previous year, and market share was up.

The improved sales of Prowess could be credited to Denise Washington, the brand manager responsible for cat foods at Nupath. Washington had joined Nupath less than two years ago as an assistant brand manager after leaving a similar job at a consumer products firm. She was one of the few women in marketing management at Nupath and had a promising career with the company. Ornath was pleased with Washington's work and tried to let her know this in the annual performance reviews. He now had an excellent opportunity to reward her by offering the recently vacated position of market research coordinator. Although technically only a lateral transfer with a modest salary increase, the marketing research coordinator job would give Washington broader experience in some high-profile work, which would enhance her career with Nupath. Few people were aware that Ornath's own career had been boosted by working as marketing research coordinator at Nupath several years before.

Denise Washington had also seen the latest sales figures on Prowess cat food and was expecting Ornath's call to meet with her that morning. Ornath began the conversation by briefly mentioning the favorable sales figures, and then explained that he wanted Washington to take the marketing research coordinator job. Washington was shocked by the news. She enjoyed brand management and particularly the challenge involved with controlling a product that directly affected the company's profitability. Marketing research coordinator was a technical support position—a "backroom" job—far removed from the company's bottom-line activities. Marketing research was not the route to top management in most organizations, Washington thought. She had been sidelined.

After a long silence, Washington managed a weak "Thank you, Mr. Ornath." She was too bewildered to protest. She wanted to collect her thoughts and reflect on what she had done wrong. Also, she did not know her boss well enough to be openly critical. Ornath recognized Washington's surprise, which he naturally assumed was her positive response to hearing of this wonderful career opportunity. He, too, had been delighted several years earlier about his temporary transfer to marketing research to round out his marketing experience. "This move will be good for both you and Nupath," said Ornath as he escorted Washington from his office.

Washington had several tasks to complete that afternoon, but was able to consider the day's events that evening. She was one of the top women in brand management at Nupath and feared that she was being sidelined because the company didn't want women in top management. Her previous employer had made it quite clear that women "couldn't take the heat" in marketing management and tended to place women in technical support positions after a brief term in lower brand management jobs. Obviously Nupath was following the same game plan. Ornath's comments that the coordinator job would be good for her was just a nice way of saying that Washington couldn't go any further in brand management at Nupath. Washington was now faced with the difficult decision of confronting Ornath and trying to change Nupath's sexist practices or submitting her resignation.

Discussion Questions

1. What symptom(s) exist in this case to suggest that something has gone wrong?

2. What are the root causes that have led to these symptoms?

3. What actions should the organization take to correct these problems?

© Copyright 2000. Steven L. McShane. ▪

How Al Dunlap self-destructed

BusinessWeek

Sunbeam CEO Albert J. Dunlap stormed out of a board meeting in Rockefeller Center, leaving a conference room filled with puzzled and incredulous directors. Most of them thought "Chainsaw Al" was becoming unglued. Bad media coverage about Sunbeam's poor financial situation concerned Dunlap to such an extent that he was convinced the board was out to get him. Sunbeam's board did fire Dunlap, but not until his wild behavior became too much. At an earlier meeting, for example, Dunlap aggressively chastised a board member who had challenged him. Even Dunlap's family had experienced enough of his style. "He got exactly what he deserved," said his sister.

This *Business Week* article describes the events leading up to Dunlap's firing as CEO of Sunbeam. The article provides enough detail to provide an idea about Dunlap's personality. It also reveals how Dunlap misperceived the board's actions which, ironically, led to the actions that Dunlap feared they had already planned. Read through this *Business Week* article at www.mhhe.com/mcshane1e and prepare for the discussion questions below.

Discussion Questions

1. Use the Big Five personality dimensions to describe Al Dunlap's personality. In your opinion, is this personality profile characteristic of an effective leader?

2. This article is a tale of misperceptions. Discuss the perceptual problems that Dunlap and others experienced.

Source: J. A. Byrne, "How Al Dunlap Self-Destructed," *Business Week*, July 6, 1998, pp. 58–63. ■

Black, white, and angry: Racial diversity in the workplace

According to a special NBC poll hardly anyone in this country believes that he or she is getting a fair shake. Nearly half of whites and ⅗ of Black Americans say that they think the system is stacked against them.

Is the system against me?

White	Black
Agree 45%	Agree 58%
Disagree 47%	Disagree 33%
Not Sure 8%	Not Sure 9%

As for job opportunities, there's a big split. Three-fourths of whites think that they are treated equal.

Nearly ¾ of blacks think that they're not. NBC's Joe Johns went to Pasadena, a community with one of the most diverse work forces in the country for an in-depth look at race in the workplace.

Equal job opportunities?

White	Black
Fair and Equal 74%	Fair and Equal 25%
Unequal 20%	Unequal 72%
Not Sure 7%	Not Sure 2%

City workers in Pasadena, California number 131,000, including 61,000 white and 23,000 blacks. Pasadena takes pride in the diversity of its work force. In the most recent survey, 56 percent of the people who worked for the city full time were minorities. On the surface, city workers black and white said they get along pretty well on the job, including those at public works. Gerald King, a line mechanic, said, "It's not really a matter of black and white, it's a matter of everybody, we're a team."

However, when it comes to the daily realities of blacks and whites working together, it's not always about teamwork. Michael Kennedy a black worker in the street department said, "I had a white guy down here this year call me a nigger, that guy right there in that sweeper right there. I went to public action with him and he got four days off work with no pay."

Indeed, for many, dealing with racial issues on the job is not easy. In the finance department at city hall there are more minority employees than whites. Carol Woodward said some whites feel they have to be extra careful with blacks. Woodward, a white woman, said, "I have found some people are worried about offending others with things that they don't think another race would be offended by." Jenny Dennis is concerned because she thinks some people link her race to her job performance. Dennis, a black woman, noted, "I feel that I have to work doubly hard because they are already assuming that I'm going to fail."

In Pasadena's fire department, one of California's most integrated, there are 139 firefighters. There are 111 who are white, 28 are black. Some white city workers argue that the city rewards failure by giving bad candidates good jobs under affirmative action. Mike Barilla, a firefighter paramedic, said, "You know they haven't got the qualifications. There are some people who have

failed and been given a second chance. Whereas persons of the other race who have failed, they've been sent home."

Captain Roy Francis has been a fireman for 15 years. He says some whites feel their race holds them back. Francis said, "Some of them feel that they don't have a chance because they've got this wall up against them. They're white."

Gerda Steele, a black talk show host and diversity consultant, said, "As the playing field becomes more level for everyone, I think a lot of whites feel that it's not as level for them because they have to compete and be able to prove their worth like everybody else." And as the battle heats up over affirmative action, the fear is that there will be even more tension between blacks and whites at work. Pasadena is, like much of America, black, white, and angry.

Discussion Questions

1. In general, what perceptions and assumptions do you think white workers have about black workers? Black workers about white workers?

2. People develop mental models based on their and others' experience. How do you think the Pasadena city workers can change their erroneous mental models about racial differences?

3. Using social identity theory, explain how whites and blacks have developed their perceptions of each other. What key factors influence the current generation's perspectives? ◼

TEAM EXERCISE

Perceptions in a diverse workforce: The Royal Bank of Canada vignettes

Purpose

This exercise is designed to help you understand perceptual issues when working in a diverse workforce.

Instructions

The instructor will play a few vignettes portraying actual events at the Royal Bank of Canada. For each vignette, the class will follow these steps:

Step 1: Watch the vignette, keeping in mind the questions presented below.

Step 2: The instructor will stop the videotape at the appropriate place and the class will discuss the vignette, guided by the following questions (the instructor may ask additional questions):

  a. What is your reaction to this incident?
  b. What is the main issue in this vignette?
  c. What perceptual problems might exist here?
  d. What solutions, if any, would you recommend?

Step 3: After discussing the vignette, the instructor will play the video follow-up so that the class can hear what the Royal Bank of Canada recommends in this situation.

Step 4: Repeat the previous steps for subsequent vignettes in the video program. ◼

SELF-ASSESSMENT EXERCISE

Personality assessment: Jung's psychological types

Purpose

This self-assessment is designed to help you estimate your psychological type within Jung's model.

Instructions

Circle the word in each pair that most appeals to you or seems most characteristic of you. In some cases, both words may appeal to you or seem characteristic of you; in others, neither word may seem characteristic of you or be appealing. Nonetheless, please try to indicate the one word in each pair you prefer. Please work across the page (i.e., begin with the top row across) and answer as quickly as possible. As a rule of thumb, trust your first impressions. After completing this, your instructor will provide instructions on how to score it.

loud–quiet	realistic–intuitive	convincing–touching	systematic–flexible
active–reflective	blueprint–dream	objective–subjective	methodical–curious
gregarious–private	details–pattern	head–heart	organized–spontaneous
outgoing–reserved	sensible–imaginative	just–humane	deliberate–improvising
sociable–detached	practical–creative	principle–passion	exacting–impulsive
external–internal	present–future	fair–tender	definite–tolerant
do–think	factual–symbolic	clarity–harmony	decisive–open-minded
speak–write	specific–general	reason–emotion	plan–adapt
talk–read	formula–hunch	professional–warm	control–freedom
___ ___	___ ___	___ ___	___ ___

Source: B. L. Dilla, G. J. Curphy, R. L. Hughes, R. C. Ginnett, and K. A. Ashley, *Instructor's Manual to Accompany Leadership: Enhancing the Lessons of Experience* (Burr Ridge, IL: Irwin, 1993). ◼

CHAPTER SEVEN

Workplace Emotions, Values, and Ethics

Learning Objectives

After reading this chapter, you should be able to:

- Discuss the linkages between emotions and behavior.
- Outline the model of job satisfaction.
- Discuss the effect of job satisfaction on task performance and customer service.
- Describe five strategies to increase organizational commitment.
- Identify the conditions for and problems with emotional labor.
- Outline the dimensions of emotional intelligence.
- Define the five main values that vary across cultures.
- Describe three ethical principles and other factors influencing ethical behavior.
- Discuss why ethical conduct varies across cultures.

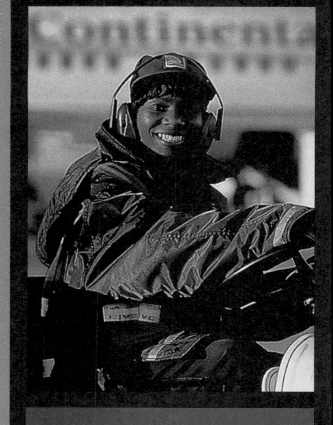

A few years ago, Zack Meza was too embarrassed to tell anyone that he worked for Continental Airlines. "You didn't dare go anywhere with a uniform on," recalls the Minneapolis reservations agent. Continental had become infamous for terrible customer service. Employees suffered through layoffs, two close calls with bankruptcy, and a former CEO whom the U.S. Department of Transportation eventually declared "unfit" to run an airline. Morale and loyalty were so low that some employees had ripped the Continental logo off their uniforms so they wouldn't be identified with the company.

Not any more. In less than three years, Continental has soared "from worst to first" in profitability, service, and morale. The Houston-based carrier has won several service awards and customers are returning in record numbers. Employees proudly wear their uniforms and Continental's company store reports brisk sales of T-shirts and other items bearing Continental's corporate logo.

Gordon Bethune, who became Continental's CEO in the mid-1990s and is credited with leading the turnaround, says that the company's success is based on a good product and employees who like to work there. "There are no successful companies long term that don't have people who like working there," Bethune explains.

Mary Ann Megna, one of Continental's veteran flight attendants, sums up the new attitude. "I've been merged, acquired, furloughed and everything else," she says. "Finally, I've been happy."[1]

ontinental Airlines depends on the emotions, attitudes, and values of its employees to serve customers and make the airline profitable. This chapter explores the dynamics of these three concepts. We begin by learning about emotions in the workplace and their relationship to attitudes and individual behavior in organizational settings. This also covers a basic model of work attitudes. We then look at two work attitudes—job satisfaction and organizational commitment—with particular emphasis on their implications for organizational behavior. Our attention then turns to the emerging organizational behavior topic of managing emotions. We consider the implications of emotional labor as well as the concept of emotional intelligence.

In the latter part of this chapter, we explore individual values at work. The five most commonly studied cultural values are discussed. Then, we look at ethical values and behavior, including specific ethical values, other factors that influence ethical conduct, why ethical behavior varies across cultures, and specific strategies that companies use to improve ethical behavior at work.

Emotions in the Workplace

Emotions permeate organizational life.[2] A team leader is alarmed that critical supplies have not yet arrived. A new employee is proud to tell friends about her new job. A nurse feels sympathy for a patient whose family has not visited the hospital. In each incident, someone has experienced one or more emotions. There are many different emotions, although scholars have organized them into the six categories shown in Exhibit 7.1.[3] These include anger, fear, joy, love, sadness, and surprise. All except one (surprise) of these general emotional categories include various specific emotional experiences. For example, researchers have found that alarm and anxiety cluster together to form the general emotional category called fear.

emotions feelings experienced toward an object, person, or event that create a state of readiness

Emotions are feelings experienced toward an object, person, or event that create a state of readiness.[4] Emotional episodes are communications to ourselves.[5] They make us aware that events have occurred that may affect important personal goals. In fact, strong emotions demand our attention and interrupt our train of thought. They also create a state of readiness to respond

Exhibit 7.1   Types of emotions in the workplace

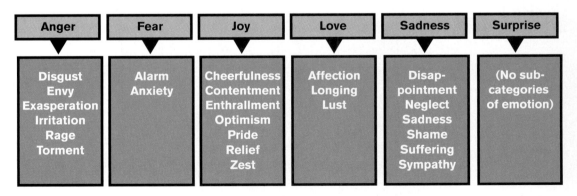

Anger	Fear	Joy	Love	Sadness	Surprise
Disgust Envy Exasperation Irritation Rage Torment	Alarm Anxiety	Cheerfulness Contentment Enthrallment Optimism Pride Relief Zest	Affection Longing Lust	Disappointment Neglect Sadness Shame Suffering Sympathy	(No subcategories of emotion)

Sources: Based on H. M. Weiss and R. Cropanzano, "Affective Events Theory: A Theoretical Discussion of the Structure, Causes, and Consequences of Affective Experiences at Work," *Research in Organizational Behavior* 18 (1996), pp. 1–74; P. Shaver, J. Schwartz, D. Kirson, and C. O'Connor, "Emotion Knowledge: Further Exploration of a Prototype Approach," *Journal of Personality and Social Psychology* 52 (1987), pp. 1061–86.

to those events. In other words, they generate the motivation to act toward the object of our attention.

Emotions are experienced through our thoughts, behaviors, and physiological reactions. A person may experience fear in a stressful situation by mentally sensing it, showing it through facial expressions, and developing a higher heartbeat. Facial expressions and other behaviors play an interactive role in the emotional experience. For example, you tend to smile when feeling joyful, and this smiling reinforces your feeling of joyfulness. Similarly, your sense of fear is maintained when you notice your heart thumping.

Emotions are directed toward someone or something. We experience joy, fear, and other emotional episodes toward tasks, customers, public speeches we present, a software program we are using, and so on. This contrasts with *moods*, which are emotional states that are not directed toward anything in particular.[6] For example, you may be in a cheerful mood, but you don't know why you have this emotion. Your cheerfulness may be caused by something at work or elsewhere, but you aren't consciously aware of this.

Emotions and Personality

positive affectivity (PA) the tendency to experience positive emotional states

extroversion a "Big Five" personality dimension that characterizes people who are outgoing, talkative, sociable, and assertive

negative affectivity (NA) the tendency to experience negative emotional states

Have you ever noticed how some co-workers seem upbeat most of the time while others are almost never happy about anything? To some extent, emotions can result from personality, not just from workplace experiences. **Positive affectivity (PA)** is the tendency to experience positive emotional states. It is very similar to **extroversion,** described in Chapter 6 as a characteristic of people who are outgoing, talkative, sociable, and assertive. In contrast, some people are high on **negative affectivity (NA),** which is the tendency to experience negative emotions.[7] Employees with high NA tend to be more distressed and unhappy because they focus on the negative aspects of life.

To what extent do these personality traits influence emotions? Some research indicates that our feelings about work can be predicted two years later from a person's PA. Studies of twins raised apart conclude that a person's heredity influences emotions and judgments about work. However, other evidence suggests that the effects of PA and NA are relatively weak.[8] Overall, it seems that PA and NA influence emotions and judgments in the workplace, but their effects are not as strong as situational factors.

Emotions, Attitudes, and Behavior

attitudes the cluster of beliefs, assessed feelings, and behavioral intentions toward an object

Emotions are related to the broader concept of **attitudes.** Attitudes represent the cluster of beliefs, assessed feelings, and behavioral intentions toward an object.[9] They are *judgments* about the attitude object. The joy we experience when receiving a promotion is an emotion. Our attitude toward promotions is more complex and long-lasting. It includes perceptions about promotions (e.g., promotions indicate that senior management values your abilities), assessed feelings (e.g., promotions are good), and intentions to receive promotions (e.g., we intend to work hard to get a promotion). As we shall see, attitudes develop from two sources: (1) our emotional experiences and (2) our perceptual process.

Emotions affect attitudes, but the two concepts are different (see Exhibit 7.2). As just noted, emotions are *experiences,* whereas attitudes are judgments. This is basically the distinction between feeling and thinking identified in Jung's psychological types (see Chapter 6). We feel emotions, whereas we think about attitudes. Moreover, emotions can be quite brief, whereas attitudes are more stable over time. The joy you experience when hearing about your promotion may last a few minutes or hours, whereas your attitude toward promotions can be stable for weeks, months, or even years.

Exhibit 7.2
Model of attitudes
and behavior

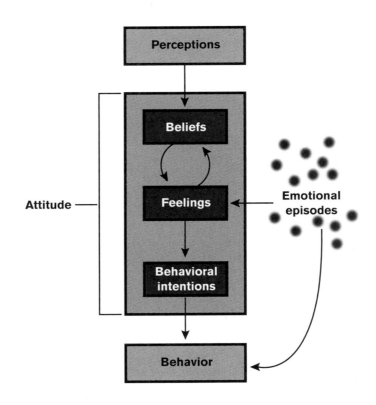

Three components of attitudes

Our definition of attitudes and the illustration in Exhibit 7.2 indicate that this concept has three components. The first component, *feelings*, represents a positive or negative assessment of our emotional experiences related to the attitude object. We experience many emotional episodes in the workplace. Today, for example, you may have been frustrated with a troublesome customer, proud that you completed a difficult task, and anxious that you might be assigned a task that you don't want. These emotions are experienced, and they shape your assessment about your job.[10] As Connections 7.1 describes, many companies try to instill more fun (joy) in the workplace so employees develop positive work attitudes. However, what is considered humorous or fun to some people is irritating to others.

The second component of attitudes, *beliefs*, provides the connection between attitudes and our perceptions. The statement "The CEO of this company values ideas from employees" is a belief because it describes a perceived characteristic of the company's top executive (the attitude object). This belief develops over time through direct experience as well as from what co-workers tell us.[11] The third component of attitudes, *behavioral intentions*, represents a motivation to engage in a particular behavior. You might hear people say that they are willing to wear their safety glasses. Others intend to look for another job. These are examples of the behavioral intentions component of attitudes.

Linking emotions to behavior

Exhibit 7.2 also shows how emotions and attitudes affect behavior. First, beliefs create feelings about something or someone. You might feel dissatisfied with your level of pay (a feeling) because you believe it is too low (a belief). The relationship between beliefs and feelings is a little more complex than this because feelings also influence beliefs.[12] You may feel frustrated in a work situation without knowing why, so you rationalize this feeling by believing that the company doesn't provide enough support. However, beliefs cause feelings most of the time.

Next, feelings influence a person's behavioral intentions. You might want to leave the organization (a behavioral intention) because you are dissatisfied with your level of pay (a feeling). In other words, you are motivated to leave the organization because of negative feelings about your low pay. Of course, people don't always want to quit their job when they have negative feelings about the size of their paycheck. Instead, some employees complain about the problem or take some action (e.g., sick leave) that seems to compensate for the

Connections 7.1 ◻ Employees Just Want to Have Fun!

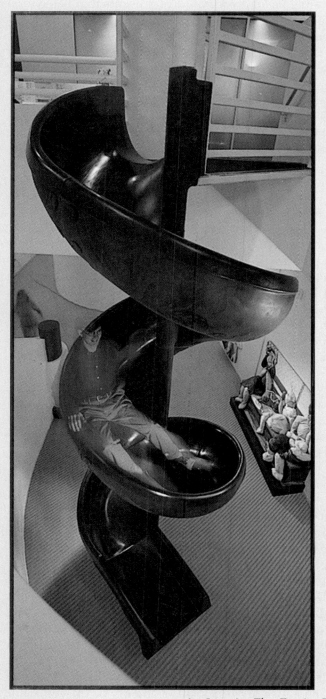

For Macromedia staff, fun is just a quick slide away.
[Mark Richards]

When work gets nasty, information systems staff at the American Association of Retired Persons (AARP) do what comes naturally. They pull out their Super Soaker water guns and start blasting unsuspecting colleagues. As others join in, the tension at AARP's Washington, D.C., headquarters turns into gales of laughter and indoor precipitation. "Laughter can be the best medicine for what ails you day to day," explains Jeanne Simia, AARP's director of information systems and customer service.

AARP isn't the only company that believes a little comic relief sparks positive emotions and work attitudes. At multimedia software firm Macromedia, employees enjoy a twisting slide connecting the second floor to the company kitchen. At Southwest Airlines, flight attendants surprise passengers by popping out of overhead luggage compartments. "We like mavericks, people with a sense of humor," explains Southwest's CEO Herb Kelleher, who is known to dress up as a leprechaun on St. Patrick's Day.

Sprint, the telecommunications company, recently held a national "Fun at Work" day in which hundreds of teams raced to see who could take the zaniest photos of themselves. "We believe employees who have fun feel appreciated and come together as a team," explains the Sprint executive who organized the event.

Of course, humor isn't a quick fix for the underlying causes of poor morale. "It's well-intentioned but kind of what you do because you can't deal with the fundamental problems," warns Scott Adams, creator of the Dilbert comic strip. Also, not everyone agrees on what constitutes fun. At Volvo's heavy truck plant in Dublin, Virginia, tardy employees are greeted by a co-worker dressed in a rooster outfit. Marshall Lineberry, an assembly worker who showed up late with a bad back, wasn't amused. He jumped on the rooster and was suspended without pay. However, Lineberry had the last laugh. He sued the company and won his case. The judge ruled that "the bird had it coming."

Sources: J. Mullich, "'Fun at Work' Is an Oxymoron, Folks," *Business First St. Louis,* November 2, 1998; R. Levering and M. Moskowitz, "The 100 Best Companies to Work for in America," *Fortune,* January 12, 1998, pp. 84–95; M. Jackson, "Bosses Are Learning That Turning Employee Frowns to Smiles Is Good for Business," *San Diego Union-Tribune,* July 21, 1997, p. C1; J. Sell, "Having Fun on the Job," *Cleveland Plain Dealer,* June 6, 1997, p. E1; K. Melymuka, "Frazzled? Let's Party!" *Computerworld,* June 16, 1997, pp. 75–77. ◻

low pay. People choose the behavioral intention that they think will work best for them.

Finally, behavioral intentions predict behavior. Generally, behavioral intentions are better than beliefs or feelings at predicting behavior. We can be more certain that employees will leave the organization if we know they intend to do so than if we only know that they are dissatisfied with low pay.[13] But behavioral intentions are not perfectly related to behavior because behavior also depends on the person's ability, role perceptions, and situational contingencies. For instance, you may be motivated to attend every day of scheduled work this month, but illness or something beyond your control prevents that behavioral intention from coming true.[14]

So far, we have described behaviors as conscious and logical consequences of emotions and attitudes. However, Exhibit 7.2 also reveals that emotions can directly influence behavior. In other words, people sometimes react to their emotions rather than their judgments (attitudes). When upset, an employee might stomp out of a meeting, bang a fist on the desk, or burst into tears. When overjoyed, an employee might embrace a co-worker or break into a little dance. These are not carefully thought out behaviors. Rather, they are automatic emotional responses that serve as coping mechanisms in that situation.[15]

cognitive dissonance a state of anxiety that occurs when an individual's beliefs, attitudes, intentions, and behaviors are inconsistent with one another

Cognitive dissonance   Before leaving this discussion of emotions and behavior, we should mention that behaviors sometimes influence beliefs and feelings rather than vice versa. This occurs when you have engaged in a behavior that is inconsistent with your previous attitudes (such as representing your firm several times on television even though you don't particularly like working there). This situation creates an uncomfortable tension, called **cognitive dissonance,** because your behavior (publicly representing your company) is inconsistent with your attitude toward the organization.

People want to reduce this dissonance, so either the behavior or attitude has to change. It's rather difficult to change past behavior, so people tend to realign their attitudes.[16] In our example, publicly representing your employer on television would likely change your negative attitude about the company to a more neutral or possibly favorable one. This is particularly likely to occur when the behavior is known to everyone, was done voluntarily, and can't be undone.

Now that we have introduced the conceptual dynamics of emotions and work attitudes, let's look more closely at two of the most important work attitudes: job satisfaction and organizational commitment.

Job Satisfaction

job satisfaction a person's evaluation of his or her job and work context

One of the most important and widely studied work attitudes is **job satisfaction.** Job satisfaction represents a person's evaluation of his or her job and work context.[17] It is an *appraisal* of the perceived job characteristics and emotional experiences at work. Satisfied employees have a favorable evaluation of their job, based on their observations and emotional experiences.

Consider what Connie Dowell says about her job. "To be honest, I love my job because of the people I work with," says the dean of information services and librarian of Connecticut College in New London. "I have a wonderful staff who work together incredibly well."[18] Dowell is providing an appraisal of her job based on perceptions as well as emotional experiences on the job.

Job satisfaction is really a collection of attitudes about specific facets of the job.[19] Employees can be satisfied with some elements of the job while simultaneously dissatisfied with others. For example, Dowell expressed her satisfaction with co-workers, whereas she may be less satisfied with workload or other aspects of the job. Different types of satisfaction will lead to different intentions and behavior. An employee might complain to the supervisor when dissatisfied with low pay but not with co-worker dissatisfaction. Overall job satisfaction is a combination of the person's feelings toward the different facets of job satisfaction.

How Satisfied Are Employees?

Surveys indicate that between 80 and 90 percent of Americans are moderately or very satisfied overall with their jobs.[20] Does this mean that Americans have high job satisfaction? Well, maybe, but probably not as high as these statistics suggest. The problem is that surveys often use a single direct question, such as "How satisfied are you with your job?" Many dissatisfied employees are reluctant to reveal their feelings in a direct question because this is tantamount to admitting that they made a poor job choice and are not enjoying life. "The employees who declare themselves satisfied with their jobs might do so only because they feel they should say they're satisfied," suggests an executive with one of the world's largest survey firms.[21]

A strong indication that overall satisfaction ratings are inflated is that people typically report much lower satisfaction levels for specific aspects of the job. For instance, only 54 percent of American workers believe they are paid fairly, 46 percent say their company promotes fairly, and 41 percent claim that senior management truly cares about them (see Exhibit 7.3). Satisfaction with co-workers seems to be one of the few ratings that comes close to overall job satisfaction (84 percent).

It's even more difficult to measure job satisfaction across countries. One major survey firm recently estimated that employees in Mexico, Brazil,

Exhibit 7.3

Job satisfaction levels among U.S. employees

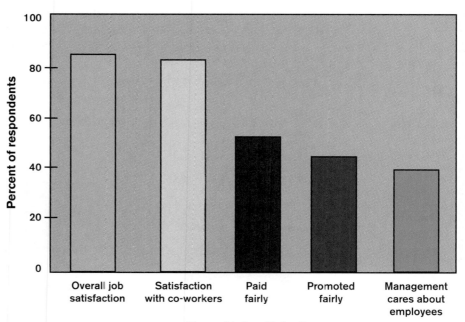

Note: Indicates percentage of employees who thought their companies were good or excellent in the category indicated.

Source: Based on Hewitt Associates, from a survey of 46,500 employees from 38 companies nationwide. Data were cited in S. Baker, "Job Satisfaction High in Survey, but Office Politics Alive and Well," *Fort Worth Star-Telegram*, March 13, 1997, p. 3. The annual Gallup survey has similar results. See D. Moore, "Public Generally Negative toward Business, but Most Workers Satisfied with Jobs," *Gallup Poll*, August 1997 (www.gallup.com).

Switzerland, Norway, and Canada are most satisfied, whereas their counterparts in Hong Kong, Japan, mainland China, and Singapore are the least satisfied. Americans placed in the middle of the pack of 22 countries on the list. The problem with these findings is that people with the same feelings toward work respond differently to these questionnaires. People in Japan and Hong Kong tend to subdue their opinions, whereas people in Brazil and Mexico are often more expressive. Also, Americans fill out a large number of questionnaires, whereas this is a novel experience for people in some countries, which may inflate their ratings.[22]

A Model of Job Satisfaction

discrepancy theory a theory that partly explains job satisfaction in terms of the gap between what a person expects to receive and what is actually received

equity theory a process motivation theory that explains how people develop perceptions of fairness in the distribution and exchange of resources

What determines the level of job satisfaction? The best explanation is provided by the model in Exhibit 7.4 that combines **discrepancy theory** and **equity theory**.[23] Discrepancy theory states that the level of job satisfaction is determined by the discrepancy between what people expect to receive and what they experience.[24] Job satisfaction or dissatisfaction results from a comparison of the amount the employee expects to receive and the perceived amount received. Job dissatisfaction occurs when the received condition is noticeably less than the expected condition. Job satisfaction improves as the person's expectations are met or exceeded—up to a point.

Equity theory is also built into Exhibit 7.4. Recall from Chapter 3 that equity occurs when the person and comparison other have similar outcome/input ratios. This is relevant to job satisfaction, because the amount we expect to receive is partly determined by our comparison with other people. For instance, the level of pay we expect to receive depends not only on how hard we work, but also on how hard other people work in this job compared to their level of pay.

Equity theory also explains why job satisfaction does not always continue to increase as the received condition exceeds expectations. As people receive much better outcomes than they expect, they typically develop feelings of guilt and a belief that organizational practices are unfair to others. At first, employees adjust their expectations upward when they are overrewarded.

Exhibit 7.4
A model of job satisfaction

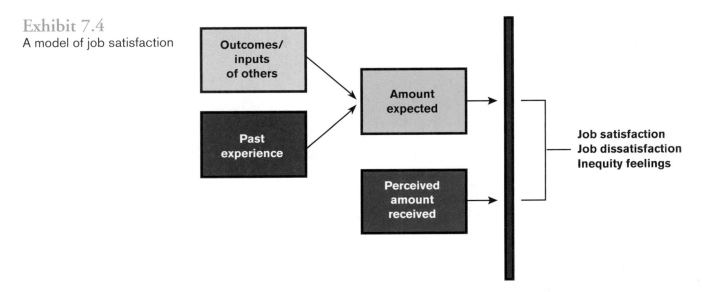

Source: Based on E. E. Lawler III, *Motivation in Work Organizations* (Monterey, CA: Brooks/Cole, 1973), p. 75.

However, if the overreward is so large that it cannot be justified, then feelings of inequity persist and dissatisfaction with organizational practices may result.

In summary, discrepancy and equity theories predict that as reality meets and exceeds expectations, job satisfaction will increase. However, job satisfaction begins to decrease when the perceived job situation is so much better than expected that the overreward creates a feeling of guilt or unfairness.

Job Satisfaction and Work Behaviors

Xerox, Nortel, and Sears are paying a lot more attention to employee satisfaction these days. In each of these firms, executive bonuses are partly determined by the level of job satisfaction indicated in annual employee surveys.[25] These bonuses consider job satisfaction because, as Continental Airlines CEO Gordon Bethune stated at the beginning of this chapter, you can't have a successful organization unless employees have sufficient levels of job satisfaction.

Organizational behavior scholars have linked job satisfaction to many types of employee behavior.[26] Employees with higher levels of job satisfaction, particularly satisfaction with the work itself, are less likely to quit their jobs, be absent from work, and experience mental or physical health problems. Joining a labor union and going on strike often result from dissatisfaction with pay or working conditions. Dissatisfied employees are also more likely to steal, deliberately sabotage company products, and engage in acts of violence against their supervisor or co-workers.[27]

Job satisfaction and task performance

Happy workers are productive workers, right? This is certainly a popular belief, but organizational behavior research consistently reports an insignificant or modest association between job satisfaction and task performance.[28] Popular opinion may prove more accurate than research on this issue. As one scholar recently admitted: "I still suspect a consistent, significant job satisfaction-task performance relationship is out there to be found."[29]

One reason why organizational behavior research reports a modest association between job satisfaction and task performance is because general attitudes don't predict specific behaviors very well. People have unique values and experiences, so they react differently to the same level of job satisfaction. One dissatisfied employee may decide to put in less work effort, whereas another maintains the same level of work effort while looking for employment elsewhere. Moreover, task performance depends on a person's ability and resources, not just work effort. Job satisfaction would also have little short term effect in jobs where employees are responsible for automated processes, such as a bottling plant or petrochemical process.

A second explanation is that job performance leads to job satisfaction (rather than vice versa), but only when performance is linked to valued rewards. Higher performers receive more rewards and, consequently, are more satisfied than low-performing employees who receive fewer rewards. The connection between job satisfaction and performance is weak because many organizations do not reward good performance.[30]

Third, the weak relationship between job satisfaction and performance may occur because satisfied employees engage in more **organizational citizenship** behaviors but not in higher levels of traditional job performance.[31] Recall from Chapter 2 that organizational citizenship behaviors include working beyond required job duties, such as assisting others with their tasks and promoting a positive work environment. Satisfied employees—particularly those who are satisfied with co-workers—are more likely to help the company beyond their normal job duties.[32]

organizational citizenship employee behaviors that extend beyond the usual job duties: avoiding unnecessary conflicts, helping others, tolerating impositions, being involved in organizational activities, and performing tasks beyond normal role requirements

Job satisfaction and customer satisfaction   Somewhat stronger than the job satisfaction-performance relationship is the relationship between job satisfaction and customer satisfaction. Southwest Airlines, Corning, Sears, and Columbia Medical Centers are among the growing list of firms that want employees to be happy because it benefits customers.[33] As John Mackey, CEO of Whole Foods, explains: "If people don't like where they're working, they're unlikely to provide good service to the customers."[34]

Satisfied employees provide better customer service. That's what Arthur Martinez, CEO of Sears, Roebuck and Co., and other executives at the Chicago-based retail giant discovered. They also developed an "employee-customer-profit" model in which employee satisfaction affects employee turnover; employee turnover affects customer satisfaction; and customer satisfaction affects the company's success. Now, one-quarter of Sears' annual bonus for managers is based on employee satisfaction ratings.[35] What factors other than job satisfaction would affect the employee–customer satisfaction relationship?
[John Thoeming]

Employee satisfaction is associated with customer satisfaction for two reasons. First, job satisfaction affects a person's general mood. Employees who are in a good mood are more likely to communicate friendliness and positive feelings, which customers appreciate. Second, satisfied employees are less likely to quit their jobs. This allows companies to provide more consistent service (customers get the same employees to serve them) and employees have more experience and better skills to serve clients.

Now that we understand the dynamics of job satisfaction, how can companies ensure that they have happy workers? The job satisfaction concept is so broad—remember there are many facets of job satisfaction—that the answer comes from every part of this textbook. Feedback, equity, rewards, leadership, corporate culture, change management, and other topics all implicitly or explicitly refer to job satisfaction as a possible outcome. We must also remember that individual differences, such as personality and personal beliefs, moderate the effects of the work environment on job satisfaction.

Organizational Commitment

organizational commitment
a person's emotional attachment to, identification with, and involvement in a particular organization

Organizational commitment refers to the employee's emotional attachment to, identification with, and involvement in a particular organization.[36] Organizational behavior scholars call this *affective commitment* because it refers to the individual's emotions toward the organization. Affective commitment is called organizational loyalty when the organization is the target of the individual's commitment. However, affective commitment can also refer to loyalty toward co-workers, customers, or a profession.[37] In this book, we will concentrate mainly on the employee's overall commitment to the organization.

Along with affective commitment, employees also have varying levels of *continuance commitment*.[38] Continuance commitment occurs when employees believe it is in their own personal interest to remain with the organization. This form of commitment is a calculative bond with the organization, rather than an emotional attachment. For example, you may have met people who do not particularly identify with the organization where they work but feel bound to remain there because it would be too costly to quit. Continuance commitment is this motivation to stay because of the high cost of leaving.[39]

Is Organizational Loyalty Declining?

Is organizational loyalty declining? According to several surveys, it is. One poll reported that 29 percent of Americans feel less loyal to their employer today than a few years ago. Another found that 86.7 percent of managers felt there was less loyalty between companies and their employees compared to five years earlier.[40] Many writers in the popular press argue that the "new deal" of employability (see Chapter 1), along with downsizing and mergers, has undermined affective commitment.[41] Companies no longer protect employee jobs, and they no longer expect loyalty in return.

© 1997 Farcus Cartoons/dist. by Universal Press Syndicate WAISGLASS/COULTHART

"It makes you miss the good ol' days when they at least pretended to value employees."

This does not mean that corporate loyalty is dead, just diminished. A Gallup survey found that over 90 percent of full-time and part-time employees feel some degree of loyalty to their employer. Moreover, international studies consistently report that Americans feel more loyal to their employer than people in most other countries. Employees in Finland, Spain, and Canada tend to be most loyal, followed by Americans, whereas those from the United Kingdom, several Asian countries, and (surprisingly) Japan tend to have relatively low levels of loyalty.[42] As we learned earlier in the chapter, these results may be distorted by the way people report their opinions in different cultures, but some of the surveys have tried to correct for this problem.

Consequences of Organizational Commitment

If organizational loyalty is truly declining, it would be bad news for employers. Research has found that employees with high levels of affective commitment are less likely to quit their jobs and be absent from work. This potentially improves customer service because long-tenure employees have better knowledge of work practices, and clients like to do business with the same employees because transactions are predictable.[43] Employees with high affective commitment tend to have higher work motivation and organizational citizenship.[44] One potential problem with a highly loyal workforce is that the organization may have very low turnover. This limits the organization's opportunity to hire new employees with new knowledge and fresh ideas.

Some firms try to build commitment by tying employees financially to the organization through low-cost loans and stock options. These "golden handcuffs" reduce turnover, but they also increase continuance commitment, not affective commitment. Evidence suggests that employees with high levels of continuance commitment have *lower* performance ratings and are *less* likely to engage in organizational citizenship behaviors![45] Thus, to build an effective workforce, employers must win employees' hearts (affective commitment) rather than tie them financially to the organization (continuance commitment).

Building Organizational Commitment

Employers are experimenting with innovative ways to build a loyal workforce. SAS Institute, a statistics software company near Raleigh, North Carolina, provides excellent fitness facilities as well as free laundry service to keep the workout clothes clean. Employees at Merck & Company can have their car's oil changed while they work. SAS, DuPont, and many other companies offer child care, flexible work arrangements, and other work/life benefits (see Chapter 5). "We now have empirical data that confirms employees who take advantage of DuPont's work/life programs are more committed than the average employee," says a DuPont executive.[46]

Employee benefits and work/life programs are just two ways that organizations improve affective commitment among employees. In fact, practicing most of the recommendations in this and other organizational behavior textbooks will improve affective commitment of employees to some extent. While many workplace experiences influence organizational commitment, the following activities have been most prominent in the literature.[47]

• *Fairness and satisfaction*—The most important ingredients for a loyal workforce are positive and equitable work experiences. New employees must believe that the company is fulfilling its obligations.[48] Organizational commitment seems to suffer when people face increased workloads in companies with record profits and senior executives earning lucrative bonuses. In contrast, companies have built commitment by sharing profits and distributing company shares to employees.

• *Job security*—Employees need to feel some permanence and mutuality in the employment relationship. Life-time employment guarantees aren't necessary, although Cisco Systems, Federal Express, Harley-Davidson, Southwest Airlines, and several other firms have maintained such policies.[49] Rather, there should be enough job security to nurture a relationship in which employees believe their effort will be rewarded eventually and generally. Job insecurity, on the other hand, fosters a more formal contractual relationship with minimal feelings of mutuality.[50] Thus, it's not surprising that layoff threats are one of the greatest blows to employee loyalty, even among those whose jobs are not immediately at risk.[51]

• *Organizational comprehension*—Affective commitment is a person's identification with the company, so it makes sense that this attitude is strengthened when employees have a solid comprehension of the company. Employees should be regularly informed about organizational activities and personally experience other parts of the company. As an executive with American Fence Corp. warns, "When people don't know what's going on in the organization, they feel very disconnected."[52]

• *Employee involvement*—Employees feel that they are part of the organization when they make decisions that guide the organization's future. Through participation, employees begin to see how the organization is a reflection of their decisions. Employee involvement also builds loyalty because giving this power is a demonstration of the company's trust in its employees.

trust a person's positive expectations about another party's intentions and actions toward them in risky situations

• *Trusting employees*—**Trust** occurs when we have positive expectations about another party's intentions and actions toward us in risky situations.[53] Trust means putting faith in the other person or group. It is also a reciprocal activity. To receive trust, you must demonstrate trust. Trust is important for organizational commitment because it touches the heart of the employment relationship (see Chapter 17). Employees identify with and feel obliged to work for an organization only when they trust its leaders.

Managing Emotions

Employees at Earl Industries, Inc., had gone out of their way to put together a proposal for a customer who was in a pinch. But when the proposal was done, the client changed its mind about what it wanted. Jerrold L. Miller, president of the Portsmouth, Virginia, ship-repair company blew up at the client's representatives. "I just had a shouting match with my best customer," says Miller, who later apologized for the incident. "I think I was right, but I didn't present it properly," he says.[54]

Like Jerrold Miller, we are sometimes overcome by our emotions. Emotions can directly influence behavior, whether it's angrily shouting at a customer or displaying subtle facial gestures of disapproval. However, we are typically expected to manage our emotions in the workplace. **Emotional labor** refers to the effort, planning, and control needed to express organizationally desired emotions during interpersonal transactions.[55] When interacting with co-workers, customers, suppliers, and others, employees are expected to abide by *display rules*. These rules are norms requiring employees to display certain emotions and withhold others. Jerrold Miller's outburst clearly violated organizational display rules. Even as company president, Miller is expected to follow a set of norms regarding the emotions presented to customers.

emotional labor the effort, planning, and control needed to express organizationally desired emotions during interpersonal transactions

Safeway employees are smiling a lot these days. They aren't happier than the rest of us; they're *required* to act happy so customers have a better shopping experience. But the emotional labor of Safeway's "smile-and-make-eye-contact" rule is too stressful for some staff. "I believe in courteous service," says a former Safeway butcher, "but Safeway has taken it to such an extreme that it's torture for most employees." A few employees have also received unwanted sexual advances from customers after giving company-mandated smiles.[57] Is Safeway's emotional labor rule unreasonable? Should employees always hide their true emotions toward customers?
[Illustration by Garrett Kallenbach]

Conditions Requiring Emotional Labor

Jobs require more emotional labor when employees have frequent voice or face-to-face contact with clients and others for long durations.[56] For instance, a tour guide must show patience and enthusiasm for several hours, requiring more effort to hide fatigue, anger, and other true emotions. Emotional labor is also more challenging where the job requires employees to display a variety of emotions (e.g., anger as well as joy) and intense emotions (e.g., showing delight rather than a weak smile). For instance, bill collectors have challenges with emotional labor because they must learn to show warmth to anxious first-time debtors and irritation (but not anger) toward debtors who seem indifferent to their financial obligations.[58]

Another consideration is the extent to which employees must abide by the display rules. Some organizations expect people to "be themselves" whereas others have strict guidelines and rules so that employees consistently display required emotions. An example of the latter is Walt Disney World, where employees are told to think of themselves as actors. Whether their role is a ticket seller or Mickey Mouse, they act out their role to satisfy the customer and fellow employees.[59] The extent that someone must follow display rules also depends on the power and personal relationship of the person receiving the service. You would closely follow display rules when meeting the owner of a client's organization, whereas more latitude might be possible when serving a friend.

There are also cross-cultural differences in emotional display norms and values. One survey reported that 83 percent of Japanese believe it is inappropriate to get emotional in a business context, compared with 40 percent of Americans, 34 percent of French, and 29 percent of Italians. In other words, Italians are more likely to accept or tolerate people who display their true emotions at work, whereas this would be considered rude or embarrassing in Japan.[60]

Customer expectations must also be taken into account. In some cultures (such as the United States), most people expect consistent emotional displays in the service provided. Customers in some other cultures give employees more latitude. Indeed, they may be offended by people who feign emotions. For instance, when McDonald's opened operations in Moscow, employees were taught to smile at customers. However, the company soon discovered that Russians do not expect this emotional display, and some customers thought the employees were mocking them.[61]

Emotional Dissonance

Comedian George Burns once said, "The secret to being a good actor is honesty. If you can fake *that*, you've got it made." Burns's humor highlights an important reality in emotional labor; namely, that it is very difficult to hide our true emotions in the workplace. Usually, they "leak" out as voice intonations, posture, and in other subtle ways.[62] As we saw with Jerrold Miller, anger toward a client will likely spill out, even where strong norms exist to discourage this. The problem is particularly true of anger, which is one of the most difficult emotions to control.

emotional dissonance the conflict experienced when the person's genuinely felt emotions are inconsistent with the emotions that must be displayed as part of one's role in an organization

Conflict between required and true emotions is called **emotional dissonance,** and it is a significant cause of stress and job burnout (see Chapter 5).[63] Emotional dissonance is most common, of course, where employees must display emotions that are quite different from their true feelings. It is also more common where emotional display rules are highly regulated and where employees do not have enough autonomy to change tasks. Ziad Altoura, an employee at the National Bank of Kuwait in London, England, experiences emotional dissonance during the busy summer months when many Kuwaitis and Gulf nationals visit London. "You must be pleasant to every customer," explains Altoura. "Nothing must show and you have to keep up that freshness throughout the day."[64]

Supporting Emotional Labor

When Nejat Sarp recently opened the Pan Pacific Hotel in Yokohama, Japan, he brought an important rule of thumb for excellent customer service. "We hire people for attitude, not for experience," says the Turkish-born Australian who was previously general manager at the Pan Pacific Gold Coast in Australia. "You can teach somebody what to do but if the attitude is not there, it doesn't work. So we hire for attitude and the result is the young, energetic team."[65]

Pan Pacific Hotel Yokohama is not the only company with a "hire for attitude, train for skills" strategy. Southwest Airlines, Doubletree Hotels, and Men's Wearhouse Inc. also believe the best way to support emotional labor is by hiring people whose emotional tendencies (e.g., positive affectivity and courteousness) match the job requirements.[66] The *Fast Company Online* feature describes how Men's Wearhouse attributes much of its success to this strategy of hiring people with an optimistic attitude.

Even with good person-job matching, many organizations rely on training so that employees learn the subtle behaviors to express appropriate emotions. Delta Airlines, for example, has employees act out their roles in training programs, then provides feedback from instructors while watching the video playback of their behaviors. Another strategy is to give employees sufficient control over the job so that they don't experience the adverse consequences of emotional labor.

Emotional Intelligence

Yip Kwok-Fun has had more than his share of emotional ups and downs lately. As chairman of the Hong Kong Telephone Company Staff Association, he has to deal with employee layoffs and economic recession. That's why Kwok-Fun is keen to take Hongkong Telecom's course on emotional intelligence. The Hong Kong government also offers this course so employees can cope more effectively with their emotions when serving disgruntled citizens. "Many of us don't know that our emotions can be controlled and therefore [we] just become victims of emotions," says the Hong Kong government's chief training officer.[67]

emotional intelligence (EI)
the ability to monitor your own and others' emotions, to discriminate among them, and to use the information to guide your thinking and actions

Emotional intelligence (EI) is the ability to monitor your own and others' emotions, to discriminate among them, and to use the information to

---

FAST COMPANY
Online

□ Men's Wearhouse Sells Suits with Soul

The only thing worse than a salesman in a slick suit is a salesman pushing a slick suit. In 1973, that insight led George Zimmer to open a store in Houston that would sell

suits differently from how they'd been sold before. Today, with 6,000 employees and 400 stores, Men's Wearhouse is the leading discount retailer of men's clothing in the United States.

How did Zimmer build a company around customers who hate buying clothes? By hiring people for their attitude rather than their skills. "We don't look for people with specific levels of education and experience," explains Shlomo Maor, associate director of training at Men's Wearhouse. "We have one criterion for hiring: optimism. We look for passion, excitement, energy. We want people who enjoy life."

Men's Wearhouse also looks for job applicants who can handle the up-and-down emotions of selling men's clothes. "You have to sell the right product to the right customer for the right reason—which often means delaying gratification and taking rejection in stride," says Maor. "That's emotional intelligence and it's what makes great salespeople great."

Men's Wearhouse became the leading U.S. discount retailer of men's clothing by hiring salespeople whose natural emotions match the job requirements.
[Jayme Maxwell, The Men's Wearhouse]

ONLINE CHECK-UP

1. This feature describes why Men's Wearhouse hires for attitude rather than skill. In your opinion, how can companies determine whether job applicants have appropriate attitudes or emotional dispositions for the job?
2. The full text of this *Fast Company* article briefly describes the training that Men's Wearhouse offers its employees. Read the full text of this article and explain how this training fits in with the practice of "hire for attitude, train for skill."
3. Shlomo Maor refers to emotional intelligence, which is also discussed in this chapter. Read through the section on emotional intelligence, then discuss how each element of emotional intelligence would help salespeople provide better customer service.

Get the full text of this *Fast Company* article at www.mhhe.com/mcshane1e

Source: Adapted from E. Ransdell, "They Sell Suits with Soul," *Fast Company*, Issue 18 (October 1998). □

guide your thinking and actions.[68] EI has its roots in the concept of social intelligence, which was introduced over 75 years ago, but scholars spent most of this time focused on cognitive intelligence. Now, many are realizing that emotional intelligence is just as important for an individual's success at work and in other social environments. Emotional intelligence includes the five dimensions illustrated in Exhibit 7.5 and described below:[69]

self-monitoring personality a personality trait referring to the extent that people are sensitive to situational cues and can readily adapt their own behavior appropriately

- *Self-awareness*—People with high self-awareness recognize and understand their moods, emotions, and needs. They perceive and anticipate how their actions affect others. Self-aware people are also comfortable talking about and admitting their limitations, so they know when to ask for help. Notice that this (as well as some other EI dimensions described here) is similar to the **self-monitoring personality** concept described in Chapter 6.

- *Self-regulation*—This is the ability to control or redirect emotional outbursts and other impulse behaviors. For example, rather than yelling at a client, you manage to remain calm and later "talk out" the emotion to a co-worker. Self-regulation includes the ability to suspend judgment—to think through the consequences of their behavior rather than acting on impulse.

- *Self-motivation*—This includes stifling impulses, directing our emotions toward personal goals, and delaying gratification. Even when people do not achieve their goals, those with high motivation remain optimistic. Motivating yourself overlaps with the self-leadership concepts of self-reinforcement and constructive thought patterns (Chapter 4).

empathy a person's ability to understand and be sensitive to the feelings, thoughts, and situation of others

- *Empathy*—In Chapter 6 we defined **empathy** as the ability to understand and be sensitive to the feelings, thoughts, and situation of others. This doesn't mean adopting other people's emotions, just being sensitized to them.

- *Social skill*—This is the ability to manage the emotions of other people. It requires social competence and skills to guide the way other people act. Social skill includes the ability to form networks of relationships and to build rapport—finding common interests and understanding with others. Social skill requires other elements of emotional intelligence, particularly empathy and self-regulation.

There is still much to learn about emotional intelligence, such as how robust are these five dimensions and how they relate to self-monitoring personality. At the same time, little is known about how to select or train people for emotional intelligence. The U.S. Air Force and a few other organizations are now using tests that select applicants with high emotional intelligence, although the quality of these tests is still uncertain.[70] Hongkong Telecom and

Exhibit 7.5
Dimensions of emotional intelligence

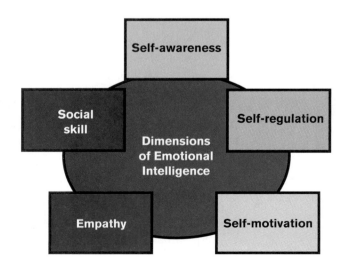

many other companies offer training in emotional intelligence because it can, to some extent, be learned. However, people don't develop emotional intelligence simply by learning about its dimensions. It requires personal coaching, plenty of practice, and frequent feedback. Emotional intelligence also increases with age; it is part of the process called maturity. Whether people are hired with high emotional intelligence or they develop it through coaching, we still need to learn whether people with high emotional intelligence are better at coping with the emotional dissonance created by emotional labor requirements.

Values at Work

values stable, long-lasting beliefs about what is important to the individual

Earlier in this chapter, we learned that beliefs are perceptions about an attitude object. People also have a higher-order set of beliefs, called **values.** Values represent stable, long-lasting beliefs about what is important. They are evaluative standards that help us define what is right or wrong, good or bad, in the world.[71] Some people value practicality, whereas others value the aesthetic. Some people value frugality, whereas others value generosity. Values differ from attitudes. Values are general beliefs about life, whereas attitudes are directed toward specific objects, events, or people. Of course, values influence our attitudes toward those attitude objects.

There are two types of values: terminal and instrumental. *Terminal values* are desired states of existence that we think are worth striving for. A world of beauty, equality, wisdom, and a comfortable life are some of the terminal values that people might hold. *Instrumental values*, on the other hand, are desirable modes of behavior that help us reach the objectives of terminal values. Some instrumental values include being polite, courageous, logical, self-controlled, and ambitious.[72] Organizational behavior researchers tend to focus on instrumental values, possibly because they shape the person's behavior and are more closely aligned with organizational values.

Values are gaining prominence in the study of organizational behavior.[73] Personal values influence our perceptions and decisions. They provide justification for our actions. Scholars have described more than 100 personal values.[74] Organizational culture values, which we discuss in Chapter 16, shape the behaviors of employees aligned with those values. Cross-cultural values, which we discuss next, partially explain how people behave differently in other countries. Ethical values, which are discussed in the last section of this chapter, lay the foundation for the appropriateness of our actions.

Cultural Differences in Values

Not long ago, several Swedish and American employees at Ericsson Telephone, the Swedish telecommunications giant, met to resolve a pressing issue. At the end of the discussion, the highest-ranking person in the room—an American—stated his position on the problem. The Americans understood that the senior executive was concluding debate by making the final decision. The Swedes, on the other hand, left the meeting feeling uneasy that no decision had been made. Scandinavians assume that decisions are made as a group, so they thought the American executive's statements were merely his opinions on the matter.[75]

Anyone who has worked long enough with people in other countries will know that values differ across cultures. As this true story illustrates, people in some cultures value group decisions while others think that a leader should take charge. Meetings in Germany usually start on time, whereas they can be a half hour late in Brazil. We need to understand cultural value differences to avoid unnecessary conflicts and subtle tensions between people from different countries. This is particularly important as companies develop global operations and information technology increases the frequency of cross-cultural communication.

individualism–collectivism
the extent to which people value their group membership and group goals (collectivism) or value their individuality and personal goals (individualism)

Five cross-cultural values   Five values account for a large portion of the differences in orientations across cultures. They include individualism–collectivism, power distance, uncertainty avoidance, achievement-nurturing orientation, and long- and short-term orientation.[76]

• *Individualism versus collectivism*—**Individualism–collectivism** refers to the degree that people value their individual goals over those of the group. There are four dimensions to this concept. First, collectivists define themselves by their group membership, whereas individualists view themselves more autonomously. Second, collectivists give group goals priority over their personal goals, whereas individualists put self-interests first. Third, collectivists experience more socially based emotions (e.g., indebtedness, friendliness) and are guided more by social norms. Individualists, on the other hand, tend to experience more socially disengaged emotions (e.g., pride, anger) and are driven more by their own beliefs and personal values. Fourth, collectivists put more emphasis on harmonious relationships, whereas individualists emphasize task achievement.[77]

power distance   the extent to which people accept unequal distribution of power in a society

• *Power distance*—**Power distance** is the extent that people accept unequal distribution of power in a society. Those with high power distance accept and value unequal power, whereas those with low power distance expect relatively equal power sharing. In high power distance cultures, employees expect to receive commands from their superiors, and conflicts are resolved through formal rules and authority. In contrast, participative management is preferred in low power distance cultures, and conflicts are resolved more through personal networks and coalitions.[78]

uncertainty avoidance   the degree to which people tolerate ambiguity (low uncertainty avoidance) or feel threatened by ambiguity and uncertainty (high uncertainty avoidance)

• *Uncertainty avoidance*—**Uncertainty avoidance** is the degree to which people tolerate ambiguity (low uncertainty avoidance) or feel threatened by ambiguity and uncertainty (high uncertainty avoidance). Employees with high uncertainty avoidance value structured situations where rules of conduct and decision making are clearly documented. They prefer direct rather than indirect or ambiguous communications. There are exceptions, however. The Japanese culture has very high uncertainty avoidance, yet, as we shall learn in Chapter 8, it relies on ambiguous and indirect communication. This occurs because there is a high power distance and collectivism in Japan. High power distance makes it less appropriate to speak forthrightly to those with higher status. The collectivist culture discourages direct communication, which can potentially disrupt harmonious relations within the group.[79]

• *Achievement versus nurturing orientation*—Achievement-oriented cultures value assertiveness, competitiveness, and materialism. As you might expect, this cultural value is strongly related to McClelland's need for achievement (see Chapter 3).[80] Recall that people with a high need for achievement desire reasonable challenges, personal responsibility, feedback, and recognition. These features also generally describe people in achievement-oriented cultures. In contrast, people in nurturing-oriented cultures emphasize relationships and the well-being of others. They focus on human interaction and caring rather than competition and personal success.

• *Long- versus short-term orientation*—People in various cultures also differ in their long- or short-term orientation. Those with a long-term orientation anchor their thoughts more in the future than in the past and present. They value thrift, savings, and persistence, whereas those with a short-term orientation place more emphasis on the past and present, such as respect for tradition and fulfilling social obligations.

Exhibit 7.6
Cultural differences in values

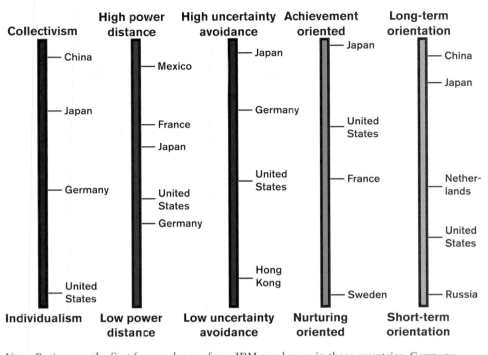

Note: Ratings on the first four scales are from IBM employees in these countries. Germany refers only to the former West Germany. Data for long- and short-term orientation are from student samples.

Sources: Based on G. Hofstede, "Cultural Constraints in Management Theories," *Academy of Management Executive* 7 (1993), pp. 81–94; G. Hofstede, "The Cultural Relativity of Organizational Practices and Theories," *Journal of International Business Studies* 14 (Fall 1983), pp. 75–89.

Exhibit 7.6 shows how Americans compare with people in other cultures on these five dimensions. In general, Americans are individualistic with a somewhat low power distance and short-term orientation. They have moderate achievement orientation and somewhat low uncertainty avoidance (i.e., they can tolerate ambiguity). We should treat this information with some caution, however. One problem is that the data for the first four scales were collected only from IBM employees in each country; data for the long- and short-term orientation scale were collected from college students. Ideally, the information should come from a representative sample of people in the country.

A second concern is that the IBM data are now almost a generation old and some cultures may have changed. For instance, there is some evidence that Japan's culture, particularly in the younger generation, has become more individualistic in recent years.[81] Another concern is that these data assume everyone in a society has similar cultural values. This may be true in a few countries, but not in diverse societies such as the United States. Still, this information provides the best comparison available of these values across cultures.[82]

Ethical Values and Behavior

Bill Daniels lost a large part of his fortune when the American Basketball Association and the team he owned, the Utah Stars, went out of business. But after regaining that wealth, Daniels knew what he had to do. He returned to Salt Lake City and began paying what he owed to former season ticket holders, vendors, and other creditors. Daniels wasn't forced to do this by a court order, and he didn't have any family ties in Utah. He simply believed it was the right thing to do.[83]

ethics the study of moral principles or values that determine whether actions are right or wrong and outcomes are good or bad

Most of us would say that Bill Daniels has strong ethical values that guide his behavior. Recall from Chapter 1 that **ethics** refers to the study of moral principles or values that determine whether actions are right or wrong and outcomes are good or bad. We rely on our ethical values to determine "the right thing to do." Daniels felt that the right thing to do was to pay back the people who lost money from his business failure. He decided this by considering various ethical principles and other factors that we discuss in this final section of the chapter.

Three Ethical Principles

Philosophers and other scholars have identified several general ethical principles, each with a few variations, that should guide our ethical conduct. We can distill most of these principles and variations down to three basic values—utilitarianism, individual rights, and distributive justice.[84]

utilitarianism a moral principle stating that decision makers should seek the greatest good for the greatest number of people when choosing among alternatives

• *Utilitarianism*—**Utilitarianism** advises us to seek the greatest good for the greatest number of people. In other words, we should choose the option providing the highest degree of satisfaction to those affected. This is sometimes known as a consequential principle because it focuses on the consequences of our actions, not on how we achieve those consequences. Unfortunately, utilitarianism can occasionally result in unethical choices because it judges morality by the results, not the means to attaining those results. Moreover, it accepts situations in which a few people may be severely oppressed to benefit others.

• *Individual rights*—This ethical value is the belief that everyone has entitlements that let them act in a certain way. Some of the most widely cited rights are freedom of movement, physical security, freedom of speech, fair trial, and freedom from torture.[85] The individual rights principle is not restricted to legal rights. A person may have a right to privacy, but employers have a right to inspect everyone's e-mail messages. One problem with individual rights is that certain individual rights may conflict with others. For example, the shareholders' right to be informed about corporate activities may ultimately conflict with an executive's right to privacy.

• *Distributive justice*—This is the ethical value of fairness that we discussed in Chapter 3. It suggests that inequality is acceptable if (1) everyone has equal access to the more favored positions in society and (2) the inequalities are ultimately in the best interest of the least well off in society. The first part means that everyone should have equal access to higher paying jobs and other valued positions in life. The second part says that some people can receive greater rewards than others if this benefits those less well off. Employees in risky jobs should be paid more if this benefits others who are less well off. The problem with this principle is that society can't seem to agree on what activities provide the greatest benefit to the least well off.

Although some people adhere to only one of these principles, we need to consider all three when making choices. We might emphasize a certain ethical value that is most consistent with our personal values, cultural values, and past experience, but all three principles should be applied to put important ethical issues to the test.

Ethical Values and Moral Development

moral development the person's level of maturity regarding ethical decision making

The development and application of ethical values depend on the individual's level of **moral development.** Throughout childhood and later years, people develop a maturity regarding ethical decision making. Exhibit 7.7 illustrates the most widely cited model of moral development.[86] At the lowest level of development (preconventional), ethical conduct is based on personal interests. Behavior is initially determined by avoiding physical punishment and obeying

Exhibit 7.7   Moral development model

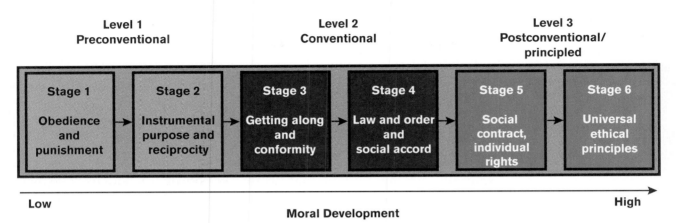

Source: Based on information in L. Kohlberg, *Essays in Moral Development*, vol. 1: *The Philosophy of Moral Development* (New York: Harper and Row, 1981).

authority (Stage 1), and later by learning to follow rules only when it is in people's self-interest or their actions will be returned in kind (Stage 2).

Most employees operate somewhere in the second level of moral development (conventional), which is characterized by the internalization of ethical rules and social expectations. In Stage 3, people engage in ethical behavior by trying to live up to the expectations of family, friends, and others who are close to them. Stage 4 extends this social contract to include the rules of law in the larger society. People who reach the highest level of moral development (postconventional/principled) create their own set of ethical values rather than relying on outside sources. In Stage 5, people develop their ethical value set by combining what others think. At Stage 6, people have chosen a more permanent composite of universal ethical principles and abide by those values, even when they are in conflict with existing laws.

This moral development model is widely used in ethics research and has good empirical support. For instance, it explains why some people have less prejudicial attitudes toward women executives.[87] However, the model might not reflect moral development for women as well as it does for men. Critics note that this model emphasizes justice and rights, whereas women apparently have a stronger ethic of care and responsibility.[88] Other studies report that women emphasize different values than men do when making choices.[89]

Moral Intensity, Ethical Sensitivity, and Situational Influences

Ethical values play an important role in ethical behavior, but we also need to consider other factors. Three central concepts in ethical behavior are the moral intensity of the issue, the individual's ethical sensitivity, and situational factors.

moral intensity the degree to which an issue demands the application of ethical principles

Moral intensity is the degree to which an issue demands the application of ethical principles. The higher the moral intensity, the more that ethical principles should provide guidance to resolve the issue. Stealing from your employer is usually considered high on moral intensity, whereas taking a client to lunch is much lower on the scale. The moral intensity of an issue is higher when the issue clearly produces good or bad consequences, others in society think it is good or evil, the issue affects people quickly, the decision maker feels close to the issue, and the person is able to influence the issue.[90]

ethical sensitivity an individual's ability to recognize the presence and determine the relative importance of an ethical issue

Even if an issue has high moral intensity, some employees might not recognize its ethical importance because they have low ethical sensitivity. **Ethical sensitivity** is a personal characteristic that enables people to recognize the presence and determine the relative importance of an ethical issue.[91] Ethically sensitive people are not necessarily more ethical. Rather, they are more likely to recognize whether an issue requires ethical consideration, and can more accurately estimate the moral intensity of the issue. Ethically sensitive people tend to have higher empathy. They also have more information about the specific situation. For example, accountants would be more ethically sensitive regarding accounting procedures than someone who has not received training in this profession.

The situation is a third important influence on ethical conduct within organizations. Some research suggests that executives are more likely to make unethical choices when they face competitive pressure or will personally gain from the unethical choice. According to one recent survey, 57 percent of American workers feel more pressure from employers and their personal situation to be unethical than they did five years ago.[92] At Digital Equipment, for example, workers under pressure to develop new ideas have invaded the computer files of co-workers to make electronic copies and claim the work as their own. Under pressure to win a Navy contract, the CEO of Bath Iron Works made copies of a file left behind by a Navy consultant that documented information about a major competitor. By reading the information rather than immediately returning the file without inspecting it, the CEO lost his job and nearly got Maine's largest employer barred from future government contracts.[93]

Situational factors explain why good people do bad things. Ethical values affect a person's motivation to act in a certain way, but environmental forces also influence individual behavior. The point here is not to justify unethical conduct. Rather, we need to recognize all of the factors that influence wrongdoing so that organizations can correct these problems in the future.

Cultural Differences in Business Ethics

When Harry Gould, Jr., visited Gould Paper's manufacturing plants in France, he asked his French counterpart to show him the books (financial statements). The French executive casually asked, "Which books do you want to see?" The executive kept three sets of records—one for his family, one for the revenue collector, and the real one. "[The French executive] didn't think anything about that," Gould recalls. "There's a cultural mind-set that has no bearing on the reality we are used to here in the United States."[94]

As Harry Gould discovered, corporate decision makers face a larger set of ethical dilemmas when they enter the global marketplace. The French executive saw little wrong with having three sets of financial records, whereas most Americans would consider this practice of falsifying information highly unethical. This isn't an isolated example. Kickbacks are illegal in the United States, whereas several European countries are just beginning to remove bribery payments as a tax deduction. Studies have reported that Australian business students are less ethically concerned than American students about padding résumés, sneaking vacations on company time, and having lavish company-paid entertainment. Singaporeans seem to be less concerned than Americans about software piracy. Hong Kong students are more willing than students in Taiwan, Japan, or Canada to treat customers unfairly.[95]

Why does ethical conduct vary across cultures? It's not that people in some cultures have lower ethical values or sensitivity. They don't. People around the world generally have similar levels of ethical sensitivity regarding stealing, physical abuse, misrepresentation, and so forth.[96] The main reason why ethical conduct varies across cultures is because people interpret the situation differently. In other words, a situation with high moral intensity in the United States might have lower intensity to people in another culture, and vice versa.[97] The French executive described earlier probably believed that false financial reporting has little effect on others and is widely practiced. These perceptions result in low moral intensity for false financial reporting. Similarly, Americans equate some forms of gift-giving as bribery, whereas people in some cultures view this as a sign of respect and part of the relationship-building process.[98]

Thus, ethical values may be similar across cultures, but people differ in their interpretation of where those ethical values should be applied. This calls for some degree of *ethical relativism*—adjusting perceptions about what is ethical to fit the culture. At the same time, we should be careful not to adjust ethical interpretations too much from one place to the next because this tends to make people less sensitive to ethical issues. In short, globalization creates an ethical balancing act.

Supporting Ethical Behavior

Almost one-half of all U.S. firms with 50 or more employees have introduced initiatives to support ethical values in the workplace. Ethical codes of conduct are the most common. Ninety-five percent of the Fortune 500 companies in the United States and 57 percent of the 500 largest companies in the United Kingdom now have codes of ethics. Even in Thailand, which has one of the worst records for business ethics, Thai Danu Bank and other firms are adopting codes of ethical conduct based on international business practices.[99]

Ethical codes establish the organization's ethical standards, but critics say that this has little effect on ethical conduct. To support this point, one survey reported that most U.S. companies have a code of ethics but only 45 percent of employees say that their company leaders abide by those ethical principles.[100] Companies must move beyond written codes to strategies that help employees alter their behavior at work. Some organizations have improved ethical behavior by changing reward systems that unintentionally encourage unethical behavior in the first place. The U.S. Internal Revenue Service recently did this after discovering that its agents' unethical conduct was traced back to an incentive scheme motivating them to collect more back taxes and penalties from taxpayers.[101]

Companies are also expanding their ethics programs with ethics audits, ethics training, hotlines, ombuds officers, ethics offices, and ethics committees. Martin Marietta uses a board game to teach employees how to sort out ethical ambiguities. Pharmaceutical giant Merck & Co. has four ombuds officers to help employees resolve ethical dilemmas.[102] Connections 7.2 describes how two health care organizations—Quorum Health Group, Inc., and Columbia/HCA Healthcare Corp.—have introduced ethics training and other initiatives to ensure that employee values and behaviors are morally correct.

Developing moral character at work   One criticism of business ethics training programs is that they focus on organizational policy issues and very little on developing moral character. Rather than just debating the merits of gift giving and conflict of interest, ethics programs should also help individuals understand hypocrisy, self-deception, and other elements of personal morality.

One way to do this is through **action learning.** Recall from Chapter 2 that action learning is experiential-based learning in which participants investigate an organizational issue. For example, one action learning issue at a Boston

action learning a form of on-site, experiential-based learning in which participants investigate an organizational problem or opportunity and propose recommendations

bank involved resolving a conflict between the human resource executive and group manager. The human resources executive wanted the group manager to hire an African-American male the next time there was an opening for a loan officer. The group manager was happy to interview African-American male applicants, but said he would hire the most qualified person. By investigating these real dilemmas, participants experience the empathy and emotion of this process and learn to combine personal morality with organizational level policy.[103]

Ethical values, cultural values, and workplace emotions have a powerful effect on individual behavior in the workplace. Throughout this chapter, it is apparent that values and emotions are shaped by the perceptual process that was discussed in Chapter 6. Another vital factor in these processes is individual and organizational communication, which we discuss in the next chapter.

Connections 7.2 ◻ Health Care Firms Instill Strong Ethical Values

Quorum Health Group, Inc., supports business ethics through training and a Help Line where an attorney answers ethics questions.
[Courtesy of Quorum Health Group, Inc.]

One of the first things that new hires learn at Quorum Health Group, Inc., is "doing the right thing." Every associate at the Brentwood, Tennessee, health care firm watches a video of the company president emphasizing the importance of ethical behavior. They also receive the company's ethical code of conduct and sign a certificate of compliance, affirming that they understand the ethics document.

Quorum takes business ethics seriously. Along with orientation sessions, many of Quorum's associates receive training on regulatory activities and other sensitive ethical issues. Posters displayed throughout Quorum's institutions remind staff that they must work ethically and do the right thing. Associates can call a 24-hour Help Line to receive answers to ethical questions or anonymously report sexual harassment and other forms of wrongdoing.

Columbia/HCA Healthcare Corp. is working quickly to catch up with Quorum's ethics initiatives. Plagued by allegations of fraud and possible Medicare overbilling, Columbia also introduced a code of conduct, ethics training, and a toll-free ethics line. Calls to the ethics line have already led to the termination of some hospital chief executives.

"I don't think we have to change personal values much," says Alan Yuspeh, Columbia's senior vice president of ethics, compliance, and corporate responsibility. "But we sure want people to know that we hope they bring their highest sense of personal values to work each day."

Source: Adapted from C. Ornstein, "A Health Care Education," *Dallas Morning News*, February 19, 1998, p. D1; C. F. Batts, "Making Ethics an Organizational Priority," *Healthcare Forum Journal* 41 (January–February 1998), pp. 38–42. ◻

Chapter Summary

Emotions are feelings experienced toward an object, person, or event that create a state of readiness. They differ from attitudes, which represent the cluster of beliefs, feelings, and behavioral intentions toward an object. Beliefs are a person's perceptions about an attitude object. Feelings are judgments about our emotional experiences associated with the target. Behavioral intentions represent a motivation to engage in a particular behavior with respect to the target. Emotions usually affect behavior through beliefs, feelings, and behavioral intentions, respectively.

Job satisfaction represents a person's evaluation of his or her job and work context. Satisfaction depends on the level of discrepancy between what people expect to receive and what they experience. Job satisfaction also increases with the perceived equity in the exchange relationship.

Job satisfaction has a weak association with task performance because general attitudes don't predict specific behaviors very well, researchers measure specific performance rather than organizational citizenship, and performance isn't always linked to valued rewards. Job satisfaction has a stronger association with customer satisfaction because it affects moods and reduces employee turnover.

Organizational commitment is a set of attitudes regarding the individual's relationship with the organization and his or her motivation to remain with the organization. Affective and continuance commitment have different effects on employee behavior. Companies build loyalty through fairness and satisfaction, some level of job security, organizational comprehension, employee involvement, and trust.

Emotional labor refers to the effort, planning, and control needed to express organizationally desired emotions during interpersonal transactions. This is more common in jobs with frequent and lengthy customer interaction, where the job requires a variety of emotions to display, and where employees must abide by the display rules. Emotional labor creates problems because true emotions tend to leak out, and conflict between expected and true emotions (emotional dissonance) causes stress and burnout.

Emotional intelligence is the ability to monitor your own and others' emotions, to discriminate among them, and to use the information to guide your thinking and actions. This includes self-awareness, self-regulation, self-motivation, empathy, and social skill.

Values represent stable, long-lasting beliefs about what is important to us. They influence our decisions and interpretation of what is ethical. Five values that differ across cultures are individualism–collectivism, power distance, uncertainty avoidance, achievement-nurturing orientation, and long- and short-term orientation.

Three values that guide ethical conduct are utilitarianism, individual rights, and distributive justice. Three other factors that influence ethical conduct are the extent that an issue demands ethical principles (moral intensity), the person's sensitivity to the presence and importance of an ethical dilemma, and situational factors that cause people to deviate from their moral values.

People from different cultures tend to act differently when faced with an ethical issue. Although ethical values differ somewhat across cultures, most of this variation is explained by the fact that unique cultural experiences cause people to see different levels of moral intensity.

Key Terms

Action learning, p. 221
Attitudes, p. 201
Cognitive dissonance, p. 204
Discrepancy theory, p. 206
Emotional dissonance, p. 212
Emotional intelligence (EI), p. 213
Emotional labor, p. 211
Emotions, p. 200
Empathy, p. 214
Equity theory, p. 206
Ethical intensity, p. 220
Ethical sensitivity, p. 220
Ethics, p. 218
Extroversion, p. 201

Individualism–collectivism, p. 216
Job satisfaction, p. 204
Moral development, p. 218
Moral intensity, p. 219
Negative affectivity (NA), p. 201
Organizational citizenship, p. 207
Organizational commitment, p. 208
Positive affectivity (PA), p. 201
Power distance, p. 216
Self-monitoring personality, p. 214
Trust, p. 210
Uncertainty avoidance, p. 216
Utilitarianism, p. 218
Values, p. 215

Discussion Questions

1. After a few months on the job, Susan has experienced several emotional episodes ranging from frustration to joy toward the work she is assigned. Use the attitude model to explain how these emotions affect Susan's level of job satisfaction with the work itself.

2. The latest employee attitude survey in your organization indicates that employees are unhappy with some aspects of the organization. However, management tends to pay attention to the single-item question asking employees to indicate their overall satisfaction with the job. The answers to this question indicate that 86 percent of staff members are very or somewhat satisfied, so management concludes that the other results refer to issues that are probably not important to employees. Explain why management's interpretation of these results may be inaccurate.

3. Universal Broadcasting Corporation is concerned about losing some of its best technical staff to competitors. Senior executives have decided that the best way to build a loyal workforce is to introduce a deferred profit-sharing plan. Employees would receive half of each year's profit share at the end of the year, but the other half would be paid out over the next two years as trailers. Anyone who leaves for any reason other than retirement or layoffs would forfeit some or all of the deferred payments. Explain what effect this plan may have on organizational commitment and employee behaviors.

4. A recent study reported that college instructors are frequently required to engage in emotional labor. Identify the situations in which emotional labor is required for this job. In your opinion, is emotional labor more troublesome for college instructors or for telephone operators working at a 911 emergency service?

5. If a co-worker told you that he or she had a high level of emotional intelligence, what would you look for to confirm that statement?

6. Your company plans to expand operations into Japan and wants you to form working relationships with Japanese suppliers. Considering only the values of individualism and uncertainty avoidance, what should you be aware of or sensitive to in your dealings with these suppliers? You may assume that your contacts hold typical Japanese values along these dimensions.

7. A major software firm set up a program whereby computer science professors would receive $200 for mentioning the firm's products at public presentations. The money is used to offset travel costs to attend these sessions. Discuss the ethical implications of this incentive.

8. Compare and contrast moral intensity and ethical sensitivity.

CASE STUDY

Rough seas on the LINK650

Professor Suzanne Baxter was preparing for her first class of the semester when Shaun O'Neill knocked lightly on the open door to her office and announced himself: "Hi, Professor, I don't suppose you remember me?" Professor Baxter had large classes, but she did remember that Shaun was a student in her organizational behavior class two years earlier. Shaun had decided to work in the oil industry for a couple of years before returning to school to complete his degree.

"Welcome back!" Baxter said as she beckoned him into the office. "I heard you were working on an oil rig in the United Kingdom. How was it?"

"Well, Professor," Shaun began, "I had worked two summers in the Texan oil fields and my family's from Ireland, so I hoped to get a job on the LINK650. It's that new WestOil drilling rig that arrived with so much fanfare in the North Sea fields two years ago. The LINK650 was built by LINK, Inc., in Texas. A standard practice in this industry is for the rig manufacturer to manage its day-to-day operations, so employees on the LINK650 are managed completely by LINK managers with no involvement from WestOil. We all know that drilling rig jobs are dangerous, but they pay well and offer generous time off. A local newspaper there said that nearly 1,000 people lined up to complete job applications for the 50 nontechnical positions. I was lucky enough to get one of those jobs.

"Everyone hired on the LINK650 was enthusiastic and proud. We were one of the chosen few and were really pumped up about working on a new rig that had received so much media attention. I was quite impressed with the recruiters—so were several other guys—because they really seemed to be concerned about our welfare out on the platform. I later discovered that the recruiters came from a consulting firm that specializes in hiring people. Come to think of it, we didn't meet a single LINK manager during that process. Maybe things would have been different if some of those LINK supervisors had interviewed us.

"Working on LINK650 was a real shock, even though most of us had some experience working in the oil fields. I'd say that none of the 50 nontechnical people hired was quite prepared for the brutal jobs on the oil rig. We did the dirtiest jobs in the biting cold winds of the North Sea. Still, during the first few months most of us wanted to show the company that we were dedicated to getting the job done. A couple of the new guys quit within a few weeks, but most of the people hired with me really got along well—you know, just like the ideas you mentioned in class. We formed a special bond that helped us through the bad weather and grueling work.

"The LINK650 supervisors were another matter. They were mean taskmasters who had worked for many years on oil rigs in the Gulf of Mexico or North Sea. They seemed to relish the idea of treating their employees the same way they had been treated before becoming managers. We put up with their abuse for the first few months, but things got worse when production on the LINK650 was stopped twice to correct mechanical problems. These setbacks embarrassed LINK's management and they put more pressure on the supervisors to get us back on schedule.

"The supervisors started to ignore equipment problems and pushed us to get jobs done more quickly without regard to safety procedures. They routinely shouted obscenities at employees in front of others. A couple of my work mates were fired and a couple of others quit their jobs. I almost lost my job one day just because my boss thought I was deliberately working slowly. He didn't realize—or care—that the fittings I was connecting were damaged. Several people started finding ways to avoid the supervisors and get as little work done as possible. Many of my co-workers developed back problems. We jokingly called it the "rigger's backache" because some employees faked their ailment to leave the rig with paid sick leave.

"On top of the lousy supervisors, we were always kept in the dark about the problems on the rig. Supervisors said that they didn't know anything, which was partly true, but they said we shouldn't be so interested in things that didn't concern us. But the rig's problems, as well as its future contract work, were a major concern to crew members who weren't ready to quit. Their job security depended on the rig's production levels and whether WestOil would sign contracts to drill new holes. Given the rig's problems, most of us were concerned that we would be laid off at any time.

"Everything came to a head when Bob MacKenzie was killed because someone secured a hoist improperly. I'm not sure if it was mentioned in the papers here, but it was big news around this time last year. A government inquiry concluded that the person responsible wasn't properly trained and that employees were being pushed to finish jobs without safety precautions. Anyway, while the inquiry was going on, several employees decided to unionize the rig. It wasn't long before most employees on LINK650 had signed union cards. That really shocked LINK's management and the entire oil industry because it was, I think, just the second time that a rig had ever been unionized there.

"Since then, management has been doing everything in its power to get rid of the union. It sent a "safety officer" to the rig, although we eventually realized that he was a consultant the company hired to undermine union support. Several managers were sent to special seminars on how to manage under a union workforce, although one of the topics was how to break the union.

"So you see, Professor, I joined LINK as an enthusiastic employee and quit last month with no desire to lift a finger for them. It really bothers me, because I was always told to do your best, no matter how tough the situation. It's been quite an experience."

Discussion Questions

1. Use the job satisfaction model to explain why the LINK650 employees were dissatisfied with their work.

2. Identify the various ways that employees expressed their job dissatisfaction on the LINK650.

3. Shaun O'Neill's commitment to the LINK organization dwindled over his two years of employment. Discuss the factors that affected his organizational commitment.

The return of corporate loyalty

BusinessWeek

Last year, Harry Cedarbaum was caught in a classic baby-boomer crunch. His parents, who live in Europe, needed help due to their health problems, yet Cedarbaum's demanding job didn't offer enough time. Fortunately, his employer, Booz, Allen & Hamilton Inc. in New York, offered a job rotation program that gave Cedarbaum more time to squeeze in trips to Europe. "I get several headhunter calls a week, but I made a commitment to the firm, and they made a commitment to me," says a grateful Cedarbaum. "This loyalty is an incredible thing."

This *Business Week* case study describes how Booz, Allen and other organizations have rediscovered the value of employee loyalty. The article discusses why companies are scrambling to build organizational commitment, how they are trying to strengthen this attitude, and how the employer-employee bond is different from before. Read through this *Business Week* article at

www.mhhe.com/mcshane1e and prepare for the discussion questions below.

Discussion Questions

1. What strategies are companies using to build organizational loyalty? Will any of them increase continuance commitment rather than affective commitment?

2. This *Business Week* case study says that organizational loyalty has been "retooled." What does this mean and how does the new loyalty compare with the previous version?

3. What problems do companies face while trying to improve organizational loyalty?

Source: A. Bernstein, "We Want You to Stay. Really," *Business Week*, June 22, 1998, pp. 67–70. ■

In depth: buy American: merger between Chrysler and Mercedes Benz

 How are Americans feeling about Mercedes, a huge German company buying Chrysler, an American automobile icon? Almost 25 million Americans drive affordable American-made Chryslers compared to half a million Mercedes. But this merger goes beyond loyalty with a lot of people, especially in Detroit, the motor city.

For 73 years, Chrysler workers have walked through the gates of an American institution and built more than 109 million cars and trucks for this country and the world. But today in Detroit over an all-American breakfast of bacon and eggs, workers and car owners heard the news—the Germans are taking over Chrysler. One Chrysler worker said, "Things are changing so much. It's a new time, a new day."

Actually, it's a new way of doing business. Chrysler who makes the Jeep, the vehicle the Americans rode to

victory in WWII, is allied with the German company that made cars for the Nazi high command. Another Chrysler worker said, "You have these two companies that formerly made war materiel that they shot at one another, are now coming together."

In 1925, Walter Chrysler took two failing car companies and started his own. Over the years Chrysler produced the DeSoto, the Plymouth, tail fins and aerodynamic styling, and eventually the minivan. But in the mid-1970s the rise in gas prices and the Japanese auto industry drove Chrysler to the edge of bankruptcy. With a $1.2 billion loan from the federal government, Lee Iacocca steered the carmaker out of trouble by wrapping the company in the American flag. Today's news of merger has revived the buy American feeling among some consumers like Theodore Wise of Chicago who can't forget Daimler's association with the Nazis. Wise remarked, "It's not Chrysler anymore, the way I understand it. It ceases to be Chrysler and becomes a German product. And if so, I would not purchase it."

But the reality is that most American-made cars, even Chrysler's minivan and sedans, have some foreign parts. The notion of a pure American car has gone the way of the tail fin. And so too has the historic notion of a purely American company like Chrysler.

Discussion Questions

1. Several Chrysler employees expressed reservations about being acquired by Daimler. How do you think this merger will affect attitudes about quality and workmanship?

2. Explain how cognitive dissonance may play a role in the merger of Chrysler and Daimler.

3. When an organization merges with another, the merger is often followed by restructuring and lay-offs. What effect do you think announcement of the merger had on employee loyalty to the company? ■

Ethical dilemmas in employment

Purpose

This exercise is designed to help you apply ethical principles to real moral dilemmas that employers and employees have faced.

Instructions

The following incidents are adapted from real events and ultimately require someone to make a decision with strong moral implications. For each incident, indicate what you would do and identify one of the three ethical principles described in this chapter to explain your decision.

When everyone is done, students will form small teams and compare their decisions and justifications for each incident. If possible, try to reach a consensus on the appropriate action for each incident, but leave enough time to discuss each incident. Finally, the class will discuss each incident, beginning with a tally of the actions that each student initially wrote down and the group results. The subsequent discussion should look at the dominant ethical principle as well as the role of personal values in ethical decision making.

The case of the illegal application form

You want to apply for a professional job at a midsized manufacturing company. As part of the hiring process, you are given an application form that asks, among other things, about your age and marital status. Requesting this information is a clear violation of human rights. If you bring this fact to the employer's attention, however, there is a concern that the employer might think you won't be a loyal employee or that you aren't a team player. If you leave those sections blank, the employer might come to the same conclusion or think that you have something to hide. You don't know much about the quality of the employer, but getting this job is important to your career. What would you do?

The case of questionable objectivity

You are owner of a highly rated talk radio station. The popular radio personality on the morning phone-in show, Judy Price, is married to John Price, a lawyer who entered politics a few years ago and is now a prominent politician. There is increasing concern from the board of directors that the radio station's perceived objectivity

227

would be compromised if Ms. Price remains on the air as a news commentator while her husband holds such a public position. Some co-workers doubt that Judy Price would publicly criticize her husband or his party's policies, although they don't know for certain. Ms. Price says that her job comes first and that any attempt to remove her would represent a form of discrimination on the basis of marital status. There are no other on-air positions available for her at this station. What would you do?

The case of the awkward office affair

As head of human resources, you have learned from two employees that one of the office administrators, Sandi, is having an affair with Jim, an employee in shipping and receiving. Jim is single, but Sandi is married and her husband also works in the company's shipping and receiving department. You have spoken privately to Sandi, who admits to the affair but doesn't think that her husband knows about it. Moreover, she retorted that the company has no right to snoop into her private life and that she will see a lawyer if the company does anything against her. So far, there haven't been any signs of office disruption because the few employees who know about the affair have not communicated it through the grapevine. However, morale problems could develop if the news spreads. The two employees who initially told you about the affair believe strongly in marriage fidelity and feel that Jim, Sandi, or both should leave the company. Finally, there is the concern that Sandi's husband might have an altercation with Jim, and that the company could be liable for the consequences. What would you do? ■

SELF-ASSESSMENT EXERCISE

Individualism–collectivism scale

Purpose

This self-assessment is designed to help you to identify your level of individualism and collectivism.

Instructions

Read each of the statements below and circle the response that you believe best indicates how well these statements describe you. Then use the scoring key to calculate your results for each scale. This exercise is completed alone so students assess themselves honestly without concerns of social comparison. However, class discussion will focus on the individualism–collectivism values.

Scoring Key

Individualism: Add up the results for odd numbered items (i.e., 1, 3, 5, 7, 9, 11, 13, 15). Maximum score is 40. Higher scores indicate more individualism.
Collectivism: Add up the results for even numbered items (i.e., 2, 4, 6, 8, 10, 12, 14, 16). Maximum score is 40. Higher scores indicate more collectivism.

Source: T. M. Singelis, H. C. Triandis, D. P. S. Bhawuk, M. J. Gelfand, "Horizontal and Vertical Dimensions of Individualism and Collectivism: A Theoretical and Measurement Refinement," *Cross-Cultural Research* 29 (August 1995), pp. 240–75.

Individualism–Collectivism Scale

Circle the number that best indicates how well these statements describe you.	Does not describe me at all ▼	Does not describe me very well ▼	Describes me somewhat ▼	Describes me well ▼	Describes me very well ▼
1. I often do "my own thing." ...	1	2	3	4	5
2. The well-being of my co-workers is important to me.	1	2	3	4	5
3. One should live one's life independently of others.	1	2	3	4	5
4. If a coworker gets a prize, I would feel proud.	1	2	3	4	5
5. I like my privacy.	1	2	3	4	5
6. If a relative were in financial difficulty, I would help within my means.	1	2	3	4	5
7. I prefer to be direct and forthright when discussing issues with people.	1	2	3	4	5
8. It is important to maintain harmony within my group. ...	1	2	3	4	5
9. I am a unique individual.	1	2	3	4	5
10. I like sharing little things with my neighbors.	1	2	3	4	5
11. What happens to me is my own doing.	1	2	3	4	5
12. I feel good when I cooperate with others.	1	2	3	4	5
13. When I succeed, it is usually because of my abilities.	1	2	3	4	5
14. My happiness depends very much on the happiness of those around me.	1	2	3	4	5
15. I enjoy being unique and different from others in many ways.	1	2	3	4	5
16. To me, pleasure is spending time with others.	1	2	3	4	5 □

CHAPTER EIGHT

Communicating in Organizational Settings

Learning Objectives

After reading this chapter, you should be able to:

- Explain the importance of communication and diagram the communication process.
- Identify four common communication barriers.
- Describe problems with communicating through electronic mail.
- Discuss how the law of telecosm will affect organizational communication.
- Explain how nonverbal communication relates to emotional labor and emotional contagion.
- Identify two conditions requiring a channel with high data-carrying capacity.
- Summarize four communication strategies in organizational hierarchies.
- Discuss the degree to which men and women communicate differently.
- Outline the key elements of active listening.
- Summarize the key features of persuasive communication.

"Hi Jack, I've worked out a klugey solution to the UI issue," an employee e-mails to a colleague in the next cubicle. "We need to get granular on this. Unfortunately, I'm OOF next week, so you'll have to burn up a few cycles on it. I'm worried that the bluebadges on this project will go totally nonlinear when they realize the RTM date is slipping."

Welcome to the world of Microspeak—the unofficial language of Microsoft. Employees at the world's largest software company have acquired a lexicon that would baffle researchers at *Webster's Dictionary*. Microsoft staffers eat their own dog food, dislike weasel users, and avoid getting caught in reality distortion fields. This all makes sense to insiders, but not to people raised in the English language!

Most of this dialogue occurs in cyber media rather than "fiber media" (paper) or facemail (face-to-face). That's not to say that Microsoft employees never meet. They do, in small groups around whiteboards in someone's office to share insights, resolve problems, and confirm deadlines. In fact, Microsoft makes sure that employees work at the same location so they can communicate and solve problems quickly in face-to-face meetings.

"All of us [are] here, with very minor exceptions, on one site, so that whatever interdependencies exist, you can go see that person face-to-face," explains Microsoft CEO and cofounder Bill Gates.[1]

Microsoft provides a collaborative workplace where employees communicate in Microspeak through e-mail and small group meetings.
[Peter Sibbald/Sygma]

At the beginning of this book, we said that organizations are people who interact with each other to achieve some purpose. Employees are the organization's brain cells, and communication represents the nervous system that carries this information and shared meaning to vital parts of the organizational body. Microsoft and other organizations require innovative strategies to keep these communication pathways open. Smaller businesses may have fewer structural bottlenecks, but they too can suffer from subtle communication barriers.

communication the process by which information is transmitted and understood between two or more people

Communication refers to the process by which information is transmitted and *understood* between two or more people. We emphasize the word *understood* because transmitting the sender's intended meaning is the essence of good communication. Corporate leaders spend almost 80 percent of their day communicating, so it isn't surprising that leadership performance is closely related to their communication skills.[2]

Buckman Labs is a pioneer in knowledge management. Yet, the Memphis-based specialty chemical company claims that its real strength is facilitating communication across the organization. "[W]e have designed a system and built a culture that facilitates the communication of whatever is needed across all of the organization's boundaries," explains CEO Robert Buckman. This isn't easy for a company with operations in 90 countries and whose employees spend much of their time visiting customers. Buckman met the challenge by distributing notebook computers so that people can communicate from anywhere. The company also developed a worldwide information database and network, called K'netix, that allows employees to search out and share information quickly and efficiently. For example, a Buckman Labs representative in Indonesia won a $6 million proposal, partly because he requested vital information and received it within eight hours from the United States and Europe.[3] What additional ways might Buckman Labs and other companies improve communication across their global operations?
[Courtesy of Buckman Labs]

knowledge management
any structured activity that improves an organization's capacity to acquire, share, and utilize knowledge that enhances its survival and success

Communication plays an important role in **knowledge management,** particularly in minimizing the "silos of knowledge" problem that undermines an organization's potential.[4] This relates to the increasing importance of communication in decision making. As organizational environments become more complex, decision makers need information from many people to perceive problems, recognize new product ideas, and identify emerging customer needs. Canon, the Japanese optics and electronics company, recognized this through its emphasis on "heart-to-heart and mind-to-mind communication." This corporate philosophy encourages employees worldwide to share information on customers and products so that they can make more informed choices about corporate actions. British Telecom does the same thing. By encouraging ongoing communication, employees create "knowledge moments"—instances where shared knowledge results in better decisions.[5]

Another vital function of communication is to coordinate work activities.[6] Through dialogue, co-workers develop common mental models—working models of the world (see Chapter 6)—so they can synchronize interdependent work activities through common expectations and assumptions.[7] Lastly, communication is the glue that bonds people together. It fulfills the need for affiliation and, as part of the dynamics of social support, eases work-related stress. Moreover, employees identify more with the organization when they feel connected to co-workers and receive information about their organization.[8]

This chapter begins by presenting a model of the communication process and discussing several communication barriers. Next, the different types of communication channels, including computer-mediated communication, are described, followed by factors to consider when choosing a communication medium. This chapter then presents some options for communicating in organizational hierarchies and describes the pervasive organizational grapevine. The latter part of the chapter examines cross-cultural and gender differences in communication, strategies to improve interpersonal communication, and persuasive communication.

A Model of Communication

The communication model presented in Exhibit 8.1 provides a useful "conduit" metaphor for thinking about the communication process.[9] According to this model, communication flows through channels between the sender and receiver. The sender forms a message and encodes it into words, gestures, voice intonations, and other symbols or signs. Next, the encoded message is transmitted to the intended receiver through one or more communication channels (media). The receiver senses the incoming message and decodes it into something meaningful. Ideally, the decoded meaning is what the sender had intended.

In most situations, the sender looks for evidence that the other person received and understood the transmitted message. This feedback may be a formal acknowledgment, such as a "Yes, I know what you mean," or indirect evidence from the receiver's subsequent actions. Notice that feedback repeats the communication process. Intended feedback is encoded, transmitted, received, and decoded from the receiver to the sender of the original message.

This model recognizes that communication is not a free-flowing conduit.[10] Rather, the transmission of meaning from one person to another is hampered by *noise*—the psychological, social, and structural barriers that distort and obscure the sender's intended message. If any part of the communication process is distorted or broken, the sender and receiver will not have a common understanding of the message.

Exhibit 8.1
The communication
process model

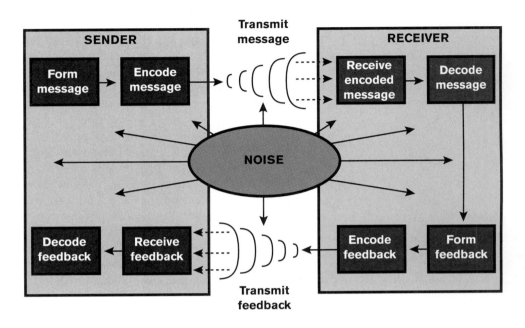

Communication Barriers (Noise)

In spite of the best intentions of sender and receiver to communicate, several barriers inhibit the effective exchange of information. As Exhibit 8.1 illustrates, these barriers are called "noise" in the communications conduit, and they occur throughout the process. We will refer to many communication barriers in this chapter, but four pervasive problems are perceptions, filtering, language, and information overload.

Perceptions

As we learned in Chapter 6, the perceptual process determines what messages we select or screen out, as well as how the selected information is organized and interpreted. This can be a significant source of noise in the communication process if the perceptions of the sender and receiver are not aligned. For example, a plant superintendent in a concrete block plant picked up a piece of broken brick while talking with the supervisor. This action had no particular meaning to the superintendent—just something to toy with during the conversation. Yet as soon as the senior manager had left, the supervisor ordered one half-hour of overtime for the entire crew to clean up the plant. The supervisor mistakenly perceived the superintendent's action as a signal that the plant was messy.[11]

Filtering

Some messages are filtered or stopped altogether on their way up or down the organizational hierarchy. Filtering may involve deleting or delaying negative information, or changing the words so that events sound more favorable. Employees and supervisors usually filter communication to create a good impression of themselves to superiors. Filtering is most common where the organization rewards employees who communicate mainly positive information and among employees with strong career mobility aspirations.[12]

Language

Words and gestures carry no inherent meaning with them. Instead, the sender must ensure that the receiver understands these symbols and signs. In reality, lack of mutual understanding is a common reason why messages are distorted. Two potential language barriers are jargon and ambiguity.

Jargon   Employees at Microsoft (and many other software companies) use a peculiar language called Microspeak to communicate their ideas. As we read in the opening story, this **jargon** includes technical language and acronyms as well as recognized words with specialized meaning in specific organizations or social groups. Jargon can improve communication efficiency when both sender and receiver understand this specialized language. It also shapes and maintains an organization's cultural values as well as symbolizes an employee's self-identity in a group (see Chapter 6).[13]

However, jargon becomes a communication barrier when the receiver doesn't understand this specialized language. For example, employees at Wacker Siltronic Corp. were breaking saw blades and causing a high rate of product defects after new machinery was introduced. Management eventually discovered that the manuals were written for engineers, and that employees were guessing (often incorrectly) the meaning of the jargon. Productivity improved and machine costs dropped after the manuals were rewritten with the jargon removed.[14]

jargon technical language of a particular occupational group or recognized words with specialized meaning in specific organizations or social groups

FARCUS is reprinted with permission from Farcus Cartoons Inc., All rights reserved.

© 1995 Farcus Cartoons/dist. by Universal Press Syndicate   WAISGLASS/COULTHART

"That's what we like about you, sir — there are no gray areas."

Ambiguity   We usually think of ambiguous language as a problem in communication because the sender and receiver interpret the same word or phrase differently. If a co-worker says, "Would you like to check the figures again?" the employee may be politely *telling* you to double-check the figures. But this message is sufficiently ambiguous that you may think the co-worker is merely *asking* if you want to do this. The result is that meaning is not transferred and both parties may become frustrated by the communication failure.

Ambiguous language is sometimes used deliberately in work settings to avoid conveying emotions and minimize conflict. Apple Computer and Southwest Airlines don't have customer service problems; they're called "issues." Microsoft doesn't warn computer users about fatal software errors; they're "undocumented behaviors." And when Microsoft Network's 2.2 million customers suffered through significant e-mail delivery problems, the company described the incident as "a partial e-mail delay."[15] Why the obfuscation? Customers tend to respond more calmly to undocumented behaviors, issues, and e-mail delays than to fatal software errors, poor customer service, and e-mail lost for weeks or forever.

Ambiguous language may be a barrier, but it is sometimes necessary where events or objects are ill-defined or lack agreement.[16] Corporate leaders often use metaphors to describe complex organizational values so that they are interpreted broadly enough to apply to diverse situations. Scholars also rely on metaphors because they convey rich meaning about complex ideas. For example, some organizational behavior scholars describe organizations as "jazz ensembles" or "machines" to reflect different variations of their complex nature.[17]

Information Overload

Every day Gayle Anderson receives about 40 voice mail messages, 30 internal e-mail messages, 20 external e-mail messages, and numerous faxes. The executive vice president of the Greater Winston-Salem Chamber of Commerce reciprocates by placing 25 phone calls, 15 e-mails, and 10 faxes of her own. "On a very, very busy day . . . you can get behind the curve," Anderson warns.[18]

Gayle Anderson is not alone. An employee working at a Fortune 1000 company typically sends and receives 190 messages and documents every day![19] This flood of messages causes **information overload.** Information overload occurs when the volume of information received exceeds the person's capacity to process it. Employees have a certain *information processing capacity,* that is, the amount of information that they are able to process in a fixed unit of time. At the same time, jobs have a varying *information load;* that is, the amount of information to be processed per unit of time.[20] As Exhibit 8.2 illustrates, information overload occurs whenever the job's information load exceeds the individual's information processing capacity.

Information overload creates noise in the communication system because information gets overlooked or misinterpreted when people can't process it fast enough. Moreover, as we learned in Chapter 5, it has become a common cause of workplace stress. One survey reports that two-thirds of managers blame information overload for interpersonal conflicts and dissatisfaction at work, and 43 percent say they suffer from "paralysis of analysis" due to the volume of information they must process.[21]

We can minimize information overload in two ways: by increasing our information processing capacity and reducing the job's information load.[22] We can increase information processing capacity by learning to read faster,

information overload a condition in which the volume of information received by an employee exceeds that person's ability to process it effectively

Exhibit 8.2
Dynamics of information overload

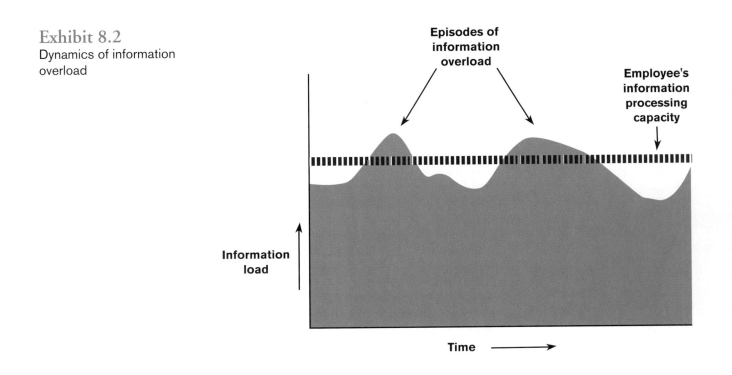

scanning documents more efficiently, and removing distractions that slow information processing speed. Time management also increases information processing capacity. When information overload is temporary, information processing capacity can increase by working longer hours.

We can reduce information load by buffering, summarizing, or omitting the information. *Buffering* occurs where assistants screen the person's messages and forward only those considered essential reading. Microsoft's Bill Gates and other CEOs depend on these "mission control" people to handle the large number of e-mail, fax, and snail mail messages they receive each day.[23] *Summarizing* condenses information into fewer words, such as the reading of abstracts and executive summaries instead of the entire document. *Omitting* is the practice of ignoring less important information. For example, some e-mail software programs have a filtering algorithm that screens out unwanted junk mail (called "spam").

Perceptions, filtering, language, and information overload are not the only sources of noise in the communication process, but they are probably the most common. Noise also occurs when we choose an inappropriate channel through which the message is sent. The next section takes a closer look at communication channels.

Communication Channels

A critical part of the communication model is the channel through which information is transmitted. There are two main types of channels: verbal and nonverbal. *Verbal communication* includes any oral or written method of transmitting meaning through words. *Nonverbal communication,* which we will discuss later, is any part of communication that does not use words.

Verbal Communication

Different forms of verbal communication should be used in different situations. Face-to-face interaction is usually better than written methods for transmitting emotions and persuading the receiver. This is because nonverbal cues accompany oral communications, such as voice intonations and use of silence. Moreover, in face-to-face settings, the sender receives immediate feedback from the receiver and can adjust the emotional tone of the message accordingly.

Written communication is more appropriate for recording and presenting technical details because ideas are easier to logically understand when written down than when communicated verbally.[24] Traditionally, written communication has been slow to develop and transmit, but electronic mail and other computer-mediated communication channels have significantly improved written communication efficiency.[25]

Electronic Mail

Electronic mail (e-mail) is revolutionizing the way we communicate in organizational settings. Today, 90 percent of large companies and over half of other companies use e-mail. According to one estimate, employees sent approximately 3 billion e-mail messages every month during the late 1990s.[26] It's easy to understand e-mail's popularity. E-mail users can quickly form, edit, and store messages. Information can be appended and transmitted to many people with a simple click of a mouse. E-mail is asynchronous (messages are sent and received at different times), so there is no need to coordinate a communication session. This technology also allows fairly random access of information; you can select any message in any order and skip to different parts of a message.

E-mail tends to be the preferred medium for coordinating work (e.g., confirming a co-worker's production schedule) and sending well-defined information for decision making. It tends to increase the volume of communication and significantly alter the flow of that information throughout the organization.[27] Specifically, it reduces some face-to-face and telephone communication but increases the flow of information to higher levels in the organization. Some social and organizational status differences still exist with e-mail, but they are less apparent than in face-to-face or telephone communication. E-mail also reduces many selective attention biases because it hides our age, race, weight, and other features that are observable in face-to-face meetings.[28]

Problems with e-mail   Anyone who has used e-mail knows that it has several problems and limitations. Perhaps the most obvious of these is that e-mail contributes to information overload. Many e-mail users are overwhelmed by hundreds of messages each week, some of which are irrelevant to them. This is because it is so easy to transmit messages. E-mails can be written and copied quickly to thousands of people through group mailbox systems. Employees receive little e-mail training, which results in ineffective message quality and usage patterns.[29]

A second concern is that e-mail seems to reduce our politeness and respect for others. This is mostly evident through the increased frequency of **flaming.** Flaming is the act of sending an emotionally charged message (called *flame-mail*) to others. This occurs because people can post e-mail messages before their emotions subside, whereas the sender of a traditional memo or letter would have time for sober second thoughts. In one recent survey, over half of the people questioned receive abusive flame-mail. Men are both the most frequent victims and perpetrators.[30]

A third problem is that it is difficult to interpret the emotional meaning behind e-mail messages. One scholar recently quipped that the result "of new information technologies within organizations has not been better communication, only faster misunderstandings."[31] For example, sarcasm is difficult to convey through e-mail because the verbal message requires contrasting nonverbal cues. E-mail aficionados try to clarify the emotional tone of their messages by combining ASCII characters to form graphic faces called "emoticons." An entire lexicon of faces (called "smileys") has developed, including those illustrated in Exhibit 8.3.

Presumably, flaming and other communication problems will become less common as employees learn the unique dynamics of e-mail. However, most of us have not yet applied the many rules and courtesies (called e-mail "netiquette") that are forming for this new medium. For example, many people are unaware that e-mail messages written in CAPITAL LETTERS are often interpreted as anger. Exhibit 8.4 offers a few basic rules in e-mail netiquette.

flaming sending an emotionally charged electronic mail message

Exhibit 8.3
Icons of emotion (emoticons) in e-mail messages

Icon	Meaning	Icon	Meaning
:-)	Happy	:-p	Tongue sticking out
:-}	Smirk	:-x	Oops!
:-(	Unhappy	{}	Hug
<:-)	Dumb question	12x-<-@	A dozen roses
0:-)	Angel (I'm being good)		

Source: Cited in R. Peck, "Learning to Speak Computer Lingo," *New Orleans Times-Picayune*, June 5, 1997, p. E1; R. Weiland, "The Message Is the Medium," *Incentive*, September 1995, p. 37.

Exhibit 8.4
Some basic e-mail
netiquette

DO fill in the "subject" line of the e-mail header with an informative description of the message.

DO keep e-mail messages to less than 25 lines—the length of a typical computer screen.

DO quote the relevant parts (but not necessarily all) of the receiver's previous message when replying to ideas in that message. (The automatic ">" indicates the original message.)

DO respond to someone's e-mail (where a reply is expected) within one day for most business correspondence.

DO switch from e-mail to telephone or face-to-face communication when the discussion gets too heated (flaming), the parties experience ongoing misunderstanding, or the issue becomes too complex.

DON'T forward private messages without the permission of the original sender.

DON'T send mass e-mails (using group lists) unless authorized to do so and the message definitely calls for this action.

DON'T send large attachments if the receiver likely has a narrow bandwidth (computer data are transmitted slowly).

DON'T use e-mail to communicate sensitive issues, such as disciplining someone, or to convey urgent information, such as rescheduling a meeting within the next hour.

DON'T write messages in ALL CAPITALS because this conveys anger or shouting. (This rule also applies to boldface text as e-mail software develops this feature.)

DON'T use emoticons excessively, and avoid them in formal business e-mails and where there is some chance that the receiver won't know their meaning.

Sources: M. M. Extejt, "Teaching Students to Correspond Effectively Electronically: Tips for Using Electronic Mail Properly," *Business Communication Quarterly* 61 (June 1998), pp. 57–67; K. Wasch, "Netiquette: Do's and Don'ts of E-Mail Use," *Association Management* 49 (May 1997), pp. 76, 115.

One last concern is that e-mail lacks the warmth of human interaction. It is clearly inappropriate to fire or lay off an employee through e-mail (although some managers have done this), because this medium does not effectively communicate empathy or social support. As employees increasingly cocoon themselves through their computers and other forms of information technology, they lose the social support of human contact that potentially keeps their stress in check. This may explain why emotional health tends to get worse when people increase the amount of time spent e-mailing and surfing the Internet.[32]

Other Computer-Mediated Communication

Internets, intranets, and other forms of computer-mediated communication have fueled the hyperfast world of corporate information sharing.[33] Some companies are experimenting with intranet videoconferencing in which people meet virtually with live audio and video images of themselves. Others use multimedia training programs that "stream" the information through the company's intranet.

Chat software is quickly becoming a valuable organizational tool for real-time communication. General Dennis Reimer, the U.S. Army's chief of staff, uses the America's Army Online chat room to discuss issues with his 350 general officers and 150 garrison commanders around the world. "The network allows me to be productive and to maintain a pulse on what is happening whether I'm in Washington or overseas," Reimer says.[34] Our *Fast Company Online* feature for this chapter reveals that online chat isn't just a passing fad; it is quickly gaining ground in organizational settings as a way to communicate with co-workers and customers.

How effective are these computer-mediated technologies for communicating in organizational settings? Each one needs to be assessed on its own merits, but most computer-mediated technologies seem to reduce time and dissolve distances. This relates to the **law of telecosm,** which says that as the web of computer networks expands, distances will shrink and eventually become irrelevant.[35] Cemex, the giant Mexican cement manufacturer, leveraged

law of telecosm a principle stating that as the web of computer networks expands, distances will shrink and eventually become irrelevant

---

FAST COMPANY Online

◻ It's (Real) Time to Chat

You use e-mail to send messages and Web pages to share information. But to swap ideas efficiently, you may need real-time chat. Blue-chip companies such as Chase Manhattan, Merrill Lynch, and IBM are experimenting with chat software to help employees communicate with co-workers and customers.

"Chat is the Internet version of an intercom," says Gregg Gallagher, who evaluates technologies and alliances for AT&T WorldNet Service. "You can summon a person quickly." Gallagher uses ICQ, a popular chat software that notifies him when specified individuals are online and lets him communicate instantly with them. Gallagher uses chat about 20 times each day, mostly for impromptu sessions rather than formal meetings. He particularly likes the software for connecting with colleagues without having to pass through the halls: "Chat saves time because I don't have to move through the building."

Online chat software is also handy for communicating with someone while carrying a conference call with other people. During a recent telephone conference call with a business partner's engineers, Gallagher learned that the engineers were reluctant to reveal a sensitive piece of information. The president of the other company happened to be available online, so Gallagher sent him a chat message while simultaneously carrying on the telephone conversation. The president cleared up the stumbling block and the conference call proceeded more smoothly. "I did it without interrupting the conversation," Gallagher recalls. "In a physical meeting, we might have had to leave the room."

ONLINE CHECK-UP

1. This *Fast Company Online* feature describes the reasons why AT&T's Gregg Gallagher uses online chat software at work. How does this communication medium differ from e-mail and Web pages? What are the problems and limitations of online chat communication in organizational settings?

2. The full-text of this *Fast Company Online* feature also describes how Hand Technologies, 1-800-FLOWERS, and Pristine Capital Management use online chat to communicate with associates and customers. What are the main reasons why they prefer this technology compared with e-mail and fax messages?

3. Speak to someone who has used online chat (even if you have also used it) to find out what they like and don't like about it. Get the class to draw up a list of features about online chat and identify items on the list that should be considered for its use in organizations.

Get the full text of this *Fast Company* article at www.mhhe.com/mcshane1e

Source: Adapted from H. Row, "It's (Real) Time to Talk," *Fast Company,* Issue 15 (June 1998). ■

the law of telecosm by installing computers in all of its cement trucks. Cement spoils in 90 minutes, which is a problem in Mexico City, where traffic jams, government inspections, and chaotic construction sites are common. But the new computer network alerts drivers to job cancellations and quickly reroutes them to another location where the cement can be used.[36] In other words, computer technology significantly reduced the time required and the relevance of the truck's distance from headquarters.

You might think that emerging computer-mediated technologies further increase information overload. However, preliminary evidence suggests that they actually *reduce* overload because we have greater control over the amount of information that flows from these sources. We decide how much information to receive from the Internet and intranet, whereas there is almost no control over the number of voice mails, e-mails, faxes, and paper-based memos we receive. This is supported by a recent survey of executives in 11 countries. Half of them (including 61 percent of those in the United States) indicated that the Internet is reducing information overload; only 19 percent claim that it is making matters worse.[37]

Nonverbal Communication

Computer-mediated communication is changing the face of organization communication, but it has not yet adequately captured the information conveyed through nonverbal communication. Nonverbal communication includes facial gestures, voice intonation, physical distance, and even silence. This communication channel is necessary where physical distance or noise prevents effective verbal exchanges and the need for immediate feedback precludes written communication.[38] But even in close face-to-face meetings, most information is communicated nonverbally.[39] Nonverbal communication is also important in **emotional labor.** Recall from Chapter 7 that emotional labor refers to the effort, planning, and control needed to express organizationally desired emotions.[40] Employees make extensive use of nonverbal cues to transmit prescribed feelings to customers, co-workers, and others.

Nonverbal communication differs from verbal communication in two ways. First, we normally know what words we say or write, whereas nonverbal cues are typically automatic and unconscious. A second distinction is that nonverbal communication is less rule bound than verbal communication. We receive a lot of formal training on how to understand spoken words, but very little to understand the nonverbal signals that accompany those words. Consequently, nonverbal cues are more ambiguous and more susceptible to misinterpretation.

emotional labor the effort, planning, and control needed to express organizationally desired emotions during interpersonal transactions

Emotional contagion   What happens when people see a co-worker accidentally bang his or her head against a filing cabinet? Chances are, they wince and put their hand on their own head as if they had hit the cabinet. This automatic and subconscious tendency to mimic and synchronize our nonverbal behaviors with other people is called **emotional contagion.**[41] Emotional contagion is not a disease. It refers to the notion that we tend to "catch" other people's emotions by continuously mimicking the facial expressions and nonverbal cues of others. For instance, listeners smile more and exhibit other emotional displays of happiness while hearing someone describe a positive event. Similarly, listeners will wince when the speaker describes an event in which they were hurt.

Emotional contagion serves three purposes. First, mimicry provides continuous feedback, communicating that we understand and empathize with the sender. To consider the significance of this, imagine if employees remain

emotional contagion the automatic and subconscious tendency to mimic and synchronize our nonverbal behaviors with other people

expressionless after watching a co-worker bang his or her head! The lack of parallel behavior conveys a lack of understanding or caring. Second, mimicking the nonverbal behaviors of other people seems to be a way of receiving emotional meaning from those people. If a co-worker is angry with a client, your tendency to frown and show anger while listening helps you share that emotion more fully. In other words, we receive meaning by expressing the sender's emotions as well as by listening to the sender's words.

Lastly, emotional contagion is a type of "social glue" that bonds people together. Social solidarity is built out of each member's awareness of a collective sentiment. Through nonverbal expressions of emotional contagion, people see others share the same emotions that we feel. This strengthens team cohesiveness by providing evidence of member similarity.

Choosing the Best Communication Channels

Employees perform better if they can quickly determine the best communication channels for the situation and are flexible enough to use different methods as the occasion requires.[42] But which communication channels are most appropriate? We partly answered this question in our evaluation of the different communication channels. However, two additional contingencies worth noting are media richness and symbolic meaning.

Media Richness

media richness the data-carrying capacity of a communication medium; the volume and variety of information that it can transmit

Communication channels can be organized into a hierarchy based on their **media richness.** This refers to their *data-carrying capacity*—the volume and variety of information that can be transmitted.[43] Face-to-face meetings have the highest data-carrying capacity because the sender can simultaneously transmit verbal and nonverbal signals, the receiver can provide immediate feedback, and the information exchange can be customized to suit the situation. In contrast, financial reports and other impersonal documents represent the leanest media because they allow only one form of data transmission (e.g., written), the sender does not receive timely feedback from the receiver, and the information exchange is standardized for everyone.

As Exhibit 8.5 shows, the most appropriate medium depends on whether the situation is nonroutine and ambiguous. Nonroutine situations require rich media because the sender and receiver have little common experience and, therefore, need to transmit a large volume of information. During unexpected emergencies, for instance, you should use face-to-face meetings to coordinate work efforts quickly and minimize the risk of misunderstanding and confusion. Lean media may be used in routine situations because the sender and receiver have common expectations through shared mental models.

Ambiguous situations also require rich media because the parties must share large amounts of information to resolve multiple and conflicting interpretations of their observations and experiences.[44] Team members require rich media communication during the early stages of a project to resolve different interpretations of the project task, each member's role, and the parameters of acceptable behavior. Similarly, research suggests that product development teams should work together in the same physical space because information technologies do not yet provide the level of media richness offered by face-to-face interaction.[45] This explains why Microsoft insists that employees work together, as we learned in the opening story to this chapter.

What happens when we choose the wrong level of media richness for the situation? When the situation is routine or clear, then using a rich medium—such as holding a special meeting—would seem like a waste of time. On the

Exhibit 8.5
A hierarchy of
media richness

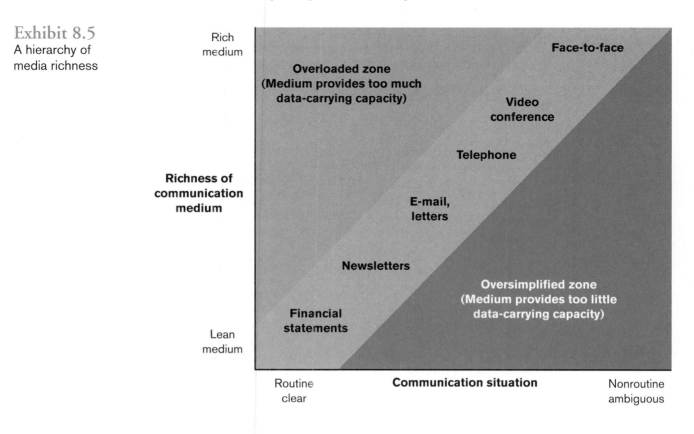

Source: Based on R. Lengel and R. L. Daft, "The Selection of Communication Media as an Executive Skill," *Academy of Management Executive* 2, no. 3 (August 1988), p. 226; R. L. Daft and R. H. Lengel, "Information Richness: A New Approach to Managerial Behavior and Organization Design," *Research in Organizational Behavior* 6, (1984), p. 199.

other hand, if a unique and ambiguous issue is handled through lean media—such as an e-mail message or a memo—then issues take longer to resolve and misunderstandings are more likely to occur.

Symbolic Meaning of the Medium

"The medium is the message."[46] This famous phrase by communications guru Marshall McLuhan means that the sender's choice of communication channel transmits meaning beyond the message content. For example, a personal meeting with an employee may indicate that the issue is important, whereas a brief handwritten note may suggest less importance.

The difficulty we face when choosing a communication medium is that its symbolic meaning may vary from one person to the next. Some people view e-mail as a symbol of professionalism, whereas others see it as evidence of the sender's efficiency. Still others might view an e-mail message as a low-status clerical activity because it involves typing.[47] Overall, we must be sensitive to the symbolic meaning of the selected communication medium to ensure that it amplifies rather than contradicts the meaning found in the message content.

Communicating in Organizational Hierarchies

Corporate leaders need to facilitate the flow of communication up, down, and across the organization. Otherwise, work units become silos of knowledge and employees feel less psychological attachment to the organization. In this section, we discuss four communication strategies: employee surveys, newsletters, management by wandering around, and workspace design.

Employee Surveys

Less than one in every three American workers believes that senior management knows what's on their minds. Employee surveys can help to communicate this information.[48] For instance, the U.S. National Research Council recently surveyed its employees regarding their job satisfaction, opinions about supervision, operating effectiveness, and training and development issues. Sears, Nortel, and other firms survey employee levels of job satisfaction as a measure of executive and corporate performance (see Chapter 7).

Federal Express (FedEx) relies on employee surveys as part of its "Survey-Feedback-Action" process of 360-degree feedback (see Chapter 2). "The first survey is always an experience for new managers," explains a FedEx executive. "But they soon realize they need it. Good communication increases the morale—and the productivity—of the group."[49]

Surveys also involve employees in corporate decisions. Allstate Insurance sends a quarterly online questionnaire to half its employees, asking about the level of comfort with diversity practices. USAA, the San Antonio–based insurance company, surveyed employees to find out how to improve corporate communications. Hong Kong's Kowloon-Canton Railway Corp. (KCRC) significantly improved service quality and performance by surveying employees about their thoughts on how the company can perform better. "A fundamental change has taken place at the KCRC because of the surveys," explains KCRC chairman and chief executive Kevin Hyde.[50]

Newsletters and E-Zines

Traditionally, companies have relied on newsletters and possibly video magazines to send information down the corporate hierarchy. For example, the British Broadcasting Corporation communicates information to employees through *Ariel*, a regular newsmagazine. Southwest Airlines and the British Post Office produce an annual report for employees, describing the company's performance and employee contributions to these results.[51]

These print media are useful for communicating some information, but they are not timely enough for most corporate news. Fortunately, electronic technologies provide faster alternatives. Los Alamos National Laboratory in New Mexico recently supplemented its monthly newsletter with a daily electronic newsletter through the organization's intranet. This *e-zine* (electronic magazine) is posted each evening so employees have the news first thing in the morning. Along with providing timely information, e-zines are less costly than print media and have more visual appeal (e.g., color graphics and video clips). The U.S. Postal Service relies on TV monitors in break rooms and cafeterias throughout nearly 400 locations to transmit the latest corporate information as well as packaged national headline news around the clock.[52]

Management by Wandering Around

management by wandering around (MBWA) the practice of getting out of the offices and learning from others in the organization through face-to-face dialogue

Cisco Systems is the world's largest manufacturer of routers and other products that run the Internet. Yet John Chambers, Cisco's CEO, doesn't communicate just through e-mail or web sites. He believes that executives need to regularly meet face-to-face with employees. In other words, they need to practice **management by wandering around (MBWA).** Coined several years ago at Hewlett-Packard, MBWA means that people should get out of their offices and learn from others in the organization through face-to-face dialogue.[53]

When Col. Gary Ambrose became commander of the 55th Wing at Offutt Air Force Base in Nebraska, his first objective was to get "out and about." Shown here near an RC-135 electronic reconnaissance aircraft, Ambrose strolls the flight line to watch maintenance crews at work. He will also sit at a randomly selected table of enlisted troops for lunch so he can hear what is on their minds. "The best way to know what is going on is to be out where the work is happening," says Ambrose, who heads the 8,000-person unit. "I put a high premium on management by wandering around. . . . Once people get used to seeing me, they will tell me things that maybe otherwise I wouldn't hear."[54] What problems might Col. Ambrose initially experience when meeting face-to-face with employees? Do you think that employees today expect more or less MBWA than employees two decades ago?
[K. Christian. Used with permission of the Omaha World-Herald.]

MBWA minimizes the previously described problem of filtering that blocks or distorts information flowing up the hierarchy. "The problem with being a CEO is that everybody between you and them wants to tell you what you want to hear," warns Brian Thompson, CEO of telecommunications firm LCI International. "So it's really just being visible to people, walking around, [and] it works."[55] AlliedSignal chairman Lawrence Bossidy practices MBWA by holding breakfast meetings several times a month with employees selected at random by computer. John Chambers and other Cisco executives attend monthly "birthday breakfasts" with several dozen employees whose birthdays fall in that month. "The birthday breakfast is the most effective vehicle for getting candid feedback from employees and for discovering potential problems," says Chambers.[56]

MBWA also provides an opportunity for executives to explain corporate decisions at a more personal level.[57] Executives at Brooklyn Union Gas Co. do this through "Straight Talk" sessions where they discuss important corporate issues with groups of about 100 employees. Cisco's John Chambers does the same thing through quarterly meetings at a nearby convention center.[58]

MBWA seems to work well in North America, but would it be equally successful in other cultures? Maybe not. As we learned in Chapter 7, some cultures emphasize a power distance between employees and their superiors. Executives who try to bypass the hierarchy or try to be equals with employees are not necessarily viewed favorably. According to one scholar, some Singaporean workers will avoid senior management so that they would not inadvertently communicate directly with them rather than through their supervisors.[59]

Work Space Design

There's nothing like a wall to prevent employees from talking to each other. That's why Alcoa abolished all private offices—even for its chief executive officer—at its new headquarters in Pittsburgh. Telecommunications giant Nortel Networks turned its former manufacturing facility near Toronto, Canada, into an open-plan cityscape headquarters. British Airways also moved to new headquarters near London with an open design that looks like a village square.[60] Most of these changes make more efficient use of space, but their main thrust is to provide direct line of sight among employees so that they share knowledge more easily.

Other companies have kept the walls up, but have rearranged the hallways to support spontaneous, horizontal communication.[61] When Corning Glass learned that its engineers got 80 percent of their ideas from face-to-face discussions with colleagues, it moved everyone into a low-rise building with informal meeting places and easy access to all areas. Engineering productivity increased by more than 10 percent in the new building. Pearl Assurance redesigned its building for the same reason. The British insurance company installed "pit-stop" areas where people can spontaneously meet and share information.

The line-of-sight communication principle also works on the plant floor. Toyota production areas typically consist of U-shaped subassembly cells so that everyone on the line can coordinate their work and solve problems more quickly through direct communication. This contrasts with the traditional

Telecommunications giant Nortel Networks recently transformed its old manufacturing facility near Toronto, Canada, into a faux cityscape for 1,300 headquarters employees. The building has a main street *(left)*, side streets and crossroads (instead of corridors), and several parks with potted trees *(right)*. Dividers (not walls) temporarily separate the offices, but even the dividers will go when employees feel more comfortable with the open setting. The governing metaphor here is to break down the walls so employees can communicate with each other more easily. "It takes walls down literally and makes managers more accessible to people," says a Nortel employee.[62] How would the physical layout of Nortel's cityscape improve communications? What problems do you think might result from this design?

[Courtesy of Nortel Networks]

I-shaped or L-shaped lines at General Motors, which make it difficult for employees to communicate with each other.[63]

Nonterritorial offices Cisco Systems, AGI, Ernst & Young, Oticon A/S, and SEI Investments have taken the open workspace concept one step further by creating **nonterritorial offices** (also called free address, hot desking, and hoteling).[64] Employees are not assigned to specific desks, offices, or workspaces. Instead, they work in any available location. Many firms introduce nonterritorial office arrangements to save space, typically where employees telecommute or are otherwise frequently away from the office. The Washington, D.C., office of Ernst & Young introduced nonterritorial offices for this reason. Employees at the accounting and consulting firm book space with a concierge the day before they arrive. A space is then made ready, complete with computer, telephone, supplies, name plate, and possibly even family pictures on the desk.[65]

Other companies introduce nonterritorial offices to improve communication and teamwork. Employees at Danish hearing-aid manufacturer Oticon A/S and the U.S. financial services firm SEI Investments have their own desks, but no fixed location to put them. Instead, the desk, chair, and belongings are on wheels so that they can be moved frequently around the building. The idea is that employees work together and share knowledge more freely than if they spend all of their time in an isolated space.[66]

It's too early to say how well these nonterritorial office designs will improve communication or productivity.[67] They may be effective where teams are temporary, require media rich communication (i.e., face-to-face), and frequent moving creates minimal disruption. However, nonterritorial offices can be cumbersome when employees spend too much time signing out equipment and finding a work space each day. Moreover, they seem to violate the inherent need for personal space. Connections 8.1 describes how advertising firm TBWA Chiat/Day has abandoned nonterritorial offices for this reason. Instead, the advertising firm has moved to a "nesting" model of office design that encourages communication, yet gives employees some privacy at work.

> **nonterritorial offices** office arrangements in which employees work at any available workstation and are not assigned to specific desks, offices, or workspaces

Communicating through the Grapevine

When St. Luke's Medical Center in Chicago radically redesigned nursing duties, the change team knew that the organizational grapevine would go into overdrive. Team members at the hospital also knew that a fair amount of that information would be erroneous, so a 24-hour rumor hotline was set up and responses were reported in regular newsletters to employees. Even with this intensive communication strategy, the rumor mill continued to buzz.[68]

Employees receive a considerable amount of information through the **grapevine,** even in the presence of well-designed formal communication structures. The grapevine is an unstructured and informal network founded on social relationships rather than organizational charts or job descriptions. Employees often receive news from the grapevine before they hear about it through formal channels; 75 percent claim that the grapevine is their first source of important information in the organization.[69]

> **grapevine** the organization's informal communication network that is formed and maintained by social relationships rather than the formal reporting relationships

Grapevine Characteristics

The grapevine has several unique features.[70] It transmits information very rapidly in all directions throughout the organization. Grapevine news is relatively accurate, possibly because the parties tend to use media-rich communication channels (e.g., face-to-face) and are motivated to communicate effectively. Nevertheless, the grapevine also distorts information by deleting fine details and exaggerating key points of the story. It transmits kernels of truth with several embellishments and consequently should not be viewed as the definitive source of organizational news.

The grapevine typically transmits information through the *cluster chain* pattern illustrated in Exhibit 8.6. Senders transmit grapevine information only to people they know and believe are interested. Some employees rarely receive grapevine information because they are not integrated with the organization's social network.

The grapevine relies on social relations, so it is more active where employees have similar backgrounds and are able to communicate easily with each other. It is also more active when employees are anxious and information from formal channels does not satisfy their need to know.[71] Even when the formal network provides some information about a particular situation, employees will participate in the grapevine because social interaction relieves some of their anxiety.

This explains why the hotline at St. Luke's Medical Center (described at the beginning of this section) did not weaken the informal grapevine. The Royal Bank of Scotland also discovered this when it conducted a full-scale review of its branch banking system. Senior management knew that the review would increase employee anxiety, so it used newsletters and other formal communications to describe the project. Yet a company survey revealed that employee reliance on the grapevine *increased* rather than decreased during the review period.[72]

Connections 8.1 □ **TBWA Chiat/Day Rethinks the Nonterritorial Office**

When advertising firm TBWA Chiat/Day moved into its binocular-shaped building near Venice Beach, California, it also plunged into the chaotic world of nonterritorial offices. Each morning, employees would sign out laptop computers and cell phones, then take whatever space met their needs on a "first-come" basis. Usually, they headed for a project room shared with others on the same client account.

This nonterritorial office structure improved communication and creativity, but it also deprived Chiat/Day's employees of any personal space. Some staffers resorted to making telephone calls in bathroom stalls and under their desks. After four years of this nomadic chaos, the company that gave us the Energizer Bunny abandoned the nonterritorial office concept and moved to a new building. Now, employees have a chunk of personal space known as a "nest." Each nest includes a telephone and computer that permanently belongs to the person assigned to that space.

Although the nonterritorial office is gone, Chiat/Day hopes to retain some of the village spirit that came with it. "People still want to belong to a community, something that's bigger than themselves," says Laurie Coots, Chiat/Day's chief marketing officer for North America. The new nest structure gives employees personal space, but they can quickly "swivel round and be right in the center of things again."

Sources: "Why Chiat/Day Is Putting Down Its Binoculars," *Creative Review*, April 1998, p. 67; A. Z. Cuneo, "California's Kovel Kresser Wagers That Imaginative New Office Plan Will Support the Agency's Staff in Producing Innovative Advertising, From Supermarket to Ad Shop," *Advertising Age*, April 20, 1998, p. 42. ■

Exhibit 8.6
Transmission pattern of
grapevine communication

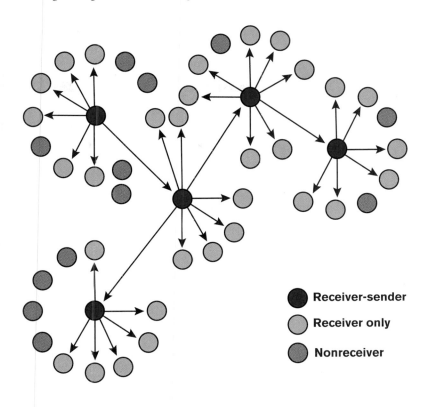

● Receiver-sender

○ Receiver only

● Nonreceiver

Grapevine Advantages and Disadvantages

Should the grapevine be encouraged, tolerated, or quashed? The difficulty in answering this question is that the grapevine has both advantages and disadvantages. One benefit is that the grapevine helps employees to make sense of their workplace when the information is not available through formal channels.[73] It is also the main conduit through which organizational stories and other symbols of the organization's culture are communicated (see Chapter 16).

Along with its informational value, the grapevine is an important social process that bonds people together and fulfills their need for affiliation.[74] Finally, because it is most active when employees are worried, the grapevine is a valuable signal for managers to take appropriate action. This may include resolving the problems behind the rumors, or communicating more fully through formal networks.

The grapevine is not always beneficial. Morale tumbles when management is slower than the grapevine in communicating information, because it suggests a lack of sincerity and concern for employees. Moreover, grapevine information may become so distorted that it escalates rather than reduces employee anxieties. This is particularly true as the original information is transmitted through several people rather than by one or two people to several listeners.

What should companies do about the grapevine? Some executives try in vain to stop the grapevine, but it will always exist. Others try to send messages down to employees through the grapevine, but this overlooks the problem that the grapevine has a selective audience and may distort important facts. A better strategy, as mentioned earlier, is to listen to the grapevine as a signal of employee anxiety, then correct the root cause of this anxiety. St. Luke's Medical Center and Royal Bank of Scotland also treat the grapevine as a competitor against which their newsletters and other formal communication programs are judged.

Cross-Cultural and Gender Communication

In Chapter 1 we learned that organizations operate in a world of increasing globalization and cultural diversity. These dynamics bring new opportunities as well as communication challenges. Employees must become more sensitive and competent in cross-cultural communication. Furthermore, they must overcome their reluctance to communicate with co-workers from another cultural group. These communication competencies are also gaining importance as companies increasingly work with clients, suppliers, and joint venture partners from other countries.

Language is the most obvious cross-cultural barrier.[75] Words are easily misunderstood in verbal communication, either because the receiver has a limited vocabulary or the sender's accent makes it difficult for the receiver to understand the sound. Many U.S. companies offer language skills training for people whose first language is not English. But what about global companies? What language do they use at corporate headquarters? At ABB Asea Brown Boveri, Ltd., the answer is simple: "Broken English," says CEO Goren Lindahl with a smile. "We discovered that one thing we all have in common is broken English. We have an acceptance across the board that we don't have to speak perfectly. The important thing is that you speak up."[76]

Mastering the same language improves one dimension of cross-cultural communication, but problems may still occur when interpreting voice intonation.[77] A deep voice symbolizes masculinity in North America, but African men often express their emotions using a high-pitched voice. Middle Easterners sometimes speak loudly to show sincerity and interest in the discussion,

Janet Powell (right) is attending an "English for Speakers of Other Languages" course to improve her language skills. Xomed Surgical Products Inc., a Jacksonville, Florida, manufacturer of medical devices, provides this course to Powell and her coworkers so they can communicate more effectively as new technology is introduced in the workplace. The company also offers training in comprehension and other basic skills.[78] How do language problems act as "noise" in the communication process?
[*Stuart Tannehill*/The Florida Times Union]

whereas Japanese people tend to speak softly to communicate politeness or humility. Different cultural norms regarding voice loudness may cause one person to misinterpret the other.

Nonverbal Differences

Probably more serious than verbal communication is misunderstanding nonverbal communication across cultures. Nonverbal communication is more important in some cultures than in others. For example, people in Japan interpret more of a message's meaning from nonverbal cues. "A lot of Japanese is either unspoken or communicated through body language," explains Henry Wallace, the Scottish-born CEO of Mazda Corp. in Japan.[79]

To avoid offending or embarrassing the receiver (particularly outsiders), Japanese people will often say what the other person wants to hear (called *tatemae*) but send more subtle nonverbal cues indicating the sender's true feelings (called *honne*).[80] A Japanese colleague might politely reject your business proposal by saying, "I will think about that," while sending nonverbal signals that he or she is not really interested. This difference explains why Japanese employees may prefer direct conversation to e-mail and other media that lack nonverbal cues. "When you talk to someone in person, you can tell if there is real understanding," explains Chikako Lane, a Japanese-born manager at Calsonic North America, a subsidiary of the Nissan Group.[81]

Most nonverbal cues are specific to a particular culture and may have a completely different meaning to people raised in other cultures.[82] For example, Americans shake their head from side to side to say "No," but this means "I understand" to some people from India. Filipinos raise their eyebrows to give an affirmative answer, yet Arabs interpret this expression (along with clicking one's tongue) as a negative response. Americans are taught to maintain eye contact with the speaker to show interest and respect, yet this is considered rude to people born in some Asian and Middle Eastern countries. Instead, they learn to show respect by looking down when a supervisor or older person is talking to them.

Even the common handshake communicates different meaning across cultures. Americans tend to appreciate a firm handshake as a sign of strength and warmth in a friendship or business relationship. In contrast, many Asians and Middle Easterners favor a loose grip and regard a firm clench as aggressive. Germans prefer one good handshake stroke, whereas anything less than five or six strokes may symbolize a lack of trust in Spain. If this isn't confusing enough, people from some cultures view any touching in public, including handshakes, as a sign of rudeness.

Silence and conversational overlaps
Silence conveys different—and sometimes the opposite—meaning in various cultures. In Japan, people tend to remain silent for a few seconds after someone has spoken, to contemplate what has just been said as a sign of respect.[83] To them, silence is an important part of communication (called *haragei*) because it preserves harmony and is more reliable than talk. Silence is shared by everyone and belongs to no one, so it becomes the ultimate form of interdependence. Moreover, the Japanese value empathy, which can only be demonstrated by understanding others without using words.

In contrast, most people in North America view silence as a *lack* of communication and often interpret long breaks as a sign of disagreement. For example, after presenting their proposal to a potential Japanese client, a group of American consultants expected to be bombarded with questions. Instead, their proposal was greeted with a long silence. As the silence continued, most of the

Americans concluded that the Japanese client disapproved, so they prepared to pack and leave. But the lead consultant gestured them to stop, because the client's face and posture seemed to indicate interest rather than rejection. He was right: When the client finally spoke, it was to give the consulting firm the job.[84]

Conversational overlaps also send different messages in different cultures. Americans usually stop talking when they are interrupted, whereas talking over the other person's speech is more common in Brazil and other Latin American countries. The reason is that talking while someone is speaking to you is considered quite rude in the United States, whereas Brazilians are more likely to interpret this as the person's interest and involvement in the conversation. Connections 8.2 describes how one Coca-Cola executive discovered cultural differences in conversational overlap during his assignment in Puerto Rico.

Gender Differences in Communication

Soon after Susan Herring joined her first Internet discussion group, she noticed that men were much more likely than women to engage in cantankerous debates with their own combative and condescending e-mail messages. To pique her curiosity, the University of Texas linguistics professor asked list group subscribers to tell her what they thought of these e-mail "flame wars." The anonymous informal poll revealed that men generally accepted this communication style and usually found the barbs entertaining. Most women, on the other hand, were offended or cautious when these debates erupted.[85]

Herring and other scholars have observed that men and women often differ in their communication styles. Whether in a corporate meeting or a virtual

---

Connections 8.2   ◻ **Coca-Cola Executive Learns That Noise to Some Is Music to Others**

George Gourlay, a senior executive at the Coca-Cola Company, recalls a meeting in Puerto Rico, attended mostly by Puerto Ricans, in which everyone seemed to be speaking at once. This seemingly incoherent babble made Gourlay uncomfortable and confused, so he used his managerial prerogative to force order in the meeting. Gourlay thought the meeting was now going well, until he noticed that the others appeared uncomfortable.

By coincidence, Gourlay took a course over the next three days in Puerto Rican culture. During the training program, the Coca-Cola manager learned that the noisy exchange with conversational overlaps in the earlier meeting was the natural way for Puerto Ricans and other Hispanics to communicate. It is normal for them to start talking while the other person is still speaking. Sometimes, three or four people would talk at the same time, thereby creating a noisy discourse to the uninitiated. By contrast, people from Germany, the United States, and a few other countries prefer a more orderly communication exchange, in which it is impolite to speak until the other person has finished.

With this knowledge in hand, Gourlay decided to adapt his style during his meetings in Puerto Rico. "I am still uncomfortable, but meetings are more productive," he admits.

Source: Adapted from G. Gourlay, "Quality's Cultural Foundation," in *Making Total Quality Happen*, F. Caropreso, ed. (New York: Conference Board, 1990), pp. 71–74. ◼

chat room, men are more likely than women to view conversations as negotiations of relative status and power.[86] They assert their power by directly giving advice to others (e.g., "You should do the following") and using combative language. For instance, from a content analysis of e-mail messages in various discussion groups, Susan Herring found that 68 percent of messages written by men included criticism, ridicule, or distancing from other participants, often while promoting the sender's own status. There is also evidence that men interrupt women far more often than the other way around and that they dominate the talk time in conversations with women.

Men tend to engage in "report talk," in which the primary function of the conversation is impersonal and efficient information exchange. This may explain why men tend to quantify information (e.g., "It took us six weeks"). Women also engage in report talk, particularly when conversing with men. But conversations among women tend to have a higher incidence of relationship building through "rapport talk." Thus, women use more intensive adverbs ("I was *so happy* that he completed the report") and hedge their statements ("It seems to be . . ."). Rather than asserting status, women use indirect requests such as "Have you considered . . . ?" Similarly, women apologize more often and seek advice from others more quickly than men. Finally, research confirms that women are more sensitive than men to nonverbal cues in face-to-face meetings.[87]

After reading some popular press books, you would think that men and women come from different planets (Mars and Venus) and require United Nations translators![88] This is not so. Although we have identified several differences, men and women mostly overlap in their verbal communication styles. Some men are very passive conversationalists, and some women are aggressive. Moreover, we know that women—and, to a less extent, men—vary their communication styles with the situation.

Both men and women usually understand each other, but there are irritants. For instance, Susan Herring and other women feel uncomfortable with aggressive male communication styles on the Internet. Female scientists have similarly complained that adversarial interaction among male scientists makes it difficult for women to participate in meaningful dialogue.[89]

Another irritant occurs when women seek empathy but receive male dominance in response. Specifically, women sometimes discuss their personal experiences and problems to develop closeness with the receiver. They look for expressions of understanding, such as "That's the way I felt when it happened to me." But when men hear problems, they quickly suggest solutions because this asserts their control over the situation. Not only does this frustrate a woman's need for common understanding, but the advice actually says: "You and I are different; you have the problem and I have the answer." Meanwhile, men become frustrated because they can't understand why women don't appreciate their advice.

Improving Interpersonal Communication

Effective interpersonal communication depends on the sender's ability to get the message across and the receiver's performance as an active listener. In this section, we outline these two essential features of effective interpersonal communication.

Getting Your Message Across

This chapter began with the statement that effective communication occurs when the other person receives and understands the message. To accomplish this difficult task, the sender must learn to empathize with the receiver, repeat the message, choose an appropriate time for the conversation, and be descriptive rather than evaluative.

empathy a person's ability to understand and be sensitive to the feelings, thoughts, and situation of others

- *Empathize*—**Empathy** involves putting yourself in the receiver's shoes when encoding the message. For instance, be sensitive to words that may be ambiguous or trigger the wrong emotional response.
- *Repeat the message*—Rephrase the key points a couple of times. The saying, "Tell them what you're going to tell them; tell them; then tell them what you've told them," reflects this need for redundancy.
- *Use timing effectively*—Your message competes with other messages and noise, so find a time when the receiver is less likely to be distracted by these other matters.
- *Be descriptive*—Focus on the problem, not the person, if you have negative information to convey. People stop listening when the information attacks their self-esteem. Also, suggest things the listener can do to improve, rather than point to him or her as a problem.

Active Listening

Listening is at least as important as talking. As one sage wisely wrote, "Nature gave people two ears but only one tongue, which is a gentle hint that they should listen more than they talk."[90] But listening is more than just hearing the other person making sounds; it is an active process of receiving and decoding those verbal messages so that they have meaning. It also requires more effort than most people realize. People interpret messages much faster than others can send them as verbal messages, so they tend to drift in and out from the conversation and are easily distracted from what others are saying. We must also keep our emotions in check so that valuable information isn't screened out. The main elements of active listening are illustrated in Exhibit 8.7 and described below. Please remember that these guidelines apply to American society; some might be contrary to communication norms in some other cultures.[91]

Don't interrupt   One of the most important features of active listening is to avoid interrupting the speaker. Give the other person an opportunity to complete the message and allow a brief pause before responding. This shows that you are thinking carefully about what the speaker has said. It also avoids the error of second-guessing what the speaker is about to say.

Exhibit 8.7
Elements of active listening

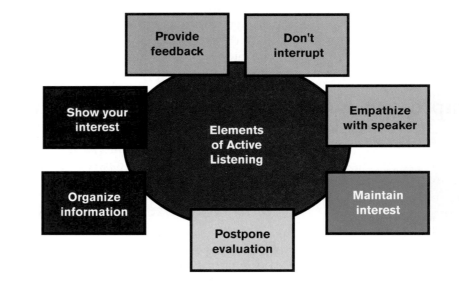

Empathize with the speaker   Empathy is just as important for listeners as it is for speakers. Recall that empathy is the ability to understand and be sensitive to the feelings, thoughts, and situation of others. This is a critical skill in active listening because the verbal and nonverbal cues from the conversation are accurately interpreted from the other person's point of view.

Maintain interest   As with any behavior, active listening requires motivation. Too often, we close our minds soon after a conversation begins because the subject is boring. Instead, try to be interested by taking the view—probably an accurate one—that there is always something of value in a conversation; it's just a matter of actively looking for it.

Postpone evaluation   It is natural to want to label a message as right-wrong or good-bad. As we learned in Chapter 6, people have a need to make sense of things quickly, so they rapidly form first impressions and fill in the missing information. However, early evaluation of what a person is saying may cause the listener to screen out important points later in the conversation. Therefore, try to stay as open-minded as possible and delay your evaluation of the message until the speaker has finished.

Organize information   Listeners easily become impatient and distracted because they can process information three times faster than the average rate of speech (450 words per minute versus 125 words per minute). To maintain interest, the active listener should concentrate on what the speaker is saying and regularly organize the information received so far into key points. In fact, it's a good idea to imagine that you must summarize what someone has said after he or she is finished.[92]

Show your interest   Along with being interested, you should motivate the speaker by showing your interest in the conversation. Eye contact and other nonverbal cues tell the speaker that you are paying attention and value the person's time. Also send back channel signals such as "Oh, really!" and "I see" during appropriate breaks in the conversation.

Provide feedback   Active listeners provide feedback by rephrasing the speaker's ideas at appropriate breaks ("So you're saying that . . . ?"). This further demonstrates your interest in the conversation and helps the speaker determine whether you understand the message.

Persuasive Communication: From Understanding to Acceptance

This chapter has mainly focused on how to get people to receive and understand messages. However, we usually want others to *accept* our information, not just *understand* it. People understand your message when they perceive the same meaning that you intended. They accept your message when it becomes part of their belief system and changes their opinions and behaviors. The elements of **persuasive communication** include characteristics of the communicator, message content, communication medium, and the audience being persuaded.[93]

persuasive communication
the process of having listeners accept rather than just understand the sender's message

Communicator Characteristics

What makes one person more persuasive than another? One important factor is the communicator's perceived expertise on the topic. Listeners mainly consider the speaker's credentials and experience, but speech pattern also influences perceived expertise. Specifically, people seem to have expertise when they talk confidently and relatively quickly, use some technical language, and avoid pauses ("umm," "uh") and hedges ("you know" and "I guess").[94]

Communicators are more persuasive if they have credibility.[95] Thus, employees are more likely to accept a new policy if it is communicated and supported by a respected peer. Trustworthiness also exists when communicators do not seem to profit from the persuasion attempt and state a few points against their position. For example, the effective persuader will acknowledge that an opposing position has one or two positive elements. Finally, people who are physically attractive or similar to us are usually more persuasive because we tend to think they have expertise and trustworthiness.[96]

Message Content

We are persuaded more by the communicator's characteristics when we don't consider the issue extremely important. When the issue is important, however, the message content becomes the critical feature of persuasive communication. The best strategy is to present all sides of the argument. Begin by introducing facts sympathetic to the audience's viewpoint, then shift into the theme of your position. Discussing only one point of view reduces your perceived trustworthiness and gives listeners the feeling of being cornered. When this happens, they react by rejecting your information.[97]

Your message should be limited to a few strong arguments because listeners are more likely to remember these points. These arguments should be repeated a couple of times, but not to the extent that you are battering listeners over the head with them.[98]

Is it better to be logical or emotional when communicating information? Generally, people should use both. Emotional appeals—such as graphically showing the unfortunate consequences of a bad decision—energize people, but they may also make them feel manipulated. Combining these emotional presentations with logical arguments tends to minimize this problem.[99] Also, emotional appeals should always be accompanied with specific recommendations to overcome the threat. In a safety campaign, for example, employees are more persuaded by graphic pictures of accident victims than by a lecture on recent accident statistics, but only if they are given explicit steps to avoid the danger.[100]

inoculation effect a persuasive communication strategy of warning listeners that others will try to influence them in the future and that they should be wary about the opponent's arguments

Finally, persuasive communicators use the **inoculation effect** to ensure that other points of view do not influence listeners. This involves warning listeners that others will try to influence them in the future and that they should be wary about the opponent's arguments. This inoculation causes listeners to generate counterarguments to the anticipated persuasion attempts. For instance, a coalition that wants the company to purchase new production equipment might warn senior management about arguments the finance department will use to try to convince them otherwise. This tends to make the finance department's subsequent persuasion attempts less effective.

Communication Medium

Earlier in this chapter we recommended using two-way verbal communication to persuade or motivate the listener. The personal nature of this medium seems to increase the credibility of the information. Furthermore, it is easier for the sender to determine whether the persuasive message is having the desired effect. Two-way communication also increases the receiver's active participation in the process. As long as this participation does not involve presenting defensive statements, the receiver is more likely to be involved in the conversation and internalize some of the information presented.

Persuasion may require written documentation, however, when dealing with technical issues. Whenever written communication is necessary for this purpose, it should be combined with direct discussions for the greatest persuasive effect. The verbal exchange could repeat highlights of the report and provide graphic images for the listener, thereby adding emotional appeal to an otherwise logical message.

Audience Characteristics

Not everyone is equally persuaded by the strategies and conditions that we have described. For example, it is more difficult to persuade people who have high self-esteem.[101] And, as we mentioned above, it is very difficult to persuade those who have been inoculated against your persuasive intent.

One guiding piece of information that you should remember from this chapter is that communication is both essential and pervasive in organizational settings. Without it, organizations would not exist because there would be no interaction among employees. Communication affects how well people perform their jobs, how much stress they experience, how satisfied they are at work, and how well they perform in teams. In fact, as we will learn over the next few chapters, effective communication becomes even more important as companies increase their reliance on teams.

Chapter Summary

Communication facilitates knowledge sharing, aids decision making, coordinates work activities, and fulfills the need for affiliation. The communication process involves forming, encoding, and transmitting the intended message to a receiver, who then decodes the message and provides feedback to the sender. Effective communication occurs when the sender's thoughts are transmitted to and understood by the intended receiver.

Several barriers create noise in the communication process. People misinterpret messages because of misperceptions. Some information is filtered out as it gets passed up the hierarchy. Jargon and ambiguous language are barriers when the sender and receiver have different interpretations of the words and symbols used. People also screen out or misinterpret messages due to information overload.

Electronic mail (e-mail) is a powerful way to communicate, and it has changed communication patterns in organizational settings. However, e-mail also contributes to information overload, tends to reduce politeness and respect in the communication process, is an ineffective channel for communicating emotions, and lacks the warmth of human interaction.

Computer-mediated communication gives employees the freedom to communicate effectively from any loca-

tion. This is part of the law of telecosm, which says that distances will shrink and eventually become irrelevant as electronic networks expand.

Nonverbal communication includes facial gestures, voice intonation, physical distance, and even silence. Employees make extensive use of nonverbal cues when engaging in emotional labor because these cues help to transmit prescribed feelings to customers, co-workers, and others. Emotional contagion refers to the automatic and unconscious tendency to mimic and synchronize our nonverbal behaviors with other people.

The most appropriate communication medium depends on its data-carrying capacity (media richness) and its symbolic meaning to the receiver. Nonroutine and ambiguous situations require rich media.

Many organizations rely on employee surveys, newsletters, management by wandering around, and work space design to facilitate communication across work units and hierarchical levels. Several firms have redesigned work spaces so employees have more line-of-sight with co-workers and better opportunities for informal communication. In any organization, employees rely on the grapevine, particularly during times of uncertainty.

Globalization and workforce diversity have brought new communication challenges. Words are easily misunderstood in verbal communication and employees are reluctant to communicate across cultures. Voice intonation, silence, and other nonverbal cues have different meaning and importance in other cultures. There are also some communication differences between men and women, such as the tendency for men to exert status and engage in report talk in conversations, whereas women use more rapport talk and are more sensitive than men to nonverbal cues.

To get a message across, the sender must learn to empathize with the receiver, repeat the message, choose an appropriate time for the conversation, and be descriptive rather than evaluative. Active listening occurs when the listener doesn't interrupt, empathizes with the speaker, maintains interest, postpones evaluation, organizes information, shows the speaker that he or she is interested in the conversation, and provides feedback to the speaker.

Persuasive communication tries to change behavior by having listeners accept rather than just understand the message. Persuasive communicators are more credible and have more perceived expertise. The message content should provide all sides of the argument, limit debate to a few strong points, repeat arguments one or two times, combine emotional appeals with logical arguments, and inoculate the listener against opposing arguments. Two-way verbal communication is more persuasive than written communication.

Key Terms

Communication, p. 232
Emotional contagion, p. 241
Emotional labor, p. 241
Empathy, p. 254
Flaming, p. 238
Grapevine, p. 247
Information overload, p. 236
Inoculation effect, p. 256

Jargon, p. 235
Knowledge management, p. 233
Law of telecosm, p. 240
Management by wandering around (MBWA), p. 244
Media richness, p. 242
Nonterritorial offices, p. 247
Persuasive communication, p. 255

Discussion Questions

1. A midsized city government intends to introduce electronic mail for office staff at its three buildings located throughout the city. Describe two benefits that the city's employees will likely experience from this medium as well as two potential problems that they may face.

2. Some cultures encourage people to be direct and precise when they communicate. Other cultures prefer more ambiguous language, even in business communication. Explain why ambiguous language may be desirable in the latter cultures and identify potential problems with ambiguity.

3. Marshall McLuhan coined the popular phrase: "The medium is the message." What does this phrase mean, and why should we be aware of it when communicating in organizations?

4. Why is emotional contagion important in organizations and what effect does the increasing reliance on e-mail have on this phenomenon?

5. Should companies try to eliminate grapevine communication? Explain your answer.

6. BankWest has just moved into one of the tallest skyscrapers in the city. Senior management is proud of its decision, because each department is neatly located on its own floor with plenty of private offices. BankWest executives have a breathtaking view from their offices on the top floor. There is even a large BankWest branch at street level. Unfortunately, other tenants occupy some floors between those leased by BankWest. Discuss the potential effects of this physical structure on communication at BankWest.

7. Explain why men and women are sometimes frustrated with each other's communication behaviors.

8. This chapter makes several distinctions between communications in Japan and the United States. Discuss three distinctions between communication in the two cultures.

Sea Pines

The coastal town of Sea Pines, Maine, retained a Boston consulting engineer to study the effect of greatly expanding the town's sewage system and discharging the treated waste into the harbor. At that time, fishermen in the town were experiencing massive lobster kills in the harbor and were concerned that the kills were caused by the effluent from the present Sea Pines sewage treatment plant. They were convinced that any expansion of the plant would further aggravate the problem. The fishermen invited Tom Stone, the engineer, to the monthly meeting of the local fishermen's organization to discuss their concerns. On the night of the meeting, the Legion Hall was filled with men in blue jeans and work jackets, many of whom were drinking beer. An account of this meeting follows, with Fred Mitchell, a local fisherman, speaking first.

Mitchell: Well, as you all know, Mr. Stone has been kind enough to meet with us tonight to explain his recommendations concerning the town's sewage disposal problem. We're all concerned about the lobster kills, like the one last summer, and I for one don't want to see any more sewage dumped into that harbor. *[Murmurs of assent are heard throughout the hall.]* So, Mr. Stone, we'd like to hear from you on what it is you want to do.

Stone: Thank you. I'm glad to get this opportunity to hear your concerns on the lobster situation. Let me say from the outset that we are still studying the problem closely and expect to make our formal recommendation to the town about a month from now. I am not prepared to discuss specific conclusions of our study, but I am prepared to incorporate any relevant comments into our study. As most of you are probably aware, we are attempting to model mathematically, or simulate, conditions in the harbor to help us predict the effects of sewage effluent in the harbor. We . . .

Mitchell: Now wait a minute. I don't know anything about models except the kind I used to make as a kid. *[Laughter.]* I can tell you that we never had lobster kills like we have now until they started dumping that sewage into the harbor a few years back. I don't need any model to tell me that. It seems to me that common sense tells you that if we've got troubles now in the summer with the lobster, then increasing the amount of sewage by 10 times the present amount is going to cause 10 times the problem.

A Fisherman: Yeah, you don't need to be an engineer to see that.

Stone: Although it's true that we're proposing to extend the sewage system in town, and that the resulting sewage flow will be about 10 times the present flow, the area of the sewage discharge will be moved to a larger area of the harbor, where it will be diluted with much more seawater than is in the present area. In addition, if the harbor is selected for the new discharge, we will design a special diffuser to mix the treated sewage effluent quickly with ocean water. As I indicated, we are attempting to use data on currents and water quality that we collected in the harbor and combine it with some mathematical equations in our computer to help us predict what the quality in the harbor will be.

Mitchell: I don't understand what you need a computer to tell you that for. I've been fishing in this area for over 35 years now, and I don't need any computer to tell me that my lobsters are going to die if that sewage goes into the harbor.

Stone: Let me say before this goes too far that we're not talking about discharging raw sewage into the harbor. The sewage is treated and disinfected before it is discharged.

Mitchell: Isn't the sewage that's being dumped into the harbor right now being treated and disinfected, Mr. Stone?

Stone: Yes, it is, but . . .

Mitchell: The lobsters still die, so it's clear to me that "treated and disinfected" doesn't solve the problem.

Stone: Our model will predict whether the treatment provided will be sufficient to maintain the water quality in the harbor at the state's standard for the harbor.

Mitchell: I don't give a damn about any state standard. I just care about my lobsters and how I'm going to put bread on the table for my kids! You engineers from Boston can come out here spouting all kinds of things about models, data, standards, and your concern for lobsters, but what it really comes down to is that it's just another job. You can collect your fees for your study, go back to your office, and leave us holding the bag.

Stone: Now wait a minute, Mr. Mitchell. My firm is well established in New England, and we didn't get that way by giving our clients that fast shuffle and making a quick exit out of town. We have no intention of leaving you with an unworkable solution to your sewage problems. We also will not solve your sewage problem and leave you with a lobster kill problem. Perhaps I have given you the wrong impression about this modeling. We regard this as one method of analysis that may be helpful in predicting future harbor conditions, but not the only method. We have over 40 years' experience in these harbor studies, and we fully intend to use this experience, *in addition to* whatever the model tells us, to come up with a reasonable solution.

Mitchell: Well, that's all well and good, but I can tell you, and I think I speak for all the lobstermen here, that if you recommend dumping that sewage into the harbor, we'll fight you all the way down the line! *[Shouts of agreement.]* Why can't you pipe the sewage out to the ocean if you're so concerned about dilution? I'm sure that your model will tell you there's enough dilution out there.

Stone: I agree that the ocean will certainly provide sufficient dilution, but the whole purpose of this study is to see if we can avoid a deep ocean outfall.

Mitchell: Why?

Stone: Because the cost of constructing a deep ocean outfall in this area is very expensive—about $700 per yard. Now, if the length of the outfall is 2,000 yards, don't you think that it makes good sense to spend a few thousand dollars studying the harbor area if we can save you millions?

Mitchell: All that money that you're going to save the town doesn't do much for the lobstermen who'll be put out of business if that sewage goes into the harbor.

Stone: As I said, we wouldn't recommend that if we thought, based on our modeling and our experience in this area, that the quality of water in the harbor would kill any lobster or any other aquatic life.

Mitchell: Well, I'm telling you again, if you try to put that stuff in our harbor, we'll fight you all the way. I think we've made our position clear on this thing, so if there are no further comments, I vote that we adjourn the meeting. *[Seconded.]*

When the meeting ended, the fishermen filed out, talking heatedly among themselves, leaving Mr. Stone standing on the platform.

Discussion Questions

1. What barriers to effective communication exist in this case? How would you overcome or minimize each of these barriers?

2. Use the model of persuasive communication to identify a more effective communication strategy that the engineering firm should consider.

Source: This case was written by Terence P. Driscoll. Reprinted from Dalmar Fisher, *Communication in Organizations* (St. Paul, MN: West Publishing, 1981). ■

CASE STUDY

The new workplace

BusinessWeek

Try looking for Paul O'Neill in his office these days and you discover that he doesn't exactly have one. The Aluminum Company of America (Alcoa) CEO and other top executives work in open cubicles and gather around a "communications center" with televisions, fax machines, newspapers, and tables to encourage impromptu meetings. Alcoa has abandoned its 31-story aluminum tower headquarters in Pittsburgh for a new three-story complex on the banks of the Allegheny. "We're going to have an opportunity to do things with the way people relate to each other. It will be freer and easier," O'Neill says.

This *Business Week* case study describes how organizations are redesigning their headquarters to improve communications and teamwork. It looks at how Procter & Gamble and other companies are removing walls to improve dialogue, and how some companies are trying out hoteling (nonterritorial offices). It also examines the

role of technology in the communication process of these new workplaces. Read through this *Business Week* article at www.mhhe.com/mcshane1e and prepare for the discussion questions below.

Discussion Questions

1. Explain how Procter & Gamble's new building improves communication among employees within teams and across organizational units.

2. How do recent improvements in computer, telephone, and other communication technologies make hoteling and other flexible work arrangements easier to implement?

3. The author of this *Business Week* case study says that hoteling (nonterritorial offices) focuses employees

more on the customer than on their offices. In your opinion, why does this occur?

Source: J. C. Hamilton, "The New Workplace," *Business Week*, April 29, 1996, pp. 106–13. ■

VIDEO CASE

Virtual companies and the Internet voicemail: Wildfire

 The number of telecommuters has more than doubled in the past five years, from four million to over nine million. Paulo Pignatelli runs The Corner Store, a computer consulting and software distribution business. Because his Web site is his store front, it allows him to do almost everything from his home in Connecticut. When he sits down at his computer every morning he's actually unlocking the door to an office in cyberspace. The Internet connects him to his research lab in Utah or his distributor in Seattle, or his clients around the world. He even connects with a client at the North Pole. Pignatelli said, "The whole business occurs electronically. We have no baggage, we have no extra fat that we need to carry." Pignatelli's wife Margo is the vice president. She said, "I'm frequently the person that people actually talk to, but they don't realize it. But I'm the person that they talk to via e-mail."

For the Pignatellis, a board meeting means a chat on the front porch. Last year The Corner Store cleared half a million dollars. This year, through continued expansion, the company expects to make over one million dollars.

The Internet is not only for small companies. Andersen Consulting in Palo Alto, California, shows Fortune 500 executives how their corporations can also profit from commerce on the Internet. Project DaVinci is a hands-on model for a joint venture which could use the Web to develop a major mining project. The model shows how each company could bring its own expertise to create a cybercorporation. Joe Carter of Andersen Consulting said, "It's not going to be an option to not be able to operate as part of the virtual enterprise. If you're not operating as a virtual enterprise ten years from now you may not be around to compete at all."

Even the conservative banking industry is jumping on the Internet. Andersen has developed a lab for an automatic teller of the future. A touch of the screen and you can talk directly with a bank representative who can pull up your file and go over it with you. As the cost of computing and communicating over the Internet drops over 50 percent every 18 months, expansion into cyberspace will become more attractive. The federal government estimates that telecommuting will increase fivefold by the year 2000, making it possible for more executives to enjoy the real rewards of their virtual efforts.

Another development in technology-mediated communications is changing the ubiquitous voice mail systems. Have you ever been annoyed by those systems where you have to select half a dozen options before you get to where you want to go? Nick Garbala, president of WildFire, thinks his company has a solution. His firm has designed an easier, friendlier approach to voice mail that he hopes will spread like wildfire.

The Wildfire system is programmed to recognize human speech. Garbala noted, "It's an electronic secretary that manages all of the users' daily telephone communications." Suppose you call someone using the Wildfire system, the machine will tell you to hold, and it will ask Nick if he wants to take the call.

Smart voice mail systems like Wildfire are part of a cutting edge technology in computing; they're called intelligent agents. Paul Saffo of the Institute for the Future says, "It's a way of interacting with a machine that seems like you're interacting with a human. With the right application that is spectacular." It isn't cheap so far. A Wildfire system costs around $50,000. Subscribing to an answering service goes for $150–$300 a month.

Discussion Questions

1. Businesses like The Corner Store have increasingly been turning to the Internet to conduct commerce. What are the potential communication advantages of doing business this way?

2. Discuss the limitations of doing business in cyberspace. For example, what problems might The Corner Store encounter that are unique to this type of business?

3. What implications does computer-mediated voice mail have regarding the emotional component of communications? ■

Cross-cultural communication: A not-so-trivial trivia game

Purpose

This exercise is designed to develop and test your knowledge of cross-cultural differences in communication and etiquette.

Instructions

Each student chooses or is assigned a partner. Each pair is then matched with another pair of students. The instructor will hand each group of four people a stack of cards with the multiple choice questions face down. These cards have questions and answers about cross-cultural differences in communication and etiquette. No books or other aids are allowed.

The exercise begins with a member of Team 1 picking up one card from the top of the pile and asking the question on that card to both people on Team 2. The information given to Team 2 includes the question and all alternatives listed on the card. Team 2 has 30 seconds to give an answer and earns one point if the correct answer is given. If Team 2's answer is incorrect, however, Team 1 earns that point. (Correct answers to each question are indicated on the card and should not be revealed until the question is correctly answered or time is up.)

Next, one member from Team 2 picks up the next card on the pile and asks the question to both members of Team 1. This procedure is repeated until all of the cards have been read or time has elapsed. The team receiving the most points wins the experiential exercise.

Important note: The textbook provides very little information pertaining to the questions in this exercise. You must rely instead on past learning, logic, and luck to win. ◼

Active listening skills inventory

Purpose

This self-assessment is designed to help you estimate your strengths and weaknesses on various dimensions of active listening.

Instructions

Think back to face-to-face conversations you have had with a co-worker or client in the office, hallway, factory floor, or other setting. Indicate the extent that each item below describes your behavior during those conversations. Answer each item as truthfully as possible so that you get an accurate estimate of where your active listening skills need improvement.

Circle the best response in the right-hand columns, indicating the extent to which each statement describes you when listening to others.

					Score
1. I keep an open mind about the speaker's point of view until he/she has finished talking.	Not at all	A little	Somewhat	Very much	_____
2. While listening, I mentally sort out the speaker's ideas in a way that makes sense to me.	Not at all	A little	Somewhat	Very much	_____
3. I stop the speaker and give my opinion when I disagree with something he or she has said.	Not at all	A little	Somewhat	Very much	_____
4. People can often tell when I'm not concentrating on what they are saying.	Not at all	A little	Somewhat	Very much	_____
5. I don't evaluate what a person is saying until he or she has finished talking.	Not at all	A little	Somewhat	Very much	_____
6. When someone takes a long time to present a simple idea, I let my mind wander to other things.	Not at all	A little	Somewhat	Very much	_____
7. I jump into conversations to present my views rather than wait and risk forgetting what I wanted to say.	Not at all	A little	Somewhat	Very much	_____
8. I nod my head and make other gestures to show I'm interested in the conversation.	Not at all	A little	Somewhat	Very much	_____
9. I can usually keep focused on what people are saying to me even when they don't sound interesting.	Not at all	A little	Somewhat	Very much	_____
10. Rather than organizing the speaker's ideas, I usually expect the person to summarize them for me.	Not at all	A little	Somewhat	Very much	_____
11. I always say things like "I see" or "uh-huh" so people know that I'm really listening to them.	Not at all	A little	Somewhat	Very much	_____
12. While listening, I concentrate on what is being said and regularly organize the information.	Not at all	A little	Somewhat	Very much	_____
13. While the speaker is talking, I quickly determine whether I like or dislike his or her ideas.	Not at all	A little	Somewhat	Very much	_____
14. I pay close attention to what people are saying even when they are explaining something I already know.	Not at all	A little	Somewhat	Very much	_____
15. I don't give my opinion until I'm sure the other person has finished talking.	Not at all	A little	Somewhat	Very much	_____

Scoring the Active Listening Skills Inventory

Step 1: Using the table on the right, assign the number corresponding to the answer you indicated for each statement. For example, if you indicated "Very much" for statement 1, then assign a "3" to the space provided to the right of the statement.

For statement items 3, 4, 6, 7, 10, 13:	For statement items 1, 2, 5, 8, 9, 11, 12, 14, 15:
Not at all = 3	Not at all = 0
A little = 2	A little = 1
Somewhat = 1	Somewhat = 2
Very much = 0	Very much = 3

Step 2: Write the scores for each item on the appropriate line below (statement numbers are in parentheses), and add up each scale. Then calculate the overall score by summing all scales.

Avoiding interruption (AI)   _____ + _____ + _____ = _____
                               (3)   (7)   (15)

Maintaining interest (MI)   _____ + _____ + _____ = _____
                               (6)   (9)   (14)

Postponing evaluation (PE)   _____ + _____ + _____ = _____
                               (1)   (5)   (13)

Organizing information (OI)   _____ + _____ + _____ = _____
                               (2)   (10)   (12)

Showing interest (SI)   _____ + _____ + _____ = _____
                               (4)   (8)   (11)

Active listening (total score):   _____

Note: This scale does not explicitly measure two other dimensions of active listening; namely, empathizing and providing feedback. Empathizing is difficult to measure and providing feedback involves behaviors similar to showing interest.

© Copyright 2000. Steven L. McShane. ◼

Team Dynamics

Learning Objectives

After reading this chapter, you should be able to:

- Define teams.
- Distinguish departmental teams from team-based organizations.
- Explain why virtual teams are becoming more common.
- Outline the model of team effectiveness.
- Identify six organizational and team environmental elements that influence team effectiveness.
- Explain the influence of the team's task, composition, and size on team effectiveness.
- Describe the five stages of team development.
- Identify four factors that shape team norms.
- List six factors that influence team cohesiveness.
- Discuss the limitations of teams.
- Explain how companies minimize social loafing.
- Summarize the four types of team building.

SEI Investments organizes employees into teams with a high degree of autonomy to complete projects and solve problems.
[Tim Hursley]

S EI Investments breaks anyone's stereotype of an investment firm. Housed in five colorful buildings in the countryside of Oaks, Pennsylvania, SEI distributes work to teams, not individuals.

The entire organization is operated by 140 self-directed teams. Some are permanent, serving large customers or important markets. However, most teams are temporary, evolving and forming around new problems and opportunities requiring immediate attention. Desks are on wheels so that employees can quickly regroup around new teams. Colorful cables spiral down from ceilings so that each desk is quickly reconnected to telephone, electricity, and intranet port in the new location. Employees work in large open areas rather than closed offices to facilitate communication among team members.

Most employees belong to one "base team" as well as three or four ad hoc teams. There is little authority to form teams—middle managers were ousted several years ago. Instead, an employee with an idea actively recruits others to form a group. "It's up to the recruiter to describe the project in a strategic and enthusiastic way," explains Rob Prucnal, a marketing team leader in the asset-management group. "But it's a soft sell. You want people to say, 'That's a team I'd like to be on. It could benefit from my insight.'"

Does the team concept work in an industry known for its rugged individualism? It does for SEI. The company handles back-office operations for 85 of the top 200 U.S. banks and its revenues have jumped 30 percent over the past three years. "This team stuff comes across as New Age mumbo jumbo," admits Richard Lieb, SEI's president of investment systems and services. "It's not. We hit the numbers."[1]

eams are replacing individuals as the basic building blocks of organizations. Companies around the globe are discovering that teams potentially make more creative and informed decisions and coordinate work without the need for close supervision.[2] At Mervyn's, the California-based department store chain, a SWAT team of skilled managers assists executives with staff shortages or problems in buying, merchandising, or advertising. At New Zealand Income Support Service, the government agency that distributes social benefits to New Zealanders, employees are grouped into teams to improve customer service. And in Germany, General Motors relies on teams to improve product quality at its Opel Eisenach plant. "The teams solve problems, eliminate waste and make suggestions—more than any other company in Germany," explains Eric Stevens, president of Opel Eisenach GmbH.[3]

teams groups of two or more people who interact and influence each other, are mutually accountable for achieving common objectives, and perceive themselves as a social entity within an organization

Teams are groups of two or more people who interact and influence each other, are mutually accountable for achieving common objectives, and perceive themselves as a social entity within an organization.[4] All teams exist to fulfill some purpose, such as assembling a product, providing a service, or making an important decision. Team members are held together by their interdependence and need for collaboration to achieve common goals. All teams require some form of communication so members can coordinate and share common objectives. Team members also influence each other, although some members are more influential than others regarding the team's goals and activities.

groups two or more people with a unifying relationship

All teams are **groups** because they consist of people with a unifying relationship. But not all groups are teams; some groups are just people assembled together.[5] For example, employees who meet for lunch are rarely called teams because they have no purpose beyond their social interaction. Although the terms "group" and "team" are used interchangeably in this book, our main focus is on teams. This is partly because most of the discussion is about task-oriented teams rather than other types of groups, and partly because the term "teams" has largely replaced "groups" in the business language.[6]

This chapter looks at the dynamics and effectiveness of work teams as well as informal groups in organizations. After introducing the different types of teams in organizational settings, we present a model of team effectiveness. Most of the chapter examines each part of this model, including team and organizational environment, team design, and the team processes of development, norms, roles, and cohesiveness. The chapter concludes by surveying the strategies to build more effective work teams.

Types of Teams and Other Groups in Organizations

There are many types of teams and other groups in organizations. Permanent work teams are responsible for a specific set of tasks in the organization. Departments may represent permanent teams, although this is not always so.[7] Exhibit 9.1(a) depicts a nonteam-oriented department where employees work alone and report individually to the immediate supervisor. This exhibit shows a group—several people are assembled together—but it is not a team. A department becomes a work team when employees are encouraged to directly interact and coordinate work activities with each other, as in Exhibit 9.1(b). The supervisor still serves as central coordinator and conduit to higher levels in the organization, but employees share information to get the work done.

team-based organizational structure a type of departmentalization with a flat span of control and relatively little formalization, consisting of self-directed work teams responsible for various work processes

SEI Investments, described in the opening story, applies work teams so completely that it is a **team-based organization**—shown in Exhibit 9.1(c). Team-based organizations rely extensively on **self-directed work teams (SDWTs)**

Exhibit 9.1
Departments as work teams

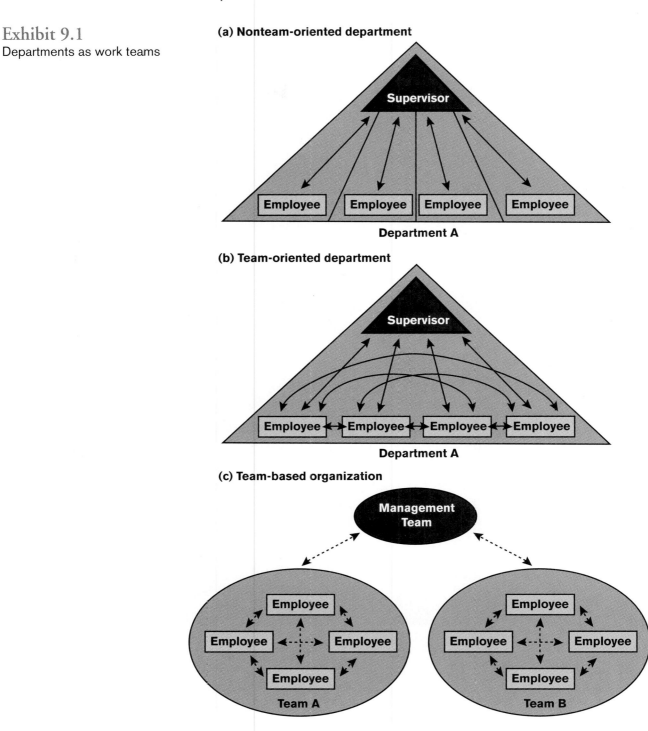

(a) Nonteam-oriented department

Supervisor

Employee | Employee | Employee | Employee

Department A

(b) Team-oriented department

Supervisor

Employee ↔ Employee ↔ Employee ↔ Employee

Department A

(c) Team-based organization

Management Team

Employee
Employee — Employee
Employee
Team A

Employee
Employee — Employee
Employee
Team B

self-directed work teams (SDWT) work groups that complete an entire piece of work requiring several interdependent tasks and have substantial autonomy over the execution of these tasks

organized around work processes rather than specialized departments as core work units.[8] These teams are fairly autonomous, as indicated by the dashed lines in Exhibit 9.1(c), so there is less need for direct supervision or someone to report continuously to the executive team. They are also *cross-functional*. This means that unlike traditional departments where employees have similar competencies (e.g., marketing, engineering), SDWTs rely on people with diverse and complementary skills, knowledge, and experience. SDWTs are described more fully in the next chapter because they represent the highest level of employee involvement.

Roberts Express has become a team-based organization. Rather than dividing employees into operations and customer service departments, the priority freight company in Akron, Ohio, organizes them into 25 autonomous customer assistance teams (CATs). Each CAT has seven to nine people and is responsible for the entire customer service process in a specific geographic area. All CATs schedule work hours and vacation days; most also arrange training schedules for their members. The longest-running teams track and analyze overhead costs for their operations. Supervisors have been replaced by facilitators who are called in by the teams for assistance. As the CATs become more comfortable with their roles, there has been less need for these facilitators.[9] What advantages would Roberts experience from this shift to a team-based organization? *[Courtesy of Roberts Express]*

quality circles small teams of employees who meet regularly to identify quality and productivity problems, propose solutions to management, and monitor the implementation and consequences of these solutions in their work area

Employees often belong to secondary teams that parallel their more permanent positions in the organization. **Quality circles** fall into this category.[10] Quality circles are small teams of employees who meet for a few hours each week to identify quality and productivity problems, propose solutions to management, and monitor the implementation and consequences of these solutions in their work area. Quality circles are usually permanent, and typically include co-workers in the same work unit.

Along with permanent teams, organizations rely on temporary teams to make decisions or complete short-term projects. Companies bring together employees from various departments to design a product, solve a client's problem, or search for new opportunities.[11] *Task forces* (also called *ad hoc* teams) are temporary teams that investigate a particular problem and disband when the decision is made. For instance, Royal Dutch/Shell Group formed a cross-functional team to improve revenues for its service stations along major highways in Malaysia. This team, which included a service station dealer, a union truck driver, and four or five marketing executives, disbanded after it had reviewed the Malaysian service stations and submitted a business plan.[12]

skunkworks cross-functional teams that are usually formed spontaneously to develop products or solve complex problems and usually in isolation from the organization and without the normal restrictions

Skunkworks are usually (but not always) temporary teams formed spontaneously to develop products or solve complex problems. They are initiated by an innovative employee (a *champion*) who borrows people and resources (called *bootlegging*) to help the organization.[13] In many cases, skunkworks are isolated from the rest of the organization, and are able to ignore the more bureaucratic rules governing other organizational units. The earliest corporate intranets at US West and other organizations started as skunkworks, championed by employees with a UNIX computer and free software from universities to create a Web server. BMW's M-series sports cars were created by a skunkworks team called the "M Group." The teams at SEI Investments also operate like skunkworks because they are formed by champions who informally encourage other employees to join. Skunkworks are responsible for several innovations at 3M Corp. One example is a special microsurface mouse pad that has become a commercial success. "Management had no idea the project was being worked on, until it was ready to be launched," explains a 3M vice president. "Some lab, some manufacturing, and some marketing people got together as an informal team to do it."[14]

Virtual Teams

A few years ago, consultants at Ernst & Young would "yell down the hallway" if they needed some advice on a problem. Now, they're connected through an intranet communication system and collaborate with colleagues around the world. They also join communities of practice—groups of people who are informally bound together through common interests and practices. All seven employees at Arizona-based Sechler CPA PC work from their homes, so team members communicate electronically. The only face-to-face meetings take place every two weeks at the home of company founder Carol Sechler. "My whole office is virtual," says Sechler.[15]

virtual teams cross-functional teams that operate across space, time, and organizational boundaries with members who communicate mainly through electronic technologies

Whether large or small, companies are seeing the emergence of **virtual teams**—cross-functional groups that operate across space, time, and organizational boundaries with members who communicate mainly through electronic technologies.[16] Some virtual teams are formed when members of permanent work units begin telecommuting or communicating with team members while visiting clients. Virtual teams also make sense when organizations want to place the best talent around the country or planet on temporary task forces or product development groups. Through electronic technologies, team members can participate in important decisions, yet remain on their home turf. Connections 9.1 illustrates how a virtual team at Sun Microsystems designed a complex electronic customer order system in just seven months without a single face-to-face meeting of all its members.

Why are virtual teams becoming more common? Emerging communications technology has certainly facilitated their development. E-mail, videoconferencing, electronic chat rooms, intranets, and networked computers let virtual teams coordinate work and make decisions fairly efficiently. In other words, they are leveraging the **law of telecosm**—making distance less relevant by expanding the web of electronic networks (see Chapter 8).[17] The shift towards knowledge-based rather than production-based work has also made virtual teamwork feasible. Employees are able to complete knowledge-based tasks from a distance through information technology, whereas production-based work activities usually require co-location of team members.[18]

law of telecosm a principle stating that as the web of computer networks expands, distances will shrink and eventually become irrelevant

Technology and knowledge-based work make virtual teams *possible,* but globalization and the benefits of knowledge sharing and teamwork make them *necessary*. As we described in Chapter 1, globalization has become the new reality in many organizations. As companies open businesses overseas or form tight alliances with companies located elsewhere in the world, there is increasing pressure to form virtual teams that coordinate these operations. Virtual teams also represent a natural extension of knowledge management because they minimize the "silos of knowledge" problem that tends to develop when employees are scattered geographically. They represent a powerful way to encourage knowledge sharing and utilization where geography limits more direct forms of collaboration. Moreover, corporate leaders are pushing for virtual teams as they discover that teams potentially make better decisions on complex issues.[19]

Informal Groups

Along with work teams, organizations consist of *informal groups* that exist primarily for the benefit of their members. Informal groups are not specifically formed by organizational decision makers, although their structure may be influenced by the existence of work teams. They shape communication patterns in the organization, particularly the grapevine described in Chapter 8. Informal groups can also interfere with the work team because members might resist team activities that conflict with the informal group's values. Some informal groups, such as the group you meet for lunch, might overlap with the work team. These groups form out of convenience and the need for affiliation.

Connections 9.1 ◻ Virtual Teams at Sun Microsystems

Sun Microsystems did something unusual when it designed a new electronic customer order system. The 15 project team members that created the system came from three different companies and three different countries, yet they completed the project in just seven months without ever meeting face-to-face. "We never had the entire team in the room at the same time," says Bill Crowley, one of the team's two coleaders.

Sun Microsystems has leapt into the world of virtual teams. After Sun's corporate leaders discovered the power of teams at Motorola and Xerox, they encouraged employees to form cross-functional teams to solve problems and build better products. These "SunTeams" were encouraged to use the intranet, videoconferencing, and other communication media so that anyone from any place could be involved.

The SunTeam that created the electronic customer order system was as diverse and dispersed as a team can get. Bill Crowley and several other Sun employees at the company's Massachusetts business unit joined forces with co-workers from Japan, the Netherlands, and the company's global headquarters in California. A representative from Motorola's operations in Texas provided a customer perspective, and Sun's major warehouse management supplier from Illinois was added to the group.

The Sun Microsystems team relied most heavily on e-mail, supplemented by weekly two-hour telephone conference calls. Videoconferencing was avoided because it was too structured for such a small group. However, the weekly telephone conferences kept everyone focused by establishing deadlines and goals for the following week. "Our strategy was that we did the work during the week outside the meeting and then came to the meeting prepared to talk about updates or problems," explained Crowley. "In retrospect, we realized that we had a formula for success."

Source: Adapted from J. Lipnack and J. Stamps, *Virtual Teams: Reaching across Space, Time, and Organizations with Technology* (New York: John Wiley, 1997), pp. 11–13, 160–67. ◼

Other groups are bound together for reasons other than social needs. For instance, you might belong to an informal group that shares a car pool and another group that plays together on the company's sports team.

coalition an informal group that attempts to influence people outside the group by pooling the resources and power of its members

A **coalition** is an informal group that attempts to influence people outside the group by pooling the resources and power of its members. By banding together, coalition members have more power than if each person worked alone to influence others. They also reinforce each other and further mobilize support for their position.[20] The coalition's mere existence can be a source of power by symbolizing the importance or level of support for the issue.

Why informal groups exist   Why do people join informal groups in organizational settings? One reason is that group membership fulfills relatedness needs (see Chapter 3). We meet friends for lunch or stop by their work areas for brief chats because this interaction satisfies our need for social interaction. Similarly, we define ourselves by our group affiliations. If we belong to work teams or informal groups that are viewed favorably by others, then we tend to view ourselves more favorably (see social identity theory in Chapter 6). We are motivated to become members of groups that are similar to ourselves because this reinforces our social identity.[21]

Some groups form because they accomplish tasks that cannot be achieved by individuals working alone. Coalitions and other task-oriented informal groups remain intact because members know they cannot achieve the same results alone. When groups are successful, it is easier to attract new members in the future. Lastly, informal groups tend to form in stressful situations because we are comforted by the physical presence of other people and are therefore motivated to be near them.[22] This explains why soldiers huddle together in battle, even though they are taught to disperse under fire. This also explains why employees tend to congregate when hearing the organization may be sold or that some people may be laid off.

A Model of Team Effectiveness

team effectiveness the extent to which the team achieves its objectives, achieves the needs and objectives of its members, and sustains itself over time

Why are some teams more effective than others? This question has challenged organizational researchers for some time and, as you might expect, numerous models of team effectiveness have been proposed over the years.[23] **Team effectiveness** refers to how the team affects the organization, individual team members, and the team's existence.[24] First, most teams exist to serve some purpose relating to the organization or other system in which the group operates. Teams at SEI Investments are given the challenge of solving problems or exploring new opportunities. Some informal groups also have task-oriented goals, such as a coalition that wants to persuade senior management to change a corporate policy.

Second, team effectiveness considers the satisfaction and well-being of its members. People join groups to fulfill their personal needs, so it makes sense that effectiveness is partly measured by this need fulfillment. Finally, team effectiveness includes the team's viability—its ability to survive. It must be able to maintain the commitment of its members, particularly during the turbulence of the team's development. Without this commitment, people leave and the team will fall apart. It must also secure sufficient resources and find a benevolent environment in which to operate.

Exhibit 9.2 presents the model of team effectiveness that we will describe over the next several pages. We begin by looking at elements of the team's and organization's environment that influence team design, processes, and outcomes.

Exhibit 9.2
A model of team
effectiveness

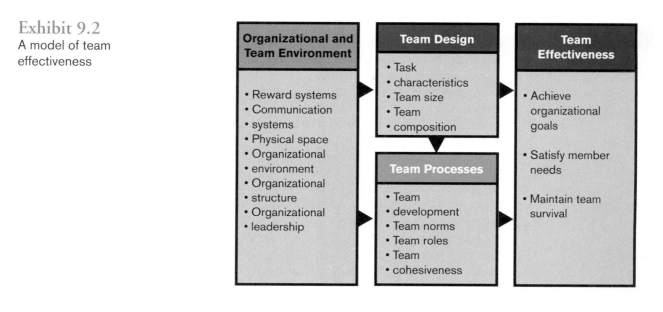

Organizational and Team Environment	Team Design	Team Effectiveness
• Reward systems • Communication • systems • Physical space • Organizational • environment • Organizational • structure • Organizational • leadership	• Task • characteristics • Team size • Team • composition	• Achieve organizational goals • Satisfy member needs • Maintain team survival
	Team Processes • Team • development • Team norms • Team roles • Team • cohesiveness	

Organizational and Team Environment

Our discussion of team effectiveness logically begins with the contextual factors that influence the team's design, processes, and outcomes. There are many elements in the organizational and team environment that influence team effectiveness. Six of the most important elements are reward systems, communication systems, physical space, organizational environment, organizational structure, and organizational leadership.

• *Reward systems*—Reward systems must be consistent with team dynamics. Recent evidence suggests that companies with the best team dynamics are more likely to have team-based rewards, merit increases partly determined by the individual's team contribution, and peer feedback systems (see Chapter 4).[25] Team members can still receive some pay based on their individual performance, but team-based rewards support the interdependence of effective teams. For instance, Coats Viyella Clothing Menswear, a Northern Ireland manufacturer of shirts, improved team dynamics by changing its reward system from individual incentives to fixed wages and team productivity bonuses.[26]

• *Communications systems*—Communication systems are important for team success.[27] An inappropriate configuration of communication systems may starve the team of information and feedback, or may result in information overload. Virtual teams particularly require the right combination of communication technologies. Telephone conferences worked well for Sun Microsystem's order system development team, described earlier, whereas videoconferences and electronic chalkboards may have been too cumbersome. Communications are also important when team members are located together. Physical space might be arranged to encourage more face-to-face dialogue. Some teams work best in open space areas that let team members communicate through signals and other nonverbal cues. The main point here is that the team's communication systems must be aligned with its task and structure.

• *Physical space*—The layout of an office or factory does more than improve communications among team members. It also influences their ability to accomplish tasks more quickly. For instance, many production teams have rearranged machinery and supplies to drastically reduce the distance needed to complete a work process. Physical space can also shape the team's perceptions about being together as a team and their sense of autonomy from other work units.[28] This is why many skunkworks are located away from other parts of the organization.

- *Organizational environment*—Teams are directly affected by the company's external environment. If the organization cannot secure resources, for instance, the team cannot fulfill its production targets. Similarly, high demand for the team's output creates feelings of success, which motivates team members to stay with the team. A competitive environment can motivate employees to work together more closely, particularly when they see teamwork as the best strategy to stay competitive.

- *Organizational structure*—Many teams fail because executives do not redesign how work is allocated across the organization. Departments are labeled as teams even where employees have little need to interact with each other. A better strategy is to form teams around work processes (such as making a product or serving a client group) so that team members need to interact frequently. Teams also work better when there are few layers of management and they have more autonomy to accomplish their work.[29] This type of structure encourages interaction with team members rather than with supervisors and other people outside the team.

- *Organizational leadership*—Teams require ongoing support from senior executives.[30] Their actions nurture team development by helping to align rewards, organizational structure, communication systems, and other elements of team context. They buffer teams from the political tactics of people who feel that the team is threatening their power. Teams are more likely to thrive in an environment where collective effort is valued more than individual effort. Again, organizational leaders establish this team-oriented value system. Organizational leadership and team-based values contributed to the successful implementation of team-based production at Campbell Soup's production facility in Maxton, North Carolina. "We really believe in [the team] approach and try to give the teams all the tools and resources to accomplish their goals," explains a Campbell Soup vice president.[31]

Team Design Features

Putting together a team is rather like creating an organization. There are several elements to consider, and the wrong combination will result in a dysfunctional rather than an effective team. Three of the main structural elements to consider when designing teams are task characteristics, team size, and team composition. As we saw earlier in the team effectiveness model (Exhibit 9.2), these design features affect team effectiveness directly as well as indirectly through team processes. For example, the skills and diversity of team members affect team cohesiveness, but they also have a direct effect on how well the team performs its task. Similarly, the type of work performed by the team (task characteristics) may influence the types of roles that emerge, but it also has a direct effect on the satisfaction and well-being of team members.

Task Characteristics

Teams are generally more effective when tasks are clear and easy to implement, because team members can learn their roles more quickly.[32] In contrast, teams with ill-defined tasks require more time to agree on the best division of labor and the correct way to accomplish the goal. These are typically more complex tasks requiring diverse skills and backgrounds, which further strain the team's ability to develop and form a cohesive unit.

task interdependence the degree to which team members must share common inputs, interact in the process of executing their work, or receive outcomes determined partly by their mutual performance

Another important task characteristic is **task interdependence.** High task interdependence exists when team members must share common inputs to their individual tasks, need to interact in the process of executing their work, or receive outcomes (such as rewards) that are partly determined by the performance of others. Teams are well suited to highly interdependent tasks because people coordinate better when working together than separately. Moreover, recent evidence indicates that task interdependence creates an additional sense of responsibility among team members which motivates them to work together rather than alone.[33] This is why SEI Investments, described in the opening story, encourages employees to form teams when creating new products or services. The design, marketing, and technical elements of the project are highly interdependent, so a cross-functional team coordinates the work more efficiently than individuals working in specialized departments.

Team Size

Microsoft is a large organization with large software development projects, yet it likes to think small about its teams. For example, most of the 450 people who worked on Microsoft's successful Windows NT operating system were assigned to small subteams with no more than 10 people responsible for a specific element. Through effective synchronization of these teams, Microsoft takes advantage of team dynamics without the coordination, cohesiveness, and communication problems that exist in large groups.[34]

St. Luke's is a highly successful British advertising agency that relies on self-directed work teams to serve clients. The London-based firm is so team oriented that it refuses to participate in industry awards that recognize individual achievement. One way that St. Luke's supports team dynamics is through the "35 rule" which says that no team shall have more than 35 members. "When any one group becomes larger than 35 people, it has to split apart, as an amoeba would," explains Andy Law, St. Luke's CEO and cofounder.[35] In your opinion, what would be the optimal size for a group of people who create advertising? What should be the smallest size of the team?

[Jonathan Player/NYT Pictures]

Some writers claim that Microsoft is following the right strategy by limiting team size to 10 people or less.[36] However, the optimal team size depends on several factors, such as the number of people required to complete the work and the amount of coordination needed to work together. The general rule is that teams should be large enough to provide the necessary competencies and perspectives to perform the work, yet small enough to maintain efficient coordination and meaningful involvement of each member.[37] Larger teams are typically less effective because members consume more time and effort coordinating their roles and resolving differences. Individuals have less opportunity to participate and, consequently, are less likely to feel that they are contributing to the team's success. Larger work units tend to break into informal subgroups around common interests and work activities, leading members to form stronger commitments to their subgroup than to the larger team.

Team Composition

When Pfizer, Inc., tried to get everyone working in teams, some employees weren't too eager. Many were near retirement and had always worked by themselves. One burly operator in his 50s said to a Pfizer team trainer: "Look lady, we barely tolerate each other here. You're out of your mind if you think you're going to get us to work in these teams you're talking about."[38]

When establishing teams, Pfizer and other companies require employees with the necessary motivation *and* competencies to work together. With respect to motivation, every member must have sufficient drive to perform the task in a team environment. Specifically, team members must be motivated to agree on the goal, work together rather than alone, and abide by the team's rules of conduct. Employees with a collectivist orientation—those who value group goals more than their own personal goals (see Chapter 7)—tend to perform better in work teams, whereas those with a strong individualist orientation tend to perform better alone.[39]

Employees must possess the skills and knowledge necessary to accomplish the team's objectives.[40] Each person needs only to possess some of the necessary skills, but the entire group must have the full set of competencies. Moreover, each team member's competencies need to be known to other team members. At Digital Equipment Corporation, one team took the time and effort to develop a skills inventory. This inventory helped everyone to know who had expertise about specific issues. By generating an understanding of each member's knowledge, the team was able to increase revenue by 56 percent within four months.[41] Along with these task competencies, team members must have the skills necessary to work with others. They must have sufficient emotional intelligence (see Chapter 7) to manage emotions, as well as conflict management skills to effectively resolve interpersonal differences.

How do companies ensure that employees have the ability and motivation to work in teams? Pfizer created a stronger team focus through intensive coaching sessions. Eventually, even Pfizer's more skeptical employees realized that teams make a difference in organizational performance. Team-based reward systems can also motivate employees to work with the team rather than focus on individual effort. However, it is often easiest to hire people at the outset who possess team-oriented competencies and values. At Anchor Hocking's team-based facility in Lancaster, Ohio, applicants are put into teams and given a project to complete, while evaluators identify those who work best in a team environment. Candidates also write an essay on what a team environment means to them. Once hired, employees at the kitchenware manufacturer attend a week-long team activity session that focuses on quality, processes, and technical issues.[42]

homogeneous teams
groups whose members have similar technical expertise, ethnicity, experiences, or values

heterogeneous teams
groups whose members have diverse personal characteristics and backgrounds

Team diversity　　Another important dimension of team composition is the diversity of team members.[43] **Homogeneous teams** include members with common technical expertise, ethnicity, experiences, or values, whereas **heterogeneous teams** have members with diverse personal characteristics and backgrounds. Heterogeneous teams experience more interpersonal conflict and take longer to develop. They are susceptible to "faultlines"—hypothetical dividing lines that may split a team into subgroups along gender, ethnic, professional, or other dimensions—that may eventually break the team apart.[44] In contrast, members of homogeneous teams experience higher satisfaction, less conflict, and better interpersonal relations. Consequently, homogeneous teams tend to be more effective on tasks requiring a high degree of cooperation and coordination, such as emergency response teams or string quartets.[45]

Although heterogeneous teams are more difficult to develop, they are generally more effective than homogeneous teams on complex projects and problems requiring innovative solutions.[46] This is because people from different backgrounds see a problem or opportunity from different perspectives. Heterogeneous team members also solve complex problems more easily because they usually have a broader knowledge base. Arnold Donald, senior vice president at Monsanto Corp., sums up this view: "Every time I have put together a diverse group of people, that team has always come up with a more breakthrough solution than any homogeneous group working on the same problem."[47] Finally, a team's diversity may give it more legitimacy or allow its members to obtain a wider network of cooperation and support in the organization.

Team composition, team size, and task characteristics affect team effectiveness directly as well as indirectly through team processes. The four team processes identified earlier in the team effectiveness model (Exhibit 9.2) include team development, team norms, team roles, and team cohesiveness.

Team Development

Team members must resolve several issues and pass through several stages of development before emerging as an effective work unit. They must get to know each other, understand their respective roles, discover appropriate and inappropriate behaviors, and learn how to coordinate their work or social activities. This is an ongoing process because teams change as new members join and old members leave. Bruce Tuckman's five-stage model of team development, shown in Exhibit 9.3, provides a general outline of how teams evolve by forming, storming, norming, performing, and eventually adjourning.[48] The model shows teams progressing from one stage to the next in an orderly fashion, but the dotted lines also illustrate that they might fall back to an earlier stage of development as new members join or other conditions disrupt the team's maturity.

Forming

The first stage of team development is a period of testing and orientation in which members learn about each other and evaluate the benefits and costs of continued membership. People tend to be polite during this stage and will defer to the existing authority of a formal or informal leader who must provide an initial set of rules and structures for interaction. Members experience a form of socialization (described in Chapter 17) as they try to find out what is expected of them and how they will fit into the team.

Storming

During the storming stage of team development, individual members become more proactive by taking on specific roles and task responsibilities. This stage

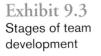

Exhibit 9.3
Stages of team development

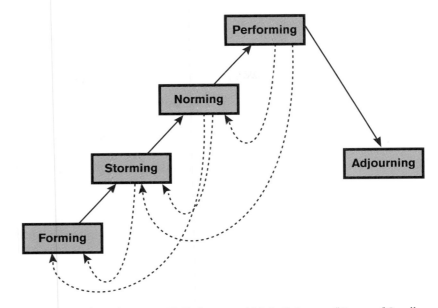

Source: Based on ideas in B. W. Tuckman and M. A. C. Jensen, "Stages of Small-Group Development Revisited," *Group and Organization Studies* 2 (1977), pp. 419–42.

is marked by interpersonal conflict as members compete for leadership and other roles in the team. Coalitions may form to influence the team's goals and means of goal attainment. Members try to establish norms of appropriate behavior and performance standards. This is a tenuous stage in the team's development, particularly when the leader is autocratic and lacks the necessary conflict-management skills.

Every work team and informal group has two sets of roles—behaviors and expectations assigned to a particular position—that help it to survive and be more productive. One set of roles helps focus the team on its objectives, such as giving and seeking information, elaborating ideas, coordinating activities, and summarizing the discussion or past events. The other set of roles tries to maintain good working relations among team members. These socio-emotional roles include resolving conflicts among team members, keeping communication channels open, reinforcing positive behaviors of other team members, and making team members aware of group process problems when they emerge.[49] During the storming stage, team members begin to sort out the specific features of these roles as well as to identify the members responsible for each role.

Norming

During the norming stage, the team develops its first real sense of cohesion as roles are established and a consensus forms around group objectives. Members have developed relatively similar mental models, so they have common expectations and assumptions about how the team's goals should be accomplished.[50] This common knowledge structure allows them to interact more efficiently, so they can move into the next stage, performing.

Performing

The team becomes more task oriented in the performing stage because it shifts from establishing and maintaining relations to accomplishing its objectives. Team members have learned to coordinate their actions and to resolve conflicts more efficiently. Further coordination improvements must occasionally be addressed, but the greater emphasis is on task accomplishment. In high-performance teams, members are highly cooperative, have a high level of trust in each other, are committed to group objectives, and identify with the team.[51]

Adjourning

Most work teams and informal groups eventually end. Task forces disband when their project is completed. Informal work groups may reach this stage when several members leave the organization or are reassigned elsewhere. Some teams adjourn as a result of layoffs or plant shutdowns. Whatever the cause of team adjournment, members shift their attention away from task orientation to a socioemotional focus as they realize that their relationship is ending.

Tuckman's model is a useful framework for thinking about how teams develop. At the same time, we must keep in mind that it is not a perfect representation of the dynamics of team development.[52] The model does not show explicitly that some teams remain in a particular stage longer than others, and that team development is a continuous process. As membership changes and new conditions emerge, teams cycle back to earlier stages in the developmental process to regain the equilibrium or balance lost by the change (as shown by the dotted lines in Exhibit 9.3). As our *Fast Company Online* feature describes, DPR Construction Inc. takes the team development process seriously. Moreover, it recognizes that team development is an ongoing process, not just something to do when project teams are formed.

Team Norms

norms informal rules and expectations that groups establish to regulate the behavior of their members

Have you ever noticed how employees in some departments almost run for the exit door the minute the work day ends, whereas people in the same jobs elsewhere seem to be competing for who can stay at work the longest? These differences are partly due to **norms**—the informal rules and expectations that groups establish to regulate the behavior of their members. Norms apply only to behavior, not to private thoughts or feelings. Moreover, norms exist only for behaviors that are important to the team.[53]

Norms guide the way team members deal with clients, how they share resources, whether they are willing to work longer hours, and many other behaviors in organizational life. Some norms ensure that employees support organizational goals, whereas other norms might conflict with organizational objectives. For example, the level of employee absence from work is partly influenced by absence norms in the workplace. In other words, employees are more likely to be absent from work if they work in teams that support this behavior.[54]

Conformity to Team Norms

Everyone has experienced peer pressure at one time or another.[55] Co-workers grimace if we are late for a meeting or make sarcastic comments if we don't have our part of the project completed on time. In more extreme situations, team members may try to enforce their norms by temporarily ostracizing deviant co-workers or threatening to terminate their membership.

Norms are also directly reinforced through praise from high-status members, more access to valued resources, or other rewards available to the team.[56] But team members often conform to prevailing norms without direct reinforcement or punishment because they identify with the group and want to align their behavior with the team's values. This effect is particularly strong in new members because they are uncertain of their status and want to demonstrate their membership in the team.

FAST COMPANY Online ◼ To Build a Great Company, Build Great Teams

DPR executive Lou Bainbridge (right) helps project participants form effective teams.

[M. Manninen. Used with permission]

Get the full text of this *Fast Company* article at www.mhhe.com/mcshane1e

"Fast" is too mild a word to describe the rise of DPR. Based in Redwood City, California, the construction company had just 12 people and $1 million in revenue in 1990; today it has 2,000 people and $1.3 billion in annual revenue. How did this upstart make it in the highly competitive construction industry? By building great teams.

DPR's founders reasoned that construction is a team sport, not a competition among architects, contractors, subcontractors, clients, and other project participants. DPR is so serious about team development that DPR executive Lou Bainbridge spends most of his time on this process. Before DPR pours the first drop of concrete, Bainbridge ensures that the project's main players have defined their goals, agreed on a schedule, established metrics of success, and even written a mission statement.

"I believe in people and in the possibility of pulling them together," says Bainbridge. "DPR provides a great laboratory for doing that."

One of Bainbridge's discoveries from this laboratory is that the best way to build great teams is to start small. "You build teams with three or four people around a table," he advises. "Then you double the number of members." By adding members slowly, you stand a better chance of pulling everyone together than if the team of 50 is formed all at once.

Bainbridge also relies on the team's tough challenges—Bainbridge calls them the "big rocks in the road"—to identify where it needs further development. "You watch a problem as it comes toward a team," Bainbridge advises. "Then you come in and coach the team through a successful resolution."

ONLINE CHECK-UP

1. Lou Bainbridge believes in building a team with a few people, then adding more later. Explain how this improves the team development process. What problems might occur through this process?

2. This *Fast Company Online* feature is part of a larger article about DPR Construction ("Building the New Economy," *Fast Company,* issue 20 [December 1998], pp. 222–36). What other team development practices are described in that article? Relate those practices to specific issues in team dynamics.

Source: Adapted from E. Ransdell, "Lou Bainbridge Builds Teams," *Fast Company,* issue 20 (December 1998). ◼

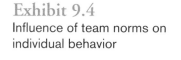

Exhibit 9.4
Influence of team norms on
individual behavior

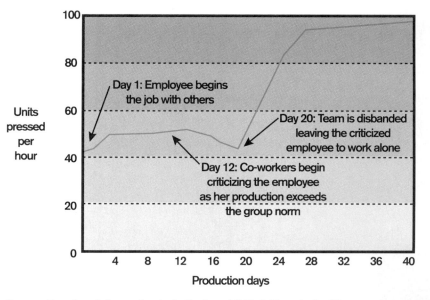

Source: Based on information in L. Coch and J. R. P. French, Jr., "Overcoming
Resistance to Change," *Human Relations* 1 (1948), pp. 512–32.

The power of conformity to team norms is revealed in the classic story of a
pajama factory employee assigned to work with a small group of pressers.[57]
The group had informally established a norm of 50 units per hour as the upper
limit of acceptable output. As Exhibit 9.4 illustrates, the newcomer quickly
reached this level and soon began to exceed it. By day 12, co-workers were
making sarcastic remarks about her excessive performance, so the employee
reduced her output to a level acceptable to the team. On day 20, the work
group was disbanded and everyone except the new employee was transferred
to other jobs. With the others gone and the team norm no longer in effect, the
employee's performance in the pressing room nearly doubled within a few
days. For the next 20 days, she maintained a performance level of 92 units per
hour compared with 45 units in the presence of co-workers.

How Team Norms Develop

Norms develop as team members learn that certain behaviors help them function more effectively.[58] Some norms develop when team members or outsiders
make explicit statements that seem to aid the team's success or survival. For
example, the team leader might frequently express the importance of treating
customers with respect and courtesy. A second factor triggering the development of a new norm is a critical event in the team's history. A team might develop a strong norm to keep the work area clean after a co-worker slips on
metal scraps and seriously injures herself.

Team norms are most strongly influenced by events soon after the team is
formed.[59] Future behaviors are influenced by the way members of a newly
formed team initially greet each other, where they locate themselves in a meeting, and so on. A fourth influence on team norms is the beliefs and values that
members bring to the team. For example, bargaining groups develop norms
about appropriate bargaining behavior based on each member's previous bargaining experience.[60]

Changing Team Norms

Although many team norms are deeply anchored, there are ways to change or
make them less influential on employee behavior. One approach is to intro-

duce performance-oriented norms as soon as the team is created. Digital Equipment Corporation asks members of newly-formed teams to think about a peak learning experience and to reflect on the norms that had contributed to it. The team discusses these experiences and selects those norms that would enable the team to be more effective. Team members then formally agree to hold themselves and each other accountable for those norms.[61]

Another strategy is to select members who will bring desirable norms to the group. If the organization wants to emphasize safety, then it should select team members who already value safety. Selecting people with positive norms may be effective in new teams, but not when adding new members to existing teams with counterproductive norms. A better strategy for existing teams is to explicitly discuss the counterproductive norm with team members using persuasive communication tactics (see Chapter 8).[62]

Team-based reward systems can sometimes weaken counterproductive norms. Unfortunately, the pressure to conform to the counterproductive norm is sometimes stronger than the financial incentive.[63] For instance, employees working in the pajama factory described earlier were paid under a piece-rate system. Most individuals in the group were able to process more units and thereby earn more money, but they all chose to abide by the group norm of 50 units per hour.

Finally, a dysfunctional norm may be so deeply ingrained that the best strategy is to disband the group and replace it with people having more favorable norms. This strategy is used at Sony's PlayStation division when a project team fails. "When you terminate a project, you have to break up the team," explains a Sony executive. "Failure usually means that the team dynamics weren't working."[64] Companies should seize the opportunity to introduce performance-oriented norms when the new team is formed, and select members who will bring desirable norms to the group.

Team Roles

role the set of behaviors that people are expected to perform because they hold certain positions in a team and organization

Everyone who works in an organization fulfills various roles. A **role** is the set of behaviors that people are expected to perform because they hold certain positions in a team and organization.[65] Employees hold one or more formally prescribed roles that guide their task-related behavior, such as how to serve clients or operate a piece of production machinery. These roles also specify what goals people are supposed to achieve and to whom they report. As we learned in Chapter 2, task performance is partly determined by accurate role perceptions; that is, how well individuals understand their prescribed roles for those tasks. We also learned in Chapter 5 that formal roles may be stressful when they are unclear—this is called **role ambiguity;** conflict with each other (*interrole conflict*); or conflict with the individual's personal values (*person-role conflict*).

role ambiguity uncertainty about job duties, performance expectations, level of authority, and other job conditions

Employees also take on certain roles when working in teams. Some of these roles are formally assigned to specific people. For example, when HMS Insurance Associates, Inc. formed teams to improve productivity and staff morale, employees volunteered for specific roles on their team. A leader was chosen to initiate discussion, keep everyone on track, and encourage participation; someone else volunteered to record and summarize the information at each meeting, and so on.[66]

Although some roles are formally prescribed with the job, many roles in team settings are not. Instead, they are informally fulfilled by various team members at different times. Exhibit 9.5 identifies several roles that facilitate team dynamics. Most team members might assume these roles at various times. However, some people prefer certain roles over others and have implicitly negotiated their right during the team development process to engage in

Exhibit 9.5   Roles for team effectiveness

Role activities	Description	Example
Task-building roles		
Initiator	Identifies goals for the meeting, including ways to work on those goals.	"The main purpose of this meeting is to solve the problem our client is having with this product."
Information seeker	Asks for clarification of ideas or further information to support an opinion.	"Jane, why do you think the client is using the product incorrectly?"
Information giver	Shares information and opinions about the team's task and goals.	"Let me tell you what some of my clients did to overcome this problem . . . "
Coordinator	Coordinates subgroups and pulls together ideas.	"Susan, will you be meeting with Shaheem's group this week to review common issues with the client?"
Evaluator	Assesses the team's functioning against a standard.	"So far, we have resolved three of the client's concerns, but we still have a tough one to wrestle with."
Summarizer	Acts as the team's memory.	Person takes notes of meeting and summarizes the discussion when requested.
Orienter	Keeps the team focused on its goals.	"We seem to be getting off on a tangent; let's focus on why the product isn't operating properly for our client."
Maintenance roles		
Harmonizer	Mediates intragroup conflicts and reduces tension.	"Courtney, you and Brad may want to look at your positions on this; they aren't as different as they seem."
Gatekeeper	Encourages and facilitates participation of all team members.	"James, what do you think about this issue?"
Encourager	Praises and supports the ideas of other team members, thereby showing warmth and solidarity to the group.	"Tracy, that's a wonderful suggestion. I think we will solve the client's problem sooner than we expected."

Sources: Adapted from information in K. D. Benne and P. Sheats, "Functional Roles of Group Members," _Journal of Social Issues_ 4 (1948), pp. 41–49.

their preferred roles. Some people like to ensure that everyone understands the ideas that co-workers have presented. Others like to encourage colleagues to participate more actively. Still others enjoy mediating conflicts that may arise among team members. The critical point, however, is that team members need to ensure that these roles are fulfilled so that the team can function effectively.

Team Cohesiveness

team cohesiveness the degree of attraction that members feel toward their team and their motivation to remain members

Team cohesiveness—the degree of attraction people feel toward the team and their motivation to remain members—is usually an important factor in a team's success.[67] Logically, employees feel cohesiveness when they believe the team will help them achieve their personal goals, fulfill their need for affiliation or status, or provide social support during times of crisis or trouble. However, cohesiveness is an emotional experience, not just a calculation of whether to stay or leave the team. It exists when team members make the team part of their social identity (see Chapter 6). Cohesiveness is the glue or _esprit de corps_ that holds the group together and ensures that its members fulfill their obligations.[68]

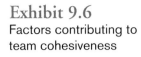

Exhibit 9.6
Factors contributing to team cohesiveness

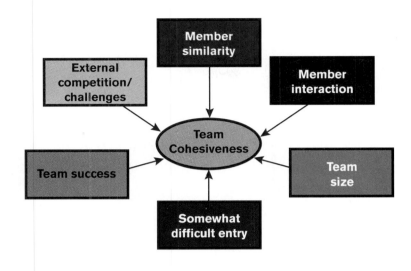

Causes of Team Cohesiveness

What makes teams cohesive? The main factors influencing team cohesiveness are identified in Exhibit 9.6. For the most part, these factors reflect the individual's identity with the group and beliefs about how team membership will fulfill personal needs.[69] Several of these factors are related to our earlier discussion of the attractiveness and development of teams. Specifically, teams become more cohesive as they reach higher stages of development and are more attractive to potential members.

Member similarity   Homogeneous teams become cohesive more easily than heterogeneous teams. As we mentioned earlier, diverse teams are susceptible to "faultlines" that psychologically impede cohesiveness, particularly during the early stages of development.[70] Employees in homogeneous teams feel more cohesive because interacting with like minds reinforces their perspective of reality and anchors their self-identity (see Chapter 6). Moreover, people who think alike find it easier to agree on team objectives, the means to fulfill those objectives, and the rules applied to maintain group behavior. This in turn leads to greater trust and less dysfunctional conflict within the group—two desirable qualities for its members.[71]

To build a more cohesive team, you would enlist employees with similar backgrounds. However, this may pose a dilemma because, as we explained earlier, heterogeneous teams are best for complex tasks or problems requiring creative solutions. Under these conditions, you need a heterogeneous team with either diverse skills or different perspectives of reality. Thus, we face a trade-off between the benefits of heterogeneity and homogeneity in team dynamics.[72]

Team size   Smaller teams tend to be more cohesive than larger teams because it is easier for a few people to agree on goals and coordinate work activities. This does not mean that the smallest teams are the most cohesive, because not having enough members prevents the team from accomplishing its objectives. Continued failure may undermine the cohesiveness as members begin to question the team's ability to satisfy their needs. Thus, team cohesiveness is potentially greatest when teams are as small as possible, yet large enough to accomplish the required tasks.

When Owens Corning moved out of its 28-story tower in Toledo, Ohio, it left behind an outdated hierarchy that interfered with the company's quest for teamwork. The fiberglass and building materials manufacturer now operates out of a new 3-story building that offers plenty of team space to improve informal communication, as this photo shows. "Today I'm not at the end of a row of offices," says an Owens Corning executive. "I'm in the middle of the team."[73] What are the advantages and potential problems with this physical space arrangement for team dynamics?
[Gary Quesada/Hedrich Blessing. Used with permission.]

Member interaction

Teams tend to be more cohesive when they perform highly interdependent tasks, are co-located (reside physically near each other), and work under other conditions that encourage direct interaction.[74] As you can see, this raises concerns about cohesiveness in the wired world of virtual teams and telecommuters. The lack of face-to-face interaction makes it difficult for team members to feel a common bond, even when they work effectively over the Internet. The problem may be worse for telecommuting employees because they are physically removed from other team members who have frequent contact. In the long run, distant workers may feel left out of an otherwise cohesive team.[75]

Even when team members work in the same area, physical structures may interfere with their level of interaction. This is why SEI Investments, described at the beginning of this chapter, and other firms have open office designs. As we learned in Chapter 8, these arrangements encourage communication and support team cohesiveness.

Somewhat difficult entry

Teams tend to be more cohesive when it is *somewhat* difficult to become a member. Notice the emphasis on the word *somewhat*—severe initiations can do more damage than good to bonding the individual to the group. An example of somewhat difficult entry would occur where applicants must pass through several interviews and selection tests before being accepted into the group. When entry to the team is somewhat difficult, teams are perceived as more prestigious to those within and outside the team. Moreover, existing team members are more willing to welcome and support new members after they have "passed the test," possibly because they have shared the same entry experience.[76]

Team success

Cohesiveness increases with the team's level of success.[77] Individuals are more likely to attach their social identity to successful teams than to those with a string of failures. Moreover, team members are more likely to believe the group will continue to be successful, thereby fulfilling their personal goals (e.g., continued employment, pay bonus). Team leaders can increase cohesiveness by regularly communicating and celebrating the team's successes.

External competition and challenges Team cohesiveness increases when members face external competition or a valued objective that is challenging. This might include the threat from an external competitor or friendly competition from other teams. Many corporate leaders try to focus employees on external competitors in order to strengthen their collective solidarity. Motorola has discovered that friendly competition among its total customer satisfaction teams can improve cohesiveness within the team and boost work performance. The British subsidiary of Armstrong World Industries also strengthens team cohesiveness through friendly competitions between its corrective action teams at an annual event called Team Expo.[78]

External threats and interteam rivalries increase cohesiveness because employees value their membership as a form of social support. They also value the team's ability to overcome the threat or competition if they can't solve the problem individually. Of course, teams remain cohesive only when members believe that working together is more effective than working alone to overcome the challenge. Teams quickly fall apart otherwise. Also, we need to be careful about the degree of external threat. Evidence suggests that teams seem to be less effective when external threats are severe.[79] Although cohesiveness tends to increase, external threats are stressful and cause teams to make less effective decisions under these conditions.

Consequences of Team Cohesiveness

Every team must have some minimal level of cohesiveness to maintain its existence.[80] In high cohesion teams, members are motivated to maintain their membership and to help the team work effectively. Compared to low cohesion teams, people in high cohesion teams spend more time together, share information more frequently, and are more satisfied with each other. They are generally more sensitive to each other's needs and develop better interpersonal relationships, thereby reducing dysfunctional conflict. When conflict does arise, members of high cohesion teams seem to resolve these differences swiftly and effectively. They also provide each other with better social support in stressful situations.[81]

Cohesiveness and team performance With better cooperation and more conformity to norms, high cohesion teams usually perform better than low cohesion teams.[82] However, the relationship is a little more complex. As we see in Exhibit 9.7, the extent that cohesiveness results in higher team

Exhibit 9.7
Effect of team cohesiveness on task performance

Team norms support company goals	**Moderately high task performance**	**High task performance**
Team norms conflict with company goals	**Moderately low task performance**	**Low task performance**

Low ⟶ **Team cohesiveness** ⟶ High

performance depends on the extent that team norms are consistent with organizational goals. Cohesive teams will likely have lower task performance when norms conflict with organizational objectives. This occurs because cohesiveness motivates employees to perform at a level more consistent with group norms. In our earlier example of the pajama factory, the new employee maintained low output because group norms discouraged high performance. If the group had low cohesiveness, she (and presumably others) would have performed at a higher level because group norms would be less influential.

The Trouble with Teams

With so much hoopla over the advantages of teams, it is easy to lose sight of the fact that teams aren't always needed.[83] Certainly, teams bring together ideas and information that one person rarely possesses alone. Yet there are also times when quick, decisive action by one person is more appropriate. Similarly, some tasks can be performed just as easily by one person as by a group. "Teams are overused," admits Philip Condit, president of Boeing. The Seattle-based aircraft manufacturer makes extensive use of teams, but knows that they aren't necessary for everything that goes on in organizations. Management guru Peter Drucker agrees: "The now-fashionable team in which everybody works with everybody on everything from the beginning rapidly is becoming a disappointment."[84]

process losses resources (including time and energy) expended toward team development and maintenance rather than the task

A second problem is that teams take time to develop and maintain. Scholars refer to these hidden costs as **process losses**—resources (including time and energy) expended toward team development and maintenance rather than the task.[85] It is much more efficient for an individual to work out an issue alone than to resolve differences of opinion with other people. The process loss problem becomes apparent when new people are added to the team. The group has to recycle through the team development process to bring everyone up to speed. The software industry even has a name for this. *Brooks's Law* says that adding more people to a late software project only makes it later.[86] Researchers point out that the cost of process losses may be offset by the benefits of teams. Unfortunately, few companies conduct a cost-benefit analysis of their team activities.[87]

A third problem is that many companies don't create an environment that allows teams to flourish. As we learned earlier in the chapter, some organizational and team environments support team dynamics, whereas other conditions do not. If companies simply put people in teams without considering the environmental factors, the effort will often be wasted.

Social Loafing

social loafing the situation in which people perform at a lower level when working in groups than when working alone

Perhaps the best known limitation of teams is the risk of productivity loss from **social loafing.** Social loafing occurs when people exert less effort (and usually perform at a lower level) when working in groups than when working alone.[88] A few scholars question whether social loafing is very common, but students can certainly report many instances of this problem in their team projects!

Social loafing is most likely to occur in large teams where individual output is difficult to identify. This particularly includes situations in which team members work alone toward a common output pool (i.e., they have low task interdependence). Under these conditions, employees aren't as worried that their performance will be noticed. Social loafing is less likely to occur when the task is interesting, because individuals have a higher intrinsic motivation to perform their duties. It is less common when the group's objective is important, possibly because individuals experience more pressure from other team members to perform well. Finally, social loafing is less common among members with a strong collectivist value, because they value group membership and believe in working toward group objectives (see Chapter 7).[89]

Minimizing social loafing

By understanding the causes of social loafing, we can identify ways to minimize this problem. Some of the strategies listed below reduce social loafing by making each member's performance more visible. Others increase each member's motivation to perform his or her tasks within the group.[90]

- *Form smaller teams*—Splitting the team into several smaller groups reduces social loafing because each person's performance becomes more noticeable and important for team performance. A smaller group also potentially increases cohesiveness so that would-be shirkers feel a greater obligation to perform fully for their team.
- *Specialize tasks*—It is easier to see everyone's contribution when each team member performs a different work activity. For example, rather than pooling their effort for all incoming customer inquiries, each customer service representative might be assigned a particular type of client.
- *Measure individual performance*—Social loafing is minimized when each member's contribution is measured. Unfortunately, individual performance is difficult to measure in some team activities, such as problem-solving projects in which the team's performance depends on one person discovering the best answer.
- *Increase job enrichment*—Social loafing is minimized when team members are assigned more motivating jobs, such as requiring more skill variety or having direct contact with clients. However, this minimizes social loafing only if members have a strong growth need strength (see Chapter 4). More generally, however, social loafing is less common among employees with high job satisfaction.
- *Select motivated employees*—Social loafing can be minimized by carefully selecting job applicants who are motivated by the task and have a collectivist value orientation. Those with a collectivist value are motivated to work harder for the team because they value their membership in the group.

Team Building

team building any formal intervention directed toward improving the development and functioning of a work team

Team building is any formal activity intended to improve the development and functioning of a work team. Most team building accelerates the team development process, which in turn might reshape team norms or strengthen cohesiveness. Team building is sometimes applied to newly established teams, but it is more common among existing teams that have regressed to earlier stages of team development. Team building is therefore most appropriate when the team experiences high membership turnover or members have lost focus of their respective roles and team objectives.[91]

Types of Team Building

There are four main types of team building: role definition, interpersonal processes, goal setting, and problem solving. A typical team-building activity includes two or more of these.[92]

Role definition

The role definition perspective examines role expectations among team members and clarifies their future role obligations to each other. Participants typically describe perceptions of their own role as well as the role expectations they have of other team members. After discussing these perceptions, team members revise their roles and present them for final acceptance.[93]

These Daewoo Motor Co. Ltd. employees are learning about teamwork and cooperation during this team-building exercise on Chebu Island in South Korea. In this exercise, employees at the Korean motorcar company are divided into two teams and each tries to control the flag. Which types of team-building processes would this exercise include? [Yun Suk-Bong. With permission of Reuters.]

This process determines whether individuals have the same role expectations that others assume of them.

Interpersonal process   Interpersonal process activities try to build trust and open communications among team members by resolving hidden agendas and misperceptions. Wilderness adventures are popular interpersonal process activities, in which teams face special challenges and threats in the woods.[94] For example, Black & Decker Corp's new design team participated in a team-building session operated by the Outward Bound group near Baltimore, Maryland. In one activity, called the Spider Web, team members had to crawl through a massive woven rope structure that hangs between two trees. Their mission was to get from one side to the other through small holes without touching the rope.[95] By solving these types of problems in unfamiliar settings, team members learn more about each other's strengths and weaknesses, and discover how interpersonal relations at work can affect each person's potential.

There are many types of team building that emphasize interpersonal process. Wilderness team building, paintball wars, and obstacle course challenges can be fun while bringing home the message that trust and respect are important elements of effective teams. Notice that these exercises also help teams develop other abilities, such as improved decision making. However, some of these fun events were designed for personal growth, not team development. Consequently, they may improve individuals, but not team dynamics.[96]

Gold of the Desert Kings is one of the most popular team-building games in North America. Developed and conducted by Eagle's Flight, this exercise places participants in a fictitious desert where they mine for gold and try to return before their water supply runs out. Each day is a few minutes in the game. What are the main team-building objectives of Gold of the Desert Kings and similar team-building games? What are the limitations of these team-building activities? *[Courtesy of Eagle's Flight, Inc.]*

dialogue a process of conversation among team members in which they learn about each other's mental models and assumptions, and eventually form a common model for thinking within the team

Another interpersonal process activity, called **dialogue,** helps team members learn about the different mental models and assumptions that each person applies when working together. Recall from Chapter 6 that mental models are working models of the world or "theories in use" that arise from our experiences and values. Dialogue is based on the idea that a team develops a "wholeness" or sense of unity when its members continually engage in conversations to understand one another. As they gain awareness of each other's models and assumptions, members eventually begin to form a common model for thinking within the team.[97]

Goal setting   As a team-building strategy, goal setting involves clarifying the team's performance goals, increasing the team's motivation to accomplish these goals, and establishing a mechanism for systematic feedback on the team's goal performance. This is very similar to the individual goal setting described in Chapter 3, except that the goals are applied to teams. Consequently, team dynamics must be addressed, such as reaching agreement on goals. Recent evidence suggests that goal setting is an important dimension of team building.[98]

Problem solving   This type of team building examines the team's task-related decision-making process and identifies ways to make it more effective.[39] Each stage of decision making is examined, such as how the team identifies problems and searches for alternatives (see Chapter 11). To improve their problem-solving skills, some teams participate in simulation games that require team decisions in hypothetical situations.[100] As well as helping team members make better decisions, these team-building activities tend to improve interpersonal processes.

Is Team Building Effective?

Team-building activities have become more popular as companies increasingly rely on teams to get the work done. As we see in Connections 9.2, some organizations are even experimenting with offbeat team-building activities in the hope that these sessions will improve team dynamics. Are these and more traditional team-building programs effective? Is the money well spent? So far, the answer is an equivocal "maybe." Recent studies suggest that some team-building activities are successful, but just as many fail to improve team effectiveness.[101]

Connections 9.2   ◘ **Team Building Takes New Twists, Turns, and Heights**

Joy Strull is afraid of heights. But that didn't stop the information systems manager at Latitude Communications from swinging on a trapeze at the San Francisco School of Circus Arts. With the guidance of a professional trapeze artist and support from co-workers, Strull held the bar with her hands and managed to latch her knees around it. Then, as onlookers chanted "Let your hands go, Joy," she let go and swung upside down for several seconds. When asked why she had gone up on the trapeze in spite of her fear, the breathless Strull replied, "Because we're a team. We're in this together."

Latitude Communications, a Santa Clara, California, hardware and software manufacturer, paid for the afternoon of trapeze swinging and other circus stunts so that its 75 employees would become more effective team members. Other companies are also trying out offbeat ways to help build more effective work groups.

Employees at one of AT&T's Silicon Valley offices were sent to Corporate Space Camp where they experienced the sensation of walking on the moon, building a structure in zero gravity, and other rudiments of astronaut training. The one-day session also included a space shuttle mission, where participants were responsible for the launch, orbit, and recovery of a space shuttle.

"The underlying message of Corporate Space Academy is the concept of teamwork, and especially how nonparticipation from even one team member could mean failure of the entire mission," says Laura Udall, an AT&T spokesperson.

Companies that aren't ready to send their teams into space or on a high-flying trapeze might consider something more earthly. In China, Coca-Cola executives participated in a team-building program that included fire walking. After stepping across the 15-foot bed of coals, managers checked their smoky feet for blisters, then broke into exuberant smiles.

Alex Kam, Coca-Cola China's human resources manager, says he wants Coke staff in China to feel part of a team and be ready to take risks. "This training forces employees to break their fear barriers—to do something they have never done before," he says.

Sources: L. Slonaker, "Counting on Training," *Dallas Morning News,* March 16, 1998, p. D4; "AT&T Has 'The Right Stuff' at Corporate Space Academy," *Business Wire,* December 17, 1997; C. Prystay, "Executive Rearmament: Tempering Asia's Executive Mettle," *Asian Business,* 32 (October 1996), pp. 18–19. ◘

WAISGLASS/COULTHART © 1997 Farcus Cartoons/dist. by Universal Press Syndicate

"Let's agree to blame this on Filmore in accounting."

Too often, team building is ineffective because it is applied incorrectly.[102] One problem with team building is that it is introduced without anyone looking at the team's needs. As we just learned, team building activities serve various purposes. Yet many companies make the unfortunate assumption that "one size fits all" in team building. We need to consider the type of team that will receive the team building. Many work teams require a great deal of coordination, so interpersonal process development may be most important. Cross-functional teams, on the other hand, often exist for a limited time to solve problems, so problem-solving training may be best for them.

Another problem is that companies tend to view team-building activities as medical inoculations that every team should receive when the team is formed. Corporate leaders forget that team building is an ongoing process, not a three-day jump start. Some experts suggest, for example, that wilderness experiences often fail because they rarely include follow-up consultation to ensure that what team members learn during these events is transferred back to the workplace.[103] Effective team development requires members to frequently return to the developmental issues and learnings. Third, we must remember that team building occurs on the job, not just in Yellowstone Park. Organizations should encourage team members to reflect on their work experiences and to experiment with just-in-time learning for team development.

Finally, there is the potential problem that team building is too effective. The activity may encourage team members to become more loyal to the team than to the larger organization.[104] Although team dynamics may improve, the high cohesiveness may result in dysfunctional conflict between the team and others in the organization. Few team-building efforts seem to have had this effect, but the risk is always present.

Chapter Summary

Teams are groups of two or more people who interact and influence each other, are mutually accountable for achieving common objectives, and perceive themselves as a social entity within an organization. All teams are groups because they consist of people with a unifying relationship, but some groups do not have the purposive interaction of teams.

A team-based organization relies on self-directed work teams rather than functional departments as the core work units. Traditional departments may be teams when employees are encouraged to interact and coordinate work activities directly with each other. Unlike traditional departments, however, team-based organizations tend to rely on cross-functional, autonomous teams with less need for supervisors in a communication or coordination role.

Virtual teams operate across space, time, and organizational boundaries with members who communicate mainly through electronic technologies. They are becoming more common due to advanced computer-based technology, the shift from physical labor to knowledge-based work, corporate globalization, and the need for greater knowledge sharing.

Team effectiveness includes the group's ability to survive, achieve its system-based objectives, and fulfill the needs of its members. The model of team effectiveness considers the team and organizational environment, team design, and team processes. The team or organizational environment influences team effectiveness directly, as well as through team design and team processes.

Six elements in the organizational and team environment that influence team effectiveness are reward systems, communication systems, physical space, organizational environment, organizational structure, and organizational leadership.

Three team design elements are task characteristics, team size, and team composition. Teams work best when tasks are clear, easy to implement, and require a high degree of interdependence. Teams should be large enough to perform the work, yet small enough for efficient coordination and meaningful involvement. Effective teams are composed of people with the competencies and motivation to perform tasks in a team environment. Heterogeneous teams operate best on complex projects and problems requiring innovative solutions.

Teams develop through the stages of forming, storming, norming, performing, and eventually adjourning.

However, some teams remain in a particular stage longer than others, and team development is a continuous process.

Teams develop norms to regulate and guide member behavior. These norms may be influenced by critical events, explicit statements, initial experiences, and members' pregroup experiences.

Cohesiveness is the degree of attraction people feel toward the team and their motivation to remain members. Cohesiveness increases with member similarity, degree of interaction, smaller team size, somewhat difficult entry, team success, and external challenges. Teams need some level of cohesiveness to survive, but high cohesive units have higher task performance only when their norms do not conflict with organizational objectives.

Teams are not necessary for all organizational activities. Moreover, they have hidden costs, known as process losses, and require particular environments to flourish. Teams often fail because they are not set up in supportive environments.

Social loafing is another potential problem with teams. This is the tendency for individuals to perform at a lower level when working in groups than when alone. Social loafing can be minimized by making each member's performance more visible and increasing each member's motivation to perform his or her tasks within the group.

Team building is any formal activity intended to improve the development and functioning of a work team. Four team-building strategies are role definition, interpersonal process, goal setting, and problem solving. Some team-building events succeed, but companies often fail to consider the contingencies of team building.

Key Terms

Coalition, p. 273
Dialogue, p. 291
Groups, p. 268
Heterogeneous teams, p. 278
Homogeneous teams, p. 278
Law of telecosm, p. 271
Norms, p. 280
Process losses, p. 288
Quality circles, p. 270
Role, p. 283
Role ambiguity, p. 283

Self-directed work teams (SDWTs), p. 268
Skunkworks, p. 271
Social loafing, p. 288
Task interdependence, p. 275
Team-based organization, p. 268
Team building, p. 289
Team cohesiveness, p. 284
Team effectiveness, p. 273
Teams, p. 268
Virtual teams, p. 271

Discussion Questions

1. During an organizational behavior course, the instructor states that the concept of "virtual teams" is just a fad that doesn't deserve any attention in this class. Explain to the instructor why his or her statement about the future of virtual teams may be incorrect.

2. If you were randomly assigned with four other students to complete a group project, what team-related problems might you experience? Describe the positive characteristics of student teams in this situation.

3. You have been put in charge of a cross-functional task force that will develop Internet banking services for retail customers. The team includes representatives from marketing, information services, customer service, and accounting, all of whom will move to the same location at headquarters for three months. Describe the evidence or behaviors that you might observe during each stage of the team's development.

4. You have just been transferred from the Kansas City office to the Denver office of your company, a national sales organization of electrical products for developers and contractors. In Kansas City, team members regularly called customers after a sale to ask whether the products arrived on time and whether they were satisfied. But when you moved to the Denver office, no one seemed to make these follow-up calls. A recently hired co-worker explained that other co-workers discouraged her from making

those calls. Later, another co-worker suggested that your follow-up calls were making everyone else look lazy. Give three possible reasons why the norms in Denver might be different from those in the Kansas City office, even though the customers, products, sales commissions, and other characteristics of the workplace are almost identical.

5. "Ideally, all work teams should have seven members, give or take one or two." Discuss the accuracy of this statement.

6. You have been assigned to a class project with five other students, none of whom you have met before. To what extent would team cohesiveness improve your team's performance on this project? What actions would you recommend to build team cohesiveness among student team members in this situation?

7. The CEO of Eastern Railway Corp. wants employees throughout the organization to perform their work in teams. According to the CEO, "teams are our solution to increasing competition and customer demands." Discuss three problems with teams that Eastern Railway's CEO may not be aware of.

8. The Johari Window, described in Chapter 6, is sometimes used as the foundation of team building. What type of team building would occur through Johari Window activities.

CASE STUDY

Treetop Forest Products Inc.

Treetop Forest Products Inc. is a sawmill operation in Oregon owned by a major forest products company, but it operates independently of headquarters. It was built 30 years ago and completely updated with new machinery five years ago. Treetop receives raw logs from the area for cutting and planing into building-grade lumber, mostly two-by-four inch and two-by-six inch pieces of standard lengths. Higher-grade logs leave Treetop's sawmill department in finished form and are sent directly to the packaging department. The remaining 40 percent of

sawmill output are cuts from lower-grade logs, requiring further work by the planing department.

Treetop has one general manager, 16 supervisors and support staff, and 180 unionized employees. The unionized employees are paid an hourly rate specified in the collective agreement, whereas management and support staff are paid a monthly salary. The mill is divided into six operating departments: boom, sawmill, planer, packaging, shipping, and maintenance. The sawmill, boom, and packaging departments operate a morning shift starting at 6 A.M. and an afternoon shift starting at 2 P.M. Employees in these departments rotate shifts every two weeks. The planer and shipping departments operate only morning shifts. Maintenance employees work the night shift (starting at 10 P.M.).

Each department, except for packaging, has a supervisor on every work shift. The planer supervisor is responsible for the packaging department on the morning shift, and the sawmill supervisor is responsible for the packaging department on the afternoon shift. However, the packaging operation is housed in a separate building from the other departments, so supervisors seldom visit the packaging department. This is particularly true for the afternoon shift, because the sawmill supervisor is the farthest distance from the packaging building.

Packaging Quality

Ninety percent of Treetop's product is sold on the international market through Westboard Co., a large marketing agency. Westboard represents all forest products mills owned by Treetop's parent company as well as several other clients in the region. The market for building-grade lumber is very price competitive, because there are numerous mills selling a relatively undifferentiated product. However, some differentiation does occur in product packaging and presentation. Buyers will look closely at the packaging when deciding whether to buy from Treetop or another mill.

To encourage its clients to package their products better, Westboard sponsors a monthly package quality award. The marketing agency samples and rates its clients' packages daily, and the sawmill with the highest score at the end of the month is awarded a plaque. Package quality is a combination of how the lumber is piled (e.g., defects turned in), where the bands and dunnage are placed, how neatly the stencil and seal are applied, the stencil's accuracy, and how neatly and tightly the plastic wrap is attached.

Treetop Forest Products won Westboard's packaging quality award several times in the past few years, and received high ratings in the months that it didn't win. However, the mill's ratings have started to decline over the past year, and several clients have complained about the appearance of the finished product. A few large customers switched to competitors' lumber, saying that the decision was based on the substandard appearance of Treetop's packaging when it arrived in their lumberyard.

Bottleneck in Packaging

The planing and sawmilling departments have increased productivity significantly over the past two years. The sawmill operation recently set a new productivity record on a single day. The planer operation has increased productivity to the point where last year it reduced operations to just one (rather than two) shifts per day. These productivity improvements are due to better operator training, fewer machine breakdowns, and better selection of raw logs. (Sawmill cuts from high-quality logs usually do not require planing work.)

Productivity levels in the boom, shipping, and maintenance departments have remained constant. However, the packaging department has recorded decreasing productivity over the past couple of years, with the result that a large backlog of finished product is typically stockpiled outside the packaging building. The morning shift of the packaging department is unable to keep up with the combined production of the sawmill and planer departments, so the unpackaged output is left for the afternoon shift. Unfortunately, the afternoon shift packages even less product than the morning shift, so the backlog continues to build. The backlog adds to Treetop's inventory costs and increases the risk of damaged stock.

Treetop has added Saturday overtime shifts as well as extra hours before and after the regular shifts for the packaging department employees to process this backlog. Last month, the packaging department employed 10 percent of the workforce but accounted for 85 percent of the overtime. This is frustrating to Treetop's management because time and motion studies recently confirmed that the packaging department is capable of processing all of the daily sawmill and planer production without overtime. Moreover, with employees earning one-and-a-half or two times their regular pay on overtime, Treetop's cost competitiveness suffers.

Employees and supervisors at Treetop are aware that people in the packaging department tend to extend lunch by 10 minutes and coffee breaks by 5 minutes. They also typically leave work a few minutes before the end of shift. This abuse has worsened recently, particularly on the afternoon shift. Employees who are temporarily assigned to the packaging department also seem to participate in this time loss pattern after a few days. Although they are punctual and productive in other departments, these temporary employees soon adopt the packaging crew's informal schedule when assigned to that department.

Discussion Questions

1. Based on your knowledge of team dynamics, explain why the packaging department is less productive than other teams at Treetop.

2. How should Treetop change the counterproductive norms that exist in the packaging group?

3. What structural and other changes would you recommend that could improve this situation in the long term?

CASE STUDY

Schwab makes investing a team sport

BusinessWeek

Joe Parascandolo recalls the day when a team representative from investment firm Charles Schwab called. The market was taking a dive and Parascandolo's options portfolio would have been hit hard if he hadn't sold the options in time. Along with saving money, Parascandolo believes that Schwab's team approach to client service beats having one broker, as other firms offer. "It's like having eight pair of eyes working for me," he says. Most of Schwab's clients don't get personal brokers. Instead, they are assigned to a small team at a call center with whom they plot investment strategy and receive other financial advice. "Your team is your concierge," says Susanne D. Lyons, president of Schwab's Specialized Investor Services unit.

This *Business Week* case study describes how Charles Schwab is redefining customer service and staving off new competition. One of its strategies—innovative for the investment industry—is to coach clients using Schwab teams. Read through this *Business Week* case study at www.mhhe.com/mcshane1e and prepare for the discussion questions below.

Discussion Questions

1. What are the advantages for clients and Charles Schwab of relying on an investment team rather than individual brokers?

2. This *Business Week* case study describes how clients receive advice from a personal team of representatives. Suppose you were put in charge of designing teams at Charles Schwab. Describe the skill mix of a typical team. What organizational and team conditions should be in place to support these teams?

Source: J. M. Laderman, "Remaking Schwab," *Business Week*, May 25, 1998, pp. 122–27. ■

VIDEO CASE

Management training outdoors

 Increasingly, Fortune 500 companies are mandating management training programs that include outdoor wilderness activities. American businesses have been training executives outdoors since the early 70s. Outward Bound uses nature to encourage team building. Their clients range from Pepsi to General Electric to local hospital executives. Don Hanson of Porter Memorial Hospital said, "Some of them came with an awful lot of anxiety and oftentimes when you have a problem at the hospital you have a level of anxiety. But I think they just transfer that and say 'Well look what we did when we were together as a team up there. Let's just figure out how to solve this problem together here.'"

Outward Bound includes briefings for clients who don't feel safe or fit to climb on the mountains. They counsel those who feel that their career could be damaged by their performance. While the Pecos River Learn-

ing Center also attracts Fortune 500 firms, their philosophy is, well, more philosophical. Their center is the creation of Larry Wilson, author of the best-seller *Changing The Game, The New Way To Sell*. Wilson said, "We define winning as going as far as you can—using all that you've got." Wilson thinks leaping off cliffs and poles helps clients transcend fears and nonproductive habits.

Wayne Townsend of General Motors, Canada, sends people to Wilson's training. He noted, "A lot of the old things that got us where we are today no longer work, and making that kind of a shift in our culture is a very significant task. And my goal is to involve the very senior people of our organization right into a conference center like this and have that cultural change happen."

Critics have claimed that the Pecos River Center doesn't tell the corporations how their employees' minds are being changed. Fundamentalists have even charged that what's really taught is theology. Wilson disputes this

297

charge, stating, "In our case, our purpose is to help organizations change, to take advantage or be able to thrive in this global market. And in order to change they're going to have to do it quickly. It's not a one seminar or one event process. It's more like an eighteen-month to a three-year process. And our goal is to help people tap into their courage and creativity to be able to see that they have other options, new ways of doing things. Because whatever got us where we are is not going to take us where we have to be."

Steve McCormick runs Colorado Outward Bound. He agrees with Wilson that the type of training they offer indeed affects how people perform at work. He stated, "Our basic goal is to help a large group of creative people remind themselves continuously of the fact that they are creative, that they can work together effectively, and that they can show effective teamwork when they need to. When given a new set of challenges, they already have within them the capability of responding to it well."

Despite the constant stream of companies utilizing this type of training, there are still many who don't believe in its effectiveness. Wilson noted, "The only way to really get you to believe it is to experience it. That is one of the advantages of this kind of learning. It's not an intellectual process, it's a intellectual, emotional, total process of new learning and breaking old patterns." Wilson pointed to an example of a woman who came to the Pecos River facility and went on to become a vice president. "In her particular case, she went on to become a vice president for her company after she realized that she had really been holding back her potential. She felt like if she could do this, she could do anything. And what it gave her was an experience of her own power, her own courage, and she realized that in all of her life that first step is what she's been holding back on. But on the other side of that step was joy and excitement and adventure and those were the things that she was really looking for."

Wilson stated that his programs are based on a deep belief in human potential. He said, "We believe that people have a lot more potential than they are using and that our competitive advantage in the future from a business is going to be able to tap into people, more of their potential. We've been training people to play the game not to lose instead of playing the game to win."

Reflecting on his training programs, McCormick stated, "We think that Outward Bound is tied into very fundamental values that have always been a part of American industry. They have to do with being an effective leader, being an effective team player, they have to do with having the ability that when you sit down to solve a problem to use your best skills and the best skills of the people who are sitting around the table."

Discussion Questions

1. Do you think the type of training provided by organizations such as the Pecos River Learning Center or Outward Bound leads to developing effective workplace teams? Explain your answer.

2. The outdoor training facilities examined in the video claim to promote teamwork in the workplace. Do you think the training as currently offered also applies to virtual teams?

3. The outdoor training facilities are designed to teach people how to work together. What elements of effective teamwork are not covered in this type of training? ◼

TEAM EXERCISE 1

Team-trust exercise

Purpose

This exercise is designed to help you understand the role of interpersonal trust in the development and maintenance of effective teams.

Instructions

Students are divided into teams of approximately 10 people. Each team receives 15 objects from the instructor. The same 15 objects are arranged in a specific way on a table at the front of the room (or elsewhere, as designated by the instructor). The table is behind a screened area so that the arrangements cannot be seen by participants from their work areas.

The goal of each team is to duplicate the *exact* arrangement (e.g., location, overlap, spacing) of the objects on the table, using its own matching set of objects, within 20 minutes (or other time limit given by the instructor). Participants are allowed one 30-second opportunity at the beginning of the exercise to view the screened table. They may not write, draw, or talk while viewing the screened table.

Each team will have *up to two saboteurs*. These are people who have been selected by the instructor (either before the exercise or through notes distributed to all participants). Saboteurs will use any reasonable method to prevent the team from producing an accurate configuration of objects in their work area (e.g., giving inaccurate information to the group). They are forbidden from revealing their identities.

At the end of the time limit, the instructor will evaluate each team's configuration and decide which one is the most accurate. The class members will then evaluate their experience in the exercise in terms of team development and other aspects of team dynamics.

This exercise is based on ideas discussed in G. Thompson and P. Pearce, "The Team-Trust Game," *Training and Development*, May 1992, pp. 42–43. ◼

Wrapping presents: A team exercise

Purpose

This exercise is designed to help students understand the importance of team development and to experience team development stages.

Instructions

Form teams with four students on each team. Several students should be assigned as judges to evaluate the results produced by each team. Observers time the performance of each team and record the team's results for each of the three task activities described below.

Each team should receive one pair of scissors, one roll or dispenser of tape, one bow (optional), and wrapping paper. (Newspaper or plain paper may substitute, but they aren't as pretty.) Each team also receives a mid-sized box, such as the boxes department stores provide when giving clothing as a gift.

Each team's objective is to wrap the box as quickly and professionally as possible. However, all team members will have their hands tied behind their backs throughout this exercise. The box will be wrapped three times with the following conditions:

First Task

With hands tied behind their backs, team members wrap the present using only the materials provided. They are allowed to talk throughout this task. Judges record the completion time when they (the judges) are satisfied with the wrapping quality. The team then removes and discards the wrapping paper and other materials from the box.

Second Task

With hands tied behind their backs *and no talking allowed*, team members wrap the present using only the materials provided. Team members must use new materials (i.e., they are not allowed to reuse wrapping paper from the first task). Judges record the completion time when they (the judges) are satisfied with the wrapping quality. The team then removes and discards the wrapping paper and other materials from the box.

Third Task

This is identical to the second task. Team members have hands tied and are not allowed to talk. Judges record the completion time when they (the judges) are satisfied with the wrapping quality.

Source: The origin of this exercise is unknown. A group of students in an organizational behavior class at Simon Fraser University presented it in a tutorial assignment. The author thanks Eleanor MacDonald for describing this exercise. ◼

SELF-ASSESSMENT EXERCISE

Team roles preferences scale

Purpose

This self-assessment is designed to help you to identify your preferred roles in meetings and similar team activities.

Instructions

Read each of the statements below and circle the response that you believe best reflects your position regarding each statement. Then use the scoring key to calculate your results for each team role. This exercise is completed alone so students assess themselves honestly without concerns of social comparison. However, class discussion will focus on the roles that people assume in team settings. This scale only assesses a few team roles.

Team roles preferences scale

Circle the number that best reflects your position regarding each of these statements.	Does not describe me at all ▼	Does not describe me very well ▼	Describes me somewhat ▼	Describes me well ▼	Describes me very well ▼
1. I usually take responsibility for getting the team to agree on what the meeting should accomplish.	1	2	3	4	5
2. I tend to summarize to other team members what the team has accomplished so far.	1	2	3	4	5
3. I'm usually the person who helps other team members overcome their disagreements.	1	2	3	4	5
4. I try to ensure that everyone gets heard on issues.	1	2	3	4	5
5. I'm usually the person who helps the team determine how to organize the discussion.	1	2	3	4	5
6. I praise other team members for their ideas more than do others in the meetings.	1	2	3	4	5
7. People tend to rely on me to keep track of what has been said in meetings.	1	2	3	4	5
8. The team typically counts on me to prevent debates from getting out of hand.	1	2	3	4	5

		1	2	3	4	5
9.	I tend to say things that make the group feel optimistic about its accomplishments.	1	2	3	4	5
10.	Team members usually count on me to give everyone a chance to speak.	1	2	3	4	5
11.	In most meetings, I am less likely than others to "put down" the ideas of team mates.	1	2	3	4	5
12.	I actively help team mates to resolve their differences in meetings.	1	2	3	4	5
13.	I actively encourage quiet team members to describe their ideas on each issue.	1	2	3	4	5
14.	People tend to rely on me to clarify the purpose of the meeting.	1	2	3	4	5
15.	I like to be the person who takes notes or minutes of the meeting.	1	2	3	4	5

Scoring

Write the scores circled for each item on the appropriate line below (statement numbers are in brackets), and add up each scale.

Encourager _____ + _____ + _____ = _____
             (6)   (9)   (11)

Gatekeeper _____ + _____ + _____ = _____
             (4)   (10)   (13)

Harmonizer _____ + _____ + _____ = _____
             (3)   (8)   (12)

Initiator _____ + _____ + _____ = _____
             (1)   (5)   (14)

Summarizer _____ + _____ + _____ = _____
             (2)   (7)   (15)

Employee Involvement and Quality Management

Learning Objectives

After reading this chapter, you should be able to:

- Identify the different forms and levels of employee involvement.
- Describe open book management.
- Outline the main features of self-directed work teams.
- Describe the sociotechnical systems theory recommendations for more successful self-directed work teams.
- Discuss the potential benefits and challenges of employee involvement.
- List the six quality management principles.
- Summarize the key features of benchmarking and concurrent engineering.
- Discuss the limitations of quality management.

S urrounded by tall prairie grass, Harley-Davidson's new assembly plant near Kansas City, Missouri, embeds the philosophy of a high-involvement organization. There are no supervisors. Instead, natural work teams of 8 to 15 employees make most day-to-day decisions through consensus. An umbrella group, representing teams and management, makes plantwide decisions.

Al Scott compares working at Harley-Davidson with his previous job as a truck driver. "Truck driving was very traditional," recalls the Harley-Davidson production employee. "I had no input. Management told us what to do and didn't ask us anything. Here [at Harley], if you make a suggestion, someone says, 'OK, now make it happen.'"

Through employee involvement, Harley-Davidson expects to continue product quality improvements. The idea is that employees know where quality problems exist and are in the best position to correct them before they get worse. "We talk about what we have done here and what we can do better," says Mark Dworak, who supplies parts to assembly employees. "Everybody is allowed to voice their opinion. I've never been anywhere like it."

"There is more pressure on employees here because they must learn to do what supervisors did," admits Karl Eberle, vice president and general manager of Harley-Davidson's Kansas City operations. Still, Harley-Davidson is taking employee involvement far beyond the traditional workplace. "There's a lot of work being done to empower the workforce," says Eberle. "But there are very few examples of where they've taken the workforce to run the factory. And that's what we've done."[1]

Harley-Davidson, Inc., relies on employee involvement and quality management to build better motorcycles.

[David Pulliam, Kansas City Star. Reprinted with permission.]

arley-Davidson has leveraged the knowledge potential of its work-force through employee involvement and quality management. This chapter discusses both topics because, as the opening story reveals, quality management goes hand-in-hand with employee participation in corporate decisions.[2] We begin by describing the forms and levels of employee involvement, including a detailed discussion of self-directed work teams and sociotechnical systems theory. Next, we discuss the potential benefits and limitations of employee involvement. The latter part of the chapter introduces quality management. We learn about the main principles (including employee involvement) behind quality management, the emerging certification standards, and two quality management practices: benchmarking and concurrent engineering. The chapter closes by discussing the limitations of quality management.

Employee Involvement

employee involvement the degree that employees share information, knowledge, rewards, and power throughout the organization

Employee involvement (also called *participative management*) refers to the degree that employees share information, knowledge, rewards, and power throughout the organization.[3] Employees have some level of activity in making decisions that were not previously within their mandate. Employee involvement extends beyond controlling resources for one's own job; it includes the power to influence decisions in the work unit and organization. The higher the level of involvement, the more power people have over the decision process and outcomes. Involved employees also receive information and possess the knowledge required to make a meaningful contribution to this decision process.

US Airways recently took employee involvement to new heights. It gave a pilot, aircraft cleaner, catering truck driver, ramp supervisor, flight attendant, mechanic, and more than a dozen other employees representing labor and management the daunting task of designing a low fare brand called MetroJet_SM. Freed from their regular jobs, team members spent just 83 days figuring out the best way to compete against low cost airlines like Southwest Airlines, which had recently entered US Airways' east coast markets. The employees priced peanuts, conducted focus groups, debated over how fast to fly the planes, timed boarding activities, and took notes while flying on competitors' airlines.[4] What are the potential advantages of employee involvement in this situation?

[Courtesy of US Airways.]

Employee involvement has increased significantly in recent years. Consider First National Bank–Employee Owned, where employees take an active role in deciding corporate strategy. The reason, as the company's name implies, is that employees own most of the Antioch, Illinois, financial institution. Employee involvement is partly credited with the dramatic turnaround of the Development Bank of Southern Africa. The bank formed an eight-person "transformation" team and 41 other teams that examined everything from interest-rate policies to gender and affirmative action issues. And at US

Airways, two dozen employees completely designed a new low fare brand, called MetroJet$_{SM}$.[5]

Why has employee participation in corporate decisions become so popular? One reason is that participation is an integral part of knowledge management. Corporate leaders are realizing that employee knowledge is a critical resource for competitive advantage, so they are encouraging employees to share this knowledge. Technology has also pushed employee involvement more than we could have imagined a decade ago. E-mail increases upward communication, most of which represents employee involvement (see Chapter 8). Other computer-mediated communication, such as the computer-networked knowledge database at Buckman Labs, also encourages employees to participate in corporate decision making.

Forms of Employee Involvement

Employee involvement exists in many forms, as we see in Exhibit 10.1.[6] *Formal participation* activities, such as the task force that designed a low fare brand at US Airways, are founded on codified policies and institutionalized practices. In other words, the company has established structures and formal expectations that support this form of participation. In contrast, *informal participation* includes casual events, such as approaching a supervisor about an idea or suggestion.

Employee involvement can also be *voluntary* or *statutory*. The City of Fort Lauderdale formed a labor-management team to solve staffing and overtime problems in the city's 911 Telecommunications Center. This team represents a voluntary and structured form of employee involvement.[7] Harley-Davidson's new production facility, described in the opening story, also encourages employee involvement without any statutory requirement. Most employee

Exhibit 10.1 Forms of employee involvement

Form of involvement	Description	Example
Formality		
Formal	Participation is codified policy or institutionalized practice	Special task force at US Airways designed a new low fare brand (MetroJet)
Informal	Casual or undocumented activities at management's discretion	Employee on the shop floor makes a suggestion to the supervisor
Legal Mandate		
Statutory	Government-legislated activities	Works councils at Volkswagen AG
Voluntary	Any participation activity that is not required by law	Labor-management task force investigating staffing problems at the City of Ft. Lauderdale's 911 Telecommunications Center
Directness		
Direct	Employees are personally involved in decisions	W. L. Gore and Associates employees have almost complete control over production decisions
Indirect	Employees participate through representation of peers	Republic Steel employees have four representatives on the Board of Directors

involvement activities in North America are voluntary, but there are exceptions. Joint health and safety committees are required by law in some jurisdictions. Statutory involvement is more widespread in Europe, where many countries have codetermination laws.

codetermination a form of employee involvement required by some governments that typically operates at both the work site as works councils and corporate level as supervisory boards

Codetermination varies from one country to the next, but it generally requires employee involvement at both the work site and corporate levels. At the corporate level, employees in Sweden, Norway, and some other European countries have up to 50 percent of the seats on supervisory boards, which advise company executives and make decisions about their salaries. At the work site, codetermination occurs through employee representation committees called *works councils*. The employer must keep the works council informed of financial performance and employment decisions within the organization. It must consult with (not just inform) the council regarding matters of employment staffing, work processes, and individual dismissals. In Germany, legislation also requires mutual agreement between the employer and the works council on work hours, use of technology, wages, health and safety, and other "social matters."[8]

The third form of employee involvement is whether it is *direct* or *representative*. Direct participation occurs when employees personally influence the decision process. For example, Harley-Davidson employees directly participate in decisions affecting their team's work process. Representative participation, on the other hand, occurs when employees are represented by peers. The supervisory boards in European codetermination fall into this category. In the United States, Republic Steel also has this structure, where employee representatives have 4 seats on the 13-member corporate board of directors. This representation occurs because employees own a large portion of outstanding shares of the company.[9] Republic Steel is not alone. As we learned in Chapter 4, many other firms have introduced employee stock ownership plans (ESOPs). In most cases, employee involvement has increased, particularly through various forms of representative participation.

Levels of Employee Involvement

There are different levels of employee involvement. These levels reflect both the degree of power over the decision and the number of decision steps over which employees can apply that power.[10] The *lowest level* of involvement is selective consultation, in which employees are asked individually for specific information or opinions about one or two aspects of the decision. They do not necessarily recommend solutions and might not even know details of the problem for which the information will be used.

quality circles small teams of employees who meet regularly to identify quality and productivity problems, propose solutions to management, and monitor the implementation and consequences of these solutions in their work area

A *moderate level* of employee involvement occurs when employees are more fully consulted either individually or in a group. They are told about the problem and offer their diagnosis and recommendations, but the final decision is still beyond their control. **Quality circles** fall into this middle level of employee involvement.[11] As we learned in Chapter 9, quality circles are small teams of employees who meet for a few hours each week to identify quality and productivity problems, propose solutions to management, and monitor the implementation and consequences of these solutions in their work area. For example, the Kowloon-Canton Railway Corporation in Hong Kong relies on cross-functional quality circles to identify ways to improve customer service.[12]

communities of practice informal groups of people who are connected by their mutual interest in a particular field of knowledge

Quality circles were most popular during the 1980s, but many have since evolved into self-directed work teams. However, computer technology has provided a medium for a similar form of participation among knowledge workers, called **communities of practice**.[13] As we learned in Chapter 9, communities of practice are groups of people informally bound together through interests and practices. Some companies have encouraged formation of these virtual teams in the hope that they will recommend ways to improve business practices. Chevron, the California-based energy company, has nurtured dozens of these virtual communities. One group debates ways to measure customer satisfaction more effectively; another considers options for improving workplace safety; several others look at strategies to improve the quality of specific production processes. Similar communities of practice operate at Monsanto and Xerox, sharing knowledge and generating new ideas to improve corporate practices.[14]

gainsharing plan a reward system that rewards team members for reducing costs and increasing labor efficiency in their work process

Gainsharing programs, which we introduced in Chapter 4, also have a moderate level of participation. Gainsharing programs calculate cost savings and pay out the same bonus to all team members using a predetermined formula. Employee participation is an essential ingredient for the success of gainsharing programs because cost savings result from the ideas that employees recommend.[15] The earliest form of gainsharing, called the Scanlon Plan, emphasized information sharing and ensured that employees learned about the financial aspects of the units or organizations. In this respect, gainsharing is similar to the recent practice of open book management.

open book management sharing financial information with employees and encouraging them to recommend ideas that improve those financial results

Open book management

An increasingly popular activity requiring a moderate level of employee involvement is **open book management.**[16] Open book management involves sharing financial information with employees and encouraging them to recommend ideas that improve those financial results. This is often (but not always) combined with either a gainsharing or employee stock ownership plan (see Chapter 4). With open book practices, employees receive monthly or quarterly financial data and operating results so they can keep track of the organization's performance. For instance, all 57 employees at the Bradshaw Manufacturing plant in Palm Bay, Florida, meet each month to examine the company's income and cash flow statements, balance sheets, and other financial documents.[17]

Many people have difficulty reading financial statements, so open book management also includes training to improve financial literacy. Employees learn the meaning and implications of income statements, balance sheets, and cash flow statements. Moreover, they learn how their work activities (e.g., unused scrap, shipment delays) influence these financial indicators. Jac Nasser, CEO of Ford Motor Company, believes that financial literacy training improves employee involvement and commitment to the organization's success. More than 50,000 employees have attended his weekly sessions in offices, factories, and lecture halls on the meaning of shareholder value, price/earnings ratios, and related concepts.[18]

A unique element of open book management is that it encourages employees to think of financial performance as a game that they can play and win. Employees and management are on the same team. Employees learn the rules of the game as well as the roles and responsibilities to help the team win. With their financial training and game-oriented perspective, employees are more likely to make meaningful recommendations that will improve the company's financial performance. "In an Open Book Management company, employees know what they're working for at the start of the year," says Ralph Burrell, president of Parallel Technologies, a Minneapolis-based computer service firm that practices open book management. "They help establish objectives and the budget, but more important, they track progress by reviewing sales and expenses at least monthly."[19]

High involvement

The highest level of involvement occurs when employees have complete power over the decision process. They discover and define problems, identify solutions, choose the best option, and monitor the results of their decision. These *high involvement* conditions are characteristic of team-based organizations, which we introduced in Chapter 9 and are described more fully in Chapter 18.[20] Team-based organizational structures rely on self-directed work teams, which we discuss next.

Self-Directed Work Teams (SDWTs)

Interconnect Devices recently took the leap toward becoming a high involvement organization. The Kansas City manufacturer of electronic devices organized its production staff into teams and gave each team responsibility for fulfilling daily production schedules. Team members divide up the task responsibilities and receive extensive training to ensure that they can perform a variety of tasks. Teams are also responsible for some quality control and equipment calibration. Teams handle most issues, so each work shift has only one supervisor, compared to four supervisors before the change. Indeed, when management tried to unilaterally reassign some employees to cope with a large order, the teams pointed out that it was their responsibility, not management's. "We made a mistake," admits an Interconnect executive. "We are new to this, too. We talked it over and they had some good ideas."[21]

Interconnect Devices is following the trend toward **self-directed work teams (SDWTs).** SDWTs are work groups that complete an entire piece of work requiring several interdependent tasks and have substantial autonomy over the execution of these tasks. By most estimates, almost half of the medium- and large-size U.S. organizations use SDWT structures for part of their operations.[22]

Although SDWTs vary somewhat from one firm to the next, most have the features listed in Exhibit 10.2.[23] First, SDWTs complete an entire piece of work, whether it's a product, a service, or part of a larger product or service. At Harley-Davidson, for example, one team might be responsible for assembling the entire engine block. Second, the tasks that individual team members perform are assigned by the team rather than by a supervisor or other external source. At Interconnect Devices, for example, senior management assigns team goals, but the teams decide how to achieve those goals. In other words, the team plans, organizes, and controls work activities with little or no direct involvement of a higher-ranking supervisor.

self-directed work teams (SDWT) work groups that complete an entire piece of work requiring several interdependent tasks and have substantial autonomy over the execution of these tasks

You won't find any bosses at W. L. Gore and Associates. The Newark, Delaware, manufacturer of Goretex and other advanced materials has taken employee involvement to the extreme. Gore associates (i.e., employees) belong to self-directed teams that make almost all the decisions in their work processes. Business plans are decided through consensus. Projects are led by people that others are willing to follow, not by managers thrust upon the group. If someone has a good idea, he or she is encouraged to form a team of associates who are willing to commit their support to the project.[24] This high level of involvement works well at Gore, but are there organizations where it might be less effective? What types of employees work best in a high involvement workplace?
[AP Wide World]

Exhibit 10.2
Attributes of self-directed
work teams

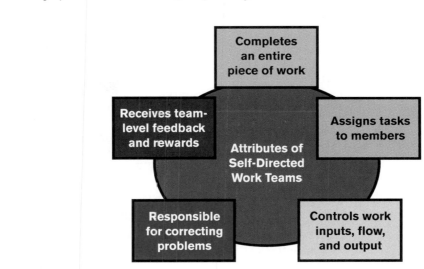

Third, SDWTs control most work inputs, flow, and output. With respect to inputs, many teams select new members and work directly with suppliers. As previously noted, they design (or help to design) the work process. For example, employees at Borg Warner Automotive in Frankfort, Illinois, design the production process that they operate.[25] With respect to outputs, teams are responsible for achieving assigned goals and for maintaining output quality. Fourth, SDWTs are responsible for correcting work flow problems as they occur. Many teams work directly with customers to resolve their concerns. Lastly, SDWTs receive team-level feedback and rewards. This recognizes and reinforces the fact that teams—not individuals—are responsible for the work, although team members may also receive individual feedback and rewards.

You may have noticed from this description that members of SDWTs have enriched and enlarged jobs (see Chapter 4). The team's work is horizontally loaded because it includes tasks required to make an entire product or provide a service. It is also vertically loaded because the team is mostly responsible for scheduling, coordinating, and planning these tasks.[26] Self-directed work teams were initially designed around production processes, but they are also found in administrative and service activities. For example, Roberts Express in Akron, Ohio, has 26 customer assistance teams that are completely responsible for serving clients and arranging package deliveries for a specific geographic area.[27] This situation is well suited to self-directed teams because members have interdependent tasks, and decisions require the employee's knowledge and experience.[28]

Conditions for Successful SDWTs

How do you create successful self-directed work teams? To answer this question, we need to look at **sociotechnical systems (STS)** theory, which is the main foundation for current SDWT practices. STS theory was introduced in the 1940s by Eric Trist and his Tavistock Institute colleagues, who had been studying the effects of technology on coal mining in the United Kingdom.[29] They suggested that organizations are open systems with two interdependent parts: (1) the social system of individual skills, needs, and interpersonal relations, and (2) the technological system of machines, tools, and production processes.

Trist and his colleagues observed that the technology introduced in coal mining led to lower (rather than higher) job performance. They analyzed the causes of this problem and established the idea that organizations need "joint optimization" between the social and technical systems of the work unit. In

sociotechnical systems (STS) a theory stating that effective work sites have joint optimization of their social and technological system, and that teams should have sufficient autonomy to control key variances in the work process

other words, they need to introduce technology in a way that creates the best structure for autonomous work teams. Moreover, Trist and his colleagues concluded that teams should be sufficiently independent so that they can control the main "variances" in the system; that is, the factors with the greatest impact on quality, quantity, and the cost of the product or service. From this overview of STS, we can identify several conditions for successful SDWTs.[30]

Primary work unit—STS theory suggests that SDWTs work best in a primary work unit, which is any work team that makes a product, provides a service, or otherwise completes an entire work process. By making an entire product or service together, the team is sufficiently independent from other work units that it can make adjustments without affecting or being affected very much by others. At the same time, employees within a primary work unit perform interdependent subtasks so they have a sense of performing a common task.[31]

Semiautonomous work groups—STS theory advocates a team-based structure in which employees in the primary work unit have sufficient autonomy to manage the work process. STS writers call it *collective self-regulation,* which means that the team can decide how to divide up work among its members as well as how to coordinate that work. Collective self-regulation is a central feature in self-directed work teams and represents a team-based version of autonomy in job enrichment (see Chapter 4).

Controlling key variances—STS theory says that productivity improves when the work team has control over "key variances." These variances represent the disturbances or interruptions that occur in a work process, such as the mixture of ingredients in soup manufacturing or the courteousness of service at an airline reservations call center. By controlling these factors, work teams control the quantity and quality of output in the work process. In contrast, STS has little advantage when the main causes of good or poor performance are mainly due to technology, supplies, or other factors beyond the team's control.

Joint optimization—Perhaps the most crucial feature of STS theory is that a balance must be struck between the social and technical systems to maximize the operation's effectiveness.[32] Production demands and social dynamics must be compatible with each other. In particular, the technological system should be implemented in a way that improves team dynamics, job enrichment, and meaningful feedback. This idea of joint optimization was quite radical in the 1940s, a time when many thought there was only one best way to install technology in the workplace and that jobs must be designed around this necessary structure. STS theory, on the other hand, says that companies have enough latitude in how technology is introduced that they can support a semiautonomous, team-based structure.

Sociotechnical system theory in practice   Sociotechnical systems theory provides valuable advice for organizations that want to introduce self-directed work teams. It clearly indicates that team-based structures will not succeed simply by putting employees into teams and giving them some team building. Such actions may adjust the social system, but the technical system will probably be incompatible. Instead, companies need to diagnose the technological structure to ensure that it supports a team-based work environment.

Hewlett-Packard, Shell Chemicals (Canada), Anchor Hocking, the University of Southern California's telecommunications group, L. L. Bean, and many other organizations have successfully applied STS principles to establish a better environment for team-based work. For example, Anchor Hocking's production facility in Ohio was recently built around STS ideas. The kitchenware company aligned technology so that several teams are able to work fairly autonomously on a specific work process. The University of Southern California's telecommunication service group identified 300 variances (causes of good or poor service) and identified 23 of them that were within the team's control and critical to the quality and quantity of service.[33] As we learn in this chapter's *Fast Company Online* (pp. 312–13), L. L. Bean applied STS principles when redesigning its order fulfillment center. Notice how the outdoor goods catalog company introduced computer technology to fit the new team-based structure, whereas the previous system forced a more individual-oriented work process.

In spite of these successes, STS is not always easy to implement. In particular, some firms have trouble finding the optimal alignment of the social and technical system. Volvo's Kalmar and Uddevalla plants in Sweden may have demonstrated this point.[34] Volvo's Kalmar plant was built in the early 1970s and was one of the earliest sociotechnically designed plants. The Uddevalla plant opened in the late 1980s. These plants replaced the traditional assembly line with fixed workstations at which teams of approximately 20 employees assemble and install components in an unfinished automobile chassis. This technological structure creates a strong team orientation, but productivity at the two Volvo plants is among the *lowest* in the automobile industry because the technological design is not sufficiently flexible. In other words, in its attempt to accommodate the social system, Volvo may have compromised technological efficiency beyond an optimal level.

Potential Benefits of Employee Involvement

For the past half century, scholars of organizational behavior have advised that self-directed work teams and other forms of employee involvement offer potential benefits for both employees and their organizations.[35] These benefits include improved decision quality, decision commitment, employee development, and employee satisfaction and empowerment.

Decision Quality

Perhaps the central reason why companies encourage employee involvement is that it can potentially improve corporate decisions. This is particularly true for complex decisions where employees possess relevant information.[36] Employees are closer to customers and production activities, so they often know where the company can save money, improve product or service quality, and realize unused opportunities.

Employee involvement may improve the quality of decisions in three ways, as Exhibit 10.3 illustrates. First, it may lead to a more accurate definition of the problem. Employees are, in many respects, the sensors of the organization's environment. When the organization's activities misalign with customer

Exhibit 10.3
How employee involvement improves decision making

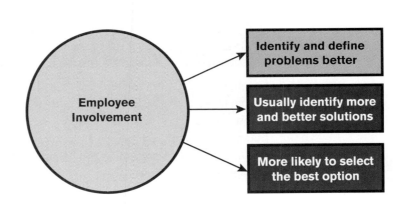

Employee Involvement

Identify and define problems better

Usually identify more and better solutions

More likely to select the best option

expectations, employees are usually the first to know. Employee involvement ensures that everyone in the organization is quickly alerted to these problems.

Second, employee involvement can potentially improve the number and quality of solutions generated to solve organizational problems. In a well-managed meeting, team members create **synergy** by pooling their knowledge to form new alternatives that no one would have designed alone. In other words, several people working together and building on each other's strengths can potentially generate more and better solutions than if these people worked alone. For example, as we noted in the previous chapter, heterogeneous teams—those whose members have diverse backgrounds—tend to be better than homogeneous teams at developing innovative solutions.[37]

Third, involving employees in decisions increases the likelihood that the best option will be selected. This occurs because several people working together tend to analyze the alternatives more carefully than if one executive made the choice alone. There is less chance that a grossly inaccurate solution will be selected when knowledgeable people are involved.

synergy the capacity of people to generate more and better solutions by working together and sharing ideas than if these people worked alone

FAST COMPANY Online

□ Sociotechnical Systems Help L. L. Bean Deliver the Goods

L. L. Bean's new order fulfillment process was designed around sociotechnical systems theory, resulting in a more efficient team-based system.
[Courtesy of L. L. Bean.]

For many years, companies flocked to L. L. Bean's distribution center in Freeport, Maine, to learn how to fulfill orders more efficiently. They saw how telephone operators at the outdoor goods catalog company would enter the customer's order into the computer, which was then relayed as a batch every 12 hours to the order fulfillment center (OFC). Pickers assembled an entire order, which was then sent to packers for wrapping.

Decision Commitment

An old maxim says that the best person to put in charge of a problem is the one most directly affected by its outcome. In other words, employees who are expected to implement organizational decisions should be involved in choosing the course of action. This participation creates psychological ownership of the decision. Rather than viewing themselves as agents of someone else's decision, staff members feel personally responsible for its success. Consequently, they tend to exhibit less resistance to change and are more motivated to implement these decisions.[38]

Employee involvement can also increase perceptions of fairness about organizational decisions.[39] If a company begins a gainsharing plan or some other reward system (see Chapter 4), individuals are more likely to believe that the reward distribution is fair if they had the opportunity to influence the rules for distributing those rewards.

But increasing demand for L. L. Bean's products placed a strain on this process. So, the company formed several teams to look at better ways to operate the order fulfillment process. While visiting the leading order-fulfillment operations in Germany and Scandinavia, one team learned that companies used advanced technology and still complied with stringent European labor laws. These companies relied on sociotechnical systems theory to fit technology around the need for self-directed work teams.

Bean's new order fulfillment process integrated sociotechnical systems by designing a team-based work process supported by technology. "The technology here is very simple," says Lou Zambello, Bean's senior vice president for operations, about the new process. "The innovative part is adapting it to create a new sociotechnical norm in the new facility. What we did before was like individual swimming in a relay race. Now we do synchronized swimming."

L. L. Bean's new sociotechnical system sends orders to the OFC as soon as the customer places an order. Team leaders use computers to track activity and assign new orders to team members who can handle the new workload. Orders are divided among pickers working in different areas of the warehouse. Bar code scanners sort the orders and offload them to packing stations. This team-based work process cuts order fulfillment from one day to about two hours.

ONLINE CHECK-UP

1. This *Fast Company Online* feature describes how L. L. Bean designed its order fulfillment system around sociotechnical systems theory. Diagram Bean's previous order fulfillment process and its new process. (You may want to read the entire article to get more details.)

2. Why does L. L. Bean's new order fulfillment process handle a larger volume of work than the previous process?

3. Using your favorite web browser and search engine, find other companies that have relied on sociotechnical design to improve quality and efficiency.

Get the full text of this *Fast Company* article at www.mhhe.com/mcshane1e

Source: Adapted from K. Kane, "L. L. Bean Delivers the Goods," *Fast Company*, Issue 10 (August 1997). ■

Employee Development

Many forms of involvement give employees the opportunity to improve their decision-making skills and prepare for higher levels of responsibility. Team decision making may offer the additional benefits of fostering teamwork and collegiality as co-workers learn more about each other and come to appreciate each other's talents.[40]

Employee Satisfaction and Empowerment

Doreen Dickey expected a lot of tedium when she was hired at Foldcraft Corp. to scrape and sand excess sealant from restaurant seats. But her employer had different ideas. The manufacturer of restaurant furniture in Kenyon, Minnesota, asked for Dickey's advice on improving the hand-sanding process. It also chose Dickey for an educational tour in Central America. The result is that Dickey and other Foldcraft employees are a lot more satisfied than if they were expected to park their brains at the door.[41]

empowerment the feeling of control and self-efficacy that emerges when people are given power in a previously powerless situation

Foldcraft Corp. and other firms have learned that employee involvement often (although not always) improves job satisfaction and feelings of **empowerment.**[42] Recall from Chapter 4 that empowerment refers to a feeling of control and self-efficacy that emerges when people are given power in a previously powerless situation.[43] Empowerment increases job satisfaction because employees feel less stress when they have some control over life's events. It also includes feelings of self-efficacy—the "can-do" belief that people have toward a specific task and, more generally, with other challenges in life.[44]

Of course, whether employees feel more satisfied and empowered depends on the situation. One factor is the type of decision. Research indicates that employees are more satisfied when involved in choosing better work methods and making other "tactical" decisions that directly affect their work lives. In contrast, involvement in corporate strategy (such as whether to launch a new product) seems to have less effect on job satisfaction.[45]

Employee involvement is a form of job enrichment, so the situational factors described in the job characteristics model must also be considered (see Chapter 4). Specifically, employee involvement is more likely to increase satisfaction when employees receive adequate training, are sufficiently happy with their work context, and have a high growth need strength. Even with these conditions, however, employee involvement may be difficult to introduce due to incompatible cultural values and various forms of resistance to change.

Overcoming Challenges to Employee Involvement

Employee involvement is not a panacea for all organizational problems. In some situations, participation may be useful but resistance to it could threaten the company's effectiveness in other ways. In other situations, involvement practices are incompatible with the needs and values of the people affected. However, where employee involvement is desirable, corporate leaders need to recognize and overcome at least three potential barriers: cultural differences, management resistance, and labor union and employee resistance.

Cultural Differences

Various forms and levels of employee involvement have been implemented in many countries. For instance, self-directed work teams and other forms of employee participation have been successfully introduced in Malaysia, Germany, Japan, India, and the Scandinavian countries.[46] Still, employee involvement is more compatible with some cultural values than with others.[47] Employee involvement is typically an interpersonal or team-based activity, so it is adopted

individualism–collectivism
the extent to which people value their group membership and group goals (collectivism) or value their individuality and personal goals (individualism)

power distance the extent to which people accept unequal distribution of power in a society

most readily in cultures with high **collectivism.** Recall from Chapter 7 that people with a collectivist value appreciate and support their membership in the group to which they belong. Consequently, they work more comfortably discussing their ideas with co-workers. In contrast, individualistic people may be less comfortable with employee involvement because of their preference to work alone.

Employee involvement also works better in low **power distance** cultures. Power distance refers to the extent that people accept unequal distribution of power in a society. Employees with low power distance usually want to be involved in corporate decisions, whereas those in high power distance cultures prefer having supervisors give them directions and answers. This may explain why employee involvement has been successful in the United States. Americans tend to be individualistic, but they also have low power distance and therefore expect to be involved in corporate decisions to some degree.

How do we overcome these cultural challenges? First, we should remember that few cultures are so extreme in either collectivism or power distance to prohibit employee involvement. Moreover, some forms of employee involvement are more problematic than others. For instance, people with high power distance may feel comfortable providing anonymous ideas (such as a suggestion system) or through a spokesperson. A third consideration is that people with fairly high power distance and high individualism may adjust over time to a workplace that espouses collectivist and low power distance values.

Management Resistance

Supervisors have difficulty making the transition to self-directed work teams.[48] Their main worry is losing power when employees gain power through participation. Some are concerned that their jobs will lose value; others worry that they won't have jobs at all. Another problem is that supervisors do not know how to become "hands-off" facilitators of several work teams rather than "hands-on" supervisors of several employees.[49] Many slip back into their command-and-control supervisory styles because they are still ultimately responsible for the team's success.

Some writers argue that senior executives are not much better.[50] Executives initiate and publicly encourage employee involvement, yet many of them are privately worried about their ability to control the process and consequences. For example, employees are encouraged to make decisions, but only within specified policies and procedures set by management. Employees are told they have more freedom, yet executives continue to use traditional resources to closely monitor employee performance. Even where self-directed work teams control the behavior of their members, executives feel some comfort in the fact that they control norms and values through selection and socialization of those teams.

Education and training are the first steps in minimizing management resistance to employee involvement. The company needs to assure these people that their careers are not threatened. They also need to receive considerable training to adjust from the old "command-and-control" style to the more ambiguous facilitator style of leadership. However, even with education and training, many companies that introduce employee involvement practices eventually have to transfer or replace supervisors and managers who cannot adjust to the new style.

Employee and Labor Union Resistance

Employees resist employee involvement for several reasons. Most have been bombarded by previous management fads and do not want to develop false hopes for the latest initiative. Employee involvement also requires new—and usually more ambiguous—role patterns and possibly new skills (e.g., working in teams). Thus, many employees feel uncomfortable as they explore their new roles, and they may be worried that they lack the skills to adapt to the new work requirements. As you will read in Connections 10.1, BP Norge experienced these problems when the Norwegian operation of British Petroleum introduced self-directed work teams on its remote North Sea oil platforms. This story also illustrates that companies can minimize employee concerns through education, training, and plenty of on-the-job feedback.

Labor unions have been strong advocates of joint health and safety committees and supported the early sociotechnical changes in Europe and India. Some labor unions in North America have also supported high involvement

Connections 10.1 ◘ BP Norge Tests the Seaworthiness of SDWTs

BP Norge encouraged employees on its North Sea oil platforms to form self-directed work teams.
[AP Wide World]

practices, but many have publicly resisted them.[51] For example, the United Brotherhood of Carpenters used labor laws dating back 50 years to prevent Efco Corp. from introducing self-directed work teams. The union argued that team practices interfered with its ability to unionize employees at the Monett, Missouri, door and window manufacturer. Similarly, a DuPont plant in New York State stopped placing its unionized employees into teams when the union local complained that this practice added new tasks for which employees are not paid.[52]

Labor union leaders have three main concerns about employee involvement.[53] First, they believe that employee involvement programs improve productivity at the price of higher stress levels among employees. This is sometimes true. SDWTs and other practices tend to give employees more tasks

An oil platform is one of the most complex workplaces in the world. It is a chemical plant, mining operation, airport, harbor, power station, hotel, and leisure center. It is also the setting in which BP Norge overcame the challenges of introducing self-directed work teams (SDWTs).

Senior executives at BP Norge, the Norwegian arm of British Petroleum, wanted to dismantle the company's hierarchy and replace it with a high involvement business model. A significant part of this process was to help BP Norge employees operate North Sea oil platforms through SDWTs. John Vemmestad, director of BP Norge, explains: "[Self-directed work teams] fit perfectly with the corporate direction, which involves pushing responsibility down to the lowest levels possible."

The transition did not occur easily, however. Some employees were skeptical that management would really give them more power. Others wanted higher status and pay for the additional responsibilities. Consequently, BP Norge held a workshop where employee and supervisor representatives discussed these issues with senior management. The company also gave people the option of not being involved in the SDWT process.

It also took a bit of nudging to get employees thinking autonomously. For example, an instrument team and electrical team at BP Norge wanted to remove the wall between their adjacent workshops. When they asked the project leader for permission, the leader told them to do what they thought was right. The two teams realized that they used the same setup lathes, so they went back to the leader for permission to move the lathes beside each other. The project leader's reply was "I'm not sure why you're asking me that." Two weeks later, the team representatives reported to the project leader, "We decided that two lathes were too many, so we only have one now." With the leader's guidance, the teams had assumed a higher level of autonomy and self-accountability.

Sources: Adapted from M. Moravec, O. J. Johannessen, and T. A. Hjelmas, "The Well-Managed SMT," *Management Review* 87 (June 1998), pp. 56–58; M. Moravec, O. J. Johannessen, and T. A. Hjelmas, "Thumbs Up for Self-Managed Teams," *Management Review* 86 (July–August 1997), p. 42. ■

and responsibilities, which may lead to greater work pressure. Second, high involvement practices require more flexibility by reversing work rules and removing job categories that unions have negotiated over the years. Labor union leaders are therefore concerned that it will be a difficult battle to regain these hard-fought union member rights. Finally, a few union leaders believe that companies use employee involvement programs as a subtle strategy to bypass the union and thereby weaken its power in the workplace.

These union fears are troublesome because employee involvement programs require union support and partnership.[54] Fortunately, there are many examples of successful labor-management initiatives that give employees more control in the workplace. In most cases, labor union resistance was minimized through the slow development of trust between corporate and labor leaders regarding the distribution of power. At the same time, labor union involvement requires labor leaders who perceive long-term value of the employee involvement activity for their membership and the labor union's survival.

Employee involvement is becoming a pervasive part of organizational life. It is difficult to think of many organizations in North America where employees are not allowed to provide their ideas or be involved in some corporate-level decisions. Part of this development occurred because employee involvement is integrated with many other organizational practices. One practice that helped to popularize employee involvement is quality management.

Quality Management

A few years ago Wagner Lighting Products had 3,700 defective products for every million produced. "We weren't very good," confesses Mark Hogan, manager of the Hampton, Virginia, company that manufactures headlights for Chrysler. Fortunately, Chrysler worked with Wagner to adopt continuous improvement and other quality management practices. The result has been a dramatic improvement in product quality and lower costs. Hogan and his employees are now horrified if they find more than one or two defects per year. "We've started doing a lot of things right," says Hogan. "We're becoming known for our quality."[55]

Two decades ago, quality was rarely mentioned and almost never studied in organizational behavior. Today, Wagner Lighting Products and other companies consider quality to be the driving force for competitive advantage. **Quality** refers to the value that the end user perceives from the product or service. A product or service has quality when its features satisfy and anticipate customer needs and expectations. This also implies reliability or conformance to a standard, because people expect the product or service to be consistently good. Quality must be defined in terms of "value" because the benefits of a product or service must be assessed against its price to the consumer. *Quality management* (also known as *total quality management*) is a philosophy and a set of guiding principles to continuously improve the organization's product or service quality.[56] The quest for quality is a journey rather than a fixed goal, and the challenge is for organizations to provide products or services that meet (or preferably surpass) customer needs and expectations at the lowest possible cost, the first time and every time.

Quality management is often considered a topic for operations research and marketing (customer service) courses. Yet, as you will see in this section, quality management also relies heavily on organizational behavior concepts. Specifically, we will discuss quality management mainly as a human process—one in which employees, suppliers, and other people possess the knowledge and creativity to discover ways to reduce costs, defects, waste, and other quality imperatives.

quality the value that the end user perceives from the product or service, including satisfying customer needs or expectations and conforming to a standard

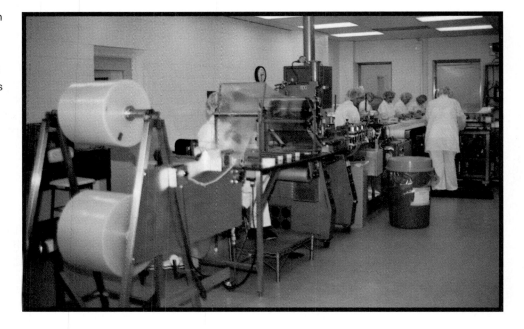

The first thing you realize when visiting Baxter Healthcare's production facility in Mountain Home, Arkansas, is how clean it is. The second observation is that this is a world-class plant where everyone takes quality seriously. Baxter has a strong belief that quality comes from high-involvement work teams and continuous performance measurement. The quality culture is so strong here that much of the plant's role has been to develop and perfect medical products and work processes before they are transferred to other plants around the world.[57] What conditions seem to help employees practice quality in the workplace?
[Courtesy of Baxter Healthcare Corporation]

This contrasts with the technological approach to quality management in which organizations introduce new technology with the expectation that this will drive out human error. Unfortunately, as General Motors discovered a few years ago, the technological approach to quality management is expensive and not always effective. General Motors spent millions of dollars on robotics in the expectation that this would solve their quality problems. It didn't. "I think GM learned some hard lessons," explains a GM executive. "There used to be a mind-set that automation was the only way to be competitive—I'll probably get my wrists slapped for saying this, but we now know that wasn't true."[58] Recent evidence suggests that U.S. firms continue to rely on technology, whereas Japanese firms rely more on the knowledge that people bring to the quality management process.[59]

Malcolm Baldrige Award and ISO Certification

Customer loyalty is the driving force behind quality management, but it is not the only force. Many U.S. companies also strive for the Malcolm Baldrige National Quality Award. Similar quality awards exist in Europe, Australia, Canada, and elsewhere. Companies apply for a Baldrige award and are judged on several criteria, such as customer focus, employee development, and work process improvements. Award winners receive favorable public recognition.

Although quality awards are valued, companies are increasingly interested in achieving one of the three ISO 9000 series certifications from the International Standards Association. ISO 9000 certification is an international standard that indicates the company performs above a minimum level of quality and competence.[60] ISO certification is so cherished that some companies raise large banners proudly identifying their ISO status. Law firms, advertising agencies, educational institutions, and other nonmanufacturing organizations have also received ISO 9000 registration.

ISO 9000 certification is primarily a documentation and auditing procedure. Companies write down how they conduct business at each step of the entire process. They execute every procedure exactly as documented. They provide objective documented evidence to an independent auditor every three years that the company's quality system meets ISO 9000 standards. After receiving certification, companies are expected to thoroughly assess their procedures annually or more often to ensure their quality system remains effective.

ISO 9000 registration requires documentation of quality processes, but this standard does not explicitly require continuous improvement, benchmarking, and other quality management principles and tools described later in this chapter. Consequently, General Motors, Ford, and Chrysler jointly developed a set of quality standards, called QS 9000, for suppliers in the automobile industry.[61] These standards include elements of ISO 9000 as well as explicit quality management practices.

Quality Management Principles

You won't find complete agreement on the principles of quality management in the literature. However, the six principles identified in Exhibit 10.4 and discussed over the next few pages capture common themes in this field.

Customer Focus

Quality is always defined in terms of customers—anyone outside or inside the organization to whom the employee supplies products, services, or information.[62] Some organizations like to say that they follow the "voice of the customer" in their quality management practices. For manufacturers, this voice comes from retailers and end users. Consulting firms listen to clients. Medical professionals have patients.

Notice that customers also exist *within* the organization. Any employee who receives work or services from another employee is a customer for that person. To reinforce this idea, Philips India engages employees in an annual exercise to determine their internal customers. They learn, for example, that manufacturing is the internal customer for the finance department when manufacturing requires support for the budgetary process.[63] By being close to internal and external customers, employees feel a stronger sense of responsibility to ensure that the product or service is defect-free. Moreover, employees who receive high-quality services from others within the organization tend to provide better service to external customers.[64]

Although it is useful to think about co-workers as customers, all employees must remain focused on their external customers because they establish the true value of the work performed. Companies focus on external customers through surveys, focus groups, and other marketing practices. As we learned in Chapter 6, some corporate executives also keep in touch with customers by

Exhibit 10.4
Quality management principles

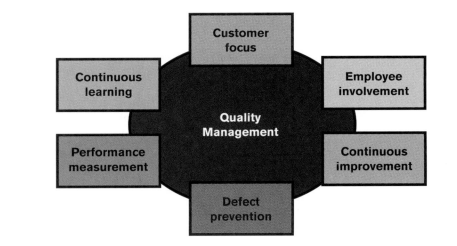

occasionally working the front lines, such as by listening to customer complaints and directly serving customers. A few companies send employees to customer locations for a few weeks to better understand their needs. Many firms invite primary customers to participate in product or service development. When developing the Boeing 777 aircraft, for example, Boeing Inc. worked closely with airlines that had placed advanced orders.

Employee Involvement for Quality

Twenty years ago, Harley-Davidson bikes had such poor quality that owners joked they needed two bikes—one to ride and one for spare parts.[65] Today, Harley-Davidson's name is synonymous with quality. And, as we learned in the opening story to this chapter, Harley continues to push the limits of quality through employee involvement.

Employee involvement is an integral part of quality management because quality is the responsibility of all employees in everything they do. Employee involvement comes in many forms, but the trend is distinctly moving toward self-directed work teams.[66] These team-based structures, which we described earlier in the chapter, give employees enough autonomy to reduce waste and improve product or service quality without the bureaucratic hurdles.

Whether companies introduce self-directed work teams or simply encourage employees to suggest work improvements, employee involvement is important for quality management because employees usually have the best information to identify quality problems and take corrective actions. Quality management is also a process of continual change, so employee involvement helps to minimize resistance to that change. Lastly, as a form of job enrichment, employee involvement may increase employee motivation and performance which in turn improves customer satisfaction.[67]

Continuous Improvement

Quality management is a never-ending process of improving work processes. Continuous improvement is often called *kaizen*, a Japanese word that literally means "good change."[68] It is also a significant part of the "lean management" philosophy that is currently sweeping the manufacturing sector.[69] No matter what title is used, the idea is to continually reduce scrap, time, distance, space, and other forms of waste in work processes. Waste exists when employees need to move raw materials long distances throughout the work facility. It exists when parts or work-in-progress are idle inventory. It exists when workstations are poorly configured, leaving large spaces and confusing arrangements for work flows.[70]

Many firms have *kaizen blitzes* to encourage the continuous improvement process. Kaizen blitzes are intense team-based events in which employees are given a fixed time to review specific work activities so that they can further reduce waste. Kaizen blitzes are action oriented because team members test and verify their ideas during the blitz. "There's a tremendous amount of implementation that goes on during the blitz," emphasizes Roger Harnishfeger, head of education programs at Dana Corp., an auto parts maker. "It's not a case where you'll learn some new techniques and maybe someday you might use them." Dana's kaizen blitz lasts about three-and-a-half days, with the first half day dedicated to instruction on basic continuous improvement concepts and practices.[71] Connections 10.2 illustrates a typical kaizen blitz at seal and gasket manufacturer Freudenberg-NOK General Partnership (FNGP).

Although most employee ideas try to improve existing processes, kaizen also involves physically moving work activities from functional departments (e.g., welding, painting) into work process flows. This often includes physically moving workstations so that everyone has a "line of sight" on the entire subprocess.

Thus, by physically designing work processes with a clear line of sight, work activities have less waste and employees tend to experience higher task identity and task significance (see Chapter 4) because they see how they are working together towards a final product or service.[72] Along with improving verbal and nonverbal communication, this arrangement makes it easier for employees to identify work practices that do not add value to customers.

One final observation about continuous improvement is that it works best in organizations that embrace knowledge management (see Chapter 1).[73] Information must flow easily to any employee so that improvements are more quickly identified and solved. Employees must learn through experience where work processes may be improved. They also study other organizations to discover ways to improve work efficiency. Companies also train employees in various statistical control methodologies and decision-making techniques so that continuous improvement may be monitored.

Defect Prevention

Quality management is built on the adage that "a stitch in time saves nine." A defect or error should stop at its source, because the cost of repair increases

Connections 10.2 ▫ Putting on a Kaizen Blitz

Seal and gasket manufacturer Freudenberg-NOK General Partnership has experienced significantly higher cost efficiencies since introducing kaizen blitzes.

[Courtesy of Freudenberg-NOK]

exponentially as the defect moves further along the process.[74] Thus, a central tenet of quality management is "do it right the first time." The only way to prevent defects or errors is to make every employee responsible for quality rather than letting defects persist until detected by inspectors or customers. The quality philosophy also pushes toward zero defects because even the smallest defect rate may have sizable consequences.

Performance Measurement

Performance measurement is the main driver for continuous improvement and defect prevention. By measuring the efficiency of work processes and organizational outcomes, quality problems become apparent and employees can see how their efforts are reducing these problems.[75] Employees are better able to reduce defects and provide continuous improvement solutions when they are trained in statistical control methods. This is also consistent with the trend toward *fact-based management;* that is, using objective rather than subjective information to assess quality and make corporate decisions.

MBNA is a classic example of how quality management companies are sticklers for performance measurement. The Wilmington, Delaware, credit

Kaizen blitzes have transformed Freudenberg-NOK General Partnership (FNGP) from a money-losing joint venture to a highly efficient manufacturer of seals and gaskets. For example, FNGP's plant in Indiana has increased productivity by 991 percent since the company introduced kaizen blitzes. Employees leave their normal duties for a week to serve on a kaizen team focusing on a particular problem, often at another work site. The idea is to identify ways to reduce waste through an intense, hands-on kaizen blitz process.

This week, Tim Stickles and Gary Chastain were given time off to work with three outsiders—a safety valve manager, a contract employee, and a journalist—to solve a valve stem seal press changeover problem at FNGP's Georgia plant. A typical changeover takes 1.5 hours, although this setup can sometime stretch to three hours or more. The kaizen team wants to reduce the changeover time to 30 minutes.

After videotaping an employee doing a changeover, Stickles and the others immediately recognize two problems: tools are poorly organized and labeled, and the employee must travel long distances to get the changeover done. The team labels these materials and moves them to a better location.

Next, two team members try out the new arrangement to see if it saves time. The changeover time is getting closer to their goal, but it's not good enough. The team decides that two employees merely get in each other's way, so they make more alterations and try the changeover using one person.

By Day Four of the kaizen blitz, the team has cut walking distance for the setup from 1,608 feet in the original videotape to just 172 feet. After a few more tryouts, the team records an operator completing the setup in less than 18 minutes. Within a day, plant managers were adopting the team's findings as a standard procedure for all valve stem seal cells in the plant.

Sources: Adapted from T. Murphy, "Kaizen Cuts Costs: GROWTTH Pays Big Dividends at Freudenberg-NOK," *Ward's Auto World* 33 (December 1997), p. 81; "Persistence with Lean Systems Can Yield 'Quantum Leaps' Year after Year, Says Freudenberg-NOK CEO," *PR Newswire*, June 2, 1997; J. P. Womack and D. T. Jones, *Lean Thinking* (New York: Simon & Schuster, 1996), pp. 90–91. ■

card company measures almost everything down to tenths of one percent. At any time of the day, employees can see the percentage of customer calls answered within the first two rings. In fact, scoreboards at MBNA facilities around the country track daily performance on fifteen standards.[76]

Continuous Learning

Employee involvement, continuous improvement, and other aspects of quality management require knowledgeable employees who are able to work in teams and adapt to new work environments. Thus, quality management requires a heavy investment in employee training and a cultural value in continuous learning. This is also consistent with our earlier connection between continuous improvement and knowledge management. Employees must continually acquire and apply knowledge to improve product and service quality.

PPG Industries Inc. has won several quality awards based in part on its emphasis on continuous learning. The Pittsburgh-based paint and resin company surveyed employees about what they needed to learn to make their jobs better and themselves more knowledgeable about the product they made. The result was a set of job-specific training modules that kept everyone up-to-date on work practices. For example, "Craters 101" teaches employees how to avoid the small holes in paint that seemed to occur in most batches.[77]

Quality Management Tools

Quality management is both a philosophy and a set of practices to improve product and service quality. In this section, we look at two of these practices: benchmarking and concurrent engineering.

Benchmarking

benchmarking a systematic and ongoing process of improving performance by measuring a product, service, or process against a partner that has mastered it

Benchmarking is a systematic and ongoing process of improving performance by measuring a product, service, or process against a partner that has mastered it.[78] Benchmarking begins by identifying and measuring performance levels, then finding benchmark companies or work units to compare these data. Benchmarked partners may include other operating units within the organization (internal benchmarking), other organizations that compete in the same product/service market (competitive benchmarking), or other organizations that are the best in a particular functional process whether or not they are competitors (functional benchmarking). Benchmarking usually involves visiting a benchmark partner to observe how a product is made or a service provided. For example, when Florida Power and Light wanted to improve the reliability of its distribution system, it visited Phillips Petroleum to study how that firm distributed oil from wellhead to tankcars. Benchmarking can also occur without the target company's knowledge. One common practice is reverse engineering, in which a competitor's product is taken apart and analyzed.

Benchmarking was developed by Xerox in 1979 and has been widely adopted by others. There are at least four reasons for its popularity. First, benchmarking is consistent with performance measurement and fact-based management. It provides objective rather than subjective standards against which to evaluate your own organization. Second, benchmarking is a form of goal setting with continually moving targets (see Chapter 3). For this reason, corporate leaders sometimes refer to benchmarked information as *stretch goals*.[79] Third, benchmarking is part of the continuous learning process and is consistent with the philosophy of knowledge management.[80] By visiting other firms, employees learn new practices through observation. This encourages them to continuously question their current work practices and to seek out new practices. Fourth, benchmarking reduces employee resistance to change because the benchmarked companies provide visible evidence that a higher standard of performance is both necessary and achievable.[81]

Concurrent Engineering

concurrent engineering the integration and concurrent development of a product or service and its associated processes, usually guided by a cross-functional team

Concurrent engineering refers to the cross-functional integration and concurrent development of a product or service and its associated processes.[82] Generally, this occurs by assigning product development to a cross-functional project team consisting of people from marketing, design, manufacturing, customer service, and other areas.

To understand concurrent engineering, consider how the development process traditionally works. As illustrated in Exhibit 10.5(a), the marketing department traditionally developed a strategy or product concept, which was passed "over the wall" to the design engineers. These designs were then sent to manufacturing engineers who figured out how to make the product or service efficiently. The manufacturing designers usually required the product designers to make several changes that minimized custom tooling. The customer service department was brought in at some later date to consider product

Exhibit 10.5
Traditional and concurrent product development

(a) Traditional serial product development

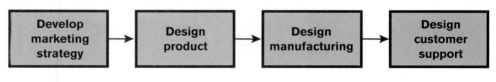

(b) Concurrent engineering product development

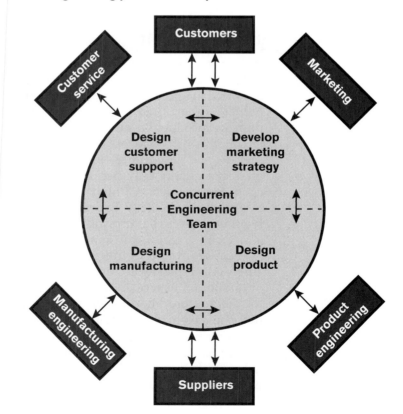

repair and parts replacement issues. Customers and suppliers were rarely involved at all.

In contrast, concurrent engineering creates a cross-functional project team—often including customers and suppliers—that simultaneously works on several phases of product or service development. Design and manufacturing engineers begin working simultaneously. Marketing and purchasing representatives are involved during this development process, not afterward. So are primary customers and suppliers. Exhibit 10.5(b) illustrates the most common form of concurrent engineering, in which the different development phases are combined.

Chrysler and other companies have benefited from concurrent engineering because their products and services are too complex for design engineers to create alone. Through cross-functional teams, concurrent engineering leverages the diverse knowledge of people from different backgrounds. This is one reason why Harley-Davidson Motor Co. has shifted to concurrent engineering at its product development center in Wisconsin. "It's crucial to have input from all these areas, as they are affected by engineering's designs at some point in the cycle," says Earl Werner, Harley-Davidson's vice president of engineering. "The more input we have up front, the better our products will be."[84]

A second benefit of concurrent engineering is that it significantly improves communication in the development process. This occurs because team members are typically "co-located"; that is, they work together in the same physical space. When co-location is combined with having people working concurrently on different phases of the project, concurrent engineering can dramatically reduce the time required to send the product or service to market.[85]

Of course, colocation isn't always feasible. For multinational projects, it may be better to have team members in their own cultural setting.[86] Information technologies increasingly make it possible for these virtual teams to work effectively at a distance (see Chapter 9). Still, until these technologies replicate face-to-face interaction, co-location will be the preferred option for product development projects.

Limitations of Quality Management

Quality management has been very successful in many organizations, but a closer look reveals that this approach also has its limitations. One major concern is that the narrow interpretation of quality management ignores stakeholders other than customers. Employees are expected to continuously improve production efficiency, yet companies tend to overlook the adverse effects this has on stress and employee health (see Chapter 5). Shareholders may also be forgotten in the quest for quality. Several companies have discovered that quality may rise, but profits may fall if they invest in quality management practices without considering shareholder return on investment. Realizing this, Federal Express and AT&T now invest only in quality management initiatives that provide a sufficient return on investment.[87]

A second reason why quality management has failed in some organizations is because it requires more commitment and dedication than executives and employees typically assume. According to one estimate, nearly three-quarters of quality management initiatives fail to produce meaningful results, mostly for this reason.[88] For instance, one British hospital failed to achieve meaningful results from quality management because the change process relied mainly on a training program. Employees learned about quality management, but the workplace systems and structures did not change. Consequently, there was no behavioral change.[89] With so many management fads passing through organizations, it is not surprising that employees have viewed quality management as another quick fix.

Overall, quality management provides an important perspective about how organizations should operate. It certainly clarifies employee and organizational goals, and leverages the benefits of employee involvement. And, although quality management may increase stress in some situations, it may also reduce stress where employees are frustrated by waste and inefficient work layout. At the same time, we must neither underestimate the challenges of implementing quality management nor ignore its potential limitations.

Chapter Summary

Employee involvement (or participation) refers to the degree that employees share information, knowledge, rewards, and power throughout the organization. It may be formal or informal, direct or indirect, and voluntary or legislated. The level of participation ranges from an employee providing information without knowing the problem to a work team having complete control over all phases of the decision process. A few companies have representative participation, in which employee representatives are on the Board of Directors.

Open book management involves sharing financial information with employees and encouraging them to recommend ideas that improve those financial results. It includes training employees how to read financial statements, and getting them to think of financial performance as a game that they can play and win.

Self-directed work teams are groups that complete an entire piece of work requiring several interdependent tasks and have substantial autonomy over the execution of these tasks. They assign tasks to team members; control most work inputs, flow, and output; are responsible for correcting problems; and receive team-level feedback and rewards.

Sociotechnical systems (STS) theory states that organizations consist of social and technical subsystems that must be jointly optimized to create the best structure for autonomous work teams. Teams should be sufficiently independent so that they can control the main "variances" in the system. STS theory suggests that self-directed work teams work best in primary work units that involve completion of an entire product or service.

Employee involvement may lead to higher decision quality, decision commitment, employee satisfaction and empowerment, and employee development in decision-making skills. Employee involvement is often resisted by management, employees, and labor unions, although this can be resolved through education, training, and trust building. Employees with high individualism and power distance are also less comfortable with some forms of employee involvement.

Quality refers to the value that the end user perceives from the product or service. Government awards and ISO certification objectives have encouraged many firms to implement quality management. The main quality management principles include customer focus, employee involvement, continuous improvement, defect prevention, performance measurement, and continuous learning.

Two popular quality management tools are benchmarking and concurrent engineering. Benchmarking is a systematic and ongoing process of improving performance by measuring a product, service, or process against a partner that has mastered that product, service, or process. Concurrent engineering refers to the cross-functional integration and concurrent development of a product or service and its associated processes.

One limitation of quality management is that it tends to overlook the needs of stakeholders other than customers. Another concern is that firms typically underestimate the amount of time and effort required to implement quality management.

Key Terms

Benchmarking, p. 324
Codetermination, p. 306
Communities of practice, p. 306
Concurrent engineering, p. 325
Employee involvement, p. 304

Empowerment, p. 314
Gainsharing plan, p. 307
Individualism–collectivism, p. 315
Open book management, p. 307
Power distance, p. 315

Discussion Questions

1. When Great West Life Assurance Co. decided to build a new headquarters, it formed a task force of employees representing different areas of the organization. The group's mandate was to identify features of the new building that would help employees do their jobs more effectively and work more comfortably. Describe the forms and level of employee involvement in this task force.

2. A chicken processing company wants to build a processing plant that represents a sociotechnically designed operation. In a traditional chicken processing plant, employees work in separate departments—cleaning and cutting, cooking, packaging, and warehousing. The cooking and packaging processes are controlled by separate workstations in the traditional plant. What changes to the social and technical systems would you make so that the proposed plant is sociotechnically designed?

3. Employee involvement applies just as well to the classroom as to the office or factory floor. Explain how student involvement in classroom decisions typically made by the instructor alone might improve decision quality. What potential problems may occur in this process?

4. Advanced Telecom Inc. has successfully introduced self-directed work teams (SDWTs) at its operations throughout the United States. The company now wants to introduce SDWTs at its plants in Singapore and Mexico. What potential cross-cultural challenges might Advanced Telecom experience as it introduces SDWTs in these countries?

5. Saturn Corp., a division of General Motors, was initially hailed as a breakthrough in employee involvement. Employees took on more responsibility, and the United Auto Workers (UAW) union, which represents Saturn employees, agreed to suspend parts of the labor agreement so that the workplace would be more flexible. However, the UAW's current leaders are having doubts about the Saturn arrangement and may want to return to a more traditional union-management relationship. Based on your knowledge of labor union resistance to employee involvement, give two possible reasons why the UAW might want to do this.

6. Some critics of quality management argue that continuous improvement is simply a form of work speedup. The more ideas that employees identify, the faster they need to work in the future. Others suggest that continuous improvement reduces work stress because it removes the waste that makes work frustrating. Debate these two points of view with others in your class. You may want to use a common example, such as the library checkout or course registration system at your college.

7. Why is employee involvement an integral part of quality management?

8. Southern Bank Corp. has been trying to develop new services involving Internet banking. However, the development requires people from several departments in Atlanta and Miami who seem to have difficulty working in a traditional development process. Describe how concurrent engineering can be applied to improve efficient service development in this situation.

CASE STUDY

Employee involvement cases

Case 1: New Machines Decision Problem

You are a manufacturing manager in a large electronics plant. The company's management is always searching for ways to increase efficiency. The company has recently installed new machines and put in a new, simplified work system, but to the surprise of everyone, including yourself, the expected increase in productivity was not realized. In fact, production has begun to drop, quality has fallen off, and the number of employee separations has risen.

You do not believe that there is anything wrong with the machines. You have had reports from other companies using them that confirm this opinion. You have also had representatives from the firm that built the machines go over them, and they report that the machines are operating at peak efficiency.

You suspect that some parts of the new work system may be responsible for the change, but this view is not widely shared among your immediate subordinates who are four first-level supervisors, each in charge of a section, and your supply manager. The drop in production has been variously attributed to poor training of the operators, lack of an adequate system of financial incentives, and poor morale. Clearly, this is an issue about which there is considerable depth of feeling among individuals and potential disagreement among your subordinates.

This morning you received a phone call from your division manager. He had just received your production figures for the last six months and was calling to express his concern. He indicated that the problem was yours to solve in any way that you thought best, but he would like to know within a week what steps you plan to take.

You share your division manager's concern over the falling productivity and know that your people are also disturbed. The problem is to decide what steps to take to rectify the situation.

Case 2: Coast Guard Cutter Decision Problem

You are the captain of a 200-foot Coast Guard cutter, with a crew of 16, including officers. Your mission is a general at-sea search and rescue. At 2:00 A.M. this morning, while en route to your home port after a routine 28-day patrol, you received word from the nearest Coast Guard station that a small plane had crashed 60 miles offshore. You obtained all the available information concerning the location of the crash, informed your crew of the mission, and set a new course at maximum speed toward the scene to commence a search for survivors and wreckage.

You have now been searching for 20 hours. Your search operation has been increasingly impaired by rough seas, and there is evidence of a severe storm building. The atmospherics associated with the deteriorating weather have made communications with the Coast Guard station impossible. A decision must be made

shortly about whether to abandon the search and place your vessel on a course that would ride out the storm—thereby protecting the vessel and your crew but relegating any possible survivors to almost certain death from exposure—or to continue a potentially futile search and the risks it would entail.

Before losing communications, you received an updated weather advisory about the severity and duration of the storm. Although your crew members are extremely conscientious about their responsibility, you believe that they would be divided on the decision of leaving or staying.

Discussion Questions (for both cases)

1. To what extent should your subordinates be involved in this decision? (Note: You may assume that neither case has time constraints that would prevent the highest level of participation.) Please choose one of the following:

   AI. You make the decision alone with no employee involvement.

   AII. Subordinates provide information that you request, but they don't offer recommendations and they might not be aware of the problem.

   CI. You describe the problem to relevant subordinates individually, getting their information and make recommendations. You make the final decision, which does not necessarily reflect the advice that subordinates have provided.

   CII. You describe the problem to subordinates in a meeting, in which they discuss information and make recommendations. You make the final decision, which does not necessarily reflect the advice that subordinates have provided.

   GII. You describe the problem to subordinates in a meeting. They discuss the problem and make a decision that you are willing to accept and implement if it has the entire team's support. You might chair this session, but you do not influence the team's decision.

2. What factors led you to choose this alternative rather than the others?

3. What problems might occur if less or more involvement occurred in this case (where possible)?

Source: Adapted from V. H. Vroom and A. G. Jago, *The New Leadership: Managing Participation in Organizations* (Englewood Cliffs, NJ: Prentice Hall, 1988). © 1987 V. H. Vroom and A. G. Jago. Used with permission of the authors. ∎

Better your business: Benchmark it

BusinessWeek

Business owners like to think they know intuitively how well their company is doing. But Elfrena S. Foord wanted hard evidence. To this financial adviser in Sacramento, winning the client's trust is everything. So the managers at Foord, Van Bruggen & Ebersole decided last year to check on what customers really thought about their service by doing some benchmarking—a process that measures a company against the standards and practices of other companies. The use of benchmarking is growing quickly among small companies as it becomes easier to do. Huge amounts of data have become accessible, on software and through the web, that allow owners to find out how rival companies are doing—and how they do it.

This *Business Week* case study describes how benchmarking is an increasingly popular business activity to improve organizational effectiveness. The case study describes how benchmarking works for financial analysts, long-haul trucking firms, hotels, and other companies. Read through this *Business Week* case study at www.mhhe.com/mcshane1e and prepare for the discussion questions below.

Discussion Questions

1. This case study suggests that the Internet can be a source of information for benchmarking. How is this done? What are the limitations of using Internet sources for benchmarking?

2. How does benchmarking relate to the quality management principles described in this textbook?

3. Use goal-setting concepts in Chapter 3 to explain why benchmarking is a potentially useful tool for improving individual and corporate performance.

Source: T. Gutner, "Better Your Business: Benchmark It," *Business Week*, April 27, 1998, p. ENT4. ▣

Focus: The power within

 The sales staff and management at a Denver furniture store have come up with a new idea for getting new customers. It's called I-Power, short for ideas power. Companies using the technique ask their employees to come up with at least two ideas a week.

At Kacey's Fine Furniture employees suggested that the trucks feature pictures of the products they sell, and that leather products that they sell be packed in foam and shrink wrapped before shipping. The employees and their bosses gather at meetings where problems are posed and solutions are offered. Rewards for good ideas range from toys and candy to cash.

I-Power also works for Board Room, Inc., a Connecticut-based publishing firm. It's used by some 1500 companies worldwide including Federal Express, Rubbermaid, and McCormick's, the world's largest spice company. It was even used by an army intelligence unit involved in the Persian Gulf War.

The I-Power system is a brain child of the Kacey's president, Martin Edelstein. He said, "I-Power makes people think and it makes them cooperate. It changes their spirit." One Kacey's employee remarked, "In this era of economic uncertainty, job insecurity, and management mistrust, it's given us a very good bond and relationship." Another said, "Today's I-Power theme is what we can do to help other departments. I've got $200 in our Dodger dollars to give away today and we're going to play our I-Power monopoly."

I-Power is a hit for major league baseball. After two depressing strike shortened seasons, the Los Angeles Dodgers are using I-Power. Labor and management have teamed up. One Dodge employee said, "If they can take time to think about what they do and ways to improve themselves, ways for the ball club to improve themselves, ways to improve customer service, then that's the real benefit of I-Power."

The history of modern business is packed with ideas, some good, some bad, that were supposed to boost employee morale, productivity, and company profits. The bottom line in most of them, including I-Power, is this: Managers, listen to your employees; they are smarter than you think.

Discussion Questions

1. I-Power is a technique for generating new ideas for workplace improvement. What level of employee involvement do you think is needed for I-Power to work?

2. I-Power requires that employees come up with two ideas per week. Besides the number of ideas to generate, what other parameters or guidelines do you think would make the ideas generated more useful?

3. What are some potential pitfalls of using I-Power in the workplace? ◼

TEAM EXERCISE

Winter survival exercise

Purpose

This exercise is designed to help you understand the potential advantages of employee involvement compared with individual decision making.

Situation

You have just crash-landed somewhere in the woods of southern Manitoba or northern Minnesota. It is 11:32 A.M. in mid-January. The small plane in which you were traveling crashed on a small lake. The pilot and co-pilot were killed. Shortly after the crash, the plane sank completely into the lake with the pilot's and copilot's bodies inside. Everyone else on the flight escaped to land dry without serious injury.

The crash came suddenly before the pilot had time to radio for help or inform anyone of your position. Since your pilot was trying to avoid the storm, you know the plane was considerably off course. The pilot announced shortly before the crash that you were 45 miles northwest of a small town that is the nearest known habitation.

You are in a wilderness area made up of thick woods broken by many lakes and rivers. The snow depth varies from above the ankles in windswept areas to more than knee-deep where it has drifted. The last weather report indicated that the temperature would reach 5 degrees Fahrenheit in the daytime and 15 degrees below 0 at night. There are plenty of dead wood and twigs in the area around the lake. You and the other surviving passengers are dressed in winter clothing appropriate for city wear—suits, pantsuits, street shoes, and overcoats. While escaping from the plane, your group salvaged the 12 items listed in the chart on pg. 332. You may assume that the number of persons in the group is the same as the number in your group, and that you have agreed to stay together.

Instructions

Your task is to rank the 12 items shown in the chart below according to their importance to your survival. In the "Individual Ranking" column, indicate the most important item with "1," going through to "12" for the least important. Keep in mind the reasons why each item is or is not important. Next, the instructor will form small teams (typically five members) and each team will rank-order the items in the second column. Team rankings should be based on consensus, and not simply an average of the individual rankings.

When the teams have completed their rankings, the instructor will provide the expert's ranking, which can be entered in the third column. Next, each student will compute the absolute difference (i.e., ignore minus signs) between the individual ranking and the expert's ranking, record this information in column four, and sum the absolute values at the bottom of column four. In column five, record the absolute difference between the team's ranking and the expert's ranking, and sum these absolute scores at the bottom. A class discussion of the absolute merits of individual versus team decision making will follow.

Winter survival tally sheet

Items	Step 1 Your individual ranking	Step 2 Your team's ranking	Step 3 Survival expert's ranking	Step 4 Difference between steps 1 and 3	Step 4 Difference between steps 2 and 3
Ball of steel wool					
Newspapers					
Compass					
Hand axe					
Cigarette lighter					
45-caliber pistol					
Section air map					
Canvas					
Shirt and pants					
Can of shortening					
Whiskey					
Chocolate bars					
			Total		
(The lower the score, the better)				Your score	Team score

Source: Adapted from "Winter Survival" in D. Johnson and F. Johnson, *Joining Together,* 3rd ed. (Englewood Cliffs, NJ: Prentice Hall, 1984). ◼

CHAPTER
ELEVEN

Decision Making in Organizations

Learning Objectives

After reading this chapter, you should be able to:

- Diagram the general model of decision making.
- Explain why people have difficulty identifying problems and opportunities.
- Identify three factors that challenge our ability to choose the best alternative.
- Outline the causes of escalation of commitment to a poor decision.
- Identify five problems facing teams when making decisions.
- Discuss three strategies to improve creativity in decision making.
- Compare and contrast the five structures for team decision making.

Early in 1994, Jeffrey P. Bezos read that the Web was growing at 2,200 percent each year. At the time, few people knew about the Internet, but the Wall Street hedge-fund manager saw immense opportunities. With no previous retail experience, Bezos quit his job and one year later launched Amazon.com. Today, Amazon.com is the world's largest online retailer of books and music.

Bezos considered 20 different products to market on the Web. He chose books because the largest stores have only a small percentage of the market and stock only a fraction of the 3 million active titles. Amazon.com operates in a virtual world, but Bezos carefully decided where to set up his online business. "Our base had to be in a city with a large pool of technical talent," says Bezos. "I narrowed it down to four places, and settled on Seattle."

Bezos made good decisions about product and location, but not everything went according to plan. Getting book details into the computer system required more manual labor than anticipated. Moreover, information about a book from one source often conflicted with data from other sources, so a computer program was developed to choose the best information. Amazon's technical staff faced the challenge of applying emerging computer technology in ways that offered customers a personalized experience. Three hundred people beta tested the site before it went officially online.

One of the great ironies of Amazon.com's success was that Bezos held many of his early meetings at the café of a major competitor because the company initially operated out of his garage. "We couldn't really bring people to our office," explains Bezos, "so we held all our early meetings in a café two miles away, which just happened to be inside a Barnes and Noble store." Barnes and Noble is the world's largest physical bookseller, but was slow to recognize the Net as a business opportunity. Now, Amazon.com is its major rival.[1]

Amazon.com, the world's largest online book and music store, is the brainchild of Jeffrey Bezos, a Wall Street investment manager who saw the Web as an opportunity for retailing.

[© Tina Hager/Focus/Matrix]

decision making a conscious process of making choices among one or more alternatives with the intention of moving toward some desired state of affairs

 o launch the world's most popular online book and music store, Jeff Bezos and his colleagues made thousands of decisions. **Decision making** is a conscious process of making choices among one or more alternatives with the intention of moving toward some desired state of affairs.[2] Some of Bezos's decisions, such as what product to sell on the Web and where to locate, followed a careful process of searching for alternatives and weighing the advantages. Other decisions, such as applying new technology to web site development, required the creative exploration of previously untested ideas.

Decisions occur in response to problems or opportunities. A *problem* is a deviation between the current and desired situation.[3] It is the gap between "what is" and "what ought to be." For example, Jeff Bezos faced several problems transferring information about each book into Amazon.com's database. The publisher's data were messier than he had expected, resulting in a much more labor intensive process. An *opportunity* is a deviation between current expectations and the recognition of a potentially better situation that is neither planned nor expected. In other words, decision makers realize that certain decisions may produce results beyond current goals or expectations. Jeff Bezos saw the Internet as an opportunity because it offered a new and potentially better way to sell books. The technology allowed him to offer more products and to customize the shopping experience more effectively than was previously possible.

This chapter explores the process of individual and team decision making in organizations. We begin by looking at each step in the general decision-making model. Then the model is examined more critically by identifying the individual and team dynamics that impede effective decision making. The latter part of the chapter examines ways to improve decision making. We discuss the all-important topic of creativity in decision making, and consider specific team structures that support the creative process as well as minimize some of the team dynamics problems described earlier in the chapter.

A General Model of Decision Making

How do people make decisions? The best place to start to answer this question is the general model of decision making shown in Exhibit 11.1.[4] As we shall see, people do not really make decisions this systematically, but the model

Exhibit 11.1
General model of decision making

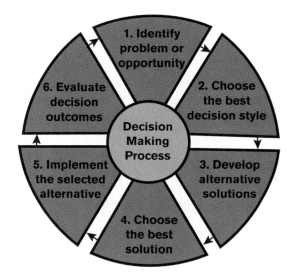

provides a useful template for our discussion of the topic. To some extent, we should also strive to follow this model.[5]

When Albert Einstein was asked how he would save the world in one hour, he replied that he would spend the first 55 minutes defining the problem and the last 5 minutes solving it. Problem identification is the first step in decision making and arguably the most important step. As mentioned above, a problem is a deviation between the current and desired situation. This deviation is a *symptom* of more fundamental causes in the organization. We need to correctly identify the problem in order to choose the best solution. This occurs by understanding the underlying causes of the symptom(s) that catches our attention. The decision process is then directed toward changing the root causes so that the symptoms are reduced or eliminated.[6]

The second step is to determine the most appropriate decision style.[7] One important question is whether this is a **programmed** or **nonprogrammed decision.**[8] A programmed decision follows standard operating procedures. There is no need to explore alternative solutions because the optimal solution has already been identified and documented. The Pentagon has thousands of standard operating procedures for everything from operating artillery to making fruitcake.[9] In contrast, new, complex, or ill-defined problems require nonprogrammed decisions. Amazon.com's Web site development consisted of several nonprogrammed decisions because employees were experimenting with new technology and Web design practices. In these cases, decision makers must search for alternatives and possibly develop a unique solution. As problems reappear, however, programmed decision routines are formed. In this respect, programmed decisions drive out nonprogrammed decisions because we strive for predictable, routine situations.

The third step in the general decision model is to develop a list of possible solutions to the problem.[10] This usually begins by searching for ready-made answers, such as practices that have worked well on similar problems. If an acceptable solution cannot be found, then decision makers try to design a custom-made solution or modify an existing one. The fourth step involves choosing the best alternative. In a purely rational process, this would involve identifying all factors against which the alternatives are judged, assigning weights reflecting the importance of those factors, rating each alternative on those factors, and calculating each alternative's total value from the ratings and factor weights.[11]

In the fifth step, decision makers must rally employees and mobilize sufficient resources to translate their decisions into action. They must consider the motivation, ability, and role perceptions of employees implementing the solution, as well as situational contingencies to facilitate its implementation (see Chapter 2). The last step in the decision model involves evaluating whether the gap has narrowed between "what is" and "what ought to be." Ideally, this information should come from systematic benchmarks so that relevant feedback is objective and easily observed.

The general model of decision making seems logical, yet it is rarely observed in organizations. Decision makers experience a number of personal limitations that make it difficult to identify problems and opportunities, choose solutions, and evaluate decision outcomes. Over the next few pages, we look at these challenges and ways to minimize them.

programmed decision the process whereby decision makers follow standard operating procedures to select the preferred solution without the need to identify or evaluate alternative choices

nonprogrammed decision the process applied to unique, complex, or ill-defined situations whereby decision makers follow the full decision-making process, including a careful search for and/or development of unique solutions

Identifying Problems and Opportunities

Problems and opportunities do not announce themselves. They are recognized and ultimately defined by the decision maker. However, people are not perfectly efficient or neutral thinking machines, so problems are often misdiagnosed and opportunities are overlooked. Two factors that interfere with identifying problems and opportunities are the decision maker's imperfect perceptions and diagnostic skills.

Perceptual Biases

People define problems or opportunities based on their perceptions, values, and assumptions. Unfortunately, selective attention mechanisms cause relevant information to be unconsciously screened out. Moreover, employees, clients, and others with vested interests can influence the decision maker's perceptions so that information is more or less likely to be perceived as a problem or opportunity. Thus, decision making is frequently marked by politics and negotiation.[12]

mental models the broad world views or "theories-in-use" that people rely on to guide their perceptions and behaviors

A broader perceptual challenge is that people see problems or opportunities through their **mental models** (see Chapter 6).[13] These working models of the world help us to make sense of our environment, but they also perpetuate assumptions that blind us to new realities. As we see in Connections 11.1, narrow mental models are the source of several famous missed opportunities.

Connections 11.1 □ Famous Missed Opportunities

Executives at several movie studios initially rejected George Lucas' film idea about life in the early 1960s. Yet *American Graffiti* eventually became one of the most popular movies of all time.

[UPI/Corbis-Bettmann]

Poor Diagnostic Skills

Perceptual problems block our ability to diagnose problems and recognize opportunities.[14] People want to make sense of situations, so they quickly define problems based on stereotypes and other unsubstantiated information. They fail to see problems or opportunities due to insufficient time or information. Decision makers also define problems poorly because the situation is complex or emotionally charged.

Another common diagnostic error is defining problems in terms of their solutions. Someone who says, "The problem is that we need more control over our suppliers," has fallen into this trap. The problem might be that suppliers aren't delivering their product in time, but this statement focuses on a solution. The tendency to focus on solutions is based on our need to reduce uncertainty; however, it can short-circuit the problem identification stage of decision making.[15]

Mental models create a road map for us to follow through life. Unfortunately, this cognitive map may leave out emerging perspectives and trends, resulting in costly decision making errors. Here are a few famous missed opportunities.

- Most of the things that make computing easy—graphical user interfaces, mice, windows, pull-down menus, laser printing, distributed computing, and Ethernet—weren't invented by Apple, Microsoft, or IBM. They were developed in the 1970s by researchers at Xerox PARC. Yet Xerox executives didn't try to market these inventions; they didn't even patent them. Xerox executives were so preoccupied with their main business (photocopiers) that they didn't see the opportunities in personal computing. Today, Xerox has only a peripheral role in the computer industry, which is much larger than the photocopier industry.
- Ken Olson founded and built Digital Equipment Corp. into one of the leading mainframe computer manufacturers. Yet, in the late 1970s, Olson proclaimed, "There is no reason for any individual to have a computer in their home." He also described a prototype of the Apple Computer as a "toy." By misperceiving the future of computing, Digital struggled to maintain any position in the microcomputer market and Olson was eventually ousted from the company he founded. Ironically, Digital was recently bought by Compaq, the leading microcomputer maker.
- In 1972, several Hollywood studios told new film director George Lucas that his low-budget movie about life in the early 1960s was commercially unacceptable. Universal Studios later changed its mind and the film, *American Graffiti*, became one of the highest-grossing movies of all time. In spite of Lucas' first success, Universal and other studios rejected the director's next project, a sci-fi movie. Twentieth Century-Fox reluctantly provided some development money, but Lucas had to raise most of the money for the project himself. The project left Lucas financially broke and dispirited, but at least he kept the picture rights. His film, *Star Wars*, became an outstanding success.
- When the World Wide Web burst onto the cyberspace scene in the early 1990s, Bill Gates wondered what all the fuss was about. Even as late as 1996, the founder and CEO of Microsoft lampooned investors for their love-in with companies that made Internet products. However, Gates eventually realized the error in his mental model of computing. Making up for lost time, Microsoft bought several Web-savvy companies and added Internet support to its Windows operating system.

Sources: S. Berglas, "Know When to Fold," *Inc.*, March 1998, p. 31; O. Port, "Xerox Won't Duplicate Past Errors," *Business Week*, September 29, 1997, p. 98; T. Abate, "Meet Bill Gates, Stand-Up Comic," *San Francisco Examiner*, March 13, 1996, p. D1; L. J. Peter, *Why Things Go Wrong* (New York: Bantam, 1984); D. Frost and M. Deakin, *I Could Have Kicked Myself* (London: André Deutsch, 1982). ■

Identifying Problems and Opportunities More Effectively

Recognizing problems and opportunities will always be a challenge, but the process can be improved through awareness of these perceptual and diagnostic limitations. By recognizing how mental models restrict a person's understanding of the world, decision makers learn to openly consider other perspectives of reality. Perceptual and diagnostic weaknesses can also be minimized by discussing the situation with colleagues. Decision makers discover blind spots in problem identification by hearing how others perceive certain information and diagnose them.[16] Opportunities also become apparent when outsiders explore this information from their different mental models. Another strategy for problem identification is to create early warning systems. If customer satisfaction ratings drop or costs increase beyond a fixed mark, executive procedures or computer programs can alert decision makers to these concerns.

To help decision makers make sense of complex information, many firms now rely on *data mining*—computer programs that search through large databases and organize this information into meaningful trends. Data mining minimizes perceptual problems that occur when people manually look for trends and patterns. For instance, executives at Hickory Farms sift through a data warehouse of 5 million customer records to find out who should receive the company's latest catalog. Most national retail chains conduct data mining to identify potential merchandise problems or recognize opportunities for better customer service.[17]

Choosing Solutions

For many years, decision making was studied mainly by economists who made several assumptions about how people choose among alternatives. They assumed that decision makers pick solutions based on well-articulated and

Kmart's eight terabyte data warehouse is one of the most impressive in the retail industry. Kmart collects information on thousands of daily customer and supplier transactions. Then Kmart executives analyze these data nuggets to spot potential problems and identify opportunities for better customer service. For example, the data analysis can show how promoting certain items may result in otherwise unexpected sales of other items.[18] How does data mining overcome human limitations of identifying problems and opportunities? What conditions are necessary to make data mining worthwhile? *[John Thoeming]*

agreed-upon organizational goals. They also assumed that decision makers are rational thinking machines who efficiently and simultaneously process facts about all alternatives and the consequences of those alternatives. Finally, these theorists assumed that decision makers always choose the alternative with the highest payoff. This rational perspective laid the foundation for popular misconceptions about how people make decisions.

Today, even the economists have cast off these unrealistic assumptions.[19] Instead, they are embracing the organizational behavior perspective that decision makers have a limited capacity to digest and analyze information. For the past 40 years organizational behavior researchers have debunked several economic assumptions about decision making in organizations, as we see in Exhibit 11.2.

Problems with Goals

We need clear goals to choose the best solution because goals provide a standard against which each alternative is evaluated. In reality, though, organizational goals are often ambiguous or in conflict with each other. The problem is compounded when organizational members disagree over the relative importance of these goals.[20] It is also doubtful that all decisions are based on organizational objectives; some decisions are made to satisfy the decision maker's personal goals even when they are incompatible with the organization's goals.

Exhibit 11.2   Traditional economic assumptions versus organizational behavior findings about choosing decision alternatives

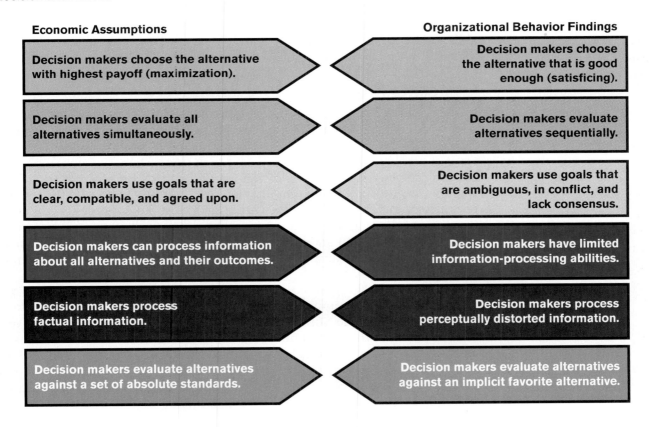

Economic Assumptions	Organizational Behavior Findings
Decision makers choose the alternative with highest payoff (maximization).	Decision makers choose the alternative that is good enough (satisficing).
Decision makers evaluate all alternatives simultaneously.	Decision makers evaluate alternatives sequentially.
Decision makers use goals that are clear, compatible, and agreed upon.	Decision makers use goals that are ambiguous, in conflict, and lack consensus.
Decision makers can process information about all alternatives and their outcomes.	Decision makers have limited information-processing abilities.
Decision makers process factual information.	Decision makers process perceptually distorted information.
Decision makers evaluate alternatives against a set of absolute standards.	Decision makers evaluate alternatives against an implicit favorite alternative.

Problems with Information Processing

People do not make perfectly rational decisions because they don't process information very well. One problem is that perceptual biases distort the selection and interpretation of information (see Chapter 6). Thus, decision makers are not aware of every piece of information because the **selective attention** process screens much of it out. Second, decision makers can't possibly think through all of the possible alternatives and their outcomes, so they engage in a limited search for and evaluation of alternatives.[21] For example, there may be dozens of computer brands to choose from, but people typically evaluate only a few of these.

Third, decision makers typically look at alternatives sequentially rather than examining all alternatives at the same time. As a new alternative comes along, it is immediately compared to an implicit favorite. An *implicit favorite* is an alternative that the decision maker prefers over the others.[22] In some cases, this option is unconsciously chosen long before the formal decision process begins. The implicit favorite becomes a comparison against which all other alternatives are judged. This might be fine, except that people unconsciously distort information to make their implicit favorite come out the winner in most comparisons.[23]

Problems with Maximization

Decision makers tend to select the alternative that is acceptable or "good enough," rather than the best possible solution. In other words, they engage in **satisficing** rather than maximizing. Satisficing occurs because it isn't possible to identify all of the possible alternatives, and information about available alternatives is imperfect or ambiguous. Satisficing also occurs because decision makers tend to evaluate alternatives one at a time against the implicit favorite and eventually select an option that is good enough to satisfy their needs or preferences. What constitutes a good enough solution depends on the availability of acceptable alternatives. Standards rise when acceptable alternatives are easily found and fall when few are available.[24]

Choosing Solutions More Effectively

It is very difficult to get around the human limitations of making choices, but a few strategies can minimize unnecessary problems. One approach is to systematically identify and weight the factors used to evaluate alternatives. A team of employees at Baxter Healthcare took this systematic approach when deciding the best work schedule. The team identified four factors (e.g., how well the schedule allows communication across shifts) and weighted the importance of each factor. Next, they rated each of seven possible schedules on those four factors and calculated the schedule's overall score.[25] This process minimizes reliance on an implicit favorite and satisficing. It also aids information processing because the calculations are made on paper rather than in our heads.

Another strategy is to use *decision support systems (DSS)*. These are computer-based programs that guide people through the decision-making process.[26] For example, software developer Cerner Corp. in Kansas City, Missouri, uses a case-based reasoning process at its help desk. Callers' problems or questions are entered in simple English and the system replies with questions and eventually solutions to the problems presented. This decision support system cut in half Cerner's backlog of unresolved client issues and increased customer satisfaction ratings to record high levels.[27]

intuition the ability to know when a problem or opportunity exists and select the best course of action without conscious reasoning

Using intuition Our intuition can assist decision making, particularly when there isn't enough time for a more organized analysis. **Intuition** is the ability to know when a problem or opportunity exists and to select the best course of action without conscious reasoning.[28] There is plenty of debate about the value of intuition. As we read in our *Fast Company Online* feature for this chapter, some executives swear by their intuition, whereas some scholars warn against this practice.

Which of these views is correct? Both. It is true that we sometimes justify biased and nonsystematic decision making as intuition. However, there is also increasing research evidence that intuition is the conduit through which people use their **tacit knowledge.** Recall from Chapter 2 that tacit knowledge is subtle information acquired through observation and experience that is not clearly understood and therefore cannot be explicitly communicated. This knowledge incorporates logical reasoning that has become habit over time. Thus, intuition allows us to draw on our vast storehouse of unconscious knowledge.[29]

tacit knowledge knowledge embedded in our actions and ways of thinking, and transmitted only through observation and experience

Consider grand chess masters who play against several people at the same time. They look at the chessboard, make their move without time to systematically evaluate the situation, and proceed to another chessboard. Chess masters make the right choice (most of the time) because they have learned patterns of chess arrangements and are able to quickly sense a pattern that threatens their position or presents an opportunity. Experienced decision makers in organizations have this same skill. They sense the best solution without consciously thinking through their preference. Certainly, we need to be careful that our "gut feelings" are not merely perceptual distortions and false assumptions, but we should also recognize the potential value of intuition in making sound choices.

Evaluating Decision Outcomes

Decision makers aren't completely honest with themselves when evaluating the effectiveness of their decisions. One concern is that after making a choice, decision makers tend to inflate the quality of the selected alternative and deflate the quality of the discarded alternatives. They ignore or suppress the importance of negative information about the selected alternative and emphasize positive information. This perceptual distortion, known as **postdecisional justification,** results from the need to maintain a positive self-identity.[30] Postdecisional justification gives people an excessively optimistic evaluation of their decisions, but only until they receive very clear and undeniable information to the contrary. Unfortunately, it also inflates the decision maker's initial evaluation of the decision, so reality often comes as a painful shock when objective feedback is finally received.

postdecisional justification justifying choices by unconsciously inflating the quality of the selected option and deflating the quality of the discarded options

Escalation of Commitment

A second problem when evaluating decision outcomes is escalation of commitment. **Escalation of commitment** is the tendency to repeat an apparently bad decision or allocate more resources to a failing course of action.[31] There are plenty of escalation examples in the public and private sectors. The Internal Revenue Service poured almost $4 billion into a new computer system before someone recently pulled the plug on the project. The U.S. Congress has granted Amtrak $20 billion in subsidies over the years, even though the passenger rail service was supposed to be self-sufficient in the 1970s and most first-time passengers today won't use Amtrak again. Escalation also occurred

escalation of commitment repeating an apparently bad decision or allocating more resources to a failing course of action

years ago when the British government continued funding the Concorde supersonic jet long after its lack of commercial viability was apparent. To this day some scholars refer to escalation of commitment as the "Concorde fallacy."[32]

FAST COMPANY
Online

▫ Decisions, Decisions

Before Deborah Rieman makes a decision, she listens to what her employees think about the issue. Then Rieman, who is Executive Director of Check Point Software Technologies in Redwood City, California, listens to her intuition.

"If I have to make a big decision, I listen to what others think," explains Rieman. "But ultimately, I listen to my intuition. I postpone a decision until I wake up one morning and know where my gut is going."

Intuition is an important part of decision making for Deborah Rieman, Executive Director of Check Point Software Technologies.
[Courtesy of Check Point Software]

Max Bazerman, a professor at Kellogg Graduate School of Management, Northwestern University, disagrees. "When making a decision, don't listen to your intuition," he warns. "Intuition will lead you astray; it's drastically overrated. The desire to follow intuition reflects the mythology of people who don't want to think rationally and systematically. They tell stories about how their intuition guided them through a decision, but they don't understand how or why. Often, when you hear about intuition, what you're really hearing is a justification of luck."

Deborah Rieman recognizes that intuition is not fully accepted by some scholars, but she believes that it provides more than logical decision processes can offer. "Some people warn against [intuition]," Rieman acknowledges. "But there's a kind of processing that happens in a far deeper place than logical processing does. Intuition offers a way to integrate and synthesize, to weigh and balance information."

ONLINE CHECK-UP

1. This *Fast Company Online* feature presents two points of view regarding intuition. Do you believe that decision makers should rely on intuition? Are there situations where intuition should be used instead of rational analysis?

2. The full text of this *Fast Company* article includes testimonials about decision making from several other people. Read the opinions of Chris Newell at Lotus Institute and Buz Mertes at GE Capital Mortgage Insurance Corp. and explain how their ideas relate to other topics in this chapter.

Get the full text of this *Fast Company* article at www.mhhe.com/mcshane1e

Source: Adapted from A. Muoio, "Decisions, Decisions—Unit of One," *Fast Company*, Issue 18 (October 1998). ▪

The London Stock Exchange started a project called Taurus to develop a new electronic system for processing stocks. Taurus was staffed by a powerful team of analysts, programmers, and strategy experts and was led by a highly respected director. The entire project was supposed to cost $75 million and take 18 months. Instead, complex issues and changing needs blew out these goals. Nearly $700 million were poured into the project before it was cancelled three years beyond its original deadline.[33] What factors likely contributed to escalation of commitment in the Taurus project? How might this problem be avoided in the future?

[Reuters/Matthew Grey/Archive Photos]

Decision makers are particularly vulnerable to escalation of commitment where the project requires large up-front costs with unknown returns until near the end of the project. This may explain why the Long Island Lighting Company built the Shoreham Nuclear Power Plant over 20 years in spite of cost overruns, regulatory delays, and changing public perceptions toward nuclear power. Originally projected to cost $70 million, the nuclear plant eventually became a $5 billion boondoggle. Long Island Lighting eventually sold the plant to the State of New York for one dollar.[34]

Causes of escalating commitment Organizational behavior scholars have identified several reasons why people are led deeper and deeper into failing projects. These include self-justification, gambler's fallacy, perceptual blinders, and closing costs.

Self-justification—Escalation of commitment often occurs because people want to present themselves in a positive light (see Chapter 12).[35] Those who are personally identified with the decision tend to persist because this demonstrates confidence in their own decision-making ability. From the decision maker's perspective, this shows leadership—"staying the course" in spite of what the critics say about the project. From another perspective, escalation is the decision maker's way of saving face—looking good to avoid the embarrassment of admitting past errors. Some cultures have a stronger emphasis on saving face than others, so escalation of commitment is probably more common in those societies.[36]

Gambler's fallacy—Many projects result in escalation of commitment because decision makers underestimate the risk and overestimate their probability of success. They become victims of the so-called "gambler's fallacy" by having inflated expectations of their ability to control problems that may arise. In other words, decision makers falsely believe that luck is on their side, so they invest more in a losing course of action.

Perceptual blinders—Escalation of commitment often occurs because decision makers do not see the problems soon enough. Through perceptual defense (see Chapter 6), they unconsciously screen out or explain away negative information. Serious problems initially look like random errors along the trend line to success. Even when people see that something is wrong, the information is sufficiently ambiguous that it can be misinterpreted or justified.

Closing costs—Even when a project's success is in doubt, decision makers will persist because the costs of ending the project are high or unknown. Terminating a major project may involve large financial penalties, a bad public image, or personal political costs. This is probably the main cause of escalation at Amtrak. Shutting down the passenger train service would cost taxpayers up to $7 billion, mainly because of a law giving Amtrak employees up to six years of severance pay.[37] This action would also have adverse political repercussions for elected officials in areas that depend on the passenger train service.[38]

Evaluating Decision Outcomes More Effectively

Probably the most effective way to minimize escalation of commitment and postdecisional justification is to separate decision choosers from decision evaluators. This tends to avoid the problem of saving face because the person responsible for evaluating the decision is not identified as the person who made the bad decision. In support of this recommendation, a recent study found that banks were more likely to take action against bad loans after the executive responsible had left.[39] In other words, problem loans were effectively managed when someone else took over the portfolio.

A second strategy is to establish a preset level at which the decision is abandoned or reevaluated.[40] This is similar to a stop-loss order in the stock market, whereby the stock is sold if it falls below a certain price. The problem with this solution is that conditions are often so complex that it is difficult to identify an appropriate point to abandon a project. However, this approach may work if a stopping point can be determined and it is implemented by someone other than the decision maker. A third strategy is to find a source of systematic and clear feedback. For example, companies might carefully survey customers during the early stages of a product launch rather than rely on less precise feedback. This reduces the problem that escalation occurs when feedback is ambiguous.[41]

Problems in Team Decision Making

Employees rarely make decisions alone. As we learned in Chapter 10, involving others in decisions has several advantages, such as improved decision quality and acceptance. However, team dynamics can also get in the way of good decisions. In this section, we look at the main problems people face when they make decisions in group settings.

Time Constraints

There's a saying that "committees keep minutes and waste hours." This reflects the fact that teams take longer than individuals to make decisions.[42] Unlike individuals, teams require extra time to organize, coordinate, and socialize. The larger the group, the more time required to make a decision. Team members need time to learn about each other and build rapport. They need to manage an imperfect communication process so that there is sufficient understanding of each other's ideas. They also need to coordinate roles and rules of order within the decision process.

production blocking a time constraint in meetings due to the procedural requirement that only one person may speak at a time

Another time constraint found in most team structures is that only one person can speak at a time.[43] This problem, known as **production blocking,** causes participants to forget what they wanted to say by the time it is their turn to speak. Team members who rehearse their lines while waiting might ignore what others are saying, even though their statements could trigger more creative ideas. These process losses, which we described in Chapter 9, cause teams to take much longer than individuals to make a decision.

Evaluation Apprehension

evaluation apprehension a person's reluctance to mention ideas that seem silly or peripheral in order to create a favorable self-image

Individuals are reluctant to mention ideas that may seem silly or not directly applicable because they believe (often correctly) that other team members are silently evaluating them. This **evaluation apprehension** is based on the individual's desire to create a favorable self-presentation and his or her need for social esteem. It is most common in meetings attended by people with different levels of status or expertise, or when members formally evaluate each other's performance throughout the year (as in 360-degree feedback). Evaluation apprehension is a problem when the group wants to generate creative ideas, because these thoughts often sound bizarre or lack logic when presented. Unfortunately, many potentially valuable ideas are never presented to the group because they initially seem ridiculous and a waste of time.

Conformity to Peer Pressure

Chapter 9 described how cohesiveness leads individual members to conform to the team's norms. This control keeps the group organized around common goals, but it may also cause team members to suppress their dissenting opinions about discussion issues, particularly when a strong team norm is related to the issue. When someone does state a point of view that violates the majority opinion, other members might punish the violator or try to persuade him or her that the opinion is incorrect. It's not surprising, then, that nearly half of the managers surveyed in a recent study say they give up in team decisions because of pressure from others to conform to the team's decision.[44] Conformity can also be subtle. To some extent, we depend on the opinions that others hold to validate our own views. If co-workers don't agree with us, then we begin to question our own opinions even without overt peer pressure.[45]

Groupthink

groupthink the tendency of highly cohesive groups to value consensus at the price of decision quality by avoiding conflict and withhold their dissenting opinions

Groupthink is the tendency of highly cohesive groups to value consensus at the price of decision quality.[46] Groupthink is based on conformity, but it goes far beyond it. There are strong social pressures on individual members to maintain harmony by avoiding conflict and disagreement. They suppress doubts about decision alternatives preferred by the majority or group leader. Team members want to maintain this harmony because their self-identity is enhanced by membership in a powerful decision-making body that speaks with one voice.[47] Team harmony also helps members cope with the stress of making crucial top-level decisions.

High cohesiveness isn't the only cause of groupthink. It is also more likely to occur when the team is isolated from outsiders, the team leader is opinionated (rather than remaining impartial), the team is under stress due to an external threat, the team has experienced recent failures or other decision-making problems, and the team lacks clear guidance from corporate policies or procedures. Several symptoms of groupthink have been identified and are summarized in Exhibit 11.3. In general, teams overestimate their invulnerability and morality, become closed-minded to outside and dissenting information, and experience several pressures toward consensus.[48]

Most research on groupthink has analyzed policy decisions that turned into fiascoes. The best-known example of groupthink is NASA's space shuttle *Challenger* explosion in 1986.[49] The technical cause of the explosion killing all seven

Exhibit 11.3
Symptoms of groupthink

Groupthink symptom	Description
Illusion of invulnerability	The team feels comfortable with risky decisions because possible weaknesses are suppressed or glossed over.
Assumption of morality	There is such an unquestioned belief in the inherent morality of the team's objectives that members do not feel the need to debate whether their actions are ethical.
Rationalization	Underlying assumptions, new information, and previous actions which seem inconsistent with the team's decision are discounted or explained away.
Stereotyping outgroups	The team stereotypes or oversimplifies the external threats upon which the decision is based; "enemies" are viewed as purely evil or moronic.
Self-censorship	Team members suppress their doubts in order to maintain harmony.
Illusion of unanimity	Self-censorship results in harmonious behavior, so individual members believe that they alone have doubts; silence is automatically perceived as evidence of consensus.
Mindguarding	Some members become self-appointed guardians to prevent negative or inconsistent information from reaching the team.
Pressuring dissenters	Members who happen to raise their concerns about the decision are pressured to fall into line and be more loyal to the team.

Source: Based on I. L. Janis, *Groupthink: Psychological Studies of Policy Decisions and Fiascoes*, 2nd ed. (Boston: Houghton Mifflin, 1982), p. 244.

crew members was a faulty O-ring seal that did not withstand the freezing temperatures the night before launch. However, a government commission pointed to a faulty decision-making process as the primary cause of the disaster. Key decision makers at NASA and the O-ring manufacturer experienced many groupthink symptoms. They were under intense pressure to launch due to previous delays and promises of the space shuttle program's success. Information about O-ring problems was withheld to avoid conflict. Engineers raised concerns about the O-rings before the launch, but they were criticized for this.

Group Polarization

group polarization the tendency for teams to make more extreme decisions (either more risky or more risk averse) than the average team member would if making the decision alone

Group polarization refers to the tendency of teams to make more extreme decisions than individuals working alone.[50] Exhibit 11.4 shows how the group polarization process operates. Individuals form initial preferences when given several alternatives. Some of these choices are riskier than others, and the average member's opinion leans one way or the other. Through open discussion, members become comfortable with more extreme positions when they realize that other team members hold similar opinions. Persuasive arguments favoring the dominant position convince doubtful members and help form a consensus around the extreme option. Finally, individuals feel less personally responsible for the decision consequences because the team has made the decision.

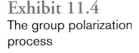

Exhibit 11.4
The group polarization
process

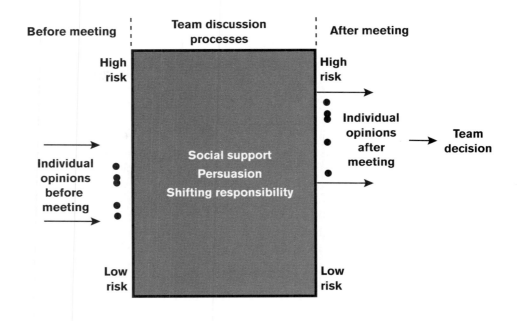

Group polarization mainly explains why teams make more *extreme* decisions, but why do they usually make riskier decisions? The answer is that decision makers often have an illusion of control. They become victims of the "gambler's fallacy" that they can beat the odds. For example, team members tend to think, "This strategy might be unsuccessful 80 percent of the time, but it will work for us!" Thus, team members are more likely to favor the risky option.[51]

Group polarization explains why some executive teams unwisely gamble assets and develop overoptimistic forecasts of success. Under some conditions, senior executives might support a "bet-your-company" solution in which most corporate assets are allocated to an investment with low probability of success. At the other extreme, teams whose members generally favor risk-averse solutions will suffer from inaction and stagnation. They will continually miss windfall opportunities and be ill-prepared for environmental changes.

Improving Team Decision Making

Team problems in decision making may be reduced in a number of ways. One approach is to ensure that neither the team leader nor any other participant dominates the process. This limits the adverse effects of conformity and lets other team members generate more ideas.[52] Another practice is to maintain an optimal team size. The group should be large enough that members possess the collective knowledge to resolve the problem, yet small enough that the team doesn't consume too much time or restrict individual input.[53] Team norms are also important to ensure that individuals engage in critical thinking rather than follow the group's implicit preferences.

Finally, groupthink, group polarization, and other team dynamics problems may be minimized by introducing more effective team structures. We will describe these team structures later in this chapter. Along with improving team dynamics, these structures potentially support more creative decision making.

Creativity in Decision Making

Henry Yuen wanted to record a baseball game on TV while out of town, but the scientist had problems setting his VCR properly. While venting his anger, Yuen had an idea. "I thought that taping a program should be as easy as dialing a telephone," he says. So he and coinventor Daniel Kwoh set out to develop a system that makes VCR recording as simple as dialing a telephone. Today, most VCR owners enjoy the fruits of Yuen's creative inspiration through VCR Plus or G-codes. Users simply punch in the appropriate number from the TV guide listing and the system does the rest.[54]

creativity developing an original product, service, or idea that makes a socially recognized contribution

Creativity refers to developing an original product, service, or idea that makes a socially recognized contribution. Creativity has been romanticized by some consultants as a special function of the brain's right hemisphere. It isn't. This myth is based on pseudosciences of the 1800s that have been proven incorrect in scientific research.[55] Others view creativity as something separate from regular decision making. Although there are unique features of creativity that we discuss in this section, creativity is really part of most nonprogrammed decisions. We use the creative process to find problems, identify alternatives, and implement solutions. Creativity is not something we save for special occasions.

Creativity Model

Creativity is a complex process, but scholars generally agree that the model presented in Exhibit 11.5 provides a reasonable representation.[56]

1. *Preparation*—Creativity is not a passive activity; rather, we gather the necessary information and concentrate on the problem or issue. For example, people are usually more creative when they take the problem apart and closely analyze each component.
2. *Incubation*—This is the stage of reflective thought. We put the problem aside (sometimes out of frustration), but our mind is still working on it unconsciously. This stage is usually aided by working (or playing) on an unrelated object or event.
3. *Insight*—At some point during the incubation stage, we become aware of a unique idea. These flashes of inspiration are fleeting and can be lost quickly if not documented. In other words, creative thoughts don't keep a particular schedule; they might come to you at any time of day or night. For this reason, many creative writers keep a journal or notebook nearby at all times, so that they can jot down these fleeting ideas before they disappear.[57]
4. *Verification*—Insights are merely rough ideas. Their usefulness still requires verification through conscious evaluation and experimentation. This is similar to the evaluating decision outcomes stage in the decision-making model described earlier in this chapter.

The flashes of inspiration identified in the creativity model are usually derived from a unique combination of previous information. For instance, Henry Yuen's inspiration for VCR Plus and G-coding came from associating VCR programming with making a telephone call. The creativity of this idea is that we don't normally think of VCRs in terms of telephone activities. This represents a special feature of creativity, known as **divergent thinking.** Divergent

divergent thinking reframing problems in a unique way and generating different approaches to the issue

Exhibit 11.5
Model of creativity in decision making

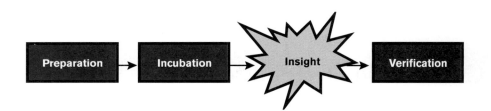

thinking involves reframing the problem in a unique way and generating different approaches to the issue. For example, one test of divergent thinking is to identify as many uses of an object as possible. Divergent thinkers are able to break away from the known uses to completely different applications. Divergent thinking contrasts with *convergent thinking*, which occurs when several people form a common mental model. For example, team building leads to convergent thinking because team members develop common norms, expectations, and beliefs.[58]

Conditions for Creativity

Minnesota Mining & Manufacturing Co. (3M) introduces an average of 10 new products every week and generates 30 percent of its annual revenues from products developed within the previous four years.[59] The company achieves these impressive goals by finding creative people and putting them in an environment that encourages innovation. In other words, 3M executives have learned that creativity is a function of both the person and the situation.

Some people are inherently more creative than others. Research indicates that creative people have strong artistic and intellectual values, tolerance of ambiguity, need for achievement, and self-confidence. They have an ability to disregard past experience and, instead, to look at problems in many different ways. People can be creative throughout their lives, although the highest level of creativity tends to occur between the ages of 30 and 40.[60]

People also tend to be more creative when they are new to a particular work environment. Industry veterans rely on entrenched mental models to frame their expectations of the future. Yet, as we learned earlier in this chapter and in Chapter 6, these mental models tend to prevent people from perceiving alternative and potentially better perspectives. In contrast, newcomers have no mental models in that environment, so they question activities that industry veterans take for granted. This is why Sony brought in people from outside the music industry to start up its highly successful Sony Music record company. "We didn't want people from the record business," explains a Sony executive. "They would just bring their old ways with them. We wanted people who would have to figure things out all over again, who would question everything, people who 'didn't know any better.'"[61]

Creative work environments   In addition to hiring creative people, organizations need to provide jobs and work environments that foster creativity.[62] Creativity flourishes when employees are given freedom deciding how to accomplish tasks and solve problems. This means that they should have sufficient autonomy for empowerment. You can see this at Rueff, the Austrian fabric printer, where the head designer wears slinky black leather and spends most of his time playing nocturnes on a grand piano. Similarly, employees at Nintendo have free rein of their time to achieve their creative goals. "We have kept quiet even when [designers] go to see a movie or play during work," explains Hiroshi Yamauchi, president of the Japanese game maker.[63]

Although employees should have freedom in the work process, some writers argue that creative productivity is higher when people engage in self-set creativity goals, feedback, and other elements of self-leadership (see Chapter 4).[64] This worked for Thomas Edison. By setting goals of one minor invention every 10 days and a major invention every six months, the inventor produced over 1,000 patents in his lifetime. Notice that self-set goals are not the same as having executives establish tight deadlines, time pressures, and performance bonuses. External pressures tend to stifle creativity because employees focus on known rather than divergent solutions to their work.

"There, there! Two, maybe three floors down. Someone has an **idea!**"

[Drawing by Leo Cullum; ©1996, The New Yorker Magazine, Inc. Used with permission.]

Supportive leadership is another critical feature for creativity and innovation. Supervisors, team leaders, and others should encourage risk taking by ensuring that employees aren't punished for behaving or thinking differently. They should reinforce the notion that errors are part of the learning process (see Chapter 2). "Our beliefs are embedded in our philosophy: failure is not fatal," explains 3M CEO Livio D. DeSimone. "Innovations are simply chance breakthroughs. And when you take a chance, there is always the possibility of a failure."[65]

Cross-pollination of ideas is another key ingredient for creativity.[66] One strategy is to have employees work on divergent projects, rather than focus their career in one product or service area. IDEO, a highly successful industrial design firm, encourages employees to consider how features of one product they've worked on might be relevant to another. For instance, while designing a quieter fan for a computer system, designers might recall how they designed a quieter vacuum cleaner a few months earlier.[67]

Cross-pollination also occurs when people with diverse skills and knowledge throughout the organization interact and share information with each other.[68] At Xerox PARC, anthropologists work with computer scientists to understand the dynamics of virtual communities. Walt Disney Corp. encourages employees to engage in "displayed thinking" by leaving their work out in the open for others to view and comment. Colleagues are encouraged to leave anonymous Post-it notes with suggestions and feedback. 3M holds corporatewide trade shows where employees learn about projects in other areas of the organization. 3M also holds Technical Forums in each geographic area to "encourage free and active interchange of information and the cross-fertilization of ideas." Du Pont, the chemical company, also does this through more than 200 active networks of researchers throughout the organization. Some networks meet regularly, whereas others share ideas and information through the intranet.[69]

Creativity Training

Some people are naturally more creative than others, but creativity can also be learned to some extent.[70] Creativity training programs help participants in three ways. First, many creativity training programs begin by making people aware that existing mental models stifle their creativity. They learn that a seemingly illogical idea may be a very good solution to a problem, but it doesn't fit our mental model. This awareness encourages participants to question their logic and open their minds to divergent thinking.

Second, creativity training programs encourage participants to spend more time understanding the problem or opportunity and, in particular, redefining it in unique ways. Just as Albert Einstein would spend most of his time trying to understand the problem, current research emphasizes problem finding in the creative process.[71] In one creativity exercise, participants read a case, identify the main problem, and then compare their problem definition with those of others in the class. They discover that the same incident can be viewed in several ways.[72]

Divergent thinking strategies A third function of creativity training is to teach people various divergent thinking strategies. Some programs teach employees how to incubate problems by playing with toys, shooting pool, or engaging in other distractions. Similarly, some firms send employees to special sessions where they perform free-thinking tasks quite different from their familiar work. For example, FöreningsSparbanken, a leading Swedish bank, used an actor to help a group of employees think of innovative applications of an automated teller machine. When the group proposed equipping the machine with more features, the actor impersonated the automated teller machine and acted out the proposed changes.[73]

A more structured divergent thinking activity is called morphological analysis. Morphology involves listing different dimensions of a system and the elements of each dimension, then looking at each combination. This encourages people to carefully examine combinations that initially seem nonsensical. Tyson Foods, the world's largest poultry producer, recently applied this activity to identify new ways to serve chicken for lunch. The marketing and research team assigned to this task focused on three categories: occasion, packaging,

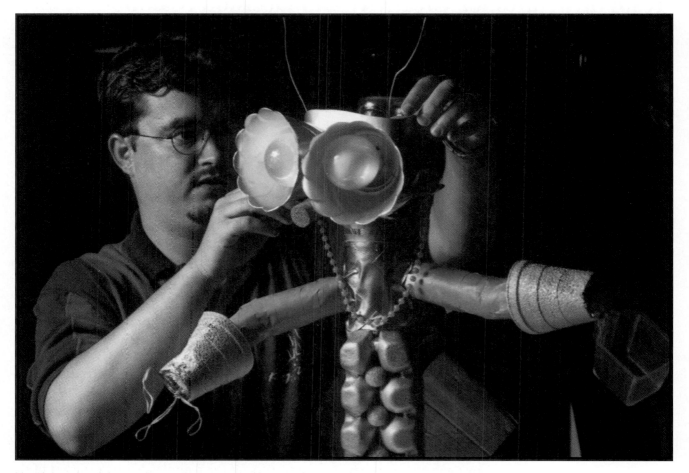

Lion Apparel took its employees to an art school where they transformed wire mesh into alligators and empty paper towel rolls into robots. The Dayton, Ohio, designer and manufacturer of firefighter clothing hopes that the creative expression developed in these art sessions will give staff members more divergent thinking back on the job. "This was a way to help them learn to think 'outside the box,'" explains Lion Apparel manager, Leise Ling. "To solve the kinds of problems they encounter every hour, they have to be able to think creatively."[74] Explain how attending an art class might improve creativity. Are there situations or conditions in which this strategy wouldn't be very effective?

[Ty Greenlees, Dayton Daily News. *Used with permission.]*

and taste. Next, the team worked through numerous combinations of items in the three categories. This created unusual ideas, such as cheese chicken pasta (taste) in pizza boxes (packaging) for concessions at baseball games (occasion). Later, the team looked more closely at the feasibility of some combinations and sent them to customer focus groups for further testing.[75]

A third divergent thinking strategy is to use metaphors to compare the situation with something else so that it is seen in a different light.[76] A telephone company used this approach to find ways to reduce damage to its pay telephones. Participants were asked to think of a telephone booth as some other object that protects—such as a bank vault or medicine capsule. Then they looked at features of these other objects that might protect telephone booths. Notice that this is similar to the incubation stage of creativity, in which decision makers put the problem in the back of their heads while focusing on a divergent object or event.

Aside from training programs, companies have experimented with different team structures to improve creativity as well as the general decision making process. The next section introduces the most popular team structures.

Team Structures for Creativity and Decision Making

Traditionally, team members meet face-to-face to suggest solutions and debate alternatives. Discussion is usually unstructured, ideas are generated and evaluated simultaneously, and there is a tendency to search for solutions before the problem is clearly understood. Consequently, traditional team structures are often marred by evaluation apprehension, production blocking, groupthink, and other problems described earlier. To minimize these problems, five alternative techniques have been proposed: constructive controversy, brainstorming, electronic brainstorming, Delphi technique, and nominal group technique.

Constructive Controversy

constructive controversy
any situation in which team members debate their different opinions regarding a problem or issue in a way that minimizes socioemotional conflict

Constructive controversy occurs when team members debate their different perceptions about an issue in a way that minimizes socioemotional conflict. Through dialogue, participants learn about other points of view, which encourages them to reexamine their basic assumptions about a problem and its possible solution. Constructive controversy is *constructive* because the discussion focuses on facts rather than people and avoids statements that threaten the esteem and well-being of other team members.[77]

How do we generate constructive controversy? First, decision-making groups should be heterogeneous.[78] As we learned in previous chapters, heterogeneous teams are better able to perceive issues and potential solutions from different perspectives. "Every time I have put together a diverse group of people, that team has always come up with a more breakthrough solution than any homogeneous group working on the same problem," says Arnold Donald, senior vice president at chemical giant Monsanto.[79]

Second, these heterogeneous team members need to meet often enough to allow meaningful discussion over contentious issues. The team's diversity won't generate constructive controversy if the team leader makes most of the decisions alone. Only through dialogue can team members better understand different perspectives, generate more creative ideas, and improve decision quality.

Third, effective teams generate constructive controversy when individual members take on different discussion roles. Some participants are action oriented, others are moderates who insist on reviewing details, one or two might be stabilizers who minimize dysfunctional conflict in the group, and so on. Some people should be **devil's advocates**—team members who challenge others to explain the logic of their preferences and who identify problems with that logic. Some scholars recommend a formal process whereby half of the group takes on the devil's advocate role during discussion.[80] However, some individuals naturally tend to fill this role without any special arrangement. Randy Powell, described in Connections 11.2, is certainly an example of this. Powell diplomatically disagreed with the CEO of Campbell Soup's Canadian operations and was respected for his different perspective of the issues.

Lastly, constructive controversy is more likely to occur when the decision is viewed from several angles. Team members should consider the effectiveness of the preferred choice under different scenarios, rather than just one or two.[81] Before buying another company, for instance, an executive team should consider the wisdom of this decision if the economy stumbles, the government changes, a supply shortage occurs, and so on. Taking different angles also means comparing the preferred alternative against many choices, not just one or two limited options. To identify these varied alternatives, effective teams engage in some form of brainstorming.

Brainstorming

In the 1950s advertising executive Alex Osborn wanted to find a better way for teams to generate creative ideas.[82] Osborn's solution, called **brainstorming,** requires team members to abide by four rules that encourage divergent thinking and minimize evaluation apprehension:

1. *No criticism*—The most important rule in brainstorming is that no one should criticize any ideas that are presented. Without criticism, team members might be more willing to suggest crazy solutions to the problem, which results in a larger number and potentially better ideas.
2. *Encourage freewheeling*—Wild and strange ideas are welcomed because these become the seeds of divergent thinking in the creative process. Crazy suggestions are sometimes crazy only because they break out of the mold set by existing mental models.
3. *Piggyback ideas*—Team members are encouraged to combine and improve on the ideas already presented because this strengthens the synergy of team processes (see Chapter 10).
4. *Encourage many ideas*—Brainstorming is based on the idea that quality increases with the number of ideas presented. This relates to the notion that divergent thinking occurs after traditional ideas have been exhausted. Therefore, the group should think of as many possible solutions as possible and go well beyond the traditional solutions to a problem.

Brainstorming is widely used at industrial design firm IDEO, where employees are explicitly reminded to follow the rules of freewheeling, piggybacking, and no criticizing. The session is always held face-to-face and is guided by a facilitator. Brainstorming has also helped project teams at pharmaceuticals firm SmithKline Beecham to think of innovative alternatives to existing action plans.[83] In spite of its popularity, however, brainstorming has several limitations. One problem is that brainstorming rules do not completely remove evaluation apprehension because employees still know that others are silently evaluating the quality of their ideas. Production blocking and related time constraints prevent all ideas from being presented. In fact, individuals working alone usually produce more potential solutions to a problem than if they work together using the brainstorming method.

On a more positive note, brainstorming rules seem to minimize negative conflict among members and improve the team's focus on the required task.

devil's advocates people who challenge others to explain the logic of their preferences and who identify problems with that logic

brainstorming a structured team decision-making process whereby team members directly interact to generate as many alternative solutions to the problem as possible, piggyback on the ideas of others, and avoid evaluating anyone's ideas during the idea-generation stage

Brainstorming participants also interact and participate directly, thereby increasing decision acceptance and team cohesiveness. Although evaluation apprehension is still a concern, mature groups may overcome this problem and

Connections 11.2   ◻ **Mavericks Like Randy Powell Create Constructive Controversy**

Randy Powell demonstrated a penchant for constructive controversy early in his career. *[Chris Wahl. Used with permission.]*

Randy Powell doesn't like to follow the crowd. Instead, the former Campbell Soup marketer (now president of coffee retailer Second Cup Limited) believes that differences of opinion should be heard and appreciated.

"Groupthink can happen," warns Powell. "What the senior person says tends to rule. I have always believed I should speak for what I believe to be true."

Powell demonstrated his penchant for constructive controversy early in his career—just one month after being hired as a brand manager at the Canadian operations of Campbell Soup Ltd. in Toronto. He had been assigned to Prego spaghetti sauce products and, during the brand review, Campbell's CEO concluded that Prego was losing out to price-cutting competitors. Powell mustered his courage and said that he disagreed with the veteran marketer. He explained that Prego's line needed more variety and a larger advertising budget. The CEO accepted Powell's reasoning.

Later, Powell's supervisor approached him and confided, "I wanted to say that, but I just didn't have the courage to step in front of [the CEO]." By the end of the day, more than a dozen colleagues congratulated Powell for speaking up.

Some time later, Campbell's CEO sent Powell and 40 other executives to a week-long New Age management session. Powell soon concluded that the consultants were off-base with their "planning back from the future" stuff. Between sessions, most of the other Campbell's executives confided that they felt the same way. The consultants heard about the dissent on the fourth day and dramatically asked participants whether they were in or out. Those who said "out" had to leave immediately.

As the consultants went around the room, every executive who privately grumbled about the session said "in." Powell was third from last. "I believed it could be political suicide to go against [the CEO] on an issue he believed to be true," Powell recalls. Every one before him had agreed to stay in. Still, when it was his turn, Powell said "out" and left the room.

The next day, the CEO called Powell into his office and told him that he respected his decision, even if he disagreed. Two months later, at 31 years of age, Powell was promoted to vice president of sales.

Source: Adapted from S. Silcoff, "The Sky's Your Limit," *Canadian Business,* April 1997, pp. 58–66. ◼

leverage the subtle benefits of face-to-face communication. For example, there is some evidence that effective brainstorming sessions create emotional contagion (see Chapter 8). Specifically, team members share feelings of optimism and excitement that may encourage a more creative climate. Clients are often involved in brainstorming sessions, so this emotional contagion may produce higher customer satisfaction than if people are working alone on the product.[84]

Electronic Brainstorming

electronic brainstorming a structured team decision-making process whereby several people individually generate ideas or make decisions through computer software that posts each participant's ideas or opinions anonymously

Chrysler, Boeing, and many other firms have worked in meeting rooms specially designed for small groups to participate in **electronic brainstorming.** With the aid of groupware (special computer software for groups), electronic brainstorming lets participants share ideas while minimizing the team dynamics problems inherent in traditional brainstorming sessions.[85] Individuals can enter ideas at any time on their computer terminal. These ideas are posted anonymously and randomly on the screens of all participants. A central convener monitors the entire input to ensure that participants stay focused on the issue. Electronic brainstorming sessions typically take place in a room with up to a few dozen computer terminals. However, participants could be located in different places and attend the "meeting" at different times if the technology is available.

Effectiveness of electronic brainstorming

The greatest benefit of electronic brainstorming is that it significantly reduces the problem of production blocking. Participants are able to document their ideas whenever they occur, rather than wait their turn to communicate.[86] This process also supports creative synergy because participants can easily develop new ideas from those generated by other people. Electronic brainstorming also minimizes the problem of evaluation apprehension because ideas are posted anonymously. "If we had to attach our names to our suggestions, I think people would be less forthcoming," insists an engineer at aircraft manufacturer Boeing Co.[87]

Electronic brainstorming is far more efficient than traditional team decision making because there is little socializing. A study of 64 electronic brainstorming groups at Boeing Co. found that total meeting time was reduced by 71 percent.[88] "You get to consider and evaluate more information in literally one-fourth of the time," says Joe O'Connor, president of Affina, a market research group based in Troy, Michigan. "You can use a two-hour session to cover more areas, or you can get a whole lot more done in less time."[89] Research confirms that electronic brainstorming generates more ideas than traditional brainstorming and participants seem to be more satisfied, motivated, and confident in the decision-making exercise than in other team structures.[90]

Despite these advantages, electronic brainstorming is perhaps too structured and technology bound for most people. Some critics have noted that the additional number of ideas generated through electronic brainstorming is not enough to justify its cost. Another concern is that organizational participants are generally less enthusiastic about electronic brainstorming sessions than students who participate in research samples.[91] It would seem odd, for example, to advise clients that they conduct an electronic brainstorm session rather than talk to each other. This reflects the problem that electronic brainstorming removes face-to-face conversation and the hidden benefits (such as emotional contagion and social bonding) that may exist through that communication medium. Lastly, we must consider the political dynamics of electronic brainstorming. Some people may feel threatened by the honesty of candid statements and by their inability to control the discussion.

Joe O'Connor attends plenty of meetings. But the president of Affina, a market research company in Troy, Michigan, can't recall any as efficient as his electronic brainstorming session at the Ameritech Center for Business Solutions. "You get to consider and evaluate more information in literally one-fourth of the time," says O'Connor. Electronic brainstorming also provides a better forum for open dialogue. "The electronic environment really nudges business cultures, which traditionally work top-down," says Rebecca Kraus (shown), director of the Ameritech Center. "When in the center, everyone has an equal voice."[93] Under what conditions is electronic brainstorming most effective? *[Courtesy of the Ameritech Center for Business Solutions, Walsh College.]*

Delphi technique a structured team decision-making process of systematically pooling the collective knowledge of experts on a particular subject to make decisions, predict the future, or identify opposing views

nominal group technique a structured team decision-making process whereby members independently write down ideas, describe and clarify them to the group, and then independently rank or vote on them

Delphi Technique

The **Delphi technique** systematically pools the collective knowledge of experts on a particular subject to make decisions, predict the future, or identify opposing views (called *dissensus*).[92] Delphi groups do not meet face-to-face; participants are often located in different parts of the world and may not know each other's identity. Moreover, like electronic brainstorming, participants do not know who "owns" the ideas submitted. Typically, Delphi group members submit possible solutions or comments regarding an issue to the central convener. The compiled results are returned to the panel for a second round of comments. This process may be repeated a few more times until consensus or dissensus emerges. Delphi technique recently helped a British electricity supply company understand how to respond to customers who don't pay their bills. It was also used by rehabilitation counselors to reach consensus on rehabilitation credentialing.[94]

Nominal Group Technique

Nominal group technique is a variation of traditional brainstorming and Delphi technique that tries to combine individual efficiencies with team dynamics.[95] The method is called *nominal* because participants form a group "in name only" during two stages of decision making. This process, shown in Exhibit 11.6, first involves the individual, then the group, and finally the individual again.

After the problem is described, team members silently and independently write down as many solutions as they can. During the group stage, participants describe their solutions to the other team members, usually in a round-robin format. As with brainstorming, there is no criticism or debate, although members are encouraged to ask for clarification of the ideas presented. In the final stage, participants silently and independently rank-order or vote on each proposed solution. Rank ordering is preferred because this forces each person to carefully review all of the alternatives presented.[96] Nominal group technique prefers voting or ranking over reaching consensus to avoid dysfunctional conflict that comes with debate.

Exhibit 11.6
Nominal group technique
process

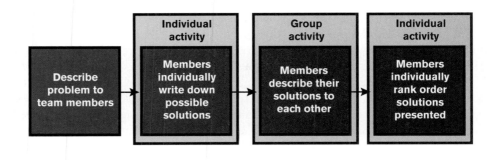

Nominal group technique tends to produce more and better quality ideas than traditional interacting groups.[97] Due to its high degree of structure, nominal group technique usually maintains a high task orientation and relatively low potential for conflict within the team. However, team cohesiveness is generally lower in nominal group decision making because the structure minimizes social interaction. Production blocking and evaluation apprehension still occur to some extent.

Throughout this chapter, we have learned various ways to overcome the problems with making decisions, either alone or in teams. Most of these problems revolve around perceptual challenges that human beings face, or team dynamics that interfere with open dialogue and objective problem solving. However, decisions are also political events because implementing decisions requires change and potential risk. In the next chapter, we look at the dynamics of power and politics in organizational settings.

Chapter Summary

Decision making is a conscious process of making choices among one or more alternatives with the intention of moving toward some desired state of affairs. This involves identifying problems and opportunities, choosing the best decision style, developing alternative solutions, choosing the best solution, implementing the selected alternative, and evaluating decision outcomes.

People have trouble identifying problems due to perceptual biases and poor diagnostic skills. These challenges are minimized by being aware of these human limitations, discussing the situation with colleagues, creating early warning systems, and using data mining to systematically identify trends.

Decision makers have difficulty choosing the best solution because organizational goals are ambiguous or in conflict, they do not process information fully or objectively, and they tend to satisfice rather than maximize. Solutions can be chosen more effectively by carefully identifying and weighting the factors used to evaluate alternatives, using decision-support systems to guide the decision process, and using intuition where we possess enough tacit knowledge on the issue.

Postdecisional justification and escalation of commitment make it difficult for people to evaluate the outcomes of their decisions. Escalation is mainly caused by self-justification, the gambler's fallacy, perceptual blinders, and closing costs. These concerns are minimized by separating decision choosers from decision evaluators, establishing a preset level at which the decision is abandoned or reevaluated, and relying on more systematic and clear feedback about the project's success.

Team decisions are impeded by time constraints, evaluation apprehension, conformity to peer pressure, groupthink, and group polarization. These problems can be minimized by ensuring that the team leader does not dominate, maintaining an optimal team size, ensuring that team norms support critical thinking, and introducing team structures that support more creative decision making.

Creativity refers to developing an original product, service, or idea that makes a socially recognized contribution. The four creativity stages are preparation, incubation, insight, and verification. Organizations improve creativity by selecting creative people, establishing a creative environment, and providing creativity training.

Creativity training programs make people aware of limited mental models, the importance of spending time thinking about the problem, and specific strategies for divergent thinking about a problem or issue.

Five team structures that potentially improve creativity and team decision making are constructive controversy, brainstorming, electronic brainstorming, Delphi technique, and nominal group technique. Constructive controversy occurs when people debate their different perceptions about an issue in a constructive manner.

Brainstorming requires team members to avoid criticizing, encourage freewheeling, and piggyback ideas. Electronic brainstorming uses computer software to share ideas while minimizing the problems of team dynamics. Delphi technique systematically pools the collective knowledge of experts on a particular subject without face-to-face meetings. In nominal group technique, participants write down ideas alone, describe these ideas in a group, then silently vote on these ideas.

Key Terms

Brainstorming, p. 355
Constructive controversy, p. 354
Creativity, p. 350
Decision making, p. 336
Delphi technique, p. 358
Devil's advocates, p. 355
Divergent thinking, p. 350
Electronic brainstorming, p. 357
Escalation of commitment, p. 343
Evaluation apprehension, p. 347
Group polarization, p. 348

Groupthink, p. 347
Intuition, p. 343
Mental models, p. 338
Nominal group technique, p. 358
Nonprogrammed decision, p. 337
Postdecisional justification, p. 343
Production blocking, p. 346
Programmed decision, p. 337
Satisficing, p. 342
Selective attention, p. 342
Tacit knowledge, p. 343

Discussion Questions

1. A school district is experiencing very high levels of teacher absenteeism. Describe three reasons why school district administrators might not realize that a problem exists or why they are unable to identify the root cause(s) of the high absenteeism.

2. A management consultant is hired by a manufacturing firm to determine the best site for its next production facility. The consultant has had several meetings with the company's senior executives regarding the factors to consider when making its recommendation. Discuss three decision-making problems that might prevent the consultant from choosing the best site location.

3. A developer received financial backing for a new financial center along a derelict section of the waterfront, a few miles from the current downtown of a large city. The idea was to build several high-rise structures, attract many tenants to those sites, and have the city extend transportation systems to the new center. Over the next decade, the developer believed that others would build in the area, thereby attracting the regional or national offices of many financial institutions. Interest from potential tenants

was much lower than initially predicted and the city did not build transportation systems as quickly as expected. Still, the builder proceeded with the original plans. Only after financial support was curtailed did the developer reconsider the project. Using your knowledge of escalation of commitment, discuss three possible reasons why the developer was motivated to continue with the project.

4. Production blocking is often identified as a problem in team decision making. Describe production blocking and identify a team structure that minimizes this problem.

5. Ancient Book Company has a problem with new book projects. Even when it is apparent to others that a book is far behind schedule and may not have much public interest, sponsoring editors are reluctant to terminate contracts with authors whom they have signed. The result is that many editors invest more time with these projects rather than on more fruitful projects. As a form of escalation of commitment, describe two methods that Ancient Book Company can use to minimize this problem.

6. The Chinese word for business is *sheng-yi,* which means "to give birth to ideas." Explain how creativity is an inherent part of business decision making.

7. A senior executive committee wants to make better decisions by practicing constructive controversy. Identify four things that the group must do to increase constructive controversy.

8. Wichita Garment Corp. wants to use brainstorming with its employees and customers to identify new uses for its products. Advise Wichita Garment's president about the rules to follow for this session.

CASE STUDY

Eastern Province Light and Power

I work as a systems and procedures analyst for the Eastern Province Light and Power Company. The systems and procedures department analyzes corporate policies, procedures, forms, equipment, and methods to simplify and standardize operations. We apply "organized common sense" to develop new practices and to improve old ones.

Requests for analysis of organizational problems are submitted to the systems and procedures department by persons of department head or higher status. Our manager places projects in line for consideration and assigns them to an analyst on the basis of availability; projects are accepted and assigned on the FIFO (first in–first out) method. Projects must undergo analysis, design, and implementation before a change in procedure is realized. What follows is a description of a problem assigned to me. I am investigating it right now.

The Problem

For some time, management had been concerned with the inventory carrying charges that accrue when material is stored in company warehouses. Not only is there a cost attached to carrying inventory for future use, but there are additional related costs such as labor to handle the inventory, warehouse usage in terms of square feet taken up in storage, and clerical time used to account for materials flowing into and out of inventory. One type of material stored is office supplies—pens, writing pads, forms, stationery, envelopes, and dozens of similar items. A desire to reduce the costs of storing these items prompted the head of the department of purchasing and material control to submit a request for a study by systems and procedures.

The request came in the required written form. It described the current procedures, estimated their costs, and invited us to explore ways of changing the procedures to reduce costs. In brief, at the time the study request was submitted, purchases of office supplies were

made through 11 vendors. The items were stored in a common warehouse area and disbursed to using departments as requested. As is customary, I convened a meeting of the requesting manager and others who seemed most directly involved in the problem.

The First Meeting

I opened the meeting by summarizing the present procedures for purchasing and storing office supplies and the estimated costs associated with these problems. I explained that we were meeting to explore ways of reducing these costs. I suggested we might try to generate as many ideas as we could without being too critical of them, and then proceed to narrow the list by criticizing and eliminating the ideas with obvious weaknesses.

Just as soon as I finished my opening remarks, the head of purchasing and material control said that we should conduct a pilot study in which we would contract with one of the regular vendors to supply each involved department directly, eliminating company storage of any inventory. The vendor would continue to sell us whatever we usually purchased from it, but would sell and deliver the items to various departments instead of to our central purchasing group. A pilot study with one vendor would indicate how such a system would work with all vendors of office supplies. If it worked well, we could handle all office supplies this way.

The head of purchasing and material control went on to explain that she had already spoken to the vice president to whom she (and, through intermediate levels, the rest of us) reported and that he recognized the potential savings that would result. She also said that she had gone over the idea with the supervisor of stores (who reported to her) and that he agreed. She wanted to know how long it would take me to carry out the pilot study. I looked at a few faces to see if anybody would say anything, but nobody did. I said I didn't know. She said, "Let's meet in a week when you've come up with a proposal." The meeting ended without anything else of real substance being said.

I felt completely frustrated. She was the highest-ranking person in the meeting. She had said what she wanted and, as if her stature wasn't enough, she had invoked the image of the vice president being in agreement with her. Nobody, including me, had said anything. No idea other than hers was even mentioned, and no comments were made about it.

I decided that I would work as hard as I could to study the problem and her proposed pilot study before the next meeting and come prepared to give the whole thing a critical review.

Between Meetings

I talked to my boss about my feeling that it seemed as though I was expected to rubber-stamp the pilot study idea. I said that I wished he would come to the next meeting. I also said that I wanted to talk to some people close to the problem, some clerks in stores, some vendors, and some buyers in purchasing to see if I could come up with any good ideas or find any problems in the pilot study area. He told me to learn all I could and that he would come to the next meeting.

My experience with other studies had taught me that sometimes the people closest to the work had expertise to contribute, so I found one stores clerk, two buyers, and two vendor sales representatives to talk to. Nobody had spoken to any of them about the pilot study and the general plan it was meant to test. This surprised me a little. Each one of these people had some interesting things to say about the proposed new way of handling office supplies. A buyer, for example, thought it would be chaotic to have 17 different departments ordering the same items. She thought we might also lose out on some quantity discounts, and it would mean 17 times the paperwork. A vendor said he didn't think any vendor would like the idea because it would increase the number of contacts necessary to sell the amount that could be sold now through one contact—the buyer in the purchasing department. A stores clerk said it might be risky to depend on a vendor to maintain inventories at adequate levels. He said, "What if a vendor failed to supply us with, say, enough mark-sensing tools for our meter readers one month, thereby causing them to be unable to complete their task and our company to be unable to get its monthly billings out on time?"

The Second Meeting

Armed with careful notes, I came to the next meeting prepared to discuss these and other criticisms. One of the stores clerks had even agreed to attend so that I could call on him for comments. But when I looked around the conference room, everyone was there except the stores clerk. The head of purchasing and material control said she had talked to the clerk and could convey any of his ideas so she had told him it wasn't necessary for him to come.

I pointed out that the stores clerk had raised a question about the company's ability to control inventory. He had said that we now have physical control of inventory, but the proposal involved making ourselves dependent on the vendor's maintaining adequate inventory. The head of purchasing and material control said, "Not to worry. It will be in the vendor's own interest to keep us well supplied." No one, including my boss, said anything.

I brought up the subject of selecting a vendor to participate in the pilot study. My boss mentioned that I had told him some vendors might object to the scheme because the additional contacts would increase their costs of sales. The head of purchasing and material control said, "Any vendor would be interested in doing business with a company as big as Eastern Province Light and Power." No further comments were made.

I mentioned that it was the practice of the systems and procedures staff to estimate independently the costs and benefits of any project before undertaking it, and also to have the internal auditing department review the proposal. I said we would need to go ahead with those steps. I asked the head of purchasing and material control to give me the name of somebody in her area I should contact to get the costs of the present system. She said that it really didn't seem necessary to go through all the usual steps in this case since she had already submitted an estimate. Besides, it was only going to be a pilot study. She said, "I think we can all agree on that and just move ahead now with the designation of a vendor." She looked around the table and nobody said anything. She said, "Fine. Let's use Moore Business Forms." Nobody said anything. She then said to me, "OK, let's get back together after you've lined things up."

Discussion Questions

1. Did this group at Eastern Province Light and Power make its decision effectively? Why or why not?

2. Identify any decision-making problems that seem to exist in this case.

3. What team structure would you recommend to make this type of decision in the future?

D. R. Hampton, *Contemporary Management* (New York: McGraw-Hill, 1981). Used with permission. ■

CASE STUDY

Flight simulators for management

BusinessWeek

William M. Connell, a group vice president at Macy's, is amused and oddly pleased. He is watching a computer screen showing awkward blocklike figures roaming about a crude layout of a department store. Developed by PricewaterhouseCoopers, this virtual world tries to simulate how real shoppers actually operate in a store. The consulting firm wants to perfect this simulation so that Macy's executives and other clients can safely test hunches, run scenarios, and preview the impact of big and small decisions without major investments or public embarrassments. Macy's, for example, is hoping the computer model will help it figure out such things as where to place cash registers and service desks to improve sales.

These flight simulators for management require more work before they represent a real department store, but Connell sees enormous potential for decision making as these models improve. "You can run a day in minutes and a month in hours," says Connell. "And if you make a wrong decision in the model, you're only dealing with a synthetic public, not the real world." This *Business Week* case study describes how consultants at Pricewater-houseCoopers are helping executives make better de-

cisions through visual complexity-based computer models. Read through this *Business Week* article at www.mhhe.com/mcshane1e and prepare for the discussion questions below.

Discussion Questions

1. Explain how these virtual reality models might help decision makers reduce some of the challenges of identifying problems and choosing alternatives.

2. This case study describes how these models might predict the behavior of shoppers, moviegoers, and competitors in the telecommunications industry. How might these models help college administrators make better decisions?

3. This case study provides an interesting description of the PricewaterhouseCoopers team that is developing these models. Looking at the team dynamics concepts in Chapter 9, discuss some of the factors that make this team cohesive.

Source: J. A. Byrne, "Flight Simulators for Management," *Business Week*, September 21, 1998, p. 80. ■

VIDEO CASE

Second City/Heavenly Ski Resort

 At the Second City Theater in Chicago where the audience expects cutting edge innovative entertainment night after night, show after show, producers and stage managers have to constantly explore questions like: "How do we find and groom the best talent?" "What technical and financial resources do we need to commit to our traveling touring companies?" and "How do we meet the needs of our corporate clients without compromising artistic integrity?"

At Heavenly Ski Resort in Lake Tahoe, Nevada, guests expect a different kind of entertainment experience. Spectacular views and well groomed slopes aren't always enough to guarantee market share in this highly

competitive industry. Managers at Heavenly have worked hard to create a world class ski resort with top notch services that are safe for the skiers and easy on the environment. They have sought answers to some questions like: "What are some ways we can increase our national exposure?" "What can we do to attract clientele year round?" and "How can we motivate seasonal employees?"

In a global economy, sound business decisions require consideration of a number of important factors that may potentially affect the company's ability to meet its goals. The quality of managerial decisions can determine a company's success or failure. A recent study concluded that managers spend approximately 50 percent of their time dealing with the consequences of bad decision making.

It's important to understand decision making as it occurs in the business world. Broadly defined, decision making is the process of choosing among alternative plans of action. In the business world this process takes place under varying conditions of certainty and risk. Decision making is more likely to be affected when approached in a series of steps that explore and evaluate alternatives. In general, the decision-making process consists of six steps:

Steps in the Decision-Making Process

1. Identify the problem
2. Generate alternative courses of action
3. Evaluate the alternatives
4. Select the best alternative
5. Implement the decision
6. Evaluate the decision

In order to evaluate a decision, managers must gather information that can shed light on its effectiveness. Although managers would prefer to follow all of these decision-making steps, time and circumstances don't always allow it. The decision-making process can also be influenced by other important factors such as intuition, emotion and stress, confidence, and risk propensity.

Although Second City and Heavenly Ski Resort are very different businesses, they are both examples of companies that have made successful decisions under conditions of risk and uncertainty. The Second City Theater has grown from its roots as a small mom-and-pop theater to a large internationally known corporate enterprise. Rather than investing all its resources into its immensely popular Old Chicago Improv Theater, Second City has decided to translate its expertise into other ventures such as television, corporate training, and other theaters in Toronto, suburban Chicago, and Detroit.

Joe Keefe, producer of Second City Communications, reflected on decision making at his firm. He said, "So much of what we do is having people approach decision-making processes from a group point of view and allowing for input. However, it's difficult many times to find the time to listen to everyone. I literally try to book time weekly where we meet with people. I meet with the directors after every project to find out what the heck happened, what did they think, how did they feel, how did the client feel? By the time you have all the information, the decision is usually self-evident. It's a matter of making certain that you get accurate information immediately, that your client response issues are done immediately, and then your intuition will tell you what's the right thing to do. About 99.99 percent of my decisions are self-evident once you have the right information."

Heavenly Ski Resort accommodates 750,000 skiers per year and competes as one of eight large Lake Tahoe area resorts, but also joins forces with them to increase the overall market. In order to remain at the forefront, marketing partnerships and investment in state-of-the-art facilities are key. Like the Second City Theater, managers at Heavenly must make decisions that affect the growth of the company in less than ideal conditions.

Malcolm Tibbets, vice president of mountain operations, reflected on decision making at his firm. "Quick decisions are going to happen every hour of the day. Looking at the business coming into the base areas, making a quick decision to open an additional lift that was not otherwise scheduled, or shutting down in order to save on cost as business is not going to warrant operation of that lift. Whether to start the snow plows at midnight or wait until 3:00 in the morning. Those kinds of things. It's constant. You have to have people in those positions who aren't afraid to make those decisions without calling six people and wasting time collecting other data. It's just part of the way business works."

Although following the six decision-making steps may lead to a sounder decision-making process, theory does not always play out in practice. Management may follow some steps but perhaps not all of them, depending on the factors affecting the decision-making process. Steve Jacobson, director of food and beverage at Heavenly said, "Most of the managers I encourage to make a decision right away and don't hold on to the problem. It's such a fast pace that I want them to just go on with the next thing, not hold back. I empower them to pretty much make their own decisions. They were hired to do the job so I let them do the job. If they do something wrong we discuss it later, but business must go on."

In their day-to-day operations, both companies experience the need to make decisions in varying conditions of certainty, uncertainty, and risk. Both companies follow the steps of the decision-making model when feasible: identifying the problem, generating alternatives, evaluating alternatives, selecting the best alternative, implementing the decision, and evaluating the decision. Factors such as intuition, emotion, and stress and confidence or risk propensity can also have an influence on the decision-making process. Awareness of the nature of decision making—its important steps and influential factors—may help managers minimize the time they spend responding to the consequences of poor decision making. This can enable managers to spend more time maximizing opportunities for growth.

Discussion Questions

1. Malcolm Tibbetts runs Heavenly Ski Resort's mountain operations. Some of the decisions he must make regard when to run snow plows, whether to open or

close lifts, and the like. Are his decisions programmed or nonprogrammed? Explain.

2. Joe Keefe of Second City mentioned that he likes to consult widely on decisions and that most of his decisions are "self-evident" by the time he makes them.

Do you think "self-evident" means that anyone who had the same information would make the same decision? Explain.

3. Who do you think makes decisions more creatively, Keefe or Tibbets? ■

TEAM EXERCISE 1

Hopping orange exercise

Purpose

To help students understand the dynamics of creativity and team problem solving.

Instructions

You will be placed in teams with an equal number of students. One student serves as the official timer for the team and must have a watch, preferably with stopwatch timer. The instructor will give each team an orange (or similar object) with a specific task involving use of the orange. (The objective is easily understood and non-threatening, and will be described by the instructor at the beginning of the exercise.) Each team will have a few opportunities to achieve the objective more efficiently. ■

TEAM EXERCISE 2

Creativity brainbusters exercise

Purpose

To help students understand the dynamics of creativity and team problem solving.

Instructions

This exercise may be completed alone or in teams of three or four people, although the latter is more fun. If teams are formed, students who already know the solutions to these problems should identify themselves and serve as silent observers. When finished (or time is up), the instructor will review the solutions and discuss the implications of this exercise. In particular, be prepared to discuss what you needed to solve these puzzles and what may have prevented you from solving them more quickly (or at all).

1. Roman Numeral Problem

Below is the Roman numeral 9. Add one single line to create a 6.

IX

2. Nine Dot Problem

Below are nine dots. Without lifting your pencil, draw no more than four straight lines that pass through all nine dots.

3. Nine Dot Problem Revisited

Referring to the nine dot exhibit above, describe how, without lifting your pencil, you could pass a pencil line through all dots with three (3) or fewer straight lines.

4. Word Search

In the following line of letters, cross out five letters so that the remaining letters, without altering their sequence, spell a familiar English word.

FCIRVEEALTETITVEERS

5. Burning Ropes

You have two pieces of rope of unequal lengths and a box of matches. In spite of their different lengths, each piece of rope takes one hour to burn; however, parts of each rope burn at unequal speeds. For example, the first half of one piece might burn in 10 minutes. Use these materials to accurately determine when 45 minutes has elapsed. ◼

SELF-ASSESSMENT EXERCISE

Decision-making style inventory

Purpose

This self-assessment is designed to help you estimate your preferred style of decision making.

Instructions

Listed below are statements describing how individuals go about making important decisions. Please indicate whether you agree or disagree with each statement. Answer each item as truthfully as possible so that you get an accurate estimate of where your active listening skills need improvement.

Please indicate the extent that you agree or disagree with the following statements about your decision-making style.	Strongly agree	Agree	Neutral	Disagree	Strongly disagree
1. I make decisions more on facts than my gut instincts.	5	4	3	2	1
2. I feel more comfortable making decisions in a logical and systematic way.	5	4	3	2	1
3. When making decisions, I rely upon my intuition more than anything else.	5	4	3	2	1
4. When I make a decision, it is more important for me to feel the decision is right than to have a rational reason for it.	5	4	3	2	1
5. I won't make a choice that doesn't feel right, even when the facts indicate it is the right choice.	5	4	3	2	1
6. My decision making tends to involve careful analysis of facts and weighting of decision criteria.	5	4	3	2	1
7. When I make a decision, I trust my inner feelings and reactions.	5	4	3	2	1
8. The best decisions I make are based on detailed analysis of factual information.	5	4	3	2	1

Scoring the decision-making style inventory

Write the scores for each item on the appropriate line below (statement numbers are in brackets), and add up each scale.

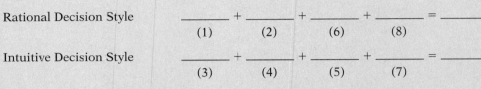

Rational Decision Style   _____ + _____ + _____ + _____ = _____
                                (1)   (2)   (6)   (8)

Intuitive Decision Style   _____ + _____ + _____ + _____ = _____
                                (3)   (4)   (5)   (7)

Sources: Inspired from ideas in C. W. Allinson and J. Hayes, J, "The Cognitive Style Index: A Measure of Intuition-Analysis for Organizational Research," *Journal of Management Studies* 33 (1996), pp. 119–35; S. G. Scott and R. A. Bruce, "Decision-Making Style: The Development and Assessment of a New Measure," *Educational & Psychological Measurement* 55 (October 1995), pp. 818–31. ■

CHAPTER TWELVE

Organizational Power and Politics

Learning Objectives

After reading this chapter, you should be able to:

- Define the meaning of power and counterpower.
- Describe the five bases of power in organizations.
- Explain how information relates to power in organizations.
- Discuss the four contingencies of power and their relationship to power bases.
- Relate the outcomes of power to the power bases applied.
- Discuss the role of power in sexual harassment.
- Summarize the advantages and disadvantages of organizational politics.
- List seven types of political activity found in organizations.
- Describe the conditions that encourage organizational politics.
- Identify ways to control dysfunctional organizational politics.

When he invited Steven Jobs *(right)* to be a special adviser at Apple Computer, Gil Amelio didn't anticipate the organizational politics that would have Jobs replacing him as Apple's CEO in just six months.

[Reuters/Lou Dematteis/Archive Photos]

Gil Amelio thought that purchasing NeXT Software, Inc., would be his masterstroke to save Apple Computer. Instead, it brought on a series of power plays that would have Steven Jobs—who founded both NeXT and Apple—replace Amelio as Apple's CEO within six months.

Steven Jobs started NeXT after he was ousted from Apple in the 1980s. NeXT never captured much of the hardware or software market, but it had a respectable operating system. By coincidence, Apple was looking for a new operating system, and Jobs convinced Amelio to buy NeXT for its system. Following the buyout, Amelio invited Jobs to serve as a special adviser, mainly to raise morale among Apple employees and customers.

But Jobs quickly became more than a cheerleader. He visited or phoned Amelio several times each week, advising on how to integrate NeXT people and products, cut costs, and redraw the organization chart. He convinced Amelio to put former NeXT people in the top positions. Within a few months, Jobs and his NeXT colleagues had the key positions for evaluating and weeding out teams of Apple employees. "NeXT is taking over from inside," said one Apple employee. "It's a Jobs-NeXT regime," said another.

Publicly, Jobs supported Amelio's leadership at Apple. "I'm giving Gil the best advice I know, and I'll keep doing so until he stops listening or tells me to go away," said Jobs soon after Apple acquired NeXT. However, Jobs and his NeXT colleagues privately ridiculed Amelio's lethargic decision making. Eventually, Jobs demonstrated his nonconfidence in Amelio more publicly by selling most of his 1.5 million Apple shares received from the NeXT purchase. This action got the attention of Apple's Board of Directors. The Board removed Amelio and invited Jobs to become Apple's "interim" CEO. Jobs then convinced Apple's current Board to resign and picked a new Board consisting of friends and allies.

Some writers believe that Amelio's days were numbered and that Jobs was the long-awaited savior for Apple. But in his biography on the experience, Gil Amelio portrayed Jobs as a conniving back-stabber "obsessed with power" who cunningly maneuvered him out of Apple. "I was . . . trapped in a web of plotting as intricate as the War of the Roses," he wrote.[1]

pple Computer isn't the only Silicon Valley firm where people engage in power and politics; in fact, every organization has some form and level of office politics. Scholars suggest that power and politics are ingrained in every decision and action.[2] Power is necessary to coordinate organizational activities, but it might also serve personal objectives that threaten the organization's survival. Moreover, organizations are rapidly changing the distribution of power. Hierarchies are being replaced by flatter structures with empowered employees.[3] Information that was once closely guarded by secretive department heads is now widely available to those who need it. These changes require a careful understanding of the dynamics of power and politics in organizations, which is the focus of this chapter.

We begin this chapter by defining power and presenting a basic model depicting the dynamics of power in organizational settings. We then discuss the five bases of power, as well as information as a power base. Next, we look at the contingencies necessary to translate those sources into meaningful power. Our discussion of power finishes with a look at how sexual harassment represents an abuse of power. The latter part of this chapter examines the dynamics of organizational politics, including the various types of political activity, the conditions that encourage organizational politics, and the ways that it can be controlled.

The Meaning of Power

power the capacity of a person, team, or organization to influence others

Power is the capacity of a person, team, or organization to influence others.[4] Power is not the act of changing others' attitudes or behavior; it is only the *potential* to do so. People frequently have power they do not use; they might not even know they have power.

The most basic prerequisite of power is that one party believes he or she is dependent on the other for something of value.[5] This relationship is shown in Exhibit 12.1, where Person A has power over Person B by controlling something that Person B needs to achieve his or her goals. You might have power over others by controlling a desired job assignment, useful information, important resources, or even the privilege of being associated with you! These dependency relationships are an inherent part of organizational life because work is divided into specialized tasks and the organization has limited resources with which to accomplish its goals. Also, power is ultimately a perception, so people might gain power simply by convincing others that they have something of value. Thus, power exists when others believe that you control resources that they want.[6]

Although power requires dependence, it is really more accurate to say that the parties are *interdependent*. One party may be more dependent than the

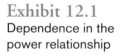

Exhibit 12.1
Dependence in the power relationship

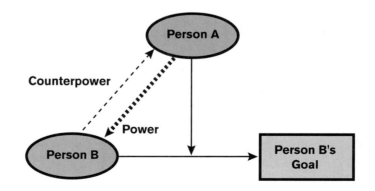

other, but the relationship exists only when both parties have something of value to the other. Exhibit 12.1 shows a dotted line to illustrate the weaker party's (Person B) power over the dominant participant (Person A). This **counterpower,** as it is known, is strong enough to maintain Person A's participation in the exchange relationship. For example, executives have power over subordinates by controlling their job security and promotional opportunities, but employees have counterpower by controlling the ability to work productively, thereby creating a positive impression of the supervisor to his or her boss. Counterpower usually motivates executives to apply their power judiciously so that the relationship is not broken.

counterpower the capacity of a person, team, or organization to keep a more powerful person or group in the exchange relationship

A Model of Power in Organizations

Power involves more than just dependence. As we see in Exhibit 12.2, the model of power includes both power sources and contingencies. It indicates that power is derived from five sources: legitimate, reward, coercive, expert, and referent. But tapping into one or more of these power bases only leads to increased power under certain conditions. These contingencies of power include the employee's or department's substitutability, centrality, discretion, and visibility. Finally, as we will discuss later, the type of power applied affects the type of influence the powerholder has over the other person or work unit.

Sources of Power in Organizations

Over 40 years ago, John French and Bertram Raven listed five sources of power within organizations: legitimate, reward, coercive, expert, and referent.[7] Many researchers have studied these five power bases and searched for others. For the most part, French and Raven's list remains intact.[8] The first three power bases are derived from the power holder's position; that is, the person receives these power bases because of the specific authority or roles he or she is assigned in the organization. The latter two sources of power originate from

Exhibit 12.2
A model of power within organizations

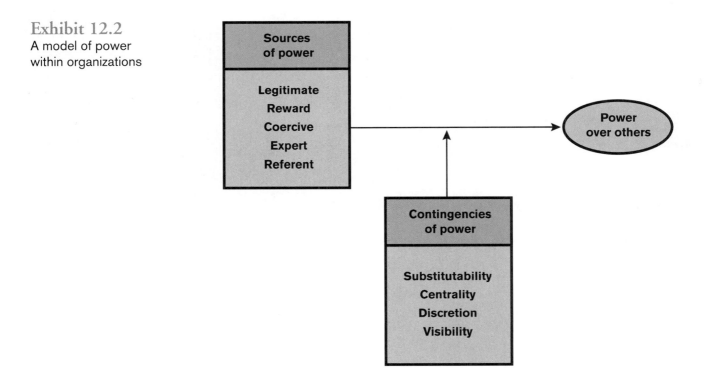

the power holder's own characteristics. In other words, people bring these power bases to the organization.[9]

Legitimate Power

legitimate power the capacity to influence others through formal authority; that is, the perceived right of people in certain roles to request certain behaviors of others

Legitimate power is an *agreement* among organizational members that people in certain roles can request specific behaviors of others. This perceived right generally comes from the person's position, such as your boss's right to require you to perform different tasks. Executives are the most obvious sources of legitimate power. However, all employees have some legitimate power, such as their right to ask others for information that will help them perform their jobs. These rights exist in formal job descriptions as well as informal rules of conduct.[10]

But obedience to authority depends on more than the rights assigned by senior executives. It also depends on employees accepting this arrangement.

The Caine Mutiny is a classic Pulitzer Prize–winning novel and film about the limits of legitimate power. Captain Queeg (Humphrey Bogart) is a hard disciplinarian who shapes up the crew of the *Caine,* a battered minesweeper during World War II. However, Queeg's judgment and focus have been impaired by too much combat. After Queeg makes several critical mistakes and forces the crew to search for missing strawberries, some of his officers fear that Queeg is a danger to himself and others. Sure enough, a beleaguered Queeg panics during a storm at sea, so two key officers—Lieutenants Keefer (Fred MacMurray) and Maryk (Van Johnson)—stage a mutiny and assume command. The story illustrates how Queeg's orders and competence tested the limits of his legitimate power over crew members. What "mutinies" have you heard about in more recent organizational settings? What commands triggered employees to refuse to obey their boss?

[Archive Photos]

Classic stories of shipboard mutinies, such as *The Caine Mutiny* and *Mutiny on the Bounty*, illustrate this point. Many incidents occur in everyday organizational life where employees question their boss's right to make them stay late, perform unsafe tasks, and other activities. Thus, legitimate power is the person's authority to make discretionary decisions as long as followers accept this discretion.[11]

power distance the extent to which people accept unequal distribution of power in a society

People in high **power distance** cultures (i.e., those who accept an unequal distribution of power—see Chapter 7) are more likely to comply with legitimate power than people in low power distance cultures. Thus, an employee in Mexico (a high power distance culture) is more likely than someone in the United States (a low power distance culture) to accept an order, particularly when the person's right to give that order is uncertain. Legitimate power is also stronger in some organizations than in others. For instance, it is not unusual for a 3M scientist to continue working on a project after being told by superiors to stop working on it. The 3M culture supports an entrepreneurial spirit, which includes ignoring your boss's authority from time to time.[12] In contrast, military organizations require strong adherence to formal authority, unless there is clear justification otherwise.

Where legitimate power is strong, those receiving the order suspend judgment and let the powerholder guide their behavior. Consider the research study in which an unknown doctor telephoned several nurses, asking them to give a certain patient in that ward 20 milligrams of Astrogen. This drug was not on the hospital's approved list and hospital rules required a written order rather than a telephone call for all such requests. Moreover, the Astrogen was locked in a special cabinet and the bottle carried a label saying that the daily dose should not exceed 10 milligrams. Nonetheless, 59 percent of the nurses tried to comply with the unknown doctor's order! (They were stopped on their way to the patient's room.)[13] These nurses suspended judgment and placed the doctor's legitimate power above hospital rules and other warnings.

Although blind compliance to authority still exists, employees are generally becoming less willing to accept legitimate power. Employees expect to be involved in decisions rather than be told what to do. As one organizational behavior scholar recently concluded, "[C]ommand managers are an endangered species in North America. Their habitat is steadily shrinking."[14] Thus, the command style of leadership that often guided employee behavior in the past must be replaced by other forms, particularly expert and referent power.

Reward Power

reward power the capacity to influence others by controlling the allocation of rewards valued by them and the removal of negative sanctions

Reward power is derived from the person's ability to control the allocation of rewards valued by others and to remove negative sanctions (i.e., negative reinforcement). Managers have formal authority that gives them power over the distribution of organizational rewards such as pay, promotions, time off, vacation schedules, and work assignments.

Employees may have reward power by extolling praise and extending personal benefits within their discretion to other co-workers. As organizations delegate responsibility and authority, work teams gain reward power over their members. In some organizations, subordinates have reward power over their bosses through the use of 360-degree feedback systems (see Chapter 2). Employee feedback affects the supervisor's promotions and other rewards, so they tend to behave differently toward employees after 360-degree feedback is introduced. "Some of our supervisors are by nature very responsive to people above them but less responsive to people at the same level or below," says Gary Dyer, president of Farm Credit Service Southwest. "I've noticed a change now [with 360-degree feedback], as they realize they're going to be evaluated by these people."[15]

Coercive Power

coercive power the capacity to influence others through the ability to apply punishment

Coercive power is the ability to apply punishment. Managers have coercive power through their authority to reprimand, demote, and fire employees. Labor unions might use coercive power tactics, such as withholding services, to influence management in collective agreement negotiations. Clients use coercive power by threatening to take their business elsewhere unless certain improvements occur. For instance, investment analysts are reluctant to give negative reviews of stocks representing their major clients (such as banks) because those clients have threatened to take their underwriting business to other investment houses.[16]

© 1992 Farcus Cartoons/dist. by Universal Press Syndicate   WAISGLASS/COULTHART

"Seeing you brought the gun, Norman, why don't you start the meeting?"

During times of low unemployment, employees have coercive power over their employers because they pose a higher risk of quitting. This explains why many companies are becoming more flexible with work hours, recreational facilities, and other benefits that employees request. "We are moving to times when employees have more power than the employer, and that changes the whole equation," acknowledges Paul Archer, marketplace president of Ikon Office Solutions, an office services business in Englewood, Colorado.[17]

Team members sometimes apply sanctions, ranging from sarcasm to ostracism, to ensure that co-workers conform to team norms.[18] An increasing number of firms rely on the coercive power of team members to control co-worker behavior.[19] As we see in Connections 12.1, organizations are leveraging this peer pressure to improve work attendance and performance, particularly in team-based structures where there are no supervisors to watch output.

Expert Power

expert power the capacity to influence others by possessing knowledge or skills that they want

For the most part, legitimate, reward, and coercive power originate from the position. In contrast, **expert power** originates from within the person. It is an individual's or work unit's capacity to influence others by possessing knowledge or skills that they want. Employees are gaining expert power in the workplace as our society moves from an industrial to a knowledge-based economy. The reason is that employee knowledge becomes the means of production, not some machine that the owner controls.[20] And without this control over production, owners are more dependent on employees to achieve their corporate objectives.

Referent Power

referent power the capacity to influence others by virtue of the admiration and identification they have of the powerholder

People have **referent power** when others identify with them, like them, or otherwise respect them. Like expert power, referent power comes from within the person. It is largely a function of the person's interpersonal skills and usually develops slowly. Referent power is typically associated with charismatic leadership. *Charisma* is defined as a form of interpersonal attraction whereby followers develop a respect for and trust in the charismatic individual.[21] This charisma may explain why, in the opening story to the chapter, Gil Amelio followed Steven Jobs's recommendations to change the organizational structure and put NeXT people in key Apple positions. Jobs is often identified as a charismatic leader.

Information and Power

Information plays an important role in organizational power.[22] One type of information power is based on control over the flow and interpretation of data given to others. In traditional hierarchies, specific employees or departments are given legitimate power to serve as gatekeepers and selectively distribute valued information. The other type of information power refers to the ability of the individual or work unit to cope with organizational uncertainties. This is a variation of expert power that has become a central concept in the literature on organizational power. Let's look more closely at these two aspects of information power.

Connections 12.1 ◘ **The Power of Peer Pressure**

After nine months, Beverly Reynolds had enough of empowered factory work at Eaton Corp.'s forge plant in South Bend, Indiana. She was particularly stressed out by the pressure to work harder. This pressure didn't come from a supervisor. It came from peers.

"They say there are no bosses here," says Randy Savage, another employee at the Eaton plant, "but if you screw up, you find one pretty fast." The 106 employees at the Eaton plant are expected to enforce the rules, so employees feel like they have a hundred bosses. If someone misses too much work or falls behind, other members of the production team are supposed to point out the problem.

Devon Products, which manufactures surgical supplies at plants in California and South Carolina, also relies on peer pressure. "You don't need to have supervisors telling someone they're tardy," explains Luke Faulstick, Devon's general manager of operations. "[Teams are] responsible for these key measures. . . . And once he gets told by that team that they're going to 'fire' him, it creates a peer environment."

NUMMI, the joint venture with General Motors and Toyota in California, was one of the early organizations to control employee behavior through peer pressure. "People try to meet the team's expectations," says one NUMMI worker, "and under peer pressure they end up pushing themselves too hard."

Of course, some employees prefer peer pressure to more traditional supervision. For example, Whole Foods is rated by *Fortune* magazine as one of the best companies to work for. Yet the health food chain relies extensively on peer pressure within each store to ensure that employees pull their weight. Moreover, Whole Foods has an elaborate system of peer store reviews, whereby employees at each store evaluate coworkers at other stores.

Sources: Based on E. Minton, "Luke Faulstick: 'Baron of Blitz' Has Boundless Vision of Continuous Improvement," *Industrial Management* 40 (January 11, 1998), p. 14; "Empowerment Torture to Some," *Tampa Tribune*, October 5, 1997, p. 6; Charles Fishman, "Whole Foods Teams," *Fast Company* (April–May 1996), pp. 104–10; "The Trouble with Teams," *The Economist*, January 1995, p. 61. ◘

Control over information flow   Some people acquire power by controlling the flow of information that others need. These communication "traffic cops" have been called "mission controllers" because they filter out and distribute information throughout the organizational hierarchy.[23] This right to control information flow is found in more bureaucratic firms and is usually accorded to certain work units or people in specific positions. The wheel formation in Exhibit 12.3 depicts this highly centralized control over information flow. The information gatekeeper in the middle of this configuration can influence others through the amount, type, and quality of information they receive.

As you can imagine, the centralized information control structure is incompatible with knowledge management and team-based organization concepts. Instead, these emerging views call for the all-channel communication structure in which all employees have relatively equal access to information. This allows employees and self-directed work teams to make better decisions. However, the all-channel network may seem rather chaotic in larger, more structured organizations, so there is a tendency to slip back into the wheel pattern.[24] Moreover, employees and work units are reluctant to give up control over information because it threatens their power base.

Coping with uncertainty   Organizations are open systems that interact with their environments by receiving inputs and transforming them into outputs (see Chapter 1). This creates varying degrees of uncertainty, that is, a lack of information about future events.[25] Uncertainty interferes with the organization's ability to carry out routine activities. Consider the troubles that Compaq Computers would face if its leaders did not know where to find tomorrow's supply of memory chips or how much demand will exist for its products next

Exhibit 12.3   Power through the control of information

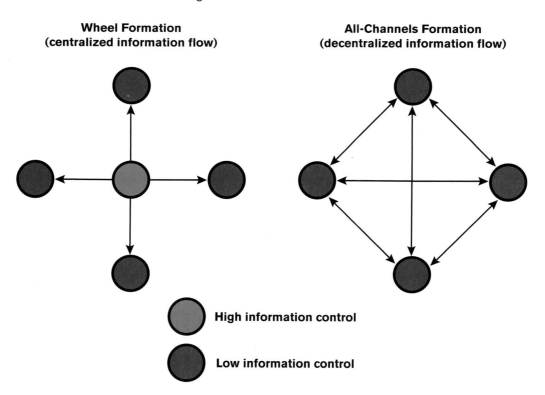

Wheel Formation
(centralized information flow)

All-Channels Formation
(decentralized information flow)

High information control

Low information control

quarter. It would be almost impossible to plan production, arrange long-term contracts with suppliers, or adjust product lines to satisfy future customer needs. Thus, to operate more efficiently and ensure continued survival, organizations need to cope with environmental uncertainties.[26]

Individuals and their work units gain power by being able to cope with uncertainties related to important organizational goals. For instance, chief executive officers increase their power over members of the Board of Directors as corporate performance improves. Presumably, Board members believe that successful CEOs have valued knowledge that helps the organization cope with its environment.[27] Coping includes any activity that effectively deals with environmental uncertainties affecting the organization. A groundbreaking study of breweries and container companies identified three general strategies to help organizations cope with uncertainty:[28]

1. *Prevention*—The most effective strategy is to prevent environmental changes and variations from occurring. For example, financial experts acquire power by preventing the organization from experiencing a cash shortage or defaulting on loans.
2. *Forecasting*—The next best strategy is to be able to predict environmental changes or variations. In this respect, marketing specialists gain power by predicting changes in consumer preferences.
3. *Absorption*—People and work units also gain power by absorbing or neutralizing the impact of environmental shifts as they occur. A classic example is the ability of maintenance crews to come to the rescue when machines break down and the production process stops.

Not many people have the job title of global trends manager. But that's what Andy Hines does at Kellogg's. "I have pretty wide latitude to bring to the company's attention the trends that I believe are important to its future," explains Hines, who is also a contributing editor at the *Futurist* magazine and coauthor of a book on how technology may shape the future. "I broker relationships with what I believe are the best futures firms and focus on bringing their best thinking into the organization to create new products and processes." It's very difficult to influence consumer trends, so Hines tries to predict what will happen.[29] What other occupational groups have power in organizational settings through their perceived ability to forecast the environment?
[John Sobczak/SKB Productions]

Contingencies of Power

Let's say that you have expert power by virtue of your ability to forecast and possibly even prevent dramatic changes in the organization's environment. Does this incredible power base mean that you have power? Not necessarily. As we saw in Exhibit 12.2, power bases generate power only under certain conditions. These conditions—called the contingencies of power—include substitutability, centrality, discretion, and visibility.[30] These are not sources of power; rather, they determine the extent to which people can leverage their power bases. You may have lots of expert power, but you won't be able to influence others with this power base if the contingency factors are not in place.

Substitutability

substitutability the extent to which those dependent on a resource have alternative sources of supply of the resource or can use other resources that would provide a reasonable substitute

Substitutability refers to the availability of alternatives. Power is strongest when someone has a monopoly over a valued resource. Conversely, power decreases as the number of alternative sources of the critical resource increases. Substitutability refers not only to other sources that offer the resource, but also to substitutions of the resource itself. For instance, labor unions are weakened when companies introduce technologies that replace the need for their union members. At one time, a strike by telephone employees would have shut down operations, but computerized systems and other technological innovations now ensure that telephone operations continue during labor strikes and reduce the need for telephone operators during normal operations. Technology is a substitute for employees and, consequently, reduces union power.

How do people and work units increase their power through nonsubstitutability? There are several ways, although not all of them are ethical. We describe some of them here for your information—not necessarily for you to practice.

Controlling tasks—Professions have legislation preventing outsiders from performing certain tasks within their domain. Lawyers keep paralegals out of certain activities, and doctors prevent nurses, midwives, and others from practicing certain interventions. Certified public accountants require public corporations to use their services in audits.

Controlling knowledge—Professions control access to the knowledge of their work domain, such as through restricted enrollment in educational programs. Knowledge is also restricted on the job. Several years ago, maintenance workers in a French tobacco processing plant had become very powerful because they controlled the knowledge required to repair the tobacco machines.[31] The maintenance manuals had mysteriously disappeared and the machines had been redesigned often enough so that only the maintenance staff knew how to fix them when they broke down (which they frequently did). Knowing the power of nonsubstitutability, maintenance staff carefully avoided documenting the repair procedures and didn't talk to production employees about their trade knowledge.

Controlling labor—Aside from their knowledge resource, people gain power by controlling the availability of their labor. Labor unions attempt to organize as many people as possible within a particular trade or industry so that employers have no other source of labor supply.[32] When unionized workers produce almost all of a particular product or service in a society, then the union has an easier time increasing wages. The current fight against outsourcing—having outside companies perform some of the work—is more than union concerns about losing jobs. It is also a fight against losing union power through substitutability. The union's power during a strike is significantly weakened when the employer can continue production through these outside contractors.

Differentiation—Differentiation occurs when an individual or work unit claims to have a unique resource, such as raw materials or knowledge, that the organization would want. By definition, the uniqueness of this resource means that no one else has it. The tactic here isn't so much the nonsubstitutability of the resource, but making organizational leaders *believe* that the resource is unique. Some people claim that consultants use this tactic. They take skills and knowledge that many consulting firms can provide and wrap them into a package (with the latest buzzwords, of course) so that it looks like a service that no one else can offer.

Centrality

centrality the degree and nature of interdependence between the powerholder and others

Employees and departments have more power as their centrality increases. **Centrality** refers to the degree and nature of interdependence between the powerholder and others.[33] There are two dimensions of centrality. One dimension refers to how many people are affected by your actions. An organization's finance department, for instance, may have considerable power because its budget activities affect virtually every other department in the organization. In contrast, employees in a branch office may affect very few people in the organization.

The other dimension of centrality refers to how quickly people are affected by your actions. Just-in-time (JIT) inventory systems—where parts or raw materials are delivered to assemblers when they are needed rather than stockpiled—have given labor unions more power for this reason. With JIT, inventory is so low that a strike by employees at one parts plant can quickly paralyze the company's entire manufacturing operations.

When employees at General Motors' (GM's) two Flint, Michigan, parts plants went on strike in 1998, they quickly shut down most of GM's assembly plants throughout North America. The Flint employees had high centrality because GM's assembly plants kept only a few days of parts on hand. The Flint workers also gained centrality by timing their strike during the busy spring car-buying season. Through their centrality, Flint employees hit GM quickly and heavily so that their demands would be met with minimal cost to them. GM held out for nearly two months, but the striking employees got much more job security and work guarantees than GM had initially offered.[34] Can you think of other strikes where union leaders did not consider the need for centrality?
[Reuters/John C. Hillery/Archive Photos]

Discretion

Discretion, the freedom to make decisions without referring to a specific rule or receiving permission from someone else, is another important contingency of power in organizations. Consider the plight of first-line supervisors. It may seem that they have legitimate power over employees, but this power is often curtailed by specific rules. They must administer programs developed from above and follow specific procedures in their implementation. They administer rewards and punishments, but must abide by precise rules regarding their distribution. Indeed, supervisors are often judged not on their discretionary skills, but on their ability to follow prescribed rules and regulations. This lack of discretion makes supervisors largely powerless even though they may have access to some of the power bases described earlier in this chapter.[35]

Visibility

Power does not flow to unknown people in the organization. Rather, employees gain power by making their sources of power known to others. If someone has unique knowledge to help others do their job better, his or her knowledge will yield power only when others are aware of it. In this respect, power derives from the individual's or work unit's reputation within and outside of the organization.[36]

Visibility increases as the number of people you interact with increases. Thus, employees become more visible—and tend to have more successful careers—by taking people-oriented jobs that require extensive contacts rather than isolated technical positions. Similarly, visibility increases with the amount of face-to-face contact rather than less personal forms of communication. People further increase their visibility by introducing themselves to senior management and by being assigned to important task forces. Along with the valuable learning experience, these committees let you work closely with—and get noticed by—senior people in the organization.

People often use public symbols as subtle (and sometimes not-so-subtle) cues to make their power sources known to others.[37] Professionals display their educational diplomas and awards on office walls to remind visitors of their expertise. Many senior executives still rely on the size of their office and related status symbols to show their legitimate power in the organization. Even the clothing we wear communicates power. Medical professionals wear white coats with a stethoscope around their neck to symbolize their legitimate and expert power in hospital settings. One study reported that women who wear jackets are initially perceived as having more legitimate and expert power than women without jackets.[38]

mentoring the process of learning the ropes of organizational life from a senior person within the company

Another way to increase visibility is through **mentoring**—the process of learning the ropes of organizational life from a more senior person within the company. Mentors give protégés more visible and meaningful work opportunities, and open doors for them to meet more senior people in the organization. Mentors also teach these newcomers political skills and tactics supported by the organization's senior decision makers.[39]

Consequences of Power

We use power to influence others, but the type of influence depends on the power source used.[40] Coercive power is generally the least desirable source because it generates resistance by the person or department being influenced. In other words, the targeted person tends to oppose the attempt to influence and actively tries to avoid carrying it out. Applying coercive power also reduces trust between the parties and increases employee dissatisfaction. Resistance and distrust also occur when other power bases are used arrogantly or in a manipulative way.

Reward and legitimate power tend to produce compliance, whereby people are motivated to implement the power holder's request for purely instrumental reasons. Suppose that your boss gives you a bonus for performing an extra task that you wouldn't otherwise accept. The reward will get you to comply with the request, but not to perform the task with enthusiasm. Commitment is the strongest form of influence, whereby people identify with the power holder's request and are motivated to implement it even when there are no extrinsic benefits in doing so. Commitment is the most common consequence of expert and referent power. For instance, employees will follow a charismatic leader and do more than is asked because this power base evokes commitment rather than compliance or resistance.

Power also affects the power holder. As we learned in Chapter 3, some people have a strong need for power and are motivated to acquire it for personal or organizational purposes. These individuals are more satisfied and committed to their jobs when they have increased responsibility, authority, and discretion. However, people who acquire too much power often abuse their position to better their personal interests and to gain more power.[41] Powerful employees tend to use their influence more often than is necessary, devalue their less powerful co-workers, and reduce their interpersonal associations with them. They also use their power to acquire more power. If unchecked, powerful employees eventually become even more powerful. In short, there appears to be some truth in Lord Acton's well-known statement that "power tends to corrupt; absolute power corrupts absolutely."[42]

Sexual Harassment: An Abuse of Power

Sexual harassment refers to unwelcome conduct of a sexual nature that detrimentally affects the work environment or leads to adverse job-related consequences for its victims (see Chapter 5).[43] As we learned in Chapter 6, sexual harassment occurs in part because people stereotype the victim as subservient and powerless. However, the harasser's power over the victim is almost always identified as a critical factor, even where the harasser is a co-worker at the same level in the organization.[44]

Abuse of power is most obvious where the harasser threatens the employee's job security or personal safety through coercive or legitimate power (known as *quid pro quo* harassment). Consider Astra USA, where female sales representatives were pressured into having sexual relations with senior executives. If they didn't comply with these requests, the women feared that they would receive the worst sales territories or get fired on some trumped-up charge of incompetence. Although women are usually the victims in *quid pro quo* cases, men have also been victims of this abuse of power. This happened in a California company where a female chief financial officer required her male subordinate to have sex with her as a condition of his employment.[45]

Abuse of power also occurs where sexual harassment takes the form of a hostile work environment. A hostile work environment involves unwelcome

conduct, such as sexual jokes, leering, and showing pornographic material. This hostile environment persists because the victim does not have sufficient power to stop the behavior. For example, Mitsubishi Motor Manufacturing of America Inc. recently settled a lawsuit in which more than 300 women employees at the company's assembly plant in Normal, Illinois, claimed they had been groped, grabbed, and pressured for sex by co-workers. The men didn't have authority over the victims, but they apparently did threaten to make their lives miserable on the job.[47]

Minimizing sexual harassment

Astra USA, Mitsubishi, and other companies accused of sexual harassment

---

sexual harassment

unwelcome conduct of a sexual nature that detrimentally affects the work environment or leads to adverse job-related consequences for its victims

Astra USA CEO Lars Bildman (shown) and other executives allegedly abused their power to get sexual favors from female employees. Older female employees at the drug manufacturer were systematically replaced with young single women. Bildman and other executives would then pressure the new recruits into sexual relations with them. "They would use their power and authority to make you think you didn't have a job if you didn't go along," says one Astra representative. Several employees who objected to the harassment were forced out of their jobs. Astra USA's parent company in Sweden eventually replaced the entire senior U.S. management group and paid a $10 million settlement to the dozens of women who experienced harassment.[46] How can organizations prevent people in positions of power from engaging in sexual harassment?

[*Laurie Swope*, Boston Herald]

pay a tremendous price in moral embarrassment, loss of goodwill, loss of talented employees, and financial penalties.[48] Some corporate leaders believe the best solution is to introduce confidential complaint procedures for people who have been sexually harassed. While certainly necessary, these are reactive procedures. Much more important are preventive strategies that reduce the likelihood of sexual harassment incidents. The importance of this preventive rather than reactive approach is reinforced by recent court judgments that have held companies liable for failing to control an individual employee's abuse of power.[49]

One way to prevent sexual harassment is to ensure that people in positions of power realize how their actions are interpreted by others. Incidents of sexual harassment may seem obvious after the fact, but many harassers really don't realize this at the time.[50] For example, men often think a comment about an employee's figure is a compliment, whereas female co-workers often feel threatened by these statements because of the unstated sanctions that the harasser might use. Moreover, executives sometimes forget they are role models for the entire organization. Their actions signal whether sexual harassment is prohibited or condoned.

A complementary strategy is to establish a clear set of rules for those in positions of power. IBM and other organizations have tried to prevent romantic relationships among employees, but this is both difficult and, according to U.S. courts, unreasonable. Instead, some firms have clear rules about sexual liaisons between people in certain reporting relationships. For instance, Autodesk has plenty of employees who have courted and married co-workers. "We have to meet people here, because we never get outside," says Heidi Hewett, who met her husband at the San Rafael, California, software maker. But Autodesk also has a golden rule that managers cannot take advantage of their authority in initiating a relationship.[51] In other words, Autodesk employees must remove themselves from a position of power if they want to form an intimate relationship with a co-worker.

Even when two people are not in a direct reporting situation, some companies take the further step of requiring them to sign a document indicating that they willingly participate in their sexual relationship. These "love forms" reduce the risk that one party later claims the relationship occurred through an abuse of power.[52]

Sexual harassment is not the only behavior that results from an abuse of power. As we mentioned earlier, powerful employees tend to use their influence to acquire more power. As we learn in the remainder of this chapter, employees engage in various types of organizational politics that may abuse their power if not directed toward organizational objectives. We will also look at the ethics of organizational politics, the conditions in which political behaviors flourish, and ways to minimize dysfunctional politics.

Organizational Politics

Charlene Pedrolie was ready for trouble when she replaced Rowe Furniture Company's old assembly line with a new team-based work structure. As Rowe's head of manufacturing, she knew there would be glitches and plenty of resistance. Naysayers in corporate office shook their heads and distanced themselves from Pedrolie's experiment. Then there were the computer people who dallied over her urgent requests for more information. Using her sharpest political skills, Pedrolie engineered the ouster of the firm's computer chief and brought in one of her pals from General Electric where she previously worked. Eventually, Pedrolie's persistence and political savvy paid off as production employees worked out the kinks in the team-based work processes.[53]

organizational politics

attempts to influence others
using discretionary behaviors
to promote personal objectives

As this true story reveals, organizational politics is widespread and can work either for or against the organization. **Organizational politics** represents attempts to influence others using discretionary behaviors to promote personal objectives.[54] It is the exercise of power to get one's own way, including the acquisition of more power, often at the expense of others. Behaviors are discretionary if they are neither formally prescribed nor prohibited by the organization. For example, the naysayers who distanced themselves from Charlene Pedrolie probably didn't do anything that was against company policy. They just kept quiet and avoided any image that aligned them with the project.

Organizational Politics: Good or Bad?

Tenneco Packaging, a world leader in packaging and automotive parts, has an unusual credo that says "Management with no fear, egos, or politics."[55] It seems to be consistent with the firm's quest for a team-based organization with high levels of trust among employees. But should companies try to prevent anyone from engaging in organizational politics? Dysfunctional politics should be discouraged, of course. For example, Rowe Furniture Company fired the head of computer systems because his actions (and inactions) undermined the change process. However, organizational politics also includes many useful activities, such as the way we dress and who we talk to. These and other political tactics sometimes help the organization achieve its objectives. Experts suggest that people need to be good politicians, particularly as they reach higher levels in the corporation.[56]

Consider the events described in the opening story to this chapter. Steven Jobs likely engaged in some degree of organizational politics to regain Apple's top post. Were these tactics good or bad? Many people would argue that Jobs took these steps guided by the belief that Apple's future was in jeopardy with Gil Amelio in charge. In other words, Steven Jobs used political tactics to gain power for the organization's benefit. Apple experienced a remarkable improvement in products and profitability just one year after Jobs took the "interim" CEO position, so his political activities possibly saved the company. The point here is that some political tactics can help organizations achieve their objectives where formally prescribed influence methods may fail.

Problems with organizational politics

Of course, organizational politics are often more of a problem than a benefit. One concern is that they consume time and disrupt work activities. They are part of the process loss that occurs in team discussions and work dynamics. This problem was recently apparent at Chester County Hospital and Nursing Center in Chester, South Carolina. Executives complained that they couldn't manage while county politicians, hospital trustees, and medical staff fought over who should control the hospital. "Because of the political infighting and division on the issue of who controls and who owns the hospital, the attention was diverted from what needed to be done," warned Austin Letson, president of regional facilities for Carolinas Healthcare System, which manages Chester County Hospital.[57]

Many political tactics reduce trust and the motivation to collaborate. When people operate in a tense political environment, they have difficulty relating to other employees. This undermines the conditions for active knowledge sharing. Several studies also report that employees who experience more organizational politics report higher stress, psychological withdrawal, and turnover. However, people tend to feel less stress and dissatisfaction as they become familiar with the work environment in which they experience the political tactics.[58]

The ethics of organizational politics   How can we tell whether a political action is good or bad? The answer may be to assess the action against the three ethical standards that we learned about in Chapter 7. Generally, a political behavior is ethical only if it satisfies all three moral principles.[59]

1. *Utilitarian rule*—Does the political tactic provide the greatest good for the greatest number of people? If it mainly benefits the individual and possibly harms the welfare of others, then the political behavior is inappropriate.

2. *Individual rights rule*—Does the political tactic violate anyone's legal or moral rights? If the political activity threatens another person's privacy, free speech, due process, or other rights, then it should not be used even if the results might be beneficial to a larger audience. For example, even if an incompetent senior executive is undermining shareholder wealth and employee job satisfaction, this does not justify wiretapping his or her telephone for embarrassing evidence that would force the executive to quit.

3. *Distributive justice rule*—Does the political activity treat all parties fairly? If the political behavior benefits those who are better off at the expense of those who are already worse off, then the activity is unethical. For example, it would be unethical for a manager to take personal credit for a subordinate's project and receive the financial benefits resulting from that performance.

Types of Political Activity

So far, we have alluded to the fact that there are various types of political games or tactics found in organizational settings. Organizational behavior scholars have conveniently grouped most of them into the seven categories illustrated in Exhibit 12.4.[60]

Attacking or Blaming Others

Probably the most direct and nastiest form of organizational politics is attacking and blaming others. This includes giving rivals a bad image in the eyes of decision makers. Not all blaming is overt. A subtle tactic occurs when people dissociate themselves from undesirable situations or use excuses to form an external attribution of the cause of the problem.[61] You might explain to your boss that a report is late because of the lack of support from another work unit or other conditions beyond your control. In other words, people try to frame their failures in terms of external attributions (see Chapter 6).

[With special permission from Ted Goff—http://www.tedgoff.com.]

Selectively Distributing Information

Information is a political tool as well as a source of

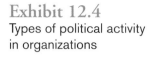

Exhibit 12.4
Types of political activity
in organizations

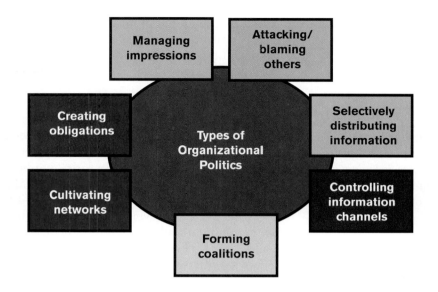

power. People strategically manage the distribution of information to shape perceptions, limit the potential performance of rivals, or further increase their power base. Consider the following incident reported by compensation consultant Graef Crystal. For several years, the CEO of a major pharmaceutical company asked Crystal to compare the CEO's base pay and bonus with other industry leaders. Each year, Crystal's report indicated that the CEO's pay was approximately in the top 25 percent. Each year, the CEO passed the report on to the Board of Directors.

But one year Crystal decided it was more accurate to include the CEO's long-term stock options in the calculations. The report now concluded that the CEO's total pay was higher than any other in the industry. A few months after he submitted the latest report, Crystal happened to see another executive from the company. When asked what the CEO did with this year's report, the executive replied: "He threw it in the wastebasket!"[62]

The pharmaceutical company CEO threw out Graef Crystal's report because he didn't want the Board of Directors to see that he was overpaid! Similarly, employees have been known to manipulate the data used to determine their pay rates. Others embellish their résumés by exaggerating past job duties and hiding negative events in their career. Job applicants have a unique advantage in selectively distributing information because prospective employers have difficulty receiving complete information from other sources.[63]

Information politics also involves hoarding information.[64] "In today's highly political corporate environment, knowledge equals power," warns Eric Austvold, director of product marketing at Infinium Software. "Getting people to understand that knowledge sharing is for the greater good of all requires significant culture change."[65] Departments are reluctant to share their knowledge sources (such as computer data or customer contacts) because they face the risk of giving up their power base. If others gain access to these information sources, then the work unit loses power as the communication pattern shifts from a wheel to an all-channel structure.

Controlling Information Channels

Through legitimate power, some people can control the interactions among employees as well as the topics of those discussions. An executive might discourage people in different work units from talking directly to each other because this might threaten the executive's power and job status. Similarly,

committee leaders might organize meeting agendas to suit their personal interests. If leaders want to avoid a decision on a particular topic, they might
place the issue near the bottom of the agenda so that the committee either
doesn't get to it or devotes little time and attention to the issue.

Forming Coalitions

coalition an informal group
that attempts to influence
people outside the group by
pooling the resources and
power of its members

In Chapter 9, we explained that a **coalition** is an informal group that attempts
to influence people outside the group by pooling the resources and power of its
members. A coalition usually forms when two or more people agree on common objectives that they cannot achieve alone, such as getting resources and
support for a new intranet system. A coalition is a political tactic because it
pools the power of several people toward a common objective that each member is unable to influence alone. By demonstrating their strength in numbers,
coalitions also create a sense that an issue has broad appeal and therefore deserves legitimate support.[66] Although coalitions are usually formed with good
intentions, one possible problem is that they put pressure on others to change,
thereby creating compliance rather than commitment to the change.[67] However, as we read in the *Fast Company Online* feature for this chapter, coalitions
can help people get things done that cannot be accomplished alone.

Cultivating Networks

networking cultivating social
relationships with others to
accomplish one's goals

"It's not what you know, but who you know that counts!" This often-heard
statement reflects the philosophy behind another political tactic known as **networking.** Networking refers to cultivating social relationships with others to
accomplish one's goals. By forming a trust network, people receive valuable information that increases their expert power in the organization.[68] Networking
also nurtures allies and sponsors, thereby making it easier to get approval for
projects and other initiatives. Finally, networking helps employees increase
their referent power, and this may lead to more favorable decisions by others
in the network.

   Networking is a natural part of the informal organization, yet it can create
a formidable barrier to those who are not actively connected to it. Women have
difficulty getting into senior management positions because they are usually
excluded from powerful networks.[69] One reason for this exclusion may be that
women are less aware of the importance of networks for career advancement.
Another explanation is that men (still the dominant powerholders in most organizations) don't feel as comfortable networking with women as they do with
other men. But perhaps the most important reason is that men don't realize
that their informal networks shut women out from information and decision
making. Edwina Woodbury, senior vice president and chief financial officer for
Avon Products Inc., sums up the problem: "It's there all the time," she said.
"How many business conversations [and] business decisions are made in the
men's room or on golf day?"[70]

Creating Obligations

The obligation to help someone who has once helped you—called the *norm of
reciprocity*—is deeply embedded in many societies. It is also a political tactic.[71]
An employee who has helped someone might later ask that person to put in a
good word or support him or her on a promotion. The indebted co-worker is
more likely to agree to this than if he or she had no debt to repay. Some organizational politicians are able to leverage these debts for a greater return than
whatever was given initially.

Managing Impressions

impression management
the practice of actively shaping our public images

Impression management is the practice of actively shaping our public images.[72] Many impression management activities are done routinely to satisfy the basic norms of social behavior. Others are political tactics because they are used deliberately to get one's way. Some political tactics described earlier—including blaming others, filtering information, and increasing the visibility of one's power base—are forms of impression management. Another well-known impression management tactic is to manage your appearance and behavior so that others develop a desired image of you.[73] For example, the way we dress is part of the impression management process.

Employees use a variety of impression management tactics, often without realizing it. For example, we make a point of attending meetings where senior executives are present, even though our time might be better spent elsewhere.

FAST COMPANY
Online

□ Using Coalitions as a Good Political Strategy

Cindy Casselman felt that Xerox needed a complete intranet system for employees to share knowledge. Unfortunately, the communications manager lacked the formal authority to put this together, and her boss would only tolerate what looked like a modest project. Moreover, some people at Xerox would feel threatened by Casselman's idea about WebBoard, a web-based information resource where employees could share information about corporate events.

Casselman's solution was to quietly assemble a coalition of people—called the Sanctioned Covert Operation group—and put together a makeshift budget. Two of Casselman's closest allies came from very different parts of Xerox. Rick Beach, a manager at Xerox Business Systems in California, saw WebBoard as an opportunity to test his group's ideas about virtual document delivery. Malcolm Kirby, a Xerox information systems expert in Rochester, New York, saw WebBoard as an opportunity to showcase Xerox's new structure of networked PCs. Casselman also got support and funding from the head of Xerox's information systems and head of its education and learning. "We were able to get some interesting people to join us," says Casselman.

As the project began to take shape, Casselman also cut a deal with her boss. He would give her time to work on the project, but only if she raised $250,000 from other areas of Xerox for its development. This was a daunting challenge, but Casselman's coalition group made it look easy. "I was shocked," admits Casselman's boss when he learned that she got the financial support. "I still don't understand how she did it."

ONLINE CHECK-UP

1. This *Fast Company Online* feature describes how Cindy Casselman relied on coalition building to accomplish a difficult project. What factors made this coalition effective here?
2. The full text of this *Fast Company* article discusses five rules for good organizational politics. Identify these five rules and determine which ones Cindy Casselman used to create WebBoard. Then relate these five rules to specific topics in this chapter.

Get the full text of this
Fast Company article at
www.mhhe.com/mcshane1e

Source: Adapted from M. Warshaw, "The Good Guy's Guide to Office Politics," *Fast Company*, no. 14 (April–May 1998). ■

We recognize that many bosses still value "face time," the physical presence suggesting that we are hard at work. Connections 12.2 points out that the trend toward telecommuting may remove employees from office politics, but it increases their career risks as they provide less face time and other impression management tactics.

Connections 12.2 ◻ **Telecommuting May Do More Than Unplug Organizational Politics**

Gary Withers, general manager of Drake International New Zealand, says that he is able to avoid office politics, now that he manages the human resource firm from his home in Queenstown rather than the firm's headquarters in Auckland.

[Southland Times, *Invercargill, New Zealand. Used with permission.*]

Conditions for Organizational Politics

Organizational politics flourish under the right conditions.[74] One of those conditions is scarce resources. When budgets are slashed, people rely on political tactics to safeguard their resources and maintain the status quo. This

The headquarters of Drake International New Zealand is located in Auckland, but you won't find its general manager there. Gary Withers leads the respected human resource firm from his home in Queenstown, hundreds of miles away on New Zealand's South Island. Withers claims that he is more productive now that he is far removed from the office politics. "I don't get involved in the office politics, which probably took up most of my time [before moving to Queenstown]," explains Withers. "If a referee was needed they always came to me—they can't do that now."

Telecommuters around the world agree that they are more productive and satisfied, partly because they are away from the interference of organizational politics. But some experts warn that many bosses still value and reward employees for their "face time." Telecommuters who think they are getting away from office politics may be forgetting one of the most important political behaviors for their career progress: impression management.

"Being removed from your company carries both risks and advantages," warns Val Arnold, senior vice president with Personnel Decisions International, a Minneapolis management and human resources consulting firm. "You need to maintain visibility and develop yourself professionally in order to succeed as a telecommuter."

Alice Campbell, director of Baxter Healthcare's Work/Life program, doesn't think that careers get unplugged when people telecommute. "I think it's a myth that people who telecommute can't or don't get promoted," she says. However, Campbell acknowledges that Baxter's telecommuters work at home only a few days each week, so they still have plenty of face time. "Typically, telecommuters only work from home one or two days a week, so it's not like they're never there."

Sources: K. Furore, "Keeping in Touch and on Track," *Chicago Tribune*, June 28, 1998, p. 1; J. K. Stewart, "Out-of-Sight Telecommuters Might Be out of Mind," *Chicago Tribune*, April 5, 1998, p. 7; S. Fea, "Boss Moves Office to Lakeside," *Southland Times* (New Zealand), February 26, 1998, p. 1. ■

happened at Exponential Technology, which was working on a superfast chip for the Apple Macintosh computer. When Apple's future became uncertain, the company hired a second group of engineers to develop a similar chip for the Intel-compatible market. But with budget restrictions, the Mac-compatible engineers did their best to run the new group out of town. "It got really ugly," recalls Exponential CEO Rick Shriner. "It came down to a battle for limited resources." To reduce the political infighting, Shriner moved the Intel group to another city.[75]

People also try to get credit for successful projects and avoid association with failures because they compete for rewards and other scarce resources. This happened a few years ago at TBWA Chiat/Day, after the advertising firm acquired more companies than it could handle. According to copywriter Bob Rice, the acquisitions resulted in a large stable of creative directors, all trying to establish their reputations in the merged company. "There were so many whispers and so much infighting [among the creative directors]," explains Rice, who now works at another agency. "It's not about the work; it's about who gets credit for it, who gets to rent the tux."[76]

Along with resource scarcity, office politics flourish when resource allocation decisions are based on ambiguous, complex, or a complete lack of rules. This occurs because decision makers are given more discretion over resource allocation, so potential recipients of those resources use political tactics to influence the factors that should be considered in the decision. Organizational change encourages political behaviors for this reason. Change creates uncertainty and ambiguity as the company moves from an old set of rules and practices to a new set. During these times, employees apply political strategies to protect their valued resources, position, and self-image. Career advancement decisions also tend to be based on complex and ambiguous decision rules. Thus, 68 percent of 46,500 U.S. employees surveyed said that political pull is important if you expect to get ahead.[77]

Organizational politics also becomes commonplace when it is tolerated and transparently supported by the organization.[78] Executives may be role models of bad corporate politicians to people further down the hierarchy. Companies sometimes inadvertently promote people who are the best politicians, not necessarily the best talent, to run the company. If left unchecked, organizational politics can paralyze an organization as people focus more on protecting themselves than fulfilling their roles. Political activity becomes self-reinforcing unless the conditions supporting political behavior are altered.

Personal Characteristics

Several personal characteristics affect a person's motivation to engage in organizational politics.[79] In Chapter 3 we learned that some people have a strong need for personal (as opposed to socialized) power. They seek power for its own sake, and use political tactics to acquire more power. People with an internal locus of control are more likely than those with an external locus of control to engage in political behaviors. This does not mean that internals are naturally political; rather, they are more likely to use influence tactics when political conditions are present because, unlike externals, they feel very much in charge of their own destiny.

Some people have strong **Machiavellian values.** Machiavellianism is named after Niccolò Machiavelli, the 16th-century Italian philosopher who wrote *The Prince*, a famous treatise about political behavior. People with high Machiavellian values believe that deceit is a natural and acceptable way to influence others. They seldom trust co-workers and frequently use power to manipulate others toward their own personal goals, even when these goals are

Machiavellian values the belief that deceit is a natural and acceptable way to influence others

unfavorable to the organization. In particular, these people tend to use cruder influence tactics, such as bypassing one's boss or being assertive.[80]

Gender differences in organizational politics   When Gil Amelio left as Apple Computer's CEO in 1997, he sent a letter to employees identifying the things he claims to have achieved during his tenure. Apple executive vice president Ellen Hancock stepped down at the same time. When interviewed, she thanked Apple employees for the opportunity to work with them and for their support in getting the company turned around.[81]

Amelio was mainly pushed out by Apple's Board of Directors whereas Hancock left voluntarily, but their actions might also reflect differences in the way men and women approach organizational politics. According to some sources, men are more likely than women to use direct impression management tactics.[82] Like Amelio, most men are comfortable advertising their achievements and taking personal credit for successes of others reporting to them. Women are more reluctant to force the spotlight on themselves, preferring instead to share the credit with others.

Men and women also seem to differ in assigning blame.[83] Research suggests that women are more likely to apologize—personally take blame—even for problems not caused by them. Men are more likely to assign blame and less likely to assume it. Some men even try to turn their errors into achievements by appearing as the white knight to save the day. This difference is consistent with our discussion of gender communication (Chapter 8); namely, that men tend to communicate and behave in ways that support their status and power.[84]

If they don't rely on blaming or impression management, then which political tactics do women tend to use? Some writers claim that women don't use any political tactics very well in organizations, and this has limited their promotional opportunities.[85] More likely, women use indirect impression management as well as forms of networking and coalition building. Of course, we must be careful not to generalize gender differences too much. Some women are very agile corporate politicians, and some men are politically inept in organizations.

Controlling Political Behavior

The conditions that fuel organizational politics also give us some clues about how to control dysfunctional political activities.[86] Here are several strategies that should keep dysfunctional politics in check:

- Ensure that there is a sufficient supply of critical resources. This is not easy, but it is possible to ensure that sufficient inventory and cash flow exist in many cases.

- Where resources are necessarily scarce, introduce clear rules and regulations to specify the use of these resources.

- Establish a free flow of information so that the organization is less dependent on a few people at the center of a communications wheel.

- Use effective organizational change management practices—particularly communication and involvement—to minimize uncertainty during the change process (see Chapter 15).

- Restructure team and organizational norms (as described in Chapter 9) to reject political tactics that appear to interfere with the organization's goals.

- Select people who have a moderately strong socialized need for power and a relatively low level of Machiavellianism.
- Provide opportunities for open and candid dialogue to resolve conflicts between employees and work units.
- Get employees to monitor the workplace and actively discourage co-workers who engage in political tactics.

Chapter Summary

Power is the capacity to influence others. It exists when one party perceives that he or she is dependent on the other for something of value. However, the dependent person must also have counterpower—some power over the dominant party—to maintain the relationship.

There are five power bases. Legitimate power is an agreement among organizational members that people in certain roles can request certain behaviors of others. Reward power is derived from the ability to control the allocation of rewards valued by others and to remove negative sanctions. Coercive power is the ability to apply punishment. Expert power is the capacity to influence others by possessing knowledge or skills that they want. People have referent power when others identify with them, like them, or otherwise respect them.

Information plays an important role in organizational power. Employees gain power by controlling the flow of information that others need, and by being able to cope with uncertainties related to important organizational goals.

Power bases are leveraged into actual power only under four conditions. Individuals and work units are more powerful when they are nonsubstitutable, quickly affect many others (centrality), have considerable discretion, and are visible.

Power is applied to influence others, but the type of influence depends on the power source. Coercive power tends to produce resistance; reward and legitimate power result in compliance; expert and referent power produce commitment. People with a high need for power feel more satisfied and committed to their jobs when they have power, but many people tend to abuse their power when given too much of it.

Sexual harassment is an abuse of power as well as evidence of prejudice. Men are often unaware that their power causes sexual harassment. Sexual harassment may be minimized by making people aware of their actions, establishing clear rules regarding intimate relationships among co-workers, and ensuring that existing relationships are voluntary.

Organizational politics attempts to influence others using discretionary behaviors that promote the individual's personal objectives. People tend to have an unfavorable view of organizational politics, but some political activities benefit the organization. Still, we must always consider the ethical implications of political behaviors.

The seven most common tactics include attacking or blaming others, selectively distributing information, controlling information channels, forming coalitions, cultivating networks, creating obligations, and managing impressions.

Organizational politics is more prevalent when scarce resources are allocated using complex and ambiguous decisions, and when the organization tolerates or rewards political behavior. Individuals with a high need for personal power, an internal locus of control, and a Machiavellian personality have a higher propensity to use political tactics. Women are less likely than men to use organizational politics, particularly direct impression management and blaming tactics, to get ahead in their career.

Dysfunctional organizational politics may be controlled by providing sufficient resources, providing clear rules for resource allocation, establishing a free flow of information, using communication and involvement during organizational change, designing norms that discourage dysfunctional politics, selecting people who are less likely to use dysfunctional politics, trying to resolve conflicts before people use political tactics against the other party, and having employees actively discourage co-workers from using dysfunctional politics.

Key Terms

Discussion Questions

1. What role does counterpower play in the power relationship? Give an example where you have counterpower at school or work.

2. You have just been hired as a brand manager of toothpaste for a large consumer products company. Your job mainly involves encouraging the advertising and production groups to promote and manufacture your product more effectively. These departments aren't under your direct authority, although company procedures indicate that they must complete certain tasks requested by brand managers. Describe the sources of power you can use to ensure that the advertising and production departments will help you make and sell toothpaste more effectively.

3. Suppose you have formal authority to allocate performance bonuses to your employees. What contingencies must exist before this source of power will translate into actual power?

4. Suppose that you have been hired by Astra AB to correct the serious sexual harassment problems at Astra USA. What would you do? You may assume that the top three or four people have been replaced, but other managers are still there and will not be fired by Astra.

5. Visibility exists in many forms in almost any setting. Without offending any individuals in your class, identify strategies that people use in the classroom to strengthen their power through visibility.

6. The author of a popular press business book recently wrote that "office politics is a demotivator that must be eliminated." He argues that when companies allow politics to determine who gets ahead, employees put their energy into political behavior rather than job performance. Discuss the author's comments about organizational politics.

7. Throughout this book, we have argued that successful companies engage in knowledge management. What political tactics were described in this chapter that directly interfere with knowledge management objectives?

8. Not long ago senior executives at a medium-sized company were deciding whether to replace the company's mainframe with a client/server system of microcomputers. During this tense time, the mainframe and microcomputer experts in the information systems department engaged in a heated battle of political infighting by openly bad-mouthing each other. Meanwhile, the people who controlled the mainframe information actively resisted the change to a client/server system, which would effectively allow users to bypass them. What strategies would you recommend to minimize these incidents of organizational politics?

Foreign exchange confrontation

I worked in the foreign exchange (FX) back office, where deals made by our 150 dealers were checked, payment instructions were added, and queries addressed. My job was to resolve problems arising from the deals. Much of the time, this meant going upstairs and talking to the dealers.

Now, you never told a dealer that he or she was wrong, even when handling those dealers who, throughout the whole of my placement, were never correct. You just briefly stated what the problem was and asked them to kindly look into it.

This particular incident involves Nick, one of the men who always "screwed up." This time he had mixed up the currencies on a deal. The payment was due in half an hour, so it was important to get him to amend the deal. I went up to see him, but Lee, also from the back office, was already talking to him about something else. Because my problem was urgent, I waited for Lee to finish. When Lee left, Nick glanced at me and then, to my surprise, left his desk and went over to another dealer, John, from whom we had heard juicy comments for quite a while. A group of dealers assembled and I could hear and see from their behavior that they were not discussing business.

I went over and discovered that the reason for their behavior was two pages from *The Sun* newspaper filled with pictures of posed naked women. Something inside me just snapped. I told Nick that my job was actually meant as a service to the dealers, to help make them aware of errors before it costs them money. I explained how much work I had to do and how much other dealers appreciated my corrections, so by ignoring me he was not only wasting my time, but his own colleagues' right to the service the back office offers. And with his error statistics, I would imagine he had better things to do than to stare at pictures of naked women.

I turned around, left my sheet of paper on his desk, and departed.

My main emotion both then and now is anger. I felt I had been patient and taken much more criticism and rude behavior than was acceptable. The way Nick ignored me to go and look at those photos in *The Sun* was the straw that broke the camel's back. I also felt helpless and vulnerable. They were discussing naked women in detail in a room with almost all men, and I knew my views were in the minority. I was afraid any reaction from me would be ridiculed. Writing about it now, I also feel proud for having had the courage to tell him off.

The foreign exchange dealers, nearly all men, were the most arrogant group of people I have ever come across in my life. If it had not been for my gradually understanding some of the reasons for their behavior, an outburst like the one I have just described would have come much earlier. You need to appreciate the fact that the FX department is, at the moment, one of the best departments resultwise in FinInter and this creates a feeling of invulnerability and extreme self-importance among those working there. I did not feel that this was a valid excuse for their behavior; still, I learned to accept it.

The back-office policy was to accept any amount of criticism from the dealers, and then let it all come out afterward when you were safely back at your desk. This policy was no good as it only helped to increase the hostility between dealers and the back office. By telling the dealer off, I had broken the main taboo in the office. Over several weeks, I realized that this earned me much respect. I had done something many of my colleagues had wanted to do for years, but dared not. The risk was smaller for me because I was there only for a short while. So, I achieved respect both from the back office and from some of the dealers. And perhaps even more importantly, I respected myself more for having done what I felt was right.

Discussion Questions

1. Describe the power bases and contingencies of power for both Nick and the "back-office" person in this case.

2. How did the back-office person's power change after her confrontation with Nick? Why?

Source: Adapted from Y. Gabriel, "An Introduction to the Social Psychology of Insults in Organizations," *Human Relations* 51 (November 1998), pp. 1329–54. ■

Saying adios to the office

BusinessWeek

Laptops, speedy modems, the Internet, and other technologies are helping people break free of the office. In particular, telecommuting—working from home with a computer connection to the office—has become a popular trend for people in many occupations. It eliminates the stress of commuting to work and frees up more time to spend with family. However, telecommuters need to adjust to the organizational power and politics of working away from the office.

This *Business Week* article describes how telecommuting liberates employees—and creates new dilemmas in organizational power and politics. Read through this *Business Week* article at www.mhhe.com/mcshane1e and prepare for the discussion questions below.

Discussion Questions

1. This article emphasizes the idea that "appearances count" in telecommuting. What does this mean in terms of organizational politics? What strategies should telecommuters use to improve their appearances?

2. According to the author of this article, what effect does telecommuting have on promotional opportunities? Explain this in terms of organizational power and politics.

3. What is probably the main concern that supervisors have in managing telecommuters? How can telecommuters minimize this problem?

Source: A. Dunkin, "Saying Adios to the Office," *Business Week*, October 12, 1998, p. 152. ■

Employers' growing control over employee off-the-job activities

 Punching in at work doesn't just mean getting ready for an eight-hour day. It also means leaving your privacy and some personal autonomy at the door. In order for an employee to get in the door at all, drug tests, credit inquiry, and background checks are not unusual. Employees' e-mail and voice mail may be monitored. Some employers have even installed hidden cameras to watch or listen to what workers think are private moments. But what about after hours?

More and more workers are being told what they can and can't do in their free time. Today, over 6,000 companies say no to smoking during or after work, and it's not just private corporations. Lewis Maltby of the American Civil Liberties Union (ACLU) said, "The city of North Miami had a policy that it would not hire anyone who smoked off duty or had smoked off duty six months before applying for the job. The ACLU challenged that policy in court and lost."

In an effort to cut insurance costs some companies discourage high risk activities like bungee jumping or even riding a motorcycle. But how far can they go? In Suffolk County, New York, there is a proposal on the table to prevent Sheriff's Deputies from drinking, even off duty. Maltby says that would be going too far. He said, "If the Suffolk County Sheriff's Department wants to make sure that the sheriffs aren't coming to work hung over, or drinking on the job, good for them; but if one of the sheriffs wants to go out with his buddies or her buddies on Saturday night and have a couple of beers it's none of the Sheriff's Department's business."

Some states are fighting to protect employees. Twenty-nine states have enacted some form of law to make sure that employees can engage in legal activities like smoking or drinking, despite objections from their employers. But with private companies, if there is no state law, there's little an employee can do. Maltby noted, "In the other 21 states your boss can run your life 24 hours a day if they want to, and there's no law against it."

The employers say it's not about running lives, it's about running businesses—that healthier employees make fewer mistakes and file fewer insurance claims. And while employees and employers want a safer workplace, the question remains—whether surrendering certain personal freedoms is the way to achieve it.

Discussion Questions

1. What type of power can employers use to influence workers' behavior beyond the organization walls? What type of power is inappropriate?

2. Do you think employees have counterpower that they can use to balance demand from employers regarding their out of the office behaviors?

3. What role does the ACLU play in the politics of employee freedom outside of the organization? ◼

TEAM EXERCISE

General Software Products: An in-basket exercise

Purpose

This exercise is designed to help you understand the dynamics and feelings of power in an organizational setting.

Instructions

Here are the steps to complete this exercise. The instructor may alter these activities.

- *Step 1:* The instructor will briefly describe what an in-basket is, including the time constraints. Each student receives a package with copies of e-mails and memos. (Note: Instead of working individually, your instructor may decide to assign the in-basket exercise to teams. If so, the following steps still apply, but Step 2 would refer to teams.)

- *Step 2:* Read the "In-Basket Setting" below. Then you have 25 minutes to go through the in-basket, regardless of how many items you actually complete. Please respond to each item in the package.

- *Step 3:* Immediately after completing the in-basket exercise, each student will complete the attitude scale provided by the instructor.

- *Step 4:* The instructor will debrief students on the exercise.

IN-BASKET SETTING

Students take the role of J. Carter, a personal computer (PC) software department manager in General Software

Products, one of the companies owned by General Holding Corporation. You are requested to respond to several e-mails, letters, and memos that have been left in your in-basket. General Holding Corp. is a large company that competes in the computer industry. Please act as if you are J. Carter, department manager for PC Software at General Software Products.

General Software develops a wide variety of software products. You, J. Carter, have just been promoted from the position of Computer Games Group manager. The previous department manager for PC Software, Sam White, died suddenly of a heart attack three weeks ago and, as many predicted (including yourself), you were appointed to the position. This new promotion represents a natural progression for someone fast-tracking through management levels at General Software Products. Your new position also carries with it membership in the firm's Software Steering Committee. This committee meets with the firm's chief executive officer, David Brown, to discuss key strategic policy decisions.

Source: D. Eylon and S. Herman, "Exploring Empowerment: One Method for the Classroom," *Journal of Management Education* 23 (February 1999), pp. 80–94. Used with permission of the authors. ◼

SELF-ASSESSMENT EXERCISE

Perceptions of politics scale (POPS)

Purpose

This self-assessment is designed to help you to assess the degree to which you view your work or school environment as politically charged.

Instructions

Listed below are statements that might or might not describe the school where you are attending classes. These statements refer to the administration of the school, not the classroom. Please indicate whether you agree or disagree with each statement by circling the number of your choice. Then calculate your score using the scoring guidelines below.

	Strongly agree	Agree	Neutral	Disagree	Strongly disagree
1. Administrators at this school tend to build themselves up by tearing others down.	5	4	3	2	1
2. Employees at this school are encouraged to speak out frankly even when they are critical of well-established ideas.	5	4	3	2	1
3. There is no place for "yes-men" here; good ideas are desired even if it means disagreeing with superiors.	5	4	3	2	1
4. Agreeing with powerful administrators is the best alternative in this organization.	5	4	3	2	1
5. At this school, there has always been an influential group of administrators whom no one ever crosses.	5	4	3	2	1
6. Sometimes it is easier to remain quiet than to fight the system at this school.	5	4	3	2	1
7. It is best not to rock the boat in this organization.	5	4	3	2	1
8. At this school, telling employees what they want to hear is sometimes better than telling the truth.	5	4	3	2	1
9. At this school, employees have to follow what they are told than to make up their own mind. . . .	5	4	3	2	1

Scoring the Perceptions of Politics Scale (POPS)

To calculate your score on the Perceptions of Politics Scale, assign the appropriate number to each question from the scoring key below. Then add up the numbers.

For statement items 1, 4, 5, 6, 7, 8, 9		For statement items 2, 3	
Strongly agree	= 5	Strongly agree	= 1
Agree	= 4	Agree	= 2
Neutral	= 3	Neutral	= 3
Disagree	= 2	Disagree	= 4
Strongly disagree	= 1	Strongly disagree	= 5

Write the scores for each item on the appropriate line below (statement numbers are in brackets), and add up each scale.

General political behavior   ___ + ___   = _____
                              (1)   (5)   (Subtotal A)

Go along to get ahead   ___ + ___ + ___ + ___ + ___ + ___ + ___ = _____
                           (2)   (3)   (4)   (6)   (7)   (8)   (9)   (Subtotal B)

Total Score: _____ + _____   = _____
                           (Subtotal A)   (Subtotal B)   (Total)

Source: Adapted from K. M. Kacmar, "Further Validation of the Perceptions of Politics Scale (POPS): A Multiple Sample Investigation," *Journal of Management* 23 (1997), pp. 627–58. ■

Organizational Conflict and Negotiation

Learning Objectives

After reading this chapter, you should be able to:

- Distinguish task-related from socioemotional conflict.
- Discuss the advantages and disadvantages of conflict in organizations.
- Identify six sources of organizational conflict.
- Outline the five interpersonal styles of conflict management.
- Summarize six structural approaches to managing conflict.
- Outline four situational influences on negotiations.
- Compare and contrast the three types of third-party dispute resolution.

Andersen Consulting and Arthur Andersen were supposed to cooperate and maintain unity as sister firms. Instead, the accounting and management consulting businesses are locked in a vicious divorce battle.
[AP Wide World]

The double doors on Arthur Andersen's corporate seal symbolize a unified organization. This sense of unity was supposed to continue when, in 1989, the accounting firm formed Andersen Consulting as a separate entity for its management consulting business. Today, the accounting and management consulting businesses are engaged in a vicious divorce battle.

One reason for the rift is that Andersen Consulting is now more profitable than Arthur Andersen, so its partners must hand over more than $100 million annually to the accounting partners. Andersen Consulting partners also became incensed when the accounting group created its own business consulting unit and bid on projects that were supposed to be the sole territory of Andersen Consulting.

Some observers say that problems began years ago when the management consultants were no longer required to spend two years in the accounting practice. This psychological distance increased when the management and accounting practices formed separate entities. "There's no cultural connection between the firms," says an industry observer.

Whatever the cause, the conflict has led to a battle of words and actions. The top managing partners of the two businesses no longer share adjoining offices. The two companies don't even link their web sites. When Andersen Consulting went public with its complaints, partners at Arthur Andersen stated that the management consulting group was trying to "inflict pain," so they increased their resolve to make them pay a hefty price for leaving. Meanwhile, Andersen Consulting claims that the accountants are trying to put them "out of business."

The two Andersen businesses failed to settle the dispute through arbitration, and are now heading toward a difficult and potentially costly separation. "The War of the Roses puts it lightly," says a former partner of the strained relationship.[1]

onflict may occur anywhere two or more people interact with each other. It can either energize the organization or, as we saw at Andersen, degenerate into a war of words and actions. This chapter looks at the dynamics of conflict in organizational settings. We begin by defining conflict, describing the conflict cycle, and discussing the consequences and sources of conflict in the workplace. Five conflict management styles are then described, followed by a discussion of the structural approaches to conflict management. The last two sections of this chapter introduce two procedures for resolving conflict: negotiation and third-party resolution.

What Is Conflict?

conflict the process in which one party perceives that its interests are being opposed or negatively affected by another party

Conflict is a process in which one party perceives that its interests are being opposed or negatively affected by another party.[2] Conflict is a perception, so it exists whenever someone believes or feels that another person or group might obstruct its efforts. This may be a mild disagreement between two people regarding the best choice in a decision. Or it may be the foundation of an all-out war between two nations.

The conflict process actually begins with the conditions that create conflict.[3] In this chapter, we will describe these sources of conflict, such as scarce resources and task interdependence. At some point, these conditions lead one or both parties to perceive that conflict exists. This perception generates feelings of conflict toward the other party. For example, you may feel angry with another employee because you realize that he or she needs the same resources that you require for your work. Perceptions and feelings of conflict usually lead to *manifest conflict*—behaviors that indicate the person's conflict toward the other party. These conflict episodes may range from subtle nonverbal behaviors to warlike aggression against the other person. Conflict aftermath refers to the relationship and situation after each conflict episode. The conflict episode may motivate the parties to alter the conditions, clarify misperceptions about their conflict, or escalate the conflict to the next stage.

Task-Related versus Socioemotional Conflict

When asked what Toyota Motor Company does to make such great cars, one engineer replied, "Lots of conflict."[4] Toyota executives know that conflict is not always bad. Successful organizations encourage mild forms of conflict without having it escalate into an emotional battle between employees or corporate divisions. The key is to keep conflict task related and prevent it from escalating to a socioemotional state.[5] When conflict is task related, the parties view the conflict experience as something separate from them. It is an object "out there" that must be addressed. This conflict is potentially healthy and valuable because it makes people rethink their perspectives of reality. As long as the conflict remains focused on the issue, new ideas may emerge and the conflict remains controlled.

Unfortunately, conflict often becomes personal. Rather than focusing on the issue, each party starts to see the other person as the problem. This socioemotional dimension is apparent at Arthur Andersen and Andersen Consulting because each side believed the other was deliberately trying to undermine its success. With socioemotional conflict, differences are viewed as personal attacks rather than attempts to resolve an issue. The discussion becomes emotionally charged, so that perceptual biases are introduced and information processing is impeded.

Conflict escalation cycle   The conflict process is often described as a series of conflict episodes that potentially link together into an escalation cycle or spiral.[6] It doesn't take much to start this conflict cycle—just an inappropriate comment, a misunderstanding, or an undiplomatic action. These behaviors send a signal to the other party that some sort of conflict exists. If the first party did not intend to demonstrate conflict, then the second party's response may create that perception.

If the conflict remains task related, both parties may resolve it through logical analysis. However, the communication process has enough ambiguity that a few words may trigger an emotional response and set the stage for socioemotional conflict. The perceptual process then adopts an "us-them" frame of reference, so that the other party's actions are more likely to receive a negative interpretation. These distorted beliefs and emotions reduce the motivation to communicate with the other side, making it more difficult to discover common ground and ultimately resolve the conflict.[7] Unfortunately, the parties then rely more on stereotypes and emotions to reinforce their perceptions of the other party. As we shall learn in this chapter, some structural conditions increase the likelihood of conflict escalation. Employees who are more confrontational and less diplomatic also tend to escalate conflict.[8]

Consequences of Organizational Conflict

There is a natural tendency to suppress conflict. While suppression may be appropriate for socioemotional conflict, task related conflict should be

Meyocks & Priebe Advertising encourages constructive controversy. The West Des Moines, Iowa, firm wants its 75 employees to evaluate ideas critically and ensure that dominant participants do not overwhelm these spirited meetings. "We thrive on conflict," says Ted Priebe, president of Meyocks & Priebe. "We actually encourage confrontation as part of our culture. Often there's spirited discussions on what to show the client. It's kind of fun."[9] What conditions must apply to ensure that conflict in these meetings remains task oriented and doesn't become socioemotional? *[Courtesy of Meyocks & Priebe Advertising]*

conflict management
interventions that alter the level and form of conflict in ways that maximize its benefits and minimize its dysfunctional consequences

encouraged under some conditions.[10] Thus, **conflict management** refers to interventions that alter the level and form of conflict in ways that maximize its benefits and minimize its dysfunctional consequences.

It has been said that if two people agree, one of them is unnecessary. This means that conflict is good (potentially) and that agreement is redundant. This is the concept of constructive controversy that we introduced in Chapter 11. Task-related conflict helps people to recognize problems, identify a variety of solutions, and understand the issues involved.[11] Conflict is a catalyst for change and improved decision making. It occurs when people offer new perspectives and these emerging views are debated.[12]

Conflict between groups or organizations potentially improves team dynamics within those units. Teams increase their cohesiveness and task orientation when they face an external threat. Under conditions of moderate conflict, this motivates team members to work more efficiently toward these goals, thereby increasing the team's productivity.

There is of course a darker side to conflict in organizations. When intergroup conflict becomes emotionally charged, teams become so cohesive that they are no longer motivated to seek outside information. In other words, a high level of socioemotional conflict may lead to groupthink, the tendency of highly cohesive groups to value consensus at the price of decision quality.[13]

At an individual level, socioemotional conflict increases the levels of frustration, job dissatisfaction, and stress. In the longer term, this leads to higher turnover or absenteeism.[14] These symptoms are showing up among executives at Walt Disney Corp. Disney CEO Michael Eisner apparently supports an environment where executives battle each other over scarce resources. The idea is to bring out constructive controversy, but some insiders claim that several executives left the animation and entertainment firm because constant conflict wore them down.[15] Connections 13.1 (pp. 406–7) provides another illustration of the adverse consequences of conflict at the CAMI and Subaru-Isuzu automobile plants. Conflict in these firms generates an "us versus them" perception that leads to the tactics described.

Sources of Conflict in Organizations

What are the main sources of conflict in organizations? We often hear about "personality conflicts" in which people have divergent personal values and dispositions. Although personality differences certainly influence conflict, this phrase often masks the underlying causes of conflict behavior and perceptions. Instead, organizational research has identified six conditions, shown in Exhibit 13.1 and described over the next few pages, under which conflict tends to germinate and flourish. In a given situation, more than one of these six factors may be contributing to conflict.

Goal Incompatibility

A common source of conflict is goal incompatibility. As the name implies, goal incompatibility occurs when people or work units have goals that interfere with each other. Financial rewards for goal accomplishment further entrench the perceived conflict because employees are more motivated to pursue their own goals.[16]

Goal incompatibility partly explains why conflicts occur between investment analysts and corporate finance staff in investment banks.[17] Analysts try to provide objective and independent advice to investors regarding whether certain securities should be purchased or sold. Meanwhile, the corporate

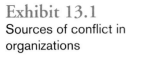

Exhibit 13.1
Sources of conflict in organizations

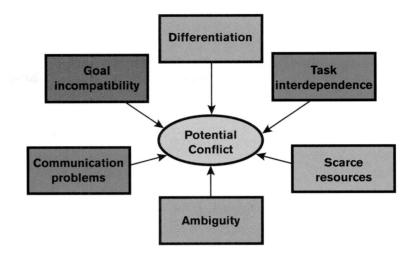

finance department within the same bank competes for capital offerings and mergers and acquisitions. Conflicts due to goal incompatibility occur when the bank's investment analysts discourage investors from buying securities that the bank's finance department is offering to the public.

Differentiation

BBK&M, a small consulting firm in Orem, Utah, has only four part-time partners, but their diverse backgrounds are enough to spark the occasional tension. "We have two [partners] from around here, one from Venezuela, and one from Ireland," explains Nathan Hatch, one of BBK&M's partners. "One is a computer scientist with an M.B.A., one has his M.B.A. in finance, and two of us have marketing backgrounds. Combine that with the cultural mix and we have the potential for some interesting controversy."[18]

Conflicts at BBK&M are caused mainly by differentiation. Differentiation occurs when people hold divergent beliefs and attitudes due to their unique backgrounds, experiences, or training. For example, BBK&M's partners have divergent technical backgrounds, so they tend to see problems in a particular way and have difficulty understanding each other's perspectives. Organizations unwittingly fuel conflict by hiring people for their technical knowledge and encouraging them to become even more specialized.

BBK&M's partners also experience some conflict arising from cultural differences. People from different cultural backgrounds may have difficulty understanding or accepting each other's beliefs and values toward organizational decisions and events. Moreover, behaviors of people from different backgrounds are more easily misinterpreted. Quite often, we rely on traditional stereotypes to explain the behaviors of people whom we seldom meet (such as Malaysian executives who work at a distance from their American counterparts), thereby increasing the perception of conflict.[19]

Finally, we should mention that differentiation explains why conflict is a common problem following mergers and acquisitions. Employees in the merged organizations often hold divergent corporate values, so they fight over the 'right way' to do things. This occurred when Japan's Mitsui Bank and Taiyo Kobe Bank merged to form Sakura Bank. Executives at the two banks had such divergent views on issues that they refused to work together, even on basic operational matters. "They wouldn't even sit down in the same room together," complains an American banker who tried to work with Sakura's executives.[20]

Task Interdependence

task interdependence the degree to which team members must share common inputs, interact in the process of executing their work, or receive outcomes determined partly by their mutual performance

Conflict tends to increase with the level of **task interdependence.** Recall from Chapter 9 that task interdependence exists when team members must share common inputs to their individual tasks, need to interact in the process of executing their work, or receive outcomes (such as rewards) that are partly determined by the performance of others.[21] The higher the level of task interdependence, the greater the risk of conflict, because there is a greater chance that each side will disrupt or interfere with the other side's goals.[22] Exhibit 13.2 (p. 408) illustrates the three levels of task interdependence.[23]

- *Pooled interdependence*—This is the lowest level of interdependence (other than independence), in which work units operate independently except for reliance on a common resource or authority. Students experience pooled interdependence when they are lined up at the laser printers trying to get their assignments completed just before a class deadline. The same thing happens in organizations. Corporate divisions must share scarce resources provided by headquarters, thereby increasing potential conflict.

Connections 13.1 ◼ **Revenge of the Andons: Conflict at Subaru-Isuzu and CAMI**

Rather than being a model of cooperative labor-management relations, this Subaru-Isuzu automobile plant may have become a battlefield of industrial conflict.

[*Patty Espich*/The Indianapolis Star & News]

- *Sequential interdependence*—This occurs where the output of one person or unit becomes the direct input for another person or unit. Sequential interdependence is found in fish processing plants. Fish are handled by the slitter, then passed to the gutter, who then pass their work to the slimers, who then send their work to the grader.[24]
- *Reciprocal interdependence*—This is the highest level of interdependence, in which work output is exchanged back and forth among individuals or work units. Reciprocal interdependence exists between bus drivers and maintenance crews in many public transportation companies. Drivers are dependent on the maintenance crews to keep the buses in good repair, whereas the maintenance crews are dependent on the drivers to operate the vehicles wisely so that their work is minimized.

Scarce Resources

Scarce resources generate conflict because scarcity motivates people to compete with others who also need those resources to achieve their objectives.[25] This occurs at Sony's video game group, where the artists who develop Spawn

The Subaru-Isuzu plant in Indiana and the General Motors-Suzuki plant (CAMI) in Ontario, Canada, were supposed to be models of cooperative labor-management relations. Instead, understaffing and the stress of continuous improvement *(kaizen)* may have created battlefields of industrial conflict.

Employees are hitting back with andons—the yellow and red cords at each workstation that management provided to improve productivity. When an employee pulls the yellow andon, a repetitive song starts playing and the workstation number is lighted on a large board above the assembly line. This alerts the team leader that help is needed at that station. The red andon cord stops the entire assembly line, so employees are discouraged from pulling it unless a team leader is not available to solve the problem with the line moving.

Employees at CAMI rebelled against understaffing by frequently pulling the red andons. "One of the things we did out at the CAMI plant . . . was to get people to pull those damn andon cords," explains Rob Pelletier, a former CAMI employee. "If you're short people, stop the line. They put those cords there, not us."

For example, one CAMI team was understaffed because management refused to replace an injured employee. In retaliation, the team started pulling the red andons whenever they got behind a little. "They pulled that cord 87 times in one day," says Pelletier. "The new person was on that line the next day."

Employees at the Subaru-Isuzu automobile plant also use the andon cords to fight back. One production team even discovered how to stop the assembly line without management tracing their location. Whenever a team member fell behind and no team leader or group leader was in sight, the group executed its secret strategy and the entire car line stopped. This gave everyone an opportunity to catch up or take a break. It was also entertaining to watch management desperately trying to find the source of the line stoppage. On one shift, the team stopped the line several times for a total of 20 minutes!

Sources: L. Graham, "Yosh!" *Across the Board* 32 (October 1995), pp. 37–41; J. Rinehart, C. Huxley, and D. Robertson "Worker Commitment and Labour Management Relations under Lean Production at CAMI," *Industrial Relations* (Laval) 49 (1994), pp. 750–75; Canadian Auto Workers, *Working Lean: Challenging Work Reorganization* (Toronto: CAW, 1993), video. ∎

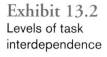

Exhibit 13.2
Levels of task
interdependence

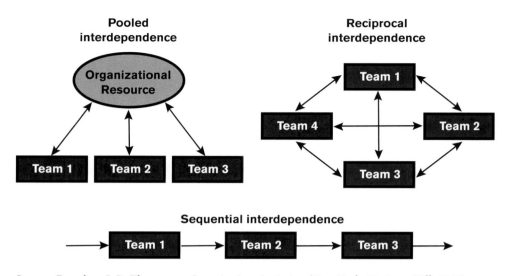

Source: Based on J. D. Thompson, *Organizations in Action* (New York: McGraw-Hill, 1967), pp. 54–56.

and other sci-fi games must compete for resources with the artists who develop sports-related games like NFL GameDay. Differentiation partly explains this conflict. "We call them the 'Ghouls and Goblins' and they call us the 'Dumb Jocks,'" laughs Chris Whaley, who heads the sports group. But the conflict is aggravated because both groups share a limited budget. "Teams are competing for internal resources for marketing dollars, support for their products," explains a Sony executive. "And they know how much that matters."[26]

Ambiguity

Ambiguity breeds conflict because the uncertainty increases the risk that one party intends to interfere with the other party's goals. Ambiguity also encourages political tactics and, in some cases, employees enter a free-for-all battle to win decisions in their favor. When rules exist, on the other hand, everyone knows what to expect from each other and have agreed to abide by those rules.

Communication Problems

Conflict often occurs due to the lack of opportunity, ability, or motivation to communicate effectively. Let's look at each of these causes. First, when two parties lack the opportunity to communicate, they tend to use stereotypes to explain past behaviors and anticipate future actions. Unfortunately, stereotypes are sufficiently subjective that emotions can negatively distort the meaning of an opponent's actions, thereby escalating perceptions of conflict. Moreover, without direct interaction, the two sides have less psychological empathy for each other.

Second, some people lack the necessary skills to communicate in a diplomatic, nonconfrontational manner. When one party communicates its disagreement in an arrogant way, opponents are more likely to heighten their perception of the conflict. Arrogant behavior also sends a message that one side intends to be competitive rather than cooperative. This may lead the other party to reciprocate with a similar conflict management style.[27] Consequently, as we explained earlier, ineffective communication often leads to an escalation in the conflict cycle.

Ineffective communication can also lead to a third problem: less motivation to communicate in the future. For example, an accountant was verbally abused by an information services manager soon after the accountant was hired. Since then, he has avoided the manager, leaving some problems undetected and unresolved. Another employee reported that the relationship with his manager deteriorated to such an extent that for five months they communicated only by e-mail.[28] These reactions aren't surprising. Socioemotional conflict is uncomfortable, so people are less motivated to interact with others in a conflicting relationship. Unfortunately, less communication can further escalate the conflict because there's less opportunity to empathize with the opponent's situation and opponents are more likely to rely on distorted stereotypes of the other party. Indeed, conflict tends to further distort these stereotypes through the process of social identity (see Chapter 6).[29] We begin to see competitors less favorably so that our self-identity remains strong during these uncertain times.

The lack of motivation to communicate also explains (along with differentiation, described earlier) why conflict is more common in cross-cultural relationships. People tend to feel uncomfortable or awkward interacting with co-workers from different cultures, so they are less motivated to engage in dialogue with them.[30] With limited communication, people rely more on stereotypes to fill in missing information. They also tend to misunderstand each other's verbal and nonverbal signals, further escalating the conflict.

Interpersonal Conflict Management Styles

win–win orientation a person's belief that the parties will find a mutually beneficial solution to their conflict

win–lose orientation a person's belief that the conflicting parties are drawing from a fixed pie, so his or her gain is the other person's loss

The six structural factors described above set the stage for conflict. However, conflict is an interpersonal process, so we also need to consider the perceptions, expectations, and values that people bring to the relationship. Some people enter a conflict with a **win–win orientation.** This is the perception that the parties will find a mutually beneficial solution to their disagreement. They believe that the resources at stake are expandable rather than fixed if the parties work together to find a creative solution. Other people enter a conflict with a **win–lose orientation.** They adopt the belief that the parties are drawing from a fixed pie, so the more one party receives, the more the other party forfeits.

Conflict tends to escalate when the parties develop a win–lose orientation because they rely on power and politics to gain advantage. A win–lose orientation may occasionally be appropriate when the conflict really is over a fixed resource, but few organizational conflicts are due to perfectly opposing interests with fixed resources. To varying degrees, the opposing groups can gain by believing that their positions aren't perfectly opposing and that creative solutions are possible. For instance, a supplier and customer may initially think they have opposing interests—the supplier wants to receive more money for the product, whereas the customer wants to pay less money for it. Yet, further discussion may reveal that the customer would be willing to pay more if the product could be provided earlier than originally arranged. The vendor may actually value that earlier delivery because it reduces inventory costs. By looking at the bigger picture, both parties can often discover common ground.

Adopting a win–win or win–lose orientation influences the way we approach the conflict, including our actions toward the other person. Researchers have categorized five interpersonal styles of approaching the other party in a conflict situation. As we see in Exhibit 13.3, each approach can be placed in a two-dimensional grid reflecting the person's motivation to satisfy his or her own interests (called *assertiveness*) and to satisfy the other party's interests (called *cooperativeness*).[31] Collaboration is the only style that represents a purely win-win orientation. The other four styles represent variations of the win–lose approach.[32] For effective conflict management, we should learn to apply different conflict management styles to different situations.[33]

• *Collaborating*—Collaboration is trying to find a mutually beneficial solution for both parties through problem solving. An important feature of

Exhibit 13.3
Interpersonal conflict
management styles

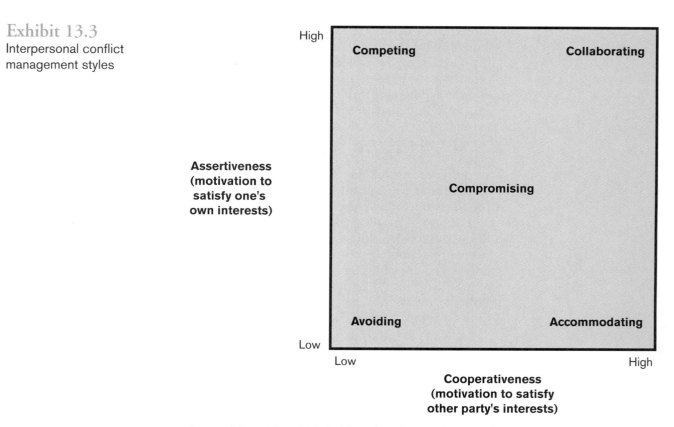

Source: Adapted from T. L. Ruble and K. Thomas, "Support for a Two-Dimensional Model of Conflict Behavior," *Organizational Behavior and Human Performance* 16 (1976), p. 145.

collaboration is information sharing so that both parties can identify common ground and potential solutions that satisfy both (or all) of them.

• *Avoiding*—Avoidance is trying to smooth over or avoid conflict situations altogether. For example, some employees will rearrange their work area or tasks to minimize interaction with certain co-workers.[34]

• *Competing*—Competition is trying to win the conflict at the other's expense. This style has the strongest win–lose orientation because it has the highest level of assertiveness and lowest level of cooperativeness.

• *Accommodating*—Accommodation involves giving in completely to the other side's wishes, or at least cooperating with little or no attention to your own interests.

• *Compromising*—Compromise is trying to reach a middle ground with the other party. You look for a position in which your losses are offset by equally valued gains.

Choosing the Best Conflict Management Style

Most people have a preferred conflict management style, but they will use different styles under different conditions. The skill of conflict management is to apply the right style for the situation. In other words, we need to recognize the contingency approach to conflict management.

The collaborative style is usually the preferred approach to conflict resolution, but it is the most appropriate approach only under certain conditions. Specifically, it is best when the parties do not have perfectly opposing interests and when they have enough trust and openness to share information. Collaborating is usually desirable because organizational conflicts are rarely win–lose situations. There is usually some opportunity for mutual gain if the parties search for creative solutions.[35]

You might think that avoiding is an ineffective conflict management strategy, but it may be the best approach when the issue is trivial or as a temporary tactic to cool down heated disputes. However, conflict avoidance should not be a long-term solution because it increases the other party's frustration.

The competing style to conflict resolution is usually inappropriate because organizational relationships rarely involve complete opposition. However, competing may be necessary when you know you are correct and the dispute requires a quick solution. It may also be necessary where the other party would take advantage of more cooperative strategies. For example, we tend to shift from the collaborating to the competing style when we see that the other party uses the information we provide to benefit themselves rather than to find a mutually agreeable solution.

The accommodating style may be appropriate when the other party has substantially more power or the issue is not as important to you as to the other party. On the other hand, accommodating behaviors may give the other side unrealistically high expectations, thereby motivating them to seek more from you in the future. In the long run, accommodating may produce more conflict rather than resolve it.

The compromising style may be best when there is little hope for mutual gain through problem solving, both parties have equal power, and both are under time pressure to settle their differences. However, compromise rarely produces the best solution because the parties overlook options for mutual gain.

Cultural and Gender Differences in Conflict Management Styles

Although the conflict style we choose is partly influenced by the type of dispute, it is also affected by personal characteristics, including cultural background. Culture determines the values and interests on which conflict is defined. Cultural values cause some people to perceive a conflict where others do not. Moreover, even where two people from different cultures perceive the same conflict, their conflict management style may differ because conflict styles must be consistent with the person's personal and cultural value system.[36]

People from collectivist cultures—where group goals are valued more than individual goals—tend to collaborate or avoid conflict with other team members. People from individualistic cultures compromise or compete with co-workers more frequently. Collectivists tend to collaborate more than individualists within the group because they identify themselves with the team's common goals and are therefore motivated to maintain harmonious relations. However, this collaboration extends mainly within the social group. People from collectivist cultures can be just as competitive as individualists with people outside their group.[37]

Cultural similarity of the two parties also seems to influence the conflict management style used. Specifically, research on international joint ventures has found that a collaborative style to conflict resolution is more commonly used where the partners view themselves as being culturally alike.[38] They discuss concerns more quickly and openly, seek their partner's opinions, and explain their course of action more fully than when dealing with culturally divergent partners. As you might expect, the collaborative conflict management approach results in better joint venture performance.

Some writers suggest that men and women tend to rely on different conflict management styles.[39] Generally speaking, women pay more attention than men to the relationship between the parties. Consequently, they tend to adopt a collaborative style in business settings, and are more willing to compromise to protect the relationship. Men tend to be more competitive and take a short-term orientation to the relationship. Of course, we must be cautious about these observations because gender has a weak influence on conflict management style.

Structural Approaches to Conflict Management

The conflict management styles described above focus on how to approach the other party in a conflict situation, but conflict management also involves altering the underlying structural causes of potential conflict. The main structural approaches are identified in Exhibit 13.4. Although this section discusses ways to reduce conflict, we should keep in mind that conflict management sometimes calls for increasing conflict. This occurs mainly by reversing the strategies described over the next few pages.[40]

Emphasizing Superordinate Goals

superordinate goals
common objectives held by conflicting parties that are more important than their conflicting departmental or individual goals

One way to minimize conflict is by focusing everyone on **superordinate goals.** Superordinate goals are common objectives held by conflicting parties that are more important than the departmental or individual goals on which the conflict is based. For instance, USAA keeps its 9,000 employees focused on the superordinate goal of serving customers. The successful insurance firm headquartered in San Antonio, Texas, reinforces this goal in weekly pep rallies and other meetings so that employees keep their minds on the company's larger mission.[41]

Focusing attention on superordinate goals is particularly useful where conflict is caused by goal incompatibility and differentiation. By increasing commitment to corporatewide goals, employees feel less conflict with co-workers regarding competing individual or departmental level goals.[42] Superordinate goals offset the problem of differentiation because they establish a common frame of reference. Heterogeneous team members still perceive different ways to achieve corporate objectives, but the superordinate goal strategy ensures that they mutually understand and agree upon the objectives themselves.

How effective are superordinate goals in conflict management? According to a recent study of top management teams, the most effective decision-

Exhibit 13.4
Structural approaches to conflict management

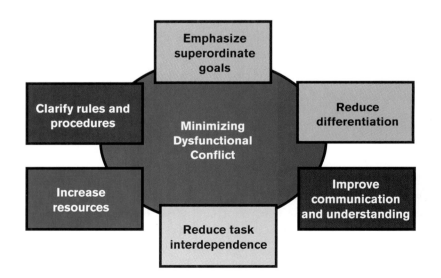

DaimlerChrysler is a pioneer in concurrent engineering, in which engineers work concurrently with purchasing, manufacturing, finance, and outside suppliers to develop the next generation of vehicles. Along with cutting development costs, concurrent engineering reduces dysfunctional conflict because team members focus on the superordinate goal to develop a better automobile design. "We have worked very hard at eliminating the adversarial relationship that once existed between internal functions," explains a DaimlerChrysler executive. "We now believe we work together as one team with a common objective: to provide the best possible vehicle to the customer."[44] What other structural sources of conflict are minimized through concurrent engineering teams? *[Alan Levenson/Tony Stone Images]*

making groups consistently apply this strategy.[43] They frame their decisions as collaborations, thereby drawing attention and commitment away from sub-level goals. Moreover, the study found that superordinate goals minimize socioemotional conflict. Team members are more likely to support common objectives even though they might disagree on the means to achieve those objectives.

Reducing Differentiation

Superordinate goals offset differentiation by establishing a common frame of reference, but they don't actually remove any of the underlying diversity that people bring to the relationship. To reduce differentiation, we must alter or re-move the conditions that create these differences in the first place. Some firms, such as Honda of America, try to reduce differentiation by having everyone wear the same work clothes. This may reduce the "us" versus "them" differences that exist in more hierarchical organizations. However, differentiation is mainly based on unique experiences and values, not just the symbols of these differences.

To fundamentally reduce differentiation, some firms encourage and rein-force a generalist rather than specialist career orientation. For example, many Japanese companies move people around to different jobs, departments, and regions so that they eventually develop common experiences with other senior decision makers in the organization.[45] Similarly, W. L. Gore and Associates re-duces differentiation by moving employees around to different teams. The manufacturer of GoreTex and other products introduced this team rotation system after it became apparent that employees were becoming too commit-ted to their own team's goals. "You can get a little too focused on your own team and forget the good of the whole company," admits one of Gore's team members.[46]

Improving Communication and Understanding

Communication is critical to effective conflict management. By improving the opportunity, ability, and motivation to share information, the parties develop less extreme perceptions of each other than if they rely on stereotypes and

Embassy Suites relied on dialogue to reduce conflict between housekeeping and engineering staff. Housekeepers are supposed to notify engineers when a TV remote control battery is dead, but they rarely bothered because they thought that engineering ignored the work orders. Embassy Suites arranged a special dialogue session to discuss these matters. At the meeting, housekeepers were surprised to learn that engineers treated the work orders very seriously but it often took a week to get the necessary parts. This discussion corrected a long misunderstanding between the two groups.[47] What structural source of conflict did dialogue help to overcome? Would dialogue be less effective for any other sources of conflict? [John Thoeming]

dialogue a process of conversation among team members in which they learn about each other's mental models and assumptions, and eventually form a common model for thinking within the team

intergroup mirroring a structured conflict management intervention in which the parties discuss their perceptions of each other and look for ways to improve their relationship by correcting misperceptions

emotions. Direct communication provides a better understanding of the other party's work environment and resource limitations. Ongoing communication is particularly important where the need for technical expertise makes it difficult to reduce differentiation.[48]

Some companies introduce **dialogue** meetings, in which the disputing parties discuss their differences. In Chapter 9, we learned that dialogue helps participants to understand each other's mental models and fundamental assumptions so that they can create a common mental model for the team.[49]

Dialogue can also occur informally, simply by giving the parties more opportunity to interact with each other. Oticon Holdings A/S, the Danish hearing-aid company, has kept dysfunctional conflict to a minimum in this way. Its open office design allows more communication and understanding across technical specialties. "When people move around and sit next to different people, they learn something about what others are doing," explains Poul Erik Lyregaard, Oticon's R&D leader. "They also learn to respect what those people do. It's hard to maintain 'enemy pictures' in this company—they're not 'those bloody fools in marketing.' You know too much about what people do."[50]

Intergroup mirroring When relations between two or more work teams or departments are openly hostile, it may be advisable to introduce **intergroup mirroring** with the assistance of a trained facilitator.[51] The basic objective is for the conflicting groups to express their perceptions, discuss their differences, and then work out strategies to improve the relationship. The process is unique because both sides share their images of themselves and each other so that distortions and misunderstandings are revealed and ultimately corrected.

Intergroup mirroring is usually a multiday retreat that begins with the parties identifying and prioritizing their relationship problems. Next, the two groups separately list three sets of perceptions. One list describes the group's perception of itself. The second list describes how the group perceives the other group. The third list describes the group's beliefs about how the other group perceives it. The "mirroring" activity in intergroup mirroring occurs when the two sides meet again to exchange their perceptions of each other. After discussing these perceptions, the two sides jointly review their relationship problems, usually in small groups that combine both sides. Finally, the participants establish goals and action plans to correct their perceptual distortions and establish more favorable relationships in the future. This typically includes future meetings that review and evaluate progress.

Reducing Task Interdependence

Another way to minimize dysfunctional conflict is to reduce the level of interdependence between the parties. If cost effective, this might occur by dividing the shared resource so that each party has exclusive use of part of it. Sequentially or reciprocally interdependent jobs might be combined so that they form a pooled interdependence. For example, rather than having one employee serve customers and another operate the cash register, each employee could handle both customer activities.

Another way to reduce task interdependence is to introduce buffers between people. Buffers might take the form of resources, such as adding more inventory between people who perform sequential tasks. We also find human buffers in organizations—people who intervene between highly interdependent people or work units.[52] Mobil Oil relies on coordinating councils to work with upstream (drilling) and downstream (processing and marketing) work units. These two groups have significantly different perspectives of the oil business, so the coordination councils minimize the need for direct communication and thereby reduce the potential for escalating conflict between the upstream and downstream employees.[53] The *Fast Company Online* feature for this chapter further illustrates how team leaders are human buffers who minimize dysfunctional conflict between younger employees and older executives.

Increasing Resources

An obvious way to reduce conflict due to resource scarcity is to increase the amount of resources available. Corporate decision makers might quickly dismiss this solution because of the costs involved. However, they need to carefully compare these costs with the costs of dysfunctional conflict arising out of resource scarcity.

Clarifying Rules and Procedures

Some conflicts arise from ambiguous decision rules regarding the allocation of scarce resources. Consequently, these conflicts can be minimized by establishing rules and procedures. "I think the key to avoiding conflict is to be up front and tell people what you expect," advises Hubert Hawkins, manager of Car Painters near Fort Worth, Texas. "Whether it's overtime, cleanup, tools, parts—whatever—if you make it clear up front, it minimizes misunderstandings and leads to a good working environment."[54] As we learn in Connections 13.2, information systems people at Armstrong Worldwide, Inc. learned this lesson when conflicts emerged between their information systems people and consultants from Booz Allen & Hamilton, Inc.

One way to clarify rules is to establish a schedule for sharing scarce resources. If two departments are fighting over the use of a new laboratory, a schedule might be established that allocates the lab exclusively to each team at certain times of the day or week. In some respects, the schedule reduces resource interdependence by dividing it up among those who need it to fulfill their goals. By redefining the terms of interdependence, the strategy of clarifying rules is part of the larger process of negotiation.

Resolving Conflict through Negotiation

Think back through yesterday's events. Maybe you had to work out an agreement with other students about what tasks to complete for a team project.

FAST COMPANY
Online

▪ Stop the Fight

In most organizations today, you can hear the sounds of two generations colliding. In one corner, the forty-somethings view the new workforce entrants as know-it-all kiddies—the webheads who can't run their own lives, let alone a company. In the other corner, the twenty-somethings see their over-the-hill counterparts as utterly clueless about technology and dangerously out of touch with markets.

To keep the peace between these two generations, companies rely on savvy team leaders who buffer the young upstarts and provide a means of indirect communication between both groups. That's what Mark Benerofe does. The 39-year-old executive in charge of The Station, Sony's popular web site, protects his crew of programmers from out-of-touch executives.

"If there's one thing I've learned from youth culture, it's that playing the hierarchical game is dumb," says Benerofe. "You have to share knowledge. And you have to earn your stripes." Benerofe has earned his stripes with his hard-working programmers. He was one of the youngest executive producers at CNN, the youngest director at Prodigy, and a hard-charging manager at Microsoft, where he initiated the MSNBC partnership.

But in the youth-obsessed world of the web, Benerofe is also a gray hair. So, he occasionally feels the same conflict that he tries to buffer from his staff. Recently, when he lunched with a young programmer at a Chinese restaurant, Benerofe had to explain the menu: "He was such a kid, he didn't know anything but chow mein." Then, in the middle of lunch, the programmer, skeptical of his companion's Net credentials, asked, "Do you have an e-mail account?" Benerofe couldn't help himself: "Since you were in diapers!" he replied.

ONLINE CHECK-UP
1. This *Fast Company Online* feature describes conflicts between young programmers and older managers at Sony. Look through this chapter to identify the structural sources that likely cause this conflict.
2. The full text of this *Fast Company* article describes other conflicts at iVillage, Philips Mobile Computing Group, and I-Traffic. Are these conflicts similar to those described at Sony? This feature describes buffering as a solution to this conflict, but what other conflict management strategies should be considered in these companies?

Get the full text of this *Fast Company* article at www.mhhe.com/mcshane1e

Source: Adapted from P. Kruger, "Stop the Fight," *Fast Company*, Issue 17 (September 1998). ▪

Connections 13.2 ◻ **Armstrong and Booz Allen Sort Out Their Differences**

Robyn Alspach *(shown)* and other staff at Armstrong Worldwide, Inc., learned that conflict can be minimized by clarifying rules.
[Nick Kelsh]

Armstrong Worldwide, Inc., didn't expect so much conflict when the flooring and building materials company brought in consultants from Booz Allen & Hamilton, Inc., to implement a client/server network. "[These conflicts] created a large amount of stress and some turnover for us," says Robyn Alspach, Armstrong's information systems development manager.

Armstrong discovered three sources of conflict during the contract with Booz Allen. First, although Armstrong had no plans to outsource its information systems activities, employees in that area were worried that they would be replaced by consultants. To some extent, this made them reluctant to give the consultants information about Armstrong's operations. "They think, 'Everything could get outsourced, so why should I share with them?'" Alspach explains.

A second source of conflict is who should lead the project—the people at Armstrong or Booz Allen? Booz Allen was given the leadership role, but this decision simply added to the tension. The problem was that Armstrong's information systems people would be responsible for the system long after the consultants from Booz Allen were gone, so they felt somewhat trapped by the consultants' power.

Scheduling was a third major source of conflict. Booz Allen consultants preferred working 12-hour days, Monday through Thursday, then flying home on Friday. This didn't sit well with Armstrong's people, who lived nearby and therefore favored a traditional schedule.

Armstrong and Booz Allen tried to minimize these conflicts by spelling out as much as possible in the contract about each party's responsibilities and roles. Issues that were unclear or overlooked in the contract were clarified by joint discussion between two senior executives at the companies. With the benefit of hindsight, Robyn Alspach offers the following advice: "You have to plan for the potential conflicts up front, then you have a better chance of resolving them amicably."

Source: Adapted from E. Horwitt, "Knowledge, Knowledge, Who's Got the Knowledge?" *Computerworld*, April 8, 1996, pp. 80–81, 84. ◻

negotiation any attempt by two or more conflicting parties to resolve their divergent goals by redefining the terms of their interdependence

Chances are that you shared transportation with someone, so you had to clarify the timing of the ride. Then perhaps there was the question of who was to make dinner. Each of these daily events created potential conflict, and they were resolved through negotiation. **Negotiation** occurs whenever two or more conflicting parties attempt to resolve their divergent goals by redefining the terms of their interdependence.[55] In other words, people negotiate when they think that discussion can produce a more satisfactory arrangement (at least for them) in their exchange of goods or services.

As you can see, negotiation is not an obscure practice reserved for labor and management bosses during collective bargaining. Everyone negotiates—every day. Most of the time, you don't even realize that you are in negotiations. Negotiation is particularly evident in the workplace because employees work interdependently with others. They negotiate with their supervisors over next month's work assignments, with customers over the sale and delivery schedules of their product, and with co-workers over when to have lunch. And yes, they occasionally negotiate in labor disputes and collective bargaining.

Some writers suggest that negotiations are more successful when the parties adopt a collaborative style, whereas others caution that this conflict management style is sometimes costly.[56] We know that any win–lose style (i.e., competing, accommodating) is unlikely to produce the optimal solution because the parties have not shared information necessary to discover a mutually satisfactory solution. On the other hand, we must be careful about adopting an openly collaborative style until mutual trust has been established.

The State of Wisconsin and the Wisconsin State Employees Union (WSEU) have successfully replaced their previous adversarial and confrontational relationship with a collaborative, problem-solving approach to negotiation. This "mutual gains" approach is grounded in the principle that labor and management have complementary—not competing—interests. Focusing on these interests rather than set positions has freed Wisconsin and WSEU to explore solutions that will bring about greater mutual gain. The new approach has reduced bargaining time, cleared a backlog of grievances, and improved public perceptions of the state's leadership.[59] What other conflict situations might benefit from the mutual gains process?
[Courtesy of the State of Wisconsin.]

The concern is that information is power, so information sharing gives the other party more power to leverage a better deal if the opportunity occurs. Skilled negotiators often adopt a *cautiously* collaborative style at the outset by sharing information slowly and determining whether the other side will reciprocate. In this respect, they try to establish trust with the other party.[57] They switch to one of the win–lose styles only when it becomes apparent that a win–win solution is not possible or the other party is unwilling to share information with a cooperative orientation.

Bargaining Zone Model of Negotiations

The negotiation process moves each party along a continuum with an area of potential overlap called the *bargaining zone*.[58] Exhibit 13.5 displays one possible bargaining zone situation. This linear diagram illustrates a purely win–lose situation—one side's gain will be the other's loss. However, the bargaining zone model can also be applied to situations in which both sides potentially gain from the negotiations. As this model illustrates, the parties typically establish

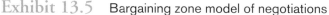

Exhibit 13.5   Bargaining zone model of negotiations

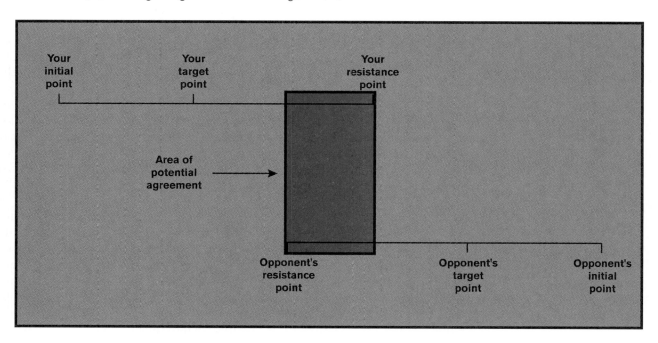

three main negotiating points. The *initial offer point* is the team's opening offer to the other party. This may be its best expectation or a pie-in-the-sky starting point. The *target point* is the team's realistic goal or expectation for a final agreement. The *resistance point* is the point beyond which the team will not make further concessions.

The parties begin negotiations by describing their initial offer point for each item on the agenda. In most cases, the participants know that this is only a starting point that will change as both sides offer concessions. In win–lose situations, neither the target nor resistance points are revealed to the other party. However, people try to discover the other side's resistance point because this knowledge helps them determine how much they can gain without breaking off negotiations.

When the parties have a win–win orientation, on the other hand, the objective is to find a creative solution that keeps everyone close to their initial offer points. They can hopefully find an arrangement by which each side loses relatively little value on some issues and gains significantly more on other issues. For example, a supplier might want to delay delivery dates, whereas delivery times are not important to the business customer. If the parties share this information, they can quickly agree to a delayed delivery schedule, thereby costing the customer very little and gaining the supplier a great deal. On other items (e.g., financing, order size), the supplier might give something with minimal loss even though it is a significant benefit to the business customer.

Situational Influences on Negotiations

What makes some negotiations work more smoothly than others? What factors influence the negotiation outcomes? In this section, we briefly describe the situational factors and negotiator behaviors that provide some answers to these questions. Four of the most important situational factors are location, physical setting, time, and audience.

Location   It is easier to negotiate on your own turf because you are familiar with the negotiating environment and are able to maintain comfortable routines.[60] Also, there is no need to cope with travel-related stress or depend on others for resources during the negotiation. Of course, you can't walk out of negotiations as easily when you are on your own turf.

Considering these strategic benefits of home turf, many negotiators agree to meet on neutral territory. Increasingly, computer technology is making it possible for two distant groups to negotiate without a location—or, more correctly, by remaining at their own location.[61] However, electronic messages are subject to misinterpretation, and conflict can easily escalate if the parties engage in flaming (see Chapter 8). Even videoconferencing is seldom used in negotiations, because it does not adequately transmit the subtle nonverbal cues that negotiators rely on for feedback about their offers and counteroffers. Negotiation requires high media richness due to the complexity and ambiguity of issues, so face-to-face meetings are usually required at some point.

Physical setting   The physical setting can be very important in negotiations.[62] The physical distance between the parties and formality of the setting can influence the parties' orientation toward each other and the disputed issues. So can the seating arrangements. People who sit face-to-face are more likely to develop a win–lose orientation toward the conflict situation. In contrast, the State of Wisconsin and the Wisconsin State Employees Union deliberately intersperse participants around the table to convey a win–win orientation.[63] Others arrange the seating so that both parties face a white board, reflecting the notion that both parties face the same problem or issue.

Time passage and deadlines   Time passage and deadlines are two important factors in negotiations. The more time people invest in negotiations, the stronger is their commitment to reaching an agreement. This increases the motivation to resolve the conflict, but it also fuels the escalation of commitment problems described in Chapter 11. For example, the more time put into negotiations, the stronger is the tendency to make unwarranted concessions so that the negotiations do not fail.

Time deadlines may be useful to the extent that they motivate the parties to complete negotiations. However, time deadlines may become a liability when exceeding deadlines is costly.[64] Negotiators make concessions and soften their demands more rapidly as the deadline approaches. Moreover, time pressure inhibits a collaborative conflict management style, because the parties have less time to exchange information or present flexible offers.

Skilled negotiators try to keep their own time limits flexible. For example, one Brazilian company invited a group of Americans to negotiate a contract the week before Christmas. The Brazilians knew that the Americans would want to return to the United States by Christmas, so they delayed agreement until the last minute to extract more concessions from their visitors. The final agreement definitely favored the Brazilians.[65]

Audience characteristics   Most negotiators have audiences—anyone with a vested interest in the negotiation outcomes, such as senior management, other team members, or the general public. Negotiators tend to act differently when their audience observes the negotiation or has detailed information about the process, compared to situations in which the audience sees only the end results.[66] When the audience has direct surveillance over the proceedings, negotiators tend to be more competitive, less willing to make concessions, and more likely to engage in political tactics against the other party.[67] This "hardline" behavior shows the audience that the negotiator is working for their interests. With their audience watching, negotiators also have more interest in saving face. Sometimes, audiences are drawn into the negotiations by acting as a source of indirect appeals. The general public often takes on this role when groups negotiate with governments.[68]

Negotiator Behaviors

Negotiator behaviors play an important role in resolving conflict. Four of the most important behaviors are setting goals, gathering information, communicating effectively, and making concessions.

Planning and goal setting
Research has consistently reported that people have more favorable negotiation outcomes when they plan and set goals.[69] In particular, negotiators should carefully think through their initial offer, target, and resistance points. They need to check their underlying assumptions as well as stated and unstated goals and values. This typically involves some level of internal negotiations, such as working out differences among team members before proceeding to negotiate with the other party.[70]

Gathering information
"Seek to understand before you seek to be understood." This popular philosophy from management guru Stephen Covey applies to effective negotiations. It means that we should spend more time listening than talking during negotiations. In particular, gather information by listening closely to the other party and asking them for details of their position.[71] Some people negotiate in teams and make each member responsible for listening intently to specific issues related to their expertise. This potentially improves the information-gathering process, although it also introduces problems of coordination among several people.[72] With more information about the opponent's interests and needs, negotiators are better able to discover low-cost concessions or proposals that will satisfy the other side.

Communicating effectively
Earlier in this chapter, we noted that poor communication tends to ignite a conflict escalation cycle that leads to socioemotional conflict. That certainly applies to negotiations, where both sides listen closely to each other for hidden meaning.[73] Studies report that effective negotiators communicate in a way that maintains effective relationships between the parties. Specifically, they focus on issues rather than people, so socioemotional conflict is minimized. Effective negotiators also avoid irritating statements such as "I think you'll agree that this is a generous offer." Third, effective communicators are masters of persuasive communication. This does not involve misleading the other party. Rather, as we learned in Chapter 8, negotiators structure the content of their message so that it is accepted by others, not merely understood.[74]

Making concessions
Concessions are important because they (1) enable the parties to move toward the area of potential agreement, (2) symbolize each party's motivation to bargain in good faith, and (3) tell the other party of the relative importance of the negotiating items.[75] How many concessions should you make? This varies with the other party's expectations and the level of trust between you. For instance, many Chinese negotiators are wary of people who change their position during negotiations. Similarly, some writers warn that Russian negotiators tend to view concessions as a sign of weakness, rather than a sign of trust.[76] Generally, the best strategy is to be moderately tough and give just the right number of concessions to communicate sincerity and motivation to resolve the conflict.[77] Being too tough can undermine relations between the parties; giving too many concessions implies weakness and encourages the other party to use power and resistance.

Third-Party Conflict Resolution

third-party conflict resolution any attempt by a relatively neutral person to help the parties resolve their differences

The opening story to this chapter described the conflict between Andersen Consulting and Arthur Andersen, but it didn't provide much detail about the strategies used by the two units to resolve their differences. First, they tried to improve relations through communication and by changing the organizational structure to reduce interdependence. Next, they tried to negotiate new terms of interdependence, including complete separation. When it became apparent that neither structural change nor negotiations were effective, the parties decided to seek a third-party conflict resolution strategy in the form of binding arbitration. **Third-party conflict resolution** is any attempt by a relatively neutral person to help the parties resolve their differences. This may range from formal labor arbitration to informal managerial interventions to resolve disagreements among employees.

There are four main objectives in third-party conflict resolution.[78] One objective is *efficiency*. Those who take the third-party role try to resolve the dispute quickly and with minimum expenditure of organizational resources. Second, the conflict resolution should be *effective*, meaning that the process should find the best long-term solution that will correct the underlying causes of the conflict. Third, this process should have *outcome fairness*. This ensures that the parties feel the solution provided by the third-party intervention is fair. Although outcome fairness is similar to effectiveness, they are not the same because people sometimes think that a solution is fair even though it does not work well in the long term.

procedural fairness perceptions of fairness regarding the dispute resolution process, whether or not the outcome is favorable to the person

Finally, third-party conflict resolution should ensure that the parties feel that the dispute resolution process is fair, whether or not the outcome is favorable to them. This objective, known as **procedural fairness,** is particularly important when the third party makes a binding decision to resolve the dispute. In these situations, procedural fairness increases when the third party isn't biased (i.e., doesn't have a vested interest toward one party), is well informed about the facts of the situation, and has listened to all sides of the dispute. It also increases when the decision can be appealed to a higher authority and the third party applies existing policies consistently.[79]

Types of Third-Party Intervention

There are generally three types of third-party dispute resolution activities: mediation, arbitration, and inquisition. These activities can be classified by their level of control over the process and control over the decision (see Exhibit 13.6).[80]

• *Mediation*—Mediators have high control over the intervention process. Indeed, their main purpose is to manage the process and context of interaction between the disputing parties. However, the parties still make the final decision about how to resolve their differences. Thus, mediators have little or no control over the conflict resolution decision. Some organizations, including United Technologies and Texaco, have an ombuds officer to mediate conflicts between management and employees, such as allegations of employment discrimination.[81] Texaco introduced an ombuds office, along with mediation and voluntary arbitration, after the oil company was accused of racial discrimination. "The establishment of an impartial, confidential Ombuds Program will complement the existing resources available to Texaco employees for problem resolution, all of which are designed to maintain a positive and productive environment," says Texaco chairman and CEO Peter Bijur.[82]

• *Arbitration*—Arbitrators make a binding decision on the conflicting parties and consequently have high control over the final decision. However,

Exhibit 13.6
Types of third-party intervention

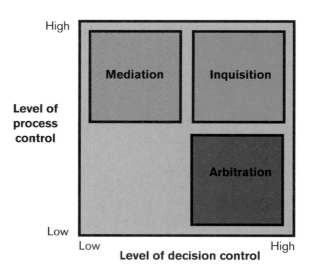

When Buddy's Natural Chickens, Inc., opened its plant in Gonzales, Texas, the poultry farming and processing company experienced a rash of workers' compensation claims and other grievances. Before these conflicts could escalate and undermine morale, Buddy's introduced alternative dispute resolution (ADR). This third-party conflict resolution program begins with informal, face-to-face talks between managers and employees and moves on, as necessary, to mediation and arbitration. So far, the 80-employee firm has had only two cases involving an outside mediator. No complaints have gone to arbitration.[84] Why wouldn't this ADR process include inquisition?
[B. Daemmrich. Used with permission.]

arbitrators have low process control because the process is largely determined by existing due process rules.[83] Arbitration is commonly applied as the final stage of grievances by unionized employees, but it is finding its way into other forms of conflict. For example, Andersen Consulting and Arthur Andersen relied on arbitration to resolve their dispute.

• *Inquisition*—Inquisitors control all discussion about the conflict. Like arbitrators, they have high decision control because they choose the form of conflict resolution. However, they also have high process control because they choose which information to examine, how to examine it, and generally decide how the conflict resolution process shall be handled.

Choosing the Best Third-Party Intervention Strategy

When trying to resolve workplace disputes, people in positions of authority (e.g., managers) sometimes adopt a mediator role; at other times they serve as arbitrators. However, research suggests managers usually adopt an inquisitional approach whereby they dominate the intervention process as well as

make a binding decision.[85] The inquisitional approach is popular because it is consistent with the decision-oriented nature of managerial jobs, gives them control over the conflict process and outcome, and tends to resolve disputes efficiently.

However, the inquisitional approach to third-party conflict resolution is usually the least effective in organizational settings.[86] One problem is that leaders who take an inquisitional role tend to collect limited information about the problem using this approach, so their imposed decision may produce an ineffective solution to the conflict. Moreover, employees tend to think that the procedures and outcomes of inquisitions are unfair because they have little control over this approach.

Which third-party intervention is most appropriate in organizations? The answer depends partly on the situation. For everyday disputes between two employees, the mediation approach is usually best because this gives employees more responsibility for resolving their own disputes. The third-party representative merely establishes an appropriate context for conflict resolution. Although not as efficient as other strategies, mediation potentially offers the highest level of employee satisfaction with the conflict process and outcomes.[87] When employees cannot resolve their differences, arbitration seems to work best because the predetermined rules of evidence and other processes create a higher sense of procedural fairness. Moreover, arbitration is preferred where the organization's goals should take priority over individual goals.

Whether resolving conflict through third-party dispute resolution or direct negotiation, we need to recognize that many solutions come from the sources of conflict that were identified earlier in this chapter. This may seem obvious, but in the heat of conflict, people often focus on each other rather than the underlying causes. Recognizing these conflict sources is the role of effective leadership, which we discuss in the next chapter.

Chapter Summary

Conflict is the process in which one party perceives that its interests are being opposed or negatively affected by another party. When conflict is task related, the parties view the conflict experience as something separate from them. Conflict is much more difficult to resolve when it rises to a socioemotional state of tension. The conflict process often escalates through a series of episodes and shifts from task related to socioemotional.

Conflict management maximizes the benefits and minimizes the dysfunctional consequences of conflict. Conflict is beneficial for introducing new ideas, making people think more fully about issues, and increasing cohesiveness (when the conflict is with another group). The main problems with conflict are that it may lead to job stress, dissatisfaction, and turnover. Dysfunctional intergroup conflict may undermine decision making.

Conflict tends to increase under conditions of goal incompatibility, differentiation, task interdependence, scarce resources, ambiguity, and communication problems. Conflict is more common in a multicultural workforce because of greater differentiation and communication problems among employees.

There are five interpersonal conflict management styles: avoiding, competing, accommodating, compromising, and collaborating. Collaborating is the only style that represents a purely win–win orientation—the belief that the parties will find a mutually beneficial solution to the conflict. The four other styles adopt some variation of a win–lose orientation—the belief that one party will lose if the other wins. Women and people with high collectivism tend to use a collaborative or avoidance style more than men and people with a high individualism.

Structural approaches to conflict management include emphasizing superordinate goals, reducing differentiation, improving communication and understanding, reducing task interdependence, increasing resources, and clarifying rules and procedures. These elements can also be altered to stimulate conflict.

Negotiation occurs whenever two or more conflicting parties attempt to resolve their divergent goals by redefining the terms of their interdependence. Negotiations are influenced by several situational factors, including location, physical setting, time passage and deadlines, and audience. Important negotiator behaviors include planning and goal setting, gathering information, communicating effectively, and making concessions.

Third-party conflict resolution is any attempt by a relatively neutral person to help the parties resolve their differences. The main objectives are to resolve the dispute efficiently and effectively, and to ensure that the parties feel that the process and outcome of dispute resolution are fair. The three main forms of third-party dispute resolution are mediation, arbitration, and inquisition. Managers tend to use an inquisitional approach, although mediation and arbitration are more appropriate, depending on the situation.

Key Terms

Conflict, p. 402
Conflict management, p. 404
Dialogue, p. 414
Intergroup mirroring, p. 414
Negotiation, p. 418
Procedural fairness, p. 422

Superordinate goals, p. 412
Task interdependence, p. 406
Third-party conflict resolution, p. 422
Win–lose orientation, p. 409
Win–win orientation, p. 409

Discussion Questions

1. Distinguish task-related from socioemotional conflict and explain where these two forms fit into the conflict escalation cycle.

2. The president of Creative Toys Inc. read about cooperation in Japanese companies and has vowed to bring this same philosophy to the company. The goal is to avoid all conflict, so that employees would work cooperatively and be happier at Creative Toys. Discuss the merits and limitations of the president's policy.

3. Conflict among managers emerged soon after a Swedish company was bought by a French company. The Swedes perceived the French management as hierarchical and arrogant, whereas the French thought the Swedes were naive, cautious, and lacking an achievement orientation. Describe an intergroup mirroring intervention that would reduce dysfunctional conflict in this situation. What conditions might make the intergroup mirroring process difficult here?

4. This chapter describes three levels of task interdependence that exist in interpersonal and intergroup relationships. Identify examples of these three levels in your work or school activities. How do these three levels affect potential conflict for you?

5. Jane has just been appointed as purchasing manager of Eagle Technologies, Inc. The previous purchasing manager, who recently retired, was known for his "winner-take-all" approach to suppliers. He continually fought for more discounts and was skeptical about any special deals that suppliers would propose. A few suppliers refused to do business with Eagle Technologies, but senior management was confident that the former purchasing manager's approach minimized the company's costs. Jane wants to try a more collaborative approach to working with suppliers. Will her approach work? How should she adopt a more collaborative approach in future negotiations with suppliers?

6. Suppose that Andersen Consulting and Arthur Andersen were advised by an arbitrator or other authority that they must work out their differences rather than split into two separate companies. Describe two other ways that the sister firms could reduce their conflict through superordinate goals.

7. Suppose that you head one of five divisions in a multinational organization and are about to begin this year's budget deliberations at headquarters. What are the characteristics of your audience in these negotiations and what effect might they have on your negotiation behavior?

8. Managers tend to use an inquisitional approach to resolving disputes between employees and departments. Describe the inquisitional approach and discuss its appropriateness in organizational settings.

Maelstrom Communications

Sales manager Roger Todd was fuming. Thanks to, as he put it, "those nearsighted addleheads in service," he had nearly lost one of his best accounts. When told of Todd's complaint, senior serviceperson Ned Rosen retorted, "That figures. Anytime Mr. Todd senses even the remotest possibility of a sale, he immediately promises the customer the world on a golden platter. We can't possibly provide the service they request under the time constraints they give us and do an acceptable job."

Feelings of this sort were common in the departments in which Roger and Ned worked at Maelstrom Communications. It seemed that sales and service, the two dominant functions in the company, never saw eye-to-eye on anything. The problems dated well back into the history of the company, even before Roger or Ned were hired some years ago.

Maelstrom Communications is a franchised distributionship belonging to a nationwide network of communications companies that sell products such as intercom, paging, sound, and interconnect telephone systems. Maelstrom competes directly with the Bell System companies in the telephone hardware market. Equipment installation and maintenance service are an integral part of the total package Maelstrom offers.

Modern telephone system hardware is highly sophisticated and few, if any, system users have the technological know-how to do their own equipment servicing. An excellent service record is crucial to the success of any company in the field. After the direct sale of a Maelstrom system, the sales force maintains contacts with customers. There is nothing the salespeople dislike so much as hearing that a customer hasn't received the type of service promised at the time of sale. On the other hand, service technicians complain of being hounded by the salespeople whenever a preferred customer needs a wire spliced. As Ned Rosen put it, "I can't remember the last time a service request came through that *wasn't* an emergency from a preferred customer."

Maelstrom's owner and president, Al Whitfield, has a strong sales background and views sales as the bread-and-butter department of the company. He is in on all major decisions and has final say on any matter brought to his attention. He spends most of his time working with sales and marketing personnel, and rarely concerns himself with the day-to-day activities of the service department unless a major problem crops up.

Next in line in Maelstrom's corporate hierarchy is the vice president in charge of production, Lawrence Henderson. Henderson is responsible for the acquisition and distribution of all job-related equipment and materials and for the scheduling of all service department activities. His sympathies lie primarily with the service department.

Each week Whitfield, Henderson, and all members of the sales force hold a meeting in Maelstrom's conference room. The sales personnel present their needs to Henderson so that equipment can be ordered and jobs scheduled. Service requests reported to salespeople from customers are also relayed to Henderson at this point. Once orders for service have been placed with production, sales personnel receive no feedback on the disposition of them (unless a customer complains to them directly) other than at these weekly meetings. It is common for a salesperson to think all is well with his or her accounts when, in fact, customers are receiving delayed service or none at all. When an irate customer phones the sales representative to complain, it sets in motion the machinery that leads to disputes such as the one between Roger Todd and Ned Rosen.

It has become an increasingly common occurrence at Maelstrom for sales personnel to go to Henderson to complain when their requests are not met by the service department. Henderson has exhibited an increasing tendency to side with the service department and to tell the salespeople that existing service department priorities must be adhered to and that any sales requests will have to wait for rescheduling. At this point, a salesperson's only recourse is to go to Whitfield, who invariably agrees with the salesperson and instructs Henderson to take appropriate action. All of this is time consuming and only serves to produce friction between the president and the vice president in charge of production.

Discussion Questions

1. What situational conditions have created the conflict in this case?

2. What actions should the organization take to manage the conflict more effectively?

Source: Written by Daniel Robey in collaboration with Todd Anthony. Used with permission. ■

Lost in space at Boeing

BusinessWeek

Marriage counselors always warn young couples that money troubles are the biggest threats to a happy union. Boeing Co. can tell you it's not so good for corporate marriages either. Almost from the time Boeing completed its merger with McDonnell Douglas Corp., the company has been racking up write-downs caused by production problems and product cancellations. These financial woes haven't helped relations between president Harry C. Stonecipher, the hard-nosed former McDonnell Douglas CEO who joined Boeing in the merger, and Ronald B. Woodard, head of Boeing's commercial aviation unit. The two have disagreed publicly over the cause of the problems. It didn't help that Woodard was in line to be president until Stonecipher came aboard, either. Insiders say that the two clashed from the start.

This *Business Week* case study describes the conditions and events that have contributed to conflict between these two executives, and likely others, at Boeing. Read through this *Business Week* case study at www.mhhe.com/mcshane1e and prepare for the discussion questions below.

Discussion Questions

1. What sources of conflict seem to exist that contribute to the conflict described in this *Business Week* case study?

2. If you were putting together a merger between Boeing and McDonnell Douglas, what actions would you take to minimize potential conflict?

Source: A. Bernstein, A. Reinhardt, and S. Browder, "Lost in Space at Boeing," *Business Week*, April 27, 1998, pp. 42–43. ■

VIDEO CASE

Saturn

 There's something revolutionary going on in the peaceful town of Springhill, Tennessee. This is the home of Saturn Corporation, a different kind of car company whose mission is to build world class cars that are the leaders in quality, cost, and customer satisfaction and to do it in a whole new way. Saturn was brought to life by General Motors and the United Auto Workers (UAW) who, working together as equal partners, designed Saturn to be a model of American manufacturing excellence.

Owen Bieber, president of the International UAW, said, "Saturn represents more than an automobile and a new plant. What makes this new company unique is that it is a bold experiment in giving workers a chance to demonstrate what they can do if they are truly involved in all aspects of decision making and regarded as co-equals with management. And that's what we demonstrate here this morning. That's what this car demonstrates."

Kay Panek, a member of the steering columns team, emphasized the role of the workers. She said, "This is our chance as workers of America to prove to the world that we are not only as good, but that we are better. Our quality will be better, is better, and we are going to do it by working together. It's not going to be us and them, we're going to do it together. We're succeeding, and I can only see complete success down the road."

The Saturn team is committed to keeping Saturn world class in every way. Powertrains and body components move by conveyers to the centrally located vehicle systems facility for final assembly. Team members assemble interior and exterior components of the car on a traveling production line. Special lifts raise or lower the vehicle to place it in the most accessible position for team members to do their jobs. Every build operation is ergonomically designed to reduce worker fatigue and increase efficiency. There are few robots in vehicle systems. The Saturn team believes that people not machines are the best judges of world class quality.

Saturn believes that it takes more than a good car to compete in the world class arena—it takes a dedicated team of committed individuals who are continually striving to make their product better. The Saturn/UAW partnership has created that team, and training is the way to keep the team on the cutting edge of automobile manufacturing. The Saturn training and development center contains extensive facilities, offering a wide range of classes including advanced college degree programs. Every team member spends at least 100 hours a year in company-paid training learning the skills that will help Saturn beat the competition.

Denise Tanguay-Hoyer, professor of Management at Eastern Michigan University, commented on the Saturn way of doing business: "There are a lot of organizations that have traditional adversarial labor-management relations. The role of the union officials really has been seen to be a table-pounding grievance handler—someone who comes in as a very strong representative of whatever the members want within reason and in a very assertive, aggressive way presents that to management, in fact demands it from management many times. At Saturn that relationship is very different. That's not to say there is no conflict. It's not to say that there are not employee grievances at Saturn, but the union role there is viewed first as an advocate for the members but very closely second as a partner with the corporate management of Saturn."

Morris Hayes, chairman of the UAW Local 1810, supported professor Tanguay-Hoyer's comments. He said, "What we have done is tried to instill a basic philosophy to the people that come here through training and role modeling and leadership to make sure that people understand that disagreement is all right. We have some finality to it though. Once an issue is raised, there must be a decision made. What we are doing is representing everybody, not individuals. What we've done here at Saturn is organized ourselves in such a way that we can maximize representation and I think by an overwhelming margin people recognize that."

Professor Tanguay-Hoyer said, "One example of the partnership in the early days was the fact that when selection and hiring decisions were made for the shop floor production people those decisions were made jointly by the union and management. One of the agreements was that the people hired would be UAW members from other plants in other cities, or perhaps people who were already on layoff. Given that those people already had some years work experience in what might be called a more traditionally managed auto plant there was clearly a lot of change expected of them when they came into the new culture at Saturn. So these people had to be willing to be team members that were going to be put into what are called semi-autonomous work groups.

That means that they would not have a supervisor, that they would be managing themselves as a team making decisions themselves."

Commenting on the unique labor-management relationship at Saturn, local UAW leader Morris Hayes said: "Here at Saturn we have what we call a living agreement which is something that has been talked about in industry and unions for some time. Basically, the difference between a living agreement and what you typically have in a labor agreement in industry in America is that the traditional agreement has a starting date and an ending date and you must have another agreement in place or extend that one or go on strike. Here at Saturn our agreement doesn't have an end date. At any time that we find that something isn't working or that something needs to be fixed, we are able to go in through the language of the agreement and fix it. We use facilitators. We have little cards with our philosophy on it and often times you will see somebody pull this card out and say 'Wait a minute you are deviating from the philosophy here. Let's not forget what we are trying to accomplish here. It's not just this decision, we've got to accomplish it within the context of the Saturn mission and philosophy.' So this is going to be a continual struggle."

Tanguay-Hoyer concluded, "I think in our society in the United States the lines have been drawn very clearly between management and labor. In fact, there are many variables that we can look at that tell us that the resistance to unions on the part of management is even stronger now than it has been in the recent past. But at Saturn, given that background context, one of the things that they have had to decide is how they are going to create their own new roles. And that is really what they are doing. They are out on the frontier and exploring what kinds of new roles make sense and evolving a partnership that will work. The union has to do the same thing internally. They have to evolve roles and relationships that will work and will serve the members."

Discussion Questions

1. Each employee at Saturn receives 100 hours of training each year. How does this training help reduce conflict between employees and management?

2. Explain what is meant by the term "living agreement." Can you site any other examples of such an agreement? What are the advantages of a living agreement? Disadvantages? What is the role of negotiations in a living agreement?

3. Discuss the role of effective communications in creating Saturn's work environment. In what ways does communication within Saturn differ from other large manufacturing operations? What role does that play in conflict management? ■

Ugli orange role play

Purpose

This exercise is designed to help you understand the dynamics of interpersonal and intergroup conflict as well as the effectiveness of negotiation strategies under specific conditions.

Instructions

The instructor will divide the class into an even number of small teams, with one participant left over for each team formed (e.g., six observers if there are six teams). One-half of the teams will take the role of Dr. Roland and the other half will be Dr. Jones. Teams will receive the appropriate materials from the instructor. Members within each team are given 15 minutes to learn their roles and decide upon negotiating strategy. After reading their roles and discussing strategy, each Dr. Jones team is matched with a Dr. Roland team to conduct negotiations for the time stated by the instructor.

Observers will receive observation forms from the instructor, and two observers will be assigned to watch the paired teams during prenegotiations and subsequent negotiations. At the end of the negotiations, the observers will describe the process and outcomes in their negotiating session. The instructor will then invite the negotiators to describe their experiences and the implications for conflict management.

Source: This exercise was developed by Dr. Robert J. House, Wharton Business School, University of Pennsylvania. ■

SELF-ASSESSMENT EXERCISE

Conflict management style orientation scale

Purpose

This self-assessment is designed to help you to identify your preferred conflict management style.

Instructions

Read each of the statements below and circle the response that you believe best reflects your position regarding each statement. Then use the scoring key to calculate your results for each management style. This exercise is completed alone so students assess themselves honestly without concerns of social comparison. However, class discussion will focus on the different conflict management styles and the situations in which each is most appropriate.

Circle the number that best indicates how well these statements describe you.	Rarely ▼				Always ▼
1. If someone disagrees with me, I vigorously defend my side of the issue.	1	2	3	4	5
2. I go along with suggestions from co-workers, even if I don't agree with them.	1	2	3	4	5
3. I give-and-take so that a compromise can be reached.	1	2	3	4	5
4. I keep my opinions to myself rather than openly disagree with people.	1	2	3	4	5
5. In disagreements or negotiations, I try to find the best possible solution for both sides by sharing information.	1	2	3	4	5
6. I try to reach a middle ground in disputes with other people.	1	2	3	4	5
7. I accommodate the wishes of people who have different points of view than my own.	1	2	3	4	5
8. I avoid openingly debating issues where there is disagreement.	1	2	3	4	5
9. In negotiations, I hold on to my position rather than give in.	1	2	3	4	5
10. I try to solve conflicts by finding solutions that benefit both me and the other person.	1	2	3	4	5
11. I let co-workers have their way rather than jeopardize our relationship.	1	2	3	4	5
12. I try to win my position in a discussion.	1	2	3	4	5
13. I like to investigate conflicts with co-workers so that we can discover solutions that benefit both of us.	1	2	3	4	5
14. I believe that it is not worth the time and trouble discussing my differences of opinion with other people.	1	2	3	4	5
15. To reach an agreement, I give up some things in exchange for others.	1	2	3	4	5

Scoring Key

Write the scores circled for each item on the appropriate line below (statement numbers are in brackets), and
add up each scale. Higher scores indicate that you are
stronger on that conflict management style.

Competing	_____	+	_____	+	_____	=	_____
	(1)		(9)		(12)		

Accommodating	_____	+	_____	+	_____	=	_____
	(2)		(7)		(11)		

Compromising	_____	+	_____	+	_____	=	_____
	(3)		(6)		(15)		

Avoiding	_____	+	_____	+	_____	=	_____
	(4)		(8)		(14)		

Collaborating	_____	+	_____	+	_____	=	_____
	(5)		(10)		(13)		

Sources: Adapted from items in M. A. Rahim, "A Measure of
Styles of Handling Interpersonal Conflict," *Academy of
Management Journal* 26 (June 1983), pp. 368–76; K. W.
Thomas and R. H. Kilmann, Thomas-Kilmann Conflict Mode
Instrument (Sterling Forst, NY: Xicom, 1977). ◼

Organizational Leadership

Learning Objectives

After reading this chapter, you should be able to:

- Define leadership.
- List seven competencies of effective leaders.
- Describe people-oriented and task-oriented leadership styles.
- Outline the path-goal theory of leadership.
- Discuss the importance of Fiedler's contingency model of leadership.
- Contrast transactional with transformational leadership.
- Describe the four elements of transformational leadership.
- Identify three reasons why people inflate the importance of leadership.
- Discuss similarities and differences in the leadership styles of women and men.

I f anyone can shake up Ford Motor Company's stodgy corporate culture, it is Jacques (Jac) Nasser. A few years ago, the Lebanese-born Australian rescued Ford of Australia by freshening the product lineup, restoring product quality, and trimming payroll by nearly 50 percent. "He took a company that was literally nonviable and left it viable," says John Ogden, who took the top Australian job after Nasser. And, Ogden adds, he maintained employee morale throughout this difficult transition.

Now Ford's CEO in Detroit, Nasser is transforming the automaker into a more nimble organization focused on shareholder value. Nasser has led the change effort by personally conducting information sessions to over 50,000 employees in offices and factories around the world. He explains about the need to cut costs, add shareholder value, and become a more entrepreneurial organization.

Nasser supports his vision of Ford's future through his actions. For example, he moved the heads of manufacturing, marketing, and finance to the same location so they can make quicker decisions about new product lines. His aggressive leadership style sets him apart from the more cautiously bureaucratic executives typically found at Ford. "I have high personal standards, and I set the same standards for my team," he acknowledges.

Nasser shrugs off concerns that he is a tough taskmaster, stating that Ford needs a leader who can prepare the company for a more competitive future. "I am an agent of change," says Nasser. "I don't believe in stagnation." Even adversaries agree that Ford will benefit from Nasser's leadership talents. "Jac Nasser's a very charismatic leader with lots of ideas and energy," says the president of a rival automobile firm.[1]

Jac Nasser (holding cowboy hat) is transforming Ford Motor Company from a cautious bureaucratic business into a nimble enterprise focused on shareholder value

[R. Cook. Used with permission of Reuters.]

433

y most accounts, Jac Nasser is an effective organizational leader. He inspires Ford's employees and creates an environment for them to work more effectively toward organizational objectives. Nasser also continually communicates his vision of Ford's future in a way that builds commitment to that future state.

What is leadership? Some people say that we can't define leadership, but we know it when we see it. Others argue that leadership can only be defined as someone who has followers. Leaders are not people in specific positions. Rather, leaders are defined by the people they serve. Recent commentaries note that scholars do not sufficiently agree on the definition of leadership.[2] As one respected scholar acknowledged, "Leadership is one of the most observed and least understood phenomena on earth."[3]

leadership the process of influencing people and providing an environment for them to achieve team or organizational objectives

With these caveats in mind, we will cautiously define **leadership** as the process of influencing people and providing an environment for them to achieve team or organizational objectives. Effective leaders help groups of people define their goals and find ways to achieve them.[4] They use power and persuasion to ensure that followers have the motivation and role clarity to achieve specified goals. Leaders also arrange the work environment—such as allocating resources and altering communication patterns—so that employees can achieve corporate objectives more easily.

However leadership is defined, only 8 percent of executives in the largest U.S. firms think they have enough of it in their organization.[5] Most are concerned about a lack of leadership talent. But leadership isn't restricted to the executive suite. Anyone in the organization may be a leader. Effective self-directed work teams, for example, consist of members who share leadership responsibilities or otherwise allocate this role to a responsible coordinator. Successful technology champions—employees who overcome technical and organizational obstacles to introduce technological change in their area of the organization—are effective leaders because they influence co-workers and transform the environmental conditions that have prevented the innovation from being introduced. Indeed, studies report that one of the most common reasons why technology champions fail is that they lack the competencies or behaviors we associate with effective leadership.[6] Overall, we should avoid the idea that leaders are people in certain positions. Anyone may be a leader at an appropriate time and place.

Perspectives of Leadership

Leadership has been contemplated since the days of Greek philosophers and it is one of the most popular research topics among organizational behavior scholars. As we describe the leadership of Jac Nasser—or any other leader in the private or public sector—it becomes apparent that there are many ways to understand leadership in organizational settings. Although some leadership perspectives are currently more popular than others, each helps us to more fully understand this complex issue.

This chapter looks at the different leadership perspectives outlined in Exhibit 14.1. Some scholars have studied the traits or competencies of great leaders, whereas others have looked at their behaviors. More recent studies have looked at leadership from a contingency approach by considering the appropriate leadership behaviors in different settings. Currently, the most popular perspective is that leaders transform organizations through their vision, communication, and ability to build commitment. Finally, an emerging perspective suggests that leadership is mainly a perceptual bias. We distort reality and attribute events to leaders because we feel more comfortable believing that a competent individual is at the organization's helm.

Exhibit 14.1
Perspectives of leadership

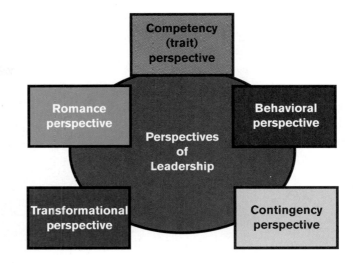

Literally dozens of theories have developed within the five leadership perspectives shown in Exhibit 14.1. Don't worry. We won't present every theory because this would undermine your capacity and willingness to understand the critical issues in leadership. Although the field of organizational behavior tends to retain leadership theories long after their validity has been put into doubt, our objective is to emphasize the handful of theories that seem to have the strongest research support.

Competency (Trait) Perspective of Leadership

As CEO of Mattel, Jill Barad is described as a fierce competitor with an unerring self-confidence. For instance, soon after completing her first career assignment on an obscure product at Mattel (plastic worms), she stormed into the CEO's office and demanded "What . . . do I have to do to get a decent assignment around here?" Barad is also considered an intelligent visionary whose instinct for what kids like has made Barbie dolls one of the most successful toys over the past two decades. Barad has a no-nonsense style, but she is also known for her infectious enthusiasm. "You can't help but be sucked up by her energy," says Shelly Lazarus, CEO of Ogilvy & Mather Worldwide Inc., Mattel's advertising agency.[7]

From these accounts, it seems that Jill Barad is an effective leader because she possesses certain leadership competencies. Recall from Chapter 2 that **competencies** are the underlying characteristics of people that lead to superior performance.[8] These include the person's knowledge, natural and learned abilities, values, and personality traits. Since the beginning of recorded civilization, people have been interested in personal characteristics that distinguish great leaders from the rest of us. Early interest focused on personality traits and physical appearance. (The competency perspective is still called the *trait perspective* of leadership in many organizational behavior textbooks because early writers concentrated on personality and physical traits rather than broader competencies.) The ancient Egyptians demanded authority, discrimination, and justice from their leaders. The Greek philosopher Plato called for prudence, courage, temperance, and justice.[9]

For the first half of the 20th century, organizational behavior scholars used scientific methods to determine whether certain personality traits and physical characteristics (particularly, the person's height and weight) actually distinguish leaders from lesser souls. A major review in the late 1940s concluded

competencies the abilities, values, personality traits, and other characteristics of people that lead to superior performance

Jill Barad is well known for her leadership competencies. The CEO of Mattel, Inc., has unwavering drive, a high degree of self-confidence, keen intelligence, and a detailed knowledge of the toy industry. Are these personal characteristics sufficient for effective leadership? Moreover, are people like Jill Barad born as great leaders, or can companies develop leadership skills?

[AP Wide World]

that no consistent list of traits could be distilled from the hundreds of studies conducted up to that time. A subsequent review suggested that a few traits are consistently associated with effective leaders, but most are unrelated to effective leadership.[10] These conclusions caused many scholars to give up their search for personal characteristics that distinguish effective leaders.

Since the 1980s, management consultants and a few organizational behavior scholars have popularized competency-based selection and reward practices. Competencies, as we mentioned, encompass a broader range of personal characteristics—such as knowledge, abilities, and values—that were not considered by earlier studies on leadership traits. This new generation of leadership experts argues that the earlier studies focused too much on the abstract personality traits and physical appearance of leaders. The recent literature on leadership identifies seven competencies that are characteristic of effective leaders (see Exhibit 14.2).[11]

• *Drive*—This refers to the inner motivation that leaders possess to pursue their goals. Leaders have a high need for achievement (see Chapter 3). This inspires an unbridled inquisitiveness and a need for constant learning. You can see this in Jill Barad through her unwavering tenacity and energy at Mattel.

• *Leadership motivation*—As we learned in Chapter 3, leaders have a strong need for power because they want to influence others. However, they tend to have a need for "socialized power" because their motivation is constrained by a strong sense of altruism and social responsibility.[12] In other words, effective leaders try to gain power so that they can influence others to accomplish goals that benefit the team or organization.

Exhibit 14.2
Seven competencies of effective leaders

Leadership competency	Description
Drive	The leader's inner motivation to pursue goals.
Leadership motivation	The leader's need for socialized power to accomplish team or organizational goals.
Integrity	The leader's truthfulness and tendency to translate words into deeds.
Self-confidence	The leader's belief in his or her own leadership skills and ability to achieve objectives.
Intelligence	The leader's above-average cognitive ability to process enormous amounts of information.
Knowledge of the business	The leader's understanding of the company's environment to make more intuitive decisions.
Emotional intelligence	The leader's ability to monitor his or her own and others' emotions, discriminate among them, and use the information to guide his or her thoughts and actions.

Sources: Most elements of this list were derived from S. A. Kirkpatrick and E. A. Locke, "Leadership: Do Traits Matter?" *Academy of Management Executive* 5 (May 1991), pp. 48–60. Several of these ideas are also discussed in H. B. Gregersen, A. J. Morrison, and J. S. Black, "Developing Leaders for the Global Frontier," *Sloan Management Review* 40 (Fall 1998), pp. 21–32; R. J. House and R. N. Aditya, "The Social Scientific Study of Leadership: Quo Vadis?" *Journal of Management* 23 (1997), pp. 409–73.

- *Integrity*—This refers to the leader's truthfulness and tendency to translate words into deeds. Several studies have reported that followers consistently identify integrity as the most important leadership characteristic. Leaders will only have followers when trust is maintained through the leader's integrity.[13]

- *Self-confidence*—Leaders believe in their leadership skills and ability to achieve objectives. They also use impression management tactics (see Chapter 12) to convince followers of their confidence. This confidence is certainly apparent in Jill Barad and Jac Nasser.

- *Intelligence*—Leaders have above-average cognitive ability to process enormous amounts of information. Leaders aren't necessarily geniuses; rather, they have a superior ability to analyze alternative scenarios and identify potential opportunities.

- *Knowledge of the business*—Leaders need to know the business environment in which they operate. This knowledge gives them an intuitive understanding of which decisions to make and whose ideas make sense for the organization's survival and success. Jill Barad has demonstrated this competency from her astute knowledge of the toy industry. This business "savvy" enables leaders to recognize opportunities and understand their organization's capacity to capture those opportunities.

- *Emotional intelligence*—Effective leaders have a high level of **emotional intelligence.** Recall from Chapter 7 that people with high emotional intelligence monitor their own and others' emotions, discriminate among them, and use the information to guide their thoughts and actions.[14] Emotional intelligence requires a strong **self-monitoring personality** (see Chapter 6) because leaders must be sensitive to situational cues and readily adapt their own behavior appropriately.[15] It also requires the ability to empathize with others and possess the social skills necessary to build rapport as well as network with

emotional intelligence the ability to monitor your own and others' emotions, to discriminate among them, and to use the information to guide your thinking and actions

self-monitoring personality a personality trait referring to the extent that people are sensitive to situational cues and can readily adapt their own behavior appropriately

Don't look for Kim Jung Tae in his office. The CEO of South Korea's Housing and Commercial Bank (HCB) is busy traveling throughout the company's nearly 500 branches and offices, instilling a new way of thinking about banking. "Our bank has to survive doing retail business," explains Kim. "That means customer satisfaction." Kim's marketing savvy and years of experience in the financial services industry make him well suited to lead HCB. Kim also has a strong drive and enough self-confidence to get paid in stock options rather than salary.[16] What competencies seem to make Kim Jung Tae an effective leader? Do you think there are cultural differences in the traits of an effective leader?
[Courtesy of South Korea's Housing and Commercial Bank]

others. Moreover, the contingency leadership perspective described later in this chapter assumes that effective leaders are high self-monitors so they can adjust their behavior to match the situation.

Competency (Trait) Perspective Limitations and Practical Implications

One concern with the competency perspective is that it assumes great leaders have the same personal characteristics and all of them are equally important in all situations. This is probably a false assumption; leadership is far too complex to have a universal list of traits that apply to every condition. Some competencies might not be important all of the time, although researchers have not yet explored this issue.

A few scholars have also warned that some personal characteristics might only influence our perception that someone is a leader, not whether the individual really makes a difference to the organization's success.[17] People who exhibit integrity, self-confidence, and other traits are called leaders because they act like leaders. Moreover, some personality traits are subjective enough that they may really be due to the follower's stereotype of leadership rather than the leader's actual characteristics. For example, we might see a successful person, call that person a leader, and then attribute to that person several unobservable traits that we consider essential for great leaders. We will discuss this perceptual distortion more fully toward the end of the chapter. At this point, you should be aware that our knowledge of leadership competencies may be partly due to perceptual distortions.

Aside from these limitations, the competency perspective offers practical implications for organizations. It recognizes that some people possess personal characteristics that offer them a higher potential to be great leaders. The most obvious implication of this is that organizations are relying increasingly on competency-based methods to hire people for future leadership positions.[18] Leadership talents are important throughout the organization, so this recommendation should extend to all levels of hiring, not just senior executives. Companies also need to determine which behaviors represent these competencies so that employees with leadership talents are identified early for promotion.

The competency perspective of leadership does not necessarily imply that great leaders are born. On the contrary, competencies only indicate leadership potential. People with these characteristics become effective leaders only after they have developed and mastered the necessary leadership behaviors. People with somewhat lower leadership competencies may become very effective leaders because they have leveraged their potential more fully. This means that companies must do more than hire people with certain competencies. They must also develop their potential through leadership development programs and practical experience in the field.

Behavioral Perspective of Leadership

In the 1940s and 1950s, scholars from Ohio State University launched an intensive research investigation to answer the question: What behaviors make leaders effective? Questionnaires were administered to subordinates, asking them to rate their supervisors on a large number of behaviors. These studies, along with similar research at the University of Michigan and Harvard University, distilled two clusters of leadership behaviors from more than 1,800 leadership behavior items.[19]

One cluster represented people-oriented behaviors. This included showing mutual trust and respect for subordinates, demonstrating a genuine concern for their needs, and having a desire to look out for their welfare. Leaders with a strong people-oriented style listen to employee suggestions, do personal favors for employees, support their interests when required, and treat employees as equals. Craig Weatherup, CEO of PepsiCo Inc., has a reputation for favoring this leadership style. He encourages executives to spend time with their families. He has called spouses of executives kept away from home on special projects to thank them for their support. And when PepsiCo laid off some people, Weatherup invited those who complained to sit in meetings where he patiently explained why the cutbacks were necessary.[20]

The other cluster represented a task-oriented leadership style and included behaviors that define and structure work roles. Task-oriented leaders assign employees to specific tasks, clarify their work duties and procedures, ensure that they follow company rules, and push them to reach their performance capacity. Jac Nasser frequently practices this style. He establishes stretch goals for executives who report to him and challenges them to push beyond those high standards. Nasser seems to know how far to challenge employees. As Connections 14.1 describes, some people are effective task-oriented leaders, whereas others carry this style to an extreme.

After identifying the two clusters of leader behavior, researchers associated them with specific measures of leadership effectiveness. The early studies concluded that people-oriented leadership is associated with higher job satisfaction among subordinates, as well as lower absenteeism, grievances, and turnover. However, job performance was lower than it was for employees with task-oriented leaders.[21] Task-oriented leadership, on the other hand, was associated with lower job satisfaction as well as higher absenteeism and turnover among subordinates. But this leadership style also seems to increase productivity and team unity. College students apparently value task-oriented instructors because they want clear course objectives and well-prepared lectures that abide by the course objectives.[22]

The "Hi-Hi" Leadership Hypothesis

Behavioral leadership scholars initially thought that people-oriented and task-oriented leadership were at opposite ends of a behavior spectrum. In other words, they believed that a strong task-oriented leader was necessarily a weak people-oriented leader. But researchers later concluded that these styles are independent of each other. Some people are high or low on both styles, others

Connections 14.1 ▫ **When Taskmasters Become Bad Bosses**

David Gilmore (center), head of the public housing authority in Washington, D.C., knows how far to stretch employees without breaking them.
[Carol Guzy. Used with permission of the Washington Post.*]*

David Gilmore admits that he can be tough on employees. "I am occasionally a tyrant," confesses the head of the public housing authority in the nation's capital. But Gilmore believes that his task-oriented leadership pushes employees just enough to achieve higher performance, and no further. "I try to stretch them as far as they will go without breaking," he says.

Employees at the Washington, D.C., public housing authority agree with Gilmore's self-assessment, but that doesn't stop them from teasing the taskmaster. Not long ago, they bought Gilmore a poster from *The Caine Mutiny* and superimposed his face over that of Humphrey Bogart as Captain Queeg. It was an apt comparison. Rather than obsessively rolling silver balls, Gilmore likes to stretch a rubber band from one index finger to the other.

Unfortunately, not everyone has a friendly tyrant for a boss. At a Chicago insurance company, Robert (who didn't want his last name known) has a tough boss who regularly threatens and insults employees. "My boss would snap at us all the time and call us idiots," says the claims representative. "He also would threaten, 'Do the work right, or you're out of here.'"

Two former employees at a New York advertising agency were so fed up with their abusive task-oriented boss that they sued the company. "While yelling at me from a distance of approximately one inch from my face, [my boss] asked me how I could be so &*%#! stupid," recalls one complainant. And in Massachusetts, the executive director of a city water and sewage department was suspended for being so demanding and abusive that he made employees cry.

Sources: Adapted from K. Sopranos, "Who's Afraid of the Big Bad Boss?" *Chicago Tribune,* June 21, 1998, p. C1; V. Loeb, "Resident Expert," *Washington Post,* May 7, 1998, p. B1; R. Holland, "Celano Called Tough Boss," *Quincy Patriot Ledger* (MA), December 19, 1997, p. C17; J. Steinhauer, "If the Boss Is Out of Line, What's the Legal Boundary?" *New York Times,* March 27, 1997, p. D1. ▪

are high on one style and low on the other, and most are somewhere in between.

With the revised assumption that leaders could be both people-oriented and task-oriented, behavioral leadership scholars hypothesized that the most effective leaders exhibit high levels of both types of behavior. This became known as the **"hi-hi" leadership hypothesis.**[23] Effective leaders, it was thought, should have a high people-oriented style and a high task-oriented style.

A popular leadership program that grew out of the "hi-hi" leadership hypothesis is the **Leadership Grid®** (formerly known as the *Managerial Grid*).[24] Participants begin by assessing their own leadership style on the grid (see Exhibit 14.3), then develop skills to move toward the best leadership style. According to the model, the best leadership style is team management (9,9 in the upper right-hand corner of the grid). This equates to "hi-hi" leadership in which leaders have high levels of concern for people and production. People with 9,9 scores tend to rely on commitment, participation, and conflict resolution to get results.

The Leadership Grid also labels people with less than perfect scores. Authority-compliance managers (9,1) try to maximize productivity through power and authority. Country club managers (1,9) focus on developing good feelings among employees even when production suffers. Middle-of-the-road managers (5,5 in the center of the grid) try to maintain the status quo by adopting a middle-of-the-road approach. Impoverished managers (1,1) do the minimum required to fulfill their leadership role and keep their job.

When the Leadership Grid was first introduced in the early 1960s, it adopted the "hi-hi" leadership hypothesis; namely, that leaders are most

"hi-hi" leadership hypothesis a proposition stating that effective leaders exhibit high levels of both people-oriented and task-oriented behaviors

Leadership Grid® a leadership model developed by Blake and Mouton that assesses an individual's leadership effectiveness in terms of his or her concern for people and concern for production

Exhibit 14.3
The Leadership Grid® figure

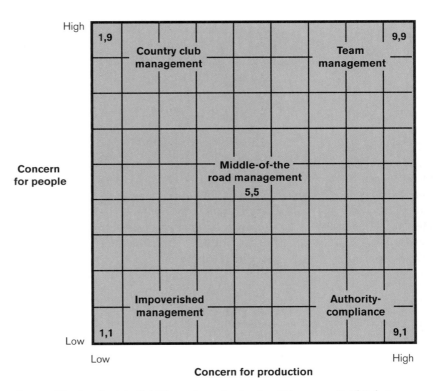

Source: The Leadership Grid figure from *Leadership Dilemmas—Grid Solutions,* by Robert R. Blake and Anne Adams McCanse. Houston: Gulf Publishing Company, p. 29. Copyright © 1991, by Scientific Methods, Inc. Reproduced by permission of the owners.

effective when they have both a high concern for people and a high concern for production (i.e., team management). While still aiming participants at this ideal level, the most recent version of the Leadership Grid program states that effective leaders have the *capacity* for high levels of both dimensions, but they should choose appropriate levels of both dimensions for the specific situation. This revision adopts the contingency perspective, which we discuss in the next section of this chapter.

Limitations of the Behavioral Leadership Perspective

The Leadership Grid probably distanced itself from the hi-hi leadership hypothesis for the same reasons that scholars have moved away from the behavioral perspective of leadership.[25] One concern is that studies supporting the hi-hi leadership hypothesis relied on very subjective questionnaire items, so it was easy for stereotyping and other biases to falsely link effective leaders with high levels of both styles.[26] Followers may have concluded that someone is a great leader and this positive halo caused them to rate the leader highly on the people-oriented and task-oriented items in the questionnaire.

Contemporary leadership scholars have also moved away from the behavioral perspective because it is a universal approach. It ignores the possibility that the best leadership style may depend on the situation.[27] This severely limits the predictive value of the behavioral perspective, so it has been largely set aside in favor of contingency theories of leadership, which we describe next.

Contingency Perspective of Leadership

The contingency perspective of leadership is based on the idea that the most appropriate leadership style depends on the situation. Most (although not all) contingency leadership theories assume that effective leaders must be both insightful and flexible.[28] They must be able to adapt their behaviors and styles to the immediate situation. This isn't easy to do, however. Leaders typically have a preferred style. It takes considerable effort to learn when and how to alter one's style to match the situation. As we noted earlier, leaders must have a high emotional intelligence, particularly a self-monitoring personality so they can diagnose the circumstances and match their behaviors accordingly.

Path-Goal Theory of Leadership

path-goal leadership theory a contingency theory of leadership based on expectancy theory of motivation that includes four leadership styles as well as several employee and situational contingencies

Several contingency theories have been proposed over the years, but **path-goal leadership theory** has withstood scientific critique better than the others. The theory has its roots in the expectancy theory of motivation (see Chapter 3). Early research by Martin Evans incorporated expectancy theory into the study of how leader behaviors influence employee perceptions of expectancies (paths) between employee effort and performance (goals). Based on this perspective, Robert House and other scholars developed and refined path-goal theory as a contingency leadership model.[29]

Path-goal theory states that effective leaders influence employee satisfaction and performance by making their need satisfaction contingent on effective job performance. Thus, leaders strengthen the performance-to-outcome expectancy and the value of those outcomes by ensuring that employees who perform their jobs well have a higher degree of need fulfillment than employees who perform poorly. Second, path-goal theory states that effective leaders strengthen the effort-to-performance expectancy by providing the information, support, and other resources necessary to help employees complete their tasks.[30]

Consider the "grassroots leadership" style of D. Michael Abrashoff. The U.S. Naval officer ensures that the work to be done is important and that the crew's needs are met along the way. Abrashoff takes the view that leaders support employees, not the other way around. As we read in the *Fast Company Online* feature, Abrashoff's grassroots leadership style incorporates many elements of the path-goal leadership model.

FAST COMPANY
Online

◻ Grassroots Leadership

The USS *Benfold* is one of the U.S. Navy's most advanced warships with a crack crew of 300 highly skilled sailors. But its real secret weapon is the leadership style of Commander D. Michael Abrashoff. Abrashoff (who was recently promoted to a top naval post) relies on what he calls a "grassroots leadership" in which the Navy's rigid hierarchy is turned upside down. The highest boss is no longer the guy with the most stripes—it's the sailors who do the work. Moreover, Abrashoff empowers his crew with responsibility and authority to get the job done without waiting for approval on every little detail.

Grassroots leadership takes the view that leaders should make sure employees have the resources to get the job done and are able to fulfill their own needs along the way. Abrashoff begins this process by meeting face-to-face with all crew members to understand their background and goals for the future. "Ultimately, I consider it my job to improve my little 300-person piece of society," Abrashoff explains. "And that's as much a part of the bottom line as operational readiness is."

Grassroots leadership is also about making sure the work is worth doing. Soon after his arrival as the *Benfold's* commander, Abrashoff interviewed every crew member to distinguish mission-critical tasks from non-value-added chores. He soon discovered that the most demoralizing chores were sanding down rust and repainting the ship. So the commander replaced rusting bolts with stainless steel hardware and had a commercial firm repaint the ship with a special rust inhibitor. The result: Crew members now spend more time learning more enjoyable work.

Grassroots leadership has had remarkable results. During Abrashoff's 20-month tour of duty, the USS *Benfold* became the best ship in the Pacific Fleet and received a prestigious award as the most combat-ready ship in the entire fleet. The crew returned one-third of the Benfold's repair and maintenance budget and all of the career sailors signed on for a second tour of duty.

ONLINE CHECK-UP

1. This *Fast Company Online* feature describes how D. Michael Abrashoff relies on what he calls "grassroots leadership." Explain how this leadership model incorporates various path-goal leadership practices.
2. In the full text of this *Fast Company* article, Abrashoff describes six principles of grassroots leadership. Discuss these principles and relate them to communication, quality management, organizational commitment, and employee involvement.
3. Check through your favorite web search engine to find examples of grassroots leadership. What are the common features of this leadership?

Get the full text of this *Fast Company* article at www.mhhe.com/mcshane1e

Source: P. LaBarre, "The Agenda—Grassroots Leadership," *Fast Company,* Issue 23 (April 1999). ◼

Exhibit 14.4
Path-goal leadership theory

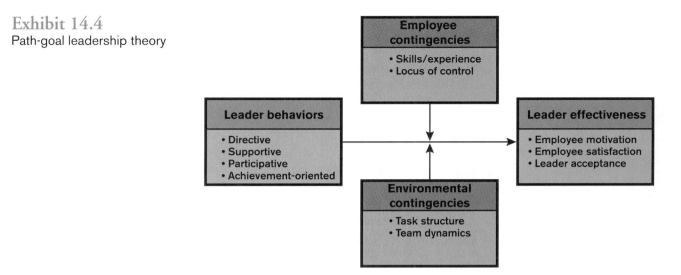

As Exhibit 14.4 illustrates, path-goal theory considers four leadership styles and several contingency factors leading to three indicators of leader effectiveness.

Leadership styles   Path-goal theory suggests that leaders motivate and satisfy employees in a particular situation by adopting one or more of the four leadership styles described below:[31]

1. *Directive*—These are clarifying behaviors that provide a psychological structure for subordinates. The leader clarifies performance goals, the means to reach those goals, and the standards against which performance will be judged. It also includes judicious use of rewards and disciplinary actions. Directive leadership is the same as task-oriented leadership described earlier and echoes our discussion in Chapter 2 on the importance of clear role perceptions in employee performance.

2. *Supportive*—These behaviors provide psychological support for subordinates. The leader is friendly and approachable, makes the work more pleasant, treats employees with equal respect, and shows concern for the status, needs, and well-being of employees. Supportive leadership is the same as people-oriented leadership described earlier and reflects the benefits of social support to help employees cope with stressful situations (see Chapter 5).

3. *Participative*—These behaviors encourage and facilitate subordinate involvement in decisions beyond their normal work activities. The leader consults with employees, asks for their suggestions, and takes these ideas into serious consideration before making a decision. Participative leadership relates to the employee involvement concepts and issues described in Chapter 10.

4. *Achievement-oriented*—These behaviors encourage employees to reach their peak performance. The leader sets challenging goals, expects employees to perform at their highest level, continuously seeks improvement in employee performance, and shows a high degree of confidence that employees will assume responsibility and accomplish challenging goals. Achievement-oriented leadership applies goal-setting theory (see Chapter 3) as well as positive expectations in self-fulfilling prophecy (see Chapter 6).

The path-goal model contends that effective leaders are capable of selecting the most appropriate behavioral style (or styles) for that situation. Leaders might simultaneously use more than one style at a time. For example, they might be both supportive and participative in a specific situation.

Contingencies of Path-Goal Theory

As a contingency theory, path-goal theory states that each of these four leadership styles will be effective in some situations but not in others. The path-goal leadership model specifies two sets of situational variables that moderate the relationship between a leader's style and effectiveness: (1) employee characteristics and (2) characteristics of the employee's work environment. Several contingencies have already been studied within the path-goal framework, and the model is open for more variables in the future.[32] However, we will examine only four contingencies here (see Exhibit 14.5).

Skill and experience   A combination of directive and supportive leadership is best for employees who are—or perceive themselves to be—inexperienced and unskilled. Directive leadership gives subordinates information about how to accomplish the task, whereas supportive leadership helps them to cope with the uncertainties of unfamiliar work situations. Directive leadership is detrimental when employees are skilled and experienced because it introduces too much supervisory control. This is one of the complaints against Jill Barad's leadership style. Although the Mattel CEO has several traits found in effective leaders (as we described earlier), she is also known for her extreme hands-on approach. In a recent makeover of the Barbie doll, for example, Barad quickly demanded changes to the face, hair, and clothing. "It is a blatant problem," complains one former executive about Barad's directive style. "Why is the chairman looking at every design concept?"[33] Generally, the participative and achievement-oriented leadership styles are more effective where employees are skilled and experienced.

locus of control a personality trait referring to the extent that people believe what happens to them is within their control

Locus of control   Recall from Chapter 6 that people with an internal **locus of control** believe that they have control over their work environment. Consequently, these employees prefer participative and achievement-oriented leadership styles and may become frustrated with a directive style. In contrast, people with an external locus of control believe that their performance is due more to luck and fate, so they tend to be more satisfied with directive and supportive leadership.

Task structure   Directive leadership should be adopted when the task is nonroutine, because this style minimizes role ambiguity that tends to occur in

Exhibit 14.5   Selected contingencies of path-goal theory

	Directive	Supportive	Participative	Achievement-oriented
Employee contingencies				
Skill-Experience	Low	Low	High	High
Locus of Control	External	External	Internal	Internal
Environmental contingencies				
Task Structure	Nonroutine	Routine	Nonroutine	?
Team Dynamics	Negative norms	Low cohesion	Positive norms	?

these complex work situations, particularly for inexperienced employees.[34] This style is ineffective when employees have routine and simple tasks because the manager's guidance serves no purpose and may be viewed as unnecessarily close control. Employees in highly routine and simple jobs may require supportive leadership to help them cope with the tedious nature of the work and lack of control over the pace of work. Participative leadership is preferred for employees performing nonroutine tasks because the lack of rules and procedures gives them more discretion to achieve challenging goals. This style is ineffective for employees in routine tasks because they lack discretion over their work.

Team dynamics   Cohesive teams with performance-oriented norms act as a substitute for most interventions by leaders. High team cohesiveness substitutes for supportive leadership, whereas performance-oriented team norms substitute for directive and possibly achievement-oriented leadership. Thus, when team cohesiveness is low, leaders should use the supportive style. Leaders should apply a directive style to counteract team norms that oppose the team's formal objectives. For example, the team leader may need to use legitimate power if team members have developed a norm to "take it easy" rather than get a project completed on time.

Recent Extensions of Path-Goal Theory

The original path-goal theory relates primarily to dyadic relations between a supervisor and employee.[35] Yet leadership also applies to the work unit and organization. Recognizing this gap, Robert House, an early developer of the original path-goal theory, extended the model in the late 1990s by adding leadership styles that apply more to work units and organizations than to individual relations.[36] One of these is *networking,* which recognizes that leaders play an important political role. They represent the work unit and engage in political networking activities (see Chapter 12) to legitimize the work unit and maintain positive influences on other areas of the organization. Another is *value-based leadership,* which includes articulating a vision of the future, displaying passion for this vision, demonstrating self-confidence in the attainment of the vision, communicating the vision, and acting in ways consistent with the vision. This is the same as the transformational leadership perspective that we will describe later in this chapter.

Practical Implications and Limitations of Path-Goal Theory

Path-goal theory clearly reinforces the idea that effective leaders vary their style with the situation. There are times to give directions, times to empathize with followers, times to use stretch goals, and times to involve people in decision making. Path-goal theory also offers a fairly precise set of contingency factors to guide our use of leadership styles. As a result, this theory provides practical advice on when to use various leadership styles.

Path-goal theory has received considerably research support, certainly more than other contingency leadership models.[37] It also has the ability to expand by adding more contingency variables as they are identified through research.[38] For example, the locus of control contingency was added a few years after the original model was introduced. However, some contingencies and leadership styles in the path-goal leadership model have received relatively little scholarly investigation.[39] For example, you probably noticed that some cells in Exhibit 14.5 have question marks. The reason is that we do not yet know how those leadership styles apply to those contingencies. The recently expanded model adds new leadership styles and contingencies, but they have not yet been tested.

Another concern is that as path-goal theory expands, the model may become too complex for practical use. Although the expanded model provides a closer representation of the complexity of leadership, it may become too cumbersome for training people in leadership styles. Few people would be able to remember all the contingencies and appropriate leadership styles for those contingencies. In spite of these limitations, path-goal theory remains a relatively complete and robust contingency leadership theory.

Other Contingency Theories

At the beginning of this chapter, we noted that numerous leadership theories have developed over the years. Most of them are found in the contingency perspective of leadership. Some overlap with the path-goal model in terms of leadership styles, but most use simpler and more abstract contingencies. We will very briefly mention only two here because of their popularity and historical significance to the field.

Situational leadership model

One of the most popular contingency theories among trainers is the **situational leadership model,** developed by Paul Hersey and Ken Blanchard.[40] The model suggests that effective leaders vary their style with the "readiness" of followers. (An earlier version of the model called this "maturity.") Readiness refers to the employee's or work team's ability and willingness to accomplish a specific task. Ability refers to the extent that the follower has the skills and knowledge to perform the task without the leader's guidance. Willingness refers to the follower's self-motivation and commitment to perform the assigned task. The model compresses these distinct concepts into a single situational condition.

The situational leadership model also identifies four leadership styles—telling, selling, participating, and delegating—that Hersey and Blanchard distinguish in terms of the amount of directive and supportive behavior provided. For example, "telling" has high task behavior and low supportive behavior. The situational leadership model uses the same template as the Leadership Grid shown earlier, except the four quadrants represent a leadership style that may be appropriate under different circumstances.

In spite of its popularity, at least three reviews have concluded that the situational leadership model lacks empirical support.[41] Only one part of the model apparently works; namely, that leaders should use "telling" (i.e., directive style) when employees lack motivation and ability. (Recall that path-goal theory also says this.) The model's elegant simplicity is attractive and entertaining, but other parts don't represent reality very well. The most recent review also concluded that the theory has logical and internal inconsistencies.

Fiedler's contingency model

The earliest contingency theory of leadership, called **Fiedler's contingency model,** was developed by Fred Fiedler and his associates.[42] According to this model, leader effectiveness depends on whether the person's natural leadership style is appropriately matched to the situation. The theory examines two leadership styles that essentially correspond to the people-oriented and task-oriented styles described previously. Unfortunately, Fiedler's model relies on a questionnaire that does not measure either leadership style very well.

Fiedler's model suggests that the best leadership style depends on the level of *situational control;* that is, the degree of power and influence that the leader possesses in a particular situation. Situational control is affected by three

situational leadership model Hersey and Blanchard's model stating that leaders should tell, sell, participate, or delegate, depending on the "readiness" of followers

Fiedler's contingency model Fiedler's leadership theory stating that the best leadership style depends on the level of situational control and that the situation should be arranged to fit the leader's natural style

factors in the following order of importance: leader-member relations, task structure, and position power.[43] Leader-member relations is the degree to which employees trust and respect the leader and are willing to follow his or her guidance. Task structure refers to the clarity or ambiguity of operating procedures. Position power is the extent to which the leader possesses legitimate, reward, and coercive power over subordinates. These three contingencies form the eight possible combinations of *situation favorableness* from the leader's viewpoint. Good leader-member relations, high task structure, and strong position power create the most favorable situation for the leader because he or she has the most power and influence under these conditions.

Fiedler has gained considerable respect for pioneering the first contingency theory of leadership. However, his theory has faired less well. As mentioned, the leadership style scale used by Fiedler has been widely criticized. There is also no scientific justification for placing the three situational control factors in a hierarchy. Moreover, it seems that leader-member relations is actually an indicator of leader effectiveness (as in path-goal theory) rather than as a situational factor. Finally, the theory considers only two leadership styles whereas other models present a more complex and realistic array of behavior options. These concerns explain why the theory has limited empirical support.[44]

Changing the situation to match the leader's natural style

Fiedler's contingency model may become a historical footnote, but it does make an important and lasting contribution by suggesting that leadership style is related to the individual's personality and, consequently, is relatively stable over time. Leaders might be able to alter their style temporarily, but they tend to use a preferred style in the long term. This contrasts with most other contingency leadership theories that assume leaders can comfortably change their style to match a given situation.

If leadership style is influenced by a person's personality, then organizations should engineer the situation to fit the leader's dominant style, rather than expect leaders to change their style with the situation. A directive leader might be assigned inexperienced employees who need direction rather than seasoned people who work less effectively under a directive style. Alternatively, companies might transfer supervisors to workplaces where their dominant style fits best. For instance, directive leaders might be parachuted into work teams with counterproductive norms, whereas leaders who prefer a supportive style should be sent to departments in which employees face work pressures and other stressors.

Leadership substitutes

So far, we have looked at theories that recommend using different leadership styles in various situations. But one theory, called **leadership substitutes,** identifies contingencies that either limit the leader's ability to influence subordinates or make that particular leadership style unnecessary. When substitute conditions are present, employees are effective without a formal leader who applies a particular style. Although the leadership substitute model requires further refinement, there is general support for the overall notion that some conditions neutralize or substitute for leadership styles.[45]

Several conditions have been identified in the literature that possibly substitute for task-oriented or people-oriented leadership. For example, performance-based reward systems keep employees directed toward organizational goals, so they probably replace or reduce the need for task-oriented leadership. Task-oriented leadership is also less important when employees are skilled and experienced. Notice how these propositions are similar to path-goal

leadership substitutes
characteristics of the employee, task, or organization that either limit the leader's influence or make it unnecessary

leadership theory, namely that directive leadership is unnecessary—and may be detrimental—when employees are skilled or experienced.[46]

Leadership substitutes have become more important as organizations remove supervisors and shift toward team-based structures. An emerging concept is that effective leaders help team members learn to lead themselves through leadership substitutes.[47] Some writers suggest that co-workers are powerful leader substitutes in these organizational structures. Co-workers instruct new employees, thereby providing directive leadership. They also provide social support, which reduces stress among fellow employees (see Chapter 5). Teams with norms that support organizational goals may substitute for achievement-oriented leadership, because employees encourage (or pressure) co-workers to stretch their performance levels.

Self-leadership has also been discussed as a potentially valuable leadership substitute in self-directed work teams.[48] Recall from Chapter 4 that self-leadership is the process of influencing oneself to establish the self-direction and self-motivation needed to perform a task.[49] It includes self-set goals, self-reinforcement, constructive thought processes, and other activities that influence the person's own motivation and behavior. As employees become more

self-leadership the process of influencing oneself to establish the self-direction and self-motivation needed to perform a task, including personal goal setting, constructive thought patterns, designing natural rewards, self-monitoring, and self-reinforcement

This self-directed work team at General Electric is able to perform its work without a traditional supervisory leader. It does this through leadership substitutes, including guidance from co-workers, formal training and socialization, and hiring people who practice self-leadership. What conditions are necessary for these teams to lead themselves without direct supervision?
[Courtesy of General Electric]

proficient in self-leadership, they presumably require less supervision to keep them focused and energized toward organizational objectives.

Transformational Perspective of Leadership

transformational leadership a leadership perspective that explains how leaders change teams or organizations by creating, communicating, and modeling a vision for the organization or work unit, and inspiring employees to strive for that vision

Andy Stefanovich is founder and CEO of Opus Event Marketing in Richmond, Virginia. But that's not what his business card says. The title on the card reads "in charge of what's next."[50] The label is appropriate because Stefanovich is a **transformational leader.** Through his vision and actions, Opus Event Marketing has become one of the leading event management firms in the United States. Other transformational leaders such as Carly Fiorina (Hewlett-Packard), Jack Welch (GE), Herb Kelleher (Southwest Airlines), and Richard Branson (Virgin) dot the corporate landscape.[51] These leaders are agents of change. They developed a vision for the organization or work unit, inspired and collectively bonded employees to that vision, and gave them a "can do" attitude that made the vision achievable.[52]

transactional leadership leadership that helps organizations achieve their current objectives more efficiently by linking job performance to valued rewards and ensuring that employees have the resources needed to get the job done

Transformational versus Transactional Leadership

Transformational leadership is different from **transactional leadership.** Transactional leadership is "managing"—helping organizations achieve their current objectives more efficiently, such as linking job performance to valued rewards and ensuring that employees have the resources needed to get the job done.[53] The contingency and behavioral theories described earlier adopt the transactional perspective because they focus on leader behaviors that improve employee performance and satisfaction.

AES, the successful global power company, wants leaders who are both transactional and transformational. "We need people who can both lead and manage," says Dennis W. Bakke (left), CEO and cofounder of the company. "The traditional idea is that a manager takes what is there and makes certain it works well, while a leader takes a visionary look at what is already known to discover something new. But the world changes so much that you can no longer just manage 'what is there.' Leadership that doesn't consider practical execution is ridiculous. It's not either/or. It is much better to think about those two abilities together."[54] How can AES and other organizations ensure that people maintain a balance between transformational and transactional leadership? Or do you think that these roles should occur in different people?

[Courtesy of The AES Corporation]

In contrast, transformational leadership is about "leading"—changing the organization's strategies and culture so that they have a better fit with the surrounding environment.[55] Transformational leaders are agents of change who energize and direct employees to a new set of corporate values and behaviors. Jac Nasser is like that. As we learned in the opening story to this chapter, Nasser is transforming the Ford Motor Company into a more nimble company focused on shareholder value.

Should organizations have transactional or transformational leaders? The answer is that they need both. Transactional leadership improves organizational efficiency, whereas transformational leadership steers organizations onto a better course of action. Unfortunately, too many leaders get trapped in the daily managerial activities that represent transactional leadership.[56] They lose touch with the transformational aspect of effective leadership. Without transformational leaders, organizations stagnate and eventually become seriously misaligned with their environments.

Transformational versus Charismatic Leadership

Another important distinction is between transformational and charismatic leadership. These concepts have generated some controversy and confusion among leadership experts.[57] A few writers use the words "charismatic" and "transformational leadership" interchangeably, as if they have the same meaning.[58] However, charismatic leadership differs from transformational leadership. As we learned in Chapter 12, *charisma* is a form of interpersonal attraction whereby followers develop a respect for and trust in the charismatic individual. Charismatic leadership therefore extends beyond behaviors to personal traits that provide referent power over followers.[59] Transformational leadership, on the other hand, is mainly about behaviors that people use to lead the change process. The remainder of this section will focus on transformational leadership because it offers more specific behavioral implications.

Elements of Transformational Leadership

There are several descriptions of transformational leadership, but most include the four elements illustrated in Exhibit 14.6. These elements include creating a strategic vision, communicating the vision, modeling the vision, and building commitment toward the vision.

Creating a strategic vision   Transformational leaders are the brokers of dreams.[60] They shape a strategic vision of a realistic and attractive future that bonds employees together and focuses their energy toward a superordinate organizational goal.[61] Visions represent the substance of transformational

Exhibit 14.6
Elements of transformational leadership

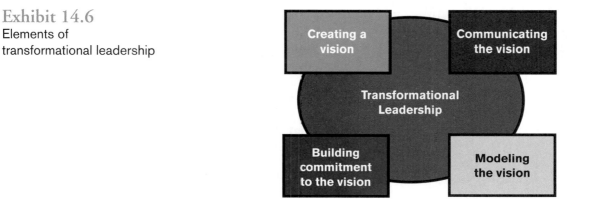

leadership. They reflect a future for the company or work unit that is ultimately accepted and valued by organizational members. Notice that leadership vision is not a mission statement plastered on someone's wall. Rather, it is part of the corporate meaning—the organization's goals and reason why it exists. Strategic visions might originate with the leader, but they are just as likely to emerge from employees, clients, suppliers, or other constituents. They typically begin as abstract ideas that become progressively clearer through critical events and discussions with staff about strategic and operational plans.[62]

There is some evidence that visions are the most important part of transformational leadership.[63] Visions offer the motivational benefits of goal setting, but they are more than mundane goals. Visions are compelling future states that bond employees and motivate them to strive for those objectives. Visions are typically described in a way that distinguishes them from the current situation, yet makes the goal both appealing and achievable.

Communicating the vision
If vision is the substance of transformational leadership, then communicating that vision is the process. Effective leaders are able to communicate meaning and elevate the importance of the visionary goal to employees.[64] They frame messages around a grand purpose with an emotional appeal that captivates employees and other corporate stakeholders. Framing helps transformational leaders establish a common mental model so that the group or organization will act collectively toward the desirable goal.[65] For example, Arthur Blank, cofounder of Home Depot, likes to remind employees that they are "in the business of making people's dreams come true."[66] Blank helps employees see their role toward customers in a different light, one that is much more meaningful and motivating than selling hammers and nails.

Transformational leaders also bring their visions to life through symbols, metaphors, stories, and other vehicles that transcend plain language.[67] Metaphors borrow images of other experiences, thereby creating a richer meaning of the vision that has not yet been experienced. When McDonald's faced the difficult challenge of opening restaurants in Moscow during the 1980s, the leader of that initiative reminded his team members that they were establishing "hamburger diplomacy." And in the mid-1800s, when ocean transportation was treacherous, Samuel Cunard emphasized that he was creating an "ocean railway." At the time, railroads provided one of the safest forms of transportation, and Cunard's metaphor reinforced the notion to employees and passengers alike that Cunard Lines would provide equally safe transportation across the Atlantic.[68]

Modeling the vision
Transformational leaders not only talk about a vision, they enact it. They "walk the talk" by stepping outside the executive suite and doing things that symbolize the vision.[69] Moreover, transformational leaders are reliable and persistent in their actions. They stay on course, thereby legitimizing the vision and providing further evidence that they can be trusted. Walking the talk is important because employees and other stakeholders are executive watchers who look for behaviors to symbolize values and expectations. The more consistent these behaviors are with statements, the more employees will believe and follow these statements. Moreover, walking the talk builds trust. As we shall learn in Chapter 17, one way to have others build trust in you is through the consistency of your behavior. By walking the talk, leaders are acting consistently and, consequently, tend to build greater employee trust in them.[70]

Leaders walk the talk through significant events, but they also alter mundane activities—meeting agendas, office locations, executive schedules—so

Coca-Cola CEO Doug Ivester is well known for walking the talk. He will visit local shops in Shanghai (or any other city where he happens to be staying) to see how widely the bubbly soft drink is available and how well it is presented to consumers. He consistently looks for places where Coke is not yet available, or where it is not presented effectively. And he expects everyone else to do the same. When he was head of Coca-Cola USA, Ivester had a camera crew videotape all of the places between Atlanta and Rome, Georgia, where Coke was not available. These actions reinforce Ivester's message to all Coke executives—get close to the market to be on the alert for new opportunities.[71] What problems do corporate leaders face when they try to enact their vision of the future by "walking the talk"? [© Fritz Hoffmann/Network/SABA]

they are consistent with the vision and its underlying values. "The first principle of leadership is authenticity," advises Hatim Tyabji, former CEO of Verifone Inc. "Watch what I do, not what I say." Percy Barnevik, chairman of the giant electrical systems manufacturer ABB, agrees. "The most important thing is to live that way yourself," he says. "If you talk about speed in action, yet procrastinate on difficult decisions, you are not believable. I and the members of my executive committee must 'walk the talk' and live up to what we say."[72]

Building commitment toward the vision Transforming a vision into reality requires employee commitment. Transformational leaders build this commitment in several ways. Their words, symbols, and stories build a contagious enthusiasm that energizes people to adopt the vision as their own. Leaders demonstrate a "can do" attitude by enacting their vision and staying on course. Their persistence and consistency reflect an image of honesty, trust, and integrity. Finally, leaders build commitment by involving employees in the process of shaping the organization's vision.

Evaluating the Transformational Leadership Perspective

Organizational behavior studies report that transformational leaders do make a difference. Subordinates are more satisfied and loyal under transformational leaders. They also perform their jobs better, engage in more organizational citizenship behaviors, and make better or more creative decisions.[73] One recent study reported that organizational commitment and financial performance may have increased in branches of a bank where the branch manager completed a transformational leadership training program.[74]

Transformational leadership is currently the most popular leadership perspective, but it faces a number of challenges. One problem is that some transformational leadership writers define this concept in terms of the leader's success.[75] They suggest that leaders are transformational when they successfully bring about change, rather than whether they engage in certain behaviors we call transformational. A related concern is that qualitative studies of transformational leaders only investigate people who are successful. A better strategy is to compare successful with unsuccessful leaders and distinguish their use of transformational behaviors.

A third problem is that the transformational leadership model still implies a universal rather than contingency approach to leadership. Only very recently have writers begun to explore the idea that transformational leadership is more appropriate in some situations than others.[76] For instance, transformational leadership is probably more appropriate when organizations need to adapt than when environmental conditions are stable. Transactional leadership would be more suitable, on the other hand, when the organization requires greater efficiency. Preliminary evidence suggests that the general concept of transformational leadership is relevant and appropriate across cultures. However, there may be specific elements of transformational leadership, such as the way visions are formed and communicated, that are more appropriate in North America than other cultures.[77]

Finally, we need to remember that establishing and communicating a broad corporate vision does not replace the practical value of hard goals and results. The problem is determining how and when to reduce the transformational leader's lofty ideals into measurable progress. Sir David Simon, chairman of British Petroleum, echoed this concern: "I'm not too happy about this floating in vision territory," he says. "I like to know the how and the what. I am very nervous of visions that end in superlatives (the 'we will be best' type)—I like deliverables."[78]

Romance Perspective of Leadership

The competency, behavior, contingency, and transformational leadership perspectives make the basic assumption that leaders "make a difference." Certainly, there is evidence that senior executives do influence organizational performance.[79] However, leaders might have less influence than most of us would like to believe. Some leadership experts suggest that three perceptual processes cause people to inflate the importance of leadership in explaining organizational events. These processes, collectively called the "romance of leadership," include attribution errors, stereotyping, and the need for situational control.[80]

Attributing Leadership

fundamental attribution error the tendency to incorrectly attribute the behavior of other people to internal more than to external factors

People have a strong need to attribute the causes of events around them so they can feel more confident about how to control them in the future. As we described in Chapter 6, the **fundamental attribution error** is a common perceptual bias in this attribution process. Fundamental attribution error is the tendency of people to attribute the behavior of other people to their own motivation and ability rather than to situational contingencies. In the context of leadership, it causes employees to believe that organizational events are due more to the motivation and ability of their leaders than to environmental conditions. Leaders are given credit or blame for the company's success or failure because employees do not readily see the external forces that also influence these events. Leaders reinforce this belief by taking credit for organizational successes.[81]

Stereotyping Leadership

There is some evidence that people rely on leadership stereotypes to make sense of organizational events. Almost everyone has a set of shared expectations regarding what an effective leader should look and act like.[82] These preconceived ideas influence perceptions about whether someone is an effective leader. By relying on these stereotypes, employees and other stakeholders evaluate a leader's effectiveness more on his or her appearance and actions than on actual outcomes. Part of the reason why this occurs is that the outcome of a leader's actions may not be known for months or years. Consequently, employees depend on immediate information to decide whether the leader is effective. If the leader fits the mold, then employees are more confident that the leader is effective.

Need for Situational Control

A third perceptual distortion of leadership suggests that people want to believe leaders make a difference. There are two basic reasons for this belief.[83] First, leadership is a useful way for us to simplify life events. It is easier to explain organizational successes and failures in terms of the leader's ability than by analyzing a complex array of other forces. For example, there are usually many reasons why a company fails to change quickly enough in the marketplace, yet we tend to simplify this explanation down to the notion that the company president or some other corporate leader was ineffective.

Second, there is a strong tendency in the United States and similar cultures to believe that life events are generated more from people than from uncontrollable natural forces.[84] This illusion of control is satisfied by believing that events result from the rational actions of leaders. In short, employees feel better believing that leaders make a difference, so they actively look for evidence that this is so.

The romance of leadership perspective questions the importance of leadership, but it also provides valuable advice to improve leadership effectiveness. This approach highlights the truth that leadership is a perception of followers as much as the actual behaviors and characteristics of people calling themselves leaders. Potential leaders must be sensitive to this, understand what followers expect, and act accordingly. Individuals who do not make an effort to fit leadership prototypes will have more difficulty bringing about necessary organizational change.[85]

Gender Issues in Leadership

Do women lead differently than men? This question has captured the interest of many organizational behavior scholars and is the subject of ongoing public debate as more women enter leadership roles at work. As we read in Connections 14.2, many people do see a difference, but others don't think gender is a factor in leadership.

Several writers argue that women have an interactive style that includes more people-oriented and participative leadership.[86] They suggest that women are more relationship oriented, cooperative, nurturing, and emotional in their leadership roles. They further assert that these qualities make women particularly well suited to leadership roles at a time when companies are adopting a stronger emphasis on teams and employee involvement. These arguments are consistent with sex role stereotypes, namely that men tend to be more task oriented whereas women are more people oriented.

Are these stereotypes true? Do women adopt more people-oriented and participative leadership styles? The answer, according to organizational behavior research, is that these stereotypes of female leaders are mostly false. Leadership studies in field settings have generally found that male and female leaders do not differ in their levels of task-oriented or people-oriented leadership. The main explanation why men and women do not differ on these styles is that real-world jobs require similar behavior from male and female job incumbents.[87]

One leadership style that women do adopt more readily than their male counterparts is employee involvement. Scholars explain that women are possibly more participative because their upbringing has made them more egalitarian and less status oriented. There is also some evidence that women have somewhat better interpersonal skills than men, and this translates into their relatively greater use of the participative leadership style. Finally, women might be more participative because subordinates expect them to be so, based on their own sex stereotypes. If a female manager tries to be more autocratic, subordinates are more likely to complain (or use some other power base) because they expect the female manager to be participative.[88]

Connections 14.2   ◾ Do Women Lead Differently?

A decade ago, Bree Bowman's male supervisor at Pacific Bell wouldn't move her into a data communications center management job. He said her leadership style wasn't tough enough to negotiate with union officials. "He said that if I spent five minutes with the union, I'd be in tears," she says, "only he wasn't that polite about it."

Fortunately, Bowman ignored his comments and was offered the position (reluctantly) by her next supervisor. Using a less confrontational leadership style, she boosted morale and productivity among the 158 datacom technicians. Today, Bowman is a more senior executive and a model of effective leadership at the California-based telephone company. "Before, [information systems] was a real command-and-control environment," recalls Diana Whitehead, chief information officer at Pacific Bell, and Bowman's mentor. "And today, it's much more collaborative and teams-driven. And that requires a diverse leadership team."

Does a diverse leadership team mean that women and men use different leadership styles? Some people think so. They claim that Bowman and other female leaders are more people oriented and tend to shun the old command-and-control style. "More and more there's a need to develop alliances," explains Stentor CEO Carol Stephenson. "The result is that the feminine style of leadership is valued more than ever before."

Gail Graham also senses that some leadership styles don't work as well for women. "I was aware that there were some styles that men advised that wouldn't work for me," says the marketing director for Pittsburgh-based PNC Bank. For this reason, Graham regrets that she hasn't had the guidance of a female mentor. "I wanted to have someone understand about leadership styles from a woman's perspective."

But not everyone is convinced that men and women lead differently. "If there are differences in how a male or female would run this plant," says Honda of America executive Susan Insley, "I believe the differences would be based on the person and the skills they bring to the job, not their gender."

Sources: S. Ginzberg, "Crashing through the Glass Ceiling with Teamwork," *Washington Post*, January 18, 1998, p. H5; L. Goff, "Gender Bender," *Computerworld*, June 1997, pp. 60–66; C. Stephenson, "The Female Model of Leadership," *Canadian Speeches* 10 (March 1997), pp. 59–64; B. S. Moskal, "Glass Ceiling, Beware!" *Industry Week*, April 18, 1994, pp. 13–15. ◾

Not long ago, the delivery department at BT Office Products had the highest turnover rate and lowest morale in the Arlington, Texas, company. But that changed for the better when Cay Cole *(center)* became department manager. "The guy who ran things before relied on the old style of management—you know the 'me boss, you servant' attitude," recalls Jim Miller, BT's former chairman of the board. Miller says that while Cole can be tough when necessary, she tends to involve employees more than her male predecessors. Darrell Dixson *(right)* and Tammie Thurmon *(left)* appreciate Cole's more participative leadership style. "I like the way she always lets us know what is going on," says Dixon. "And it goes the other way. She listens to us and gets our perspective."[89] Is the tendency for female leaders to be more participative than their male counterparts a benefit or liability today compared to 20 years ago?

[Lisa Means]

A disturbing finding is that people evaluate female leaders slightly less favorably than equivalent male leaders, and this difference is almost completely due to sex stereotype bias. Specifically, women are evaluated negatively when they adopt a stereotypically male leadership style (i.e., directive) and occupy traditionally male-dominated positions. Men tend to give female leaders lower ratings than do other women, and male subordinates have lower acceptance of female supervisors as role models.[90] These negative evaluations suggest that women "pay the price" for entering traditionally male leadership jobs and for adopting a male-stereotypic leadership style.[91] It also lends further support to our earlier point on why women adopt a more participative style.

Mattel CEO Jill Barad seems to face this problem. Her leadership style has been criticized by some for being more direct and confrontational than one would expect from a woman. But supporters argue that her style is similar to successful male leaders. "These people calling [Barad] abrasive, have they met

Ted Turner? Have they met Michael Eisner?" asks Geraldine Laybourne, president of Disney/ABC Cable Networks. "Compared to most CEOs, she is not abrasive. But maybe compared to their wives she is."[92]

The debate regarding leadership differences between men and women isn't over yet. Meanwhile, we should be careful about perpetuating the apparently false assumption that women leaders are less task oriented or more people oriented. By holding these assumptions, many corporate decision makers have shifted women into staff roles—such as human resources, public relations, and customer service—and out of line management jobs that most frequently lead to senior management positions.

Remember, too, that our implicit assumptions about how female leaders should act may result in unfair negative evaluations of them under conditions in which the leader must adopt a stereotypically male style. This is consistent with our discussion in the previous section on the romance of leadership. Leaders must be sensitive to the expectations that followers have about how leaders should act, and that negative evaluations may go to leaders who deviate from those expectations.

Chapter Summary

Although leadership is difficult to define, it is often described as the process of influencing people and providing an environment for them to achieve team or organizational objectives. Leaders use power and persuasion to motivate followers, and arrange the work environment so that they do the job more effectively.

The competency perspective tries to identify the characteristics of effective leaders. Recent writing suggests that leaders have drive, leadership motivation, integrity, self-confidence, above-average intelligence, knowledge of the business, and high emotional intelligence.

The behavioral perspective of leadership identifies two clusters of leader behavior: people oriented and task oriented. People-oriented behaviors include showing mutual trust and respect for subordinates, demonstrating a genuine concern for their needs, and having a desire to look out for their welfare. Task-oriented behaviors include assigning employees to specific tasks, clarifying their work duties and procedures, ensuring that they follow company rules, and pushing them to reach their performance capacity. The "hi–hi" leadership hypothesis states that the most effective leaders exhibit high levels of both types of behaviors, but this hypothesis has since been cast into doubt.

The contingency perspective of leadership takes the view that effective leaders diagnose the situation and adapt their style to fit that situation. The path-goal model is the prominent contingency theory that identifies four leadership styles—directive, supportive, participative, and achievement-oriented—and several contingencies relating to the characteristics of the employee and of the situation. A recent extension of path-goal theory adds more leadership styles and moves the model from a dyadic to a team and organizational level.

Two other contingency leadership theories include the situational leadership model and Fiedler's contingency theory. Neither theory has much research support. However, a lasting element of Fiedler's theory is that leaders have natural styles and, consequently, companies need to change the leader's environment to suit his or her style. Leadership substitutes identify contingencies that either limit the leader's ability to influence subordinates or make that particular leadership style unnecessary. This idea will become more important as organizations remove supervisors and shift toward team-based structures.

Transformational leaders create a strategic vision, communicate that vision through framing and use of metaphors, model the vision by "walking the talk" and acting consistently, and build commitment toward the vision. This contrasts with transactional leadership, which links job performance to valued rewards and ensures that employees have the resources needed to get the job done. The contingency and behavioral perspectives adopt the transactional view of leadership.

According to the romance perspective, people inflate the importance of leadership through attribution, stereotyping, and a fundamental need for human control.

Women generally do not differ from men in the degree of people-oriented or task-oriented leadership. However, female leaders more often adopt a participative style. Research also suggests that people evaluate female leaders slightly less favorably than equivalent male leaders, but this is mainly due to sex stereotype biases.

Key Terms

Competencies, p. 435
Emotional intelligence, p. 437
Fiedler's contingency model, p. 447
Fundamental attribution error, p. 454
"Hi-hi" leadership hypothesis, p. 441
Leadership, p. 434
Leadership Grid®, p. 441
Leadership substitutes, p. 448

Locus of control, p. 445
Path-goal leadership theory, p. 442
Self-leadership, p. 449
Self-monitoring personality, p. 437
Situational leadership model, p. 447
Transactional leadership, p. 450
Transformational leadership, p. 450

Discussion Questions

1. Your organization wants to develop a competency-based approach to executive selection. Which leadership perspective mainly applies to this practice? Also, based on leadership research, identify four competencies that your organization will probably identify in effective executives.

2. Think about your favorite teacher. What people-oriented and task-oriented leadership behaviors did he or she use effectively? In general, do you think students prefer an instructor who is more people oriented or task oriented? Explain your preference.

3. Your employees are skilled and experienced customer service representatives who perform nonroutine tasks, such as solving unique customer problems or special needs with the company's equipment. Use path-goal theory to identify the most appropriate leadership style(s) you should use in this situation. Be sure to explain your answer fully and discuss why other styles are inappropriate.

4. Discuss the accuracy of the following statement: "Contingency theories don't work because they assume leaders can adjust their style to the situation. In reality, people have a preferred leadership style that they can't easily change."

5. Is it possible to be a transformational leader and have poor communication skills? Why or why not?

6. Transformational leadership is currently the most popular perspective of leadership. However, it is far from perfect. Discuss three concerns with transformational leadership.

7. Identify a current political leader (e.g., U.S. president, mayor of your city) and his or her recent accomplishments. Now, using the romance of leadership perspective, think of ways that the leader's accomplishments may be overstated. In other words, explain why they may be due to factors other than the leader.

8. You hear two people debating the merits of women as leaders. One person claims that women make better leaders than men because women are more sensitive to their employees' needs and involve them in organizational decisions. The other person counters that although these leadership styles may be increasingly important, most women have trouble gaining acceptance as leaders when they face tough situations in which a more autocratic style is required. Discuss the accuracy of the comments made in this discussion.

Leadership in whose eyes?

Two senior managers, John Waisglass and Sammi Intar, are discussing Tegan Upton, the company president who joined the organization last year. Waisglass says: "I think Upton is great. She has given us a clearer sense of what we want to be as an organization. I feel much better about working here since she took over. Haven't you noticed the difference? Upton is visible and approachable. She's listened to everyone's ideas and pulled them into something that we can aim for. Upton also does what she says. Remember in one of our first meetings with her that we agreed to spend more time with our clients? Soon after, Upton was personally calling on clients and sending production people out with sales staff to hear about any customer complaints. I was skeptical at first, thinking that Upton's actions were temporary. But she's maintained this focus. And I now hear employees throughout the company using that buzzword of hers—"customer connections"—meaning that our actions must be connected to the customer's needs. She's great!"

Sammi Intar replies: "I don't know, John. I want to believe that Upton is good for this company, but I can't.

She doesn't look like a leader. Just listen to her. She sounds like Mickey Mouse with a cold. And the way she walks into a room doesn't look to me like someone who should be running a $100 million business. I've heard a few clients notice this—not many, mind you, just a few. They seem to shrug it off, pointing to some good things that our company has done for them since she took over. But my clients can go elsewhere if they have to. For me, this company is a career. Even though Upton has been doing some good things and our results have been good, I get very concerned about the future with her in charge."

Discussion Question

John Waisglass and Sammi Intar are relying on two different perspectives of leadership in their judgment of Tegan Upton. Describe these two perspectives, using specific comments to illustrate the features of each model. ◼

How Jack Welch runs GE

BusinessWeek

If leadership is an art, then surely Jack Welch, chairman and CEO of General Electric (GE), has proved himself a master painter. Few have personified corporate leadership more dramatically. Fewer still have so consistently delivered on the results of that leadership. For 17 years, while big companies and their chieftains tumbled like dominoes in an unforgiving global economy, Welch has led GE to one revenue and earnings record after another. "The two greatest corporate leaders of this century are Alfred Sloan of General Motors and Jack Welch of GE," says Noel Tichy, a longtime GE observer and University of Michigan management professor. "And Welch would be the greater of the two because he set a new, contemporary paradigm for the corporation that is the model for the 21st century."

This *Business Week* case study describes the leadership talents and style of General Electric CEO Jack Welch. It describes the personal characteristics that seem to make Welch one of America's greatest corporate leaders. The article also examines how Welch motivates and inspires people to be more creative and stretch their current capacity to perform. Read through this *Business Week* case study at www.mhhe.com/mcshane1e and prepare for the discussion questions below.

Discussion Questions

1. What personal characteristics of Jack Welch are described in this *Business Week* case study that seem to represent his leadership competencies?

2. Jack Welch is often described as a transformational leader. What evidence does this case study provide to support or weaken this view?

3. The romance perspective of leadership suggests that leaders take more credit than they deserve for organizational success. Does the romance perspective seem to occur for Jack Welch at GE?

Source: J. A. Byrne "How Jack Welch Runs GE," *Business Week,* June 8, 1998. ▨

VIDEO CASE

IBM

 For every business, solid leadership and management are keys to success. Companies benefit from managers who understand the operations of the business and the marketplace it serves. To provide the right guidance a manager must focus on four foundations of management:

- Organizing
- Leading
- Planning
- Controlling

Organizing allows for the supervision and management of complex operations. It also fosters an increased sense of responsibility among employees. This aids in team building, an essential part of the organizing function.

Leading involves creating a vision and guiding employees to achieve goals. This is perhaps the most vital management function. As competition accelerates one of these goals inevitably involves a belief in the culture of service. The manager must inspire his employees to make customer satisfaction a priority.

Planning is necessary for charting the best course through the marketplace.

Controlling the organization is achieved through sound fiscal supervision. When a company is financially healthy it is in a better position to seize new opportunities as they arise. Inspiration and smart management of these vital areas can raise a company from a state of decline to one of vitality. And few companies in the 90's were more in need of corporate resurrection than computer giant IBM.

When Lou Gerstner was called in to heal IBM, the patient was failing fast. Now just six years later IBM, Big Blue, is healthy again.

Turning around a corporation the size of IBM meant Gerstner had to create a new vision for the computer giant's future. But he also knew that more than vision was needed to get the job done. Walter Scott, professor at the J. L. Kellogg Graduate School of Management, Northwestern University, said "When Gerstner came in he disclaimed the need for vision in the company, but clearly he had to be generating a strong sense of purpose within the organization. And that purpose had to be something that they would execute. He had to change the whole atmosphere in the organization to have people executing against customer needs which they certainly had forgotten how to do over a period of time."

Gerstner's approach to the turnaround was based on his attention to the four management functions. When Gerstner first arrived he assessed his existing staff and made a number of changes. He knew the key to success was in forming the right management team. Hiring bright, talented people became his first priority. Several key positions once held by insiders now went to persons from outside the computer industry, bringing new perspectives to a corporation that had become bogged down by outdated ways of doing business. In many cases these new executives had worked with Gerstner at other companies. The IBM chief was able to rely on them to take control of their own areas.

Gerstner came to IBM with a history of guiding and motivating employees to work effectively. Hiring outside the company carries risk. Employee morale can be weakened if insiders believe that only outsiders will get decision-making positions. As a leader Gerstner understood this. He also knew that outsiders would bring fresh perspectives to a company that had become stagnant. He was able to overcome the morale issue by creating an open atmosphere of communication among all his employees. Opinions were requested and responded to—often over the IBM corporate intranet system.

Gerstner also needed to create a new culture of service at IBM. This meant that he had to set up new goals for the company that were responsive to the needs of consumers. IBM had lost touch with its customers. To get back their business, the company had to devise better lines of communication with them. Among Gerstner's first moves was to push IBM feet first into the fledgling intranet industry. The intranet is an in-house information system designed to move information and communication rapidly through the workplace. Before Gerstner's arrival IBM would have created the hardware for this system, but would not have provided support. Now, by installing the hardware along with the customized business solutions, IBM is improving relations with its customers. All IBM service and consulting contracts keep the company involved with the customer long after the system is in place.

Throughout his tenure Gerstner has always provided sound fiscal supervision, something which was desperately needed. When Gerstner arrived at IBM he was faced with a difficult financial question. How could a company with $60 billion in annual revenues be operating in the red? The answer was painfully simple—IBM was bloated. The company was top heavy with management and its expenses were out of control. Gerstner, working with chief financial officer Jerry York, set out on an ambiguous cost cutting program. By tightening expenses, dropping unprofitable lines, and cutting back on employees, the two were able to trim the annual budget by nearly $6 billion within 3 years. By 1996, Big Blue was reporting a profit for the first time in three years.

By focusing on the four management functions, and emphasizing customer service, Lou Gerstner led the turnaround at IBM. The once arrogant Big Blue is now a leader in customer service as well as hardware manufacturing. And this new customer image will keep the company growing into the twenty-first century.

Discussion Questions

1. Leadership typically involves creating a vision for a company. What is the most effective way for a leader to develop such a vision? How should a vision be communicated?

2. This video describes controlling primarily in terms of sound fiscal management. What are the other aspects of controlling? Why are these important?

3. Gerstner hired people from outside the computer industry to fill key executive positions. Explain how that strategy can be helpful. What happens to people who remain in the same industry for a long period of time? ◼

TEAM EXERCISE

Leadership diagnostic analysis

Purpose

To help students learn about the different path-goal leadership styles and when to apply each style.

Instructions

The exercise begins with students individually writing down two incidents in which someone has served as an effective manager or leader over them. The leader and situation might be from work, a sports team, a student work group, or any other setting where leadership could emerge. For example, students might describe how their supervisor in a summer job pushed them to reach higher performance goals than they would have done otherwise. Each incident should state the actual behaviors that the leader used, not simply general statements (e.g., "My boss sat down with me and we agreed on specific targets and deadlines. Then he said several times over the next few weeks that I was capable of reaching those goals"). Each incident requires only two or three sentences.

After everyone has written their two incidents, the instructor will form small groups (typically between four or five students). Each team will answer the following questions for each incident presented in that team:

1. Which path-goal theory leadership style(s) (i.e., directive, supportive, participative, or achievement-oriented) did the leader apply in this incident?

2. Ask the person who wrote the incident about the conditions that made this leadership style (or styles, if more than one was used) appropriate in this situation? The team should list these contingency factors clearly and, where possible, connect them to the contingencies described in path-goal theory. (Note: the team might identify path-goal leadership contingencies that are not described in the book. These, too, should be noted and discussed.)

After diagnosing the incidents presented by team members, each team will describe to the entire class its most interesting incident and its diagnosis of that incident. Other teams will critique the diagnosis. Any leadership contingencies not mentioned in the textbook should also be presented and discussed. ◼

SELF-ASSESSMENT EXERCISE

Leadership dimensions instrument

Purpose

This assessment is designed to help you to understand two important dimensions of leadership and to identify which of these dimensions is more prominent in your supervisor, team leader, coach, or other person to whom you are accountable.

Instructions

Read each of the statements below and circle the response that you believe best describes your supervisor.

You may substitute "supervisor" with anyone else to whom you are accountable, such as a team leader, CEO, course instructor, or sports coach. Then use the scoring key to calculate the results for each leadership dimension. After completing this assessment, be prepared to discuss in class the distinctions between these leadership dimensions.

My supervisor . . .	Strongly agree ▼	Agree ▼	Neutral ▼	Disagree ▼	Strongly disagree ▼
1. Focuses attention on irregularities, mistakes, exceptions, and deviations from what is expected of me.	1	2	3	4	5
2. Engages in words and deeds that enhance his/her image of competence.	1	2	3	4	5
3. Monitors performance for errors needing correction.	1	2	3	4	5
4. Serves as a role model for me.	1	2	3	4	5
5. Points out what I will receive if I do what is required.	1	2	3	4	5
6. Instills pride in being associated with him/her.	1	2	3	4	5
7. Keeps careful track of mistakes.	1	2	3	4	5
8. Can be trusted to help me overcome any obstacle.	1	2	3	4	5
9. Tells me what to do to be rewarded for my efforts.	1	2	3	4	5
10. Makes me aware of strongly held values, ideals, and aspirations which are shared in common.	1	2	3	4	5
11. Is alert for failure to meet standards.	1	2	3	4	5
12. Mobilizes a collective sense of mission.	1	2	3	4	5
13. Works out agreements with me on what I will receive if I do what needs to be done.	1	2	3	4	5
14. Articulates a vision of future opportunities.	1	2	3	4	5
15. Talks about special rewards for good work.	1	2	3	4	5
16. Talks optimistically about the future.	1	2	3	4	5

Scoring Key

Write the scores circled for each item on the appropriate line below (statement numbers are in brackets), and add up each scale. Higher scores indicate that the leader is stronger on that leadership style.

Transactional Leadership: Add up scores for the odd numbered items (i.e., 1, 3, 5, 7, 9, 11, 13, 15). Maximum score is 40. Higher scores indicate that your supervisor has a strong inclination toward transactional leadership.

Transformational Leadership: Add up scores for the even numbered items (i.e., 2, 4, 6, 8, 10, 12, 14, 16). Maximum score is 40. Higher scores indicate that your supervisor has a strong inclination toward transformational leadership.

Source: Items and dimensions are adapted from D. N. Den Hartog, J. J. Van Muijen, and P. L. Koopman, "Transactional versus Transformational Leadership: An Analysis of the MLQ," *Journal of Occupational & Organizational Psychology* 70 (March 1997), pp. 19–34. Den Hartog et al. label transactional leadership as "rational-objective leadership" and label transformational leadership as "inspirational leadership." Many of their items may have originated from B. M. Bass and B. J. Avolio, *Manual for the Multifactor Leadership Questionnaire* (Palo Alto, CA: Consulting Psychologists Press, 1989). ■

Organizational Change and Development

Learning Objectives

After reading this chapter, you should be able to:

- Identify four forces for change in the business environment.
- Describe the elements of Lewin's force field analysis model.
- Outline six reasons why people resist organizational change.
- Discuss six strategies to minimize resistance to change.
- Outline the role of change agents.
- Define organization development.
- Discuss three things consultants need to determine in a client relationship.
- Explain how appreciative inquiry differs from the more traditional approach to OD.
- Discuss four ethical issues in organization development.

Royal Dutch/Shell's top executives created a more responsive organization by working directly with frontline employees rather than through layers of management.

[John Thoeming]

In the mid-1990s, senior executives at Royal Dutch/Shell realized that the giant Anglo-Dutch oil company had to change. Although still profitable, Shell was not responsive enough to global customers, and new competitors were grabbing market share. Shell's executives in London and The Hague spent two years reorganizing, downsizing, and educating several layers of management, but this top-down approach had minimal effect. Managers in charge of Shell's operations for a particular country resisted changes that threatened their autonomy, and headquarters managers couldn't break out of the routines that worked well in the past.

So Steve Miller, head of Shell's worldwide oil products business, decided to change the company from the bottom up. He and his executive team held several five-day workshops, each attended by six country teams of frontline people (e.g., gas station managers, truck drivers, marketing professionals). Participants at these "retailing boot camps" learned about worrisome competitive trends in their regions and were taught powerful marketing tools to identify new opportunities. The teams then returned home to study their market and develop proposals for improvement. For example, a team in South Africa proposed ways to increase liquid gas market share. Another team developed plans to increase gasoline sales in Malaysia.

Four months later, the teams returned for a second workshop where each proposal was critiqued by Miller's executive team in "fishbowl" sessions with the other teams watching. Videotapes from these sessions became powerful socialization tools for other employees back in the home country. Each team had 60 days to put its ideas into action, then return for a third workshop to analyze what worked and what didn't.

These workshops, along with field tours and several other grassroots activities, had a tremendous effect. Frontline employees developed an infectious enthusiasm and a stronger business approach to challenging the competition. "I can't overstate how infectious the optimism and energy of these committed employees was on the many managers above them," says Miller. The change process also resulted in solid improvements in profitability and market share in most regions where employees had attended the sessions.[1]

hange is difficult enough in small firms. At Shell and other large organizations, it requires monumental effort and persistence. Organizational change is also very messy. Although Steve Miller's change process sounds like a well-executed strategy, he later said that it was a "scary" experience with uncertain consequences. Even in successful firms, leaders need to overcome (or bypass) resistance to change. They need to give up control and move people out of their comfortable routines.

This chapter examines ways to bring about meaningful change in organizations. After considering some of the more significant forces for organizational change, we introduce Lewin's model of change and its component parts. This includes sources of resistance to change, ways to minimize this resistance, and stabilizing desired behaviors. The latter part of this chapter introduces the field of organization development (OD). In particular, we review the OD process, emerging OD strategies, and issues relating to OD effectiveness.

External Forces for Change

Today's business environment is changing so rapidly that it leaves everyone breathless. "The velocity of change is so rapid, so quick, that if you don't accept the change and move with the change, you're going to be left behind," says Ford CEO Jacques Nasser. W. Allen Schaffer, head of managed care at CIGNA Healthcare, Inc., agrees. "The pace of change is stunning," he says. "We have to reevaluate our strategic assumptions every six months."[2]

To illustrate the amount of churn and upheaval in the business environment, consider *Business Week*'s latest list of top-performing companies: Microsoft, Dell Computer, GAP, Oracle, and EMC.[3] Twenty years ago, these companies were either junior start-ups or nonexistent. Today, they are leaders in growth and profitability. And unless these firms anticipate and adapt to continual change, few of them will be on the list 20 years from now. As open systems (see Chapter 1), successful organizations monitor their environments and take appropriate steps to maintain a compatible fit with the new external conditions. This adaptability requires continual change. It is an ongoing process because environmental change does not end.

There are many forces for change in the external environment, but the prominent forces are computer technology, global and local competition, and demographics. Not surprisingly, most of these are emerging organizational behavior issues that we discussed in the opening chapter of this book.

Computer Technology

Computer technology seems to be the main reason why organizations are experiencing such dramatic and rapid environmental change. More specifically, the systems of networks that connect computers throughout the planet have dramatically reduced time and dissolved distances. As we learned in Chapter 8, this relates to the **law of telecosm,** which says that as the web of computer networks expands, distances will shrink and eventually become irrelevant.[4]

A few years ago "e-commerce" was a spelling mistake. Now, Amazon.com, Charles Schwab, and other companies are leveraging the power of the Internet to offer a variety of electronic commerce experiences. Intranets have also made it easy and inexpensive to transfer information throughout the organization.[5] Employees use intranet systems to directly access job-related information, bypassing supervisors who previously served as conduits. Suppliers are hooked up to computer-based networks—called *extranets*—to accelerate just-in-time delivery of goods. Major clients are also hooked up to the organization's product database for direct ordering and delivery.[6]

law of telecosm a principle stating that as the web of computer networks expands, distances will shrink and eventually become irrelevant

How do organizations survive? By continually changing with the external environment. Just look at Nokia, the Finnish conglomerate that is currently an industry leader in cellular telephones. Nokia may be a high-tech firm today, but it started in 1865 as a pulp and paper company in a mill town near Helsinki *(see photo, taken around 1890)*. *[Courtesy of the National Board of Antiquities, Finland]* In the 1920s the company bought into the rubber and cable business. Many Finns still associate Nokia with the rubber snow boots they wore as children. In the 1960s Nokia invested in electronics and was soon making televisions and computer screens. A decade later, it began producing mobile phones—weighing a hefty 22 pounds! Today, Nokia's sleek mobile phones weigh less than one-quarter pound.[8] What factors do you think helped Nokia anticipate new opportunities and change the organization to realize those opportunities? *[Courtesy of Nokia]*

Computer technology does more than open up business opportunities. It forces corporate leaders to rethink how their organizations are configured, as well as what competencies and expectations employees must have in these emerging organizational forms.[7] It facilitates telecommuting and opens up new employment relationships with employees. It places more emphasis on knowledge management rather than physical presence and manufacturing capacity as a driver of competitive advantage. As we learned in Chapter 1 and will explain further in Chapter 18, e-commerce, extranets, and other forms of networked computer technology are also creating new organizational structures in which small businesses are able to compete on a global level through network alliances.

Global and Local Competition

Increasing global and local competition are also powerful forces for organizational change.[9] Competitors are just as likely to be located in a distant part of the world than within your country. Emerging trading blocs in North America, Europe, the Asia-Pacific region, and other areas add another dimension to these competitive forces. As we learned in the opening story to this chapter, Shell's need for change arose mainly because new competitors were threatening the oil company's survival in France and other key markets.

Technology has played a role in increasing global and local competition. A few years ago, no one would have guessed that Internet upstart Amazon.com would be a threat to bookstore giants Barnes & Noble and Borders. AT&T executives would not have predicted that WorldCom would become a major competitor. And few could imagine that cable companies would somehow be competing with telephone companies.

Government deregulation and privatization have also fueled competition. Energy companies in several U.S. states now compete where they previously held monopolies. Post offices in Australia and the United Kingdom have also been forced to reinvent themselves as their governments open up some mail services to the private sector. Government-owned telephone companies in Singapore, Canada, and other countries have been transformed into private or semiprivate enterprises.[10]

Global and domestic competition often leads to corporate restructuring. To increase their competitiveness, companies reduce layers of management, sell entire divisions of employees, and reduce payroll through downsizing.

Raytheon, Gillette, Levi Strauss, and many other firms have closed plants and laid off thousands of employees due to increased competition and other pressures to increase efficiency.[11]

Global competition has also fueled an unprecedented number of mergers and acquisitions in recent years. Daimler-Benz merged with Chrysler; British Petroleum merged with Amoco and Arco; General Electric acquires dozens of companies each year. Mergers potentially improve a company's competitive advantage through greater efficiency and global reach, but they also require dramatic changes in the way people work. When America Online acquired Netscape, for instance, Netscape's employees worried about losing their jobs and their Californian way of life.[12]

Demography

While firms adjust to global competition, they are also adapting to changes in the workforce. Employees are more educated and consequently expect more

A decade ago, the auto industry was dominated by the "Big Three" U.S. automakers. Today, it's the "Global Five"—General Motors, Ford, DaimlerChrysler, Toyota, and Volkswagen. Only two (GM and Ford) are headquartered in the United States, and even they have significant investments in other parts of the world. The merger of Chrysler with Germany's Daimler-Benz illustrates how global competition has created turbulent change. The two companies struggled throughout the merger process with different cultural values, government regulations, and overlapping product development projects. However, the process has also generated improvements on both sides of the Atlantic Ocean. For example, Daimler is learning Chrysler's efficient production methods at its recently built plant in Rastatt, Germany (shown in photo).[13] What changes typically occur within organizations during mergers and acquisitions?

[AP Wide World]

involvement and interesting work. Generation-X employees are less intimidated by management directives and they work to live more than live to work. In Japan, corporate leaders must adjust to a younger workforce that is more individualistic. In Singapore, once considered a country with a high respect for authority, younger employees are starting to openly question and debate with senior executives. Meanwhile, in many parts of the world, companies employ a far more diverse workforce than they did a few decades ago (see Chapter 1). These changes have put pressure on organizational leaders to alter work practices, develop more compatible structures and rewards, and discover new ways to lead.

Lewin's Force Field Analysis Model

force field analysis Lewin's model of systemwide change that helps change agents diagnose the forces that drive and restrain proposed organizational change

It is easy to see that these environmental forces push companies to change the way they operate. What is more difficult to see is the complex interplay of these forces against other organizational dynamics. Psychologist Kurt Lewin developed the force field analysis model to help us understand how the change process works (see Exhibit 15.1).[14] Although developed over 50 years ago, Lewin's **force field analysis** model remains the prominent way of viewing this process.

One side of the force field model represents the *driving forces* that push organizations toward a new state of affairs. We began this chapter by describing several driving forces in the external environment: computer technology, global and local competition, and demographics. Along with these external forces are driving forces that seem to originate from within the organization, such as competition across divisions of the company and the leader's need to impose his or her image on the organization.

unfreezing the first part of the change process whereby the change agent produces a disequilibrium between the driving and restraining forces

refreezing the latter part of the change process in which systems and conditions are introduced that reinforce and maintain the desired behaviors

The other side of Lewin's model represents the *restraining forces* that maintain the status quo. These restraining forces are commonly called "resistance to change" because they appear as employee behaviors that block the change process. Stability occurs when the driving and restraining forces are roughly in equilibrium; that is, they are of approximately equal strength in opposite directions.

Lewin's force field model emphasizes that effective change occurs by **unfreezing** the current situation, moving to a desired condition, and then **refreezing** the system so that it remains in this desired state. Unfreezing involves producing a disequilibrium between the driving and restraining forces. As we

Exhibit 15.1
Lewin's force field
analysis model

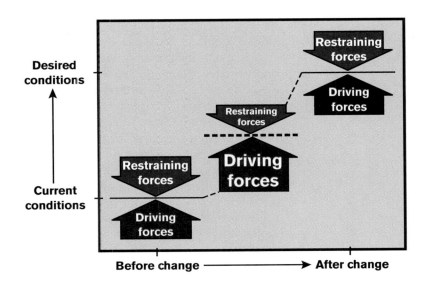

will describe later, this may occur by increasing the driving forces, reducing the restraining forces, or having a combination of both. Refreezing occurs when the organization's systems and structures are aligned with the desired behaviors. They must support and reinforce the new role patterns and prevent the organization from slipping back into the old way of doing things. This stabilization does not occur automatically; rather, organizational leaders must continuously restabilize the desired behaviors. Over the next few pages, we use Lewin's model to understand why change is blocked and how the process can evolve more smoothly.

Restraining Forces

When BP Norge introduced self-directed work teams (SDWTs) on its North Sea drilling rigs, the Norwegian subsidiary of British Petroleum faced more resistance from employees than from the infamous North Sea weather. Many skeptical employees claimed that previous attempts to create SDWTs didn't work. Others were convinced that they already had SDWTs, so why change anything? Several people complained that SDWTs required more responsibility, so they wanted more status and pay. Still others were worried that they lacked the skills to operate in SDWTs. Some BP Norge supervisors were slow to embrace SDWTs because they didn't want to give away their cherished power.[15]

BP Norge isn't the only organization in which employees seem to block the change process.[16] According to one recent survey, 43 percent of U.S. executives identify employee resistance as the main reason why their organization is not more productive.[17] This resistance takes many forms, including passive noncompliance, complaints, absenteeism, turnover, and collective action (e.g., strikes, walkouts). Some organizational behavior scholars point out that these actions do not necessarily represent employee resistance to change. Employees usually appreciate the need for change and actively embrace it when it does not threaten their own situation.[18] Rather, these behaviors indicate that restraining forces still exist in the organizational system. For example, resistance occurs because rewards discourage rather than encourage desired behaviors. Similarly, employee norms and roles may be incompatible with the desired state of affairs. These incompatible systems and structures produce obstacles to change, which manifest themselves in employee behavior.[19]

From this perspective, employee "resistance" represents symptoms of underlying restraining forces that need to be removed. Some employees are worried about the *consequences* of change, such as how the new conditions will take away their power and status. Others are concerned about the *process* of change itself, such as the effort required to break old habits and learn new skills. The main reasons why people create obstacles to change include direct costs, saving face, fear of the unknown, breaking routines, incongruent organizational systems, and incongruent team dynamics (see Exhibit 15.2).[20] We describe each briefly in the following paragraphs.

• *Direct costs*—People tend to block actions that result in higher direct costs or lower benefits than the existing situation. For instance, supervisors at BP Norge resisted self-directed work teams because they believed they would lose power as the change process empowered employees.

• *Saving face*—Some people resist change as a political strategy to "prove" that the decision is wrong or that the person encouraging change is incompetent. For example, senior executives in a manufacturing firm bought a computer system other than the one recommended by the information systems department. Soon after the system was in place, several information systems employees let minor implementation problems escalate to demonstrate that senior management had made a poor decision.

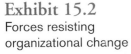

Exhibit 15.2
Forces resisting
organizational change

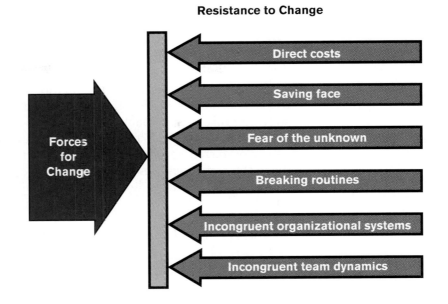

- *Fear of the unknown*—People resist change because they are worried that they cannot adopt the new behaviors. This fear of the unknown increases the *risk* of personal loss. This happened at a company where the owner wanted sales staff to telephone rather than personally visit prospective customers. These employees had little experience in telephone sales, so they argued against the need for using telephone calls. Some didn't even show up for the training program that taught them how to make telephone sales. "The sales-people were afraid of failing," explained the owner. "Each of them was very successful in the field, but they had never been exposed to a formalized telephone lead development program."[21]

- *Breaking routines*—In Chapter 1, we described how organizations need to unlearn, not just learn.[22] This means that employees need to abandon the behavioral routines that are no longer appropriate. Unfortunately, people are creatures of habit. They like to stay within the comfort zones by continuing routine role patterns that make life predictable.[23] Consequently, many people resist organizational changes that force employees out of their comfort zones and require investing time and energy learning new role patterns.

- *Incongruent organizational systems*—Rewards, selection, training, and other control systems ensure that employees maintain desired role patterns. Yet the organizational systems that maintain stability also discourage employees from adopting new ways.[24] The implication, of course, is that organizational systems must be altered to fit the desired change. Unfortunately, control systems can be difficult to change, particularly when they have supported role patterns that worked well in the past.[25]

- *Incongruent team dynamics*—As we learned in Chapter 9, teams develop and enforce conformity to a set of norms that guide behavior. However, conformity to existing team norms may discourage employees from accepting organizational change. Team norms that conflict with the desired changes need to be altered.

Unfreezing, Changing, and Refreezing

According to Lewin's force field analysis model, effective change occurs by unfreezing the current situation, moving to a desired condition, and then refreezing the system so that it remains in this desired state. Unfreezing occurs when the driving forces are stronger than the restraining forces. This occurs by making the driving forces stronger, weakening or removing the restraining forces, or a combination of both. With respect to the first option, driving forces must certainly increase enough to motivate change. However, change rarely occurs by increasing driving forces alone because the restraining forces often adjust to counterbalance the driving forces. It is rather like the coils of a mattress. The harder corporate leaders push for change, the stronger the restraining forces push back. This antagonism threatens the change effort by producing tension and conflict within the organization.

The preferred option is to both increase the driving forces and reduce or remove the restraining forces. Increasing the driving forces creates an urgency for change, whereas reducing the restraining forces minimizes resistance to change.

Creating an Urgency for Change

Driving forces represent the booster rockets that push employees out of their comfort zones. They energize people to face the risks that change presents to them. Driving forces must be real, not contrived; otherwise, employees will doubt the change agent's integrity. Some threats are well known to employees. PepsiCo employees never forget about their archrivals at Coca-Cola. Bay Networks staff members are frequently reminded of competitive threats from Cisco Systems. However, many driving forces are unknown to employees beyond the top ranks of the organization. Thus, the change process must begin by informing employees about competitors, changing consumer trends, impending government regulations, and other driving forces.[26]

James Donald had to communicate the urgency for change when he took over Pathmark Stores. The New Jersey–based supermarket chain was in financial trouble, but few of the company's 28,000 employees knew about these problems. To get employees ready for change and to avoid bankruptcy, Donald prepared a video that told everyone about Pathmark's tremendous financial debt. Some employees quit, fearing that the company wasn't going to make it. But the remaining 99 percent quickly developed a commitment to get the company back to health.[27]

Customer driven change   Another powerful driver of change is customer expectations.[28] Dissatisfied customers represent a compelling force for change because of the adverse consequences for the organization's survival and success. Customers also provide a human element that further energizes employees to change current behavior patterns. Greg Brenneman and Gordon Bethune relied on customer complaints to motivate change at Continental Airlines. The executives took on the painful task of listening to customer complaints, and they communicated these problems to employees.[29]

Joel Kocher, CEO of Micron Electronics, also engaged in customer-driven change in his previous job as an executive with Power Computing. At a large employee meeting, Kocher read an angry customer letter. Then, to everyone's surprise, he brought the customer who wrote the letter into the meeting. "We actually brought the customer to the meeting, to personalize it for every single person in the room," says Kocher. "And it was very, very interesting to see the metamorphosis that occurred within the context of these several hundred people when you actually had a customer talking about how their foul-up had hurt this person and hurt their business."[30]

Reducing the Restraining Forces

Effective change involves more than making employees aware of the driving forces. It also involves reducing or removing the restraining forces.

In the mid-1980s, the city of Hampton, Virginia, had a stagnant population and declining business base. Alarmed at these problems, Hampton's city council and new city manager communicated their concerns to employees. They also worked with employees to develop a vision statement for the change effort—"the most livable city in Virginia"—along with specific action plans to implement that vision. The vision statement appeared everywhere—even on employee paychecks—and the action plans were applied throughout the organization. To reinforce this customer focus, the city conducted annual citizen satisfaction surveys and tied the survey results to employee bonuses. If satisfaction reaches certain levels, every city worker got a bonus check. The results of customer-driven change are apparent in Hampton today. "My job description is recycling manager, but my duty is customer service for the citizens of Hampton," says a Hampton employee.[31] Are there situations where companies should not rely on customers to drive change?

[Courtesy of the City of Hampton, Virginia.]

Exhibit 15.3 identifies six ways to overcome employee resistance. The first four—communication, training, employee involvement, and stress management—try to reduce the restraining forces and, if feasible, should be attempted first.[32] However, negotiation and coercion are necessary for people who will clearly lose something from the change and when the speed of change is critical.

Communication   Communication is the highest priority and first strategy required for any organizational change. It reduces the restraining forces by keeping employees informed about what to expect from the change effort. Although time consuming and costly, communication can potentially reduce fear of the unknown and develop team norms that are more consistent with the change effort.[33]

Du Pont recognized the importance of communication when it decided to outsource most of its 3,100 information systems (IS) employees to Computer Systems Corp. and other IS service firms. The chemical giant informed everyone of this decision six months before the change, and it continuously communicated with them throughout the process using e-mail, videos, and face-to-face meetings. By the time the transition took place, employees had a deeply embedded knowledge about what was happening and how it would affect them personally. The result was that 97 percent of Du Pont's IS staff went along with the change. "The communication was so thorough that, by the time we got the offer letter, it was an absolute nonevent," says an outsourced Du Pont employee.[34]

Exhibit 15.3   Methods for dealing with resistance to change

Strategy	Example	When used	Problems
Communication	Customer complaint letters shown to employees.	When employees don't feel an urgency for change, or don't know how the change will affect them.	Time consuming and potentially costly.
Training	Employees learn how to work in teams as company adopts a team-based structure.	When employees need to break old routines and adopt new role patterns.	Time consuming and potentially costly.
Employee involvement	Company forms task force to recommend new customer service practices.	When the change effort needs more employee commitment, some employees need to save face, and/or employee ideas would improve decisions about the change strategy.	Very time consuming. Might also lead to conflict and poor decisions if employees' interests are incompatible with organizational needs.
Stress management	Employees attend sessions to discuss their worries about the change.	When communication, training, and involvement do not sufficiently ease employee worries.	Time consuming and potentially expensive. Some methods may not reduce stress for all employees.
Negotiation	Employees agree to replace strict job categories with multiskilling in return for increased job security.	When employees will clearly lose something of value from the change and would not otherwise support the new conditions. Also necessary when the company must change quickly.	May be expensive, particularly if other employees want to negotiate their support. Also tends to produce compliance but not commitment to the change.
Coercion	Company president tells managers to "get on board" the change or leave.	When other strategies are ineffective and the company needs to change quickly.	Can lead to more subtle forms of resistance, as well as long-term antagonism with the change agent.

Sources: Adapted from J. P. Kotter and L. A. Schlesinger, "Choosing Strategies for Change," *Harvard Business Review* 57 (March–April 1979), pp. 106–14; P. R. Lawrence, "How to Deal with Resistance to Change," *Harvard Business Review* (May–June 1954), pp. 49–57.

Training   The opening story to this chapter described how Steve Miller and other Royal Dutch/Shell executives brought about meaningful change by putting a cross-section of frontline employees through "retailing boot camps." These week-long sessions not only generated an urgency to change, but also taught employees valuable skills for the desired future. Retail boot camps and other forms of training are necessary so that employees learn the required skills and knowledge under the new conditions. When a company introduces a new sales database, for instance, representatives need to learn how to adapt their previous behavior patterns to benefit from the new system. Training is time consuming, but as employees learn new role patterns, they experience less stress and feel more comfortable with breaking previous routines.

Employee involvement   Employee involvement can be an effective way to reduce the restraining forces because it creates a psychological ownership of the decision (see Chapter 10). Rather than viewing themselves as agents of someone else's decision, staff members feel personally responsible for its success. Employee involvement also minimizes resistance to change by reducing problems of saving face and fear of the unknown.[35]

It's fairly easy for small organizations to involve everyone in the change process. But how do you apply employee involvement when there are thousands of employees? The answer is to involve as many people as possible through **search conferences.** Search conferences are large group sessions, usually lasting a few days, in which participants identify environmental trends and determine ways to adapt to those trends.[36] Search conferences are often known as "putting the entire system in the room" because they attempt to congregate representatives throughout the organization's entire system. This means involving as many employees as possible, along with others associated with the organization. For instance, Eicher Motors, a large manufacturer of light commercial vehicles in central India, holds an annual three-day search conference that includes a representation of suppliers, buyers, and shareholders as well as all employees.[37]

Various types of organizations, including Ford Motor Company, the U.S. Forest Service, a high school, and a religious order, have used search conferences to assist the change process.[38] Connections 15.1 describes how Keene State College and PECO Energy successfully involved most employees in the change process through these large group activities. Of course, search conferences and other forms of employee involvement require follow-up action by organizational leaders. If employees do not see meaningful decisions and actions resulting from these meetings, they begin to question the credibility of the process and are more cynical of similar change strategies in the future.

Stress management   For most of us, organizational change is a stressful experience.[39] It threatens our self-esteem and creates uncertainty about our future. Communication, training, and employee involvement can reduce some of these stressors, but companies sometimes need to introduce formal stress management programs to help employees cope with the changes. The Kerr Drug chain recognized this problem when it acquired 164 stores from J. C. Penney Co. Store managers and pharmacists had to install and operate new systems almost overnight without creating a disturbance to customers. They also had to adjust to Kerr's more customer-oriented culture. To help everyone cope, Kerr installed a toll-free telephone line, appropriately called "1-(800)-I've-Had-It." Employees who called this number received informational or emotional support from human resource professionals at Kerr Drugs. "Sometimes they needed only a pat on the back or a hug because we were putting too many demands on them," explains Diane Eliezer, Kerr's director of marketing.[40]

Negotiation   Organizational change is, in large measure, a political activity.[41] People have vested interests and apply their power to ensure that the emerging conditions are consistent with their personal values and needs. Consequently, negotiation may be necessary for employees who will clearly lose out from the change activity. This negotiation offers certain benefits to offset some of the cost of the change.

Consider the experience of GE Capital Fleet Services. When the company removed two levels of management, it faced serious resistance from supervisors who worried that they would lose their status. After several months, senior executives negotiated with the supervisors and eventually created an intermediate manager position to overcome this resistance. "In our case, the decision to delayer was nonnegotiable," recalls a GE Capital manager. "As time was

---

search conferences

systemwide group sessions, usually lasting a few days, in which participants identify environmental trends and establish strategic solutions for those conditions

Connections 15.1 ◻ **Keene State College and PECO Energy Get Everyone Involved in Change**

Keene State College involved 350 faculty, staff, and administrators in the process of identifying shared and achievable goals for the learning institution's future.

[Courtesy of Keene State College, NH]

Keene State College in New Hampshire brought together 350 faculty, staff, and administrators to identify shared and achievable goals for the learning institution's future. Administrators at the college concluded that the three day search conference—called "Speak Out"—would yield more meaningful ideas and generate more commitment to strategic decisions than if these decisions were made only by senior decision makers.

"Instead of appointing a committee to write an institutional plan," said Keene State College's president when opening the conference, "I am asking each of you to 'speak out' about the things you want changed and the things you value."

Keene State's participants discussed more than 100 issues during the sessions, some in small groups of three people, others in packed rooms with people spilling out the door. As Day Three came to a close, everyone voted on the top 10 to 15 issues. Over 100 people then grouped the dozens of discussion topics and mapped their relationships to one another.

PECO Energy, the Philadelphia-based electrical utility, required more than one search conference to restructure its human resource (HR) management group. With the help of consultants, four conferences were held over a five-month period to create a vision statement as well as design and implementation plan for the HR function. Each conference was attended by a broad cross-section of 200 employees, so that nearly 800 people participated altogether. Between these conferences, the company's other 7,000 employees contributed their ideas through videotapes, memos, and faxes.

The PECO Energy activity was structured with a specific agenda. Other search conferences merely gather the organization's representatives in a common location and let them determine the agenda. Most gatherings, however, create "max-mix" teams, whereby each table consists of a representation of people from different departments and levels of the organization.

Sources: P. D. Tolchinsky, "Still on a Winning Streak," *Workforce* 76 (September 1997), pp. 97–102; W. Kaschub, "PECO Energy Redesigns HR," *HR Focus* 74 (March 1997), p. 3; S. E. Brigham, "Large-Scale Events: New Ways of Working across the Organization," *Change* 28 (November 1996), pp. 28–34. ◼

subsequently to show, however, we should have been prepared to negotiate on the number of layers to be eliminated."[42]

Coercion Gordon Bethune and Greg Brenneman orchestrated a dramatic turnaround of Continental Airlines, but not everyone was ready for the change process. Fifty of the 61 executive officers were replaced with about 20 new people soon after Bethune and Brenneman became CEO and president, respectively.[43] This is not an isolated example. One survey reported that two-thirds of senior management in large U.S. firms were replaced by the time the businesses were revived.[44]

We don't want to give you the impression that firing people is a valuable way to change organizations. On the contrary, this is a risky strategy because survivors (employees who are not fired) may have less trust in corporate leaders and engage in more political tactics to protect their own job security. More generally, various forms of coercion may change behavior through compliance, but it won't develop commitment to the change effort (see Chapter 12).

At the same time, coercion may be necessary when speed is essential and other tactics are ineffective. For example, it may be necessary to remove several members of an executive team who are unwilling or unable to change their existing mental models of the ideal organization. This is also a radical form of organizational "unlearning" (see Chapter 1) because when executives leave, they take knowledge of the organization's past routines with them. This potentially opens up opportunities for new practices to take hold.[45]

Changing to the Desired Future State

Organizational change takes many forms. In our example of the Du Pont information systems employees who were outsourced, the actual changes were probably quite subtle at first. The outsourced employees still worked at Du Pont and probably kept their same desks, but their paychecks came from another company. Eventually, the change required new behaviors, such as calling their new employer rather than Du Pont about employment issues. Change was more dramatic at Royal Dutch/Shell. The company laid off many people and changed the organizational structure. When those actions didn't work, a representation of frontline employees diagnosed marketing opportunities and later implemented these ideas. Overall, change results in new behaviors that employees must learn and internalize.

Refreezing the Desired Conditions

After unfreezing and changing behavior patterns, we need to refreeze desired behaviors so that people do not slip back into their old work practices.[46] Refreezing occurs when organizational systems and team dynamics are realigned with the desired changes. Numerous systems and structures can "nail down" desired patterns of behavior. Organizational structure, which we discuss more fully in Chapter 18, anchors new roles and behavior patterns. For example, companies that want to encourage decisions and actions that support customer service would redesign the organization around customers rather than specialized knowledge groups (e.g., marketing, engineering).

Organizational rewards are powerful systems that refreeze behaviors. If the change process is supposed to encourage efficiency, then rewards should be realigned to motivate and reinforce efficient behavior. Information systems play a complementary role in the change process, particularly as conduits for feedback.[47] Feedback mechanisms help employees learn how well they are moving toward the desired objectives, and they provide a permanent architecture to support the new behavior patterns in the long term. The adage "What gets measured, gets done" applies here. Employees concentrate on the new priorities when they receive a continuous flow of feedback about how well they are achieving those goals.

The dramatic turnaround of Continental Airlines illustrates how rewards and feedback refreeze desired behavior patterns. As we learned in Chapter 7, Continental had one of the worst performance records in the U.S. airline industry. It was particularly notorious for late arrivals and departures. To change Continental "from worst to first," incoming president Greg Brenneman offered every employee $65 for each month that the U.S. Department of Transportation (DOT) placed Continental in the top five airlines for on-time performance. Within months, the airline was regularly finishing first. The reward system—which cost $3 million in each successful month—aligned employees to the desired goals and the DOT's on-time performance feedback became symbolically meaningful. Both became important ingredients to refreeze Continental employees around efficiency and customer service.[48]

Strategic Visions, Change Agents, and Diffusing Change

Kurt Lewin's force field analysis model provides a rich understanding of the dynamics of organizational change. But the model overlooks three important ingredients in effective change processes: strategic visions, change agents, and diffusing change. Every successful change requires a clear, well-articulated vision of the desired future state. Indeed, a recent survey of executives in large U.S. firms found that the most important feature of successful change efforts was a clear vision of the proposed change.[49] This minimizes employee fear of the unknown and provides a better understanding about what behaviors employees must learn for the future state.[50] Strategic visions represent the goals that clarify role perceptions and thereby guide future behavior.

In the opening story, Steve Miller relied on retail boot camps to communicate and build commitment to his vision of Royal Dutch/Shell's future. When the city of Hampton, Virginia, began its change process, it formed a clear vision to become "the most livable city in Virginia." This image was understood and internalized by involving employees in the change process and continually communicating the vision statement. Departmental managers also worked out specific action plans to implement that vision. Moreover, employees were put into cross-department task forces responsible for moving the city toward this vision.

Change Agents

change agent anyone who possesses enough knowledge and power to guide and facilitate the change effort

transformational leadership a leadership perspective that explains how leaders change teams or organizations by creating, communicating, and modeling a vision for the organization or work unit, and inspiring employees to strive for that vision

Organizational change also requires change agents to help form, communicate, and build commitment toward the desired future state. A **change agent** is anyone who possesses enough knowledge and power to guide and facilitate the change effort. Some organizations rely on external consultants to serve as change agents. However, change agents are typically people within the organization who possess the leadership competencies necessary to bring about meaningful change. Corporate executives certainly need to be change agents. However, as companies rely increasingly on self-directed work teams, every employee may become a change agent at one time or another.

Effective change agents are **transformational leaders** (see Chapter 14).[51] They form a vision of the desired future state, communicate that vision in ways that are meaningful to others, behave in ways that are consistent with the vision, and build commitment to the vision. Jacques Nasser, CEO of Ford Motor Company, has a reputation as a transformational leader. As we noted earlier, he effectively changed Ford Australia a few years ago and is now engaging Ford employees worldwide to become more proactive and entrepreneurial.[52]

Diffusion of Change

It is often better to test the transformation process with a pilot project, then diffuse what has been learned from this experience to other parts of the organization. The reason is that pilot projects are more flexible and less risky than centralized, organizationwide programs.[53] How are the results of pilot projects successfully diffused to other parts of the organization? Organizational behavior scholars offer several recommendations.[54] Generally, diffusion is more likely to occur when the pilot project is successful within one or two years and receives visibility (e.g., favorable news media coverage). These

Roberts Express, the expedited delivery service firm in Akron, Ohio, started its team-based organizational structure with a pilot project. Seven employees from operations, customer service, and safety/recruiting agreed to form a pilot team, representing the first cross-functional customer service unit. As problems were ironed out, the company expanded this process by forming other teams. Today, the entire work process is operated by self-directed teams.[55] Are there situations in which starting change with a pilot project would be difficult or inappropriate?

[Courtesy of Roberts Express]

conditions tend to increase top management support for the change program and persuade other employees to support the change effort in their operations. Successful diffusion also depends on labor union support and active involvement in the diffusion process.

Another important condition is that the diffusion strategy isn't described too abstractly, because this makes the instructions too vague to introduce the change elsewhere. Neither should the strategy be stated too precisely, because it might not seem relevant to other areas of the organization. Finally, without producing excessive turnover in the pilot group, people who have worked under the new system should be moved to other areas of the organization. These employees transfer their knowledge and commitment of the change effort to work units that have not yet experienced it.

Organization Development

organization development (OD) a planned systemwide effort, managed from the top with the assistance of a change agent, that uses behavioral science knowledge to improve organizational effectiveness

So far, we have discussed the dynamics of change that occur every day in organizations. However, an entire field of study, called **organization development (OD),** tries to understand how to manage planned change in organizations. OD is a planned systemwide effort, managed from the top with the assistance of a change agent, that uses behavioral science knowledge to improve organizational effectiveness.[56]

Organization development relies on many of the organizational behavior concepts described in this book, such as team dynamics, perceptions, job design, and conflict management. OD also takes an open systems perspective because it recognizes that organizations have many interdependent parts and must adapt to their environments. Thus, OD experts try to ensure that all parts of the organization are compatible with the change effort, and that the change activities help the company fit its environment.[57]

action research a data-based, problem-oriented process that diagnoses the need for change, introduces the OD intervention, and then evaluates and stabilizes the desired changes

Most OD activities rely on **action research** as the primary blueprint for planned change. As depicted in Exhibit 15.4, action research is a data-based, problem-oriented process that diagnoses the need for change, introduces the OD activity, and then evaluates and stabilizes the desired changes.[58]

Action research is a highly participative process, involving the client throughout the various stages.[59] It typically includes an action research team consisting of people both affected by the organizational change and having the power to facilitate it. This participation is a fundamental philosophy of OD, but it also increases commitment to the change process and provides valuable information to conduct organizational diagnosis and evaluation. Let's look at the main elements of the action research process.

Exhibit 15.4   The action research approach to organization development

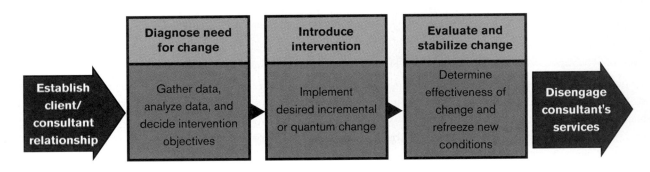

The Client-Consultant Relationship

The organization development process begins by forming a relationship between the client and consultant. External consultants might become change agents, but they are usually retained as facilitators to assist an internal change agent (usually a senior executive or team leader). Consultants need to determine three things when forming a client relationship in organization development: the client's readiness for change, the consultant's power base, and the consultant's role in the relationship.

First, consultants need to determine the client's readiness for change, including whether people are motivated to participate in the process, are open to meaningful change, and possess the abilities to complete the process. They watch out for people who enter the process with preconceived answers before the situation is fully diagnosed, or who intend to use the change effort to their personal advantage (e.g., closing down a department or firing a particular employee).

Second, consultants need to establish their power base in the client relationship.[60] Effective consultants rely on expertise and perhaps referent power to have any influence on the participants (see Chapter 12). However, they *should not* use reward, legitimate, or coercive power, because these bases may weaken trust and neutrality in the client-consultant relationship.

Lastly, consultants need to agree with their clients on the most appropriate role in the relationship.[61] This might range from providing technical expertise on a specific change activity to facilitating the change process. Many OD experts prefer the latter role, commonly known as **process consultation**.[62] Process consultation involves helping the organization solve its own problems by making it aware of organizational processes, the consequences of those processes, and the means by which they can be changed. Rather than providing expertise about the content of the change—such as how to introduce a quality management program—process consultants help participants learn how to solve their own problems by guiding them through the change process.[63]

> **process consultation** a method of helping the organization solve its own problems by making it aware of organizational processes, the consequences of those processes, and the means by which they can be changed

Diagnose the Need for Change

Action research is a problem-oriented activity that carefully diagnoses the problem (or opportunity) through systematic analysis of the situation. *Organizational diagnosis* involves gathering and analyzing data about an ongoing system. Organizational diagnosis is important because it establishes the appropriate direction for the change effort.[64]

Data collection may occur through interviews, survey questionnaires, direct observation, analysis of documents, or any combination of these. The consultant typically organizes and interprets the data, then presents it to the client to identify symptoms, problems, and possible solutions. These results also become drivers for change. They motivate participants to support the change process because it allows them to see the need for change. The data analysis should be neutral and descriptive to avoid perceptual defensiveness. The information should also relate to factors over which participants have control.

Along with gathering and analyzing data, the diagnostic process involves agreement upon specific prescriptions for action, including the appropriate change method and the schedule for these actions. This process, known as *joint action planning*, ensures that everyone knows what is expected of them and that standards are established to properly evaluate the process after the transition.[65]

Introduce Change

incremental change an
evolutionary approach to
change in which existing
organizational conditions are
fine-tuned and small steps are
taken toward the change
effort's objectives

Organization development is a process of altering specific system variables identified in the organizational diagnosis and planning stages. These changes might alter tasks, strategic organizational goals, system controls (e.g., rewards), attitudes, or interpersonal relationships.

An important issue is the appropriate amount of change. **Incremental change** is an evolutionary strategy whereby the change agent fine-tunes the existing organization and takes small steps toward the change effort's objectives.[66] Continuous improvement (described in Chapter 10) usually applies incremental change, because it attempts to make small improvements to existing work processes. Incremental change is generally less threatening and stressful to employees because they have time to adapt to the new conditions. Moreover, any problems in the process can be corrected while the change process is occurring, rather than afterwards.[67]

quantum change a
revolutionary approach
to change in which the
organization breaks out of
its existing ways and moves
toward a totally different
configuration of systems and
structures

However, incremental change may be inadequate where companies face extreme environmental turbulence. Instead, companies may require **quantum change** in which they create a totally different configuration of systems and structures.[68] "We are at the beginning of a revolutionary time in business," warns Mort Meyerson, CEO of Perot Systems. "Many companies that have enjoyed decades of fabulous success will find themselves out of business in the next five years if they don't make revolutionary changes."[69]

Although restructuring, reengineering, and other forms of quantum change are sometimes necessary, they also present risks. One problem is that quantum change usually includes the costly task of altering organizational systems and structures. Many costs, such as getting employees to learn completely different roles, are not apparent until the change process has started. Another problem is that quantum change is usually traumatic and rapid, so change agents rely more on coercion and negotiation than employee involvement to build support for the change effort.[70] As we learn in the *Fast Company Online* feature in this chapter, Hewlett-Packard's Barbara Waugh believes that change is usually most effective when change agents create the right conditions for change, then start slow and work small.

Evaluate and Stabilize Change

Organization development activities can be very expensive, so measuring their effectiveness makes a great deal of sense. To evaluate an OD process, we need to recall its objectives that were developed during the organizational diagnosis and action planning stages. But even when these goals are clearly stated, the effectiveness of an OD activity might not be apparent for several years. It is also difficult to separate the effects of the activity from external factors (e.g., improving economy, introduction of new technology).

If the activity has the desired effect, then the change agent and participants need to stabilize the new conditions. This refers to the refreezing process that we described earlier. Rewards, information systems, team norms, and other conditions are redesigned so that they support the new values and behaviors. Even with stabilizing systems and structures in place, the desired conditions may erode without the ongoing support of a change champion. For example, ALCOA's magnesium plant in Addy, Washington, became a model of efficiency under the guidance of its plant manager and human resource manager. Then, ALCOA transferred both of them to other turnaround projects and reduced the number of department heads at the plant. This unintentionally had the effect of removing the change champions and undermining the previous four years of change effort. ALCOA "stripped away the leadership that could have supported the change efforts afterwards," says one of the original change agents.[71]

Emerging Trends in Organization Development

Organization development includes any planned change intended to make a firm more effective. In theory, this means that OD covers almost every area of organizational behavior, as well as many aspects of strategic and human resource management. In practice, OD consultants have favored one perspective and level of process more than others at various periods in OD's history.

When the field of organization development emerged in the 1940s and 1950s, OD practitioners focused almost exclusively on interpersonal and small group dynamics. Few OD activities were involved with macrolevel organizationwide changes. The field was equated with various forms of sensitivity training. **Sensitivity training** is an unstructured and agendaless session in which a small group of people meet face-to-face, often for a few days, to learn more about themselves and their relations with others.[72] Learning occurs as participants disclose information about themselves and receive feedback from others during the session.

sensitivity training an unstructured and agendaless session in which participants become more aware through their interactions of how they affect others and how others affect them

Today, the reverse is true.[73] OD processes now are mostly aimed at improving service quality, corporate restructuring, and knowledge management. They are typically organizationwide, affecting organizational systems and structures with less emphasis on individual emotions and values.[74] And although surveys

---

FAST COMPANY
Online

▫ Start Slow and Work Small

Barbara Waugh's official title is Worldwide Personnel Manager at HP Labs, a division of Hewlett-Packard. But her real job is to help the 1,200 scientists, engineers, and support staff engage in continual change. Most of us would call her a change agent, but Waugh disagrees. "The notion of a 'change agent' is problematic," she says. "You don't manage change. You help to create the conditions for it. You help people to do what they already want to do."

This point of clarification is a reflection of Waugh's two guiding principles for change. First, it would be up to the people of HP Labs to move the organization forward; she couldn't do the job for them. Second, deep-seated change could occur only as a result of incremental improvement: If you want to make a big difference, then you need to help people achieve little victories.

In other words, quantum change isn't part of Waugh's toolkit. "The way we've done it here is to start slow and work small. At some point, it begins to multiply, and you get transformation—almost before you realize it." That's why Waugh and HP Labs have spent the past five years cultivating more than 100 small, achievable, grassroots initiatives, all designed to make measurable improvements inside HP Labs. "It's better to do something small and conventional that can actually make a difference than to do something big and far-out that isn't going to go anywhere," explains Waugh.

ONLINE CHECK-UP

1. This *Fast Company Online* feature describes Barbara Waugh's preference for incremental rather than quantum change. Explain her reasoning for this approach. Are there situations in which incremental change is inappropriate?

2. The full text of this *Fast Company* article describes several other activities that are part of Barbara Waugh's change initiatives. Identify these strategies and discuss their importance for minimizing resistance to change.

Get the full text of this *Fast Company* article at www.mhhe.com/mcshane1e

Source: Adapted from K. Mieszkowski, "Change: Barbara Waugh," *Fast Company*, issue 20 (December 1998). ▪

suggest that OD consultants still value their humanistic roots, there is also increasing awareness that the field's values have shifted more to a bottom-line focus.

There are numerous OD activities. Some are discussed elsewhere in this book, such as job design (Chapter 4), team building (Chapter 9), intergroup mirroring (Chapter 13), and changing organizational culture (Chapter 16). In this section, we briefly discuss two emerging OD activities: parallel learning structures and appreciative inquiry.

Parallel Learning Structures

Executives at Europcar wanted to make the company's vehicle rental process more customer friendly and efficient. But the European vehicle rental company operated as a set of independent fiefdoms in each country. The only way to change this dispersed organization was to create a parallel learning structure in the form of a task force that represented these far-reaching and independent units. The Greenway Project, as it was called, brought together 100 representatives from Europcar's operations across the continent to design and implement a better car rental process. In spite of opposition from country managers protecting their turf, the Greenway project made significant progress over the 18-month mandate. Its members became committed to the new structure. Moreover, Greenway's members made the subsequent structural change easier because they became change champions throughout the system.[75]

parallel learning structure
a highly participative social structure constructed alongside (i.e., parallel to) the formal organization with the purpose of increasing the organization's learning

The Greenway Project relied on an organization development process known as a parallel learning structure. **Parallel learning structures** are highly participative arrangements, composed of people from most levels of the organization who follow the action research model to produce meaningful organizational change. They are social structures developed alongside the formal hierarchy with the purpose of increasing the organization's learning.[76] Ideally, parallel learning structure participants are sufficiently free of the constraints of the larger organization that they may solve organizational issues more effectively.

The Greenway Project served as a parallel learning structure because it operated alongside the existing organization. Royal Dutch/Shell's retail boot camp teams, described at the beginning of this chapter, also represented a form of parallel structure because they worked outside the normal structure. These teams represented various countries and established a more entrepreneurial approach to getting things done at Shell. Shell separated these people from the traditional hierarchy so that it was easier to instill new attitudes, role patterns, and work behaviors. These teams became committed to the desired values and behaviors and later transmitted them to co-workers in the larger organization.

Appreciative Inquiry

The action research process described earlier in this chapter is based on the traditional problem-solving model. OD participants focus on problems with the existing organizational system and identify ways to correct those problems. Unfortunately, this deficiency model of the world—in which something is wrong that must be fixed—focuses on the negative dynamics of the group or system rather than its positive opportunities.

appreciative inquiry an organization development intervention that directs the group's attention away from its own problems and focuses participants on the group's potential and positive elements

Appreciative inquiry tries to break out of the problem-solving mentality by reframing relationships around the positive and the possible.[77] It takes the view that organizations are creative entities in which people are capable of building synergy beyond their individual capabilities. To avoid dwelling on the group's own shortcomings, the process usually directs its inquiry toward successful events and successful organizations. This external focus becomes a form of behavioral modeling, but it also increases open dialogue by redirecting the group's attention away from its own problems. Appreciative inquiry is especially useful when participants are aware of their "problems" or already suffer from enough negativity in their relationships. The positive orientation of appreciative inquiry enables groups to overcome these negative tensions and build a more hopeful perspective of their future by focusing on what is possible.

Exhibit 15.5 outlines the four main stages of appreciative inquiry.[78] The process begins with *discovery*—identifying the positive elements of the observed events or organization. This might involve documenting positive customer experiences elsewhere in the organization. Or it might include interviewing members of another organization to discover its fundamental strengths. As participants discuss their findings, they shift into the *dreaming* stage by envisioning what might be possible in an ideal organization. By directing their attention to a theoretically ideal organization or situation, participants feel safer revealing their hopes and aspirations than if they were discussing their own organization or predicament.

As participants make their private thoughts public to the group, the process shifts into the third stage, *designing*. Designing involves the process of **dialogue** (see Chapter 9) in which participants listen with selfless receptivity to each others' models and assumptions and eventually form a collective model for thinking within the team.[79] In effect, they create a common image of what should be. As this model takes shape, group members shift the focus back to their own situation. In the final stage of appreciative inquiry, *delivering*, participants establish specific objectives and direction for their own organization based on their model of what will be.

Appreciative inquiry is a relatively new approach to organization development, but several organizations have already applied its basic principles. One of these is DPR, the fast-growing construction company in Redwood City, California. DPR begins the first five minutes of its problem-solving meetings by highlighting the project's successes. "There's nothing like a whiteboard covered with wins," explains DPR executive Lou Bainbridge. "It raises the energy level of your meetings and reminds people that they can succeed together."[80]

dialogue a process of conversation among team members in which they learn about each other's mental models and assumptions, and eventually form a common model for thinking within the team

Exhibit 15.5   The appreciative inquiry process

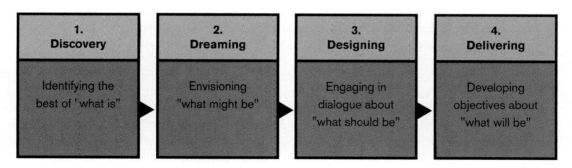

Source: Based on D. Whitney and C. Schau, "Appreciative Inquiry: An Innovative Process for Organization Change," *Employment Relations Today* 25 (Spring 1998), pp. 11–21; F. J. Barrett and D. L. Cooperrider, "Generative Metaphor Intervention: A New Approach for Working with Systems Divided by Conflict and Caught in Defensive Perception," *Journal of Applied Behavioral Science* 26 (1990), p. 229.

Effectiveness of Organization Development

Is organization development effective? Considering the incredible range of organization development activities, answering this question is not easy. Nevertheless, a few studies have generally reported that some OD processes have a moderately positive effect on employee productivity and attitudes. According to some reviews, team building and intergroup mirroring produce the most favorable results when a single activity is applied.[81] Others report that self-directed work teams are very effective.[82] One of the most consistent findings is that OD has its greatest effectiveness when it includes two or more change processes.

Cross-Cultural Concerns with Organization Development

One significant concern with OD techniques originating from the United States is that they conflict with cultural values in other countries.[83] Some scholars argue that OD in North America assumes a particular model of change that is different from organizational change philosophies held by people in other cultures.[84] The North American model of change is linear, as shown earlier in the force field analysis, and is punctuated by tension and conflict. Until recently, OD practitioners also embraced a humanistic approach with intergroup mirroring, sensitivity training, and other interpersonal processes. These practices are based on assumptions that open dialogue and conflict based on direct communication are good for individuals and organizations.

However, the linear and open conflict assumptions about change are not held in cultures with high power distance, saving face, and collectivism (a high need to maintain harmony). Instead, people in some countries work well with Confucian assumptions, namely that change is a natural cyclical process with harmony and equilibrium as the objectives.[85] This does not mean that OD is ineffective elsewhere. Rather, it suggests that the field needs to develop a more contingency-oriented perspective toward the cultural values of its participants.

Ethical Concerns with Organization Development

The field of organization development also faces ethical concerns with respect to some processes.[86] One ethical concern is that OD activities potentially increase management's power by inducing compliance and conformity in organizational members. This power shift occurs because OD initiatives create uncertainty and reestablish management's position in directing the organization. Moreover, because OD is a systemwide activity, it requires employee participation rather than allowing individuals to get involved voluntarily. Indeed, one of the challenges of OD consultants is to gain the support of those who are reluctant to engage in the process.

A second ethical concern is that OD activities may threaten the individual's privacy rights. The action research model is built on the idea of collecting information from organizational members, yet this requires employees to provide personal information that they may not want to divulge.[87] Some OD processes, such as sensitivity training, further threaten individual privacy rights by requiring participants to reveal their private lives. Consider the session attended by Jim Morgan, a copywriter for an advertising agency in London, England. "I saw adults 'confessing' (via a large PA system) to complete strangers about childhood sexual abuse, incidents where they were nearly murdered and all manner of dark secrets and fears, crying uncontrollably as they did so."[88]

A third concern with some OD activities is that they undermine the individual's self-esteem. The unfreezing process requires participants to disavow their existing beliefs, sometimes including their own competence at certain tasks or interpersonal relations. Sensitivity training and intergroup mirroring may involve direct exposure to personal critique by co-workers as well as public disclosure of one's personal limitations and faults. A more extreme example apparently occurred at SaskTel. As we read in Connections 15.2, consultants working at the government-owned telephone company in Saskatchewan, Canada, used OD tactics that allegedly included public ridicule and control over employees who participated in the project.

A fourth ethical dilemma facing OD consultants is their role in the client relationship. Generally, they should occupy "marginal" positions with the clients they are serving. This means that they must be sufficiently detached from the organization to maintain objectivity and avoid having the client become too dependent on them.[89] However, this can be a difficult objective to satisfy because of the politics of organizational change. OD consultants and clients have their own agendas, and these are not easily resolved without moving beyond the marginal positions that change agents should ideally attain.

The organization development practices described in this section facilitate the change process, and Lewin's force field analysis model provides a valuable

Connections 15.2 ▫ Organization Development Behind Closed Doors at SaskTel

It all seemed quite normal on the surface. A group of employees and managers at SaskTel, the telephone provider in Saskatchewan, Canada, would form a cross-functional team under the guidance of Symmetrix, a U.S. consulting firm. Instead, according to participants, the organization development process may have wandered over the line of ethical conduct.

Symmetrix used a "greenhouse approach" by isolating the SaskTel employees in an office suite with paper taped over its glass walls so that no one could see inside. Participants say they were quarantined in small cubicles and were prevented from talking to each other. Moreover, Symmetrix refused to give reasons for assignments or why employees had to work long hours with tight deadlines at various times.

The project was supposed to last six weeks. Instead, it ended one year later, after participants united and forced SaskTel to get rid of Symmetrix. Of the 20 SaskTel employees who were involved in the project, nearly half took stress leave. The employees' union hired a university professor to evaluate the Symmetrix project. That report, along with internal documents, shocked SaskTel's board and ended the consultant's contract.

Symmetrix claims that the process was working and that the insults were the result of "political hoopla" and union-management problems. But employees say the problems were real. "There was always a manipulative pressure on the group to submit," says Gord Young, a SaskTel installer who participated in most of the Symmetrix project. "Team members regularly received insults in front of the group," recalls Kathryn Markus, a seven-year SaskTel manager. "The isolation, long hours, and purposeless activity left me feeling abandoned, betrayed, and frightened." Markus hasn't worked since she left the project.

Source: "Perils of Public Sector Work: A Case Study," *Consultants News,* April 1996, p. 5; S. Parker, Jr., "SaskTel Dials the Wrong Number," *Western Report,* February 26, 1996, pp. 14–17. ▫

template for understanding how the change process works. Still, you can see from reading this chapter that organizational change is easier said than done. Many corporate leaders have promised more change than they were able to deliver because they underestimated the time and challenges involved with this process. Probably the most difficult area of change is corporate culture, which we study in the next chapter.

Chapter Summary

Organizations face numerous forces for change because they are open systems that need to adapt to changing environments. Some current environmental dynamics include computer technology, globalization, competition, and demographics.

Lewin's force field analysis model states that all systems have driving and restraining forces. Change occurs through the process of unfreezing, changing, and refreezing. Unfreezing involves producing a disequilibrium between the driving and restraining forces. Refreezing occurs when the organization's systems and structures are aligned with the desired behaviors.

Almost all organizational change efforts face one or more forms of employee resistance. The main reasons why people resist change are direct costs, saving face, fear of the unknown, breaking routines, incongruent organizational systems, and incongruent team dynamics

Resistance to change may be minimized by keeping employees informed about what to expect from the change effort (communicating), teaching employees valuable skills for the desired future (training), involving them in the change process, helping employees cope with the stress of change, negotiating trade-offs with those who will clearly lose from the change effort, and using coercion sparingly and as a last resort.

A change agent is anyone who possesses enough knowledge and power to guide and facilitate the change effort. Change agents rely on transformational leadership to develop a vision, communicate that vision, and build commitment to the vision of a desirable future state.

Organization development (OD) is a planned systemwide effort, managed from the top with the assistance of a change agent, that uses behavioral science knowledge to improve organizational effectiveness.

When forming a client relationship, OD consultants need to determine the readiness for change, establish their power base in the client relationship, and understand their appropriate role in the change process. An important issue is whether change should be evolutionary (incremental change) or revolutionary (quantum change).

Appreciative inquiry focuses participants on the positive and possible. It tries to break out of the problem-solving mentality that dominates OD through the action research model. The four stages of appreciative inquiry include discovery, dreaming, designing, and delivering.

Organization development activities, particularly those with multiple parts, have a moderately positive effect on employee productivity and attitudes. However, there are some cross-cultural concerns with OD processes. Moreover, there are ethical concerns with some OD activities, including increasing management's power over employees, threatening individual privacy rights, undermining individual self-esteem, and making clients dependent on the OD consultant.

Key Terms

Action research, p. 482
Appreciative inquiry, p. 486
Change agent, p. 480
Dialogue, p. 487
Force field analysis, p. 471
Incremental change, p. 484
Law of telecosm, p. 468
Organization development (OD), p. 482

Parallel learning structures, p. 486
Process consultation, p. 483
Quantum change, p. 484
Refreezing, p. 471
Search conferences, p. 477
Sensitivity training, p. 485
Transformational leadership, p. 480
Unfreezing, p. 471

Discussion Questions

1. Chances are that the school you are attending is currently undergoing some sort of change to adapt more closely to its environment. Discuss the external forces that are driving these changes. What internal drivers for change also exist?

2. Use Lewin's force field analysis to describe the dynamics of organizational change at Royal Dutch/Shell described in the opening vignette to this chapter.

3. Senior management of a large multinational corporation is planning to restructure the organization. Currently, the firm is decentralized around geographical areas so that the executive responsible for each area has considerable autonomy over manufacturing and sales. The new structure will transfer power to the executives responsible for different product groups; the executives responsible for each geographic area will no longer be responsible for manufacturing in their area but will retain control over sales activities. Describe two types of resistance senior management might encounter from this organizational change.

4. Read again the organizational change process at Keene State College (Connections 15.1). Then explain how this process reduced resistance to change.

5. Web Circuits, Inc., is a manufacturer of computer circuit boards for high-technology companies. Senior management wants to introduce value-added management practices to reduce production costs and remain competitive. A consultant has recommended that the company start with a pilot project in one department. When the pilot project succeeds, the company can diffuse these practices to other areas of the organization. Discuss the merits of this recommendation and identify three conditions (other than the pilot project's success) that would make diffusion of the change effort more successful.

6. You are an organization development consultant who has been asked by the president of Southern Textiles, Inc., to explore "issues" that may account for poor sales in the company's Pacific-Northwest division. Before accepting this role, what three things should you consider when forming the client relationship? How would you determine whether the client-consultant is well suited to organization development?

7. Suppose that you are vice president of branch services at Humongus BankCorp. You notice that several branches have consistently low customer service ratings even though there are no apparent differences in resources or staff characteristics. Describe an appreciative inquiry process in one of these branches that might help to overcome these problems.

8. This chapter suggests that some organization development activities face ethical concerns. Yet, several OD consultants actively use these processes because they believe they benefit the organization and do less damage to employees than it seems on the surface. For example, some OD activities try to open up the employee's hidden area (see Johari Window in Chapter 6) so that there is better mutual understanding with co-workers. Discuss the merits of this argument and identify where you think OD should limit this process.

CASE STUDY

TransAct Insurance Corporation

TransAct Insurance Corporation (TIC) provides automobile insurance throughout the southeastern United States. Last year a new president was brought in by TIC's Board of Directors to improve the company's competitiveness and customer service. After spending several months assessing the situation, the new president introduced a strategic plan to improve TIC's competitive position. He also replaced three vice presidents. Jim Leon was hired as vice president of claims, TIC's largest division with 1,500 employees, 50 claims center managers, and 5 regional directors.

Jim immediately met with all claims managers and directors, and visited employees at TIC's 50 claims centers. As an outsider, this was a formidable task, but his strong interpersonal skills and uncanny ability to remember names and ideas helped him through the process. Through these visits and discussions, Jim discovered that the claims division had been managed in a relatively authoritarian, top-down manner. He could also see that morale was extremely low and employee-management relations were guarded. High workloads and isolation (claims adjusters work in tiny cubicles) were two other common complaints. Several managers acknowledged that the high turnover among claims adjusters was partly due to these conditions.

Following discussions with TIC's president, Jim decided to make morale and supervisory leadership his top priority. He initiated a divisional newsletter with a tear-off feedback form for employees to register their comments. He announced an open-door policy in which any claims division employee could speak to him directly and confidentially without going first to the immediate supervisor. Jim also fought organizational barriers to initiate a flextime program so that employees could design work schedules around their needs. This program later became a model for other areas of TIC.

One of Jim's most pronounced symbols of change was the "Claims Management Credo" outlining the philosophy that every claims manager would follow. At his first meeting with the complete claims management team, Jim presented a list of what he thought were important philosophies and actions of effective managers. The management group was asked to select and prioritize items from this list. They were told that the resulting list would be the division's management philosophy and all managers would be held accountable for abiding by its principles. Most claims managers were uneasy about this process, but they also understood that the organization was under competitive pressure and that Jim was using this exercise to demonstrate his leadership.

The claims managers developed a list of 10 items, such as encouraging teamwork, fostering a trusting work environment, setting clear and reasonable goals, and so on. The list was circulated to senior management in the organization for their comment and approval and sent back to all claims managers for their endorsement. Once this was done, a copy of the final document was sent to every claims division employee. Jim also announced plans to follow up with an annual survey to evaluate each claims manager's performance. This worried the managers, but most of them believed that the credo exercise was a result of Jim's initial enthusiasm and that he would be too busy to introduce a survey after settling into the job.

One year after the credo had been distributed, Jim announced that the first annual survey would be conducted. All claims employees were to complete the survey and return it confidentially to the human resources department where the survey results would be compiled for each claims center manager. The survey asked the extent to which the manager had lived up to each of the 10 items in the credo. Each form also provided space for comments.

Claims center managers were surprised that the survey Jim had promised a year ago would be conducted, but they were even more worried about Jim's statement that the results would be shared with employees. What "results" would employees see? Who would distribute these results? What happens if a manager gets poor ratings from his or her subordinates? "We'll work out the details later," said Jim in response to these questions. "Even if the survey results aren't great, the information will give us a good baseline for next year's survey."

The claims division survey had a high response rate. In some centers, every employee completed and returned a form. Each report showed the claims center manager's average score for each of the 10 items and how many employees rated the manager at each level of the five-point scale. The reports also included every comment made by employees at that center.

No one was prepared for the results of the first survey. Most managers received moderate or poor ratings on the 10 items. Very few managers averaged above 3.0 (out of a five-point scale) on more than a couple of items. This suggested that, at best, employees were ambivalent about whether their claims center manager had abided by the 10 management philosophy items. The comments were even more devastating than the ratings. Comments ranged from mildly disappointed to extremely critical of their claims manager. Employees also described their long-standing frustration with TIC, high workloads, and isolated working conditions. Several people bluntly stated that they were skeptical about the changes that Jim had promised. "We've heard the promises before, but now we've lost faith," wrote one claims adjuster.

The survey results were sent to each claims manager, the regional director, and employees at the claims center. Jim instructed managers to discuss the survey data and comments with their regional manager and directly with employees. The claims center managers, who thought employees only received average scores, were shocked to learn that the reports included individual comments. Some managers went to their regional director, complaining that revealing the personal comments would ruin their careers. Many directors sympathized, but the results were already available to employees.

When Jim heard about these concerns, he agreed that the results were lower than expected and that the comments should not have been shown to employees. After discussing the situation with the regional directors, he decided that the discussion meetings between claims managers and their employees should proceed as planned. To delay or withdraw the reports would undermine the credibility and trust that Jim was trying to develop with employees. However, the regional director in that area attended the meeting in each claims center to minimize direct conflict between the claims center manager and employees.

Although many of these meetings went smoothly, a few created harsh feelings between managers and their employees. The source of some comments was easily identified by their content, and this created a few delicate moments in several sessions. A few months after these meetings, two claims center managers quit and three others asked for transfers back to nonmanagement positions in TIC. Meanwhile, Jim wondered how to manage this process more effectively, particularly since employees expected another survey the following year.

Discussion Questions

1. Identify the forces pushing for change and the forces restraining the change effort in this case.

2. Was Jim Leon successful at bringing about change? Why or why not?

3. What should Jim Leon do now?

CASE STUDY

The taming of France Telecom

BusinessWeek

When Michel Bon took charge of France Telecom a few years ago, privatization of the phone monopoly was the government's *bête noire*. Each time officials made a move, militant unions staged massive strikes, forcing the government into a humiliating retreat. Bon's predecessor quit after just five days, making Bon the third president in three months. Unions struck within weeks of his arrival. Their ominous message to the newcomer: "Don't even think about privatizing." But Bon surprised everyone. Within nine months, the smooth-talking marketer from the retailing industry gained union support and put the privatization plans back on track.

This *Business Week* case study describes how privatization and deregulation are driving France Telecom and other telecommunications companies to change the way they do business. It highlights how Michel Bon not only privatized France Telecom, but is working to make the former government monopoly more competitive. Read through this *Business Week* case study at www.mhhe.com/mcshane1e and prepare for the discussion questions below.

Discussion Questions

1. Use Lewin's force field analysis model to depict the driving and restraining forces for privatization and competitive behavior at France Telecom.

2. What actions did Bon take to minimize resistance to change? Identify these strategies in terms of the options described in Exhibit 15.3.

Source: G. Edmondson, "The Taming of France Telecom," *Business Week*, January 27, 1997. ■

VIDEO CASE

Harley-Davidson

 Harley-Davidson is the only company currently making motorcycles in the United States. There once were more than 100 manufacturers. However, just over a decade ago, Harley was hemorrhaging. Poorly-built bikes and a customer-be-damned attitude had its share of the motorcycle market going down faster than the Titanic. It was literally hours away from declaring bankruptcy.

Fourteen men, including now president and CEO Jeffrey Bluestein, bought the company when it was on its deathbed. Perhaps the most important thing he did was begin listening to what loyal Harley owners wanted. A bike that didn't leak, and a bike that didn't fall apart. And today they are still listening. Bluestein said, "We try to adapt the best of the new with the best of the old. And of course our customers are experts at doing that themselves."

The results of the new Harley have been well documented, but the phenomenal success of Harley continues to build. It has almost reached cult proportions. Harley currently holds 65 percent of the big bike market, and has experienced an 80 percent increase in revenue. All Harley's bikes are sold before they are even built. And in the last year or so everything that has a Harley name on it has worked.

The face lift also had a profound effect on the faces of the people riding the big machine. Dick Knight and his wife Anita certainly don't fit the stereotypical greaser image, but they are part of the new breed. Sometimes they are called Rubs—Rich Urban Bikers. But to the Knights riding is a family affair, and their daughter Lisa, who just bought her first Harley, represents the newest change for Harley: one in four is a woman buyer. The Knights are certainly well-to-do, but when they get on their bikes that all goes away. The motorcycle is an equalizer of both rich and poor. Dick Knight said, "Harley riders have something in common and it doesn't make any difference what kind of an economic background you come from. If you ride a Harley you've got a brother out there that rides a Harley also." About 100,000 Harley riders traveled to Milwaukee for the company's 95th birthday celebration in June of 1998.

Several thousand bikers traveled to Milwaukee from both coasts. They were on the road for about a week, and while much of the time is a lot of fun and games, there is a serious side to it. Harley is a big supporter of Muscular Dystrophy, and by the end of a week they will have raised more than a million dollars for MD.

Discussion Questions

1. What role does the customer play in the turnaround at Harley-Davidson?

2. How does the Harley "image" affect its internal operations?

3. How can a company like Harley-Davidson include employees in the change process? ■

TEAM EXERCISE

Applying Lewin's force field analysis

Purpose

This exercise is designed to help you understand how to diagnose situations using force field analysis and to identify strategies to facilitate organizational change.

Instructions

This exercise involves diagnosing the situation described below, identifying the forces for and against change, and recommending strategies to reduce resistance to change. The exercise is described as a team activity, although the instructor may choose to have it completed individually. Also, the instructor may choose a situation other than the one presented here.

Step 1: Students will form teams of four or five people and everyone will read the following situation. (Note: If your school currently has a full trimester system, then imagine the situation as though your school currently has a two-semester system):

Your college has two semesters (beginning in September and January) as well as a six-week "summer school" from early May to mid-June. Instructors typically teach their regular load of courses during the two semesters. Summer school is mainly taught by part-time contract faculty, although some full-time faculty teach for extra pay. After carefully reviewing costs, student demand, and competition from other institutions, senior administration has decided that your college should switch to a trimester curriculum. In a trimester system, courses are taught in three equal semesters—September to December, January to April, and May to early August. Faculty with research obligations must teach any two semesters in which their courses are offered; teaching-only faculty teach courses in all three semesters. Senior administration has determined that this change will make more efficient use of college resources, particularly because it will allow the institution to admit more students without building additional classrooms or other facilities. Moreover, market surveys indicate that over 50 percent of current students would continue their studies in the revised summer semester (i.e., second trimester) and the institution would attract more full-fee students from other countries. The Faculty Association has not yet had time to state its position on this proposed change.

Force field analysis model

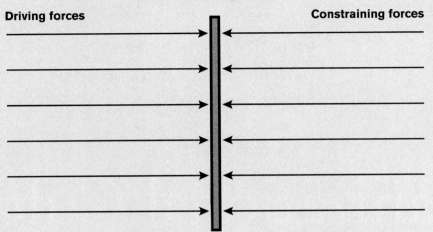

Driving forces   **Constraining forces**

Step 2: Using Lewin's force field analysis model (above), identify the forces that seem to support the change and the forces that are likely to oppose the change to a trimester system. Team members should consider all possible sources of support and resistance, not just those stated in the situation above.

Step 3: For each source of resistance, identify one or more strategies that would manage change most effectively. Recall from the textbook that the change management strategies include communication, training, employee involvement, stress management, negotiation, and coercion.

Step 4: The class will discuss each team's results. ■

Organizational Culture

Learning Objectives

After reading this chapter, you should be able to:

- Describe the elements of organizational culture.
- Discuss the importance of organizational subcultures.
- List four categories of artifacts through which corporate culture is communicated.
- Identify three functions of organizational culture.
- Discuss the conditions under which cultural strength improves corporate performance.
- Discuss the effect of organizational culture on business ethics.
- Compare and contrast four strategies for merging organizational cultures.
- Identify five strategies to strengthen an organization's culture.

To an outsider, PeopleSoft is one of the loopiest places on the planet. The Pleasanton, California, business management software company has nerf ball shootouts and minigolf tournaments in the hallways. Dress-down day is every day of the week. A white collar is usually a T-shirt. The bagels and gourmet coffee are free. Having fun is so ingrained that many employees—called PeoplePeople—say it's the best place to have a bad day.

PeopleSoft also values egalitarianism—treating everyone with respect and minimal status differences. Executives don't have secretaries, special perks, or grandiose offices. "Don't kiss up and slap down," PeopleSoft cofounder Dave Duffield reminds everyone. In other words, give the bagel delivery guy the same respect as the company president.

PeopleSoft is also extreme on technology and flexible customer service. Job applicants use an automated voice response system to accept their job offer. On the first day of work, newcomers are outfitted with a notebook computer and a backpack. They also receive tools for posting personal web pages on the company intranet. "There's an unstated expectation that this is how things are done at the company," says Steve Zarate, PeopleSoft's chief information officer.

This corporate culture has contributed to PeopleSoft's success. The company has grown faster than SAP and Oracle and is now the second largest provider of business management software (after SAP). "Our true competence is our culture," explains Dave Duffield. "That's what attracts people and keeps them here. It also helps sell customers. Customers want to work with companies that are competent, trustworthy, and fun."[1]

Nerf ball shootouts and minigolf tournaments in the hallways reveal some of PeopleSoft's corporate culture.

[K. Miller. Used with permission.]

eopleSoft has a distinctive organizational culture. Moreover, it is a culture that seems to work well for the computer software firm's competitiveness. **Organizational culture** is the basic pattern of shared assumptions, values, and beliefs considered to be the correct way of thinking about and acting on problems and opportunities facing the organization. It defines what is important and unimportant in the company. You might think of it as the organization's DNA—invisible to the naked eye, yet a powerful template that shapes what happens in the workplace.[2]

This chapter begins by examining the elements of organizational culture and how culture is deciphered through artifacts. This is followed by a discussion of the relationship between organizational culture and corporate performance, including the effects of cultural strength, fit, and adaptability. Then we turn to the issue of mergers and corporate culture. The last section of this chapter looks at specific strategies for maintaining a strong organizational culture.

organizational culture the basic pattern of shared assumptions, values, and beliefs governing the way employees within an organization think about and act on problems and opportunities

Elements of Organizational Culture

As we see in Exhibit 16.1, the assumptions, values, and beliefs that represent organizational culture operate beneath the surface of organizational behavior. They are not directly observed, yet their effects are everywhere. Assumptions represent the deepest part of organizational culture because they are unconscious and taken for granted. Assumptions are the shared **mental models** that we discussed in Chapter 6—the broad worldviews or theories-in-use that people rely on to guide their perceptions and behaviors.

Consider two organizations with different "absence cultures."[3] Absence cultures exist where employees have a shared understanding about taking time away from regularly scheduled work. In one company, employees assume that sick leave is their right to use, whether or not they are sick. At another company, sick leave is reserved for real illnesses; people would not imagine taking paid time off unless they were truly sick. In both firms, assumptions about taking sick leave are ingrained, taken for granted.

An organization's cultural beliefs and values are somewhat easier to decipher than assumptions because people are aware of them. *Beliefs* represent the individual's perceptions of reality. **Values** are more stable, long-lasting beliefs about what is important. They help us define what is right or wrong, or good or bad, in the world (see Chapter 7).[4] In some organizations, playing nerf ball and wearing T-shirts is considered inappropriate and evidence of poor

mental models the broad world views or "theories-in-use" that people rely on to guide their perceptions and behaviors

values stable, long-lasting beliefs about what is important to the individual

Exhibit 16.1
Elements of organizational culture

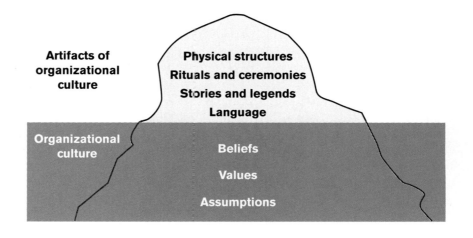

performance. But PeopleSoft's values support the fun side of work and the egalitarianism of casual dress code.

We can't determine an organization's cultural values just by asking employees and other people about them. Values are socially desirable, so what people say they value (called *espoused values*) may differ from what they truly value (*enacted values*).[5] Espoused values do not represent an organization's culture. Rather, they establish the public image that corporate leaders want to display. Enacted values, on the other hand, are values-in-use. They are the values that guide individual decisions and behavior in the workplace.

Content of Organizational Culture

Organizations differ in their cultural content; that is, the relative ordering of beliefs, values, and assumptions. Consider the following companies and their apparent dominant cultures:

- *Nokia Corp.*—Responsive and collegial best describes the corporate culture of Nokia Corp. The Helsinki, Finland, conglomerate is a leader in popular cellular telephones. But don't expect employees to personally take credit for their own successes. Unlike the "me first" cultures found in other high technology firms, Nokia emphasizes understated collegiality. "We don't snap our suspenders," says Nokia CEO Jorma Ollila.[6]

- *Amazon.com*—Frugality is clearly a corporate value at Amazon.com. Beyond the online bookseller's popular web site is a drab 1960s four-story headquarters in downtown Seattle. Everyone's desks are made from doors (total cost: $130). Monitors are propped up on telephone books to avoid paying for monitor stands. Extra chairs are considered an extravagance. "By watching your overhead you can spend more on business expansion," explains Amazon.com founder and CEO Jeff Bezos.[7]

- *Mattel, Inc.*—Mattel makes Barbie dolls, but its corporate culture is so competitive that some say that it looks more like a war zone for GI Joe. "It has always been a place where people are pitted against each other," says a former Mattel executive. "It's a shark pond. You throw people in and see if they can swim fast enough to stay alive."[8]

Responsive and collegial. Frugal. Competitive. How many corporate cultural values are there? No one knows for certain. There are dozens of individual and cross-cultural values, so there are likely to be just as many organizational values. Some writers and consultants have attempted to classify organizational cultures into a few categories with catchy labels such as "clubs" and "fortresses." Although these typologies might reflect the values of a few organizations, they oversimplify the diversity of cultural values in organizations. Worse, they tend to distort rather than clarify our attempts to diagnose corporate culture.

Organizational Subcultures

When discussing organizational culture, we are actually referring to the *dominant culture;* that is, the themes shared most widely by the organization's members. However, organizations are also comprised of *subcultures* located throughout its various divisions, geographic regions, and occupational groups.[9] Some subcultures enhance the dominant culture by espousing parallel assumptions, values, and beliefs; others are called *countercultures* because they directly oppose the organization's core values.

Subcultures, particularly countercultures, potentially create conflict and dissension among employees, but they also serve two important functions. First, they maintain the organization's standards of performance and ethical behavior. Employees who hold countercultural values are an important source

Hewlett Packard (HP) is a global organization with a corporate culture that is spread to employees around the world. Whether at HP's Far East distribution center in Singapore *(shown at right)* or at research labs in Cupertino, California, employees live by five well-established values known as "The HP Way." These values include trust and respect for individuals, a focus on achievement and contribution, the conduct of business with uncompromising integrity, achievement of common objectives through teamwork, and encouragement of flexibility and innovation.[10] How might HP and other companies with global operations instill a common culture in several countries? What challenges would they experience?
[Courtesy of Hewlett-Packard]

of surveillance and evaluation of the dominant order.[11] They encourage constructive controversy and more creative thinking about how the organization should interact with its environment. Subcultures prevent employees from blindly following one set of values and thereby help the organization to abide by society's ethical values.

The second function of subcultures is that they are the spawning grounds for emerging values that keep the firm aligned with the needs of customers, suppliers, society, and other stakeholders. Companies eventually need to replace their dominant values with ones that are more appropriate for the changing environment. If subcultures are suppressed, the organization may take longer to discover and adopt values aligned with the emerging environment.

Deciphering Organizational Culture through Artifacts

artifacts the observable symbols and signs of an organization's culture, including its physical structures, ceremonies, language, and stories

We can't see an organization's cultural assumptions, values, and beliefs directly. Instead, as Exhibit 16.1 illustrated, organizational culture is deciphered indirectly through **artifacts.** Artifacts are the observable symbols and signs of an organization's culture, such as the way visitors are greeted, the physical layout, and how employees are rewarded.[12] "You show your corporate culture in everything—the way the building looks, the way people act, the names of the conference rooms," said Joe Kraus, a cofounder of Excite, an Internet gateway and search engine company in Redwood City, California.[13]

Understanding an organization's culture requires painstaking assessment of many artifacts because they are subtle and often ambiguous.[14] The process is very much like an anthropological investigation of a newfound society. Some scholars extract organizational values from the narratives of everyday corporate life.[15] Others survey employees, observe workplace behavior, and study written documents. We probably need to do all of these things to accurately assess an organization's culture. We should be cautious about public statements regarding a company's culture because they are often the company's own public relations pronouncements of its espoused values. With this in mind, let's consider four broad categories of artifacts: organizational stories and legends, rituals and ceremonies, language, and physical structures and symbols.

Organizational Stories and Legends

Many years ago, so the story goes, a security guard stopped IBM CEO Thomas Watson, Jr., as he was about to enter an area without his identification badge. Watson explained who he was, but the guard insisted that a badge must be worn in secured areas of the building. Rather than discipline the guard, Watson praised him and used this experience to tell others about performing their job well. Stories and legends like this about past corporate incidents serve as powerful social prescriptions of the way things should (or should not) be done. They provide human realism to individual performance standards and use role models to demonstrate that organizational objectives are attainable.

Not all stories and legends are positive. Contrast the IBM story with the following incident at Revlon Corporation. Charles Revson, CEO of the cosmetics manufacturer, seldom arrived at work much before noon, yet he insisted that everyone else arrive on time and complete a sign-in sheet to prove their promptness. One day, Revson picked up the sign-in sheet, but a new receptionist stopped him under strict orders that the sheet must not be removed. After some argument, Revson asked: "Do you know who I am?" When the receptionist answered that she didn't, Revson responded: "Well, when you pick up your final pay check this afternoon, ask 'em to tell ya.'" The lessons here? IBM's story advises employees to obey rules, whereas the Revlon story says "Obey rulers!"[16]

Four Seasons Hotels and Resorts hires, trains, and rewards employees for superior customer service. Yet founder Isadore Sharp will tell you that the company's legendary service is also ingrained in Four Seasons' corporate culture. There is certainly evidence of the customer service value in stories and legends. One story recounts an incident in which rock star Rod Stewart called Four Seasons staff while he was a guest to find someone to play the bagpipes in his suite. The employees were able to find a willing bagpipe player, even though Stewart phoned in the request at midnight![17] In what ways do these stories and legends support organizational culture?
[Courtesy of Four Seasons Hotels and Resorts.]

Organizational stories and legends are most effective at communicating cultural values when they describe real people, are assumed to be true, and are known by employees throughout the organization. Organizational culture stories are also prescriptive—they advise people what to do or not to do.[18] Research on organizational stories reveals that they tend to answer one or more of the following questions: How does the boss react to mistakes? What events are so important that people get fired? Who, if anyone, can break the rules? How do people rise to the top of this organization? How much help can employees expect from the organization for transfers and other events? How will the organization deal with crises?[19]

Rituals and Ceremonies

Soon after moving from IBM to Digital Equipment Corporation (now part of Compaq Computer Corp.) several years ago, Peter DeLisi noticed that Digital employees seemed to fight a lot with each other. "Shouting matches were a frequent occurrence, and I came to conclude that Digital people didn't like one another," recalls the marketing executive.[20] Eventually, DeLisi learned that Digital employees didn't dislike each other, but were engaging in the ritual of "pushing back"—defending ideas until truth ultimately prevailed. These apparent conflicts were rituals that reinforced the computer firm's value in constructive conflict. **Rituals** are the programmed routines of daily organizational life that dramatize the organization's culture. Along with shouting matches at Digital, rituals include how visitors are greeted, how often senior executives visit subordinates, how people communicate with each other, how much time employees take for lunch, and so on.

Ceremonies are more formal artifacts than rituals. Ceremonies are planned activities conducted specifically for the benefit of an audience. This would include publicly rewarding (or punishing) employees, or celebrating the launch of a new product or newly won contract.[21] Many firms deliberately use ceremonies to reinforce and communicate the organization's core values. For instance, all 75 employees at Fitzgerald Communications, Inc., received wallet-sized cards describing the company's core values: true partnerships, never compromising integrity, and engaging in direct communication. Twice each year, the Cambridge, Massachusetts, public relations firm holds an award ceremony honoring employees who have best exemplified those values.[22]

Organizational Language

The language of the workplace speaks volumes about the company's culture. For instance, when Monsanto Company CEO Robert Shapiro met with American Home Products CEO John Stafford about a possible merger, Monsanto employees referred to "Bob," whereas American Home Products executives addressed "Mr. Stafford."[23] Monsanto's egalitarian culture and American Home's hierarchical culture were soon evident to everyone in these meetings.

Language also highlights values held by organizational subcultures. This was recently apparent to consultants working at Whirlpool. They kept hearing employees talk about the home appliance company's "PowerPoint culture." This phrase, named after Microsoft's presentation software, was used by employees as a critique of Whirlpool's hierarchical culture in which communication is one way (from executives to employees) and employees have limited opportunity to voice opinions or concerns to company executives.[24]

Corporate culture might also be represented in the phrases, metaphors, and other special vocabularies used by organizational leaders.[25] Consider the "grocery store" metaphor that General Electric CEO Jack Welch often uses. He wants everyone to think of GE not as an electrical manufacturing colossus, but

rituals the programmed routines of daily organizational life that dramatize the organization's culture

ceremonies planned activities conducted specifically for the benefit of an audience that symbolize organizational culture

[DILBERT reprinted by permission of United Feature Syndicate, Inc.]

as a small business where customer service and the constant search for new opportunities keep the "shop" in business.[26] Of course, metaphors and catchphrases often reflect the leader's espoused values, not necessarily values-in-use. Moreover, when leaders spew out jargon that is inconsistent with the dominant culture, employees are more likely to play "buzzword bingo" than to adopt the new value system.[27]

Physical Structures and Symbols

British Airways (BA) is changing its corporate culture by changing its headquarters building. The old multistory headquarters near London's Heathrow Airport reinforced hierarchical and bureaucratic values that the airline was trying to cast off. The new headquarters is designed with a central village square and work units spreading out from it. Executives are located with their units, not cloistered on a separate executive floor. In the words of British Airways CEO Bob Ayling, "move the office, change the culture."

Physical structures and spaces, such as British Airways' village square headquarters, often symbolize the company's underlying values and beliefs.[28] The size, shape, location, and age of buildings might suggest the organization's emphasis on teamwork, risk aversion, flexibility, or any other set of values. "We have a firm belief that the physical layout of the building reflects the culture," says Gary Bromberger, director of worldwide facilities for Bell & Howell's mail processing division in Durham, North Carolina. Bell & Howell replaced its warren of boxy offices with a more collaborative open space. "It's a very human building," says another Bell & Howell executive. "That's the epitome of who we are."[29]

Bell & Howell and British Airways are part of the recent wave in which corporate leaders are redesigning the workplace to fit the culture (or create a new one). How far are companies taking the symbolism? The headquarters of Oakley, Inc., might give you some idea. As we read in this chapter's *Fast Company Online* feature, the eyewear and footwear manufacturer has built a structure that almost screams out its cultural message.

Even if the building doesn't make much of a statement, there is a treasure trove of physical artifacts inside. Desks, chairs, cafeteria food, and wall hangings are just a few of the items that might convey cultural meaning.

Amazon.com's frugal culture is apparent from its homemade desks. People-Soft's fun and egalitarian culture can be seen from the wall posters showing fun-seeking employees, not executives or products. Husky Injection Molding

FAST COMPANY Online   □ The Empire Strikes Back

Oakley, Inc.'s headquarters symbolizes a corporate culture in which employees believe they are at war with competitors.
[Courtesy of Oakley, Inc.]

Oakley, Inc., the maker of high-end, ultrahip eyewear and footwear, is at war. That's the impression you get when visiting its corporate headquarters in Foothill Ranch, California. In fact, the architecture suggests that Oakley's war is more intergalactic than a local skirmish.

Oakley's combat-ready headquarters symbolizes a corporate culture that attacks such rivals as Nike with gladiator glee. The lobby of the two-year-old, $40-million building looks like a bomb shelter. Its huge, echoing vault is straight out of *Star Wars*. Sleek pipes, watertight doors, and towering metallic walls studded with oversize bolts suggest a place that is routinely subjected to laser fire and floods. Ejection seats from a B-52 bomber furnish the waiting area. A full-size torpedo lies in a rack behind the receptionist's armored desk.

Oakley's culture is also apparent in its annual report, which reads more like the *Art of War* than a financial report. "We've always had a fortress mentality," says Colin Baden, Oakley's vice president of design. "What we make is gold, and people will do anything to get it, so we protect it."

ONLINE CHECK-UP

1. This *Fast Company Online* feature illustrates how Oakley's building design represents and reinforces the company's fortress mentality. What other activities might occur at Oakley to communicate this corporate culture?
2. Go to Oakley's web site (www.oakley.com). What organizational culture values do you decipher from the web site's design, the annual report's language (available at the web site), the company's products, and other artifacts at this site?

Get the full text of this *Fast Company* article at www.mhhe.com/mcshane1e

Source: Adapted from P. Roberts, "The Empire Strikes Back," *Fast Company*, Issue 22 (February–March 1999). ■

Systems, a leading supplier of plastic molding technology, has an extremely health-conscious culture. This explains why employees pay for coffee but get herbal tea free in Husky's cafeteria.[30] Each of these artifacts potentially conveys meaning about the company's culture.

Organizational Culture and Performance

Nucor Steel is a stunning success story at a time when most other U.S. steel companies are struggling to stay in business. The secret, according to Nucor's CEO Ken Iverson, is the steel firm's corporate culture. "Without a doubt, Nucor's culture is its most important source of competitive advantage, and it always will be," explains Iverson.[31]

Does organizational culture affect corporate performance? Ken Iverson thinks so, as do many writers on this subject.[32] Generally, they argue that culture serves three important functions. First, corporate culture is a deeply embedded form of social control that influences employee decisions and behavior.[33] Culture is pervasive and operates unconsciously. You might think of it as an automatic pilot, directing employees in ways that are consistent with organizational expectations.

Second, corporate culture is the "social glue" that bonds people together and makes them feel part of the organizational experience.[34] Employees are motivated to internalize the organization's dominant culture because it fulfills their need for social identity. This is increasingly important in organizations with global and virtual workforces because culture is one of the few means to tie these people together. For example, NovaCare, Inc., has 17,000 people dispersed in 2,000 client locations across the United States. It depends on its corporate culture to keep these far-flung employees together. "Our culture is the only thing—except for our name—that connects all of these people in all of these units," explains NovaCare CEO John H. Foster.[35]

Finally, corporate culture assists the sense-making process.[36] It helps employees understand organizational events. They can get on with the task at hand rather than spend time trying to figure out what is expected of them. Employees can also communicate more efficiently and reach higher levels of cooperation with each other because they share common mental models of reality.

Organizational Culture Strength and Fit

Each of these functions of organizational culture assumes that a strong culture is better than a weak one. A *strong organizational culture* exists when most employees across all subunits hold the dominant values. The values are also institutionalized through well-established artifacts, thereby making it difficult for those values to change. Finally, strong cultures are long lasting. In many cases, they can be traced back to the beliefs and values established by the company's founder.[37] In contrast, companies have weak cultures when the dominant values are short lived, poorly communicated, and held mainly by a few people at the top of the organization.

Our discussion so far suggests that companies with strong cultures should have higher performance, but studies have found only a modestly positive relationship.[38] One reason for the weak relationship is that a strong culture increases organizational performance only when the cultural content is appropriate for the organization's environment (see Exhibit 16.2). Companies that operate in a highly competitive environment might be better served with a culture that engenders efficiency. Companies in environments that require dedicated employees will be more successful with an employee-oriented culture. When a firm's culture does not fit its environment, on the other hand,

Exhibit 16.2
Organizational culture
and performance

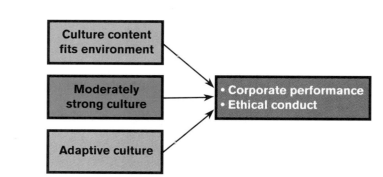

employees have difficulty anticipating and responding to the needs of customers or other dominant stakeholders.

A second concern is that a company's culture might be so strong that employees focus blindly on the mental model shaped by that culture. For example, when an organization's culture emphasizes customer service intensely, employees tend to see problems as customer service problems, even though some are really problems about efficiency or technology. Thus, strong cultures might cause decision makers to overlook or incorrectly define subtle misalignments between the organization's activities and the changing environment.[39]

Finally, very strong cultures tend to suppress dissenting subcultural values. In the long term, this prevents organizations from nurturing new cultural values that should become dominant values as the environment changes. For this reason, corporate leaders need to recognize that healthy organizations have subcultures with dissenting values that may produce dominant values in the future.

Adaptive Cultures

So far, we have explained that strong cultures are more effective when the cultural values are aligned with the organization's environment. We have also indicated that no corporate culture should be so strong that it blinds employees to alternative viewpoints or completely suppresses dissenting subcultures. Along with these points, we should add that organizations are more likely to succeed when they have an adaptive culture.[40] An **adaptive culture** focuses employees on the changing needs of customers and other stakeholders, and supports initiative and leadership to keep pace with these changes.

An adaptive culture is focused outwardly rather than inwardly. This means that senior executives are more interested in the satisfaction of customers and others than in their own well-being. The underlying mental model is that the organization will survive and succeed through continuous change. Organizations with adaptive cultures are readily identifiable by their uncanny ability to shift directions with the market. Nokia has moved from toilet paper and rubber boots to cellular telephones. Hewlett-Packard has shifted from engineering instruments to computer systems and peripherals. Monsanto has transformed from synthetic fibers and carpets to life sciences. Each of these firms has maintained an adaptive culture in which employees believe that change is a necessary and inevitable part of organizational life.

Organizational Culture and Business Ethics

Along with other forms of performance, an organization's culture can potentially influence ethical conduct.[41] Kickbacks and other forms of corruption in the International Olympic Committee (IOC) have been attributed to its organizational culture. "This culture was made possible by the closed nature of the

adaptive culture an organizational culture that focuses employees on the changing needs of customers and other stakeholders, and supports initiative and leadership to keep pace with these changes

IOC and by the absence of ethical and transparent financial controls of its operation," concluded a U.S. Senate committee. "We do not excuse or condone those from Salt Lake City who did the giving. What they did was wrong. But . . . they did not invent this culture; they joined one that was already flourishing."[42]

Fortunately, leaders can develop—with considerable effort and persistence—a culture that supports ethical conduct. Lockheed Martin provides a good example of this. The aerospace giant was created in the mid-1990s from the merger of 16 companies. Some of these firms had previously been accused of unethical conduct in government procurement contracts. When these diverse cultures were integrated, senior executives wanted to be sure that the emerging culture emphasized ethical conduct. To accomplish this, they adopted six core values that represented both the company's culture and its ethical standards: honesty, integrity, respect, trust, responsibility and citizenship.[43]

Although organizational culture can support ethical values, it can also become the source of ethical problems. As we mentioned earlier, corporate culture is a form of control because it guides employee decisions and behavior. All organizations require some control to ensure that employee actions are aligned with organizational objectives. However, a few organizations imprint their cultural values so strongly on employees that they risk becoming corporate cults that rob a person's individualism. These strong cultures may discourage dissent and, consequently, undermine constructive controversy. Thus, an organization's culture should be consistent with society's

For more than 100 years, Shiseido's corporate culture has valued beauty and knowledge. "For us, beauty is art and knowledge is science," explains Akira Gemma, president of Japan's largest cosmetics company. "It is who we are. It is our corporate culture." But after complaints in the mid-1990s about its sales methods, Shiseido is also trying to make business ethics part of its corporate culture. A new set of corporate values called "The Shiseido Code" was developed and several hundred employees have become its standard-bearers in Shiseido's 250 Japanese offices. When the ethics code was distributed, the company designated two months as "a period of reflection" during which employees were asked to reflect on all their past activities in the light of business ethics. Shiseido hopes that these practices, along with training and communication, will embed the ethics code in the company's culture.[44] What factors suggest that Shiseido might eventually be successful at creating a more ethical culture? [John Thoeming]

ethical values and the culture should not be so strong that it undermines individual freedom.

Merging Organizational Cultures

Before SmithKline merged with the British-based Beecham Group a few years ago, the Philadelphia-based drug manufacturer wanted to find out whether the corporate cultures of the two firms were sufficiently similar to make the merger succeed. A consulting firm interviewed hundreds of managers from both organizations to determine the extent to which they had compatible values and were motivated to make the merger work. During the merger, over 2,000 people from both firms were divided into more than 200 teams to figure out how to integrate their respective structures, systems, and cultures. "From the very beginning, they were learning how to work together," said Joanne Lawrence, who headed the culture change initiative.[45]

The SmithKline Beecham merger is considered a stellar example of how to decide on and implement a merger or acquisition from a corporate cultural perspective. Unfortunately, it is also the exception. Companies typically look at financial or marketing issues when deciding to merge with or acquire another firm, but few of them conduct due-diligence audits on their respective corporate cultures. Yet, attempting to merge two organizations with distinct values and beliefs could result in a cultural collision that threatens the success of an otherwise strategically compatible merger.[46] One survey reported that over two-thirds of executives in major U.S. companies identified integrating organizational cultures as the top challenge in a merger.[47]

The corporate world is littered with mergers that failed because of clashing organizational cultures. WordPerfect held over half of the word processing market when Novell, Inc. purchased it. But Novell's culture undermined WordPerfect's strengths in customer service and quick decision making. Two years later, Novell sold WordPerfect at a $1 billion loss, both suffering from the cultural conflicts of their short-lived liaison.[48]

The recent merger of NationsBank and BankAmerica is also showing signs that their cultures are different. NationsBank has an aggressive culture—the company awards a crystal hand grenade for those with peak performance and decisive action. In comparison, BankAmerica's more bureaucratic culture values discussion and contemplation before making choices. As you might expect, NationsBank people are impatient with the amount of time that their BankAmerica counterparts spend in meetings. "They have procedures to discuss procedures," grumbles one NationsBank executive.[49] As we read in Connections 16.1, similar corporate culture clashes may have occurred when British Petroleum merged with Amoco.

bicultural audit diagnosing cultural relations between companies in a potential merger and determining the extent to which cultural clashes will likely occur

Organizational leaders can minimize these cultural collisions and fulfill their duty of due diligence by conducting a bicultural audit. A **bicultural audit** diagnoses cultural relations between the companies and determines the extent to which cultural clashes will likely occur.[50] The process begins with interviews, questionnaires, focus groups, and observation of cultural artifacts to identify cultural differences between the merging companies. This includes carefully examining the artifacts of each organization—the office layout, how they bill customers, how decisions are made, how information is shared, and so on. Next, the audit data are analyzed to determine which differences between the two firms will result in conflict and which cultural values provide common ground on which to build a cultural foundation in the merged organization. The final stage of the bicultural audit involves identifying strategies and preparing action plans to bridge the two organizations' cultures.

Strategies to Merge Different Organizational Cultures

In some cases, the bicultural audit results in a decision to end merger talks because the two cultures are too different to merge effectively. For instance, in spite of its earlier merger success with Beecham, SmithKline later walked

Connections 16.1 □ **BP and Amoco Merger Creates Risk of Culture Clash**

BP's merger with Amoco resulted in a few culture clashes. Now Sir John Browne *(shown on screen)* is hoping that the acquisition of ARCO will not add further disruption. *[P. Morgan. Used with permission of Reuters.]*

Amoco and British Petroleum (BP) executives were all smiles when they announced that merging the two oil firms wouldn't result in clashing corporate cultures. "This is not going to be a difficult merger to put together in cultural terms," predicted a BP executive at the time.

But many industry experts disagreed. "The people who succeed [at BP] are people who take the initiative," said an industry consultant. In contrast, Amoco's culture rewarded those who are cautious and contemplative. "They have had a tendency to try to avoid making the huge mistakes," said another oil industry expert, "and in that sense are a bit more conservative and traditional in defining what the solutions are."

BP and Amoco called the merger "an alliance of equals," but BP's executives took most of the top positions and the new company has mostly adopted BP's culture. This deculturation of Amoco might not be so bad. Consultants believe that BP's cultural values are more compatible with the current environment. Says one consultant, "[BP] is arguably the role model for the industry in terms of creating a culture that is intensely focused on generating returns for the shareholder and demanding the level of performance from their people to achieve that."

Still, BP's aggressive style worries many people at Atlantic Richfield (ARCO), the Los Angeles–based oil company that BP acquired soon after the Amoco deal. ARCO was known for its community-minded culture, donating millions of dollars to local charities each year. It's uncertain whether that culture will remain intact for much longer. "We don't know what the new corporate culture will be or if things will change," says the head of the United Way in Los Angeles.

Sources: G. J. Wilcox, "L.A. to Lose More Than ARCO's Logo," *Daily News of Los Angeles*, April 1, 1999, p. N1; R. Gough and C. Cole, "BP, Amoco Merger Creates World's Third Largest Oil Company," *Octane Week*, August 17, 1998; J. King, "BP, Amoco Merger Marries IT Opposites," *Computerworld*, August 17, 1998, pp. 1, 76; R. Gribbon, "BP's Bumpy Path to World's Biggest Deal," *Daily Telegraph* (London), August 15, 1998, p. 27; S. L. Gaines, "Culture of Amoco, Industry May Be Forever Changed," *Chicago Tribune*, August 13, 1998, p. N1. □

away from merger talks with Glaxo Wellcome PLC because of "insurmountable differences" over management philosophy and corporate culture.[51] However, even with substantially different cultures, two companies may form a workable union if they apply the appropriate merger strategy. The four main strategies for merging different corporate cultures are assimilation, deculturation, integration, and separation (see Exhibit 16.3).[52]

Assimilation   Assimilation occurs when employees at the acquired company willingly embrace the cultural values of the acquiring organization. This tends to occur when the acquired company has a weak culture that is dysfunctional, whereas the acquiring company's culture is strong and focused on clearly defined values. Sun Microsystems has acquired many smaller organizations using this strategy. It refuses to digest larger firms because it is much more difficult to apply Sun's aggressive culture.[53] Culture clash is rare with assimilation because the acquired firm's culture is weak and employees are looking for better cultural alternatives.

Deculturation   Assimilation is rare. Employees usually resist organizational change, particularly when they include throwing away personal and cultural values. Under these conditions, some acquiring companies apply a *deculturation* strategy by imposing their culture and business practices on the acquired organization. The acquiring firm strips away artifacts and reward systems that support the old culture. People who cannot adopt the acquiring company's culture are often terminated. This recently occurred when Taylor Corp., a Minnesota-based conglomerate, acquired Current Inc., a midsized greeting card catalog retailer in Colorado Springs. For years, Current employees enjoyed a familylike culture with generous benefits and close relations with the company founders. "It was a very positive and personable type of culture," recalls a former Current executive. But soon after Taylor took over, Current employees had to reapply for their own jobs and pass a drug test. Some cherished employee benefits were also taken away.[54]

Deculturation may be necessary when the acquired firm's culture doesn't work but employees aren't convinced of this. However, this strategy rarely

Exhibit 16.3
Strategies for merging different organizational culture

Merger strategy	Description	Works best when:
Assimilation	Acquired company embraces acquiring firm's culture.	Acquired firm has a weak culture.
Deculturation	Acquiring firm imposes its culture on unwilling acquired firm.	Rarely works—may be necessary only when acquired firm's culture doesn't work but employees don't realize it.
Integration	Combining two or more cultures into a new composite culture.	Existing cultures can be improved.
Separation	Merging companies remain distinct entities with minimal exchange of culture or organizational practices.	Firms operate successfully in different businesses requiring different cultures.

Source: Based on ideas in A. R. Malekazedeh and A. Nahavandi, "Making Mergers Work by Managing Cultures," *Journal of Business Strategy*, May–June 1990, pp. 55–57.

works because it increases the risk of socioemotional conflict (see Chapter 13). Employees from the acquired firm resist the cultural intrusions from the buying firm, thereby delaying or undermining the merger process. This happened when AT&T acquired NCR Corp. After a nasty takeover battle, AT&T antagonized NCR employees by changing NCR's name to AT&T Global Information Solutions, installing AT&T executives to run the acquired firm, and generally trying to make NCR's culture become more like AT&T's. The merger strategy failed. AT&T eventually divested NCR (which returned to its original name) after piling up nearly $4 billion in losses at the cash register and computer systems company based in Dayton, Ohio.[55]

Integration A third strategy is to integrate the corporate cultures of both organizations. This involves combining two or more cultures into a new composite culture that preserves the best features of the previous cultures. Raytheon is applying an integration strategy as the defense and aerospace conglomerate develops a new culture for the half-dozen companies that recently merged or were acquired.[56] Integration is most effective when the companies have relatively weak cultures or when their cultures include several overlapping values. Integration also works best when people realize that their existing cultures are ineffective and are therefore motivated to adopt a new set of dominant values. However, integration is slow and potentially risky because there are many forces preserving the existing cultures.

Separation A separation strategy occurs where the merging companies agree to remain distinct entities with minimal exchange of culture or organizational practices. Insignia Financial Group, a South Carolina real estate firm, has applied a separation strategy to its more than 30 acquisitions over the past decade. "When we buy the companies, we leave the infrastructure in place," says Henry Horowitz, Insignia's executive managing director. "We're buying a successful company. Why would we want to disrupt something that works? And the morale becomes terrible if you start decimating."[57]

Separation is most appropriate when the two merging companies are in unrelated industries because the most appropriate cultural values tend to differ by industry. Unfortunately, few acquired firms remain independent for long because executives in the acquiring firm want to control corporate decisions. Therefore, it's not surprising that only 15 percent of acquisitions leave the purchased organization as a stand-alone unit.[58]

Changing and Strengthening Organizational Culture

Whether merging two cultures or reshaping the firm's existing values, corporate leaders need to understand how to change and strengthen the organization's dominant culture. Indeed, some organizational scholars conclude that the only way to ensure any lasting change is to realign cultural values with those changes. In other words, changes "stick" when they become "the way we do things around here."[59]

Changing organizational culture requires the change management toolkit that we learned about in Chapter 15. Corporate leaders need to make employees aware of the urgency for change. Then they need to "unfreeze" the existing culture by removing artifacts that represent that culture and "refreeze" the new culture by introducing artifacts that communicate and reinforce the new values.

Executives at Hitachi are changing their bureaucratic and inflexible corporate culture by altering artifacts that communicate and reinforce those values. The Japanese electronics manufacturer has abolished daily morning exercises because executives believe that this reinforced a group mentality at the expense of individual initiative. To encourage a more open and communicative culture, Hitachi's employees are encouraged to dress in polo shirts and other casual wear rather than in formal business attire. The company is also breaking the long tradition of calling each other by title. Instead, employees are now asked to call each other by name. "Even when employees talk to the chairman or the president, they should use their names," says a representative from the office of Hitachi's president.[60]

Strengthening Organizational Culture

Artifacts communicate and reinforce the new corporate culture, but we also need to consider ways to further strengthen that culture. Five approaches commonly cited in the literature are the actions of founders and leaders, introducing culturally consistent rewards, maintaining a stable workforce, managing the cultural network, and selecting and socializing new employees (see Exhibit 16.4).

Wayne Leonard is turning Entergy around by unraveling its button-down conservative culture that paid little attention to service. Since his arrival as CEO, Leonard has held several meetings with the New Orleans–based power company's 13,000 employees, warning them about the urgent need to change the culture. "This was a company that saw itself as being better than the people it served," Leonard warned New Orleans area workers in one meeting. Leonard encourages a more open dialogue culture by personally answering employee e-mail and wearing casual sweaters and the occasional black T-shirt. "There is a psychology to dressing," Leonard explains. "Dressing one way for work and another way for play makes you think that work isn't meant to be fun and enjoyable." Changing a company's culture is a slow process, but observers say that the new culture is already taking shape.[61] What other changes could Leonard make to encourage a more customer focused, open dialogue culture?
*[Ellis Lucia/*The Times Picayune*]*

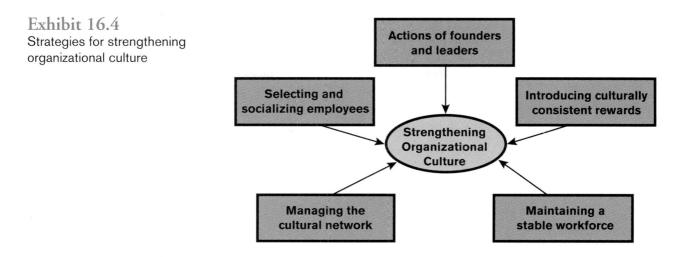

Exhibit 16.4
Strategies for strengthening organizational culture

Actions of founders and leaders   Founders establish an organization's culture.[62] In the opening story to this chapter, we saw the powerful influence of PeopleSoft, Inc., cofounder Dave Duffield. "The culture of any start-up is driven by the founder," says a PeopleSoft executive. "We are what Dave Duffield is."[63] Founders develop the systems and structures that support their personal values. Founders are often visionaries whose energetic style provides a powerful role model for others to follow. The founder's cultural imprint often remains with the organization for decades. Wal-Mart, the discount retailer, has a deeply embedded customer satisfaction value long after its founder Sam Walton passed away.

In spite of the founder's effect, subsequent leaders can break the organization away from the founder's values if they apply the transformational leadership concepts described in Chapter 14. Transformational leaders strengthen organizational culture by communicating and enacting their vision of the future.[64] Cultural values are particularly reinforced when leaders behave in ways that are consistent with the vision ("walking the talk"). James Preston did this when he became CEO of Avon. He dismantled the boys' club culture by promoting women into more senior positions and removing macho rituals (such as the annual hunting trip) that previously existed. Today, 44 percent of Avon's senior vice presidents are women.[65]

Introducing culturally consistent rewards   Reward systems strengthen corporate culture when they are consistent with cultural values.[66] Aggressive cultures might offer more performance-based individual incentives, whereas paternalistic cultures would more likely offer employee assistance programs, medical insurance, and other benefits that support employee well-being. Home Depot relies on rewards to strengthen its corporate culture. Employees at the Atlanta-based home improvement retail chain receive stock incentives which the company hopes will support a value system of customer service and entrepreneurship. "We've always wanted this to be part of our culture," explains Home Depot CEO and cofounder Arthur Blank, "that associates feel that they own the stores, that they own the merchandise, that they have total responsibility for the customers in their aisles, and that they create the value."[67]

Maintaining a stable workforce   An organization's culture is embedded in the minds of its employees. Organizational stories are rarely written down; rituals and celebrations do not usually exist in procedure manuals; organizational metaphors are not found in corporate directories. Thus, organizations depend on a stable workforce to communicate and reinforce the dominant beliefs and values. The organization's culture can literally disintegrate during periods of high turnover and precipitous downsizing because the corporate memory leaves with these employees. Corporate culture also weakens during periods of rapid expansion or mergers because it takes time for incoming employees to learn about and accept the dominant corporate values and assumptions.[68] For this reason, some organizations keep their culture intact by moderating employment growth and correcting turnover problems.

Managing the cultural network

Organization culture is learned, so an effective network of cultural transmission is necessary to strengthen the company's underlying assumptions, values, and beliefs. According to Max De Pree, CEO of furniture manufacturer Herman Miller Inc., every organization needs "tribal storytellers" to keep the organization's history and culture alive.[69] The cultural network exists through the organizational grapevine. It is also supported through frequent opportunities for interaction so that employees can share stories and reenact rituals. Senior executives must tap into the cultural network, sharing their own stories and creating new ceremonies and other opportunities to demonstrate shared meaning. Company magazines and other media can also strengthen organizational culture by communicating cultural values and beliefs more efficiently.

Selecting and socializing employees

When Terri Wolfe interviews applicants for employment at Patagonia, she is looking for more than their ability to fill the vacant positions. The human resources director of the Ventura, California, outdoor clothing company also wants to see whether their values are compatible with the company's values. "I screen for corporate culture fit," Wolfe explains.[70] Patagonia and a flock of other organizations strengthen their corporate cultures by hiring people with beliefs, values, and assumptions similar to those cultures. They realize that a good fit of personal and organizational values makes it easier for employees to adopt the corporate culture. A good person-organization fit also improves job satisfaction and organizational loyalty because new hires with values compatible to the corporate culture adjust more quickly to the organization.[71]

Job applicants are also paying more attention to corporate culture during the hiring process. According to one recent survey, job applicants ask corporate culture questions more than any other topic, aside from pay and benefits.[72] They realize that as employees, they must feel comfortable with the company's values, not just the job duties and hours of work.

Kathy Wheeler learned this important point the hard way. A few years ago, the Hewlett-Packard engineer accepted a career opportunity at Apple Computer. Apple's headquarters are only two miles away from HP, but its corporate culture is on another planet. HP's culture emphasizes collaboration, consensus, and advanced engineering technology, whereas Apple's culture applauds marketers rather than engineers, and slick user interfaces rather than advanced technology. Fourteen months later, Wheeler was back at HP. "I admire Apple to a large extent," says Wheeler. "But I wouldn't work there again because of the cultural issues."[73] The point here is that you need to look at corporate culture artifacts when deciding whether to join a particular organization. By diagnosing the company's dominant culture, you are more likely to determine whether its values are compatible with your own.

Along with selecting people with compatible values, companies maintain strong cultures through the effective socialization of new employees. **Organizational socialization** refers to the process by which individuals learn the values, expected behaviors, and social knowledge necessary to assume their roles

organizational socialization
the process by which individuals learn the values, expected behaviors, and social knowledge necessary to assume their roles in the organization

in the organization.[74] By communicating the company's dominant values, job candidates and new hires are more likely to internalize these values quickly and deeply.

We will learn more about the organizational socialization process in the next chapter (Chapter 17) on employment relations and career dynamics. At this point, you should know that socialization partially includes the process of learning about the company's culture and adopting its set of values. This process begins long before the first day of work. People learn about the organization's culture through recruiting literature, advertising, and news media reports about the company. During the recruitment process, some companies provide information about "the way things are done around here." Even if this information is not forthcoming, applicants might learn from employees, customers, and others who regularly interact with the organization.

By the first day of work, newcomers have a fairly clear (although not necessarily accurate) perception about the company's culture. These perceptions are tested against everyday experiences. To some extent, newcomers align their values with the organization to minimize conflict. Like Kathy Wheeler, however, some employees eventually leave the organization when they realize how much their personal values differ from the organization's culture.[75]

Throughout this chapter, we have learned that organizational culture is pervasive and powerful. For corporate leaders, it is either a force for change or an insurmountable barrier to it. For employees, it is either the glue that bonds people together or drives them away from the organization. So many artifacts communicate and reinforce the existing culture that it requires a monumental effort to replace the current values. Transformational leadership and effective management of change can assist in this process, but it is a challenge that no leader should take lightly.

Chapter Summary

Organizational culture is the basic pattern of shared assumptions, values, and beliefs that govern behavior within a particular organization. Assumptions are the shared mental models or theories-in-use that people rely on to guide their perceptions and behaviors. *Beliefs* represent the individual's perceptions of reality. *Values* are more stable, long-lasting beliefs about what is important. They help us define what is right or wrong, or good or bad, in the world. Culture content refers to the relative ordering of beliefs, values, and assumptions.

Organizations have subcultures as well as the dominant culture. Some subcultures enhance the dominant culture, whereas countercultures have values that oppose the organization's core values. Subcultures maintain the organization's standards of performance and ethical behavior. They are also the source of emerging values that replace aging core values.

Artifacts are the observable symbols and signs of an organization's culture. Four broad categories of artifacts include organizational stories and legends, rituals and ceremonies, language, and physical structures and sym-

bols. Understanding an organization's culture requires painstaking assessment of many artifacts because they are subtle and often ambiguous.

Organizational culture has three main functions: (1) It is a deeply embedded form of social control; (2) it is also the "social glue" that bonds people together and makes them feel part of the organizational experience; and (3) corporate culture helps employees make sense of the workplace.

Companies with strong cultures generally perform better than those with weak cultures, but only when the cultural content is appropriate for the organization's environment. Also, the culture should not be so strong that it drives out dissenting values that may form emerging values for the future. Organizations should have adaptive cultures so that employees focus on the need for change and support initiatives and leadership that keeps pace with these changes.

Organizational culture relates to business ethics in two ways. First, corporate cultures can support ethical values of society, thereby reinforcing ethical conduct.

Second, some cultures are so strong that they rob a person's individualism and discourage constructive controversy.

Mergers should include a bicultural audit to diagnose the compatibility of the organizational cultures. The four main strategies for merging different corporate cultures are integration, deculturation, assimilation, and separation.

Organizational culture is very difficult to change. However, this may be possible by creating an urgency for change and replacing artifacts that support the old culture with artifacts aligned more with the desired future culture. Organizational culture may be strengthened through the actions of founders and leaders, the introduction of culturally consistent rewards, maintenance of a stable workforce, management of the cultural network, and selection and socialization of employees.

Key Terms

Adaptive culture, p. 506
Artifacts, p. 500
Bicultural audit, p. 508
Ceremonies, p. 502
Mental models, p. 498

Organizational culture, p. 498
Organizational socialization, p. 514
Rituals, p. 502
Values, p. 498

Discussion Questions

1. Superb Consultants Inc. have submitted a proposal to analyze the cultural values of your organization. The proposal states that Superb has developed a revolutionary new survey to tap the company's true culture. The survey takes just 10 minutes to complete and accurate results can be based on a small sample of employees. Discuss the merits and limitations of this proposal.

2. Some people suggest that the most effective organizations have the strongest cultures. What do we mean by the "strength" of organizational culture? What possible problems are there with a strong organizational culture?

3. Identify four types of artifacts used to communicate organizational culture. Why are artifacts used for this purpose?

4. Acme Corp. is planning to acquire Beta Corp., which operates in a different industry. Acme's culture is entrepreneurial and fast paced, whereas Beta employees value slow, deliberate decision making by consensus. Which merger strategy would you recommend to minimize culture shock when Acme acquires Beta? Explain your answer.

5. Under what conditions is assimilation likely to occur when two companies merge? Your answer should clearly describe the assimilation strategy.

6. Explain how transformational leadership strengthens corporate culture.

CASE STUDY

Hillton's transformation

Twenty years ago, Hillton was a small city (about 70,000 residents) that served as an outer suburb to a large Midwest metropolitan area. The city government treated employees like family and gave them a great deal of autonomy in their work. Everyone in the municipal organization, including the two labor unions representing employees, agreed implicitly that the leaders and supervisors of the organization should rise through the ranks based on their experience. Few people were ever hired from the outside into middle or senior positions. The rule of employment at Hillton was to learn the job skills, maintain a reasonably good work record, and wait your turn for promotion.

Hillton has grown rapidly since the mid-1960s. As the population grew, so did the municipality's workforce to keep pace with the increasing demand for municipal services. This meant that employees were promoted fairly quickly and were almost assured guaranteed employment. Until recently, Hillton had never laid off any employee. The organization's culture could be described as one of entitlement and comfort. Neither the elected city councilors nor city manager bothered the departmental managers about their work. There were few cost controls because the rapid growth placed more emphasis on keeping up with the population expansion. The public gradually became somewhat more critical of the city's poor service, including road construction at inconvenient times and the apparent lack of respect some employees showed taxpayers.

During the expansion years, Hillton put most of its money into "outside" (also called "hard") municipal services. These included road building, utility construction and maintenance, fire and police protection, recreational facilities, and land use control. This emphasis occurred because an expanding population demanded more of these services and most of Hillton's senior officials came from the outside services group. For example, Hillton's city manager was formerly a road development engineer. The "inside" workers (e.g., taxation, community services) tended to have less seniority and their departments were given less priority.

As commuter and road systems developed, Hillton attracted more upwardly mobile professionals into the community. Some infrastructure demands continued, but the new suburban dwellers wanted more of the "soft" services, such as libraries, social activities, and community services. They also began complaining about the way the municipality was being run. The population had more than tripled between the 1960s and 1990s, and it was increasingly apparent that the organization needed more corporate planning, information systems, organization development, and cost-control systems. In various ways, residents voiced their concerns that the municipality was not providing the quality of management that they expected from a city of its size.

In 1996, a new mayor and council replaced most of the previous incumbents, mainly on the election platform of improving the municipality's management structure. The new council gave the city manager, along with two other senior managers, an early retirement buyout package. Rather than promoting from the lower ranks, the council decided to fill all three positions with qualified candidates from large municipal corporations in the region. The following year, several long-term managers left Hillton and at least half of those positions were filled by people from outside the organization.

In less than two years, Hillton had eight senior or departmental managers hired from other municipalities who played a key role in changing the organization's value system. These eight managers became known (often with negative connotations) as the "professionals." They worked closely with each other to change the way middle- and lower-level managers had operated for many years. They brought in a new computer system and emphasized cost controls where managers previously had complete autonomy. Promotions were increasingly based on merit rather than seniority.

These managers frequently announced in meetings and newsletters that municipal employees must provide superlative customer service, and that Hillton will become one of the most customer-friendly places for citizens and those who do business with the municipality. To this end, these managers were quick to support the public's increasing demand for more "soft" services, including expanded library services and recreational activities. And when population growth flattened out in the late 1990s, the city manager and other professionals gained council support to lay off a number of outside workers due to lack of demand for hard services.

One of the most significant changes was that the "outside" departments no longer held dominant positions in city management. Most of the "professional" managers had worked exclusively in administrative and related inside jobs. Two had master of business administration degrees. This led to some tension between the professional managers and the older outside managers.

Even before the layoffs, managers of outside departments resisted the changes more than others. These managers complained that their employees with the highest seniority were turned down for promotions. They argued for an increased budget and warned that infrastructure deterioration would cause liability problems. Informally, the outside managers were supported by the labor union representing outside workers. The union leaders tried to bargain for more job guarantees whereas the union representing inside workers focused more on improving wages and benefits. Leaders of the outside union made several statements in the local media that the city had "lost its heart" and that the public would suffer from the actions of the new professionals.

Discussion Questions

1. Contrast Hillton's earlier corporate culture with the emerging set of cultural values.

2. Considering the difficulty in changing organizational culture, why does Hillton's management seem to be relatively successful at this transformation?

3. Identify two other strategies that the city might consider to reinforce the new set of corporate values.

CASE STUDY

MetLife's cultural transformation

BusinessWeek

At Metropolitan Life Insurance Co. (MetLife), tradition still plays a weighty role. Just visit its ornate boardroom in New York City. The room lies deep within the fortresslike building that MetLife built a century ago. It boasts 27-foot ceilings painted with 18-karat gold, a massive mahogany fireplace, and solemn portraits of past chief executives with patrician names like Haley Fiske. Now, MetLife directors are calling upon the new CEO, Robert H. Benmosche, to turn this sleepy organization into a nimble, performance-oriented public company. He must get 41,000 employees to shake the "Mother Met" mentality and teach 10,100 agents how to sell more than whole life insurance, which is declining in popularity.

This *Business Week* case study describes MetLife's current corporate culture as well as the culture that MetLife's directors think the company needs to compete in the next millennium. Read through this *Business Week* case study at www.mhhe.com/mcshane1e and prepare for the discussion questions.

Discussion Questions

1. Describe MetLife's current corporate culture. What factors contributed to these cultural values?

2. Use the force field model of organizational change described in this chapter and in Chapter 15 to explain how Robert Benmosche should change MetLife's corporate culture.

3. This article describes some of the actions that Robert Benmosche is taking to change MetLife's culture. How do his actions fit into the transformational leadership model discussed in Chapter 14?

Source: L. N. Spiro, "Metlife's Fighter Pilot," *Business Week*, December 14, 1998, pp. 124–26. ▪

VIDEO CASE

Dog days: Companies encouraging employees to take pets to work

It's early morning in San Rafael, California and software executive Steve Wong is off for work. So is his dog, Grimmy. Why does he do it? Wong says, "When it gets a little stressful, I can take her for a long walk, and if it gets really stressful I take her for a longer walk."

Welcome to Autodesk, a San Rafael software company where doggie treats are as common as CD ROM's,

and where its not unusual to see highly paid executives sharing halls with a dog on deadline. Roughly a hundred pets are here every day. For some owners, like Steve Wong, it's workplace therapy, for others a chance to work long hours guilt free. One employee said, "You probably don't cut off as early because you want to run home and let the dog out, feed the dog, that kind of thing. You don't do that because you've got it here with you."

It's a perk that has attracted new employees and makes leaving a difficult decision. One employee remarked, "What would it be like working somewhere where you do not have that?" Another said, "I would not like it."

There are rules—no barking, no fleas, no meetings. And there's the three strikes and you're out rule. If a dog is caught relieving itself inside the building three times, then doggy has to stay home. But dogs usually behave, gathering around the water cooler, or visiting offices that are known for their treats. It also seems that pets are bringing people closer together. One woman employee noted, "I probably wouldn't have half of the visitors that I have if I didn't have the dog." And while dogs seems to dominate this company's image, even having conference rooms named after them. In the dog eat dog world of computer software there is one place where not every bark has a bite.

Discussion Questions

1. What corporate cultural values are expressed at AutoDesk?

2. Do you think the dogs in the AutoDesk workplace are cultural artifacts? Explain.

3. What role does AutoDesk's policy about allowing dogs in the workplace play in maintaining a stable work force? ■

Assessing organizational culture: A metaphor exercise

Purpose

Both parts of this exercise are designed to help you understand, assess, and interpret organizational culture using metaphors.

Part A: Assessing Your College's Culture

Instructions

A metaphor is a figure of speech that contains an implied comparison between a word or phrase that is ordinarily used for one thing but can be applied to another. Metaphors also carry a great deal of hidden meaning—they say a lot about what we think and feel about that object. Therefore, this activity asks you to use several metaphors to define the organizational culture of your college. (Alternatively, the instructor might ask students to assess another organization that most students know about.)

Step 1. The class will be divided into teams of four to six members.

Step 2. Each team will reach consensus on which words or phrases should be inserted in the blanks of the statements presented below. This information should be recorded on a flip chart or overhead transparency for class presentation. The instructor will provide 15 to 20 minutes for teams to determine which words best describe the culture of the college.

If our college were an animal, it would be a _____ because _____.

If our college were a food, it would be _____ because _____.

If our college were a place, it would be _____ because _____.

If our college were a season, it would be _____ because _____.

If our college were a television show or movie, it would be _____ because _____.

Step 3. The class will listen to each team present the metaphors that it believes symbolizes the culture. For example, a team that picks winter for a season might mean they are feeling cold or distant about the college and its people.

Step 4. The class will discuss the discussion questions for Part A below.

Discussion Questions for Part A

1. How easy was it for your group to reach consensus regarding these metaphors? What does that imply about the culture of your college?

2. How do you see these metaphors in action? In other words, what are some critical college behaviors or other artifacts that reveal the presence of your culture?

3. Think of another organization to which you belong (e.g., workplace, religious congregation). What are its dominant cultural values, how do you see them in action, and how do they affect the effectiveness of that organization?

Part B: Analyzing and Interpreting Cultural Metaphors

Purpose

Previously, you completed a metaphor exercise to describe the corporate culture of your college. That ex-

ercise gave you a taste of how to administer such a diagnostic tool and draw inferences from the results generated. This activity builds on that experience and is designed to help refine your ability to analyze such data and make suggestions for improvement.

Instructions

Five work teams (four to seven members; mixed gender in all groups) of an organization located in Cincinnati completed the metaphor exercise similar to the exercise in Part A. Their responses are shown in the table below. Working in teams, analyze the information in this table and answer these questions:

Discussion Questions for Part B

1. In your opinion, what are the dominant cultural values in this organization? Explain your answer.

2. What are the positive aspects of this type of culture?

3. What are the negative aspect of this type of culture?

4. In your opinion, what is this organization's main business? Explain your answer.

5. These groups all reported to one manager. What advice would you give to him or her about this unit?

Metaphor results of five teams in a Cincinnati organization					
Team	Animal	Food	Place	TV show	Season
1	Rabbit	Big Mac	Casino	*48 Hours* (movie)	Spring
2	Horse	Taco	Racetrack	*Miami Vice*	Spring
3	Elephant	Ribs	Circus	*Roseanne*	Summer
4	Eagle	Big Mac	Las Vegas	CNN	Spring
5	Panther	Chinese	New York	*LA Law*	Racing

Source: Adapted from D. L. Luechauer and G. M. Shulman, "Using a Metaphor Exercise to Explore the Principles of Organizational Culture," *Journal of Management Education* 22 (December 1998), pp. 736–44. Used with permission of the authors. ■

SELF-ASSESSMENT EXERCISE

Corporate culture preference scale

Purpose

This self-assessment is designed to help you to identify a corporate culture that fits most closely with your personal values and assumptions.

Instructions

Read each pair of the statements in the Corporate Culture Preference Scale and circle the statement that best describes the organization in which you would prefer to work. Then use the scoring key to calculate your results for each subscale. This exercise is completed alone so students assess themselves honestly without concern for social comparison. However, the class discussion will focus on the importance of matching job applicants to the organization's dominant values.

Corporate culture preference scale

I would prefer to work in an organization:

1a. Where employees work well together in teams.	**OR**	1b. That produces highly respected products or services.
2a. Where top management maintains a sense of order in the workplace.	**OR**	2b. That listens to customers and responds quickly to their needs.
3a. Where employees are treated fairly.	**OR**	3b. Where employees continuously search for ways to work more efficiently.
4a. Where employees adapt quickly to new work requirements.	**OR**	4b. Where corporate leaders work hard to keep employees happy.
5a. Where senior executives receive special benefits not available to other employees.	**OR**	5b. Where employees are proud when the organization achieves its performance goals.
6a. Where employees who perform the best get paid the most.	**OR**	6b. Where senior executives are respected.
7a. Where everyone gets their jobs done like clockwork.	**OR**	7b. That is on top of new innovations in the industry.
8a. Where employees receive assistance to overcome any personal problems.	**OR**	8b. Where employees abide by company rules.
9a. That is always experimenting with new ideas in the marketplace.	**OR**	9b. That expects everyone to put in 110 percent for peak performance.
10a. That quickly benefits from market opportunities.	**OR**	10b. Where employees are always kept informed of what's happening in the organization.
11a. That can respond quickly to competitive threats.	**OR**	11b. Where most decisions are made by the top executives.
12a. Where management keeps everything under control.	**OR**	12b. Where employees care for each other.

Scoring Key

In this scoring key, write in a "1" if you circled the item (indicated by number in the key) and "0" if you did not. Then add up the scores for each subscale. The maximum score for each subscale is 6 and the minimum is 0. The higher the score, the more you are likely to feel comfortable in that type of culture.

Control culture	____ + (2a)	____ + (5a)	____ + (6b)	____ + (8b)	____ + (11b)	____ = _____ (12a)
Performance culture	____ + (1b)	____ + (3b)	____ + (5b)	____ + (6a)	____ + (7a)	____ = _____ (9b)
Relationship culture	____ + (1a)	____ + (3a)	____ + (4b)	____ + (8a)	____ + (10b)	____ = _____ (12b)
Responsive culture	____ + (2b)	____ + (4a)	____ + (7b)	____ + (9a)	____ + (10a)	____ = _____ (11a)

Explanation of Subscales

These subscales may be found in many organizations, but they represent only four of the many possible organizational culture values. Also, keep in mind that none of these subscales is inherently good or bad. Each is effective in different situations.

Control culture. This culture values the role of senior executives to lead the organization. Its goal is to keep everyone aligned and under control.

Performance culture. This culture values individual and organizational performance and strives for effectiveness and efficiency.

Relationship culture. This culture values nurturing and well-being. It considers open communication, fairness, teamwork, and sharing a vital part of organizational life.

Responsive culture. This culture values its ability to keep in tune with the external environment, including being competitive and realizing new opportunities.

Employment Relationship and Career Dynamics

Learning Objectives

After reading this chapter, you should be able to:

- Discuss the two types of psychological contract.
- Identify the three levels of trust in organizational settings.
- Discuss the two primary functions of organizational socialization.
- Describe the stages of organizational socialization.
- Explain how realistic job previews and socialization agents assist the socialization process.
- Describe the main features of Holland's theory of occupational choice.
- List Driver's four career concepts.
- Identify three conditions that would encourage lateral career development.
- Explain why boundaryless careers have become more common.
- Explain why the contingent workforce is growing.
- Discuss the issues surrounding job performance of contingent workers.

Ana Witherow gave up the security of full-time employment to become a "free agent" in the contingent workforce.

[Courtesy of Ana Witherow, Capital Performance]

ary Miller has been a busy guy lately. He works three days a week as chief financial officer (CFO) for a Dallas clinical research firm, then fills the other two days as CFO at another firm. Later this year he will probably be working for two other employers.

Miller isn't a job hopper. He is one of the growing number of professionals who work as "free agents" in the contingent workforce. Miller is a partner in Tatum CFO Partners, an Atlanta-based firm that supplies financial executives to small to midsize businesses. These firms can't afford full-time CFOs on the payroll, so they are happy to hire Miller and other Tatum partners as temporary, part-time hired guns.

Ana Witherow also gave up a traditional full-time job two years ago to become a free agent. Today, she markets her expertise as an interim controller for start-up companies in the San Francisco area. Witherow typically works with two start-up firms at a time, and stays on the payroll only for about six months or until a full-time controller is hired. "I love working with different companies, meeting different people, and really making an impact," says Witherow.

Not everyone, however, is cut out for contingent work. As Gary Miller points out, it requires a new perspective of employment and security. "I would argue that you don't have security in today's job world," warns Miller. "But if you perceive security as being with one organization . . . you wouldn't fit this mold."[1]

ary Miller and Ana Witherow are part of the growing trend toward free agent careers, in which employees contract their time and competencies to different companies. These people aren't consultants who bill their clients. They work as employees for a limited time or for a few days of the week. The opening story paints a glowing picture of contingent work, but most people in this segment of the labor force would rather have permanent jobs. As we will find out in this chapter, contingent work may offer some economic benefits, but hidden costs are also revealed from the perspective of organizational behavior.

Before exploring the contingent workforce and other emerging career trends, we need to understand certain basic features of all employment relationships. This chapter begins with the most fundamental element: the psychological contract. We consider the types of contracts, how contracts change, and the importance of trust in employment relationships. Next, this chapter examines the process of employee socialization, including the stages of socialization and specific socialization strategies. We then turn to the topic of career development, including models of occupational choice and career patterns, as well as the emerging trends toward lateral and boundaryless career development. This chapter closes with a detailed look at the dynamics and implications of the contingent workforce.

The Psychological Contract

When Maggie Starley was hired as an AT&T telephone operator in 1971, she assumed the company would employ her for most of her life. After all, AT&T was a bastion of job security in an era when people could expect a reasonably long career with one firm. But times have changed. In the mid-1990s, AT&T laid off Starley and thousands of other employees during a dramatic downsizing. Although Starley now has a better-paying job with Bell Atlantic, her assumptions about employment relationships are quite different. "Don't think you've got a job locked," warns Starley, "because there's no such thing as job security anymore."[2]

psychological contract the individual's beliefs about the terms and conditions of a reciprocal exchange agreement between that person and another party

Maggie Starley and millions of other people are adjusting to a significantly different **psychological contract** between employers and employees than existed 30 years ago. The psychological contract refers to the individual's beliefs about the terms and conditions of a reciprocal exchange agreement between that person and another party.[3] The psychological contract is inherently perceptual, so one person's understanding of the contract may differ from the other party's understanding. In employment relationships, psychological contracts consist of beliefs about what the employee believes he or she is entitled to receive and is obliged to offer the employer in return. For example, Maggie Starley and other AT&T employees believed they would have job security in exchange for loyalty.[4]

Cross-Cultural Perspectives of Psychological Contracts

Although organizational behavior scholars define psychological contracts as reciprocal exchanges, this has a somewhat legalistic slant that is held more strongly in the United States than in some other cultures.[5] In some cultures, employees assume that employment is a venue for social interaction rather than an economic relationship with the employer. In other cultures, employees believe the organization must provide for them no matter what they contribute in return. In each situation, employees believe that they are owed certain conditions of work, yet their obligations to the employer are less clear.

Consider the psychological contract in Mexico, which is influenced by high power distance value as well as mutual obligations traced back to the Mexican Constitution of 1917 and the revolution during that time.[6] Mexicans tend to view a job as a social right, not just an exchange for money and labor. Companies have a strong obligation to provide "life, health, dignity and liberty," compared to the more paternalistic employment relationship assumed in some other cultures. As a high power distance culture, Mexican employees are also more receptive to the legitimate power of supervisors than employees in the United States and other low power distance countries. Overall, we must be sensitive to cultural differences in the psychological contracting process as well as interpretations and assumptions about the content of those contracts.

Types of Psychological Contracts

As Exhibit 17.1 illustrates, psychological contracts range along a continuum from transactional to relational.[7] *Transactional contracts* are primarily short-term economic exchanges. Responsibilities are well defined around a fairly narrow set of obligations that do not change over the life of the contract. People hired in temporary positions and as consultants tend to have transactional contracts. To some extent, new employees also form transactional contracts until they develop a sense of continuity with the organization.

Relational contracts, on the other hand, are rather like marriages; they are long-term attachments that encompass a broad array of subjective mutual obligations. Relational contracts are also dynamic, meaning that the parties expect that mutual obligations are not necessarily balanced in the short run. For example, employees who work overtime in transactional contracts expect appropriate payment, whereas those in relational contracts assume that the employer will eventually reciprocate in some unspecified way. Not surprisingly, organizational citizenship behaviors are more likely to prevail under relational than transactional contracts. Permanent employees are more likely to believe they have a relational contract.

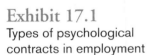

Exhibit 17.1

Types of psychological contracts in employment

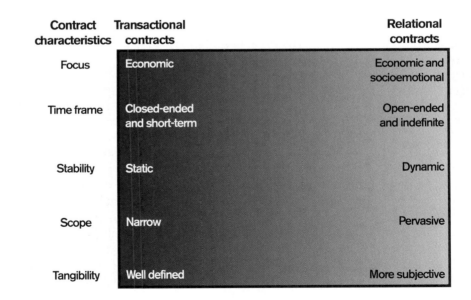

Contract characteristics	Transactional contracts	Relational contracts
Focus	Economic	Economic and socioemotional
Time frame	Closed-ended and short-term	Open-ended and indefinite
Stability	Static	Dynamic
Scope	Narrow	Pervasive
Tangibility	Well defined	More subjective

Source: Based on information in D. M. Rousseau and J. M. Parks, "The Contracts of Individuals and Organizations," *Research in Organizational Behavior* 15 (1993), pp. 1–43.

Trust and the Psychological Contract

Any relationship—including an employment relationship—depends on a certain degree of trust between the parties.[8] Recall from Chapter 7 that **trust** occurs when we have positive expectations about another party's intentions and actions toward us in risky situations. A high level of trust occurs when the other party's actions affect you in situations where you are vulnerable, but you believe they will not adversely affect your needs.

There are many trust relationships in organizations.[9] Employees learn to trust their co-workers, team leaders, subordinates, suppliers, and customers. Organizational behavior scholars also refer to *institutional trust,* which is the employee's trust in the organization's CEO and top management. Along with whom to trust, there are three types of trust, each representing a different level and form of relationship.[10]

1. *Calculus-based trust*   This minimal level of trust refers to an expected consistency of behavior based on deterrence. Each party believes that the other will deliver on its promises because punishments will be administered if they fail. For example, most of us trust our employer enough to expect a paycheck at the end of the work period because we believe the company will face government sanctions if employees don't receive payment.

2. *Knowledge-based trust*   Knowledge-based trust is grounded on the other party's predictability. This predictability develops from meaningful communication and past experience. The better you know someone's past actions, the more accurately you can predict what that person will do in the future. Similarly, the more consistent the leader's behavior—the more he or she "walks the talk"—the more employees are willing to trust that person.[11]

3. *Identification-based trust*   This third type of trust is based on mutual understanding and emotional bond between the parties. Identification occurs when one party thinks like, feels like, and responds like the other party. High-performance teams exhibit this level of trust. To some extent, employees can have a high level of identification-based trust in organizations with strong cultures. By identifying with the company's dominant values, employees understand what to expect and what is expected of them.

Calculus-based trust is the weakest of the three because it is easily broken by a violation of expectations and the subsequent application of sanctions against the violating party. It is difficult to develop a strong level of trust based on the threat of punishment if one party fails to deliver on its promises. Generally, calculus-based trust alone cannot sustain a relational type of psychological contract.

Knowledge-based trust is more stable than calculus-based trust because it is developed over time. Suppose an employer hires someone from outside the company rather than promotes from within, as it almost always did in the past. A trusting employee "knows" that this is probably an exception because it deviates from the employer's past actions. Identification-based trust is the most robust of all three. Because the individual identifies with the organization (or any other party), he or she is more likely to forgive transgressions. Moreover, we are reluctant to acknowledge a violation of this high-level trust because it strikes at the heart of our self-image.

Trust is important in the employment relationship because it affects the type of psychological contract. When employees experience psychological contract violations, they lose trust in the employer and are less likely to engage in organizational citizenship behaviors.[12] If violations continue, the loss of trust shifts the employee's psychological contract from being open and dynamic to precise and static. In other words, loss of trust moves the psychological contract from relational to transactional. As the CEO of Eastman Chemical recently warned,

Terry Akre *(right)* put in 37 years as a technician at AT&T, waking up at 5:30 A.M. each day to be on the job by 7:30 A.M. Then he was laid off without any warning. Terry's son Daniel *(left)*, who was 18 at the time, vowed never to let that happen to him. "I said then and there, I'm going to 'employ' my employers," Akre recalls. So Akre, a top-performing salesman, has worked for seven employers since graduating from college in 1987. He left on good terms with most employers. Each job hop resulted in higher pay or more challenging work.[13] How does Daniel Akre's psychological contract differ from his father's? What level of trust do you think he has with his employer compared with the trust his father had in AT&T?
[Photo: K. Wade. Used with permission of the San Francisco Chronicle.*]*

"Somehow, we have lost some of the trust that employees need to have in us to achieve greatness. We have to reearn their trust—that's the key to gaining competitive advantage."[14]

Psychological Contract Dynamics

Psychological contracts evolve over time, particularly for people in relational contracts. These changes are typically mutual accommodations to the existing contract. The parties believe the original contract is still in place and has minor additions or modifications. How much change can occur to the original contract, yet still maintain this sense of continuity? The answer depends on the flexibility of the employer and employee, which is largely determined by the degree of trust between them.[15]

Along with these minor adjustments over time, some people experience radical transformations of their psychological contract. These transformations occur when one party—usually the employer—wants to significantly change the employee's expectations regarding rewards, career development, corporate culture, or other important elements of the employment relationship. Some parts of the original contract usually remain, but other features are sufficiently different that the parties believe they are entering into a new relationship.

From security to employability

The most dramatic transition in recent years is the shift away from a psychological contract that emphasizes job security in return for loyalty. The old contract established the expectation that if you were loyal to the company, the company would be loyal to you by providing job security and managing your career development.[16] Many employees could expect lifelong career progression through the ranks with ever-increasing salaries. Although this paternalistic contract didn't exist for everyone (e.g., construction, forestry), it was considered the norm in banking and other office-related businesses.

The emerging psychological contract, called **employability,** says that employees must take responsibility for their own careers by continually developing new competencies for future work opportunities within and beyond the organization. In this "new deal," jobs are temporary events and organizations are no longer perceived as paternalistic institutions that take care of their employees. Rather, they are customers to whom employees must be able to offer valuable skills and knowledge. From this perspective, individuals must anticipate future organizational needs and develop new competencies accordingly. In other words, new challenges and learning opportunities are the currency of employability.[17]

Some firms have dramatically shattered the security-based psychological contract by making employees reapply for their own jobs. This recently occurred when Wisconsin Power & Light Co. merged with Iowa-based IES Industries and Interstate Power Co. Employees who held duplicate positions had to compete with co-workers from the other companies for those positions. Similarly, hundreds of employees at Ireland's Northern Bank were given the option of accepting a layoff package or reapplying for available jobs, including their own.[18] Other firms, such as Consumers Energy Co., have taken a gentler approach by educating employees about the shifting contractual relationship.[19]

Some people might argue that the psychological contract pendulum will swing from employability back to job security contracts again as low unemployment gives employees enough power to push for more job guarantees. Yet employability is not only a consequence of high unemployment in the early 1990s; it is also a consequence of dramatic changes in the business environment described in Chapter 15. Global competition, deregulation, and computer technologies have made it difficult for employers to provide the job security that was possible in more stable conditions. Organizations need employability to remain flexible and adaptive.

Consequences of employability

How has the trend toward employability affected employees? To some extent, it varies from one generation to the next. Baby-boomer employees tend to experience more stress as they psychologically adjust to a world without job security. They also develop a more transactional than relational contract because the shift to employability violates some fundamental assumptions and expectations about the psychological contract. "I'm a prime baby boomer," says Allen Janacek, a former marketing manager for Mobil Oil. "And I'm like so many, I grew up in an era that encouraged loyalty—stay with one employer and grow. But now suddenly somehow the rules have changed."[20]

In contrast, a few writers suggest that the rules haven't changed for Generation-X employees.[21] Few Gen-Xers have worked under a psychological contract that emphasizes job security, so they adjust more readily to

---

employability The "new deal" employment relationship in which the job is a temporary event and employees are expected to continuously learn skills that will keep them employed in a variety of work activities

employability. Indeed, younger employees say the old psychological contract would be stifling—rather like serving time—because there was less opportunity to steer one's career through personal achievement. Of course, we can't say that every Gen-Xer wants the new deal psychological contract, but it seems that they are more comfortable with the career risks and opportunities that employability offers. Even so, organizations need to clarify the psychological contract before people join the organization. As we learn next, one of the best ways to form an accurate psychological contract is through effective socialization of new employees.

Organizational Socialization

Intel Corp. approaches new employees like everything else—as a source of competitive advantage. The world's largest computer chip manufacturer sends new hires a complete package of materials about the company before they begin their first day. On Day One, recruits learn about Intel's corporate strategy and get a clear message about performance expectations. A month later, they spend an entire day learning about Intel's corporate culture. At the six-month mark, employees experience a two-hour review of how they have adjusted and how much they have learned about Intel.[22]

organizational socialization
the process by which individuals learn the values, expected behaviors, and social knowledge necessary to assume their roles in an organization

Intel and other organizations pay attention to the **organizational socialization** process so that employees adjust quickly and appropriately to their new situation. Organizational socialization is the process by which individuals learn the values, expected behaviors, and social knowledge necessary to assume their roles in the organization.[23] The effectiveness of this socialization process may increase or hinder job performance and job satisfaction, whether the recruits are unskilled and new to the work force or are highly skilled and have many years of work experience.[24] Cisco Systems discovered this when it recently surveyed new employees. As our *Fast Company Online* feature describes, the Internet network company introduced activities that significantly helped newcomers adjust to the workplace and learn the ropes more quickly.

Socialization as a Learning Process

Organizational socialization is a process of both learning and change. It is a learning process because newcomers try to make sense of the company's physical workplace, social dynamics, and strategic/cultural environment. They learn about what is expected of them, how they fit into the organization, and what they should expect to receive in return for their effort, loyalty, and job performance.[25] For example, we just noted that both Intel and Cisco Systems ensure that new employees learn about performance expectations, business objectives, and corporate cultural values. Overall, organizational behavior research has identified six content dimensions of organizational socialization (see Exhibit 17.2, p. 533):

1. *Performance proficiency* Newcomers need to learn what is required to perform the assigned work. This includes learning role perceptions of the job as well as understanding which competencies need to be mastered over time.

2. *People* Newcomers need to form successful and satisfying relationships with other people from whom they can learn the ropes.[26] These socialization agents provide reliable sources of information as well as social support to minimize the stress of the adjustment process.

3. *Politics* Newcomers need to know who holds power in the organization so that they can accomplish their work and avoid the cross-fire of organizational politics. They need to learn new behavior patterns that help them gain power and deal effectively with political tactics aimed at them.

4. *Language*   Newcomers need to learn technical jargon so that information is acquired from co-workers and communicated to them more easily. They also need to understand the shared meaning of slang and other terms that convey the organizational culture.

5. *Organizational goals and values*   Newcomers need to understand the company's espoused goals as well as its underlying cultural values and beliefs. They need to understand the unstated rules and rituals of the organization, along with the norms of the immediate work group.

FAST COMPANY
Online

◻ Cisco Gives New Employees a Fast Start

Beau Parnell, Cisco System's director of human resource development, calls a new employee's first day "the most important eight hours in the world." His personal mission, he says, is to help Cisco achieve "the fastest time to productivity for new hires in the industry."

Cisco Systems gives new employees a Fast Start by ensuring that their work space is ready and that they have a buddy who teaches them the ropes.

[Courtesy of Cisco Systems]

That requires work—and technology. Last year employee surveys at Cisco Systems showed that some new hires felt like lost baggage rather than the company's most precious asset. Their phones didn't work. They had computers but no software. They had software but no idea how to use it. Amazingly, in a company synonymous with the Internet, they weren't getting e-mail addresses for two weeks.

When the problem became known, Parnell got clearance to develop a collection of employee-orientation initiatives called Fast Start. One initiative was computer software that tracks the hiring process and alerts facilities teams just before a new recruit arrives. As a result, every new employee now starts with a fully functional work space and a full day of training in desktop tools (computers, telephones, voice mail).

But Fast Start doesn't just eliminate headaches. It opens people's eyes to life inside the company. Each new hire gets assigned a "buddy" (a peer in the company) who answers questions about how Cisco works. New employees take a two-day course called "Cisco Business Essentials," which covers company history, the networking market, and Cisco's business units. Two weeks after new hires start, their managers receive an automatically generated e-mail reminding them to review departmental initiatives and personal goals.

ONLINE CHECK-UP

1. The full text of this *Fast Company* article also describes socialization activities at Netscape Communications and MEMC Electronic Materials. How do these differ from the activities described at Cisco? Do they fulfill different objectives in the socialization process?

2. Evaluate Cisco's web site regarding information for job applicants (www.cisco.com). Is the information realistic, or does it seem to be more marketing hype that might lead to reality shock on the job? Does the site give you much information about what it is like to work at Cisco?

Get the full text of this *Fast Company* article at www.mhhe.com/mcshane1e

Source: Adapted from B. Birchard, "Hire Great People Fast," *Fast Company,* Issue 10 (July 1997), p. 132. ◼

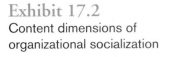

Exhibit 17.2
Content dimensions of
organizational socialization

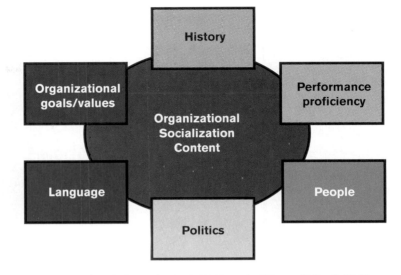

Source: Based on information in G. T. Chao, A. O'Leary-Kelly, S. Wolf,
H. J. Klein, and P. D. Gardner, "Organizational Socialization: Its Content
and Consequences," *Journal of Applied Psychology* 79 (1994), pp. 450–63.

6. *History*   Newcomers need to learn about the organization's past as well
as the stories, legends, and rituals that derive from that history. Similarly, they
need to understand the past experiences of co-workers and key decision makers, along with recent events in the organization before they arrived.

Socialization as a Change Process

Organizational socialization is also a process of change, because individuals
need to adapt to their new work environment.[27] They develop new work roles,
adopt new team norms, and practice new behaviors. To varying degrees, newcomers also acquire the values and assumptions of the organization's dominant culture as well as the local subculture. Some people quickly internalize
the company's culture; a few others rebel against these attempts to change
their mental models and values. Ideally, newcomers adopt a level of creative individualism in which they accept the essential elements of the organization's
culture and team norms, yet maintain a healthy individualism that challenges
the potentially dysfunctional elements of organizational life.

Socialization is a continuous process, beginning long before the first day of
employment and continuing throughout one's career within the company.
However, it is most intense when people cross organizational boundaries, such
as when they first join a company, move to a new department or regional
branch office, get transferred to (or back from) an international assignment, or
get promoted to a higher level in the firm. For each of these transitions, employees need to learn about and adjust to an entirely new work context as well
as learn role-specific behaviors.[28]

Stages of Socialization

The organizational socialization process can be divided into three stages: preemployment socialization, encounter, and role management (see Exhibit 17.3).
These stages parallel the individual's transition from outsider, to newcomer,
and then to insider.[29]

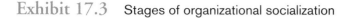

Exhibit 17.3   Stages of organizational socialization

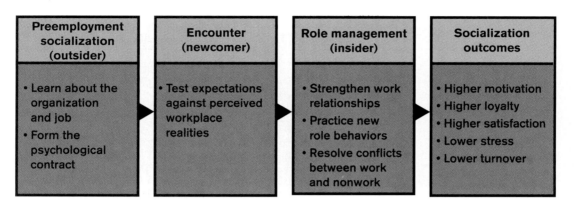

Stage 1: Preemployment Socialization

Think back to the months and weeks before you began working in a new job (or attending a new school). You actively searched for information about the company, formed expectations about working there, and felt some anticipation about fitting into that environment. The preemployment socialization stage encompasses all of the learning and adjustment that occurs prior to the first day of work in a new position.

Much of the socialization adjustment process occurs prior to the first day of work.[30] This is not an easy process, however. Individuals are outsiders, so they must rely on friends, employment interviews, recruiting literature, and other indirect information to form expectations about what it is like to work in the organization. The employer also forms a set of expectations about the job applicant, such as the unique skills and vitality that he or she will bring to the organization.

Conflicts when exchanging information   Job applicants and employers need an open exchange of accurate information during preemployment socialization to ensure that they form accurate expectations. Unfortunately, as Exhibit 17.4 illustrates, four conflicts make it difficult for both parties to send or receive accurate information.[31]

Conflict A occurs between the employer's need to attract qualified applicants and the applicant's need for complete information to make accurate employment decisions. Many firms use a "flypaper" approach by describing only positive aspects of the job and company, causing applicants to accept job offers on the basis of incomplete or false expectations.

Conflict B occurs between the applicant's need to look attractive to employers and the organization's need for complete information to make accurate selection decisions. The problem is that applicants sometimes emphasize favorable employment experiences and leave out less favorable events in their careers. This provides employers with inaccurate data, thereby distorting their expectations of the job candidate and weakening the quality of organizational selection decisions.

Conflict C occurs when applicants avoid asking important career decision questions because they convey an unfavorable image. For instance, applicants usually don't like to ask about starting salaries and promotion opportunities because it makes them sound greedy or overaggressive. Yet, unless the employer presents this information, applicants might fill in the missing

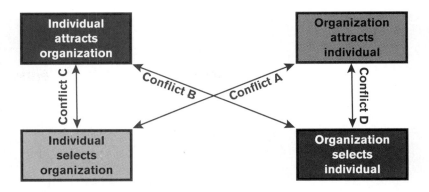

Source: L. W. Porter, E. E. Lawler III, and J. R. Hackman, *Behavior in Organizations* (New York: McGraw-Hill, 1975), p. 134. Reprinted by permission.

Exhibit 17.4
Information exchange conflicts during preemployment socialization

information with false assumptions that produce an inaccurate psychological contract.

Finally, conflict D occurs when employers avoid asking certain questions or using potentially valuable selection devices because they might put the organization in a bad light. For instance, some employers refuse to use aptitude or ability tests because they don't want to give the impression that the organization treats employees like mice running through a maze. Unfortunately, without the additional information, employers may form a less accurate opinion of the job candidate's potential as an employee.

In spite of these conflicts, job applicants do manage to discover some information about the organization. They learn from casual acquaintances with current and former employees. They receive some information from brochures, advertisements, and public news about the company. Job applicants also learn from their visits to the organization. For example, after leaving a senior marketing position at Sun Microsystems, Peter Kestenbaum arranged to interview with a start-up company in New York. When he arrived in his $1,000 suit, he found everyone was wearing sandals and shorts. There was no receptionist, so Kestenbaum had to wander through the place to find the person he was supposed to meet. But the deciding factor was the restrooms. They were so filthy that Kestenbaum was convinced that the company would not fit his style.[32]

postdecisional justification
justifying choices by unconsciously inflating the quality of the selected option and deflating the quality of the discarded options

Postdecisional justification Both employers and job applicants further distort their perceptions of the psychological contract through the process of **postdecisional justification** that was described in Chapter 11. To maintain a positive self-identity, new hires tend to subconsciously increase the importance of favorable elements of the job and justify or completely forget about some negative elements. At the same time, they reduce the quality of job offers that they turned down. Employers often distort their expectations of new hires in the same way. The result is that both parties develop higher expectations of each other than they will actually experience during the encounter stage.

Stage 2: Encounter

The first day on the job typically marks the beginning of the encounter stage of organizational socialization. During this stage, newcomers test their prior expectations with the perceived realities. Unfortunately, many employers fail this test. One survey reported that new hires in hotel administration have more

At the Irvine police headquarters, lead dispatcher Cristine Gaiennie takes an emergency call while Joshua Goldmark identifies a police cruiser nearest to the incident. It's a struggle to keep these jobs staffed because new hires experience the reality shock of working on traumatic incidents. A recently hired dispatcher at Irvine lasted one day. On average, more than one-third of 911 operators quit within their first year.
*[Don Bartlett/*Los Angeles Times]

reality shock the experience of sudden entry into a new work environment and perceived discrepancies between what the newcomer believes should occur and what actually occurs

negative than positive first day experiences, including unprofessional orientation sessions, beginning work without adequate instruction, and being assigned menial work. In some cases, new employees arrived to discover that their supervisor and co-workers had forgotten they were starting that day! Similarly, human resource executives in Australia indicate that the most common reason why recently hired employees quit is that their expectations had not been met.[33]

These findings indicate that newcomers usually experience some degree of **reality shock** when they begin the employment relationship. Reality shock refers to the experience of sudden entry into a new work environment and perceived discrepancies between what the newcomer believes should occur and what actually occurs.[34] Newcomers rarely have the benefit of gradual exposure to the new workplace. Rather, they are immediately inundated with unfamiliar signals. Reality shock is also the discovery of discrepancies between what newcomers anticipate and what they actually experience. The larger the gap, the more the employee believes that his or her psychological contract has been violated. Reality shock is a specific application of discrepancy theory (described in Chapter 7) in which the perceived reality falls significantly short of the newcomer's preemployment expectations. Reality shock might occur on the first day of work, or it may be more subtle, such as the newcomer's eventual realization that the company's emphasis on profits over safety are at odds with his or her own values.

Reality shock sometimes occurs because the employer is unable to live up to its promises. However, reality shock just as often results from the problems of the preemployment socialization stage described earlier. New hires inadvertently develop an inaccurate psychological contract due to information exchange conflicts, and they further distort their beliefs about the new work situation through the process of postdecisional justification. Whatever the cause, reality shock can be stressful, particularly for new hires who have made a significant investment or sacrifice to join the organization (such as moving to another city or turning down other potentially good jobs). Reality shock impedes the socialization process because the newcomer's energy is directed toward managing the stress rather than learning and accepting organizational knowledge and roles.[35]

Stage 3: Role Management

During the role management stage in the socialization process, employees settle in as they make the transition from newcomers to insiders. They strengthen relationships with co-workers and supervisors, practice new role behaviors, and adopt attitudes and values consistent with their new position and organization.

Role management also involves resolving the conflicts between work and nonwork activities. In particular, employees must redistribute their time and energy between work and family, reschedule recreational activities, and deal with changing perceptions and values in the context of other life roles. They must address any discrepancies between their existing values and those emphasized by the organizational culture. New self-identities are formed that are more compatible with the work environment.

Managing the Socialization Process

Organizational socialization has a profound effect on individual performance, organizational commitment, and turnover, so companies should consider various ways to guide this process. Two important strategies are providing realistic job previews and effectively engaging socialization agents.

Realistic Job Previews

Many companies use a flypaper approach to recruiting: They exaggerate positive features of the job and neglect to mention the undesirable elements in the hope that the best applicants will get "stuck" on the organization. In reality, as was described earlier, this strategy tends to produce a distorted psychological contract that eventually leads to lower trust and higher turnover.[36]

realistic job previews (RJPs) giving job applicants a realistic balance of positive and negative information about the job and work context

Rather than selling the job with distorted information, companies should provide **realistic job previews (RJPs)**—giving job applicants a realistic balance of positive and negative information about the job and work context.[37] For example, one public transit company shows job applicants a video depicting angry riders, knife attacks, and other abuses that bus drivers must endure on their routes. Applicants then meet with a union representative who explains, among other things, that new drivers are typically assigned night shifts and the poorest routes. Finally, applicants are given the opportunity to drive a bus.

Although RJPs scare away some applicants, they tend to reduce turnover and increase job performance because RJPs help applicants develop more accurate preemployment expectations that minimize reality shock.[38] RJPs represent a type of vaccination by preparing employees for the more challenging and troublesome aspects of work life. Moreover, applicants self-select themselves when given realistic information. For example, applicants who don't like working with people tend to withdraw their job application when the RJP reveals how frequently they interact with customers. There is also some evidence that RJPs increase organizational loyalty. A possible explanation for this is that companies providing candid information are easier to trust. They also show respect for the psychological contract and concern for employee welfare.[39]

Socialization Agents

Organizations also improve the socialization process by effectively involving supervisors, co-workers, and other socialization agents.[40] Newcomers tend to ask supervisors for technical information as well as performance feedback and information about job duties. Supervisors also improve the socialization process by giving newcomers reasonably challenging first assignments, buffering them from excessive demands, and helping them form social ties with co-workers.[41]

Co-workers are important socialization agents because they are easily accessible, can answer questions when problems arise, and serve as role models for appropriate behavior. Consequently, Cisco Systems, Ametek, Sun Microsystems, and other firms rely on a "buddy system" whereby newcomers are assigned to a co-worker for sources of information and social support. Generally, new employees tend to receive this information and support when co-workers integrate them into the work team. Co-workers also aid the socialization process by being flexible and tolerant in their interactions with these new hires.

Newcomers who quickly form social relations with co-workers tend to have a less traumatic socialization experience and are less likely to quit their jobs within the first year of employment.[42] However, co-workers sometimes engage in hazing—the practice of fooling or intimidating newcomers as a practical joke or initiation ritual. Connections 17.1 describes how employees at a McDonald's restaurant haze new employees by asking them to look for "steam mix." This initiation seems innocent enough and certainly provides

Team member Bob Ragard *(right)* helps Scott Whitney, a new Ametek Aerospace employee, assemble a surface mount at the company's plant in Binghamton, New York. The manufacturer of aerospace parts relies on Ragard and his co-workers to serve as socialization agents in a formal "buddy" system. Sun Microsystems Inc. also recognizes that co-workers are potentially valuable socialization agents. Buddy co-workers are called "SunVisors" and are expected to help newcomers learn the ropes and adjust to their new work environment.[43] Although co-workers provide timely information and support, what problems can occur when organizations rely heavily on these socialization agents? *[Beth Kaplan,* Binghamton Press & Sun-Bulletin*]*

entertainment for other staff members, but it can further stress new hires and interfere with their need to form social bonds with co-workers.

Organizational socialization is a continuous process as employees make adjustments through different jobs and organizations. As we learn in the next section, we must also view careers as dynamic and multiorganizational processes in this rapidly changing environment.

Organizational Careers

If changing jobs is one of life's greatest stresses, then someone forgot to tell Marcy Keenan. A year ago, the high-technology marketer was a regional sales manager at start-up Internet company @Home. Keenan's salary doubled when she moved to a better job at Netscape Communications. Now, she is taking a position as director of sales at software start-up Kana Communications. The

Connections 17.1 ▪ Separating the Steam from the Haze

"We need more steam mix for our hamburger buns," a veteran employee calls out to the new hire at a McDonald's restaurant. "Get another package of mix, please."

For the newly hired McDonald's employee, this is just another task to learn in the confusing world of fast-food restaurants. For seasoned employees, it is a ritual for newcomers that usually brings hilarity to the otherwise serious work-oriented setting.

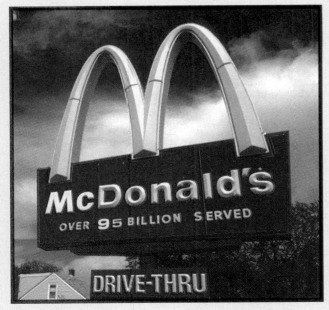

[John Thoeming]

Some new employees get the joke immediately, but most scurry to the food storage area in search of the elusive package of steam mix. They check among the stacks of hamburger buns and in the freezer around the boxes of french fries for any package that says "steam mix" on it. After 5 or 10 minutes, the discouraged recruits return empty-handed and ask for further directions.

Sometimes, if it isn't too busy, co-workers might say: "It's the big bag clearly marked 'Steam Mix'—the one with the picture of a kettle on it." Occasionally, the hazing might go one step further. With a straight face, an employee might reply, "Oh, that's right. We're out of steam mix. Here, take this bucket and go next door to Wendy's Hamburgers. We often borrow some of their mix."

Eager to please their fellow employees, newcomers jaunt across the parking lot with a McDonald's bucket in hand and politely ask a Wendy's employee for some of their steam mix. A few Wendy's staff members have learned to play along with the game by telling the visitor that their steam mix is different than what McDonald's uses. More often, the new McDonald's worker is politely reminded that steam comes from boiled water and doesn't require any other ingredients.

Across the parking lot, co-workers watch the embarrassed (and occasionally angry) newcomer return with the empty McDonald's bucket. Somehow, the hazing ritual never loses its appeal, maybe because it provides a welcome break from the work. We haven't heard of anyone quitting over the experience, although most newcomers are cautious whenever co-workers ask them to retrieve anything from the storage area.

Source: Based on information provided to Steven L. McShane by a student who survived this hazing ritual and watched many others experience it. ▪

latest jump involves a 30 percent pay cut, but gives her a boatload of stock options.[44]

career a sequence of work-related experiences that people participate in over the span of their working lives

Marcy Keenan may be your above-average job hopper, but her career pattern is becoming more the norm than the exception. A **career** is not simply moving up a career ladder within one organization. It is a sequence of work-related experiences that people participate in over the span of their working lives.[45] A person's career might include moving across the organization (i.e., laterally) or temporarily moving down the hierarchy to acquire new skills. Increasingly, Marcy Keenan and other people are extending their careers across organizational boundaries.[46]

Effective career development improves employee satisfaction and self-esteem, minimizes stress, and strengthens the employee's psychological and physical health. Effective career development benefits organizations because employees adapt more quickly to changing organizational needs.[47] In this section, we explore the prominent career development concepts, starting with Holland's model of occupational choice and following through to the emerging trends in lateral and boundaryless career paths.

Holland's Theory of Occupational Choice

After completing law school, Glenn Miller launched his career as an administrative legal assistant to a New Jersey Superior Court judge. He then took a position with a small law firm. About six months into his second job, Miller realized that he hated law. However, he was fascinated with advertising and felt that he had the talent and interest to enter this entirely different line of work. Soon after, Miller made the dramatic career jump from lawyer to junior copy editor at a prominent New York advertising agency.[48]

Glenn Miller and many other people have discovered that a career is not just about matching your skills with a job. It is a complex alignment of personality, values, and competencies with the requirements of work and conditions of the work environment. Miller may have become a talented lawyer, but his personality and values were mismatched with that line of work. He wanted more creative tasks in a less structured environment.

John Holland, a career development scholar, was an early proponent of the notion that career success depends on the degree of fit between the person and his or her work environment.[49] Specifically, Holland's theory of occupational choice states that the degree of congruence between an individual's personality traits and the work environment has a significant effect on the person's performance, satisfaction, and length of time in that career. Moreover, a person's occupational choice is an expression of his or her personality.[50] Thus, we would expect that medical doctors have similar traits and interests, which differ from the traits and interests of, say, marketing analysts. With similar personality characteristics, people in a particular occupational group will respond in similar ways to problems and situations.

Holland's six types

Holland's theory contends that six types or "themes" represent characteristics of both the work environment and the personality traits and interests of people working in those environments. These six categories include realistic, investigative, artistic, social, enterprising, and conventional. Exhibit 17.5 defines these types of people and work environments, along with sample occupations representing those environments.

Before trying to categorize your occupational preference, you should be aware that few people fall squarely into only one type. Instead, Holland refers to a person's degree of *differentiation;* that is, the extent to which the individual

Exhibit 17.5   Holland's six types of personality and work environment

Holland type	Personality traits	Work environment characteristics	Sample occupations
Realistic	Practical, shy, materialistic, stable	Work with hands, machines, or tools; focus on tangible results	Assembly worker; dry cleaner, mechanical engineer
Investigative	Analytic, introverted, reserved, curious, precise, independent	Work involves discovering, collecting, and analyzing; solving problems	Biologist, dentist, systems analyst
Artistic	Creative, impulsive, idealistic, intuitive, emotional	Work involves creation of new products or ideas, typically in an unstructured setting	Journalist, architect, advertising executive
Social	Sociable, outgoing, conscientious, need for affiliation	Work involves serving or helping others; working in teams	Social worker, nurse, teacher, counselor
Enterprising	Confident, assertive, energetic, need for power	Work involves leading others; achieving goals through others in a results-oriented setting	Salesperson, stockbroker, politician
Conventional	Dependable, disciplined, orderly, practical, efficient	Work involves systematic manipulation of data or information	Accountant, banker, administrator

Sources: Based on information in D. H. Montross, Z. B. Leibowitz, and C. J. Shinkman, *Real People, Real Jobs* (Palo Alto, CA: Davies-Black, 1995); J. H. Greenhaus, *Career Management* (Chicago: Dryden, 1987).

fits into one or several types. A highly differentiated person is aligned with a single category, whereas most people relate to two or more categories.

Since most people have more than one career type, Holland developed a hexagonal model that helps people determine the consistency of their personality with the career model (see Exhibit 17.6). *Consistency* refers to the extent that a person is aligned with similar rather than dissimilar types. Similar types are adjacent to each other in the hexagon, whereas dissimilar types are opposite. For instance, individuals with enterprising personalities are more similar to social people than to investigative people. Those who mainly fit into the enterprising category but also relate to the social type are considered consistent, whereas enterprising people who also relate to the investigative type are inconsistent.

"Big Five" personality dimensions most personality traits are represented by five abstract personality dimensions: conscientiousness, emotional stability, openness to experience, agreeableness, and extroversion

Practical implications of Holland's theory   There is ongoing debate regarding how well Holland's model represents reality.[51] Holland's personality types represent only the **"Big Five" personality dimensions** of openness and extroversion (see Chapter 6). This begs the question of whether Holland's types are incomplete because the other three personality dimensions are not represented. Also, research has reported that Holland's model should look more like a skewed polygon than a hexagon. In other words, some opposing categories are less opposite than others. Aside from these concerns, research using

Exhibit 17.6
Holland's hexagon model

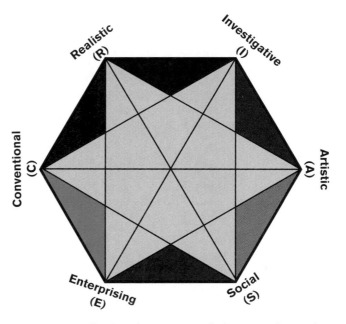

Source: J. L. Holland, *Making Vocational Choices: A Theory of Vocational Personalities and Work Environments,* 2nd ed. (Englewood Cliffs, NJ: Prentice Hall, 1985).

Holland's concepts has found that job stress is related to a lack of congruence between personality and work environment.[52]

Holland's model of occupational choice has laid the foundation for many career development activities in use today. If you take a vocational interest test, there is a good chance that the results are presented around Holland's six dimensions. The idea that an individual's personality should be congruent with the work environment is now well established in research and practice. Holland's hexagonal model (Exhibit 17.6) helps to identify the degree of congruence between an individual's dominant personality type and his or her work environment. Someone who fits mostly into the realistic category would, of course, be most congruent with a realistic environment. The adjacent environments (conventional and investigative) would offer the next best degree of congruence. The lowest congruence occurs for realistic people working in a social environment. Overall, Holland's theory emphasizes the point that effective career development involves finding a good "fit" between the individual's personality and the work environment.

Driver's Career Concepts

Holland's theory views career success in terms of congruence. Another view, developed by organizational behavior scholar Michael Driver, is that careers develop various patterns over time, and these patterns influence the individual's need fulfillment. Driver developed a conceptual framework that identifies four career concepts, each representing a distinct pattern of career activity over time. Most people have careers that combine two or possibly three of these patterns, but each career concept provides a benchmark for comparison.[53]

The *linear career concept* is the traditional view that career success is measured by the amount of movement up the corporate ladder. It equates upward movement with increasing responsibility and authority. The linear career concept has been the dominant view of career success in the United States, but other career concepts are gaining acceptance. The *expert career concept* identifies the best career as one involving a lifelong commitment to some occupational field or specialty. This pattern is well established among professors, medical experts, and other professionals. The *spiral career concept* advocates changing occupations or specialties every 7 to 10 years. Ideally, the person shifts from one area into an allied area (e.g., from engineering to product development) so that the individual builds on previous experience rather than throws it away. Last, Driver identifies the *transitory career concept* in which the individual has a consistently inconsistent career pattern. The person views his or her career as a smorgasbord of work experiences rather than a set of strategic steps of progression.

Driver's career concept model contributes to our understanding of career development by pointing out that career patterns influence the type of need fulfillment the career will offer. The linear career concept fulfills the need for power and status. The expert pattern suits those who emphasize expertise and security. Those who value personal growth may prefer the spiral pattern, and those who want independence and novelty would be fulfilled through the transitory career concept. The implication is that none of the four patterns is universally better than the others. The appropriateness of each pattern depends on the individual's needs and motives.

Driver's career concept model is also useful because it represents some emerging trends in career development.[54] While most career theories assume a certain degree of career stability or predictability (notably the linear and expert patterns), Driver's model recognizes that less traditional patterns also exist. These less traditional patterns have become more common in today's rapidly changing environment. As the next section explains, the spiral career concept has become popular as organizations emphasize lateral career development.

Lateral Career Development

lateral career development
the view that career success occurs when employees fulfill their personal needs in different jobs across the organization rather than by moving through the organizational hierarchy

The traditional career path up the corporate ladder is not as common as it once was. Instead, many firms now define career success in terms of **lateral career development** rather than how many steps employees have taken up the corporate hierarchy.[55] The idea behind lateral career development is that people can fulfill their personal needs in different jobs across the organization. Employees must think about their careers as a "lattice" rather than a ladder. They must also redefine career success in terms of the variety of challenging work assignments a person completes across the few organizational levels that still remain.

One reason for lateral career development is that many organizations have transformed their tall hierarchies into flattened team-based structures. Employees tend to move to different projects across the organization rather than to higher management levels. Hewlett-Packard (HP) encourages lateral career development for this reason. For example, John Toppel is currently an HP global account sales manager, but he previously opened and managed HP's sales offices in Hong Kong and Switzerland, and managed an HP manufacturing plant in Mexico. "Nobody gets pigeonholed here," says Toppel. Sally Dudley, who has held 14 varied positions at HP, agrees: "Those who have spent most of their careers at HP—and most of us have—don't identify with doing the same thing," says the 24-year HP veteran.[56]

A second reason for the increasing emphasis on lateral career development is that it is consistent with the shift from job status to competency-based rewards. Promotions through the traditional corporate ladder tend to reinforce job status, whereas lateral career development helps people learn new competencies and remain competitive in the labor market. This is also aligned with the trend toward employability rather than job security. Employees must anticipate future demand for skills and knowledge, and manage their careers accordingly by seeking out work opportunities that develop those competencies.

Consider Glaxo Wellcome in the United Kingdom, Volkswagen in Germany, IBM in the United States, and Michelin Tires in France. Each of these firms has developed fewer and wider pay grades to reflect the fewer promotional opportunities in the organization (see Chapter 4).[57] These companies now advise employees to broaden their knowledge and experience through lateral career paths. The result is a more flexible workforce with multiple skills.

A third reason why organizations encourage lateral career development is because much of the existing career ladder is filled with baby boomers who aren't going anywhere.[58] Lateral career development helps employees to fulfill their personal needs in different jobs across the organization when promotional opportunities are limited. As Connections 17.2 describes, this is the main reason why Mitsui Group, Japan's largest trading company, introduced lateral career development. Notice how lateral career development at Mitsui Group does more than just improve career satisfaction. It also improves knowledge management and minimizes potential conflict among divisions.

Encouraging lateral career development   Many people have difficulty adjusting to lateral career development. Baby boomers, in particular, have learned to praise the linear career concept in which career success is defined

Connections 17.2   ■ **Lateral Career Development at Japan's Mitsui Group**

When Naohiko Kumagai became CEO of Mitsui Group a few years ago, the firm's 12,000 employees were specialized within one of 76 independent divisions. Young people at Japan's largest trading company were frustrated by the lack of career development opportunities.

"When I became president, most management positions were filled," explains Kumagai, "and because of the age of our workforce, few were opening up. It's easy to imagine the thoughts racing through the minds of today's young employee—namely, the near impossibility of climbing the corporate ladder in the years ahead."

Kumagai took two dramatic steps to improve career opportunities. First, he aggressively encouraged early retirement so that some upward career mobility could occur. This was widely criticized because it broke the lifetime employment condition that is found in most large Japanese firms. Second, he introduced a lateral career development program so employees would feel more satisfied with their career success.

The lateral career development strategy involves rotating employees across divisions—a dramatic action in a company where employees rarely moved outside their specialized divisional knowledge. The program applies to all employees, not just managers, who have at least six years employment with Mitsui.

Kumagai believes the lateral career development program gives employees new perspectives and allows them to share ideas with co-workers throughout Mitsui Group's wide network of business units. "We want to expand our employees' concept of what it means to work for our company, and to expose them to different operations," he says.

Source: Adapted from C. M. Farkas and P. De Backer, *Maximum Leadership* (New York: Henry Holt, 1996), pp. 185–90. ■

in terms of how high you go up the corporate hierarchy. It is frustrating for them to shift to a spiral pattern in which career success occurs laterally through different projects and skill areas. Employees are also reluctant to engage in lateral career development because it involves the risk of leaving their long-time jobs and departments. Moreover, they may face interference from supervisors who don't want to see their prized staff move elsewhere.

To encourage lateral career development, companies need to regularly communicate new job openings and help employees with career self-assessments. For instance, Apple Computer offers its employees a comprehensive career resource library, networking group meetings to learn about other areas of the company, and computer-based job postings.[59] Employees also need to work out a self-development orientation toward careers. Raychem does this by offering career seminars that encourage employees to think of themselves as self-employed and to explore many career options. The Menlo Park, California, electronics company has a career development center where employees explore their potential through self-assessments, career workshops, and referrals to career resources. Employees compare their current competencies with current and future market demands.[60]

Boundaryless Careers

Forty years ago in his best-selling book *Organization Man*, William H. Whyte painted a picture of American white-collar career success in terms of secure employment with slow, steady promotions through several professional and management layers. These people devoted their entire lives to the same company, slowly working their way up the corporate ladder.[61] Some people still follow this structured model of career development, but most do not. Instead, there is a growing trend toward the **boundaryless career**—the idea that careers operate across company and industry boundaries rather than within a single organizational hierarchy.[62] It is the view that careers unfold throughout one's life, not necessarily throughout one company.

boundaryless career the idea that careers operate across company and industry boundaries rather than just within a single organizational hierarchy

Marcy Keenan, mentioned at the beginning of this section on careers, and many other high-tech employees in California's Silicon Valley advance their careers by job-hopping rather than waiting for the next great challenge with their current employer. In Silicon Valley's hyperpaced high-tech firms, one of every four employees switches jobs each year. This is 60 percent more job-hopping than 10 years ago and is currently twice the national average. Some observers note that many high-tech workers have embraced the boundaryless career to such an extent that they think they work for one large organization called "Silicon Valley."[63]

Reasons why people adopt boundaryless careers Boundaryless careers are more common today than 10 years ago, but this does not imply that employees enjoy changing jobs. On the contrary, by a two-to-one margin, high-tech job-hoppers would rather stay with one employer for 20 years than have 5 jobs for 4 years each.[64] This suggests that the boundaryless career is more a function of necessity than motivation. The trend toward boundaryless careers accelerated with massive corporate downsizing over the past decade.[65] These layoffs and early retirements forced people to realign their careers with other organizations. From this painful experience, many people developed the attitude that it is better to accept career opportunities as they come along rather than remain loyal to one employer.

A related explanation for the rise in boundaryless careers is that many psychological contracts have shifted from job security to employability. As we mentioned earlier in this chapter, the "new deal" rewards people who take control of their own career development.[66] But moving away from a loyalty-based contract also weakens the internal labor market. Thus, employees are more likely to seek career development opportunities outside the organization. And while job-hopping was once a liability, recruiters are now developing a more favorable attitude toward this type of career path. "There was a point when jumping around was viewed more negatively than it is today," said Phyllis Bruner, director of regional recruitment at American Express in Phoenix. "It's not uncommon today to see lots of job changes."[67]

Some industries are adjusting to boundaryless careers by forming alliances that encourage employees to move around the industry. The San Francisco Hotels Partnership Project is one example. This alliance of twelve first-class hotels and two labor unions gives people the opportunity to develop their career across hotels within the alliance without the risks associated with job-hopping. The agreement benefits employers by developing a more flexible workforce while keeping this valuable talent within the alliance.[68] For employees who lack industry alliances, a variation of boundaryless careers is to join the contingent workforce, which we discuss next.

Contingent Workforce

The world's largest employer isn't General Motors or IBM. It's Manpower Inc., a temporary services agency that provides contingent workers in almost any occupation a company would want. Manpower annually provides 2 million temps to over 250,000 employers around the globe.[69] Manpower is riding the trend toward a contingent workforce. **Contingent work** is any job in which the individual does not have an explicit or implicit contract for long-term employment, or one in which the minimum hours of work can vary in a nonsystematic way.[70]

contingent work any job in which the individual does not have an explicit or implicit contract for long-term employment, or one in which the minimum hours of work can vary in a nonsystematic way

Some contingent workers are hired directly by an organization for a fixed time. Others are hired or retained by an employment agency and work for a client organization on a day-to-day basis. Contingent workers also include self-employed people who contract their services directly with an organization. Most definitions of contingent workers exclude people in permanent part-time employment because their employment is stable and long term. However, it would include part-timers who are mainly "on call" because their work hours can vary considerably from one month to the next.

How many people are in the contingent workforce? No one agrees on the answer. The U.S. Bureau of Labor Statistics estimates that six million people—about five percent of the labor force—are in "alternative work arrangements."[71] However, this excludes on-call part-time staff and leased employees (those who work in one organization but are employed by another), and may underestimate the number of temporary and subcontracted workers. Other studies estimate that contingent workers represent up to one-quarter of the U.S. workforce. The correct number is probably somewhere in between. However, we do know that temporary workers are the fastest growing segment of the nonpermanent workforce. Today 91 percent of U.S. companies use some form of temporary help. This trend is growing even more quickly in Europe, where labor laws make it difficult to lay off or fire permanent employees.[72]

Why Contingent Work Is Growing

The main reason for the growing contingent workforce is that it provides companies with greater numerical and skill flexibility.[73] It is easier to increase or decrease the size of the workforce through contingent work contracts than by hiring and firing permanent employees. For instance, United HealthCare hires up to 1,000 on-call staff during peak periods at its phone centers in San

Antonio, Texas; Chesapeake, Virginia; and West Chester, Pennsylvania. "It's a very good way for us to staff the spikes in our business," says a United Health-Care executive.[74]

With respect to skill flexibility, organizations respond faster to market demands by temporarily contracting skilled people than by retraining current staff in the new skills. This is particularly important in dynamic environments where skill requirements may shift suddenly. Free agents bring to the organization valuable knowledge that is immediately applied and shared with others. This knowledge can also have a catalytic effect on the knowledge-creation process because permanent employees learn the foundations for further knowledge acquisition.[75]

Organizations also have increased their reliance on contingent workers to reduce costs.[76] Temporary, on-call, and contract workers typically receive fewer employer-paid benefits. Many contract employees receive lower wages than permanent staff while stationed side-by-side performing the same work.

When Big Sky Bread Co. recently outsourced its 15 employees, it reduced its administrative workload and gave the leased staff more benefits. Douglas Ryer, co-owner and manager of the Longwood, Florida, company, claims that by leasing employees, he reduced insurance premiums and employees were able to receive health benefits that his small business could not afford. "It has cut our insurance premiums drastically," says Ryer, shown here wrapping loaves along with lease-employee June Morton. "So the cost of employee leasing about equals the savings. And we can offer our employees benefits that a major corporation would."[77] In spite of these mutual benefits, what problems might Big Sky Bread Co. experience with this contingent workforce? [*Dennis Wall*/The Orlando Sentinel]

Small employers sometimes reduce their costs by leasing their former employees. Employees are outsourced to a large professional employment organization (employee-lease agency) which can offer more benefits at a lower cost than a small business would receive. The small business owner also reduces administrative costs.

Contingent work is also increasing because technology has made it easier for people in some professions to contract out their services without worrying about commuting or travel. In other words, people who are confident in their technical skills are more willing and able to enter self-employment through telecommuting. Some writers speculate that information technology will produce a new regime of electronically connected free-lancers—called e-lancers—who join together into temporary organizations. This is not as bizarre as it seems. As we will learn in Chapter 18, we already see examples of these "virtual organizations," each relying on a contract workforce.[78]

Types of Contingent Workers

Contingent workers generally fall into three camps (see Exhibit 17.7). The largest group, representing approximately two-thirds of all contingent workers, are those who want permanent employment but have not been able to secure such a position.[79] These "temporary temporaries" have been the primary focus of media attention. Many have been laid off or contracted out and cannot regain permanent employment. Some have outdated skills; others are young people who lack work experience. These people accept contract work to meet basic economic needs, gain work experience, and find leads to more permanent employment.

Gary Miller and Ana Witherow, described in the opening story to this chapter, are part of a smaller but growing cadre of professional contingent workers known as "free agents." Free agents are less interested in permanent employment and possess valued competencies that make them confident in their independence. They recognize that their career success depends on maintaining up-to-date knowledge and skills rather than a paternalistic employment

Exhibit 17.7
Types of contingent workers

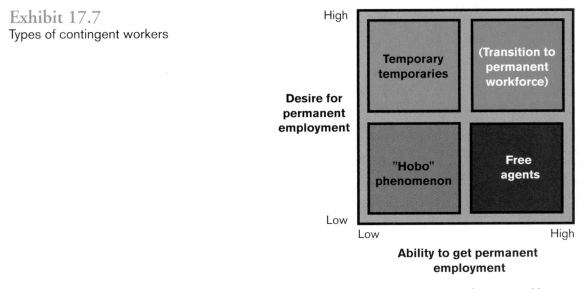

Note: Those who want permanent employment and have high demand skills tend to leave the contingent workforce quickly, so they are defined in parentheses.

relationship.[80] Free agents are typically found in technical fields, such as accounting or information systems management. These professional contingents have not completely rejected organizational life. Many eventually return to permanent employment to avoid the nuisance of continuously marketing themselves. However, they have sufficient expert power in the labor market to make this choice of permanent employment, whereas most contingent workers lack the skills and expertise.

Finally, some people in the contingent workforce lack both the motivation and ability to obtain permanent employment. These people would be responsible for the "hobo phenomenon" described in Chapter 2. They are unwilling or unable to abide by the confined work schedules and organizational control systems of permanent employment. They lack the skills or experience to command much power over work opportunities. However, work opportunities beyond basic needs are not important to them because they reject the idea that long-term employment is a sign of career success.[81]

Contingent Workforce Concerns

Although contingent work seems to provide certain economic benefits to organizations, these calculations usually ignore the organizational behavior side of the equation.[82] One concern is that contingent workers tend to have a transactional psychological contract.[83] This creates a static relationship whereby people are less willing to perform beyond the strict performance guidelines. Contingent workers also tend to feel more stress because of uncertainty about future employment opportunities. Marcus Courtney, who has been a contract worker for Microsoft Corp. and Adobe Systems, explains: "I was constantly looking for another job, and every day when I came to work, I wondered if my assignment was going to end."[84]

Another concern is that both contingent and permanent employees may feel tension and inequity when they work side by side.[85] Contingent workers experience underreward inequity when they perform similar duties, yet receive significantly lower compensation, benefits, and job security than permanent workers. At the same time, permanent staff may experience feelings of overreward inequity, which weakens their psychological attachment to the organization. One company excluded its temporary workers from the "employee of the month" awards even though some of them had been working there longer than the award winners. Many of the permanent staff recognized this inequity and viewed the company less favorably.

Job performance of contingent workers Job performance is one of the major concerns with a contingent workforce. Typically, temporary employees are less familiar with procedures and the organization's culture. Kellogg's, the cereal company, discovered this when it contracted out maintenance staff at its Botany plant in Australia. "It took contract electricians and fitters six months, on a steep learning curve, to come up to full competence," admits a Kellogg's executive.[86]

Contingent workers also tend to have less training and work experience, which has led to lower quality and higher accident rates.[87] For example, the primary cause of the 1996 ValuJet crash in the Florida Everglades was that unskilled contract workers had mislabeled dangerous cargo. Other firms have experienced increased property loss after hiring contingent workers. For instance, one university replaced its security department with a contracted security firm, but fired the firm just three months later. The institution discovered that several employees at the contracted firm were stealing from the offices they were supposed to protect!

Against these criticisms are arguments that contingent workers may be more productive than permanent employees under certain conditions. Many professionals are contracted precisely because they have better skills and experience than permanent employees. To increase their probability of future contract or permanent employment, some contingent workers may also be highly motivated to perform the job well. This particularly applies to professionals because their "reputational capital" affects future contract opportunities. Although professionals may have low commitment to the contracting organization, they typically have a strong sense of loyalty and obligation to the standards of their profession.

Adjusting to a Contingent Workforce

How can organizations minimize the organizational problems with contingent workers? To begin with, permanent employees will feel more secure in their employment relationship if the company carefully explains the use of contingent workers and how it affects permanent staff. Feelings of inequity are reduced by giving contingent workers the same respect and treatment as permanent staff.[88] Where possible, they should receive similar pay and prorated benefits. If this isn't possible, then it may be better to staff an entire work activity with either temps or core staff, not both. This reduces feelings of inequity because the two groups are less likely to compare with each other.

Careful selection of temporary employees is another way to minimize problems, particularly with high turnover and risk of theft. For example, one recent study of temporary service workers at a theme park reported that those with a high work ethic had higher organizational commitment and were less likely to quit before their contract ended.[89] Overall, the contingent workforce has become another element in career dynamics and employment relationships. Organizational behavior scholars will continue to explore the ramifications of this shifting workforce on the psychological contract and organizational outcomes.

Whether you are part of the contingent workforce or a permanent employee with one organization for most of your life, you should keep in mind that career dynamics have changed dramatically as organizations adapt to today's rapidly changing business environment. The psychological contract has definitely shifted toward employability, so career self-management is essential for long-term career success. You need to anticipate opportunities and develop new skills accordingly. But before jumping into a new job or work project, you must also keep in mind that your success is partly determined by how well you can match your personality and personal needs to jobs that fit those characteristics.

Chapter Summary

The psychological contract is a set of perceived mutual obligations about the employer's and employee's exchange relationship. Contracts vary in terms of whether the exchange relationship is mainly transactional or relational. Many organizations are replacing the "job-for-life" psychological contract with a "new deal" based on employability.

Trust is an important factor in the employment relationship. There are three levels of trust: calculus-based, knowledge-based, and identification-based. Knowledge-based and identification-based trust are stronger and more flexible than calculus-based trust.

Organizational socialization is the process by which individuals learn the values, expected behaviors, and social knowledge necessary to assume their roles in the organization. It is a learning process because newcomers need to acquire information about performance proficiency, people, politics, language, organizational goals and values, and history. Socialization is also a process of change as newcomers develop new work roles, adopt new team norms, and practice new behaviors.

Employees typically pass through three socialization stages. Preemployment socialization occurs before the first day and includes conflicts between the organization's and applicant's need to collect information and attract the other party. Encounter begins on the first day and typically involves adjusting to reality shock. Role management involves resolving work-nonwork conflicts and settling in the workplace.

To manage the socialization process, organizations should introduce realistic job previews (RJPs) and recognize the value of socialization agents in the process. RJPs give job applicants a realistic balance of positive and negative information about the job and work context. Socialization agents provide information and social support during the socialization process.

A career is a sequence of work-related experiences in which people participate over the span of their working lives. Holland's theory of occupational choice states that the degree of congruence between an individual's personality traits and the work environment affects career performance, satisfaction, and longevity. Holland's theory includes six personality types and work environments: realistic, investigative, artistic, social, enterprising, and conventional. Individuals are differentiated if they fit mainly in one of these categories and they are consistent if they relate to adjacent rather than opposite types.

Driver's theory includes four career concepts: linear, expert, spiral, and transitory. The theory states that careers develop various patterns over time, and these patterns influence the individual's need fulfillment.

Companies are encouraging lateral career development, rather than the traditional climb up the corporate ladder. This is because there are fewer steps on the corporate ladder, baby boomers block upward mobility of employees farther down the hierarchy, and the traditional ladder reinforces job status.

Boundaryless careers operate across company and industry boundaries. They are becoming more common due to corporate downsizing and the shift from job security to employability contracts.

Contingent work is any job in which the individual does not have an explicit or implicit contract for long-term employment or one in which the minimum hours of work can vary in a nonsystematic way. Contingent work is growing because companies want more flexibility and lower payroll costs, and many are outsourcing noncore work activities.

There are several concerns about contingent work, including the shift toward transactional contracts, the risk of inequity feelings, and lower training and experience. However, contingent workers may be more productive if they are motivated to work toward permanent employment or maintain their reputational capital.

Key Terms

"Big Five" personality dimensions, p. 541
Boundaryless career, p. 545
Career, p. 540
Contingent work, p. 546
Employability, p. 530
Lateral career development, p. 543

Organizational socialization, p. 531
Postdecisional justification, p. 535
Psychological contract, p. 526
Realistic job previews (RJPs), p. 537
Reality shock, p. 536
Trust, p. 528

Discussion Questions

1. Jack Santoni works on the field production crew at Gusher Drilling Co. When he joined the company five years ago, the supervisor who hired him said Jack could use the company's old pickup truck on weekends. Now the company plans to sell the truck and won't replace it, leaving Jack without a vehicle on the weekends. Discuss the implications of this action on Jack's psychological contract with Gusher Drilling.

2. Many organizations are moving toward a psychological contract based on employability. What does this mean, and how does it differ from the psychological contract in which most employees believed a few decades ago? Do you think this employability contract will continue, or revert to a security-based contract in the future?

3. Organizational socialization is a process of learning and change. What does this mean, and how do organizations facilitate both for new employees?

4. After three months on the job, you feel that the company has violated the psychological contract. The job is not as exciting as you originally expected, and your current boss is no better than the supervisor in your previous job. The people who interviewed you are concerned about your feelings, but say that they didn't misrepresent either the job or the fact that some supervisors are not as good as others here. Explain how your perceived psychological contract may have been distorted during preemployment socialization.

5. Cisco Systems, Ametek, and other companies rely on a "buddy" system to socialize new employees. What are the advantages of relying on this type of socialization agent? What problems can you foresee (or have you personally experienced) with co-worker socialization practices?

6. You have just completed a vocational test which concludes that you have an enterprising personality along with fairly high levels of the artistic and investigative type in Holland's model. Assuming that this vocational test is accurate, what are its implications for your career?

7. Although companies encourage lateral career development, many baby-boomer employees still prefer the opportunity to climb the corporate ladder. Do you think that these employees are correct in thinking that "real" career development occurs only when you are promoted? Will Generation-X employees develop a similar attachment to promotions later in their career?

8. WestCrude, a major oil company, has just decided that its core competency is in exploring and drilling for oil deposits, and that it will outsource most of its support services such as human resources and information systems. This will result in a large contingent workforce in these functions. What issues should WestCrude consider before moving to a contingent workforce?

CASE STUDY

Quantor Corp.'s contingent workforce

Quantor Corp., a large manufacturer of computer printers and other peripherals, established a task force three years ago to determine the most appropriate use of contingent workers throughout the company. The company had started to rely on contract, part-time, and temporary help agencies to fill temporary jobs. At the time, this represented less than 1 percent of Quantor's workforce, and the company wanted to review these practices to ensure consistency and effectiveness.

After reviewing current ad hoc practices, the task force concluded that Quantor needed contingent workers when demand for the company's products expanded rapidly or a new product was launched. Quantor needed this workforce flexibility because of uncertain production demand beyond the short term. At the same time, the task force warned that treating contingent workers the same as permanent employees would undermine the benefits of flexibility, create false hopes of permanent employment among contingent workers, and possibly create feelings of inequity between the two groups. Thus, policies were introduced to treat contingent workers differently from permanent employees.

Quantor's task force established two contingent worker categories: on-call and on-contract. On-call people are employed by Quantor as part-time staff. They work a full day, but only up to two-thirds of the days of a full-time permanent employee. Their managers can alter their work schedules at will to suit production demands. On-contract people are employed full-time by Quantor for a fixed period, usually six months. Their contract may be renewed up to three times for a maximum employment of two years.

On-call and on-contract employees received no employee benefits other than the government-mandated minimum vacation and holiday pay. Benefits therefore represented approximately 10 percent of their total pay, compared to nearly 40 percent for permanent employees. However, contingent workers earned the midpoint of the pay grade for their job group, which was 15 percent above the entry rate. This rate was paid even when the contingent worker lacked experience in the job.

Quantor's Contingent Workforce Problems

Three years after Quantor's task force recommendations, the contingent workforce policy was in trouble. Current practices succeeded in creating a more flexible workforce, and there was some evidence that using contingent workers increased profitability. However, these practices created unanticipated problems that became apparent as the percentage of contingent workers increased.

One problem was that few people wanted only contract employment. Most were seeking full-time permanent work and were using their contingent position as a stepping-stone to those jobs at Quantor. The result was that many contract workers remained for the entire two-year maximum period and beyond. The company was reluctant to apply the task force's recommendation of not renewing contracts beyond two years because of the perceived arbitrariness of this action as well as the loss of knowledge to the organization. Several contract staff members asked the company for an employee-paid benefit package (benefits are mainly employer-paid for permanent employees). However, Quantor rejected this because it would add further permanence to the contract workers' employment relationship.

Quantor's managers also began to complain about the company policy that contingent workers could not be offered permanent employment. They appreciated the opportunity to select permanent employees based on observations of their performance in on-contract or on-call

positions. Quantor's task force had warned against this practice because it might create inequities and raise false expectations about the likelihood of permanent employment. Managers acknowledged this risk, but the inability to permanently hire good contract staff was frustrating to them.

The third problem was that Quantor's treatment of contingent workers was incompatible with its organizational culture. Quantor had a strong culture based on the philosophy of employee well-being. The company had a generous benefits package, supportive leadership, and a belief system that made employees a top priority in corporate decisions. The company did not treat contingent workers in a way that was consistent with this philosophy. Yet if Quantor treated contingent workers the same as permanent staff members, then flexibility would be lost. For example, managers would continue renewing contract workers even when their employment was not essential, and would be reluctant to schedule on-call people at awkward times.

Quantor's team orientation was also incompatible with its use of contingent workers. Permanent staff members frequently gathered to discuss organizational and group decisions. Contingent workers were not invited to these team activities because they might be working at Quantor for only a few more months. This barrier created some awkward moments for managers as contingent workers continued working while permanent employees went to meetings and team sessions.

As these problems intensified, senior management formed another task force to reexamine Quantor's contingent workforce policy. The company needed contingent workers, but it was increasingly apparent that the current practices were not working.

Discussion Questions

1. Identify the problems that Quantor experienced with its contingent workforce practices. Also identify other possible contingent workforce problems that have not been explicitly mentioned in this case.

2. Discuss the problems with contingent workers at Quantor in terms of the psychological contract and organizational commitment.

3. What alternative strategies might allow Quantor to include a contingent workforce with fewer problems? ■

The corporate samurai are getting less loyal

BusinessWeek

Fumitako Konno is prime material for Japan's corporate world. Young and ambitious, Konno has the credentials from Keio University that companies from Sony to Mitsui prefer when hiring junior executives. But Konno doesn't think a lifetime job at some Japanese company will give him the thorough grounding in management that he craves. So he's joining Andersen Consulting. And he cheerfully anticipates working for several different firms, both Japanese and foreign, in the decades to come.

Bit by bit, Japan's well-known psychological contract of lifetime employment is changing. Employees are leading the change by focusing on their careers and skills, not on staying put at one company. After years of rebuffs, headhunters are finally getting their calls returned. Companies are also shifting the contract by talking about rewarding workers based on their contributions, not just seniority. This *Business Week* case study describes how employment relationships in Japan are slowly changing. Read through this *Business Week* article at www.mhhe.com/mcshane1e and prepare for the discussion questions below.

Discussion Questions

1. Compare and contrast the traditional psychological contract in large Japanese firms with the emerging contract.

2. What evidence suggests that the psychological contract is changing in Japan?

3. What factors have contributed to changes in Japan's psychological contract?

Source: M. Tanikawa, "The Corporate Samurai Are Getting Less Loyal," *Business Week*, March 16, 1998. ■

VIDEO CASE

The changing workplace: Freelance copywriter Lorraine Duffy Merkl

The number of temporary workers in America has soared by more than 400 percent in the last two decades. The majority are women. Temporary workers fill many job categories and they've become a permanent fixture in the workforce. Lorraine Duffy Merkl, a freelance copywriter, is a temporary employee. Merkl reflected on her work life, "My husband and I always said when we had a family that I would be a stay at home mom and, luckily, the kind of job I have allows me to stay at home and be a mom, and to make my own schedule. I like that. I like the fact that I can just really concentrate on my work even though I don't actually work on the premises. I don't see it as isolating at all because I'm not home alone, I'm home with my child. I could even be working more, but then that defeats the purpose of me staying home to be with my son. If I'm gonna be with people all day, I'd rather be with him all day than anyone else."

Merkl continued, "I like the diversity of the type of jobs that I get. It's very different than when you work on staff. When you work on staff you're kind of at the mercy of the agency, whatever business they have and they tell you to work on. The way I work now is I have a long list of companies that I want to work for and I go to them. And it's great because if they give me work, then I'm working for a company on an assignment that I really like, and if they don't I just move on to the next. I also work with a temporary staffing agency and they have opened doors for me with companies that I would never have thought to go to."

Sara Horowitz, executive director of the nonprofit organization for temporary workers, called Working Today, said, "The temp agencies have grown astronomically. People do all different kinds of work. There are emergency room doctors, lawyers, as well as clerical workers. It just ranges across the economic spectrum."

There is a legal distinction between a temporary employee and an independent contractor. Temporary workers generally have more legal protection than an independent contractor, as Horowitz noted, "An independent contractor is somebody who comes in and does a specific project, is more like a business person, and is really not covered by any of the labor laws in this country. A temp is an employee of the agency, and the agency then supposedly provides those kinds of protections. But it is very hard when you are a temp because you go from assignment to assignment. So, if there is a problem, you typically leave rather than seek a legal remedy."

So what does an organization do to fill these gaps for people? Horowitz said, "It's really interesting. What we've found is that there's a two-tiered workforce. The first tier are the people who are working at full time jobs that come with benefits and legal protections. The second tier tends to be people who are temping—independent contractors, freelancers, consultants. They don't have the benefits, typically. They are really the new kind of workforce and it's the fastest growing segment. And Working Today supports this new kind of workforce. We do two things. One is we realize that people like Lorraine Merkl are really going out in the market and buying things themselves. We do group purchases for things like office supplies and we have a national health insurance plan."

Some of the potential pitfalls of temporary employment include lack of benefits and lack of job security. Horowitz added, "It's also very hard to predict where your earnings are going to be in two years. When you get a regular paycheck you know how you're going to pay your mortgage or your kids' college payment or your rent. Lorraine has to go out there and make sure she gets those jobs. There is also poor legal protection and not feeling like you're part of a team if you're not going into the same office every day. But there certainly is flexibility. Lorraine enjoys that. No office politics and the ability to follow your dreams."

Despite its lifestyle benefits, temporary work isn't for everyone. Merkl noted, "I think you have to be motivated and you can't be shy because you have to be able to call people up and ask for work and follow up. I look for a job every single day. You just can't sit back and say I have five people who consistently give me work because one of those people could quit and go some place else or they could decide to hire somebody full time. So, I always have to keep making new contacts."

Discussion Questions

1. How has the rise of temporary work affected the psychological contract in the American workplace? What type of psychological contract does the temporary worker have with employers?

2. Explain how temporary workers affect an organization's socialization process.

3. Explain the temporary worker's career from the perspective of Driver's four career concepts. ◼

TEAM EXERCISE 17.1

Organizational socialization diagnostic exercise

Purpose

To help students understand the socialization strategies that organizations should use for new employees, and to learn about the impediments to forming an accurate psychological contract.

Instructions

The instructor will form teams (typically four or five people). Each team will follow these steps:

Step 1: Each team member will describe one particularly memorable positive or negative experience encountered when entering an organization. (Students with limited organizational experience may describe entry to school.) Entry to the organization would include any interaction with the company up to, including, and a short while after the first day of work. The incident might describe how the individual was greeted during the first day of work, how the company kept him or her informed before the first day of work, how the company did (or didn't) tell the person about negative aspects of the work or job context, and so forth. The team will consider all of these experiences, but will pick the most interesting one for description in class.

Step 2: Based on these experiences, the team will develop a list of strategies that companies should use to improve the organizational entry process. Some experiences will reflect effective management of this process. Other experiences will indicate what companies have done ineffectively, so the team must identify strategies to avoid those problems.

Step 3: In class, one person from each team will describe his or her organizational entry experience. (This person is chosen in Step 1.) The team will explain what the company did well or poorly with respect to that incident. After each team has presented one anecdote, the class will discuss other ideas from the team discussion. ◻

TEAM EXERCISE 17.2

Truth in advertising

Purpose

This team activity is designed to help you to diagnose the degree to which recruitment advertisements and brochures provide realistic previews of the job and/or organization.

Instructions

The instructor will place students into teams and give them copies of recruiting brochures and/or advertisements. The instructor might assign one lengthy brochure; alternatively, several newspaper advertisements may be assigned. All teams should receive the same materials so that everyone is familiar with the items and will be able to compare results. Teams will evaluate the recruiting material(s) and answer the following questions for each item:

1. What information in the text of this brochure/advertisement identifies conditions or activities in this organization or job that some applicants may not like?
2. If there are photographs or images or people at work, do they show only positive conditions? Do any show conditions or events that some applicants may not like?
3. After reading this item, would you say that it provides a realistic preview of the job and/or organization? ◻

SELF-ASSESSMENT EXERCISE

Matching Holland's career types

Purpose

This self-assessment is designed to help you to understand Holland's career types.

Instructions

Holland's theory identifies six different types of environments and occupations in which people work. Few jobs fit purely in one category, but all have a dominant type. Your task is to circle the letter representing the Holland type that you believe best fits each of the occupations listed below. A brief description of each work environment is described below. When finished, the instructor will provide the correct answers. Add up the number of occupations that you matched correctly to determine your score.

Descriptions of Holland's Six Work Environments

R Realistic—Work with hands, machines, or tools; focus on tangible results.

I Investigative—Work involves discovering, collecting, and analyzing; solving problems.

A Artistic—Work involves creation of new products or ideas, typically in an unstructured setting.

S Social—Work involves serving or helping others; working in teams.

E Enterprising—Work involves leading others; achieving goals through others in a results-oriented setting.

C Conventional—Work involves systematic manipulation of data or information.

Interpreting Your Score

Number correct	Interpretation
26–30	Excellent understanding of Holland's career types
21–25	Good understanding of Holland's career types
16–20	Fair understanding of Holland's career types
11–15	Need to look more closely at Holland's descriptions
Less than 11	Career counseling might not be your calling!

	Holland category					
Occupation	Realistic	Investigative	Artistic	Social	Enterprising	Conventional
Actuary	R	I	A	S	E	C
Archeologist	R	I	A	S	E	C
Buyer	R	I	A	S	E	C
Computer operator	R	I	A	S	E	C
Corporate executive	R	I	A	S	E	C
Corporate trainer	R	I	A	S	E	C
Dietitian	R	I	A	S	E	C
Economist	R	I	A	S	E	C
Elementary school teacher	R	I	A	S	E	C
Fashion model	R	I	A	S	E	C
Fire fighter	R	I	A	S	E	C
Foreign exchange trader	R	I	A	S	E	C
Jeweler	R	I	A	S	E	C
Life insurance agent	R	I	A	S	E	C
Lobbyist	R	I	A	S	E	C
Mathematics teacher	R	I	A	S	E	C
Medical illustrator	R	I	A	S	E	C
Minister/priest/rabbi	R	I	A	S	E	C
Pediatrician	R	I	A	S	E	C
Pharmacist	R	I	A	S	E	C
Pilot	R	I	A	S	E	C
Production manager	R	I	A	S	E	C
Professional athlete	R	I	A	S	E	C
Public relations director	R	I	A	S	E	C
Recreation leader	R	I	A	S	E	C
School administrator	R	I	A	S	E	C
Sculptor	R	I	A	S	E	C
Tax auditor	R	I	A	S	E	C
Veterinarian	R	I	A	S	E	C
Wine maker	R	I	A	S	E	C ■

CHAPTER
EIGHTEEN

Organizational Structure and Design

Learning Objectives

After reading this chapter, you should be able to:

- Describe the two fundamental requirements of organizational structures.
- Explain why firms can have flatter structures than previously believed.
- Discuss the dynamics of centralization and formalization as organizations get larger.
- Contrast functional structures with divisional structures.
- Outline the features and advantages of the matrix structure.
- Describe four features of team-based organizational structures.
- Discuss the merits of the network structure.
- Summarize three contingencies of organizational design.
- Explain how organizational strategy relates to organizational structure.

The writing was on the wall for Chiat/Day's 35 employees in London, England. The Los Angeles-based advertising company had been acquired by a larger firm, which planned to lay off most of the people at Chiat/Day's London office. But the entire London office rebelled before the transition took place. They held a retreat to design their concept of the ideal organization. Then the London employees negotiated a deal that would let them apply that ideal model to their newly formed advertising agency, called St. Luke's.

Named after the patron saint of creativity, St. Luke's is fashioned after a medieval guild. All of the original employees (and most of the 100 people now employed there) are company owners and receive equal shares each year. A five-member board elected by employees governs the agency. Other committees monitor finances, resources (including salaries), and quality control.

St. Luke's has a very flat, team-based organizational structure. There aren't any bosses or corporate layers—only apprentices and practitioners. "We wanted to do something radical," explains David Abraham, one of St. Luke's founders. "Many ad agencies have a very hierarchical structure and exist only to benefit shareholders that you never meet or owners with little direct involvement, so we created a corporate structure to match our ideals."

The converted toffee factory in London where St. Luke's makes its headquarters doesn't have any offices. The main work spaces are client rooms with visual themes to support creative thinking. For example, employees responsible for the Clarks shoe account meet in the Clarks room, which looks and smells like a shoe store.

It hasn't been easy for some employees to adjust to St. Luke's unique organizational structure. "Working without a formal structure presents pressures—ambiguity is stressful," explains Abraham. Still, Britain's most unusual ad agency has become its most successful. In its first three years of operation, St. Luke's attracted Coca-Cola, IKEA, Clarks Shoes, and other major clients, and was recently named ad agency of the year in the United Kingdom.[1]

British advertising agency St. Luke's has become a model of a team-based organization with minimal hierarchy or formalization.

[JJonathan Player/NYT Pictures]

organizational structure
the division of labor as well as
the patterns of coordination,
communication, work flow, and
formal power that direct
organizational activities

organizational design the
creation and modification of
organizational structures

here is something of a revolution occurring in how organizations are structured. Driven by global competition and facilitated by computer-based information technology, St. Luke's and many other companies are throwing out the old organizational charts and experimenting with new designs that will hopefully improve coordination, sharing knowledge, and employee focus on critical objectives. **Organizational structure** refers to the division of labor as well as the patterns of coordination, communication, work flow, and formal power that direct organizational activities.[2] An organizational structure reflects its culture and power relationships.[3] Our knowledge of this subject provides the tools to engage in **organizational design;** that is, to create and modify organizational structures.

We begin this chapter by considering the two fundamental processes in organizational structure: division of labor and coordination. This is followed by a detailed investigation of the four main elements of organizational structure: span of control, centralization, formalization, and departmentalization. The latter part of this chapter examines the contingencies of organizational design, including organizational size, technology, external environment, and strategy.

Division of Labor and Coordination

All organizational structures include two fundamental requirements: the division of labor into distinct tasks and the coordination of that labor so employees are able to accomplish common goals.[4] Recall from Chapter 1 that organizations are groups of people who work interdependently toward some purpose.[5] To efficiently accomplish their goals, these goals typically divide the work into manageable chunks, particularly when there are many different tasks to perform. They also introduce various coordinating mechanisms to ensure that everyone is working effectively toward the same objectives.

Division of Labor

job specialization the result
of division of labor in which
each job now includes a
narrow subset of the tasks
required to complete the
product or service

Division of labor refers to the subdivision of work into separate jobs assigned to different people. As we learned in Chapter 4, subdivided work leads to **job specialization,** because each job now includes a narrow subset of the tasks necessary to complete the product or service. Launching a space shuttle at NASA, for example, requires tens of thousands of specific tasks that are divided among thousands of people. Tasks are also divided vertically, such as having supervisors coordinate work while employees perform the work.

Work is divided into specialized jobs because it potentially increases work efficiency.[6] Job incumbents can master their tasks quickly because work cycles are very short. Less time is wasted changing from one task to another. Training costs are reduced because employees require fewer physical and mental skills to accomplish the assigned work. Finally, job specialization makes it easier to match people with specific aptitudes or skills to the jobs for which they are best suited.

Coordinating Work Activities

As soon as people divide work among themselves, coordinating mechanisms are needed to ensure that everyone works in concert.[7] Every organization, from the two-person corner convenience store to the largest corporate entity, uses one or more of the following coordinating mechanisms: informal communication, formal hierarchy, and standardization (see Exhibit 18.1).

Exhibit 18.1
Coordinating mechanisms in organizations

Form of coordination	Description	Subtypes
Informal communication	Sharing information on interdependent tasks; forming common mental models to synchronize work activities	• Direct communication • Liaison roles • Integrator roles
Formal hierarchy	Assigning legitimate power to individuals, who then use this power to direct work processes and allocate resources	• Direct supervision • Corporate structure
Standardization	Creating routine patterns of behavior or output	• Standardized skills • Standardized processes • Standardized output

Source: Based on information in D. A. Nadler and M. L. Tushman, *Competing by Design: The Power of Organizational Architecture* (New York: Oxford University Press, 1997), chap. 6; H. Mintzberg, *The Structuring of Organizations* (Englewood Cliffs, NJ: Prentice Hall, 1979), chap. 1; J. Galbraith, *Designing Complex Organizations* (Reading, MA: Addison-Wesley, 1973), pp. 8–19.

Coordination through informal communication   Informal communication is a coordinating mechanism in all organizations.[8] This includes sharing information on interdependent tasks as well as forming common mental models so that employees can synchronize work activities using the same mental road map.[9] Informal communication permits considerable flexibility because employees transmit a large volume of information through face-to-face communication and other media-rich channels (see Chapter 8). Consequently, informal communication is a vital coordinating mechanism in nonroutine and ambiguous situations.

Coordination through informal communication is easiest in small firms and work units where employees face few communication barriers. Emerging electronic communication technologies have expanded the ability of this coordinating mechanism to operate in large organizations, even where employees are scattered around the globe. Larger organizations can also encourage coordination through informal communication by forming temporary cross-functional teams and moving team members into a common physical area (called *co-locating*). **Concurrent engineering** teams, which we discussed in Chapter 10, are usually more successful than traditional product development processes because employees from different work areas are co-located and thereby coordinate their work through informal communication.

Larger organizations also encourage coordination through informal communication by assigning *liaison roles* to employees, who are expected to communicate and share information with co-workers in other work units. Where coordination is required among several work units, companies create *integrator roles*. These people are responsible for coordinating a work process by encouraging employees in each work unit to share information and informally coordinate work activities. Integrators do not have authority over the people involved in that process, so they must rely on persuasion and commitment. Brand managers at Procter & Gamble coordinate work between marketing,

concurrent engineering the integration and concurrent development of a product or service and its associated processes, usually guided by a cross-functional team

W. L. Gore & Associates Inc. avoids hierarchies and formal supervision. Instead, the maker of Gore-Tex and other high-tech fabrics encourages informal communication by limiting the size of each facility to about 200 people and ensuring that each unit is self-sufficient. The company also avoids job titles so its 6,500 employees can communicate openly with anyone else. "People sometimes get concerned and worried that there is no structure and no organization, and I don't think that is true at all," says Arthur Chase, a senior Gore associate. He explains that project leaders serve as integrators by coordinating the work of various individuals and work units.[10] If Gore coordinates mainly through informal communications, would this coordinating mechanism work well at a General Motors assembly plant?

[W. L. Gore and Associates, Inc.]

production, and design groups. Project leaders at Gore, Technicon, and other companies also serve as integrators by encouraging people from various work units to work together on the project.

Coordination through formal hierarchy

Informal communication is the most flexible form of coordination, but it can be time-consuming. Consequently, as organizations grow, they develop a second coordinating mechanism in the shape of a formal hierarchy. Hierarchy assigns legitimate power to individuals, who then use this power to direct work processes and allocate resources (see Chapter 12). In other words, work is coordinated through direct supervision.

Any organization with a formal structure coordinates work to some extent through the formal hierarchy. For instance, team leaders at Microsoft coordinate work by ensuring that employees in their group remain on schedule and that their respective tasks are compatible with tasks completed by others in the group. The team leader has direct authority to reassign people to different work activities and to resolve conflicts by dictating solutions. The formal hierarchy also coordinates work among executives through the division of organizational activities. If the organization is divided into geographic areas, the structure gives the regional group leaders legitimate power over executives responsible for production, customer service, and other activities in those areas. If the organization is divided into product groups, then the heads of those groups have the right to coordinate work across regions.

The formal hierarchy has traditionally been applauded as the optimal coordinating mechanism for large organizations. Henri Fayol, a French industrialist who wrote in the early 1900s on the subject, argued that organizations are most effective where managers exercise their authority and employees receive orders from only one supervisor. Coordination should occur through the chain of command; that is, up the hierarchy and across to the other work unit.[11] This approach to coordination is practiced at the British conglomerate Rentokil Initial. With eight levels of management and a strict chain of command, Rentokil operates like a military organization. "I don't encourage people to pick up the phone directly to me because that is attempting to bypass their boss," warns Rentokil CEO Sir Clive Thompson.[12]

Coordination through formal hierarchy may have been possible with classic organizational theorists, but it is often a very inefficient coordinating mechanism. As we shall learn later in this chapter, there are limits to how many employees a supervisor can coordinate. Furthermore, the chain of command is rarely as fast or accurate as direct communication between employees. And, as recent scholars have warned, today's educated and individualistic workforce is less tolerant of rigid structures and legitimate power.[13]

Coordination through standardization Standardization—creating routine patterns of behavior or output—is the third means of coordination. Many organizations standardize work activities through job descriptions and procedures. This coordinates work requiring routine and simple tasks, but not in complex and ambiguous situations. In these situations, companies might coordinate work by standardizing the individual's or team's goals and product or service output (e.g., customer satisfaction, production efficiency). For instance, to coordinate the work of salespeople, companies assign sales targets rather than specific behaviors.

When work activities are too complex to standardize through procedures or goals, companies often coordinate work effort by extensively training employees or hiring people who have learned precise role behaviors from educational programs. This form of coordination is useful in hospital operating rooms. Surgeons, nurses, and other operating room professionals coordinate their work more through training than goals or company rules.

Elements of Organizational Structure

The division of labor and coordination of work represent the fundamental requirements of organizations. These requirements relate to four basic elements of organizational structure. This section introduces three of them: span of control, centralization, and formalization. The fourth element—departmentalization—is presented in the next section.

Span of Control

span of control the number of people directly reporting to the next level in the hierarchy

Span of control refers to the number of people reporting directly to the next level in the hierarchy. As we mentioned earlier, Henri Fayol strongly recommended the formal hierarchy as the primary coordinating mechanism.

The work of this medical team at UCLA Medical Center in California is divided into specialized jobs so that each person has the required competencies for each position. To some extent, surgical work is coordinated through informal communication. However, much of the work activity can occur without discussion because team members also coordinate through standardization of skills. Through extensive training, each medical professional has learned precise role behaviors so that his or her task activities are coordinated with others on the surgical team. What other types of organizations make extensive use of standardization of skills to coordinate work?

[Mark Harmel/Tony Stone Images]

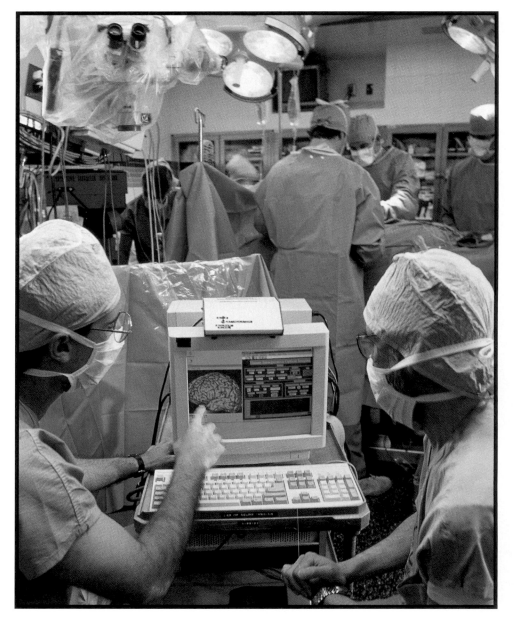

Consequently, he and other theorists in the early 1900s prescribed a relatively narrow span of control, typically no more than 20 employees per supervisor and 6 supervisors per manager. These prescriptions were based on the assumption that managers simply cannot monitor and control any more subordinates closely enough.

Today, we know better. The best performing U.S. manufacturing facilities currently have an average of 31 employees per supervisor. This is a much wider span of control than past scholars had recommended. Yet these operations plan to stretch this span to an average of 75 employees per supervisor over the next few years.[14]

What's the secret here? Did Fayol and others miscalculate the optimal span of control? The answer is that early scholars thought in terms of Fredrick Taylor's scientific management model (see Chapter 4). They believed that employees should "do" the work, whereas supervisors and other management personnel should monitor employee behavior and make most of the decisions. This division of labor limited the span of control. It is very difficult to directly supervise 75 people. It is much easier to *oversee* 75 subordinates who are grouped into several self-directed work teams. Employees manage themselves, thereby releasing supervisors from the time-consuming tasks of monitoring behavior.

Vancom Zuid-Limburg, a joint venture that operates a public bus company in the Netherlands, illustrates this point. Vancom has about 40 bus drivers for each manager, whereas other bus companies have 8 drivers per manager. Vancom is able to operate with a much wider span of control because bus drivers are organized into self-directed work teams that manage their own schedules and budgets.[15]

The underlying principle here is that the span of control depends on the presence of other coordinating mechanisms.[16] Self-directed work teams replace direct supervision with informal communication and specialized knowledge. This also explains why dozens of surgeons and other medical professionals may report to the head surgeon in a major hospital. The head surgeon doesn't engage in much direct supervision because the standardized skills of medical staff coordinates the unit's work. A wider span of control is possible when employees perform similar tasks or have routine jobs. In these situations, the organization relies more on standardization of work processes to coordinate work, thereby reducing the need for hands-on supervision.

Tall and flat structures   The Development Bank of South Africa recently increased employee productivity by restructuring and flattening the organization. In particular, the government-owned financial institution slashed the number of managers from 74 to 27 and cut out one of its four management layers. "[T]he essence of transformation was not to shift the chairs, but to ensure that some of the chairs came out of the room," says a bank executive.[17]

The Development Bank of South Africa joins a long list of companies that are moving toward flatter organizational structures. Royal Mail, which delivers mail throughout Great Britain, went from 16 layers of management to 6. Varian X-Ray Tube Products reduced its five management tiers to three. St. Luke's, the British advertising agency described in the opening vignette for this chapter, has only two layers.[18] This trend toward delayering—moving from a tall to flat structure—is partly in response to the recommendations of management gurus. For example, Tom Peters challenged corporate leaders to cut the number of layers to three within a facility and to five within the entire organization.[19]

The main arguments in favor of delayering are that it potentially cuts overhead costs and puts decision makers closer to frontline staff and information about customer needs. "American corporations have come to realize that they need to have fewer layers of management if they are to communicate daily with their organizations and if they are to become closer to

8-26
© 1996 Farcus Cartoons/dist. by UPS   WAISGLASS/COULTHART

"That reminds me . . . Harris, they want to see you in Personnel."

the customer," advises Lawrence A. Bossidy, CEO of AlliedSignal.[20] However, some organizational experts warn that corporate leaders may be cutting out too much hierarchy. They argue that the much-maligned "middle managers" serve a valuable function by controlling work activities and managing corporate growth. For example, Nike can't launch and coordinate major retail initiatives in sportswear and accessories without middle managers. Moreover, companies will always need hierarchy because someone has to make quick decisions and represent a source of appeal over conflicts.[21]

Before leaving this topic, we should point out that the size of an organization's hierarchy depends on two factors: the average span of control and the number of people employed by the organization. As shown in Exhibit 18.2, a tall structure has many hierarchical levels, each with a relatively narrow span of control, whereas a flat structure has few levels, each with a wide span of control.[22] Larger organizations that depend on hierarchy for coordination necessarily develop taller structures. For instance, Microsoft is considered a high-involvement organization, yet it has at least seven levels of corporate hierarchy to coordinate its 25,000 or more employees.[23]

Centralization and Decentralization

centralization the degree that formal decision authority is held by a small group of people, typically those at the top of the organizational hierarchy

Centralization and decentralization represents a second element of organizational design. **Centralization** means that formal decision authority is held by a small group of people, typically those at the top of the organizational hierarchy. Most organizations begin with centralized structures, as the founder makes most of the decisions and tries to direct the business toward his or her

Exhibit 18.2   Span of control and tall/flat structures

**Tall structure/
Narrow span of control**

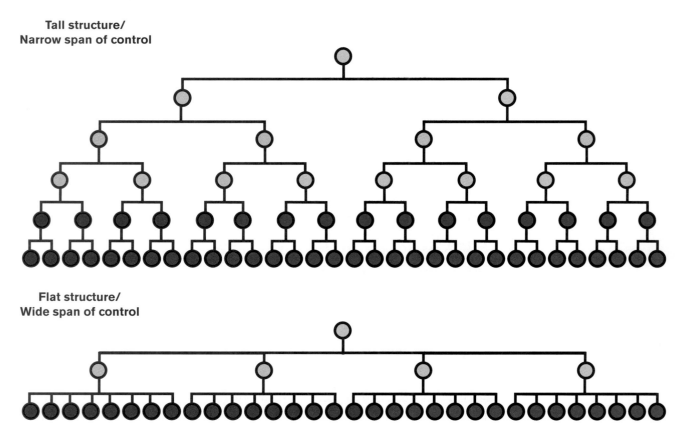

**Flat structure/
Wide span of control**

vision. But as organizations grow, they become more complex. Work activities are divided into more specialized functions, a broader range of products or services is introduced, and operations expand into different regions or countries.

Under these conditions, the founder and senior executives lack the necessary time and expertise to process all the decisions that significantly influence the business. Consequently, growing organizations become *decentralized;* that is, they disperse authority and power throughout the organization. This is what happened at Rosenbluth Travel. As our *Fast Company Online* feature for this chapter describes, Rosenbluth had to adapt quickly to a changing environment. The best way to do that was to decentralize into an organizational structure based on the family farm.

Organizational and environmental complexity push organizations toward decentralization, but some corporate leaders further encourage this process. They have learned that decentralized organizations are potentially more entrepreneurial and responsive to the local environments in which they operate. Tenneco, a leading packaging and automobile parts company, relies on a decentralized organizational structure for this reason. Responsibility has been pushed down to its 77 corrugated packaging plants so that each one will be responsive to the local market. "The business model we're trying to build is to give everyone a free hand to develop the future of their plant and division," explains Paul Stecko, Tenneco's chief operating officer. "We have 77 corrugated facilities in the U.S. We don't have one strategy for this division, we have 77 competitive strategies."[24]

Organizational complexity may encourage decentralization, but other forces push for centralization. Senior executives centralize to increase their power over organizational events. They particularly try to gain decision-making control during times of turbulence and organizational crisis. Yet, when the problems are over, these leaders are reluctant to decentralize decision making to lower levels.

Centralization may improve consistency and reduce costs if, as we noted above, it doesn't reduce local flexibility. This is the main reason why companies are moving toward shared services—centralizing human resources, accounting, information systems, and other support functions in one unit rather than having them scattered around different divisions or countries.[25] Similarly, Procter & Gamble is one of many organizations that have centralized marketing activities that were previously dispersed across various geographic divisions. Brand managers and other marketing people are still employed in each region, but most decisions are made at corporate headquarters so that the product or service is delivered consistently and at a lower marketing cost.[26]

Formalization

formalization the degree that organizations standardize behavior through rules, procedures, formal training, and related mechanisms

Have you ever wondered why a McDonald's hamburger in Atlanta tastes the same as one in Kuala Lumpur, Malaysia? The reason is that the fast-food company has engineered out all variation through formalization. **Formalization** is the degree to which organizations standardize behavior through rules, procedures, formal training, and related mechanisms.[27] In other words, formalization represents the establishment of standardization as a coordinating mechanism.

McDonald's Restaurants has a formalized structure because it prescribes every activity in explicit detail. Each McDonald's franchise must dole out five perfect drops of mustard, a quarter ounce of onions, and two pickles—three if they're small—on each hamburger. Drink cups are filled with ice up to a point just below the arches on their sides. Cooking and bagging fries are explained in 19 steps. Employees who work on the grill must put the hamburger patties in six rows of six patties each. A Big Mac is supposed to be assembled in 25 seconds from the time it appears on the order screen.[28]

Older companies tend to become more formalized because work activities become routinized, making them easier to document into standardized practices. Larger companies formalize as a coordinating mechanism, because direct supervision and informal communication among employees are not as efficient. External influences, such as government safety legislation and strict accounting rules, also encourage formalization.

Problems with formalization   Formalization may increase efficiency, but it can also create problems. Rules and procedures reduce organizational flexibility, so employees follow prescribed behaviors even when the situation clearly calls for a customized response. Some work rules become so convoluted that organizational efficiency would decline if they were actually followed as prescribed. Labor unions sometimes call work-to-rule strikes, in which their members closely follow the formalized rules and procedures

FAST COMPANY Online ▫ Rosenbluth International Adopts a Decentralized Family Farm Structure

Rosenbluth International became more responsive to customer needs by reorganizing around a family farm model of decentralized decision making.

[© Rosenbluth International, Inc., 1998]

established by an organization. This tactic increases union power, because the company's productivity falls significantly when employees follow the rules that are supposed to guide their behavior.

Another concern is that although employees with very strong security needs and a low tolerance for ambiguity like working in highly formalized organizations, others become alienated and feel powerless in these structures. Finally, rules and procedures have been known to take on a life of their own in some organizations. They become the focus of attention rather than the organization's ultimate objectives of producing a product or service and serving its dominant stakeholders.

Mechanistic versus Organic Structures

mechanistic structure an organizational structure with a narrow span of control and high degrees of formalization and centralization

You may have noticed that organizations seem to cluster around their span of control, centralization, and formalization. Some companies, such as McDonald's, have a **mechanistic structure.**[29] Mechanistic structures are characterized by a narrow span of control and a high degree of formalization and

Hal Rosenbluth has piloted his great-grandfather's modest travel business into the third largest travel agency in the world. In 1993, however, the airlines limited travel agents' commissions, so Rosenbluth had to convince business clients to pay the travel agency for value-added service rather than receive a large fee from Rosenbluth for the privilege of serving them. "We must meet our current and future clients' needs more consistently, more effectively, and a lot faster," Rosenbluth told employees at the time.

To provide more value-added service, Rosenbluth International reorganized around a family farm model of decentralized decision making. The idea came to him while helping a farmer friend in North Dakota. "What I'm beginning to see," says Rosenbluth, "is that the family farm is the most efficient type of unit I've ever run across, because everybody on the farm has to be fully functional and multifaceted. And what I'm looking for is an organizational design that can communicate that change."

With that in mind, Rosenbluth broke his company into more than 100 business units, each functioning as a farm serving specific regions and clients. Corporate headquarters became the equivalent of the farm town, where "stores" like human resources and accounting dole out what the farmers need. On the Rosenbluth farm, decision making and learning would be localized. It was an attempt to re-create the spirit of the young, supersonic Rosenbluth environment; if the whole company was too big to be a farm, at least each unit could be one.

ONLINE CHECK-UP

1. This *Fast Company Online* feature describes how Rosenbluth International redesigned the organization around the model of a family farm. How would the family farm model benefit Rosenbluth in this environment?
2. The full text of this *Fast Company* article explains how Rosenbluth International relies on technology and employee orientation to support its new organizational structure. How do technology and employee socialization practices fit into the family farm metaphor of organizational structure?

Source: R. Walker, "Back to the Farm," *Fast Company,* Issue 7 (February 1997). ■

Get the full text of this *Fast Company* article at www.mhhe.com/mcshane1e

centralization. They have many rules and procedures, limited decision making at lower levels, tall hierarchies of people in specialized roles, and vertical rather than horizontal flows of communication. Tasks are rigidly defined and altered only when sanctioned by higher authorities.

organic structure an organizational structure with a wide span of control, little formalization, and highly decentralized decision making

Companies with an **organic structure** have the opposite characteristics. They have a wide span of control, little formalization, and decentralized decision making. Tasks are fluid, adjusting to new situations and organizational needs. The organic structure values knowledge and takes the view that information may be located anywhere in the organization rather than among senior executives. Thus, communication flows in all directions with little concern for the formal hierarchy.

Mechanistic structures operate best in stable environments because they rely on efficiency and routine behaviors. However, as we have emphasized throughout this book, most organizations operate in a world of dramatic change. New technology, globalization, a changing workforce, and other factors have strengthened the need for a more organic structure that is flexible and responsive to these changes. Organic structures are also more consistent with knowledge management because they emphasize information sharing rather than hierarchy and status.

Traditional Forms of Departmentalization

Span of control, centralization, and formalization are important elements of organizational structure, but most people think about organizational charts when the discussion of organizational structure arises. The organizational chart represents the fourth element in the structuring of organizations, called **departmentalization.** Departmentalization specifies how employees and their activities are grouped together. It is a fundamental strategy for coordinating organizational activities because it influences organizational behavior in the following ways.[30]

departmentalization an element of organizational structure specifying how employees and their activities are grouped together, such as by function, product, geographic location, or some combination

• Departmentalization establishes a system of common supervision between positions and units within the organization. It establishes formal work teams, as we learned in Chapter 9. Departmentalization typically determines which positions and units must share resources. Thus, it establishes interdependencies between employees and subunits.

• Departmentalization usually creates common measures of performance. Members of the same work team, for example, share common goals and budgets, giving the company standards against which to compare subunit performance.

• Departmentalization encourages coordination through informal communication between people and subunits. With common supervision and resources, members within each configuration typically work near each other, so they can use frequent and informal interaction to get the work done.

There are almost as many organizational charts as there are businesses, but we can identify four pure types of departmentalization: simple, functional, divisional, and matrix. Few companies fit exactly into any of these categories, but they represent a useful framework for discussing more complex hybrid forms of departmentalization. Later in this chapter, we will introduce two emerging forms of departmentalization: team-based and network structures.

Simple Structure

Most companies begin with a *simple structure*.[31] They employ only a few people and typically offer only one distinct product or service. There is minimal hierarchy—usually just employees reporting to the owners. Employees are

When Opus Event Marketing was launched in the early 1990s, cofounders Andy Stefanovich and his sister Christine Rochester did most of the work. When they landed a contract with Virginia Lottery, for example, the duo designed the promotional display, dropped off display tents, and staffed events themselves. Later, the Richmond, Virginia, firm hired a few employees who performed whatever tasks were required. But as more employees were added and the company expanded into different services, Opus shifted from a simple structure to a more complex functional structure. Employees now perform more specialized roles in public relations, merchandising, promotions, and other functions.[32] Why would Opus and most other firms move away from the simple structure as they get larger and diversify?

[Courtesy of Opus Marketing]

grouped into broadly defined roles because there are insufficient economies of scale to assign them to specialized roles. Simple structures are flexible, yet they usually depend on the owner's direct supervision to coordinate work activities. Consequently, this structure is very difficult to operate under complex conditions. For instance, as Opus Event Marketing expanded into diverse marketing services, it added professionals to coordinate more specialized roles. In doing so, the Richmond, Virginia, company evolved away from the simple structure.

Functional Structure

A **functional structure** organizes employees around specific knowledge or other resources. Employees with marketing expertise are grouped into a marketing unit, those with production skills are located in manufacturing, engineers are found in product development, and so on. Organizations with functional structures are typically centralized to coordinate their activities effectively. Coordination through standardization of work processes is the most common form of coordination used in a functional structure. Most organizations use functional structures at some level or at some time in their development.

Advantages and disadvantages

An important advantage of functional structures is that they foster professional identity and clarify career paths. They permit greater specialization so that the organization has expertise in each area. Direct supervision is easier because managers have backgrounds in that functional area and employees approach them with common problems and issues. Finally, functional structures create common pools of talent that typically serve everyone in the organization. This creates an economy of scale that would not exist if functional specialists were spread over different parts of the organization.[33]

Functional structures also have limitations. Because people are grouped together according to common interests and backgrounds, these designs promote differentiation among functions. For this reason, functional structures tend to have higher dysfunctional conflict and poorer coordination with other work units. A related concern is that functional structures tend to emphasize subunit goals over superordinate organizational goals. Employees in purchasing, accounting, engineering, and other functional units are less likely to give priority to the company's product or service than to the goals of their specific department. Unless people are transferred from one function to the next, they fail to develop a broader understanding of the business. Together, these problems require substantial formal controls and coordination when functional structures are used.

Divisional Structure

A **divisional structure** groups employees around geographic areas, clients, or outputs (products/services). Divisional structures are sometimes called *strategic business units* (SBUs) because they are normally more autonomous than functional structures and may operate as subsidiaries rather than as departments of the enterprise.

Exhibit 18.3 illustrates the three pure forms of divisional structure.[34] *Geographic divisionalized structures* organize employees around distinct areas of the country or globe. Exhibit 18.3(*a*) displays the geographic divisional structure at McDonald's restaurants in the United States. *Product/service structures* organize work around distinct outputs. Exhibit 18.3(*b*) illustrates this type of structure at Hewlett-Packard. The computer manufacturer has divided the workforce into five divisions, ranging from software and services to laserjet products. *Client structures* organize work activities around specific customers. Exhibit 18.3(*c*) highlights some of the industry segments around which Andersen Consulting staff are organized.

Advantages and disadvantages

The divisional form is a building block structure, because it accommodates growth relatively easily. Related products

Exhibit 18.3 Three types of divisional structure

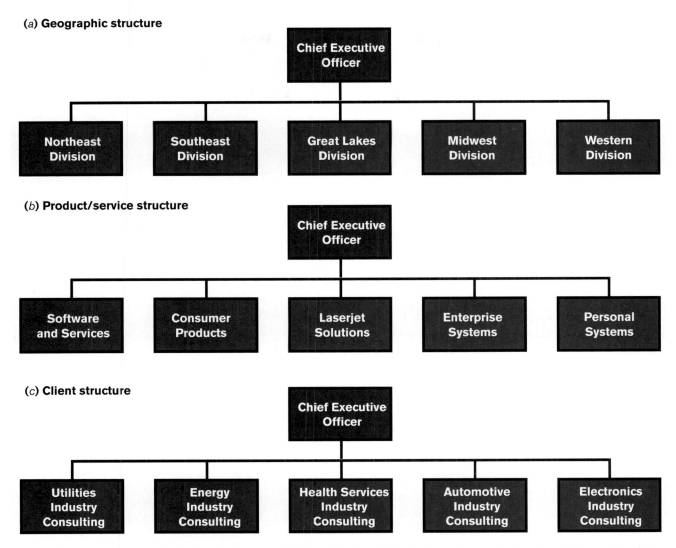

(a) Geographic structure

Chief Executive Officer

- Northeast Division
- Southeast Division
- Great Lakes Division
- Midwest Division
- Western Division

(b) Product/service structure

Chief Executive Officer

- Software and Services
- Consumer Products
- Laserjet Solutions
- Enterprise Systems
- Personal Systems

(c) Client structure

Chief Executive Officer

- Utilities Industry Consulting
- Energy Industry Consulting
- Health Services Industry Consulting
- Automotive Industry Consulting
- Electronics Industry Consulting

Note: (a) shows the geographic divisional structure of McDonald's Corp. USA; (b) shows the product/service divisions at Hewlett-Packard; (c) shows five of the industry customer groups at Andersen Consulting.

or clients can be added to existing divisions with little need for additional learning, whereas increasing diversity may be accommodated by sprouting a new division. Organizations typically reorganize around divisional structures as they expand into distinct products, services, and domains of operation, because coordinating functional units becomes too unwieldy with increasing diversity.[35] The main advantage of divisional structures is that they give employees more flexibility and output focus than functional structures.

Organizations tend to adopt divisional structures as they grow and become more complex, but this structural configuration is not perfect. The most common complaint is that divisional structures increase the amount of duplication and underutilization of resources. This structure creates "silos of knowledge" because functional specialists are spread throughout the various business units. Consequently, new knowledge and practices in one part of the organization are not shared elsewhere. Connections 18.1 describes how Mobil Oil seems to have reversed its short-lived geographical organizational structure for this reason. Notice, too, that Mobil did not completely return to a functional

With Bill Gates watching, Microsoft Corp. President Steve Ballmer tells employees by means of television monitors about a major restructuring of the software giant. Microsoft employees were previously organized around products and technology. The new structure organizes them into four customer groups: consumers, knowledge workers, software developers, and business enterprise. A fifth division is responsible for home and retail products. "This new structure is part of the reinvention of Microsoft," said Ballmer during the announced reorganization.[36] How would organizing employees around customers rather than products improve Microsoft's competitiveness? Should all large enterprises have a divisional structure organized around customers rather than products or regions?
[Photo: Reuters/Anthony Bolante/Archive Photos]

matrix structure a type of departmentalization that overlays a divisionalized structure (typically a project team) with a functional structure

structure. It is very difficult for large and complex organizations to completely abandon the divisional form.

Along with the problem of duplication, divisional structures tend to reduce cooperation across groups. The opening story to Chapter 13 provides a classic example of this problem. Arthur Andersen Worldwide divided its organization into separate consulting (Andersen Consulting) and accounting (Arthur Andersen) units. Over time, the groups became more independent of each other to the point where they eventually went through a vicious divorce battle.[37]

Matrix Structure

You can see from our discussion so far that organizations face a dilemma when they grow and become more complex. When organizations adopt a functional structure, employees develop strong expertise but tend to be less responsive to product and customer needs. When organizations adopt a divisionalized structure, employees apply their knowledge more effectively around products and clients. However, this structure creates silos of knowledge and often results in wasteful duplication.

The **matrix structure** offers a potential solution to this dilemma by combining or overlaying two structures. The idea behind this combination is to leverage the benefits of both types of structure. The most common form of matrix structure occurs in project-based organizations. As Exhibit 18.4 illustrates, employees are assigned to a cross-functional project team, yet also belong to a permanent functional unit to which they return when a project is completed.

General Electric's business in India (Godrej-GE) relied on a project-based matrix structure to design and build a high-capacity refrigerator plant. Project team members regularly communicated with their functional departments on technical issues, yet they worked on-site throughout the construction period and reported to the project team leader on time-related issues. This arrangement created a balance of power between the project and functional heads so that neither the project nor functional goals became more important than the other.[38]

The second form of matrix structure is found in multinational corporations that balance power between two divisional groups. ABB Asea Brown Boveri has this structure as it overlays a geographic- with a product-based divisional structure. The product-based structure lets the Swiss-based electrical systems manufacturer exploit global economies of scale, whereas the geographic structure keeps knowledge close to the needs of individual countries.[39]

Notice that employees have two bosses within a matrix structure. For example, the head of ABB's combustion engineering group in Connecticut reports to both the U.S. country manager and the global manager of ABB's Power Engineering business. Some companies give these managers equal power; more often, each has authority over different elements of the employee's or work unit's tasks.[40] However, only a small percentage of people report to two bosses in these multinational matrix structures. At ABB, for example, only about 500 plant managers and group leaders have matrix roles. The other 200,000 ABB employees work in direct authority (functional or divisional) structures below the matrix structure.

Advantages and disadvantages Matrix structures usually optimize the use of resources and expertise, making them ideal for project-based organizations with fluctuating workloads.[41] When properly managed, they improve communication efficiency, project flexibility, and innovation compared to purely functional designs. Matrix structures focus technical specialists on the goals of serving clients and creating marketable products. Yet, by maintaining

Connections 18.1 ◘ Mobil Flip-Flops Between "Mini-Mobils" and Functional Structures

For many years Mobil Oil organized employees into functional departments. Some worked in upstream departments, exploring for oil and producing it. Others worked in downstream departments, refining and marketing the oil to customers. The problem was that employees focused more on their specialization than on serving clients. Mobil's solution was to reorganize around 11 geographic divisions. Each of these "mini-Mobils" included both upstream and downstream operations and operated as an independent business. The intention was to make the company more entrepreneurial and provide more unified service to clients in the region.

"When you talk to one person, that person has a perception of all of Mobil's operations in that region," explained a Mobil Oil executive at the time, "whereas before, you'd find that people had a very specific functional focus."

Eighteen months after creating these mini-Mobils, the company returned to a more functional structure that also included some geographic differentiation. The new structure includes upstream and downstream divisions for the Americas and the rest of the world. "We think now is a good time to return to a more functional structure, which permits us to better drive shareholder value," explains Mobil CEO Eugene A. Renna.

Why did Mobil change its structure so quickly? Most likely, the mini-Mobil structure created too much duplication because resources were replicated across each of the 11 units. Divisionalized structures also tend to create "silos of knowledge" whereby knowledge in one unit is unknown to people in another division who might need that knowledge. Mobil's new hybrid structure may not be ideal, but it tries to blend the advantages of both functional and divisional organizational forms.

Sources: "Mobil Announces Organizational Realignment," *Business Wire*, February 11, 1998; T. Brown, B. Massoudi, and A. Rupple, "Restoring 'Functional Excellence' through Best Practices," *Oil & Gas Investor*, Second Quarter 1997, pp. 8–10; J. S. DeMott, "The Key Issue: Managing Bigness," *Worldbusiness*, September–October 1996, pp. 30–33. ◘

Exhibit 18.4   A simplified matrix structure

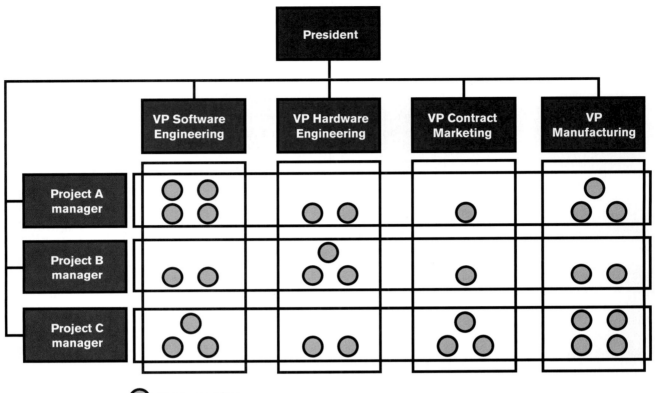

a link to their functional unit, employees are able to interact and coordinate with others in their technical specialty.

In spite of these advantages, matrix structures require more coordination than functional or pure divisional structures. The existence of two bosses can also dilute accountability. Royal Dutch/Shell is moving away from a matrix design for these reasons.[42] Matrix structures also tend to generate conflict, organizational politics, and stress.[43] In project-based firms, for example, project leaders must have sufficient leadership and conflict-resolution skills to coordinate people with diverse functional backgrounds. They also need good negotiation and persuasive communication skills to gain support from functional leaders. Employees who feel comfortable in structured bureaucracies tend to have difficulty adjusting to the relatively fluid nature of matrix structures. Stress is a common symptom of poorly managed matrix structures, because employees must cope with two managers with potentially divergent needs and expectations.

Hybrid Structure

Very few organizations adopt a purely functional, divisional, or matrix structure. Instead, they combine some parts of various designs into a hybrid structure. Research suggests that multinational corporations need to develop structures and systems that maintain some balance of power and effectiveness across functional, product, geographic, and client-focused units.[44] In other words, they must ensure that functional managers do not dominate product

Nortel Networks keeps changing its organizational structure. In the 1980s, the network equipment giant had three geographic businesses. This structure worked well in the era of regional telephone monopolies, but it created inefficient duplication of marketing and product development. As the telecommunications industry globalized, Nortel reorganized around a hybrid structure with three product groups and four geographically based subsidiaries. This increased global efficiency, but customers somehow got lost in the equation. Today, Nortel is structured around four client groups (e.g., wireless) and two geographical groups. "Nortel's new structure reinforces the tie-in with the market and with our customers," explains a Nortel executive.[45] Why wasn't Nortel's new structure applied in the 1980s?
[Courtesy of Nortel Networks]

managers, product managers do not dominate regional managers, and so forth.

Emerging Forms of Departmentalization

All organizations include one or more of the previously described forms of departmentalization. However, due to changes in the workforce and information technology, two new forms of departmentalization are emerging: team-based and network structures.[46] Although they typically exist within or in conjunction with traditional departmentalization, team-based and network structures have unique features and someday may become the dominant structural design in some industries.

Team-Based (Lateral) Structure

Harley Davidson, Inc., has reinvented the wheel. More specifically, the motorcycle company designed three overlapping circles to represent its new organizational structure: a Create Demand Circle, a Produce Products Circle, and a Support Circle. In the center where the three circles intersect, Harley has a Leadership and Strategy Council. Each circle represents a team (or set of teams) responsible for specific work processes. Eastman Chemical Co. has a similar structure, but its organizational chart looks like a pizza with pepperoni sprinkled over it. Each pepperoni represents a cross-functional team responsible for managing a business, a geographic area, or a core competence in a specific technology or area.[47]

team-based organizational structure a type of departmentalization with a flat span of control and relatively little formalization, consisting of self-directed work teams responsible for various work processes

Harley Davidson and Eastman Chemical are two examples of the **team-based organizational structure** that we introduced in Chapter 9. Some writers call it a *lateral structure* because, with few organizational levels, it is very flat (like a pizza) and relies on extensive lateral communication. Others refer to it as a *circle structure* (similar to Harley's wheels), because the organization has several circles of activity with free-floating teams operating within each domain.[48] The team-based organization is also known as a *cluster structure*, because it is composed of a cluster of teams. Exhibit 18.5 illustrates two perspectives of team-based organizations.

No matter what name is used or how it is drawn, the team-based structure has a few distinguishing features from other organizational forms. First, it uses self-directed work teams rather than individuals as the basic building block of organizations. Second, teams are typically organized around work processes, such as making a specific product or serving a specific client group. At St. Luke's, described at the beginning of this chapter, client accounts are assigned to teams rather than to individual employees in different departments. Contrast this to a typical advertising agency where the client works with an account manager, who then coordinates with people located in several functional departments—art, copywriting, design, and so on.[49]

A third distinguishing feature of team-based organizational structures is that they have a very flat hierarchy, usually with no more than two or three

Exhibit 18.5   Two perspectives of a team-based (lateral) structure

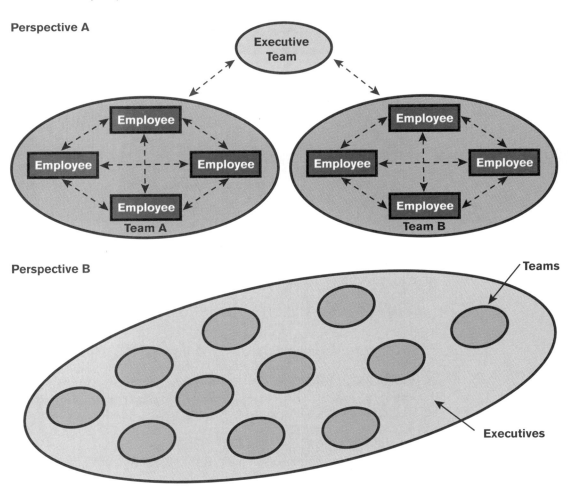

management levels. Most supervisory activities are delegated to the team by having members take turns as the coordinator. Finally, this type of structure has very little formalization. Almost all day-to-day decisions are made by team members rather than someone farther up the organizational hierarchy. Teams are given relatively few rules about how to organize their work. Instead, the executive team typically assigns output goals to the team, such as the volume and quality of product or service, or productivity improvement targets for the work process. Teams are then encouraged to use available resources and their own initiative to achieve those objectives.

Team-based structures are usually found within larger divisionalized forms. For example, several manufacturing facilities in Pratt & Whitney, General Electric, and Nortel are organized around a team-based structure, but each unit is part of a larger divisionalized structure. However, St. Luke's and a few other innovative companies are experimenting with a team-based structure from the top to the bottom of the organization. SEI Investments, described in the opening story to Chapter 10, is another organization that relies exclusively on a team-based structure. Connections 18.2 describes how Oticon A/S, the Danish hearing aid manufacturer, also operates a highly flexible team-based

Connections 18.2 ◻ Oticon Holding A/S Turns to Spaghetti

Oticon Holding A/S has been transformed from a sleepy Danish hearing aid manufacturer to a nimble trendsetter. Oticon's secret is a radical organizational structure that replaced departments with project teams. A hundred or so projects exist at any one time, and most people work on several projects at once. This is an open market system where project leaders compete for resources, and employees compete for a place on desirable projects.

Lars Kolind, Oticon's president, likes to call this structure "the spaghetti organization"—a continuously changing chaotic tangle of human relationships. "To keep a company alive, one of the jobs of top management is to keep it dis-organized," Kolind declares approvingly.

The spaghetti organization replaced formal communication with informal dialogue. Incoming mail is scanned into a network computer system and then shredded. Anyone can access almost any document; project teams are encouraged to share knowledge by tapping into each other's files. Everyone walks around with mobile telephones clipped to their waist.

The most obvious feature of Oticon's new structure is the office design that supports it. The new building (a refurbished soft drink plant) is an open space with uniform workstations. Each person has a computer and a birch desk on wheels, an "organization of 1,000 birch trees" as Kolind likes to call it. This allows any employee to move his or her "office" anywhere else in the building in just five minutes.

The spaghetti structure has significantly improved creativity and knowledge sharing. Oticon is now a leader in hearing aid technology and has gained in market share and profitability. In spite of the chaos, employees seem better off, not burned out. "There's a paradox here," Kolind says. "We're developing products twice as fast as anybody else. But when you look around, you see a very relaxed atmosphere. We're not fast on the surface; we're fast underneath."

Sources: P. Labarre, "This Organization Is Dis-Organization," *Fast Company*, Issue 3 (1997); "The Revolution at Oticon: Creating a 'Spaghetti' Organization," *Research-Technology Management* 39 (September–October 1996), p. 54; P. LaBarre, "The Dis-organization of Oticon," *Industry Week*, July 18, 1994, pp. 22–28. ◼

structure with almost no hierarchy. The CEO of the Danish hearing aid manufacturer calls it a "spaghetti organization" because it is a chaotic interconnection of people working freely on different projects.

Advantages and disadvantages   The team-based structure is a relatively new organizational form, but it has quickly become a popular way to organize employees. One reason for this popularity is that team-based structures are usually more responsive to global competition.[50] Teams empower employees and reduce reliance on a managerial hierarchy. Employees with a high growth need are more motivated and satisfied with this arrangement, and the company reduces overhead costs.

Team-based structures are also increasingly popular because they tend to improve communication and cooperation across traditional boundaries. With greater autonomy, this structure also allows quicker and more informed decision making.[51] Some hospitals have shifted from functional departments to cross-functional teams for this reason. Teams composed of nurses, radiologists, anesthetists, a pharmacology representative, a rehabilitation therapist, and other specialists communicate and coordinate more efficiently, thereby reducing delays and errors.[52]

These benefits are partly (or sometimes completely!) offset by several known problems with team-based structures. One concern is that this structure is more costly to maintain. Teamwork takes more effort to coordinate than the old command-and-control hierarchical system. Employees may experience more stress due to increased ambiguity in their roles. Team leaders also experience more stress due to increased conflict, loss of functional power, and unclear career progression ladders.[53]

Network Structure

To the outside world, Cisco Systems is one company. But the world's leading provider of business-to-business computer networks is really a constellation of suppliers, contract manufacturers, assemblers, and other partners connected through an intricate web of computer technology. Cisco's network springs into action as soon as a customer places an order, usually through the Internet. Suppliers send the required materials to assemblers who ship the product directly to the client, usually the same day. Seventy percent of Cisco's product is outsourced this way. In many cases, Cisco employees never touch the product. "Partnerships are key to the new world strategies of the 21st century," says a Cisco senior vice president. "Partners collapse time because they allow you to take on more things and bring them together quicker."[54]

network structure an alliance of several organizations for the purpose of creating a product or serving a client

Cisco is a living example of the **network structure.** A network structure (also known as a *virtual corporation* or *modular structure*) is an alliance of several organizations for the purpose of creating a product or serving a client.[55] As Exhibit 18.6 illustrates, this collaborative structure typically consists of several satellite organizations beehived around a "hub" or "core" firm. The core firm coordinates the network process and provides one or two other core competencies, such as marketing or product development. For instance, Cisco mainly designs new products. Nike, another network organization, provides marketing expertise for its sports footwear and apparel.

The core firm might be the first contact with customers, but most of the product or service delivery and support activities are farmed out to satellite organizations located anywhere in the world. Extranets (web-based networks with partners) and other technologies ensure that information flows easily and openly between the core firm and its satellites. For instance, Nokia, the Finnish conglomerate, entered the U.S. video display market with only five

Exhibit 18.6
A network structure

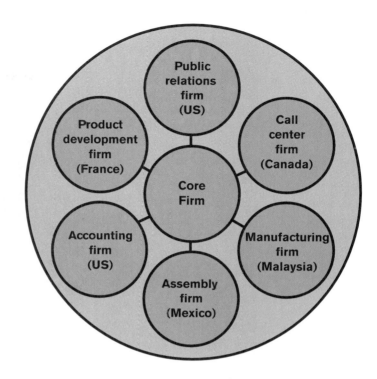

employees. All of the major tasks—marketing, sales, logistics, and technical support—were contracted out to specialists around the country. This diverse network was then connected through information technology to a common database.[56]

One of the main forces pushing toward a network structure is the recognition that an organization has only a few *core competencies*. A core competency is a knowledge base that resides throughout an organization and provides a strategic advantage. Exxon's core competency is its ability to distribute and market oil products. Most people think of Yahoo! as a search engine, but the internet company's core competency is really internet-based marketing. Yahoo! relies on another company, Inktomi, for its search product.[57]

As companies discover their core competency, they outsource noncritical tasks to other organizations that have a core competency at performing those tasks. Many firms have outsourced information systems for this reason. Several have their accounting, payroll, and even their manufacturing done by outside firms. Product development firms might rely on marketing firms to launch their products. Many companies rely on independent sales agencies to provide sales support in certain territories. Each of these relations represents a form of network organization structure.

affiliate networks network organizations where the satellite companies have a special affiliation with the core firm, such as investment or start-up support

Affiliate networks Some network organizations are called **affiliate networks** because they have a special historical or financial affiliation with the core company. Affiliates may be former departments or divisions of the core firm that have been spun off to form independent businesses. Other affiliates are recent start-ups that receive financial support from the core firm. In either case, affiliate networks have a special relationship with the core firm that distinguishes them from arm's-length network structures.

NEC is one of many firms that has nurtured the development of affiliate networks in an effort to improve innovation and market responsiveness. The Japanese computer and electronics company developed an intrapreneurship program for research staff and offered them venture capital funding as

IBM, Mitsubishi, Hewlett-Packard, and Ericsson design and market cell phones, pagers, modems, fax machines, and other well-known products. But they leave the manufacturing expertise to companies like Solectron. Solectron's core competence is manufacturing electronic products, so it represents the manufacturing arm of the network structure. Solectron sometimes buys the manufacturing plant from the brand name company, then uses the facility to make the other firm's products. Solectron then fills any excess capacity to make products for other clients.[58] What risks and opportunities does this network structure arrangement create for the brand name companies? Should all organizations outsource their noncore work?

*[Bob Padgett/*Washington Post*]*

incentives to develop their own businesses. One of these affiliates is Authentic Limited, which supplies flat speakers for NEC's personal computers. Another is Signafy Inc., which develops digital watermarking technology for copyright protection. In each case NEC is a shareholder, but the affiliate is a separate corporate entity.[59]

Microsoft Corp. also provides start-up funding for several affiliate companies, such as Teledesic, a satellite-based telecommunications company. However, many affiliates were launched by former Microsoft employees with generous stock options earned at the software giant. These "Baby Bills" (named after Microsoft CEO Bill Gates) became affiliates by working with—rather than competing against—Microsoft on emerging technology.[60]

Cellular organizations   The network structures that exist at Cisco Systems, Nike, Dell Computer, and other firms generally perform a set of standardized production tasks for all clients. When you order a computer from Dell, the network partners follow the same set of transactions as the next person who orders a computer. The specific computer configuration may change, but the relationships among the partners and the production process are fairly standardized until the partnership is reconfigured every few years.

In contrast, some network structures—called **cellular organizations**—form unique partnership teams that provide customized products or services, usually to specific clients, for a limited time.[61] When an opportunity emerges, a unique combination of partners in the network structure forms a special team that works on the assignment until it is completed. These network structures are called cellular organizations because they reshape themselves quickly to fit immediate needs. They are also self-organizing, meaning that they rearrange their own communication patterns and roles to fit the situation. The relationship between the partners is mutually determined rather than imposed by a core firm. In this respect, cellular firms are the ultimate *virtual corporation*.

Technical and Computer Graphics (TCG), a privately held information technology company in Sydney, Australia, comes close to a pure cellular organizational structure. TCG is really a consortium of 13 companies that specialize in computer hardware or software design and implementation. When any one of the partners begins to form a business opportunity, it contracts with some of the other TCG companies to assist in that process. This unique combination provides a customized expertise and ensures that the knowledge gained from

cellular organizations a highly **flexible** network structure in which partners provide customized products or services, usually to specific clients, for a limited time

the project is disseminated throughout TCG. The project team disbands when the project is completed.[62]

Advantages and disadvantages For several years scholars have argued that organizational leaders must develop a metaphor of organizations as plasmalike organisms rather than rigid machines.[63] Network structures come close to the organism metaphor because they offer the flexibility to realign their structure with changing environmental requirements. If customers demand a new product or service, the core firm forms new alliances with other firms offering the appropriate resources. For example, by finding partners with available plant facilities, Cisco Systems expanded its business much more rapidly than if it built its own production facilities. When Cisco's needs change, it isn't saddled with nonessential facilities and resources.

Network structures also offer the efficiencies that tend to occur when organizations focus on their core competencies compared to having all activities performed in-house by different departments.[64] The core firm coordinates the network structure and focuses on a core competency while outsourcing other activities to partners who possess appropriate competencies for those tasks. In this respect, the core firm becomes globally competitive as it shops worldwide for subcontractors with the best people and the best technology at the best price. Indeed, the pressures of global competition have made network structures more vital, and computer-based information technology has made them possible.[65]

A potential disadvantage of network structures is that they expose the core firm to the same market forces used to get the best resources. Other companies may bid up the subcontractors' price in any functional area, whereas the short-term cost would be lower if the company hired its own employees to provide this function. Another problem is that although information technology makes worldwide communication much easier, it will never replace the degree of control organizations have when manufacturing, marketing, and other functions are in-house. The core firm can use arm's-length incentives and contract provisions to maintain the subcontractor's quality, but these actions are relatively crude compared to those used to maintain performance of in-house employees.

Contingencies of Organizational Design

Organizational theorists and practitioners are interested not only in the elements of organizational structure, but also in the contingencies that determine or influence the optimal design. In this section, we introduce four contingencies of organizational design: size, technology, environment, and strategy.

Organizational Size

Larger organizations have considerably different structures than smaller organizations.[66] As the number of employees increases, job specialization increases due to a greater division of labor. Larger firms also have more elaborate coordinating mechanisms to manage the greater division of labor. They are more likely to use standardization of work processes and outputs to coordinate work activities. These coordinating mechanisms create an administrative hierarchy and greater formalization. Informal communication has traditionally decreased as a coordinating mechanism as organizations get larger. However, emerging computer technologies and increased emphasis on empowerment have caused informal communication to regain its importance in large firms.[67]

Larger organizations also tend to be more decentralized. As we noted earlier in this chapter, neither founders nor senior managers have sufficient time or expertise to process all the decisions that significantly influence the business as it grows. Therefore, decision-making authority is pushed down to lower levels, where incumbents are able to cope with the narrower range of issues under their control.[68]

Technology

Based on the open systems model (see Chapter 1), we know that an organization's structure needs to be aligned with its dominant technology. Two important technological contingencies that influence the best type of organizational structure are the variety and analyzability of work activities.[69] *Variety* refers to the number of exceptions to standard procedure that can occur in the team or work unit. *Analyzability* refers to the extent that the transformation of input resources to outputs can be reduced to a series of standardized steps.

Some jobs are routine, meaning that employees perform the same tasks all of the time and rely on set rules (standard operating procedures) when exceptions do occur. Almost everything is predictable. These situations, such as automobile assembly lines, have high formalization and centralization as well as standardization of work processes. When employees perform tasks with high variety and low analyzability, they apply their skills to unique situations with little opportunity for repetition. Research project teams operate under these conditions. These situations call for an organic structure, one with low formalization, highly decentralized decision-making authority, and coordination mainly through informal communication among team members.

High-variety and high-analyzability tasks have many exceptions to routines, but these exceptions can usually be resolved through standard procedures. Maintenance groups and engineering design teams experience these conditions. Work units that fall into this category should use an organic structure, but it is possible to have somewhat greater formalization and centralization due to the analyzability of problems.

Skilled tradespeople tend to work in situations with low variety and low analyzability. Their tasks involve few exceptions but the problems that arise are difficult to resolve. This situation allows for more centralization and formalization than a purely organic structure, but coordination must include informal communication among the skilled employees so that unique problems can be resolved.

External Environment

The best structure for an organization depends on its external environment. The external environment includes anything outside the organization, including most stakeholders (e.g., clients, suppliers, government), resources (e.g., raw materials, human resources, information, finances), and competitors. Four relatively distinct characteristics of external environments influence the type of organizational structure best suited to a particular situation: dynamism, complexity, diversity, and hostility.[70]

• *Dynamic versus stable environments*   Dynamic environments have a high rate of change, leading to novel situations and a lack of identifiable patterns. Organic structures are better suited to this type of environment so that the organization can adapt more quickly to changes.[71] Network and team-based structures seem to be most effective in dynamic environments, because they usually have these features. In contrast, stable environments are characterized by regular cycles of activity and steady changes in supply and demand for inputs and outputs. Events are more predictable, enabling the firm to apply rules and procedures. Thus, more mechanistic structures tend to work best under these conditions.

- *Complex versus simple environments* Complex environments have many elements whereas simple environments have few things to monitor. For instance, a multinational corporation has a complex environment because it has many stakeholders. Decentralized structures seem to be better suited to complex environments, because these subunits are close to their local environment and are able to make more informed choices.

- *Diverse versus integrated environments* Organizations located in diverse environments have a greater variety of products or services, clients, and regions. In contrast, an integrated environment has only one client, product, and geographic area. The more diversified the environment, the more the firm needs to use a divisionalized form aligned with that diversity. If it sells a single product around the world, a geographic divisionalized form would align best with the firm's geographic diversity. As we noted earlier with Nortel, global firms with several products and client groups have a continuous dilemma concerning which form of diversity is most important.

- *Hostile versus munificent environments* Firms located in a hostile environment face resource scarcity and more competition in the marketplace. Hostile environments are typically dynamic ones because they reduce the predictability of access to resources and demand for outputs. Organic structures tend to be best in hostile environments. However, when the environment is extremely hostile—such as a severe shortage of supplies or lower market share—organizations tend to temporarily centralize so that decisions can be made more quickly and executives feel more comfortable being in control.[72] Ironically, centralization may result in lower-quality decisions during organizational crises, because top management has less information, particularly when the environment is complex.

Organizational Strategy

organizational strategy the way the organization positions itself in its setting in relation to its stakeholders given the organization's resources, capabilities, and mission

strategic choice the idea that an organization interacts with its environment rather than being totally determined by it

Although size, technology, and environment influence the optimal organizational structure, these contingencies do not necessarily determine structure. Instead, there is increasing evidence that corporate leaders formulate and implement strategies that shape both the characteristics of these contingencies as well as the organization's resulting structure. **Organizational strategy** refers to the way the organization positions itself in its setting in relation to its stakeholders, given the organization's resources, capabilities, and mission.[73] **Strategic choice** refers to the idea that an organization interacts with its environment instead of being totally determined by it.[74] In other words, organizational leaders take steps to define and manipulate their environments, rather than let the organization's fate be entirely determined by external influences.

The notion of strategic choice can be traced back to the work of Alfred Chandler in the early 1960s.[75] Chandler's proposal was that structure follows strategy. He observed that organizational structures follow the growth strategy developed by the organization's decision makers. Moreover, he noted that organizational structures change only after decision makers decide to do so. This recognizes that the link between structure and the contingency factors described earlier is mediated by organizational strategy.

Chandler's thesis that structure follows strategy has become the dominant perspective of business policy and strategic management. An important aspect of this view is that organizations can choose the environments in which they want to operate. Some businesses adopt a *differentiation strategy* by bringing unique products to the market or attracting clients who want customized goods and services. They try to distinguish their outputs from those provided by other firms through marketing, providing special services, and innovation. Others adopt a *cost leadership strategy*, in which they maximize productivity and are thereby able to offer popular products or services at a competitive price.[76]

The organizational strategy that we select determines the best organizational structure to adopt.[77] Organizations with a cost leadership strategy should adopt a mechanistic, functional structure with high levels of job specialization and standardized work processes. This is similar to the routine technology category described earlier because it maximizes production and service efficiency. A differentiation strategy, on the other hand, requires more customized relations with clients. A matrix or team-based structure with less centralization and formalization is most appropriate here so that technical specialists are able to coordinate their work activities more closely with the client's needs. Overall, it is now apparent that organizational structure is influenced by size, technology, and environment, but the organization's strategy may reshape these elements and loosen their connection to organizational structure.

Organizational Design and Organizational Behavior

At some point in your career, you will likely face difficult decisions about how an organization should be structured. This is much more than drawing boxes and lines on an organization chart; it requires critical decisions about how people work together. And as you grapple with these decisions, keep in mind that restructuring an organization relates to almost every topic in organizational behavior. An organization's structure influences the ability of employees to acquire and share knowledge. It affects their motivation and the alignment of rewards to organizational objectives. Ineffective structures are sources of employee stress and misperceptions about customers and co-workers. Our knowledge of teams from Chapters 9 and 10 can improve organizational structures, particularly emerging forms. We must also keep in mind that every organizational configuration has implications for power, politics, conflict, and resistance to change.

Overall, you can see how organizational behavior topics are interrelated. It is difficult to discuss motivation without referring to personality. We can't understand communication without noting power and politics. Leadership embraces change. Change embraces knowledge management. And as you apply organizational behavior concepts throughout your career, remember that organizations are the people in them. They are human entities—full of life, sometimes fragile, always exciting.

Chapter Summary

Organizational structure refers to the division of labor as well as the patterns of coordination, communication, work flow, and formal power that direct organizational activities. All organizational structures divide labor into distinct tasks and coordinate that labor to accomplish common goals. The primary means of coordination are information communication, formal hierarchy, and standardization.

The four basic elements of organizational structure include span of control, centralization, formalization, and departmentalization. At one time, scholars suggested that firms should have a tall hierarchy with a narrow span of control. Today most organizations have the opposite because they rely on informal communication and standardization, rather than direct supervision, to coordinate work processes.

Centralization means that formal decision authority is held by a small group of people, typically senior executives. Many companies decentralize as they become larger and more complex because senior executives lack the necessary time and expertise to process all the decisions that significantly influence the business.

Companies also tend to become more formalized over time because work activities become routinized. Formalization increases in larger firms because standardization works more efficiently than informal communications and direct supervision.

A functional structure organizes employees around specific knowledge or other resources. This fosters greater specialization and improves direct supervision, but makes it more difficult for people to see the organization's larger picture or to coordinate across departments. A divisional structure groups employees around geographic areas, clients, or outputs. This structure accommodates growth and focuses employee attention on products or customers rather than tasks. However, this structure creates silos of knowledge and duplication of resources.

The matrix structure combines two structures to leverage the benefits of both types of structure. However, this approach requires more coordination than functional or pure divisional structures, may dilute accountability, and increases conflict.

One emerging form of departmentalization is the team-based structure. This structure is very flat with low formalization that organizes self-directed teams around work processes rather than functional specialties.

A network structure is an alliance of several organizations for the purpose of creating a product or serving a client. Cellular organizations are network structures that can quickly reorganize themselves to suit the client's requirements.

The best organizational structure depends on the firm's size, technology, and environment. Generally, larger organizations are decentralized and more formalized, with greater job specialization and elaborate coordinating mechanisms. The work unit's technology, including variety of work and analyzability of problems, influences whether to adopt an organic or mechanistic structure. We need to consider whether the external environment is dynamic, complex, diverse, or hostile.

Although size, technology, and environment influence the optimal organizational structure, these contingencies do not necessarily determine structure. Rather, organizational leaders formulate and implement strategies to define and manipulate their environments. These strategies, rather than the other contingencies, directly shape the organization's structure.

Key Terms

Affiliate networks, p. 581
Cellular organizations, p. 582
Centralization, p. 566
Concurrent engineering, p. 561
Departmentalization, p. 570
Divisional structure, p. 572
Formalization, p. 567
Functional structure, p. 572
Job specialization, p. 560
Matrix structure, p. 574

Mechanistic structure, p. 569
Network structure, p. 580
Organic structure, p. 570
Organizational design, p. 560
Organizational strategy, p. 585
Organizational structure, p. 560
Span of control, p. 563
Strategic choice, p. 585
Team-based organizational structure, p. 578

Discussion Questions

1. Why are organizations moving toward flatter structures?

2. CyberTech makes four types of products, each of which is sold to different types of clients. For example, one product is sold exclusively to automobile repair shops, whereas another is used mainly in hospitals. Customer expectations and needs are surprisingly similar throughout the world. However, the company has separate marketing, product design, and manufacturing facilities in North America, Europe, Asia, and South America because, until recently, each jurisdiction had unique regulations governing the production and sales of this product. However, several governments have begun the process of deregulation, and trade agreements have opened several

markets to foreign-made products. Which form of departmentalization might be best for CyberTech if deregulation and trade agreements occur?

3. Why don't all organizations group people around product-based divisions?

4. Several global organizations have tried implementing a matrix structure to balance the power of their functional and divisional groups. However, many of these firms experienced problems and eventually switched to a hybrid form of divisionalized structure. Identify some of the problems that these companies may have experienced with a matrix structure.

5. St. Luke's has a team-based structure from top to bottom. Is this typical? Could such a structure exist at AT&T or a national mail service?

6. Some writers believe that a network structure is an effective design for global competition. Is this true, or are there situations where this organizational structure may be inappropriate?

7. Suppose that you have been hired as a consultant to diagnose the external environment of your college. How would you describe the college's external environment? Is the college's existing structure appropriate for this environment?

8. What do we mean by "structure follows strategy"?

CASE STUDY

The rise and fall of PMC AG

Founded in 1930, PMC AG is a German manufacturer of high-priced sports cars. During the early years, PMC was a small consulting engineering firm that specialized in solving difficult automotive design problems for clients. At the end of World War II, however, the son of PMC's founder decided to expand the business beyond consulting engineering. He was determined that PMC would build its own precision automobiles.

In 1948, the first PMC prototypes rolled out of the small manufacturing facility. Each copy was hand made by highly skilled craftspeople. For several years, parts and engine were designed and built by other companies and assembled at the PMC plant. By the 1960s, however, PMC had begun to design and build its own parts.

PMC grew rapidly during the 1960s to mid-1980s. The company designed a completely new car in the early 1960s, launched a lower-priced model in 1970, and added a midpriced model in 1977. By the mid-1980s PMC had become very profitable as its name became an icon for wealthy entrepreneurs and jetsetters. In 1986, the year of highest production, PMC sold 54,000 cars, nearly two-thirds of which were sold in North America.

PMC's Structure

PMC's organizational structure expanded with its success. During the early years, the company consisted only of an engineering department and a production department. By the 1980s employees were divided into more than 10 functional departments representing different stages of the production process as well as upstream (e.g., design, purchasing) and downstream (e.g., quality control, marketing) activities. Employees worked exclusively in one department. It was almost considered mutiny for an employee to voluntarily move into another department.

PMC's production workers were organized into a traditional hierarchy. Frontline employees reported to work group leaders, who reported to supervisors, who reported to group supervisors in each area. Group supervisors reported to production managers, who reported to production directors, who reported to PMC's executive vice president of manufacturing. At one point in time, nearly 20 percent of production staff members was involved in supervisory tasks. In the early 1990s, for example, there were 48 group supervisors, 96 supervisors, and 162 work group leaders supervising about 2,500 frontline production employees.

PMC's Craft Tradition

PMC had a long tradition and culture that supported craft expertise. This appealed to Germany's skilled workforce because it gave employees an opportunity to test and further develop their skills. PMC workers were encouraged to master long work cycles, often as much as 15 minutes per unit. Their ideal was to build as much of the automobile as possible on their own. For example, a few masters were able to assemble an entire engine. Their reward was to personally sign their name on the completed component.

The design engineers worked independently of the production department, with the result that production employees had to adjust designs to fit the available parts. Rather than being a nuisance, the production employees viewed this as a challenge that would further test their well-developed craft skills. Similarly, manufacturing engineers occasionally redesigned the product to fit manufacturing capabilities.

To improve efficiency, a moving track assembly system was introduced in 1977. Even then, the emphasis on craft skills was apparent. Employees were encouraged to quickly put all the parts on the car, knowing that highly skilled troubleshooting craftspeople would discover and repair defects after the car came off the line. This was much more costly and time consuming than assembling the vehicle correctly the first time, but it provided yet another challenging set of tasks for skilled craftspeople. And to support their position, PMC vehicles were known for their few defects by the time they were sold to customers.

The End of Success?

PMC sports cars filled a small niche in the automobile market for those who wanted a true sports car just tame enough for everyday use. PMCs were known for their superlative performance based on excellent engineering technology, but they were also becoming very expensive. Japanese sports cars were not quite in the same league as a PMC. However, the cost of manufacturing the Japanese vehicles was a small fraction of the cost of manufacturing a vehicle at PMC.

This cost inefficiency hit PMC's sales during the late 1980s and early 1990s. First, the German currency appreciated against the U.S. dollar, which made PMC sports cars even more expensive in the North American market. By 1990, PMC was selling half the number of cars it sold just four years earlier. Then the North American recession hit, driving PMC sales down further. In 1993, PMC sold just 14,000 vehicles, compared with 54,000 in 1986. Although sales rebounded to 20,000 by 1995, the high price tag put PMCs out of reach for many potential customers. It was clear to PMC's founding family that changes were needed, but they weren't sure where to begin.

Discussion Questions

1. Describe PMC's organizational structure in terms of the four organizational design features (i.e., span of control, centralization, formalization, and departmentalization).

2. Describe an organizational structure that, in your opinion, would reduce costs and improve production efficiency at PMC.

3. This case touches on quality management issues (see Chapter 10). Identify some quality management practices that PMC should consider to improve its competitiveness.

Source: Written by Steven L. McShane based on information from several sources about "PMC." The company name and some details of actual events have been altered to provide a fuller case discussion. ■

CASE STUDY

Procter & Gamble's hottest new product: P&G

BusinessWeek

Visitors at Washington State's Clark County Fair got a peek at Procter & Gamble's (P&G) latest product—itself. P&G's sales force was out distributing coffee samples at the Pancake Feed. Behind this unusual display of grass-roots marketing is P&G's new corporate structure and vision, called Organization 2005. Battered by disappointing revenue growth and demanding retail customers, senior executives at the consumer products company visited the CEOs of a dozen major companies, including Kellogg Co. and 3M, in search of advice. The message from all was clear: Be simpler and move faster.

To meet this challenge, P&G shuffled its hierarchy and created a new product-development process designed to speed innovative offerings to the global market. This *Business Week* case study describes P&G's new corporate structure and explains why the company had to change its organizational design. Read through this

Business Week case study at www.mhhe.com/mcshane1e and prepare for the discussion questions below.

Discussion Questions

1. Describe Procter & Gamble's new organizational structure in terms of the four elements of organizational structure described in this chapter.

2. What environmental factors put pressure on P&G to change its structure and work practices?

3. What problems would you anticipate from P&G's emerging organizational structure?

Source: P. Galuszka and E. Neuborne, "P&G's Hottest New Product: P&G," *Business Week,* October 5, 1998, pp. 92–93. ■

VIDEO CASE

Big Apple Bagel/St. Louis Bread Co.

In the past, a corporation was structured much like the military with a formal chain of command and division of labor. Over time, many companies came to realize that this type of bureaucratic structure can cause breakdowns in communications and lower efficiency levels. Manufacturers of products in relatively unchanging environments often take a mechanistic approach to production. In such environments employees strictly adhere to their job descriptions. Companies that rely on their ability to continuously introduce new innovations usually take a more organic approach, giving employees more room to make decisions and communicate outside the chain of command. Some companies may choose to radically modify or reengineer their structure. Big Apple Bagels and Saint Louis Bread Company are two rapidly growing businesses that share a similar market. However, each organization is structured quite differently.

Whatever the structure of an organization, to be successful it must be responsive to its customers. Many companies are finding that changing the way in which they are organized improves their responsiveness. For example, they may choose to simplify their structure and reduce the layers of management—thus reducing the layers in the chain of command. Another option is to widen spans of control. The traditional organization had a tall structure and a narrow span of control, which meant managers had few subordinates who reported directly to them. By contrast, a company with a flat organizational structure has a wide span of control with fewer reporting levels.

Many companies are empowering their employees and letting them make decisions on their own rather than insisting that they report to various levels of management. When Paul Stolzer opened the first Big Apple Bagel store in 1985 he had no idea that, in the short span of seven years, his small store would grow into a franchise that boasts 75 stores with more opening all the time. As Mr. Stolzer said, "The stores have changed quite extensively over the years. Initially, the stores were set up as strictly bagel bakeries where the predominate products were bagels and cream cheese. We've progressed to a more aggressive stature and added a few more dimensions to our operation in that we have dining facilities, a more extensive sandwich menu, a strong coffee program, and we are still progressing. That's an evolution that never ends."

One thing that hasn't changed is Big Apple's open door policy. From top management to line workers, communication lines are wide open. Jim Lentz, director of training, said, "At Big Apple Bagels we have an open door policy between the franchisee and the franchiser and the ultimate consumer in that we encourage people to come up with suggestions, ideas, and new products. We're never farther than a phone call or stop away. We are continually in the franchisee's stores to make sure that their operations meet our specifications."

In 1987 Ken Rosenthal opened his first Saint Louis Bread Company store in Kirkwood, Missouri, with used baking equipment. Today, St. Louis Bread Company operates over 50 stores. The growth happened quickly, but not without careful planning. This growth forced the company to change its organizational structure. Originally it was a small store with 17 employees. When it became a large chain employing over 1,000 people a more traditional organizational structure was needed.

By mid-1992 St. Louis Bread was growing at a frantic pace. The partners decided it was time to slow down and take a breath. They began to realize that the opportunistic approach wouldn't work anymore. They had reached a point where the controls and information systems they had in place were inadequate for a larger operation. New equipment was purchased to automate processes on the line. Point of purchase cash registers were installed to track everything from sales per hour to sales per stock keeping unit to sales by stores.

David S. Hutkin, president of St. Louis Bread Co., said, "The organization of St. Louis Bread Company was not atypical of many organizations. We have a hierarchical structure in terms of someone who is ultimately accountable for the results of the business. We do fight vigorously to maintain a flat organization. There aren't a lot of layers between the president and the people who are in the grinds, if you will, day in and day out, taking care of our customers. I think we have succeeded because of the efforts put into that."

In November of 1993, Au Bon Pain, the dominant bakery café chain in the country, acquired St. Louis Bread Company. Au Bon Pain stores were all in suburban areas. St. Louis Bread Company would enable them to tap into the urban market. Kenneth J. Rosenthal, founder and executive vice president of St. Louis Bread Company, said, "Our organizational structure hasn't changed dramatically. It really hasn't changed since the acquisition. We've continued to run the company very independent of our parent company and we are still building stores and expanding the concept. As far as the organization, basically, we are still doing the same things that we were doing before."

A company like Big Apple Bagels is considered to be a boundaryless organization. In such an organization the corporate structure is more horizontal than vertical. Boundaryless businesses are typically organized around core customer-oriented processes such as communication, customer contact, and managing quality. In order to enjoy the benefits that a horizontal organization offers certain boundaries must be overcome. Even a relatively boundaryless company has an authority boundary. Some people lead, others follow. To overcome problems that may arise management must learn how to lead and still remain open to criticism. Their subordinates need to be trained and encouraged not only to follow, but to challenge their superiors if there is an issue worth reconsidering. Three types of boundaries must be overcome:

- Task Boundary
- Political Boundary
- Identity Boundary

The task boundary develops out of the "it's not my job" mentality. A task boundary can be overcome by defining who does what when employees from different departments divide up work. The political boundary derives from the differences in political agendas that often separate employees and can cause conflict. It's closely related to the identity boundary. The identity boundary emerges due to an employee tendency to identify with those individuals or groups with whom they have shared experiences. To overcome identity boundaries, employees and management need to be trained to gain an understanding of the business as a whole and avoid the "us versus them" mentality. A good way to do this is by forming cross-functional teams in which tasks are shared and cross training simply happens.

The new boundaryless organization relies on self-managed work teams. It reduces internal boundaries that separate functions and create hierarchical levels. A horizontal corporation is structured around customer-oriented processes. Lines of communication are very open allowing front-line employees to communicate directly with those at the management and executive levels. Not all organizations are structured the same way. There are factors to consider such as organizational size, culture, and production volume. These factors may indicate that, under some circumstances, a tall organizational structure may be more appropriate than a flat structure. Companies in the future may change or alter the way they operate, but customer satisfaction, quality, and efficiency will always be the primary goals.

Discussion Questions

1. Although it is fashionable today to encourage flat organizational structures, the tall structure still has merit for some organizations. Explain why an organization would choose a tall over a flat structure.

2. When an organization grows in size and complexity organizational structure changes often become necessary. How can an organization maintain a "small company" feel as it grows?

3. Explain the meaning of the term "boundaryless organization." What is the value of boundaries in an organization? ◼

Organizational structure and design: The Club Ed exercise

Purpose

This exercise is designed to help you understand the issues to consider when designing organizations at various stages of growth.

Instructions

Students are placed in teams (typically four or five people). Each team works through each of the steps below. The instructor will facilitate discussion and advise teams when to begin the next step. This exercise may be continued over two class sessions.

Step 1: Determined never to shovel snow again, you are establishing a new resort business on a small Caribbean island. The resort is under construction and is scheduled to open one year from now. You decide it is time to draw up an organizational chart for this new venture, called Club Ed. What services will you provide? What jobs and tasks are required for this business? Your team will draw Club Ed's organizational chart. Be prepared to present your design and answer the following questions:

1. What type of structure have you drawn? Why is it appropriate?
2. What problems are you trying to address with this structure?
3. How does this structure relate to Club Ed's strategy?

Step 2: Your instructor will select one or two groups to present their designs and lead the class discussion.

Step 3: It is now seven years later. Your resort has been wildly successful. Through profits and investment from a silent partner, Club Ed now owns several resorts—two in the Caribbean, two in Mexico, and one in the South Pacific. Draw an up-to-date organizational chart and answer the questions above in Step 1.

Step 4: Your instructor will select one or two groups to present their designs and lead the class discussion.

Step 5: Ten years later, you and your partners own 80 Club Ed resorts in North, Central, and South America, the Caribbean, and South Pacific. The company also operates a cruise ship. Draw an up-to-date organizational chart for Club Ed and answer the questions above in Step 1.

Step 6: Your instructor will select one or two groups to present their designs and lead the class discussion.

Step 7: Ten more years have passed. The Club now has 112 resorts and three cruise ships. A recent customer profile shows that almost 50 percent of its customers are repeat business and are more than 40 years old. The three "S's" (sun, sand, and sex) marketing theme is out of date in a world where AIDS and fears of skin cancer are all too real. This has contributed to fewer guests over each of the past three years. Moreover, North America and Europe are entering a recession, which will further reduce demand for Club Ed's services. How does Club Ed adapt to these new realities? Diagram the company's organizational chart and answer the questions above in Step 1. In particular, be prepared to discuss Club Ed's new structure in terms of its new business strategy.

Step 8: Your instructor will select one or two groups to present their designs and lead the class discussion.

Discussion Questions

1. How does Club Ed's organizational structure change as it grows and diversifies? What factors drive these structural changes?

2. How can Club Ed structure itself as an adaptive organization? Does it always have to react to environmental changes or are there some ways it can be proactive?

Source: Adapted from C. Harvey and K. Morouney, *Journal of Management Education* 22 (June 1998), pp. 425–29. Used with permission of the authors. ∎

SELF-ASSESSMENT EXERCISE

Identifying your preferred organizational structure

Purpose

This exercise is designed to help you understand how an organization's structure influences the personal needs and values of people working in that structure.

Instructions

Personal needs and values influence how comfortable you are working in different organizational structures. You might prefer an organization with clearly defined rules or no rules at all. You might prefer a firm where almost any employee can make important decisions, or where important decisions are screened by senior executives. Read the statements below and indicate the extent to which you would like to work in an organization with the stated characteristic. When finished, use the scoring key to calculate your results. This self-assessment is completed alone. However, class discussion will focus on the elements of organizational design and their relationship to personal needs and values.

Organizational structure preference scale					
I would like to work in an organization where . . .					**Score**
1. A person's career ladder has several steps toward higher status and responsibility.	Not at all	A little	Somewhat	Very much	_____
2. Employees perform their work with few rules to limit their discretion.	Not at all	A little	Somewhat	Very much	_____
3. Responsibility is pushed down to employees who perform the work.	Not at all	A little	Somewhat	Very much	_____
4. Supervisors have few employees, so they work closely with each person.	Not at all	A little	Somewhat	Very much	_____
5. Senior executives make most decisions to ensure that the company is consistent in its actions.	Not at all	A little	Somewhat	Very much	_____
6. Jobs are clearly defined so there is no confusion over who is responsible for various tasks.	Not at all	A little	Somewhat	Very much	_____
7. Employees have their say on issues, but senior executives make most of the decisions.	Not at all	A little	Somewhat	Very much	_____
8. Job descriptions are broadly stated or nonexistent.	Not at all	A little	Somewhat	Very much	_____
9. Everyone's work is tightly synchronized around top management operating plans.	Not at all	A little	Somewhat	Very much	_____
10. Most work is performed in teams without close supervision.	Not at all	A little	Somewhat	Very much	_____
11. Work gets done through informal discussion with co-workers rather than through formal rules.	Not at all	A little	Somewhat	Very much	_____
12. Supervisors have so many employees that they can't watch anyone very closely.	Not at all	A little	Somewhat	Very much	_____

13.	Everyone has clearly understood goals, expectations, and job duties.	Not at all	A little	Somewhat	Very much	_____
14.	Senior executives assign overall goals, but leave daily decisions to frontline teams.	Not at all	A little	Somewhat	Very much	_____
15.	Even in a large company, the CEO is only three or four levels above the lowest position.	Not at all	A little	Somewhat	Very much	_____

Scoring the organizational structure preference scale

Step 1. Using the table below, assign the number corresponding to the answer you indicated for each statement. For example, if you indicated "Very much" for statement 1, then write "3" in the space provided to the right of the statement.

For statement items 2, 3, 4, 8, 10, 11, 14, 15	For statement items 1, 5, 6, 7, 9, 12, 13
Not at all = 3	Not at all = 0
A little = 2	A little = 1
Somewhat = 1	Somewhat = 2
Very much = 0	Very much = 3

Step 2. Write the scores for each item on the appropriate line below (statement numbers are in parentheses), and add up each scale. Then calculate the overall score by summing all scales.

Tall hierarchy (H) _____ + _____ + _____ + _____ + _____ = _____
                        (1)   (4)   (10)   (12)   (15)   (H)

Formalization (F) _____ + _____ + _____ + _____ + _____ = _____
                        (2)   (6)   (8)   (11)   (13)   (F)

Centralization (C) _____ + _____ + _____ + _____ + _____ = _____
                        (3)   (5)   (7)   (9)   (14)   (C)

Total score* _____ + _____ + _____   = _____
                    (H)   (F)   (C)   (Total)

*A higher total score indicates preference for mechanistic organizations, whereas lower scores indicate preference for more organic organizations.

© Copyright 2000. Steven L. McShane. ■

- **Case 1. Arctic Mining Consultants**
- **Case 2. A Window on Life**
- **Case 3. Montville Hospital Dietary Department**
- **Case 4. Perfect Pizzeria**

CASE 1

Arctic Mining Consultants

Tom Parker enjoyed working outdoors. At various times in the past, he worked as a ranch hand, high steel rigger, headstone installer, and prospector. Now 43 years old, Parker is a geological field technician and field coordinator with Arctic Mining Consultants. He has specialized knowledge and experience in all nontechnical aspects of mineral exploration, including claim staking, line cutting and grid installation, soil sampling, prospecting, and trenching. He is responsible for hiring, training, and supervising field assistants for all of Arctic Mining Consultants' programs. Field assistants are paid a fairly low daily wage (no matter how long they work, which may be up to 12 hours or more) and are provided meals and accommodation. Many of the programs are operated by a project manager who reports to Parker.

Parker sometimes acts as a project manager, as he did on a job that involved staking 15 claims near Eagle Lake, Alaska. He selected John Talbot, Greg Boyce, and Brian Millar, all of whom had previously worked with Parker, as the field assistants. To stake a claim, the project team marks a line with flagging tape and blazes (trail markers) along the perimeter of the claim, cutting a claim post every 500 yards (called a "length"). The 15 claims would require almost 60 miles of line in total. Parker had budgeted seven days (plus mobilization and demobilization) to complete the job. This meant that each of the four stakers (Parker, Talbot, Boyce, and Millar) would have to complete a little over seven "lengths" each day. The following is a chronology of the project.

Day 1

The Arctic Mining Consultants crew assembled in the morning and drove to Eagle Lake, from where they were flown by helicopter to the claim site. On arrival, they set up tents at the edge of the area to be staked and agreed on a schedule for cooking duties. After supper, they pulled out the maps and discussed the job—how long it would take, the order in which the areas were to be staked, possible helicopter landing spots, and areas that might be more difficult to stake.

Parker pointed out that with only a week to complete the job, everyone would have to average seven and one-half lengths per day. "I know that is a lot," he said, "but you've all staked claims before and I'm confident that each of you is capable of it. And it's only for a week. If we get the job done in time, there's a $300 bonus for each man." Two hours later, Parker and his crew members had developed what seemed to be a workable plan.

Day 2

Millar and Boyce completed six lengths each, Talbot and Parker eight each. Parker was not pleased with Millar's or Boyce's production. However, he didn't make an issue of it, thinking that they would develop their "rhythm" quickly.

Day 3

Millar completed five and one-half lengths, Boyce four, and Talbot seven. Parker, who was nearly twice as old as the other three, completed eight lengths. He also had enough time remaining to walk over and check the quality of the stakes that Millar and Boyce had completed, then walk back to his own area for a helicopter pickup back to the tent site.

That night Parker exploded with anger. "I thought I told you that I wanted seven and a half lengths a day!" he shouted at Boyce and Millar. Boyce said that he was slowed down by unusually thick underbrush in his assigned area. Millar said that he had done his best and would try to pick up the pace. Parker did not mention

595

that he had inspected their work. He explained that as far as he was concerned, the field assistants were supposed to finish their assigned area for the day, no matter what.

Talbot, who was sharing a tent with Parker, talked to him later. "I think that you're being a bit hard on them. I know that it has been more by luck than anything else that I've been able to do my quota. Yesterday I only had five lengths done after the first seven hours and there was only one hour before I was supposed to be picked up. Then I hit a patch of really open bush, and was able to do three lengths in 70 minutes. Why don't I take Millar's area tomorrow and he can have mine? Maybe that will help."

"Conditions are the same in all of the areas," replied Parker, rejecting Talbot's suggestion. "Millar just has to try harder."

Day 4

Millar did seven lengths and Boyce completed six and a half. When they reported their production that evening, Parker grunted uncommunicatively. Parker and Talbot did eight lengths each.

Day 5

Millar completed six lengths, Boyce six, Talbot seven and one-half, and Parker eight. Once again Parker blew up, but he concentrated his diatribe on Millar. "Why don't you do what you say you are going to do? You know that you have to do seven and one-half lengths a day. We went over that when we first got here, so why don't you do it? If you aren't willing to do the job, then you never should have taken it in the first place!"

Millar replied that he was doing his best, that he hadn't even stopped for lunch and didn't know how he could possibly do any better. Parker launched into him again, "You have got to work harder! If you put enough effort into it, you will get the area done!"

Later Millar commented to Boyce, "I hate getting dumped on all the time! I'd quit if it didn't mean that I'd have to walk 50 miles to the highway. Besides, I need the bonus money. Why doesn't he pick on you? You don't get any more done than me; in fact, you usually get less. Maybe if you did a bit more he wouldn't be so bothered about me."

"I only work as hard as I have to," Boyce replied.

Day 6

Millar raced through breakfast, was the first one to be dropped off by the helicopter, and arranged to be the last one picked up. That evening the production figures were Millar eight and one-quarter lengths, Boyce seven, and Talbot and Parker eight each. Parker remained silent when the field assistants reported their performance for the day.

Day 7

Millar was again the first out and last in. That night, he collapsed in an exhausted heap at the table, too tired to eat. After a few moments, he announced in an abject tone, "Six lengths. I worked like a dog all day and I only got a lousy six lengths!" Boyce completed five lengths, Talbot seven, and Parker seven and one-quarter.

Parker was furious. "That means we have to do a total of 34 lengths tomorrow if we are to finish this job on time!" With his eyes directed at Millar, he added, "Why is it that you never finish the job? Don't you realize that you are part of a team, and that you are letting the rest of the team down? I've been checking your lines and you're doing too much blazing and wasting too much time making picture-perfect claim posts! If you worked smarter, you'd get a lot more done!"

Day 8

Parker cooked breakfast in the dark. The helicopter drop-offs began as soon as morning light appeared on the horizon. Parker instructed each assistant to complete eight lengths and, if they finished early, to help the others. Parker said that he would finish the other 10 lengths. Helicopter pickups were arranged for one hour before dark.

By noon, after working as hard as he could, Millar had completed only three lengths. "Why bother," he thought to himself, "I'll never be able to do another five lengths before the helicopter comes, and I'll catch the same amount of abuse from Parker for doing six lengths as for seven and a half." So he sat down and had lunch and a rest. "Boyce won't finish his eight lengths either, so even if I did finish mine, I still wouldn't get the bonus. At least I'll get one more day's pay this way."

That night, Parker was livid when Millar reported that he had completed five and one-half lengths. Parker had done ten and one-quarter lengths, and Talbot had completed eight. Boyce proudly announced that he finished seven and one-half lengths, but sheepishly added that Talbot had helped him with some of it. All that remained were the two and one-half lengths that Millar had not completed.

The job was finished the next morning and the crew demobilized. Millar has never worked for Arctic Mining Consultants again, despite being offered work several times by Parker. Boyce sometimes does staking for Arctic, and Talbot works full time with the company.

A window on life

For Gilbert LaCrosse, there is nothing quite as beautiful as a handcrafted wood-framed window. LaCrosse's passion for windows goes back to his youth in Eau Claire, Wisconsin, where an elderly carpenter taught him how to make residential windows. He learned about the characteristics of good wood, the best tools to use, and how to choose the best glass from local suppliers. LaCrosse apprenticed with the carpenter in his small workshop and, when the carpenter retired, was given the opportunity to operate the business himself.

LaCross hired his own apprentice as he built up business in the local area. His small operation soon expanded as the quality of windows built by LaCrosse Industries Co. became better known. Within eight years the company employed nearly 25 people and the business had moved to larger facilities to accommodate the increased demand in Wisconsin. In these early years LaCrosse spent most of his time in the production shop, teaching new apprentices the unique skills that he had mastered and applauding the journeymen for their accomplishments. He would constantly repeat the point that LaCrosse products had to be of the highest quality because they gave families a "window on life."

After 15 years, LaCross Industries employed more than 200 people. A profit-sharing program was introduced to give employees a financial reward for their contribution to the organization's success. Due to the company's expansion, headquarters had to be moved to another part of the city, but the founder never lost touch with the workforce. Although new apprentices were now taught entirely by the master carpenters and other craftspeople, LaCrosse would still chat with plant and office employees several times each week.

When a second work shift was added, LaCrosse would show up during the evening break with coffee and boxes of doughnuts and discuss how the business was doing and how it became so successful through quality workmanship. Production employees enjoyed the times when he would gather them together to announce new contracts with developers from Chicago and New York. After each announcement, LaCrosse would thank everyone for making the business a success. They knew that LaCrosse quality had become a standard of excellence in window manufacturing across the eastern part of the country.

It seemed that almost every time he visited, LaCrosse would repeat the now well-known phrase that LaCrosse products had to be of the highest quality because they provided a window on life to so many families. Employees never grew tired of hearing this from the company founder. However, it gained extra meaning when LaCrosse began posting photos of families looking through LaCrosse windows. At first, LaCrosse would personally visit developers and home owners with a camera in hand. Later, as the "window on life" photos became known by developers and customers, people would send in photos of their own families looking through elegant front windows made by LaCrosse Industries. The company's marketing staff began using this idea, along with LaCrosse's famous phrase, in their advertising. After one such marketing campaign, hundreds of photos were sent in by satisfied customers. Production and office employees took time after work to write personal letters of thanks to those who had submitted photos.

As the company's age reached the quarter-century mark, LaCrosse, now in his mid-50s, realized that the organization's success and survival depended on expansion to other parts of the United States. After consulting with employees, LaCrosse made the difficult decision to sell a majority share to Build-All Products, Inc., a conglomerate with international marketing expertise in building products. As part of the agreement, Build-All brought in a vice president to oversee production operations while LaCrosse spent more time meeting with developers. LaCrosse would return to the plant and office at every opportunity, but often this would be only once a month.

Rather than visiting the production plant, Jan Vlodoski, the new production vice president, would rarely leave his office in the company's downtown headquarters. Instead, production orders were sent to supervisors by memorandum. Although product quality had been a priority throughout the company's history, less attention had been paid to inventory controls. Vlodoski introduced strict inventory guidelines and outlined procedures on using supplies for each shift. Goals were established for supervisors to meet specific inventory targets. Whereas employees previously could have tossed out several pieces of warped wood, they would now have to justify this action, usually in writing.

Vlodoski also announced new procedures for purchasing production supplies. LaCrosse Industries had a highly trained purchasing staff who worked closely with senior craftspeople when selecting suppliers, but Vlodoski wanted to bring in Build-All's procedures. The new purchasing methods removed production leaders from the decision-making process and, in some cases, resulted in trade-offs that LaCrosse's employees would not have made earlier. A few employees quit at this time, saying that they did not feel comfortable about producing a window that would not stand the test of time. However, there were few jobs for carpenters, so most staff members remained with the company.

After one year, inventory expenses decreased by approximately 10 percent, but the number of defective windows returned by developers and wholesalers had increased markedly. Plant employees knew that the number of defective windows would increase as they used somewhat lower-quality materials to reduce inventory costs. However, they heard almost no news about the seriousness of the problem until Vlodoski sent a memo to all production staff saying that quality must be maintained. During the latter part of the first year under Vlodoski, a few employees had the opportunity to personally ask LaCrosse about the changes and express their concerns. LaCrosse apologized, saying that because of his travels to new regions, he had not heard about the problems, but he would look into the matter.

Exactly 18 months after Build-All had become majority shareholder of LaCrosse Industries, LaCrosse called together five of the original staff in the plant. The company founder looked pale and shaken as he said that Build-All's actions were inconsistent with his vision of the company and, for the first time in his career, he did not know what to do. Build-All was not pleased with the arrangement either. Although LaCrosse windows still enjoyed a healthy market share and were competitive for the value, the company did not quite provide the minimum 18 percent return on equity that the conglomerate expected. LaCrosse asked his long-time companions for advice.

© Copyright. Steven L. McShane. ■

CASE 3

Montville Hospital dietary department

Introduction

Rene Marcotte briskly walked home from her part-time job with the Montville Hospital dietary department. "Mom," she said as she entered the house, "they may have to close down the hospital! The Montville Department of Health has just found the dietary department's sanitary conditions to be substandard. Mrs. DeMambro, our chief supervisor, said that we are really going to have to get to work and clean the place or the hospital is in trouble!"

The Hospital

As Rene continued to tell her mother about this latest event, she thought about her part-time job at the hospital, which she had had now for almost a year. Montville Hospital was a 400-bed community general hospital located in suburban Montville outside New York City. Montville itself was a racially mixed community of low- and middle-income working families. However, Montville, along with most hospitals, was operating under severe financial pressure and needed constantly to find ways to reduce costs. It offered a range of medical services but, due to the nature of the Montville population, it had an appreciable number of elderly terminal patients. The hospital was well thought of by the community both as a place of treatment and as a source of employment. Through the years it had received strong financial support from the community and had grown as the community had grown. It currently was building a new wing to keep up with expanding demand, and this added to its tight financial situation.

The Dietary Department

The dietary department, where Rene worked, was located in the wing that had been added during the previous expansion project a little more than 10 years ago. This department employed approximately 100 employees (mostly female) and was under the direction of Mr. Thomas Ellis, food service director. The department employed cooks, dieticians, and "kitchen workers" (of whom Rene was one). The department had two major responsibilities—namely, the planning, preparation, and serving of three meals a day to every patient and the operation of an employees' cafeteria. Since most of the patients required special diets, such as salt-free meals, the food for each was quite different, although cooked in a common kitchen.

Rene well remembered her initial contact with the department. When applying for a job, she was first "screened" by the hospital personnel office, then sent to be interviewed by Mrs. Kelley, the chief dietary supervisor, and, after a second interview by Mrs. Kelley, given a "tour" through the kitchen facilities by one of the supervisors. She never saw Mr. Ellis or Mrs. Johnston, the chief dietician. As she later learned, Mrs. Kelley did all of the hiring and firing, while salary and raises were determined by the payroll department. Rene felt as if Mr. Ellis were some kind of "god," when she eventually heard of his existence two weeks after starting work.

Upon being hired, Rene was put right to work with no formal instructions in standards or procedures. She, like every other new employee, was expected to learn by watching others and asking her peers. Rene, who undertook the job with a deep sense of responsibility, well remembers one of the older kids saying to her, "Hurry up; you're taking too long; don't bother to clean up those spots of spilled soup."

Along with Rene, the majority of the employees were kitchen workers (diet aides, dishwashers, and porters). Ninety-five percent were female. Twenty-five were full-timers working 40 hours per week, and 50 to 60 were part-timers, as was Rene.

Ten years ago the dietary department was smaller and under the direction of one of the current dieticians. There were no food service director and no chief dietary supervisor positions. While the kitchen was centralized at that time, tray preparation was not. This was done in a kitchenette located on each floor of the hospital. The workers moved from floor to floor, serving food from bulk containers onto individual trays on each floor. The dishroom also was separated physically. When the new wing was built, everything was centralized into one location from which carts of setup trays are sent out to each floor. Now, only the diet aides went to the floors and only for the purpose of distributing and collecting trays from the patients.

The full-time employees

The full-time employees were mostly older women (40 to 65 years of age) who had been working in the department for a long time, some for 15 to 20 years. All lived in Montville, most had a high school education, many were married, and most were helping to augment the family income so their children could be the first in their family to go to college. With few exceptions, they worked a morning shift from either 6:30 A.M. to 3:00 P.M. or 8:00 A.M. to 4:30 P.M.

Most of the women had worked in this organization back in the old days before the hospital expanded and the kitchen was rebuilt. They had many stories to tell about how it used to be and how much easier and less chaotic their jobs had been before the change. One woman, who had recently been reemployed, had worked in the same dietary department 20 years ago as a teenager. She was amazed at how different everything was and said now she felt she was in another world from the job she used to know and love 20 years ago. The women, however, took great pride in their work (many had been doing the same job for years). Each woman had her own assigned task, which she did every day, and there was little shifting around of positions. The dessert or salad makers never learned much about the work routine of the tray coverers, silverware sorters, or juice-setter-uppers. Every woman was set in a specific routine during a day's work. This routine was heavily controlled by the tight time schedule everyone had to follow. There was no fooling around, even though the working atmosphere was very congenial and everyone was on a first-name basis, including the supervisors. There was considerable conversation among the women while they worked, but it did not distract them from doing their jobs—perhaps because management required the workers to completely finish their assigned tasks before leaving for home, even if it meant working overtime, without extra pay.

There was a striking cross section of cultural backgrounds among these full-time employees. There were about equal numbers of whites, blacks, and Asians, and many were immigrants. Many spoke Spanish and very little English. Although a language barrier existed between many of the employees, feelings of mutual respect and friendliness were maintained. Malicious gossip due to racial or ethnic differences was uncommon, and the women helped each other when necessary to finish their jobs on time.

The women often expressed their concern about not getting their jobs done on time, especially when they were working the assembly line. This assembly line consisted of sending a tray down a belt, along which, at certain intervals, each worker put a specific item on the tray as designated by the menu for each patient. After each tray was completed, it was put in an electric cart with each cart containing trays for different floors of the hospital. The carts were then pulled (by men porters) into elevators and transferred to the designated floors. At this time, pairs of diet aides (not working on the line) were sent to the floors to deliver the trays to the patients. Speed and efficiency in delivering trays were very important. If the trays were sent up and then left standing for a long time before delivery to each patient, the food got cold and the dietary department received patient complaints directed at the dieticians. The complaints were relayed to the supervisor, who in turn reprimanded the diet aide(s) responsible for the cold food. This temporarily disrupted the informal and friendly working relationship between the diet aides and their supervisor, whom they liked and respected, causing uncomfortable guilt feelings for the diet aides. As a result, reprimands were seldom necessary among the full-timers.

At the same time, the diet aides were expected to meet certain established standards governing such matters as size of portion, cleanliness of kitchen facilities, and cleanliness in food handling and preparation. At times, indeed rather often, the standards were overlooked under the pressure of time. For instance, if the line was to be started at exactly 11:00 A.M. and if by that time the desserts were not wrapped or covered as required by sanitary regulations, the line might begin anyway, and the desserts went to the patients unwrapped.

The full-time employees received pay raises designated by a set scale based on continuing length of employment. Starting salary was about average for this type of work. They were allowed a certain number of sick days per year as well as paid vacations (the length of which were based on the numbers of years of employment). The uniforms they were required to wear were provided (three per person) by the hospital and could be laundered free of charge at the hospital laundry service. Also, the workers paid very little money, if anything at all, for meals eaten at work. Technically, they were supposed to pay in full for meals, but seldom did because of the lack of consistent control.

Work performance was evaluated on the basis of group effort. Individual effort usually was not singled out and rewarded in any tangible way. However, supervisors often would compliment an individual on how nice a salad plate looked or how quickly and efficiently a worker delivered the patients' trays. For instance, the woman who prepared fancy salad plates and sandwiches could take pride in the way they looked. Furthermore, the aides recognized that their work could affect a patient's well-being and therefore could be important, and sometimes a patient was a former hospital staff member or neighbor known by the aides. When delivering a tray, a diet aide might chat with a patient and discover particular likes or dislikes, which, when reported to the dietician, sometimes led to a revision in the patient's diet.

Extra care often was taken in arranging food on the tray in an attractive manner to please the patient. Sometimes this dedication produced minor problems, such as a diet aide violating certain rules to do something extra for a patient or promoting her own version of efficiency in doing a task. This type of individual initiative (and creativity) was not encouraged. Management set down rigid guidelines for performing all tasks as the only correct way, since they had worked out for so many years. Any recommendations for changes in these techniques were approached with caution by management. The equipment also had changed little in the past decade.

The part-time employees

There were 50 to 60 part-time employees in the dietary department whose level of pay was appreciably less than that of the full-timers. They were divided into two teams (team A and team B); each team worked on alternate days of the week and on alternate weekends, a device adopted on the advice of some efficiency experts as a way of avoiding having to pay overtime to anyone. There was no specific supervisor for each team; instead, each might have one of two supervisors depending on the day and/or week. Two different shifts exist for the part-timers: 3:30 to 6:30 and 4:00 to 8:00 (the kitchen closed at 8:00 P.M.), but on average all part-timers including Rene worked a 16-hour week. Their duties were the same as the full-timers, except that part-timers served and cleaned up after dinner instead of after breakfast and lunch. The majority of these workers were young, mostly high school age (16 to 18 years), working for extra money and because friends were working. Most had not worked in the hospital very long, because there was a constant turnover as individuals left to go to college, and so on, but other kids were readily available to take their places. There were also several older women, working on a part-time basis, who had been with the organization for many years.

The part-timers' situation exhibited a striking contrast to that of full-timers. There were no permanent task assignments; each night a part-timer did something different, and the kids often asked to do this or that different task. As a group, the night shift was not as unified in spirit or congeniality as the day shift (full-timers). The younger workers tended to form cliques apart from the older women and gossip and poke fun at non-English-speaking workers.

Most of the teenagers also took their work much less seriously than the older women (the full-timers), doing only what was required at the minimal level. As was the case with the full-timers, they worked on a tight schedule and their working behavior was heavily controlled by it. However, they seemed more anxious to get their work done as soon as possible. Once they had finished, they were free to leave no matter what time it was at no loss of pay—that is, if everyone was finished at, say, 7:45 P.M., all could leave yet still be paid until 8:00 P.M. It was not uncommon for work areas to become messy, for hands to be left unwashed, and for food to be handled and touched even though it shouldn't be. They also tended to devise their own ways for doing the job, partially to promote efficiency and decrease the time needed for completion. It was not uncommon to hear a more experienced teenage part-timer tell a newcomer, "Oh, come on, we don't have to do it that way. Don't be so eager; relax and enjoy yourself." The supervisor seemed to have little control over the teenagers. They ignored her comments or talked back to her and continued doing things their own way. The working atmosphere was informal and friendly, with everyone on a first-name basis except for the supervisor. At times there was a high pitch of excitement among the kids as everyone kidded one another, sang songs, and generally socialized together. At times this led to mistakes being made, which infuriated the supervisor but didn't bother the kids, as they had little respect for her.

Conflict existed between the supervisor and the teenagers about wearing the required hairnets (especially the boys) and aprons and such procedures as not eating during work. They seldom took reprimands seriously, saying that they "hated their job" but needed the money. In general, however, these young diet aides did complete their required tasks in the time allotted, although the quality was often substandard. There was not a total lack of concern for quality because, if so, they would have lost their jobs, and they knew this; but quality was maintained most strongly only when "it didn't take too long."

There did exist some conflict between the older and younger workers during the night shift. The older women did not approve of the young people's attitudes, even though those older women who worked at night did not exhibit as much pride in their work as their daytime counterparts. They resented the teenagers' new and different ways of doing jobs, which was especially evident when an older woman was assigned to work with a teenager for the evening.

The management   There were several people involved with the management staff of the dietary department. As the food service director, Mr. Ellis was the man to whom everyone else was ultimately responsible. He was an older man, hired by the hospital about five years previously. A flashy dresser, he wore no uniform and spent most of the day in his office. He rarely talked to anyone in the department except the chief dietician and the chief dietary supervisor. He communicated to the rest of the employees by means of memos posted on a bulletin board in the kitchen. His memos usually contained instructions, telling the workers to change or improve some facet of their jobs. He also relayed messages down the ranks via the supervisors to the workers. About once a day he would walk through the kitchen in a very formal manner, apparently observing what was going on. The diet aides (and supervisors) became very conscious of their actions as he walked by, hoping they were doing everything right. When questioned about this man, the workers expressed feelings of curiosity mixed with an element of fear. The only time a diet aide came into direct contact with him was on payday, when she entered his office to receive her check after he signed it. One recently hired employee said that she thought that his main job was signing paychecks. There was obviously much confusion by workers concerning who this man really was. He was the mystery man of management to them.

A second management person was the chief dietician, Mrs. Johnston, a woman in her late 30s. Her job was mainly administrative in nature, acting as a consultant to the dieticians and assisting them when the workload was heavy or someone was out sick. She also helped out in the kitchen once in a while if the kitchen staff was especially shorthanded. In general, however, she tended to remain relatively formal and distant from the workers, although when she had suggestions to make, she often went directly to the workers instead of using memos. Her relationship with the four dieticians was informal and friendly, and she was highly respected by them for her technical excellence as a dietician.

The chief dietary supervisor (CDS), Mrs. Kelly (about age 44), was in charge of hiring and firing. She also was responsible for making up employee schedules week by week, especially those involving the scheduling of the part-time workers. Workers went to her with gripes and requests for favors and special days off. She was generally sympathetic to employee problems, having been one of them about six years ago before she became the chief supervisor. In general, she was relatively informal with the workers, although not on a first-name basis. The employees respected her, and her authority was rarely questioned or challenged by any of the workers. She seemed to be regarded as the real boss, rather than the two people who ranked above her.

These three people constituted the main power structure in the dietary department. They tended to keep to themselves socially as well as physically. They never ate with the workers and seldom communicated with them except about their work. If any changes, plans, or decisions were to be made, they were made by these three people, the final say being had by the food service director. The supervisors were then told of any new policy and expected to inform the workers and implement the change. The CDS seemed to act as a middleman between the director and the workers. When she (or the director) felt that the workers were "sloughing off," a staff meeting would be called and she would exhort everyone to shape up. For instance, a meeting was called after an unusually large number of complaints were received about patients receiving cold food. The CDS said, "We are here to help these patients get well as best we can—they are sick and deserve the best possible care. They won't eat cold food, and that slows down their recovery. Keeping the food warm is more important than whether or not you want to hurry to get the day's work done."

Other members of the management staff included the supervisors, whose main responsibilities involved the diet aides and other kitchen workers. The supervisors, in all cases former diet aides, worked in the kitchen. They assigned jobs, made sure they got done, maintained discipline and order (hopefully), and helped out when needed. In general, they saw that everything ran smoothly. Altogether there were three supervisors, one of whom was part-time. They took turns covering the weekends and thus had contact with all employees, although they worked with one group most of the time.

The cooks and dieticians were the other members of the department. The cooks' job was to prepare the food according to standard recipes and to put it on the serving line at meal times. They did their jobs efficiently and effectively. They kept to themselves, eating together and not mingling with the diet aides. The dieticians also kept to themselves both physically and socially. They had their own office and ate together. Little was seen of them by the workers; when approached, however, they seemed quite friendly.

The Current Problem

The state board of health makes periodic, unannounced visits to the dietary department to determine whether it meets certain sanitary standards. Although the hospital believes that the board of health interprets the regulations too strictly, there is little it can do except make efforts to satisfy any criticisms made by the inspectors.

In the past, the director of the dietary department managed to find out when the inspectors were coming and prepared for the visit by a frantic two- to three-day major cleanup campaign. Historically, this has resulted in Montville passing the inspection. However, over the past two or three months, the inspectors have become

more successful in making their visits a complete surprise. Frantic efforts to clean up took place the last time during the brief time it took the inspectors to get from their car to the kitchen. As a result, the department recently failed the inspection and was given a limited amount of time to correct the situation or face being shut down. The department did pass a reinspection, but only because a lot of extra pressure was put on workers to do extra cleaning during and after working hours (for overtime pay) for several days. If the organization should fail inspection repeatedly, it will be required to shut down indefinitely. The impact of this would be catastrophic for the hospital as a whole, since it must provide food for both patients and employees! Rene wondered what the hospital would do about the situation and how it might affect her job situation.

Source: S. Fink, S. Jenks, and R. Willits, *Designing and Managing Organizations,* 1983, pp. 568–75. Reproduced by permission of Richard D. Irwin, Inc., Burr Ridge, IL. ■

CASE 4

Perfect Pizzeria

Perfect Pizzeria in Southville, deep in southern Illinois, is the chain's second-largest franchise. Company headquarters is located in Phoenix, Arizona. Although the business is prospering, it has employee and managerial problems.

Each operation has one manager, an assistant manager, and from two to five night managers. The managers of each pizzeria work under an area supervisor. There are no systematic criteria for being a manager or becoming a manager trainee. The franchise has no formalized training period for the manager and no college education is required. The managers for whom the case observer worked during a four-year period were relatively young (ages 24 to 27), and only one had completed college. They came from the ranks of night managers, assistant managers, or both. The night managers were chosen for their ability to perform the duties of the regular employees. The assistant managers worked a two-hour shift during the luncheon period five days a week to gain knowledge about bookkeeping and management. Those becoming managers remained at that level unless they expressed interest in investing in the business.

The employees were mostly college students, with a few high school students performing the less challenging jobs. Because Perfect Pizzeria was located in an area

with few job opportunities, it had a relatively easy task of filling its employee quotas. All the employees, with the exception of the manager, were employed part time. Consequently, they earned only the minimum wage.

The Perfect Pizzeria system is devised so that food and beverage costs and profits are set up according to a percentage. If the percentage of food unsold or damaged in any way is very low, the manager gets a bonus. If the percentage is high, the manager does not receive a bonus; instead, he or she receives only the normal salary.

There are many ways in which the percentage can fluctuate. Because the manager cannot be in the pizzeria 24 hours a day, some employees make up for their paychecks by helping themselves to the food. When a friend comes in to order a pizza, extra ingredients are put on the friend's pizza. Occasional nibbles by 18 to 20 employees throughout the day at the meal table also raise the percentage figure. An occasional bucket of sauce may be spilled or a pizza accidentally burned. Sometimes the wrong size pizza may be made.

In the event of an employee mistake or a burned pizza by the oven person, the expense is supposed to be covered by the individual. Because of peer pressure, the night manager seldom writes up a bill for the erring employee. Instead, the establishment takes the loss and the error goes unnoticed until the end of the month when the inventory is taken. That's when the manager finds out that the percentage is high and there will be no bonus.

In the present instance, the manager took retaliatory measures. Previously, each employee was entitled to a free pizza, salad, and all the soft drinks he or she could drink for every six hours of work. The manager raised this figure to 12 hours of work. However, the employees had received these six-hour benefits for a long time. Therefore, they simply took advantage of the situation whenever the manager or the assistant was not in the building. Although the night managers theoretically had complete control of the operation in the evenings, they did not command the respect that the manager or assistant manager did because night managers received the same pay as the regular employees, could not reprimand other employees, and were basically the same age or sometimes even younger than the other employees.

Thus, apathy grew within the pizzeria. There seemed to be a further separation between the manager and his workers, who started out as a closely knit group. The manager made no attempt to alleviate the problem, because he felt it would iron itself out. Either the dissatisfied employees would quit or they would be content to put up with the new regulations. As it turned out, there was a rash of employee dismissals. The manager had no problem in filling the vacancies with new workers, but the loss of key personnel was costly to the business.

With the large turnover, the manager found he had to spend more time in the building, supervising, and sometimes taking the place of inexperienced workers. This was in direct violation of the franchise regulation, which stated that a manager would act as a supervisor and at no time take part in the actual food preparation. Employees were not placed under strict supervision with the manager working alongside them. The operation no longer worked smoothly because of differences between the remaining experienced workers and the manager concerning the way that a particular function should be performed.

Within a two-month period, the manager was again free to go back to his office and leave his subordinates in charge of the entire operation. During this two-month period, in spite of the differences between experienced workers and the manager, the percentage of unsold and damaged food had returned to the previous low level and the manager received a bonus each month. The manager felt that his problems had been resolved and that conditions would remain the same, since the new personnel had been properly trained.

It didn't take long for the new employees to become influenced by the other employees. Immediately after the manager had returned to his supervisory role, the percentage of unsold and damaged food began to rise. This time the manager took a bolder step. He cut out most benefits that the employees had—no free pizzas, salads, or drinks. With the job market at an even lower ebb than usual, most employees were forced to stay. The appointment of a new area supervisor made it impossible for the manager to "work behind the counter," because the supervisor was centrally located in Southville.

The manager tried still another approach to alleviate the problem of the rising percentage of unsold and damaged food and to maintain his bonus. He placed a notice on the bulletin board, stating that if the percentage remained at a high level, a lie detector test would be given to all employees. All those found guilty of taking or purposefully wasting food or drinks would be immediately terminated. This did not have the desired effect on the employees, because they knew if they were subjected to the test, all would be found guilty and the manager would have to dismiss all of them. This would leave him in a worse situation than ever.

Even before the following month's percentage was calculated, the manager knew it would be high. He had evidently received information from one of the night managers about the employees' feelings toward the notice. What he did not expect was that the percentage would reach an all-time high. That is the state of affairs at the present time.

Source: J. E. Dittrich and R. A. Zawacki, *People and Organizations* (Plano, TX: Business Publications, 1981), pp. 126–28. Used by permission of Irwin/McGraw-Hill.

Theory building and the scientific method

People need to make sense of their world, so they form theories about the way the world operates. A **theory** is a general set of propositions that describes interrelationships among several concepts. We form theories for the purpose of predicting and explaining the world around us.[1] What does a good theory look like? First, it should be stated as clearly and simply as possible so that the concepts can be measured and there is no ambiguity regarding the theory's propositions. Second, the elements of the theory must be logically consistent with each other, because we cannot test anything that doesn't make sense. Finally, a good theory provides value to society; it helps people to understand their world better than without the theory.[2]

Theory building is a continuous process that typically includes the inductive and deductive stages shown in Exhibit A.1.[3] The inductive stage draws on personal experience to form a preliminary theory, whereas the deductive stage uses the scientific method to test the theory.

The inductive stage of theory building involves observing the world around us, identifying a pattern of relationships, and then forming a theory from these personal observations. For example, you might casually notice that new employees want their supervisor to give direction, whereas this leadership style irritates long-term employees. From these observations, you form a theory about the effectiveness of directive leadership. (See Chapter 14 for a discussion of this leadership style.)

Positivism versus Interpretivism

Research requires an interpretation of reality, and researchers tend to perceive reality in one of two ways. A common view, called **positivism,** is that reality exists independent of people. It is "out there" to be discovered and tested. Positivism is the foundation for most quantitative research (i.e., statistical analysis). It assumes that we can measure variables and those variables have fixed relationships with other variables. For example, the positivist perspective says that we could study whether a supportive style of leadership reduces stress. If we find evidence of this, then someone else studying leadership and stress would "discover" the same relationship.

Interpretivism takes a different view of reality. It suggests that reality comes from shared meaning among people in that environment. For example, supportive leadership is a personal interpretation of reality, not something that can be measured across time and people. Interpretivists rely mainly

Exhibit A.1   The theory building process

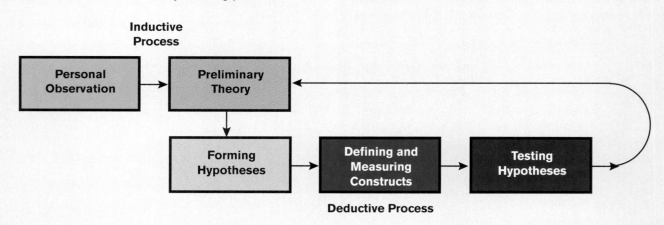

on qualitative data, such as observation and non-directive interviews. They particularly listen to the language people use to understand the common meaning that people have toward various events or phenomena. For example, they might argue that you need to experience and observe supportive leadership to study it effectively. Moreover, you can't really predict relationships because the specific situation shapes reality.[4]

Most OB scholars identify themselves somewhere between the extreme views of positivism and interpretivism. Many believe that inductive research should begin with an interpretivist angle. We should enter a new topic with an open mind and search for shared meaning among people in that situation. In other words, researchers should let the participants define reality rather than let the researcher's preconceived notions shape that reality. This process involves gathering qualitative information and letting this information shape theory.[5] After the theory emerges, researchers shift to a positivist perspective by quantitatively testing relationships in that theory.

Theory Testing: The Deductive Process

Once a theory has been formed, we shift into the deductive stage of theory building. This process includes forming hypotheses, defining and measuring constructs, and testing hypotheses (see Exhibit A.1). **Hypotheses** make empirically testable declarations that certain variables and their corresponding measures are related in a specific way proposed by the theory. For instance, to find support for the directive leadership theory described earlier, we need to form and then test a specific hypothesis from that theory. One such hypothesis might be: "New employees are more satisfied with supervisors who exhibit a directive rather than nondirective leadership style." Hypotheses are indispensable tools of scientific research because they provide the vital link between the theory and empirical verification.

Defining and measuring constructs   Hypotheses are testable only if we can define and then form measurable indicators of the concepts stated in those hypotheses. Consider the hypothesis in the previous paragraph about new employees and directive leadership. To test this hypothesis, we first need to define the concepts, such as "new employees," "directive leadership," and "supervisor." These are known as **constructs** because they are abstract ideas constructed by the researcher that can be

linked to observable information. Organizational behavior scholars developed the construct called *directive leadership* to help them understand the different effects that leaders have over followers. We can't directly see or hear directive leadership; instead, we rely on indirect indicators that it exists, such as observing someone giving directions, maintaining clear performance standards, and ensuring that procedures and practices are followed.

As you can see, defining constructs well is very important, because these definitions become the foundation for finding or developing acceptable measures of those constructs. We can't measure directive leadership if we only have a vague idea about what this concept means. The better the definition, the better our chances of applying a measure that adequately represents that construct. However, even with a good definition, constructs can be difficult to measure because the empirical representation must capture several elements in the definition. A measure of directive leadership must be able to identify not only the people who give directions, but also those who maintain performance standards and ensure that procedures are followed.

Testing hypotheses   The third step in the deductive process is to collect data for the empirical measures of the variables. Following our directive leadership example, we might conduct a formal survey in which new employees indicate the behavior of their supervisors and their attitudes toward their supervisor. Alternatively, we might design an experiment in which people work with someone who applies either a directive or nondirective leadership style. When the data have been collected, we can use various procedures to test our hypotheses statistically.

A major concern in theory building is that some researchers might inadvertently find support for their theory simply because they use the same information that was used to form the theory during the inductive stage. Consequently, the deductive stage must collect new data that are completely independent of the data used during the inductive stage. For instance, you might decide to test your theory of directive leadership by studying employees in another organization. Moreover, the inductive process may have relied mainly on personal observation, whereas the deductive process might use survey questionnaires. By studying different samples and using different measurement tools, we minimize the risk of conducting circular research.

Using the Scientific Method

Earlier, we said that the deductive stage of theory building follows the scientific method. The **scientific method** is a systematic, controlled, empirical, and critical investigation of hypothetical propositions about the presumed relationships among natural phenomena.[6] There are several elements to this definition, so let's look at each one. First, scientific research is systematic and controlled because researchers want to rule out all but one explanation for a set of interrelated events. To rule out alternative explanations, we need to control them in some way, such as keeping them constant or removing them entirely from the environment.

Second, we say that scientific research is empirical because researchers need to use objective reality—or as close as they can get to it—to test theory. They measure observable elements of the environment, such as what a person says or does, rather than rely on their own subjective opinion to draw conclusions. Moreover, scientific research analyzes these data using acceptable principles of mathematics and logic.

Finally, scientific research involves critical investigation. This means that the study's hypotheses, data, methods, and results are openly described so that other experts in the field can properly evaluate this research. It also means that scholars are encouraged to critique and build upon previous research. Eventually, the scientific method encourages the refinement and the replacement of a particular theory with one that better suits our understanding of the world.

Selected Issues in Organizational Behavior Research

There are many issues to consider in theory building, particularly when we use the deductive process to test hypotheses. Some of the more important issues are sampling, causation, and ethical practices in organizational research.

Sampling in Organizational Research

When finding out why things happen in organizations, we typically gather information from a few sources and then draw conclusions about the larger population. If we survey several employees and determine that older employees are more loyal to their company, then we would like to generalize this statement to all older employees in our population, not just those whom we surveyed. Scientific inquiry generally requires researchers to engage in **representative sampling**—that is, sampling a population in such a way that we can extrapolate the results of that sample to the larger population.

One factor that influences representativeness is whether the sample is selected in an unbiased way from the larger population. Let's suppose that you want to study organizational commitment among employees in your organization. A casual procedure might result in sampling too few employees from the head office and too many located elsewhere in the country. If head office employees actually have higher loyalty than employees located elsewhere, then the biased sampling would cause the results to underestimate the true level of loyalty among employees in the company. If you repeat the process again next year but somehow overweight employees from the head office, the results might wrongly suggest that employees have increased their organizational commitment over the past year. In reality, the only change may be the direction of sampling bias.

How do we minimize sampling bias? The answer is a *random sample*. A randomly drawn sample gives each member of the population an equal probability of being chosen, so there is less likelihood that a subgroup within that population dominates the study's results.

The same principle applies to random assignment of subjects to groups in experimental designs. If we want to test the effects of a team development training program, we need to randomly place some employees in the training group and randomly place others in a group that does not receive training. Without this random selection, each group might have different types of employees, so we wouldn't know whether the training explains the differences between the two groups. Moreover, if employees respond differently to the training program, we couldn't be sure that the training program results are representative of the larger population. Of course, random sampling does not necessarily produce a perfectly representative sample, but we do know that this is the best approach to ensure unbiased selection.

The other factor that influences representativeness is sample size. Whenever we select a portion of the population, there will be some error in our estimate of the population values. The larger the sample, the less error in our estimate. Let's suppose that you want to find out how employees in a 500-person firm feel about smoking in the workplace. If you asked 400 of those employees, the information would provide a very good estimate of how the entire workforce in that organization feels. If you survey only 100 employees, the estimate might deviate more from the true population. If you ask only 10 people, the estimate could be quite different from what all 500 employees feel.

Notice that sample size goes hand in hand with random selection. You must have a sufficiently large sample size for the principle of randomization to work effectively. In our example of attitudes toward smoking, we would do a poor job of random selection if our sample consisted of only 10 employees from the 500-person organization. The reason is that these 10 people probably wouldn't capture the diversity of employees throughout the organization. Indeed, the more diverse the population, the larger the sample size should be, to provide adequate representation through random selection.

Causation in Organizational Research

Theories present notions about relationships among constructs. Often, these propositions suggest a causal relationship; namely, that one variable has an effect on another variable. When discussing causation, we refer to variables as being independent or dependent. Independent variables are the presumed causes of dependent variables, which are the presumed effects. In our earlier example of directive leadership, the main independent variable (there might be others) would be the supervisor's directive or nondirective leadership style, because we presume that it causes the dependent variable (satisfaction with supervision).

In laboratory experiments (described later), the independent variable is always manipulated by the experimenter. In our research on directive leadership, we might have subjects (new employees) work with supervisors who exhibit directive or nondirective leadership behaviors. If subjects are more satisfied under the directive leaders, then we would be able to infer an association between the independent and dependent variables.

Researchers must satisfy three conditions to provide sufficient evidence of causality between two variables.[7] The first condition of causality is that the variables are empirically associated with each other. An association exists whenever one measure of a variable changes systematically with a measure of another variable. This condition of causality is the easiest to satisfy, because there are several well-known statistical measures of association. A research study might find, for instance, that

heterogeneous groups (in which members come from diverse backgrounds) produce more creative solutions to problems. This might be apparent because the measure of creativity (such as the number of creative solutions produced within a fixed time) is higher for teams that have a high score on the measure of group heterogeneity. They are statistically associated or correlated with each other.

The second condition of causality is that the independent variable precedes the dependent variable in time. Sometimes, this condition is satisfied through simple logic. In our group heterogeneity example, it doesn't make sense to say that the number of creative solutions caused the group's heterogeneity, because the group's heterogeneity existed before it produced the creative solutions. In other situations, however, the temporal relationship among variables is less clear. One example is the ongoing debate about job satisfaction and organizational commitment. Do companies develop more loyal employees by increasing their job satisfaction, or do changes in organizational loyalty cause changes in job satisfaction? Simple logic does not answer these questions; instead, researchers must use sophisticated longitudinal studies to build up evidence of a temporal relationship between these two variables.

The third requirement for evidence of a causal relationship is that the statistical association between two variables cannot be explained by a third variable. There are many associations that we quickly dismiss as being causally related. For example, there is a statistical association between the number of storks in an area and the birthrate in that area. We know that storks don't bring babies, so something else must cause the association between these two variables. The real explanation is that both storks and birthrates have a higher incidence in rural areas.

In other studies, the third variable effect is less apparent. Many years ago, before polio vaccines were available, a study in the United States reported a surprisingly strong association between consumption of a certain soft drink and the incidence of polio. Was polio caused by drinking this pop, or did people with polio have an unusual craving for this beverage? Neither. Both polio and consumption of the soft drink were caused by a third variable: climate. There was a higher incidence of polio in the summer months and in warmer climates, and people drink more liquids in these climates.[8] As you can see from this example, researchers have a difficult time supporting causal inferences, because third variable effects are sometimes difficult to detect.

Ethics in Organizational Research

Organizational behavior researchers need to abide by the ethical standards of the society in which the research is conducted. One of the most important ethical considerations is the individual subject's freedom to participate in the study. For example, it is inappropriate to force employees to fill out a questionnaire or attend an experimental intervention for research purposes only. Moreover, researchers have an obligation to tell potential subjects about any potential risks inherent in the study so that participants can make an informed choice about whether or not to be involved.

Finally, researchers must be careful to protect the privacy of those who participate in the study. This usually includes letting people know when they are being studied as well as guaranteeing that their individual information will remain confidential (unless publication of identities is otherwise granted). Researchers maintain anonymity through careful security of data. The research results usually aggregate data in numbers large enough that they do not reveal the opinions or characteristics of any specific individual. For example, we would report the average absenteeism of employees in a department rather than state the absence rates of each person. When sharing data with other researchers, it is usually necessary to code each case in such a way that individual identities are not known.

Research Design Strategies

So far, we have described how to build a theory, including the specific elements of empirically testing that theory within the standards of scientific inquiry. But what are the different ways to design a research study so that we get the data necessary to achieve our research objectives? There are many strategies, but they mainly fall under three headings: laboratory experiments, field surveys, and observational research.

Laboratory Experiments

A **laboratory experiment** is any research study in which independent variables and variables outside the researcher's main focus of inquiry can be controlled to some extent. Laboratory experiments are usually located outside the everyday work environment, such as a classroom, simulation lab, or any other artificial setting in which the researcher can manipulate the environment. Organizational behavior researchers sometimes conduct experiments in the workplace (called *field experiments*) in which the independent variable is manipulated. However, the researcher has less control over the effects of extraneous factors in field experiments than in laboratory situations.

Advantages of laboratory experiments

There are many advantages to laboratory experiments. By definition, this research method offers a high degree of control over extraneous variables that would otherwise confound the relationships being studied. Suppose we want to test the effects of directive leadership on the satisfaction of new employees. One concern might be that employees are influenced by how much leadership is provided, not just the type of leadership style. An experimental design would allow us to control how often the supervisor exhibited this style so that this extraneous variable does not confound the results.

A second advantage of lab studies is that the independent and dependent variables can be developed more precisely than in a field setting. For example, the researcher can ensure that supervisors in a lab study apply specific directive or nondirective behaviors, whereas real-life supervisors would use a more complex mixture of leadership behaviors. By using more precise measures, we are more certain that we are measuring the intended construct. Thus, if new employees are more satisfied with supervisors in the directive leadership condition, we are more confident that the independent variable was directive leadership rather than some other leadership style.

A third benefit of laboratory experiments is that the independent variable can be distributed more evenly among participants. In our directive leadership study, we can ensure that approximately half of the subjects have a directive supervisor, whereas the other half have a nondirective supervisor. In natural settings, we might have trouble finding people who have worked with a nondirective leader and, consequently, we couldn't determine the effects of this condition.

Disadvantages of laboratory experiments

With these powerful advantages, you might wonder why laboratory experiments are the least appreciated form of organizational behavior research.[9] One obvious limitation of this research method is that it lacks realism and, consequently, the results might be different in the real world. One argument is that laboratory experiment subjects are less involved than their counterparts in an actual work situation. This is sometimes true although many lab studies have highly motivated participants. Another criticism is that the extraneous variables controlled in the lab setting might produce a different effect of the independent variable on the dependent variables. This might also be true, but remember that the experimental design controls variables in accordance with the theory and its hypotheses. Consequently, this concern is really a critique of the theory, not the lab study.

Finally, there is the well-known problem that participants are aware they are being studied and this causes them to act differently than they normally would. Some participants try to figure out how the researcher wants them to behave and then deliberately try to act that way. Other participants try to upset the experiment by doing just the opposite of what they believe the researcher expects. Still others might act unnaturally simply because they know they are being observed. Fortunately, experimenters are well aware of these potential problems and are usually (although not always) successful at disguising the study's true intent.

Field Surveys

Field surveys collect and analyze information in a natural environment—an office, factory, or other existing location. The researcher takes a snapshot of reality and tries to determine whether elements of that situation (including the attitudes and behaviors of people in that situation) are associated with each other as hypothesized. Everyone does some sort of field research. You might think that people from some states are better drivers than others, so you "test" your theory by looking at the way people with out-of-state license plates drive. Although your methods of data collection might not satisfy scientific standards, this is a form of field research because it takes information from a naturally occurring situation.

Advantages and disadvantages of field surveys
One advantage of field surveys is that the variables often have a more powerful effect than they would in a laboratory experiment. Consider the effect of peer pressure on the behavior of members within the team. In a natural environment, team members would form very strong cohesive bonds over time, whereas a researcher would have difficulty replicating this level of cohesiveness and corresponding peer pressure in a lab setting.

Another advantage of field surveys is that the researcher can study many variables simultaneously, thereby permitting a fuller test of more complex theories. Ironically, this is also a disadvantage of field surveys, because it is difficult for the researcher to contain his or her scientific inquiry.

There is a tendency to shift from deductive hypothesis testing to more inductive exploratory browsing through the data. If these two activities become mixed together, the researcher can lose sight of the strict covenants of scientific inquiry.

The main weakness with field surveys is that it is very difficult to satisfy the conditions for causal conclusions. One reason is that the data are usually collected at one point in time, so the researcher must rely on logic to decide whether the independent variable really preceded the dependent variable. Contrast this with the lab study in which the researcher can usually be confident that the independent variable was applied before the dependent variable occurred. Increasingly, organizational behavior studies use longitudinal research to provide a better indicator of temporal relations among variables, but this is still not as precise as the lab setting. Another reason why causal analysis is difficult in field surveys is that extraneous variables are not controlled as they are in lab studies. Without this control, there is a higher chance that an unknown variable might explain the relationship between the hypothesized independent and dependent variables.

Observational Research

In their study of brainstorming and creativity, Robert Sutton and Andrew Hargadon observed 24 brainstorming sessions at IDEO, a product design firm in Palo Alto, California. They also attended a dozen "Monday morning meetings," conducted 60 semi-structured interviews with IDEO executives and designers, held hundreds of informal discussions with these people, and read through several dozen magazine articles about the company.[10]

Sutton and Hargadon's use of observational research and other qualitative methods was quite appropriate for their research objectives, which were to reexamine the effectiveness of brainstorming beyond the number of ideas generated. Observational research generates a wealth of descriptive accounts about the drama of human existence in organizations. It is a useful vehicle for learning about the complex dynamics of people and their activities, such as brainstorming. (The results of Sutton and Hargadon's study are discussed in Chapter 11.)

Participant observation takes the observation method one step further by having the observer take part in the organization's activities. This gives the researcher a fuller understanding of the experience compared to just watching others participate in those activities.

In spite of its intuitive appeal, observational research has a number of weaknesses. The main problem is that the observer is subject to the perceptual screening and organizing biases that we discuss in Chapter 6. There is a tendency to overlook the routine aspects of organizational life, even though they may prove to be the most important data for research purposes. Instead, observers tend to focus on unusual information, such as activities that deviate from what the observer expects. Because observational research usually records only what the observer notices, valuable information is often lost.

Another concern with the observation method is that the researcher's presence and involvement may influence the people whom he or she is studying. This can be a problem in short-term observations, but in the long term people tend to return to their usual behavior patterns. With ongoing observations, such as Sutton and Hargadon's study of brainstorming sessions at IDEO, employees eventually forget that they are being studied.

Finally, observation is usually a qualitative process, so it is more difficult to empirically test hypotheses with the data. Instead, observational research provides rich information for the inductive stages of theory building. It helps us to form ideas about the way things work in organizations. We begin to see relationships that lay the foundation for new perspectives and theory. We must not confuse this inductive process of theory building with the deductive process of theory testing. ■

Vroom-Jago decision tree

he Vroom-Jago model guides decision makers through the characteristics of a problem (called *problem attributes*) to determine the most appropriate level of employee involvement for that problem. There are five levels of employee involvement specified in the model. They are:

AI: You make the decision alone with no employee involvement.

AII: Subordinates provide information that you request, but they don't offer recommendations and they might not be aware of the problem.

CI: You describe the problem to relevant subordinates individually, getting their information and recommendations. You make the final decision, which does not necessarily reflect the advice that subordinates have provided.

CII: You describe the problem to subordinates in a meeting, in which they discuss information and recommendations. You make the final decision, which does not necessarily reflect the advice that subordinates have provided.

GII: You describe the problem to subordinates in a meeting. They discuss the problem and make a decision that you are willing to accept and implement if it has the entire team's support. You might chair this session, but you do not influence the team's decision.

The Vroom-Jago model consists of four decision trees. Two trees pertain to decisions affecting a team of employees, whereas the other two focus on individual problems. Within each pair, one emphasizes time efficiency and the other emphasizes employee development. Exhibit B.1 describes the time-driven decision tree for team issues, because it is most frequently used in organizational settings. It consists of eight problem attributes that distinguish the characteristics of each decision situation. Each problem attribute is phrased as a question, and the appropriate answer directs the decision maker along a different path in the decision tree.

The decision maker begins at the left side of the decision tree and must first decide whether the problem has a high- or low-quality dimension. Most decisions have a quality requirement because some alternatives are more likely than others to achieve organizational objectives. However, where all of the alternatives are equally good (or bad), the decision maker would select the low-importance route in the decision tree. The decision maker would then be asked whether subordinate commitment is important to the decision. This process continues until the path leads to the recommended participation level, ranging from AI to GII.

Exhibit B.1
Vroom-Jago time-driven
decision tree

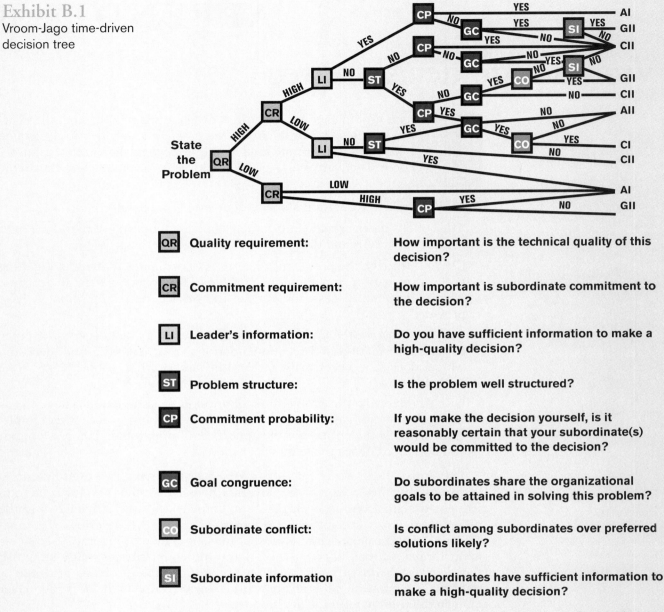

	QR	Quality requirement:	How important is the technical quality of this decision?
	CR	Commitment requirement:	How important is subordinate commitment to the decision?
	LI	Leader's information:	Do you have sufficient information to make a high-quality decision?
	ST	Problem structure:	Is the problem well structured?
	CP	Commitment probability:	If you make the decision yourself, is it reasonably certain that your subordinate(s) would be committed to the decision?
	GC	Goal congruence:	Do subordinates share the organizational goals to be attained in solving this problem?
	CO	Subordinate conflict:	Is conflict among subordinates over preferred solutions likely?
	SI	Subordinate information	Do subordinates have sufficient information to make a high-quality decision?

Source: V. H. Vroom and A. G. Jago, *The New Leadership: Managing Participation in Organizations* (Englewood Cliffs, N.J.: Prentice Hall, 1988), p. 184. © 1987 V. H. Vroom and A. G. Jago. Used with permission of the authors. ▪

GLOSSARY

The number after each definition indicates the chapter in which the term receives the fullest description.

A

ability   The natural aptitudes and learned capabilities required to successfully complete a task. (2)

action learning   A form of on-site, experiential-based learning in which participants investigate an organizational problem or opportunity and propose recommendations. (2)

action research   A data-based, problem-oriented process that diagnoses the need for change, introduces the organization development (OD) intervention, and evaluates and stabilizes the desired changes. (15)

adaptive culture   An organizational culture that focuses employees on the changing needs of customers and other stakeholders, and supports initiative and leadership to keep pace with these changes. (16)

affiliate networks   Network organizations where the satellite companies have a special affiliation with the core firm, such as investment or start-up support. (18)

agency theory   An economic theory that assumes company owners (principals) and employees (agents) have different goals and interests, so rewards and other control systems are required to align the agent's goals with those of the principals. (4)

appreciative inquiry   An organization development intervention that directs the group's attention away from its own problems and focuses participants on the group's potential and positive elements. (15)

artifacts   The observable symbols and signs of an organization's culture, including its physical structures, ceremonies, language, and stories. (16)

attitudes   The cluster of beliefs, assessed feelings, and behavioral intentions toward an object. (7)

attribution process   A perceptual process used to interpret the causes of behavior in terms of the person (internal attributions) or the situation (external attributions). (6)

autonomy   The degree to which a job gives employees the freedom, independence, and discretion to schedule their work and determine the procedures used in completing it. (4)

B

behavior modification   A theory that explains learning in terms of the antecedents and consequences of behavior. (2)

benchmarking   A systematic and ongoing process of improving performance by measuring a product, service, or process against a partner that has mastered it. (10)

"Big Five" personality dimensions   Most personality traits are represented by five abstract personality dimensions: conscientiousness, emotional stability, openness to experience, agreeableness, and extroversion. (6)

boundaryless career   The idea that careers operate across company and industry boundaries rather than just within a single organizational hierarchy. (17)

brainstorming   A structured team decision-making process whereby team members interact directly to generate as many alternative solutions to the problem as possible, piggyback on the ideas of others, and avoid evaluating anyone's ideas during the idea-generation stage. (11)

C

career   A sequence of work-related experiences that people participate in over the span of their working lives. (17)

cellular organizations   A highly flexible network structure in which partners provide customized products or services, usually to specific clients, for a limited time. (18)

centrality   The degree and nature of interdependence between the power holder and others. (12)

centralization   The degree to which formal decision authority is held by a small group of people, typically those at the top of the organizational hierarchy. (18)

ceremonies

ceremonies   Planned activities symbolizing organizational culture that are conducted specifically for the benefit of an audience. (16)

change agent   Anyone who possesses enough knowledge and power to guide and facilitate the change effort. (15)

coalition   An informal group that attempts to influence people outside the group by pooling the resources and power of its members. (9)

codetermination   A form of employee involvement required by some governments that typically operates at the work site as works councils and at the corporate level as supervisory boards. (10)

coercive power   The capacity to influence others through the ability to apply punishment. (12)

cognitive dissonance   A state of anxiety that occurs when an individual's beliefs, attitudes, intentions, and behaviors are inconsistent with one another. (7)

communication   The process by which information is transmitted and understood between two or more people. (8)

communities of practice   Informal groups of people connected by their mutual interest in a particular field of knowledge. (10)

competencies   The abilities, values, personality traits, and other characteristics of people that lead to superior performance. (2)

concurrent engineering   The integration and concurrent development of a product or service and its associated processes, usually guided by a cross-functional team. (10)

conflict   The process in which one party perceives that its interests are being opposed or negatively affected by another party. (13)

conflict management   Interventions that alter the level and form of conflict in ways that maximize its benefits and minimize its dysfunctional consequences. (13)

conscientiousness   A "Big Five" personality dimension that characterizes people who are careful, dependable, and self-disciplined. (6)

constructive controversy Any situation in which team members debate different opinions about a problem or issue in a way that minimizes socioemotional conflict. (11)

constructs Abstract ideas constructed by researchers that can be linked to observable information. (Appendix A)

content theories of motivation Theories that explain the dynamics of employee needs, such as why people have different needs at different times. (3)

contingency approach The idea that a particular action may have different consequences in different situations; that no single solution is best in all circumstances. (1)

contingent work Any job in which the individual does not have an explicit or implicit contract for long-term employment, or one in which the minimum hours of work can vary in a nonsystematic way. (17)

continuous reinforcement A schedule that reinforces behavior every time it occurs. (2)

counterpower The capacity of a person, team, or organization to keep a more powerful person or group in the exchange relationship. (12)

creativity Developing an original product, service, or idea that makes a socially recognized contribution. (11)

cross-functional teams Groups that overlay a more permanent structure, usually functional departments. (9)

D

decision making A conscious process of making choices among one or more alternatives with the intention of moving toward some desired state of affairs. (11)

Delphi technique A structured team decision-making process of systematically pooling the collective knowledge of experts on a particular subject to make decisions, predict the future, or identify opposing views. (11)

departmentalization An element of organizational structure specifying how employees and their activities are grouped together, such as by function, product, geographic location, or some combination. (18)

devil's advocates People who challenge others to explain the logic of their preferences and who identify problems with that logic. (11)

dialogue A process of conversation among team members in which they learn about each other's mental models and assumptions, and eventually form a common model for thinking within the team. (9)

discrepancy theory A theory that partly explains job satisfaction in terms of the gap between what a person expects to receive and what is actually received. (7)

divergent thinking Reframing problems in a unique way and generating different approaches to an issue. (11)

divisional structure A type of departmentalization that groups employees around outputs, clients, or geographic areas. (18)

E

effort-to-performance (E→P) expectancy An individual's perceived probability that a particular level of effort will result in a particular level of performance. (3)

electronic brainstorming A structured team decision-making process whereby several people individually generate ideas or make decisions through computer software that posts each participant's ideas or opinions anonymously. (11)

emotional contagion The automatic and subconscious tendency to mimic and synchronize our nonverbal behaviors with other people. (8)

emotional dissonance The conflict experienced when the person's genuinely felt emotions are inconsistent with the emotions that must be displayed as part of one's role in an organization. (7)

emotional intelligence The ability to monitor our own and others' emotions, to discriminate among them, and to use the information to guide your thinking and actions. (7)

emotional labor The effort, planning, and control needed to express organizationally desired emotions during interpersonal transactions. (7)

emotions Feelings experienced toward an object, person, or event that create a state of readiness. (7)

empathy A person's ability to understand and be sensitive to the feelings, thoughts, and situation of others. (6)

employability The "new deal" employment relationship in which the job is a temporary event and employees are expected to continuously learn skills that will keep them employed in a variety of work activities. (17)

employee assistance programs (EAPs) Counseling services that help employees cope with personal or organizational stressors and adopt more effective coping mechanisms. (5)

employee involvement The degree that employees share information, knowledge, rewards, and power throughout an organization. (10)

employee stock ownership plan (ESOP) A reward system that encourages employees to buy shares of the company. (4)

empowerment The feeling of control and self-efficacy that emerges when people are given power in a previously powerless situation. (4)

environmental scanning Receiving information from the external and internal environments so that more effective strategic decisions can be made. (1)

equity theory A process motivation theory that explains how people develop perceptions of fairness in the distribution and exchange of resources. (3)

ERG theory Alderfer's content motivation theory of three instinctive needs arranged in a hierarchy, in which people progress to the next higher need when a lower one is fulfilled, and regress to a lower need if unable to fulfill a higher one. (3)

escalation of commitment Repeating an apparently bad decision or allocating more resources to a failing course of action. (11)

ethical sensitivity An individual's ability to recognize the presence and determine the relative importance of an ethical issue. (7)

ethics The study of moral principles or values that determine whether actions are right or wrong and outcomes are good or bad. (7)

evaluation apprehension A person's reluctance to mention ideas that seem silly or peripheral in order to create a favorable self-image. (11)

existence needs A person's physiological and physically related safety needs, such as the need for food, shelter, and safe working conditions. (3)

expectancy theory A process motivation theory stating that work effort is directed toward behaviors that people believe will lead to desired outcomes. (3)

expert power The capacity to influence others by possessing knowledge or skills that they want. (12)

extinction Occurs when a target behavior decreases because no consequence follows it. (2)

extroversion A "Big Five" personality dimension that characterizes people who are outgoing, talkative, sociable, and assertive. (6)

F

feedback   Any information that people receive about the consequences of their behavior. (2)

Fiedler's contingency model   Fiedler's leadership theory stating that the best leadership style depends on the level of situational control and that the situation should be arranged to fit the leader's natural style. (14)

field survey   Any research design in which information is collected in a natural environment. (Appendix A)

fixed interval schedule   A schedule that reinforces behavior after it has occurred a fixed period of time. (2)

fixed ratio schedule   A schedule that reinforces behavior after it has occurred a fixed number of times. (2)

flaming   Sending an emotionally charged electronic mail message. (8)

force field analysis   Lewin's model of systemwide change that helps change agents diagnose the forces that drive and restrain proposed organizational change. (15)

formalization   The degree that organizations standardize behavior through rules, procedures, formal training, and related mechanisms. (18)

frustration-regression process   A process whereby a person who is unable to satisfy a higher need becomes frustrated and regresses back to the next lower need level. (3)

functional structure   A type of departmentalization that organizes employees around specific skills or other resources. (18)

fundamental attribution error   The tendency to incorrectly attribute the behavior of other people to internal more than to external factors. (6)

G

Gainsharing plan   A reward system that rewards team members for reducing costs and increasing labor efficiency in their work process. (4)

general adaptation syndrome   A model of the stress experience, consisting of three stages: alarm reaction, resistance, and exhaustion. (5)

goals   The immediate or ultimate objectives that employees are trying to accomplish from their work effort. (3)

goal setting   The process of motivating employees and clarifying their role perceptions by establishing performance objectives. (3)

grafting   The process of acquiring knowledge by hiring individuals or buying entire companies. (1)

grapevine   An organization's informal communication network that is formed and maintained by social relationships rather than the formal reporting relationships. (8)

group   Two or more people with a unifying relationship. (9)

group polarization   The tendency for teams to make more extreme decisions (either more risky or more risk averse) than the average team member would if making the decision alone. (11)

groupthink   The tendency of highly cohesive groups to value consensus at the price of decision quality by avoiding conflict and withholding their dissenting opinions. (11)

growth needs   A person's self-esteem achieved through personal achievement as well as self-actualization. (3)

H

halo effect   A perceptual error whereby our general impression of a person, usually based on one prominent characteristic, biases our perception of that person's other characteristics. (6)

heterogeneous teams   Groups whose members have diverse personal characteristics and backgrounds. (9)

hi-hi leadership hypothesis   A proposition stating that effective leaders exhibit high levels of both people-oriented and task-oriented behaviors. (14)

homogeneous teams   Groups whose members have similar technical expertise, ethnicity, experiences, or values. (9)

hypotheses   Statements making empirically testable declarations that certain variables and their corresponding measures are related in a specific way proposed by a particular theory. (Appendix A)

I

implicit learning   Acquiring information about the environment through experience without any conscious attempt to do so. (2)

impression management   The practice of actively shaping our public images. (12)

incremental change   An evolutionary approach to change in which existing organizational conditions are fine-tuned and small steps are taken toward the objectives of the change effort. (15)

individualism-collectivism   The extent to which people value their group membership and group goals (collectivism) or value their individuality and personal goals (individualism). (7)

informal group   Two or more people who interact primarily to meet their personal (rather than organizational) needs. (9)

information overload   A condition in which the volume of information received by an employee exceeds that person's ability to process it effectively. (8)

inoculation effect   A persuasive communication strategy of warning listeners that others will try to influence them in the future and that they should be wary about the opponents' arguments. (8)

intellectual capital   The knowledge that resides in an organization, including its human, structural, and customer capital. (1)

intergroup mirroring   A structured conflict management intervention in which the parties discuss their perceptions of each other and look for ways to improve their relationship by correcting misperceptions. (13)

interpretivism   The view held in many qualitative studies that reality comes from shared meaning among people in that environment. (Appendix A)

introversion   A "Big Five" personality dimension that characterizes people who are quiet, shy, and cautious. (6)

intuition   The ability to know when a problem or opportunity exists and select the best course of action without conscious reasoning. (11)

J

jargon   Technical language of a particular occupational group or recognized words with specialized meaning in specific organizations or social groups. (8)

job burnout   The process of emotional exhaustion, depersonalization, and reduced personal accomplishment resulting from prolonged exposure to stress. (5)

job characteristics model   A job design model that relates five core job dimensions to three psychological states and several personal and organizational consequences. (4)

job design   The process of assigning tasks to a job, including the interdependency of those tasks with other jobs. (4)

job enlargement   Increasing the number of tasks employees perform within their job. (4)

job enrichment   Assigning responsibility for scheduling, coordinating, and planning work to employees who actually make the product or provide the service. (4)

job evaluation   Systematically evaluating the worth of jobs within an organization by measuring their required skill, effort, responsibility, and working conditions. Job evaluation results create a hierarchy of job worth. (4)

job feedback   The degree to which employees can tell how well they are doing based on direct sensory information from the job itself. (4)

job rotation   The practice of moving employees from one job to another, typically for short periods of time. (4)

job satisfaction   A person's evaluation of his or her job and work context. (7)

job specialization   The result of division of labor in which each job now includes a subset of the tasks required to complete the product or service. (4)

Johari window   A model of personal and interpersonal understanding that encourages disclosure and feedback to increase the open area and reduce the blind, hidden, and unknown areas of oneself. (6)

K

knowledge management   Any structured activity that improves an organization's capacity to acquire, share, and utilize knowledge that enhances its survival and success. (1)

L

laboratory experiment   Any research study in which independent variables and variables outside the researcher's main focus of inquiry can be controlled to some extent. (Appendix A)

lateral career development   The view that career success occurs when employees fulfill their personal needs in different jobs across the organization rather than by moving through the organizational hierarchy. (17)

law of effect   A principle stating that the likelihood that an operant behavior will be repeated depends on its consequences. (2)

law of telecosm   A principle stating that as the web of computer networks expands, distances will shrink and eventually become irrelevant. (8)

leadership   The process of influencing people and providing an environment for them to achieve team or organizational objectives. (14)

Leadership Grid®   A model of leadership developed by Blake and Mouton that assesses an individual's leadership effectiveness in terms of his or her concern for people and production. (14)

leadership substitutes   Characteristics of the employee, task, or organization that either limit the leader's influence or make it unnecessary. (14)

learning   A relatively permanent change in behavior (or behavior tendency) that occurs as a result of a person's interaction with the environment. (2)

legitimate power   The capacity to influence others through formal authority; that is, the perceived right of people in certain roles to request certain behaviors of others. (12)

locus of control   A personality trait referring to the extent that people believe what happens to them is within their control. (6)

M

Machiavellian values   The belief that deceit is a natural and acceptable way to influence others. (12)

management-by-objectives (MBOs)   A participative goal-setting process in which organizational objectives are cascaded down to work units and individual employees. (3)

management by wandering around   The practice of leaving one's office and learning from others in the organization through face-to-face dialogue. (8)

matrix structure   A type of departmentalization that overlays a divisionalized structure (typically a project team) with a functional structure. (18)

mechanistic structure   An organizational structure with a narrow span of control and high degrees of formalization and centralization. (18)

media richness   The data-carrying capacity of a communication medium; the volume and variety of information that it can transmit. (8)

mental imagery   Mentally practicing a task and visualizing its successful completion. (4)

mental models   The broad world views or "theories-in-use" that people rely on to guide their perceptions and behaviors. (6)

methods-time measurement   The process of systematically observing, measuring, and timing physical movements to identify more efficient work behaviors. (4)

moral development   A person's level of maturity regarding ethical decision making. (7)

moral intensity   The degree to which an issue demands the application of ethical principles. (7)

motivation   The forces within a person that affect his or her direction, intensity, and persistence of voluntary behavior. (3)

motivator-hygiene theory   Herzberg's theory stating that employees are primarily motivated by growth and esteem needs, not by lower-level needs. (3)

Myers-Briggs Type Indicator (MBTI)   A personality test based on Jung's theory that identifies people into 16 types based on how they focus their attention, collect information, process and evaluate information, and orient themselves to the outer world. (6)

N

need for achievement (nAch)   A learned need in which people want to accomplish reasonably challenging goals through their own efforts, like to be successful in competitive situations, and desire unambiguous feedback regarding their success. (3)

need for affiliation (nAff)   A learned need in which people seek approval from others, conform to their wishes and expectations, and avoid conflict and confrontation. (3)

need for power (nPow)   A learned need in which people want to control their environment, including people and material resources, to benefit either themselves (personalized power) or others (socialized power). (3)

needs   Deficiencies that energize or trigger behaviors to satisfy a person's needs. (3)

needs hierarchy theory   Maslow's content motivation theory of five instinctive needs arranged in a hierarchy, whereby people are motivated to fulfill a higher need as a lower one becomes gratified. (3)

negative affectivity (NA)   The tendency to experience negative emotional states. (7)

negative reinforcement   Occurs when the removal or avoidance of a consequence increases or maintains the frequency or future probability of a behavior. (2)

negotiation Any attempt by two or more conflicting parties to resolve their divergent goals by redefining the terms of their interdependence. (13)

networking Cultivating social relationships with others to accomplish one's goals. (12)

network structure An alliance of several organizations for the purpose of creating a product or serving a client. (18)

nominal group technique A structured team decision-making process whereby members independently write down ideas, describe and clarify them to the group, and then independently rank or vote on them. (11)

nonprogrammed decision The process applied to unique, complex, or ill-defined situations whereby decision makers follow the full decision-making process, including a careful search for and/or development of unique solutions. (11)

nonterritorial offices Office arrangements in which employees work at any available workstation and are not assigned to specific desks, offices, or workspaces. (8)

norms Informal rules and expectations that groups establish to regulate the behavior of their members. (9)

O

open systems Organizations and other "systems" with interdependent parts that work together to continually monitor and transact with the external environment. (1)

organic structure An organizational structure with a wide span of control, little formalization, and highly decentralized decision making. (18)

organizational behavior The study of what people think, feel, and do in and around organizations. (1)

organizational citizenship Employee behaviors that extend beyond the usual job duties: avoiding unnecessary conflicts, helping others, tolerating impositions, being involved in organizational activities, and performing tasks beyond normal role requirements. (2, 7)

organizational commitment A person's emotional attachment to, identification with, and involvement in a particular organization. (7)

organizational culture The basic pattern of shared assumptions, values, and beliefs governing the way employees within an organization think about and act on problems and opportunities. (16)

organizational design The creation and modification of organizational structures. (18)

organizational memory The storage and preservation of an organization's intellectual capital. (1)

organizational politics Attempts to influence others using discretionary behaviors to promote personal objectives. (12)

organizational socialization The process by which individuals learn the values, expected behaviors, and social knowledge necessary to assume their roles in an organization. (17)

organizational strategy The way an organization positions itself in its setting in relation to its stakeholders given the organization's resources, capabilities, and mission. (18)

organizational structure The division of labor as well as the patterns of coordination, communication, work flow, and formal power that direct organizational activities. (18)

organization development (OD) A planned systemwide effort, managed from the top with the assistance of a change agent, that uses behavioral science knowledge to improve organizational effectiveness. (15)

organizations Groups of people who work interdependently toward some purpose. (1)

P

parallel learning structure A highly participative social structure constructed alongside (i.e., parallel to) a formal organization with the purpose of increasing the organization's learning. (15)

path-goal leadership theory A contingency theory of leadership based on expectancy theory of motivation that includes four leadership styles and several employee and situational contingencies. (14)

perception The process of receiving information about and making sense of our environment; includes deciding which information to notice and how to categorize and interpret it. (6)

perceptual defense A psychological process that involves subconsciously screening out large blocks of information that threaten the person's beliefs and values. (6)

perceptual grouping The perceptual organization process of placing people and objects into recognizable and manageable patterns or categories. (6)

performance-to-outcome (P→O) expectancy An individual's perceived probability that a specific behavior or performance level will lead to specific outcomes. (3)

personality The relatively stable pattern of behaviors and consistent internal states that explain a person's behavioral tendencies (6)

persuasive communication The process of having listeners accept rather than just understand a sender's message. (8)

positive affectivity (PA) The tendency to experience positive emotional states. (7)

positive reinforcement Occurs when the introduction of a consequence increases or maintains the frequency or future probability of a behavior. (2)

positivism The view held in quantitative research that reality exists independent of people. (Appendix A)

postdecisional justification Justifying choices by unconsciously inflating the quality of the selected option and deflating the quality of the discarded options. (11)

power The capacity of a person, team, or organization to influence others. (12)

power distance The extent to which people accept unequal distribution of power in a society. (7)

prejudice Unfounded negative emotions toward people belonging to a particular stereotyped group. (6)

primacy effect A perceptual error in which we quickly form an opinion of people based on the first information we receive about them. (6)

procedural fairness Perceptions of fairness regarding the dispute resolution process, whether or not the outcome is favorable to the person. (13)

process consultation A method of helping the organization solve its own problems by making it aware of organizational processes, the consequences of those processes, and the means by which they can be changed. (15)

process losses Resources (including time and energy) expended toward team development and maintenance rather than the task. (9)

process theories of motivation Theories that describe the processes through which need deficiencies are translated into behavior. (3)

production blocking A time constraint in meetings due to the procedural requirement that only one person may speak at a time. (11)

profit sharing   A reward system in which a designated group of employees receives a share of corporate profits. (4)

programmed decision   The process whereby decision makers follow standard operating procedures to select the preferred solution without the need to identify or evaluate alternative choices. (11)

projection bias   A perceptual error in which we tend to believe that other people hold the same beliefs and attitudes that we do. (6)

psychological contract   The individual's beliefs about the terms and conditions of a reciprocal exchange agreement between that person and another party. (17)

punishment   Occurs when a consequence decreases the frequency or future probability of a behavior. (2)

Q

quality   The value that the end user perceives from the product or service, including satisfying customer needs or expectations and conforming to a standard. (10)

quality circles   Small teams of employees who meet regularly to identify quality and productivity problems, propose solutions to management, and monitor the implementation and consequences of these solutions in their work area. (9)

quantum change   A revolutionary approach to change in which an organization breaks out of its existing ways and moves toward a totally different configuration of systems and structures. (15)

R

realistic job previews   Giving job applicants a realistic balance of positive and negative information about the job and work context. (17)

reality shock   The experience of sudden entry into a new work environment and perceived discrepancies between what the newcomer believes should occur and what actually occurs. (17)

recency effect   A perceptual error in which the most recent information dominates our perception about a person. (6)

referent power   The capacity to influence others by virtue of one's admiration for and identification with the power holder. (12)

refreezing   The latter part of the change process in which systems and conditions are introduced that reinforce and maintain the desired behaviors. (15)

relatedness needs   A person's need to interact with other people and receive public recognition, and to feel secure around people (i.e., interpersonal safety). (3)

representative sampling   Sampling a population in a way that allows us to extrapolate the results to a larger population. (Appendix A)

reward power   The capacity to influence others by controlling the allocation of rewards valued by them and the removal of negative sanctions. (12)

rituals   The programmed routines of daily organizational life that dramatize an organization's culture. (16)

role   The set of behaviors that people are expected to perform because they hold positions in a team and organization. (9)

role ambiguity   Uncertainty about job duties, performance expectations, level of authority, and other job conditions. (5)

role conflict   A situation whereby people experience competing demands, such as having job duties that are incompatible with personal values or receiving contradictory messages from different people. (5)

role perceptions   A person's beliefs about what behaviors are appropriate or necessary in a particular situation, including the specific tasks that make up the job, their relative importance, and the preferred behaviors to accomplish those tasks. (2)

S

satisfaction-progression process   A process whereby a person becomes motivated to fulfill a higher need as a lower need is gratified. (3)

satisficing   Selecting a solution that is satisfactory or "good enough" rather than optimal or "the best." (11)

scientific management   The process of systematically determining how work should be partitioned into its smallest possible elements and how the process of completing each task should be standardized to achieve maximum efficiency. (4)

scientific method   A set of principles and procedures that help researchers to systematically understand previously unexplained events and conditions. (Appendix A)

search conferences   Systemwide group sessions, usually lasting a few days, in which participants identify the environmental trends and establish strategic solutions for those conditions. (15)

selective attention   The process of filtering (selecting and screening out) information received by our senses. (6)

self-directed work teams (SDWTs)   Work groups that complete an entire piece of work requiring several interdependent tasks and have substantial autonomy over the execution of these tasks. (10)

self-efficacy   A person's belief that he or she has the ability, motivation, and situational contingencies to complete a task successfully. (2)

self-fulfilling prophecy   A phenomenon in which an observer's expectations of someone cause that person to act in a way that is consistent with the observer's expectation. (6)

self-leadership   The process of influencing oneself to establish the self-direction and self-motivation needed to perform a task, including personal goal setting, constructive thought patterns, designing natural rewards, self-monitoring, and self-reinforcement. (4)

self-monitoring   A personality trait referring to the extent that people are sensitive to situational cues and can readily adapt their own behavior appropriately. (6)

self-serving bias   A perceptual error whereby people tend to attribute their own success to internal factors and their failures to external factors. (6)

self-talk   Talking to yourself about your thoughts or actions, for the purpose of increasing self-efficacy and navigating through the decisions required to get a job done effectively. (4)

sensitivity training   An unstructured and agendaless session in which participants become more aware through their interactions of how they affect others and how others affect them. (15)

sexual harassment   Unwelcome conduct of a sexual nature that detrimentally affects the work environment or leads to adverse job-related consequences for its victims. (5)

shaping   Initially reinforcing crude approximations of the ideal behavior, then increasing reinforcement standards until only the ideal behavior is rewarded. (2)

situational contingencies   Environmental conditions beyond the employee's immediate control that constrain or facilitate employee behavior and performance. (2)

situational leadership model Hersey and Blanchard's model stating that leaders should tell, sell, participate, or delegate, depending on the "readiness" of followers. (14)

skill-based pay (SBP) Pay structures in which employees earn higher pay rates with the number of skill modules they have mastered. (4)

skill variety The degree to which a job requires employees to use different skills and talents to complete a variety of work activities. (4)

skunkworks Cross-functional teams that are usually formed spontaneously to develop products or solve complex problems and usually in isolation from the organization and without the normal restrictions. (9)

social identity theory A theory that explains self-perception and social perception in terms of our unique characteristics (personal identity) as well as membership in various social groups (social identity). (6)

social learning theory A theory stating that learning mainly occurs by observing others and then modeling the behaviors that lead to favorable outcomes and avoiding behaviors that lead to punishing consequences. (2)

social loafing The situation in which people perform at a lower level when working in groups than when working alone. (9)

social responsibility A person's or organization's moral obligation toward others who are affected by his or her actions. (1)

sociotechnical design A theory stating that effective work sites have joint optimization of their social and technological system, and that teams should have sufficient autonomy to control key variances in the work process. (10)

span of control The number of people directly reporting to the next level in the hierarchy. (18)

stereotyping The process of using a few observable characteristics to assign people to a preconceived social category, and then assigning less observable traits to those people based on their membership in the group. (6)

strategic choice The idea that an organization interacts with its environment rather than being totally determined by it. (18)

stress An adaptive response to a situation that is perceived as challenging or threatening to the person's well-being. (5)

stressors Any environmental conditions that place a physical or emotional demand on the person. (5)

substitutability The extent to which those dependent on a resource have alternative sources of supply of the resource or can use other resources that would provide a reasonable substitute. (12)

superordinate goals Common objectives held by conflicting parties that are more important than their conflicting departmental or individual goals. (13)

synergy The capacity of people to generate more and better solutions by working together and sharing ideas than if these people worked alone. (10)

T

tacit knowledge Knowledge embedded in our actions and ways of thinking, and transmitted only through observation and experience. (2)

task identity The degree to which a job requires completion of a whole or identifiable piece of work. (4)

task interdependence The degree to which team members must share common inputs, interact in the process of executing their work, or receive outcomes determined partly by their mutual performance. (9)

task performance Goal-directed activities that are under the individual's control. (2)

task significance The degree to which the job has a substantial impact on the organization and/or larger society. (4)

team-based organizational structure A type of departmentalization with a flat span of control and relatively little formalization, consisting of self-directed work teams responsible for various work processes. (18)

team building Any formal intervention directed toward improving the development and functioning of a work team. (9)

team cohesiveness The degree of attraction that members feel toward their team and their motivation to remain members. (9)

team effectiveness The extent to which the team achieves its objectives, satisfies the needs and objectives of its members, and sustains itself over time. (9)

teams Groups of two or more people who interact and influence each other, are mutually accountable for achieving common objectives, and perceive themselves as a social entity within an organization. (9)

telecommuting Performing work at home or another location away from the office, usually with a computer or other telecommunications connection to the office (also called *teleworking*). (1)

theory A general set of propositions that describes interrelationships among several concepts. (Appendix A)

third-party conflict resolution Any attempt by a relatively neutral person to help the parties resolve their differences. (13)

transactional leadership Leadership that helps organizations achieve their current objectives more efficiently by linking job performance to valued rewards and ensuring that employees have the resources needed to get the job done. (14)

transformational leadership A leadership perspective that explains how leaders change teams or organizations by creating, communicating, and modeling a vision for the organization or work unit, and inspiring employees to strive for that vision. (14)

trust Positive expectations about another party's intentions and actions toward us in risky situations. (17)

Type A behavior pattern A behavior pattern associated with people having premature coronary heart disease; Type A's tend to be impatient, lose their temper, talk rapidly, and interrupt others. (5)

Type B behavior pattern A behavior pattern of people with low risk of coronary heart disease; Type B's tend to work steadily, take a relaxed approach to life, and be even-tempered. (5)

U

uncertainty avoidance The degree to which people tolerate ambiguity (low uncertainty avoidance) or feel threatened by ambiguity and uncertainty (high uncertainty avoidance). (7)

unfreezing The first part of the change process whereby the change agent produces a disequilibrium between the driving and restraining forces. (15)

utilitarianism A moral principle stating that decision makers should seek the greatest good for the greatest number of people when choosing among alternatives. (7)

V

valence The anticipated satisfaction or dissatisfaction that an individual feels toward an outcome. (3)

values   Stable, long-lasting beliefs about what is important to the individual. (7)

variable interval schedule   A schedule that reinforces behavior after it has occurred for a variable period of time around some average. (2)

variable ratio schedule   A schedule that reinforces behavior after it has occurred a varying number of times around some average. (2)

virtual teams   Cross-functional teams that operate across space, time, and organizational boundaries with members who communicate mainly through electronic technologies. (9)

W

win-lose orientation   A person's belief that the conflicting parties are drawing from a fixed pie, so his or her gain is the other person's loss. (13)

win-win orientation   A person's belief that the parties will find a mutually beneficial solution to their conflict. (13)

360-degree feedback   Performance feedback received from a full circle of people around an employee. (2)

NOTES

Chapter One

1. C. Zinko, "Silicon Valley Companies Reward Workers With Celebrations," *San Francisco Chronicle*, October 8, 1998, p. A17; A. Kupfer, "The Real King of the Internet," *Fortune*, September 7, 1998, pp. 84–93; J. A. Byrne, "The Corporation of the Future," *Business Week*, August 31, 1998; J. Flower, "The Cisco Mantra," *Wired Magazine*, 5 (March 1997).

2. M. Warner, "Organizational Behavior Revisited," *Human Relations* 47 (October 1994), pp. 1151–66.

3. L. E. Greiner, "A Recent History of Organizational Behavior," in *Organizational Behavior*, S. Kerr, ed. (Columbus, OH: Grid, 1979), pp. 3–14.

4. B. Schlender, "The Three Faces of Steve," *Fortune*, November 9, 1998, pp. 96–104.

5. R. N. Stern and S. R. Barley, "Organizations as Social Systems: Organization Theory's Neglected Mandate," *Administrative Science Quarterly* 41 (1996), pp. 146–62; D. Katz and R. L. Kahn, *The Social Psychology of Organizations* (New York: Wiley, 1966), chap. 2.

6. J. Pfeffer, *New Directions for Organization Theory* (New York: Oxford University Press, 1997), pp. 7–9.

7. S. E. Zahn, "No Kudos for Chek Lap Kok Airport," *World Trade* 11 (October 1998), p. 32; "Best Laid Plans," *Air Transport World*, Fall 1998, p. 8; "What Went Wrong?: Learning from the Foul-ups at Chek Lap Kok," *Asiaweek*, July 27, 1998, p. 1; J. J. Kosowatz, "Building a New Gateway to China," *Scientific American* 277 (December 1997), pp. 102–11; S. T. Martin, "Happier Landings for Hong Kong," *St. Petersburg Times*, June 26, 1997, p. E1; L. Woellert, "Hong Kong Outgrows Its Airport," *Washington Times*, January 17, 1997, p. A14.

8. A. Etzioni, *Modern Organizations*, (Englewood Cliffs, NJ: Prentice-Hall, 1964) p. 1.

9. P. R. Lawrence, "Historical Development of Organizational Behavior," in *Handbook of Organizational Behavior*, L. W. Lorsch, ed. (Englewood Cliffs, NJ: Prentice Hall, 1987), pp. 1–9; D. S. Pugh, "Modern Organizational Theory: A Psychological and Sociological Study," *Psychological Bulletin* 66 (1966), pp. 235–51. For a contrary view of the role of practicality on OB research, see A. P. Brief and J. M. Dukerich, "Theory in Organizational Behavior: Can It Be Useful?" *Research in Organizational Behavior* 13 (1991), pp. 327–52.

10. M. S. Myers, *Every Employee a Manager* (New York: McGraw Hill, 1970).

11. R. Barner, "The New Millennium Workplace: Seven Changes that Will Challenge Managers—and Workers," *The Futurist* 30 (March 1996), pp. 14–18.

12. L. Chong, "Cisco Now Making All the Connections," *New Straits Times*, September 21, 1998; R. L. Brandt, "John Chambers—On the Future of Communications and the Failure of Deregulation," *Upside* 10 (October 1998), pp. 122–33.

13. K. Ohlson, "Leadership in an Age of Mistrust," *Industry Week*, February 2, 1998, pp. 36–46; M. F. R. Kets de Vries, "Charisma in Action: The Transformational Abilities of Virgin's Richard Branson and ABB's Percy Barnevik," *Organizational Dynamics*, 26 (Winter 1998), pp. 6–21; S. Reed and A. Sains, "No More Boardrooms as Usual in Sweden?" *Business Week*, February 2, 1998.

14. For a discussion of globalization in smaller firms, see P. Haapaniemi and W. R. Hill, "Not Just For the Big Guys!" *Chief Executive*, September, 1998, pp. 62–73.

15. K. Doler, "Interview: Jeff Bezos, Founder and CEO of Amazon.com Inc.," *Upside* 10 (September 1998), pp. 76–80; J. Littman, "Driven to Succeed: The Yahoo Story," *Upside* 10 (September 1998), pp. 70–75.

16. V. Fung "Fast, Global, and Entrepreneurial: Supply Chain Management, Hong Kong Style: An Interview with Victor Fung," *Harvard Business Review* 76 (September–October 1998), pp. 102–14; P. Engardio, "How Can Asia Rebound from the Crisis?" *Business Week*, December 1, 1997.

17. K. L. Newman and S. D. Nollen, "Culture and Congruence: The Fit between Management Practices and National Culture," *Journal of International Business Studies* 27 (1996); pp. 753–78. Early warnings came from A. R. Negandhi and B. D. Estafen, "A Research Model to Determine the Applicability of American Management Knowhow in Different Cultures and/or Environment," *Academy of Management Journal* 8 (1965), pp. 309–18.

18. P. R. Sparrow, "Reappraising Psychological Contracting: Lessons for the Field of Human-Resource Development from Cross-Cultural and Occupational Psychology Research," *International Studies of Management & Organization* 28 (Spring 1998), pp. 30–63; R. Schuler and N. Rogovsky, "Understanding Compensation Practice Variations across Firms: The Impact of National Culture," *Journal of International Business Studies* 29 (1998), pp. 159–77.

19. Haapaniemi and Hill, "Not Just For the Big Guys!"

20. A. Siedsma, "Cultural Diversity in the Business Driver's Seat," *San Diego Business Journal*, July 7, 1997, p. 17.

21. C. Bowman, "BLS Projections to 2006: A Summary," *Monthly Labor Review*, November 1997, pp. 3–5.

22. D. Mangan, "Remember When . . . A Women Doctor was a Rarity?" *Medical Economics* 75 (May 11, 1998), pp. 225–226; P. M. Flynn, J. D. Leeth, and E. S. Levy, :"The Accounting Profession in Transition," *CPA Journal* 67 (May 1997), pp. 42–45.

23. B. Tulgan, *Managing Generation X* (Oxford: Capstone, 1996).

24. Most writers explicitly identify Generation-X as people born immediately after the baby boom generation ended (1964) through to the mid-1970s. This is also known as the "Baby Bust" generation because they represent the period of low birth rates. B. Losyk, "Generation X: What They Think and What They Plan to Do," *The Futurist*, 31 (March–April 1997), pp. 29–44.

25. J. A. Conger, "How Generational Shifts Will Transform Organizational

Life," in F. Hesselbein, M. Goldsmith and R. Beckhard, eds., *The Organization of the Future* (San Francisco: Jossey-Bass, 1997), pp. 17–24.

26. D. C. Lau and J. K. Murnighan, "Demographic Diversity and Faultlines: The Compositional Dynamics of Organizational Groups," *Academy of Management Review* 23 (April 1998), pp. 325–40; G. Robinson and K. Dechant, "Building a Business Case for Diversity," *Academy of Management Executive* 11 (August 1997), pp. 21–31; J. R. W. Joplin and C. S. Daus, "Challenges of Leading a Diverse Workforce," *Academy of Management Executive* 11 (August 1997), pp. 32–47.

27. T. L. Sager, "Partnering-Diversity," *Metropolitan Corporate Counsel*, July 1997, p. 26; see also M. J. Reid, "Profit Motivates Corporate Diversity," *San Francisco Examiner*, March 15, 1998, p. W42.

28. S. D. Friedman, P. Christensen, J. DeGroot, "Work and Life: The End of the Zero-Sum Game," *Harvard Business Review* 76 (November–December 1998), pp. 119–29.

29. J. King, "All Work, No Play? Gen X-ers: No Way," *Computerworld*, May 5, 1997, pp. 1–2.

30. "What Blacks Think of Corporate America," *Fortune*, July 6, 1998, pp. 140–43.

31. P. Cappelli et al, *Change at Work* (New York: Oxford University Press, 1997); M. G. Evans, H. P. Gunz, and R. M. Jalland, "The Aftermath of Downsizing: A Cautionary Tale of Restructuring and Careers," *Business Horizons* 39 (March 1996), pp. 62–66; D. Yankelovich, "Got to Give to Get," *Mother Jones* (July 1997), pp. 60–63; C. C. Heckscher, *White-Collar Blues: Management Loyalties in an Age of Corporate Restructuring* (New York: Basic Books, 1995).

32. A. E. Polivka, "Contingent and Alternative Work Arrangements, Defined," *Monthly Labor Review* 119 (October 1996), pp. 3–10. For further discussion of the meaning of contingent work, see S. Nollen and H. Axel, *Managing Contingent Workers* (New York: AMACOM, 1996), pp. 4–9.

33. S. B. Gould, K. J. Weiner, and B. R. Levin, *Free Agents: People and Organizations Creating a New Working Community* (San Francisco: Jossey-Bass, 1997).

34. A. Dunkin, "Saying Adios to the Office," *Business Week*, October 12, 1998.

35. T. A. Stewart, "Gray Flannel Suit? Moi?" *Fortune*, March 16, 1998, pp. 76–82.

36. A. Tergesen, "Making Stay-at-Homes Feel Welcome," *Business Week*, October 12, 1998, pp. 155–57.

37. J. A. Challenger, "There Is No Future for the Workplace," *Futurist* 32 (October 1998), pp. 16–20; Dunkin, "Saying Adios to the Office"; A. Mahlon, "The Alternative Workplace: Changing Where and How People Work," *Harvard Business Review* (May–June 1998), pp. 121–30.

38. J. Lipnack and J. Stamps, *Virtual Teams: Reaching Across Space, Time, and Organizations with Technology* (New York: John Wiley, 1997), pp. 5–8; D. J. Armstrong and P. Cole, "Managing Distances and Differences in Geographically Distributed Work Groups," in S. E. Jackson and M. N. Ruderman, eds., *Diversity in Work Teams: Research Paradigms for a Changing Workplace* (Washington, DC: American Psychological Association, 1995), pp. 187–215.

39. W. C. Taylor, "At Verifone, It's a Dog's Life," in *Handbook of the Business Revolution* (New York: Fast Company, 1997), pp. 12–17.

40. J. A. Byrne "The Corporation of the Future," *Business Week*, August 31, 1998, pp. 102–104.

41. W. J. Mitchell, "Do We Still Need Skyscrapers?" *Scientific American*, 277 (December 1997), pp. 112–13.

42. "Teamwork Grows ROOTS in China," *Industry Week*, October 19, 1998 pp. 26–27.

43. For several examples, see: R. S. Wellins, W. C. Byham, and G. R. Dixon, *Inside Teams* (San Francisco: Jossey-Bass, 1994).

44. L. Rittenhouse, "Dennis W. Bakke— Empowering a Workforce with Principles," *Electricity Journal*, January 1998, pp. 48–59.

45. L. Swick, "Team-Based Organization: The Fruits of Employee Empowerment," *Hospital Materiel Management Quarterly* 19 (November 1997), pp. 1–3.

46. G. Lawton, "Fighting Back Against the Bribery Culture," *Chemistry and Industry*, December 7, 1998, p. 957; "Eastman Chemical Pleads Guilty to Price Fixing," *Chemical Engineering*, 105 (November 1998), p. 54; K. Eichenwald, "Former Archer Daniels Executives Are Found Guilty of Price Fixing," *New York Times*, September 18, 1998, p. A1.

47. Ohlson, "Leadership in an Age of Mistrust."

48. M. D. Somerson, "Doctors Find Gifts an Ethical Minefield," *Columbus Dispatch*, January 24, 1999, p. A1.

49. M. N. Zald, "More Fragmentation? Unfinished Business in Linking the Social Sciences and the Humanities," *Administrative Science Quarterly* 41 (1996), pp. 251–61.

50. C. Hardy, "The Contribution of Political Science to Organizational Behavior," in J. W. Lorsch, ed., *Handbook of Organizational Behavior* (Englewood Cliffs, NJ: Prentice Hall, 1987), pp. 96–108.

51. J. Pfeffer, *New Directions for Organization Theory: Problems and Prospects* (New York: Oxford University Press, 1997), p. 192–93.

52. T. S. Kuhn, *The Structure of Scientific Revolutions* (Chicago: University of Chicago Press, 1970).

53. H. L. Tosi and J. W. Slocum, Jr., "Contingency Theory: Some Suggested Directions," *Journal of Management* 10 (1984), pp. 9–26.

54. D. M. Rousseau and R. J. House, "Meso Organizational Behavior: Avoiding Three Fundamental Biases," in C. J. Cooper and D. M. Rousseau, eds., *Trends in Organizational Behavior*, vol. 1, (Chichester, UK: John Wiley, 1994), pp. 13–30.

55. P. M. Senge, "Leading Learning Organizations: The Bold, the Powerful, and the Invisible," in F. Hesselbein, M. Goldsmith, and R. Beckhard, eds., *The Leader of the Future* (San Francisco: Jossey-Bass, 1996), pp. 41–57.

56. A. Waring, *Practical Systems Thinking* (Boston: International Thomson Business Press, 1997); K. Ellis et al., eds., *Critical Issues in Systems Theory and Practice* (New York: Plenum, 1995); P. M. Senge, *The Fifth Discipline: The Art and Practice of the Learning Organization* (New York: Doubleday Currency, 1990), chap. 4; F. E. Kast and J. E. Rosenweig, "General Systems Theory: Applications for Organization and Management," *Academy of Management Journal*, 15, 1972, pp. 447–65.

57. M. L. Tushman, M. B. Nadler, and D. A. Nadler, *Competing by Design: The Power of Organizational Architecture* (New York: Oxford University Press, 1997).

58. G. F. B. Probst, "Practical Knowledge Management: A Model That Works," *Prism* (Second Quarter 1998), pp. 17–23; G. Miles, Grant, R. E. Miles, V. Perrone, and L. Edvinsson, "Some Conceptual and Research Barriers to the Utilization of Knowledge," *California Management Review* 40 (Spring 1998), pp. 281–288; E. C. Nevis, A. J. DiBella, and J. M. Gould, "Understanding Organizations as Learning Systems," *Sloan Management Review* 36 (Winter 1995), pp. 78–85; G. Huber, "Organizational Learning: The Contributing Processes and Literature." *Organizational Science* 2 (1991), pp. 88–115.

59. D. Ulrich, M. Von Glinow, and T. Jick, "High Impact Learning: Building and Diffusing Learning Capability," *Organizational Dynamics* 22 (Autumn 1993), pp. 52–66.

60. Cited in A. T. Young, "Ethics in Business," *Vital Speeches of the Day* 58 (September 15, 1992), pp. 725–30.

61. T. A. Stewart, *Intellectual Capital: The New Wealth of Organizations* (New York: Doubleday Currency, 1997); H. Saint-Onge, "Tacit Knowledge: The Key to the Strategic Alignment of Intellectual Capital," *Strategy & Leadership* 24 (March/April 1996), pp. 10–14; G. Petrash, "Dow's Journey to a Knowledge Value Management Culture," *European Management Journal* 14 (August 1996), pp. 365–73.

62. D. J. Skyrme and D. M. Amidon, "New Measures Of Success," *Journal of Business Strategy*, January–February 1998, pp. 20–24.

63. There is no complete agreement on the meaning of organizational learning, and the relationship between organizational learning and knowledge management is still somewhat ambiguous. For writing on organizational learning, see: Huber, "Organizational Learning"; P. M. Senge, *The Fifth Discipline: The Art and Practice of the Learning Organization* (New York: Doubleday Currency, 1990), pp. 3–5.

64. S. Caudron, "Five Critical Competencies," *Industry Week*, October 19, 1998, pp. 12–14.

65. R. Karpinski, "Microsoft Buys Vermeer Technologies," *CommunicationsWeek*, January 22, 1996, p. 29; P. Keefe, "PC Software Pioneer Ends Missionary Work," *Computerworld*, October 5, 1987, pp. 41, 48.

66. Huber, "Organizational Learning."

67. Byrne, "The Corporation of the Future."

68. C. W. Wick and L. S. Leon, "From Ideas to Actions: Creating a Learning Organization," *Human Resource Management* 34 (Summer 1995), pp. 299–311; Ulrich, Jick, and Von Glinow, "High Impact Learning." This is similar to "Synthetic Learning" described in D. Miller, "A Preliminary Typology of Organizational Learning: Synthesizing the Literature," *Journal of Management* 22 (1996), pp. 485–505.

69. C. O'Dell and C. J. Grayson, "If Only We Knew What We Know: Identification and Transfer of Internal Best Practices," *California Management Review* 40 (Spring 1998), pp. 154–74.

70. R. Ruggles, "The State of the Notion: Knowledge Management in Practice," *California Management Review* 40 (Spring 1998), pp. 80–89; G. S. Richards and S. C. Goh, "Implementing Organizational Learning: Toward a Systematic Approach," *The Journal of Public Sector Management*, Autumn 1995, pp. 25–31.

71. I. Nonaka and H. Takeuchi, *The Knowledge-Creating Company: How Japanese Companies Create the Dynamics of Innovation* (New York: Oxford University Press, 1995).

72. G. H. Anthes, "Learning How to Share," *Computerworld*, February 23, 1998, pp. 75–77.

73. R. Madhavan and R. Grover, "From Embedded Knowledge to Embodied Knowledge: New Product Development as Knowledge Management," *Journal of Marketing* 62 (October 1998), pp. 1–12; C. J. Grayson and C. O'Dell, "Mining Your Hidden Resources," *Across the Board* 35 (April 1998), pp. 23–28; W. D. Hitt, "The Learning Organization: Some Reflections on Organizational Renewal," *Leadership & Organization Development Journal* 16, no. 8 (1995), pp. 17–25.

74. O'Dell and Grayson, "If Only We Knew What We Know."

75. S. Greengard, "Will Your Culture Support KM?" *Workforce* 77 (October 1998), pp. 93–94; M. Groves, "Asset Values Shifting as Firms Begin to Account for Employee Brainpower," *Los Angeles Times*, January 18, 1998, p. D5.

76. P. Galagan, "Smart Companies; Knowledge Management," *Training &

Development* 51 (December 1997), pp. 20–24.

77. J. Kurtzman, "A Mind Is a Terrible Thing to Waste," *Chief Executive*, April 1996, p. 20.

78. J. Schmitt, "High-Tech Job Hopping," *USA Today*, August 21, 1998. p. B1.

79. Stewart, *Intellectual Capital*, chap. 7.

80. T. Davenport and L. Prusak, *Working Knowledge: How Organizations Manage What They Know* (Boston: Harvard Business School Press, 1998).

81. M. E. McGill and J. W. Slocum, Jr., "Unlearn the Organization," *Organizational Dynamics* 22, no. 2 (1993), pp. 67–79.

Chapter Two

1. F. W. Timmerman, Jr., "ECHO System Helps USAA Listen—and Respond—to Customer Feedback," *Journal of Retail Banking Services* 20 (June 1998), pp. 29–33; M. Clark, "Is This the Ideal Place to Work?" *The Virginian-Pilot* (Norfolk), February 1, 1998, p. D1; R. B. Lieber, "Why Employees Love These Companies," *Fortune*, January 12, 1998, pp. 72–74; W. Wilhelm and B. Rossello, "The Care and Feeding of Customers," *Management Review* 86 (March 1997), pp. 19–23.

2. Cite in A. Haasen, "Opel Eisenach GmbH—Creating a High-Productivity Workplace," *Organizational Dynamics* 24 (Winter 1996), pp. 80–85.

3. C. C. Pinder, *Work Motivation* (Glenview, IL: Scott, Foresman, 1984), pp. 7–10; and E. E. Lawler III, *Motivation in Work Organizations* (Monterey, CA: Brooks/Cole, 1973), pp. 2–5.

4. J. Kochanski, "Competency-Based Management," *Training & Development*, October 1997, pp. 40–44; Hay Group et. al., *Raising the Bar: Using Competencies to Enhance Employee Performance* (Scottsdale, AZ: American Compensation Association, 1996); L. M. Spencer and S. M. Spencer, *Competence at Work: Models for Superior Performance* (New York: John Wiley, 1993).

5. "Should Competencies Be Used to Determine Pay for Performance?" *Pay for Performance Report*, September 1996, p. 1.

6. B. Birchard, "Hire Great People Fast," *Fast Company*, no. 10 (July 1997), p. 132.

7. J. R. Edwards, "Person-Job Fit: A Conceptual Integration, Literature Review, and Methodological Critique," *International Review of Industrial and Organizational Psychology* 6 (1991), pp. 283–357; J. E. Hunter and R. F. Hunger, "Validity and Utility of Alternative Predictors of Job Performance," *Psychological Bulletin* 96 (1984), pp. 72–98.

8. J. W. Johnson, "Linking Employee Perceptions of Service Climate to Customer Satisfaction," *Personnel Psychology* 49 (1996), pp. 831–51; A. Sharma and D. Sarel, "The Impact of Customer Satisfaction Based Incentive Systems on Salespeople's Customer Service Response: An Empirical Study," *Journal of Personal Selling & Sales Management* 15 (Summer 1995), pp. 17–29; R. A. Guzzo, R. D. Jette, and R. A. Katzell, "The Effects of Psychological Based Intervention Programs on Worker Productivity: A Meta-Analysis," *Personnel Psychology* 38 (1985), pp. 275–91.

9. S. P. Brown and R. A. Peterson, "The Effect of Effort on Sales Performance and Job Satisfaction," *Journal of Marketing* 58 (April 1994), pp. 70–80; D. N. Behrman and W. D. Perreault, Jr., "A Role Stress Model of the Performance and Satisfaction of Industrial Salespersons," *Journal of Marketing* 48 (1984), pp. 9–21.

10. S. B. Bacharach and P. Bamberger, "Beyond Situational Constraints: Job Resources Inadequacy and Individual Performance at Work," *Human Resource Management Review* 5 (1995), pp. 79–102; K. F. Kane, ed., "Special Issue: Situational Constraints and Work Performance," *Human Resource Management Review* 3 (Summer 1993), pp. 83–175.

11. J. H. Sheridan, "Lockheed Martin Corp.," *Industry Week*, no. 247 (October 19, 1998), pp. 54–56.

12. D. J. Nahorney, "You Can't Eat an Elephant in One Bite?" *Managers Magazine* 70 (July 1995), pp. 16–20.

13. D. Yankelovich, "Got to Give to Get," *Mother Jones* 22 (July 1997), pp. 60–63.

14. W. J. Holstein and B. Murray, "Give Us Your Wired, Your Highly Skilled," *U.S. News & World Report*, October 5, 1998, p. 53.

15. M. Irvine, "Perks Rise to Another Level," *Arizona Republic*, September 19, 1998; L. Uchitelle, "Bonuses Spread as a Hiring Lure," *San Jose Mercury News*, June 10, 1998; N. Munk, "The New Organization Man," *Fortune*, March 16, 1998, pp. 63–74.

16. Munk, "The New Organization Man," p. 68.

17. E. Roche, "Leading by Example," *Datamation* 44 (January 1998), p. 126.

18. S. M. Jacoby, "Most Workers Find a Sense of Security in Corporate Life," *Los Angeles Times*, September 7, 1998, p. B5.

19. E. Roche, "Send Your Staff Home," *Datamation* 44 (February 1998), p. 94; M. Hofman, "Tackling Turnover: Staying Power," *Inc.*, January 1998, p. 74.

20. R. W. Griffeth and P. W. Hom, "The Employee Turnover Process," *Research in Personnel and Human Resource Management* 13 (1995), pp. 245–93.

21. S. J. Hartman, A. C. Yrle, and A. R. Yrle, "Turnover in the Hotel Industry: Is There a Hobo Phenomenon at Work?" *International Journal of Management* 13 (1996), pp. 340–48; T. A. Judge and S. Watanabe, "Is the Past Prologue? A Test of Ghiselli's Hobo Syndrome," *Journal of Management* 21 (1995), pp. 211–29.

22. S. R. Rhodes and R. M. Steers, *Managing Employee Absenteeism* (Reading, MA: Addison-Wesley, 1990).

23. D. Sefton, "Healthy Workers Tap Sick Days for Family Time," *Times Union* (Albany, NY), November 30, 1998, p. C1.

24. S. Shellenbarger, "Busy Staffers Are Taking More Time Off of Work," *The Wall Street Journal*, September 23, 1998; D. A. Harrison and J. J. Martocchio, "Time for Absenteeism: A 20-Year Review of Origins, Offshoots, and Outcomes," *Journal of Management* 24 (Spring 1998), pp. 305–50; R. D. Hackett and P. Bycio, "An Evaluation of Employee Absenteeism as a Coping Mechanism among Hospital Nurses," *Journal of Occupational & Organizational Psychology* 69 (December 1996), pp. 327–38; J. J. Bardsley and S. R. Rhodes, "Using the Steers-Rhodes (1984) Framework to Identify Correlates of Employee Lateness," *Journal of Business & Psychology* 10 (Spring 1996), pp. 351–65; R. G. Ehrenberg, R. A. Ehrenberg, D. I. Rees, and E. L. Ehrenberg, "School District Leave Policies, Teacher Absenteeism, and Student Achievement," *Journal of Human Resources* 26 (Winter 1991), pp. 72–105.

25. J. P. Campbell, R. A. McCloy, S. H. Oppler, and C. E. Sager, "A Theory of Performance," in N. Schmitt, W. C. Borman, and Associates, eds., *Personnel Selection in Organizations* (San Francisco: Jossey-Bass, 1993), pp. 35–70.

26. S. T. Hunt, "Generic Work Behavior: An Investigation into the Dimensions of Entry-Level, Hourly Job Performance," *Personnel Psychology* 49 (1996), pp. 51–83.

27. C. I. Barnard, *The Functions of the Executive* (Cambridge: Harvard University Press, 1938), pp. 83–84; and D. Katz and R. L. Kahn, *The Social Psychology of Organizations* (New York: John Wiley, 1966), pp. 337–40.

28. P. M. Podsakoff, M. Ahearne, and S. B. MacKenzie, "Organizational Citizenship Behavior and the Quantity and Quality of Work Group Performance," *Journal of Applied Psychology* 82 (1997), pp. 262–70; D. W. Organ, "The Motivational Basis of Organizational Citizenship Behavior," *Research in Organizational Behavior* 12 (1990), pp. 43–72. The discussion of altruism is also based on R. N. Kanungo and J. A. Conger, "Promoting Altruism as a Corporate Goal," *Academy of Management Executive* 7, no. 3 (1993), pp. 37–48.

29. P. Cappelli and N. Rogovsky, "Employee Involvement and Organizational Citizenship: Implications for Labor Law Reform and 'Lean Production,'" *Industrial and Labor Relations Review* 51 (July 1998), pp. 633–53; R. H. Moorman, G L. Blakley, and B. P. Niehoff, "Does Perceived Organizational Support Mediate the Relationship between Procedural Justice and Organizational Citizenship Behavior?" *Academy of Management Journal* 41 (1998)), pp. 351–57; Organ, "The Motivational Basis of Organizational Citizenship Behavior," pp. 60–63.

30. Kanungo and Conger, "Promoting Altruism as a Corporate Goal," p. 42.

31. T. A. Stewart, "Gray Flannel Suit? Moi?" *Fortune*, March 16, 1998, pp. 76–82.

32. D. M. Harris and R. L. DeSimone, *Human Resource Development* (Fort Worth, TX: Harcourt Brace, 1994), p. 54; B. Bass and J. Vaughn,

Training in Industry: The Management of Learning (Belmont, Calif.: Wadsworth, 1966), p. 8; W. McGehee and P. W. Thayer, *Training in Business and Industry* (New York: John Wiley, 1961), pp. 131–34.

33. G. G. B. Probst, "Practical Knowledge Management: A Model That Works," *Prism* (Second Quarter 1998), pp. 17–23; G. Miles, R. E. Miles, V. Perrone, and L. Edvinsson, "Some Conceptual and Research Barriers to the Utilization of Knowledge," *California Management Review* 40 (Spring 1998), pp. 281–88; E. C. Nevis, A. J. DiBella, and J. M. Gould, "Understanding Organizations as Learning Systems," *Sloan Management Review* 36 (Winter 1995), pp. 73–85; G. Huber, "Organizational Learning: The Contributing Processes and Literature," *Organizational Science* 2 (1991), pp. 88–115.

34. D. Ulrich, T. Jick, and M. Von Glinow, "High Impact Learning: Building and Diffusing Learning Capability," *Organizational Dynamics* 22 (Autumn 1993), pp. 52–66.

35. R. Madhavan and R. Grover, "From Embedded Knowledge to Embodied Knowledge: New Product Development as Knowledge Management," *Journal of Marketing* 62 (October 1998), pp. 1–12; D. Leonard and S. Sensiper, "The Role of Tacit Knowledge in Group Innovation," *California Management Review* 40 (Spring 1998), pp. 112–132; I. Nonaka and H. Takeuchi, *The Knowledge-Creating Company* (New York: Oxford University Press, 1995); R. K. Wagner and R. J. Sternberg, "Practical Intelligence in Real-World Pursuits: The Role of Tacit Knowledge," *Journal of Personality and Social Psychology* 49 (1985), pp. 436–58.

36. M. J. Kerr, "Tacit Knowledge as a Predictor of Managerial Success: A Field Study," *Canadian Journal of Behavioral Science* 27 (1995), pp. 36–51.

37. R. G. Miltenberger, *Behavior Modification: Principles and Procedures* (Pacific Grove, CA: Brooks/Cole, 1997); J. Komaki, T. Coombs, and S. Schepman, "Motivational Implications of Reinforcement Theory," in R. M. Steers, L. W. Porter, and G. A. Bigley, eds., *Motivation and Leadership at Work* (New York: McGraw-Hill, 1996), pp. 34–52; H. P. Sims and

P. Lorenzi, *The New Leadership Paradigm: Social Learning and Cognition in Organizations* (Newbury Park, CA: Sage, 1992), part II; Pinder, *Work Motivation*, chap. 9.

38. W. F. Dowling, "Conversation with B. F. Skinner," *Organizational Dynamics*, Winter 1973, pp. 31–40.

39. B. F. Skinner, *The Behavior of Organisms* (New York: Appleton-Century-Crofts, 1938).

40. F. Luthans and R. Kreitner, *Organizational Behavior Modification and Beyond* (Glenview, Ill.: Scott, Foresman, 1985), pp. 85–88; and T. K. Connellan, *How to Improve Human Performance* (New York: Harper & Row, 1978), pp. 48–57.

41. Miltenberger, *Behavior Modification*, chaps. 4–6.

42. T. C. Mawhinney and R. R. Mawhinney, "Operant Terms and Concepts Applied to Industry," in *Industrial Behavior Modification: A Management Handbook*, R. M. O'Brien, A. M. Dickinson, and M. P. Rosow, eds. (New York: Pergamon Press, 1982), p. 117; R. Kreitner, "Controversy in OBM: History, Misconceptions, and Ethics," in *Handbook of Organizational Behavior Management*, L. W. Frederiksen, ed. (New York: John Wiley, 1982), pp. 76–79.

43. Luthans and Kreitner, *Organizational Behavior Modification and Beyond*, pp. 53–54.

44. K. D. Butterfield, L. K. Trevino, and G. A. Ball, "Punishment from the Manager's Perspective: A Grounded Investigation and Inductive Model," *Academy of Management Journal* 39 (1996), pp. 1479–1512; L. K. Trevino, "The Social Effects of Punishment in Organizations: A Justice Perspective," *Academy of Management Review* 17 (1992), pp. 647–76.

45. B. S. Klaas and H. N. Wheeler, "Managerial Decision Making about Employee Discipline: A Policy-Capturing Approach," *Personnel Psychology* 43 (1990), pp. 117–34.

46. Butterfield et al., "Punishment from the Manager's Perspective"; G. Eden, "Progressive Discipline: An Oxymoron?" *Relations Industrielles* 47 (1992), pp. 511–27; Luthans and Kreitner, *Organizational Behavior Modification and Beyond*, pp. 139–44; J. M. Beyer and H. M. Trice, "A Field Study of the Use and Perceived Effects of Discipline in Controlling Work Performance," *Academy of*

Management Journal 27 (1984), pp. 743–64.

47. D. N. Campbell, R. L. Fleming, and R. C. Grote, "Discipline Without Punishment—at Last," *Harvard Business Review* 63 (July–August 1985), pp. 162–74.

48. G. P. Latham and V. L. Huber, "Schedules of Reinforcement: Lessons from the Past and Issues for the Future," *Journal of Organizational Behavior Management* 13 (1992), pp. 125–49.

49. R. Kreitner and F. Luthans, "A Social Learning Approach to Behavioral Management: Radical Behavioralists 'Mellow Out,'" *Organizational Dynamics*, Autumn 1984, pp. 47–65.

50. Miltenberger, *Behavior Modification*, chap. 10; L. Grant and E. Evans, *Principles of Behavior Analysis* (New York: HarperCollins, 1994); Pinder, *Work Motivation*, p. 198.

51. G. Masek, "Dana Corp.," *Industry Week*, 247 (October 19, 1998), p. 48.

52. Alexander D. Stajkovic and F. Luthans, "A Meta-Analysis of the Effects of Organizational Behavior Modification on Task Performance, 1975–95," *Academy of Management Journal* 40 (1997), pp. 1122–49.

53. J. Austin, M. L. Kessler, J. E. Riccobono, and J. S. Bailey, "Using Feedback and Reinforcement to Improve the Performance and Safety of a Roofing Crew," *Journal of Organizational Behavior Management* 16 (1996), pp. 49–75; T. LaFleur and C. Hyten, "Improving the Quality of Hotel Banquet Staff Performance," *Journal of Organizational Behavior Management* 15 (1995), pp. 69–93.

54. G. A. Merwin, J. A. Thomason, and E. E. Sanford, "A Methodological and Content Review of Organizational Behavior Management in the Private Sector: 1978–1986," *Journal of Organizational Behavior Management* 10 (1989), pp. 39–57.

55. P. Drucker, *Management: Tasks, Responsibilities, Practices* (New York: Harper & Row, 1974).

56. Latham and Huber, "Schedules of Reinforcement," pp. 132–33.

57. Pinder, *Work Motivation*, pp. 230–32; T. C. Mawhinney, "Philosophical and Ethical Aspects of Organizational Behavior Management: Some Evaluative Feedback," *Journal of Organizational Behavior Management* 6 (Spring 1984), pp. 5–31; and F. L. Fry, "Operant Conditioning in Organizational Settings: Of Mice or

Men?" *Personnel* 51 (July–August 1974), pp. 17–24.

58. L. Csoka, *Closing the Human Performance Gap: A Research Report* (New York: Conference Board, 1994).

59. A. N. Kluger and A. DeNisi, "The Effects of Feedback Interventions Performance: A Historical Review, A Meta-Analysis, and a Preliminary Feedback Intervention Theory," *Psychological Bulletin* 119 (March 1996), pp. 254–284; A. A. Shikdar and B. Das, "A Field Study of Worker Productivity Improvements," *Applied Ergonomics* 26 (1995), pp. 21–27; L. M. Sama and R. E. Kopelman, "In Search of a Ceiling Effect on Work Motivation: Can Kaizen Keep Performance 'Risin'?" *Journal of Social Behavior & Personality* 9 (1994), pp. 231–37.

60. M. D. Cooper and R. A. Phillips, "Reducing Accidents Using Goal Setting and Feedback: A Field Study," *Journal of Occupational & Organizational Psychology* 67 (1994), pp. 219–40; K. N. Wexley and G. P. Latham, *Developing and Training Human Resources in Organizations*, 2nd ed. (New York: HarperCollins, 1991), pp. 77–80.

61. R. Waldersee and F. Luthans, "The Impact of Positive and Corrective Feedback on Customer Service Performance," *Journal of Organizational Behavior* 15 (1994), pp. 83–95; P. K. Duncan and L. R. Bruwelheide, "Feedback: Use and Possible Behavioral Functions," *Journal of Organizational Behavior Management* 7 (Fall 1985), pp. 91–114; J. Annett, *Feedback and Human Behavior* (Baltimore: Penguin, 1969).

62. R. McDonald, "Transition to PowerPC: RAM Doubler 1.5," *TidBITS*, no. 236 (July 25, 1994) (Web-zine: http://king.tidbits.com).

63. K. Kein, "Searching 360 Degrees for Employee Evaluation," *Incentive*, October 1996, pp. 40–42; M. Marchetti, "Pepsi's New Generation of Employee Feedback," *Sales & Marketing Management*, August 1996, pp. 38–39.

64. M. London and J. W. Smither, "Can Multisource Feedback Change Perceptions of Goal Accomplishment, Self-Evaluations, and Performance-Related Outcomes? Theory-Based Applications and Directions for Research," *Personnel Psychology* 48 (1995), pp. 803–39. For a discussion of multisource

feedback, see M. Edwards and A. Ewan, *360 Feedback: The Powerful New Model for Employee Assessment & Performance Improvement* (New York: AMACOM, 1996); D. Antonioni, "Designing an Effective 360-Degree Appraisal Feedback Process," *Organizational Dynamics*, Autumn 1996, pp. 24–38.

65. P. G. Dominick, R. R. Reilly, and J. W. McGourty, "The Effects of Peer Feedback on Team Member Behavior," *Group & Organization Management* 22 (December 1997), pp. 508–20.

66. R. Y. Bergstrom, "Cells in Steel Country," *Production*, February 1995, pp. 51–54.

67. D. M. Herold, R. C. Linden, and M. L. Leatherwood, "Using Multiple Attributes to Assess Sources of Performance Feedback," *Academy of Management Journal* 30 (December 1987), pp. 826–35.

68. M. London, "Giving Feedback: Source-Centered Antecedents and Consequences of Constructive and Destructive Feedback," *Human Resource Management Review* 5 (1995), pp. 159–88; D. Antonioni, "The Effects of Feedback Accountability on 360-Degree Appraisal Ratings," *Personnel Psychology* 47 (1994), pp. 375–90; S. J. Ashford and G. B. Northcraft, "Conveying More (or Less) Than We Realize: The Role of Impression Management in Feedback Seeking," *Organizational Behavior and Human Decision Processes* 53 (1992), pp. 310–34; E. W. Morrison and R. J. Bies, "Impression Management in the Feedback-Seeking Process: A Literature Review and Research Agenda," *Academy of Management Review* 16 (1991), pp. 522–41.

69. G. B. Northcraft and S. J. Ashford, "The Preservation of Self in Everyday Life: The Effects of Performance Expectations and Feedback Context on Feedback Inquiry," *Organizational Behavior and Human Decision Processes* 47 (1990), pp. 42–64.

70. R. D. Pritchard, P. L. Roth, S. D. Jones, and P. G. Roth, "Implementing Feedback Systems to Enhance Productivity: A Practical Guide," *National Productivity Review* 10 (Winter 1990–1991), pp. 57–67.

71. P. M. Posakoff and J. Fahr, "Effects of Feedback Sign and Credibility on Goal Setting and Task Performance," *Organizational Behavior and Human Decision Processes* 44 (1989), pp. 45–67.

72. R. D. Guzzo and B. A. Gannett, "The Nature of Facilitators and Inhibitors of Effective Task Performance," *Facilitating Work Effectiveness*, F. D. Schoorman and B. Schneider, eds. (Lexington, MA: Lexington Books, 1988), p. 23; R. C. Linden and T. R. Mitchell, "Reactions to Feedback: The Role of Attributions," *Academy of Management Journal* 28 (June 1985), pp. 291–308.

73. S. Robinson and E. Weldon, "Feedback Seeking in Groups: A Theoretical Perspective," *British Journal of Social Psychology* 32 (1993), pp. 71–86; S. J. Ashford and L. L. Cummings, "Feedback as an Individual Resource: Personal Strategies of Creating Information," *Organizational Behavior and Human Performance* 32 (1983), pp. 370–98; S. J. Ashford, "Feedback Seeking in Individual Adaptation: A Resource Perspective," *Academy of Management Journal* 29 (1986), pp. 465–87.

74. W. S. Brown, "The Rising Rate of Snooping," *Journal of Commerce*, August 7, 1997, p. 8a; R. Grant, "Work Monitored Electronically," *HRMagazine*, May 1992, pp. 81–86; E. Kallman, "Electronic Monitoring of Employees: Issues and Guidelines," *Journal of Systems Management* 44, no. 6 (June 1993), pp. 17–21.

75. M. Drummond, "Are You Watched at Work? Right to Privacy Stops at the Door," *Dayton Daily News*, March 8, 1998, p. 1A.

76. J. M. Mishra and S. M. Crampton, "Employee Monitoring: Privacy in the Workplace?" *SAM Advanced Management Journal* 63 (June 1998), pp. 4–14; B. E. Bohling, "Workplace Video Surveillance," *Monthly Labor Review* 120 (July 1997), p. 41; L. Wirthman, "New Software Can Catch Workers Goofing Off, But Some Say Such Surveillance Goes Too Far," *Orange County Register* (CA), July 20, 1997, p. K07; C. D. Creps and L. M. Bolduan, "Is Somebody Watching? Employee Communications and Privacy," *Risk Management* 44 (April 1997), p. 22; K. A. Jenero and L. D. Mapes-Riordan, "Electronic Monitoring of Employees and the Elusive 'Right to Privacy,'" *Employee Relations Law Journal* 18 (Summer 1992), pp. 71–102.

77. K. D. Grimsley "35% of Firms Found to Monitor Workers Electronically," *Washington Post*, May 24, 1997,

p. F01; International Labour Organization, *Conditions of Work Digest: Monitoring and Surveillance in the Workplace* 12, no. 1 (Geneva: International Labour Office, 1993).

78. D. Lyon, *The Electronic Eye: The Rise of the Surveillance Society* (Minneapolis: University of Minnesota Press, 1994); B. P. Niehoff and R. H. Moorman, "Justice as a Mediator of the Relationship Between Methods of Monitoring and Organizational Citizenship Behavior," *Academy of Management Journal* 36 (1993), pp. 527–56; J. Chalykoff and T. A. Kochan, "Computer-Aided Monitoring: Its Influence on Employee Job Satisfaction and Turnover," *Personnel Psychology* 42 (1989), pp. 807–34.

79. A. Bandura, *Social Foundations of Thought and Action: A Social Cognitive Theory* (Englewood Cliffs, NJ: Prentice Hall, 1986).

80. A. Pescuric and W. C. Byham, "The New Look of Behavior Modeling," *Training & Development* 50 (July 1996), pp. 24–30; H. P. Sims, Jr., and C. C. Manz, "Modeling Influences on Employee Behavior," *Personnel Journal*, January 1982, pp. 58–65.

81. A. Bandura, *Self-Efficacy: The Exercise of Control* (New York: W. H. Freeman, 1996); M. E. Gist and T. R. Mitchell, "Self-Efficacy: A Theoretical Analysis of Its Determinants and Malleability," *Academy of Management Review* 17 (1992), pp. 183–211; R. F. Mager, "No Self-Efficacy, No Performance," *Training* 29 (April 1992), pp. 32–36.

82. L. K. Trevino, "The Social Effects of Punishment in Organizations: A Justice Perspective," *Academy of Management Review* 17 (1992), pp. 647–76; M. E. Schnake, "Vicarious Punishment in a Work Setting," *Journal of Applied Psychology* 71 (1986), pp. 343–45.

83. M. Foucault, *Discipline and Punish: The Birth of the Prison* (Harmondsworth, England: Penguin, 1977).

84. Trevino, "The Social Effects of Punishment in Organizations," pp. 647–76; M. E. Schnake, "Vicarious Punishment in a Work Setting," *Journal of Applied Psychology* 71 (1986), pp. 343–45.

85. A. W. Logue, *Self-Control: Waiting Until Tomorrow for What You Want Today.* (Englewood Cliffs, NJ: Prentice Hall, 1995); A Bandura, "Self-Reinforcement: Theoretical and Methodological Considerations," *Behaviorism* 4 (1976), pp. 135–55.

86. C. A. Frayne, "Improving Employee Performance through Self-Management Training," *Business Quarterly* 54 (Summer 1989), pp. 46–50.

87. S. Gherardi, D. Nicolini, F. Odella, "Toward a Social Understanding of How People Learn in Organizations," *Management Learning* 29 (September 1998), pp. 273–97; Ulrich, Jick and von Glinow, "High Impact Learning."

88. L. J. Perelman, "Kanban to Kanbrain," *Forbes ASAP*, June 6, 1994, pp. 85–95.

89. International Forest Products Limited, *1995 Environmental Report* (Vancouver, B.C.: International Forest Products Company, 1996), p. 7.

90. R. P. DeShon and R. A. Alexander, "Goal Setting Effects on Implicit and Explicit Learning of Complex Tasks," *Organizational Behavior and Human Decision Processes* 65 (1996), pp. 18–36; C. A. Seger, "Implicit Learning," *Psychological Bulletin* 115 (1994), pp. 163–96.

91. A. C. Edmondson, "Learning from Mistakes Is Easier Said than Done: Group and Organizational Influences on the Detection and Correction of Human Error," *Journal of Applied Behavioral Science* 32 (1996), pp. 5–28; C. D'Andrea-O'Brien and A. F. Buono, "Building Effective Learning Teams: Lessons from the Field," *SAM Advanced Management Journal* 61 (Summer 1996), pp. 4–10.

92. G. Dutton, "Enhancing Creativity," *Management Review*, November 1996, pp. 44–46.

93. P. Froiland, "Action Learning: Taming Real Problems in Real Time," *Training*, January 1994, pp. 27–34; R. W. Revans, "What Is Action Learning?" *Journal of Management Development* 15, no. 3 (1982), pp. 64–75.

94. R. M. Fulmer, P. Gibbs, and J. B. Keys, "The Second Generation Learning Organizations: New Tools for Sustaining Competitive Advantage," *Organizational Dynamics* 27 (Autumn 1998), pp. 6–20.

95. T. T. Baldwin, C. Danielson, and W. Wiggenhorn, "The Evolution of Learning Strategies in Organizations: From Employee Development to Business Redefinition," *Academy of Management Executive* 11 (November 1997), pp. 47–58.

Chapter Three

1. Adapted from N. Munk, "The New Organization Man," *Fortune,* March 16, 1998, pp. 63–74; B. Tiernan, "Generation Xers, Employers Adapt to Changes," *Tulsa World,* November 30, 1997, p. E1; Roberta Maynard, "A Less-Stressed Work Force," *Nation's Business,* November, 1996, pp. 50–51.

2. C. C. Pinder, *Work Motivation* (Glenview, IL: Scott, Foresman, 1984), pp. 7–10; E. E. Lawler III, *Motivation in Work Organizations* (Monterey, CA: Brooks/Cole, 1973), pp. 2–5.

3. B. Losyk, "Generation X: What They Think and What They Plan to Do," *The Futurist* 31 (March–April 1997), pp. 29–44; B. Tulgan, *Managing Generation X: How to Bring Out the Best in Young Talent* (Oxford: Capstone, 1996).

4. D. J. McNerney, "Creating a Motivated Workforce," *HR Focus,* August 1996, pp. 1, 4–6; B. Tulgan, "Correcting the 'Slacker Myth': Managing Generation X in the Work Place," *Manage,* July 1996, pp. 14–16.

5. A. H. Maslow, "A Theory of Human Motivation," *Psychological Review* 50 (1943), pp. 370–96; A. H. Maslow, *Motivation and Personality* (New York: Harper & Row, 1954).

6. M. A. Wahba and L. G. Bridwell, "Maslow Reconsidered: A Review of Research on the Need Hierarchy Theory," *Organizational Behavior and Human Performance* 15 (1976), pp. 212–40.

7. C. P. Alderfer, *Existence, Relatedness, and Growth* (New York: Free Press, 1972).

8. J. P. Wanous and A. A. Zwany, "A Cross-Sectional Test of Need Hierarchy Theory," *Organizational Behavior and Human Performance* 18 (1977), pp. 78–97.

9. F. Herzberg, B. Mausner, and B. Snyderman, *The Motivation to Work* (New York: John Wiley, 1959).

10. A. K. Korman, *Industrial and Organizational Psychology* (Englewood Cliffs, NJ: Prentice Hall, 1971), p. 149; N. King, "Clarification and Evaluation of the Two Factor Theory of Job Satisfaction," *Psychological Bulletin* 74 (1970), pp. 18–31.

11. J. L White, "Wide Open Spaces, Roomy Workplaces," *Arizona Republic,* July 18, 1998; S. Caudron, "Be Cool!" *Workforce* 77 (April 1998), pp. 50–61; "Microsoft Headquarters

Evokes Ambience of Campus, but 'It's Just an Office Park,'" *Chronicle of Higher Education,* April 24, 1998.

12. The motivational value of money is effectively argued in T. Kinni, "Why We Work," *Training* 35 (August 1998), pp. 34–39.

13. R. M. Steers and L. W. Porter, *Motivation and Work Behavior,* 5th ed. (New York: McGraw-Hill, 1991), p. 413.

14. D. C. McClelland, *The Achieving Society* (New York: Van Nostrand Reinhold, 1961); M. Patchen, *Participation, Achievement, and Involvement on the Job* (Englewood Cliffs, NJ: Prentice-Hall, 1970).

15. For example, see: J. Langan-Fox and S. Roth, "Achievement Motivation and Female Entrepreneurs," *Journal of Occupational and Organizational Psychology* 68 (1995), pp. 209–18; H. A. Wainer and I. M. Rubin, "Motivation of Research and Development Entrepreneurs: Determinants of Company Success, Part I," *Journal of Applied Psychology* 53 (June 1969), pp. 178–84.

16. D. C. McClelland, "Retrospective Commentary," *Harvard Business Review* (January–February 1995), pp. 138–39; D. McClelland and R. Boyatzis, "Leadership Motive Pattern and Long-Term Success in Management," *Journal of Applied Psychology* 67 (1982), pp. 737–43.

17. McClelland, *The Achieving Society;* R. deCharms and G. H. Moeller, "Values Expressed in American Children's Readers: 1800–1950," *Journal of Abnormal and Social Psychology* 64 (1962), pp. 136–42.

18. Adapted from H. Wee, "Young Entrepreneurs at Work," *Daily News of Los Angeles,* July 14, 1998.

19. R. J. House and R. N. Aditya, "The Social Scientific Study of Leadership: Quo Vadis?" *Journal of Management* 23 (1997), pp. 409–73; D. C. McClelland and D. H. Burnham, "Power Is the Great Motivator," *Harvard Business Review* 73 (January–February 1995), pp. 126–39 (reprinted from 1976).

20. McClelland and Burnham, "Power Is the Great Motivator."

21. D. G. Winter, "A Motivational Model of Leadership: Predicting Long-term Management Success from TAT Measures of Power Motivation and Responsibility," *Leadership Quarterly* 2 (1991), pp. 67–80.

22. House and Aditya, "The Social Scientific Study of Leadership: Quo Vadis?"

23. D. C. McClelland and D. G. Winter, *Motivating Economic Achievement* (New York: Free Press, 1969); and D. Miron and D. McClelland, "The Impact of Achievement Motivation Training on Small Business," *California Management Review* 21 (1979), pp. 13–28.

24. Munk, "The New Organization Man," *Fortune,* pp. 63–74.

25. A. Kohn, *Punished by Rewards* (Boston: Houghton Mifflin, 1993).

26. D. A. Nadler and E. E. Lawler, "Motivation: A Diagnostic Approach," in *Perspectives on Behavior in Organizations,* 2nd ed., J. R. Hackman, E. E. Lawler III, and L. W. Porter, eds. (New York: McGraw-Hill, 1983), pp. 67–78; and V. H. Vroom, *Work and Motivation* (New York: John Wiley, 1964).

27. K. Lewin, "Psychology of Success and Failure," *Occupations* 14 (1936), pp. 926–30.

28. Lawler's version of expectancy theory is described in J. P. Campbell, M. D. Dunnette, E. E. Lawler, and K. E. Weick, *Managerial Behavior, Performance, and Effectiveness* (New York: McGraw-Hill, 1970), pp. 343–48; Lawler, *Motivation in Work Organizations,* chap. 3; Nadler and Lawler, "Motivation: A Diagnostic Approach," pp. 67–78.

29. Nadler and Lawler, "Motivation: A Diagnostic Approach," pp. 70–73.

30. Lawler, *Motivation in Work Organizations,* pp. 53–55.

31. K. A. Karl, A. M. O'Leary-Kelly, and J. J. Martoccio, "The Impact of Feedback and Self-Efficacy on Performance in Training," *Journal of Organizational Behavior* 14 (1993), pp. 379–94; T Janz, "Manipulating Subjective Expectancy through Feedback: A Laboratory Study of the Expectancy-Performance Relationship," *Journal of Applied Psychology* 67 (1982), pp. 480–85.

32. J. B. Fox, K. D. Scott, and J. M. Donohoe, "An Investigation into Pay Valence and Performance in a Pay-for-Performance Field Setting," *Journal of Organizational Behavior* 14 (1993), pp. 687–93.

33. W. Van Eerde and H. Thierry, "Vroom's Expectancy Models and Work-Related Criteria: A Meta-Analysis," *Journal of Applied Psychology* 81 (1996), pp. 575–86; T. R. Mitchell, "Expectancy Models

of Job Satisfaction, Occupational Preference and Effort: A Theoretical, Methodological, and Empirical Appraisal," *Psychological Bulletin* 81 (1974), pp. 1053–77.

34. D. D. Baker, R. Ravichandran, and D. M. Randall, "Exploring Contrasting Formulations of Expectancy Theory," *Decision Sciences* 20 (1989), pp. 1–13; Vroom, *Work and Motivation,* pp. 14–19.

35. K. C. Snead and A. M. Harrell, "An Application of Expectancy Theory to Explain a Manager's Intention to Use a Decision Support System," *Decision Sciences* 25 (1994), pp. 499–513; M. E. Tubbs, D. M. Boehne, and J. G. Dahl, "Expectancy, Valence, and Motivational Force Functions in Goal-Setting Research: An Empirical Test," *Journal of Applied Psychology* 78 (1993), pp. 361–73; J. A. Shepperd, "Productivity Loss in Performance Groups: A Motivation Analysis," *Psychological Bulletin* 113 (January 1993) pp. 67–81; T. P. Summers and W. H. Hendrix, "Development of a Turnover Model that Incorporates a Matrix Measure of Valence-Instrumentality-Expectancy Perceptions," *Journal of Business & Psychology* 6 (1991), pp. 227–45; C. C. Pinder, *Work Motivation: Theory, Issues, and Applications* (Glenview, IL: Scott, Foresman, 1984), pp. 144–47.

36. J. S. Adams, "Toward an Understanding of Inequity," *Journal of Abnormal and Social Psychology* 67 (1963), pp. 422–36; R. T. Mowday, "Equity Theory Predictions of Behavior in Organizations," in *Motivation and Work Behavior,* 5th ed., R. M. Steers and L. W. Porter, eds. (New York: McGraw-Hill, 1991), pp. 111–31.

37. G. Blau, "Testing the Effect of Level and Importance of Pay Referents on Pay Level Satisfaction," *Human Relations* 47 (1994), pp. 1251–68; C. T. Kulik and M. L. Ambrose, "Personal and Situational Determinants of Referent Choice," *Academy of Management Review* 17 (1992), pp. 212–37; J. Pfeffer, "Incentives in Organizations: The Importance of Social Relations," in *Organization Theory: From Chester Barnard to the Present and Beyond,* O. E. Williamson, ed. (New York: Oxford University Press, 1990), pp. 72–97.

38. P. P. Shah, "Who Are Employees' Social Referents? Using A Network

Perspective to Determine Referent Others," *Academy of Management Journal* 41 (June 1998), pp. 249–68; K. S. Law and C. S. Wong, "Relative Importance of Referents on Pay Satisfaction: A Review and Test of a New Policy-Capturing Approach," *Journal of Occupational and Organizational Psychology* 7l (March 1998), pp. 47–60.

39. T. P. Summers and A. S. DeNisi, "In Search of Adams' Other: Reexamination of Referents Used in the Evaluation of Pay," *Human Relations* 43 (1990), pp. 497–511.

40. J. S. Adams, "Inequity in Social Exchange," in *Advances in Experimental Psychology*, L. Berkowitz, ed. (New York: Academic Press, 1965), pp. 157–89.

41. J. Barling, C. Fullagar, and E. K. Kelloway, *The Union and Its Members: A Psychological Approach* (New York: Oxford University Press, 1992).

42. L. Greenberg and J. Barling, "Employee Theft," in C. L. Cooper and D. M. Rousseau, eds., *Trends in Organizational Behavior* 3 (1996), pp. 49–64.

43. J. Greenberg, "Cognitive Reevaluation of Outcomes in Response to Underpayment Inequity," *Academy of Management Journal* 32 (1989), pp. 174–84; E. Hatfield and S. Sprecher, "Equity Theory and Behavior in Organizations," *Research in the Sociology of Organizations* 3 (1984), pp. 94–124.

44. R. Folger and R. A. Baron, "Violence and Hostility at Work: A Model of Reactions to Perceived Injustice," in G. R. VandenBos and E. Q. Bulatao, eds., *Violence on the Job: Identifying Risks and Developing Solutions* (Washington: American Psychological Association, 1996); J. Greenberg, "Stealing in the Name of Justice: Informational and Interpersonal Moderators of Theft Reactions to Underpayment Inequity," *Organizational Behavior and Human Decision Processes* 54 (1993), pp. 81–103; R. D. Bretz, Jr. and S. L. Thomas, "Perceived Equity, Motivation, and Final-Offer Arbitration in Major League Baseball," *Journal of Applied Psychology* 77 (1993), pp. 280–87.

45. R. P. Vecchio and J. R. Terborg, "Salary Increment Allocation and Individual Differences," *Journal of Organizational Behavior* 8 (1987), pp. 37–43.

46. J. Rawls, *A Theory of Justice* (Cambridge, MA: Harvard University Press, 1971). For recent discussion of justice and ethics, see: M. Schminke, M. L. Ambrose, and T. W. Noel, "The Effect of Ethical Frameworks on Perceptions of Organizational Justice," *Academy of Management Journal*, 40 (October 1997), pp. 1190–1207.

47. "Volvo's New Man," *Fortune*, March 8, 1993, p. 135.

48. For recent research on the effectiveness of goal setting, see: L. A. Wilk and W. K. Redmon, "The Effects of Feedback and Goal Setting on the Productivity and Satisfaction of University Admissions Staff," *Journal of Organizational Behavior Management* 18 (1998), pp. 45–68; K. H. Doerr and T. R. Mitchell, "Impact of Material Flow Policies and Goals on Job Outcomes," *Journal of Applied Psychology* 81 (1996), pp. 142–52; A. A. Shikdar and B. Das, "A Field Study of Worker Productivity Improvements," *Applied Ergonomics* 26 (February 1995), pp. 21–27; M. D. Cooper and R. A. Phillips, "Reducing Accidents Using Goal Setting and Feedback: A Field Study," *Journal of Occupational & Organizational Psychology* 67 (1994), pp. 219–40.

49. "Reinvention Revolution: Report from the Federal-Front Lines," *Government Executive*, April 1997; I. Villelabeitia, "La Palma Schedules Goal-Setting Workshop," *Orange County Register*, January 16, 1997, p. 3; L. Struebing, "Measuring for Excellence," *Quality Progress* 29 (December 1996), pp. 25–28.

50. T. H. Poister and G. Streib, "MBO in Municipal Government: Variations on a Traditional Management Tool," *Public Administration Review* 55 (1995), pp. 48–56.

51. E. A. Locke and G. P. Latham, *A Theory of Goal Setting and Task Performance* (Englewood Cliffs, NJ: Prentice Hall, 1990); A. J. Mento, R. P. Steel, and R. J. Karren, "A Meta-Analytic Study of the Effects of Goal Setting on Task Performance: 1966–1984," *Organizational Behavior and Human Decision Processes* 39 (1987), pp. 52–83; M. E. Tubbs, "Goal-Setting: A Meta-Analytic Examination of the Empirical Evidence," *Journal of Applied Psychology* 71 (1986), pp. 474–83.

52. I. R. Gellatly and J. P. Meyer, "The Effects of Goal Difficulty on Physiological Arousal, Cognition,

and Task Performance," *Journal of Applied Psychology* 77 (1992), pp. 694–704; A. Mento, E. A. Locke, and H. Klein, "Relationship of Goal Level to Valence and Instrumentality," *Journal of Applied Psychology* 77 (1992), pp. 395–405.

53. K. R. Thompson, W. A. Hochwarter, and N. J. Mathys, "Stretch Targets: What Makes Them Effective?" *Academy of Management Executive* 11 (August 1997), pp. 48–60; S. Sherman, "Stretch Goals: The Dark Side of Asking for Miracles," *Fortune*, November 13, 1995, pp. 231–32.

54. H. J. Klein, "Further Evidence of the Relationship between Goal Setting and Expectancy Theory," *Organizational Behavior and Human Decision Processes* 49 (1991), pp. 230–57.

55. M. E. Tubbs, "Commitment as a Moderator of the Goal-Performance Relation: A Case for Clearer Construct Definition," *Journal of Applied Psychology* 78 (1993), pp. 86–97.

56. "Goal-Driven Incentives," *Inc.*, August 1996, p. 91.

57. G. P. Latham, D. C. Winters, and E. A. Locke, "Cognitive and Motivational Effects of Participation: A Mediator Study," *Journal of Organizational Behavior* 15 (1994), pp. 49–63.

58. J. Chowdhury, "The Motivational Impact of Sales Quotas on Effort," *Journal of Marketing Research* 30 (1993), pp. 28–41; Locke and Latham, *A Theory of Goal Setting and Task Performance*, chap. 6 and 7; E. A. Locke, G. P. Latham, and M. Erez, "The Determinants of Goal Commitment," *Academy of Management Review* 13 (1988), pp. 23–39.

59. Adapted from L. Struebing, "Measuring for Excellence," *Quality Progress* 29 (December 1996), pp. 25–28.

60. P. M. Wright, "Goal Setting and Monetary Incentives: Motivational Tools that Can Work Too Well," *Compensation and Benefits Review*, May–June 1994, pp. 41–49.

61. F. M. Moussa, "Determinants and Process of the Choice of Goal Difficulty," *Group & Organization Management* 21 (1996), pp. 414–38.

62. R. P. DeShon and R. A. Alexander, "Goal Setting Effects on Implicit and Explicit Learning of Complex Tasks," *Organizational Behavior and Human*

Decision Processes 65 (1996), pp. 18–36.

63. G. Audia, K. G. Brown, A. Kristof-Brown, and E. A. Locke, "Relationship of Goals and Microlevel Work Processes to Performance on a Multipath Manual Task," *Journal of Applied Psychology* 81 (1996), pp. 483–97.

64. D. S. Elenkov, "Can American Management Concepts Work in Russia? A Cross-Cultural Comparative Study," *California Management Review* 40 (Summer 1998), pp. 133–56; N. J. Adler, *International Dimensions of Organizational Behavior*, 3rd ed. (Cincinnati, OH: South-Western, 1997), chap. 6; G. Hofstede, "Motivation, Leadership, and Organization: Do American Theories Apply Abroad?" *Organizational Dynamics*, Summer 1980, pp. 42–63.

65. A. Sagie, D. Elizur, and H. Yamauchi, "The Structure and Strength of Achievement Motivation: A Cross-Cultural Comparison," *Journal of Organizational Behavior* 17 (September 1996). pp. 431–44; D. Elizur, I. Borg, R. Hunt, and I. M. Beck, "The Structure of Work Values: A Cross-Cultural Comparison," *Journal of Organizational Behavior* 12 (1991), pp. 21–38.

66. D. S. Elenkov, "Can American Management Concepts Work in Russia?"; N. A. Boyacigiller and N. J. Adler, "The Parochial Dinosaur: Organizational Science in a Global Context," *Academy of Management Review* 16 (1991), pp. 262–90; Adler, *International Dimensions of Organizational Behavior*, chap. 6.

67. D. H. B. Welsh, F. Luthans, and S. M. Sommer, "Managing Russian Factory Workers: The Impact of U.S.-Based Behavioral and Participative Techniques," *Academy of Management Journal* 36 (1993), pp. 58–79; T. Matsui and I. Terai, "A Cross-Cultural Study of the Validity of the Expectancy Theory of Motivation," *Journal of Applied Psychology* 60 (1979), pp. 263–65.

68. K. I. Kim, H. J. Park, and N. Suzuki, "Reward Allocations in the United States, Japan, and Korea: A Comparison of Individualistic and Collectivistic Cultures," *Academy of Management Journal* 33 (1990), pp. 188–98.

Chapter Four

1. C. Palmeri, "Making the Grandkids Happy," *Forbes*, August 25, 1997, pp. 60–62; Jeff Richgels, "Rewarding Workers Pays Off in Many Ways," *Capital Times* (Madison, WI), January 1, 1997, p. C1; G. Miller, "Holiday Bonus for Workers: $100 Million," *Los Angeles Times*, December 15, 1996, p. A1.

2. M. C. Bloom and G. T. Milkovich, "Issues in Managerial Compensation Research," in C. L. Cooper and D. M. Rousseau, eds., *Trends in Organizational Behavior*, vol. 3 (Chichester, UK: John Wiley, 1996), pp. 23–47.

3. S. Desker-Shaw, "Revving Up Asia's Workers," *Asian Business* 32 (February 1996), pp. 41–44.

4. H. Y. Park, "A Comparative Analysis of Work Incentives in U.S. and Japanese Firms," *Multinational Business Review* 4 (Fall 1996), pp. 59–70.

5. M. Geiger, "NewAge Industries: A Lesson in Old-Fashioned Caring," *Philadelphia Business Journal*, June 9, 1997.

6. G. T. Milkovich and J. M. Newman, *Compensation*, 4th ed. (Homewood, IL: Irwin, 1993), chap. 4.

7. S. L. McShane, "Two Tests of Direct Gender Bias in Job Evaluation Ratings," *Journal of Occupational Psychology* 63 (1990), pp. 129–40.

8. F. F. Reichheld, *The Loyalty Effect* (Boston: Harvard Business School Press, 1996), p. 137; M. Quaid, *Job Evaluation: The Myth of Equitable Assessment* (Toronto: University of Toronto Press, 1993).

9. L. M. Spencer and S. M. Spencer, *Competence at Work: Models for Superior Performance* (New York: John Wiley, 1993).

10. D. Hofrichter, "Broadbanding: A 'Second Generation' Approach," *Compensation & Benefits Review* 25 (September–October 1993), pp. 53–58.

11. E. E. Lawler III, "From Job-Based to Competency-Based Organizations," *Journal of Organizational Behavior* 15 (1994), pp. 3–15; R. L. Bunning, "Models for Skill-Based Pay Plans," *HR Magazine* 37 (February 1992), pp. 62–64; and G. E. Ledford, Jr., "The Design of Skill-Based Pay Plans," in *The Compensation Handbook*, M. L. Rock and L. A. Berger, eds. (New York: McGraw-Hill, 1991), pp. 199–217.

12. C. T. Crumpley, "Skill-Based Pay Replaces Traditional Ranking," *Kansas City Star*, June 30, 1997, p. B6.

13. E. E. Lawler III, G. E. Ledford, Jr., and L. Chang, "Who Uses Skill-Based Pay, and Why," *Compensation and Benefits Review* 25 (March–April 1993), pp. 22–26.

14. E. E. Lawler III, "Competencies: A Poor Foundation for The New Pay," *Compensation & Benefits Review*, November–December 1996, pp. 20, 22–26.

15. S. Chandler, "Sears' System of Rewards Has Ups and Downs," *Chicago Tribune*, February 15, 1998, p. C1.

16. "Corporate Restructuring Sweeps Japan," *Focus Japan* 23 (March 1996), pp. 1–2.

17. E. B. Peach and D. A. Wren, "Pay for Performance from Antiquity to the 1950s," *Journal of Organizational Behavior Management*, 1992, pp. 5–26.

18. S. D. Shaw "Revving Up Asia's Workers," *Asian Business* 32 (February 1996), pp. 41–44.

19. G. Koretz, "How Piecework Rates Goosed Output," *Business Week*, February 17, 1997, p. 25; D. R. Francis, "Incentive Pay Boosts Output on Shop Floor," *Christian Science Monitor*, December 23, 1996, p. 1.

20. J. S. DeMatteo, L. T. Eby, and E. Sundstrom, "Team-Based Rewards: Current Empirical Evidence and Directions for Future Research," in B. M. Staw and L. L. Cummings, eds., *Research in Organizational Behavior* 20 (1998), pp. 141–83; P. Pascarella, "Compensating Teams," *Across the Board* 34 (February 1997), pp. 16–23; D. G. Shaw and C. E. Schneier, "Team Measurement and Rewards: How Some Companies Are Getting it Right," *Human Resource Planning* 18 (1995), pp. 34–49.

21. K. Hein, "Lodging Free Advice," *Incentive* 170 (September 1996), pp. 34–38.

22. S. Wilson, "Counties Try Productivity Bonuses," *Washington Post*, March 26, 1998, p. M1.

23. C. T. Geer, "Turning Employees into Stakeholders," *Forbes*, December 1, 1997, p. 154.

24. M. Jarman, "Stock Plans for Workers," *Arizona Republic*, June 14, 1998; D. Bencivenga, "Employee-Owners Help Bolster the Bottom Line," *HRMagazine* 42 (February 1997), pp. 78–83.

25. R. P. Sanders and J. Thompson, "Live Long and Prosper," *Government Executive*, April 1997, pp. 50–53;

B. Friel, "Privatized Investigators' Success," *The Daily Fed*, March 28, 1997.

26. Bencivenga, "Employee-Owners Help Bolster the Bottom Line"; J. M. Newman and M. Waite, "Do Broad-Based Stock Options Create Value?" *Compensation and Benefits Review*, 30 (July 1998), pp. 78–86.

27. S. G. Ogden, "Profit Sharing and Organizational Change," *Accounting, Auditing & Accountability Journal* 8 (1995), pp. 23–47.

28. J. Chelius and R. S. Smith, "Profit Sharing and Employment Stability," *Industrial and Labor Relations Review* 43 (1990), pp. 256s–73s.

29. A. Kohn, "Challenging Behaviorist Dogma: Myths about Money and Motivation," *Compensation and Benefits Review*, 30 (March 1998), pp. 27, 33; A. Kohn, *Punished by Rewards* (Boston: Houghton Mifflin, 1993).

30. B. Nelson, *1001 Ways to Reward Employees* (New York: Workman Publishing, 1994), p. 148.

31. For two classic OB articles on this, see: J. L. Pearce, "Why Merit Pay Doesn't Work: Implications from Organizational Theory," in D. B. Balkin and L. R. Gomez-Mejia, eds., *New Perspectives on Compensation* (Englewood Cliffs, NJ: Prentice Hall, 1987), pp. 169–78; W. C. Hamner, "How to Ruin Motivation with Pay," *Compensation Review* 7, no. 3 (1975), pp. 17–27.

32. T. Kinni, "Why We Work," *Training* 35 (August 1998), pp. 34–39. For an early summary of research supporting the motivational value of performance-based rewards, see: E. E. Lawler III, *Pay and Organizational Effectiveness: A Psychological View* (New York: McGraw-Hill, 1971).

33. T. J. Keefe, G. R. French, and J. L. Altmann, "Incentive Plans Can Link Employee and Company Goals," *Compensation and Benefits Review*, January–February 1994, pp. 27–33; E. L. Pavlik and A. Belkaoui, *Determinants of Executive Compensation* (New York: Quorum, 1991); K. M. Eisenhardt, "Agency Theory: An Assessment and Review," *Academy of Management Review* 14 (1989), pp. 57–74. For a discussion of agency theory with more behaviorist views, see J. H. Davis, F. D. Schoorman, and L. Donaldson, "Toward a Stewardship Theory of Management," *Academy of*

Management Review 22 (1997), pp. 20–47.

34. Watson Wyatt Worldwide. News release (October 1997). Also see Towers Perrin Inc., "Towers Perrin 1997 Workplace Index Reveals Growing Concerns in Employer Delivery On 'The New Deal' Contract," September 15, 1997 (News release at www.towersperrin.com).

35. K. M. Bartol and D. C. Martin, "When Politics Pays: Factors Influencing Managerial Compensation Decisions," *Personnel Psychology* 43 (1990), pp. 599–614.

36. Chandler, "Sears' System of Rewards Has Ups and Downs."

37. DeMatteo et al, "Team-Based Rewards."

38. R. Wageman, "Interdependence and Group Effectiveness," *Administrative Science Quarterly* 40 (1995), pp. 145–80.

39. H. Syedain, "The Rewards of Recognition," *Management Today*, May 1995, pp. 72–74.

40. S. Kerr, "On the Folly of Rewarding A, While Hoping for B," *Academy of Management Journal* 18 (1975), pp. 769–83.

41. D. R. Spitzer, "Power Rewards: Rewards that Really Motivate," *Management Review*, May 1996, pp. 45–50.

42. This definition is more consistent with popular use of the word "job" and with *Webster's College Dictionary*. However, some scholars have used this definition for a "position" and have defined a "job" as a group of similar positions. See K. Pearlman, "Job Families: A Review and Discussion of Their Implications for Personnel Selection," *Psychological Bulletin* 87 (January 1980), pp. 1–28.

43. M. Bensaou and M. Earl, "The Right Mind-Set for Managing Information Technology," *Harvard Business Review* 76 (September–October 1998), pp. 118–28; B. B. Arnetz, "Technological Stress: Psychophysiological Aspects of Working with Modern Information Technology," *Scandinavian Journal of Work and Environmental Health* 23, Suppl. 3 (1997), pp. 97–103; J. W. Medcof, "The Effect of Extent of Use and Job of the User upon Task Characteristics," *Human Relations* 42 (1989), pp. 23–41, R. J. Long, *New Office Information Technology: Human and Managerial Implications* (London: Crom Helm, 1987).

44. G. L. Dalton, "The Collective Stretch: Workforce Flexibility," *Management Review* 87 (December 1998), pp. 54–59; C. Hendry and R. Jenkins, "Psychological Contracts and New Deals," *Human Resource Management Journal* 7 (1997), pp. 38–44.

45. M. Hequet, "Worker Involvement Lights Up Neon," *Training*, June 1994, pp. 23–29.

46. A. Smith, *The Wealth of Nations* (1776; reprint, London: Dent, 1910).

47. M. A. Campion, "Ability Requirement Implications of Job Design: An Interdisciplinary Perspective," *Personnel Psychology* 42 (1989), pp. 1–24; H. Fayol, *General and Industrial Management*, trans. C. Storrs (London: Pitman, 1949); E. E. Lawler III, *Motivation in Work Organizations* (Monterey, CA: Brooks/Cole, 1973), chap. 7.

48. For a review of Taylor's work and life, see R. Kanigel, *The One Best Way: Frederick Winslow Taylor and the Enigma of Efficiency* (New York: Viking, 1997); see also C. R. Littler, "Taylorism, Fordism, and Job Design," in *Job Design: Critical Perspectives on the Labor Process*, D. Knights, H. Willmott, and D. Collinson, eds. (Aldershot, UK: Gower, 1985), pp. 10–29; F. W. Taylor, *The Principles of Scientific Management* (New York: Harper Bros., 1911).

49. F. B. Gilbreth, *Primer of Scientific Management* (New York: Van Nostrand Reinhold, 1912).

50. A. A. Shikdar and B. Das, "A Field Study of Worker Productivity Improvements," *Applied Ergonomics* 26 (1995), pp. 21–27; W. J. Duncan, *Great Ideas in Management* (San Francisco: Jossey-Bass, 1989), chap. 4.

51. E. E. Lawler III, *High-Involvement Management* (San Francisco: Jossey-Bass, 1986), chap. 6; and C. R. Walker and R. H. Guest, *The Man on the Assembly Line* (Cambridge: Harvard University Press, 1952).

52. A. Markels, "Power to the People," *Fast Company*, Issue 13 (February–March 1998), p. 161.

53. W. F. Dowling, "Job Redesign on the Assembly Line: Farewell to Blue-Collar Blues?" *Organizational Dynamics*, Autumn 1973, pp. 51–67; Lawler, *Motivation in Work Organizations*, p. 150.

54. M. Keller, *Rude Awakening* (New York: Harper Perennial, 1989), p. 128.

55. C. S. Wong and M. A. Campion, "Development and Test of a Task Level Model of Motivational Job Design," *Journal of Applied Psychology* 76 (1991), pp. 825–37; R. W. Griffin, "Toward an Integrated Theory of Task Design," *Research in Organizational Behavior* 9 (1987), pp. 79–120.

56. F. Herzberg, B. Mausner, and B. B. Snyderman, *The Motivation to Work* (New York: John Wiley, 1959).

57. R. M. Steers and L. W. Porter, *Motivation and Work Behavior*, 5th ed. (New York: McGraw-Hill, 1991), p. 413.

58. J. R. Hackman and G. Oldham, *Work Redesign* (Reading, MA: Addison-Wesley, 1980).

59. G. Johns, J. L. Xie, and Y. Fang, "Mediating and Moderating Effects in Job Design," *Journal of Management* 18 (1992), pp. 657–76.

60. P. E. Spector, "Higher-Order Need Strength as a Moderator of the Job Scope–Employee Outcome Relationship: A Meta Analysis," *Journal of Occupational Psychology* 58 (1985), pp. 119–27.

61. P. Osterman, "How Common Is Workplace Transformation and Who Adopts It?" *Industrial and Labor Relations Review* 47 (1994), pp. 173–88.

62. M. Treanor, "Remittance Processing System Supports Company Objectives," *Inform* 11 (November 1997), pp. 26–27; T. L. Besser, *Team Toyota: Transplanting the Toyota Culture to the Camry Plant in Kentucky* (Albany: State University of New York Press, 1996).

63. "Cross-Trained Employees," *Food Management*, June 1996, pp. 32, 35.

64. M. Sczech and D. Attenello, "NationsBank Reengineers to Achieve Leadership in International Services," *National Productivity Review* 14 (Spring 1995), pp. 89–96.

65. N. G. Dodd and D. C. Ganster, "The Interactive Effects of Variety, Autonomy, and Feedback on Attitudes and Performance," *Journal of Organizational Behavior* 17 (1996), pp. 329–47; M. A. Campion and C. L. McClelland, "Follow-up and Extension of the Interdisciplinary Costs and Benefits of Enlarged Jobs," *Journal of Applied Psychology* 78 (1993), pp. 339–51.

66. This point is emphasized in C. Pinder, *Work Motivation* (Glenview, IL: Scott, Foresman, 1984), p. 244; and F. Herzberg, "One More Time: How Do You Motivate Employees?" *Harvard Business Review* 46 (January–February 1968), pp. 53–62. For a full discussion of job enrichment, also see R. W. Griffin, *Task Design: An Integrative Approach* (Glenview, IL: Scott Foresman, 1982); J. R. Hackman, G. Oldham, R. Janson, and K. Purdy, "A New Strategy for Job Enrichment," *California Management Review* 17, no. 4 (1975), pp. 57–71.

67. J. A. Conger and R. N. Kanungo, "The Empowerment Process: Integrating Theory and Practice," *Academy of Management Review* 13 (1988), pp. 471–82.

68. R. C. Liden and S. Arad, "A Power Perspective of Empowerment and Work Groups: Implications for Human Resource Management Research," *Research in Personnel and Human Resource Management* 14 (1996), pp. 205–51; G. M. Spreitzer, "Psychological Empowerment in the Workplace: Dimensions, Measurement, and Validation," *Academy of Management Journal* 38 (1995), pp. 1442–65.

69. J. Godard, "When Do Workplace Reform Programs Appear to Work? Some Preliminary Findings," Paper presented at the Organizational Practices and the Changing Employment Relationship Conference, University of British Columbia, October 18–19, 1996; A. J. H. Thorlakson and R. P. Murray, "An Empirical Study of Empowerment in the Workplace." *Group & Organization Management* 21 (March 1996), pp. 67–83.

70. Hackman and Oldham, *Work Redesign*, pp. 137–38.

71. S. L. Paulson, "Training for Change," *American Gas* 79 (December–January 1998), pp. 26–29.

72. Osterman, "How Common Is Workplace Transformation and Who Adopts It?"

73. Y. Fried and G. R. Ferris, "The Validity of the Job Characteristics Model: A Review and Meta-Analysis," *Personnel Psychology* 40 (1987), pp. 287–322; B. T. Loher, R. A. Noe, N. L. Moeller, and M. P. Fitzgerald, "A Meta-Analysis of the Relation of Job Characteristics to Job Satisfaction," *Journal of Applied Psychology* 70 (1985), pp. 280–89.

74. D. E. Bowen and E. E. Lawler III, "The Empowerment of Service Workers: What, Why, How, and When," *Sloan Management Review*, Spring 1992, pp. 31–39.

75. C-S. Wong, C. Hui, and K. S. Law, "A Longitudinal Study of the Job Perception–Job Satisfaction Relationship: A Test of the Three Alternative Specifications," *Journal of Occupational and Organizational Psychology* 71 (June 1998), pp. 127–46.

76. G. van der Vegt, B. Emans, and E. van de Vliert, "Motivating Effects of Task and Outcome Interdependence in Work Teams," *Group & Organization Management* 23 (June 1998), pp. 124–43.

77. D. I. Levine, *Reinventing the Workplace* (Washington, DC: Brookings Institution, 1995), pp. 63–66, 86.

78. P. Kraft, "To Control and Inspire: US Management in the Age of Computer Information Systems and Global Production," in M. Wardell, P. Meiksins, and T. Steiger, eds., *Labor and Monopoly Capital in the Late Twentieth Century: The Braverman Legacy and Beyond* (Albany: State University of New York Press, in press); R. Hodson, "Dignity in the Workplace under Participative Management: Alienation and Freedom Revisited," *American Sociological Review*, 61 (1996), pp. 719–38; Pinder, *Work Motivation*, pp. 257–58.

79. "Bodies for Hire—The Contracting Out Debate," *Workplace Change* (Australia), April 1996, pp. 1–3.

80. Campion, "Ability Requirement Implications of Job Design: An Interdisciplinary Perspective," p. 20; and R. B. Dunham, "Relationships of Perceived Job Design Characteristics to Job Ability Requirements and Job Value," *Journal of Applied Psychology* 62 (1977), pp. 760–63.

81. R. Martin and T. D. Wall, "Attentional Demand and Cost Responsibility as Stressors in Shopfloor Jobs," *Academy of Management Journal* 32 (1989), pp. 69–86; D. P. Schwab and L. L. Cummings, "Impact of Task Scope on Employee Productivity: An Evaluation Using Expectancy Theory," *Academy of Management Review* 1 (1976), pp. 23–35.

82. C. Bunish, "Reviewing the Review Process," *Business Marketing* 82 (December 1997), p. 41.

83. C. P. Neck and C. C. Manz, "Thought Self-Leadership: The Impact of Mental Strategies Training on Employee Cognition, Behavior, and Affect," *Journal of Organizational Behavior* 17 (1996), pp. 445–67.

84. C. C. Manz and H. P. Sims, Jr., *Superleadership: Leading Others to Lead Themselves* (Englewood Cliffs, NJ: Prentice Hall, 1989); C. C. Manz, "Self-Leadership: Toward an Expanded Theory of Self-Influence Processes in Organizations," *Academy of Management Review* 11 (1986), pp. 585–600.

85. A. M. Saks, R. R. Haccoun, and D. Laxer, "Transfer Training: A Comparison of Self-Management and Relapse Prevention Interventions," *ASAC 1996 Conference Proceedings, Human Resources Division* 17, no. 9 (1996), pp. 81–91; M. E. Gist, A. G. Bavetta, and C. K. Stevens, "Transfer Training Method: Its Influence on Skill Generalization, Skill Repetition, and Performance Level," *Personnel Psychology* 43 (1990), pp. 501–23.

86. H. P. Sims, Jr., and C. C. Manz, *Company of Heroes: Unleashing the Power of Self-Leadership* (New York: John Wiley, 1996).

87. A. Morin, "Self-Talk and Self-Awareness: On the Nature of the Relation," *Journal of Mind and Behavior* 14 (1993), pp. 223–34; C. P. Neck and C. C. Manz, "Thought Self-Leadership: The Influence of Self-Talk and Mental Imagery on Performance," *Journal of Organizational Behavior* 13 (1992), pp. 681–99.

88. Neck and Manz, "Thought Self-Leadership: The Impact of Mental Strategies Training on Employee Cognition, Behavior, and Affect."

89. V. D. Mayo and J. Tanaka-Matsumi, "Think Aloud Statements and Solutions of Dysphoric Persons on a Social Problem-Solving Task," *Cognitive Therapy and Research* 20 (1996), pp. 97–113.

90. Early scholars seem to distinguish mental practice from mental imagery, whereas recent literature combines mental practice with visualizing positive task outcomes within the meaning of mental imagery. For a recent discussion of this concept, see: C. P. Neck, G. L. Stewart, and C. C. Manz, "Thought Self-Leadership as a Framework for Enhancing the Performance of Performance Appraisers," *Journal of Applied Behavioral Science* 31 (September 1995), pp. 278–302; W. P. Anthony, R. H. Bennett III, E. N. Maddox, and W. J. Wheatley, "Picturing the Future: Using Mental Imagery to Enrich Strategic Environmental Assessment,"

Academy of Management Executive 7, no. 2 (1993), pp. 43–56.

91. J. E. Driscoll, C. Cooper, and A. Moran, "Does Mental Practice Enhance Performance?" *Journal of Applied Psychology* 79 (1994), pp. 481–92.

92. C. Salter, "This Is Brain Surgery," *Fast Company*, Issue 13 (February–March 1998), pp. 147–50.

93. Manz, "Self-Leadership: Toward an Expanded Theory of Self-Influence Processes in Organizations."

94. A. W. Logue, *Self-Control: Waiting Until Tomorrow for What You Want Today* (Englewood Cliffs, NJ: Prentice Hall, 1995).

95. A. M. Saks and B. E. Ashforth, "Proactive Socialization and Behavioral Self-Management," *Journal of Vocational Behavior* 48 (1996), pp. 301–23; Neck and Manz, "Thought Self-Leadership: The Impact of Mental Strategies Training on Employee Cognition, Behavior, and Affect."

96. S. Ming and G. L. Martin, "Single-Subject Evaluation of a Self-Talk Package for Improving Figure Skating Performance," *Sport Psychologist* 10 (1996), pp. 227–38.

97. G. L. Stewart, K. P. Carson, and R. L. Cardy, "The Joint Effects of Conscientiousness and Self-Leadership Training on Employee Self-Directed Behavior in a Service Setting," *Personnel Psychology* 49 (1996), pp. 143–64.

Chapter Five

1. D. Simpson and D. W. Patterson, "Technology Can Be Harmful to Your Mental Health," *News & Record* (Greensboro, NC), June 3, 1997, p. D1; D. W. Patterson and D. Simpson, "Technology's Touch: What Is the Information Age Doing to Connect and Disconnect Mankind?" *News & Record* (Greensboro, NC), June 1, 1997, p. D1; K. Kwong, "Saturday Review," *South China Morning Post*, May 10, 1997, p. 1; Pitney Bowes, "Are Workers Overwhelmed by Communications?" Company news release, May 1997.

2. From the American Institute of Stress, www.stress.org

3. J. Lawlor, "Aaarrgh!!! Have Your Salespeople Had Enough?" *Sales & Marketing Management* 149 (March 1997), pp. 46–53; R. Lally, "Managing Technostress," *Computerworld* 42

(October 1997), pp. 5–6; Cross-National Collaborative Group, "The Changing Rate of Major Depression: Cross-National Comparisons," *JAMA: The Journal of the American Medical Association* 268 (December 2, 1992), pp. 3098–3105.

4. B. Shutan, "High Anxiety: Employers Battling Stress-Related Claims," *Employee Benefit News*, November 1, 1998; R. S. DeFrank and J. M. Ivancevich, "Stress on the Job: An Executive Update," *Academy of Management Executive* 12 (August 1998), pp. 55–66.

5. N. Chowdhury and S. Menon, "Beating Burnout," *India Today*, June 9, 1997, p. 86; R. Rees, "This is the Age of the Strain," *Sunday Times* (London), May 18, 1997.

6. J. C. Quick and J. D. Quick, *Organizational Stress and Prevention Management* (New York: McGraw-Hill, 1984); M. T. Matteson and J. M. Ivancevich, *Managing Job Stress and Health* (New York: Free Press, 1982).

7. J. C. Quick, J. D. Quick, D. L. Nelson, and J. J. Hurrell, Jr., *Preventive Stress Management in Organizations* (Washington, DC: American Psychological Association, 1997).

8. S. Sauter and L. R. Murphy, eds., *Organizational Risk Factors for Job Stress* (Washington, DC: American Psychological Association, 1995).

9. H. Selye, *Stress without Distress* (Philadelphia: J. B. Lippincott, 1974).

10. S. E. Taylor, R. L. Repetti, and T. Seeman, "Health Psychology: What Is an Unhealthy Environment and How Does It Get Under the Skin?" *Annual Review of Psychology* 48 (1997), pp. 411–47.

11. Quick and Quick, *Organizational Stress and Prevention Management*, p. 3.

12. S. Melamed and S. Bruhis, "The Effects of Chronic Industrial Noise Exposure on Urinary Cortisol, Fatigue, and Irritability: A Controlled Field Experiment," *Journal of Occupational and Environmental Medicine* 38 (1996), pp. 252–56.

13. M. Siegall and L. L. Cummings, "Stress and Organizational Role Conflict," *Genetic, Social, and General Psychology Monographs* 12 (1995), pp. 65–95; E. K. Kelloway and J. Barling, "Job Characteristics, Role Stress and Mental Health," *Journal of Occupational Psychology* 64 (1991), pp. 291–304; R. L. Kahn, D. M. Wolfe, R. P. Quinn, J. D. Snoek, and R. A. Rosenthal, *Organizational*

Stress: Studies in Role Conflict and Ambiguity (New York: John Wiley, 1964).

14. G. R. Cluskey and A. Vaux, "Vocational Misfit: Source of Occupational Stress among Accountants," *Journal of Applied Business Research* 13 (Summer 1997), pp. 43–54; A. Kristof, "Person-Organization Fit: An Integrative Review of Its Conceptualizations, Measurement, and Implications," *Personnel Psychology* 49 (1996) pp. 1–50; J. R. Edwards, "An Examination of Competing Versions of the Person-Environment Fit Approach to Stress," *Academy of Management Journal* 39 (1996), pp. 292–339; B. E. Ashforth and R. H. Humphrey, "Emotional Labor in Service Roles: The Influence of Identity," *Academy of Management Review* 18 (1993), pp. 88–115.

15. A. M. Saks and B. E. Ashforth, "Proactive Socialization and Behavioral Self-Management," *Journal of Vocational Behavior* 48 (1996), pp. 301–23; D. L. Nelson and C. Sutton, "Chronic Work Stress and Coping: A Longitudinal Study and Suggested New Directions," *Academy of Management Journal* 33 (1990), pp. 859–69.

16. "Beating Stress Can Be Full-Time Occupation," *Chicago Tribune*, December 1, 1996, p. W8.

17. L. D. Sargent and D. J. Terry, "The Effects of Work Control and Job Demands on Employee Adjustment and Work Performance," *Journal of Occupational and Organizational Psychology* 71 (September 1998), pp. 219–36; M. G. Marmot, H. Bosma, H. Hemingway, E. Brunner, and S. Stansfeld, "Contribution of Job Control and Other Risk Factors to Social Variations in Coronary Heart Disease Incidence," *Lancet* 350 (July 26, 1997), pp. 235–39; P. M. Elsass and J. F. Veiga, "Job Control and Job Strain: A Test of Three Models," *Journal of Occupational Health Psychology* 2 (July 1997), pp. 195–211; B. B. Arnetz, "Technological Stress: Psychophysiological Aspects of Working with Modern Information Technology," *Scandinavian Journal of Work and Environment Health* 23 (1997, Supplement 3), pp. 97–103; R. Karasek and T. Theorell, *Healthy Work: Stress, Productivity, and the Reconstruction of Working Life* (New York: Basic Books, 1990).

18. DeFrank and Ivancevich, "Stress on the Job: An Executive Update"; R. Andre, "Diversity Stress as Morality Stress," *Journal of Business Ethics* 14 (1995), pp. 489–96.

19. D. F. Elloy and A. Randolph, "The Effect of Superleader Behavior on Autonomous Work Groups in a Government Operated Railway Service," *Public Personnel Management* 26 (Summer 1997), pp. 257–72.

20. J. T. Madore, C. Mason-Draffen, and R. Feigenbaum, "When Work Turns Ugly," *Newsday*, April 5, 1998, p. A4.

21. J. L. Thomas, "Harassment Is Worse, Fire Case Plaintiff Says," *Kansas City Star*, February 19, 1998, p. A1; T. Jackman, "Women Tell of Insults, Abuse," *Kansas City Star*, December 10, 1997, p. A1; T. Jackman, "Sexual Harassment Lasted for Years, Fire Captain Says," *Kansas City Star*, November 4, 1997, p. A1.

22. V. Schultz, "Reconceptualizing Sexual Harassment," *Yale Law Journal* 107 (April 1998), pp. 1683–1805. Several U.S. court cases have discussed these two causes for action, including: *Lehman v. Toys 'R' Us Inc.* (1993) 132 N.J. 587; 626 A. (2nd) 445; *Meritor Savings Bank v. Vinson*. 477 U.S. 57 (1986) (U.S.S.C.).

23. C. M. Solomon, "Don't Forget the Emotional Stakes," *Workforce* 77 (October 1998), pp. 52–58; C. S. Piotrkowski, "Gender Harassment, Job Satisfaction, and Distress among Employed White and Minority Women," *Journal of Occupational Health Psychology* 3 (January 1998), pp. 33–43.

24. J. H. Neuman and R. A. Baron, "Workplace Violence and Workplace Aggression: Evidence Concerning Specific Forms, Potential Causes, and Preferred Targets," *Journal of Management* 24 (May 1998), pp. 391–419.

25. G. Lardner, Jr., "Violence at Work Is Largely Unreported," *Washington Post*, July 27, 1998, p. A2.

26. J. Barling, "The Prediction, Experience, and Consequences of Workplace Violence," in G. R. VandenBos and E. Q. Bulatao, eds., *Violence on the Job: Identifying Risks and Developing Solutions* (Washington, DC: American Psychological Association, 1996), pp. 29–49.

27. J. K. Hall and P. E. Spector, "Relationships of Work Stress

28. B. Shutan, "High Anxiety: Employers Battling Stress-Related Claims," *Employee Benefit News*, November 1, 1998; C. A. Duffy and A. E. McGoldrick, "Stress and the Bus Driver in the UK Transport Industry," *Stress and Work* 4 (1990), pp. 17–27.

29. J. Guynn, "Work Shouldn't Hurt," *Sacramento Bee*, November 15, 1998, p. E2; J. MacFarland, "Many Are Called, But What Are the Choices: Working in New Brunswick's 1-800 Call Centers," *New Maritimes* 14 (July–August 1996), pp. 10–19.

30. B. L. Galperin, "Impact of Privatization on Stress in Different Cultures," *Proceedings of the Annual ASAC Conference, International Business Division* 17, no. 8 (1996), pp. 8–16; P. H. Mirvis and M. L. Marks, *Managing the Merger: Making It Work* (Englewood Cliffs, NJ: Prentice Hall, 1992), chap. 5.

31. G. A. Adams, L. A. King, and D. W. King, "Relationships of Job and Family Involvement, Family Social Support, and Work-Family Conflict with Job and Life Satisfaction," *Journal of Applied Psychology* 81 (August 1996), pp. 411–20; S. Lewis and C. L. Cooper, "Balancing the Work/Home Interface: A European Perspective," *Human Resource Management Review* 5 (1995), pp. 289–305; K. J. Williams and G. M. Alliger, "Role Stressors, Mood Spillover, and Perceptions of Work-Family Conflict in Employed Parents," *Academy of Management Journal* 37 (1994), pp. 837–68.

32. P. Dryden, "Network Pros Often Chained to Their Jobs," *Computerworld*, October 6, 1997, p. 1.

33. M. Jamal and V. V. Baba, "Shiftwork and Department-Type Related to Job Stress, Work Attitudes and Behavioral Intentions: A Study of Nurses," *Journal of Organizational Behavior* 13 (1992), pp. 449–64; C. Higgins, L. Duxbury, and R. Irving, "Determinants and Consequences of Work—Family Conflict," *Organizational Behavior and Human Decision Processes* 51 (February 1992), pp. 51–75.

34. C. S. Rogers, "The Flexible Workplace: What Have We Learned?" *Human Resource Management* 31 (Fall 1992), pp. 183–99; L. E. Duxbury and C. A. Higgins, "Gender

Measures for Employees with the Same Job," *Work and Stress* 5 (1991), pp. 29–35.

Differences in Work—Family Conflict," *Journal of Applied Psychology* 76 (1991), pp. 60–74; A. Hochschild, *The Second Shift* (New York: Avon, 1989).

35. D. L. Morrison and R. Clements, "The Effect of One Partner's Job Characteristics on the Other Partner's Distress: A Serendipitous, But Naturalistic, Experiment," *Journal of Occupational and Organizational Psychology* 70 (December 1997), pp. 307–24; M. P. Leiter and M. J. Durup, "Work, Home, and In-Between: A Longitudinal Study of Spillover," *Journal of Applied Behavioral Science* 32 (1996), pp. 29–47; W. Stewart and J. Barling, "Fathers' Work Experiences Effect on Children's Behaviors via Job-Related Affect and Parenting Behaviors," *Journal of Organizational Behavior* 17 (1996), pp. 221–32.

36. A. S. Wharton and R. J. Erickson, "Managing Emotions on the Job and at Home: Understanding the Consequences of Multiple Emotional Roles," *Academy of Management Review* 18 (1993), pp. 457–86; S. E. Jackson and C. Maslach, "After-Effects of Job-Related Stress: Families as Victims," *Journal of Occupational Behavior* 3 (1982), pp. 63–77.

37. International Labor Office, *World Labor Report* (Geneva: ILO, 1993), chap. 5; Karasek and Theorell, *Healthy Work*.

38. Quick et al., *Preventive Stress Management in Organizations*, chap. 3.

39. J. A. Roberts, R. S. Lapidus, and L. B. Chonko, "Salespeople and Stress: The Moderating Role of Locus of Control on Work Stressors and Felt Stress," *Journal of Marketing Theory & Practice* 5 (Summer 1997), pp. 93–108; J. Schaubroeck and D. E. Merritt, "Divergent Effects of Job Control on Coping with Work Stressors: The Key Role of Self-Efficacy," *Academy of Management Journal* 40 (June 1997), pp. 738–54; A. O'Leary and S. Brown, "Self-Efficacy and the Physiological Stress Response," in J. E. Maddux, ed., *Self-Efficacy, Adaptation, and Adjustment: Theory, Research, and Application* (New York: Plenum Press, 1995.)

40. S. C. Segerstrom, S. E. Taylor, M. E. Kemeny, and J. L. Fahey, "Optimism Is Associated with Mood, Coping, and Immune Change in Response to Stress," *Journal of Personality &*

Social Psychology 74 (June 1998), pp. 1646–55.

41. K. R. Parkes, "Personality and Coping as Moderators of Work Stress Processes: Models, Methods and Measures," *Work & Stress* 8 (April 1994), pp. 110–29; S. J. Havlovic and J. P. Keenen, "Coping with Work Stress: The Influence of Individual Differences," in P. L. Perrewé, ed., Handbook on Job Stress [special issue], *Journal of Social Behavior and Personality* 6 (1991), pp. 199–212.

42. B. C. Long and S. E. Kahn, eds., *Women, Work, and Coping: A Multidisciplinary Approach to Workplace Stress* (Montreal: McGill-Queen's University Press, 1993); E. R. Greenglass, R. J. Burke, and M. Ondrack, "A Gender-Role Perspective of Coping and Burnout," *Applied Psychology: An International Review* 39 (1990), pp. 5–27; T. D. Jick and L. F. Mitz, "Sex Differences in Work Stress," *Academy of Management Review* 10 (1985), pp. 408–20.

43. M. Friedman and R. Rosenman, *Type A Behavior and Your Heart* (New York: Knopf, 1974); for a more recent discussion, see P. E. Spector and B. J. O'Connell, "The Contribution of Personality Traits, Negative Affectivity, Locus of Control and Type A to the Subsequent Reports of Job Stressors and Job Strains," *Journal of Occupational and Organizational Psychology* 67 (1994), pp. 1–11; K. R. Parkes, "Personality and Coping as Moderators of Work Stress Processes: Models, Methods and Measures," *Work & Stress* 8 (April 1994), pp. 110–29.

44. M. Jamal and V. V. Baba, "Type A Behavior, Its Prevalence and Consequences among Women Nurses: An Empirical Examination," *Human Relations* 44 (1991), pp. 1213–28; T. Kushnir and S. Melamed, "Work-Load, Perceived Control and Psychological Distress in Type A/B Industrial Workers," *Journal of Organizational Behavior* 12 (1991), pp. 155–68.

45. M. Jamal, "Type A Behavior and Job Performance: Some Suggestive Findings," *Journal of Human Stress* 11 (Summer 1985), pp. 60–68; C. Lee, P. C. Earley, and L. A. Hanson, "Are Type As Better Performers?" *Journal of Organizational Behavior* 9 (1988), pp. 263–69.

46. E. Greenglass, "Type A Behaviour and Occupational Demands in

Managerial Women," *Canadian Journal of Administrative Sciences* 4 (1987), pp. 157–68.

47. B. Allee-Walsh, "Back on the Tightrope," *New Orleans Times-Picayune*, July 21, 1996, p. C4.

48. R. J. Benschop et al., "Cardiovascular and Immune Responses to Acute Psychological Stress in Young and Old Women: A Meta-Analysis," *Psychosomatic Medicine* 60 (May–June 1998), pp. 290–96; H. Bosma, R. Peter, J. Siegrist, and M. Marmot, "Two Alternative Job Stress Models and the Risk of Coronary Heart Disease," *American Journal of Public Health* 88 (January 1998), pp. 68–74; Taylor et. al., "Health Psychology," *Annual Review of Psychology*; S. Cohen and T. B. Herbert, "Health Psychology," *Annual Review of Psychology* 47 (1996), pp. 113–42.

49. S. Cohen, D. A. Tyrrell, and A. P. Smith, "Psychological Stress and Susceptibility to the Common Cold," *New England Journal of Medicine* 325 (August 29, 1991), pp. 654–56.

50. D. K. Sugg, "Study Shows Link between Minor Stress, Early Signs of Coronary Artery Disease," *Baltimore Sun*, December 16, 1997, p. A3.

51. H. M. Weiss and R. Cropanzano, "Affective Events Theory: A Theoretical Discussion of the Structure, Causes, and Consequences of Affective Experiences at Work," *Research in Organizational Behavior* 18 (1996), pp. 1–74.

52. R. C. Kessler, "The Effects of Stressful Life Events on Depression," *Annual Review of Psychology* 48 (1997), pp. 191–214.

53. S. Roan, "The Breaking Point," *Los Angeles Times*, June 5, 1996, p. E1.

54. R. T. Golembiewski, R. A. Boudreau, B. C. Sun, and H. Luo, "Estimates of Burnout in Public Agencies: Worldwide, How Many Employees Have Which Degrees of Burnout, and with What Consequences?" *Public Administration Review* 58 (January–February 1998), pp. 59–65.

55. R. T. Lee and B. E. Ashforth, "A Meta-Analytic Examination of the Correlates of the Three Dimensions of Job Burnout," *Journal of Applied Psychology* 81 (1996) pp. 123–33; R. J. Burke, "Toward a Phase Model of Burnout: Some Conceptual and Methodological Concerns," *Group and Organization Studies* 14 (1989), pp. 23–32; and C. Maslach, *Burnout:*

The Cost of Caring (Englewood Cliffs, NJ: Prentice Hall, 1982).

56. C. L. Cordes and T. W. Dougherty, "A Review and Integration of Research on Job Burnout," *Academy of Management Review* 18 (1993), pp. 621–56.

57. R. T. Lee and B. E. Ashforth, "A Further Examination of Managerial Burnout: Toward an Integrated Model," *Journal of Organizational Behavior* 14 (1993), pp. 3–20.

58. Jamal, "Job Stress and Job Performance Controversy: An Empirical Assessment"; G. Keinan, "Decision Making under Stress: Scanning of Alternatives under Controllable and Uncontrollable Threats," *Journal of Personality and Social Psychology* 52 (1987), pp. 638–44; S. J. Motowidlo, J. S. Packard, and M. R. Manning, "Occupational Stress: Its Causes and Consequences for Job Performance," *Journal of Applied Psychology* 71 (1986), pp. 618–29.

59. R. D. Hackett and P. Bycio, "An Evaluation of Employee Absenteeism as a Coping Mechanism among Hospital Nurses," *Journal of Occupational & Organizational Psychology* 69 (December 1996), pp. 327–38; V. V. Baba and M. J. Harris, "Stress and Absence: A Cross-Cultural Perspective," *Research in Personnel and Human Resources Management, Supplement 1* (1989), pp. 317–37.

60. DeFrank and Ivancevich, "Stress on the Job: An Executive Update"; Neuman and Baron, "Workplace Violence and Workplace Aggression."

61. C. Tarricone, "At Electric Boat: 'We're in Disbelief,'" *Providence Journal-Bulletin*, December 14, 1998, p. B1; J. Hughes and M. Robinson, "2 Die as Hearing Turns Violent; State Worker Opens Fire on Questioners," *Denver Post*, December 9, 1998, p. A1; G. Puit and J. Schoenmann, "Worker Goes Berserk, Kills Using Bulldozer," *Las Vegas Review-Journal*, November 11, 1998, p. A1.

62. M. A. Diamond, "Administrative Assault: A Contemporary Psychoanalytic View of Violence and Aggression in the Workplace," *American Review of Public Administration* 27 (September 1997), pp. 228–47.

63. Neuman and Baron, "Workplace Violence and Workplace Aggression"; L. Berkowitz, *Aggression: Its Causes, Consequences, and Control* (New York: McGraw-Hill, 1993).

64. B. Schulte, "Relax, Take a Breath, Live Longer," *Las Vegas Review-Journal*, October 20, 1997, p. A1.

65. Siegall and Cummings, "Stress and Organizational Role Conflict"; Havlovic and Keenen, "Coping with Work Stress: The Influence of Individual Differences."

66. T. Newton, J. Handy, and S. Fineman, *Managing Stress: Emotion and Power at Work* (Newbury Park, CA: Sage, 1995).

67. N. Terra, "The Prevention of Job Stress by Redesigning Jobs and Implementing Self-Regulating Teams," in L. R. Murphy, ed., *Job Stress Interventions* (Washington, DC: American Psychological Association, 1995); T. D. Wall and K. Davids, "Shopfloor Work Organization and Advanced Manufacturing Technology," *International Review of Industrial and Organizational Psychology* 7 (1992), pp. 363–98; Karasek and Theorell, *Healthy Work*.

68. A. Brice, "Pressed for Time," *Atlanta Journal and Constitution*, January 18, 1998, p. B2.

69. S. Shellenbarger, "Concern Rises over Work-Life Conflict," *Orange County Register* (CA), September 29, 1997, p. D18.

70. "Study Corporate Culture Significantly Impacts Employee Use of Work/Life Benefits," *PR Newswire*, March 11, 1998; J. Landauer, "Bottom-Line Benefits of Work/Life Programs," *HR Focus* 74 (July 1997), p. 3.

71. K. Mayer, "Lilly's Family Views Win Awards," *Lafayette Business Digest*, December 1, 1997, p. 1.

72. B. S. Watson, "Share and Share Alike," *Management Review* 84 (October 1995), pp. 50–52.

73. S. G. Stern, "Corporate Programs Help to Avoid Job Burnout," *American Banker*, February 1998, p. 7.

74. E. J. Hill, B. C. Miller, S. P. Weiner, J. Colihan, "Influences of the Virtual Office on Aspects of Work and Work/Life Balance," *Personnel Psychology* 51 (Autumn 1998), 667–83; A. Mahlon, "The Alternative Workplace: Changing Where and How People Work," *Harvard Business Review* 76 (May–June 1998), pp. 121–30.

75. S. Kim, "Toward Understanding Family Leave Policy in Public Organizations: Family Leave Use and Conceptual Framework for the Family Leave Implementation Process," *Public Productivity & Management Review* 22 (September 1998), pp. 71–87.

76. S. Gelston, "Firms Invest in Child Care," *Boston Herald*, February 21, 1997.

77. K. Hein, "Cigna Offers Employees 'Fast Break' Stress Relief," *Incentive*, July 1996, p. 6.

78. C. Trela, "Happy and Productive," *OC Metro* (Orange County, CA), May 22, 1997, p. 26.

79. "Firms Take Sabbatical from Sabbaticals," *San Jose Mercury News*, October 13, 1998; J. Schmit, "Sleep and a Social Life Take a Back Seat," *USA Today*, December 12, 1996.

80. "Asian Nations Graded for Stress," *Daily Commercial News*, April 25, 1996, p. B1; J. M. Brett, L. K. Stroh, and A. H. Reilly, "Job Transfer," *International Review of Industrial and Organizational Psychology* 7 (1992), pp. 323–62.

81. A. M. Saks and B. E. Ashforth, "Proactive Socialization and Behavioral Self-Management." *Journal of Vocational Behavior* 48 (1996), pp. 301–23; M. Waung, "The Effects of Self-Regulatory Coping Orientation on Newcomer Adjustment and Job Survival," *Personnel Psychology* 48 (1995), pp. 633–50; J. E. Maddux, ed., *Self-Efficacy, Adaptation, and Adjustment: Theory, Research, and Application* (New York: Plenum Press, 1995).

82. M. Barrier, "How Exercise Can Pay Off," *Nation's Business*, February, 1997, p. 41; K. Johnson, "Southwest Texas State University Offers Practical Education to Government Workers," *Austin American-Statesman*, June 6, 1997.

83. L. E. Falkenberg, "Employee Fitness Programs: Their Impact on the Employee and the Organization," *Academy of Management Review* 12 (1987), pp. 511–22; R. J. Shephard, M. Cox, and P. Corey, "Fitness Program Participation: Its Effect on Workers' Performance," *Journal of Occupational Medicine* 23 (1981), pp. 359–63.

84. Shutan, "High Anxiety."

85. A. S. Sethi, "Meditation for Coping with Organizational Stress," in *Handbook of Organizational Stress Coping Strategies*, A. S. Sethi and R. S. Schuler, eds. (Cambridge, MA: Ballinger, 1984), pp. 145–65; and Matteson and Ivancevich, *Controlling Work Stress*, pp. 160–66.

86. S. MacDonald and S. Wells, "The Prevalence and Characteristics of

Employee Assistance, Health Promotion and Drug Testing Programs in Ontario," *Employee Assistance Quarterly* 10 (1994), pp. 25–60.

87. B. N. Uchino, J. T. Cacioppo, and J. K. Kiecolt-Glaser, "The Relationship between Social Support and Physiological Processes: A Review with Emphasis on Underlying Mechanisms and Implications for Health," *Psychological Bulletin* 119 (May 1996), pp. 488–531; M. R. Manning, C. N. Jackson, and M. R. Fusilier, "Occupational Stress, Social Support, and the Costs of Health Care," *Academy of Management Journal* 39 (June 1996), pp. 738–50; J. M. George, T. F. Reed, K. A. Ballard, J. Colin, and J. Fielding, "Contact with AIDS Patients as a Source of Work-Related Distress: Effects of Organizational and Social Support," *Academy of Management Journal* 36 (1993), pp. 157–71.

88. J. S. House, *Work Stress and Social Support* (Reading, MA: Addison-Wesley, 1981); S. Cohen and T. A. Wills, "Stress, Social Support, and the Buffering Hypothesis," *Psychological Bulletin* 98 (1985), pp. 310–57.

89. S. Schachter, *The Psychology of Affiliation* (Stanford, CA: Stanford University Press, 1959).

Chapter Six

1. L. Hawkins, "High-Tech Boom is Bust for Older Workers," *Austin American-Statesman* (Texas), April 5, 1998, p. A1; B. Sharkey, "The Age of Discrimination: Hollywood—Speed Limit: 55," *Mediaweek*, June 30, 1997; K. D. Grimsley, "Bosses Who Don't Trust Anyone over 40," *Sacramento Bee*, February 23, 1997, p. F3.

2. Plato, *The Republic*, trans. D. Lee (Harmondsworth, UK: Penguin, 1955), part VII, sec. 7.

3. S. Buggs, "Big Blue No Longer One Color in Cultural Rainbow," *Raleigh News and Observer* (NC), March 4, 1998, p. D1.

4. S. F. Cronshaw and R. G. Lord, "Effects of Categorization, Attribution, and Encoding Processes on Leadership Perceptions," *Journal of Applied Psychology* 72 (1987), pp. 97–106.

5. W. Burkan, "Developing Your Wide-Angle Vision; Skills for Anticipating the Future," *Futurist*, 32 (March 1998), pp. 35–38. Splatter vision is

also used by fighter pilots and professional bird watchers; for example, see: E. Nickens, "Window on the Wild," *Backpacker* 25 (April 1997), pp. 28–32.

6. R. H. Fazio, D. R. Roskos-Ewoldsen, and M. C. Powell, "Attitudes, Perception, and Attention," in P. M. Niedenthal and S. Kitayama, eds., *The Heart's Eye: Emotional Influences in Perception and Attention* (San Diego, CA: Academic Press, 1994), pp. 197–216.

7. D. Goleman, *Vital Lies, Simple Truths: The Psychology of Deception* (New York: Touchstone, 1985); M. Haire and W. F. Grunes, "Perceptual Defenses: Processes Protecting an Organized Perception of Another Personality," *Human Relations* 3 (1950), pp. 403–12.

8. J. M. Beyer et al., "The Selective Perception of Managers Revisited," *Academy of Management Journal* 40 (June 1997), pp. 716–37; C. N. Macrae and G. V. Bodenhausen, "The Dissection of Selection in Person Perception: Inhibitory Processes in Social Stereotyping," *Journal of Personality & Social Psychology* 69 (1995), pp. 397–407; J. P. Walsh, "Selectivity and Selective Perception: An Investigation of Managers' Belief Structures and Information Processing," *Academy of Management Journal* 31 (1988), pp. 873–96; D. C. Dearborn and H. A. Simon, "Selective Perception: A Note on the Departmental Identification of Executives," *Sociometry* 21 (1958), pp. 140–44.

9. C. Argyris and D. A. Schön, *Organizational Learning II* (Reading, MA: Addison-Wesley, 1996); D. Nicolini and M. B. Meznar, "The Social Construction of Organizational Learning: Conceptual and Practical Issues in the Field," *Human Relations* 48 (1995), pp. 727–46; P. M. Senge, *The Fifth Discipline: The Art and Practice of the Learning Organization* (New York: Doubleday Currency, 1990), chap. 10; P. N. Johnson-Laird, *Mental Models* (Cambridge: Cambridge University Press, 1984).

10. Mental models are widely discussed in the philosophy of logic; for example, see: J. L. Aronson, "Mental Models and Deduction," *American Behavioral Scientist* 40 (May 1997), pp. 782–97.

11. Burkan, "Developing Your Wide-Angle Vision:" "What Are Mental

Models?" *Sloan Management Review* 38 (Spring 1997), p. 13; P. Nystrom and W. Starbuck, "To Avoid Organizational Crises, Unlearn," *Organizational Dynamics* 12 (Winter 1984), pp. 53–65.

12. T. Abate, "Meet Bill Gates, Stand-Up Comic," *San Francisco Examiner*, March 13, 1996, p. D1; P. J. H. Schoemaker "Scenario Planning: A Tool for Strategic Thinking," *Sloan Management Review* 36 (Winter 1995), pp. 25–40.

13. B. E. Ashforth and F. Mael, "Social Identity Theory and the Organization," *Academy of Management Review* 14 (1989), pp. 20–39; H. Tajfel, *Social Identity and Intergroup Relations* (Cambridge: Cambridge University Press, 1982).

14. K. E. Weick, *Sensemaking in Organizations* (Thousand Oaks, CA: Sage, 1995), p. 20.

15. J. E. Dutton, J. M. Dukerich, and C. V. Harquail, "Organizational Images and Member Identification," *Administrative Science Quarterly* 39 (June 1994), pp. 239–63.

16. G. Brenneman, "Right Away and All at Once: How We Saved Continental," *Harvard Business Review* 76, September–October 1998, pp. 162–79.

17. J. W. Jackson and E. R. Smith, "Conceptualizing Social Identity: A New Framework and Evidence for the Impact of Different Dimensions," *Personality & Social Psychology Bulletin* 25 (January 1999), pp. 120–35.

18. W. G. Stephan and C. W. Stephan, *Intergroup Relations* (Boulder, CO: Westview, 1996), chap. 1; L. Falkenberg, "Improving the Accuracy of Stereotypes Within the Workplace," *Journal of Management* 16 (1990), pp. 107–18; D. L. Hamilton, S. J. Sherman, and C. M. Ruvolo, "Stereotype-Based Expectancies: Effects on Information Processing and Social Behavior," *Journal of Social Issues* 46 (1990), pp. 35–60.

19. S. Madon et al., "The Accuracy and Power of Sex, Social Class, and Ethnic Stereotypes: A Naturalistic Study in Person Perception," *Personality & Social Psychology Bulletin* 24 (December 1998), pp. 1304–18; L. Jussim, C. McCauley, and Y. T. Lee, "Why Study Stereotype Accuracy and Inaccuracy?" in Y. T. Lee, L. Jussim,

and C. McCauley, eds., *Stereotype Accuracy: Toward an Appreciation of Group Differences* (Washington, DC: American Psychological Association, 1995), pp. 1–23. For early discussion of stereotypes, see W. Lippmann, *Public Opinion* (New York: Macmillan, 1922).

20. D. L. Stone and A. Colella, "A Model of Factors Affecting the Treatment of Disabled Individuals in Organizations," *Academy of Management Review* 21 (1996), pp. 352–401.

21. C. Stangor and L. Lynch, "Memory for Expectancy-Congruent and Expectancy-Incongruent Information: A Review of the Social and Social Development Literatures," *Psychological Bulletin* 111 (1992), pp. 42–61; C. Stangor, L. Lynch, C. Duan, and B. Glass, "Categorization of Individuals on the Basis of Multiple Social Features," *Journal of Personality and Social Psychology* 62 (1992), pp. 207–18.

22. W. Hermann "Policewomen Out in Force," *Arizona Republic*, June 28, 1999, p. A1.

23. P. J. Oaks, S. A. Haslam, and J. C. Turner, *Stereotyping and Social Reality* (Cambridge, MA: Blackwell, 1994).

24. C. N. Macrae, A. B. Milne, and G. V. Bodenhausen, "Stereotypes as Energy-Saving Devices: A Peek Inside the Cognitive Toolbox," *Journal of Personality and Social Psychology* 66 (1994), pp. 37–47; S. T. Fiske, "Social Cognition and Social Perception," *Annual Review of Psychology* 44 (1993), pp. 155–94.

25. Z. Kunda and P. Thagard, "Forming Impressions from Stereotypes, Traits, and Behaviors: A Parallel-Constraint Satisfaction Theory," *Psychological Review* 103 (1996), pp. 284–308.

26. S. O. Gaines and E. S. Reed, "Prejudice: From Allport to DuBois," *American Psychologist* 50 (February 1995), pp. 96–103; L. Jussim and T. E. Nelson, "Prejudice, Stereotypes, and Labeling Effects: Sources of Bias in Person Perception," *Journal of Personality & Social Psychology* 68 (February 1995), pp. 228–46.

27. H. Chiang, "Employees Sue Wonder Bread—Bias Alleged," *San Francisco Chronicle*, June 16, 1998.

28. "What Blacks Think of Corporate America," *Fortune*, July 6, 1998, pp. 140–43.

29. A. P. Brief et. al., "Beyond Good Intentions: The Next Steps toward Racial Equality in the American Workplace," *Academy of Management Executive* 11 (November 1997), pp. 59–72; M. J. Monteith, "Self-Regulation of Prejudiced Responses: Implications for Progress in Prejudice-Reduction Efforts," *Journal of Personality and Social Psychology* 65 (1993), pp. 469–85.

30. P. M. Buzzanell, "Reframing the Glass Ceiling as a Socially Constructed Process: Implications for Understanding and Change," *Communication Monographs* 62 (December 1995), pp. 327–54; M. E. Heilman, "Sex Stereotypes and Their Effects in the Workplace: What We Know and What We Don't Know," *Journal of Social Behavior & Personality* 10 (1995) pp. 3–26.

31. R. F. Maruca, "Says Who?" *Harvard Business Review* 75 (November–December 1997), pp. 15–17; "Balancing Briefcase and Baby," *Daily Commercial News*, March 4, 1996, p. B1.

32. L. Everett, D. Thorne, and C. Danehower, "Cognitive Moral Development and Attitudes toward Women Executives," *Journal of Business Ethics* 15 (November 1996), pp. 1227–35; J. M. Norris and A. M. Wylie, "Gender Stereotyping of the Managerial Role among Students in Canada and the United States," *Group & Organization Management* 20 (1995), pp. 167–82; R. J. Burke, "Canadian Business Students' Attitudes towards Women as Managers," *Psychological Reports* 75 (1994), pp. 1123–29; S. Coate and G. C. Loury, "Will Affirmative-Action Policies Eliminate Negative Stereotypes?" *American Economic Review* 83 (1993), pp. 1220–40; C. L. Owen and W. D. Todor, "Attitudes toward Women as Managers: Still the Same," *Business Horizons* 36 (March–April 1993), pp. 12–16; V. E. Schein and R. Mueller, "Sex Role Stereotyping and Requisite Management Characteristics: A Cross Cultural Look," *Journal of Organizational Behavior* 13 (1992), pp. 439–47; O. C. Bremmer, J. Tomkiewicz, and V. E. Schein, "The Relationship between Sex Role Stereotypes and Requisite Management Characteristics Revisited," *Academy of Management Journal* 32 (1989), pp. 662–69.

33. S. T. Fiske and P. Glick, "Ambivalence and Stereotypes Cause Sexual Harassment: A Theory with Implications for Organizational Change," *Journal of Social Issues* 51 (1995), pp. 97–115; K. Deaux, "How Basic Can You Be? The Evolution of Research on Gender Stereotypes," *Journal of Social Issues* 51 (1995) pp. 11–20.

34. E. Rosell and K. Miller, "Firefighting Women and Sexual Harassment." *Public Personnel Management* 24 (Fall 1995), pp. 339–50.

35. H. H. Kelley, *Attribution in Social Interaction* (Morristown, NJ: General Learning Press, 1971).

36. H. H. Kelley, "The Processes of Causal Attribution," *American Psychologist* 28 (1973), pp. 107–28; J. M. Feldman, "Beyond Attribution Theory: Cognitive Processes in Performance Appraisal," *Journal of Applied Psychology* 66 (1981), pp. 127–48.

37. J. D. Ford, "The Effects of Causal Attributions on Decision Makers' Responses to Performance Downturns," *Academy of Management Review* 10 (1985), pp. 770–86; M. J. Martinko and W. L. Gardner, "The Leader/Member Attribution Process," *Academy of Management Review* 12 (1987), pp. 235–49.

38. B. Bemmels, "Attribution Theory and Discipline Arbitration," *Industrial and Labor Relations Review* 44 (April 1991), pp. 548–62.

39. J. M. Crant and T. S. Bateman, "Assignment of Credit and Blame for Performance Outcomes," *Academy of Management Journal* 36 (1993), pp. 7–27.

40. J. Martocchio and J. Dulebohn, "Performance Feedback Effects in Training: The Role of Perceived Controllability," *Personnel Psychology* 47 (1994), pp. 357–73; D. R. Norris and R. E. Niebuhr, "Attributional Influences on the Job Performance—Job Satisfaction Relationship," *Academy of Management Journal* 27 (1984), pp. 424–31.

41. H. J. Bernardin and P. Villanova, "Performance Appraisal," in *Generalizing from Laboratory to*

Field Settings, E. A. Locke, ed. (Lexington, MA: Lexington Books, 1986), pp. 43–62; and S. G. Green and T. R. Mitchell, "Attributional Processes of Leader-Member Interactions," *Organizational Behavior and Human Performance* 23 (1979), pp. 429–58.

42. J. R. Bettman and B. A. Weitz, "Attributions in the Board Room: Causal Reasoning in Corporate Annual Reports," *Administrative Science Quarterly* 28 (1983), pp. 165–83.

43. P. Rosenthal and D. Guest, "Gender Difference in Managers' Causal Explanations for Their Work Performance: A Study in Two Organizations," *Journal of Occupational & Organizational Psychology* 69 (1996) pp. 145–51.

44. For a summary of cross-cultural attribution research, see Stephan and Stephan, *Intergroup Relations*, pp. 124–25.

45. B. McElhinny, "Printing Plant Makes Its Mark," *Charleston Daily Mail*, May 6, 1997, p. D1.

46. J. M. Darley and K. C. Oleson, "Introduction to Research on Interpersonal Expectations," in *Interpersonal Expectations: Theory, Research, and Applications* (Cambridge: Cambridge University Press, 1993), pp. 45–63; D. Eden, *Pygmalion in Management* (Lexington, MA: Lexington Books, 1990); L. Jussim, "Self-Fulfilling Prophecies: A Theoretical and Integrative Review," *Psychological Review* 93 (1986), pp. 429–45.

47. Similar models are presented in R. H. G. Field and D. A. Van Seters, "Management by Expectations (MBE): The Power of Positive Prophecy," *Journal of General Management* 14 (Winter 1988), pp. 19–33; D. Eden, "Self-Fulfilling Prophecy as a Management Tool: Harnessing Pygmalion," *Academy of Management Review* 9 (1984), pp. 64–73.

48. M. J. Harris and R. Rosenthal, "Mediation of Interpersonal Expectancy Effects: 31 Meta-Analyses," *Psychological Bulletin* 97 (1985), pp. 363–86.

49. D. Eden, "Interpersonal Expectations in Organizations," in *Interpersonal Expectations*, pp. 154–78.

50. A. Bandura, *Self-Efficacy: The Exercise of Control* (W. H. Freeman, 1996); M. E. Gist and T. R. Mitchell,

"Self-Efficacy: A Theoretical Analysis of Its Determinants and Malleability," *Academy of Management Review* 17 (1992), pp. 183–211.

51. P. D. Blanck, "Interpersonal Expectations in the Courtroom: Studying Judges' and Juries' Behavior," in *Interpersonal Expectations*, pp. 64–87; J. B. Rosser, Jr., "Belief: Its Role in Economic Thought and Action," *American Journal of Economics & Sociology* 52 (1993), pp. 355–68; R. Rosenthal and L. Jacobson, *Pygmalion in the Classroom: Teacher Expectation and Student Intellectual Development* (New York: Holt, Rinehart & Winston, 1968).

52. J-F. Manzoni, "The Set-Up-to-Fail Syndrome," *Harvard Business Review* 76 (March–April 1998), pp. 101–13; J. S. Livingston, "Retrospective Commentary," *Harvard Business Review* 66 (September–October 1988), p. 125.

53. For a review of organizational studies of self-fulfilling prophecy, see: Eden, "Interpersonal Expectations in Organizations," in *Interpersonal Expectations: Theory, Research, and Applications.*

54. D. Eden and A. B. Shani, "Pygmalion Goes to Boot Camp: Expectancy, Leadership, and Trainee Performance," *Journal of Applied Psychology* 67 (1982), pp. 194–99.

55. S. Oz and D. Eden, "Restraining the Golem: Boosting Performance by Changing the Interpretation of Low Scores," *Journal of Applied Psychology* 79 (1994), pp. 744–54; D. Eden, "OD and Self-Fulfilling Prophecy: Boosting Productivity by Raising Expectations," *Journal of Applied Behavioral Science* 22 (1986), pp. 1–13.

56. T. Hill, P. Lewicki, M. Czyzewska, and A. Boss, "Self-Perpetuating Development of Encoding Biases in Person Perception," *Journal of Personality and Social Psychology* 57 (1989), pp. 373–87; C. L. Kleinke, *First Impressions: The Psychology of Encountering Others* (Englewood Cliffs, NJ: Prentice Hall, 1975).

57. D. D. Steiner and J. S. Rain, "Immediate and Delayed Primacy and Recency Effects in Performance Evaluation," *Journal of Applied Psychology* 74 (1989), pp. 136–42; R. L. Heneman and K. N. Wexley, "The Effects of Time

Delay in Rating and Amount of Information Observed in Performance Rating Accuracy," *Academy of Management Journal* 26 (1983), pp. 677–86.

58. Adapted from "Lasting Impressions," *Inc.* 20 (July 1998), p. 126.

59. W. H. Cooper, "Ubiquitous Halo," *Psychological Bulletin* 90 (1981), pp. 218–44; K. R. Murphy, R. A. Jako, and R. L. Anhalt, "Nature and Consequences of Halo Error: A Critical Analysis," *Journal of Applied Psychology* 78 (1993), pp. 218–25.

60. S. Kozlowski, M. Kirsch, and G. Chao, "Job Knowledge, Ratee Familiarity, Conceptual Similarity, and Halo Error: An Exploration," *Journal of Applied Psychology* 71 (1986), pp. 45–49; H. C. Min, "Country Image: Halo or Summary Construct?" *Journal of Marketing Research* 26 (1989), pp. 222–29.

61. W. K. Balzer and L. M. Sulsky, "Halo and Performance Appraisal Research: A Critical Examination," *Journal of Applied Psychology* 77 (1992), pp. 975–85; H. J. Bernardin and R. W. Beatty, *Performance Appraisal: Assessing Human Behavior at Work* (Boston: Kent, 1984).

62. G. G. Sherwood, "Self-Serving Biases in Person Perception: A Reexamination of Projection as a Mechanism of Defense," *Psychological Bulletin* 90 (1981), pp. 445–59.

63. G. Robinson and K. Dechant, "Building a Business Case for Diversity," *Academy of Management Executive* 11 (August 1997), pp. 21–31; R. Rousseau, "Employing the New America," *Restaurants & Institutions*, March 15, 1997, pp. 40–52.

64. J. R. W. Joplin and C. S. Daus, "Challenges of Leading a Diverse Workforce," *Academy of Management Executive*, August 1997, pp. 32–47.

65. M. J. Reid, "Profit Motivates Corporate Diversity," *San Francisco Examiner*, March 15, 1998, p. W42.

66. M. J. Reid, ibid.

67. M. J. Brown, "Let's Talk About It, Really Talk about It," *Journal for Quality & Participation* 19 no. 6 (1996), pp. 26–33; E. H. Schein, "On Dialogue, Culture, and Organizational Learning," *Organizational Dynamics*, Autumn 1993, pp. 40–51; and P. M. Senge,

The Fifth Discipline (New York: Doubleday Currency, 1990), pp. 238–49.

68. G. Flynn, "The Harsh Reality of Diversity Programs," *Workforce* 77 (December 1998), pp. 26–33.

69. M. G. Fine, *Building Successful Multicultural Organizations* (Westport, CT: Quorum, 1995), pp. 114–16.

70. G. Egan, *The Skilled Helper: A Model for Systematic Helping and Interpersonal Relating* (Belmont, CA: Brooks/Cole, 1975); D. B. Fedor and K. M. Rowland, "Investigating Supervisor Attributions of Subordinate Performance," *Journal of Management* 15 (1989), pp. 405–16.

71. D. Goleman, "What Makes a Leader?" *Harvard Business Review* 76 (November–December 1998), pp. 92–102.

72. S. Mycek, "Up Close and Personal: Taking a Community Plunge Puts You in Touch with Real People, Real Needs," *Trustee* 50 (October 1997), pp. 8–13.

73. L. Beamer, "Learning Intercultural Communication Competence," *Journal of Business Communication* 29 (1992), pp. 285–303; and D. Landis and R. W. Brislin, eds., *Handbook of Intercultural Training* (New York: Pergamon, 1983).

74. T. W. Costello and S. S. Zalkind, *Psychology in Administration: A Research Orientation* (Englewood Cliffs, NJ: Prentice Hall, 1963), pp. 45–46.

75. J. Luft, *Group Processes* (Palo Alto, CA: Mayfield Publishing, 1984). For a variation of this model, see J. Hall, "Communication Revisited," *California Management Review* 15 (Spring 1973), pp. 56–67.

76. L. C. Miller and D. A. Kenny, "Reciprocity of Self-Disclosure at the Individual and Dyadic Levels: A Social Relations Analysis," *Journal of Personality and Social Psychology* 50 (1986), pp. 713–19.

77. M. Maccoby, "Teams Need Open Leaders," *Research-Technology Management* 38 (January 1995), pp. 57–59.

78. J. Carlton, "Think Different: Jobs Cuts a Mean Figure," *The Wall Street Journal*, April 14, 1998; A. Gore, "Necessary Roughness," *MacWorld*, December 1997, p. 23; L. Picarille, "Steve Jobs," *Computer Reseller News*, November 16, 1997, pp. 51–52.

79. R. T. Hogan, "Personality and Personality Measurement," in M. D. Dunnette and L. M. Hough, eds., *Handbook of Industrial and Organizational Psychology*, 2nd ed., vol. 2 (Palo Alto, CA: Consulting Psychologists Press, 1991), pp. 873–919; see also W. Mischel, *Introduction to Personality* (New York: Holt, Rinehart & Winston, 1986).

80. H. M. Weiss and S. Adler, "Personality and Organizational Behavior," *Research in Organizational Behavior* 6 (1984), pp. 1–50.

81. W. Revelle, "Personality Processes," *Annual Review of Psychology* 46 (1995), pp. 295–328.

82. R. M. Guion and R. F. Gottier, "Validity of Personality Measures in Personnel Selection," *Personnel Psychology* 18 (1965), pp. 135–64; see also N. Schmitt, R. Z. Gooding, R. D. Noe, and M. Kirsch, "Meta-Analyses of Validity Studies Published between 1964 and 1982 and the Investigation of Study Characteristics," *Personnel Psychology* 37 (1984), pp. 407–22.

83. P. G. Irving, "On the Use of Personality Measures in Personnel Selection," *Canadian Psychology* 34 (April 1993), pp. 208–14.

84. K. M. DeNeve and H. Cooper, "The Happy Personality: A Meta-Analysis of 137 Personality Traits and Subjective Well-Being," *Psychological Bulletin* 124 (September 1998), pp. 197–229; M. K. Mount and M. R. Barrick, "The Big Five Personality Dimensions: Implications for Research and Practice in Human Resources Management," *Research in Personnel and Human Resources Management* 13 (1995), pp. 153–200; B. M. Bass, *Stogdill's Handbook of Leadership: A Survey of Theory and Research*, 3rd ed. (New York: Free Press, 1990); J. L. Holland, *Making Vocation Choices: A Theory of Careers* (Englewood Cliffs, NJ: Prentice Hall, 1973).

85. R. D. Gatewood and H. S. Feild, *Human Resource Selection*, 3rd Ed. (Fort Worth, TX: Harcourt Brace and Company, 1994), chap. 15.

86. T. A. Stewart, "Escape from the Cult of Personality Tests," *Fortune*, March 16, 1998, p. 80.

87. This historical review and the trait descriptions in this section are discussed in R. J. Schneider and

L. M. Hough, "Personality and Industrial/Organizational Psychology," *International Review of Industrial and Organizational Psychology* 10 (1995), pp. 75–129; M. K. Mount and M. R. Barrick, "The Big Five Personality Dimensions: Implications for Research and Practice in Human Resources Management," *Research in Personnel and Human Resources Management* 13 (1995), pp. 153–200; J. M. Digman, "Personality Structure: Emergence of the Five-Factor Model," *Annual Review of Psychology* 41 (1990), pp. 417–40.

88. I. R. Gellatly, "Dispositional Determinants of Task Performance: Focus on the Big Five Factor of Conscientiousness," *Proceedings of the Annual ASAC Conference*, Human Resources Division 17, no. 9 (1996), pp. 43–52; M. K. Mount, M. R. Barrick, and J. P. Strauss, "Validity of Observer Ratings of the Big Five Personality Factors," *Journal of Applied Psychology* 79 (1994), pp. 272–80; R. P. Tett, D. N. Jackson, and M. Rothstein, "Personality Measures as Predictors of Job Performance: A Meta-Analytic Review," *Personnel Psychology* 44 (1991), pp. 703–42.

89. J. M. Howell and C. A. Higgins, "Champions of Change: Identifying, Understanding, and Supporting Champions of Technological Innovations," *Organizational Dynamics*, Summer 1990, pp. 40–55.

90. K. P. Carson and G. L. Stewart, "Job Analysis and the Sociotechnical Approach to Quality: A Critical Examination," *Journal of Quality Management* 1 (1996), pp. 49–64; Mount and Barrick, "The Big Five Personality Dimensions," pp. 177–78.

91. I. B. Myers, *The Myers-Briggs Type Indicator*. (Palo Alto, CA: Consulting Psychologists Press, 1987); C. G. Jung, *Psychological Types*, trans. by H. G. Baynes, revised by R. F. C. Hull (originally published in 1921; Princeton, NJ: Princeton University Press, 1971).

92. D. W. Salter and N. J. Evans, "Test-Retest of the Myers-Briggs Type Indicator: An Examination of Dominant Functioning," *Educational & Psychological Measurement* 57 (August 1997), pp. 590–97; W. L. Gardner and M. J.

Martinko, "Using the Myers-Briggs Type Indicator to Study Managers: A Literature Review and Research Agenda," *Journal of Management* 22 (1996), pp. 45–83; R. Zemke, "Second Thoughts About the MBTI," *Training,* April 1992, pp. 42–47; M. H. McCaulley, "The Myers-Briggs Type Indicator: A Measure for Individuals and Groups," *Measurement and Evaluation in Counseling and Development* 22 (1990), pp. 181–95.

93. G. N. Landrum, *Profiles of Genius* (New York: Prometheus, 1993).

94. Gardner and Martinko, "Using the Myers-Briggs Type Indicator to Study Managers."

95. C. Caggiano, "Psycho Path," *Inc.* 20 (July 1998), pp. 76–85.

96. J. M. Howell and B. J. Avolio, "Transformational Leadership, Transactional Leadership, Locus of Control, and Support for Innovation: Key Predictors of Consolidated-Business-Unit Performance," *Journal of Applied Psychology* 78 (1993), pp. 891–902; P. E. Spector, "Behavior in Organizations as a Function of Employee's Locus of Control," *Psychological Bulletin* 91 (1982), pp. 482–97; P. J. Andrisani and C. Nestel, "Internal-External Control as a Contributor to and Outcome of Work Experience," *Journal of Applied Psychology* 61 (1976), pp. 156–65.

97. D. Miller and J.-M. Toulouse, "Chief Executive Personality and Corporate Strategy and Structure in Small Firms," *Management Science* 32 (1986), pp. 1389–1409; D. Miller, M. F. R. Ket de Vries, and J.-M. Toulouse, "Top Executive Locus of Control and Its Relationship to Strategy-Making, Structure, and Environment," *Academy of Management Journal* 25 (1982), pp. 237–53.

98. M. Snyder, *Public Appearances/ Private Realities: The Psychology of Self-Monitoring* (New York: W. H. Freeman, 1987).

99. M. Kilduff and D. V. Day, "Do Chameleons Get Ahead? The Effects of Self-Monitoring on Managerial Careers," *Academy of Management Journal* 37 (1994), pp. 1047–60; R. J. Ellis and S. E. Cronshaw, "Self-Monitoring and Leader Emergence: A Test of Moderator Effects," *Small Group Research* 23 (1992), pp. 113–29; S. J. Zaccaro, R. J. Foti,

and D. A. Kenny, "Self-Monitoring and Trait-Based Variance in Leadership: An Investigation of Leader Flexibility across Multiple Group Situations," *Journal of Applied Psychology* 76 (1991), pp. 308–15.

100. H. A. Simon, *Administrative Behavior* (New York: Free Press, 1957), p. xv.

Chapter Seven

1. G. Brenneman, "Right Away and All at Once: How We Saved Continental," *Harvard Business Review* 76 (September–October 1998), pp. 162–79; G. Flynn, "A Flight Plan for Success," *Workforce* 76 (July 1997), pp. 72–77; D. Van De Mark, "Continental Airlines' Comeback," *CNNFN Business Unusual,* March 6, 1997; Transcript 97030601FN-l17; S. McCartney, "With Gordon Bethune at Controls, Continental Lifts Employees' Morale," *Denver Post,* May 19, 1996, p. G3.

2. B. E. Ashforth and R. H. Humphrey, "Emotion in the Workplace: A Reappraisal," *Human Relations* 48 (1995), pp. 97–125.

3. For a fuller discussion of specific emotions, see R. Pekrun and M. Frese, "Emotions in Work and Achievement," *International Review of Industrial and Organizational Psychology* 7 (1992), pp. 153–200.

4. This definition is based on material in H. M. Weiss and R. Cropanzano, "Affective Events Theory: A Theoretical Discussion of the Structure, Causes, and Consequences of Affective Experiences at Work," *Research in Organizational Behavior* 18 (1996), pp. 1–74; S. Kitayama and P. M. Niedenthal, "Introduction," in P. M. Niedenthal and S. Kitayama, *The Heart's Eye: Emotional Influences in Perception and Attention* (San Diego, CA: Academic Press, 1994), pp. 6–7.

5. K. Oatley and J. M. Jenkins, "Human Emotions: Function and Dysfunction," *Annual Review of Psychology* 43 (1992), pp. 55–85.

6. J. M. George and A. P. Brief, "Motivational Agendas in the Workplace: The Effects of Feelings on Focus of Attention and Work Motivation," *Research in Organizational Behavior* 18 (1996), pp. 75–109; J. M. George, "Mood

and Absence," *Journal of Applied Psychology* 74 (1989), pp. 317–24.

7. T. A. Judge, E. A. Locke, and C. C. Durham, "The Dispositional Causes of Job Satisfaction: A Core Evaluations Approach," *Research in Organizational Behavior* 19 (1997), pp. 151–88; A. P. Brief, A. H. Butcher, and L. Roberson, "Cookies, Disposition, and Job Attitudes: The Effects of Positive Mood-Inducing Events and Negative Affectivity on Job Satisfaction in a Field Experiment," *Organizational Behavior and Human Decision Processes* 62 (1995), pp. 55–62.

8. J. Schaubroeck, D. C. Ganster, and B. Kemmerer, "Does Trait Affect Promote Job Attitude Stability?" *Journal of Organizational Behavior* 17 (1996), pp. 191–96; R. D. Arvey, B. P. McCall, T. L. Bouchard, and P. Taubman, "Genetic Differences on Job Satisfaction and Work Values," *Personality and Individual Differences* 17 (1994), pp. 21–33; B. M. Staw and J. Ross, "Stability in the Midst of Change: A Dispositional Approach to Job Attitudes," *Journal of Applied Psychology* 70 (1985), pp. 469–80.

9. J. M. George and G. R. Jones, "Experiencing Work: Values, Attitudes, and Moods," *Human Relations* 50 (April 1997), pp. 393–416; J. M. Olson and M. P. Zama, "Attitudes and Attitude Change," *Annual Review of Psychology* 44 (1993), pp. 117–54; M. Fishbein and I. Ajzen, *Belief, Attitude, Intention, and Behavior* (Reading, MA: Addison-Wesley, 1975).

10. Weiss and Cropanzano, "Affective Events Theory."

11. M. D. Zalesny and J. K. Ford, "Extending the Social Information Processing Perspective: New Links to Attitudes, Behaviors, and Perceptions," *Organizational Behavior and Human Decision Processes* 52 (1992), pp. 205–46; G. Salancik and J. Pfeffer, "A Social Information Processing Approach to Job Attitudes and Task Design," *Administrative Science Quarterly* 23 (1978), pp. 224–53.

12. For a full discussion of several theories on this topic, see K. T. Strongman, *The Psychology of Emotion: Theories of Emotion in Perspective,* 4th ed. (Chichester, UK: John Wiley, 1996), chap. 6.

13. D. M. Irvine and M. G. Evans, "Job Satisfaction and Turnover among

Nurses: Integrating Research Findings Across Studies," *Nursing Research* 44 (1995) pp. 246–53.

14. Pinder, *Work Motivation*, pp. 88–89.

15. Weiss and Cropanzano, "Affective Events Theory," pp. 52–57.

16. L. Festinger, *A Theory of Cognitive Dissonance* (Evanston, IL: Row, Peterson, 1957); and G. R. Salancik, "Commitment and the Control of Organizational Behavior and Belief," in *New Directions in Organizational Behavior*, B. M. Staw and G. R. Salancik, eds. (Chicago: St. Clair, 1977), pp. 1–54.

17. Weiss and Cropanzano, "Affective Events Theory." The definition of job satisfaction is still being debated. This definition captures the most popular view that job satisfaction is an evaluation and represents both beliefs and feelings. For details, see A. P. Brief, *Attitudes in and around Organizations* (Thousand Oaks, CA: Sage, 1998), chaps. 2 and 4.

18. H. Ubinas, "Most Americans Say They'd Take This Job and Love It," *Hartford Courant*, September 1, 1997, p. A1.

19. E. A. Locke, "The Nature and Causes of Job Satisfaction," in *Handbook of Industrial and Organizational Psychology*, M. Dunnette, ed. (Chicago: Rand McNally, 1976), pp. 1297–1350.

20. "'We're Dispensable,' Workers Are Realizing," *Memphis Commercial Appeal*, September 13, 1998; L. Lavelle, "Layoffs Breed Era of Skepticism," *Bergen County Record* (NJ), September 4, 1998, p. B1; D. Moore, "Public Generally Negative toward Business, But Most Workers Satisfied with Jobs," *Gallup Poll*, August 1997 (from www.gallup.com); M. Stepanek, "Poll Finds Workers Secure, Loyal," *Raleigh News and Observer*, August 30, 1997, p. A8; S. Baker, "Job Satisfaction High in Survey, But Office Politics Alive and Well," *Fort Worth Star-Telegram*, March 13, 1997, p. 3.

21. S. MacDonald, "Do You Really Enjoy Your Work?" *The Times* (London), January 15, 1998.

22. These data are from the following source. The problems with the data are described in the article by an executive in the firm that conducted this survey. See G. Law, "If You're Happy & You Know It, Tick the Box," *Management-Auckland* 45

(March 1998), pp. 34–37. The problems with measuring work attitudes across cultures is also discussed in K. Bae and C. Chung, "Cultural Values and Work Attitudes of Korean Industrial Workers in Comparison with Those of the United States and Japan," *Work and Occupations* 24 (February 1997), pp. 80–96.

23. E. E. Lawler III, *Motivation in Work Organizations* (Belmont, CA: Wadsworth, 1973), pp. 66–69, 74–77.

24. D. B. McFarlin and R. W. Rice, "The Role of Facet Importance as a Moderator in Job Satisfaction Processes," *Journal of Organizational Behavior* 13 (1992), pp. 41–54.

25. A. J. Rucci, S. P. Kirn, and R. T. Quinn, "The Employee-Customer-Profit Chain at Sears," *Harvard Business Review* 76 (January–February 1998), pp. 83–97; W. Bole, "Workers Getting Say in CEOs' Pay," *Orlando Sentinel*, September 14, 1997, p. H1; M. Kerr, "Developing a Corporate Culture for the Maximum Balance between the Utilization of Human Resources and Employee Fulfillment in Canada," *Canada-United States Law Journal* 22 (1996), pp. 169–76.

26. For a review, see P. E. Spector, *Job Satisfaction: Application, Assessment, Causes, and Consequences* (Thousand Oaks, CA: Sage, 1997); Brief, *Attitudes In and Around Organizations*, chap. 2.

27. R. D. Hackett and P. Bycio, "An Evaluation of Employee Absenteeism as a Coping Mechanism among Hospital Nurses," *Journal of Occupational & Organizational Psychology* 69 (December 1996), pp. 327–38; J. Barling, "The Prediction, Psychological Experience, and Consequences of Workplace Violence," in G. R. VandenBos and E. Q. Bulatao, *Violence on the Job* (Washington, DC: American Psychological Association, 1996), pp. 29–49; S. D. Bluen, "The Psychology of Strikes," *International Review of Industrial and Organizational Psychology* 9 (1994), pp. 113–45; P. Y. Chen and P. E. Spector, "Relationships of Work Stressors with Aggression, Withdrawal, Theft and Substance Use: An Exploratory Study," *Journal*

of Occupational & Organizational Psychology 65 (1992), pp. 177–84.

28. B. M. Staw and S. G. Barsade, "Affect and Managerial Performance: A Test of the Sadder-but-Wiser vs. Happier-and-Smarter Hypotheses," *Administrative Science Quarterly* 38 (1993), pp. 304–31; M. T. Iaffaldano and P. M. Muchinsky, "Job Satisfaction and Job Performance: A Meta-Analysis," *Psychological Bulletin* 97 (1985), pp. 251–73; D. P. Schwab and L. L. Cummings, "Theories of Performance and Satisfaction: A Review," *Industrial Relations* 9 (1970), pp. 408–30.

29. Brief, *Attitudes in and around Organizations*, p. 43.

30. E. E. Lawler III and L. W. Porter, "The Effect of Performance on Job Satisfaction," *Industrial Relations* 7 (1967), pp. 20–28.

31. C. D. Fisher and E. A. Locke, "The New Look in Job Satisfaction Research and Theory," in Cranny et al., eds., *Job Satisfaction*, pp. 165–94; P. M. Podsakoff, S. B. MacKenzie, and C. Hui, "Organizational Citizenship Behaviors and Managerial Evaluations of Employee Performance: A Review and Suggestions for Future Research," *Research in Personnel and Human Resources Management* 11 (1993), pp. 1–40; D. W. Organ, "The Motivational Basis of Organizational Citizenship Behavior," *Research in Organizational Behavior* 12 (1990), pp. 43–72.

32. D. S. Bolon, "Organizational Citizenship Behavior among Hospital Employees: A Multidimensional Analysis Involving Job Satisfaction and Organizational Commitment," *Hospital & Health Services Administration* 42 (Summer 1997), pp. 221–41.

33. R. Verrier, "Staff Morale a Priority, Hospitals' New Chief Says," *St. Petersburg Times*, January 10, 1997, p. 1; S. H. Shapoff, "Why Corning Breathes TQM," *Financial Executive* 12 (November–December 1996), pp. 26–28; R. Hallowell, L. A. Schlesinger, and J. Zornitsky, "Internal Service Quality, Customer and Job Satisfaction: Linkages and Implications for Management," *Human Resource Planning* 19, no. 2 (1996), pp. 20–31; A. Payne, *Advances in Relationship Marketing*

(London: Kogan Page, 1995), pp. 46–48.

34. R. M. Breyer, "Whole Foods Makes List of Best Places to Work," *Austin American-Statesman,* December 20, 1997, p. D1.

35. A. J. Rucci, S. P. Kirn, and R. T. Quinn, "The Employee-Customer-Profit Chain at Sears," *Harvard Business Review* 76 (January–February 1998), pp. 83–97; S. Chandler, "Sears' System of Rewards Has Ups and Downs," *Chicago Tribune,* February 15, 1998, p. C1.

36. R. T. Mowday, L. W. Porter, and R. M. Steers, *Employee Organization Linkages: The Psychology of Commitment, Absenteeism, and Turnover* (New York: Academic Press, 1982).

37. T. E. Becker, R. S. Billings, D. M. Eveleth, and N. L. Gilbert, "Foci and Bases of Employee Commitment: Implications for Job Performance," *Academy of Management Journal* 39 (1996), pp. 464–82.

38. J. P. Meyer, "Organizational Commitment," *International Review of Industrial and Organizational Psychology* 12 (1997), pp. 175–228. Along with affective and continuance commitment, Meyer identifies "normative commitment," which refers to employee feelings of obligation to remain with the organization. This commitment has been excluded so that students focus on the two most common perspectives of commitment.

39. R. D. Hackett, P. Bycio, and P. A. Hausdorf, "Further Assessments of Meyer and Allen's (1991) Three-Component Model of Organizational Commitment," *Journal of Applied Psychology* 79 (1994), pp. 15–23.

40. "Employees' Morale Plummets," *Management Services* 41 (February 1997), p. 6; Angus Reid Interactive, "Loyalty at Work," Angus Reid Group/Bloomberg Business News Poll, press release, October 17, 1996 (www.angusreid.com); P. Houston, "The Smartest Ways to Build Loyalty," *Working Woman* 17 (April 1992), pp. 72–74, 100–1.

41. D. Yankelovich, "Got to Give to Get," *Mother Jones* 22 (July 1997), p. 60; J. Laabs, "Employee Commitment," *Personnel Journal,* August 1996, pp. 58–66; C. C. Heckscher, *White-Collar Blues:*

Management Loyalties in an Age of Corporate Restructuring (New York: Basic Books, 1995).

42. M. Stepanek, "Poll Finds Workers Secure, Loyal," *Raleigh News and Observer* (NC), August 30, 1997, p. A8; Walker Information, *The International Employee Commitment Project* (Indianapolis: Walker Information, 1997) from www.walkernet.com; Bae and Chung, "Cultural Values and Work Attitudes of Korean Industrial Workers in Comparison with Those of the United States and Japan"; "Japanese Worker Loyalty Overrated, Survey Says," *Japan Weekly Monitor,* September 9, 1996.

43. F. F. Reichheld, *The Loyalty Effect* (Boston: Harvard Business School Press, 1996), chap. 4.

44. D. S. Bolon, "Organizational Citizenship Behavior among Hospital Employees: A Multidimensional Analysis Involving Job Satisfaction and Organizational Commitment," *Hospital & Health Services Administration* 42 (Summer 1997), pp. 221–41; Meyer, "Organizational Commitment," pp. 203–15; J. P. Meyer, S. V. Paunonen, I. R. Gellatly, R. D. Goffin, and D. N. Jackson, "Organizational Commitment and Job Performance: It's the Nature of the Commitment That Counts," *Journal of Applied Psychology* 74 (1989), pp. 152–56.

45. A. A. Luchak and I. R. Gellatly, "Employer-Sponsored Pensions and Employee Commitment," *Proceedings of the Annual ASAC Conference, Human Resource Management Division* 17, no. 9 (1996), pp. 64–71; H. L. Angle and M. B. Lawson, "Organizational Commitment and Employees' Performance Ratings: Both Type of Commitment and Type of Performance Count," *Psychological Reports* 75 (1994), pp. 1539–51; L. M. Shore and S. J. Wayne, "Commitment and Employee Behavior: Comparison of Affective Commitment and Continuance Commitment with Perceived Organizational Support," *Journal of Applied Psychology* 78 (1993), pp. 774–80; Meyer et al., "Organizational Commitment and Job Performance: It's the Nature of the Commitment That Counts."

46. C. Fishman, "Sanity Inc." *Fast Company,* no. 21 (January 1999),

pp. 85–96; R. Gerena-Morales, "The Best Places to Work," *Bergen County Record* (NJ), January 25, 1998, p. B1; J. Landauer, "Bottom-Line Benefits of Work/Life Programs," *HR Focus* 74 (July 1997), p. 3.

47. J. P. Meyer and N. J. Allen, *Commitment in the Workplace: Theory, Research, and Application* (Thousand Oaks, CA: Sage, 1997), chap. 4.

48. E. W. Morrison and S. L. Robinson, "When Employees Feel Betrayed: A Model of How Psychological Contract Violation Develops," *Academy of Management Review* 22 (1997), pp. 226–56.

49. S. Branch, "The 100 Best Companies to Work for in America," *Fortune,* January 11, 1999, pp. 118–44; R. Levering and M. Moskowitz, "The 100 Best Companies to Work for in America," *Fortune,* January 12, 1998, pp. 84–95.

50. Shore and Wayne, "Commitment and Employee Behavior"; D. M. Rousseau and J. M. Parks, "The Contracts of Individuals and Organizations," *Research in Organizational Behavior* 15 (1993), pp. 1–43; and D. J. Koys, "Human Resource Management and a Culture of Respect: Effects on Employees' Organizational Commitment," *Employee Responsibilities and Rights Journal* 1 (1988), pp. 57–68.

51. C. Hendry, Chris and R. Jenkins, "Psychological Contracts and New Deals," *Human Resource Management Journal* 7 (1997), pp. 38–44; D. M. Noer, *Healing the Wounds* (San Francisco: Jossey-Bass, 1993); S. Ashford, C. Lee, and P. Bobko, "Content, Causes, and Consequences of Job Insecurity: A Theory-Based Measure and Substantive Test," *Academy of Management Journal* 32 (1989), pp. 803–29.

52. I. M. Botero, "Boosters and Busters of Employee Morale," *Phoenix Business Journal,* June 14, 1996, p. 37.

53. R. J. Lewicki and B. B. Bunker, "Developing and Maintaining Trust in Work Relationships," in R. M. Kramer and T. R. Tyler, eds., *Trust in Organizations: Frontiers of Theory and Research* (Thousand Oaks, CA: Sage, 1996), pp. 114–39; S. L. Robinson, "Trust and Breach of the Psychological Contract,"

Administrative Science Quarterly 41 (1996), pp. 574–99; B. S. Frey, "Does Monitoring Increase Work Effort? The Rivalry with Trust and Loyalty," *Economic Inquiry* 31 (1993), pp. 663–70; J. K. Butler, Jr., "Toward Understanding and Measuring Conditions of Trust: Evolution of a Conditions of Trust Inventory," *Journal of Management* 17 (1991), pp. 643–63; J. M. Kouzes and B. Z. Posner, *The Leadership Challenge* (San Francisco: Jossey-Bass, 1987), pp. 146–52.

54. S. Nelton, "Emotions in the Workplace," *Nation's Business,* February 1996, pp. 25–30.

55. J. A. Morris and D. C. Feldman, "The Dimensions, Antecedents, and Consequences of Emotional Labor," *Academy of Management Review* 21 (1996), pp. 986–1010; B. E. Ashforth and R. H. Humphrey, "Emotional Labor in Service Roles: The Influence of Identity," *Academy of Management Review* 18 (1993), pp. 88–115.

56. J. A. Morris and D. C. Feldman, "Managing Emotions in the Workplace," *Journal of Managerial Issues* 9 (Fall 1997), pp. 257–74.

57. "Safeway Employees Announce the Filing of a Charge with the Equal Employment Opportunity Commission," *Business Wire,* November 16, 1998; K. D. Grimsley, "Service With a Forced Smile," *Washington Post,* October 18, 1998, p. A1.

58. R. I. Sutton, "Maintaining Norms about Expressed Emotions: The Case of Bill Collectors," *Administrative Science Quarterly* 36 (1991), pp. 245–68.

59. S. Fish and F. Jamerson, eds., *Inside the Mouse: Work and Play at Disney World* (Durham, NC: Duke University Press, 1995).

60. E. Forman, "'Diversity Concerns Grow as Companies Head Overseas,' Consultant Says," *Fort Lauderdale Sun-Sentinel,* June 26, 1995.

61. Ashforth and Humphrey, "Emotional Labor in Service Roles: The Influence of Identity," p. 91.

62. R. Buck, "The Spontaneous Communication of Interpersonal Expectations," in *Interpersonal Expectations: Theory, Research, and Applications* (Cambridge: Cambridge University Press, 1993), pp. 227–41. The quotation from George Burns also comes from this source; however, this line has also been attributed to Groucho Marx.

63. A. S. Wharton, "The Psychosocial Consequences of Emotional Labor," *Annals of the American Academy of Political & Social Science* 561 (January 1999), pp. 158–76; J. A. Morris and D. C. Feldman, "Managing Emotions in the Workplace," *Journal of Managerial Issues* 9 (Fall 1997), pp. 257–74; P. K. Adelmann, "Emotional Labor as a Potential Source of Job Stress," in S. Sauter and L. R. Murphy, eds., *Organizational Risk Factors for Job Stress* (Washington, DC: American Psychological Association, 1995), chap. 24.

64. "Ziad Altoura: Yoga Makes Him Giggly," *Sunday Times* (London), May 18, 1997.

65. I. Anai, "Here to Stay," *Daily Yomiuri* (Japan), November 21, 1997, p. 17.

66. P. Carbonara, "Hire for Attitude, Train for Skill," *Fast Company,* no. 4 (August 1996), p. 73; K. Frieberg and J. Frieberg, *Nuts! Southwest Airlines' Crazy Recipe for Business and Personal Success.* (Austin, TX: Bard Press, 1996), Chap. 6.

67. L. Yeung, "Stress-Busters Strive for Balance," *South China Morning Post,* October 18, 1998, p. 2; J. Cheung, "'Emotions' Class for Civil Servants," *South China Morning Post,* September 14, 1998, p. 3.

68. J. D. Mayer and P. Salovey, "The Intelligence of Emotional Intelligence," *Intelligence* 17 (1993), pp. 433–42.

69. D. Goleman, "What Makes a Leader?" *Harvard Business Review* 76 (November–December 1998), pp. 92–102.

70. "Unconventional Smarts," *Across the Board* 35 (January 1998), pp. 22–23.

71. A. Sagie and D. Elizur, "Work Values: A Theoretical Overview and a Model of Their Effects," *Journal of Organizational Behavior* 17 (1996), pp. 503–14; W. H. Schmidt and B. Z. Posner, *Managerial Values in Perspective* (New York: American Management Association, 1983).

72. M. Rokeach, *Understanding Human Values* (New York: Free Press, 1979).

73. B. M. Meglino and E. C. Ravlin, "Individual Values in Organizations: Concepts, Controversies, and Research," *Journal of Management,* 24 (May 1998), pp. 351–89; P. McDonald and J. Gandz, "Getting Value from Values," *Organizational Dynamics,* Winter 1992, pp. 64–77.

74. M. Rokeach, *The Nature of Human Values* (New York: Free Press, 1973); F. Kluckhorn and F. L. Strodtbeck, *Variations in Value Orientations* (Evanston, IL: Row, Peterson, 1961).

75. A. Gove, "Culture Club," *Red Herring,* November 1998.

76. K. L. Newman and S. D. Nolan, "Culture and Congruence: The Fit between Management Practices and National Culture," *Journal of International Business Studies* 27 (1996), pp. 753–79; G. Hofstede, "Cultural Constraints in Management Theories," *Academy of Management Executive* 7 (1993), pp. 81–94; G. Hofstede, *Culture's Consequences: International Differences in Work-Related Values* (Beverly Hills, CA: Sage, 1980).

77. F. S. Niles, "Individualism-Collectivism Revisited," *Cross-Cultural Research* 32 (November 1998), pp. 315–41; C. P. Earley and C. B. Gibson, "Taking Stock in Our Progress on Individualism-Collectivism: 100 Years of Solidarity and Community," *Journal of Management* 24 (May 1998), pp. 265–304; W. G. Stephan and C. W. Stephan, *Intergroup Relations* (Boulder, CO: Westview, 1996), pp. 119–21; J. A. Wagner III, "Studies of Individualism-Collectivism: Effects of Cooperation in Groups," *Academy of Management Journal* 38 (1995), pp. 152–72; H. C. Triandis, *Individualism and Collectivism* (Boulder, CO: Westview, 1995).

78. M. Erez and P. Christopher Earley, *Culture, Self-Identity, and Work* (New York: Oxford University Press, 1993), pp. 126–27.

79. Erez and Earley, *Culture, Self-Identity, and Work,* p. 127.

80. G. Hofstede, *Cultures and Organizations: Software of the Mind* (New York: McGraw-Hill, 1991), p. 124. Hofstede used the terms *masculinity* and *femininity* for achievement and nurturing orientation, respectively. We have adopted the latter to minimize the sexist perspective of these concepts. The achievement and nurturing orientation labels are also used in

G. R. Jones, J. M. George, and C. W. L. Hill, *Contemporary Management* (New York: Irwin/McGraw-Hill, 1998), pp. 112–13.

81. C. W. Stephan, W. G. Stephan, I. Saito, and S. M. Barnett, "Emotional Expression in Japan and the United States: The Nonmonolithic Nature of Individualism and Collectivism," *Journal of Cross-Cultural Psychology* 29 (November 1998), pp. 728–48; D. Matsumoto, T. Kudoh, and S. Takeuchi, "Changing Patterns of Individualism and Collectivism in the United States and Japan," *Culture and Psychology* 2 (1996), pp. 77–107.

82. For counterarguments to these criticisms, see G. Hofstede, "Attitudes, Values and Organizational Culture: Disentangling the Concepts," *Organization Studies* 19 (June 1998), pp. 477–92.

83. J. Evensen, "Ethical Behavior in Business and Life Is Its Own Reward," *Deseret News* (Salt Lake City), October 19, 1997.

84. W. H. Shaw and V. Barry, *Moral Issues in Business*, 5th ed. (Belmont, CA: Wadsworth, 1992), chaps. 1–3; and M. G. Velasquez, *Business Ethics*, 2nd ed. (Englewood Cliffs, NJ: Prentice Hall, 1988), chap. 2.

85. R. Berenbeim, "The Search for Global Ethics," *Vital Speeches of the Day* 65 (January 1999), pp. 177–78.

86. L. Kohlberg, *Essays in Moral Development*, vol. 1: *The Philosophy of Moral Development* (New York: Harper and Row, 1981).

87. L. Everett, D. Thorne, and C. Danehower, "Cognitive Moral Development and Attitudes toward Women Executives," *Journal of Business Ethics* 15 (November 1996), pp. 1227–35.

88. T. I. White, "Sexual Harassment: Trust and the Ethic of Care," *Business and Society Review*, 100–1 (January 1998), pp. 9–20; T. I. White, "Business, Ethics, and Carol Gilligan's 'Two Voices,'" *Business Ethics Quarterly* 2 (1992), pp. 51–61.

89. J. J. Hoffman, "Are Women Really More Ethical Than Men? Maybe It Depends on the Situation," *Journal of Managerial Issues* 10 (Spring 1998), pp. 60–73; S. Galbraith and H. Stephenson, "Decision Rules Used by Male and Female Business Students in Making Ethical Value Judgments: Another Look," *Journal of Business Ethics* 12 (1993), pp. 227–33.

90. A. Singhapakdi, S. Vitell, and K. Kraft, "Moral Intensity and Ethical Decision Making of Marketing Professionals," *Journal of Business Research* 36 (1996), 248–55; S. A. Morris and R. A. McDonald, "The Role of Moral Intensity in Moral Judgments: An Empirical Investigation," *Journal of Business Ethics* 14 (1995), pp. 715–26; T. J. Jones, "Ethical Decision Making by Individuals in Organizations: An Issue Contingent Model," *Academy of Management Review* 16 (1991), pp. 366–95.

91. J. R. Sparks and S. D. Hunt, "Marketing Researcher Ethical Sensitivity: Conceptualization, Measurement, and Exploratory Investigation," *Journal of Marketing* 62 (April 1998), pp. 92–109.

92. J. Evensen, "Ethical Behavior in Business and Life Is Its Own Reward"; S. A. Morris, K. A. Rehbein, J. C. Hosseini, and R. L. Armacost, "A Test of Environmental, Situational, and Personal Influences on the Ethical Intentions of CEOs," *Business and Society* 34 (1995), pp. 119–46. For a discussion of the situational effects on ethical conduct, see C. J. Thompson, "A Contextualist Proposal for the Conceptualization and Study of Marketing Ethics," *Journal of Public Policy and Marketing* 14 (1995), pp. 177–91.

93. D. Jones, "Balancing Ethics and Technology," *USA Today*, April 27, 1998, p. A1; N. R. Brooks, "The Often-Thin Line between Cheating and Competing," *Los Angeles Times*, November 3, 1997, p. D9.

94. P. Haapaniemi and W. R. Hill, "Not Just for the Big Guys!" *Chief Executive*, September 1998, pp. 62–73.

95. G. Lawton, "Fighting Back Against the Bribery Culture," *Chemistry and Industry*, December 7, 1998, p. 957; T. H. Stevenson and C. D. Bodkin, "A Cross-National Comparison of University Students' Perceptions Regarding the Ethics and Acceptability of Sales Practices," *Journal of Business Ethics* 17 (January 1998), pp. 45–55; T. Jackson and M. C. Artola, "Ethical Beliefs and Management Behavior: A Cross-Cultural Comparison," *Journal of Business Ethics* 16 (August 1997), pp. 1163–73; S. J. Carroll and M. J. Gannon, *Ethical Dimensions of International Management* (Thousand Oaks, CA: Sage, 1997); M-K. Nyaw and I. Ignace, "A Comparative Analysis of Ethical Beliefs: A Four Country Study," *Journal of Business Ethics* 13 (1994), pp. 543–55; W. R. Swinyard, H. Rinne, and A. K. Kau, "The Morality of Software Piracy: A Cross-Cultural Analysis," *Journal of Business Ethics* 9 (1990), pp. 655–64.

96. S. J. Vitell, S. L. Nwachukwu, and J. H. Barnes, "The Effects of Culture on Ethical Decision-Making: An Application of Hofstede's Typology," *Journal of Business Ethics* 12 (1993), pp. 753–60; R. Abratt, D. Nel, and N. S. Higgs, "An Examination of the Ethical Beliefs of Managers Using Selected Scenarios in a Cross-Cultural Environment," *Journal of Business Ethics* 11 (1992), pp. 29–35; S. Lysonski and W. Gaidis, "A Cross-Cultural Comparison of the Ethics of Business Students," *Journal of Business Ethics* 10 (1991), pp. 141–50.

97. This point relates to the attitude-behavior model described earlier in the chapter. See J. Weber and J. Gillespie, "Differences in Ethical Beliefs, Intentions, and Behaviors," *Business and Society* 37 (December 1998), pp. 447–67.

98. P. F. Buller, J. J. Kohls, and K. S. Anderson, "A Model for Addressing Cross-Cultural Ethical Conflicts," *Business and Society* 36 (June 1997), pp. 169–93.

99. Institute of Business Ethics, *Report on Business Ethics Codes 1998* (www.ibe.org.uk); "Ethical Business Practices Hit the Spotlight," *Emerging Markets Datafile: Nation*, January 7, 1998; J. Alexander, "On the Right Side," *Worldbusiness* 3 (January–February 1997), pp. 38–41.

100. H. Q. Langenderfer, "Ethics Are Hard to Instill When Core Values Missing," *Chapel Hill Herald* (NC), June 23, 1998, p. 4; M. A. Clark and S. L. Leonard, "Can Corporate Codes of Ethics Influence Behavior?" *Journal of Business Ethics* 17 (April 1998), pp. 619–30.

101. A. E. Tenbrunsel, "Misrepresentation and

Expectations of Misrepresentation in an Ethical Dilemma: The Role of Incentives and Temptation," *Academy of Management Journal* 41 (June 1998), pp. 330–39; J. Settel and N. B. Kurland, "Can We Create a Conflict-Free Commission Payment System?" *Business and Society Review* 100–1 (January 1998), pp. 33–44; E. Jansen and M. A. Von Glinow, "Ethical Ambivalence and Organizational Reward Systems," *Academy of Management Review* 10 (1985), pp. 814–22.

102. L. Lavelle, "Doing the Right Thing," *Bergen County Record* (NJ), March 22, 1998, p. B1; G. A. Johnston, "Can Nice Guys Finish First?" *Executive Excellence* 14 (June 1997), pp. 9–10.

103. R. P. Nielson, "Can Ethical Character Be Stimulated and Enabled? An Action-Learning Approach to Teaching and Learning Organizational Ethics," *Business Ethics Quarterly* 8 (July 1998), pp. 581–604.

Chapter Eight

1. Adapted from information in K. Barnes, "The Microsoft Lexicon" (www.cinepad.com/mslex.htm); S. Greenhouse, "Braindump on the Blue Badge: A Guide to Microspeak," *New York Times*, August 13, 1998, p. G1; M. A. Cusumano, "How Microsoft Makes Large Teams Work like Small Teams," *Sloan Management Review* 39 (Fall 1997), pp. 9–20. The opening quotation is fictitious, but uses phrases actually found in Microsoft e-mail. Roughly translated, it says: "Hi Jack, I've worked out a rough solution to the user interface problem. We need to examine the finer details. Unfortunately, I'm away next week, so you need to devote time and energy to this problem. I'm worried that the permanent Microsoft employees on this project will get really angry when they realize that we are getting behind on the released-to-manufacturing date." ("OOF" means "out of office feature" in e-mail that sends a vacation message response to all incoming e-mail.)

2. L. E. Penley, E. R. Alexander, I. E. Jernigan, and C. L. Henwood, "Communication Abilities of Managers: The Relationship to Performance," *Journal of Management* 17 (1991), pp. 57–76; H. Mintzberg, *The Nature of Managerial Work* (New York: Harper & Row, 1973); E. T. Klemmer and F. W. Snyder, "Measurement of Time Spent Communicating," *Journal of Communication* 22 (June 1972), pp. 142–58.

3. R. Grenier and G. Metes, "Wake Up and Smell the Syzygy," *Business Communications Review* 28 (August 1998), pp. 57–60; "We Are the World," *CIO* 9 (August 1996), p. 24.

4. S. Greengard, "Will Your Culture Support KM?" *Workforce* 77 (October 1998), pp. 93–94; M. N. Martinez, "The Collective Power of Employee Knowledge," *HRMagazine* 43 (February 1998), pp. 88–94; R. K. Buckman, "Knowledge Sharing at Buckman Labs," *Journal of Business Strategy*, January–February 1998, pp. 11–15.

5. R. T. Barker and M. R. Camarata, "The Role of Communication in Creating and Maintaining a Learning Organization: Preconditions, Indicators, and Disciplines," *Journal of Business Communication* 35 (October 1998), pp. 443–67.

6. G. Calabrese, "Communication and Co-operation in Product Development: A Case Study of a European Car Producer," *R & D Management* 27 (July 1997), pp. 239–52; C. Downs, P. Clampitt, and A. L. Pfeiffer, "Communication and Organizational Outcomes," in *Handbook of Organizational Communication*, G. Goldhaber and G. Barnett, eds. (Norwood, NJ: Ablex, 1988), pp. 171–211.

7. V. L. Shalin and G. V. Prabhu, "A Cognitive Perspective on Manual Assembly," *Ergonomics* 39 (1996), pp. 108–27; I. Nonaka and H. Takeuchi, *The Knowledge-Creating Company* (New York: Oxford University Press, 1995).

8. L. K. Lewis and D. R. Seibold, "Communication During Intra-organizational Innovation Adoption: Predicting User's Behavioral Coping Responses to Innovations in Organizations," *Communication Monographs* 63, no. 2 (1996), pp. 131–57; S. G. Strauss and J. E. McGrath, "Does the Medium Matter? The Interaction of Task Type and Technology on Group Performance and Member Reactions," *Journal of Applied Psychology* 79 (1994), pp. 87–97;

R. T. Mowday, L. W. Porter, and R. M. Steers, *Employee-Organization Linkages* (New York: Academic Press, 1982); R. J. Burke and D. S. Wilcox, "Effects of Different Patterns and Degrees of Openness in Superior-Subordinate Communication on Subordinate Satisfaction," *Academy of Management Journal* 12 (1969), pp. 319–26.

9. C. E. Shannon and W. Weaver, *The Mathematical Theory of Communication* (Urbana: University of Illinois Press, 1949). For a more recent discussion, see: K. J. Krone, F. M. Jablin, and L. L. Putnam, "Communication Theory and Organizational Communication: Multiple Perspectives," in *Handbook of Organizational Communication: An Interdisciplinary Perspective*, F. M. Jablin, L. L. Putnam, K. H. Roberts, and L. W. Porter, eds. (Newbury Park, CA: Sage, 1987), pp. 18–40.

10. S. Axley, "Managerial and Organizational Communication in Terms of the Conduit Metaphor," *Academy of Management Review* 9 (1984), pp. 428–37.

11. M. Meissner, "The Language of Work," in R. Dubin, ed.. *Handbook of Work, Organization, and Society* (Chicago: Rand McNally, 1976), pp. 205–79.

12. M. J. Glauser, "Upward Information Flow in Organizations: Review and Conceptual Analysis," *Human Relations* 37 (1984), pp. 613–43.

13. L. Larwood, "Don't Struggle to Scope Those Metaphors Yet," *Group and Organization Management* 17 (1992), pp. 249–54; and L. R. Pondy, P. J. Frost, G. Morgan, and T. C. Dandridge, eds., *Organizational Symbolism* (Greenwich, CT: JAI Press, 1983).

14. M. Kaeter, "Quality through Clarity," *Quality*, May 1993, pp. 19–22.

15. J. Gleick, "A Bug by Any Other Name," *New York Times Magazine*, June 17, 1997.

16. A. Markham, "Designing Discourse: A Critical Analysis of Strategic Ambiguity and Workplace Control," *Management Communication Quarterly* 9 (1996), pp. 389–421; Larwood, "Don't Struggle to Scope Those Metaphors Yet"; R. Mead, *Cross-Cultural Management Communication* (Chichester, UK: John Wiley, 1990), pp. 130–37;

E. M. Eisenberg, "Ambiguity as a Strategy in Organizational Communication," *Communication Monographs* 51 (1984), pp. 227–42; R. Daft and J. Wiginton, "Language and Organization," *Academy of Management Review* 4 (1979), pp. 179–91.

17. M. F. R. Kets de Vries, "Creative Leadership: Jazzing Up Business," *Chief Executive*, no. 121 (March 1997), pp. 64–66; G. Morgan, *Images of Organization*, 2nd ed. (Thousand Oaks, CA: Sage, 1997); L. L. Putnam, Nelson Phillips, and P. Chapman, "Metaphors of Communication and Organization," in S. R. Clegg, C. Hardy, and W. R. Nord, eds., *Handbook of Organization Studies* (London: Sage, 1996), pp. 373–408.

18. D. Simpson and D. W. Patterson "Technology Can Be Harmful to Your Mental Health," *Greensboro News & Record* (NC), June 3, 1997, p. D1; D. W. Patterson and D. Simpson, "Technology's Touch: What Is the Information Age Doing to Connect and Disconnect Mankind?" *Greensboro News & Record* (NC), June 1, 1997, p. D1.

19. K. D. Grimsley "Workers Bombarded by Messages," *Spokane.net*, May 24, 1998; Pitney Bowes, Inc. "Are Workers Overwhelmed by Communications?" News release (www.pitneybowes.com), May 1997.

20. A. G. Schick, L. A. Gordon, and S. Haka, "Information Overload: A Temporal Approach," *Accounting, Organizations & Society* 15 (1990), pp. 199–220; K. Alesandrini, *Survive Information Overload* (Burr Ridge, IL: Business One-Irwin, 1993).

21. J. Kaye, "The Devil You Know," *Computer Weekly*, March 19, 1998, p. 46; D. Shenk, "Data Smog: Surviving the Info Glut," *Technology Review* 100 (May–June 1997), pp. 18–26.

22. Schick et al., "Information Overload," pp. 209–14; C. Stohl and W. C. Redding, "Messages and Message Exchange Processes," in *Handbook of Organizational Communication: An Interdisciplinary Perspective*, Jablin et al., eds., pp. 451–502.

23. Pitney Bowes, "Study Finds Growth of Communication Options Is Fundamentally Changing Work," News release (www.pitneybowes.com), April 8,

1997. Bill Gates personally answers e-mail from Microsoft employees, but relies on the buffer to sort e-mail and respond to messages from outside the company.

24. L. Porter and K. Roberts, "Communication in Organizations," in *Handbook of Industrial and Organizational Psychology*, M. Dunnette, ed. (Chicago: Rand McNally, 1976), pp. 1553–89.

25. J. H. E. Andriessen, "Mediated Communication and New Organizational Forms," *International Review of Industrial and Organizational Psychology* 6 (1991), pp. 17–70.

26. J. L. Locke, "Q: Is E-Mail Degrading Public and Private Discourse?; Yes: Electronic Mail Is Making Us Rude, Lonely, Insensitive and Dishonest," *Insight on the News*, October 19, 1998, p. 24; J. Hunter and M. Allen, "Adaptation to Electronic Mail," *Journal of Applied Communication Research*, August 1992, pp. 254–74; M. Culnan and M. L. Markus, "Information Technologies," in *Handbook of Organizational Communication: An Interdisciplinary Perspective*, Jablin et al., eds., pp. 420–43.

27. C. S. Saunders, D. Robey, and K. A. Vaverek, "The Persistence of Status Differentials in Computer Conferencing," *Human Communications Research* 20 (1994), pp. 443–72; D. A. Adams, P. A. Todd, and R. R. Nelson, "A Comparative Evaluation of the Impact of Electronic and Voice Mail on Organizational Communication," *Information & Management* 24 (1993), pp. 9–21.

28. M. M. Extejt, "Teaching Students to Correspond Effectively Electronically: Tips for Using Electronic Mail Properly," *Business Communication Quarterly* 61 (June 1998), pp. 57–67.

29. Hein, "Communication Breakdown"; V. Frazee, "Is E-Mail Doing More Harm than Good?" *Personnel Journal* 75 (May 1996), p. 23.

30. A. Gumbel, "How E-Mail Puts Us in a Flaming Bad Temper," *The Independent* (London), January 3, 1999, p. 14; J. Kaye, "The Devil You Know," *Computer Weekly*, March 19, 1998, p. 46; S. Kennedy, "The Burning Issue of Electronic Hate Mail," *Computer Weekly*, June 5,

1997, p. 22; D. Asbrand, "E-Mail 'Flame' Messages Can Ignite Office Angst," *InfoWorld*, December 6, 1993, p. 74; J. Goode and M. Johnson, "Putting Out the Flames: The Etiquette of E-Mail," *Online*, November 1991, pp. 61–65.

31. A. D. Shulman, "Putting Group Information Technology in Its Place: Communication and Good Work Group Performance," in Clegg et al., eds., *Handbook of Organization Studies*, pp. 373–408.

32. J. Jacons, "An Unhappy, Wired World out There," *Tulsa World*, September 5, 1998.

33. C. Meyer and S. Davis, *Blur: The Speed of Change in the Connected Economy* (Reading, MA: Addison-Wesley, 1998); P. Bordia "Face-to-Face versus Computer-Mediated Communication: A Synthesis of the Experimental Literature," *Journal of Business Communication* 34 (January 1997), pp. 99–120.

34. A. Mahlon, "The Alternative Workplace: Changing Where and How People Work," *Harvard Business Review* 76, May–June 1998, pp. 121–30.

35. J. S. Brown, "Seeing Differently: A Role for Pioneering Research," *Research Technology Management* 41 (May–June 1998), pp. 24–33; in particular, see comments by George Gilder, who is credited with developing the law of telecosm, in "Is Bigger Better?" *Fast Company*, Issue 17 (September 1998).

36. K. Ohlson, "Leadership in an Age of Mistrust," *Industry Week*, February 2, 1998, pp. 37–46.

37. "New Age Heralds End of Information Overload," *Financial News*, December 8, 1998.

38. R. E. Rice and D. E. Shook, "Relationships of Job Categories and Organizational Levels to Use of Communication Channels, Including Electronic Mail: A Meta-Analysis and Extension," *Journal of Management Studies* 27 (1990), pp. 195–229; Sitkin et al., "A Dual-Capacity Model of Communication Media Choice in Organizations," p. 584.

39. T. E. Harris, *Applied Organizational Communication: Perspectives, Principles, and Pragmatics* (Hillsdale, NJ: Lawrence Erlbaum Associates, 1993), chap. 5; A. Mehrabian, *Silent Messages*, 2nd

ed. (Belmont, CA: Wadsworth, 1981).

40. J. A. Morris and D. C. Feldman, "The Dimensions, Antecedents, and Consequences of Emotional Labor," *Academy of Management Review* 21 (1996), pp. 986–1010.

41. B. Parkinson, *Ideas and Realities of Emotion* (London: Routledge, 1995), pp. 182–83; E. Hatfield, J. T. Cacioppo, and R. L. Rapson, *Emotional Contagion* (Cambridge: Cambridge University Press, 1993).

42. R. L. Daft, R. H. Lengel, and L. K. Tevino, "Message Equivocality, Media Selection, and Manager Performance: Implications for Information Systems," *MIS Quarterly* 11 (1987), pp. 355–66.

43. R. Lengel and R. Daft, "The Selection of Communication Media as an Executive Skill," *Academy of Management Executive* 2 (1988), pp. 225–32; G. Huber and R. Daft, "The Information Environments of Organizations," in *Handbook of Organizational Communication: An Interdisciplinary Perspective*, Jablin et al., eds., pp. 130–64; R. Daft and R. Lengel, "Information Richness: A New Approach to Managerial Behavior and Organization Design," *Research in Organizational Behavior* 6 (1984), pp. 191–233.

44. R. E. Rice, "Task Analyzability, Use of New Media, and Effectiveness: A Multi-Site Exploration of Media Richness," *Organization Science* 3 (1992) pp. 475–500; J. Fulk, C. W. Steinfield, J. Schmitz, and J. G. Power, "A Social Information Processing Model of Media Use in Organizations," *Communication Research* 14 (1987), pp. 529–52.

45. R. Madhavan and R. Grover, "From Embedded Knowledge to Embodied Knowledge: New Product Development as Knowledge Management," *Journal of Marketing* 62 (October 1998), pp. 1–12; D. Stork and A. Sapienza, "Task and Human Messages over the Project Life Cycle: Matching Media to Messages," *Project Management Journal* 22 (December 1992), pp. 44–49.

46. M. McLuhan, *Understanding Media: The Extensions of Man* (New York: McGraw-Hill, 1964).

47. S. B. Sitkin, K. M. Sutcliffe, and J. R. Barrios-Choplin, "A Dual-Capacity Model of Communication Media Choice in Organizations," *Human Communication Research* 18 (June 1992), pp. 563–98; J. Schmitz and J. Fulk, "Organizational Colleagues, Media Richness, and Electronic Mail: A Test of the Social Influence Model of Technology Use," *Communication Research* 18 (1991), pp. 487–523.

48. S. Baker, "Job Satisfaction High in Survey, But Office Politics Alive and Well," *Fort Worth Star-Telegram*, March 13, 1997, p. 3; B. Schneider, S. D. Ashworth, A. C. Higgs, and L. Carr, "Design, Validity, and Use of Strategically Focused Employee Attitude Surveys," *Personnel Psychology* 49 (1996), pp. 695–705; T. Geddie, "Surveys Are a Waste of Time . . . until You Use Them," *Communication World*, April 1996, pp. 24–26; D. M. Saunders and J. D. Leck, "Formal Upward Communication Procedures: Organizational and Employee Perspectives," *Canadian Journal of Administrative Sciences* 10 (1993), pp. 255–68.

49. D. Stellfox, "Survey Firm Finds NRC Employees' Job Views Are Close to National Norms," *Inside N.R.C.* 20 (July 6, 1998), p. 8; K. Mark, "No More Pink Slips," *Human Resources Professional*, November 1996, pp. 21–23; R. V. Lindahl, "Automation Breaks the Language Barrier," *HRMagazine* 41 (March 1996), pp. 79–83.

50. F. Santiago, "Diversity Awareness Makes Inroads into Corporate Culture," *Houston Chronicle*, February 16, 1997, p. 3; T. Geddie, "Surveys Are a Waste of Time and Money . . . ," pp. 24–26; M. Allix, "Surveys Plumb Corporate Depths," *Asian Business*, November 1996.

51. J. Walsh, "BBC Extends Air Time for Employees," *People Management* 4 (February 19, 1998), p. 11; P. Schofield, "Smart Moves: Knowledge Is Power," *The Independent* (London), February 8, 1998, p. 2; "Airline Rises to Internal Communications Challenges," *PR News*, January 22, 1996.

52. "Modernize Your Agency's Internal Communications," *Federal Human Resources Week*, April 13, 1998; "Postal Service Targets Employees with New Communication Systems," *PR News* 53, no.15 (April 14, 1997).

53. T. Peters and R. Waterman, *In Search of Excellence* (New York: Harper & Row, 1982), p. 122; W. Ouchi, *Theory Z* (New York: Avon Books, 1981), pp. 176–77.

54. J. P. Donlon et. al., "In Search of the New Change Leader," *Chief Executive*, November 1997, pp. 64–75.

55. S. Branch, "The 100 Best Companies to Work for in America," *Fortune*, January 11, 1999, pp. 118–44; M. Goldberg, "Cisco's Most Important Meal of the Day," *Fast Company*, no. 13 (February 1998), p. 56.

56. M. Young and J. E. Post, "Managing to Communicate, Communicating to Change: How Leading Companies Communicate with Employees," *Organizational Dynamics* 22 (Summer 1993), pp. 31–43.

57. J. Gertzen, "Commander Strives to Know His Troops," *Omaha World Herald*, February 20, 1997, p. 1.

58. M. G. Katz, "So, What's My Motivation? Employee Incentives in a Changing Industry," *American Gas*, February 1998, pp. 28–32.

59. M. Maruyama, *Mindscapes in Management* (Aldershot, UK: Dartmouth, 1994), pp. 33–34.

60. "Places to Linger," *The Economist* 348 (August 1, 1998), pp. 55–56; M. Jackson, "Walls Come Tumbling Down," *Akron Beacon Journal*, May 21, 1998; K. A. Edelman, "Take Down the Walls! Open Office," *Across the Board* 34 (March 1997), pp. 32–38; G. Levitch, "Pizzas and Piazzas: Workplace of the Future," *Globe and Mail* (Toronto), October 12, 1996, p. C7.

61. L. Chadderdon, "Nortel Switches Cities," *Fast Company*, no. 16 (August 1998).

62. L. Stuart, "Why Space Is the New Frontier," *The Guardian* (London), October 31, 1998, p. 24; J. Kroho, Jr., "What Makes an Office Work?" *Across the Board*, May 1993, pp. 16–23; T. Peters, *Liberation Management: Necessary Disorganization for the Nanosecond Nineties* (New York: Knopf, 1992), pp. 379–80; T. H. Walker, "Designing Work Environments That Promote Corporate Productivity," *Site Selection and Industrial Development*, April 1992, pp. 8–10.

63. A. Goldman, "Implications of Japanese Total Quality Control for Western Organizations: Dimensions of an Intercultural Hybrid," *Journal of Business Communication* 30

(1993), pp. 29–47; J. P. Womack, D. T. Jones, and D. Roos, *The Machine That Changed the World* (New York: Rawson, 1990), p. 79.

64. T. Petzinger Jr., "Elimination of Permanent Desks Has Some Office Workers Fuming," *Chicago Tribune*, April 13, 1997, p. H5; J. Macht, "When the Walls Come Tumbling Down," *Inc. Technology* 17 (September 1995), pp. 70–72; F. Becker, "A Workplace by Any Other Name: The Unassigned Office," *Facilities Design & Management* 12 (July 1993), pp. 50–53.

65. A. K. Stone, "Office as Hotel," *Washington Business Journal*, February 1, 1999.

66. S. Kirsner, "Every Day, It's a New Place," *Fast Company*, April–May, 1998, pp. 130–34; J. S. Russell, "A Company Headquarters Planned for Flexibility," *New York Times*, September 7, 1997, p. 7; P. LaBarre, "The Dis-Organization of Oticon," *Industry Week*, July 18, 1994, pp. 23–28.

67. T. Davis, "The Influence of the Physical Environment in Offices," *Academy of Management Review* 9, no. 2 (1984), pp. 271–83; S. B. Bacharach and M. Aitken, "Communications in Administrative Bureaucracies," *Academy of Management Journal* 20 (1977), pp. 365–77.

68. A. Minnick and K. Pischke-Winn, "Work Redesign: Making It a Reality," *Nursing Management*, October 1996, pp. 61–65.

69. "Survey Finds Good and Bad Points on Worker Attitudes," *Eastern Pennsylvania Business Journal*, May 5, 1997, p. 13.

70. G. Kreps, *Organizational Communication* (White Plains, NY: Longman, 1986), pp. 202–6; W. L. Davis and J. R. O'Connor, "Serial Transmission of Information: A Study of the Grapevine," *Journal of Applied Communication Research* 5 (1977), pp. 61–72; K. Davis, "Management Communication and the Grapevine," *Harvard Business Review* 31 (September–October 1953), pp. 43–49.

71. R. L. Rosnow, "Inside Rumor: A Personal Journey," *American Psychologist* 46 (May 1991), pp. 484–96; C. J. Walker and C. A. Beckerle, "The Effect of State Anxiety on Rumor Transmission," *Journal of Social Behavior &*

Personality 2 (August 1987), pp. 353–60.

72. N. Fitzgerald, "Spread the Word," *The Accountant's Magazine* 97 (February 1993), pp. 32–33.

73. D. Krackhardt and J. R. Hanson, "Informal Networks: The Company Behind the Chart," *Harvard Business Review* 71 (July–August 1993), pp. 104–11; H. Mintzberg, *The Structuring of Organizations* (Englewood Cliffs, NJ: Prentice Hall, 1979), pp. 46–53.

74. M. Noon and R. Delbridge, "News from Behind My Hand: Gossip in Organizations," *Organization Studies* 14 (1993), pp. 23–36.

75. G. Dutton, "One Workforce, Many Languages," *Management Review* 87 (December 1998), pp. 42–47.

76. Ohlson, "Leadership in an Age of Mistrust."

77. A. Hall and D. J. Hall "Cultural Crossroads," *Wisconsin State Journal* (*Madison*), March 29, 1998, p. B1.

78. E. Daniels, "Back to School," *Florida Times-Union* (*Jacksonville*), May 24, 1999, p. 14.

79. F. Cunningham, "A Touch of the Tartan Treatment for Mazda," *The Scotsman*, October 14, 1997, p. 27.

80. R. M. March, *Reading the Japanese Mind* (Tokyo: Kodansha, 1996), chap. 1; H. Yamada, *American and Japanese Business Discourse: A Comparison of Interaction Styles* (Norwood, NJ: Ablex, 1992), p. 34.

81. "E-Mail, Bloody E-Mail," *Training*, January 1996, p. 12.

82. R. Axtell, *Gestures: The Do's and Taboos of Body Language Around the World* (New York: John Wiley, 1991); P. Harris and R. Moran, *Managing Cultural Differences* (Houston: Gulf, 1987); and P. Ekman, W. V. Friesen, and J. Bear, "The International Language of Gestures," *Psychology Today*, May 1984, pp. 64–69.

83. H. Yamada, *Different Games, Different Rules* (New York: Oxford University Press, 1997), pp. 76–79; H. Yamada, *American and Japanese Business Discourse*, chap. 2; D. Tannen, *Talking from 9 to 5* (New York: Avon, 1994), pp. 96–97; D. C. Barnlund, *Communication Styles of Japanese and Americans: Images and Realities* (Belmont, CA: Wadsworth, 1988).

84. D. Goleman, "What Makes a Leader?" *Harvard Business Review* 76 (November–December 1998), pp. 92–102.

85. S. Herring, "Gender Differences in Computer-Mediated Communication: Bringing Familiar Baggage to the New Frontier," paper presented at the American Library Association Annual Conference, Miami, Florida, June 27, 1994.

86. M. Crawford, *Talking Difference: On Gender and Language* (Thousand Oaks, CA: Sage, 1995), pp. 41–44; Tannen, *Talking from 9 to 5*; D. Tannen, *You Just Don't Understand: Men and Women in Conversation* (New York: Ballantine Books, 1990); S. Helgesen, *The Female Advantage: Women's Ways of Leadership* (New York: Doubleday, 1990).

87. A. Mulac et al., "'Uh-Huh. What's That All About?' Differing Interpretations of Conversational Backchannels and Questions as Sources of Miscommunication across Gender Boundaries," *Communication Research* 25 (December 1998), pp. 641–68; G. H. Graham, J. Unruh, and P. Jennings, "The Impact of Nonverbal Communication in Organizations: A Survey of Perceptions," *Journal of Business Communication* 28 (1991), pp. 45–61; J. Hall, "Gender Effects in Decoding Nonverbal Cues," *Psychological Bulletin* 68 (1978), pp. 845–57.

88. This stereotypic notion is prevalent throughout J. Gray, *Men Are from Mars, Women Are from Venus* (New York: HarperCollins, 1992). For a critique of this view, see Crawford, *Talking Difference*, chap. 4; D. J. Canary, T. M. Emmers-Sommer, *Sex and Gender Differences in Personal Relationships* (New York: Guilford Press, 1997), chap. 1.

89. P. Tripp-Knowles "A Review of the Literature on Barriers Encountered by Women in Science Academia," *Resources for Feminist Research* 24 (Spring–Summer 1995) pp. 28–34.

90. Cited in K. Davis and J. W. Newstrom, *Human Behavior at Work: Organizational Behavior*, 7th ed. (New York: McGraw-Hill, 1985), p. 438.

91. J. Brownell, *Building Active Learning Skills* (Englewood Cliffs, NJ: Prentice Hall, 1986); A. Mikalachki, "Does Anyone

Listen to the Boss?" *Business Horizons*, March–April 1982, pp. 34–39.

92. S. Silverstein, "On the Job, But Do They Listen?" *Los Angeles Times*, July 19, 1998.

93. A. P. Brief, *Attitudes in and around Organizations* (Thousand Oaks, CA: Sage, 1998), pp. 69–84; K. K. Reardon, *Persuasion in Practice* (Newbury Park, CA: Sage, 1991); P. Zimbardo and E. B. Ebbeson, *Influencing Attitudes and Changing Behavior* (Reading, MA: Addison-Wesley, 1969).

94. J. Cooper and R. T. Coyle, "Attitudes and Attitude Change," *Annual Review of Psychology* 35 (1984), pp. 395–426; and N. MacLachlan, "What People Really Think about Fast Talkers," *Psychology Today* 113 (November 1979), pp. 112–17.

95. J. A. Conger, *Winning 'Em Over: A New Model for Managing in the Age of Persuasion* (New York: Simon & Schuster, 1998).

96. D. B. Freeland, "Turning Communication into Influence," *HR Magazine* 38 (September 1993), pp. 93–96; M. Snyder and M. Rothbart, "Communicator Attractiveness and Opinion Change," *Canadian Journal of Behavioural Science* 3 (1971), pp. 377–87.

97. E. Aronson, *The Social Animal* (San Francisco: W. H. Freeman, 1976), pp. 67–68; and R. A. Jones and J. W. Brehm, "Persuasiveness of One- and Two-Sided Communications as a Function of Awareness That There Are Two Sides," *Journal of Experimental Social Psychology* 6 (1970), pp. 47–56.

98. D. G. Linz and S. Penrod, "Increasing Attorney Persuasiveness in the Courtroom," *Law and Psychology Review* 8 (1984), pp. 1–47; R. B. Zajonc, "Attitudinal Effects of Mere Exposure," *Journal of Personality and Social Psychology Monograph* 9 (1968), pp. 1–27; and R. Petty and J. Cacioppo, *Attitudes and Persuasion: Classic and Contemporary Approaches* (Dubuque, Iowa: W. C. Brown, 1981).

99. Conger, *Winning 'Em Over*.

100. Zimbardo and Ebbeson, *Influencing Attitudes and Changing Behavior*.

101. M. Zellner, "Self-Esteem, Reception, and Influenceability," *Journal of Personality and Social Psychology* 15 (1970), pp. 87–93.

Chapter Nine

1. S. Kirsner, "Every Day, It's a New Place," *Fast Company*, April–May, 1998, pp. 130–34; J. S. Russell, "A Company Headquarters Planned for Flexibility," *New York Times*, September 7, 1997, p. 7.

2. J. Pfeffer, "Seven Practices of Successful Organizations," *California Management Review* 40 (1998), pp. 96–124.

3. P. Carbonara, "Mervyn's Call in the SWAT Team," *Fast Company*, April–May 1998, pp. 54–55; D. T. Kurylko, "Once-Grimy Eisenach Becomes Opel's Jewel," *Automotive News*, November 11, 1996, p. 42a; A. Haasen, "Opel Eisenach GMBH—Creating a High-Productivity Workplace," *Organizational Dynamics* 24 (Winter 1996), pp. 80–85; P. McDonald and A. Sharma, "Toward Work Teams Within a New Zealand Public Service Organization," paper presented at the 1994 International Conference on Self-Managing Work Teams, University of North Texas, Denton, April 1994.

4. S. G. Cohen and D. E. Bailey, "What Makes Teams Work: Group Effectiveness Research from the Shop Floor to the Executive Suite," *Journal of Management* 23 (May 1997), pp. 239–90; M. A. West, "Preface: Introducing Work Group Psychology," in M. A. West, ed., *Handbook of Work Group Psychology* (Chichester, UK: John Wiley, 1996), p. xxvi; S. A. Mohrman, S. G. Cohen, and A. M. Mohrman, Jr., *Designing Team-Based Organizations: New Forms for Knowledge Work* (San Francisco: Jossey-Bass, 1995), pp. 39–40; R. M. McIntyre and E. Salas, "Measuring and Managing for Team Performance: Emerging Principles from Complex Environments," in R. A. Guzzo, E. Salas, and Associates, eds., *Team Effectiveness and Decision Making in Organizations* (San Francisco: Jossey-Bass, 1995), pp. 9–45; J. R. Katzenbach and K. D. Smith, "The Discipline of Teams," *Harvard Business Review* 71 (March–April 1993), pp. 111–20; M. E. Shaw, *Group Dynamics*, 3rd ed. (New York: McGraw-Hill, 1981), p. 8.

5. David Nadler similarly distinguishes *crowds* from *groups* and *teams*. See D. A. Nadler, "From Ritual to Real Work: The Board as a Team," *Directors and Boards* 22 (Summer 1998), pp. 28–31.

6. The preference for using the term *team* rather than *group* is also discussed in Cohen and Bailey, "What Makes Teams Work."

7. G. E. Huszczo, *Tools for Team Excellence* (Palo Alto, CA: Davies-Black, 1996), pp. 9–15; R. Likert, *New Patterns of Management* (New York: McGraw-Hill, 1961), pp. 106–8.

8. Mohrman, Cohen, and Mohrman, *Designing Team-Based Organizations*, p. 6; J. H. Shonk, *Team-Based Organizations: Developing a Successful Team Environment* (Burr Ridge, IL: Business One Irwin, 1992).

9. C. Salter, "Roberts Rules the Road," *Fast Company*, Issue 17 (September 1998); J. Childs, "Five Years and Counting: The Path to Self-Directed Work Teams," *Hospital Materiel Management Quarterly*, May 1997, pp. 34–43.

10. N. S. Bruning and P. R. Liverpool, "Membership in Quality Circles and Participation in Decision Making," *Journal of Applied Behavioral Science* 29 (March 1993), pp. 76–95; S. D. Saleh, Z. Guo, and T. Hull, "The Use of Quality Circles in the Automobile Parts Industry," *Proceedings of the Annual ASAC Conference, Organizational Behaviour Division* 9, pt. 5 (1988), pp. 95–104.

11. Mohrman, Cohen, and Mohrman, *Designing Team-Based Organizations*, chap. 2; R. S. Wellins, W. C. Byham, and G. R. Dixon, *Inside Teams* (San Francisco: Jossey-Bass, 1994), pp. 9–10.

12. R. Pascale, "Change How You Define Leadership, and You Change How You Run a Company," *Fast Company*, April–May 1998, pp. 110–20.

13. T. Peters, *Thriving on Chaos* (New York: Alfred A. Knopf, 1987), pp. 211–18; T. Kidder, *Soul of a New Machine* (Boston: Little, Brown, 1981); T. Peters and N. Austin, *A Passion for Excellence* (New York: Random House, 1985), chaps. 9 and 10.

14. S. Zesiger, "Dial 'M' for Mystique," *Fortune*, January 12, 1998, p. 175; R. Hertzberg, "No Longer a Skunkworks," *Internet World*, November 3, 1997; R. Lim, "Innovation, Innovation, Innovation," *Business Times*

(Singapore), October 27, 1997, p. 18.

15. N. Shachtman, "Group Think," *InformationWeek On-Line*, June 1, 1998; J. Newberg, "Offices No Longer Restricted to a Fixed Site," *Arizona Republic*, April 21, 1998, p. 4; B. Manville and N. Foote, "Harvest Your Workers' Knowledge," *Datamation* 42 (July 1996), pp. 78–80.

16. J. Lipnack and J. Stamps, *Virtual Teams: Reaching Across Space, Time, and Organizations with Technology* (New York: John Wiley, 1997), pp. 5–8; D. J. Armstrong and P. Cole, "Managing Distances and Differences in Geographically Distributed Work Groups," in S. E. Jackson and M. N. Ruderman, eds., *Diversity in Work Teams: Research Paradigms for a Changing Workplace* (Washington, DC: American Psychological Association, 1995), pp. 187–215.

17. J. S. Brown, "Seeing Differently: A Role for Pioneering Research," *Research Technology Management* 41 (May–June 1998), pp. 24–33; in particular, see comments by George Gilder, who is credited with developing the law of telecosm, in "Is Bigger Better?" *Fast Company*, Issue 17 (September 1998).

18. A. M. Townsend, S. M. DeMarie, and A. R. Hendrickson, "Virtual Teams: Technology and the Workplace of the Future," *Academy of Management Executive* 12 (August 1998), pp. 17–29.

19. J. A. Wagner III, C. R. Leana, E. A. Locke, and D. M. Schweiger, "Cognitive and Motivational Frameworks in U.S. Research on Participation: A Meta-Analysis of Primary Effects," *Journal of Organizational Behavior* 18 (1997), pp. 49–65.

20. W. B. Stevenson, J. L. Pearce, and L. W. Porter, "The Concept of 'Coalition' in Organization Theory and Research," *Academy of Management Review* 10 (1985), pp. 256–68; Shaw, *Group Dynamics*, pp. 105–10.

21. B. E. Ashforth and F. Mael, "Social Identity Theory and the Organization," *Academy of Management Review* 14 (1989), pp. 20–39; L. N. Jewell and H. J. Reitz, *Group Effectiveness in Organizations* (Glenview, IL: Scott, Foresman, 1981).

22. A. S. Tannenbaum, *Social Psychology of the Work Organization* (Belmont, CA: Wadsworth, 1966), p. 62; S. Schacter, *The Psychology of Affiliation* (Stanford, CA: Stanford University Press, 1959), pp. 12–19.

23. M. A. West, C. S. Borrill, and K. L. Unsworth, "Team Effectiveness in Organizations," *International Review of Industrial and Organizational Psychology* 13 (1998), pp. 1–48; R. A. Guzzo and M. W. Dickson, "Teams in Organizations: Recent Research on Performance and Effectiveness," *Annual Review of Psychology* 47 (1996), pp. 307–38; P. S. Goodman, E. Ravlin, and M. Schminke, "Understanding Groups in Organizations," *Research in Organizational Behavior* 9 (1987), pp. 121–73.

24. M. A. West, C. S. Borrill, and K. L. Unsworth, "Team Effectiveness in Organizations," *International Review of Industrial and Organizational Psychology*, 13 (1998), pp. 1–48; Mohrman, Cohen, and Mohrman, *Designing Team-Based Organizations*, pp. 58–65; J. E. McGrath, "Time, Interaction, and Performance (TIP): A Theory of Groups," *Small Group Research* 22 (1991), pp. 147–74; G. P. Shea and R. A. Guzzo, "Group Effectiveness: What Really Matters?" *Sloan Management Review* 27 (1987), pp. 33–46.

25. "Team Incentives Prominent among 'Best-Practice' Companies," *Quality* 35 (April 1996), p. 20; for a discussion of the role of rewards in team dynamics, see J. S. DeMatteo, L. T. Eby, and E. Sundstrom, "Team-Based Rewards: Current Empirical Evidence and Directions for Future Research," in B. M. Staw and L. L. Cummings, eds., *Research in Organizational Behavior* 20 (1998), pp. 141–83; A. Barua, C. H. S. Lee, and A. B. Whinston, "Incentives and Computing Systems for Team-Based Organizations," *Organization Science* 6 (1995), pp. 487–504; R. L. Heneman and C. von Hippel, "Balancing Group and Individual Rewards: Rewarding Individual Contributions to the Team," *Compensation & Benefits Review* 27 (July–August, 1995), pp. 63–68.

26. F. Burlage, "Master the Art of Kaizen," *The European*, February 20, 1997, p. 12.

27. P. Bordia, "Face-to-Face versus Computer-Mediated Communication: A Synthesis of the Experimental Literature," *Journal of Business Communication* 34 (January 1997), pp. 99–120; A. D. Shulman, "Putting Group Information Technology in Its Place: Communication and Good Work Group Performance," in S. R. Clegg, C. Hardy, and W. R. Nord, eds., *Handbook of Organization Studies* (London: Sage, 1996), pp. 357–74; J. E. McGrath and A. B. Hollingshead, *Groups Interacting with Technology* (Thousand Oaks, CA: Sage, 1994).

28. G. Bushe, S. J. Havlovic, and G. Coetzer, "Exploring Empowerment from the Inside-Out (Part Two)," *Journal for Quality and Participation* 19 (June 1996), pp. 78–85.

29. R. Wageman, "Case Study: Critical Success Factors for Creating Superb Self-Managing Teams at Xerox," *Compensation and Benefits Review* 29 (September–October 1997), pp. 31–41; D. Dimancescu and K. Dwenger, "Smoothing the Product Development Path," *Management Review* 85 (January 1996), pp. 36–41.

30. D. G. Ancona and D. E. Caldwell, "Demography and Design: Predictors of New Product Team Performance," *Organization Science* 3 (August 1992), pp. 331–41.

31. S. Berne, "Self-Directed Teams Soup Up Operations," *Prepared Foods* 166 (September 1997), p. 32.

32. M. A. Campion, E. M. Papper, and G. J. Medsker, "Relations between Work Team Characteristics and Effectiveness: A Replication and Extension," *Personnel Psychology* 49 (1996), pp. 429–52; S. Worchel and S. L. Shackelford, "Groups Under Stress: The Influence of Group Structure and Environment on Process and Performance," *Personality & Social Psychology Bulletin* 17 (1991), pp. 640–47; E. Sundstrom, K. P. De Meuse, and D. Futrell, "Work Teams: Applications and Effectiveness," *American Psychologist* 45 (1990), pp. 120–33.

33. G. van der Vegt, B. Emans, and E. van de Vliert, "Motivating Effects of Task and Outcome Interdependence in Work Teams," *Group & Organization Management* 23 (June 1998), pp. 124–43; R. C. Liden, S. J. Wayne, and L. K. Bradway, "Task Interdependence as a Moderator of the Relation

between Group Control and Performance," *Human Relations* 50 (1997), pp. 169–81; R. Wageman, "Interdependence and Group Effectiveness," *Administrative Science Quarterly* 40 (1995), pp.145–80; M. A. Campion, G. J. Medsker, and A. C. Higgs, "Relations between Work Group Characteristics and Effectiveness: Implications for Designing Effective Work Groups," *Personnel Psychology* 46 (1993), pp. 823–50; M. N. Kiggundu, "Task Interdependence and the Theory of Job Design," *Academy of Management Review* 6 (1981), pp. 499–508.

34. M. A. Cusumano "How Microsoft Makes Large Teams Work like Small Teams," *Sloan Management Review* 39 (Fall 1997), pp. 9–20.

35. A. Muoio, "Growing Smart," *Fast Company*, no. 16 (August 1998); A. R. Sorkin, "Gospel According to St. Luke's," *New York Times*, February 12, 1998, p. D1.

36. G. R. Hickman and A. Creighton-Zollar, "Diverse Self-Directed Work Teams: Developing Strategic Initiatives for 21st Century Organizations," *Public Personnel Management* 27 (Summer 1998), pp. 187–200.

37. J. R. Katzenbach and D. K. Smith, *The Wisdom of Teams: Creating the High-Performance Organization* (Boston: Harvard University Press, 1993), pp. 45–47; and G. Stasser, "Pooling of Unshared Information during Group Discussion," in S. Worchel, W. Wood, and J. A. Simpson, eds., *Group Process and Productivity* (Newbury Park, CA: Sage, 1992), pp. 48–67.

38. R. S. Wellins, W. C. Byham, and G. R. Dixon, *Inside Teams: How 20 World-Class Organizations Are Winning through Teamwork* (San Francisco: Jossey-Bass, 1994), pp. 94–95.

39. L. T. Eby and G. H. Dobbins, "Collectivist Orientation in Teams: An Individual and Group-Level Analysis," *Journal of Organizational Behavior* 18 (1997), pp. 275–95; P. C. Earley, "East Meets West Meets Mideast: Further Explorations of Collectivistic and Individualistic Work Groups," *Academy of Management Journal* 36 (1993), pp. 319–48.

40. R. Klimoski and R. G. Jones, "Staffing for Effective Group Decision Making: Key Issues in Matching People and Teams," in Guzzo, Salas, and Associates, eds., *Team Effectiveness and Decision Making in Organizations,* pp. 291–332; Mohrman, Cohen, and Mohrman, *Designing Team-Based Organizations*, pp. 248–54; M. J. Stevens and M. A. Campion, "The Knowledge, Skill and Ability Requirements for Teamwork: Implications for Human Resources Management," *Journal of Management* 20 (1994) pp. 503–30; A. P. Hare, *Handbook of Small Group Research*, 2nd ed. (New York: Free Press, 1976), pp. 12–15.

41. C. D'Andrea-O'Brien and A. F. Buono, "Building Effective Learning Teams: Lessons from the Field," *SAM Advanced Management Journal* 61 (Summer 1996), pp. 4–9.

42. "New Anchor Hocking Plant Incorporates 'Socio-Tech' Work Environment Philosophy," *Business Wire*, October 19, 1995.

43. D. C. Hambrick, S. C. Davison, S. A. Snell, and C. C. Snow, "When Groups Consist of Multiple Nationalities: Towards a New Understanding of the Implications," *Organization Studies* 19 (1998), pp. 181–205; S. G. Baugh and G. B. Graen, "Effects of Team Gender and Racial Composition on Perceptions of Team Performance in Cross-Functional Teams," *Group & Organization Management* 22 (September 1997), pp. 366–83; F. J. Milliken and L. L. Martins, "Searching for Common Threads: Understanding the Multiple Effects of Diversity in Organizational Groups," *Academy of Management Review* 21 (1996), pp. 402–33; J. E. McGrath, J. L. Berdahl, and H. Arrow, "Traits, Expectations, Culture, and Clout: The Dynamics of Diversity in Work Groups," in Jackson and Ruderman, eds., *Diversity in Work Teams*, pp. 17–45.

44. D. C. Lau and J. K. Murnighan, "Demographic Diversity and Faultlines: The Compositional Dynamics of Organizational Groups," *Academy of Management Review* 23 (April 1998), pp. 325–40.

45. S. M. Colarelli and A. L. Boos, "Sociometric and Ability-Based Assignment to Work Groups: Some Implications for Personnel Selection," *Journal of Organizational Behavior* 13 (1992), pp. 187–96; D. G. Ancona and D. F. Caldwell, "Demography and Design: Predictors of New Product Team Performance," *Organization Science* 3 (1992), pp. 321–41; J. K. Murnighan and D. Conlon, "The Dynamics of Intense Work Groups: A Study of British String Quartets," *Administrative Science Quarterly* 36 (1991), pp. 165–86.

46. K. Y. Williams and C. A. O'Reilly III, "Demography and Diversity in Organizations: A Review of 40 Years of Research," *Research in Organizational Behavior* 20 (1998); B. Daily, A. Wheatley, S. R. Ash, and R. L. Steiner, "The Effects of a Group Decision Support System on Culturally Diverse and Culturally Homogeneous Group Decision Making," *Information & Management* 30 (1996), pp. 281–89; W. E. Watson, K. Kumar, and L. K. Michaelson, "Cultural Diversity's Impact on Interaction Process and Performance: Comparing Homogeneous and Diverse Task Groups," *Academy of Management Journal* 36 (1993), pp. 590–602.

47. L. Tucci, "Owens Drake Consulting Fosters Systematic Change," *St. Louis Business Journal*, May 25, 1998.

48. B. W. Tuckman and M. A. C. Jensen, "Stages of Small-Group Development Revisited," *Group and Organization Studies* 2 (1977), pp. 419–42; for a humorous and somewhat cynical discussion of team dynamics through these stages, see H. Robbins and M. Finley, *Why Teams Don't Work* (Princeton, NJ: Peterson's/Pacesetters, 1995), chap. 21.

49. Likert, *New Patterns of Management*, pp. 172–77.

50. J. A. Cannon-Bowers, S. I. Tannenbaum, E. Salas, and C. E. Volpe, "Defining Competencies and Establishing Team Training Requirements," in Guzzo, Salas, and Associates, eds., *Team Effectiveness and Decision Making in Organizations*, pp. 333–80.

51. C. Argyris, *Interpersonal Competence and Organizational Effectiveness* (Homewood, IL: Irwin, 1962).

52. D. L. Miller, "Synergy in Group Development: A Perspective on Group Performance," *Proceedings of the Annual ASAC Conference, Organizational Behavior Division* 17, pt. 5 (1996), pp. 119–28; S. Worchel, D. Coutant-Sassic, and M. Grossman, "A Developmental

Approach to Group Dynamics: A Model and Illustrative Research," in *Group Process and Productivity*, ed. Worchel et al., pp. 181–202; C. J. G. Gersick, "Time and Transition in Work Teams: Toward a New Model of Group Development," *Academy of Management Journal* 31 (1988), pp. 9–41.

53. D. C. Feldman, "The Development and Enforcement of Group Norms," *Academy of Management Review* 9 (1984), pp. 47–53; L. W. Porter, E. E. Lawler, and J. R. Hackman, *Behavior in Organizations* (New York: McGraw-Hill, 1975), pp. 391–94.

54. I. R. Gellatly, "Individual and Group Determinants of Employee Absenteeism: Test of a Causal Model," *Journal of Organizational Behavior* 16 (1995), pp. 469–85; G. Johns, "Absenteeism Estimates by Employees and Managers: Divergent Perspectives and Self-Serving Perceptions," *Journal of Applied Psychology* 79 (1994), pp. 229–39.

55. B. Latané, "The Psychology of Social Impact," *American Psychologist* 36 (1981), pp. 343–56; and C. A. Kiesler and S. B. Kiesler, *Conformity* (Reading, MA: Addison-Wesley, 1970).

56. Porter, Lawler, and Hackman, *Behavior in Organizations*, pp. 399–401.

57. L. Coch and J. R. P. French, Jr., "Overcoming Resistance to Change," *Human Relations* 1 (1948), pp. 512–32.

58. Feldman, "The Development and Enforcement of Group Norms," pp. 50–52.

59. Katzenbach and Smith, *The Wisdom of Teams*, pp. 121–23.

60. K. L. Bettenhausen and J. K. Murnighan, "The Development of an Intragroup Norm and the Effects of Interpersonal and Structural Challenges," *Administrative Science Quarterly* 36 (1991), pp. 20–35.

61. D'Andrea-O'Brien and Buono, "Building Effective Learning Teams," *SAM Advanced Management Journal*.

62. R. S. Spich and K. Keleman, "Explicit Norm Structuring Process: A Strategy for Increasing Task-Group Effectiveness," *Group & Organization Studies* 10 (March 1985), pp. 37–59.

63. D. I. Levine, "Piece Rates, Output Restriction, and Conformism," *Journal of Economic Psychology* 13 (1992), pp. 473–89.

64. P. Roberts, "Sony Changes the Game," *Fast Company*, no. 10 (1997), p. 116.

65. D. Katz and R. L. Kahn, *The Social Psychology of Organizations* (New York: John Wiley, 1966), chap. 7; J. W. Thibault and H. H. Kelley, *The Social Psychology of Groups* (New York: John Wiley, 1959), chap. 8.

66. D. Antrim, "Improvement Teams," *Rough Notes* 142 (February 1999), p. 100.

67. D. Vinokur-Kaplan, "Treatment Teams That Work (and Those That Don't): An Application of Hackman's Group Effectiveness Model to Interdisciplinary Teams in Psychiatric Hospitals," *Journal of Applied Behavioral Science* 31 (1995), pp. 303–27; Shaw, *Group Dynamics*, pp. 213–26; Goodman et al., "Understanding Groups in Organizations," pp. 144–46.

68. S. Lembke and M. G. Wilson, "Putting the 'Team' into Teamwork: Alternative Theoretical Contributions for Contemporary Management Practice," *Human Relations* 51 (July 1998), pp. 927–44; B. E. Ashforth and R. H. Humphrey, "Emotion in the Workplace: A Reappraisal," *Human Relations* 48 (1995), pp. 97–125; P. R. Bernthal and C. A. Insko, "Cohesiveness without Groupthink: The Interactive Effects of Social and Task Cohesiveness," *Group and Organization Management* 18 (1993), pp. 66–87.

69. A. Lott and B. Lott, "Group Cohesiveness as Interpersonal Attraction: A Review of Relationships with Antecedent and Consequent Variables," *Psychological Bulletin* 64 (1965), pp. 259–309.

70. Lau and Murnighan, "Demographic Diversity and Faultlines."

71. S. E. Jackson, "Team Composition in Organizational Settings: Issues in Managing an Increasingly Diverse Work Force," in *Group Process and Productivity*, ed. Worchel et al., pp. 138–73; J. Virk, P. Aggarwal, and R. N. Bhan, "Similarity versus Complementarity in Clique Formation," *Journal of Social Psychology* 120 (1983), pp. 27–34.

72. J. A. Alexander, R. Lichtenstein, K. Jinnett, T. A. D'Aunno, and E. Ullman, "The Effects of Treatment Team Diversity and Size on Assessments of Team Functioning," *Hospital & Health Services Administration* 41 (1996), pp. 37–53.

73. D. Bencivenga, "A Humanistic Approach to Space," *HRMagazine* 43 (March 1998), pp. 68–76; M. Jackson, "Walls Come Tumbling Down," *Akron Beacon Journal*, May 21, 1998.

74. M. B. Pinto, J. K. Pinto, and J. E. Prescott, "Antecedents and Consequences of Project Team Cross-Functional Cooperation," *Management Science* 39 (1993), pp. 1281–96; W. Piper, M. Marrache, R. Lacroix, A. Richardson, and B. Jones, "Cohesion as a Basic Bond in Groups," *Human Relations* 36 (1983), pp. 93–108.

75. E. J. Hill, B. C. Miller, S. P. Weiner and J. Colihan, "Influences of the Virtual Office on Aspects of Work and Work/Life Balance," *Personnel Psychology* 51 (Autumn 1998), pp. 667–83; S. B. Gould, K. J. Weiner, and B. R. Levin, *Free Agents: People and Organizations Creating a New Working Community* (San Francisco: Jossey-Bass, 1997), pp. 158–60.

76. J. E. Hautaluoma and R. S. Enge, "Early Socialization into a Work Group: Severity of Initiations Revisited," *Journal of Social Behavior & Personality* 6 (1991) pp. 725–48; E. Aronson and J. Mills, "The Effects of Severity of Initiation on Liking for a Group," *Journal of Abnormal and Social Psychology* 59 (1959), pp. 177–81.

77. B. Mullen and C. Copper, "The Relation between Group Cohesiveness and Performance: An Integration," *Psychological Bulletin* 115 (1994), pp. 210–27; Shaw, *Group Dynamics*, p. 215.

78. "Business Excellence at Armstrong World Industries," *IRS Employment Review*, October 1996, pp. 13–16; B. Carroll, "Team Competition Spurs Continuous Improvement at Motorola," *National Productivity Review* 14 (Autumn 1995), pp. 1–9.

79. M. Rempel and R. J. Fisher, "Perceived Threat, Cohesion, and Group Problem Solving in Intergroup Conflict," *International Journal of Conflict Management* 8 (1997), pp. 216–34.

80. J. M. McPherson and P. A. Popielarz, "Social Networks and Organizational Dynamics," *American Sociological Review* 57

(1992), pp. 153–70; Piper et al., "Cohesion as a Basic Bond in Groups," pp. 93–108.

81. C. A. O'Reilly III, D. F. Caldwell, and W. P. Barnett, "Work Group Demography, Social Integration, and Turnover," *Administrative Science Quarterly* 34 (1989), pp. 21–37.

82. R. D. Banker, J. M. Field, R. G. Schroeder, and K. K. Sinha, "Impact of Work Teams on Manufacturing Performance: A Longitudinal Study," *Academy of Management Journal* 39 (1996), pp. 867–90; D. Vinokur-Kaplan, "Treatment Teams That Work (And Those That Don't): An Application of Hackman's Group Effectiveness Model to Interdisciplinary Teams in Psychiatric Hospitals," *Journal of Applied Behavioral Science* 31 (September 1995), pp. 303–27; Mullen and Copper, "The Relation between Group Cohesiveness and Performance," *Psychological Bulletin*; C. R. Evans and K. L. Dion, "Group Cohesion and Performance: A Meta-Analysis," *Small Group Research* 22 (1991), pp. 175–86.

83. Robbins and Finley, *Why Teams Don't Work*, chap. 20; "The Trouble with Teams," *The Economist*, January 14, 1995, p. 61; A. Sinclair, "The Tyranny of Team Ideology," *Organization Studies* 13 (1992), pp. 611–26.

84. P. Panchak, "The Future Manufacturing," *Industry Week* 247 (September 21, 1998), pp. 96–105; B. Dumaine, "The Trouble with Teams," *Fortune*, September 5, 1994, pp. 86–92.

85. I. D. Steiner, *Group Process and Productivity* (New York: Academic Press, 1972).

86. Cusumano, "How Microsoft Makes Large Teams Work like Small Teams."

87. D. Dunphy and B. Bryant, "Teams: Panaceas or Prescriptions for Improved Performance?" *Human Relations* 49 (1996), pp. 677–99.

88. M. Erez and A. Somech "Is Group Productivity Loss the Rule or the Exception? Effects of Culture and Group-Based Motivation," *Academy of Management Journal* 39 (1996), pp. 1513–37; S. J. Karau and K. D. Williams, "Social Loafing: A Meta-Analytic Review and Theoretical Integration," *Journal of Personality and Social Psychology* 65 (1993),

pp. 681–706; J. M. George, "Extrinsic and Intrinsic Origins of Perceived Social Loafing in Organizations," *Academy of Management Journal* 35 (1992), pp. 191–202; R. Albanese and D. D. Van Fleet, "Rational Behavior in Groups: The Free-Riding Tendency," *Academy of Management Review* 10 (1985), pp. 244–55.

89. Erez and Somech "Is Group Productivity Loss the Rule or the Exception?" pp. 1513–37; P. C. Earley, "Social Loafing and Collectivism: A Comparison of the U.S. and the People's Republic of China," *Administrative Science Quarterly* 34 (1989), pp. 565–81.

90. T. A. Judge and T. D. Chandler, "Individual-Level Determinants of Employee Shirking," *Relations Industrielles* 51 (1996), pp. 468–86; J. M. George, "Asymmetrical Effects of Rewards and Punishments: The Case of Social Loafing," *Journal of Occupational and Organizational Psychology* 68 (1995), pp. 327–38; R. E. Kidwell and N. Bennett, "Employee Propensity to Withhold Effort: A Conceptual Model to Intersect Three Avenues of Research," *Academy of Management Review* 19 (1993), pp. 429–56; J. A. Shepperd, "Productivity Loss in Performance Groups: A Motivation Analysis," *Psychological Bulletin* 113 (1993), pp. 67–81.

91. W. G. Dyer, *Team Building: Issues and Alternatives*, 2nd ed. (Reading, MA: Addison-Wesley, 1987); and S. J. Liebowitz and K. P. De Meuse, "The Application of Team Building," *Human Relations* 35 (1982), pp. 1–18.

92. E. Sundstrom, K. P. De Meuse, and D. Futrell, "Work Teams: Applications and Effectiveness," *American Psychologist* 45 (1990), p. 128; M. Beer, *Organizational Change and Development: A Systems View* (Santa Monica, CA: Goodyear, 1980), pp. 143–46.

93. Beer, *Organizational Change and Development*, p. 145.

94. J. J. Laabs, "Team Training Goes Outdoors," *Personnel Journal*, June 1991, pp. 56–63.

95. A. Seybert, "The Great Outdoors—Corporate Style," *Baltimore Business Journal*, March 7, 1997, p. 21.

96. Robbins and Finley, *Why Teams Don't Work*, chap. 17.

97. M. J. Brown, "Let's Talk about It, Really Talk about It," *Journal for Quality & Participation* 19, no. 6 (1996) pp. 26–33; E. H. Schein, "On Dialogue, Culture, and Organizational Learning," *Organizational Dynamics*, Autumn 1993, pp. 40–51; and P. M. Senge, *The Fifth Discipline* (New York: Doubleday Currency, 1990), pp. 238–49.

98. G. Coetzer, "A Study of the Impact of Different Team Building Techniques on Work Team Effectiveness," unpublished MBA research project, Simon Fraser University, British Columbia, 1993.

99. T. G. Cummings and C. G. Worley, *Organization Development & Change*, 6th ed. (Cincinnati: South-Western, 1997), pp. 218–19; P. F. Buller and C. H. Bell, Jr., "Effects of Team Building and Goal Setting on Productivity: A Field Experiment," *Academy of Management Journal* 29 (1986), pp. 305–28.

100. C. J. Solomon, "Simulation Training Builds Teams through Experience," *Personnel Journal* 72 (June 1993), pp. 100–6.

101. R. W. Woodman and J. J. Sherwood, "The Role of Team Development in Organizational Effectiveness: A Critical Review," *Psychological Bulletin* 88 (1980), pp. 166–86; Sundstrom et al., "Work Teams: Applications and Effectiveness," p. 128.

102. Huszczo, *Tools for Team Excellence*, pp. 50–58.

103. P. McGraw, "Back from the Mountain: Outdoor Management Development Programs and How to Ensure the Transfer of Skills to the Workplace," *Asia Pacific Journal of Human Resources* 31 (Spring 1993), pp. 52–61; G. E. Huszczo, "Training for Team Building," *Training and Development Journal* 44 (February 1990), pp. 37–43.

104. R. W. Boss and H. L. McConkie, "The Destructive Impact of a Positive Team-Building Intervention," *Group & Organization Studies* 6 (1981), pp. 45–56.

Chapter Ten

1. D. Fields, "Harley Teams Shoot for Better Bike," *Akron Beacon Journal*, June 15, 1998; M. Savage, "Harley Irons Out an Innovative Way of Working," *Milwaukee Journal*

Sentinel, May 25, 1998, p. 12; L. Ziegler, "Labor's Role at New Harley Plant," National Public Radio, "All Things Considered" program, February 25, 1998; C. Eberting, "The Harley Mystique Comes to Kansas City," *Kansas City Star*, January 6, 1998, p. A1.

2. E. E. Lawler, "Far from the Fad Crowd," *People Management*, October 24, 1996, pp. 38–40.

3. G. C. McMahon and E. E. Lawler III, "Effects of Union Status on Employee Involvement: Diffusion and Effectiveness," *Research in Organizational Change and Development* 8 (1995), pp. 47–76; V. H. Vroom and A. G. Jago, *The New Leadership: Managing Participation in Organizations* (Englewood Cliffs, NJ: Prentice Hall, 1988), p. 15.

4. D. Adams, "MetroJet Carries Workers' Ideas," *Akron Beacon Journal*, May 28, 1998; S. Carey, "US Air 'Peon' Team Pilots Start-Up of Low-Fare Airline," *The Wall Street Journal*, March 24, 1998, p. B1.

5. B. Simon, "Bank Leads by Example in Transformation," *Business Day* (South Africa), July 30, 1998, p. 17; C. Brenner, "Pride in Ownership Is Byword for Bank's Employees," *Waukegan News-Sun* (IL), February 11, 1997, p. A3.

6. A. M. Berg, "Participatory Strategies in Quality Improvement Programs," *Public Productivity & Management Review* 21 (September 1997), pp. 30–43; D. I. Levine, *Reinventing the Workplace* (Washington, DC: Brookings Institution, 1995), chap. 3; E. A. Locke and D. M. Schweiger, "Participation in Decision-Making: One More Look," *Research in Organizational Behavior* 1 (1979), pp. 265–339.

7. M. S. Milinski, "Obstacles to Sustaining a Labor-Management Partnership: A Management Perspective," *Public Personnel Management* 27 (Spring 1998), pp. 11–21.

8. J. T. Addison, "Nonunion Representation in Germany," *Journal of Labor Research*, 20 (Winter 1999), pp. 73–92; G. Strauss, "Collective Bargaining, Unions, and Participation," in F. Heller, E. Pusic, G. Strauss, and B. Wilpert, eds., *Organizational Participation: Myth and Reality* (New York: Oxford University Press, 1998), pp. 97–143; Levine, *Reinventing the Workplace*, pp. 47–48.

9. "Republic Steels Remakes Workplace through ESOP," *Employee Benefit Plan Review* 51 (July 1996), pp. 48–50.

10. R. C. Liden and S. Arad, "A Power Perspective of Empowerment and Work Groups: Implications for Human Resources Management Research," *Research in Personnel and Human Resources Management* 14 (1996), pp. 205–51; R. C. Ford and M. D. Fottler, "Empowerment: A Matter of Degree," *Academy of Management Executive* 9 (August 1995), pp. 21–31; R. W. Coye and J. A. Belohlav, "An Exploratory Analysis of Employee Participation," *Group & Organization Management* 20 (1995), pp. 4–17; Vroom and Jago, *The New Leadership*.

11. N. S. Bruning and P. R. Liverpool, "Membership in Quality Circles and Participation in Decision Making," *Journal of Applied Behavioral Science* 29 (March 1993), pp. 76–95; S. D. Saleh, Z. Guo, and T. Hull, "The Use of Quality Circles in the Automobile Parts Industry," *Proceedings of the Annual ASAC Conference, Organizational Behaviour Division* 9, pt. 5 (1988), pp. 95–104.

12. Information comes from the Kowloon-Canton Railway Corporation web site.

13. J. Liedtka, "Linking Competitive Advantage with Communities of Practice," *Journal of Management Inquiry* 8 (March 1999), pp. 5–16.

14. C. O'Dell and C. J. Grayson, "If Only We Knew What We Know: Identification and Transfer of Internal Best Practices," *California Management Review* 40 (Spring 1998), pp. 154–74; C. J. Grayson and C. O'Dell, "Mining Your Hidden Resources," *Across the Board* 35 (April 1998), pp. 23–28; B. Manville and N. Foote, "Harvest Your Workers' Knowledge," *Datamation* 42 (July 1996), pp. 78–80.

15. P. E. Rossler and C. P. Koelling, "The Effect of Gainsharing on Business Performance at a Papermill," *National Productivity Review* 12 (Summer 1993), pp. 365–82; C. R. Gowen, III, "Gainsharing Programs: An Overview of History and Research," *Journal of Organizational Behavior Management* 11, no. 2 (1990), pp. 77–99; F. G. Lesieur, ed., *The Scanlon Plan: A Frontier in Labor-Management Cooperation* (Cambridge: MIT Press, 1958).

16. J. Case, "Opening the Books," *Harvard Business Review* 75 (March–April 1997), pp. 118–27; T. R. V. Davis, "Open-Book Management: Its Promise and Pitfalls," *Organizational Dynamics*, Winter 1997, pp. 7–20; J. Case, *Open Book Management: The Coming Business Revolution* (New York: HarperBusiness, 1995).

17. P. Dillon, "Open Book Policy Pays Off at Palm Bay Firm," *Orlando Business Journal*, August 3, 1998.

18. S. Zesiger, "Jac Nasser Is Car Crazy," *Fortune*, June 22, 1998, pp. 79–82.

19. R. Burrell, "Opening the Books Pays Off Handsomely," *CityBusiness* (Minneapolis-St. Paul), January 20, 1997.

20. D. E. Yeatts and C. Hyten, *High-Performing Self-Managed Work Teams: A Comparison of Theory and Practice* (Thousand Oaks, CA: Sage, 1998); S. A. Mohrman, S. G. Cohen, and A. M. Mohrman, Jr., *Designing Team-Based Organizations: New Forms for Knowledge Work* (San Francisco: Jossey-Bass, 1995); Lawler, *High-Involvement Management*, chaps. 11 and 12; L. C. Plunkett and R. Fournier, *Participative Management: Implementing Empowerment* (New York: John Wiley, 1991).

21. E. Palmer, "Self-Directed Team Effort Working Well," *Kansas City Star*, September 22, 1997, p. B6.

22. S. G. Cohen, G. E. Ledford, Jr., and G. M. Spreitzer, "A Predictive Model of Self-Managing Work Team Effectiveness," *Human Relations* 49 (1996), pp. 643–76.

23. The SDWT attributes discussed here are discussed in Yeatts and Hyten, *High-Performing Self-Managed Work Teams*; B. L. Kirkman and D. L. Shapiro, "The Impact of Cultural Values on Employee Resistance to Teams: Toward a Model of Globalized Self-Managing Work Team Effectiveness," *Academy of Management Review* 22 (July 1997), pp. 730–57; Mohrman et al., *Designing Team-Based Organizations*.

24. A. Dominguez, "Employees Flourish at No-Boss Firm," *Salt Lake City Deseret News*, July 4, 1998; M. Kaplan. "You Have No Boss," *Fast Company*, Issue 11 (November 1997), p. 226.

25. G. Taninecz, "Borg-Warner Automotive," *Industry Week*, October 19, 1998, p. 44.

26. P. S. Goodman, R. Devadas, and T. L. G. Hughson, "Groups and Productivity: Analyzing the

Effectiveness of Self-Managing Teams," in *Productivity in Organizations*, J. P. Campbell, R. J. Campbell, and Associates, eds. (San Francisco: Jossey-Bass, 1988), pp. 295–327.

27. J. Childs, "Five Years and Counting: The Path to Self-Directed Work Teams," *Hospital Materiel Management Quarterly* 18 (May 1997), pp. 34–43.

28. D. Tjosvold, *Teamwork for Customers* (San Francisco: Jossey-Bass, 1993); D. E. Bowen and E. E. Lawler III, "The Empowerment of Service Workers: What, Why, How, and When," *Sloan Management Review*, Spring 1992, pp. 31–39.

29. E. L. Trist, G. W. Higgin, H. Murray, and A. B. Pollock, *Organizational Choice* (London: Tavistock, 1963). The origins of SDWTs from sociotechnical systems research is also noted in R. Beckham, "Self-Directed Work Teams: The Wave of the Future?" *Hospital Materiel Management Quarterly* 20 (August 1998), pp. 48–60.

30. The main components of sociotechnical systems are discussed in M. Moldaschl and W. G. Weber, "The 'Three Waves' of Industrial Group Work: Historical Reflections on Current Research on Group Work," *Human Relations* 51 (March 1998), pp. 347–88; W. Niepce and E. Molleman, "Work Design Issues in Lean Production from a Sociotechnical Systems Perspective: Neo-Taylorism or the Next Step in Sociotechnical Design?" *Human Relations* 51 (March 1998), pp. 259–87.

31. E. Ulich and W. G. Weber, "Dimensions, Criteria, and Evaluation of Work Group Autonomy," in M. A. West, ed., *Handbook of Work Group Psychology* (Chichester, UK: John Wiley, 1996), pp. 247–82.

32. C. C. Manz and G. L. Stewart, "Attaining Flexible Stability by Integrating Total Quality Management and Socio-Technical Systems Theory," *Organization Science* 8 (1997), pp. 59–70; K. P. Carson and G. L. Stewart, "Job Analysis and the Sociotechnical Approach to Quality: A Critical Examination," *Journal of Quality Management* 1 (1996), pp. 49–65.

33. D. Zell, *Changing by Design: Organizational Innovation at Hewlett-Packard* (Ithaca, NY: ILR Press, 1997); "New Anchor Hocking Plant Incorporates 'Socio-Tech' Work Environment Philosophy," *Business Wire*, October 19, 1995; R. Reese, "Redesigning for Dial Tone: A Socio-Technical Systems Case Study," *Organizational Dynamics* 24 (Autumn 1995), pp. 80–90.

34. P. S. Adler and R. E. Cole, "Designed for Learning: A Tale of Two Auto Plants," *Sloan Management Review* 34 (Spring 1993), pp. 85–94; O. Hammarström and R. Lansbury, "The Art of Building a Car: The Swedish Experience Re-examined," *New Technology, Work and Employment* 2 (Autumn 1991), pp. 85–90; J. P. Womack, D. T. Jones, and D. Roos, *The Machine That Changed the World* (New York: Macmillan, 1990). For more favorable evaluations of Volvo's plants, see I. Magaziner and M. Patinkin, *The Silent War* (New York: Random House, 1988); P. G. Gyllenhammar, *People at Work* (Reading, MA: Addison-Wesley, 1977).

35. R. Likert, *New Patterns of Management* (New York: McGraw-Hill, 1961); D. McGregor, *The Human Side of Enterprise* (New York: McGraw-Hill, 1960); C. Argyris, *Personality and Organization* (New York: Harper & Row, 1957).

36. J. A. Wagner III, C. R. Leana, E. A. Locke, and D. M. Schweiger, "Cognitive and Motivational Frameworks in U.S. Research on Participation: A Meta-Analysis of Primary Effects," *Journal of Organizational Behavior* 18 (1997), pp. 49–65; G. P. Latham, D. C. Winters, and E. A. Locke, "Cognitive and Motivational Effects of Participation: A Mediator Study," *Journal of Organizational Behavior* 15 (1994), pp. 49–63; Cotton, *Employee Involvement*, chap. 8; S. J. Havlovic, "Quality of Work Life and Human Resource Outcomes," *Industrial Relations* 30 (1991), pp. 469–79; K. I. Miller and P. R. Monje, "Participation, Satisfaction, and Productivity: A Meta-Analytic Review," *Academy of Management Journal* 29 (1986), pp. 727–53.

37. K. Y. Williams and C. A. O' Reilly III, "Demography and Diversity in Organizations: A Review of 40 Years of Research," *Research in Organizational Behavior* 20 (1998).

38. J. P. Walsh and S-F. Tseng, "The Effects of Job Characteristics on Active Effort at Work," *Work & Occupations* 25 (February 1998), pp. 74–96; K. T. Dirks, L. L. Cummings, and J. L. Pierce, "Psychological Ownership in Organizations: Conditions under Which Individuals Promote and Resist Change," *Research in Organizational Change and Development* 9 (1996), pp. 1–23.

39. C. L. Cooper, B. Dyck, and N. Frohlich, "Improving the Effectiveness of Gainsharing: The Role of Fairness and Participation," *Administrative Science Quarterly* 37 (1992), pp. 471–90.

40. Vroom and Jago, *The New Leadership*, pp. 151–52.

41. G. P. Zachary, "Search for Meaning Spreads to Shop Floor," *The Wall Street Journal*, January 8, 1997.

42. The limits of employee involvement for improving employee satisfaction are discussed in J. A. Wagner III, C. R. Leana, E. A. Locke, and D. Schweiger, "Cognitive and Motivational Frameworks in U.S. Research on Participation: A Meta-Analysis of Primary Effects," *Journal of Organizational Behavior* 18 (1997), pp. 49–65; V. Smith, "Employee Involvement, Involved Employees: Participative Work Arrangements in a White-Collar Service Occupation," *Social Problems* 43 (May 1996), pp. 166–79; D. J. Glew, A. M. O'Leary-Kelly, R. W. Griffin, and D. D. Van Fleet, "Participation in Organizations: A Preview of the Issues and Proposed Framework for Future Analysis," *Journal of Management* 21 (1995), pp. 395–421.

43. J. A. Conger and R. N. Kanungo, "The Empowerment Process: Integrating Theory and Practice," *Academy of Management Review* 13 (1988), pp. 471–82.

44. A. Bandura, *Self-Efficacy: The Exercise of Control* (W. H. Freeman, 1996); M. E. Gist and T. R. Mitchell, "Self-Efficacy: A Theoretical Analysis of Its Determinants and Malleability," *Academy of Management Review* 17 (1992), pp. 183–211; R. F. Mager, "No Self-Efficacy, No Performance," *Training* 29 (April 1992), pp. 32–36.

45. A. Sagie and M. Koslowsky, "Organizational Attitudes and Behavior as a Function of Participation in Strategic and Tactical Change Decisions: An Application of Path-Goal Theory," *Journal of Organizational Behavior* 15 (1994), pp. 37–47.

46. Berg, "Participatory Strategies in Quality Improvement Programs"; A. A. Aziz, "A Grip on Employee Absenteeism," *New Straits Times* (Malaysia), June 20, 1996, p. 3; A. Haasen, "Opel Eisenach GMBH—Creating a High-Productivity Workplace," *Organizational Dynamics* 24 (January 1996), pp. 80–85; T. Murakami, "Introducing Team Working—A Motor Industry Case Study from Germany," *Industrial Relations Journal* 26 (1995), pp. 293–305; R. S. Wellins, W. C. Byham, and G. R. Dixon, *Inside Teams* (San Francisco: Jossey-Bass, 1994), pp. 262–71.

47. B. L. Kirkman and D. L. Shapiro, "The Impact of Cultural Values on Employee Resistance to Teams: Toward a Model of Globalized Self-Managing Work Team Effectiveness," *Academy of Management Review* 22 (July 1997), pp. 730–57; C. Pavett and T. Morris, "Management Styles within a Multinational Corporation: A Five Country Comparative Study," *Human Relations* 48 (1995) pp. 1171–91; M. Erez and P. C. Earley, *Culture, Self-Identity, and Work* (New York: Oxford University Press, 1993), pp. 104–12.

48. D. I. Levine, *Reinventing the Workplace* (Washington, D.C.: Brookings Institution, 1995), pp. 63–66, 86; C. C. Manz, D. E. Keating, and A. Donnellon, "Preparing for an Organizational Change to Employee Self-Management: The Managerial Transition," *Organizational Dynamics* 19 (Autumn 1990), pp. 15–26.

49. G. T. Fairhurst, S. Green, and J. Courtright, "Inertial Forces and the Implementation of a Socio-Technical Systems Approach: A Communication Study," *Organization Science* 6 (1995), pp. 168–85; Manz et al., "Preparing for an Organizational Change to Employee Self-Management," pp. 23–25.

50. C. Argyris, "Empowerment: The Emperor's New Clothes," *Harvard Business Review* 76 (May–June 1998), pp. 98–105; C. Hardy and S. Leiba-O'Sullivan, "The Power behind Empowerment: Implications for Research and Practice," *Human Relations* 51 (April 1998), pp. 451–83.

51. S. Wood and L. de Menezes, "High Commitment Management in the U.K.: Evidence from the Workplace Industrial Relations Survey, and Employers' Manpower and Skills Practices Survey," *Human Relations* 51 (April 1998), pp. 485–515; I. Goll and N. B. Johnson, "The Influence of Environmental Pressures, Diversification Strategy, and Union/Nonunion Setting on Employee Participation," *Employee Responsibilities and Rights Journal* 10 (1997), pp. 141–54; R. Hodson, "Dignity in the Workplace under Participative Management: Alienation and Freedom Revisited," *American Sociological Review* 61 (1996), pp. 719–38.

52. M. H. LeRoy, "Are Employers Constrained in the Use of Employee Participation Groups by Section 8(a)(2) of the National Labor Relations Act?" *Journal of Labor Research* 20 (Winter 1999), pp. 53–71; H. Allerton "The TEAM Act," *Training & Development* 50 (October 1996), p. 9; R. King, "Dupont Plant Settles Worker Team Dispute," *Plastics News*, May 27, 1996, p. 8; G. C. Armas "Plant's Worker Teams Ignite Debate," *St. Louis Post-Dispatch*, February 10, 1996, p. A6.

53. R. Yonatan and H. Lam, "Union Responses to Quality Improvement Initiatives: Factors Shaping Support and Resistance," *Journal of Labor Research* 20 (Winter 1999), p. 20; Levine, *Reinventing the Workplace*, pp. 66–69; L. D. Ketchum and E. Trist, *All Teams Are Not Created Equal: How Employee Empowerment Really Works* (Newbury Park, CA: Sage, 1992); M. Parker and J. Slaughter, *Choosing Sides: Unions and the Team Concept* (Boston: South End Press, 1988); T. A. Kochan, H. C. Katz, and R. B. McKersie, *The Transformation of American Industrial Relations* (New York: Basic Books, 1986), chaps. 6–7.

54. E. C. Rosenthal "Sociotechnical Systems and Unions: Nicety or Necessity," *Human Relations* 50 (May 1997), pp. 585–604; R. E. Allen and K. L. Van Norman, "Employee Involvement Programs: The Noninvolvement of Unions Revisited," *Journal of Labor Research* 17 (Summer 1996), pp. 479–95; B. Gilbert, "The Impact of Union Involvement on the Design and Introduction of Quality of Working Life," *Human Relations* 42 (1989), pp. 1057–78; T. A. Kochan, H. C. Katz, and R. B. McKersie, *The Transformation of American Industrial Relations* (New York: Basic Books, 1986), pp. 238–45.

55. L. Chappell, "Transplants Ushered in Quality Revolution," *Automotive News*, April 27, 1998, p. N8.

56. For discussions on the meaning of quality and total quality management, see A. Rao et al., *Total Quality Management: A Cross Functional Perspective* (New York: John Wiley, 1996), chap. 2; M. Zairi and P. Leonard, *Practical Benchmarking: The Complete Guide* (London: Chapman & Hall, 1994), pp. 14–21; W. H. Schmidt and J. P. Finnigan, *The Race Without a Finish Line* (San Francisco: Jossey-Bass, 1992); B. Brocka and M. S. Brocka, *Quality Management: Implementing the Best Ideas of the Masters* (Burr Ridge, IL: Business One-Irwin, 1992), chap. 1.

57. W. H. Miller, "Baxter Healthcare Corp.," *Industry Week*, October 19, 1998, pp. 38–40.

58. R. Laver, "The Future of the Car," *Maclean's*, April 15, 1991, p. 45.

59. P. B. Doeringer, C. Evans-Klock, and D. Terkla, "Hybrids of Hodgepodges? Workplace Practices of Japanese and Domestic Startups in the United States," *Industrial and Labor Relations Review* 51 (January 1998), pp. 171–86. Similarly, M. Bensaou and M. Earl, "The Right Mind-Set for Managing Information Technology," *Harvard Business Review* 76 (September–October 1998), pp. 118–28, found that Japanese firms try to ensure that technology fits the people using it (called *chowa*), whereas U.S. firms tend to focus on technology's benefits independent of the human element.

60. M. V. Uzumeri, "ISO 9000 and Other Metastandards: Principles for Management Practice?" *Academy of Management Executive* 11 (February 1997), pp. 21–36.

61. "Navigating the Road to QS 9000," *Plant*, July 15, 1996, p. 23.

62. D. L. Goetsch and S. B. Davis, *Introduction to Total Quality*, 2nd ed. (Upper Saddle River, NJ: Prentice Hall, 1997), chap. 7; M. E. Milakovich, *Improving Service Quality* (Delray Beach, FL: St. Lucie Press, 1995), pp. 16–23; R. L. Flood, *Beyond TQM* (Chichester, UK: John Wiley, 1993).

63. G. Skaria, S. Khann, and P. Kawatra, "Customerising the Corporation," *Business Today*, January 7, 1997, pp. 30–37.

64. R. Hallowell, L. A. Schlesinger, and J. Zornitsky, "Internal Service

Quality, Customer and Job Satisfaction: Linkages and Implications for Management," *Human Resource Planning* 19, no. 2 (1996), pp. 20–31.

65. D. Machan, "Is the Hog Going Soft?" *Forbes*, March 10, 1997, pp. 114–15.

66. R. D. Banker, J. M. Field, R. G. Schroeder, and K. K. Sinha, "Impact of Work Teams on Manufacturing Performance: A Longitudinal Study," *Academy of Management Journal* 39 (1996), pp. 867–90.

67. L. D. Fredendall and T. L. Robbins, "Modeling the Role of Total Quality Management in the Customer Focused Organization," *Journal of Managerial Issues* 7 (Winter 1995), pp. 403–19.

68. F. Burlage, "Master the Art of Kaizen," *The European*, February 20, 1997, p. 12.

69. Niepce and Molleman, "Work Design Issues in Lean Production from a Sociotechnical Systems Perspective."

70. J. P. Womack and D. T Jones, *Lean Thinking* (New York: Simon & Schuster, 1996).

71. L. A. Klaus, "Kaizen Blitz Proves Effective for Dana Corporation," *Quality Progress* 31 (May 1998), p. 8.

72. T. J. McCoy, *Creating An 'Open Book' Organization* (New York: AMACOM, 1996), chaps. 6–7; R. Y. Bergstrom, "Cells in Steel Country," *Production*, February 1995, pp. 50–54.

73. E. A. Locke and V. K. Jain, "Organizational Learning and Continuous Improvement," *International Journal of Organizational Analysis* 3 (January 1995), pp. 45–68.

74. P. B. Crosby, *The Eternally Successful Organization* (New York: McGraw-Hill, 1988); P. B. Crosby, *Quality Is Free* (New York: McGraw-Hill, 1979).

75. Milakovich, *Improving Service Quality*, chap. 6.

76. J. Martin, "Are You as Good as You Think You Are?" *Fortune*, September 30, 1996, pp. 142–47.

77. C. Newman, "Manufacturing Plants Fine Tune 'Quality' Initiatives of the Early '90s," *Pittsburgh Business Times*, June 1, 1998.

78. M. Zairi and P. Leonard, *Practical Benchmarking: The Complete Guide* (London: Chapman & Hall, 1994); E. F. Glanz and L. K. Dailey, "Benchmarking," *Human Resource Management* 31 (Spring/Summer 1992), pp. 9–20.

79. C. Frank, "From the Rust Belt to the Baldrige Award," *Journal for Quality and Participation* 19 (December 1996), pp. 46–51.

80. Grayson and O'Dell, "Mining Your Hidden Resources."

81. R. K. Reger, L. T. Gustafson, S. M. DeMarie, and J. V. Mullane, "Reframing the Organization: Why Implementing Total Quality Is Easier Said Than Done," *Academy of Management Review* 19 (1994), pp. 565–84.

82. M. L. Swink, J. C. Sandvig, and V. A. Mabert, "Customizing Concurrent Engineering Processes: Five Case Studies," *Journal of Product Innovation Management* 13 (1996), pp. 229–44; W. I. Zangwill, *Lightning Strategies for Innovation: How the World's Best Firms Create New Products* (New York: Lexington, 1993); J. V. Owen, "Concurrent Engineering," *Manufacturing Engineering* 109 (November 1992), pp. 69–73.

83. C. Terwiesch and C. H. Loch, "Measuring the Effectiveness of Overlapping Development Activities," *Management Science* 45 (April 1999), pp. 455–65.

84. T. Minahan, "Harley-Davidson Revs up Development Process," *Purchasing* 124 (May 1998), p. 44S18.

85. A. L. Patti, J. P. Gilbert, and S. Hartman, "Physical Co-location and the Success of New Product Development Projects," *Engineering Management Journal* 9 (September 1997), pp. 31–37.

86. F. Rafii, "How Important Is Physical Collocation to Product Development Success?" *Business Horizons* 38 (January 1995), pp. 78–84.

87. R. Reed, D. J. Lemak, and J. C. Montgomery, "Beyond Process: TQM Content and Firm Performance," *Academy of Management Review* 21 (1996), pp. 173–202; R. C. Hill, "When the Going Gets Rough: A Baldrige Winner on the Line," *Academy of Management Executive* 7 (August 1993), pp. 75–79; M. M. Steeples, *The Corporate Guide to the Malcolm Baldrige National Quality Award*, 2nd ed. (Homewood, IL: Business One-Irwin, 1993), pp. 293–99.

88. M. Brown, D. Hitchcock, and M. Willard, *Why TQM Fails and What to Do About It* (Burr Ridge, IL: Richard D. Irwin, 1994).

89. U. Nwabueze and G. K. Kanji, "The Implementation of Total Quality Management in the NHS: How to Avoid Failure," *Total Quality Management* 8 (October 1997), pp. 265–80.

Chapter Eleven

1. R. D. Hof, "Amazon.Com: The Wild World of E-Commerce," *Business Week*, December 14, 1998, p. 106; S. Homer, "Damn! What a Nice, Bookish Tycoon," *The Independent* (London), November 16, 1998, p. 13; K. Doler, "Interview: Jeff Bezos, Founder and CEO of Amazon.com Inc.," *Upside* 10 (September 1998), pp. 76–80.

2. F. A. Shull, Jr., A. L. Delbecq, and L. L. Cummings, *Organizational Decision Making* (New York: McGraw-Hill, 1970), p. 31. See also J. G. March, "Understanding How Decisions Happen in Organizations," in Z. Shapira, ed., *Organizational Decision Making* (New York: Cambridge University Press, 1997), pp. 9–32.

3. B. M. Bass, *Organizational Decision Making* (Homewood, IL: Richard D. Irwin, 1983), chap. 3; W. F. Pounds, "The Process of Problem Finding," *Industrial Management Review* 11 (Fall 1969), pp. 1–19; C. Kepner and B. Tregoe, *The Rational Manager* (New York: McGraw-Hill, 1965).

4. This model is adapted from several sources: H. Mintzberg, D. Raisinghani, and A. Théorét, "The Structure of 'Unstructured' Decision Processes," *Administrative Science Quarterly* 21 (1976), pp. 246–75; H. A. Simon, *The New Science of Management Decision* (New York: Harper & Row, 1960); Kepner and Tregoe, *The Rational Manager*; W. C. Wedley and R. H. G. Field, "A Predecision Support System," *Academy of Management Review* 9 (1984), pp. 696–703.

5. J. W. Dean, Jr., and M. P. Sharfman, "Does Decision Process Matter? A Study of Strategic Decision-Making Effectiveness," *Academy of Management Journal* 39 (1996), pp. 368–96.

6. P. F. Drucker, *The Practice of Management* (New York: Harper & Brothers, 1954), pp. 353–57.

7. Wedley and Field, "A Predecision Support System," p. 696; Drucker, *The Practice of Management*, p. 357; and L. R. Beach and T. R. Mitchell, "A Contingency Model for the

Selection of Decision Strategies," *Academy of Management Review* 3 (1978), pp. 439–49.

8. I. L. Janis, *Crucial Decisions* (New York: Free Press, 1989), pp. 35–37; Simon, *The New Science of Management Decision,* pp. 5–6.

9. J. D. Malone, "Technology vs. Bureaucracy: Common Sense Government in the Post-Industrial Age," *Vital Speeches* 63 (June 1, 1997), pp. 492–94.

10. Mintzberg, Raisinghani, and Théorét, "The Structure of 'Unstructured' Decision Processes," pp. 255–56.

11. B. Fischhoff and S. Johnson, "The Possibility of Distributed Decision Making," in Shapira, *Organizational Decision Making,* pp. 216–37.

12. J. E. Dutton, "Strategic Agenda Building in Organizations," in Shapira, *Organizational Decision Making,* pp. 81–107; M. Lyles and H. Thomas, "Strategic Problem Formulation: Biases and Assumptions Embedded in Alternative Decision-Making Models," *Journal of Management Studies* 25 (1988), pp. 131–45; I. I. Mitroff, "On Systematic Problem Solving and the Error of the Third Kind," *Behavioral Science* 9 (1974), pp. 383–93.

13. P. M. Senge, *The Fifth Discipline: The Art and Practice of the Learning Organization* (New York: Doubleday Currency, 1990), chap. 10.

14. D. Domer, *The Logic of Failure* (Reading, MA: Addison-Wesley, 1996); M. Basadur. "Managing the Creative Process in Organizations," in M. A. Runco, ed., *Problem Finding, Problem Solving, and Creativity* (Norwood, NJ: Ablex, 1994), pp. 237–68.

15. P. C. Nutt, "Preventing Decision Debacles," *Technological Forecasting and Social Change* 38 (1990), pp. 159–174.

16. P. C. Nutt, *Making Tough Decisions* (San Francisco: Jossey-Bass, 1989).

17. C. Elliott, "Give Your Data a Workout," *InternetWeek,* June 1, 1998, p. 32.

18. K. A. Zimmermann, "Kmart to Quadruple Size of Data Warehouse," *Daily News Record,* July 1, 1998, p. 13.

19. J. Conlisk, "Why Bounded Rationality?" *Journal of Economic Literature* 34 (1996), pp. 669–700;

B. L. Lipman, "Information Processing and Bounded Rationality: A Survey," *Canadian Journal of Economics* 28 (1995), pp. 42–67.

20. L. T. Pinfield, "A Field Evaluation of Perspectives on Organizational Decision Making," *Administrative Science Quarterly* 31 (1986), pp. 365–88.

21. H. A. Simon, *Administrative Behavior,* 2nd ed. (New York: Free Press, 1957), pp. xxv, 80–84; and J. G. March and H. A. Simon, *Organizations* (New York: John Wiley, 1958), pp. 140–41.

22. P. O. Soelberg, "Unprogrammed Decision Making," *Industrial Management Review* 8 (1967), pp. 19–29; and H. A. Simon, "A Behavioral Model of Rational Choice," *Quarterly Journal of Economics* 69 (1955), pp. 99–118.

23. J. E. Russo, V. H. Medvec, and M. G. Meloy, "The Distortion of Information during Decisions," *Organizational Behavior & Human Decision Processes* 66 (1996), pp. 102–10.

24. H. A. Simon, *Models of Man: Social and Rational* (New York: John Wiley, 1957), p. 253.

25. L. Blake, "Group Decision Making at Baxter," *Personnel Journal,* January 1991, pp. 76–82.

26. A. Rangaswamy and G. L. Lilien, "Software Tools for New Product Development," *Journal of Marketing Research* 34 (1997), pp. 177–84.

27. G. H. Anthes, "Learning How to Share," *Computerworld* 32 (February 23, 1998), pp. 75–77.

28. O. Behling and N. L. Eckel, "Making Sense Out of Intuition," *Academy of Management Executive* 5 (February 1991), pp. 46–54; Nutt, *Making Tough Decisions,* p. 54; ; H. A. Simon, "Making Management Decisions: The Role of Intuition and Emotion," *Academy of Management Executive* (February 1987), pp. 57–64; W. H. Agor, "The Logic of Intuition," *Organizational Dynamics* (Winter 1986), pp. 5–18.

29. E. N. Brockmann and W. P. Anthony, "The Influence of Tacit Knowledge and Collective Mind on Strategic Planning," *Journal of Managerial Issues* 10 (Summer 1998), pp. 204–22; D. Leonard and S. Sensiper, "The Role of Tacit Knowledge in Group Innovation," *California Management Review* 40 (Spring 1998), pp. 112–32.

30. R. N. Taylor, *Behavioral Decision Making* (Glenview, IL: Scott, Foresman, 1984), pp. 163–66.

31. D. R. Bobocel and J. P. Meyer, "Escalating Commitment to a Failing Course of Action: Separating the Role of Choice and Justification," *Journal of Applied Psychology* 79 (1994), pp. 360–63; G. Whyte, "Escalating Commitment in Individual and Group Decision Making: A Prospect Theory Approach," *Organizational Behavior and Human Decision Processes* 54 (1993), pp. 430–55; G. Whyte, "Escalating Commitment to a Course of Action: A Reinterpretation," *Academy of Management Review* 11 (1986), pp. 311–21.

32. P. Ayton and H. Arkes, "Call It Quits," *New Scientist,* June 20, 1998 (online); J. Vranich, "All Aboard for a Tax Ripoff," *Chicago Tribune,* December 23, 1997, p. 19; R. J. Samuelson, "The Parable of Amtrak," *Newsweek,* November 3, 1997, p. 57; "When Government Buys Computers," *Washington Post,* March 20, 1997, p. A26.

33. H. Drummond, *Escalation in Decision Making* (New York: Oxford University Press, 1997).

34. D. Main and R. G. Rambo, "Avoiding Entrapment; Decision-Making Phenomenon Associated with Research and Development Projects," *CPA Journal* 68 (March 1998), pp. 24–27.

35. F. D. Schoorman and P. J. Holahan, "Psychological Antecedents of Escalation Behavior: Effects of Choice, Responsibility, and Decision Consequences," *Journal of Applied Psychology* 81 (1996), pp. 786–93.

36. S. W. Geiger, C. J. Robertson, and J. G. Irwin, "The Impact of Cultural Values on Escalation of Commitment," *International Journal of Organizational Analysis* 6 (April 1998), pp. 165–76; D. K. Tse, K. Lee, I. Vertinsky, and D. A. Wehrung, "Does Culture Matter? A Cross-Cultural Study of Executives' Choice, Decisiveness, and Risk Adjustment in International Marketing," *Journal of Marketing* 52 (1988), pp. 81–95.

37. K. Jenkins, Jr., "Is Amtrak Headed for a Political Train Wreck?" *U.S. News & World Report,* November 3, 1997, pp. 34, 36.

38. L. Dean, "Amtrak's Losses Still Outnumber Its Friends," *St. Louis Post-Dispatch,* July 10, 1998, p. A6.

39. B. M. Staw. K. W. Koput, and S. G. Barsade "Escalation at the Credit Window: A Longitudinal Study of Bank Executives' Recognition and Write-Off of Problem Loans," *Journal of Applied Psychology*, 82 (1997), pp. 130–42.

40. W. Boulding, R. Morgan, and R. Staelin, "Pulling the Plug to Stop the New Product Drain," *Journal of Marketing Research* 34 (1997), pp. 164–76; I. Simonson and B. M. Staw, "De-Escalation Strategies: A Comparison of Techniques for Reducing Commitment to Losing Courses of Action," *Journal of Applied Psychology* 77 (1992), pp. 419–26.

41. D. Ghosh, "De-Escalation Strategies: Some Experimental Evidence," *Behavioral Research in Accounting* 9 (1997), pp. 88–112.

42. V. H. Vroom and A. G. Jago, *The New Leadership* (Englewood Cliffs, NJ: Prentice Hall, 1988), pp. 28–29.

43. R. B. Gallupe, W. H. Cooper, M. L. Grisé, and L. M. Bastianutti, "Blocking Electronic Brainstorms," *Journal of Applied Psychology* 79 (1994), pp. 77–86; M. Diehl and W. Stroebe, "Productivity Loss in Idea-Generating Groups: Tracking Down the Blocking Effects," *Journal of Personality and Social Psychology* 61 (1991), pp. 392–403.

44. P. W. Mulvey, J. F. Veiga, P. M. Elsass, "When Teammates Raise a White Flag," *Academy of Management Executive* 10 (February 1996), pp. 40–49.

45. S. Plous, *The Psychology of Judgment and Decision Making* (Philadelphia: Temple University Press, 1993), pp. 200–2.

46. Janis, *Crucial Decisions*, pp. 56–63; I. L. Janis, *Groupthink: Psychological Studies of Policy Decisions and Fiascoes*, 2nd ed. (Boston: Houghton Mifflin, 1982).

47. M. E. Turner and A. R. Pratkanis, "Threat, Cohesion, and Group Effectiveness: Testing a Social Identity Maintenance Perspective on Groupthink," *Journal of Personality and Social Psychology* 63 (1992), pp. 781–96.

48. M. Rempel and R. J. Fisher, "Perceived Threat, Cohesion, and Group Problem Solving in Intergroup Conflict," *International Journal of Conflict Management* 8 (1997), pp. 216–34.

49. G. Moorhead, R. Ference, and C. P. Neck, "Group Decision Fiascoes Continue: Space Shuttle *Challenger* and a Revised Groupthink Framework," *Human Relations* 44 (1991), pp. 539–50; Janis, *Crucial Decisions*, pp. 76–77.

50. C. McGarty, J. C. Turner, M. A. Hogg, B. David, and M. S. Wetherell, "Group Polarization as Conformity to the Prototypical Group Member," *British Journal of Social Psychology* 31 (1992), pp. 1–20; D. Isenberg, "Group Polarization: A Critical Review and Meta-Analysis," *Journal of Personality and Social Psychology* 50 (1986), pp. 1141–51; D. G. Myers and H. Lamm, "The Group Polarization Phenomenon," *Psychological Bulletin* 83 (1976), pp. 602–27.

51. D. Friedman, "Monty Hall's Three Doors: Construction and Deconstruction of a Choice Anomaly," *American Economic Review* 88 (September 1998), pp. 933–46; D. Kahneman and A. Tversky, "Prospect Theory: An Analysis of Decision under Risk," *Econometrica* 47 (1979), pp. 263–91.

52. Janis, *Crucial Decisions*, pp. 244–49.

53. F. A. Schull, A. L. Delbecq, and L. L. Cummings, *Organizational Decision Making* (New York: McGraw-Hill, 1970), pp. 144–49.

54. A. MacKensie "Innovate or Be Damned," *Asian Business*, January 1995, pp. 30–34.

55. T. Hines, "Left Brain/Right Brain Mythology and Implications for Management and Training," *Academy of Management Review* 12 (1987), pp. 600–6.

56. B. Kabanoff and J. R. Rossiter, "Recent Developments in Applied Creativity," *International Review of Industrial and Organizational Psychology* 9 (1994), pp. 283–324.

57. V. Parv, "The Idea Toolbox: Techniques for Being a More Creative Writer," *Writer's Digest* 78 (July 1998), p. 18.

58. Leonard and Sensiper "The Role of Tacit Knowledge in Group Innovation."

59. K. Cottrill, "Reinventing Innovation," *Journal of Business Strategy*, March–April 1998, pp. 47–51; M. J. Kiernan, "Get Innovative or Get Dead," *Business Quarterly* 61 (Autumn 1996), pp. 51–58; T. A. Stewart, "3M Fights Back," *Fortune*, February 5, 1996, pp. 94–99.

60. M. Michalko, "Thinking Like a Genius: Eight Strategies Used by the Supercreative, from Aristotle and Leonardo to Einstein and Edison," *The Futurist* 32 (May 1998), pp. 21–25; J. S. Dacey, "Peak Periods of Creative Growth across the Lifespan," *Journal of Creative Behavior* 23 (1989), pp. 224–47; F. Barron and D. M. Harrington, "Creativity, Intelligence, and Personality," *Annual Review of Psychology* 32 (1981), pp. 439–76.

61. P. Roberts, "Sony Changes the Game," *Fast Company*, no. 10 (1997), p. 116.

62. G. R. Oldham and A. Cummings, "Employee Creativity: Personal and Contextual Factors at Work," *Academy of Management Journal* 39 (1996), pp. 607–34; C. E. Shalley, "Effects of Coaction, Expected Evaluation, and Goal Setting on Creativity and Productivity," *Academy of Management Journal* 38 (1995), pp. 483–503; R. M. Burnside, "Improving Corporate Climates for Creativity," in *Innovation and Creativity at Work*, M. A. West and J. L. Farr, eds. (Chichester, UK: John Wiley, 1990), pp. 265–84.

63. A. van de Vliet, "Perish Not the Thought," *Management Today*, April 1997, 70–73; C. M. Farkus and P. DeBacker, *Maximum Leadership* (New York: Henry Holt, 1996), pp. 154–55.

64. Michalko, "Thinking Like a Genius."

65. D. Maitra, "Livio D. Desimone: We Do Not See Failures as Failure," *Business Today* (India), June 22, 1998, p. 66.

66. A. G. Robinson and S. Stern, *Corporate Creativity, How Innovation and Improvement Actually Happen* (San Francisco: Berrett-Koehler, 1997).

67. R. I. Sutton and A. Hargadon, "Brainstorming Groups in Context: Effectiveness in a Product Design Firm," *Administrative Science Quarterly* 41 (1996), pp. 685–718.

68. T. M. Amabile, R. Conti, H. Coon, J. Lazenby, and M. Herron, "Assessing the Work Environment for Creativity," *Academy of Management Journal* 39 (1996), pp. 1154–84; R. W. Woodman, J. E. Sawyer, and R. W. Griffin, "Toward a Theory of Organizational Creativity," *Academy of Management Review* 18 (1993), pp. 293–321; T. M. Amabile, "A Model of Creativity and Innovation in Organizations," *Research in Organizational Behavior* 10 (1988), pp. 123–67.

69. Cottrill, "Reinventing Innovation"; D. Leonard and S. Strauss, "Putting Your Company's Whole Brain to Work," *Harvard Business Review* 75 (July–August 1997), pp. 110–13; K. A. Edelman, "Take Down the Walls! Open Office," *Across the Board* 34 (March 1997), pp. 32–38; G. Dutton, "Enhancing Creativity," *Management Review,* November 1996, pp. 44–46.

70. B. Kabanoff and P. Bottiger, "Effectiveness of Creativity Training and Its Relation to Selected Personality Factors," *Journal of Organizational Behavior* 12 (1991), pp. 235–48; and L. H. Rose and H. T. Lin, "A Meta-Analysis of Long-Term Creativity Training Programs," *Journal of Creative Behavior* 18 (1984), pp. 11–22.

71. S. Z. Dudek and R. Côté, "Problem Finding Revisited," in Runco, ed., *Problem Finding, Problem Solving, and Creativity,* pp. 130–50.

72. M. Basadur, G. B. Graen, and S. G. Green, "Training in Creative Problem Solving: Effects on Ideation and Problem Finding and Solving in an Industrial Research Organization," *Organizational Behavior and Human Performance* 30 (1982), pp. 41–70.

73. A. Gove, "Corporate Consulting Gets Kao'd," *Red Herring,* January 1999 (online).

74. K. W. Jesse, "A Creative Approach to Doing Business," *Dayton Daily News,* June 19, 1998, p. C1.

75. J. Neff, "At Eureka Ranch, Execs Doff Wing Tips, Fire Up Ideas," *Advertising Age,* March 9, 1998, pp. 28–29.

76. W. J. J. Gordon, *Synectics: The Development of Creative Capacity* (New York: Harper & Row, 1961).

77. A. C. Amason, "Distinguishing the Effects of Functional and Dysfunctional Conflict on Strategic Decision Making: Resolving a Paradox for Top Management Teams," *Academy of Management Journal* 39 (1996), pp. 123–48; G. Katzenstein, "The Debate on Structured Debate: Toward a Unified Theory," *Organizational Behavior and Human Decision Processes* 66 (1996), pp. 316–32; D. Tjosvold, *Team Organization: An Enduring Competitive Edge* (Chichester, UK: John Wiley, 1991).

78. K. M. Eisenhardt, J. L. Kahwajy, and L. J. Bourgeois III, "Conflict and Strategic Choice: How Top Management Teams Disagree," *California Management Review* 39 (Winter 1997), pp. 42–62.

79. L. Tucci, "Owens Drake Consulting Fosters Systematic Change," *St. Louis Business Journal,* May 25, 1998 (online).

80. J. S. Valacich and C. Schwenk. "Structuring Conflict in Individual, Face-to-Face, and Computer-Mediated Group Decision Making: Carping versus Objective Devil's Advocacy," *Decision Sciences* 26 (1995), pp. 369–93; D. M. Schweiger, W. R. Sandberg, and P. L. Rechner, "Experiential Effects of Dialectical Inquiry, Devil's Advocacy, and Consensus Approaches to Strategic Decision Making," *Academy of Management Journal* 32 (1989), pp. 745–72.

81. P. J. H. Schoemaker, "Disciplined Imagination: From Scenarios to Strategic Options," *International Studies of Management & Organization* 27 (Summer 1997), pp. 43–70.

82. A. F. Osborn, *Applied Imagination* (New York: Charles Scribner, 1957).

83. T. Keelin, "How SmithKline Beecham Makes Better Resource-Allocation Decisions," *Harvard Business Review* 76 (March–April 1998), pp. 45–57; D. Leonard and J. F. Rayport, "Spark Innovation through Empathic Design," *Harvard Business Review* 75 (November–December 1997), pp. 102–8.

84. Sutton and Hargadon, "Brainstorming Groups in Context," *Administrative Science Quarterly;* P. B. Paulus and M. T. Dzindolet, "Social Influence Processes in Group Brainstorming," *Journal of Personality and Social Psychology* 64 (1993), pp. 575–86; B. Mullen, B. C. Johnson, and E. Salas, "Productivity Loss in Brainstorming Groups: A Meta-Analytic Integration." *Basic and Applied Psychology* 12 (1991), pp. 2–23.

85. Gallupe et al., "Blocking Electronic Brainstorms."

86. P. Bordia, "Face-to-Face versus Computer-Mediated Communication: A Synthesis of the Experimental Literature," *Journal of Business Communication* 34 (1997), pp. 99–120; J. S. Valacich, A. R. Dennis, and T. Connolly, "Idea Generation in Computer-Based Groups: A New Ending to an Old Story," *Organizational Behavior and Human Decision Processes* 57 (1994), pp. 448–67; R. B. Gallupe, W. H. Cooper, M. L. Grisé, and L. M. Bastianutti, "Blocking Electronic Brainstorms," *Journal of Applied Psychology* 79 (1994), pp. 77–86.

87. M. Schrage, "Anonymous E-Mail Fans Flames of Corporate Conflict," *Computerworld,* June 9, 1997, p. 33.

88. W. M. Bulkeley, "'Computerizing' Dull Meetings Is Touted as an Antidote to the Mouth That Bored," *The Wall Street Journal,* January 28, 1992, pp. B1–B2.

89. J. J. Smith, "Meeting Center Allows Everyone in Business Meeting to Get Ideas Across," *Detroit News,* September 23, 1997, p. S12.

90. B. Daily, A. Wheatley, S. R. Ash, and R. L. Steiner, "The Effects of a Group Decision Support System on Culturally Diverse and Culturally Homogeneous Group Decision Making," *Information & Management* 30 (1996), pp. 281–89; R. B. Gallupe, A. R. Dennis, W. H. Cooper, J. S. Valacich, L. M. Bastianutti, and J. F. Nunamaker, Jr., "Electronic Brainstorming and Group Size," *Academy of Management Journal* 35 (June 1992), pp. 350–69; R. B. Gallupe, L. M. Bastianutti, and W. H. Cooper, "Unblocking Brainstorms," *Journal of Applied Psychology* 76 (1991), pp. 137–42.

91. B. Kabanoff and J. R. Rossiter, "Recent Developments in Applied Creativity," *International Review of Industrial and Organizational Psychology* 9 (1994), pp. 283–324.

92. H. A. Linstone and M. Turoff, eds., *The Delphi Method: Techniques and Applications* (Reading, MA: Addison-Wesley, 1975).

93. A. Mindell, "Electronic Format Recharges Meetings," *Crain's Detroit Business,* October 27, 1997, p. 17.

94. C. Critcher and B. Gladstone, "Utilizing the Delphi Technique in Policy Discussion: A Case Study of a Privatized Utility in Britain," *Public Administration* 76 (Autumn 1998), pp. 431–49; S. R. Rubin et al., "Research Directions Related to Rehabilitation Practice: A Delphi Study," *Journal of Rehabilitation* 64 (Winter 1998), p. 19.

95. A. L. Delbecq, A. H. Van de Ven, and D. H. Gustafson, *Group Techniques for Program Planning: A Guide to Nominal Group and Delphi Processes* (Middleton, WI: Green Briar Press, 1986).

96. A. B. Hollingshead, "The Rank-Order Effect in Group Decision Making," *Organizational Behavior and Human*

Decision Processes 68 (1996), pp. 181–93.

97. S. Frankel, "NGT + MDS: An Adaptation of the Nominal Group Technique for Ill-Structured Problems," *Journal of Applied Behavioral Science* 23 (1987), pp. 543–51; and D. M. Hegedus and R. Rasmussen, "Task Effectiveness and Interaction Process of a Modified Nominal Group Technique in Solving an Evaluation Problem," *Journal of Management* 12 (1986), pp. 545–60.

Chapter Twelve

1. D. Kirkpatrick, "The Second Coming of Apple," *Fortune*, November 9, 1998, pp. 86–92; J. Carlton, "Thinking Different," *The Wall Street Journal*, April 14, 1998; J. Mardesich, "Office Gossip Points at Jobs as Mastermind of a Coup," *San Jose Mercury*, July 10, 1997; Brent Schlender, "Something's Rotten in Cupertino," *Fortune*, March 3, 1997, pp. 100–8; J. Pearlstein, "Rumors Fly as Staffers Brace for Apple Cuts," *MacWeek*, February 28, 1997.

2. C. Hardy and S. Leiba-O'Sullivan, "The Power Behind Empowerment: Implications for Research and Practice," *Human Relations* 51 (April 1998), pp. 451–83; R. Farson, *Management of the Absurd* (New York: Simon & Schuster, 1996), chap. 13; R. M. Cyert and J. G. March, *A Behavioral Theory of the Firm* (Englewood Cliffs, NJ: Prentice Hall, 1963).

3. R. C. Liden and S. Arad, "A Power Perspective of Empowerment and Work Groups: Implications for Human Resources Management Research," *Research in Personnel and Human Resource Management* 14 (1996), pp. 205–51.

4. For a discussion of the definition of power, see: J. Pfeffer, *New Directions in Organizational Theory* (New York: Oxford University Press, 1997), chap. 6; J. Pfeffer, *Managing with Power* (Boston: Harvard Business School Press, 1992), pp. 17, 30; H. Mintzberg, *Power in and around Organizations* (Englewood Cliffs, NJ: Prentice Hall, 1983), chap. 1.

5. A. M. Pettigrew, *The Politics of Organizational Decision-Making* (London: Tavistock, 1973); R. M. Emerson, "Power-Dependence Relations," *American Sociological Review* 27 (1962), pp. 31–41; R. A. Dahl, "The Concept of Power,"

Behavioral Science 2 (1957), pp. 201–18.

6. D. J. Brass and M. E. Burkhardt, "Potential Power and Power Use: An Investigation of Structure and Behavior," *Academy of Management Journal* 36 (1993), pp. 441–70; K. M. Bartol and D. C. Martin, "When Politics Pays: Factors Influencing Managerial Compensation Decisions," *Personnel Psychology* 43 (1990), pp. 599–614.

7. P. P. Carson and K. D. Carson, "Social Power Bases: A Meta-Analytic Examination of Interrelationships and Outcomes," *Journal of Applied Social Psychology* 23 (1993), pp. 1150–69; P. Podsakoff and C. Schreisheim, "Field Studies of French and Raven's Bases of Power: Critique, Analysis, and Suggestions for Future Research," *Psychological Bulletin* 97 (1985), pp. 387–411; J. R. P. French and B. Raven, "The Bases of Social Power," in D. Cartwright, ed., *Studies in Social Power* (Ann Arbor: University of Michigan Press, 1959), pp. 150–67.

8. For example, see S. Finkelstein, "Power in Top Management Teams: Dimensions, Measurement, and Validation," *Academy of Management Journal* 35 (1992), pp. 505–38.

9. G. Yukl and C. M. Falbe, "Importance of Different Power Sources in Downward and Lateral Relations," *Journal of Applied Psychology* 76 (1991), pp. 416–23.

10. G. A. Yukl, *Leadership in Organizations*, 3rd ed. (Englewood Cliffs, NJ: Prentice Hall, 1994), p. 13; B. H. Raven, "The Bases of Power: Origins and Recent Developments," *Journal of Social Issues* 49 (1993), pp. 227–51.

11. C. Hardy and S. R. Clegg, "Some Dare Call It Power," in S. R. Clegg, C. Hardy, and W. R. Nord, eds., *Handbook of Organization Studies* (London: Sage, 1996), pp. 622–41; C. Barnard, *The Function of the Executive* (Cambridge: Harvard University Press, 1938).

12. I. Nonaka and H. Takeuchi, *The Knowledge-Creating Company* (New York: Oxford University Press, 1995), pp. 138–39.

13. D. Koulack, "When It's Healthy to Doubt the Doctor," *Globe & Mail* (Toronto), February 17, 1993, p. A20.

14. J. A. Conger, *Winning 'em Over* (New York: Simon & Shuster, 1998), appendix A.

15. H. Lancaster, "Job Reviews Are More Valuable When More Join In," *The Wall Street Journal*, July 1996.

16. M. Siconolfi, "Firms Freeze Out Stock Bashers," *Globe & Mail* (Toronto), August 3, 1995, p. B8.

17. L. Eisaguirre, "Welcome to the '90s, Boss," *Colorado Business* 25 (March 1998), pp. 20–22.

18. R. Hodson, "Group Relations at Work: Solidarity, Conflict, and Relations with Management," *Work & Occupations* 24 (November 1997), pp. 426–52.

19. G. Sewell, "The Discipline of Teams: The Control of Team-Based Industrial Work through Electronic and Peer Surveillance," *Administrative Science Quarterly* 43 (June 1998), pp. 397–428.

20. P. Panchak, "The Future Manufacturing," *Industry Week*, September 21, 1998, pp. 96–105.

21. J. D. Kudisch and M. L. Poteet, "Expert Power, Referent Power, and Charisma: Toward the Resolution of a Theoretical Debate," *Journal of Business & Psychology* 10 (Winter 1995), pp. 177–95.

22. Yukl and Falbe, "Importance of Different Power Sources in Downward and Lateral Relations."

23. Pitney Bowes, Inc., "Study Finds Growth of Communication Options Is Fundamentally Changing Work," news release, April 8, 1997 (www.pitneybowes.com).

24. D. J. Brass, "Being in the Right Place: A Structural Analysis of Individual Influence in an Organization," *Administrative Science Quarterly* 29 (1984), pp. 518–39; N. M. Tichy, M. L. Tuchman, and C. Frombrun, "Social Network Analysis in Organizations," *Academy of Management Review* 4 (1979), pp. 507–19; H. Guetzkow and H. Simon, "The Impact of Certain Communication Nets upon Organization and Performance in Task-Oriented Groups," *Management Science* 1 (1955), pp. 233–50.

25. C. S. Saunders, "The Strategic Contingency Theory of Power: Multiple Perspectives," *The Journal of Management Studies* 27 (1990), pp. 1–21; D. J. Hickson, C. R. Hinings, C. A. Lee, R. E. Schneck, and J. M. Pennings, "A Strategic Contingencies' Theory of Intraorganizational Power," *Administrative Science Quarterly* 16 (1971), pp. 216–27.

26. J. D. Thompson, *Organizations in Action* (New York: McGraw-Hill, 1967); Cyert and March, *A Behavioral Theory of the Firm*.

27. C. M. Daily and J. L. Johnson, "Sources of CEO Power and Firm Financial Performance: A Longitudinal Assessment," *Journal of Management* 23 (March 1997), p. 97.

28. C. R. Hinings, D. J. Hickson, J. M. Pennings, and R. E. Schneck, "Structural Conditions of Intraorganizational Power," *Administrative Science Quarterly* 19 (1974), pp. 22–44.

29. "The Art of Gazing over the Horizon," *Financial Times*, February 8, 1999, p. 14.

30. Hickson et al., "A Strategic Contingencies' Theory of Intraorganizational Power"; Hinings et al., "Structural Conditions of Intraorganizational Power"; and R. M. Kanter, "Power Failure in Management Circuits," *Harvard Business Review* 57 (July–August 1979), pp. 65–75.

31. M. Crozier, *The Bureaucratic Phenomenon* (London: Tavistock, 1964).

32. M. F. Masters, *Unions at the Crossroads: Strategic Membership, Financial, and Political Perspectives* (Westport, CT: Quorum Books, 1997).

33. Brass and Burkhardt, "Potential Power and Power Use," pp. 441–70; Hickson et al., "A Strategic Contingencies' Theory of Intraorganizational Power," pp. 219–21; J. D. Hackman, "Power and Centrality in the Allocation of Resources in Colleges and Universities," *Administrative Science Quarterly* 30 (1985), pp. 61–77.

34. B. Koenig, "GM to Shut Most of Its U.S. Plants," *Indianapolis News*, June 26, 1998, p. D10; P. Kaplan, "GM Dealers Fear Strike May Cause Car Shortage," *Washington Times*, June 19, 1998, p. B9; D. W. Nauss, "Strike at GM Facility Forces 5 Plants to Shut," *Los Angeles Times*, June 9, 1998, p. 1.

35. Kanter, "Power Failure in Management Circuits," p. 68; B. E. Ashforth, "The Experience of Powerlessness in Organizations," *Organizational Behavior and Human Decision Processes* 43 (1989), pp. 207–42.

36. M. L. A. Hayward and W. Boeker, "Power and Conflicts of Interest in Professional Firms: Evidence from Investment Banking," *Administrative Science Quarterly* 43 (March 1998), pp. 1–22.

37. Raven, "The Bases of Power," pp. 237–39.

38. L. E. Temple and K. R. Loewen. "Perceptions of Power: First Impressions of a Woman Wearing a Jacket," *Perceptual and Motor Skills* 76 (1993), pp. 339–48.

39. B. R. Ragins, "Diversified Mentoring Relationships in Organizations: A Power Perspective," *Academy of Management Review* 22 (1997), pp. 482–521; G. R. Ferris, D. D. Frink, D. P. S. Bhawuk, J. Zhou, and D. C. Gilmore, "Reactions of Diverse Groups to Politics in the Workplace," *Journal of Management* 22 (1996), pp. 23–44.

40. C. M. Falbe and G. Yukl, "Consequences for Managers of Using Single Influence Tactics and Combinations of Tactics," *Academy of Management Journal* 35 (1992), pp. 638–52.

41. D. Kipnis, *The Powerholders* (Chicago: University of Chicago Press, 1976); G. R. Salancik and J. Pfeffer, "The Bases and Use of Power in Organizational Decision Making: The Case of a University," *Administrative Science Quarterly* 19 (1974), pp. 453–73.

42. G. E. G. Catlin, *Systematic Politics* (Toronto: University of Toronto Press, 1962), p. 71.

43. V. Schultz, "Reconceptualizing Sexual Harassment," *Yale Law Journal* 107 (April 1998), pp. 1683–1805.

44. D. E. Terpstra, "The Effects of Diversity on Sexual Harassment: Some Recommendations on Research," *Employee Responsibilities and Rights Journal* 9 (1996), pp. 303–13; J. A. Bargh and P. Raymond, "The Naive Misuse of Power: Nonconscious Sources of Sexual Harassment," *Journal of Social Issues* 51 (1995) pp. 85–96; R. A. Thacker and G. R. Ferris, "Understanding Sexual Harassment in the Workplace: The Influence of Power and Politics with the Dyadic Interaction of Harasser and Target," *Human Resource Management Review* 1 (1991), pp. 23–37.

45. D. Greenberg and S. Perkins, "When Employees Cry Foul," *Outlook* 65 (March 1997), p. 26.

46. L. H. Coady, "Astra U.S.A. Will Pay $9.85 Million to Settle EEOC Suit," *Sexual Harassment Litigation Reporter*, February 6, 1998, p. 1; K. N. Gilpin, "Firm to Pay $10 Million in Settlement of Sex Case," *New York Times*, February 6, 1998, p. 16; M. Maremont, "Abuse of Power," *Business Week*, May 13, 1996, pp. 86–98.

47. K. D. Grimsley, "Mitsubishi Settles for $34 Million," *Washington Post*, June 12, 1998, p. A1.

48. For a discussion of the ethical implications of sexual harassment, see T. I. White, "Sexual Harassment: Trust and the Ethic of Care," *Business and Society Review,* January 1998, pp. 9–20; J. Keyton and S. C. Rhodes, "Sexual Harassment: A Matter of Individual Ethics, Legal Definitions, or Organizational Policy?" *Journal of Business Ethics* 16 (February 1997), pp. 129–46.

49. M. Verespej, "New Boundaries for Sexual Harassment," *Industry Week*, May 6, 1998, pp. 6–7.

50. T. L. Tang and S. L. McCollum, "Sexual Harassment in the Workplace," *Public Personnel Management* 25 (1996), pp. 53–58; Bargh and Raymond, "The Naive Misuse of Power," pp. 85–96.

51. J. Lardner, D. Lackaff, K. Roebuck, and S. Hammel, "Cupid's Cubicles," *U.S. News & World Report*, December 14, 1998, pp. 44–54.

52. H. Pauly, "Sex and the Workplace: Companies Revisit the Rules," *Chicago Sun-Times*, August 26, 1998 (online).

53. T. Petzinger Jr., *The New Pioneers: The Men and Women Who Are Transforming the Workplace and Marketplace* (New York: Simon & Schuster, 1999), chap. 1.

54. K. M. Kacmar and G. R. Ferris, "Politics at Work: Sharpening the Focus of Political Behavior in Organizations," *Business Horizons* 36 (July–August 1993), pp. 70–74; A. Drory and T. Romm, "The Definition of Organizational Politics: A Review," *Human Relations* 43 (1990), pp. 1133–54; P. J. Frost and D. C. Hayes, "An Exploration in Two Cultures of a Model of Political Behavior in Organizations," in *Organizational Influence Processes*, R. W. Allen and L. W. Porter, eds. (Glenview, IL: Scott, Foresman, 1983), pp. 369–92.

55. K. Ohlson, "Leadership in an Age of Mistrust," *Industry Week*, February 2, 1998, pp. 37–46.

56. T. H. Davenport, R. G. Eccles, and L. Prusak, "Information Politics," *Sloan Management Review,* Fall 1992, pp. 53–65; Pfeffer, *Managing with Power,* chap. 17.

57. A. J. Skerritt, "Management Problems Lead to Split," *Rock Hill Herald* (SC), June 24, 1998, p. A4.

58. J. C. Howes, A. A. Grandey, and P. Toth, "The Relationship of Organizational Politics and Support to Work Behaviors, Attitudes, and Stress," *Journal of Organizational Behavior* 18 (March 1997), pp. 159–80; G. R. Ferris and D. D. Frink, "Reactions of Diverse Groups to Politics in the Workplace," *Journal of Management* 22 (Spring 1996), pp. 23–44; P. Kumar and R. Ghadially, "Organizational Politics and Its Effects on Members of Organizations," *Human Relations* 42 (1989), pp. 305–14.

59. M. Velasquez, D. J. Moberg, and G. F. Cavanaugh, "Organizational Statesmanship and Dirty Politics: Ethical Guidelines for the Organizational Politician," *Organizational Dynamics* 11 (1983), pp. 65–79.

60. R. W. Allen, D. L. Madison, L. W. Porter, P. A. Renwick, and B. T. Mayes, "Organizational Politics: Tactics and Characteristics of Its Actors," *California Management Review* 22 (Fall 1979), pp. 77–83; V. Murray and J. Gandz, "Games Executives Play: Politics at Work," *Business Horizons,* December 1980, pp. 11–23.

61. B. E. Ashforth and R. T. Lee, "Defensive Behavior in Organizations: A Preliminary Model," *Human Relations* 43 (1990), pp. 621–48.

62. G. S. Crystal, *In Search of Excess* (New York: W. W. Norton, 1991), pp. 12–13.

63. N. Gupta and G. D. Jenkins, Jr., "The Politics of Pay," *Compensation and Benefits Review* 28 (March–April 1996), pp. 23–30; S. L. McShane, "Applicant Misrepresentation in Résumés and Interviews," *Labor Law Journal* 45 (January 1994), pp. 15–24.

64. For examples and discussion of these information "turf wars," see A. Simmons, *Territorial Games: Understanding & Ending Turf Wars* (New York: AMACOM, 1998).

65. S. Greengard, "Will Your Culture Support KM?" *Workforce* 77 (October 1998), pp. 93–94.

66. E. A. Mannix, "Organizations as Resource Dilemmas: The Effects of Power Balance on Coalition Formation in Small Groups," *Organizational Behavior and Human Decision Processes* 55 (1993), pp. 1–22; A. T. Cobb, "Toward the Study of Organizational Coalitions: Participant Concerns and Activities in a Simulated Organizational Setting," *Human Relations* 44 (1991), pp. 1057–79; W. B. Stevenson, J. L. Pearce, and L. W. Porter, "The Concept of 'Coalition' in Organization Theory and Research," *Academy of Management Review* 10 (1985), pp. 256–68.

67. Falbe and Yukl, "Consequences for Managers of Using Single Influence Tactics and Combinations of Tactics," pp. 638–52.

68. D. Krackhardt and J. R. Hanson, "Informal Networks: The Company behind the Chart," *Harvard Business Review* 71 (July–August 1993), pp. 104–11; and R. E. Kaplan, "Trade Routes: The Manager's Network of Relationships," *Organizational Dynamics,* Spring 1984, pp. 37–52.

69. R. J. Burke and C. A. McKeen, "Women in Management," *International Review of Industrial and Organizational Psychology* 7 (1992), pp. 245–83; B. R. Ragins and E. Sundstrom, "Gender and Power in Organizations: A Longitudinal Perspective," *Psychological Bulletin* 105 (1989), pp. 51–88.

70. "Balancing Briefcase and Baby," *Daily Commercial News,* March 4, 1996, p. B1.

71. A. R. Cohen and D. L. Bradford, "Influence without Authority: The Use of Alliances, Reciprocity, and Exchange to Accomplish Work," *Organizational Dynamics* 17, no. 3 (1989), pp. 5–17.

72. A. Rao and S. M. Schmidt, "Upward Impression Management: Goals, Influence Strategies, and Consequences," *Human Relations* 48 (1995), pp. 147–67; R. A. Giacalone and P. Rosenfeld, eds., *Applied Impression Management* (Newbury Park, CA: Sage, 1991); and J. T. Tedeschi, ed., *Impression Management Theory and Social Psychological Research* (New York: Academic Press, 1981).

73. W. L. Gardner III, "Lessons in Organizational Dramaturgy: The Art of Impression Management," *Organizational Dynamics* 21 (Summer 1992), pp. 33–46; R. C. Liden and T. R. Mitchell, "Ingratiatory Behaviors in Organizational Settings," *Academy of Management Review* 13 (1988), pp. 572–87; and A. MacGillivary, S. Ascroft, and M. Stebbins, "Meritless Ingratiation," *Proceedings of the Annual ASAC Conference, Organizational Behaviour Division* 7, pt. 7 (1986), pp. 127–35.

74. C. Hardy, *Strategies for Retrenchment and Turnaround: The Politics of Survival* (Berlin: Walter de Gruyter, 1990), chap. 14; J. Gandz and V. V. Murray, "The Experience of Workplace Politics," *Academy of Management Journal* 23 (1980), pp. 237–51.

75. P. Dillon, "Failure IS an Option," *Fast Company,* Issue 22 (February–March, 1999), pp. 154–71.

76. B. Dunlap, "Inside Out: Former TBWA Chiat/Day Inc. Staffers," *Shoot* 50 (December 12, 1997), p. 54.

77. S. Baker, "Job Satisfaction High in Survey, But Office Politics Alive and Well," *Fort Worth Star-Telegram,* March 13, 1997, p. 3

78. G. R. Ferris, G. S. Russ, and P. M. Fandt, "Politics in Organizations," in R. A. Giacalone and P. Rosenfeld, eds., *Impression Management in the Organization* (Hillsdale, NJ: Erlbaum, 1989), pp. 143–70; H. Mintzberg, "The Organization as Political Arena," *Journal of Management Studies* 22 (1985), pp. 133–54.

79. R. J. House, "Power and Personality in Complex Organizations," *Research in Organizational Behavior* 10 (1988), pp. 305–57; L. W. Porter, R. W. Allen, and H. L. Angle, "The Politics of Upward Influence in Organizations," *Research in Organizational Behavior* 3 (1981), pp. 120–22.

80. S. M. Farmer, J. M. Maslyn, D. B. Fedor, and J. S. Goodman, "Putting Upward Influence Strategies in Context," *Journal of Organizational Behavior* 18 (1997), pp. 17–42; P. E. Mudrack, "An Investigation into the Acceptability of Workplace Behaviors of a Dubious Ethical Nature," *Journal of Business Ethics* 12 (1993), pp. 517–24; and R. Christie and F. Geis, *Studies in Machiavellianism* (New York: Academic Press, 1970).

81. K. Ryer, "Hancock Speaks," *MacWeek,* July 11, 1997 (online); "Amelio Says His Good-byes," *Macworld Daily,* July 11, 1997 (online).

82. D. Tannen, *Talking from 9 to 5* (New York: Avon, 1995), pp. 137–41, 151–52.

83. Ibid., chap. 2.

84. M. Crawford, *Talking Difference: On Gender and Language* (Thousand Oaks, CA: Sage, 1995), pp. 41–44; D. Tannen, *You Just Don't Understand: Men and Women in Conversation* (New York: Ballentine Books, 1990); S. Helgesen, *The Female Advantage: Women's Ways of Leadership* (New York: Doubleday, 1990).

85. S. Mann, "Politics and Power in Organizations: Why Women Lose Out," *Leadership & Organization Development Journal* 16 (1995), pp. 9–15; L. Larwood and M. M. Wood, "Training Women for Management: Changing Priorities," *Journal of Management Development* 14 (1995), pp. 54–65. A recent popular press book even serves as a guide for women to learn organizational politics; see: H. Rubin, *The Princessa: Machiavelli for Women* (New York: Doubleday/Currency, 1996).

86. G. R. Ferris et al., "Perceptions of Organizational Politics: Prediction, Stress-Related Implications, and Outcomes," *Human Relations* 49 (1996), pp. 233–63.

Chapter Thirteen

1. R. O. Crockett, "Andersen vs. Andersen: Next Stop, Splitsville," *Business Week*, January 18, 1999, online; M. Petersen, "How the Andersens Turned into the Bickersons," *New York Times*, March 15, 1998, sect. 3, pp. 1, 13; "A Family Feud," *Management Consultant International*, February 1998, p. 7; M. Krantz, "Divorce Case: Andersen vs. Andersen," *Investor's Business Daily*, December 18, 1997, p. A6; J. Johnsson, "Accounting Giant Andersen Pushed to End Infighting," *Crain's Detroit Business*, October 27, 1997, p. 40.

2. J. A. Wall and R. R. Callister, "Conflict and Its Management," *Journal of Management* 21 (1995), pp. 515–58; D. Tjosvold, *Working Together to Get Things Done* (Lexington, MA: Lexington, 1986), pp. 114–15.

3. L. Pondy, "Organizational Conflict: Concepts and Models, *Administrative Science Quarterly* 12 (1967), pp. 296–320.

4. A. C. Ward, "Another Look at How Toyota Integrates Product Development," *Harvard Business Review* (July–August 1998), pp. 36–49.

5. A. C. Amason, "Distinguishing the Effects of Functional and Dysfunctional Conflict on Strategic Decision Making: Resolving a Paradox for Top Management Teams," *Academy of Management Journal* 39 (1996), pp. 123–48; K. A. Jehn, "A Multimethod Examination of the Benefits and Detriments of Intragroup Conflict," *Administrative Science Quarterly* 40 (1995), pp. 256–82.

6. J. M. Brett, D. L. Shapiro, and A. L. Lytle, "Breaking the Bonds of Reciprocity in Negotiations," *Academy of Management Journal* 41 (August 1998), pp. 410–24; G. E. Martin and T. J. Bergman, "The Dynamics of Behavioural Response to Conflict in the Workplace," *Journal of Occupational & Organizational Psychology* 69 (December 1996), pp. 377–87; G. Wolf, "Conflict Episodes," in *Negotiating in Organizations*, M. H. Bazerman and R. J. Lewicki, eds. (Beverly Hills, CA: Sage, 1983), pp. 135–40; Pondy, "Organizational Conflict: Concepts and Models," pp. 296–320.

7. H. Witteman, "Analyzing Interpersonal Conflict: Nature of Awareness, Type of Initiating Event, Situational Perceptions, and Management Styles," *Western Journal of Communications* 56 (1992), pp. 248–80; F. J. Barrett and D. L. Cooperrider, "Generative Metaphor Intervention: A New Approach for Working with Systems Divided by Conflict and Caught in Defensive Perception," *Journal of Applied Behavioral Science* 26 (1990), pp. 219–39.

8. Wall and Callister, "Conflict and Its Management," pp. 526–33.

9. S. Armour, "Moderate Amounts of Conflict Contribute to Healthy Workplace," *Des Moines Register*, May 20, 1997, p. 8.

10. Amason, "Distinguishing the Effects of Functional and Dysfunctional Conflict on Strategic Decision Making."

11. L. L. Putnam, "Productive Conflict: Negotiation as Implicit Coordination," *International Journal of Conflict Management* 5 (1994), pp. 285–99; D. Tjosvold, *The Conflict-*

Positive Organization (Reading, MA: Addison-Wesley, 1991); R. A. Baron, "Positive Effects of Conflict: A Cognitive Perspective," *Employee Responsibilities and Rights Journal* 4 (1991), pp. 25–36.

12. K. M. Eisenhardt, J. L. Kahwajy, and L. J. Bourgeois III, "Conflict and Strategic Choice: How Top Management Teams Disagree," *California Management Review* 39 (Winter 1997), pp. 42–62; J. K. Bouwen and R. Fry, "Organizational Innovation and Learning: Four Patterns of Dialog between the Dominant Logic and the New Logic," *International Studies of Management and Organizations* 21 (1991), pp. 37–51.

13. Rempel and R. J. Fisher, "Perceived Threat, Cohesion, and Group Problem Solving in Intergroup Conflict," *International Journal of Conflict Management* 8 (1997), pp. 216–34.

14. R. R. Blake and J. S. Mouton, *Solving Costly Organizational Conflicts* (San Francisco: Jossey-Bass, 1984).

15. F. Rose, "The Eisner School of Business," *Fortune*, July 6, 1998, pp. 29–30.

16. R. E. Walton and J. M. Dutton, "The Management of Conflict: A Model and Review," *Administrative Science Quarterly* 14 (1969), pp. 73–84.

17. M. L. A. Hayward and W. Boeker, "Power and Conflicts of Interest in Professional Firms: Evidence from Investment Banking," *Administrative Science Quarterly* 43 (March 1998), pp. 1–22.

18. S. Haddock, "No More Politics as Usual," *Deseret News*, Salt Lake City, July 12, 1998.

19. D. C. Hambrick, S. C. Davison, S. A. Snell, and C. C. Snow, "When Groups Consist of Multiple Nationalities: Towards a New Understanding of the Implications," *Organization Studies* 19 (1998), pp. 181–205; L. H. Pelled, "Demographic Diversity, Conflict, and Work Group Outcomes: An Intervening Process Theory," *Organization Science* 7 (1996), pp. 615–31.

20. N. McGrath, P. Janssen, and D. Hulme, "Scheming Workers Can Ruin Business," *Asian Business* 31 (September 1995) pp. 50–52.

21. R. C. Liden, S. J. Wayne, and L. K. Bradway, "Task Interdependence as a Moderator of the Relation between Group Control and Performance," *Human Relations* 50 (February

1997), pp. 169–81; R. Wageman, "Interdependence and Group Effectiveness," *Administrative Science Quarterly* 40 (1995), pp.145–80; M. A. Campion, G. J. Medsker, and A. C. Higgs, "Relations between Work Group Characteristics and Effectiveness: Implications for Designing Effective Work Groups," *Personnel Psychology* 46 (1993), pp. 823–50; M. N. Kiggundu, "Task Interdependence and the Theory of Job Design," *Academy of Management Review* 6 (1981), pp. 499–508.

22. P. C. Earley and G. B. Northcraft, "Goal Setting, Resource Interdependence, and Conflict Management," in M. A. Rahim, ed., *Managing Conflict: An Interdisciplinary Approach* (New York: Praeger, 1989), pp. 161–70.

23. J. D. Thompson, *Organizations in Action* (New York: McGraw-Hill, 1967), pp. 54–56.

24. K. H. Doerr, T. R. Mitchell, and T. D. Klastorin, "Impact of Material Flow Policies and Goals on Job Outcomes," *Journal of Applied Psychology* 81 (1996), pp. 142–52.

25. W. W. Notz, F. A. Starke, and J. Atwell, "The Manager as Arbitrator: Conflicts over Scarce Resources," in Bazerman and Lewicki, eds., *Negotiating in Organizations*, pp. 143–64.

26. P. Roberts, "Sony Changes the Game," *Fast Company*, Issue 10 (1997), p. 116.

27. Brett et al., "Breaking the Bonds of Reciprocity in Negotiations"; R. A. Baron, "Reducing Organizational Conflict: An Incompatible Response Approach," *Journal of Applied Psychology* 69 (1984), pp. 272–79.

28. K. D. Grimsley, "Slings and Arrows on the Job," *Washington Post*, July 12, 1998, p. H1; "Flame Throwers," *Director* 50 (July 1997), p. 36.

29. J. W. Jackson and E. R. Smith, "Conceptualizing Social Identity: A New Framework and Evidence for the Impact of Different Dimensions," *Personality & Social Psychology Bulletin* 25 (January 1999), pp. 120–35.

30. D. C. Dryer and L. M. Horowitz, "When Do Opposites Attract? Interpersonal Complementarity versus Similarity," *Journal of Personality and Social Psychology* 72 (1997), pp. 592–603.

31. K. W. Thomas, "Conflict and Conflict Management," in M. D. Dunnette, ed., *Handbook of Industrial and Organizational Psychology* (Chicago: Rand McNally, 1976), pp. 889–935. For similar models see R. R. Blake and J. S. Mouton, *The Managerial Grid* (Houston: Gulf Publications, 1964); M. A. Rahim, "A Measure of Styles of Handling Interpersonal Conflict," *Academy of Management Journal* 26 (1983), pp. 368–76.

32. R. J. Lewicki and J. A. Litterer, *Negotiation* (Burr Ridge, IL: Richard D. Irwin, 1985), pp. 102–6.

33. K. W. Thomas, "Toward Multi-Dimensional Values in Teaching: The Example of Conflict Behaviors," *Academy of Management Review* 2 (1977), pp. 484–90.

34. Jehn, "A Multimethod Examination of the Benefits and Detriments of Intragroup Conflict," p. 276.

35. Tjosvold, *Working Together to Get Things Done*, chap. 2; D. W. Johnson, G. Maruyama, R. T. Johnson, D. Nelson, and S. Skon, "Effects of Cooperative, Competitive, and Individualistic Goal Structures on Achievement: A Meta-Analysis," *Psychological Bulletin* 89 (1981), pp. 47–62; R. J. Burke, "Methods of Resolving Superior-Subordinate Conflict: The Constructive Use of Subordinate Differences and Disagreements," *Organizational Behavior and Human Performance* 5 (1970), pp. 393–441.

36. M. A. Rahim and A. A. Blum, eds., *Global Perspectives on Organizational Conflict* (Westport, CT: Praeger, 1995); M. Rabie, *Conflict Resolution and Ethnicity* (Westport, CT: Praeger, 1994).

37. C. C. Chen, X. P. Chen, and J. R. Meindl, "How Can Cooperation Be Fostered? The Cultural Effects of Individualism-Collectivism," *Academy of Management Review* 23 (1998), pp. 285–304; S. M. Elsayed-Ekhouly and R. Buda, "Organizational Conflict: A Comparative Analysis of Conflict Styles across Cultures," *International Journal of Conflict Management* 7 (1996), pp. 71–81; D. K. Tse, J. Francis, and J. Walls, "Cultural Differences in Conducting Intra- and Inter-Cultural Negotiations: A Sino-Canadian Comparison," *Journal of International Business Studies* 25 (1994), pp. 537–55; S. Ting-Toomey et al., "Culture, Face Management, and Conflict Styles of Handling Interpersonal Conflict: A Study in Five Cultures," *International Journal of Conflict Management* 2 (1991), pp. 275–96.

38. L. Xiaohua and R. Germain, "Sustaining Satisfactory Joint Venture Relationships: The Role of Conflict Resolution Strategy," *Journal of International Business Studies* 29 (March 1998), pp. 179–96.

39. L. Karakowsky, "Toward an Understanding of Women and Men at the Bargaining Table: Factors Affecting Negotiator Style and Influence in Multi-Party Negotiations," *Proceedings of the Annual ASAC Conference, Women in Management Division* (1996), pp. 21–30; W. C. King, Jr., and T. D. Hinson, "The Influence of Sex and Equity Sensitivity on Relationship Preferences, Assessment of Opponent, and Outcomes in a Negotiation Experiment," *Journal of Management* 20 (1994), pp. 605–24; R. Lewicki, J. Litterer, D. Saunders, and J. Minton, eds., *Negotiation: Readings, Exercises, and Cases* (Burr Ridge, IL: Richard D. Irwin, 1993).

40. E. Van de Vliert, "Escalative Intervention in Small Group Conflicts," *Journal of Applied Behavioral Science* 21 (Winter 1985), pp. 19–36.

41. J. R. W. Joplin and C. S. Daus, "Challenges of Leading a Diverse Workforce," *Academy of Management Executive*, August 1997, pp. 32–47.

42. M. B. Pinto, J. K. Pinto, and J. E. Prescott, "Antecedents and Consequences of Project Team Cross-Functional Cooperation," *Management Science* 39 (1993), pp. 1281–97; M. Sherif, "Superordinate Goals in the Reduction of Intergroup Conflict," *American Journal of Sociology* 68 (1958), pp. 349–58.

43. K. M. Eisenhardt, J. L. Kahwajy, and L. J. Bourgeois III, "How Management Teams Can Have a Good Fight," *Harvard Business Review*, July–August 1997, pp. 77–85.

44. T. Minahan, "Platform Teams Pair with Suppliers to Drive Chrysler to Better Designs," *Purchasing*, May 7, 1998, p. 44S3.

45. M. Zimmerman, *How to Do Business with the Japanese* (New York: Random House, 1985), pp. 170, 200; W. G. Ouchi, *Theory Z* (New York: Avon, 1982), pp. 25–32.

46. "American Factories Halt Their Assembly Lines," *Globe and Mail* (Toronto), January 7, 1995, p. D4.

47. "Two (Very Different) Success Stories," *Harvard Business Review*, January–February 1995, pp. 71–72.

48. R. J. Fisher, E. Maltz, and B. J. Jaworski, "Enhancing Communication between Marketing and Engineering: The Moderating Role of Relative Functional Identification," *Journal of Marketing* 61 (July 1997), pp. 54–70.

49. W. N. Isaacs, "Taking Flight: Dialog, Collective Thinking, and Organizational Learning," *Organizational Dynamics*, Autumn 1993, pp. 24–39; E. H. Schein, "On Dialog, Culture, and Organizational Learning," *Organizational Dynamics*, Autumn 1993, pp. 40–51; P. M. Senge, *The Fifth Discipline* (New York: Doubleday Currency, 1990), pp. 238–49.

50. P. Labarre "This Organization Is Dis-Organization," *Fast Company* (online), Issue 3 (1997).

51. Blake and Mouton, *Solving Costly Organizational Conflicts*, chap. 6; R. R. Blake and J. S. Mouton, "Overcoming Group Warfare," *Harvard Business Review*, November–December 1984, pp. 98–108.

52. P. R. Lawrence and J. W. Lorsch, *Organization and Environment* (Burr Ridge, IL.: Richard D. Irwin, 1969).

53. J. S. DeMott, "The Key Issue: Managing Bigness," *Worldbusiness*, September–October 1996, pp. 30–33.

54. B. Pletcher, "When Managers Play Referee: Workplace Conflict Approaches Vary," *Fort Worth Star-Telegram*, May 4, 1998, p. 13.

55. D. G. Pruitt and P. J. Carnevale, *Negotiation in Social Conflict* (Buckingham, England: Open University Press, 1993), p. 2; J. A. Wall, Jr., *Negotiation: Theory and Practice* (Glenview, IL: Scott, Foresman, 1985), p. 4.

56. For a critical view of collaboration in negotiation, see J. M. Brett, "Managing Organizational Conflict," *Professional Psychology: Research and Practice* 15 (1984), pp. 664–78.

57. R. E. Fells, "Overcoming the Dilemmas in Walton and McKersie's Mixed Bargaining Strategy," *Industrial Relations* (Laval) 53 (Spring 1998), pp. 300–25; R. E. Fells, "Developing Trust in Negotiation," *Employee Relations* 15 (1993), pp. 33–45.

58. R. Stagner and H. Rosen, *Psychology of Union-Management Relations* (Belmont, CA: Wadsworth, 1965), pp. 95–96, 108–10; R. E. Walton and R. B. McKersie, *A Behavioral Theory of Labor Negotiations: An Analysis of a Social Interaction System* (New York: McGraw-Hill, 1965), pp. 41–46.

59. M. Beil and J. E. Litscher, "Consensus Bargaining in Wisconsin State Government: A New Approach to Labor Negotiation," *Public Personnel Management* 27 (Spring 1998), pp. 39–50.

60. J. W. Salacuse and J. Z. Rubin, "Your Place or Mine? Site Location and Negotiation," *Negotiation Journal* 6 (January 1990), pp. 5–10; Lewicki and Litterer, *Negotiation*, pp. 144–46.

61. B. C. Herniter, E. Carmel, and J. F. Nunamaker, Jr., "Computers Improve Efficiency of the Negotiation Process," *Personnel Journal*, April 1993, pp. 93–99.

62. Lewicki and Litterer, *Negotiation*, pp. 146–51; B. Kniveton, *The Psychology of Bargaining* (Aldershot, England: Avebury, 1989), pp. 76–79.

63. Beil and Litscher, "Consensus Bargaining in Wisconsin State Government."

64. Pruitt and Carnevale, *Negotiation in Social Conflict*, pp. 59–61; Lewicki and Litterer, *Negotiation*, pp. 151–54.

65. N. J. Adler, *International Dimensions of Organizational Behavior*, 2nd ed. (Belmont, CA: Wadsworth, 1991), p. 191.

66. B. M. Downie, "When Negotiations Fail: Causes of Breakdown and Tactics for Breaking the Stalemate," *Negotiation Journal*, April 1991, pp. 175–86.

67. Pruitt and Carnevale, *Negotiation in Social Conflict*, pp. 56–58; Lewicki and Litterer, *Negotiation*, pp. 215–22.

68. V. V. Murray, T. D. Jick, and P. Bradshaw, "To Bargain or Not to Bargain? The Case of Hospital Budget Cuts," in Bazerman and Lewicki, *Negotiating in Organizations*, pp. 272–95.

69. R. L. Lewicki, A. Hiam, and K. Olander, *Think Before You Speak: The Complete Guide to Strategic Negotiation* (New York : John Wiley, 1996); G. B. Northcraft and M. A. Neale, "Joint Effects of Assigned Goals and Training on Negotiator Performance," *Human Performance* 7 (1994), pp. 257–72.

70. S. Doctoroff, "Reengineering Negotiations," *Sloan Management Review* 39 (Spring 1998), pp. 63–71.

71. M. A. Neale and M. H. Bazerman, *Cognition and Rationality in Negotiation* (New York: Free Press, 1991), pp. 29–31; and L. L. Thompson, "Information Exchange in Negotiation," *Journal of Experimental Social Psychology* 27 (1991), pp. 161–79.

72. L. Thompson, E. Peterson, and S. E. Brodt, "Team Negotiation: An Examination of Integrative and Distributive Bargaining," *Journal of Personality and Social Psychology* 70 (1996), pp. 66–78; Lewicki and Litterer, *Negotiation*, pp. 177–80; and Adler, *International Dimensions of Organizational Behavior*, pp. 190–91.

73. L. L. Putnam and M. E. Roloff, eds., *Communication and Negotiation* (Newbury Park, CA: Sage, 1992).

74. L. Hall, ed., *Negotiation: Strategies for Mutual Gain* (Newbury Park, CA: Sage, 1993); and D. Ertel, "How to Design a Conflict Management Procedure That Fits Your Dispute," *Sloan Management Review* 32 (Summer 1991), pp. 29–42.

75. Lewicki and Litterer, *Negotiation*, pp. 89–93.

76. P. Brethour, "Toronto Firm Takes to Heart Cultural Lessons," *Globe and Mail* (Toronto), August 30, 1996, p. B6; Adler, *International Dimensions of Organizational Behavior*, pp. 180–81.

77. Kniveton, *The Psychology of Bargaining*, pp. 100–1; J. Z. Rubin and B. R. Brown, *The Social Psychology of Bargaining and Negotiation* (New York: Academic Press, 1976), chap. 9; Brett, "Managing Organizational Conflict," pp. 670–71.

78. B. H. Sheppard, R. J. Lewicki, and J. W. Monton, *Organizational Justice: The Search for Fairness in the Workplace* (New York: Lexington Books, 1992).

79. R. Folger and J. Greenberg, "Procedural Justice: An Interpretive Analysis of Personnel Systems," *Research in Personnel and Human Resources Management* 3 (1985), pp. 141–83.

80. L. L. Putnam, "Beyond Third Party Role: Disputes and Managerial Intervention," *Employee Responsibilities and Rights Journal* 7 (1994), pp. 23–36; Sheppard et al., *Organizational Justice*.

81. K. McCullough, "More and More Executives Find that Formal Ethics Program Benefits Their Company's Bottom Line," *CNBC Management Today*, October 19, 1996, program transcript; "An Ombudsperson Can Improve Management-Labor Relations," *Personnel Journal*, August 1993, p. 62.

82. "Carole A. Young Named Corporate Ombuds Director," *Business Wire,* January 30, 1998; "Texaco Chief Executive Says Company Made Excellent Progress in First Six Months of Diversity Plan," *Business Wire,* July 29, 1997.

83. M. A. Neale and M. H. Bazerman, *Cognition and Rationality in Negotiation* (New York: Free Press, 1991), pp. 140–42.

84. M. Barrier, "A Working Alternative for Settling Disputes," *Nation's Business* 86 (July 1998), pp. 43–46.

85. B. H. Sheppard, "Managers as Inquisitors: Lessons from the Law," in Bazerman and Lewicki, eds., *Negotiating in Organizations,* pp. 193–213.

86. Tjosvold, *The Conflict-Positive Organization,* pp. 112–13; R. Karambayya and J. M. Brett, "Managers Handling Disputes: Third Party Roles and Perceptions of Fairness," *Academy of Management Journal* 32 (1989), pp. 687–704.

87. J. P. Meyer, J. M. Gemmell, and P. G. Irving, "Evaluating the Management of Interpersonal Conflict in Organizations: A Factor-Analytic Study of Outcome Criteria," *Canadian Journal of Administrative Sciences* 14 (1997), pp. 1–13.

Chapter Fourteen

1. S. Wetlaufer, "Driving Change: An Interview with Ford Motor Company's Jacques Nasser," *Harvard Business Review* 77 (March–April 1999), pp. 76–88; S. Zesiger, "Jac Nasser Is Car Crazy," *Fortune,* June 22, 1998, pp. 79–82; R. L. Simison, "Ford Exec Has 1 Speed," *Fort Lauderdale Sun-Sentinel,* February 15, 1998, p. F2; W. J. Holstein, "A Driven Man at Ford," *U.S. News & World Report,* January 19, 1998; K. Yung, "Ford's Progress Comes with Pain," *Detroit News,* September 14, 1997, p. C1; D. C. Smith and G. Gardner, "Nasser: Savior or Slasher?" *Ward's Auto World* 33 (February 1997), pp. 27–35.

2. R. A. Barker, "How Can We Train Leaders If We Do Not Know What Leadership Is?" *Human Relations* 50 (1997), pp. 343–62; R. Farson, *Management of the Absurd* (New York: Simon & Schuster, 1996), chap. 28; P.C. Drucker, "Forward," in F. Hesselbein et al., *The Leader of the Future* (San Francisco: Jossey-Bass, 1997).

3. J. M. Burns, *Leadership* (New York: Harper & Row, 1978), p. 2.

4. D. Miller, M. F. R. Ket de Vries, and J. M. Toulouse, "Top Executive Locus of Control and Its Relationship to Strategy-Making, Structure, and Environment," *Academy of Management Journal* 25 (1982), pp. 237–53; P. Selznick, *Leadership in Administration* (Evanston, IL: Row, Peterson, 1957), p. 37.

5. M. Groves, "Cream Rises to the Top, but from a Small Crop," *Los Angeles Times,* June 8, 1998.

6. C. A. Beatty, "Implementing Advanced Manufacturing Technologies: Rules of the Road," *Sloan Management Review,* Summer 1992, pp. 49–60; J. M. Howell and C. A. Higgins, "Champions of Technological Innovation," *Administrative Science Quarterly* 35 (1990), pp. 317–41.

7. K. Morris, "The Rise of Jill Barad," *Business Week,* May 25, 1998, pp. 112–19; L. Bannon, "Helping Barbie Bounce Back," *Orange County Register* (CA), March 6, 1997, p. C1.

8. J. Kochanski, "Competency-Based Management," *Training & Development,* October 1997, pp. 40–44; Hay Group et. al., *Raising the Bar: Using Competencies to Enhance Employee Performance* (Scottsdale, AZ: American Compensation Association, 1996); L. M. Spencer and S. M. Spencer, *Competence at Work: Models for Superior Performance* (New York: John Wiley, 1993).

9. T. Takala, "Plato on Leadership," *Journal of Business Ethics* 17 (May 1998), pp. 785–98.

10. R. M. Stogdill, *Handbook of Leadership* (New York: Free Press, 1974), chap. 5.

11. Most elements of this list were derived from S. A. Kirkpatrick and E. A. Locke, "Leadership: Do Traits Matter?" *Academy of Management Executive* 5 (May 1991), pp. 48–60. Several of these ideas are also discussed in H. B. Gregersen, A. J. Morrison, and J. S. Black, "Developing Leaders for the Global Frontier," *Sloan Management Review* 40 (Fall 1998), pp. 21–32; R. J. House and R. N. Aditya, "The Social Scientific Study of Leadership: Quo Vadis?" *Journal of Management* 23 (1997), pp. 409–73; R. J. House and M. L. Baetz, "Leadership: Some Empirical Generalizations and New Research Directions," *Research in Organizational Behavior* 1 (1979), pp. 341–423.

12. House and Aditya, "The Social Scientific Study of Leadership."

13. J. M. Kouzes and B. Z. Posner, *Credibility: How Leaders Gain and Lose It, Why People Demand It* (San Francisco: Jossey-Bass, 1993).

14. D. Goleman, "What Makes a Leader?" *Harvard Business Review* 76 (November–December 1998), pp. 92–102; J. D. Mayer and P. Salovey, "The Intelligence of Emotional Intelligence," *Intelligence* 17 (1993), pp. 433–42.

15. J. A. Kolb, "The Relationship between Self-Monitoring and Leadership in Student Project Groups," *Journal of Business Communication* 35 (April 1998), pp. 264–82; S. J. Zaccaro, R. J. Foti, and D. A. Kenny, "Self-Monitoring and Trait-Based Variance in Leadership: An Investigation of Leader Flexibility across Multiple Group Situations," *Journal of Applied Psychology* 76 (1991), pp. 308–15; S. E. Cronshaw and R. J. Ellis, "A Process Investigation of Self-Monitoring and Leader Emergence," *Small Group Research* 22 (1991), pp. 403–20; S. J. Zaccaro, R. J. Foti, and D. A. Kenny, "Self-Monitoring and Trait-Based Variance Is Leadership: An Investigation of Leader Flexibility across Multiple Group Situations," *Journal of Applied Psychology* 76 (1991), pp. 308–15; G. H. Dobbins, W. S. Long, E. J. Dedrick, and T. C. Clemons, "The Role of Self-Monitoring and Gender on Leader Emergence: A Laboratory and Field Study," *Journal of Management* 16 (1990), pp. 609–18.

16. L. Nakarmi, "Here Come the Mavericks," *Asiaweek,* April 9, 1999; "Korea's Kim Jung Tae," *Business Week,* June 29, 1998, p. 66.

17. R. G. Lord and K. J. Maher, *Leadership and Information Processing: Linking Perceptions and Performance* (Cambridge, MA: Unwin Hyman, 1991).

18. W. C. Byham, "Grooming Next-Millennium Leaders," *HRMagazine* 44 (February 1999), pp. 46–50; R. Zemke and S. Zemke, "Putting Competencies to Work," *Training* 36 (January 1999), pp. 70–76.

19. G. A. Yukl, *Leadership in Organizations,* 3rd ed. (Englewood Cliffs, NJ: Prentice Hall, 1994), pp. 53–75; R. Likert, *New Patterns of*

Management (New York: McGraw-Hill, 1961).

20. N. Deogun, "Is Craig Weatherup Too Nice for Pepsi-Cola's Own Good?" *The Wall Street Journal*, March 19, 1997.

21. A. K. Korman, "Consideration, Initiating Structure, and Organizational Criteria—A Review," *Personnel Psychology* 19 (1966), pp. 349–62; E. A. Fleishman, "Twenty Years of Consideration and Structure," in *Current Developments in the Study of Leadership*, E. A. Fleishman and J. C. Hunt, eds. (Carbondale, IL: Southern Illinois University Press, 1973), pp. 1–40.

22. V. V. Baba, "Serendipity in Leadership: Initiating Structure and Consideration in the Classroom," *Human Relations* 42 (1989), pp. 509–25.

23. R. L. Kahn, "The Prediction of Productivity," *Journal of Social Issues* 12, no. 2 (1956), pp. 41–49; P. Weissenberg and M. H. Kavanagh, "The Independence of Initiating Structure and Consideration: A Review of the Evidence," *Personnel Psychology* 25 (1972), pp. 119–30; Stogdill, *Handbook of Leadership*, chap. 11.

24. R. R. Blake and A. A. McCanse, *Leadership Dilemmas—Grid Solutions* (Houston: Gulf Publishing Company, 1991); and R. R. Blake and J. S. Mouton, "Management by Grid Principles or Situationalism: Which?" *Group and Organization Studies* 7 (1982), pp. 207–10.

25. L. L. Larson, J. G. Hunt, and R. N. Osborn, "The Great Hi-Hi Leader Behavior Myth: A Lesson from Occam's Razor," *Academy of Management Journal* 19 (1976), pp. 628–41; A. K. Korman, "Consideration, Initiating Structure, and Organizational Criteria—A Review," *Personnel Psychology* 19 (1966), pp. 349–62.

26. G. N. Powell and D. A. Butterfield, "The 'High-High' Leader Rides Again!" *Group & Organization Studies* 9 (1984), pp. 437–50.

27. S. Kerr, C. A. Schriesheim, C. J. Murphy, and R. M. Stogdill, "Towards a Contingency Theory of Leadership Based upon the Consideration and Initiating Structure Literature," *Organizational Behavior and Human Performance* 12 (1974), pp. 62–82.

28. R. Tannenbaum and W. H. Schmidt, "How to Choose a Leadership Pattern," *Harvard Business Review* 51 (May–June 1973), pp. 162–80.

29. M. G. Evans, "The Effects of Supervisory Behavior on the Path-Goal Relationship," *Organizational Behavior and Human Performance* 5 (1970), pp. 277–98; M. G. Evans, "Extensions of a Path-Goal Theory of Motivation," *Journal of Applied Psychology* 59 (1974), pp. 172–78; R. J. House, "A Path-Goal Theory of Leader Effectiveness," *Administrative Science Quarterly* 16 (1971), pp. 321–38.

30. R. J. House and T. R. Mitchell, "Path-Goal Theory of Leadership," *Journal of Contemporary Business*, Autumn 1974, pp. 81–97.

31. R. J. House, "Path-Goal Theory of Leadership: Lessons, Legacy, and a Reformulated Theory," *Leadership Quarterly* 7 (1996), pp. 323–52.

32. J. C. Wofford and L. Z. Liska, "Path-Goal Theories of Leadership: A Meta-Analysis," *Journal of Management* 19 (1993), pp. 857–76; and J. Indvik, "Path-Goal Theory of Leadership: A Meta-Analysis," *Academy of Management Proceedings*, 1986, pp. 189–92.

33. Morris, "The Rise of Jill Barad."

34. R. T. Keller, "A Test of the Path-Goal Theory of Leadership with Need for Clarity as a Moderator in Research and Development Organizations," *Journal of Applied Psychology* 74 (1989), pp. 208–12.

35. J. M. Jermier, "The Path-Goal Theory of Leadership: A Subtextural Analysis," *Leadership Quarterly* 7 (1996), pp. 311–16.

36. House, "Path-Goal Theory of Leadership: Lessons, Legacy, and a Reformulated Theory."

37. Wofford and Liska, "Path-Goal Theories of Leadership: A Meta-Analysis"; Yukl, *Leadership in Organizations*, pp. 102–4; Indvik, "Path-Goal Theory of Leadership: A Meta-Analysis."

38. House and Baetz, "Leadership: Some Empirical Generalizations and New Research Directions."

39. C. A. Schriesheim and L. L. Neider, "Path-Goal Leadership Theory: The Long and Winding Road," *Leadership Quarterly* 7 (1996), pp. 317–21.

40. P. Hersey and K. H. Blanchard, *Management of Organizational Behavior: Utilizing Human Resources*, 7th ed. (Upper Saddle River, NJ: Prentice Hall, 1996), chap. 8.

41. C. L. Graeff, "Evolution of Situational Leadership Theory: A Critical Review," *Leadership Quarterly* 8 (1997), pp. 153–70; W. Blank, J. R. Weitzel, and S. G. Green, "A Test of the Situational Leadership Theory," *Personnel Psychology* 43 (1990), pp. 579–97; R. P. Vecchio, "Situational Leadership Theory: An Examination of a Prescriptive Theory," *Journal of Applied Psychology* 72 (1987), pp. 444–51.

42. F. E. Fiedler, *A Theory of Leadership Effectiveness* (New York: McGraw-Hill, 1967); and F. E. Fiedler and M. M. Chemers, *Leadership and Effective Management* (Glenview, IL: Scott, Foresman, 1974).

43. F. E. Fiedler, "Engineer the Job to Fit the Manager," *Harvard Business Review* 43 (September–October 1965), pp. 115–22.

44. For a summary of criticisms, see Yukl, *Leadership in Organizations*, pp. 197–98.

45. P. M. Podsakoff and S. B. MacKenzie, "Kerr and Jermier's Substitutes for Leadership Model: Background, Empirical Assessment, and Suggestions for Future Research," *Leadership Quarterly* 8 (1997), pp. 117–32; P. M. Podsakoff, B. P. Niehoff, S. B. MacKenzie, and M. L. Williams, "Do Substitutes Really Substitute for Leadership? An Empirical Examination of Kerr and Jermier's Situational Leadership Model," *Organizational Behavior and Human Decision Processes* 54 (1993), pp. 1–44.

46. This observation has also been made by C. A. Schriesheim, "Substitutes-for-Leadership Theory: Development and Basic Concepts," *Leadership Quarterly* 8 (1997), pp. 103–8.

47. D. F. Elloy and A. Randolph, "The Effect of Superleader Behavior on Autonomous Work Groups in a Government Operated Railway Service," *Public Personnel Management* 26 (Summer 1997), pp. 257–72.

48. C. Manz and H. Sims, *Superleadership: Getting to the Top by Motivating Others* (San Francisco: Berkley Publishing, 1990).

49. C. P. Neck and C. C. Manz, "Thought Self-Leadership: The Impact of Mental Strategies Training on Employee Cognition, Behavior, and Affect," *Journal of Organizational Behavior* 17 (1996), pp. 445–67.

50. M. O. Howard, "Play-Doh Might Enhance Productivity," *Richmond Times Dispatch*, July 1, 1998, p. 22.

51. Carly Fiorina led the hugely successful public offering of Lucent Technologies and was recently named by *Fortune* magazine as the most powerful woman in American business; see P. Sellers, "The 50 Most Powerful Women in American Business," *Fortune*, October 12, 1998, pp. 76–98. For literature on the other leaders, see R. Slater, *Jack Welch and the GE Way: Management Insights and Leadership Secrets of the Legendary CEO* (New York: McGraw-Hill, 1998); K. Freiberg and J. Freiberg, *Nuts!: Southwest Airlines' Crazy Recipe for Business and Personal Success* (New York: Bantam Doubleday Dell, 1996).

52. J. M. Howell and B. J. Avolio, "Transformational Leadership, Transactional Leadership, Locus of Control, and Support for Innovation: Key Predictors of Consolidated-Business-Unit Performance," *Journal of Applied Psychology* 78 (1993), pp. 891–902; J. A. Conger and R. N. Kanungo, "Perceived Behavioral Attributes of Charismatic Leadership," *Canadian Journal of Behavioral Science* 24 (1992), pp. 86–102; J. Seltzer and B. M. Bass, "Transformational Leadership: Beyond Initiation and Consideration," *Journal of Management* 16 (1990), pp. 693–703.

53. B. J. Avolio and B. M. Bass, "Transformational Leadership, Charisma, and Beyond," in J. G. Hunt, H. P. Dachler, B. R. Baliga, and C. A. Schriesheim, eds., *Emerging Leadership Vistas* (Lexington, MA: Lexington Books, 1988), pp. 29–49.

54. L. Rittenhouse, "Dennis W. Bakke—Empowering a Workforce with Principles," *Electricity Journal*, January 1998, pp. 48–59.

55. J. Kotter, *A Force for Change* (Cambridge: Harvard Business School Press, 1990); W. Bennis and B. Nanus, *Leaders: The Strategies for Taking Charge* (New York: Harper & Row, 1985), p. 21; A. Zaleznik, "Managers and Leaders: Are They Different?" *Harvard Business Review* 55 (September–October 1977), pp. 67–78.

56. W. Bennis, *An Invented Life: Reflections on Leadership and Change* (Reading, MA: Addison-Wesley, 1993); D. Tjosvold and M. M. Tjosvold, *The Emerging Leader* (New York: Lexington Books, 1993), p. 25.

57. B. S. Pawar and K. K. Eastman, "The Nature and Implications of Contextual Influences on Transformational Leadership: A Conceptual Examination," *Academy of Management Review* 22 (1997), pp. 80–109.

58. J. A. Conger and R. N. Kanungo, "Toward a Behavioral Theory of Charismatic Leadership in Organizational Settings," *Academy of Management Review* 12 (1987), pp. 637–47; R. J. House, "A 1976 Theory of Charismatic Leadership," in J. G. Hunt and L. L. Larson, eds., *Leadership: The Cutting Edge* (Carbondale, IL: Southern Illinois University Press, 1977), pp. 189–207.

59. Y. A. Nur, "Charisma and Managerial Leadership: The Gift That Never Was," *Business Horizons* 41 (July 1998), pp. 19–26; J. E. Barbuto, Jr., "Taking the Charisma Out of Transformational Leadership," *Journal of Social Behavior & Personality* 12 (September 1997), pp. 689–97.

60. L. Sooklal, "The Leader as a Broker of Dreams," *Human Relations* 44 (August 1991), pp. 833–55.

61. J. M. Stewart, "Future State Visioning—A Powerful Leadership Process," *Long Range Planning* 26 (December 1993), pp. 89–98; Bennis and Nanus, *Leaders*, pp. 27–33, 89; J. M. Kouzes and B. Z. Posner, *The Leadership Challenge* (San Francisco: Jossey-Bass, 1987), chap. 5.

62. T. J. Peters, "Symbols, Patterns, and Settings: An Optimistic Case for Getting Things Done," *Organizational Dynamics* 7 (Autumn 1978), pp. 2–23.

63. S. A. Kirkpatrick and E. A. Locke, "Direct and Indirect Effects of Three Core Charismatic Leadership Components on Performance and Attitudes," *Journal of Applied Psychology* 81 (1996), pp. 36–51.

64. J. A. Conger, "Inspiring Others: The Language of Leadership," *Academy of Management Executive* 5 (February 1991), pp. 31–45.

65. G. T. Fairhurst and R. A. Sarr, *The Art of Framing: Managing the Language of Leadership* (San Francisco: Jossey-Bass, 1996).

66. R. S. Johnson, "Home Depot Renovates," *Fortune*, November 23, 1998, pp. 200–6.

67. Fairhurst and Sarr, *The Art of Framing*, chap. 5; J. Pfeffer, "Management as Symbolic Action: The Creation and Maintenance of Organizational Paradigms," *Research in Organizational Behavior* 3 (1981), pp. 1–52.

68. L. Black, "Hamburger Diplomacy," *Report on Business Magazine* 5 (August 1988), pp. 30–36; S. Franklin,. *The Heroes: A Saga of Canadian Inspiration* (Toronto: McClelland and Stewart, 1967), p. 53.

69. M. E. McGill and J. W. Slocum, Jr., "A Little Leadership, Please?" *Organizational Dynamics* 39 (Winter 1998), pp. 39–49; N. H. Snyder and M. Graves, "Leadership and Vision," *Business Horizons* 37 (January 1994), pp. 1–7; D. E. Berlew, "Leadership and Organizational Excitement," in *Organizational Psychology: A Book of Readings*, D. A. Kolb, I. M. Rubin, and J. M. McIntyre, eds. (Englewood Cliffs, NJ: Prentice Hall, 1974), pp. 410–23.

70. E. M. Whitener, S. E. Brodt, M. A. Korsgaard, and J. M. Werner, "Managers as Initiators of Trust: An Exchange Relationship Framework for Understanding Managerial Trustworthy Behavior," *Academy of Management Review* 23 (July 1998), pp. 513–30; Bennis and Nanus, *Leaders*, pp. 43–55; Kouzes and Posner, *Credibility: How Leaders Gain and Lose It, Why People Demand It.*

71. B. Morris, "Doug Is It," *Fortune*, May 25, 1998, pp. 70–84.

72. M. F. R. Kets de Vries "Charisma in Action: The Transformational Abilities of Virgin's Richard Branson and ABB's Percy Barnevik," *Organizational Dynamics* 26 (Winter 1998), pp. 6–21; M. F. R. Kets de Vries, "Creative Leadership: Jazzing Up Business," *Chief Executive*, March 1997, pp. 64–66; F. Basile, "Hotshots in Business Impart Their Wisdom," *Indianapolis Business Journal*, July 21, 1997, p. A40.

73. J. J. Sosik, S. S. Kahai, and B. J. Avolio, "Transformational Leadership and Dimensions of Creativity: Motivating Idea Generation in Computer-Mediated Groups," *Creativity Research Journal* 11 (1998), pp. 111–21; P. Bycio, R. D. Hackett, and J. S. Allen, "Further Assessments of Bass's (1985) Conceptualization of Transactional and Transformational Leadership," *Journal of Applied Psychology* 80 (1995), pp. 468–78; W. L. Koh, R. M. Steers, and J. R. Terborg, "The Effects of Transformational Leadership on Teacher Attitudes and Student Performance in Singapore," *Journal of Organizational Behavior* 16 (1995), pp. 319–33; Howell and Avolio, "Transformational Leadership,

74. J. Barling, T. Weber, and E. K. Kelloway, "Effects of Transformational Leadership Training on Attitudinal and Financial Outcomes: A Field Experiment," *Journal of Applied Psychology* 81 (1996), pp. 827–32.

75. A. Bryman, "Leadership in Organizations," in S. R. Clegg, C. Hardy, and W. R. Nord, eds., *Handbook of Organization Studies* (Thousand Oaks, CA: Sage, 1996), pp. 276–92.

76. Pawar and Eastman, "The Nature and Implications of Contextual Influences on Transformational Leadership."

77. K. Boehnke, A. C. DiStefano, J. J. DiStefano, and N. Bontis, "Leadership for Extraordinary Performance," *Business Quarterly* 61 (Summer 1997), pp. 56–63.

78. M. Johnson, "Taking the Lid Off Leadership," *Management Review*, November 1996, pp. 59–61.

79. For a review of this research, see House and Aditya, "The Social Scientific Study of Leadership: Quo Vadis?"

80. R. J. Hall and R. G. Lord, "Multi-level Information Processing Explanations of Followers' Leadership Perceptions," *Leadership Quarterly* 6 (1995), pp. 265–87; R. Ayman, "Leadership Perception: The Role of Gender and Culture," in M. M. Chemers and R. Ayman, eds., *Leadership Theory and Research: Perspectives and Directions* (San Diego, CA: Academic Press, 1993), pp. 137–66; J. R. Meindl, "On Leadership: An Alternative to the Conventional Wisdom," *Research in Organizational Behavior* 12 (1990), pp. 159–203.

81. G. R. Salancik and J. R. Meindl, "Corporate Attributions as Strategic Illusions of Management Control," *Administrative Science Quarterly* 29 (1984), pp. 238–54; J. M. Tolliver, "Leadership and Attribution of Cause: A Modification and Extension of Current Theory," *Proceedings of the Annual ASAC Conference, Organizational Behavior Division* 4, pt. 5 (1983), pp. 182–91.

82. S. F. Cronshaw and R. G. Lord, "Effects of Categorization, Attribution, and Encoding Processes on Leadership Perceptions," *Journal of Applied Psychology* 72 (1987),

pp. 97–106; J. W. Medcof and M. G. Evans, "Heroic or Competent? A Second Look," *Organizational Behavior and Human Decision Processes* 38 (1986), pp. 295–304.

83. Meindl, "On Leadership: An Alternative to the Conventional Wisdom," p. 163.

84. J. Pfeffer, "The Ambiguity of Leadership," *Academy of Management Review* 2 (1977), pp. 102–12; and Yukl, *Leadership in Organizations*, pp. 265–67.

85. Cronshaw and Lord, "Effects of Categorization, Attribution, and Encoding Processes on Leadership Perceptions," pp. 104–5.

86. S. H. Appelbaum and B. T. Shapiro, "Why Can't Men Lead Like Women?" *Leadership and Organization Development Journal* 14 (1993), pp. 28–34; J. B. Rosener, "Ways Women Lead," *Harvard Business Review* 68 (November–December 1990), pp. 119–25; and J. Grant, "Women as Managers: What They Can Offer to Organizations," *Organization Dynamics*, Winter 1988, pp. 56–63.

87. G. N. Powell, "One More Time: Do Female and Male Managers Differ?" *Academy of Management Executive* 4 (August 1990), pp. 68–75; G. H. Dobbins and S. J. Platts, "Sex Differences in Leadership: How Real Are They?" *Academy of Management Review* 11 (1986), pp. 118–27.

88. A. H. Eagly and B. T. Johnson, "Gender and Leadership Style: A Meta-Analysis," *Psychological Bulletin* 108 (1990), pp. 233–56.

89. N. Wood, "Venus Rules," *Incentive* 172 (February 1998), pp. 22–27.

90. M. Javidan, B. Bemmels, K. S. Devine, and A. Dastmalchian, "Superior and Subordinate Gender and the Acceptance of Superiors as Role Models," *Human Relations* 48 (1995), pp. 1271–84.

91. A. H. Eagly, S. J. Karau, and M. G. Makhijani, "Gender and the Effectiveness of Leaders: A Meta-Analysis," *Psychological Bulletin* 117 (1995), pp. 125–145; M. E. Heilman and C. J. Block, "Sex Stereotypes: Do They Influence Perceptions of Managers?" *Journal of Social Behavior & Personality* 10 (1995), pp. 237–52; R. L. Kent and S. E. Moss, "Effects of Sex and Gender Role on Leader Emergence," *Academy of Management Journal* 37 (1994), pp. 1335–46; A. H. Eagly, M. G. Makhijani, and B. G. Klonsky,

"Gender and the Evaluation of Leaders: A Meta-Analysis," *Psychological Bulletin* 111 (1992), pp. 3–22.

92. Morris, "The Rise of Jill Barad."

Chapter Fifteen

1. R. T. Pascale, "Leading from a Different Place," in J. A. Conger, G. M. Spreitzer, and E. E. Lawler III, eds., *The Leader's Change Handbook* (San Francisco: Jossey-Bass, 1999), pp. 301–20; D. J. Knight, "Strategy in Practice: Making It Happen," *Strategy & Leadership* 26 (July–August 1998), pp. 29–33; R. T. Pascale, "The Agenda—Grassroots Leadership," *Fast Company*, no. 14 (April–May 1998), pp. 110–20; J. Guyon, "Why Is the World's Most Profitable Company Turning Itself Inside Out?" *Fortune*, August 4, 1997, pp. 120–25.

2. D. Hoewes, "Future Hinges on Global Teams," *Detroit News*, December 21, 1998; T. E. Backer, "Managing the Human Side of Change in VA's Transformation," *Hospital & Health Services Administration*, 42 (September 1997), p. 433.

3. N. Byrnes, "The Best Performers," *Business Week*, March 29, 1999, pp. 98–100.

4. J. S. Brown, "Seeing Differently: A Role for Pioneering Research," *Research Technology Management* 41 (May–June 1998), pp. 24–33; in particular, see comments by George Gilder, who is credited with developing the law of telecosm, in "Is Bigger Better?" *Fast Company*, no. 17 (September 1998). For a general discussion of computer technology and organizational change, see C. Meyer and S. Davis, *Blur: The Speed of Change in the Connected Economy* (Reading, MA: Addison-Wesley, 1998). For an excellent discussion of computer networks, see K. Kelly, "New Rules for the New Economy," *Wired*, September 1997.

5. D. Tapscott and A. Laston, *Paradigm Shift* (New York: McGraw-Hill, 1993); W. H. Davidow and M. S. Malone, *The Virtual Corporation* (New York: HarperBusiness, 1992).

6. D. Tapscott, A. Lowy, and D. Ticoll, eds., *Blueprint to the Digital Economy: Wealth Creation in the Era of E-Business* (New York: McGraw-Hill, 1998).

7. J. W. Gurley, "A Dell for Every Industry," *Fortune,* October 12, 1998, pp. 167–72.

8. K. Lyytinen and S. Goodman, "Finland: The Unknown Soldier on the IT Front," *Communications of the ACM* 42 (March 1999), pp. 13–17; S. Baker, "Can CEO Ollila Keep the Cellular Superstar Flying High?" *Business Week,* August 10, 1998, pp. 54–61; J. Dromberg, "Nokia's Line to the Top Slot," *Independent* (London), August 9, 1998, p. 5.

9. R. Bettis and M. Hitt, "The New Competitive Landscape," *Strategic Management Journal* 16 (1995), pp. 7–19.

10. R. L. Brandt, "John Chambers—On the Future of Communications and the Failure of Deregulation," *Upside* 10 (October 1998), pp. 122–33; S. Ellis, "A New Role for the Post Office: An Investigation into Issues behind Strategic Change at Royal Mail," *Total Quality Management* 9 (May 1998), pp. 223–34; S. L. Paulson, "Training for Change," *American Gas* 79 (December–January 1998), pp. 26–29.

11. J. Muller, "Raytheon's Job Cuts Will Total 14,000; 1,200 Slots in State Targeted as Defense Firm Streamlines," *Boston Globe,* October 8, 1998, p. A1; "Gillette to Cut 4,700 Jobs, Shut Factories," Reuters, September 28, 1998.

12. "Similar Goals May Smooth Differences in Netscape-AOL Merger," Dow Jones Newswires, March 17, 1999.

13. D. Hoewes, "Future Hinges on Global Teams," *Detroit News,* December 21, 1998; D. Phillips, "Daimler-Benz Has Much to Learn from Chrysler," *Detroit News,* June 4, 1998.

14. K. Lewin, *Field Theory in Social Science* (New York: Harper & Row, 1951).

15. M. Moravec, O. J. Johannessen, and T. A. Hjelmas, "Thumbs Up for Self-Managed Teams," *Management Review* 86 (July–August 1997), pp. 42–47.

16. D. A. Nadler, *Champions of Change* (San Francisco: Jossey-Bass, 1998), chap. 5; P. Strebel, "Why Do Employees Resist Change?" *Harvard Business Review* 74 (May–June 1996), pp. 86–92; R. Maurer, *Beyond the Wall of Resistance: Unconventional Strategies to Build Support for Change* (Austin, TX: Bard Books, 1996); C. Hardy, *Strategies for Retrenchment and Turnaround: The Politics of Survival* (Berlin: Walter de Gruyter, 1990), chap. 13.

17. C. O. Longenecker, D. J. Dwyer, and T. C. Stansfield, "Barriers and Gateways to Workforce Productivity," *Industrial Management* 40 (March–April 1998), pp. 21–28.

18. J. P. Kotter, "Leading Change: Why Transformation Efforts Fail," *Harvard Business Review* 73 (March–April 1995), pp. 59–67.

19. E. B. Dent and S. G. Goldberg, "Challenging 'Resistance to Change,'" *Journal of Applied Behavioral Science* 35 (March 1999), pp. 25–41.

20. D. A. Nadler, "The Effective Management of Organizational Change," in *Handbook of Organizational Behavior,* J. W. Lorsch, ed. (Englewood Cliffs, NJ: Prentice Hall, 1987), pp. 358–69; D. Katz and R. L. Kahn, *The Social Psychology of Organizations,* 2nd ed. (New York: John Wiley, 1978).

21. "Making Change Work for You—Not Against You," *Agency Sales Magazine* (June 1998), pp. 24–27.

22. M. E. McGill and J. W. Slocum, Jr., "Unlearn the Organization," *Organizational Dynamics* 22 no. 2 (1993), pp. 67–79.

23. R. Katz, "Time and Work: Toward an Integrative Perspective," *Research in Organizational Behavior* 2 (1980), pp. 81–127.

24. D. Nicolini and M. B. Meznar, "The Social Construction of Organizational Learning: Conceptual and Practical Issues in the Field," *Human Relations* 48 (1995), pp. 727–46.

25. D. Miller, "What Happens after Success: The Perils of Excellence," *Journal of Management Studies* 31 (1994), pp. 325–58.

26. T. G. Cummings, "The Role and Limits of Change Leadership," in Conger, Spreitzer, and Lawler, eds., *The Leader's Change Handbook,* pp. 301–20.

27. J. P. Donlon et al., "In Search of the New Change Leader," *Chief Executive,* November 1997, pp. 64–75.

28. L. D. Goodstein and H. R. Butz, "Customer Value: The Linchpin of Organizational Change," *Organizational Dynamics* 27 (Summer 1998), pp. 21–34.

29. G. Brenneman, "Right Away and All at Once: How We Saved Continental," *Harvard Business Review* 76 (September–October 1998), pp. 162–79.

30. A. Gore, "Joel Kocher: Power COO Says It's Time to Evolve," *MacUser,* April 1997.

31. D. Osborne and P. Plastrik "A Lesson in Reinvention," *Governing Magazine,* February 1997, p. 26; D. Osborne and P. Plastrik "The O'Neill Factor," *Washington Post,* July 13, 1997, p. W8.

32. J. P. Kotter and L. A. Schlesinger, "Choosing Strategies for Change," *Harvard Business Review* 57 (March–April 1979), pp. 106–14.

33. V. D. Miller and J. R. Johnson, "Antecedents to Willingness to Participate in a Planned Organizational Change," *Journal of Applied Communication Research* 22 (1994) pp. 59–80; L. C. Caywood and R. P. Ewing, *The Handbook of Communications in Corporate Restructuring and Takeovers* (Englewood Cliffs, NJ: Prentice Hall, 1992).

34. J. Moad, "Du Pont's People Deal," *PC Week,* September 29, 1997, p. 75.

35. J. P. Walsh and S-F. Tseng, "The Effects of Job Characteristics on Active Effort at Work," *Work & Occupations* 25 (February 1998), pp. 74–96; K. T. Dirks, L. L. Cummings, and J. L. Pierce, "Psychological Ownership in Organizations: Conditions under Which Individuals Promote and Resist Change," *Research in Organizational Change and Development* 9 (1996), pp. 1–23.

36. B. B. Bunker and B. T. Alban, *Large Group Interventions: Engaging the Whole System for Rapid Change* (San Francisco: Jossey-Bass, 1996); M. Emery and R. E. Purser, *The Search Conference: A Powerful Method for Planning Organizational Change and Community Action* (San Francisco: Jossey-Bass, 1996).

37. R. Dubey, "The CEO Who Walked Away," *Business Today* (India), May 22, 1998.

38. "Making Organizational Changes Effective and Sustainable," *Educating for Employment,* August 7, 1998; D. Coghlan, "The Process of Change through Interlevel Dynamics in a Large-Group Intervention for a Religious Organization," *Journal of Applied Behavioral Science* 34 (March 1998), pp. 105–19; R. Larson, "Forester Defends 'Feel-Good' Meeting," *Washington Times,* November 28, 1997, p. A9.

39. P. H. Mirvis and M. L. Marks, *Managing the Merger* (Englewood Cliffs, NJ: Prentice Hall, 1992).

40. D. K. Cassal, "Taking Over 164 Stores, Kerr Drug Quickly Sets Up Shop," *Drug Topics,* December 8, 1997, pp. 106–7.

41. R. Greenwood and C. R. Hinings, "Understanding Radical Organizational Change: Bringing Together the Old and the New Institutionalism," *Academy of Management Review* 21 (1996), pp. 1022–54.

42. J. Dibbs, "Organizing for Empowerment," *Business Quarterly* 58 (Autumn 1993), pp. 97–102.

43. G. Brenneman, "Right Away and All at Once." G. Flynn, "A Flight Plan for Success," *Workforce* 76 (July 1997), p. 72.

44. J. Lublin, "Curing Sick Companies Better Done Fast," *Globe and Mail* (Toronto), July 25, 1995, p. B18.

45. Nicolini and Meznar, "The Social Construction of Organizational Learning."

46. T. G. Cummings and E. F. Huse, *Organization Development and Change,* 4th ed. (St. Paul, MN: West Publishing, 1989), pp. 477–85; P. Goodman and J. Dean, "Creating Long-Term Organizational Change," in *Change in Organizations,* P. Goodman and Associates, eds. (San Francisco: Jossey-Bass, 1982), pp. 226–79; W. W. Burke, *Organization Development: A Normative View* (Reading, MA: Addison-Wesley, 1987), pp. 124–25.

47. R. H. Miles, "Leading Corporate Transformation: Are You Up to the Task?" in Conger, Spreitzer, and Lawler, eds., *The Leader's Change Handbook,* pp. 221–67; L. D. Goodstein and H. R. Butz, "Customer Value: The Linchpin of Organizational Change," *Organizational Dynamics* 27 (Summer 1998), pp. 21–34.

48. Brenneman, "Right Away and All at Once: How We Saved Continental."

49. B. McDermott and G. Sexton, "Sowing the Seeds of Corporate Innovation," *Journal for Quality and Participation* 21 (November–December 1998), pp. 18–23.

50. D. A. Nadler, "Implementing Organizational Changes," in D. A. Nadler, M. L. Tushman, and N. G. Hatvany, eds., *Managing Organizations: Readings and Cases* (Boston: Little, Brown, 1982), pp. 440–59.

51. J. P. Kotter, "Leading Change: The Eight Steps to Transformation," in Conger, Spreitzer, and Lawler, eds., *The Leader's Change Handbook,* pp. 221–67; J. P. Kotter, "Leading Change: Why Transformation Efforts Fail," *Harvard Business Review* 73 (March–April 1995), pp. 59–67.

52. S. Wetlaufer, "Driving Change: An Interview with Ford Motor Company's Jacques Nasser," *Harvard Business Review* 77 (March–April 1999), pp. 76–88; S. Zesiger, "Jac Nasser Is Car Crazy," *Fortune,* June 22, 1998, pp. 79–82.

53. M. Beer, R. A. Eisenstat, and B. Spector, *The Critical Path to Corporate Renewal* (Boston: Harvard Business School Press, 1990).

54. R. E. Walton, *Innovating to Compete: Lessons for Diffusing and Managing Change in the Workplace* (San Francisco: Jossey-Bass, 1987); Beer et al., *The Critical Path to Corporate Renewal,* chap. 5; and R. E. Walton, "Successful Strategies for Diffusing Work Innovations," *Journal of Contemporary Business,* Spring 1977, pp. 1–22.

55. J. Childs, "Five Years and Counting: The Path to Self-Directed Work Teams," *Hospital Materiel Management Quarterly* 18 (May 1997), pp. 34–43.

56. R. Beckhard, *Organization Development: Strategies and Models* (Reading, MA: Addison-Wesley, 1969), chap. 2. See also Cummings and Huse, *Organization Development and Change,* pp. 1–3.

57. Burke, *Organization Development,* pp. 12–14.

58. W. L. French and C. H. Bell, Jr., *Organization Development: Behavioral Science Interventions for Organization Improvement,* 4th ed. (Englewood Cliffs, NJ: Prentice Hall, 1990), chap. 8. For a recent discussion of action research model, see J. B. Cunningham, *Action Research and Organization Development* (Westport, CT: Praeger, 1993).

59. A. B. Shani and G. R. Bushe, "Visionary Action Research: A Consultation Process Perspective," *Consultation: An International Journal* 6, no. 1 (1987), pp. 3–19.

60. M. L. Brown, "Five Symbolic Roles of the Organizational Development Consultant: Integrating Power, Change, and Symbolism," *Proceedings of the Annual ASAC Conference, Organizational Behavior Division* 14, pt. 5 (1993), pp. 71–81; D. A. Buchanan and D. Boddy, *The Expertise of the Change Agent: Public Performance and Backstage Activity* (New York: Prentice Hall, 1992); L. E. Greiner and V. E. Schein, *Power and Organization Development: Mobilizing Power to Implement Change* (Reading, MA: Addison-Wesley, 1988).

61. D. F. Harvey and D. R. Brown, *An Experiential Approach to Organization Development,* 5th ed. (Upper Saddle River, NJ: Prentice Hall, 1996), chap. 4.

62. M. Beer and E. Walton, "Developing the Competitive Organization: Interventions and Strategies," *American Psychologist* 45 (February 1990), pp. 154–61.

63. E. H. Schein, *Process Consultation: Its Role in Organization Development* (Reading, MA: Addison-Wesley, 1969).

64. For a case study of poor diagnosis, see M. Popper, "The Glorious Failure," *Journal of Applied Behavioral Science* 33 (March 1997), pp. 27–45.

65. Beer, *Organization Change and Development,* pp. 101–2.

66. D. A. Nadler, "Organizational Frame Bending: Types of Change in the Complex Organization," in R. H. Kilmann, T. J. Covin, and Associates, eds., *Corporate Transformation: Revitalizing Organizations for a Competitive World* (San Francisco: Jossey-Bass, 1988), pp. 66–83.

67. T. Y. Choi, M. Rungtusanatham, and J. S. Kim, "Continuous Improvement on the Shop Floor: Lessons from Small to Midsize Firms," *Business Horizons* 40 (November–December 1997), pp. 45–50; J. M. Kouzes and B. Z. Posner, *The Leadership Challenge* (San Francisco: Jossey-Bass, 1988), chap. 10; and C. Lindblom, "The Science of Muddling Through," *Public Administration Review* 19 (1959), pp. 79–88.

68. C. R. Hinings and R. Greenwood, *The Dynamics of Strategic Change* (Oxford, England: Basil Blackwell, 1988), chap. 6; D. Miller and P. H. Friesen, "Structural Change and Performance: Quantum versus Piecemeal-Incremental Approaches," *Academy of Management Journal* 25 (1982), pp. 867–92.

69. M. Meyerson, "Everything I Thought I Knew about Leadership Is Wrong," *Fast Company,* Issue #2 (1996).

70. P. A. Strassmann, "The Hocus-Pocus of Reengineering," *Across the Board* 31 (June 1994), pp. 35–38.

71. S. R. Olberding, "Turnaround Drama Instills Leadership," *Journal for Quality & Participation* 21 (January–February 1998), pp. 52–55.

72. Cummings and Huse, *Organization Development and Change*, pp. 158–61.

73. A. H. Church and W. W. Burke, "Practitioner Attitudes about the Field of Organization Development," *Research in Organizational Change and Development*, 8 (1995), pp. 1–46.

74. A. H. Church, W. W. Burke, and D. F. Van Eynde, "Values, Motives, and Interventions of Organization Development Practitioners," *Group and Organization Management* 19 (1994), pp. 5–50.

75. R. T. Pascale, "Europcar's 'Greenway' Reengineering Project," *Planning Review*, May–June 1994, pp. 18–19.

76. E. M. Van Aken, D. J. Monetta, and D. S. Sink, "Affinity Groups: The Missing Link in Employee Involvement," *Organizational Dynamics* 22 (Spring 1994), pp. 38–54; G. R. Bushe and A. B. Shani, *Parallel Learning Structures* (Reading, MA: Addison-Wesley, 1991).

77. D. Whitney and D. L. Cooperrider, "The Appreciative Inquiry Summit: Overview and Applications," *Employment Relations Today* 25 (Summer 1998), pp. 17–28.

78. D. Whitney and C. Schau, "Appreciative Inquiry: An Innovative Process for Organization Change," *Employment Relations Today* 25 (Spring 1998), pp. 11–21; F. J. Barrett and D. L. Cooperrider, "Generative Metaphor Intervention: A New Approach for Working with Systems Divided by Conflict and Caught in Defensive Perception," *Journal of Applied Behavioral Science* 26 (1990), pp. 219–39.

79. G. R. Bushe and G. Coetzer, "Appreciative Inquiry as a Team-Development Intervention: A Controlled Experiment," *Journal of Applied Behavioral Science* 31 (1995), pp. 13–30; L. Levine, "Listening with Spirit and the Art of Team Dialogue," *Journal of Organizational Change Management* 7 (1994), pp. 61–73.

80. E. Ransdell, "Lou Bainbridge Builds Teams," *Fast Company*, Issue 20 (December 1998), p. 228.

81. G. A. Neuman, J. E. Edwards, and N. S. Raju, "Organizational Development Interventions: A Meta-Analysis of Their Effects on Satisfaction and Other Attitudes," *Personnel Psychology* 42 (1989), pp. 461–89; R. A. Guzzo, R. D. Jette, and R. A. Katzell, "The Effects of Psychologically Based Intervention Programs on Worker Productivity: A Meta-Analysis," *Personnel Psychology* 38 (1985), pp. 275–91.

82. R. J. Long, "The Effects of Various Workplace Innovations on Productivity: A Quasi-Experimental Study," *Proceedings of the Annual ASAC Conference, Personnel and Human Resources Division* 11, pt. 9 (1990), pp. 98–107.

83. C.-M. Lau, "A Culture-Based Perspective of Organization Development Implementation," *Research in Organizational Change and Development* 9 (1996), pp. 49–79.

84. T. C. Head and P. F. Sorenson, "Cultural Values and Organizational Development: A Seven-Country Study," *Leadership and Organization Development Journal* 14 (1993), pp. 3–7; J. M. Putti, "Organization Development Scene in Asia: The Case of Singapore," *Group and Organization Studies* 14 (1989), pp. 262–70; A. M. Jaeger, "Organization Development and National Culture: Where's the Fit?" *Academy of Management Review* 11 (1986), pp. 178–90.

85. R. J. Marshak, "Lewin Meets Confucius: A Review of the OD Model of Change," *Journal of Applied Behavioral Science* 29 (1993), pp. 395–415.

86. C. M. D. Deaner, "A Model of Organization Development Ethics," *Public Administration Quarterly* 17 (1994), pp. 435–46; M. McKendall, "The Tyranny of Change: Organizational Development Revisited," *Journal of Business Ethics* 12 (February 1993), pp. 93–104.

87. G. A. Walter, "Organization Development and Individual Rights," *Journal of Applied Behavioral Science* 20 (1984), pp. 423–39.

88. "How I Dressed Up as a Sheep and Learned to Love My Boss (and Workmates)," *Evening Standard* (London), July 29, 1997, p. 19.

89. Burke, *Organization Development*, pp. 149–51; Beer, *Organization Change and Development*, pp. 223–24.

Chapter Sixteen

1. J. Guynn, "Executive Describes Pain at California-Based PeopleSoft after Layoffs," *Contra Costa Times*, January 30, 1999 (online); S. McManis, "A Man and His Money," *San Francisco Chronicle*, November 22, 1998, p. 1; J. Hibbard, "Cultural Breakthrough," *Information Week*, September 21, 1998 (online); "Making Work Fun," *Minneapolis Star Tribune*, August 18, 1998, p. E9; E. Brown, "PeopleSoft: Tech's Latest Publicly Traded Cult," *Fortune*, May 25, 1998, p. 155; P. Roberts, "Humane Technology," *Fast Company*, Issue 14 (April–May 1998), pp. 122–28; D. Bartholomew, "Successful? Try, Try Again," *Industry Week*, February 2, 1998, pp. 56–62; R. Levering and M. Moskowitz, "The 100 Best Companies to Work for in America," *Fortune*, January 12, 1998, pp. 84–95.

2. T. O. Davenport, "The Integration Challenge: Managing Corporate Mergers," *Management Review* 87 (January 1998), pp. 25–28; E. H. Schein, "What Is Culture?" in P. J. Frost, L. F. Moore, M. R. Louis, C. C. Lundberg, and J. Martin, eds., *Reframing Organizational Culture* (Beverly Hills, CA: Sage, 1991), pp. 243–53; A. Williams, P. Dobson, and M. Walters, *Changing Culture: New Organizational Approaches* (London: Institute of Personnel Management, 1989).

3. J. J. Martocchio, "The Effects of Absence Culture on an Individual's Absence Taking," *Human Relations* 47 (1994), pp. 243–62; N. Nicholson and G. Johns, "The Absence Culture and the Psychological Contract: Who's in Control of Absence?" *Academy of Management Review* 10 (1985), pp. 397–407.

4. A. Sagie and D. Elizur, "Work Values: A Theoretical Overview and a Model of Their Effects," *Journal of Organizational Behavior* 17 (1996), pp. 503–14; W. H. Schmidt and B. Z. Posner, *Managerial Values in Perspective* (New York: American Management Association, 1983).

5. B. M. Meglino and E. C. Ravlin, "Individual Values in Organizations: Concepts, Controversies, and Research," *Journal of Management*, 24 (May 1998), pp. 351–89; C. Argyris and D. A. Schön, *Organizational Learning: A Theory of Action Perspective* (Reading, MA: Addison-Wesley, 1978).

6. S. Baker, "Can CEO Ollila Keep the Cellular Superstar Flying High?" *Business Week*, August 10, 1998, pp. 54–61.

7. K. Doler, "Interview: Jeff Bezos, Founder and CEO of Amazon.com Inc.," *Upside* 10 (September 1998), pp. 76–80.

8. K. Morris, "The Rise of Jill Barad," *Business Week*, May 25, 1998, p. 112.

9. S. Sackmann, "Culture and Subcultures: An Analysis of Organizational Knowledge," *Administrative Science Quarterly* 37 (1992), pp. 140–61; J. Martin and C. Siehl, "Organizational Culture and Counterculture: An Uneasy Symbiosis," *Organizational Dynamics*, Autumn 1983, pp. 52–64; J. S. Ott, *The Organizational Culture Perspective* (Pacific Grove, CA: Brooks/Cole, 1989), pp. 45–47; T. E. Deal and A. A. Kennedy, *Corporate Cultures* (Reading, MA: Addison-Wesley, 1982), pp. 138–39.

10. HP's values are described at its web site *(www.hp.com)* and in J. Y. Wind and J. Main, *Driving Change* (New York: Free Press, 1998), p. 104.

11. A. Sinclair, "Approaches to Organizational Culture and Ethics," *Journal of Business Ethics* 12 (1993), pp. 63–73.

12. M. O. Jones, *Studying Organizational Symbolism: What, How, Why?* (Thousand Oaks, CA: Sage, 1996); Ott, *The Organizational Culture Perspective*, chap. 2; J. S. Pederson and J. S. Sorensen, *Organisational Cultures in Theory and Practice* (Aldershot, England: Gower, 1989), pp. 27–29.

13. "Making Work Fun," *Minneapolis Star Tribune*, August 18, 1998, p. E9.

14. A. Furnham and B. Gunter, "Corporate Culture: Definition, Diagnosis, and Change," *International Review of Industrial and Organizational Psychology* 8 (1993), pp. 233–61; E. H. Schein, "Organizational Culture," *American Psychologist*, February 1990, pp. 109–119; Ott, *The Organizational Culture Perspective*, chap. 2; W. J. Duncan, "Organizational Culture: 'Getting a Fix' on an Elusive Concept," *Academy of Management Executive* 3 (1989), pp. 229–36.

15. J. C. Meyer, "Tell Me a Story: Eliciting Organizational Values from Narratives," *Communication Quarterly* 43 (1995), pp. 210–24.

16. T. A. Stewart, "The Cunning Plots of Leadership," *Fortune*, September 7, 1998, pp. 165–66. Details of the Revlon story can be found in A. Brown, *Organisational Culture* (London: Pitman, 1995), p. 15.

17. K. Foss, "Isadore Sharp," *Foodservice and Hospitality*, December 1989, pp. 20–30; and J. DeMont, "Sharp's Luxury Empire," *Maclean's*, June 5, 1989, pp. 30–33.

18. R. Zemke, "Storytelling: Back to a Basic," *Training* 27 (March 1990), pp. 44–50; A. L. Wilkins, "Organizational Stories as Symbols Which Control the Organization," in L. R. Pondy, P. J. Frost, G. Morgan, and T. C. Dandridge, eds., *Organizational Symbolism* (Greenwich, CT: JAI Press, 1984), pp. 81–92; J. Martin and M. E. Powers, "Truth or Corporate Propaganda: The Value of a Good War Story," in Pondy et al., *Organizational Symbolism*, pp. 93–107.

19. J. Martin et. al., "The Uniqueness Paradox in Organizational Stories," *Administrative Science Quarterly* 28 (1983), pp. 438–53.

20. P. S. DeLisi, "A Modern-Day Tragedy: The Digital Equipment Story," *Journal of Management Inquiry* 7 (June 1998), pp. 118–30.

21. J. M. Beyer and H. M. Trice, "How an Organization's Rites Reveal Its Culture," *Organizational Dynamics* 15, no. 4 (1987), pp. 5–24; L. Smirchich, "Organizations as Shared Meanings," in Pondy et al., *Organizational Symbolism*, pp. 55–65.

22. "Fitzgerald Family Values," *Fast Company*, Issue 14 (April–May 1998), p. 194.

23. D. Barboza, "Monsanto Visionary in a Cubicle," *New York Times*, March 3, 1999, p. C1.

24. R. E. Quinn and N. T. Snyder, "Advanced Change Theory: Culture Change at Whirlpool Corporation," in J. A. Conger, G. M. Spreitzer, and E. E. Lawler III, eds., *The Leader's Change Handbook* (San Francisco: Jossey-Bass, 1999), pp. 162–93.

25. L. A. Krefting and P. J. Frost, "Untangling Webs, Surfing Waves, and Wildcatting," in P. J. Frost, L. F. Moore, M. R. Louis, C. C. Lundberg, and J. Martin, eds., *Organizational Culture* (Beverly Hills, CA: Sage, 1985), pp. 155–68.

26. J. A. Byrne, "How Jack Welch Runs GE," *Business Week*, June 8, 1998.

27. For a discussion of buzzword bingo, see M. Precker, "Synergy, Paradigm, Bingo!" *Dallas Morning News*, July 19, 1998, p. F1.

28. J. M. Kouzes and B. Z. Posner, *The Leadership Challenge* (San Francisco: Jossey-Bass, 1995), pp. 230–31.

29. R. Bickley, "Bell and Howell's Transformation Lets in the Light," *Raleigh News and Observer*, September 27, 1998, p. E1.

30. Guynn, "Executive Describes Pain at California-Based PeopleSoft after Layoffs"; Doler, "Interview: Jeff Bezos, Founder and CEO of Amazon.com Inc."; D. Menzies, "What Do You Mean There Are No More Donuts?" *Financial Post Magazine*, December 1996, p. 10.

31. B. McDermott and G. Sexton, "Sowing the Seeds of Corporate Innovation," *Journal for Quality and Participation* 21 (November–December 1998), pp. 18–23.

32. C. Siehl and J. Martin, "Organizational Culture: A Key to Financial Performance?" in *Organizational Climate and Culture*, B. Schneider, ed. (San Francisco: Jossey-Bass, 1990), pp. 241–81; J. B. Barney, "Organizational Culture: Can It Be a Source of Sustained Competitive Advantage?" *Academy of Management Review* 11 (1986), pp. 656–65; V. Sathe, *Culture and Related Corporate Realities* (Homewood, IL: Richard D. Irwin, 1985), chap. 2; Deal and Kennedy, *Corporate Cultures*, chap. 1.

33. C. A. O'Reilly and J. A. Chatman, "Culture as Social Control: Corporations, Cults, and Commitment," *Research in Organizational Behavior* 18 (1996), pp. 157–200.

34. B. Ashforth and F. Mael, "Social Identity Theory and the Organization," *Academy of Management Review* 14 (1989), pp. 20–39.

35. J. P. Donlon, "The Virtual Organization," *Chief Executive* 125 (July 1997), pp. 58–66.

36. S. G. Harris, "Organizational Culture and Individual Sensemaking: A Schema-Based Perspective," *Organization Science* 5 (1994), pp. 309–21; M. R. Louis, "Surprise and Sensemaking: What Newcomers Experience in Entering Unfamiliar Organizational Settings," *Administrative Science Quarterly* 25 (1980), pp. 226–51.

37. G. S. Saffold III, "Culture Traits, Strength, and Organizational Performance: Moving beyond

'Strong' Culture," *Academy of Management Review* l3 (1988), pp. 546–58; Williams et al., *Changing Culture*, pp. 24–27.

38. J. P. Kotter and J. L. Heskett, *Corporate Culture and Performance* (New York: Free Press, 1992); G. G. Gordon and N. DiTomasco, "Predicting Corporate Performance from Organizational Culture," *Journal of Management Studies* 29 (1992), pp. 783–98; D. R. Denison, *Corporate Culture and Organizational Effectiveness* (New York: John Wiley, 1990).

39. E. H. Schein, "On Dialogue, Culture, and Organizational Learning," *Organization Dynamics*, Autumn 1993, pp. 40–51.

40. J. Kotter, "Cultures and Coalitions," *Executive Excellence* 15 (March 1998), pp. 14–15; Kotter and Heskett, *Corporate Culture and Performance.*

41. S. J. Carroll and M. J. Gannon, *Ethical Dimensions of International Management* (Thousand Oaks, CA: Sage, 1997), chap. 5; A. Sinclair, "Approaches to Organisational Culture and Ethics," *Journal of Business Ethics* 12 (1993), pp. 63–73.

42. "Olympics Report Deplores 'Culture of Improper Gift-Giving,'" *Commercial Appeal* (Memphis), March 2, 1999, p. A1.

43. J. Davidson, "The Business of Ethics," *Working Woman* 23 (February 1998), pp. 68–71.

44. J. Mizuo, "Business Ethics and Corporate Governance in Japanese Corporations," *Business and Society Review*, March 1999, p. 65; "Shiseido," *Forbes* (supplement), January 11, 1999, p. S6.

45. S. Silverstein and D. Vrana, "After Back-Slapping Wanes, Mega-Mergers Often Fail," *Los Angeles Times*, April 19, 1998, p. 1; Davenport, "The Integration Challenge."

46. G. A. Walter, "Culture Collisions in Mergers and Acquisitions," in Frost et al., *Organizational Culture*, pp. 301–14; A. F. Buono and J. L. Bowditch, *The Human Side of Mergers and Acquisitions* (San Francisco: Jossey-Bass, 1989), chap. 6; E. H. Schein, *Organizational Culture and Leadership* (San Francisco: Jossey-Bass, 1985), pp. 33–36.

47. P. Troiano, "Post-Merger Challenges," *Management Review* 88 (January 1999), p. 6.

48. "Business 'Cultures' at War," *Electronic News* 44 (August 3, 1998),

pp. 50–51; D. Clark, "Sadder But Wiser, Novell Refocuses," *Globe and Mail* (Toronto), January 12, 1996, p. B4.

49. P. L. Moore, "Infighting Lurks behind Smiles of Bank Merger," *Arkansas Democrat-Gazette* (Little Rock), July 19, 1998, p. G1.

50. M. Raynaud and M. Teasdale, "Confusions and Acquisitions: Post-Merger Culture Shock and Some Remedies," *IABC Communication World*, May/June 1992, pp. 44–45. A corporate culture audit is also recommended for joint ventures. For details, see K. J. Fedor and W. B. Werther, Jr., "The Fourth Dimension: Creating Culturally Responsive International Alliances," *Organizational Dynamics* 25 (Autumn 1996), pp. 39–53.

51. T. Buerkle, "The Chemistry Just Wasn't There," *International Herald Tribune*, February 25, 1998, p. 1. GE Capital has also walked away from acquisitions when it became apparent that the acquired firm's cultural values were incompatible. See R. N. Ashkenas, L. J. DeMonaco, and S. C. Francis "Making the Deal Real: How GE Capital Integrates Acquisitions," *Harvard Business Review* 76 (January–February 1998), pp. 165–76.

52. A. R. Malekazedeh and A. Nahavandi, "Making Mergers Work by Managing Cultures," *Journal of Business Strategy*, May–June 1990, pp. 55–57.

53. A. Levy, "Mergers Spread Despite Failures," *Cleveland Plain Dealer*, August 9, 1998, p. H1.

54. J. Bean, "Taylor Corp.–Current Inc. Merger's Effect on Business Culture Is Debated," *Gazette Telegraph* (Colorado Springs), March 22, 1999.

55. Silverstein and Vrana, "After Back-Slapping Wanes, Mega-Mergers Often Fail."

56. A. Muradian, "Picard's Departure as Raytheon CEO the End of an Era," *Defense Daily*, December 7, 1998.

57. J. Harrington, "When Merger Mania Leads to Road Rage," *Midwest Real Estate News*, March 1998.

58. "Mergers and Acquisitions May Be Driven by Business Strategy—But Often Stumble over People and Culture Issues," *PR Newswire*, August 3, 1998.

59. J. P. Kotter, "Leading Change: The Eight Steps of Transformation," in Conger, Spreitzer, and Lawler, eds.,

The Leader's Change Handbook, pp. 87–99.

60. "Hitachi to Allow Casual Clothes, Drop Honorifics," *Daily Yomiuri* (Japan), April 16, 1999.

61. K. Darce, "Entergy Recharges," *New Orleans Times-Picayune*, March 21, 1999, p. F1.

62. E. H. Schein, "The Role of the Founder in Creating Organizational Culture," *Organizational Dynamics* 12, no. 1 (Summer 1983), pp. 13–28.

63. "Where PeopleSoft Is Headed," *Contra Costa Times* (California), March 22, 1999 (online).

64. Schein, *Organizational Culture and Leadership*, chap. 10; T. J. Peters, "Symbols, Patterns, and Settings: An Optimistic Case for Getting Things Done," *Organizational Dynamics* 7, no. 2 (Autumn 1978), pp. 2–23.

65. A. Kingston, "Avon's Calling," *Globe & Mail* (Toronto), July 31, 1998; Y. Gault, "Current Chief's Lead Place Three Females as Top Candidates," *Crain's New York Business*, June 2, 1997.

66. J. Kerr and J. W. Slocum, Jr., "Managing Corporate Culture through Reward Systems," *Academy of Management Executive* 1 (May 1987), pp. 99–107; Williams et al., *Changing Cultures*, pp. 120–24; K. R. Thompson and F. Luthans, "Organizational Culture: A Behavioral Perspective," in *Organizational Climate and Culture*, pp. 319–44.

67. "Get Rich? Work at Home Depot," *Baltimore Sun*, July 27, 1998.

68. W. G. Ouchi and A. M. Jaeger, "Type Z Organization: Stability in the Midst of Mobility," *Academy of Management Review* 3 (1978), pp. 305–14; K. McNeil and J. D. Thompson, "The Regeneration of Social Organizations," *American Sociological Review* 36 (1971), pp. 624–37.

69. M. De Pree, *Leadership Is an Art* (East Lansing: Michigan State University Press, 1987).

70. C. M. Solomon, "A Day in the Life of Terri Wolfe: Maintaining Corporate Culture," *Workforce* 77 (June 1998), pp. 94–96.

71. A. L. Kristof, "Person-Organization Fit: An Integrative Review of Its Conceptualizations, Measurement, and Implications," *Personnel Psychology* 49 (1996), pp. 1–49; J. A. Chatman, "Matching People and Organizations: Selection and

Socialization in Public Accounting Firms," *Administrative Science Quarterly* 36 (1991), pp. 459–84.

72. Robert Half International, "Corporate Culture Rivals Company Benefits in Importance to Job Applicants," news release, May 1, 1996.

73. M. Siegal, "The Perils of Culture Conflict," *Fortune*, November 9, 1998, pp. 257–62.

74. J. Van Maanen, "Breaking In: Socialization to Work," in *Handbook of Work, Organization, and Society*, R. Dubin, ed. (Chicago: Rand McNally, 1976), p. 67.

75. C. A. O'Reilly III, J. Chatman, and D. F. Caldwell, "People and Organizational Culture: A Profile Comparison Approach to Assessing Person-Organization Fit," *Academy of Management Journal* 34 (1991), pp. 487–516.

Chapter Seventeen

1. J. Applegate, "Skilled Workers for Rent," *Bergen Record* (NJ), July 20, 1998; D. Kunde, "Not Mere Temps," *Chicago Tribune*, May 31, 1998, p. 7.

2. B. Rudolph, *Disconnected: How Six People from AT&T Discovered the New Meaning of Work in a Downsized Corporate America* (New York: Free Press, 1998); M. Thomas, "Your Job Security Has Been Retired," *Binghamton Press* (NY), October 5, 1998.

3. D. M. Rousseau, "Psychological and Implied Contracts in Organizations," *Employee Responsibility and Rights Journal* 2 (1989), pp. 121–39; see also E. W. Morrison and S. L. Robinson, "When Employees Feel Betrayed: A Model of How Psychological Contract Violation Develops," *Academy of Management Review* 22 (1997), pp. 226–56.

4. S. L. Robinson, M. S. Kraatz, and D. M. Rousseau, "Changing Obligations and the Psychological Contract: A Longitudinal Study," *Academy of Management Journal* 37 (1994), pp. 137–52; D. M. Rousseau and J. M. Parks, "The Contracts of Individuals and Organizations," *Research in Organizational Behavior* 15 (1993), pp. 1–43.

5. P. R. Sparrow, "Reappraising Psychological Contracting: Lessons for the Field of Human-Resource Development from Cross-Cultural and Occupational Psychology Research," *International Studies of Management & Organization* 28 (Spring 1998), pp. 30–63.

6. M. E. De Forest, "Hecho en Mexico: Tips for Success," *Apparel Industry Magazine*, 59 (September 1998), pp. 98–106.

7. J. McLean Parks and D. L. Kidder, "'Till Death Us Do Part . . .' Changing Work Relationships in the 1990s," in C. L. Cooper and D. M. Rousseau, eds., *Trends in Organizational Behavior*, vol. 1 (Chichester, England: John Wiley, 1994), pp. 112–36.

8. S. L. Robinson, "Trust and Breach of the Psychological Contract," *Administrative Science Quarterly* 41 (1996), pp. 574–99. For a discussion of the antecedents of trust, see E. M. Whitener, S. E. Brodt, M. A. Korsgaard, and J. M. Werner, "Managers as Initiators of Trust: An Exchange Relationship Framework for Understanding Managerial Trustworthy Behavior," *Academy of Management Review* 23 (July 1998), pp. 513–30.

9. R. D. Costigan, S. S. Ilter, and J. J. Berman, "A Multi-Dimensional Study of Trust in Organizations," *Journal of Managerial Issues* 10 (Fall 1998), pp. 303–17.

10. D. M. Rousseau, S. B. Sitkin, R. S. Burt, and C. Camerer, "Not So Different after All: A Cross-Discipline View of Trust," *Academy of Management Review* 23 (July 1998), pp. 393–404; R. J. Lewicki and B. B. Bunker, "Developing and Maintaining Trust in Work Relationships," in R. M. Kramer and T. R. Tyler, eds., *Trust in Organizations: Frontiers of Theory and Research* (Thousand Oaks, CA: Sage, 1996), pp. 114–39.

11. Whitener et al, "Managers as Initiators of Trust"; W. Bennis and B. Nanus, *Leaders: The Strategies for Taking Charge* (New York: Harper & Row, 1985), pp. 43–55; J. M. Kouzes and B. Z. Posner, *Credibility: How Leaders Gain and Lose It, Why People Demand It* (San Francisco: Jossey-Bass, 1993).

12. S. L. Robinson and E. W. Morrison, "Psychological Contracts and OCB: The Effect of Unfulfilled Obligations on Civic Virtue Behavior," *Journal of Organizational Behavior* 16 (1995), pp. 289–98.

13. I. DeBare, "Keeping a Packed Bag at Work," *San Francisco Chronicle*, April 30, 1999.

14. K. Ohlson, "Leadership in an Age of Mistrust," *Industry Week*, February 2, 1998, pp. 37–39.

15. D. M. Rousseau, "Changing the Deal While Keeping the People," *Academy of Management Executive* 10 (February 1996), pp. 50–61.

16. C. Hendry and R. Jenkins, "Psychological Contracts and New Deals," *Human Resource Management Journal* 7 (1997), pp. 38–44; P. Herriot and C. Pemberton, *New Deals: The Revolution in Managerial Careers* (New York: John Wiley, 1995), chap. 3; W. H. Whyte, *The Organization Man* (New York: Simon and Schuster, 1956), p. 129.

17. J. C. Meister, "The Quest for Lifetime Employability," *Journal of Business Strategy* 19 (May–June 1998), pp. 25–28; T. A. Stewart, "Gray Flannel Suit? Moi?" *Fortune*, March 16, 1998, pp. 76–82; A. Rajan, "Employability in the Finance Sector: Rhetoric vs. Reality," *Human Resource Management Journal* 7 (1997), pp. 67–78.

18. E. O'Gorman, "Further Revamp at Northern Bank to Cost over 200 Jobs," *Irish Times*, August 25, 1998, p. 14; J. Newman, "WPL Transforms in Merger," *Wisconsin State Journal*, November 30, 1997, p. E1.

19. T. Moran and C. Zielinski, "Experts Say There's Security in Employability, Not a Job," *Crain's Detroit Business*, September 1, 1997, p. L6.

20. K. D. Grimsley, "Bosses Who Don't Trust Anyone over 40," *Sacramento Bee*, February 23, 1997, p. F3.

21. P. Herriot and C. Pemberton, "Facilitating New Deals," *Human Resource Management Journal* 7 (1997), pp. 45–56; P. R. Sparrow, "Transitions in the Psychological Contract: Some Evidence from the Banking Sector," *Human Resource Management Journal* 6 (1996), pp. 75–92.

22. K. Mieszkowski, "Get with the Program!" *Fast Company*, no. 13 (February–March 1998), pp. 28–30.

23. J. Van Maanen, "Breaking In: Socialization to Work," in *Handbook of Work, Organization, and Society*, R. Dubin, ed. (Chicago: Rand McNally, 1976), p. 67.

24. C. L. Adkins, "Previous Work Experience and Organizational Socialization: A Longitudinal Examination," *Academy of Management Journal* 38 (1995),

pp. 839–62; T. N. Bauer and S. G. Green, "The Effect of Newcomer Involvement in Work-Related Activities: A Longitudinal Study of Socialization," *Journal of Applied Psychology* 79 (1994), pp. 211–23.

25. E. F. Holton III, "New Employee Development: A Review and Reconceptualization," *Human Resource Development Quarterly* 7 (Fall 1996), pp. 233–52; G. T. Chao, A. O'Leary-Kelly, S. Wolf, H. J. Klein, and P. D. Gardner, "Organizational Socialization: Its Content and Consequences," *Journal of Applied Psychology* 79 (1994), pp. 450–63.

26. J. T. Mignerey, R. B. Rubin, and W. I. Gorden, "Organizational Entry: An Investigation of Newcomer Communication Behavior and Uncertainty," *Communication Research* 22 (1995), pp. 54–85.

27. B. E. Ashforth and A. M. Saks, "Socialization Tactics: Longitudinal Effects on Newcomer Adjustment," *Academy of Management Journal* 39 (1996), pp. 149–78; C. D. Fisher, "Organizational Socialization: An Integrative View," *Research in Personnel and Human Resources Management* 4 (1986), pp. 101–45; and N. Nicholson, "A Theory of Work Role Transitions," *Administrative Science Quarterly* 29 (1984), pp. 172–91.

28. C. C. Pinder and K. G. Schroeder, "Time to Proficiency Following Job Transfers," *Academy of Management Journal* 30 (1987), pp. 336–53; and N. J. Adler, *International Dimensions of Organizational Behavior* (Belmont, CA: Wadsworth, 1991), chap. 8.

29. Van Maanen, "Breaking In," pp. 67–130; L. W. Porter, E. E. Lawler III, and J. R. Hackman, *Behavior in Organizations* (New York: McGraw-Hill, 1975), pp. 163–67; and D. C. Feldman, "The Multiple Socialization of Organization Members," *Academy of Management Review* 6 (1981), pp. 309–18.

30. Ashforth and Saks, "Socialization Tactics"; Bauer and Green, "Effect of Newcomer Involvement in Work-Related Activities," pp. 211–23.

31. Porter et al., *Behavior in Organizations*, chap. 5.

32. J. Stites, "Going from the Corporate World to Silicon Alley Can Prove Tough," *New York Times*, August 31, 1998, p. 3.

33. E. Hannan, "Staff Turnover Tops $4b," *The Age* (Melbourne), June 7,

1998; C. A. Young and C. C. Lundberg, "Creating a Good First Day on the Job," *Cornell Hotel and Restaurant Administration Quarterly* 37 (December 1996), pp. 26–33; S. L. Robinson and D. M. Rousseau, "Violating the Psychological Contract: Not the Exception But the Norm," *Journal of Organizational Behavior* 15 (1994), pp. 245–59.

34. M. R. Louis, "Surprise and Sensemaking: What Newcomers Experience in Entering Unfamiliar Organizational Settings," *Administrative Science Quarterly* 25 (1980), pp. 226–51.

35. D. L. Nelson, "Organizational Socialization: A Stress Perspective," *Journal of Occupational Behavior* 8 (1987), pp. 311–24.

36. E. W. Morrison and S. L. Robinson, "When Employees Feel Betrayed: A Model of How Psychological Contract Violation Develops," *Academy of Management Review* 22 (1997), pp. 226–56.

37. J. A. Breaugh, *Recruitment: Science and Practice* (Boston: PWS-Kent, 1992), chap. 7; J. P. Wanous, *Organizational Entry*, 2nd ed. (Reading, MA: Addison-Wesley, 1992), chap. 3; A. M. Saks and S. F. Cronshaw, "A Process Investigation of Realistic Job Previews: Mediating Variables and Channels of Communication," *Journal of Organizational Behavior* 11 (1990), pp. 221–36.

38. J. M. Phillips, "Effects of Realistic Job Previews on Multiple Organizational Outcomes: A Meta-Analysis," *Academy of Management Journal* 41 (December 1998), pp. 673–90.

39. J. P. Wanous and A. Colella, "Organizational Entry Research: Current Status and Future Directions," *Research in Personnel and Human Resources Management* 7 (1989), pp. 59–120.

40. C. Ostroff and S. W. J. Koslowski, "Organizational Socialization as a Learning Process: The Role of Information Acquisition," *Personnel Psychology* 45 (1992), pp. 849–74; N. J. Allen and J. P. Meyer, "Organizational Socialization Tactics: A Longitudinal Analysis of Links to Newcomers' Commitment and Role Orientation," *Academy of Management Journal* 33 (1990), pp. 847–58; F. M. Jablin, "Organizational Entry, Assimilation, and Exit," in F. M. Jablin, L. L.

Putnam, K. H. Roberts, and L. W. Porter, eds., *Handbook of Organizational Communication*, (Beverly Hills, CA.: Sage, 1987), pp. 679–740.

41. E. W. Morrison, "Newcomer Information Seeking: Exploring Types, Modes, Sources, and Outcomes," *Academy of Management Journal* 36 (1993), pp. 557–89; Fisher, "Organizational Socialization," pp. 135–36; Porter et al., *Behavior in Organizations*, pp. 184–86.

42. S. L. McShane, "Effect of Socialization Agents on the Organizational Adjustment of New Employees," Paper presented at the Annual Conference of the Western Academy of Management, Big Sky, Montana, March 1988.

43. "Work Week: Welcome to the Jungle," *Wall Street Journal Interactive Edition*, October 13, 1998; M. Thomas, "Factories Move toward Team Lineups," *Binghamton Press* (NY), July 29, 1998.

44. Adapted from J. Schmitt, "High-Tech Job Hopping," *USA Today*, August 21, 1998, p. B1.

45. M. B. Arthur, D. T. Hall, and B. S. Lawrence, "Generating New Directions in Career Theory: The Case for a Transdisciplinary Approach," in *Handbook of Career Theory*, M. B. Arthur, D. T. Hall, and B. S. Lawrence, eds. (Cambridge: Cambridge University Press, 1989), pp. 7–25.

46. M. B. Arthur, "The Boundaryless Career: A New Perspective for Organizational Inquiry," *Journal of Organizational Behavior* 15 (1994), pp. 295–306.

47. D. T. Hall, *Careers in Organizations* (Glenview, IL: Scott, Foresman, 1976), pp. 93–97.

48. Adapted from D. H. Montross, Z. B. Leibowitz, and C. J. Shinkman, *Real People, Real Jobs* (Palo Alto, CA: Davies-Black, 1995), pp. 121–23.

49. J. Holland, *Making Vocational Choices: A Theory of Careers* (Englewood Cliffs, NJ: Prentice Hall, 1973).

50. G. D. Gottfredson and J. L. Holland, "A Longitudinal Test of the Influence of Congruence: Job Satisfaction, Competency Utilization, and Counterproductive Behavior," *Journal of Counseling Psychology* 37 (1990), pp. 389–98.

51. J. Arnold, "The Psychology of Careers in Organizations," *International Review of Industrial*

and Organizational Psychology 12 (1997), pp. 1–37.

52. For example, see G. R. Cluskey and A. Vaux, "Vocational Misfit: Source of Occupational Stress among Accountants," *Journal of Applied Business Research* 13 (Summer 1997), pp. 43–54.

53. K. R. Brousseau and M. J. Driver, "Enhancing Informed Choice: A Career-Concepts Approach to Career Advisement," *Selections* 10 (Spring 1994), pp. 24–31.

54. K. R. Brousseau, M. J. Driver, K. Eneroth, and R. Larsson, "Career Pandemonium: Realigning Organizations and Individuals," *Academy of Management Executive* 10 (November 1996), pp. 52–66.

55. D. T. Hall and J. Richter, "Career Gridlock: Baby Boomers Hit the Wall," *Academy of Management Executive* 4 (August 1990), pp. 7–22.

56. Schmitt, "High-Tech Job Hopping"; Stewart, "Gray Flannel Suit? Moi?"

57. P. Baker, "A Sideways Move Could Bring You Out of Your Shell," *The Observer* (London), March 22, 1998, p. 8; "De-Layered Pay Systems Encourage Employees to Move Sideways," *Universal News Services*, January 24, 1997.

58. B. Kaye and C. Farren, "Up Is Not the Only Way," *Training & Development* 50 (February 1996), pp. 48–53.

59. S. Caudron, "Apple Computer Leaves No Stone Unturned in Employee Career Management," *Personnel Journal* 73 (April 1994), p. 64E.

60. J. C. Meister, "The Quest for Lifetime Employability," *Journal of Business Strategy* 19 (May–June 1998), pp. 25–28.

61. Whyte, *Organization Man,*

62. M. B. Arthur and D. M. Rousseau, *The Boundaryless Career: A New Employment Principle for a New Organizational Era* (New York: Oxford University Press, 1996); M. B. Arthur, "The Boundaryless Career: A New Perspective for Organizational Inquiry," *Journal of Organizational Behavior* 15 (1994), pp. 295–306.

63. Schmit, "High-Tech Job Hopping"; K. Kelly, "New Rules for the New Economy," *Wired Magazine* 5 (September 1997).

64. Stewart, "Gray Flannel Suit? Moi?"

65. *New York Times. The Downsizing of America* (New York: Times Books, 1996); R. J. Defillippi and M. B. Arthur, "The Boundaryless Career:

A Competency-Based Perspective," *Journal of Organizational Behavior* 15 (1994), pp. 307–24.

66. B. O'Reilly, "The New Deal: What Companies and Employees Owe One Another," *Fortune*, June 13, 1994, pp. 44–52.

67. M. Jarman, "Job Hopping Acceptable," *Arizona Republic*, July 26, 1998.

68. A. Bernhardt and T. Bailey, "Improving Worker Welfare in the Age of Flexibility," *Challenge* 41 (September–October 1998), pp. 16–44.

69. Facts about Manpower, Inc. are from its website: www.manpower.com. This observation is also noted in T. W. Malone and R. J. Laubacher, "The Dawn of the E-lance Economy," *Harvard Business Review* 76 (September–October 1998), pp. 144–52.

70. A. E. Polivka, "Contingent and Alternative Work Arrangements, Defined," *Monthly Labor Review* 119 (October 1996), pp. 3–10. For further discussion of the meaning of contingent work, see S. Nollen and H. Axel, *Managing Contingent Workers* (New York: AMACOM, 1996), pp. 4–9.

71. S. Hipple, "Contingent Work: Results from the Second Survey," *Monthly Labor Review* 121 (November 1998), pp. 22–35.

72. For a discussion of contingent work, including estimates of the American workforce percentage in this category, see K. Barker and K. Christensen, eds., *Contingent Work: American Employment in Transition* (Ithaca, NY: ILR Press, 1998). Contingent work in Europe is discussed in G. Edmondson et al., "A Tidal Wave of Temps," *Business Week*, November 24, 1997; Sparrow, "Reappraising Psychological Contracting."

73. C. von Hippel, S. L. Mangum, D. B. Greenberger, R. L. Heneman, and J. D. Skoglind, "Temporary Employment: Can Organizations and Employees Both Win?" *Academy of Management Executive* 11 (February 1997), pp. 93–104.

74. R. J. Grossman, "Short-Term Workers Raise Long-Term Issues," *HRMagazine* 43 (April 1998), pp. 80–89.

75. S. F. Matusik and C. W. L. Hill, "The Utilization of Contingent Work, Knowledge Creation, and Competitive Advantage," *Academy of*

Management Review 23 (October 1998), pp. 680–97.

76. J. Larson, "Temps Are Here to Stay," *American Demographics* 18 (February 1996), pp. 26–30.

77. S. Hagstrom, "Employment Agencies Offer New Lease on Life," *Orlando Sentinel,* March 23, 1998, p. 27.

78. Malone and Laubacher, "The Dawn of the E-lance Economy."

79. von Hippel et al., "Temporary Employment"; A. E. Polivka, "Into Contingent and Alternative Employment: By Choice?" *Monthly Labor Review* 119 (October 1996), pp. 55–74. A recent U.S. Government study revealed that the percentage of contingent workers who want permanent employment is dropping. However, most of these people still prefer permanent employment. See "Gains in Job Security," *Monthly Labor Review* 121 (March 1998), pp. 74–75.

80. S. B. Gould, K. J. Weiner, and B. R. Levin, *Free Agents: People and Organizations Creating a New Working Community* (San Francisco: Jossey-Bass, 1997); von Hippel, et al., "Temporary Employment," pp. 94–96; W. J. Byron, "Coming to Terms with the New Corporate Contract," *Business Horizons* 38 (January 1995), pp. 8–15.

81. S. J. Hartman, A. C. Yrle, and A. R. Yrle, "Turnover in the Hotel Industry: Is There a Hobo Phenomenon at Work?" *International Journal of Management* 13 (1996), pp. 340–48; T. A. Judge and S. Watanabe, "Is the Past Prologue? A Test of Ghiselli's Hobo Syndrome," *Journal of Management* 21 (1995), pp. 211–29.

82. J. Pfeffer, *New Directions in Organizational Theory* (New York: Oxford University Press, 1997), pp. 18–20.

83. K. M. Beard and J. R. Edwards, "Employees at Risk: Contingent Work and the Psychological Experience of Contingent Workers," in C. L. Cooper and D. M. Rousseau, eds., *Trends in Organizational Behavior,* vol. 2 (Chichester, England: John Wiley, 1995), pp. 109–26.

84. B. Cole-Gomolski, "Reliance on Temps Creates New Problems," *Computerworld* (August 31, 1998), pp. 1, 85.

85. Beard and Edwards, "Employees at Risk," pp. 118–19.

86. "Bodies for Hire—The Contracting Out Debate," *Workplace Change* (Australia), April 1996, pp. 1–3.

87. D. M. Rousseau and C. Libuser, "Contingent Workers in High Risk Environments," *California Management Review* 39 (Winter 1997), pp. 103–23; G. LaBarr, "Contingent Worker Safety: A Full-Time Job in a Part-Time World," *Occupational Hazards* 10 (October 1997), pp. 92–100.

88. D. C. Feldman and H. I. Doerpinghaus, "Managing Temporary Workers: A Permanent HRM Challenge," *Organizational Dynamics* 23 (Fall 1994), pp. 49–63.

89. A. M. Saks, P. E. Mudrack, and B. E. Ashforth, "The Relationship between the Work Ethic, Job Attitudes, Intentions to Quit, and Turnover for Temporary Service Workers," *Canadian Journal of Administrative Sciences* 13 (1996), pp. 226–36.

Chapter Eighteen

1. J. P. Flintoff, "Keeping Faith in St Luke," *Guardian* (London), September 19, 1998, p. 22; F. Jebb, "Don't Call Me Sir," *Management Today*, August 1998, pp. 44–47; H. Jones, "Selling Space," *Design Week*, April 10, 1998, pp. 18–21; A. R. Sorkin, "Gospel According to St. Luke's," *New York Times*, February 12, 1998, pp. D1, D7; S. Caulkin, "The Advertising Gospel According to St Luke's," *Observer* (London), August 24, 1997, p. 8; M. Carter, "In St Luke's We Trust," *The Independent* (London), April 21, 1997, p. 6.

2. A. G. Bedeian and R. F. Zammuto, *Organizations: Theory and Design* (Hinsdale, IL: Dryden, 1991), pp. 117–18.

3. S. Ranson, R. Hinings, and R. Greenwood, "The Structuring of Organizational Structure," *Administrative Science Quarterly* 25 (1980), pp. 1–14.

4. H. Mintzberg, *The Structuring of Organizations* (Englewood Cliffs, NJ: Prentice Hall, 1979), pp. 2–3.

5. D. Katz and R. L. Kahn, *The Social Psychology of Organizations* (New York: John Wiley, 1966), chap. 2.

6. H. Fayol, *General and Industrial Management*, transl. C. Storrs (London: Pitman, 1949); E. E. Lawler III, *Motivation in Work Organizations* (Monterey, CA: Brooks/Cole, 1973), chap. 7; and M. A. Campion, "Ability Requirement Implications of Job Design: An Interdisciplinary Perspective," *Personnel Psychology* 42 (1989), pp. 1–24.

7. A. N. Maira, "Connecting across Boundaries: The Fluid-Network Organization," *Prism*, First Quarter 1998, pp. 23–26; D. A. Nadler and M. L. Tushman, *Competing by Design: The Power of Organizational Architecture* (New York: Oxford University Press, 1997), chap. 6; Mintzberg, *Structuring of Organizations*, pp. 2–8.

8. C. Downs, P. Clampitt, and A. L. Pfeiffer, "Communication and Organizational Outcomes," in *Handbook of Organizational Communication*, G. Goldhaber and G. Barnett, eds. (Norwood, NJ: Ablex, 1988), pp. 171–211; H. C. Jain, "Supervisory Communication and Performance in Urban Hospitals," *Journal of Communication* 23 (1973), pp. 103–17.

9. V. L. Shalin and G. V. Prabhu, "A Cognitive Perspective on Manual Assembly," *Ergonomics* 39 (1996), pp. 108–27; I. Nonaka and H. Takeuchi, *The Knowledge-Creating Company* (New York: Oxford University Press, 1995).

10. D. Anfuso, "Core Values Shape W. L. Gore's Innovative Culture," *Workforce* 78 (March 1999), pp. 48–53; M. Kaplan, "You Have No Boss," *Fast Company*, Issue 11 (November 1997), p. 226; D. M. Price, "Gore-Tex Gets Hip," *Minneapolis Star Tribune*, May 5, 1997, p. D1.

11. Fayol, *General and Industrial Management*, p. 24.

12. F. Jebb, "Rentokil Initial: A Place for Everyone and Everyone in Their Place," *Management Today*, August 1998, p. 46.

13. J. A. Conger, *Winning 'Em Over* (New York: Simon & Schuster, 1998), appendix A.

14. J. H. Sheridan, "Lessons from the Best," *Industry Week*, February 20, 1995, pp. 13–22.

15. J. Pfeffer, "Seven Practices of Successful Organizations," *California Management Review* 40 (Winter 1998), pp. 96–124.

16. D. D. Van Fleet and A. G. Bedeian, "A History of the Span of Management," *Academy of Management Review* 2 (1977), pp. 356–72; Mintzberg, *Structuring of Organizations*, chap. 8; and D. Robey, *Designing Organizations*, 3d ed. (Burr Ridge, IL: Richard D. Irwin, 1991), pp. 255–59.

17. B. Simon, "Bank Leads by Example in Transformation," *Business Day* (South Africa), July 30, 1998, p. 17.

18. S. Ellis, "A New Role for the Post Office: An Investigation into Issues behind Strategic Change at Royal Mail," *Total Quality Management* 9 (May 1998), pp. 223–34; R. H. Kluge, "An Incentive Compensation Plan with an Eye on Quality," *Quality Progress* 29 (December 1996), pp. 65–68.

19. T. Peters, *Thriving on Chaos* (New York: Alfred A. Knopf, 1987), p. 359.

20. L. A. Bossidy, "Reality-Based Leadership," *Executive Speeches* 13 (August–September 1998), pp. 10–15.

21. P. Panchak, "The Future Manufacturing," *Industry Week* 247 (September 21, 1998), pp. 96–105. For a thorough critique of delayering, see L. Donaldson and F. G. Hilmer, "Management Redeemed: The Case against Fads That Harm Management," *Organizational Dynamics* 26 (Spring 1998), pp. 6–20.

22. Mintzberg, *Structuring of Organizations*, p. 136.

23. The number of layers at Microsoft is inferred from an example in Jebb, "Don't Call Me Sir."

24. K. Ohlson, "Leadership in an Age of Mistrust," *Industry Week*, February 2, 1998, pp. 37–46.

25. D. F. Barker, N. Godley, and R. M. Curtice, "Creating a Successful Shared-Services Organization," *Prism*, First Quarter 1998, pp. 71–74.

26. P. Galuszka, "Procter's Latest Gamble," *Business Week*, September 14, 1998, p. 58; A. Richards, "Brand New Days; Brand Managers," *Marketing*, December 4, 1997, pp. 26–27.

27. Mintzberg, *Structuring of Organizations*, chap. 5.

28. B. Victor and A. C. Boynton, *Invented Here* (Boston: Harvard Business School Press, 1989), chap. 2; M. Hamstra, "McD Speeds Up Drive-Thru with Beefed Up Operations," *Nation's Restaurant News*, April 6, 1998, p. 3; G. Morgan, *Creative Organization Theory: A Resourcebook* (Newburg Park, CA: Sage, 1989), pp. 271–73; K. Deveny, "Bag Those Fries, Squirt That Ketchup, Fry That Fish," *Business Week*, October 13, 1986, p. 86.

29. T. Burns and G. Stalker, *The Management of Innovation* (London: Tavistock, 1961).

30. Mintzberg, *Structuring of Organizations*, p. 106.

31. Ibid., chap. 17.

32. J. Tupponce, "Special Events Spark Company's Creativity," *Richmond Times Dispatch*, March 23, 1998, p. D7.

33. Robey, *Designing Organizations*, pp. 186–89.

34. M. Hamstra, "McD's to Decentralize U.S. Management Team," *Nation's Restaurant News*, June 2, 1997, p. 1.

35. Robey, *Designing Organizations*, pp. 191–97; Bedeian and Zammuto, *Organizations: Theory and Design*, pp. 162–68.

36. "Microsoft Splits into Five Groups in Reorganization," *Reuters*, March 29, 1999; "Microsoft Plans Realignment to Focus on Customers," *Reuters*, February 8, 1999.

37. M. Petersen, "How the Andersens Turned into the Bickersons," *New York Times*, March 15, 1998, sec. 3, pp. 1, 13; "A Family Feud," *Management Consultant International*, February 1998, p. 7; M. Krantz, "Divorce Case: Andersen vs. Andersen," *Investor's Business Daily*, December 18, 1997, p. A6; J. Johnsson, "Accounting Giant Andersen Pushed to End Infighting," *Crain's Detroit Business*, October 27, 1997, p. 40.

38. V. B. Sen, N. Majumdar, and G. Chakravorthy, "Competing on Time," *Business Today* (India), September 7, 1997.

39. M. F. R. Kets de Vries, "Charisma in Action: The Transformational Abilities of Virgin's Richard Branson and ABB's Percy Barnevik," *Organizational Dynamics* 26 (Winter 1998), pp. 6–21; D. A. Nadler and M. L. Tushman, *Competing by Design* (New York: Oxford University Press, 1997), chap. 6.

40. H. F. Kolodny, "Managing in a Matrix," *Business Horizons*, March–April 1981, pp. 17–24; S. M. Davis and P. R. Lawrence, *Matrix* (Reading, MA: Addison-Wesley, 1977).

41. K. Knight, "Matrix Organization: A Review," *Journal of Management Studies*, May 1976, pp. 111–30.

42. C. Herkströter, "Royal Dutch/Shell: Rewriting the Contracts," in G. W. Dauphinais and C. Price, eds., *Straight from the CEO* (New York: Simon & Schuster, 1998), pp. 86–93.

43. G. Calabrese, "Communication and Co-operation in Product Development: A Case Study of a European Car Producer," *R & D Management* 27 (July 1997), pp. 239–52; J. L. Brown and N. M. Agnew, "The Balance of Power in a Matrix Structure," *Business Horizons*, November–December 1982, pp. 51–54.

44. C. A. Bartlett and S. Ghoshal, "Managing across Borders: New Organizational Responses," *Sloan Management Review*, Fall 1987, pp. 43–53.

45. B. Rayner, "Life's Getting Complex," *Electronic Business* 22 (December 1996), pp. 49–51; "A World of Networks: Building the Foundation for the Future," *Telesis*, October 1995, pp. 6–15; "Nortel Splits Operating Roles," *Globe & Mail* (Toronto), December 23, 1993, p. B3; L. Surtees, "Power Shifts at Northern Telecom," *Globe & Mail* (Toronto), February 14, 1991, pp. B1–B2.

46. J. R. Galbraith, E. E. Lawler III, & Associates, *Organizing for the Future: The New Logic for Managing Complex Organizations* (San Francisco: Jossey-Bass, 1993).

47. G. Imperato, "Harley Shifts Gears," *Fast Company* 9 (1997); J. A. Byrne, "Congratulations, You're Moving to a New Pepperoni," *Business Week*, December 20, 1993, pp. 80–81.

48. J. R. Galbraith, *Competing with Flexible Lateral Organizations* (Reading, MA: Addison-Wesley, 1994); J. B. Rieley, "The Circular Organization: How Leadership Can Optimize Organizational Effectiveness," *National Productivity Review* 13 (Winter 1993–1994), pp. 11–19; J. A. Byrne, "The Horizontal Corporation," *Business Week*, December 20, 1993, pp. 76–81; R. Tomasko, *Rethinking the Corporation* (New York: AMACOM, 1993); D. Quinn Mills with G. Bruce Friesen, *Rebirth of the Corporation* (New York: John Wiley, 1991), pp. 29–30.

49. L. D. Goodstein and H. R. Butz, "Customer Value: The Linchpin of Organizational Change," *Organizational Dynamics* 27 (Summer 1998), pp. 21–34.

50. R. Bettis and M. Hitt, "The New Competitive Landscape," *Strategic Management Journal* 16 (1995), pp. 7–19.

51. P. C. Ensign, "Interdependence, Coordination, and Structure in Complex Organizations: Implications for Organization Design," *Mid-Atlantic Journal of Business* 34 (March 1998), pp. 5–22.

52. L. Y. Chan and B. E. Lynn, "Operating in Turbulent Times: How Ontario's Hospitals Are Meeting the Current Funding Crisis," *Health Care Management Review* 23 (June 1998), pp. 7–18; M. M. Fanning, "A Circular Organization Chart Promotes a Hospital-Wide Focus on Teams," *Hospital & Health Services Administration* 42 (June 1997), pp. 243–54.

53. W. F. Joyce, V. E. McGee, and J. W. Slocum Jr., "Designing Lateral Organizations: An Analysis of the Benefits, Costs, and Enablers of Nonhierarchical Organizational Forms," *Decision Sciences* 28 (Winter 1997), pp. 1–25.

54. J. A. Byrne, "The Corporation of the Future," *Business Week*, August 31, 1998, pp. 102–4.

55. C. Baldwin and K. Clark, "Managing in an Age of Modularity," *Harvard Business Review* 75 (September–October 1997), pp. 84–93; W. Powell, K. W. Koput, and L. Smith-Doerr, "Interorganizational Collaboration and the Locus of Innovation: Networks of Learning in Biotechnology," *Administrative Science Quarterly* 41 (1996), pp. 116–45; R. E. Miles and C. C. Snow, "The New Network Firm: A Spherical Structure Built on a Human Investment Philosophy," *Organizational Dynamics* 23, no. 4 (1995), pp. 5–18; R. E. Miles and C. C. Snow, "Causes of Failure in Network Organizations," *California Management Review* 34 (Summer 1992), pp. 53–72; H. F. Kolodny, "Some Characteristics of Organizational Designs in New/High Technology Firms," in L. R. Gomez-Mejia and M. W. Lawless, eds., *Organizational Issues in High Technology Management* (Greenwich, CT: JAI Press, 1990), pp. 165–76; W. Powell, "Neither Market nor Hierarchy: Network Forms of Organization," *Research in Organizational Behavior* 12 (1990), pp. 295–336.

56. T. W. Malone and R. J. Laubacher, "The Dawn of the E-lance Economy," *Harvard Business Review* 76 (September–October 1998), pp. 144–52.

57. J. Hagel III and M. Singer, "Unbundling the Corporation," *Harvard Business Review* 77 (March–April 1999), pp. 133–41. For a discussion of core competencies,

see G. Hamel and C. K. Prahalad, *Competing for the Future* (Boston: Harvard Business School Press, 1994), chap. 10.

58. D. Einstein, "Solectron's Acquisition Strategy Pays Off Big in Revenue Growth," *San Francisco Chronicle*, April 26, 1999.

59. R. Nathan, "NEC Organizing for Creativity, Nimbleness," *Research Technology Management* 41 (July–August 1998), pp. 4–6.

60. J. Matthews, "'Baby Bills' Follow Leader to Success," *Baltimore Sun*, August 14, 1998; J. F. Moore, "The Rise of a New Corporate Form," *Washington Quarterly* 21 (Winter 1998), pp. 167–81.

61. L. Fried, *Managing Information Technology in Turbulent Times* (New York: John Wiley, 1995); W. H. Davidow and M. S. Malone, *The Virtual Corporation* (New York: HarperBusiness, 1992).

62. R. E. Miles, C. C. Snow, J. A. Mathews, G. Miles, and H. J. Coleman, Jr., "Organizing in the Knowledge Age: Anticipating the Cellular Form," *Academy of Management Executive* 11 (November 1997), pp. 7–20.

63. G. Morgan, *Imagin-I-Zation: New Mindsets for Seeing, Organizing and Managing* (Thousand Oaks, CA: Sage, 1997); G. Morgan, *Images of Organization*, 2nd ed. (Newbury Park: Sage, 1996).

64. P. M. J. Christie and R. Levary, "Virtual Corporations: Recipe for Success," *Industrial Management* 40 (July 1998), pp. 7–11; H. Chesbrough and D. J. Teece, "When Is Virtual Virtuous? Organizing for Innovation," *Harvard Business Review* 74 (January–February 1996), pp. 65–73.

65. C. Meyer and S. Davis, *Blur: The Speed of Change in the Connected Economy* (Reading, MA: Addison-Wesley, 1998).

66. Mintzberg, *Structuring of Organizations*, chap. 13; D. S. Pugh and C. R. Hinings, eds., *Organizational Structure: Extensions and Replications* (Farnborough, England: Lexington Books, 1976).

67. T. A. Stewart, *Intellectual Capital: The New Wealth of Organizations* (New York: Doubleday/Currency, 1997), chap. 10.

68. Robey, *Designing Organizations*, p. 102.

69. C. Perrow, "A Framework for the Comparative Analysis of Organizations," *American Sociological Review* 32 (1967), pp. 194–208.

70. Mintzberg, *Structuring of Organizations*, chap. 15.

71. Burns and Stalker, *The Management of Innovation*; P. R. Lawrence and J. W. Lorsch, *Organization and Environment* (Burr Ridge, IL: Richard D. Irwin, 1967); D. Miller and P. H. Friesen, *Organizations: A Quantum View* (Englewood Cliffs, NJ: Prentice Hall, 1984), pp. 197–98.

72. Mintzberg, *Structuring of Organizations*, p. 282.

73. R. H. Kilmann, *Beyond the Quick Fix* (San Francisco: Jossey-Bass, 1984), p. 38.

74. J. Child, "Organizational Structure, Environment, and Performance: The Role of Strategic Choice," *Sociology* 6 (1972), pp. 2–22.

75. A. D. Chandler, *Strategy and Structure* (Cambridge: MIT Press, 1962).

76. M. E. Porter, *Competitive Strategy* (New York: Free Press, 1980).

77. D. Miller, "Configurations of Strategy and Structure," *Strategic Management Journal* 7 (1986), pp. 233–50.

Appendix A

1. F. N. Kerlinger, *Foundations of Behavioral Research* (New York: Holt, Rinehart & Winston, 1964), p. 11.

2. J. B. Miner, *Theories of Organizational Behavior* (Hinsdale, IL: Dryden, 1980), pp. 7–9.

3. Ibid. pp. 6–7.

4. J. Mason, *Qualitative Researching* (London: Sage, 1996).

5. A. Strauss and J. Corbin, eds., *Grounded Theory in Practice* (London: Sage, 1997); B. G. Glaser and A. Strauss, *The Discovery of Grounded Theory: Strategies for Qualitative Research* (Chicago: Aldine, 1967).

6. Kerlinger, *Foundations of Behavioral Research*, p. 13.

7. P. Lazarsfeld, *Survey Design and Analysis* (New York: Free Press, 1955).

8. This example is cited in D. W. Organ and T. S. Bateman, *Organizational Behavior*, 4th ed., Burr Ridge, IL: Richard D. Irwin, 1991), p. 42.

9. Ibid. p. 45

10. R. I. Sutton and A. Hargadon, "Brainstorming Groups in Context: Effectiveness in a Product Design Firm," *Administrative Science Quarterly* 41 (1996), pp. 685–718.

COMPANY INDEX

NAME INDEX

SUBJECT INDEX